LAW, MEDICINE, AND MEDICAL TECHNOLOGY

CASES AND MATERIALS

THIRD EDITION

by

LARS NOAH
Professor of Law
University of Florida

FOUNDATION PRESS
2012

THOMSON REUTERS™

1 New York Plaza, 34th Floor
New York, NY 10004
Phone Toll Free 1–877–888–1330
Fax 646–424–5201
foundation–press.com

Printed in the United States of America

ISBN 978–1–60930–102–6

Mat #41227471

To my daughter, Sigrid

PREFACE

The desire to take medicine is perhaps the greatest feature which distinguishes man from animals.

—William Osler (1925)

In its broadest sense, the word "technology" refers to the application of knowledge.* In that respect, medicine has always centered on technology. With accelerating advances in biomedical knowledge, the number of therapeutic interventions continues to multiply. Instead of concerns about generating the information, the challenge has become how best to manage—in terms of both filtering and disseminating—the increasing quantity and complexity of clinically-relevant research findings.

In a narrower sense, the word "technology" refers to the objects produced by the application of scientific knowledge. Medicine involves the use of technology alongside the application of professional skill and judgment in the treatment of patients, and we may find ourselves in the midst of a radical transformation in the delivery of health care in this country. Of course, physicians have long made use of various instruments and medications, at first quite primitive but now increasingly complex. See Audrey B. Davis, Medicine and Its Technology: An Introduction to the History of Medical Instrumentation (1981). Even so, the health care system has always emphasized the provision of professional services.

Dramatic changes in health care financing have shaken this tradition in recent years, but continuing technological advances also threaten to overtake the classic service-oriented paradigm. As one physician observed:

> Technology will confound almost any attempt to change the health care system or redirect its fundamental goals. Further, if there is one thing that can be singled out as the engine of the medical cost inflation now occurring everywhere in the world, it is the seemingly irresistible spread of technology into every level of medicine.... [L]ike the broom in *The Sorcerer's Apprentice*, technologies come to have a life of their own, not only because of their own properties but also because of certain universal human traits. Technologies come

* See XVII Oxford English Dictionary 705 (2d ed. 1989) ("A particular practical or industrial art."). For a discussion of the difficulties in defining medical technology, see Michael H. Shapiro, Is Bioethics Broke?: On the Idea of Ethics and Law "Catching Up" with Technology, 33 Ind. L. Rev. 17, 38–39 & n.43 (1999); see also Einer Elhauge, The Limited Regulatory Potential of Medical Technology Assessment, 82 Va. L. Rev. 1525, 1530 n.14 (1996) ("The technology assessment literature generally defines 'medical technology' as including not only machinery, devices, and drugs but also medical practices and procedures. This definition ... somewhat confusingly seems to eliminate any distinction between technology and health care.").

> into being to serve the purposes of their users, but ultimately their users redefine their own goals in terms of the technology.

Eric J. Cassell, Doctoring: The Nature of Primary Care Medicine 62–63 (1997); see also Daniel Callahan, Taming the Beloved Beast: Medical Technology Costs Are Destroying Our Health Care System (2009); Annetine Gelijns & Nathan Rosenberg, The Dynamics of Technological Change in Medicine, Health Aff., Summer 1994, at 29.

In 2010, this country spent approximately $400 billion on prescription drugs, medical devices, and diagnostic equipment. There is more to the subject, however, than expense. Technological advances challenge existing institutional relationships as well as mechanisms of supervision and control. In concluding his chapter on this technological imperative in medicine, Dr. Cassell noted a paradox: "Despite the enormous power of modern medical technology . . . , the power of the medical profession is at a low point. Doctors had greater public power in 1950, when technological power was modest." Id. at 79; see also George J. Annas, Some Choice: Law, Medicine, and the Market ch. 5 (1998) (offering a critical assessment of the enthusiasm for new medical technology). One theme running through these materials focuses on the interactions between health care providers and medical technologies, whether defined broadly as biomedical knowledge or more narrowly as the products utilized in the treatment of patients.

Of course, technological advances offer tremendous promise for promoting patient welfare. The story of past successes—ranging from the development of antibiotics, vaccines, chemotherapy agents, artificial joints, pacemakers, and magnetic resonance imaging (MRI) devices—is by now familiar. In the near future, persons may have implanted microprocessors that can monitor numerous physiological parameters on a continuous real-time basis; expert systems might allow computers to download this information and provide a differential diagnosis; and gene therapies might allow for the delivery of precisely tailored biological treatments. See Bruce N. Kuhlik, The Regulation of Drugs and Biologics: Fifty Years into the Future, 55 Food & Drug L.J. 21, 22 (2000); Scott Hensley, New Race Heats up to Turn Gene Information into Drug Discoveries, Wall St. J., June 26, 2000, at B1 (reporting that the completion of the Human Genome Project may lead to improved therapies). In 1999, recognizing these possibilities, more than 40 medical journals from around the world devoted one entire issue of their publications to the growing significance of medical technologies in health care. See David H. Mark & Richard M. Glass, Editorial, Impact of New Technologies in Medicine: A Global Theme Issue, 282 JAMA 1875 (1999); Caralee E. Caplan & John Hoey, Editorial, Impact of New Technologies in Medicine: Progress and Pitfalls, 160 Can. Med. Ass'n J. 66 (1999).

This is not a book designed for futurists, however, and I do not mean to suggest that the medical profession will be further marginalized, though the roles of health care providers no doubt will continue to evolve in the face of technological advances. Medical technology is already, and has been for some time, an essential aspect of modern medicine. Unfortunately, existing textbooks fail to give the subject adequate attention. For instance, one of the leading health law casebooks devotes essentially no attention to the regulation of drugs and medical devices by the Food and Drug Administration (FDA) or to the transmission of biomedical knowledge. See Barry R. Furrow et al., Health Law: Cases, Materials & Problems (6th ed.2008). To be sure, issues concerning the control of medical technologies appear sporadically throughout this and similar texts, but the emphasis rests squarely on the service aspects of this industry: licensing chapters focus on state regulation of health care professionals rather than federal regulation of health care products; the tort law chapters focus on medical malpractice rather than products liability; the health care financing chapters focus on payment for services rather than medical equipment; and the materials about informed consent focus on the transmission of knowledge that occurs vertically (between physicians and patients) rather than horizontally (among clinical researchers and health care providers). In short, the subject of health law must concern itself with more than just efforts at supervising the provision of medical services.

Moreover, anyone with an interest in issues relating to the control of medical technologies will struggle to find any comprehensive treatment of these sorts of questions in other texts. For instance, one of the leading casebooks on products liability devotes all of forty pages to a focused discussion of the special tort law principles governing prescription drugs and medical devices. See James A. Henderson, Jr. & Aaron D. Twerski, Products Liability: Problems & Process 540–80 (6th ed.2008). Again, issues involving such products receive sporadic attention elsewhere in this and similar texts, but the subject deserves more thorough treatment than is possible in a general course on products liability. Similarly, administrative law texts often use the activities of the FDA to illustrate questions of agency procedure and judicial review. See, e.g., Peter L. Strauss et al., Gellhorn & Byse's Administrative Law: Cases & Comments (11th ed.2011). Even so, sustained attention to this powerful agency can only be found in a specialized but infrequently offered course. See Peter Barton Hutt et al., Food and Drug Law: Cases & Materials (3d ed.2007).

This casebook attempts to blend the best of all of these fields by focusing on the regulation of medical technology. I intentionally use the word "regulation" broadly to encompass not just legislative and administrative agency controls on the creation and use of such technology but also less direct controls mediated through the systems of tort law, insurance, and intellectual property regimes, among others. Although organized thematically rather than sequentially in reference to a product's life-cycle, these materials consider the many ways in which society attempts to manage the production and application of medical technologies, tracing the research and development process from laboratory bench to ultimate use in the treatment of patients. Although students would benefit from some prior exposure to the numerous doctrinal subjects addressed—ranging across administrative law, constitutional law (esp. First Amendment issues), products liability and medical malpractice, insurance, antitrust, intellectual property, and bioethics—not to mention the scientific issues that arise, I have tried to design the materials in a way that persons with widely different backgrounds will find equally accessible and hopefully valuable. I also hope that the Problems scattered throughout the book, including one lengthier exercise focused on questions of an attorney's professional responsibilities, will facilitate use in the classroom.

A note on editing: Deletions from materials are indicated by asterisk ellipses except when the omitted material consists only of subheadings, citations, or footnotes. Some citations within judicial opinions have been modified as appropriate to approximate the formatting guidelines of *The Bluebook: A Uniform System of Citation.*

ACKNOWLEDGEMENTS

American Law Institute, Restatement of Torts, Second, Copyright © 1965, 1977 by The American Law Institute. Reprinted with permission of The American Law Institute. American Law Institute, Restatement of Torts, Third: Products Liability, Copyright © 1998 by The American Law Institute. Reprinted with permission of The American Law Institute.

American Medical Association, Code of Medical Ethics, Opinion 8.135: Managed Care Cost Containment Involving Prescription Drugs. Source: Council on Ethical and Judicial Affairs, Code of Medical Ethics: Current Opinions. Copyright © 1996 by the American Medical Association. Reprinted with Permission of the American Medical Association.

Danzon, Patricia M. and Li–Wei Chao, Does Regulation Drive Out Competition in Pharmaceutical Markets?, 43 J.L. & Econ. 311 (2000). Copyright © 2000 by the University of Chicago. All rights reserved. Reprinted with permission of the University of Chicago and Patricia M. Danzon.

Goldberg, Steven, The Changing Face of Death: Computers, Consciousness, and Nancy Cruzan, 43 Stan. L. Rev. 659 (1991). Copyright © 1991 by the Board of Trustees of the Leland Stanford Junior University. Reprinted with permission of the Stanford Law Review.

Hall, Mark A., Rationing Health Care at the Bedside, 69 N.Y.U. L. Rev. 693 (1994). Copyright © 1994 by New York University Law Review. Reprinted with permission of New York University Law Review.

Heyman, Philip B. and Lance Liebman, The Social Responsibilities of Lawyers, 216–34 (1988). Copyright © 1988 by Foundation Press. Reprinted with permission of Foundation Press, publisher.

Hutt, Peter Barton, The Transformation of United States Food and Drug Law, Journal of the Association of Food & Drug Officials, Sept. 1996, at 1. Copyright © 1996 by the Association of Food and Drug Officials. Reprinted with permission of the Association of Food and Drug Officials.

Makow, Lawrence S., Note, Medical Device Review at the Food and Drug Administration: Lessons from Magnetic Resonance Spectroscopy and Biliary Lithotripsy, 46 Stan. L. Rev. 709 (1994). Copyright © 1994 by the Board of Trustees of the Leland Stanford Junior University. Reprinted with permission of the Stanford Law Review.

Malinowski, Michael J. and Robin J. R. Blatt, Commercialization of Genetic Testing Services: The FDA, Market Forces, and Biological Tarot Cards, 71 Tul. L. Rev. 1211 (1997). Copyright © 1997 by Tulane Law Review Association. Reprinted with the permission of the Tulane Law Review Association.

Marshall, Edward A., Note, Medical Malpractice in the New Eugenics: Relying on Innovative Tort Doctrine to Provide Relief When Gene Therapy Fails, 35 Ga. L. Rev. 1277 (2001). Copyright © 2001 by the Georgia Law Review. Reprinted with permission of the Georgia Law Review.

Merrill, Richard A., The Importance and Challenges of "Mutual Recognition," 29 Seton Hall L. Rev. 736 (1998). Copyright © 1998 by the Seton Hall University School of Law. Reprinted with permission of the Seton Hall Law Review.

Noah, Lars, Administrative Arm–Twisting in the Shadow of Congressional Delegations of Authority, 1997 Wis. L. Rev. 873. Copyright © 1997 by The Board of Regents of the University of Wisconsin system. Reprinted with permission of the Wisconsin Law Review.

Noah, Lars, Assisted Reproductive Technologies and the Pitfalls of Unregulated Biomedical Innovation, 55 Fla. L. Rev. 603 (2003). Copyright © 2003 by the Florida Law Review. Reprinted with permission of the Florida Law Review.

Noah, Lars, Deputizing Institutional Review Boards to Police (Audit?) Biomedical Research, 25 J. Legal Med. 267 (2004). Copyright © 2004 by Taylor & Francis. Reprinted with permission of the Journal of Legal Medicine.

Noah, Lars, The Little Agency That Could (Act with Indifference to Constitutional and Statutory Strictures), 93 Cornell L. Rev. 901 (2008). Copyright © 2008 by the Cornell Law Review. Reprinted with permission of the Cornell Law Review.

Noah, Lars, Managing Biotechnology's [R]evolution: Has Guarded Enthusiasm Become Benign Neglect?, 11 Va. J.L. & Tech. 4 (2006). Copyright © 2006 by the Virginia Journal of Law & Technology Association. Reprinted with permission of the Virginia Journal of Law & Technology Association.

Noah, Lars, Pigeonholing Illness: Medical Diagnosis as a Legal Construct, 50 Hastings L.J. 241 (1999). Copyright © 2001 by University of California, Hastings College of the Law. Reprinted with permission of the Hastings Law Journal.

Noah, Lars, Platitudes About "Product Stewardship" in Torts: Continuing Drug Research and Education, 15 Mich. Telecomm. & Tech. L. Rev. 359 (2009). Copyright © 2009 by the Michigan Telecommunications & Technology Law Review. Reprinted with permission of the Michigan Telecommunications & Technology Law Review.

Noah, Lars, A Postmodernist Take on the Human Embryo Research Debate, 36 Conn. L. Rev. 1133 (2004). Copyright © 2004 by the Connecticut Law Review. Reprinted with permission of the Connecticut Law Review.

Noah, Lars, Rewarding Regulatory Compliance: The Pursuit of Symmetry in Products Liability, 88 Geo. L.J. 2147 (2000). Copyright © 2000 by the Georgetown Law Journal Association. Reprinted with permission of the Georgetown Law Journal Association.

Noah, Lars, Sham Petitioning as a Threat to the Integrity of the Regulatory Process, 74 N.C. L. Rev. 1 (1995). Copyright © 1995 by the North Carolina Law Review Association. Reprinted with permission of the North Carolina Law Review Association.

Noah, Lars, This Is Your Products Liability Restatement on Drugs, 74 Brook. L. Rev. 839 (2009). Copyright © 2009 by the Brooklyn Law Review. Reprinted with permission of the Brooklyn Law Review.

Noah, Lars, Treat Yourself: Is Self–Medication the Prescription for What Ails American Health Care?, 19 Harv. J.L. & Tech. 359 (2006). Copyright © 2006 by the Harvard Journal of Law & Technology. Reprinted with permission of the Harvard Journal of Law & Technology.

Noah, Lars, Triage in the Nation's Medicine Cabinet: The Puzzling Scarcity of Vaccines and Other Drugs, 54 S.C. L. Rev. 741 (2003). Copyright © 2003 by the South Carolina Law Review. Reprinted with permission of the South Carolina Law Review.

Noah, Lars, Truth or Consequences?: Commercial Free Speech vs. Public Health Promotion (at the FDA), 21 Health Matrix 31 (2011). Copyright © 2011 by Health Matrix: Journal of Law–Medicine. Reprinted with permission of Health Matrix.

Note, Will Health Care Economic Information Lead to Therapeutic–Class Warfare or Welfare?, 111 Harv. L. Rev. 2384 (1998). Copyright © 1998 by the Harvard Law Review Association. Reprinted with permission of the Harvard Law Review Association.

Rokosz, Gregory J., Human Cloning: Is the Reach of FDA Authority Too Far a Stretch?, 30 Seton Hall L. Rev. 464 (2000). Copyright © 2000 by the Seton Hall University School of Law. Reprinted with permission of the Seton Hall Law Review.

Saver, Richard S., Note, Reimbursing New Technologies: Why Are the Courts Judging Experimental Medicine?, 44 Stan. L. Rev. 1095 (1992). Copyright © 1992 by the Board of Trustees of the Leland Stanford Junior University. Reprinted with permission of the Stanford Law Review.

Shapiro, Michael H., Is Bioethics Broke?: On the Idea of Ethics and Law "Catching Up" with Technology, 33 Ind. L. Rev. 17 (1999). Copyright © 1999 by the Trustees of Indiana University. Reprinted with permission of the Indiana Law Review and Michael H. Shapiro.

Siegel, Laurel R., Comment, Re–Engineering the Laws of Organ Transplantation, 49 Emory L.J. 917 (2000). Copyright © 2000 by the Emory Law Journal. Reprinted with permission of the Emory Law Journal.

Sorum, Paul C., Limiting Cardiopulmonary Resuscitation, 57 Alb. L. Rev. 617 (1994). Copyright © 1994 by the Albany Law Review. Reprinted with permission of the Albany Law Review.

SUMMARY OF CONTENTS

TABLE OF CONTENTS

TABLE OF CASES

Principal cases are in bold type. Non-principal cases are in roman type. References are to Pages.

Law, Medicine, and Medical Technology

PART I

GOVERNMENT REGULATION

CHAPTER 1

FDA Control: Preliminaries

A. History and Overview

Peter Barton Hutt, *The Transformation of United States Food and Drug Law*

J. Ass'n Food & Drug Officials, Sept. 1996, at 1.

* * * [B]etween 1850 and 1900 virtually every state enacted some form of food and drug statute. Although resources were obviously limited and the science needed to police the food and drug industry was unsophisticated by current standards, our basic concepts of protecting the public health from adulterated and misbranded food and drugs find their origin in this formative era. * * * At the [turn of the century], however, there was a powerful obstacle in the way. A majority of Congress firmly believed that regulation of the manufacture and sale of food and drugs within the United States involved local matters that the Constitution left entirely to the states. Only the import and export of food and drugs was regarded as within the jurisdiction of the federal government. * * * State food and drug officials were early supporters of federal legislation. As a result of the increasingly national scope of our growing economy, they recognized the need for a federal leadership role to set national policy and standards that would be used throughout the country. * * *

Regulation of biological products represents the oldest form of government regulation of business in our country. * * * [I]n 1901 contaminated smallpox vaccine caused an outbreak of tetanus in Camden and a lot of tetanus-infected diphtheria antitoxin resulted in the death of several children in Saint Louis. * * * Congress promptly enacted the Biologics Act of 1902. The 1902 Act represented a remarkable turning point in the history of food and drug regulation, even though it was not appreciated at the time. For the first time in history, a statute required premarket approval by the government of a category of consumer products before any product within that category could lawfully be marketed. The 1902 Act required government approval of a product license application and an establishment license application for every biological drug intended for human use. Never before—and indeed, not for more than another fifty years—did Congress impose a similar regulatory requirement upon any other category of products. Equally remarkable, the 1902 Act explicitly authorized the Treasury Department to inspect any biologics establishment during all reasonable hours. This was the first federal law authorizing inspection of private manufacturing premises by the federal government. * * * It was to take seventy years before regulation of human biological products would be integrated into FDA regulatory responsibilities. * * *

The Federal Food, Drug and Cosmetic Act * * * was enacted in 1938 to replace the 1906 [Pure Food and Drugs] Act * * * * As a result of the numerous amendments to the 1938 Act during the past fifty-eight years, the statute today consists of very lengthy and complex provisions that have never been subjected to a comprehensive review and rationalization. Each amendment has been negotiated on an ad hoc basis, reflecting the prevailing balance of power in Congress and the Administration at the moment, without consideration of the need for consistency in language or policy throughout the entire statute. Different words are used to mean the same thing in different parts of the statute, different types of authority are granted with respect to similar matters, different enforcement powers are provided for comparable violations, and the relationship among all of the provisions in the statute is increasingly ambiguous. * * *

[T]he legislation that has often been most important in establishing national policy on food and drug regulation has been created in the aftermath of a major product disaster. As is often true under these conditions, the legislation has been shaped as much by public emotion as by rational policy design. There has often been insufficient congressional analysis and legislative history to guide FDA, the regulated industry and the courts in the intended meaning and application of the resulting statutory language.

The relation of any federal agency with Congress is always tenuous. Congress has two functions with respect to a regulatory program. First, it creates the agency and authorizes the program. Second, it conducts oversight to determine any weakness or limitations and to recommend changes in both legislative and administrative policy. * * * Since 1960, there have been far more oversight hearings than legislative hearings regarding FDA. Virtually every aspect of the agency's work has been subjected to intense investigation.

For the first two decades of these oversight hearings, on all but one occasion the hearing was conducted to criticize FDA for failing to take adequate regulatory action against a product that the committee concluded was unlawful or for approval of a new product that the committee thought was unsafe or ineffective. On only one occasion was FDA criticized for not approving a new drug with sufficient speed. On literally hundreds of other occasions the agency was subjected to withering criticism for failing to protect against unsafe and ineffective products. This congressional criticism had a profound impact on FDA employees at all levels. Already risk averse by nature, they became even more conservative in implementing the FDA premarket approval authority. * * * After such a long time during which the congressional focus was on the failure of FDA adequately to protect the public against harm, FDA was ill-prepared to respond to charges that the agency was failing to promote the public health by fostering the prompt availability of new products. * * *

For roughly the first half of its existence, until 1940, FDA [defined broadly to include its predecessor agencies] remained a component of USDA. The agency was transferred from USDA to the Federal Security Agency in 1940 and to the Department of Health, Education and Welfare when it was formed in 1953, which later became the Department of Health and Human Services in 1979. From 1930 to the present, it has retained its present designation: the Food and Drug Administration. * * * FDA is our oldest federal regulatory agency, and for decades it was the only federal agency charged with jurisdiction over a broad range of consumer products. The Environmental Protection Agency, the Occupational Safety and Health Administration and the Consumer Product Safety Commission are all of relatively recent origin, created during 1970–1972. FDA thus towers over the field of regulation in the United States as our most venerable and respected regulatory institution. * * * Yet FDA has never been a large government agency by federal standards and has commanded only a rather modest annual appropriation. [In 1995, the agency received almost $900 million in appropriations and employed more than 9500 individuals.] * * * [I]t is likely that user fees and other innovative sources of revenue for FDA will continue to be explored in the future. * * *

The history of progress in food and drug regulation over the past century is largely the history of the development of science, not the enactment of statutory provisions. The 1938 Act contains broad statutory mandates that are meaningless without the infusion of scientific knowledge that permits the development of specific operational rules. * * * Development of some of the most important principles of toxicology can be attributed to FDA scientists. * * * FDA has long struggled with its identity as a "regulatory" or "law enforcement" agency on the one hand or as a "science" agency on the other hand. * * *

Lars Noah, *The Little Agency That Could (Act with Indifference to Constitutional and Statutory Strictures)*

93 CORNELL L. REV. 901 (2008).

More than a century ago, Congress inaugurated federal regulation of foods and drugs. By today's standards, the 1906 Act looked terribly anemic, running just five pages in length. Thirty years later, reacting to difficulties with enforcing the original statute (as tragically revealed by a series of fatalities caused by a product called Elixir sulfanilamide), Congress replaced it with the Food, Drug, and Cosmetic Act (FDCA). Although more comprehensive, the new statute continued to eschew details in favor of broad prohibitions against adulteration and misbranding. The original FDCA filled only fifteen pages in the *U.S. Code*. In the intervening years, Congress has both tinkered with the original language and appended brand new powers and requirements, so that the amended version of the FDCA in the latest edition of the *U.S. Code* occupies 230 pages. What started as a fairly simple regime of after-the-fact policing aimed at substandard foods and drugs has morphed into a complex set of product licensing requirements.

In delegating this authority, Congress has demanded much from the Food and Drug Administration, making the agency responsible for twenty-five percent of all consumer goods sold in the United States, but the legislature has not always supplied the regulatory tools and appropriations needed to fulfill this mandate. Throughout its history, however, the FDA has had an enviable record of success in the courts because judges have shown tremendous deference to its expertise in implementing its public health mission. * * * Although it has not fared as well in recent years, the FDA remains one of the most respected agencies in the federal government. This respect translates into important clout for an agency that lacks the size and resources of other regulatory bodies. Nonetheless, because of the controversial issues that have confronted the agency, it has gone without permanent leadership for much of the last decade. * * *

The FDA has shown tremendous creativity in construing the reach of its authority, as, for example, it did one decade ago in announcing that it would control human cloning experiments. The agency must, of course, grapple with advances in science and technology that Congress could not have anticipated many decades earlier, including the advent of genetically modified foods, bioengineered drugs, nanotechnology, tissue engineering and regenerative medicine, gene therapy, and pharmacogenomics. Conversely, the FDA has at times tried to escape the occasionally precise (and, to its mind, inflexible) directives issued by Congress.

In the early 1970s, the FDA's Chief Counsel [Peter Barton Hutt] expressed the view that the agency's enabling statute represented a broad "constitution," authorizing it to protect the public health by any necessary and proper means, rather than a limited and precise delegation of power from Congress. * * * His successor in that office [Richard A. Merrill], though writing many years after leaving government service, analogized the FDCA to an unfinished set of architectural blueprints. As explained by one of the chief congressional "architects" of detailed amendments to the original statutory provisions governing medical devices, however, the greater specificity of this legislation sought "to make clear that Congress wanted the agencies to follow the congressional mandate more carefully and not go off on bureaucratic binges pursuing bureaucratic whims." During the 1990s, the FDA asserted the authority to regulate tobacco products as medical devices, and some commentators invoked the constitutional metaphor to defend this creative effort against claims that the agency had overstepped the limits on its jurisdiction. * * * In the course of invalidating the agency's restrictions on cigarette advertising, the Supreme Court sensibly declined to view the FDCA as akin to an adaptable constitution. * * *

Necessity may be the mother of invention, but, over the course of a century of struggling to protect the public health with its limited statutory powers and often inadequate resources, the FDA evidently has institutionalized a practice of cavalierly ignoring legal constraints. At times, the agency's creativity has received belated endorsement from Congress or the courts, though, on other occasions, members of these branches have condemned it for showing excessive initiative. Most of the FDA's decisions, however, escape any such scrutiny, which means that nothing other than humility and self-restraint stand in the way of regulatory overreaching. It seems that whenever, in the course of pursuing its vision of the public good, this little agency found that it could get away with doing something, the FDA blithely disregarded its obligation of fidelity to constitutional and statutory constraints. Even if we applaud the ends that the agency sought to achieve, such a pattern of behavior represents a serious affront to the rule of law.

NOTES AND QUESTIONS

1. *Statutory evolution.* In 1997, Congress enacted the Food and Drug Administration Modernization Act (FDAMA), Pub. L. No. 105–115, 111 Stat. 2296. In 2007, Congress enacted the Food and Drug Administration Amendments Act (FDAAA), Pub. L. No. 110–85, 121 Stat. 823. These two laws represented the most significant sets of amendments to the 1938 statute in decades, though, consistent with the recent pattern of legislative micro-management, the amendments tinkered with rather than transformed the FDCA. Less sweeping changes were made to the drug and device provisions of the statute in 1992 and 2002 (and can be expected again in 2012), and it is no coincidence that amendments now appear at five year intervals: the user fee legislation of 1992 (further discussed in Chap. 3(A)(1)) sunsets every five years, forcing Congress to reauthorize this increasingly critical source of revenue for the agency and, depending on how the political winds blow, give it the opportunity to make sundry other changes. This feature also has created a peculiar bargaining dynamic between the agency and industry insofar as Congress leaves these parties to hash out the terms of new user fee legislation. See Anna W. Mathews, Drug Firms Use Financial Clout to Push Industry Agenda at FDA, Wall St. J., Sept. 1, 2006, at A1; Cindy Skrzycki, FDA's User–Fee Habit, Wash. Post, Apr. 3, 2007, at D1; see also 72 Fed. Reg. 1743, 1745 (2007) (describing the process used for the development of legislative recommendations). Relevant provisions of the statute as amended over the years can be found at www.fda.gov/RegulatoryInformation/Legislation, and they also are reproduced in appropriate parts of the text or in excerpted judicial opinions (though they may have been amended subsequent to the decision).*

2. *Further commentary.* See Margaret A. Hamburg & Joshua M. Sharfstein, The FDA as a Public Health Agency, 360 New Eng. J. Med. 2493 (2009); Peter Barton Hutt, The State of Science at the Food and Drug

* A note on numbering: The original sections of the Act were renumbered as codified in Title 21 of the United States Code, usually by adding a "3" at the beginning and dropping the middle "0" of the three digit section number (so FDCA § 301 becomes 21 U.S.C. § 331). Where there is no "0" in the middle (or at the end) of the original, the codified section numbers attach letters (so FDCA § 510 becomes 21 U.S.C. § 360, and FDCA § 511 becomes 21 U.S.C. § 360a).

Administration, 60 Admin. L. Rev. 431 (2008); Richard A. Merrill, The Architecture of Government Regulation of Medical Products, 82 Va. L. Rev. 1753 (1996); Andrew C. von Eschenbach, Continuing the Restoration and Transformation of the FDA, 13 J. Health Care L. & Pol'y 203 (2010); Kara W. Swanson, Food and Drug Law as Intellectual Property Law: Historical Reflections, 2011 Wis. L. Rev. 329; Symposium, U.S. Food and Drug Regulation in Its First Century and Beyond, 93 Cornell L. Rev. 901 (2008); see also Rob Stein, Ailing FDA May Need a Major Overhaul, Officials and Groups Say, Wash. Post, Nov. 26, 2008, at A2.

B. PRODUCT CATEGORIES AND INTENDED USE

The FDA regulates a wide range of consumer products, including food, food additives, dietary supplements, human and animal drugs, medical devices, and cosmetics. The lines of demarcation between these product categories are often unclear and sharply contested because the classification will dictate whether the FDA has any jurisdiction and then what types of regulatory controls it might impose on the product. Cosmetics face the weakest controls (only after-the-fact policing for adulteration and misbranding) and new drugs face the most rigorous controls (including thorough premarket review in addition to after-the-fact policing), with dietary supplements, foods, color additives, food additives, and medical devices arrayed between these two extremes (and roughly in that order). Although this casebook focuses on human drugs and medical devices, the growing interest in unconventional therapies necessitates some discussion of dietary supplements, and the other product categories will be mentioned as necessary to illuminate definitional disputes.

1. DRUGS

United States v. An Article of Drug . . . Bacto–Unidisk

394 U.S. 784 (1969).

■ Warren, Chief Justice:

* * * Various antibiotics, known more commonly as "wonder drugs" under such familiar names as penicillin, aureomycin, terramycin, tetracycline, and streptomycin, have proved very useful since World War II in treating numerous infectious diseases. Produced biologically, however, these drugs tend to vary greatly in their quality and potency unless developed, and thereafter tested, under very carefully controlled conditions. Consequently, Congress enacted § 507 of the Food, Drug, and Cosmetic Act, directing the Secretary of Health, Education, and Welfare to promulgate regulations establishing such standards of identity, potency, quality, and purity as necessary to ensure the "safety" and "efficacy" of those antibiotics. At present, more than 30 antibiotic drugs are listed with accompanying regulations covering more than 700 pages in the Code of Federal Regulations.

With the proliferation of the various types of antibiotics, doctors found a need for a screening test to help choose which antibiotic to use in treating a particular infection. A diffusion test, using antibiotic sensitivity discs like the one in question here, soon became a widely employed screening method. In this test, a round paper disc, which has been impregnated with a specific antibiotic, is placed in contact with sample cultures, or isolates, of a patient's virus, grown in a special culture medium (agar) from a specimen of the patient's fluid (blood, spinal fluid, sputum, urine, etc.). In those places impregnated with an antibiotic to which the patient's infection is sensitive, no new isolate will grow, leaving a clear area (an "inhibition zone"); in those places impregnated with a drug to which the infection is resistant, the isolate will grow, leaving no clear area. The disc is used, in conjunction with a patient's specimen, in laboratory work exclusively, and never comes in contact with any part of the patient's body itself.

The discs had been in general use for some four years when, in 1960, the Secretary of Health, Education, and Welfare determined to regulate them pursuant to § 507. After notice and an opportunity for public participation, the Commissioner of Food and Drugs, under authority delegated by the Secretary, promulgated regulations requiring pre-clearance, batch-testing, and certification of antibiotic sensitivity discs. The Commissioner's action, the regulations noted, followed "numerous complaints by the medical profession, hospitals, and laboratory technicians" and a resulting extensive survey of the use of the discs. That study found the discs unreliable in their statements of potency with resulting loss of safety and efficacy, and thus found it "vital for the protection of the public health" to adopt the regulations (25 Fed. Reg. 9370).

This case arose in May 1962 as an in rem seizure proceeding against an interstate shipment of a number of cases of sensitivity discs, manufactured by Difco Laboratories, Inc., under the trade name of "Bacto–Unidisk." In condemning the product pursuant to § 301 et seq. of the Food, Drug, and Cosmetic Act, the United States claimed, inter alia, that the product, as a "drug" within the meaning of the Act, had not been certified nor exempted from certification as required by § 507 and the regulations thereunder and was therefore misbranded under § 502. The seizure was proper only if the Secretary's regulations subjecting the discs to the pre-market clearance requirements were authorized by the Act. Since the scope of the Secretary's pre-market regulatory power over antibiotic drugs under § 507 depends ultimately on the Act's general definition of "drug" in § 201(g), the validity of the disc regulations allegedly violated turned on the coverage of the drug definition:

> For the purposes of this chapter—
>
> (g)(1) The term "drug" means (A) articles recognized in the official United States Pharmacopoeia, official Homeopathic Pharmacopoeia of the United States, or official National Formulary, or any supplement to any of them; and (B) articles intended for use in the diagnosis, cure, mitigation, treatment, or prevention of disease in man or other animals; and (C) articles (other than food) intended to affect the structure

> or any function of the body of man or other animals; and (D) articles intended for use as a component of any article specified in clauses (A), (B), or (C) of this paragraph; but does not include devices or their components, parts, or accessories.

If, on the other hand, the product was a "device," only the misbranding, adulteration, and labeling provisions of §§ 501 and 502 applied, and the Secretary's disc certification regulations were invalidly promulgated. Although a "device" expressly cannot be a "drug" under the last phrase of the drug definition above, a device is given almost a parallel definition in § 201(h):

> The term "device" ... means instruments, apparatus, and contrivances, including their components, parts, and accessories, intended (1) for use in the diagnosis, cure, mitigation, treatment, or prevention of disease in man or other animals; or (2) to affect the structure or any function of the body of man or other animals.

Finally, it was established at trial that of the various definitions given above, the operative ones in this case were § 201(g)(1)(B) of the drug provision and § 201(h)(1) of the parallel device definition; the essential question underlying the validity of the regulations, then, was whether the Bacto–Unidisks were "articles intended for use in the diagnosis, cure, mitigation, treatment, or prevention of disease in man or other animals." * * *

Although there was some testimony below debating the precise extent of the public health dangers posed by the sensitivity discs, the courts below declined to substitute their judgment for that of the Commissioner of Food and Drugs by determining whether his action was really necessary to protect the public health from a purely medical viewpoint. Rather, the courts below quite properly confined the inquiry to an examination of whether the disc regulations, even if medically unwise, were authorized by the Act, and more specifically, by the Act's definition of "drug." * * *

Respondent's primary contention here is that the sensitivity discs are not subject to any of the provisions of the Act because Congress did not intend it to cover articles used so indirectly in the "cure, mitigation, (and) treatment" of disease. Respondent uses the same two-step analysis relied on by the courts below: (1) Congress did not intend to write the drug definition more broadly than does the medical profession, and (2) the medical concept of drug is limited to articles that are administered to man either internally or externally. Alternatively, respondent argues, even if the Act's "intended for use" language does cover the discs, they must clearly be classified as devices. In view of the legislative history discussed below and the broad, remedial purpose of the Act itself, however, we hesitate to give the critical language such a narrow, restrictive reading in the absence of congressional direction to do so, and we therefore reject the contention that the discs do not properly fall within the purview of the Act. For the same basic reasons, we furthermore reject the argument that the discs, once found to come under the Act's coverage, must be classified specifically as devices and not drugs.

We need not stop to parse the language of the Act's definition of drug, for the district court found, and the parties do not disagree here, that a literal reading of the words "intended for use in the . . . cure, mitigation, (or) treatment" of disease "clearly has application" to the Bacto–Unidisk. Although respondent again urges that the disc itself does not "treat" a patient in the same way an antibiotic does in terms of personal application, the disc plays at least some role in the selection of the appropriate drug. Thus, the essential question for our determination is whether Congress intended the definition of drug to have the broad coverage the courts below and the parties agree its words allow. Viewing the structure, the legislative history, and the remedial nature of the Act, we think it plain that Congress intended to define "drug" far more broadly than does the medical profession. The reason for including a separate, almost parallel, definition of "devices" in the Act is, as the legislative history shows, relevant to congressional intent. It is therefore helpful to consider both the question of the Act's initial application and the question of the drug-device dichotomy at the same time. * * *

[T]he word "drug" is a term of art for the purposes of the Act, encompassing far more than the strict medical definition of that word. If Congress had intended to limit the statutory definition to the medical one, it could have so stated explicitly, or simply have made reference to the official United States Pharmacopoeia (or the National Formulary), as it did in the first of the three subsections of § 201(g)(1), and let the definition rest there. The historical expansion of the statute's definition, furthermore, clearly points out Congress' intention of going beyond the medical usage. * * *

The enactment of the 1938 Federal Food, Drug, and Cosmetic Act illustrates the expansion of the definition of drug. One of the changes contemplated in S. 2800, an early version of the Act, defined "drug" to include

> (1) all substances and preparations recognized in the United States Pharmacopoeia, Homeopathic Pharmacopoeia of the United States, or National Formulary or supplements thereto; and (2) all substances, preparations, and devices intended for use in the cure, mitigation, treatment, or prevention of disease in man or other animals; and (3) all substances and preparations, other than food, and all devices intended to affect the structure or any function of the body.

Senator Copeland of New York, who sponsored the Act, remarked about the inclusion of the word "devices" in his prepared statement introducing S. 2800 as follows:

> The present law defines drugs as substances or mixtures of substances intended to be used for the cure, mitigation, or prevention of disease. This narrow definition permits escape from legal control of all therapeutic or curative devices like electric belts, for example. It also permits the escape of preparations which are intended to alter the structure or some function of the body, as, for example, preparations intended to reduce excessive weight. There are many worthless and

some dangerous devices and preparations falling within these classifications. S. 2800 contains ample authority to control them.

The definition was revised in S. 5, 74th Cong., 1st Sess. (1935), to include substances, preparations, and devices intended for diagnostic purposes, as well as for cure, mitigation, treatment, or prevention of disease. As the inclusion of the word "diagnosis" came before the Senate for consideration, a controversy developed on the floor, aimed more at the word "devices," which was not then before the Senate, than at the word "diagnosis." * * *

As a result of the criticism on the Senate floor, Senator Copeland proposed an amendment to add a definition of "device" to parallel that of drug, an amendment which was included when the bill was returned to the Senate Committee on Commerce and later agreed to by the Senate without debate. The ultimate effect of the various amendments, of course, was still to include devices under the control of the Act for the first time, the goal Senator Copeland had originally set out to achieve. As Congressman Chapman of Kentucky explained to the House after the bill had passed the Senate, "For the first time it is proposed in a bill before Congress to control therapeutic devices.... There are hundreds of worthless contrivances being sold to and used by gullible people. Suffice it to say that a fake contraption for the cure of consumption is just as serious a menace to health as is a worthless drug sold for the same disease." 80 Cong. Rec. 10,236 (1936). * * * Thus, it is clear that two parallel definitions were provided for semantic reasons only; for the purposes of the Act, the two definitions had the same effect of subjecting both drugs and devices to the adulteration and misbranding provisions. No practical significance to the distinction between the two words arose until the pre-market clearance provisions, similar to the certification regulations for antibiotics enacted in 1945, were added after a drug tragedy in the fall of 1937.[17] The excepting clause of § 201(g)(1), stating clearly that a drug cannot be a device, was also added in 1938.*

The historical expansion of the definition of drug, and the creation of a parallel concept of devices, clearly show, we think, that Congress fully intended that the Act's coverage be as broad as its literal language indicates—and, equally clearly, broader than any strict medical definition might otherwise allow. Strong indications from legislative history that Congress intended the broad coverage the district court thought "ridiculous" should satisfy us that the lower courts erred in refusing to apply the Act's language as written. But we are all the more convinced that we must give effect to congressional intent in view of the well-accepted principle that remedial legislation such as the Food, Drug, and Cosmetic Act is to be given a liberal construction consistent with the Act's overriding purpose to protect the public health * * * *

17. This was the "Elixir–Sulfanilamide" tragedy of September–October, 1937, where nearly 100 persons died as the result of consuming an untested drug.

* In 1990, Congress amended the statute to, among other things, delete the exclusion of devices from the drug definition.

Respondent's alternative contention, that even if its product does fall within the purview of the Act, it is plainly a "device" and therefore by definition necessarily not a "drug," must also be rejected, we believe, in light of the foregoing analysis. At the outset, it must be conceded that the language of the statute is of little assistance in determining precisely what differentiates a "drug" from a "device": to the extent that both are intended for use in the treatment, mitigation and cure of disease, the former is an "article" and the latter includes "instruments," "apparatus," and "contrivances." Despite the obvious areas of overlap in definition, we are not entirely without guidance in determining the propriety of the Secretary's decision below, given the overall goals of the Act and its legislative history.

More specifically, as we have previously held in an analogous situation where the statute's language seemed insufficiently precise, the "natural way" to draw the line "is in light of the statutory purpose." Since the patient will tend to derive less benefit and perhaps some harm from a particular antibiotic if, though the drug itself was properly batch-tested, it was not the proper antibiotic to use, it was entirely reasonable for the Secretary to determine that the discs, like the antibiotics they serve, are drugs and similarly subject to pre-clearance certification under § 507. An opposite conclusion might undercut the value of testing the antibiotics themselves, for such testing would be a useless exercise if the wrong drug were ultimately administered * * * as the result of an unreliable disc.

Furthermore, the legislative history, read in light of the statute's remedial purpose, directs us to read the classification "drug" broadly, and to confine the device exception as nearly as is possible to the types of items Congress suggested in the debates, such as electric belts, quack diagnostic scales, and therapeutic lamps, as well as bathroom weight scales, shoulder braces, air conditioning units, and crutches. In upholding the Secretary's determination here, without deciding the precise contours of the "device" classification, we need only point out that the exception was created primarily for the purpose of avoiding the semantic incongruity of classifying as drugs (1) certain quack contraptions and (2) basic aids used in the routine operation of a hospital—items characterized more by their purely mechanical nature than by the fact that they are composed of complex chemical compounds or biological substances. Finally, we are supported in the decision to uphold the FDA's determination that the sensitivity discs fall under the coverage of the Act and specifically under the drug provision thereof by the knowledge that the classification of these discs as drugs may not be as contrary to common medical usage as the district court and respondent would have us believe.[20]

---

20. See W. Dorland's Illustrated Medical Dictionary 449 (24th ed., 1965), where "drug" is defined as: "Any chemical compound or any non-infectious biological substance, not used for its mechanical properties, which may be administered to or used on or for patients, either human or animal, as an aid in the diagnosis, treatment or prevention of disease or other abnormal condition, for the relief of pain or suffering, or to control or improve any physiological or pathological condition."

In upholding the Secretary's construction of the Act, we are not unmindful of our warning that "[i]n our anxiety to effectuate the congressional purpose of protecting the public, we must take care not to extend the scope of the statute beyond the point where Congress indicated it would stop." 62 Cases of Jam v. United States, 340 U.S. 593, 600 (1951). Our holding here simply involves an obvious corollary to that principle, that we must take care not to narrow the coverage of a statute short of the point where Congress indicated it should extend.

United States v. Article of Drug . . . Ova II

414 F.Supp. 660 (D.N.J.1975), aff'd mem., 535 F.2d 1248 (3d Cir.1976).

■ BIUNNO, DISTRICT JUDGE:

This case involves the question whether a kit of chemicals and equipment, marketed in interstate commerce by Faraday Laboratories, Inc. under the name "Ova II," is a "drug" within the meaning of the Federal Food, Drug and Cosmetic Act. The kit is marketed with literature indicating its use for the purpose of performing, in the home, a "preliminary screening test" by which a human female, having some reason to suspect that she may be pregnant, may obtain an indication of probability that she is or is not pregnant. The United States (FDA) filed a complaint for forfeiture and condemnation of several thousand kits seized within the jurisdiction of the court, and Faraday, as claimant, resists that action. * * * Both sides agree that if it comes within any of the definitions of a "drug," it is also a "new drug" as defined by 21 U.S.C. § 321(p), and may not be marketed in interstate commerce without first filing a "new drug application" on the basis of which FDA determines that it is "safe and effective," 21 U.S.C. § 355. * * *

Turning to the Ova II kit, the facts are that it consists of two glass vials, and two bottles of solutions. Bottle A contains a solution of hydrochloric acid (HCl). Bottle B contains a solution of sodium hydroxide (NaOH). Use of the kit involves taking a quantity of fresh urine and reacting it with both solutions in the two vials, with differences between them in respect to the number of drops added and the time sequence of the addition. The presence or absence of distinct visual differences in the darkness of the two quantities of urine so treated forms the basis for the indication (distinct differences of color indicates absence of pregnancy, essentially similar color and saturation indicates pregnancy). This test is in glass, outside the body, using body fluids available by ordinary bodily processes (i.e., "in vitro" to use the technical term). The test does not involve the injection or ingestion of any material in the human body itself (i.e., "in vivo").

Items which are "drugs" as contemplated by the statute fall into two major functional categories. One such category is the "diagnostic" function. The other is the "treatment" function, in the broadest sense that embraces prevention and alleviation of pain or discomfort as well as "cure." Those items related to the treatment function are necessarily "in vivo." Something must be done, or applied to or placed within the body itself to provide treatment. At least in this country, treatment outside the body, as by inserting pins in a doll, is not considered to be treatment. Those items related to the diagnostic function may be either "in vivo" or "in vitro." The test of a urine sample for the presence of sugar is "in vitro," and is a means for diagnosing the disease of diabetes. The presence of certain enzymes in the blood, with the test performed "in vitro" may indicate heart disease in the form of a myocardial infarction. On the other hand, the Schick Test, which involves the intradermal injection of a dilute toxin, is an "in vivo" diagnostic procedure to determine susceptibility or immunity to diphtheria. Similarly, scratch tests which involve the tearing of the skin surface and the application of allergens are another example of "in vivo" diagnostic procedures for allergies and sensitivity to various substances. * * *

In the ordinary sense of the word "drugs," it would be rational to limit its meaning to items used or applied for diagnostic purposes to those employed "in vivo" and not for those employed "in vitro." There can be little question that for the entire array, this distinction will usually be valid. But an overlap between these two areas arises by reason of the decision in *United States v. An Article of Drug . . . Bacto–Unidisk*, 394 U.S. 784 (1969). * * * Careful analysis of all the opinions in the case indicates that this conclusion reached to the outer boundaries of what might be found to be encompassed by the definition "drug." The fundamental rationale of the conclusion rests on the context within which the disc was used. The activating circumstances would necessarily involve the existence of a patient known to be ill, i.e., suffering from a disease, and that an infection was involved. Also involved is the circumstance that the identity of the infecting organism was not known. Without an item like the disc, a treating physician might be obliged to try one antibiotic after another, by way of "challenge and response" to find out what treatment would be effective. The disc, which applied a whole spectrum of antibiotics to a cultured specimen of the infected material offered a diagnostic tool for simultaneous testing of what would be effective.

On the face of the statutory language, the disc doubtless fell more clearly within the exception of a "device" carved out of the definition of a "drug." At best, the question was on the edges of the outer boundaries. The Supreme Court accepted a generous and broad construction, no doubt influenced by the life-and-death risks involved in achieving a correct diagnosis to identify the specific infection at the earliest possible moment, so that effective treatment might begin without avoidable delay. Considerations of like nature are non-existent here. The condition of pregnancy, as such, is a normal physiological function of all mammals and cannot be considered a disease of itself. Pregnancy is an execution of an inherent bodily function and implies no ailment, illness or disease. * * * A test for pregnancy, then, is not a test for the diagnosis of disease. It is no more than a test for news, which may be either good news or bad news depending on whether pregnancy is wanted or not. * * *

The key point is that no pregnancy test, including those recognized by FDA as not only "safe and effective" but also considered by it as the most "safe and effective" (a quality not required by the Act), is fully 100% reliable, and even if they were 100% reliable would disclose no more than that pregnancy exists or does not exist. No presently known pregnancy test is designed to or capable of differentiating between a pregnancy as such and an ailment or disease arising out of the pregnancy such as an abnormal pregnancy (i.e., tubal) or a pregnancy not indicated (i.e., in a female with hypertension or mental illness), or a disease (i.e., toxemia of pregnancy). These ailments or diseases have other symptoms, other conditions or history, and the like, that must be separately diagnosed. Neither Ova II nor any other pregnancy test attempts to do so. In the context of the issues here, the fact that there may be ailments or diseases related to pregnancy or associated with it is not an element that may be considered.

On the central question, then, the court is satisfied that there is no genuine issue on any material fact, and that Faraday is entitled to judgment as a matter of law. This determination rests on the view that the Ova II kit is not a "drug" within any rational sense that may be attributed to the term as defined. There is no dispute that FDA has the burden of persuasion. Taking each of the three definitions of a "drug," as set out in 21 U.S.C. § 321(g)(1), it is plain that the Ova II kit does not fall within any of them.

The first definition, i.e., recognition of an item in the U.S. Pharmacopeia, National Formulary, etc., cannot be taken literally. In the first place, none of these compendium publications is more than a privately sponsored set of standards of strength and purity, for medicinal use, which may properly carry labeling such as "U.S.P." or "N.F.," and the like. The overwhelming mass of items for which there are monographs are substances or chemicals whose use for medicinal purposes calls for a high degree of adherence to uniform standards of strength and purity. * * *

These compendiums and pharmacopeiae, being privately published, make changes from time to time. And thus the question arises whether they can have the force of law without running afoul of the principle that a legislative body may not lawfully delegate its functions to a private citizen or organization. Limited delegation of legislative functions to governmental agencies within the boundaries of an expressed norm, standard or guide is well recognized; but a delegation to private groups, and without such boundaries, is quite another matter. * * *

Since the Congress will not be presumed to have enacted an invalid statute, the first definition, i.e., recognition in the U.S.P. or other named compendium must be read [more narrowly] * * * * Under this interpretation, the Ova II kit is not a drug under 21 U.S.C. § 321(g)(1)(A), despite the fact that it contains sodium hydroxide and hydrochloric acid, since it is not labeled "U.S.P." etc., and is not marketed for medicinal use.

The second definition, namely articles related to the diagnosis of disease, etc., does not apply to the Ova II kit because its purpose is to indicate the existence or non-existence of pregnancy, which is not of itself a disease, and because no other pregnancy test attempts or purports to do anything more than Ova II does. The third definition, articles intended to affect the structure or any function of the body is obviously not applicable to any article which is used "in vitro," and in no way inserted in, injected in, ingested by or applied to the body. * * * In arriving at these conclusions and determinations, the court has not considered the implications of pending legislation, such as S.510, passed by the U.S. Senate on April 17, 1975 even though it would define a "device" as embracing in vitro reagents intended for use in the diagnosis of "conditions" (i.e., pregnancy), other than disease. * * * Summary judgment will be entered accordingly in favor of Faraday.

NOTES AND QUESTIONS

1. *Drugs vs. devices*. In *Bacto–Unidisk*, the Court cited a lower court decision upholding the FDA's decision to classify a ligature product (using nylon suture material to tie off blood vessels during surgery) as drugs rather than devices. See AMP Inc. v. Gardner, 275 F.Supp. 410 (S.D.N.Y. 1967), aff'd, 389 F.2d 825 (2d Cir.1968); see also Jay M. Zitter, Annotation, What Is "Drug" Within Meaning of § 201(g)(1) of Federal Food, Drug, and Cosmetic Act, 127 A.L.R. Fed. 141 (1995 & 2011 Supp.). For a contemporary version of antibiotic sensitivity discs, consider the following technology: a gene sequencing test for HIV designed to help physicians select from more than a dozen AIDS drugs those to which the patient's particular virus is least likely to develop resistance. See Andrew Pollack, When Gene Sequencing Becomes a Fact of Life, N.Y. Times, Jan. 17, 2001, at C1. Is this a drug? Could the FDA assert jurisdiction over a textbook on antibiotic therapies because it too is intended for use in the treatment of patients (and, if the information is incorrect, it would defeat the purpose of demanding pre-clearance of antibiotics)? Finally, notwithstanding the judge's attempt in *Ova II* to distinguish *Bacto–Unidisk*, might antibiotic sensitivity discs (or newer in vitro diagnostic tools) be used to help physicians measure a patient's microbial flora—not with the intent to select a particular antibiotic but perhaps to recommend dietary changes that would promote the repopulation of the large intestine with beneficial bacteria after a course of antibiotics for an infection? Cf. Rick Weiss, Legion of Little Helpers in the Gut Keeps Us Alive, Wash. Post, June 5, 2006, at A6 (reporting that new DNA probes have allowed researchers to identify the diverse array of intestinal microbes, and noting that in the future such testing might help physicians anticipate diseases by detecting subtle changes in the ratios of various bacteria); id. (adding that 90% of the cells in the human body are bacterial though, because they are so much smaller than human cells, they account for "only" about three pounds of body weight). Is pregnancy testing really so different?!

2. *The U.S. Pharmacopeia and National Formulary*. In a lengthy appendix to the *Ova II* opinion elaborating on the nature of pharmacopeiae, the court noted that "their status generally is not unlike that of legal publications such as the Restatements and Model Codes adopted by the American

Law Institute, or the Uniform Acts and Codes published by the Commissioner on Uniform Laws and approved by the House of Delegates of the American Bar Association." Even so, the concern that the first clause of the drug definition might represent an unconstitutional delegation of governmental authority to private parties has not troubled other courts that have faced this objection more directly. See James O. Freedman, Delegation of Power and Institutional Competence, 43 U. Chi. L. Rev. 307, 333 (1976) ("In these cases, the private party's decision to include or exclude a particular drug is invariably made according to pre-existing professional standards in order to serve a particular professional need, rather than as a response to the legislation that gives such decisions a coincidental public effect."). When it created a tax deduction for the costs of "medical care," Congress defined that phrase using language identical to the second and third clauses of the "drug" definition. See Revenue Act of 1942, § 127, 56 Stat. 798, 825–26 (codified as amended at 26 U.S.C. § 23(x)). The compendial recognition clauses in the FDCA's drug and device definitions have fallen into disuse.

3. *Structure-or-function claims.* The courts have sustained FDA enforcement actions against products such as starch blockers (made from kidney beans) or guar gum when they are marketed as weight loss aids that interfere with digestion because such claims reflect an intent to affect the structure or function of the body and trigger drug status. See American Health Prods. Co. v. Hayes, 744 F.2d 912, 913 (2d Cir.1984); Nutrilab, Inc. v. Schweiker, 713 F.2d 335, 338–39 (7th Cir.1983); United States v. Undetermined Quantities of "Cal–Ban 3000," 776 F.Supp. 249, 253–55 (E.D.N.C.1991); see also United States v. Undetermined Quantities of Bottles of an Article of Veterinary Drug, 22 F.3d 235, 239–40 (10th Cir.1994) (holding that a pet food additive containing subtherapeutic doses of an antibiotic and promoted as a way to reduce the odors resulting from intestinal bacteria qualified as a drug under both the "disease" and the "structure or function" clauses in the statutory definition); cf. E.R. Squibb & Sons, Inc. v. Bowen, 870 F.2d 678, 682–83 (D.C.Cir.1989) (noting that "the 'structure or ... function' definition, unlike the 'disease in man' definition, is relatively narrow, and was not intended to encompass all articles that might have some remote physical effect upon the body").

4. *Drugs vs. cosmetics.* Courts have sustained FDA enforcement actions against cosmetic products as unapproved new drugs when accompanied by claims that they affect the structure or function of the body. See United States v. An Article of Drug ... "Line Away," 415 F.2d 369, 372 (3d Cir.1969) (finding drug connotations in advertising claims for skin lotion containing bovine albumin); United States v. An Article ... Sudden Change, 409 F.2d 734, 739–42 (2d Cir.1969) (holding that a "face lift without surgery" claim for a lotion that had only a temporary physiological effect on the skin triggered drug status because some gullible consumers might take it literally); United States v. Kasz Enter., Inc., 855 F.Supp. 534, 539–40 (D.R.I.1994) (herbal shampoo marketed as promoting hair growth); cf. United States v. An Article of Drug ... "Helene Curtis Magic Secret," 331 F.Supp. 912, 917 (D.Md.1971) (holding that claims that a "pure protein'' skin lotion could smooth facial wrinkles and cause an ''astringent sensation'' did not convert it into a drug). See generally Victoria Farren, Note, Removing the Wrinkle in Cosmetics and Drug Regulation: A Notice Rating System and Education Proposal for Anti–Aging Cosmeceuticals, 16 Elder L.J. 375 (2009); Amity Hartman, Note, FDA's Minimal Regulation of Cosmetics and the Daring Claims of Cosmetic Companies That Cause Consumers Economic Harm, 36 W. St. U. L. Rev. 53 (2008). In the early 1990s, a company introduced a thigh cream product containing aminophylline for topical application (aminophylline is an ingested anti-asthmatic prescription drug whose labeling warns of risks such as ventricular arrhythmias, convulsions, and death). See Pamela A. Simon et al., Skin Reactions to Topical Aminophylline, 273 JAMA 1737 (1995). Around the same time, several companies began marketing products containing alpha-hydroxy acids for reducing the appearance of wrinkles, and the FDA undertook investigations because of concerns that high concentrations could cause skin damage. See Laura A. Heymann, The Cosmetic/Drug Dilemma: FDA Regulation of Alpha–Hydroxy Acids, 52 Food & Drug L.J. 357 (1997).

5. *Intended use.* A product is regulated according to claims made for it rather than its composition. The mere presence of a chemically active substance would not satisfy this definition; the intended use of the substance must serve a diagnostic or therapeutic purpose or otherwise affect the structure or function of the body. Conversely, a chemically inert substance can qualify as a drug depending on the claims made for it. Thus, bottled water, which would normally be regulated by FDA as a food (and also by the EPA under a different statute) might be regulated (1) as a drug if labeled as a cure for cancer, (2) as a medical device (accessory) if labeled as a sterilizing agent for surgical instruments, or (3) as a cosmetic if labeled as a skin softener. See Bradley v. United States, 264 F. 79, 81–82 (5th Cir.1920) (holding that curative claims for mineral water made it a ''drug''). More plausible classification problems arise with items like toothpastes (cosmetic or drug, depending, for instance, on whether anticavity claims are made, while denture cleansers are regarded as medical devices). The intended use of a product typically is determined by its labeling and any other promotional claims made by the seller. See, e.g., United States v. Article of Drug ... B–Complex Cholinos Capsules, 362 F.2d 923, 925–26 (3d Cir.1966) (radio broadcasts); Nature Food Centres, Inc. v. United States, 310 F.2d 67, 70 (1st Cir.1962) (public lectures); V.E. Irons, Inc. v. United States, 244 F.2d 34, 44 (1st Cir.1957) (oral representations made by authorized sales distributors); United States v. General Nutrition, Inc., 638 F.Supp. 556, 563–64 (W.D.N.Y.1986) (same); Hanson v. United States, 417 F.Supp. 30, 35 (D.Minn.), aff'd, 540 F.2d 947 (8th Cir.1976).

6. *Other puzzles*. The reference to ''disease'' in the definitions of drug and device may pose difficult questions of its own. See Lars Noah, Pigeonholing Illness: Medical Diagnosis as a Legal Construct, 50 Hastings L.J. 241 (1999) [excerpted in Chap. 11(D)(3)]. The term connotes some sort of departure from normal physiological or psychological functioning. See Oxford Medical Companion 207 (1994) (''Any sickness, ailment, or departure from the generally accepted norm of good health ....''); Stedman's Medical Dictionary 492 (26th ed. 1995) (''An interruption, cessation, or disorder of body functions, systems, or organs.''). Recall that, in *Ova II*, the court rejected the FDA's argument that pregnancy qualifies as a disease. Note also that Congress added the structure-or-function clause in 1938 so that the agency could regulate weight loss products. Nowadays, of course, many in the public health community characterize obesity as a disease—indeed, one of rather large proportions. See Chap. 11(D)(3). In the course of regulating nailbiting and thumbsucking deterrents as non-prescription drug products, the FDA rejected an argument made by the sellers that these were simply bad habits rather than diseases. See 58 Fed. Reg. 46,749, 46,750 (1993).

PROBLEM #1. *THE BATTLE AGAINST BAD BREATH*

Your client has developed a new mouthwash product. It contains an antibacterial agent, but the bacteriostatic action in the mouth is entirely superficial. One of your competitors claims in labeling that its mouthwash product ''stops bad breath,'' which the FDA has accepted as a simple deodorancy claim—because it suggests that the product only masks odors—and, therefore, subject to regulation as a cosmetic. See 59 Fed. Reg. 6084, 6088 (1994). Another competitor claims in labeling that its mouthwash ''kills the germs that cause bad breath,'' which the FDA historically had allowed as making an appropriately qualified antibacterial claim also subject only to cosmetic regulation. See William Gilbertson, FDA OTC Drug Standards Versus Cosmetic Standards, 21 Drug Info. J. 379, 382 (1987). Your client, anxious to attract customers of these other well-established products, has proposed a number of items for its labeling: (1) ''contains a powerful new antimicrobial chemical;'' (2) ''kills germs,'' (3) ''fights halitosis,'' and/or (4) ''kills germs that cause the common cold.'' Could the FDA subject this product to regulation as a drug? Cf. Francesca L. Kritz, Thin Defense, Wash. Post, Sept. 21, 2004, at F3 (describing the Kleenex Anti–Viral tissue, which claims to reduce the transmission of a user's cold and flu viruses to others).

2. Dietary Supplements

As noted above, the FDA occasionally brought enforcement actions against sellers of dietary supplements by arguing that the intended use of these products fit within the ''drug'' definition. Thus, courts found that vitamins accompanied by therapeutic claims qualified as drugs. See, e.g., United States v. ''Vitasafe Formula M,'' 226 F.Supp. 266, 278 (D.N.J.1964), rev'd, 345 F.2d 864 (3d Cir.1965); see also United States v. Articles of Drug ... ''Cal's Tupelo Blossom'' ... , 344 F.2d 288, 289 (6th Cir.1965) (honey); United States v. Hohensee, 243 F.2d 367, 369–71 (3d Cir.1957) (tea). The agency also has used its food additive authority to regulate dietary supplements. See Lars Noah & Richard A. Merrill, Starting from Scratch?: Reinventing the Food Additive Approval Process, 78 B.U. L. Rev. 329, 346–49 (1998). Increasing interest in ''functional foods'' has blurred the line between traditional foods and pharmaceuticals. See Margaret W. Pressler, The New Apple a Day: Selling the Health Benefits of Enriched "Phoods," Wash. Post, June 26, 2004, at E1. Some products have recognized applications in the treatment of patients with special dietary needs, and the FDA has regulated such "medical foods" as a separate category. See 21 U.S.C. § 360ee(b)(3); Symposium, Medical Foods: Their Past, Present, and Future Regulation, 44 Food Drug Cosm. L.J. 461 (1989).

The FDCA now allows labels of food products to include limited health claims that otherwise would transform the article into a drug (e.g., foods high in calcium "may help reduce the risk of osteoporosis"). See 21 U.S.C. §§ 321(g)(1)(D), 343(r); see also United States v. Undetermined Quantities ... Exachol, 716 F.Supp. 787, 793–96 (S.D.N.Y.1989); Mara A. Michaels, Comment, FDA Regulation of Health Claims Under the Nutrition Labeling and Education Act of 1990: A Proposal for a Less Restrictive Scientific Standard, 44 Emory L.J. 319 (1995); Marc Kaufman, FDA Eases Rules on Touting Food as Healthful, Wash. Post, July 11, 2003, at A1 (reporting that the agency now allows "qualified health claims" based on weaker scientific evidence); cf. Lyndsey Layton, FDA Cracking Down on Food–Packaging Claims, Wash. Post, Mar. 4, 2010, at A8 (reporting agency objections that labeling for foods such as Cheerios, Diamond Walnuts, and POM Wonderful pomegranate juice had included unauthorized drug claims). At least initially, the agency resisted authorizing any health claims for dietary supplements.

Whitaker v. Thompson

353 F.3d 947 (D.C.Cir.2004).

■ WILLIAMS, SENIOR CIRCUIT JUDGE:

* * * Dr. Julian Whitaker and others [petitioned the FDA in 1999] to approve their intended marketing of "saw palmetto," an extract from the pulp and seed of the dwarf American palm, *Serenoa repens*, under a label that they argued was a "health claim." Whitaker proposed a label stating: "Consumption of 320 mg daily of Saw Palmetto extract may improve urine flow, reduce nocturia and reduce voiding urgency associated with mild benign prostatic hyperplasia (BPH)." BPH is a non-cancerous enlargement of the prostate that affects almost half of men over 50.

The FDA denied the petition. In explaining the decision, it drew a distinction between claims regarding use of a product to maintain health and to "prevent" disease, on the one hand, and claims that a product could "treat" a disease, on the other. The former could qualify as "health claims," but the latter would always be considered "drug claims." As BPH is classified as a disease despite its comparative ubiquity, and the proposed label indicated an intent to treat it, the FDA decided that saw palmetto could not be marketed under that label without approval as a drug. * * *

The general purpose of the NLEA appears to have been to allow the dissemination—subject to a regulatory approval process—of certain dietary and health information on food products without requiring that those products be regulated as drugs. Specifically, the NLEA amended the FDCA to authorize the sale of dietary supplements pursuant to "health claims" that "characterize[] the relationship of any nutrient ... to a disease or health-related condition," 21 U.S.C. § 343(r)(1)(B), so long as the dietary supplement is "subject to a procedure and standard, respecting the validity of such claim, established by regulation of the Secretary," id. § 343(r)(5)(D). Whitaker insists, with some justification, that the label he proposed fits within the plain terms of the "health claim" definition.

Thus, although the consequences of classification as a "drug claim" or a "health claim" are quite substantial, Congress has given definitions that at least partially overlap. And it has given little guidance as to how the FDA should sort out claims that seem to fit both definitions. On the one hand, as the FDA points out, the statutory definition of "dietary supplement" plainly contemplates that dietary supplements may fall under the § 321(g) definition of "drugs": it says that a dietary supplement shall be deemed to be a "food" "[e]xcept for purposes of [§ 321(g)]," which defines "drugs" and "counterfeit drugs." 21 U.S.C. § 321(ff). On the other hand, the last sentence of § 321(g)(1), which defines drugs, explicitly states that a "dietary supplement for which a [health claim under § 343(r)] is made ... is not a drug ... solely because the label or the labeling contains such a statement." Id. § 321(g)(1). * * *

The FDA gave several reasons for classifying claims regarding cure, mitigation, or treatment of an existing disease ("treatment claims") as drug claims and for exempting only health claims that concern reducing the risk of contracting a disease ("prevention claims"). First, the agency reasoned that the legislative history of the NLEA demonstrated an understanding that the health claim provision was intended for claims of prevention rather than ones of treatment. The agency noted statements in the legislative history indicating that the purpose of the health claims provision was to promote long-term health maintenance and prevention of disease, but found nothing suggesting that legislators enacting this provision contemplated treatment of a person's existing disease with dietary supplements. Indeed, all the specific examples of "health claims" mentioned in the NLEA's legislative history involved prevention rather than treatment.

Second, the FDA looked to research mandated by Congress when it adopted the NLEA. At that time Congress instructed the FDA, in adopting regulations to implement § 343(r), to investigate ten specific possible health claims, all of which involved prevention—"reduction of the risk of a chronic disease"—rather than treatment. Third, the FDA noted that the health claims provision was enacted against a backdrop of longstanding application of drug regulation to foods and dietary supplements that made treatment claims—an assertion Whitaker does not dispute. The agency inferred that Congress meant the "solely" sentence of § 321(g)(1) to preserve this practice.

Finally, the FDA invoked policy concerns to support a distinction between treatment and prevention claims. It argued that, because the health of diseased populations is particularly vulnerable, greater regulation may be justified for products intended for their consumption. Moreover, it argued that treatment claims for symptoms of a disease might lull people with those symptoms into a "false sense of security," leading them to delay a visit to a doctor that might result, for example, in a diagnosis of prostate cancer rather than BPH. Finally, in a statement looking only at possible benefits of its classification decision (and not any of the possible drawbacks), the FDA said that if products could escape regulation as drugs by qualifying as "dietary supplements" that make treatment claims, the protections of the drug approval system could be undermined and incentives to research a substance's health effects would be diminished.

None of these is a knock-down argument, and we doubt that any of them would be sufficient to overcome a strong textual or structural inference in favor of a different interpretation. Certainly there is nothing in the two statutory definitions that would obviously equate claims of "treatment" with drug claims and of "prevention" with health claims. But given our finding that the statute is ambiguous on the critical question of how to classify a claim that meets the statutory definitions both of a drug claim and of a health claim, the legislative history and statutory context invoked by FDA are enough to render its interpretation reasonable.

Whitaker also attacks the FDA's distinction between prevention and treatment claims as arbitrary and capricious. First, he argues that there is no sharp distinction between "prevention" and "treatment"; the two categories may often overlap. They may, of course, but that does not render the distinction either unworkable or irrational. The existence of dawn and dusk, as has often been said, doesn't make it absurd to distinguish between day and night. Second, Whitaker claims that the FDA failed to explain adequately how it could square its decision not to allow Whitaker's claim that saw palmetto extract alleviates symptoms of BPH with the agency's prior approval of a "health claim" that low-fat diets lower cholesterol. See 21 C.F.R. § 101.75(e)(3). But here the FDA plausibly explains that the reference to the lower cholesterol consequences of low-fat diets merely clarifies the mechanism by which heart disease is prevented; the FDA did not authorize a claim that a low-fat diet could treat hypercholesterolaemia. So the cholesterol example doesn't show an irrationality in the FDA's attempted distinction. * * *

NOTES AND QUESTIONS

1. *Health claims.* The court also rejected the petitioner's First Amendment objection to the agency's action, concluding that "it is constitutionally permissible for the FDA to use speech, in the form of labeling, to infer intent for purposes of determining that Whitaker's proposed sale of saw palmetto extract would constitute the forbidden sale of an unapproved drug." Id. at 953; see also Alliance for Natural Health U.S. v. Sebelius, 786 F.Supp.2d 1 (D.D.C.2011) (sustaining, with a couple of exceptions, the FDA's denial of a petition to allow qualified health claims linking vitamins

C and E with reductions in the risk of various cancers); Margaret Gilhooley, The Impact and Limits of the Constitutional Deregulation of Health Claims on Foods and Supplements: From Dementia to Nuts to Chocolate to Saw Palmetto, 56 Mercer L. Rev. 683 (2005). Chapter 4(C) gives extended treatment to First Amendment issues. Although some research is emerging to suggest that certain dietary supplements may have some therapeutic value, a number of other supplements seem to represent a return to the era of snake oil. See Franklin G. Miller et al., Ethical Issues Concerning Research in Complementary and Alternative Medicine, 291 JAMA 599 (2004); Charles A. Morris & Jerry Avorn, Internet Marketing of Herbal Products, 290 JAMA 1505 (2003); January W. Payne, When Put to the Test, Americans' Most Trusted Supplements Failed, Wash. Post, June 20, 2006, at F1; Lindsey Tanner, Many Go on Taking Discredited Remedies, Seattle Times, Feb. 27, 2006, at A5 (reporting that studies have found no therapeutic value to glucosamine, chondroitin, saw palmetto, echinacea, St. John's wort, or shark cartilage); David Templeton, FDA Wants Disputed Eggs to Stay off the Table, Pitt. Post–Gazette, May 18, 2006, at A1 (reporting that the agency secured convictions against sellers of powdered eggs from vaccinated chickens sold as dietary supplements but with numerous therapeutic claims); see also FTC v. National Urological Group, Inc., 645 F.Supp.2d 1167 (N.D.Ga.2008) (sustaining charges of deceptive advertising for dietary supplements), aff'd mem., 356 F.App'x 358 (11th Cir. 2009); Cassandra B. Robertson, Separating Snake Oil from Therapeutic Supplements: The Nexus Between Litigation and Regulation in the Dietary Supplement Industry, 35 U. Tol. L. Rev. 317 (2003) (recommending in part greater use of state consumer protection laws).

2. *Deregulating market introduction.* In the early 1990s, the FDA seriously began to consider broad-based rulemaking to deal with the growing market for dietary supplements. See 58 Fed. Reg. 33,690 (1993). In its infinite wisdom, Congress quickly reacted to the FDA's announcement (and aggressive lobbying by supplement manufacturers and consumers) by exempting such products from all but the most basic statutory requirements. In 1994, Congress enacted the Dietary Supplement Health and Education Act (DSHEA), Pub. L. No. 103–417, 108 Stat. 4325, in order to limit the agency's power to regulate dietary supplements as either food additives or new drugs. Although most commentators have criticized at least some aspects of DSHEA, a few vigorously defend its deregulatory approach as promoting consumer autonomy. See Michael H. Cohen, U.S. Dietary Supplement Regulation: Belief Systems and Legal Rules, 11 Hastings Women's L.J. 3 (2000); Joshua H. Beisler, Note, Dietary Supplements and Their Discontents: FDA Regulation and the Dietary Supplement Health and Education Act of 1994, 31 Rutgers L.J. 511 (2000).

3. *DSHEA's safe harbors.* In part, DSHEA grew out of the FDA's initial resistance to approving any health claims for dietary supplements as authorized by the NLEA in 1990. Congress therefore reminded the agency to issue regulations allowing supplement companies to make health claims that otherwise would trigger drug status. More significantly, DSHEA authorized structure-or-function claims for dietary supplements so long as they included certain disclaimers. See 21 U.S.C. §§ 343(r)(6), 343–2; see also Laura A.W. Khatcheressian, Regulation of Dietary Supplements: Five Years of DSHEA, 54 Food & Drug L.J. 623 (1999). Popular supplements now include gingko biloba (memory), glucosamine chondroitin ("may help promote healthy joints"), St. John's Wort (mental well-being), and echinacea ("may help promote a healthy immune system"). The agency had proposed broadening a definition of the term "disease" in connection with its rules governing dietary supplement labeling, apparently in an attempt to narrow the range of structure-or-function claims that Congress had exempted from drug regulation. See 63 Fed. Reg. 23,624, 23,626 (1998); see also 72 Fed. Reg. 29,337 (2007) (announcing the availability of a draft guidance entitled "Complementary and Alternative Medicine Products and Their Regulation by the FDA").

United States v. Lane Labs–USA, Inc.

324 F.Supp.2d 547 (D.N.J.2004).

■ BASSLER, DISTRICT JUDGE:

* * * Lane Labs sells the products at issue in this action directly to consumers, both in and outside of New Jersey, through Lane Labs' CompassioNet division. BeneFin is a product distributed in either powder or caplet form, containing shark cartilage. MGN–3, distributed in capsule form, is a polysaccharide dietary fiber formula made from rice bran (hemicellulose B) that is produced by the hydrolysis of rice bran with the enzymatic extract of Shiitake mushroom. The main ingredient in MGN–3 is arabinoxylan. SkinAnswer is a skin cream that is applied topically and labeled as containing glycoalkaloid, an extract of sand brier. * * *

William Lane, Ph.D. is defendant Andrew Lane's father and has worked as a paid consultant for Lane Labs since at least 1997. * * * Dr. Lane has written a myriad of articles, books, papers and pamphlets and has participated in interviews in which he touted the positive effects of BeneFin, SkinAnswer and MGN–3. Many of these sources are available to consumers over the Internet. Specifically, Dr. Lane has promoted shark cartilage, particularly BeneFin, as an effective treatment for cancer. Dr. Lane has claimed glycoalkaloids, such as SkinAnswer, are safe and effective treatments for skin cancer. Dr. Lane has also made assertions that MGN–3 is a safe and effective treatment for cancer and Human Immunodeficiency Virus (HIV).

In addition to the many articles Dr. Lane has written on the alleged benefits of the products, he has co-authored three books on shark cartilage as an effective treatment for cancer—*Sharks Don't Get Cancer*, *Sharks Don't Get Cancer: How Shark Cartilage Could Save Your Life*, and *Sharks Still Don't Get Cancer: The Continuing Story of Shark Cartilage Therapy*. Dr. Lane has also produced one videotape on the same subject, *Shark Cartilage: A Promise Kept*, and one book on how glycoalkaloid cream can help treat skin cancer, *The Skin Cancer Answer*.

The government claims that part of Dr. Lane's role as a paid consultant for Lane Labs has been to promote the products as treatments for cancer and HIV through his position as "researcher-spokesperson." The government further argues that the relationship between Lane Labs and Dr. Lane is so closely intertwined and financially mutually beneficial that any claims about the products made by Dr. Lane may be attributed to defendants. However, defendants contend that Dr. Lane has been compensated by Lane Labs only for his "critical" role in discovering the existence of the products and forming business relationships with various distributors * * * *

Mamdooh Ghoneum, Ph.D. has also worked closely with Lane Labs. Dr. Ghoneum is an Associate Professor and Chief of Research in the Department of Otolaryngology at Charles D. Drew University. Dr. Ghoneum is one of the leading researchers of MGN–3. He has written many scientific abstracts and articles summarizing his research findings and discussing MGN–3 as a possible effective treatment for cancer, HIV and Acquired Immune Deficiency Syndrome (AIDS). Lane Labs has an agreement with Dr. Ghoneum such that defendants pay Dr. Ghoneum a royalty of 9.5 percent for every kilogram of MGN–3 that Lane Labs purchases from Daiwa, the Japanese distributor. * * *

The government asserts that Dr. Ghoneum's role in Lane Labs' business has been that of "researcher-spokesperson." The government contends defendants purposefully and consistently link the products with statements, articles and research by Dr. Ghoneum through promotional mailings, the Internet, and statements by defendants' employees. Therefore, the government argues that the promotional claims made by Dr. Ghoneum may also be attributed to defendants. * * * Defendants point to Dr. Ghoneum's deposition testimony in which he testified that Lane Labs had no control over the content of his writing or research. Defendants also highlight that much of Dr. Ghoneum's research was published prior to 1998, before he had any financial relationship with Lane Labs. * * *

In 1994, Congress amended the FDCA by enacting DSHEA, which established a new regulatory category for dietary supplements. The DSHEA amendments to the FDCA distinguish drugs from dietary supplements. Pursuant to DSHEA, the term "dietary supplement" is defined as:

> [A] product (other than tobacco) intended to supplement the diet that bears or contains one or more of the following dietary ingredients: (A) a vitamin; (B) a mineral; (C) an herb or other botanical; (D) an amino acid; (E) a dietary substance for use by man to supplement the diet by increasing the total dietary intake; or (F) a concentrate, metabolite, constituent, extract, or combination of any ingredient described in clause (A), (B), (C), (D), or (E).

21 U.S.C. § 321(ff)(1). One purpose of DSHEA was "to narrow the reach of the FDA's preauthorization scheme out of concern over excessive regulation of dietary supplements and the suppression of truthful information." Nutritional Health Alliance v. Shalala, 144 F.3d 220, 224 (2d Cir.1998). * * *

DSHEA expanded the types of claims dietary supplement manufacturers are permitted to place on their products without first obtaining approval from the FDA. The type of claims allowed by DSHEA include: (1) statements asserting "a benefit related to a classical nutrient deficiency disease and disclos[ing] the prevalence of such disease in the United States"; (2) statements commonly known as "structure-function claims" that "describe the role of a nutrient or dietary ingredient intended to affect the structure or function in humans [and] characterize the documented mechanism by which a nutrient or dietary ingredient acts to maintain such structure or function"; and (3) declarations of "general well-being from consumption of a nutrient or dietary ingredient." 21 U.S.C. § 343(r)(6)(A).

These types of claims are permissible under DSHEA only if the manufacturer of the dietary supplement has "substantiation" that the "statement is truthful and not misleading" and if the label contains the following disclaimer in boldface type: "This statement has not been evaluated by the Food and Drug Administration. This product is not intended to diagnose, treat, cure, or prevent any disease." Id. § 343(r)(6)(B)–(C). Although DSHEA permits these three types of claims without preapproval from the FDA, manufacturers are specifically prohibited from making any claim that the dietary supplement diagnoses, mitigates, treats, cures or prevents a specific disease or class of diseases. "If the manufacturer of a dietary supplement proposes to make [such] a statement . . . in the labeling of the dietary supplement, the manufacturer shall notify the Secretary no later than 30 days after the first marketing of the dietary supplement with such statement that such a statement is being made." Id. § 343(r)(6).

DSHEA also permits natural products companies to publicize the health benefits of dietary supplements without prior FDA approval. Under DSHEA's exemption for "third-party literature," manufacturers may, "in connection with the sale of a dietary supplement," provide consumers with publications such as articles, books or abstracts from scientific publications. This type of material is not defined as labeling under the statute when it is used in connection with the sale of a dietary supplement to consumers and it:

(1) is not false or misleading;

(2) does not promote a particular manufacturer or brand of a dietary supplement;

(3) is displayed or presented, or is displayed or presented with other such items on the same subject matter, so as to present a balanced view of the available scientific information on a dietary supplement;

(4) if displayed in an establishment, is physically separate from the dietary supplements; and

(5) does not have appended to it any information by sticker or any other method.

Id. § 343–2(a). Assuming these five provisions are met, third-party literature provided to consumers regarding the health benefits of dietary supplements is permissible.

Notwithstanding DSHEA's attempt to clarify the types of claims dietary supplement manufacturers may make without FDA approval, some confusion arises when the language of § 343(r)(6) is compared to that of § 321(g)(1). Section 321(g)(1)(C) defines drugs as "articles (other than food) intended to affect the structure or any function of the body of man or other animals." However, pursuant to § 343(r)(6)(A) of DSHEA, manufacturers of dietary supplements may make structure-function claims describing how a particular nutrient or dietary supplement is "intended to affect the structure or function in humans." From this language alone it is unclear how a dietary supplement may make a permissible structure-function claim pursuant to DSHEA without falling under FDCA's definition of a drug.

Section 321(g)(1) further explains these seemingly contradictory provisions.

> A food or dietary supplement for which a claim, subject to sections 343(r)(1)(B) and 343(r)(3) of this title or sections 343(r)(1)(B) and 343(r)(5)(D) of this title, is made in accordance with the requirements of section 343(r) of this title is not a drug solely because the label or the labeling contains such a claim. A food, dietary ingredient, or dietary supplement for which a truthful and not misleading statement is made in accordance with section 343(r)(6) of this title is not a drug under clause (C) solely because the label or the labeling contains such a statement.

Therefore, it does not follow that a product with a label that makes a permissible structure-function claim pursuant to § 343(r)(6)(A) is necessarily a drug under the definition in § 321(g)(1)(C). As long as the claim is "truthful and not misleading" under § 321(g)(1), and under a similar provision in § 343(r)(6)(B), manufactures of dietary supplements may make claims about how the supplement affects the structure or function of the body.

However, given that § 343(r)(6) does specifically preclude manufacturers from claiming that a product diagnoses, mitigates, treats, cures, or prevents a specific disease or class of diseases, any claim of this sort necessarily places that product under the scope of the FDCA's definition of a drug. See 21 U.S.C. § 321(g)(1) (presenting an alternative definition of drugs as "articles intended for use in the diagnosis, cure, mitigation, treatment, or prevention of disease"). * * *

[T]he issue before this court is not, as defendants contend, Lane Labs' subjective intent in marketing the products. Rather, the "intended use" referred to within the FDCA framework contemplates "the objective intent of those persons legally responsible for the labeling of drugs." 21 C.F.R. § 201.128 ("The intent is determined by such persons' expressions or may be shown by the circumstances surrounding the distribution of the article."). Various other courts, when considering similar FDCA enforcement actions, have upheld this objective standard. E.g., United States v. Kasz Enterprises, Inc., 855 F.Supp. 534, 542 (D.R.I.1994) ("It is the objective intent of the vendor, not the vendor's subjective explanations and disclaimers, which determines the intended use of a product, as gleaned not only from the vendor's statements, but from any relevant source, such as promotional material, advertising, labeling and other circumstances surrounding the distribution of the article."); United States v. Storage Spaces Designated Nos. "8" & "49", 777 F.2d 1363, 1366 (9th Cir.1985) ("[I]ntent may be derived or inferred from labeling, promotional material, advertising, or any other relevant source."). * * *

In fact, many of the materials at issue in this action blatantly claimed that the given product was an effective treatment for cancer or HIV/AIDS, both of which the parties stipulate are diseases not capable of self-diagnosis or self-treatment. For example, much of the material written by Dr. Lane, including his books and the "Having My Say" article, have espoused the theory that shark cartilage is an effective treatment for cancer. Defendants have used Dr. Lane's name and picture in its packaging and have distributed his written work with the products. In addition, defendants have provided links to Dr. Lane's articles and interviews through its publishedresearch.com website.

Lane Labs has similarly distributed mailings to customers and potential customers that include articles by Dr. Ghoneum, such as "One Sizeable Step for Immunology, One Giant Leap for Cancer Patients," in which Dr. Ghoneum advocates that MGN–3 is a promising treatment for cancer and HIV/AIDS. Furthermore, defendants have used Dr. Ghoneum's endorsement on advertisements for its products, specifically MGN–3. Defendants' publishedresearch.com website also provides links to abstracts written by Dr. Ghoneum. In addition to the materials authored by Drs. Lane and Ghoneum, defendants have distributed third-party promotional literature—such as the "A New Chapter in Healing" article by Dr. Williams and the Health & Healing newsletter edited by Dr. Whitaker—that specifically make claims about the ability of the products to treat, cure, and mitigate diseases. * * *

The government argues, and this court agrees, that by claiming that the products cure and treat cancer and HIV/AIDS, the materials in question contained misleading statements. No approved or peer-reviewed studies have been conducted providing results that confirm this contention. In fact, even defendants admit that the products have not been proven to effectively treat or cure cancer or HIV/AIDS. Section 343–2(a) also mandates that permissible third-party literature may not promote a particular manufacturer or brand of a dietary supplement. This statutory provision has been repeatedly violated by defendants. As detailed above, much of the promotional literature distributed by defendants push Lane Labs' products by name, even providing pricing, ordering information, and links to Lane Labs' websites. * * *

The government correctly asserts that defendants' DSHEA arguments have no applicability to this court's determination of whether SkinAnswer has been marketed as a drug. One requirement for a product to be considered a dietary supplement is that it must be "ingested." Accordingly, the provisions of DSHEA do not apply to SkinAnswer, because it is not a dietary supplement, but rather it is cream that users apply topically. The government has provided ample evidence of the various ways defendants have marketed SkinAnswer as a treatment or cure for skin cancer. For instance, the Health Professional Information Kit distributed by defendants as late as August 2001, nearly two years after the commencement of this action, included Dr. Whitaker's Health & Healing newsletter. Dr. Whitaker not only made recommendations about using glycoalkaloids to treat skin cancer, but SkinAnswer was the glycoalkaloid product he specifically recommended. This is just one of many examples of defendants' use and distribution of third-party literature to market SkinAnswer. Given that SkinAnswer does not fall under the purview of DSHEA, defendants cannot even argue that the dissemination of these promotional materials was permissible under federal law. * * *

This court has found that the products are drugs under § 321(g)(1)(B). Since defendants have not obtained FDA approval for the products, nor have the products been proven safe and effective, nor do the products contain adequate labeling, the products are unapproved new drugs and misbranded drugs * * * *

PROBLEM #2. *JAVA JUNKIES*

Imagine that the FDA decides to tackle coffee as an unapproved new drug product (after all, caffeine is an active ingredient in products currently regulated as drugs, consumers show mild signs of addiction (i.e., symptoms of withdrawal when cutting down), and it may cause chronic health risks). See Gwendolyn Prothro, The Caffeine Conundrum: Caffeine Regulation in the United States, 27 Cumb. L. Rev. 65, 70–74 (1996); Michael Stroh, Kicking Caffeine, Balt. Sun, Nov. 5, 2004, at 1F (asserting that "caffeine is the most popular mind-altering drug in the world"). Sellers respond that they make no therapeutic (vascular headache or Parkinson's disease) or structure-or-function (wakefulness) claims, it's formulated as a traditional food product (drink) rather than as a pill, and there's no evidence of exclusive consumer use for a drug effect (many people like the taste, and it does provide calories). How would a court rule? What if the FDA instead went after energy drinks, which often contain higher doses of caffeine plus various vitamins, minerals and herbal ingredients? See Joseph G. Hoflander, Note, A Red Bull Instead of a Cigarette: Should the FDA Regulate Energy Drinks?, 45 Val. U. L. Rev. 689 (2011); Nausheen Rokerya, Note, Caffeine: The New "Energy" Crisis—The Dietary Supplement Health and Education Act of 1994 and Its Implications for Caffeine Regulation, 75 Brook. L. Rev. 627 (2009).

NOTES AND QUESTIONS

1. *Elusive intended uses.* Toward the end of its lengthy opinion, the court in *Lane Labs* made the following observation: "The government does not dispute that, had defendants complied with the FDCA from the outset, defendants could have marketed shark cartilage and arabinoxylane as dietary supplements and glycoalkaloid skin cream as a cosmetic.'' 324 F.Supp.2d at 580–81. It decided, however, that the company's past marketing infractions meant that Lane Labs could no longer sell these products even if brought into compliance with DSHEA. A different aspect of the court's order was affirmed on appeal. See United States v. Lane Labs–USA, Inc., 427 F.3d 219, 223 n.2 (3d Cir.2005). Could another entrepreneur, with no financial (or familial) connections to Dr. Lane, sell a shark cartilage supplement with labeling devoid of any problematic claims but hoping to tap into the hype about its cancer-fighting properties (in other words, does a seller's subjective intent play any role in deciding how to categorize a product)? See David Brown, FDA Warns About Fraudulent Cancer Treatments, Wash. Post, June 18, 2008, at A6 (reporting that the agency had sent warning letters to dozens of online sellers of ''shark cartilage, turmeric extract, flaxseed oil, dried mushrooms, herbal teas and irritating skin salves made from bloodroot,'' adding that ''[m]any of the products may continue to be sold as legal 'dietary supplements,' as long as claims that they can treat or prevent cancer are eliminated''). Long before enactment of DSHEA, the FDA had attempted to regulate high-dose vitamin A & D products as drugs, but the courts found no objective evidence of an intended therapeutic use. See National Nutritional Foods Ass'n v. Mathews, 557 F.2d 325 (2d Cir.1977) (holding that lack of nutritional usefulness and potential toxicity at high doses coupled with widespread use for therapeutic purposes did not convert these vitamins into drugs in the absence of claims made by the sellers).

In contrast, and notwithstanding DSHEA, a court sustained the FDA's determination that Cholestin, a product derived from red yeast rice and intended to promote healthy cholesterol levels, was an unapproved new drug because it contained a natural substance that was chemically identical to the active ingredient lovastatin in a cholesterol-lowering prescription drug (Mevacor®). See Pharmanex v. Shalala, 221 F.3d 1151 (10th Cir.2000). In another case, a court sustained the FDA's claim that a vitamin supplement sold in a noningestible form was an unapproved new drug rather than either a food or a dietary supplement: ''Although vitamin B–12 may commonly be used as a food, gels containing vitamin B–12 that are administered through the nose hardly meet the every day definition of food and are not commonly used as food, anymore than an enema containing vitamin B–12 meets the everyday definition of food.'' United States v. Ten Cartons . . . Ener–B Nasal Gel, 888 F.Supp. 381, 391, 390–98 (E.D.N.Y.), aff'd, 72 F.3d 285, 287 (2d Cir.1995) (per curiam). In one curious case, federal agents arrested individuals for selling balloons filled with nitrous oxide (laughing gas) outside of a rock concert on charges of violating the drug misbranding provisions of the FDCA, and a reviewing court accepted the government's argument that, even in the absence of any representations by the sellers, one could infer an intended use (to affect the structure or function of the body) from the totality of the circumstances surrounding the sale. See United States v. Travia, 180 F.Supp.2d 115, 119 (D.D.C.2001) (''This case is obviously unique in that, if the government's allegations are true, the sellers did not need to label or advertise their product, as the environment provided the necessary information between buyer and seller."); see also Meza v. Southern Cal. Physicians Ins. Exch., 73 Cal.Rptr.2d 91, 94 (Ct.App.1998) (concluding that melaleuca oil used by a physician to treat warts qualified as a drug even though the seller made no therapeutic claims). Some supplement manufacturers use print or broadcast advertising that mimics the format required for prescription pharmaceuticals—would that suffice to demonstrate an intended drug use?

2. *New dietary supplement ingredients.* A company wishing to sell a supplement containing a "new dietary ingredient" (defined as one not available prior to October 15, 1994) must file a notification with the FDA 75 days before market introduction, which would have to demonstrate only that "[t]here is a history of use or other evidence of safety," 21 U.S.C. § 350b(a)(2), but, if the agency found the notification inadequate, it could prevent marketing only by initiating formal enforcement proceedings. See Scott Bass & Emily Marden, The New Dietary Ingredient Safety Provision of DSHEA: A Return to Congressional Intent, 31 Am. J.L. & Med. 285 (2005); Ashish R. Talati, New Dietary Ingredient Notifications: A Comprehensive Review and Strategies for Avoiding FDA Objections, 62 Food & Drug L.J. 387 (2007).

3. *Safety concerns.* In addition to representing possible economic frauds, some dietary supplements may pose serious health hazards. See James D. Lewis & Brian L. Strom, Balancing Safety of Dietary Supplements with the Free Market, 136 Annals Internal Med. 616 (2002); Peter A.G.M. De Smet, Herbal Remedies, 347 New Eng. J. Med. 2046 (2002); Carter Anne McGowan, Note, Learning the Hard Way: L–Tryptophan, the FDA, and the Regulation of Amino Acids, 3 Cornell J.L. & Pub. Pol'y 383 (1994); Justin Gillis, Herbal Remedies Turn Deadly for Patients, Wash. Post, Sept. 5, 2004, at A1; Marc Kaufman, FDA Seeks to Halt Sales of Supplement: Agency Warns Distributors as It Reports Andro Poses Long–Term Health Risk, Wash. Post, Mar. 12, 2004, at A3; January W. Payne, Antioxidant Pills Questioned, Again, Wash. Post, Oct. 12, 2004, at F1 (describing a meta-analysis of several studies evaluating the supposed cancer prevention properties of antioxidant supplements which concluded that such products may not prevent cancer and may in fact increase the risk of death). For instance, supplements may interact dangerously with prescription drugs. See Jane Spencer, The Risks of Mixing Drugs and Herbs, Wall St. J., June 22, 2004, at D1. Contamination also poses concerns. See Robert B. Saper et al., Heavy Metal Content of Ayurvedic Herbal Medicine Products, 292 JAMA 2868 (2004) (finding contaminants (such as lead, mercury, or arsenic) in 20% of herbal products sampled, at levels sufficiently high to pose a risk of toxicity if ingested according to labeled dosing recommendations); see also 72 Fed. Reg. 34,752 (2007) (FDA's good manufacturing practice rules); Alliance for Natural Health U.S. v. Sebelius, 775 F.Supp.2d 114 (D.D.C.2011) (rejecting an industry challenge to these regulations); Richard Potomac, Comment, Are You Sure You Want to Eat That?: U.S. Government and Private Regulation of Domestically Produced and Marketed Dietary Supplements, 23 Loy. Consumer L. Rev. 54 (2010).

4. *Administrative impotence?* In the face of these questions about the safety and effectiveness of dietary supplements, a number of commentators have bemoaned the FDA's lack of regulatory authority. See, e.g., Margaret Gilhooley, Deregulation and the Administrative Role: Looking at Dietary Supplements, 62 Mont. L. Rev. 85 (2001); Stephanie Kauflin, Comment, Dietary Supplements: Is Availability Worth the Risks? Proposed Alternatives to the Present DSHEA Scheme, 33 Seton Hall L. Rev. 411 (2003); Lauren J. Sloane, Note, Herbal Garden of Good and Evil: The Ongoing Struggles of Dietary Supplement Regulation, 51 Admin. L. Rev. 323 (1999); see also Eric Lipton, Support Is Mutual for Senator and Makers of Supplements, N.Y. Times, June 21, 2011, at A1 ("[M]any public health experts argue that ... [Senator Orrin] Hatch has hindered regulators from preventing dangerous products from being put on the market ... [and] is the person in Washington most responsible for the proliferation of products that make exaggerated claims about health benefits."). After the agency finally decided to flex its purportedly atrophied muscles (in response to dangers posed by a popular class of dietary supplements), it secured a potentially important victory in the courts.

Nutraceutical Corp. v. von Eschenbach

459 F.3d 1033 (10th Cir.2006).

■ EAGAN, DISTRICT JUDGE:

* * * [Plaintiffs] manufacture and sell Ephedra, a product containing ephedrine-alkaloid dietary supplements ("EDS"). In 2004, the FDA issued a regulation which banned all EDS sales in the United States market. Nutraceutical brought this action challenging the regulation as unlawful. * * * The district court determined that the risk-benefit analysis employed by the FDA to support an EDS ban was contrary to the intent of Congress and that the FDA had failed to prove by a preponderance of the evidence that EDS pose an unreasonable risk of illness or injury at 10 milligrams or less a day. See Nutraceutical Corp. v. Crawford, 364 F.Supp.2d 1310 (D.Utah 2005). * * *

Ephedrine alkaloids are a class of structurally-related chemical stimulants that occur naturally in some botanicals. In the 1980s and 1990s, manufacturers promoted the sale of EDS for weight loss and athletic performance enhancement. In the 1990s, the FDA received numerous adverse event reports (AERs) which documented harmful side effects, including heart attacks, strokes, seizures, and death, associated with EDS intake. Based on the circumstantial evidence of the AERs, the FDA began to investigate the effects of EDS. * * *

The administrative record grew to over 130,000 pages, approximately 19,000 AERs were collected, and extensive public notice and comment resulted in over 48,000 comments. After seven years of investigating EDS, the FDA adopted a regulation which banned EDS at all dosage levels from the national market. 69 Fed. Reg. 6788 (2004). In the final rule, the FDA concluded that "[t]he best clinical evidence for a benefit ... supports only a modest short-term weight loss, insufficient to positively affect cardiovascular risk factors or health conditions associated with being overweight or obese." Id. at 6789. Based on this risk-benefit analysis, the FDA determined that all EDS present an "unreasonable risk of illness or injury" under all ordinary or recommended conditions of use. * * *

Courts are to review agency actions under DSHEA using the "traditional tools of statutory construction." Challenges by private parties to FDA rules promulgated under DSHEA are reviewed pursuant to the Administrative Procedure Act (APA) and "the normal rules for judicial deference regarding agency action apply." NVE, Inc. v. HHS, 436 F.3d 182, 196 (3d Cir.2006) [(reviewing another challenge to the EDS rule)]. * * *

In 1994, Congress enacted DSHEA to clarify that dietary supplements, absent declarations promoting the supplements as drugs, would be regulated in a manner similar to food products. Accordingly, in the interest of public health, Congress imposed a duty on the FDA to keep adulterated dietary supplements off the market. Pub. L. No. 103–417, 108 Stat. 4325, 4326 (1994) (instructing the FDA to "take swift action against [dietary supplements] that are unsafe or adulterated"). DSHEA classifies a dietary supplement as adulterated if it "presents a significant or unreasonable risk of illness or injury." 21 U.S.C. § 342(f)(1). The FDA understood "[t]he plain meaning of 'unreasonable' . . . [to] connote[] comparison of the risks and benefits of the product." 69 Fed. Reg. at 6823. We agree. The plain language of the statute directs the FDA to restrict distribution of dietary supplements which pose any risk that is unreasonable in light of its potential benefits. See Merck KGaA v. Integra Lifesciences I, Ltd., 545 U.S. 193 (2005) (unanimously finding that "unreasonable risk," as used in another FDCA provision, 21 U.S.C. § 355(i)(3)(B)(i), "involves a comparison of the risks and the benefits").

Congress enacted DSHEA in an effort to improve public access to dietary supplements based on the belief that there may be a positive relationship between dietary supplement use, reduced health-care expenses, and disease prevention. The FDCA should not be read too restrictively but in [a] manner consistent with the statute's overriding purpose to protect public health. Accordingly, DSHEA should receive a liberal construction where the FDA has taken remedial steps in response to a perceived public health problem.

According to the district court, by injecting a risk-benefit analysis, the FDA required Nutraceutical to make a showing of the benefits of its product. However, at no time has the FDA required manufacturers of EDS to provide data on the benefits of their products. Rather, the FDA has assumed its responsibility of gathering data, soliciting comments, and conducting the risk-benefit analysis.[5] Congress expressly placed the burden

5. The district court compared the language of DSHEA to the statutory language governing medical devices and drugs and concluded that, unlike manufacturers of medical devices and drugs, manufacturers of dietary supplements do not need to prove effectiveness prior to taking their product to market. The district court is correct. However, the district court confused effectiveness with safety. The FDA did not ban EDS for failing to deliver

of proof on the government to determine whether a dietary supplement is adulterated. Accordingly, EDS were allowed to enter the market without findings of safety or effectiveness. The FDA did not impose a pre-market requirement for the sale of EDS. For example, Nutraceutical has been selling EDS since 1988. As dictated by the statutory scheme, the FDA assumed the duty of post-market surveillance and imposed the EDS ban following numerous AERs, public notice and comment, and significant scientific review. * * * The burden remains on the agency to show that risks associated with a dietary supplement outweigh benefits and are, therefore, unreasonable. Thus, a risk-benefit analysis does not undermine congressional intent by improperly shifting the burden of proof onto manufacturers of dietary supplements.

Under the rules of statutory construction, courts consider the whole act and evaluate terms in context. The rule against surplusage encourages courts to give meaning to every word used in a statute to realize congressional intent. In effect, this rule embodies the belief that Congress would not have included superfluous language. Thus, in DSHEA, an "unreasonable risk" has a meaning independent from a "significant risk." The plain meaning of a "significant risk" is a great danger. "Unreasonable risk" is a distinct term and requires more than evaluation of the significance of risk. "A risk could be significant but reasonable if the benefits were great enough to outweigh the risks." 69 Fed. Reg. at 6823. In other words, an "unreasonable risk" is relative to the circumstances; the potential risk is more "unreasonable" if the potential benefit is smaller. The district court erred by conflating the terms "significant" and "unreasonable," thereby rendering "unreasonable" superfluous. In contrast to "significant risk," "unreasonable risk" accounts for whether the benefits justify the risks. The use of "unreasonable" to qualify risk in addition to "significant" makes it clear that Congress intended to integrate a risk-benefit analysis in the former. * * *

In determining that EDS pose an "unreasonable risk of illness or injury," the FDA found that the weight loss and other health benefits possible from the use of EDS were dwarfed by the potential long-term harm to the user's cardiovascular system. The agency went on to enact a complete ban on the product after making a finding that any amount of EDS had negative ramifications on the cardiovascular system and, based on the FDA's analysis, EDS provided no benefits so great as to justify such risk. * * *

The review of scientific literature is properly in the province of the FDA, to which this court grants deference based on its expertise. * * * We find that the FDA correctly followed the congressional directive to analyze the risks and benefits of EDS in determining that there is no dosage level of EDS acceptable for the market. Summary judgment for plaintiffs was therefore improper, and summary judgment for defendants should have been entered. * * *

---

promised health gains or for ineffectiveness; the FDA banned EDS because they were determined to be unsafe.

NOTES AND QUESTIONS

1. *Making it stick.* In resolving subsequent FDA enforcement actions against ephedra supplements, courts rejected collateral attacks on the rule. See United States v. 5 Unlabeled Boxes, 572 F.3d 169 (3d Cir.2009); Hi–Tech Pharms., Inc. v. Crawford, 544 F.3d 1187 (11th Cir.2008). See generally Phil B. Fontanarosa et al., The Need for Regulation of Dietary Supplements—Lessons from Ephedra, 289 JAMA 1568 (2003); Melissa Davenport, Note, Risky Business: The FDA Bans Ephedra, and Gets a Leg up on the Dietary Supplement Industry, 5 Geo. J.L. & Pub. Pol'y 635 (2007). Alternatives to ephedra appear to pose similar risks. See Christine A. Haller et al., Hemodynamic Effects of Ephedra–Free Weight–Loss Supplements in Humans, 118 Am. J. Med. 998 (2005).

2. *Beyond ephedra.* Should the tradition of giving a liberal construction to remedial legislation apply to DSHEA, and in which direction would that point here? Do you really think that this interpretation comports with the design of the Congress that enacted the statute? Does it empower the agency to crack down on other dubious dietary supplements in the future? Consider the following take on the FDA's interpretation of DSHEA's adulteration provision:

> [T]he next supplement manufacturer that faces an adulteration charge will try to argue that its purported risks are "reasonable" because the product's benefits outweigh its risks. The FDA then could choose to focus on the "significant risk" prong of the standard and claim that, whatever the product's benefits, it carries significant risks.... If supplement manufacturers manage to substantiate their permitted structure-or-function claims, then they avoid the risk of a misbranding charge because the label is accurate, but, if it also serves as a signal of potentially hazardous pharmacological activity (as suggested previously), then, in a perverse fashion, persuasive evidence of efficacy could lead to an adulteration charge under the "significant risk" provision, while leaving the manufacturer unable to defend itself on the basis of the product's usefulness. If ensnared by this "Catch–22," the manufacturer would retain the option of submitting an application for new drug approval to the FDA after first undertaking clinical trials to demonstrate its product's safety and efficacy. Of course, this avenue is precisely what dietary supplement manufacturers sought to avoid when they lobbied Congress to enact DSHEA, but, at least to the extent that these companies want to make strong claims of utility for their products, the FDA should force them to satisfy new drug approval requirements when supplements pose genuine risks to go with the promise of real therapeutic benefit.

Lars Noah, A Drug by Any Other Name ... ?: Paradoxes in Dietary Supplement Risk Regulation, 17 Stan. L. & Pol'y Rev. 165, 190 (2006); see also David Brown, FDA Signals Scrutiny of Dietary Supplements, Wash. Post, Dec. 16, 2010, at A4 ("[S]ince 2007 the agency [claims that it] has identified about 300 pharmaceutical products 'masquerading as dietary supplements.' ... Supplements sold with promises that they act quickly—

weight loss in a month, an erection within minutes—are hints that they contain pharmaceutical compounds.").

3. *Further commentary.* See Peter J. Cohen, Science, Politics, and the Regulation of Dietary Supplements: It's Time to Repeal DSHEA, 31 Am. J.L. & Med. 175 (2005); Rahi Azizi, Comment, "Supplementing" the DSHEA: Congress Must Invest the FDA with Greater Regulatory Authority over Nutraceutical Manufacturers by Amending the Dietary Supplement Health and Education Act, 98 Cal. L. Rev. 439 (2010); Andrew L.T. Green, Note, Spreading the Blame: Examining the Relationship Between DSHEA and the Baseball Steroid Scandal, 90 B.U. L. Rev. 399 (2010); Richard E. Nowak, Note, DSHEA's Failure: Why a Proactive Approach to Dietary Supplement Regulation Is Needed to Effectively Protect Consumers, 2010 U. Ill. L. Rev. 1045.

3. MEDICAL DEVICES

Alabama Tissue Center v. Sullivan

975 F.2d 373 (7th Cir.1992).

■ SHABAZ, DISTRICT JUDGE:

Six not-for-profit heart valve allograft processors filed a petition for review with this court contesting the "Notice of Applicability of a Final Rule" (NAFR) * * * stat[ing] that replacement heart valve allografts are subject to the final rule issued by the FDA on May 13, 1987, which requires the filing of a pre-market approval application (PMA) for all preamendment replacement heart valves and their equivalents. A heart valve allograft is a human heart valve which has been processed and preserved so it can be stored until needed for implantation into a human recipient. * * *

The FDC Act defines "device" as:

> [A]n instrument, apparatus, implement, machine, contrivance, implant, in vitro reagent, or other similar or related article, including any component, part, or accessory, which is—
>
> (1) recognized in the official National Formulary, or the United States Pharmacopeia, or any supplement to them,
>
> (2) intended for use in the diagnosis of disease or other conditions, or in the cure, mitigation, treatment, or prevention of disease, in man or other animals, or
>
> (3) intended to affect the structure or any function of the body of man or other animals, and
>
> which does not achieve its primary intended purposes through chemical action within or on the body of man or other animals and which is not dependent upon being metabolized for the achievement of any of its principal intended purposes.

21 U.S.C. § 321(h). * * * The 1980 regulation defines "replacement heart valves" as:

> [A] device intended to perform the function of any of the heart's natural valves. This device includes valves constructed of prosthetic materials, biologic valves (e.g., porcine valves), or valves constructed of a combination of prosthetic and biologic materials.

21 C.F.R. § 870.3925(a). * * *

In 1989, perhaps with some reason for doing so, the FDA began notifying the industry of its intent to subsequently regulate heart valve allografts, believing it to be within its authority pursuant to the prior regulation. For example, in October 1989 the Center for Devices and Radiological Health of the FDA participated in a workshop on human heart valves sponsored by the American Association of Tissue Banks. Further, on August 20 and 21, 1990, the Circulatory System Devices Panel, an advisory committee of the FDA, held a public hearing to assist the heart valve allograft processors in subsequently complying with the premarket approval. The FDA's proposed guidelines concerning the regulation of heart valve allografts were discussed at this meeting.

On June 26, 1991 the FDA published the NAFR. The summary of the NAFR states:

> The Food and Drug Administration (FDA) is issuing a notice to clarify that replacement heart valve allografts, devices, are subject to a final rule that was issued by FDA on May 13, 1987, requiring the filing of a premarket approval application (PMA) for all preamendment replacement heart valves, and those substantially equivalent to replacement heart valves. PMAs or investigational device exemptions (IDEs) will be required as described herein.

56 Fed. Reg. 29,177. * * *

Petitioners contend that a heart valve allograft is not a "device." This court, as reinforced by the Supreme Court, has allowed liberal construction of the FDC Act consistent with its purpose of protecting the public health. See United States v. 25 Cases, More or Less, of an Article of Device, 942 F.2d 1179, 1183 (7th Cir.1991). "The FDA has consistently interpreted 'device' in a very expansive manner." Id. at 1182.

Congress has provided a detailed definition of "device" at 21 U.S.C. § 321(h) to include an "implant." At issue is whether heart valve allografts are "implants." We are analyzing the term "implant" within the medical context, because our concern is with the provisions of the FDC Act which regulate medical devices. "Implant" is defined as "an object or material, such as an alloplastic or radioactive material or tissue, partially or totally inserted or grafted into the body for prosthetic, therapeutic, diagnostic, or experimental purposes." Dorland's Illustrated Medical Dictionary 824 (27th ed. 1988). Further, the act of implanting, or "implantation," is stated as:

> 2. the insertion of an organ or tissue, such as skin, nerve, or tendon, in a new site in the body.
>
> 3. the insertion or grafting into the body of biological, living, inert, or radioactive material.

Id. Heart valve allografts can reasonably be construed to be implants within these definitions. Petitioners argue that the definition of "device" was intended only to include man-made or artificial "implants." However, the ordinary meaning of "implant" does not support this argument. Further, a heart valve allograft is tissue which undergoes a cryopreservation process so that it has a considerable shelf life. Accordingly, heart valve allografts appear to be artificial "implants." We find that the FDA's interpretation of the statutory definition of "device" is permissible.

Further, petitioners contend that the definition of replacement heart valve in the 1980 regulation does not include heart valve allografts, because they are not "biologic valves." * * * The definition of "replacement heart valve" clearly encompasses matters relating to human organisms. Petitioners claim that "biologic valves" only refer to animal valves and not human valves primarily because the definition lists animal valves as an example of "biologic valves." The list and example contained in the definition are clearly not intended to be all inclusive. A reasonable inference cannot be drawn that the regulation sought to exclude human heart valve allografts particularly when such allografts have been in use for almost thirty years. Accordingly, the FDA's interpretation of its regulation is consistent with its regulation. * * *

United States v. Bowen

172 F.3d 682 (9th Cir.1999).

■ GRABER, CIRCUIT JUDGE:

Defendant repairs the SteriSafe Handpiece Sterilizer (SteriSafe), which is used to sterilize dental handpieces. He also manufactures the SteriDot High Purity Water Ampule (SteriDot), an accessory used with SteriSafe. The government brought this action, claiming that both products are adulterated * * * and that SteriDot also is misbranded in violation of the FDCA. The district court agreed and enjoined defendant from introducing into, or receiving from, interstate commerce any SteriSafes or SteriDots. * * *

Defendant argues that the district court erred by concluding that SteriSafe and SteriDot are "devices" as defined in 21 U.S.C. § 321(h). * * * Under the plain wording of the statute, an instrument that sterilizes dental handpieces satisfies the "device" requirement. Specifically, "[t]he sterilizing of a medium implies complete destruction of all germs in it." Webster's New Int'l Dictionary 2472 (unabridged 2d ed. 1954). A germ is "any microorganism, esp., any of the pathogenic bacteria; a microbe; a disease germ." Id. at 1051. Thus, a sterilization instrument's purpose is to destroy disease-causing germs. Because SteriSafe sterilizes dental handpieces, it is "an instrument . . . which is . . . intended for use in the . . . mitigation . . . or prevention of disease[] in man." Additionally, the term "device" includes any accessory to an instrument intended for use in the prevention of disease. * * *

Congress had two purposes in enacting the FDCA: (1) to regulate products that actually prevent disease, and (2) to regulate products that falsely claim that they prevent disease. Because of those dual concerns, the only question under the FDCA is whether the intended use of the product is to prevent disease, not whether the product actually prevents disease. See United States v. Article ... Consisting of 216 Cartoned Bottles, 409 F.2d 734, 739 (2d Cir.1969) ("Regardless of the actual physical effect of a product, it will be deemed a drug for purposes of the Act where the labeling and promotional claims show intended uses that bring it within the drug definition."). Accordingly, this court has applied the FDCA to instruments that do not actually prevent disease. See Church of Scientology of Cal. v. Richardson, 437 F.2d 214, 217 (9th Cir.1971) (holding that a Scientology "E-meter" was a device, even though the plaintiff admitted that "the devices are ineffective for any medical therapeutic purpose"); Drown v. United States, 198 F.2d 999, 1002–03, 1006 (9th Cir.1952) (holding that a machine that allegedly eliminated lumps from women's breasts was governed by the FDCA, even though "expert witnesses expressed the unanimous belief that appellant's instruments are useless for diagnosis or treatment of any human ailment"). * * *

United States v. An Undetermined Number of Unlabeled Cases

21 F.3d 1026 (10th Cir.1994).

■ MOORE, CIRCUIT JUDGE:

Clinical Reference Laboratory, Inc. appeals a grant of summary judgment holding certain urine and saliva specimen containers used in HIV-testing are adulterated "devices" subject to seizure * * * * CRL employs a series of laboratory protocols to help life insurance companies screen applicants for various health risks. One of these protocols detects HIV–1 antibodies in saliva and urine specimens. Formerly, to obtain the necessary samples, CRL purchased specimen containers, repackaged them into kits which included instruction sheets, and forwarded them along with consent forms to insurers to collect specimens. CRL reported its HIV findings to the insurance companies as either "non-reactive" for normal results or "inconclusive" for any other result.

The FDA maintains AIDS tests which do not use blood products or serum violate the Act. Furthermore, specimen containers used in these disapproved tests must receive premarket approval by the FDA. Accordingly, the FDA told CRL to cease distribution of the containers used in detecting HIV antibodies or face enforcement action. In response, CRL filed an action requesting declaratory and injunctive relief on the grounds the FDA lacked authority to regulate the containers. The FDA countered with its own action seeking to seize and condemn the containers. * * *

CRL contends the specimen containers do not qualify as devices regulated by the Act because CRL neither used them nor intended to use them for medical diagnosis as the containers were not part of a prelude to medical treatment. Essentially, CRL argues the containers' use for insurance risk assessment and CRL's subsequent actions removed the containers from the statute's reach. CRL maintains it did not provide a firm answer about the presence of HIV and reported findings only to the insurer. Moreover, CRL expressly informed applicants the test did not furnish a medical diagnosis. All of these actions, CRL claims, are inconsistent with the meaning of "diagnosis."

The Act includes in its definition of "device" an article "intended for use in the diagnosis of disease or other conditions, or in the cure, mitigation, treatment, or prevention of disease." 21 U.S.C. § 321(h)(2). To qualify as a device under the statute, an article must serve either a diagnostic or therapeutic purpose. The definition does not define the term "diagnosis" nor limit diagnostic devices to those used prior to medical treatment. * * * The plain meaning of "diagnosis" disregards context and bears no connection to medical treatment. A diagnosis is "the art or act of identifying a disease from its signs and symptoms" or alternatively an "investigation or analysis of the cause or nature of a condition, situation, or problem." Webster's Third New International Dictionary 622 (1981). Therefore, the Act regulates as a "device" an article intended for use in diagnosis regardless of whether medical treatment will follow.

CRL used the specimen containers as part of a protocol which seeks to identify the presence of HIV antibodies. The fact CRL's results were inconclusive does not eliminate the diagnostic nature of CRL's inquiry. Also, the fact insurance companies rather than health professionals considered CRL's findings to make business rather than medical decisions does not erase the diagnostic character of CRL's activities or the containers' use. Therefore, we conclude the specimen containers at issue are devices within the meaning of 21 U.S.C. § 321(h)(2) and subject to FDA regulation. * * * [The court held, however, that such devices were not properly subject to premarket approval requirements and, therefore, were not adulterated.]

■ COOK, SENIOR DISTRICT JUDGE (dissenting in part):

The statute in question provides that a device must be intended for use in the diagnosis of disease or in the cure, mitigation, treatment, or prevention of disease. The government concedes that it does not claim that a device which has no medical application could "qualify as a device under the FDCA." There is no evidence present in the record that the containers involved here had any medical application. They were used only to "transport the specimens to the lab for analysis." Again, the government characterizes them as "generic collection containers." They were used, along with other materials, merely to contain and transport the specimens from one location to another, where, upon arriving at their destination, a totally independent and separate testing protocol was applied. It is the testing protocol which is the diagnosis. Under the facts of this case, the containers played no part in the protocol of diagnosis.

If an item's participation in the mere transportation and containment of a specimen means that the item constitutes a "device" under the statute and regulations, then it could be argued that all means of transportation and containment so used would also qualify as a "device." If the containers were required to be of special design as part of the protocol, a stronger argument could be made that they serve a use in diagnosis. From the evidence before us, these containers were perfectly ordinary. The conclusion that these ordinary containers were "used" in diagnosis can only be reached in the most attenuated sense, in the same way that a truck or airplane might be "used" in the transportation and/or containment process. The majority quite rightly says that the act must be liberally construed consistent with its overriding purpose to protect the public health. However, the majority's reading goes beyond liberality to all-inclusiveness.

NOTES AND QUESTIONS

1. *Devices vs. biological products.* Another court found procedural flaws with the FDA's announcement that its PMA requirement for heart valves applied to allografts. See Northwest Tissue Ctr. v. Shalala, 1 F.3d 522, 536 (7th Cir.1993). The agency subsequently withdrew its notice. See 59 Fed. Reg. 52,078 (1994). The court in *Alabama Tissue Center* interpreted the term "implant" in the definition of "device" rather broadly by referring to medical dictionaries. Are whole organs or tissue transplants potentially subject to FDA regulation as devices? In testifying before Congress one decade earlier, the FDA disclaimed having any such authority. See Hearing Before the Subcomm. on Investigations & Oversight of the House Comm. on Sci. & Tech., 98th Cong. (1983). The Public Health Service Act, which the FDA also implements, defines the term "biological product" as "a virus, therapeutic serum, toxin, antitoxin, vaccine, blood, blood component or derivative, allergenic product, or analogous product ... applicable to the prevention, treatment, or cure of a disease or condition of human beings." 42 U.S.C. § 262(i); see also Loge v. United States, 662 F.2d 1268, 1272 (8th Cir.1981) (interpreting the scope of an earlier version of this definition); Gary E. Gamerman, Regulation of Biologics Manufacturing, 49 Food & Drug L.J. 213 (1994). Nowadays, the FDA regulates vaccines in a manner similar to new drugs, but it regulates the blood supply in an entirely different fashion. Blood is sometimes referred to as a liquid organ, and one could interpret the reference to any "analogous product" as covering other types of human tissues (bone marrow, kidney, liver, skin, cornea, ova, etc.). See United States v. Loran Med. Sys., Inc., 25 F.Supp.2d 1082, 1085–86 (C.D.Cal.1997) (holding that the FDA could regulate fetal cells injected to stimulate insulin production as either a biological product or a drug, and explaining that "Congress conferred upon the FDA broad statutory authority to regulate products analogous to toxins, antitoxins, vaccines, blood, etc."). How would the agency classify an artificial blood substitute? And how about "xenotransplants" (i.e., organs and tissues from other animals)? These issues receive closer attention in Chapter 11(B).

2. *Combination products.* Recognizing that some technologies would not fit neatly into just one of the statutory definitions, Congress amended the FDCA in 1990 to provide, among other things, that a "combination product" should be regulated according to its "primary mode of action." 21 U.S.C. § 353(g); see also Matthew Avery & Dan Liu, Bringing Smart Pills to Market: FDA Regulation of Ingestible Drug/Device Combination Products, 66 Food & Drug L.J. 329 (2011); Susan B. Foote & Robert J. Berlin, Can Regulation Be as Innovative as Science and Technology? The FDA's Regulation of Combination Products, 6 Minn. J.L. Sci. & Tech. 619 (2005); Kevin Edler, Comment, Getting a Handle on Hybrid Devices: The FDA and Industries' Struggles with Regulatory Approval of Drug–Eluting Stents and Possible Solutions for Future Combination Devices, 12 Tul. J. Tech. & Intell. Prop. 221 (2009). Thus, transdermal nicotine patches or metered dose inhalers would be regulated as drugs even though their delivery mechanism would qualify as a device. In addition, courts have insisted that the FDA maintain consistency in the classification of comparable products sold by different companies. See Bracco Diagnostics, Inc. v. Shalala, 963 F.Supp. 20, 28 (D.D.C.1997) (enjoining inconsistent review of injectable contrast agents for use with ultrasound equipment, some as drugs and others as devices). Cosmetics that also qualify as drugs or devices must abide by the requirements applicable to both types of products. See 21 U.S.C. § 359. Thus, skin creams claiming protection against damaging UV rays must satisfy cosmetic ingredient labeling rules as well as the OTC drug monograph for sunscreens. See Patrick R. Jones, Note, Protecting the Consumer from Getting Burned: The FDA, the Administrative Process, and the Tentative Final Monograph on Over-the-Counter Sunscreens, 20 Am. J.L. & Med. 317 (1994). The FDA briefly considered deregulating decorative contact lenses (i.e., colored lenses that do not correct vision) by classifying these prescription devices as cosmetics. See Megan Garvey, Health Concerns Tinge Use of Cosmetic Lenses, L.A. Times, Aug. 26, 2002, § 1, at 1. Congress responded by amending the statute to require that all contact lenses be regulated as medical devices. See Pub. L. No. 109–96, 119 Stat. 2119 (2005) (codified at 21 U.S.C. § 360j(n)).

3. *Some other atypical medical devices.* See United States v. 25 Cases, More or Less, of an Article of Device, 942 F.2d 1179, 1180–83 (7th Cir.1991) (breast self-examination devices); United States v. An Article of Device, 731 F.2d 1253, 1255–58 (7th Cir.1984) (chiropractic instrument that supposedly detected low levels of electromagnetic radiation emanating from the body); United States v. 23, More or Less, Articles, 192 F.2d 308, 310 (2d Cir.1951) (self-help phonograph records); Holistic Candlers & Consumer Ass'n v. FDA, 770 F.Supp.2d 156 (D.D.C.2011) ("ear candles"); United States v. One Unlabeled Unit ... Thor of Genesis I, 885 F.Supp. 1025, 1027–28 (N.D.Ohio 1995) (vinyl covered bed with 24 audio speakers mounted on its sides and promoted as generating micro-massage for relaxation and various health benefits); United States v. Various Articles of Device, 814 F.Supp. 31 (E.D.Tenn.1992) (disinfectants); United States v. 22 Rectangular ... MD–200, 714 F.Supp. 1159, 1164 (D.Utah 1989) (sterilizer machine for surgical instruments); see also Rita Rubin, Maggots and Leeches: Good Medicine, USA Today, July 8, 2004, at 4D (reporting that the FDA had just cleared requests to market both of these peculiar "devices"). See generally Gary E. Gamerman, Note, Intended Use and Medical Devices: Distinguishing Nonmedical "Devices" from Medical "Devices" Under 21 U.S.C. § 321(h), 61 Geo. Wash. L. Rev. 806 (1993); Jay M. Zitter, Annotation, What Is "Device" Within Meaning of § 201(h) of Federal Food, Drug, and Cosmetic Act, 129 A.L.R. Fed. 343 (1996 & 2011 Supp.). Are items published in medical journals and textbooks subject to regulation as devices because they represent "articles" intended for use in the diagnosis and treatment of disease (and do not depend on chemical action or metabolism to achieve their purpose)? Cf. Frank D. Nguyen, Comment, Regulation of Medical Expert Systems: A Necessary Evil?, 34 Santa Clara L. Rev. 1187, 1208–11, 1230–32 (1994) (proposing alternatives to FDA regulation of software as a medical device); FDA Aims to Regulate Medical Apps, Boston Globe, July 20, 2011, at B6 ("Tools that let smartphones monitor blood sugar or work as stethoscopes may face the same regulatory scrutiny as heart stents and ultrasound machines."). Notice that the statutory definition, as amended in 1976, covers articles used to diagnose "conditions" as well as diseases, thereby resolving the regulatory status of pregnancy test kits left open in *Ova II*. See 44 Fed. Reg. 10,133 (1979); see also James W. Hulse et al., How Broad Is the FDA's Authority over Research and Investigational IVDs?, 48 Food & Drug L.J. 285 (1993). Notice also that, while the statute only uses the term "devices," the legislative history and FDA officials routinely refer to "medical devices." Does that affect your reaction to the classification of specimen containers used solely for insurance underwriting purposes?

4. *Tobacco products as drugs and/or devices*. In a pair of early enforcement actions, the FDA successfully argued that cigarettes labeled with therapeutic or weight loss claims were unapproved new drugs. See United States v. 354 Bulk Cartons ... Trim Reducing–Aid Cigarettes, 178 F.Supp. 847, 851 (D.N.J.1959) (holding that cigarettes purporting to reduce appetite affect both the structure (body weight) and function (appetite) of the body); United States v. 46 Cartons ... Fairfax Cigarettes, 113 F.Supp. 336, 337 (D.N.J.1953) (holding that the FDA could regulate cigarettes as drugs where their labeling clearly suggested that they would reduce the risk of upper respiratory infections). In 1980, a court rejected an effort by a public interest group to force the FDA to regulate all tobacco products as drugs. See Action on Smoking & Health v. Harris, 655 F.2d 236, 240 (D.C.Cir. 1980) (holding that cigarettes are not drugs simply because they affect the structure or function of the body unless they were intended to be used for this purpose, though leaving open the possibility that such intent could be inferred if consumers used cigarettes almost exclusively for such purposes).

In 1996, the FDA issued a rule restricting the advertising of tobacco products to minors. See 61 Fed. Reg. 44,396, 44,616–18 (1996). The agency claimed that nicotine qualified as a drug because the tobacco industry had intended to capitalize on its addictive potential, and it classified tobacco products as drug-delivery systems subject to regulation as "restricted" medical devices. For a summary and criticism of this curious assertion of jurisdiction, see Lars Noah, Regulating Cigarettes: (Non)sense and Sensibility, 22 S. Ill. U. L.J. 677 (1998); see also Symposium, Are the Risks Worth Regulating?: Tobacco v. the FDA, 47 Duke L.J. 1013 (1998). In the end, a closely divided Supreme Court refused to defer to the agency's construction of the FDCA as allowing it to reach tobacco products. See FDA v. Brown & Williamson Tobacco Corp., 529 U.S. 120 (2000); see also id. at 131–32 (declining to address the industry's argument that only claims made to consumers could provide the basis for finding an intended drug or device use); Lars Noah, Interpreting Agency Enabling Acts: Misplaced Metaphors in Administrative Law, 41 Wm. & Mary L. Rev. 1463, 1529–30 (2000) (arguing that courts should not defer to agency interpretations of statutory ambiguities that expand jurisdiction). See generally Jeffrey R. Lax & Mathew D. McCubbins, The FDA, the Courts, and the Regulation of Tobacco, 15 J. Contemp. Legal Issues 163 (2006). Congress eventually granted the FDA limited authority over tobacco products, but definitional quandaries remain.

Sottera, Inc. v. FDA

627 F.3d 891 (D.C.Cir.2010).

■ WILLIAMS, SENIOR CIRCUIT JUDGE:

Sottera, Inc., which does business as NJOY, is an importer and distributor of "electronic cigarettes" or "e-cigarettes," a product that enables users to inhale vaporized nicotine. The question before us is whether Congress has authorized the FDA to regulate e-cigarettes under the drug/device provisions of the FDCA or under the Family Smoking Prevention and Tobacco Control Act of 2009, Pub. L. No. 111–31, 123 Stat. 1776. We think that the statutes, properly read in light of the Supreme Court's decision in *FDA v. Brown & Williamson,* 529 U.S. 120 (2000), locate the product under the Tobacco Act.

Electronic cigarettes are battery-powered products that allow users to inhale nicotine vapor without fire, smoke, ash, or carbon monoxide. Designed to look like a traditional cigarette, each e-cigarette consists of three parts: the nicotine cartridge, the atomizer or heating element, and the battery and electronics. The plastic cartridge serves as the mouthpiece and contains liquid nicotine, water, propylene glycol, and glycerol. The atomizer vaporizes the liquid nicotine, and the battery and electronics power the atomizer and monitor air flow. When the user inhales, the electronics detect the air flow and activate the atomizer; the liquid nicotine is vaporized, and the user inhales the vapor.

NJOY has imported and distributed e-cigarettes since 2007. The liquid nicotine in each e-cigarette is derived from natural tobacco plants, and NJOY claims that its product is marketed and labeled for "smoking pleasure," rather than as a therapeutic or smoking cessation product. On April 15, 2009 the FDA ordered that a shipment of NJOY's e-cigarettes be denied entry into the United States, asserting that the e-cigarettes appeared to be adulterated, misbranded, or unapproved drug-device combinations under the FDCA. Also in April 2009, another importer and distributor of e-cigarettes, Smoking Everywhere, Inc., sought a preliminary injunction barring the FDA and various officials from denying their products entry into the United States and from regulating e-cigarettes under the drug/device provisions of the FDCA. NJOY joined as an intervenor-plaintiff and filed its own complaint and request for a preliminary injunction.

Smoking Everywhere and NJOY argued that the FDA can regulate electronic cigarettes, as they propose to market them, only under the Tobacco Act, claiming that the Supreme Court's opinion in *Brown & Williamson* foreclosed FDCA drug/device jurisdiction over tobacco products marketed without claims of therapeutic effect. The district court agreed and granted the injunction. See Smoking Everywhere, Inc. v. FDA, 680 F.Supp.2d 62 (D.D.C.2010). While this appeal was pending, Smoking Everywhere voluntarily dismissed its complaint against the FDA, leaving NJOY as the sole appellee. * * *

Under the FDCA, the FDA has authority to regulate articles that are "drugs," "devices," or drug/device combinations. 21 U.S.C. § 321(g)(1) defines drugs to include "(B) articles intended for use in the diagnosis, cure, mitigation, treatment, or prevention of disease in man or other animals; and (C) articles (other than food) intended to affect the structure or any function of the body of man or other animals." The statute defines devices similarly, see id. § 321(h)(2) & (3); products that are "combination[s] of a drug, device, or biological product" are regulated as combination products, see id. § 353(g)(1). Until 1996, the FDA had never attempted to regulate tobacco products under the FDCA (with one exception, irrelevant for reasons discussed below) unless they were sold for therapeutic uses * * * *

Reflecting on the history and structure of tobacco regulation, *Brown & Williamson* concluded,

> Congress has affirmatively acted to address the issue of tobacco and health, relying on the representations of the FDA that it had no authority to regulate tobacco. It has created a distinct scheme to regulate the sale of tobacco products, focused on labeling and advertising, and premised on the belief that the FDA lacks such jurisdiction under the FDCA. As a result, Congress' tobacco-specific statutes preclude the FDA from regulating tobacco products as customarily marketed.

529 U.S. at 156. *Brown & Williamson* therefore did not preclude the FDA from regulating only those products for which Congress had passed specific statutes. Rather, it recognized that Congress had consciously developed a statutory scheme for tobacco and health that distinguished tobacco products as customarily marketed from ones marketed for therapeutic purposes. * * * The Tobacco Act is wholly consistent with this reading of *Brown & Williamson*. Written to address the regulatory gap that the case identified, the Tobacco Act provides the FDA with regulatory authority over tobacco products without requiring therapeutic claims. Besides leaving the FDA's authority under the drug/device provisions of the FDCA undisturbed, see 21 U.S.C. § 321(rr)(2) & § 387a(c)(1), the act broadly defines tobacco products as extending to "any product made or derived from tobacco," id. § 321(rr)(1). * * *

The FDA has also offered a consequentialist argument, namely, that understanding *Brown & Williamson* in this fashion leaves the FDA severely thwarted in any effort to nudge e-cigarettes toward relatively healthful forms (or at least away from relatively unhealthful ones). Whether such a consequentialist argument should play any role in our interpretation of *Brown & Williamson* is questionable, but no matter. In fact the Tobacco Act gives the FDA broad regulatory authority over tobacco products, including, for instance, authority to impose restrictions on their sale, and on the advertising and promotion of such products, see 21 U.S.C. § 387f(d), to regulate the mode of manufacture of tobacco products, see id. § 387f(e), and to establish standards for tobacco products, see id. § 387g. To the extent that Congress believed *Brown & Williamson* left an insufficiently regulative environment for cigarettes, smokeless tobacco, cigars, and other tobacco products, it found the Tobacco Act an adequate remedy.

Together, *Brown & Williamson* and the Tobacco Act establish that the FDA cannot regulate customarily marketed tobacco products under the FDCA's drug/device provisions, that it can regulate tobacco products marketed for therapeutic purposes under those provisions, and that it can regulate customarily marketed tobacco products under the Tobacco Act. As to NJOY's likelihood of success on the merits, the firm claims that its electronic cigarettes use a liquid nicotine mixture derived from tobacco and that its products are not marketed for therapeutic uses; the FDA appears not to challenge either claim. Still, the district court noted that the factual record on NJOY is meager and that the FDA may establish that NJOY does in fact make therapeutic claims regarding its electronic cigarettes. * * * Given the likelihood of NJOY's success on the merits, the irreparable harm to NJOY's business, and the FDA's unquestioned Tobacco Act authority to mitigate any public harm, the district court did not abuse its discretion in granting the preliminary injunction. * * * Of course, in the event that Congress prefers that the FDA regulate e-cigarettes under the FDCA's drug/device provisions, it can always so decree.

■ GARLAND, CIRCUIT JUDGE (concurring in judgment):

Although I join my colleagues in the disposition of this case, I do so based on different reasoning. I do not read *FDA v. Brown & Williamson*, 529 U.S. 120 (2000), as barring the FDA from regulating "electronic cigarettes" under the FDCA because I do not believe the Supreme Court intended its use of the term "tobacco products" to extend to products that do not contain tobacco. The Tobacco Control Act of 2009, however, expressly extends to products that are merely "derived from" tobacco. Accordingly, at least in the absence of a contrary agency interpretation entitled to *Chevron* deference, I read the Tobacco Control Act as requiring the FDA to regulate products like electronic cigarettes under that Act, rather than under the FDCA.

In *Brown & Williamson*, the Supreme Court held that the FDA lacks authority to regulate "tobacco products" under the drug/device provisions of the FDCA, unless those products are marketed with therapeutic claims. On its face, the natural meaning of the term "tobacco product" is a product—like cigarettes or chewing tobacco—that *contains* tobacco. Although it is true that the liquid nicotine in NJOY's electronic cigarettes is *derived from* tobacco, it seems less natural to regard that fact as sufficient to transform NJOY's plastic cartridges—which contain no tobacco—into a tobacco product. As NJOY acknowledges, its reading leads to the counterintuitive conclusion that a syringe filled with injectable nicotine is a tobacco product as well. * * *

This reading is consistent with the context in which the Court decided *Brown & Williamson*. In that case, the Court upheld a challenge to a 1996 FDA rule asserting authority to regulate the sale of cigarettes and smokeless tobacco under the FDCA. Because all of the products at issue in the rule contained tobacco, the Court had no occasion to opine upon the FDA's authority to regulate a product, like electronic cigarettes, that does not. * * *

But the most telling indication that the holding of *Brown & Williamson* does not extend to electronic cigarettes is that the Court's reasoning does not apply to products that do not contain tobacco. The Supreme Court's chief rationale for its holding had two premises. First, the Court determined that, "if tobacco products were 'devices' under the FDCA, the FDA would be required to remove them from the market." 529 U.S. at 135. It reached this conclusion because the FDA may only approve a product for marketing under the FDCA if it is safe and effective for its intended use, and the FDA had "exhaustively documented" that tobacco products are unsafe for any pharmacological use. Id. at 133–35. Second, the Court found that Congress had "foreclosed the removal of tobacco products from the market" through "tobacco-specific legislation" passed subsequent to the FDCA. Id. at 137, 143. Thus, the Court concluded: "If they cannot be used safely for any therapeutic purpose, and yet they cannot be banned, they simply do not fit" within the FDCA's regulatory scheme. Id. at 143.

Neither premise holds true for pure nicotine or for a tobacco-free product that delivers nicotine. First, unlike products containing tobacco, which the FDA has found to be associated with "cancer, respiratory illnesses, and heart disease," id. at 134–35, the FDA has *not* found that nicotine or tobacco-free products that deliver nicotine are inherently unsafe. To the contrary, the FDA has approved several such products marketed with therapeutic claims, determining that they satisfy the FDCA safety requirements that *Brown & Williamson* determined "tobacco products" could not meet. Indeed, the FDA states that "it may well be possible for a manufacturer of 'electronic cigarettes' . . . to satisfy the FDCA's safety, effectiveness, and labeling requirements and obtain FDA approval."

Second, the "tobacco-specific legislation" the Court found dispositive in *Brown & Williamson* simply does not address products that deliver nicotine but contain no tobacco. As the Court explained, Congress had "directly addressed the problem of tobacco and health through legislation on six occasions since 1965." 529 U.S. at 137. Those statutes impose labeling and advertising requirements that "create a distinct regulatory scheme for cigarettes and smokeless tobacco." Id. at 155. Moreover, Congress has declared that "[t]he marketing of tobacco constitutes one of the greatest basic industries of the United States," id. at 137 (quoting 7 U.S.C.

§ 1311(a)), making it "highly unlikely" that the legislature would have subjected the industry to a regulatory regime that could substantially or entirely shut it down, id. at 160. "[T]he collective premise of these statutes," the Court said, is "that cigarettes and smokeless tobacco will continue to be sold in the United States." Id. at 139.

This "collective premise" does not extend to products, like electronic cigarettes, that contain only nicotine. None of the statutes the Court referenced regulate such products, and the statutory labeling requirements and advertising restrictions the Court cited do not apply to electronic cigarettes. Nor can it be said that FDA regulation of a novel product like electronic cigarettes would threaten the health of the American tobacco industry. As NJOY avers, it "imports one hundred percent of its supply of e-cigarettes from overseas manufacturers, and, upon information and belief, there is no domestic manufacturer of e-cigarettes or their component parts."

Finally, the *Brown & Williamson* Court also noted that, "[i]n adopting each statute, Congress . . . acted against the backdrop of the FDA's consistent and repeated statements that it lacked authority under the FDCA to regulate *tobacco* absent claims of therapeutic benefit by the manufacturer." 529 U.S. at 144 (emphasis added). * * * But the backdrop of pre–1996 statements to which the Court referred did not include statements that the FDA lacked authority over a product like nicotine, which is merely derived from tobacco. * * * [I]n fact, as noted above, in 1987 the FDA had asserted authority to regulate a product that is materially indistinguishable from electronic cigarettes—the Favor Smokeless Cigarette—apparently without challenge.

In sum, I see nothing in the words, context, or rationale of *Brown & Williamson* that supports interpreting that case as barring the FDA from regulating electronic cigarettes under the drug/device provisions of the FDCA. Although I agree with my colleagues that these considerations do not justify reading *Brown & Williamson* as merely a "carve-out from the FDCA for cigarettes and smokeless tobacco," they do justify reading it as a carve-out only for products that contain tobacco. The Supreme Court had no reason to opine on the status of a product that contains no tobacco, and there is no indication in the opinion that it meant to do so. As my colleagues' opinion rests on the supposition that it did, I cannot join their rationale.

But *Brown & Williamson* is not the end of the story. In 2009, Congress passed the Tobacco Control Act, which states: "Tobacco products . . . shall be regulated by the Secretary under this [Act] and shall not be subject to the provisions of [the drug/device subchapter of the FDCA]." 21 U.S.C. § 387a(a). Moreover, unlike *Brown & Williamson*, which used the term "tobacco products" without defining it, the Tobacco Control Act includes a definition: "The term 'tobacco product' means any product made *or derived from* tobacco that is intended for human consumption." Id. § 321(rr)(1) (emphasis added). Because the nicotine in NJOY's electronic cigarettes is "derived from" natural tobacco, it appears that the FDA may regulate it only pursuant to the provisions of the Tobacco Control Act.

The FDA disagrees with this conclusion, contending that the Tobacco Control Act does not narrow the FDA's preexisting authority under the FDCA. In support, agency counsel cites another definitional provision of the Tobacco Control Act, which states that "[t]he term 'tobacco product' does not mean an article that is a drug . . . , a device . . . , or a combination product" under the FDCA. Id. § 321(rr)(2). In the FDA's view, this provision preserves for regulation under the FDCA any product "made or derived from tobacco" that *Brown & Williamson* did not carve out of the FDCA's coverage. And because *Brown & Williamson*'s carve-out did not extend to nicotine-only products, the agency maintains that such products are not necessarily "tobacco products" within the meaning of the Tobacco Control Act.

There is no doubt that § 321(rr)(2) introduces a note of ambiguity into the analysis. But it is a stretch to conclude that, having just used one express statutory subsection to include products "derived from" tobacco within the definition of "tobacco product," § 321(rr)(1), Congress then immediately employed the next, ambiguous subsection to carve them out again. Rather, it is more likely that § 321(rr)(2) is an expression of Congress' intent to preserve *Brown & Williamson*'s holding that even a product made from tobacco—for example, a cigarette—remains a drug, device, or drug/device combination that can be regulated under the FDCA if it is marketed for therapeutic purposes. Hence, the better reading is that § 321(rr)(2) simply makes clear that products made or derived from tobacco that are marketed for therapeutic purposes are not "tobacco products" within the meaning of the Tobacco Control Act, and are therefore subject to regulation under the drug/device provisions of the FDCA.

In the usual circumstance, of course, a judge's view of the "better" reading of a statute administered by an agency is not necessarily dispositive. * * * In this case, there is no agency pronouncement that calls for *Chevron* deference. Other than its briefs, which do not qualify, the only expression of the FDA's view regarding electronic cigarettes is the agency's 2008 detention order barring the importation of NJOY's products. But that order was issued before Congress passed the Tobacco Control Act in 2009 and hence does not construe it at all. * * *

In the absence of an authoritative agency interpretation, I conclude that, unless a product derived from tobacco is marketed for therapeutic purposes, the FDA may regulate it only under the provisions of the Tobacco Control Act. Accordingly, because NJOY's electronic cigarettes are derived from tobacco, I join my colleagues' disposition. What the result would be were the FDA to offer a contrary statutory interpretation in the form of a regulation, I leave for the day the agency decides to take that step.

NOTES AND QUESTIONS

1. *Snuffing out e-cigs?* If in fact NJOY had made no therapeutic claims, what regulatory authority could the FDA exercise over the company's products under the Tobacco Act? In what sense would Judge Garland's concurrence give the agency more potential room to maneuver in the future? A few months before the appellate court announced its decision, the FDA sent warning letters to several other sellers of electronic cigarettes. See Thomas H. Maugh II, FDA Targets e-Cigarette Companies, L.A. Times, Sept. 10, 2010, at B1 ("All were warned that, because their products are marketed as stop-smoking aids, the companies must obtain preapproval by the FDA."). Does anything in the *Sottera* opinion weaken the legal basis for the agency's objections in these cases? In any event, it now appears to have backed down. See FDA to Regulate e-Cigarettes as Tobacco Items, Wash. Post, Apr. 26, 2011, at A15. A few states also have tried to crack down on such products. See Marisa Lagos, Attorney General Sues Company to Block e-Cigarette Sales in State, S.F. Chron., Jan. 14, 2010, at C1 (reporting that California and Oregon have accused Smoking Everywhere of violating state consumer protection laws). Public health experts continue to express concern about the rise in popularity of e-cigs. See Cyrus K. Yamin et al., E–Cigarettes: A Rapidly Growing Internet Phenomenon, 153 Annals Internal Med. 607 (2010).

2. *FDA's authority over tobacco product formulation.* Congress granted the agency limited authority to regulate the composition of tobacco products. See Lyndsey Layton, Kessler Calls for Nicotine Reduction: Former FDA Chief Wants Agency to Use Its Power to Cut Cigarette Cravings, Wash. Post, June 17, 2010, at A19 ("While the new law prevents the FDA from banning cigarettes or reducing nicotine levels to zero, it does permit the agency to lower levels of the drug. The amount of nicotine in a cigarette should drop from about 10 milligrams to less than 1 milligram, [David] Kessler said."); Duff Wilson, Firms Told to Divulge All Changes to Tobacco, N.Y. Times, Jan. 6, 2011, at B3 ("Federal regulators ... outlined rules for the tobacco industry that for the first time require disclosure of any changes to their products and that detail how to seek permission to market new products .... Any tobacco product changed after Feb. 15, 2007, when the legislation was introduced in Congress, must be reviewed by the agency.... Companies may apply for a fast track review of new products that are 'substantially equivalent' to earlier products."); see also BBK Tobacco & Foods, LLP v. FDA, 672 F.Supp.2d 969 (D.Ariz.2009) (dismissing as unripe objections to guidance documents interpreting new section 907(a)(1)(A) of the FDCA, which bans cigarettes that contain a characterizing flavor, as also applicable to rolling paper or filters intended for use as components in roll-your-own cigarettes); Michael Felberbaum, Smokeless Products Face FDA Test: Tobacco Maker First in Line for Regulatory Review, Boston Globe, Sept. 29, 2010, at C9 (reporting that a small company has sought FDA permission to market its tobacco lozenges as less harmful than cigarettes, adding that the agency "has not yet ironed out its guidelines for approval of such ['modified-risk'] products"); Dahleen Glanton, Blacks Divided over Possible FDA Ban of Menthol Cigarettes, Wash. Post, Jan. 2, 2011, at A5 ("[FDA] is considering whether to ban the sale of menthol cigarettes, which for decades were heavily marketed to minorities.... According to the NAACP, the FDA discriminated against African American children by banning the sale of clove and fruit-flavored cigarettes in 2009 while exempting menthol-flavored cigarettes."); David Kesmodel,

Glaxo Aims to Snuff out "Dissolvable" Tobacco Items, Wall St. J., Sept. 28, 2010, at B1 (explaining that manufacturers of smoking cessation drug products have urged the FDA to remove dissolvable smokeless-tobacco products (lozenges, strips and sticks) from the market because they might appeal to kids, though noting that these items aren't marketed "as quit-smoking devices, but as options that smokers might use in certain situations, such as where smoking is prohibited").

3. *FDA's authority over tobacco product marketing*. Congress directed the agency to enhance the classic Surgeon General's warning labels. See Duff Wilson, U.S. Selects Cigarette Warning Images, N.Y. Times, June 22, 2011, at B1 ("[T]he graphic images will include photos of horribly damaged teeth and lungs and a man exhaling smoke through a tracheotomy opening in his neck.... The [color] images are to cover the upper half of the front and back of cigarette packages produced after September 2012, as well as 20 percent of the space in cigarette advertisements."). The FDA also imposed significant restrictions on marketing. See Lyndsey Layton, New FDA Rules Will Greatly Restrict Tobacco Advertising and Sales, Wash. Post, Mar. 19, 2010, at A8; Nate Ryan, Tobacco Era in NASCAR Ending, USA Today, June 2, 2010, at 7C; see also Duff Wilson, Color Coding, N.Y. Times, Feb. 19, 2010, at B1 ("[C]igarette companies will no longer be allowed to use words like 'light' or 'mild' on packages to imply that some cigarettes are safer than others. But in a move that critics say simply skirts the new rules, tobacco companies plan to use packaging to make those same distinctions: light colors for light cigarettes."). The industry lodged First Amendment objections to these rules with only limited success. See Commonwealth Brands, Inc. v. United States, 678 F.Supp.2d 512 (W.D.Ky. 2010), app. pending (6th Cir.); see also Matt Shechtman, Comment, Smoking out Big Tobacco: Can the Family Smoking Prevention and Tobacco Control Act Equip the FDA to Regulate Tobacco Without Infringing on the First Amendment?, 60 Emory L.J. 705 (2011). See generally Chap. 4(C).

4. *Further commentary*. See Kevin G. Barker, Comment, Thank You for Regulating: Why Philip Morris's Embrace of FDA Regulation Helps the Company but Harms the Agency, 61 Admin. L. Rev. 197 (2009); Jeremy R. Singer, Comment, Taking on Tobacco: The Family Smoking Prevention and Tobacco Control Act, 34 Nova L. Rev. 539 (2010); Amy Goldstein, VA Health Chief to Lead Tobacco Center: New FDA Division Will Oversee Efforts to Regulate Products, Wash. Post, Aug. 20, 2009, at A15; see also Duff Wilson, Cigarette Giants in a Global Fight on Tighter Rules, N.Y. Times, Nov. 14, 2010, at A1 ("As sales to developing nations become ever more important to giant tobacco companies, they are stepping up efforts around the world to fight tough restrictions on the marketing of cigarettes.").

4. NEW DRUGS

United States v. 50 Boxes More or Less

909 F.2d 24 (1st Cir.1990).

■ BREYER, CIRCUIT JUDGE:

The government has seized fifty boxes of a prescription drug called Cafergot P–B Suppository, a drug that contains two active ingredients (caffeine, ergotamine) designed to stop vascular headaches such as migraine and two other active ingredients (pentobarbital, bellafoline) designed to stop nauseous side effects resulting from the first two ingredients. The government has a legal right to seize these products if (1) the drug (which we shall call "CPB") is a "new drug" and (2) its manufacturer, Sandoz Pharmaceuticals, has failed to present "substantial evidence" that the drug is "effective." CPB is a "new drug" unless it is "generally recognized, among experts ... as safe and effective for use under the conditions prescribed ... in the labeling" (i.e., unless it is what drug regulators call "GRASE"). See 21 U.S.C. § 321(p)(1). The district court, concluding that CPB is a "new drug" (i.e., not GRASE) and that Sandoz has not presented "substantial evidence" of its effectiveness, granted the government's motion for summary judgment. Sandoz appeals.

Were the law to give ordinary English-language meanings to the statutory words quoted in the preceding paragraph, the record created for summary judgment purposes would strongly support Sandoz. CPB is not a new drug; Sandoz has sold it successfully for thirty-five years. The anti-headache ingredients in CPB are the same as those in another Sandoz product approved as safe and effective by both the Food and Drug Administration and the National Academy of Sciences, and Sandoz presents evidence that the anti-nausea ingredients in CPB are effective for that purpose. Six experts in the treatment of headache pain prepared affidavits attesting to the general medical consensus, based on published reports and clinical experience, that CPB is safe and effective for the treatment of vascular headache.

The law, however, does not give the quoted words their ordinary English meanings. For example, the term "new drug" means "any drug" that is not GRASE. The term "substantial evidence" does not mean what it means elsewhere in administrative law, namely, "such relevant evidence as a reasonable mind might accept as adequate to support a conclusion." Universal Camera Corp. v. NLRB, 340 U.S. 474, 477 (1951). It means "evidence consisting of adequate and well-controlled investigations, including clinical investigations, by experts," which "adequate and well-controlled investigations" must satisfy a host of technical scientific requirements, including "a valid comparison with a control" such as an "active treatment trial" that includes "randomization and blinding of patients or investigators" (double-blind studies). See 21 U.S.C. § 355(d); 21 C.F.R. § 314.126(b)(2)(iv) (1989). Finally, and perhaps most surprisingly, the exception for drugs "generally recognized as safe and effective" is not an exception at all. In *Weinberger v. Hynson, Westcott & Dunning*, the Supreme Court held that, to qualify as GRASE, a drug must meet the same elaborate, technical, scientific testing requirements that it would have to meet to win approval as a "new drug." The Court wrote that

> the hurdle of "general recognition" of effectiveness requires at least "substantial evidence" of effectiveness for approval of an NDA [i.e.,

> "new drug" application]. In the absence of any evidence of adequate and well-controlled investigation supporting the efficacy of [a drug], a fortiori, [the drug] ... would be a "new drug" subject to the [new drug] provisions of the Act.

412 U.S. 609, 629–30 (1973). In sum, if we give the relevant statutory terms their special legal meanings, the statute permits the government to seize virtually any prescription drug by showing that the manufacturer has failed to conduct the technical scientific tests needed to obtain FDA "new drug" approval. And Sandoz concedes that neither it, nor anyone else, has tested CPB in the technical scientific manner specified in FDA regulations. This would seem sufficient basis for affirming the district court's grant of summary judgment.

Sandoz argues, however, that we should not accept the legal proposition that a drug is GRASE only if "adequate and well-controlled studies" demonstrate its "effectiveness." This legal proposition amounts to saying, in a sense, that a drug is exempt from "new drug" standards only if it meets "new drug" standards. Sandoz asks us to hold, instead, that a drug can be "generally recognized ... as ... effective" if the existing evidence to that effect, while not exactly the same as (and perhaps less costly than) technical, "well-controlled" studies, "is at least as scientifically convincing as 'substantial evidence' consisting of adequate and well-controlled studies." In support of this argument, Sandoz makes (or might make) several points.

First, its view of the meaning of GRASE makes better sense of the statute. The statute requires "substantial evidence" of "effectiveness" for approval of "new drugs," which it specifically defines as drugs that are not GRASE. Why would the statute define a category of drugs exempt from the "new drug" requirements and in the same breath make the exception virtually meaningless by applying the same requirements to drugs that are exempt?

Second, its view arguably avoids certain important policy risks. When Congress amended the drug statute in 1962, adding the requirement that all "new drugs" be proven "effective," approximately 4,000 approved "new drugs," and many times as many close imitations, were already on the market. Most of these drugs had not been proven effective by "substantial evidence" consisting of "adequate and well-controlled studies." From the perspective of health, should one read the statute to require the FDA to force all such drugs off the market, even those that were generally recognized by doctors as safe and effective (in the plain-English sense of those words) for their indicated use? If so, would those who needed such drugs not then be hurt? From the perspective of cost, should one read the statute to require the FDA to force the makers of all such drugs to undertake the special, expensive testing needed to satisfy the statutory (and FDA regulation) "substantial evidence" requirements, when a long history of safe and effective use (plus other scientific information) indicate both safety and effectiveness? Would the ultimate result not be unnecessary, and significant, increases in the price of drugs? From the perspective of law, should one read the statute to impose a requirement upon existing drugs that few could meet, thereby potentially granting to the FDA, through its discretionary power to enforce the law, the legal authority to pick and choose among existing drugs, keeping some on the market, removing others from the market, for reasons other than failure to meet the "substantial evidence" test?

Third, the Supreme Court itself has not read the law as rigidly as the above-quoted language from *Hynson* suggests. In *Weinberger v. Bentex Pharmaceuticals, Inc.*, a case decided the same day as *Hynson*, the Court wrote, "in some cases general recognition that a drug is efficacious might be made *without* the kind of scientific support necessary to obtain approval of an NDA." 412 U.S. 645, 652–53 (1973) (emphasis added). Sandoz argues that CPB is the very kind of drug the Court had in mind when it created this so-called *Bentex* exception to *Hynson*.

Fourth, the FDA itself has acted as if the GRASE exception was a genuine exception from the "substantial evidence" requirement. The FDA has promulgated regulations stating that it will certify over-the-counter (i.e., non-prescription) drugs as GRASE on the basis of evidence other than "adequate and well controlled studies," even though the statute does not distinguish between prescription and non-prescription drugs. See 21 C.F.R. § 330.10(a)(4)(ii) (1989); 37 Fed. Reg. 9469 (1972). Moreover, for at least a dozen years after the 1962 statute was enacted, the FDA took no action against many prescription drugs despite its knowledge that these drugs had not been proven "effective" by "adequate and well controlled studies." And the FDA conceded at oral argument that it still has not acted against some such drugs that were on the market before 1938. Of course, one could not reasonably expect drug manufacturers of several thousand existing drugs suddenly to produce complex, double-blind studies showing "effectiveness" nor expect the FDA to remove all such drugs from the market for lack of such studies. Yet, leaving administrative practicalities aside, the FDA's actions reveal that it did not believe the statute meant to impose the special "substantial evidence" of "effectiveness" requirement on all existing drugs, at least not immediately and not without exception.

Although we have set forth Sandoz's arguments as strongly as we can, we have done so to emphasize that even if those arguments are strong ones, we cannot accept them. For one thing, no drug manufacturer has ever won GRASE status for a drug that lacked "substantial evidence" of effectiveness by relying on the "*Bentex* exception." The *Hynson* Court, using absolute-sounding language, squarely rejected the argument that a drug could be GRASE despite a lack of "adequate and well-controlled studies" showing effectiveness. The contrary statement in *Bentex* was made in passing in a case presenting a different issue, namely, whether the FDA or the district courts have jurisdiction to determine whether a drug is a "new drug" within the meaning of the statute. This court, in an opinion written by (then senior) Justice Stewart, wrote that *Hynson* "foreclosed" the argument that Sandoz now makes. See United States v. Articles of Drug . . . 5,906 Boxes, 745 F.2d 105, 116 (1st Cir.1984). Other circuits have written in the same vein. See, e.g., United States v. 225 Cartons ... Fiorinal, 871 F.2d 409, 418–19 (3d Cir.1989); Simeon Management Corp. v. FTC, 579 F.2d 1137, 1143 (9th Cir.1978).

For another thing, the passage of time has erased many of the anomalies growing out of the *Hynson* decision. Since 1972, the FDA, acting pursuant to a court order, has systematically been applying the "adequate and well-controlled studies" requirement to almost all of the drugs that were on the market in 1962. To change the requirements for GRASE status at this late date may serve little purpose.

Finally, insofar as *Bentex* creates an exception to *Hynson*'s interpretation of the statute's language, it would seem appropriate for the agency itself to work out the contours of that exception. The FDA has, in fact, created exceptions for non-prescription drugs, but those exceptions do not apply to CPB. We do not find the sentence in *Bentex* sufficient to undo settled law, or to overturn our own circuit precedent, a precedent created after the Supreme Court wrote *Bentex* itself. If the law is to change, Sandoz must look to the Supreme Court, not to this court, to bring that change about. In our view, the district court correctly applied governing precedent.

NOTES AND QUESTIONS

1. *Old vs. new drugs.* Courts have construed the GRASE exception narrowly, explaining for instance that, even if the active ingredients are GRASE, a combination not used previously would qualify as a "new drug." See United States v. 225 Cartons ... Fiorinal ..., 871 F.2d 409, 415–20 (3d Cir.1989); United States v. Article of Drug ... Promise Toothpaste, 826 F.2d 564, 566 (7th Cir.1987); see also United States v. Atropine Sulfate 1.0 mg., 843 F.2d 860 (5th Cir.1988) (same, even if product contains a single active ingredient that qualifies as GRASE because of possible differences in inactive ingredients, dosages, or routes of administration). Occasionally, the FDA belatedly calls for new drug applications from the sellers of a drug sold before 1962 that slipped through the cracks of the retrospective review mentioned by the court. See, e.g., 69 Fed. Reg. 23,410 (2004) (giving the sellers of exocrine pancreatic insufficiency drug products four years to secure approval); see also Marc Kaufman, Unapproved Drugs Called "Threat," Wash. Post, June 9, 2006, at A12 ("The agency estimated that 2 percent of the prescription drugs now for sale have never been reviewed or formally determined to be safe and effective ...."); Rob Stein, FDA Cracks Down on Unapproved Cold and Allergy Drugs, Wash. Post, Mar. 3, 2011, at A4 ("About 500 [Rx] products that had not been formally evaluated by federal regulators will be removed from the market ...."). The GRASE exception was not designed to allow generic copies of previously approved new drugs to enter the market without securing separate FDA approval. See Tri–Bio Lab., Inc. v. United States, 836 F.2d 135, 141–42 (3d Cir.1987); see also United States v. Sandoz Pharm. Corp., 894 F.2d 825, 826–28 (6th Cir.1990) (preventing a manufacturer from relitigating a new drug issue resolved against it in a previous enforcement proceeding); United States v.

Articles of Drug ... 5,906 Boxes, 745 F.2d 105, 113–17 (1st Cir.1984) (rejecting an effort to invoke a separate grandfather clause); Cody Labs., Inc. v. Sebelius, 2010 WL 3119279, at *6, 13–15 (D.Wyo.2010) (same). See generally Jay M. Zitter, Annotation, What Is "New Drug" Within Meaning of § 201(p) of Federal Food, Drug, and Cosmetic Act, 133 A.L.R. Fed. 229 (1996 & 2011 Supp.). Chap. 3(A)(2) discusses the approval mechanism for generic products based on findings of bioequivalence.

2. *It's all relative.* In *Ova II*, the district court made the following point:

> It should be observed in passing and for context that historically, a dispute on the question whether something is "safe and effective" was normally resolved on the basis of expert testimony adduced in the course of the litigation. Under the present scheme, that method is excluded and two new alternative methods are provided. One, if the item is one which has recognition in the technical and professional literature, in the form of papers by investigators competent in the field, it is accepted as being an "old drug" which may be marketed in interstate commerce without further proof that it is "safe and effective." Two, if the item has no such body of published literature to support the proposition that it is "safe and effective," there must first be an administrative determination by FDA, as the disposition of a new drug application, that it is "safe and effective."
>
> The term "safe" and "effective," in some contexts, may be more or less absolute terms. Most people think of something as being "safe" when its use or application under any conceivable set of circumstances is not likely to cause some kind of harm or damage. They will think of something as being "effective" when its use or application invariably achieve the desired result. But in real life it may be doubted whether these terms can have any absolute meaning and in most situations, if not all, the terms express relative concepts. Thus, everyone knows that plain water may be thought of as being safe and effective for the removal of a stain of cherry-colored sugar syrup from fabric. This will be true if the fabric is ordinary cotton, or linen, or polyester and the like. But if the fabric contains a "filler," or is colored with a water-soluble dye, the use of water may damage the fabric while removing the stain. In those conditions, while effective, the use of plain water will not be safe. Similarly, in cases where water will not harm the fabric, it will not be effective if the stain contains oil or grease. For them, a solvent such as alcohol, kerosene or benzene may be needed. These may be effective, but because they give off flammable fumes, care must be taken in using them. Oxalic acid is effective for the removal of rust stains, but it is a poison and must be used with great care. Are these products "safe"? Under what conditions? Thus, it is plain that the terms are relative and not absolute, and a designation that something is "safe" or "effective" involves collateral questions such as "to whom or what," and "for what purpose," and "compared to what"?

414 F.Supp. at 661–62. These questions recur in Chapter 3 when we consider new drug approval and medical device premarket review requirements.

3. *Proving GRASE.* In defending against an enforcement action alleging the sale of an unapproved new drug, the claimant apparently bears the burden of proving that the drug is generally recognized as safe and effective. See United States v. An Article of Drug ... "Bentex Ulcerine," 469 F.2d 875, 878–80 (5th Cir.1972). A claimant cannot avoid the entry of summary judgment simply by offering doctors' testimonials about the safety and effectiveness of the drug in question. See United States v. Articles of Drug ... Hormonin, 498 F.Supp. 424, 433–35 (D.N.J.1980), aff'd mem., 672 F.2d 902 (3d Cir.1981). A claimant need not, however, prove that a consensus of favorable expert opinion exists. Even so, the FDA may respond by offering affidavits from experts who conclude that the drug is not safe and effective. See United States v. Undetermined Quantities of "Cal–Ban 3000," 776 F.Supp. 249, 256 (E.D.N.C.1991) ("If there is a dispute among experts as to a drug's safety and effectiveness, this demonstrates that there is no general recognition of its safety and effectiveness therefore making it a new drug under the FDCA."). Even without introducing such affidavits, the FDA may be entitled to summary judgment on this issue by demonstrating the absence of any studies about the drug published in the medical literature. See United States v. Seven Cardboard Cases ... "ESGIC with Codeine Capsules," 716 F.Supp. 1221, 1224–25 (E.D.Mo. 1989). Thus, when the agency challenges an assertion of GRASE status, the seller faces long odds, but does the application of the "substantial evidence" standard render the exception from "new drug" approval requirements meaningless? Assuming that double-blind clinical trials exist to support the effectiveness of a long-used drug, doesn't GRASE status at least provide some procedural benefit?

4. *Material time and extent.* Even if expert agreement exists (as reflected in the medical literature) about the safety and effectiveness of a drug, a product must also have been "used to a material extent or for a material time" to escape classification as a new drug. See 21 U.S.C. § 321(p)(2). This scope and duration requirement ensures that the expert agreement will emerge from the test of time. See Kenneth C. Baumgartner, Getting a Grip on Material Time and Extent, 49 Food & Drug L.J. 433 (1994); Gary L. Yingling, Are We on the Road to a Single Drug Approval Process?, 45 Food Drug Cosm. L.J. 235 (1990).

5. *Over-the-counter drug monographs.* Manufacturers of OTC drugs must abide by the terms of "monographs" issued as regulations by the FDA. Unlike individual licenses for new drugs, OTC monographs emerge from lengthy reviews of the available safety and effectiveness information for entire classes of active ingredients, resulting in conclusions by the agency that nonprescription drug products are not "new drugs" under specified circumstances. Monographs dictate for particular categories of products—such as antacids or internal analgesics—permissible ingredients, dosages, and labeling claims. See 21 C.F.R. pt. 330; see also Cutler v. Hayes, 818

F.2d 879 (D.C.Cir.1987) (describing the OTC drug review); Lars Noah, Treat Yourself: Is Self–Medication the Prescription for What Ails American Health Care?, 19 Harv. J.L. & Tech. 359 (2006); Gardiner Harris, New F.D.A. Rules for Sunscreens to Show the Extent of Protection, N.Y. Times, June 15, 2011, at A1 (noting that it took more than 30 years to finalize the bulk of this monograph); Rob Stein, Children's Cold Remedies Raised Questions for Years, Wash. Post, Oct. 26, 2007, at A1 (reporting that an FDA advisory committee recommended revisions in the monograph for OTC cough-cold products to discourage their use in kids younger than six); Liz Szabo, ER Visits Fall for Tots After Meds Pulled, USA Today, Nov. 22, 2010, at 10B. Persons wishing to sell OTC drug products not covered by a monograph must file a new drug application. See Farquhar v. FDA, 616 F.Supp. 190, 192 (D.D.C.1985).

6. *Hokey homeopathy*. The statute defines drugs to include "articles recognized in the ... official Homeopathic Pharmacopoeia of the United States." Homeopathic drugs typically contain infinitesimally diluted quantities of naturally occurring substances (e.g., tincture of spider), making them unlikely to pose any safety concerns (or work for that matter). See Julie Deardorff, Homeopathy: The Placebo Effect? Fans Soar, but Foes Say There's Nothing in the Medicine, Chi. Trib., Mar. 6, 2011, at A4; Chris Woolston, Homeopathic Cold Remedies Are Quite Diluted, L.A. Times, Dec. 6, 2010, at E3. As a matter of longstanding policy, the FDA generally does not interfere with the marketing of such products. See Compliance Policy Guides § 400.400; Kimberly Brown, Comment, Federal Regulation of Homeopathy: A Pathway to Consumer Protection, 29 Temp. J. Sci. Tech. & Envtl. L. 337 (2010); Amy Gaither, Comment, Over the Counter, Under the Radar: How the Zicam Incident Came About Under FDA's Historic Homeopathic Exception, 62 Admin. L. Rev. 487 (2010). Efforts to stretch this de facto exemption have, however, met with agency resistance. See United States v. Writers & Research, Inc., 113 F.3d 8, 11 (2d Cir.1997) (holding that a homeopathic drug promoted as a treatment for terminal illnesses was not exempt from new drug approval requirements); Nanci Hellmich, HCG Weight–Loss Products Are Fraudulent, FDA Says: They're Not Dangerous, They Just Don't Work, USA Today, Jan. 24, 2011, at 4D (reporting that, according to an agency announcement, human chorionic gonadotropins sold as "homeopathic" OTC drugs do not abide by the CPG's criteria).

7. *Old medical devices*. The statutory definition makes no distinction between old and new devices, but devices that were introduced before May 28, 1976, or that are "substantially equivalent" to devices marketed before that date, may remain on the market, at least until the FDA issues a regulation that requires the filing of a premarket approval (PMA) application for a particular class of device (as it did for replacement heart valves). A person wishing to introduce a new device but asserting that it is substantially equivalent to a previously marketed device must file a premarket notification (PMN) under FDCA § 510(k) to advise the agency and demonstrate that the device has the same intended use and any changes in technological characteristics raise no new safety or effectiveness questions. See 21 U.S.C. § 360(k); see also General Med. Co. v. FDA, 770 F.2d 214,

217 & n.1 (D.C.Cir.1985) (deferring to the agency's position that a switch from prescription to OTC labeling altered the intended use and prevented a finding of substantial equivalence); United States v. Article of Device ... "Stryker," 607 F.Supp. 990, 996–97 (W.D.Mich.1985) (seller was required to file a new PMN before introducing a modified device). This has become the primary mechanism for FDA review of new devices. See S. Rep. No. 101–513, at 15 (1990) ("Over 95% of the devices marketed since the passage of the [1976] Amendments have been found 'substantially equivalent' to a predicate device."); see also Chap. 3(B).

C. ADULTERATION, MISBRANDING, AND THE PRACTICE OF MEDICINE

Historically, the core provisions of the statute prohibited adulteration and misbranding of products subject to the FDA's jurisdiction. Under FDCA § 501(a), a drug or device would be deemed "adulterated" if, among other things, "it consists in whole or in part of any filthy, putrid, or decomposed substance," or "it has been prepared, packaged, or held under insanitary conditions whereby it may have been contaminated with filth, or whereby it may have been rendered injurious to health." Under FDCA § 502, a drug or medical device would be deemed "misbranded" if, among other things, "its labeling is false or misleading in any particular," its label failed to include with sufficient prominence certain identifying information (such as its established name, ingredients, identity of the seller, and quantity of contents), or its labeling failed to provide "adequate directions for use" and appropriate warnings.

Thus, in situations where the FDA finds bacterial contamination, it may allege that the drug violates the statutory prohibitions against adulteration. See United States v. Morton–Norwich Prods., Inc., 461 F.Supp. 760, 762–65 (N.D.N.Y.1978). In addition, if the product is labeled as "sterile," any such contamination would violate the misbranding prohibitions. See United States v. Torigian Lab., Inc., 577 F.Supp. 1514, 1524–25 (E.D.N.Y.), aff'd mem., 751 F.2d 373 (2d Cir.1984); see also Rheinecker v. Forest Lab., Inc., 813 F.Supp. 1307, 1311 (S.D.Ohio 1993) (holding that a drug of substandard quality could violate both the adulteration and misbranding prohibitions). Even without evidence that finished drugs or medical devices are contaminated or sub-potent, failures to abide by good manufacturing practices (GMPs) required by the FDA would constitute adulteration. See United States v. Undetermined Quantities ... Proplast, 800 F.Supp. 499, 502 (S.D.Tex.1992). The following cases focus on the misbranding provisions. Subsequent sections will revisit the adulteration issues in connection with agency efforts to implement GMP requirements.

United States v. An Article ... Acu-dot

483 F.Supp. 1311 (N.D.Ohio 1980).

■ LAMBROS, DISTRICT JUDGE:

This action is the result of a libel of information brought by the United States of America for the condemnation of numerous cases of an over-the-counter medical device called an Acu-dot, as provided for in 21 U.S.C. § 334. The American firm that markets the seized devices, Acu-dot Corp., was the sole claimant-intervenor responding to the published notice of the in rem action. The court has been very much aware throughout the pendency of this action that the economic viability of Acu-dot Corp. is exclusively founded on its ability to market the res of this action, and therefore granted claimant-intervenor's request for expedited trial. * * *

In simple terms, the Acu-dot is a small, pin-head sized magnet attached to the underside of a circular, adhesive patch. It is sold to the public in sheets of ten, packaged in a flat, cardboard box. Inside the box, in addition to the sheet of ten Acu-dots, can be found a four-page pamphlet, purporting to be instructions for the use of the device. The obverse of the cardboard box reads in this way:

ACU–DOT

Magnetic Analgesic Patch

For temporary relief of occasional minor aches and pains of muscles and joints.

Contains 10 Patches

The reverse is labelled in this way:

ACU–DOT

Magnetic Analgesic Patch

Mfg. for Acu–Dot Corp. Box F 598, Akron, Ohio 44308

Directions for use: Apply fingertip pressure to sensitive area to determine point or points of sharpest pain or discomfort. Thoroughly clean and dry area and apply an adhesive-backed ACU–DOT to each such point. Complete adhesion of the ACU–DOT is recommended. Leave ACU–DOT in place for a two- to five-day period, then procedure may be repeated as needed for continued symptomatic relief. If itching, rash or other skin irritation occurs, discontinue use. If pain or soreness persists for ten days or longer, discontinue use and consult a physician. Keep this and all medicines out of the reach of children.

FOR EXTERNAL USE ONLY

MADE IN U.S.A.

Manufactured under U.S.A. Patent No. 4162672

The pamphlet insert merely enlarges on the information presented by the outer packaging, adding, however, that the device is "Not a pill. Not a drug. Easy to use."

Libellant claims that the Acu-dots are "misbranded" * * * , specifically attack[ing] the descriptions of the devices as "magnetic analgesic patch(es)" and "for temporary relief of occasional minor aches and pains of muscles and joints." Libellant offered the testimony of three experts—one biophysicist and two medical doctors. These experts were adduced to show that none of the theories offered by claimant-intervenor were valid explanations for the mechanism by which the devices were to achieve their results. Further, each expert testified to his belief that the devices could not achieve the effect alleged by the labeling, other than through a placebo effect.

On behalf of the effectiveness of the res, claimant-intervenor presented several theories for the mechanism of the device. At various times, it was suggested that the magnetic action of the device "drew" blood to the affected area, which action had the therapeutic effect; that the blood, being composed in part of iron-based chemicals, produced an electromotive force within the body when passing through the field of the magnet, much in the way electric generators produce electricity by moving an electric wire through a magnetic field; that the pressure of the device against the skin creates therapeutic effects in a way analogous to acupuncture techniques; that the ionization of molecules in the skin area under the magnet caused the therapeutic effect claimed; and, finally, that the claimed beneficial effect of the device was achieved largely as a result of the psychosomatic placebo response.[3] These various theories were suggested by the teachings of the patent said to include the res (U.S. patent #4,162,672), by the theories presented in an article written by Kyoichi Nakagawa, M.D., one of a number of Japanese researchers attempting to analyze the mechanism of an identical device now in wide currency in Japan, and, most importantly, by the empirical results of an experiment conducted by Rocco Antenucci, M.D., an Akron area family physician who testified at the hearing.

The most impressive evidence on behalf of the res was the result of the Antenucci study. That study purported to be a double-blind comparison of the Acu-dots with non-magnetized facsimiles. Of the 70 patients receiving the facsimiles, 10 indicated some degree of pain relief. Of the 152 patients receiving the Acu-dots, 138 reported some degree of pain relief. These figures are impressive and argue strongly for the therapeutic claims.

However, each of the government witnesses was able to suggest major flaws in the conception and execution of the test protocol. Considerable doubt was also cast on the Nakagawa study and the court was finally left with this problem: libellant could demonstrate that the therapeutic claims of the device could not be explained by any reasonable theory that did not rely on a "placebo" explanation, but had no empirical evidence of the lack

3. * * * [A] placebo cannot be dismissed as "ineffective" simply because it works its effect in a way more oblique than standard therapeutic treatments. As is seen infra in this opinion, the real difficulty of this case is that a "placebo" can work only by means of the artifice of its presentation to the patient—the patient must be misled as to its inherent effectiveness. This artifice is the heart of the negative aspects of a placebo, for the composition of the placebo is largely irrelevant to its effectiveness, and a sugar pill of minimal cost to the patient should theoretically be as effective as a $500 device. The person marketing the $500 device is misleading the buyer because the seller claims that the $500 device relieves pain, when it is really the patient's belief in the device that relieves pain. The potential for abuse is obvious.

of efficacy; claimant-intervenor had very weak theoretical support for the mechanism of the device, and vested its claims in unexplained empirical evidence.

The lack of empirical evidence on the part of libellant is not an insurmountable deficiency. * * * After careful consideration of all of the evidence, this court finds that any therapeutic value of the res is the result of its placebo effect, and that this placebo effect is very strong in the case of ailments for which the device is claimed effective. Thus, the device often can achieve its claims of providing "temporary relief of occasional minor aches and pains of muscles and joints;" but this effect is the result of nothing more than sophisticated marketing chicanery.

This court hastens to affirm here its belief in the right of the American public to seek any treatment it wishes, especially when that treatment is a harmless, if ineffective, drug or device. * * * There is a difference, however, between the right to use a harmless, ineffective drug or device and a claimed right to promote and profit from the drug or device. * * *

This court resists the impulse to allow claimant to market a product that works only by means of a placebo effect on the basis that it nevertheless often achieves a relief of pain as claimed. The strong placebo effect may save the res from claims of "false labeling" under 21 U.S.C. § 352(a), but it does not protect the device from the charge that the labeling is "misleading" under 21 U.S.C. § 352(a), and that is all that is required to warrant condemnation of the res. The device's label is "misleading" because the device is not inherently effective, its results being attributable to the psychosomatic effect produced by the advertising and marketing of the device. A kiss from mother on the affected area would serve just as well to relieve pain, if mother's kisses were marketed as effectively as the Acu-dot device.

This court finds that the device is "misbranded" under 21 U.S.C. § 352, and properly subject to seizure and condemnation under 21 U.S.C. § 334, even though the claims are not technically false, because the claims are inherently misleading. * * *

NOTES AND QUESTIONS

1. *Policing against economic frauds.* Ineffective products violate the general prohibition against misbranding. See United States v. An Article of Device . . . "Toftness Radiation Detector," 731 F.2d 1253, 1259 (7th Cir. 1984) ("[A] prescription device is misbranded unless it can be used safely and effectively for the purposes for which it is intended. That is, the device has to work—if it does not work, it is misbranded."); see also United States v. Articles of Drug, 825 F.2d 1238, 1241–45 (8th Cir.1987) (passing off drugs containing caffeine as having other active ingredients); United States v. One Device Intended for Use as a Colonic Irrigator, 160 F.2d 194 (10th Cir.1947) (sustaining action against the "Tox–Eliminator"); Peter Barton Hutt, A History of Government Regulation of Adulteration and Misbranding of Medical Devices, 44 Food Drug Cosm. L.J. 99, 105 (1989) (recounting the FDA's early enforcement actions against quack devices). Scientists have, however, begun to take the placebo effect seriously as a therapeutic mechanism. See Adam J. Kolber, A Limited Defense of Clinical Placebo Deception, 26 Yale L. & Pol'y Rev. 75 (2007); Gardiner Harris, Study Finds Many Doctors Often Give Placebos, N.Y. Times, Oct. 24, 2008, at A12; Deborah Kotz, Can Chronic Medical Conditions, Including Depression, Be Treated with Placebos? Recent Studies Suggest They Can, Boston Globe, Mar. 7, 2011, at G12 (reporting one online company's plans to sell Obecalp (placebo spelled backward) for $5.95 per 50 doses). If a product is otherwise harmless, why should the FDA care that consumers may waste money on worthless treatments? Might ineffectiveness alone pose a risk to health?

2. *Protecting gullible consumers.* In assessing promotional claims directed to laypersons, the courts often ask how an unsophisticated consumer would understand the message. See V.E. Irons, Inc. v. United States, 244 F.2d 34, 39–40 (1st Cir.1957); id. at 42 ("Bearing in mind the broadly remedial purposes of the Act in preventing deception, the Congress must be taken to have meant to strike not only at palpably false claims but also at clever indirection and ambiguity in the creation of misleading impressions."); United States v. 62 Packages ... Marmola Prescription Tablets, 48 F.Supp. 878, 887 (W.D.Wis.1943) (explaining, in the course of sustaining a misbranding charge against an anti-obesity drug, that the FDCA seeks "to protect the public, the vast multitude which includes the ignorant, the unthinking and the credulous who, when making a purchase, do not stop to analyze"). Disclaimers will not cure otherwise misleading claims. See Pasadena Research Lab. v. United States, 169 F.2d 375, 383 (9th Cir.1948). Note that, in these and other enforcement cases, the FDA must prove its case by a preponderance of the evidence. See United States v. 60 28–Capsule Bottles ... "Unitrol," 325 F.2d 513, 514 (3d Cir.1963); United States v. 4 Cases ... Slim–Mint Chewing Gum, 300 F.2d 144, 148–50 (7th Cir.1962); see also United States v. 43½ Gross Rubber Prophylactics ... , 65 F.Supp. 534, 535–37 (D.Minn.1946) (sustaining seizure of entire shipment of condoms based on limited sampling that identified defects in a small percentage). What substantiation is required to avoid a misbranding charge (is it, like GRASE, "substantial evidence" of effectiveness)? Cf. FTC v. QT, Inc., 512 F.3d 858 (7th Cir.2008) (affirming judgment for the Federal Trade Commission on charges that analgesic claims in advertising for an "ionized" brass bracelet lacked substantiation); id. at 862 ("[A]ll statements about how the product works—Q–Rays, ionization, enhancing the flow of bio-energy, and the like—are blather."); id. at 863 ("[T]he placebo effect cannot justify fraud in promoting a product.").

3. *Other types of misbranding violations.* The statute specifies a number of acts that may constitute misbranding. For instance, to provide "adequate directions for use," the labeling must identify the product's intended use(s). See Alberty Food Prods. v. United States, 194 F.2d 463, 464 (9th Cir.1952). In addition, courts have interpreted the basic prohibition to imply other specific requirements. See United States v. Dino, 919 F.2d 72, 75 (8th Cir.1990) ("While the statute does not specifically state that a drug in a container without this information is 'misbranded,' we think the language 'false or misleading in any particular' includes drugs received without lot numbers or expiration dates."). Labeling issues are addressed at greater length in Chapter 4.

United States v. Evers

643 F.2d 1043 (5th Cir.1981).

■ RANDALL, CIRCUIT JUDGE:

* * * Dr. H. Ray Evers is the owner and operator of Ra–Mar Clinic, a health facility which opened in 1976 in Montgomery, Alabama. Dr. Evers and his clinic specialize in the treatment of chronic degenerative diseases. Although the clinic is not a hospital, it has a 40–bed capacity and does accept patients for treatment on a resident basis for periods of up to three or four weeks. A central part of Dr. Evers' approach to the treatment of degenerative diseases is his use of "chemo-endartectomy therapy." Dr. Evers explains this therapy as "a special treatment given by licensed medical doctors for the relief of poor circulation that has been caused by hardening of the arteries (arteriosclerosis, atherosclerosis)." Dr. Evers' approach, which he describes as "holistic" and "preventative," seeks to alleviate circulatory disorders by creating the proper balance of metals, vitamins, enzymes and other substances in the body.

The most important part of Dr. Evers' chemo-endartectomy therapy is his use of "chelation." Chelation is a chemical reaction which occurs between certain drugs and various harmful metals which are in the bloodstream. These drugs, which Dr. Evers injects intravenously, form a bond with heavy metals in a form which allows them to pass out of the body through the kidneys. Chelating drugs are ordinarily used for the treatment of heavy metal poisoning, particularly lead poisoning. According to Dr. Evers, however, this process also removes from blood vessels build-ups of calcium which are blocking the vessels and causing hardening of the arteries. Dr. Evers claims that he has used chelation therapy with tremendous success in the treatment of circulatory disorders, and with little danger to his patients.

Whether this process actually has this beneficial effect is a serious question. Dr. Evers' claims for his therapy are not generally accepted by the medical profession, and, as discussed below, the FDA has not approved any chelating drug for use in the treatment of circulatory disorders. Moreover, chelating drugs bear a serious danger: if too many heavy metals are passed into the kidneys within too short a period of time, the patient may suffer kidney failure and may die as a result. An additional danger, of course, is that patients who could benefit from a more traditional mode of treatment (probably heart by-pass surgery) will be convinced by Dr. Evers' alternative to postpone that treatment until it is too late. * * *

The focus of the government's case against Dr. Evers is not, however, the potential danger in his use of chelation therapy. Instead, the government challenges his vigorous promotion and advertising of chelating drugs for a use which has not been approved by the FDA. * * * When the Ra–Mar Clinic opened in 1976, Dr. Evers placed a full two-page advertisement in the Montgomery Advertiser. Although the ad did not explain Dr. Evers' program in any detail, it specifically listed chemo-endartectomy therapy as one of his chief methods. The more important aspect of Dr. Evers' campaign, however, consists of a booklet describing the Ra–Mar Clinic. The booklet explains chemo-endartectomy and chelation in lay terms and describes the program employed by the Ra–Mar Clinic. The booklet claims remarkable success for chelation, cites Dr. Evers' extensive experience with the process, urges the reader to try chemo-endartectomy therapy before traditional modes of treatment, and underplays the serious dangers involved in the use of chelating drugs. This booklet was apparently given to patients and prospective patients of the clinic, both in person and through the mail. * * *

Although there exists a variety of lawful chelating drugs, the government has charged Dr. Evers in this suit with the misbranding of one particular chelating drug, calcium disodium edetate (Calcium EDTA). * * * [T]he FDA-approved labeling (commonly called the package insert) for Calcium EDTA does not indicate that the drug can be used to treat circulatory diseases and does not include any instructions for the use of the drug for such purposes. In fact, the sole purpose indicated on the label for Calcium EDTA is "the reduction of blood levels and depot stores of lead in lead poisoning (acute and chronic) and lead encephalopathy." The FDA is therefore correct in its assertion that, whether or not chelation is of any beneficial effect to a patient suffering circulatory diseases, the package insert in the Calcium EDTA used by Dr. Evers provided no direction whatsoever for that use of the drug. * * *

In response to this charge, Dr. Evers (as well as certain of his patients, as intervenors) argues that as a licensed physician he has a right to prescribe any lawful drug for any purpose, whether or not that purpose has been approved by the FDA. The district court agreed with Dr. Evers and held that no misbranding could result from a doctor's prescription of a lawful drug to his own patients. The court relied for this holding on the intent of the statute, which seeks to avoid interference with "the practice of medicine;" on supposed limitations on the powers of Congress; and on the patient's constitutional right to privacy in the context of medical care.

However, the analysis urged by Dr. Evers and adopted by the district court misapprehends the thrust of the government's case against Dr. Evers, for the FDA has at no point contended, and the government does not argue on appeal, that the misbranding provisions of the Act prohibit a doctor from prescribing a lawful drug for a purpose for which the drug has not been approved by the FDA. To the contrary, the FDA has explicitly informed Dr. Evers that he could legally prescribe chelating drugs for the treatment of circulatory disorders. When Dr. Evers inquired of the FDA in early 1974 whether he could use Calcium EDTA for that purpose, the agency responded by letter that "[u]se of a locally obtained drug for an indication which is not in the package insert is considered 'the practice of medicine,' " and that Dr. Evers therefore need not seek any exception to the regulations. This advice to Dr. Evers rested on a discussion of the Act which appears in a notice of proposed rulemaking which the FDA issued in 1972 but on which it has never acted. See 37 Fed. Reg. 16,503 (1972). As the agency explained in that notice:

> Once (an approved) new drug is in a local pharmacy after interstate shipment, the physician may, as part of the practice of medicine, lawfully prescribe a different dosage for his patient, or may otherwise vary the conditions of use from those approved in the package insert, without informing or obtaining the approval of the Food and Drug Administration. This interpretation of the Act is consistent with congressional intent as indicated in the legislative history of the 1938 Act and the drug amendments of 1962. Throughout the debate leading to the enactment, there were repeated statements that Congress did not intend the Food and Drug Administration to interfere with medical practice and references to the understanding that the bill did not purport to regulate the practice of medicine as between the physician and the patient. Congress recognized a patient's right to seek civil damages in the courts if there should be evidence of malpractice, and declined to provide any legislative restrictions upon the medical profession.

Of course, while the Act was not intended to regulate the practice of medicine, it was obviously intended to control the availability of drugs for prescribing by physicians. In order to extend this control to situations like the one before us, the FDA has proposed regulations and actively has sought legislation which would restrict the availability of lawful drugs for uses for which the drugs have not been approved by the FDA. Nevertheless the government agrees with Dr. Evers that the provisions of the Act and the regulations of the FDA that are now in force do not prevent him from prescribing for uses not approved by the FDA drugs which have been approved by the FDA for some other purpose. * * *

Since the government relies for its case on Dr. Evers' promotion and advertising of chelating drugs for an unapproved use, and since the FDA itself interprets the Act to allow physicians to prescribe (while not promoting or advertising) lawful drugs for unapproved uses, we need not decide whether, as the district court apparently concluded, the Constitution prohibits federal interference with prescriptions by licensed physicians. The question before us is the narrower issue of whether Dr. Evers violated section 301(k) of the Act. In order to establish such a violation, the government must demonstrate the two elements required by that section. In terms of this case, we must find (1) that Dr. Evers held Calcium EDTA for sale after its shipment in interstate commerce, and (2) that Dr. Evers' promotion and advertising of Calcium EDTA without providing any more information than was contained on the drug's label and in the clinic's pamphlets failed to provide "adequate directions for use" and therefore constitutes misbranding under section 502(f)(1) of the Act.

The Act was intended, inter alia, to keep misbranded drugs out of the channels of interstate commerce. The flow of commerce begins with the manufacturer of the drug and ends with the consumer, that is, the patient. Accordingly, section 301 of the Act is designed to prevent misbranding at each stage of the distribution process. * * * Section 301(k) extends the Act's protection to the entire distribution process for drugs moving in interstate commerce by covering what is often the final stage in that process: the distribution by a person not himself a party to the interstate transportation of the drug. * * * A serious gap would be left in the statute if doctors who had received drugs in an intrastate transaction from a party who had in turn received them from interstate commerce were allowed to misbrand the drugs and then distribute them to their patients. Doctors holding drugs for use in their practice are clearly one part of the distribution process, and doctors may therefore hold drugs for sale within the meaning of section 301(k) of the Act.

We now turn to the second requirement of section 301(k) in the context of this case: the drug at issue must have been misbranded. In order to establish that Dr. Evers misbranded Calcium EDTA, the government relies on section 502(f)(1) of the Act. As discussed above, that section deems a drug to be misbranded "unless its labeling bears . . . adequate directions for use." * * * [I]nterpretation begins with 21 C.F.R. § 201.5 (1980), which defines "adequate directions for use" as "directions under which the layman can use a drug safely and for the purposes for which it is intended." The "intended use" of the drug is the "objective intent of the persons legally responsible for the labeling of the drug," and may be determined, for example, by "labeling claims, advertising matter, or oral or written statements by such persons or their representatives." 21 C.F.R. § 201.128. Since Dr. Evers clearly intended to use Calcium EDTA for the treatment of arteriosclerosis, these provisions would seem to require him to provide adequate directions in lay terms to his patients for the use of Calcium EDTA in the treatment of arteriosclerosis. However, * * * since Calcium EDTA is a prescription drug, there is no conceivable explanation which Dr. Evers could have given to his patients which would have complied with section 502(f)(1)'s requirement of adequate directions for lay use.

However, this does not mean that drug distributors misbrand each prescription drug which they hold for sale, for the statute provides for two important exceptions to section 502(f)(1) of the Act. In the first place, the section itself authorizes the FDA to create a regulatory exemption. The FDA has exercised this authority by creating an exception for prescription drugs. See 21 C.F.R. §§ 201.100, 201.115. In order to qualify for the prescription drug exception under these regulations, the drug's labeling must meet a number of specific full disclosure requirements. The labeling must include, for example: certain information regarding dosage, administration, and the drug's active ingredients; a warning that the drug cannot lawfully be dispensed without a prescription; an identifying number from which one may determine the manufacturing history of the particular package of the drug; a statement directed to the pharmacist specifying the type of container to be used in dispensing the drug; and, if the drug is a "new drug" within the meaning of the Act, a label which has been approved by the FDA pursuant to a new drug application under the Act. If these extensive requirements are met, the drug is completely exempt from the reach of section 502(f)(1) of the Act, and the distributor of the drug therefore need not provide "adequate directions for use" to the layman.

In the second place, the statute itself provides for an exception in section 503(b)(2) of the Act. This section states that if certain basic information is provided on the label a prescription drug shall be exempt from most of the requirements of section 502 of the Act, including that of section 502(f)(1). While the requirements of this section are somewhat more lenient than those of the regulatory exception, it provides a much narrower protection for the distributor of the drug, for it exempts the provisions of section 502 of the Act only at the point at which the drug is actually prescribed and dispensed by a licensed physician. The regulatory exemption, on the other hand, protects any person who holds the drug for sale at any point in the distribution process. * * *

The purpose of this scheme is, in brief, to require that adequate information be provided to the person who must decide whether and how to administer the drug. Where non-prescription drugs are involved, the "adequate directions for use" requirement insures full disclosure to the layman purchasing the drugs for self-treatment. But prescription drugs depend for their safety and effectiveness on the professional judgment of a licensed physician. Accordingly, the prescription drug exceptions to the "adequate directions for use" requirement contain conditions requiring adequate information for prescribing doctors. * * * It is undisputed that Dr. Evers did in fact fail to provide adequate directions for either lay or professional use; Dr. Evers does not contend that his booklets contained "adequate directions for lay use" within the meaning of the regulations, and he does not appear to have made any attempt to meet the terms of either the regulatory or the statutory exception for prescription drugs.

When each of the two elements of the offense with which Dr. Evers is charged is examined individually, Dr. Evers does indeed seem to have violated the statute. A different picture emerges, however, when the two elements are considered together. Since Calcium EDTA is a prescription drug, the FDA can establish an act of misbranding under section 502(f)(1) of the Act only by proving that Dr. Evers did not provide adequate information for use by physicians, as is required by the exceptions to that section * * * [, but] the government does not contend that Dr. Evers was distributing Calcium EDTA to other licensed physicians. The government therefore must find itself in an awkward position: while the misbranding violation it urges is based on Dr. Evers' failure to provide adequate information to licensed physicians, it seeks to include his actions within the reach of section 301(k) of the Act by virtue of his distribution to patients.

The requirement which the FDA seeks to impose is nonsensical. Since Calcium EDTA is a prescription drug, the misbranding provision under which Dr. Evers was charged requires him to provide adequate information for use by prescribing physicians. However, Dr. Evers was the only physician who used the Calcium EDTA in question. The government's application of the statute may therefore be reduced to the following proposition: Dr. Evers did not provide adequate information to himself. * * *

Although Dr. Evers was holding Calcium EDTA for sale in the sense that he was distributing it to his own patients, he was not holding it for sale to physicians. Section 301(k) of the Act cannot reasonably be read to require a physician who is holding a drug for sale only to patients to provide adequate information to physicians to whom he is not distributing the drug. * * * No legitimate purpose is served when a statutory provision requiring disclosure to one particular group of purchasers is invoked on the basis of sales made to a different group. Since Dr. Evers was holding Calcium EDTA, a prescription drug, for sale only to his patients, and since section 502(f)(1) of the Act does not require any disclosure to patients regarding prescription drugs, we conclude that Dr. Evers did not violate section 301(k) of the Act.[16] We have not been called upon in this case to consider the safety and effectiveness of Dr. Evers' use of chelation therapy; accordingly, we neither approve nor criticize his medical practices. * * *

NOTES AND QUESTIONS

1. *Prescription labeling.* See United States v. Articles of Drug, 625 F.2d 665, 672–75 (5th Cir.1980) (accepting the FDA's interpretation of the statute as requiring that prescription drugs satisfy regulatory exemptions to avoid a misbranding charge for failure to provide adequate directions for lay use); see also United States v. An Article of Device ... "Toftness Radiation Detector," 731 F.2d 1253, 1260–62 (7th Cir.1984) (holding that the claimant had the burden of proving compliance with the prescription labeling exemption applicable to devices). See generally Richard P. Shafer, Annotation, Exemption from Provision of § 502(f) of the Federal Food, Drug, and Cosmetic Act That Drug or Device Is Misbranded Unless Its Label Bears "Adequate Directions for Use," 65 A.L.R. Fed. 725 (1983 & 2011 Supp.). Chapter 4(A)(1) will revisit some of these questions.

---

16. One might argue that although Dr. Evers did not distribute Calcium EDTA to other physicians, he nevertheless "labeled" the drug to the medical community at large through his public promotional and advertising efforts, and that he therefore caused the drug to be "misbranded" because the drug's label did not meet the full disclosure requirements of the regulatory exception to section 502(f)(1) with respect to the new use advocated for the drug by Dr. Evers. * * * This approach relies on the promotion per se of the drug, and seems to ignore altogether the fact that misbranding under section 301(k) of the Act can occur only with respect to particular drugs "held for sale after shipment in interstate commerce." At base, this theory equates promotion with sale, and therefore brings into question the legality of a physician's advocacy of any medical program involving drugs not approved for the advocated use by the FDA, even when the physician does not himself sell or even dispense the drug. But the Act was intended to regulate the distribution of drugs in interstate commerce, not to restrain physicians from public advocacy of medical opinions not shared by the FDA. We believe, therefore, that a doctor who merely advocates to other doctors a lawful prescription drug for a use not approved by the FDA, and does not distribute that drug to other doctors, is not holding that drug for sale within the meaning of the statute and therefore is not in violation of section 301(k) of the Act.

2. *Interstate commerce.* The FDA's jurisdiction extends only to products that have moved in interstate commerce, but it generally has no difficulty satisfying this requirement. See Baker v. United States, 932 F.2d 813, 814–16 (9th Cir.1991) (holding that the interstate movement of ingredients used in a drug manufactured and sold only intrastate would create a sufficient connection to interstate commerce). With regard to medical devices, Congress eliminated the need to demonstrate any movement in interstate commerce. See United States v. Two Units ... of a Power Unit and a Chair, 49 F.3d 479, 481 (9th Cir.1995); see also FDAMA, Pub. L. No. 105–115, § 419, 111 Stat. 2296, 2379 (1997) (codified at 21 U.S.C. § 379a) (extending this presumption to all FDA regulated products). A drug or device is "held for sale" by a health care provider even if not resold to patients but used in the course of treatment. See United States v. Diapulse Corp. of Am., 514 F.2d 1097, 1098 (2d Cir.1975); United States v. Article of Drug ... Reserpine Tablets, 568 F.Supp. 29, 31 (D.N.J.1983); United States v. Article of Device ... Cameron Spitler, 261 F.Supp. 243, 246 (D.Neb. 1966).

3. *Practice of medicine.* As mentioned in *Evers*, once a product reaches a health care professional, the FDA has no power to regulate its use, not because the product lacks the necessary connection with interstate commerce, but because of the agency's longstanding policy against interfering with the practice of medicine. See FTC v. Simeon Mgmt. Corp., 391 F.Supp. 697, 705–07 (N.D.Cal.1975) (holding that the promotion of a treatment program by a weight loss clinic based on off-label uses of drugs did not violate the FDCA), aff'd, 532 F.2d 708, 717 (9th Cir.1976). Note that, although the phrase "practice of medicine" gets bandied about with some regularity, it lacks a fixed meaning. See Lars Noah, Ambivalent Commitments to Federalism in Controlling the Practice of Medicine, 53 U. Kan. L. Rev. 149, 161–64, 185–88 (2004); id. at 163 & n.58 (offering as an illustration the suggestion that "physicians who testify as experts in litigation engage in the practice of medicine"); id. at 185 (arguing that "the legitimate practice of medicine" may be "a contested political and social question"). Historically, states exercised primary authority over medical practitioners. See Timothy S. Jost, Oversight of the Quality of Medical Care: Regulation, Management, or the Market?, 37 Ariz. L. Rev. 825, 827–41 (1995); see also Philip M. Rosoff & Doriane L. Coleman, The Case for Legal Regulation of Physicians' Off–Label Prescribing, 86 Notre Dame L. Rev. 649 (2011). Is this sufficient oversight? Note that some physicians still use chelation therapy even though it does not appear to work. See Rob Stein, FDA Warns Companies Promoting Products Used in Chelation Procedures, Wash. Post, Oct. 15, 2010, at A3 (noting that a CDC survey found more than 100,000 adults had undergone chelation in 2006 for unapproved uses); Researchers Debunk Fringe Heart Therapy, Hous. Chron., Mar. 22, 2001, at A25; see also Gina Kolata, Drug That Stops Bleeding Shows Off–Label Dangers, N.Y. Times, Apr. 19, 2011, at D1 (reporting that 97% of use of the Factor VIIa drug NovoSeven® in hospitals occurs off-label but often appears to offer little long-term benefit and sometimes also poses an increased risk of clotting).

4. *Commercialization.* What if Dr. Evers had sold Calcium EDTA to other physicians for use in the treatment of arteriosclerosis along with detailed instructions and warnings (would he have anything to fear from the agency)? See United States v. Burzynski Cancer Research Inst., 819 F.2d 1301, 1304–05 (5th Cir.1987) (recounting FDA enforcement action against a clinic selling unapproved new drugs in interstate commerce); United States v. Hoxsey Cancer Clinic, 198 F.2d 273, 281 (5th Cir.1952) (same); Cowan v. United States, 5 F.Supp.2d 1235, 1240 (N.D.Okla.1998) (explaining, in the course of rejecting a terminally ill patient's effort to secure access to an unapproved AIDS drug containing goat neutralizing antibodies, that "[n]othing in the FDCA or the case law suggests that the exception [for physicians from the statute's registration requirements] was intended to be expanded to permit doctors to test unapproved drugs"); see also United States v. Livdahl, 356 F.Supp.2d 1289 (S.D.Fla.2005) (preliminarily enjoining defendants' continued distribution of unapproved Botulinum Toxin Type A); Al Kamen, FDA's Allergic Reaction, Wash. Post, Jan. 15, 2007, at A13 (reporting that, shortly after his election to Congress, a physician received a warning letter from the FDA for compounding and selling allergy shots to patients in two dozen states); Trine Tsouderos, FDA to Doctor: Stop Web Claims, Chi. Trib., Apr. 26, 2011, at A1 (reporting agency action against a physician whose website touted off-label uses of thermographic camera).

Retkwa v. Orentreich

579 N.Y.S.2d 577 (Sup.Ct.1991).

■ SKLAR, JUSTICE:

Defendants Norman Orentreich, MD and Orentreich Medical Group move for an order vacating a medical malpractice panel's unanimous finding of liability against the defendants, on the ground that the panel erroneously considered evidence on the issue of whether defendants violated the Federal Food, Drug and Cosmetic Act by compounding liquid silicone for injection into plaintiff's face. * * *

Defendants readily admit that the microdroplet liquid silicone which was compounded by Dr. Orentreich's staff was a class III "device" without premarket approval and was therefore deemed to be an adulterated device within the meaning of the Act. The defendants allege, however, that the nonmedical grade base silicone which was shipped by Dow Chemical [from Delaware to New York] was not such a device when shipped interstate and that therefore the requisite contact with interstate commerce was absent. Defendants further allege that the Act was not intended to regulate physicians within their own practices, whether or not the device being used was approved * * * *

It is not necessary under [21 U.S.C. § 331(k)] to show that a device was adulterated when it left the interstate sender's hand or that it became adulterated while still in interstate commerce. Nor is there a necessity to show any wrongful motive or intent on the part of the sender. Indeed, it is not even necessary that the individual or entity receiving the article in interstate commerce be involved in the misbranding or adulteration. Rather, it is sufficient if the device was held for sale after shipment in interstate commerce and then was adulterated. A device is "held for sale" within the meaning of the Act if it is, inter alia, held by a practitioner for treatment of patients.

Defendants' assertion that the nonmedical grade base silicone which was shipped interstate by Dow is not a device within the meaning of the Act is without merit. * * * It is readily apparent from the definition of the word "device" that it applies to any component of a device which was intended to affect the structure or functions of the body. Clearly defendants intended such result when the base silicone was ordered from Dow and when they compounded it and injected it. Moreover, analogous case law involving drugs supports the conclusion that the base silicone falls within the reach of the statute. For example, in *United States v. Dianovin Pharmaceuticals, Inc.*, 475 F.2d 100 (1st Cir.1973), the appeals court upheld the district court's determination that a drug manufacturer's use of the raw material vitamin K, which had been shipped in interstate commerce, in making the drug injectable vitamin K, solely for local consumption fell within the Act since articles intended for use as components of a drug were also defined as drugs * * * *

The defendants further urge that Congress did not intend that the Act interfere with the practice of medicine or prohibit the use by a physician of any product whether or not it was approved or adulterated. The defendants attempt to support their argument with case authority but a review of the cases cited reveals that the physicians in those cases were using approved drugs for unapproved uses. Indeed, I could find no authority for the proposition that the Act was inapplicable to physicians using a drug or device which was never approved for any purpose. * * * In *United States v. Algon Chem. Inc.*, 879 F.2d 1154, 1163 (3d Cir.1989), the [court] concluded that Congress intended nothing more than to preserve a physician's right to compound and prepare medicines which were legally obtained during the course of the physician's medical practice. * * *

I find that defendants' conduct in preparing and administering the silicone injections to the plaintiff falls within the "held for sale" provision of 21 U.S.C. § 331(k) and therefore has the requisite contact with interstate commerce to come within the operation of the Act. Further, the medical-practice exception to the Act does not pertain to a physician's compounding of an unapproved or illegal substance as any contrary result would defeat the intent of the protections afforded by the Act. Accordingly, the defendants' motion is denied.

United States v. Baxter Healthcare Corp.

901 F.2d 1401 (7th Cir.1990).

■ CUMMINGS, CIRCUIT JUDGE:

The federal Food and Drug Administration (FDA) challenges a program involving the reconstitution, repackaging, freezing, and distribution of already approved drugs without specific FDA approval for final products of the program as new drugs. The district court granted the FDA's motion for a preliminary injunction prohibiting Baxter Healthcare Corporation and intervenor Glaxo Specialties, Inc. from producing (so far as is relevant to this appeal) eight ready-to-use frozen antibiotic drug products pending trial on the merits. The FDA claims that Baxter and Glaxo must apply to the FDA for separate approval to combine drug powders and liquids that have already been approved by the FDA into packages that are readily usable by the hospitals, clinics, and physicians to whom they are sold. * * * Baxter and Glaxo respond that the FDA unreasonably demands more than one approval for the same drug products. The companies assert that they do not violate the FDCA in acting without separate FDA approval because by the FDA's admission the drugs which are the components of the final products have already been approved by the FDA and, the companies assert, are being combined in FDA-approved containers in the detailed manner prescribed by the FDA through manufacturing practices open to inspection by the FDA. Baxter seeks to avoid submitting the products to the FDA's new drug approval system. * * *

Baxter is a large manufacturer and distributor of health-care products incorporated in Delaware originally as Travenol Laboratories, Inc. Since July 1982, Baxter has operated or attempted to operate a Travenol Regional Compounding Center (TRC), first opening a center in Morton Grove, Illinois, later adding a second in Bridgeport, New Jersey. Baxter created the TRC program because many drugs do not leave drug manufacturers in final form for administration to patients, but instead are purchased in either lyophilized (freeze-dried) or liquid concentrate form. Hospitals have commonly responded to the need to prepare the drugs for administration to patients by operating their own centralized drug preparation programs for the reconstitution, dilution, repackaging, and in some cases freezing, of antibiotics in batches. The TRC program is designed to transform such powders and concentrates on a large scale into dosage packages suitable for immediate use by health-care providers * * * *

The FDA alleges that the TRC activities violate the FDCA because, in essence, the drug packages produced at the TRCs are new drugs which must be separately tested for safety and efficacy. The FDA states that Baxter is inappropriately relying on a labeling system intended to be used in the best professional judgment of medical professionals in the context of hospitals and clinics, not by commercial manufacturers on a large scale. Baxter and Glaxo respond that the products at issue are in no sense new drugs because they are the direct result of the reconstitution of already approved component drugs in a manner which they assert is dictated by the FDA labels. The companies assert that they can follow the labels even more reliably and efficiently than can individual hospitals or doctors. * * *

Each of the eight component drugs at issue is subject to regulation under Section 507(a) of the FDCA as an antibiotic, the infection-fighting drug defined in the FDCA as that "produced by a microorganism and which has the capacity to inhibit or destroy microorganisms in dilute solution." * * * Under Section 507, the Commissioner of the FDA has the authority to certify every batch of antibiotic drug as safe and effective:

> A batch of [antibiotic for human use] shall be certified if such drug has such characteristics of identity and such batch has such characteristics of strength, quality, and purity, as the Secretary prescribes in such regulations as necessary to adequately insure safety and efficacy of use, but shall not otherwise be certified. * * *

Section 507 of the FDCA authorizes the FDA to promulgate regulations requiring that each batch of antibiotic drug be certified. A batch is a specific homogenous quantity produced under a single order during one manufacturing cycle. In 1982, however, the FDA exempted all antibiotic drugs for human use from the batch certification requirement that had been authorized by Congress. See 21 C.F.R. § 433.1. This regulatory exemption was to apply so long as four conditions were met, only two of which are relevant here: (1) that the drug has been approved for marketing (pursuant to the approval procedures and requirements found in 21 C.F.R. Part 314), and (2) that the drug is packaged and labeled for dispensing in accordance with the applicable monograph, except where other labeling has been approved pursuant to an application. * * *

Baxter responds that it does not seek an exemption from Section 507(a) of the FDCA, but instead has complied fully with the FDCA because its drug products are in fact certified drugs. Thus the first and it would appear largely decisive question in this appeal is this: may the FDA permissibly interpret the term "antibiotic drug" in Section 507(a) as including the TRC drug products subject to a new round of certification? We conclude that it may. * * *

This may be the archetypal case calling for agency expertise. The FDA states that as a matter of science Baxter is "compounding" substances to produce drugs that differ in important, if sometimes subtle, ways from those component substances. In order to side with Baxter, we would need to find the authority to disagree with the following assertions solicited by the FDA in this case: (1) "leaching" (that is, movement of chemicals into the bag contents) from the plastic bags used as the final container for the TRC products may change the chemical composition of the TRC products with possibly harmful effects; (2) the longer than approved expiration dates for nafcillin, piperacillin, and ticarcillin may have the effect of altering the concentration of the drug, with possibly harmful effects; (3) similarly, the freezing of penicillin G and tobramycin without approval and use of an expiration date longer than that used in the insert might have the same effects; (4) a change in the method of manufacture of the component powders or liquids by their respective manufacturers "could result in the appearance of new impurities or degradation" of the TRC products, since adjustments might be required to be made by Baxter. In the view of the FDA, such concerns are not answered without adequate scientific testing to certify each drug product as a drug. Or, put in the terms of the FDCA, the drug products are "misbranded" pursuant to 21 U.S.C. § 352(*l*) because they are not antibiotics certified under 21 U.S.C. § 357(a) or exempt from certification pursuant to 21 U.S.C. § 357(c), (d). * * *

Congress has decided to treat commercial manufacturers of drugs differently from pharmacies and individual physicians in contexts closely related to that presented in this appeal. Therefore, to the extent Congress has addressed the issue, it has decided to focus governmental resources upon the commercial distributors of drugs rather than upon the trained pharmacists and physicians who must reconstitute drugs for patient use on a smaller scale. One sound argument for this choice is evident: A drug improperly compounded on a large scale will harm more patients than the same compounding mistake made on a smaller scale. * * *

As a policy choice, Congress has exempted pharmacies and physicians from the registration and inspection requirements that apply to all manufacturers of drugs. 21 U.S.C. §§ 360(g)(1), (2), 374(a)(1), (2). The FDA only follows that lead by focusing on the mass commercial distribution of drugs rather than at the individual level of hospitals and pharmacists. This does not suggest that the FDA has taken a path which is "manifestly contrary to the statute," but to the contrary suggests sound adherence to congressional intent. The methods used in small-scale drug admixture programs carried out by medical professionals may carry some of the same hazards complained of by the FDA regarding the TRC operations. But, as stated above, it is not illogical for Congress to suggest, and the FDA to effectuate the suggestion, that those hazards are most effectively met at the manufacturing level of the medical establishment. * * *

■ PELL, SENIOR CIRCUIT JUDGE (dissenting):

* * * When a single dose of an antibiotic, or a very small number of doses, are to be reconstituted, the reconstitution is done with a needle and syringe. An appropriate amount of sterile reconstituting fluid is drawn into the syringe, the needle is inserted through the stopper of the manufacturer's vial of lyophilized drug, and the reconstituting fluid is inserted into the vial. The powder and fluid are then agitated to form a solution. * * *

The single dose preparation technique for intravenous antibiotics is practiced at virtually all hospitals. Many larger hospitals, however, cannot meet their need for intravenous antibiotic drugs through the single dose preparation method. Many of these hospitals have established centralized drug preparation programs in which they reconstitute, dilute, and repackage the antibiotics in batches. It is not cost-effective for a hospital of more than 300 beds to engage in single dose reconstitution of antibiotics. Hospitals that engage in this type of centralized drug preparation do not necessarily reconstitute the antibiotics in response to an order for a specific patient. Some of these hospitals prepare batches of reconstituted antibiotics sufficient for one day's needs. Other hospitals prepare large batches intended to be used over a relatively long period of time. At least one hospital has prepared as many as 4,000 doses of reconstituted antibiotics at one time.

Hospitals that prepare single doses of reconstituted and/or diluted antibiotics may encounter numerous problems. These include: selection of the wrong drug, contamination during preparation, improper dosage, incorrect drug concentration, drug deterioration, labeling problems, and incompatible mixtures of drugs or fluids. Moreover, all hospitals experience critical care problems if prepared antibiotic drugs are not available.

Many reconstituted intravenous antibiotics have very short stability periods if maintained at room temperature, or even under refrigeration. In the 1960s and 1970s, research demonstrated that freezing could extend the stability period for most such drugs. * * * Virtually every hospital in the United States which has more than 300 beds has a pharmacy which operates an admixture program and many of these programs engage in the freezing of reconstituted antibiotics. Once freezing programs were developed, drug storage times were extended. The extensions were determined by reference to published literature, the institution's own studies, the manufacturer's labeling, or technical letters from manufacturers. Most hospitals, however, do not possess the facilities to engage in sophisticated analytical testing of these products. In fact, very few of these hospitals conduct stability testing on these frozen reconstituted antibiotics.

Baxter initiated its TRC program in 1982. The concept was that the TRC would perform the same functions as the hospital pharmacy, but more efficiently, more safely, and at a reduced price. * * * In the first seven years that the TRC has reconstituted and shipped these products, it has enjoyed an excellent safety record. During this time period, approximately seven million products have been produced at the TRCs, and there have been only 14 medical complaints. Moreover, none of these complaints have been attributed to the reconstitution and repackaging process at the TRC. * * * It is of interest to note that the FDA was informed of Baxter's intention to commence the TRC program even before it became operational. This was by letter to the district director of FDA in Chicago on June 16, 1982. FDA did not raise any regulatory objection to this program and Baxter began reconstituting drugs in July 1982. FDA investigators conducted inspections at the TRC in June 1983 and June 1985. Neither of these inspections resulted in any expressions of concern by the FDA. * * *

In the case at bar, the TRC products contain the same active and inactive ingredients as the approved product, and are of equal bioavailability and are bioequivalent to those approved products. Thus, it appears to me, the TRC products are the same "drug" as that which the FDA has approved. * * * [T]he TRC does not change anything about the product that would affect the rate and extent of absorption, and thus the TRC products are bioequivalent to the products that have already been approved by FDA. * * * They are not imitations or variations of the eight FDA antibiotics. They are the eight approved antibiotics now ready to be administered to a patient. They are simply brought farther along in their necessary preparation for use than were the drugs formerly. * * * Rather than employ this very extensive, expensive, and protracted [approval] procedure to deal specifically with the issues of stability in freezing and expiration dating, FDA is fully justified in utilizing the more specific and limited authority conferred by the CGMP regulations. * * *

I come away from reviewing this appeal with the unfortunate feeling that we have a case of bureaucratic overreaction to Baxter's declination to engage in a process which it did not deem legally necessary, in which position I fully concur. I do not intend to denigrate or minimize the importance of the [FDA] in protecting the interest of the public's safety in the use of drugs necessary in the continuation of good health. The diligence of FDA is testified to obviously by the periodic references in the media to drugs which are being administered in other parts of the world with effectiveness and apparent safety but which have not yet been approved for use in this country. I am putting aside in preparing this dissent any idea that the FDA in this case has succumbed to the necessities of its annual presentation of a budget to preserve, and ordinarily increase, that which Congress gives to it. Such budget requests, of course, are predicated to a considerable extent on justification of personnel needs, and I would be most disappointed in this respected governmental agency if it was devoting itself unnecessarily to an easily found target such as an established pharmaceutical company rather than to fly-by-night generic substitute operators. * * *

NOTES AND QUESTIONS

1. *Updates*. In 1997, as part of FDAMA, Congress codified the FDA's regulatory exemption from batch certification for antibiotics by deleting § 507. See Pub. L. No. 105–115, § 125(b)(1), 111 Stat. 2296, 2325. Thus, antibiotic products are now regulated in precisely the same fashion as drugs. That same year, the agency approved a purified form of liquid silicone for treating detached retinas. See Natasha Singer, Injecting Silicone, and Risk, N.Y. Times, Jan. 26, 2006, at G1 (reporting that this decision has allowed physicians to engage in off-label cosmetic use); cf. Anemona Hartocollis & Christina Davidson, Warning of a Cheap, Fast and Sometimes Deadly Way to Get Beautiful, N.Y. Times, Apr. 17, 2009, at A21 (reporting serious injuries associated with the growing popularity of liquid silicone injections by unlicensed practitioners).

2. *Drug compounding*. In his dissenting opinion in *Baxter*, Judge Pell described large-scale admixture programs run by hospital pharmacies—are these obviously lawful? The FDA has challenged physicians or pharmacists who compound drugs that they offer for general sale rather than solely in the treatment of a particular patient. See United States v. Sene X Eleemosynary Corp., 479 F.Supp. 970, 978–79 (S.D.Fla.1979) (rejecting practice of pharmacy defense to misbranding charges associated with large-scale compounding); see also Cabiroy v. Scipione, 767 A.2d 1078 (Pa.Super.Ct.2001) (finding that a physician's injection of unapproved liquid silicone constituted negligence per se). The resurgence in pharmacy compounding has raised concerns about product safety. See Erin Hallissy & Sabin Russell, Who's Mixing Your Drugs, S.F. Chron., June 23, 2002, at A1 (documenting serious instances of contamination); Gardiner Harris, Drugs' Cost and Safety Fuel a Fight, N.Y. Times, Apr. 5, 2011, at D5 ("[W]hile the compounds are supposed to be made specially for individuals, some compounding pharmacies operate in a legal gray area, making large batches of medicines and selling them widely. Even though many patients over the years have died after taking these medicines, the F.D.A. does not subject compounding pharmacies to the strict controls that are routine for drug manufacturers."); see also Tara Parker–Pope, New Controversy over Menopause Hormones, Wall St. J., May 2, 2006, at D1 (reporting that the FDA received thousands of adverse public comments after the manufacturer of Prempro® filed a petition asking the agency to crack down on compounded hormone products).

In *Thompson v. Western States Medical Center*, 535 U.S. 357 (2002) [excerpted in Chap. 4(C)], the Supreme Court offered the following background on pharmacy compounding and its regulation:

> Drug compounding is a process by which a pharmacist or doctor combines, mixes, or alters ingredients to create a medication tailored to the needs of an individual patient. Compounding is typically used to prepare medications that are not commercially available, such as medication for a patient who is allergic to an ingredient in a mass-produced product. It is a traditional component of the practice of pharmacy and is taught as part of the standard curriculum at most pharmacy schools. Many States specifically regulate compounding practices as part of their regulation of pharmacies. Some require all licensed pharmacies to offer compounding services. Pharmacists may provide compounded drugs to patients only upon receipt of a valid prescription from a doctor or other medical practitioner licensed to prescribe medication.... For approximately the first 50 years after the enactment of the FDCA, the FDA generally left regulation of compounding to the States. Pharmacists continued to provide patients with compounded drugs without applying for FDA approval of those drugs. The FDA eventually became concerned, however, that some pharmacists were manufacturing and selling drugs under the guise of compounding, thereby avoiding the FDCA's new drug requirements. In 1992, in response to this concern, the FDA issued a Compliance Policy Guide [No. 7132.16] ....
>
> Congress turned portions of this policy into law when it enacted the FDAMA in 1997. The FDAMA, which amends the FDCA, exempts compounded drugs from the FDCA's "new drug" requirements and other requirements provided the drugs satisfy a number of restrictions. 21 U.S.C. § 353a. First, they must be compounded by a licensed pharmacist or physician in response to a valid prescription for an identified individual patient, or, if prepared before the receipt of such a prescription, they must be made only in "limited quantities" and in response to a history of the licensed pharmacist's or physician's receipt of valid prescription orders for that drug product within an established relationship between the pharmacist, the patient, and the prescriber. Second, the compounded drug must be made from approved ingredi-

> ents that meet certain manufacturing and safety standards, and the compounded drug may not appear on an FDA list of drug products that have been withdrawn or removed from the market because they were found to be unsafe or ineffective. Third, the pharmacist or physician compounding the drug may not "compound regularly or in inordinate amounts (as defined by the Secretary) any drug products that are essentially copies of a commercially available drug product." Fourth, the drug product must not be identified by the FDA as a drug product that presents demonstrable difficulties for compounding in terms of safety or effectiveness. Fifth, in States that have not entered into a "memorandum of understanding" with the FDA addressing the distribution of "inordinate amounts" of compounded drugs in interstate commerce, the pharmacy, pharmacist, or physician compounding the drug may not distribute compounded drugs out of state in quantities exceeding five percent of that entity's total prescription orders. Finally, ... the prescription must be "unsolicited," and the pharmacy, licensed pharmacist, or licensed physician compounding the drug may "not advertise or promote the compounding of any particular drug, class of drug, or type of drug." The pharmacy, licensed pharmacist, or licensed physician may, however, "advertise and promote the compounding service."

Id. at 360–65. After the Court invalidated this provision of the statute on First Amendment grounds, the FDA issued a new guidance document setting forth its policies concerning the practice. See In re Establishment Inspection of Wedgewood Vill. Pharmacy, Inc., 270 F.Supp.2d 525, 545–50 (D.N.J.2003), aff'd, 421 F.3d 263, 272–73 (3d Cir.2005). One appellate court held, however, that the advertising prohibition was severable, which meant that the remainder of 21 U.S.C. § 353a remains operative in that jurisdiction. See Medical Ctr. Pharm. v. Mukasey, 536 F.3d 383, 401–05 (5th Cir.2008); Jesse M. Boodoo, Note, Compounding Problems and Compounding Confusion: Federal Regulation of Compounded Drug Products and the FDAMA Circuit Split, 36 Am. J.L. & Med. 220 (2010).

3. *Devices made to order*. "Custom devices" are exempt from premarket approval requirements so long as they satisfy restrictions that roughly parallel some of those imposed on compounded drugs. See 21 U.S.C. § 360j(b); 21 C.F.R. § 812.3; see also United States v. Endotec, Inc., 563 F.3d 1187, 1195–200, 1203–04 (11th Cir.2009) (discussing the application of this exemption to the defendants' ankle, knee and jaw implants); cf. John J. Smith, Physician Modification of Legally Marketed Medical Devices: Regulatory Implications Under the FDCA, 55 Food & Drug L.J. 245 (2000). In FDAMA, Congress codified the FDA's policy against interfering with the practice of medicine, though only with respect to devices. See 21 U.S.C. § 396. Congress has included similar language in numerous other statutes. See Lars Noah, Ambivalent Commitments to Federalism in Controlling the Practice of Medicine, 53 U. Kan. L. Rev. 149, 165–68 (2004).

4. *Reprocessing of single-use devices (SUDs)*. As a cost-saving measure, hospitals increasingly reuse disposable medical devices (i.e., devices labeled for single-use only). Responding to concerns about inadequate sterilization and material degradation, the FDA announced plans to regulate hospitals as device manufacturers when they engage in such reprocessing. See John J. Smith & Jennifer A. Agraz, Federal Regulation of Single–Use Medical Devices: A Revised FDA Policy, 56 Food & Drug L.J. 305 (2001); Diane Carey, Comment, Reprocessing and Reusing Single–Use Only Medical Devices: Safe Medical Practice or Risky Business?, 17 J. Contemp. Health L. & Pol'y 657 (2001); Alec Klein, FDA Asked About Oversight of Reused Medical Devices, Wash. Post, Dec. 17, 2005, at D1; see also Medical Device User Fee and Modernization Act of 2002, Pub. L. No. 107–250, §§ 301–303, 116 Stat. 1588, 1616–20. As a consequence, hospitals now leave most of the work to companies that specialize in device reprocessing. See Alec Klein, Good as New?: The Reuse of Medical Devices, Wash. Post, Dec. 11–12, 2005, at A1.

D. FDA Practice and Procedures

Peter Barton Hutt, *The Transformation of United States Food and Drug Law*

J. Ass'n Food & Drug Officials, Sept. 1996, at 1.

Neither the 1906 Act nor the 1938 Act is self-executing. Both have required FDA to implement very broad and general statutory provisions with more specific operating rules. Thus, FDA has spent the past century determining, and then making public, procedural and substantive policy statements designed to facilitate its administration of the organic statute. * * *

One of the major reasons for the use of rulemaking to replace individual court enforcement actions in the early 1970s was to achieve greater fairness and consistency in application of the law. Use of court enforcement, while clearly a permissible course of action, is inherently selective and can lead to the perception, and perhaps at times the reality, of invidious discrimination. Establishment of policy by promulgation of regulations, in contrast, assures that all affected companies have equal notice of FDA requirements and an equal opportunity for compliance. * * *

Prior to the 1970s, it was common practice simply to propose a regulation, obtain public comment and then publish a final regulation, without an explanation of the reasons for the proposal or why the changes recommended by the public comment were or were not accepted in the final regulations. FDA pioneered the use of explanatory preambles to both the proposed and the final regulations. The preamble to the proposal laid out in detail the need for the proposed regulation, any documentation appropriate for its specific provisions and an analysis of its intended interpretation and implementation. The preamble to the final regulation responded to each type of comment, stating the reasons why it was accepted or rejected. These preambles served and continue to serve to this day the purpose of educating FDA employees, the regulated industry and the general public about the important work of the agency. * * *

Because of the increasing burdens imposed by regulatory agencies on industry, Congress has responded with corresponding requirements for all federal agencies to justify their rulemaking. * * * As these requirements for the promulgation of regulations have increased, the number of regulations promulgated by FDA has decreased correspondingly. Issues that previously might have been resolved through regulations of the type promulgated by FDA during the 1970s increasingly have been handled by more informal approaches. * * * In the early 1990s, the use of guidelines by FDA * * * skyrocketed. Some courts have already found that these informal statements of policy are poorly disguised regulations and have invalidated or refused to enforce substantive guidelines implemented by FDA as though they were regulations. * * *

Under the 1906 Act, any violation constituted a misdemeanor punishable by a fine, imprisonment or both. Violative products were also subject to seizure. The 1938 Act expanded FDA's enforcement power. In addition to criminal liability and seizure, FDA was authorized to obtain a judicial injunction against any violation of the statute. FDA was also authorized to issue a written administrative notice or warning for minor violations in lieu of formal court proceedings, to conduct factory inspection and to issue publicity and other public information. FDA has not been satisfied with the enforcement powers specifically included within the 1938 Act. It has sought to expand these powers both through administrative action and through new legislation. * * *

Under the 1906 Act, FDA enforced the statute almost exclusively through seizure actions and criminal prosecution. * * * This pattern of enforcement continued under the 1938 Act but was profoundly affected by changes in statutory authority and FDA policy. First, as the 1938 Act was amended to require premarket approval for regulated products, FDA was able to enforce the statute informally through administrative decisions as part of the approval process rather than by formal court action. Second, as FDA realized that informal administrative sanctions such as regulatory/warning letters and recall requests were more efficient and effective, these informal actions also displaced formal court enforcement. Third, when FDA began to issue more and more of its policy in the form of regulations in the early 1970s and later guidelines in the early 1990s, violations by industry substantially decreased and thus the need for either informal or formal enforcement was diminished. As a result of all of these developments, the FDA enforcement statistics under the 1938 Act show an extraordinary shift from formal court action to informal administrative action * * * * FDA and the state agencies have always depended upon voluntary compliance by the vast majority of the regulated industry with food and drug laws and regulations. If there were any substantial noncompliance, neither FDA nor the state agencies would have sufficient resources to address the problem. * * *

From a policing role under the 1906 Act, FDA gradually undertook the role of sole gatekeeper to the marketplace. * * * This change in regulatory function has had the single most profound impact on FDA of any change in the history of the agency. For a product subject to premarket approval, no manufacturer may lawfully distribute the product and no member of the public has a right to obtain it unless and until FDA authorizes marketing. * * * [P]remarket approval under the 1938 Act includes no mechanism for public accountability. Citizens who wish to obtain a product have no right to participate in the process and no access to judicial review of whatever action is taken by FDA. Even the applicant is precluded from access to the courts until final action is taken on a product application. Because the premarket approval process is conducted in private without public participation and there is no right to judicial intervention or any other form of public accountability, it has become subject to increasing criticism. * * *

1. ADJUDICATION

United States v. Alcon Laboratories

636 F.2d 876 (1st Cir.1981).

■ CAMPBELL, CIRCUIT JUDGE:

The United States appeals from orders of the district court for the District of Puerto Rico in two seizure actions and a suit for injunctive relief instituted by the Food and Drug Administration (FDA) against Alcon Laboratories, Inc. and one of its products pursuant to the Federal Food, Drug, and Cosmetic Act.

Alcon manufactures and markets in suppository dosage a prescription antiemetic drug called "WANS." The drug contains pyrilamine maleate (an antihistamine) and pentobarbital sodium (a barbituate) and comes in three dosage strengths, WANS No. 1, WANS No. 2 and WANS Children. WANS has been used under medical supervision for approximately 25 years and did not become an object of FDA concern until 1978. * * *

Where the FDA believes that a drug is a "new drug" and is being marketed without approval of an NDA, it is empowered to institute seizure and injunction actions in federal district court to remedy the alleged violation of the Act. The agency may also seek criminal sanctions.

On March 17, 1978, the FDA sent Alcon a regulatory letter informing it of a report received from the agency's Neurological Drugs Advisory Committee "that children aged 6 months to seven years who were treated for nausea and vomiting with drugs containing pyrilamine maleate and pentobarbital experienced severe and sometimes fatal reactions." The Committee had concluded, the letter went on, "that there is no evidence of safety and efficacy for drugs containing pyrilamine maleate with or without a barbituate in the treatment of nausea and vomiting." Based on the Committee's report, "and because (the FDA was) unaware of substantial scientific evidence which demonstrates that a combination of these ingredients is generally recognized as safe and effective for the treatment of nausea and vomiting," the FDA advised Alcon that it considered Alcon's marketing of WANS to be in violation of the "new drug" provision of the Federal Food, Drug, and Cosmetic Act. * * * Alcon was told to reply within ten days and was warned that failure to discontinue marketing WANS would expose the company to seizure and injunction actions.

Alcon responded on April 3, 1978. It claimed that WANS was not a "new drug," objected to the FDA's departure from the ordinary sequence of its enforcement priorities on the basis of an "unsubstantiated, conclusionary indictment of the safety" of the active ingredients in WANS, and requested that it be allowed to "identify and review the data and information upon which the Agency relies, and to make a formal submission to the Agency ...." The company also offered to revise the labeling of WANS consistent with the findings of its review. Subsequent to this letter, Alcon, on its own initiative, sent the FDA proposed new labeling for WANS and information supporting the safety and efficacy of the drug. Various company officials met with agency officials on July 10 and 18, 1978, to discuss WANS.

The FDA reviewed the materials provided by Alcon and in a letter of August 4, 1978, reaffirmed its position upon the "new drug" status of WANS: "the data submitted ... contains no adequate scientific data to support the safety and efficacy of the WANS products." Though the proposed relabeling was felt to be "an improvement," it could not substitute for "scientific evidence to establish that a fixed combination of pyrilamine maleate and pentobarbital sodium is either safe or effective for the treatment of nausea and vomiting." * * * *

Alcon continued to manufacture WANS and on September 21, 1978, the FDA instituted a seizure action in federal district court alleging that the drug was a "new drug" being marketed in violation of section 505 of the Act. By court order, a large quantity of WANS suppositories (approximately 453,900) was seized. In its responsive pleadings in the seizure action, Alcon admitted that no approval of a new drug application was in effect for WANS or was being sought. The company nevertheless denied that WANS was being marketed in violation of section 505. Alcon argued that WANS is not subject to the "new drug" requirements of the Act because "it is generally recognized as safe for use under the conditions prescribed, recommended or suggested in its labeling" * * * *

Despite seizure of the suppositories, Alcon continued to manufacture and distribute WANS, thus prompting the FDA, on November 28, 1978, to institute a further action, this time seeking a temporary restraining order, a preliminary injunction and a permanent injunction against continued marketing of WANS without FDA approval. On the next day, November 29, the district court denied the FDA's request for a temporary restraining order, and consolidated the injunctive suit with the earlier seizure action. * * *

No further action was taken in the case until January 28, 1980. On that date the FDA instituted a second seizure against WANS. Large quantities of the drug were again confiscated. A month later, on February

27, 1980, the district court consolidated the latest seizure action with the pending actions * * * * The United States presently attacks three aspects of the district court's order: (1) its instruction that the FDA "defer regulatory action against the WANS preparation ... or against defendants" pending further administrative proceedings; (2) its decision to leave prior seizures of WANS "without effect;" and (3) its remand of the case to the agency. * * *

The order has the effect of forbidding the FDA from exercising in any forum its statutory power both to proceed against WANS and its producer and to seize the article pending condemnation. * * * This injunction exceeded the district court's authority. To prevent this sort of eroding of the agency's protective powers, the Supreme Court in *Ewing v. Mytinger & Casselberry, Inc.*, 339 U.S. 594 (1950), held that district courts lack jurisdiction to enjoin multiple seizure actions instituted by the FDA under the Act. * * * Alcon's argument that such a rule exposes a manufacturer to potentially devastating hardship and loss was disposed of in *Ewing*. * * *

It is the government's contention that the district court "ha(d) no authority simply to give back the seized property without determining ... whether or not the Act (was) violated." The Act provides that before trial the court shall "allow any party to a condemnation proceeding ... to obtain a representative sample of the article seized" and that after condemnation the court has discretion to order the goods sold or destroyed, 21 U.S.C. § 334(c), (d), but otherwise is silent upon the release of seized goods prior to a decision upon the FDA's claims. Rule E(5)(c) of the Supplemental Rules for Certain Admiralty and Maritime Claims, which were intended to inform seizure procedure under the Act, * * * provides for release of property if a plaintiff consents, or when "approved security as provided by law and these rules" is tendered. Neither circumstance exists here (and, indeed, in a new drug case, where the purpose of the seizure is to remove a possibly risky drug from public use, it is hard to see how the mere putting up of security would be a proper basis for release). In any event, we see little in Rule E(5) by way of a general grant of authority permitting courts to countermand administratively instituted seizures without first adjudicating the merits of the agency's claim. If the seizure is plainly frivolous, the court can act rapidly and achieve justice in that manner, but its action should ordinarily follow, not precede, an adjudication. * * *

We conclude that the district court erred in dissolving the administrative seizures of WANS without first addressing the merits of the seizure proceedings initiated by the FDA, including, as part thereof, the agency's contention that WANS is a "new drug." We therefore vacate this portion of the district court's order. The district court believed that allowing "the continued retention of the material seized would be an abuse of judicial discretion" in light of its findings that WANS "has been used for years" and that "the information which prompted the FDA to initiate these actions was not only contradictory, but also insufficient to allow a causal relation." These preliminary and necessarily tentative and incomplete findings cannot serve as a substitute for a determination on the merits. It has been said that in pursuing a seizure action, the FDA must first allege sufficient facts to state a claim and must then prove its claim by a preponderance of the evidence. A decision by a district court as to whether the FDA has met those burdens would be the proper means for adjudicating the validity of the FDA's enforcement efforts; a seizure should only be dissolved thereafter, in event of the government's failure to do so. * * *

The district court premised its decision to remand to the FDA on interrelated procedural and substantive grounds. The court was troubled by the agency's failure to conduct "a formal administrative determination of the 'new drug' status of WANS" before instituting suit against Alcon. * * * [T]he court characterized itself as ill-suited to decide the "new drug" status of WANS or to determine whether "significant new information" existed that questioned WANS' safety. Citing lack of jurisdiction, the doctrine of primary agency jurisdiction and prudential considerations, the court decided that these questions were better left to "the Agency entrusted by Congress with the necessary expertise to make a responsible determination." Accordingly, it ordered the action "remanded to the Food and Drug Administration to hold a formal administrative hearing" * * * *

[T]he imposition of a pre-enforcement hearing requirement (coupled with preliminary relief, as, to be meaningful, it would have to be) is at odds with the language and intent of the Act. To be sure, in certain circumstances a formal administrative proceeding is a precondition to agency action. For example, when the FDA issues, pursuant to 5 U.S.C. § 554(e), a declaratory order governing all drugs covered by a particular new drug application, or when it withdraws approval of a new drug application pursuant to 21 U.S.C. § 355(e), it must first hold a hearing in compliance with section 554 of the Administrative Procedure Act * * * By contrast, there is no statutory hearing requirement for FDA decisions to initiate seizure or injunction actions. Indeed, the probable cause determination necessary to institute multiple seizure actions against allegedly misbranded products is to be made "without hearing." 21 U.S.C. § 334(a)(1). As the Supreme Court has made abundantly clear, a manufacturer subjected to an FDA enforcement action has no right to raise objections in an administrative forum prior to the agency's institution of the action. This is because the imposition of any formal, pre-enforcement hearing requirement might seriously impair the effectiveness of the Act's enforcement provisions. * * *

NOTES AND QUESTIONS

1. *Seizures.* In contrast to the FDA, the Drug Enforcement Administration (DEA) utilizes an administrative forfeiture process that gives claimants resort to a judicial process only under certain circumstances. See Malladi Drugs & Pharms., Ltd. v. Tandy, 552 F.3d 885 (D.C.Cir.2009) (dismissing for failure to exhaust administrative remedies a challenge to the seizure of bulk pseudoephedrine and related substances subject to the Controlled Substances Act). The FDA's power to seize violative products instead resembles arrest and pre-trial detention of a suspected criminal (this explains some of the odd captions in the case law). See, e.g., Sara Clarke, FDA Halts Distribution of Drugs Paxil CR, Avandamet: Manufacturing Concerns Prompted the Agency to Seize Batches of the Antidepressant and Diabetes Medicines, L.A. Times, Mar. 5, 2005, at A14. The manufacturer may appear in the condemnation proceeding as a claimant in order to challenge the agency's action, but it cannot ask a court to enjoin those proceedings. See Parke, Davis & Co. v. Califano, 564 F.2d 1200, 1205–06 (6th Cir.1977). But cf. United States v. Undetermined Quantities of Drugs, 675 F.Supp. 1113, 1114–17 (N.D.Ill.1987) (ordering release of seized drugs pending resolution of a condemnation proceeding, distinguishing *Alcon* as involving non-perishable and potentially harmful drugs). The courts generally have found no merit in constitutional objections to the FDA's exercise of its authority to seize adulterated or misbranded products. See Ewing v. Mytinger & Casselberry, Inc., 339 U.S. 594, 598–600 (1950) (rejecting a Fifth Amendment procedural due process objection to the initiation of multiple seizure actions without a prior hearing); United States v. Argent Chem. Lab., Inc., 93 F.3d 572, 574–78 (9th Cir.1996) (rejecting a Fourth Amendment objection to an FDA seizure made without first obtaining a warrant from a judicial officer based on a finding of probable cause because the drug industry is pervasively regulated and its members therefore have diminished expectations of privacy); cf. United States v. Proplast II, 946 F.2d 422, 423 (5th Cir.1991) ("To balance a claimant's constitutional right to due process in a post-deprivation procedure, while at the same time accommodating the public health protection policy embodied in the [FDCA], a hearing on the merits should be scheduled at the promptest date practicable ....").

2. *Injunctions*. Seizures take violative products out of circulation but, if the manufacturer is obstinate and continues violating the statute, the FDA would have to bring repeated seizure actions. To deal with the problem of recurring infractions, the agency can request that a court issue an injunction against the manufacturer, as it did in *Alcon*. The government need not show irreparable harm or the inadequacy of remedies at law in order to receive such equitable relief. See United States v. Vital Health Prods., Ltd., 786 F.Supp. 761, 770 (E.D.Wis.1992), aff'd, 985 F.2d 563 (7th Cir.1993). But cf. United States v. Nutri-cology, Inc., 982 F.2d 394, 396, 398 (9th Cir.1992) (affirming the denial of a preliminary injunction where the government had failed to demonstrate any likelihood of success on the merits or irreparable harm); David A. Levitt, Judicial Enforcement of the Federal Food, Drug, and Cosmetic Act: Are Injunctions Always Required to Remedy Ongoing Violations?, 48 Food & Drug L.J. 227 (1993) (arguing that the courts should still balance hardship to the parties). The government need only show a reasonable likelihood that identified violations of the statute will continue. For instance, courts may grant injunctions that effectively shut down manufacturers until they bring their operations into compliance with GMPs. See United States v. Barr Lab., Inc., 812 F.Supp. 458, 487–91 (D.N.J.1993) (fashioning an injunction that directed the company to remedy several GMP violations with respect to a number of different product lines); United States v. Richlyn Lab., Inc., 827 F.Supp.

1145, 1150–52 (E.D.Pa.1992) (rejecting the defendant's argument that it was correcting problems and that the injunction was too harsh); see also United States v. Diapulse Corp., 457 F.2d 25, 29 (2d Cir.1972) ("Nor can appellant complain that the injunction is impermissible because it will put him out of business."); United States v. Syntrax Innovations, Inc., 149 F.Supp.2d 880, 882–85 (E.D.Mo.2001) (rejecting objections that an injunction against any further sale of an unapproved new drug was overbroad and vague). Courts also may craft injunctions that prohibit otherwise lawful conduct if necessary to cure the lingering effects of past transgressions such as inappropriate marketing. See United States v. Articles of Drug ... Doxylamine Succinate, 890 F.2d 1004, 1007–08 (8th Cir.1989). But cf. United States v. Diapulse Corp. of Am., 748 F.2d 56, 61–62 (2d Cir.1984) (rejecting such an injunction as overbroad).

United States v. Superpharm Corp.

530 F.Supp. 408 (E.D.N.Y.1981).

■ COSTANTINO, DISTRICT JUDGE:

This is an action under the Federal Food, Drug and Cosmetic Act to enjoin alleged violations of the Act and for other forms of relief. The suit, initiated in January, 1981, contends that Superpharm Corporation and Norman E. Rubin, president of Superpharm, engaged in the manufacture and distribution of a human drug, furosemide, in the absence of approval by the Food and Drug Administration * * * *

The government maintains that this court has the authority pursuant to section 302 of the Act to order a recall. Section 302 provides in pertinent part that "the district courts of the United States ... shall have jurisdiction, for cause shown, to restrain violations of Section 301 of this Title." In addition, the government contends that the court's general equitable power also authorizes the issuance of a recall order. * * *

An examination of the Act itself reveals that Congress specifically did not include a judicially ordered recall remedy when the Act was passed. It did, however, provide a threefold enforcement scheme: (1) injunctive relief; (2) criminal prosecution; and (3) seizure. Moreover, in reading the legislative history behind the Act when passed in 1938, it is clear that Congress considered seizures to be the most drastic remedy, and that the injunction remedy was included to temper the hardship inherent in seizures. * * * [G]iven this orientation, it is difficult to conclude that Congress intended section 302(a) to authorize judicial recalls.

In effect, the government is asking this court to do something that the FDA itself cannot do. While there are provisions in the FDA regulations which provide for recalls, recalls cannot be ordered by the FDA as they are usually undertaken voluntarily at the request of the FDA. The authorized vehicle for FDA removal of goods from the marketplace is the seizure remedy. It is simply not within the FDA's stated authority to order a manufacturer to recall its own goods.

If for medical and public safety reasons the FDA believes the removal of the restrained pharmaceutical product is imperative, they have the seizure remedy at their disposal. To order a recall under the Act would be an unwarranted act of judicial legislation because the FDA * * * would have yet another method of attacking the allegedly illegal distributions of drugs without being restricted by either the Act or the regulations promulgated thereunder. Recalls are simply not within the enforcement powers of the Act, and the court perceives no reason to expand the remedies currently in effect by including such a remedy. * * *

In the instant case, resort to ancillary remedies through equitable powers is unnecessary to enforce the spirit, as well as the letter, of the Act. The FDA's statutory remedies provide for sufficient means to enforce the Act, and the legislative history and the Act itself manifest a reluctance to expand enforcement powers to the point where they are punitive. Moreover, the seizure remedy exists if the FDA perceives a potential public danger which must be rectified immediately, or if the manufacturer or distributor refuses to remove the illegal product from the market. Although the court's duty is heightened when, in a case such as this, the public interest is involved, the government and the FDA have the tools at their disposal to solve the problem and there is no need to attempt to add to those powers when not necessary. No resort to, or expansion of, the court's equitable power is needed to remove these drugs from interstate commerce. Accordingly, the government's request for an order recalling the drugs from the marketplace is denied.

United States v. Universal Management Services, Inc.

191 F.3d 750 (6th Cir.1999).

■ SUHRHEINRICH, CIRCUIT JUDGE:

* * * As part of their business, Appellants sell and distribute a product known as the Stimulator, and also a product that connects to the Stimulator known as the Xtender. The Stimulator is essentially an electric gas grill igniter, marketed as a pain relieving device. To produce the Stimulator, Appellants purchase gas grill igniters and outfit them with finger grips. A user then places the tip of the Stimulator on his body, presses with his thumb on a plunger, and an electric current passes into that part of the body. Appellants' advertising literature states that, when applied to certain acupressure points, the Stimulator can relieve numerous kinds of pain (e.g., migraine headaches, swollen joints, allergies). The Xtender is an accessory that allows an individual to use the Stimulator to reach areas of the body otherwise difficult to reach, such as the spine. Appellants sold a total of 800,000 gas grill igniters, at a cost to the company of one dollar each, for $88.30 each.

In May 1995, U.S. Marshals seized over $1.2 million worth of Appellants' devices pursuant to seizure authority under the Federal Food, Drug & Cosmetic Act. Later that month, the Food and Drug Administration (FDA) informed Appellants that they considered the devices adulterated and subject to regulation, threatening further legal action if approval was not sought and distribution did not cease. Distribution did not cease and the government sought the injunction that is the subject of this appeal. The district court granted summary judgment for the government on December 30, 1997, and, in February 1998, rejected Appellants' Motion for Reconsideration. The resulting judgment placed a permanent injunction against the distribution of Appellants' products and ordered Appellants to offer full refunds to all customers who had purchased their devices after the May 1995 seizure. * * *

Below, the government requested its costs and any such other relief the court deemed proper, including equitable disgorgement of profits. After finding disgorgement inappropriate, the district court found that restitution was a remedy available to the FDA and appropriate. The district court awarded restitution, finding that the FDCA does not contain a clear command indicating that restitution is not a remedy available to the district court. It supported its decision on the premise that the FDCA should receive liberal construction. The restitution ordered required Appellants to offer and provide refunds to all of their customers who requested them in writing. Appellants challenge the restitution order, arguing the FDCA does not permit restitution and, if it does, restitution was inappropriate in this case.

The FDCA provides only three remedies for violations: (1) injunctive relief, 21 U.S.C. § 332; (2) criminal prosecution, 21 U.S.C. § 333; and (3) seizure, 21 U.S.C. § 334. To rule on Appellants' first contention, that the FDCA does not permit orders of restitution, we must consider the scope of injunctive relief authorized under § 332. The district court in this case was sitting as a court of equity. Restitution and disgorgement are part of courts' traditional equitable authority. Absent a clear command by Congress that a statute providing for equitable relief excludes certain forms of such relief, this court will presume the full scope of equitable powers may be exercised by the courts. * * *

[T]he remedy of seizure exists alongside an explicit authorization for injunctive relief to cure violations of the FDCA. The express provision for general equitable relief without the enumeration of any exceptions makes it difficult for this court to find any legitimate means for implicitly carving out such exceptions as we see fit. Even if Congress expressed some concern that seizure should remain the harshest relief available, there is no convincing argument that, in all cases, restitution creates a more harsh result than seizure, procedurally or substantively. Moreover, * * * these concerns are far from a clear statement of Congress's intent to exclude restitution, recalls, disgorgement, or any other traditional form of equitable relief. * * * Therefore, we hold that nothing in the FDCA precludes a court sitting in equity from ordering restitution in appropriate cases.

Next, we must determine whether restitution was an appropriate remedy on the facts of the case at bar. We review an award of restitution for an abuse of discretion. Appellants first argue that the FDA's charge itself should preclude restitution. The FDA charge, they claim, was only that Appellants marketed a product without required approval, rather than that the product didn't perform as it was intended. If the performance is not questioned and no deficiency in the same is established, they contend that there has been no detriment to consumers justifying the restitution order. In other words, Appellants contend that restitution was unwarranted because there is no evidence that consumers received anything less than what they bargained for.

The approval process exists to protect consumers' health and their pocketbooks. One of the primary goals of the FDCA is to protect consumers from economic harm. It is not the government's burden to prove that a product is not safe and effective. FDCA regulations exist to allow the public to assume that marketed devices have received the imprimatur of FDA approval. To circumvent the law by marketing illegally without approval is to deceive the public both as purchasers and users of the device. In such cases, restitution exists to make the consumer whole. Because restitution seeks to remedy the type of economic harm to consumers contemplated by the FDCA, it serves goals of the FDCA that are encompassed within the section the FDA charges Appellants violated. * * *

Appellants also claim that restitution is punitive because, unlike disgorgement which removes ill-gotten gain by forcing surrender of profits, restitution requires a return of the entire purchase price, included in which are costs and profits. Simply because disgorgement and restitution are different, however, does not make restitution punitive. Appellants, who disobeyed the law, should not have [their] expenses covered by consumers. To say that restitution is unavailable is to say that consumers must cover the costs of Appellants' production, advertising, and illegal distribution. Instead, the district court should have the discretion in a case such as this to make the consumers whole rather than allow the illegal activities to stand uncorrected to the consumer's detriment.

Despite Appellants' contentions, their violation was also more than a mere technicality. Congress set up a sophisticated statutory scheme for the regulation of medical devices, and the requirement that devices be approved or cleared by the FDA before marketing is at the heart of the scheme. Thus, Appellants' failure to achieve such clearance violates a key component of the regulatory scheme. And, in the context of public health and safety, the district court's equitable authority is broader and more flexible to support such a regulatory scheme than in ordinary litigation.

The district court did not abuse its discretion in determining restitution was appropriate in this case. The district court seemed to fairly balance the equities in the case. There is evidence that Appellants continued to distribute their product without seeking any approval even after they were put on notice of their violation by the FDA in May 1995, distributed after the district court issued a preliminary injunction, and obstructed FDA inspections. Appellants were hardly mere flies caught in the web of technical government regulation. Appellants marketed a device to the consuming public, a public that the FDCA regulatory structure seeks to protect. Appellants marketed their product in clear violation of the

FDCA. They continued to sell to the public even after the FDA notified them that their product could not be sold without FDA approval. For these reasons, the district court's order of restitution was well within its discretion. * * *

NOTES AND QUESTIONS

1. *Disgorgement hurts.* In the FDA's previous attempt to secure a restitution order, one court held that it lacked statutory authority to provide any such relief. See United States v. Parkinson, 240 F.2d 918, 922 (9th Cir.1956) ("The use of the extraordinary remedies of equity in governmental litigation should never be permitted by the courts unless clearly authorized by the statute in express terms."). By virtue of intervening decisions of the Supreme Court interpreting other statutory grants of equitable powers, however, *Parkinson* no longer holds sway. See United States v. Lane Labs–USA Inc., 427 F.3d 219, 233–36 (3d Cir.2005) (upholding a district court order that the seller of unapproved new drugs pay restitution to consumers). As that court observed:

> In the years since *Universal Management*, the FDA has negotiated three consent decrees with drug companies that included significant disgorgement amounts. In 1999, just two months after *Universal Management* was decided, Abbott Laboratories agreed to pay $100 million to the government as part of a consent decree. In October 2000, Wyeth–Ayerst agreed to pay $30 million in disgorgement as part [of] the remedial measures implemented under a consent decree. Most recently, Schering–Plough paid $500 million for equitable disgorgement as part of a consent decree.

Id. at 234; see also United States v. Rx Depot, Inc., 438 F.3d 1052, 1058–63 (10th Cir.2006); Eric M. Blumberg, Universal Management, Abbott, Wyeth, Schering–Plough, and . . .: Restitution and Disgorgement Find Another Home at the FDA, 58 Food & Drug L.J. 169 (2003); William W. Vodra & Arthur N. Levine, Anchors Away: The FDA's Use of Disgorgement Abandons Legal Moorings, 59 Food & Drug L.J. 1 (2004).

2. *Civil penalties.* Congress expressly authorized the FDA to seek civil penalties from medical device manufacturers. See 21 U.S.C. § 333(g). One court accepted as reasonable a record plea agreement for $61 million in criminal and civil fines against a company that had sold cardiac catheters with unapproved design modifications that resulted in several deaths. See United States v. C.R. Bard, Inc., 848 F.Supp. 287, 294 (D.Mass.1994); id. at 291 (noting that this amount equaled the company's gross sales of the unlawful products); Barbara Carton, Bard Former Executives Are Convicted of Concealing Data on Heart Catheters, Wall St. J., Aug. 25, 1995, at B2. The FDA also can seek civil penalties for the unlawful distribution of prescription drug samples, 21 U.S.C. § 333(b), and for statutory violations by manufacturers of radiation-emitting products, id. § 360pp(b); see also Korangy v. FDA, 498 F.3d 272 (4th Cir.2007) (upholding civil penalties of over $1 million against a radiologist and his practice for repeatedly violating certification requirements of the Mammography Quality Standards Act). Section 518(b) of the statute also authorizes refunds for devices under limited circumstances—shouldn't these cut against the court's willingness to imply parallel remedies under the authority to seek injunctive relief?

3. *Recalls*. Contrary to *Superpharm*, the *Universal Management* opinion hinted that courts also might use their equitable powers to order recalls, and a few lower courts had previously so concluded. See United States v. K–N Enters., Inc., 461 F.Supp. 988, 990–91 (N.D.Ill.1978); United States v. X–Otag Plus Tablets, 441 F.Supp. 105, 115 (D.Colo.1977), aff'd on other grds., 602 F.2d 1387, 1391 (10th Cir.1979). In 1990, Congress amended the statute to authorize recalls and other special forms of relief (such as administrative detention) against device manufacturers. See Safe Medical Devices Act, Pub. L. No. 101–629, § 8, 104 Stat. 4520 (codified at 21 U.S.C. § 360h(e)). Whether voluntary or mandatory, recalls of medical devices can raise some unusual issues not encountered with pharmaceutical products, particularly when dealing with implants. See Mitesh S. Amin et al., Management of Recalled Pacemakers and Implantable Cardioverter–Defibrillators: A Decision Analysis Model, 296 JAMA 412 (2006); Paul Gould et al., Complications Associated with Implantable Cardioverter–Defibrillator Replacement in Response to Device Advisories, 295 JAMA 1907 (2006); Kenneth Chang, When Medical Devices Fail in the Body, N.Y. Times, Aug. 7, 2001, at D1 (describing the possible need to explant part of a hip prosthesis received by thousands of patients because of a flaw discovered in the manufacturing process that left an undetectable residue of machine lubricant that would interfere with fusion to the bone).

John D. Copanos & Sons, Inc. v. FDA

854 F.2d 510 (D.C.Cir.1988).

■ GINSBURG, DOUGLAS, CIRCUIT JUDGE:

John D. Copanos & Sons, Inc., and Kanasco, Ltd., affiliated enterprises owned by John D. Copanos (hereinafter referred to collectively as Kanasco), manufacture and distribute human and veterinary drugs, including, until recently, a number of sterile injectable products. These injectable drugs were produced pursuant to a number of New Drug Applications (NDAs) and New Animal Drug Applications (NADAs) approved by the respondent Food and Drug Administration (FDA). On March 10, 1987, the FDA published a Notice of Opportunity for a Hearing (NOOH) in the *Federal Register*, proposing to withdraw Kanasco's NDAs and NADAs for sterile injectable products on the ground that the methods, facilities, and controls used to produce these drugs were inadequate to assure their identity, strength, quality, and purity. Kanasco responded to this Notice, and requested a hearing, but on August 6, 1987, the agency denied the hearing and summarily withdrew its approval of the company's applications, effectively barring Kanasco from producing the subject drugs. * * *

[The FDCA] establishes procedures whereby the FDA, "after due notice and opportunity for hearing to the applicant," can withdraw its prior approval. One of the statutory grounds for such withdrawal is that:

> the Secretary finds ... that on the basis of new information before him, evaluated together with the evidence before him when the application was approved, the methods used in, or the facilities and controls used for, the manufacture, processing and packing of such drug are inadequate to assure and preserve its identity, strength, quality, and purity and were not made adequate within a reasonable time after receipt of written notice from the Secretary specifying the matter complained of.

21 U.S.C. § 355(e) (NDAs); id. § 360b(e)(2)(B) (NADAs). The standards for determining whether a manufacturer's "methods[,] ... facilities and controls" are adequate "to assure and preserve [the] identity, strength, quality and purity" of its drugs are set forth in the FDA's "Current Good Manufacturing Practice" (CGMP) regulations. See 21 C.F.R. Part 211. Those regulations govern numerous aspects of the manufacturing process, including (1) the qualifications and responsibilities of personnel; (2) standards for the design and construction of buildings, facilities, and equipment; (3) laboratory controls; and (4) requirements for record keeping, packaging and labeling. Drugs produced in violation of these CGMP regulations are deemed to be adulterated without the agency having to show that they are actually contaminated. 21 U.S.C. § 351(a)(2)(B).

FDA has rarely withdrawn its approval of an application for failure to comply with CGMP. Indeed, Kanasco maintains, without contradiction by the agency, that the only previous withdrawal actions based on this ground were uncontested and involved animal feed applications. * * *

From late August through early October 1984, the FDA conducted a CGMP inspection of Kanasco's oral dosage form manufacturing facility. This inspection revealed numerous deficiencies in the company's manufacturing and quality control procedures, including inaccurate and even falsified manufacturing records, failure to calibrate laboratory equipment, unsanitary conditions in the manufacturing area, and production of a subpotent and impure animal drug. At the conclusion of the inspection, the FDA left with the company a Form FDA–483 listing the deficiencies noted in the inspection. See 21 U.S.C. § 374(b).

Based on the results of this inspection, the United States sought to enjoin Kanasco from the further manufacture and shipment of pharmaceuticals. The complaint and the accompanying exhibits described in detail the CGMP deficiencies revealed in the August–October inspection, noting, in particular, that "[t]here is not an adequate number of qualified personnel to perform and supervise the manufacture, processing, packing, labeling, and holding of each product." Rather than contesting the allegations in this complaint, on November 2, 1984, Kanasco agreed that it would not manufacture or ship any drugs without the prior written authorization of the FDA, and the government dismissed the complaint without prejudice. In late November, Kanasco responded by letter to the observations in the

Form FDA–483. This letter, for the most part, acknowledged the alleged deficiencies and promised corrective measures in the future. In January 1985, a consultant employed by Kanasco informed the FDA that the firm's injectable drug manufacturing operation was in compliance with CGMP.

In February and March 1985, the FDA returned to Kanasco to verify the consultant's assessment. Inspection of the facility once again revealed a variety of alleged deficiencies. * * * Kanasco again replied to the Form FDA–483 by letter, acknowledging the alleged deficiencies, disputing some of the agency's conclusions but promising improvements in the areas identified by the inspector. * * *

In May 1985, the FDA once again returned to Kanasco to evaluate the results of the company's recent media fills.* The FDA judged these tests unsatisfactory * * * * Then, in the summer of 1985, the FDA learned that, between January and June 1985, Kanasco had manufactured 23 lots—over one million vials—of injectable veterinary drugs, in violation of the 1984 Agreement. (FDA had authorized Kanasco to manufacture one batch of injectable product solely in order to test its manufacturing process.) Several thousand vials had been shipped to customers without FDA approval. In addition, the company withheld records that would have revealed the shipments.

In July 1985, FDA officials visited Kanasco to monitor the company's media fills. The Form FDA–483 prepared after this visit noted that flexible tubing had not been properly stored or sterilized, and that personnel in the aseptic fill room had touched exposed portions of their faces with gloved hands and reached across a conveyor holding previously sterilized bottles.

In the wake of these events, the government filed a second complaint for injunctive relief in the district court on August 7, 1985. On August 13, FDA returned to the company with a criminal search warrant. Based on this search, the FDA concluded that Kanasco had committed further violations of the CGMP record keeping requirements * * * *

On September 5, the district court by consent entered an interim order prohibiting Kanasco from making or distributing injectable drugs without prior judicial authorization. The court later ordered Kanasco to show cause why a permanent injunction should not be entered against it. Instead, however, on November 4, Kanasco agreed to a "Consent Decree of Permanent Injunction." Like the 1984 Agreement, the 1985 Decree prohibited the company from distributing any injectable drugs manufactured at its plant until the facility was operated and administered in accordance with CGMP. The Decree also required Kanasco to obtain the FDA's written approval of any personnel with supervisory responsibility to the manufacture of drugs. On the same day, the FDA authorized Kanasco to resume manufacturing injectable drugs "based upon the certification of [Kanasco's consultant that

* [As the court explained: "A media fill is a test procedure in which product containers are filled with sterile growth media, run through the normal production procedures, incubated, and then examined for contamination; lack of contamination provides evidence that the filling process has been 'validated.' "]

its manufacturing plants] appear to be in compliance with [CGMP]" as required by the Consent Decree. Three weeks later, however, an FDA inspection to verify the consultant's representations once again revealed potential violations of CGMP * * * *

On December 12, 1985, the FDA again sought a court order requiring Kanasco to cease the manufacture of all injectable drugs. Kanasco once again persuaded the agency, however, that the noted deficiencies had been, or would be, corrected. The FDA, again without conducting an on-site inspection, authorized the company to resume manufacturing and shipping injectable drugs, and so notified the court.

Ten months passed without incident—or inspection. When the FDA reinspected Kanasco's manufacturing facility in September 1986, it noted numerous potential violations of CGMP * * * * Kanasco's written response to the FDA's Form FDA–483 disputed a number of the agency's conclusions, particularly the determination that facilities and equipment were unvalidated. Kanasco nonetheless promised a number of improvements. The government again moved to enforce the 1985 Consent Decree. The court first temporarily enjoined Kanasco from manufacturing and shipping injectable drugs, and then by consent made the injunction permanent.

In December 1986 and January 1987, in an attempt to persuade the agency to allow its facility to reopen, Kanasco submitted to the FDA validation data relating to recent media fills. In February 1987, the FDA visited the Kanasco facility to collect data related to the recent submissions and to interview supervisory personnel. During its visits, the FDA encountered both new and familiar problems * * * *

Its patience finally exhausted, the FDA published a notice in the *Federal Register* on March 10, 1987, proposing to withdraw Kanasco's NDAs and NADAs for sterile injectable products. Seven of the NOOH's eight pages consisted of a "Regulatory History of Kanasco," recounting the above-stated chronology in greater detail. * * * The NOOH required Kanasco, if it wanted a hearing, to submit "the data, information, and analyses relied on to justify a hearing, as specified in 21 C.F.R. § 312.200," and noted that the same regulation would govern any subsequent proceedings. The notice also warned that "[a] request for a hearing may not rest upon mere allegations or denials, but must present specific facts showing that there is a genuine and substantial issue of fact that requires a hearing." Failing that, "the Commissioner of Food and Drugs will enter summary judgment against the person(s) who request the hearing, making findings and conclusions, and denying a hearing."

Kanasco both requested a hearing and moved for summary judgment. The hearing request included a number of declarations and other exhibits that, according to the company, demonstrated that it was in compliance with CGMP and that it was committed to maintaining such compliance. The motion for summary judgment was based on the argument that the agency had not complied with the requirements in 21 U.S.C. §§ 355(e) and 360b(e)(2)(B) that it provide Kanasco with proper written notice "specifying the matter complained of" and "a reasonable time after receipt of written notice" within which to make adequate any deficiencies. By a Notice published August 6, 1987, the FDA denied both the hearing request and the motion for summary judgment, and ordered that Kanasco's NDAs and NADAs be withdrawn from the market. See 52 Fed. Reg. 29,274. * * *

Section 355(e) of 21 U.S.C., which governs the withdrawal of NDA approvals, requires the FDA to provide "due notice and opportunity for hearing to the applicant." It is well settled that this provision does not guarantee the applicant a hearing in all circumstances; the agency may by regulation provide for summary withdrawal of approvals when there is no "genuine and substantial issue of fact that requires a hearing." See 21 C.F.R. § 314.200(g); Weinberger v. Hynson, Westcott & Dunning, 412 U.S. 609, 621 (1973) ("[W]e cannot impute to Congress the design of requiring, nor does due process demand, a hearing when it appears conclusively from the applicant's 'pleadings' that the application cannot succeed."). * * *

Before 1962, NDAs were approved upon a showing that a drug was "safe." The 1962 amendments to the FDC Act directed the FDA to withdraw approval of an NDA if "there is a lack of substantial evidence" that the drug is also effective for its intended use. See Drug Amendments of 1962, Pub. L. No. 87–781, § 102(e), 76 Stat. 782. The amendments defined "substantial evidence" as "consisting of adequate and well-controlled investigations, including clinical investigations, by experts qualified by scientific training and experience to evaluate the effectiveness of the drug involved." Id. § 102(d) (codified as amended at 21 U.S.C. § 355(d)).

As a result of these amendments, the FDA was required to reevaluate more than 4000 outstanding NDAs for substantial evidence that the covered drugs were "effective." For help with this task, the FDA retained the National Academy of Sciences–National Research Council (NAS–NRC), which created expert panels to review the efficacy of all approved drugs. Holders of NDAs were invited to submit to the panels any data substantiating the efficacy of their drugs. If the FDA adopted the panel's conclusion that a particular drug had not been shown to be "effective," it would publish a notice indicating its intention to withdraw approval of the NDA, and offering the applicant the opportunity for a prior hearing. In order to avoid a large number of unnecessary proceedings, however, the FDA issued regulations establishing minimal standards for what it would accept as "adequate and well-controlled investigations" and limiting the right to a hearing to those applicants who could proffer at least some evidence meeting those standards. The agency's regulations provided that

> when it clearly appears from the data in the application and from the reasons and factual analysis in the request for the hearing that there is no genuine and substantial issue of fact which precludes . . . the withdrawal of approval of the application, . . . the Commissioner will enter an order on this data, making findings and conclusions on such data.

21 C.F.R. § 130.14(b) (1971).

In *Hynson*, the Supreme Court found that this administrative summary judgment procedure satisfied the Act's requirement of "due notice and opportunity for hearing" because the agency's regulations had reduced the statutory standard to "detailed guidelines," 412 U.S. at 617, giving "[t]he drug manufacturers . . . full and precise notice of the evidence they must present to sustain their NDAs," id. at 622, while making it possible for the agency to discern "at the threshold" whether the applicant had tendered any evidence which on its face met the statutory standards. Id. at 620. In a footnote, which Kanasco emphasizes, the court noted that summary judgment might not be appropriate if the agency's regulations were not "precise" but called for "the exercise of discretion or subjective judgment," such that it "may not be possible to tell from the face of a [submission] whether the standards have been met." Id. at 621 n.17.

We have not read *Hynson* to hold, however, that precise regulations specifying the type of evidence necessary to justify a hearing are a prerequisite to due notice whenever the agency is contemplating summary action. The requirements of "due notice" must depend upon the context of the agency's action. In *Hynson*, for example, the 1962 amendments to the Act placed on applicants the burden of producing "adequate and well-controlled investigations" demonstrating efficacy in order to retain their FDA approval. The success, vel non, of the applicant's submission therefore turned upon the types of evidence that would satisfy the statutory standard of "adequate and well-controlled." The agency's notice indicating its intent to withdraw approval, however, generally failed to explain why the information provided to the NAS–NRC panel did not meet this standard. See, e.g., USV Pharm. Corp. v. HEW, 466 F.2d 455, 461 (D.C.Cir.1972) (NAS–NRC reports upon which FDA notice relied were "cryptic and conclusory, without any statement of supporting facts"). Under those circumstances, particularized regulations were necessary to provide the applicant with notice of what its submission must contain in order to warrant continued authorization to market a drug.

By contrast, the petitioners here were not confronted with any significant ambiguity regarding the type of information that would warrant a hearing before the agency. The NOOH discussed in detail the facts and evidence that formed the basis for the agency's proposed withdrawal of approval. Read in conjunction with the record of prior proceedings and the CGMP regulations, this document provided adequate notice of the type of information that Kanasco would have to submit in order to command a hearing. To take but one example, the NOOH alleged that Kanasco manufactured a drug product for human use that was required to be penicillin-free in the same area and with the same equipment used to make products containing penicillin. See 52 Fed. Reg. at 7315; see also 21 C.F.R. § 211.42(d) ("Operations relating to the manufacture, processing, and packing of penicillin shall be performed in facilities separate from those used for other drug products for human use."). Due notice of the basis for the agency's action would hardly require the FDA to specify, in regulations or in the NOOH, what types of evidence Kanasco needed to submit to raise a material issue of fact about this allegation. The answer is self-evident:

any competent evidence (e.g., affidavits or documentary exhibits) to the effect that (1) Kanasco did not in fact manufacture penicillin products using equipment also used for non-penicillin products; or (2) that the deficiency had been remedied within a reasonable time after receipt of written notice of the violation from the Secretary or his designee. We do not mean to suggest, of course, that an action withdrawing an NDA on CGMP grounds can never raise a genuine issue regarding the type of evidence that would be responsive. When the sorts of evidence that would be responsive appear to be obvious, however, as in this case, we think it is incumbent upon the petitioner to demonstrate how it was prejudiced by the lack of specific instructions telling it what to produce. Because Kanasco has failed to identify any evidence, or type of evidence, that it might have presented but for lack of notice as to its relevance, we reject the company's claim to any more specific notice than it received. * * *

The CGMP regulations on which the FDA based its withdrawal order in this case are "imprecise" in various places. See, e.g., 21 C.F.R. § 211.67 (equipment and utensils to be cleaned, maintained, and sanitized at "appropriate intervals"); id. § 211.25(a) (each employee to have the "education, training, and experience, or any combination thereof, to enable that person to perform the assigned functions"); id. § 211.46(b) (requiring equipment to assure "adequate control over air pressure" when "appropriate"). Moreover, the agency's "particularization" of these general standards has been explicitly challenged by Kanasco in a number of instances where Kanasco's non-compliance with the regulation's requirements cannot fairly be described as "manifest." There are, therefore, several "issues of fact" that are genuinely in dispute. * * * [But,] in order to warrant a hearing, it is not sufficient that Kanasco's submission raised questions of fact regarding some of the CGMP violations described in the agency's NOOH. Instead, that submission must raise a genuine issue about whether Kanasco is (1) in compliance with CGMP; and (2) corrected deficiencies within a "reasonable" time of their being brought to its attention. Kanasco's request for a hearing failed to make this showing. Turning to the second issue first, the record documents numerous instances where obvious or undisputed violations of CGMP were allowed to persist long after Kanasco had received appropriate notice from the FDA. * * * [In addition,] Kanasco failed to contest a number of "current" deficiencies noted by the FDA in its NOOH, and thus, has not shown that it brought itself, even temporarily, into compliance with CGMP. * * *

To demonstrate that it raised material issues of fact regarding these allegations, Kanasco points first to more than 1,000 pages of data documenting the numerous media fills it performed in October 1986. According to Kanasco, these data, which were incorporated by reference in its Request for Hearing, show that its manufacturing systems were properly validated. We note, however, that the agency's NOOH listed numerous methodological deficiencies in these validation data, including failure to mimic worst case, or even normal, production conditions, unexplained discrepancies regarding the order in which various procedures were alleged to have been performed, and missing raw data. The FDA further alleged that Kanasco had failed to validate a number of individual subsystems. Kanasco failed to respond to these specific allegations in its Request for Hearing. Instead, Kanasco offered only the general and unsupported statements of its experts to the effect that Kanasco's systems had in fact been validated. Because these statements fail to address the specific problems identified by the FDA, they do not create a genuine issue of fact.

Moreover, even if Kanasco's submission did create an issue of fact on the validation question, it would not be material since the company failed entirely to respond to a number of other allegations in the NOOH, including the failure to protect equipment during renovation of its plant, and the failure to store sterile containers in an appropriately classified environment. * * * In sum, the record demonstrates that in several respects Kanasco's methods, facilities and controls were "inadequate and were not made adequate within a reasonable time after receipt of written notice specifying the matter complained of." 52 Fed. Reg. at 29,307. The FDA was therefore entitled to withdraw Kanasco's NDAs and NADAs for injectable drugs without holding a hearing. * * *

NOTES AND QUESTIONS

1. *The regulatory dance.* The opinions in *Alcon*, *Universal*, and *Copanos* illustrate the difficulties that the FDA may encounter when attempting to enforce the statute. First, it must discover violations. For the most part, the agency's power to conduct inspections of drug and device establishments is well settled. See United States v. Jamieson–McKames Pharm., Inc., 651 F.2d 532, 536–40 (8th Cir.1981); Daniel H. White, Annotation, Validity of Inspection Conducted Under Provisions of the Federal Food, Drug, and Cosmetic Act Authorizing FDA Inspectors to Enter and Inspect Food, Drug, or Cosmetic Factory, Warehouse, or Other Establishment, 18 A.L.R. Fed. 734 (1974 & 2011 Supp.). The FDA's assertion of records inspection authority sometimes generates controversy. See, e.g., Wedgewood Vill. Pharmacy, Inc. v. United States, 421 F.3d 263, 269–75 (3d Cir.2005). Resource constraints present a more serious obstacle to monitoring for compliance. Second, the FDA and the regulated entity usually both prefer resolving identified deficiencies through informal mechanisms. In some situations, however, a company will disagree with the agency's charge of noncompliance or simply wants to stall. Third, when the FDA decides that it must impose sanctions, it has to abide by various formal procedures that may consume significant time and energy, hence it will often look for short-cuts such as the summary judgment method discussed in *Copanos*. Overall FDA enforcement statistics for Fiscal Year 1999 (though not limited to drugs and devices) reveal the following:

Total inspections	15,161
Violations found	1,589
Warning letters issued	1,589
Recalls (inc. voluntary)	3,736
Seizures	25
Injunctions	8
Criminal prosecutions	373

Tamar Nordenberg, FDA Takes Action to Enforce the Law, FDA Consumer, May–June 2000, at 7; see also FDA, Enforcement Statistics Summary for Fiscal Year 2010, available at http://www.fda.gov/downloads/ICECI/EnforcementActions/UCM247845.pdf (listing 10 seizures, 17 injunctions, 673 warning letters, 3800 recalls, and 13 debarments); Mary Olson, Substitution in Regulatory Agencies: FDA Enforcement Alternatives, 12 J.L. Econ. & Org. 376, 404 (1996) (observing that, between 1972 and 1992, "budget reductions and increasing applications for product approval ... led the agency to reduce its monitoring of FDA-regulated industries and to substitute less resource-intensive enforcement actions"); Mary K. Olson, Agency Rulemaking, Political Influences, Regulation, and Industry Compliance, 15 J.L. Econ. & Org. 573 (1999); Andrew Zajac, Under Obama, a Renewed FDA: The Agency Steps up Its Regulatory Activity, and the Activism Is Likely to Increase, L.A. Times, Oct. 10, 2010, at A11 ("Warning letters for misleading labeling and other violations issued by the FDA's Center for Drug Evaluation and Research jumped from 24 in 2005 and 21 in 2006 to 103 in 2009 ....").

2. *Enforcement discretion*. In *Heckler v. Chaney*, 470 U.S. 821 (1985), the Supreme Court rejected an effort by a group of death row inmates to force the FDA to take enforcement action against the use of lethal injection drugs because of alleged misbranding and new drug approval violations. The Court held that agency nonenforcement decisions are presumptively unsuitable for judicial review:

> First, an agency decision not to enforce often involves a complicated balancing of a number of factors which are peculiarly within its expertise. Thus, the agency must not only assess whether a violation has occurred, but whether agency resources are best spent on this violation or another, whether the agency is likely to succeed if it acts, whether the particular enforcement action requested best fits the agency's overall policies, and, indeed, whether the agency has enough resources to undertake the action at all. An agency generally cannot act against each technical violation of the statute it is charged with enforcing. The agency is far better equipped than the courts to deal with the many variables involved in the proper ordering of its priorities.... The Act's enforcement provisions commit complete discretion to the Secretary to decide how and when they should be exercised.

Id. at 831–32; cf. Heterochemical Corp. v. FDA, 644 F.Supp. 271, 274–76 (E.D.N.Y.1986) (holding that the agency was not entirely free to decline enforcement action against companies that it had already found in violation of statute). Enforcement discretion does not, however, permit the FDA to treat similarly-situated products or persons differently. See United States v. Diapulse Corp. of Am., 748 F.2d 56, 61–62 (2d Cir.1984); Bracco Diagnostics, Inc. v. Shalala, 963 F.Supp. 20, 28 (D.D.C.1997). But cf. United States v. Sage Pharm., Inc., 210 F.3d 475, 480 (5th Cir.2000) (holding that the FDA could target one firm for selling unapproved new drugs even though it had not yet acted against others who distributed substantially similar products). After uncovering evidence that, in response to domestic supply shortages, the FDA had cleared importation of an unapproved version of a drug used for lethal injections, the ACLU filed a lawsuit challenging the agency's action. See Andrew Welsh–Huggins, FDA Has Helped Two States Obtain Anesthetic Used in Executions, Wash. Post, Jan. 13, 2011, at A21.

3. *License withdrawal.* In *Copanos*, the FDA withdrew the companies' product licenses. As the court noted, the agency rarely does so to sanction noncompliance (the withdrawal of a license is more draconian than an injunction). The withdrawal of an NDA normally entails lengthy procedures. See Warner–Lambert Co. v. Heckler, 787 F.2d 147, 152, 162–63 (3d Cir.1986); Dan Morgan & Marc Kaufman, Lawmakers' Help for Drug Firm Tests Limits: FDA Calls Efforts for Bayer Illegal, Wash. Post, Apr. 30, 2005, at A1 (reporting that various challenges to the agency's proposed withdrawal of Baytril—an antibiotic approved for use in livestock—delayed final action for five years). How else might it have sanctioned a firm violating the statute (or what would it do next if Kanasco continued selling its now unapproved new drug products)?

United States v. Dotterweich

320 U.S. 277 (1943).

■ FRANKFURTER, JUSTICE:

This was a prosecution begun by two informations, consolidated for trial, charging Buffalo Pharmacal Company, Inc., and Dotterweich, its president and general manager, with violations of [the FDCA] * * * * Three counts went to the jury—two, for shipping misbranded drugs in interstate commerce, and a third, for so shipping an adulterated drug. The jury disagreed as to the corporation and found Dotterweich guilty on all three counts. * * *

The Food and Drugs Act of 1906 was an exertion by Congress of its power to keep impure and adulterated food and drugs out of the channels of commerce. By the Act of 1938, Congress extended the range of its control over illicit and noxious articles and stiffened the penalties for disobedience. The purposes of this legislation thus touch phases of the lives and health of people which, in the circumstances of modern industrialism, are largely beyond self-protection. Regard for these purposes should infuse construction of the legislation if it is to be treated as a working instrument of government and not merely as a collection of English words. The prosecution to which Dotterweich was subjected is based on a now familiar type of legislation whereby penalties serve as effective means of regulation. Such legislation dispenses with the conventional requirement for criminal conduct—awareness of some wrongdoing. * * *

If the 1938 Act were construed as it was below, the penalties of the law could be imposed only in the rare case where the corporation is merely an individual's alter ego. Corporations carrying on an illicit trade would be subject only to what the House Committee described as a "license fee for the conduct of an illegitimate business." A corporate officer, who even with "intent to defraud or mislead," introduced adulterated or misbranded drugs into interstate commerce could not be held culpable for conduct which was indubitably outlawed by the 1906 Act. This argument proves too much. It is not credible that Congress should by implication have exonerated what is probably a preponderant number of persons involved in acts of disobedience—for the number of non-corporate proprietors is relatively small. * * *

Hardship there doubtless may be under a statute which thus penalizes the transaction though consciousness of wrongdoing be totally wanting. Balancing relative hardships, Congress has preferred to place it upon those who have at least the opportunity of informing themselves of the existence of conditions imposed for the protection of consumers before sharing in illicit commerce, rather than to throw the hazard on the innocent public who are wholly helpless.

It would be too treacherous to define or even to indicate by way of illustration the class of employees which stands in such a responsible relation. To attempt a formula embracing the variety of conduct whereby persons may responsibly contribute in furthering a transaction forbidden by an Act of Congress, to wit, to send illicit goods across state lines, would be mischievous futility. In such matters the good sense of prosecutors, the wise guidance of trial judges, and the ultimate judgment of juries must be trusted. * * * For present purpose it suffices to say that in what the defense characterized as "a very fair charge" the district court properly left the question of the responsibility of Dotterweich for the shipment to the jury, and there was sufficient evidence to support its verdict.

■ MURPHY, JUSTICE (dissenting):

Our prime concern in this case is whether the criminal sanctions of the Federal Food, Drug, and Cosmetic Act of 1938 plainly and unmistakably apply to the respondent in his capacity as a corporate officer. He is charged with violating § 301(a) of the Act, which prohibits the introduction or delivery for introduction into interstate commerce of any adulterated or misbranded drug. There is no evidence in this case of any personal guilt on the part of the respondent. There is no proof or claim that he ever knew of the introduction into commerce of the adulterated drugs in question, much less that he actively participated in their introduction. Guilt is imputed to the respondent solely on the basis of his authority and responsibility as president and general manager of the corporation.

It is a fundamental principle of Anglo–Saxon jurisprudence that guilt is personal and that it ought not lightly to be imputed to a citizen who, like the respondent, has no evil intention or consciousness of wrongdoing. It may be proper to charge him with responsibility to the corporation and the stockholders for negligence and mismanagement. But in the absence of clear statutory authorization it is inconsistent with established canons of criminal law to rest liability on an act in which the accused did not participate and of which he had no personal knowledge. * * *

Moreover, the fact that individual liability of corporate officers may be consistent with the policy and purpose of a public health and welfare measure does not authorize this Court to impose such liability where Congress has not clearly intended or actually done so. Congress alone has the power to define a crime and to specify the offenders. It is not our function to supply any deficiencies in these respects, no matter how grave the consequences. Statutory policy and purpose are not constitutional substitutes for the requirement that the legislature specify with reasonable certainty those individuals it desires to place under the interdict of the Act.

Looking at the language actually used in this statute, we find a complete absence of any reference to corporate officers. There is merely a provision in § 303(a) to the effect that "any person" inadvertently violating § 301(a) shall be guilty of a misdemeanor. Section 201(e) further defines "person" as including an "individual, partnership, corporation, and association." The fact that a corporate officer is both a "person" and an "individual" is not indicative of an intent to place vicarious liability on the officer. Such words must be read in light of their statutory environment. Only if Congress has otherwise specified an intent to place corporate officers within the ambit of the Act can they be said to be embraced within the meaning of the words "person" or "individual" as here used.

Nor does the clear imposition of liability on corporations reveal the necessary intent to place criminal sanctions on their officers. A corporation is not the necessary and inevitable equivalent of its officers for all purposes. In many respects it is desirable to distinguish the latter from the corporate entity and to impose liability only on the corporation. In this respect it is significant that this Court has never held the imposition of liability on a corporation sufficient, without more, to extend liability to its officers who have no consciousness of wrongdoing. * * *

This fatal hiatus in the Act is further emphasized by the ability of Congress, demonstrated on many occasions, to apply statutes in no uncertain terms to corporate officers as distinct from corporations. The failure to mention officers specifically is thus some indication of a desire to exempt them from liability. In fact the history of federal food and drug legislation is itself illustrative of this capacity for specification and lends strong support to the conclusion that Congress did not intend to impose liability on corporate officers in this particular Act. * * *

[T]he framers of the 1938 Act had an intelligent comprehension of the inadequacies of the 1906 Act and of the unsettled state of the law. They recognized the necessity of inserting clear and unmistakable language in order to impose liability on corporate officers. It is thus unreasonable to assume that the omission of such language was due to a belief that the Act as it now stands was sufficient to impose liability on corporate officers. Such deliberate deletion is consistent only with an intent to allow such officers to remain free from criminal liability. Thus to apply the sanctions of this Act to the respondent would be contrary to the intent of Congress as expressed in the statutory language and in the legislative history.

The dangers inherent in any attempt to create liability without express congressional intention or authorization are illustrated by this case. Without any legislative guides, we are confronted with the problem of determining precisely which officers, employees and agents of a corporation are to be subject to this Act by our fiat. To erect standards of responsibility is a difficult legislative task and the opinion of this Court admits that it is "too treacherous" and a "mischievous futility" for us to engage in such pursuits. But the only alternative is a blind resort to "the good sense of prosecutors, the wise guidance of trial judges, and the ultimate judgment of juries." Yet that situation is precisely what our constitutional system sought to avoid. Reliance on the legislature to define crimes and criminals distinguishes our form of jurisprudence from certain less desirable ones. The legislative power to restrain the liberty and to imperil the good reputation of citizens must not rest upon the variable attitudes and opinions of those charged with the duties of interpreting and enforcing the mandates of the law.

NOTES AND QUESTIONS

1. *Strict criminal liability*. The Court in *Dotterweich* had split 5–4. In a subsequent case involving adulterated food, the Supreme Court reiterated its holding that the FDCA imposed strict criminal liability. See United States v. Park, 421 U.S. 658, 670–73 (1975) (conceding, however, that the defendant can claim that he or she was powerless to prevent or correct the alleged violation). Lower courts have upheld misdemeanor convictions of persons accused of violating the FDCA even though they lacked criminal intent. See, e.g., United States v. Torigian Lab., Inc., 577 F.Supp. 1514, 1529–31 (E.D.N.Y.), aff'd mem., 751 F.2d 373 (2d Cir.1984); see also United States v. Hodges X–Ray, Inc., 759 F.2d 557, 560–61 (6th Cir.1985) (extending this standard to another statute enforced by the FDA); Jennifer Bragg et al., Onus of Responsibility: The Changing Responsible Corporate Officer Doctrine, 65 Food & Drug L.J. 525, 527 (2010) ("[T]he doctrine [has] begun to make a comeback. Within the last three years, seven executives at two major pharmaceutical and device companies have pled guilty to FDCA misdemeanors . . . ."); Vanessa O'Connell & Michael Rothfeld, U.S. Targets Drug Execs—Law Allows Courts to Hold Corporate Officials Responsible for Pharma Violations, Wall St. J., Sept. 13, 2011, at B1. But cf. Alicia Mundy & Brent Kendall, U.S. Rebuffed in Glaxo Misconduct Case, Wall St. J., May 11, 2011, at B1 (reporting that a federal judge summarily acquitted a company's VP/Associate General Counsel who allegedly obstructed an FDA investigation into the off-label promotion of the antidepressant Wellbutrin®).

2. *Misdemeanor penalties*. The statute calls for no more than one year in prison and/or a $1,000 fine in such cases. See 21 U.S.C. § 333(a)(1). Note, however, that caps on the sanctions available under the Act refer to individual transgressions and may cumulate. See V.E. Irons, Inc. v. United States, 244 F.2d 34, 45–46 (1st Cir.1957). Furthermore, sentencing reform legislation has dramatically raised the maximum fines for these and other federal crimes. See 18 U.S.C. § 3571. Thus, a single violation may cost an individual $100,000 and a corporation $200,000. For instance, the former president, general counsel, and former medical director of Purdue Frederick each received sentences of three years probation, 400 hours of community service in drug treatment programs, and together paid $34.5 million in fines after pleading guilty to a single misbranding charge in connection with the marketing of their company's long-acting opioid analgesic. See Barry Meier, 3 Officials Are Sentenced in Case Involving OxyContin, N.Y. Times, July 21, 2007, at C4 (reporting controversy over the fact that they had avoided jail time, adding that the manufacturer's parent company received five years of probation and paid $600 million in fines and other settlements after pleading guilty to a felony charge for fraudulently claiming that the drug was less prone to abuse); see also Carrie Johnson, OxyContin Makers Admit Deception: Addiction Danger from Painkiller Was Understated, Wash. Post, May 11, 2007, at A1.

3. *Felony penalties for violations committed with an intent to defraud or mislead.* The statute calls for up to three years in prison and/or a $10,000 fine in such cases. See 21 U.S.C. § 333(a)(2). As mentioned previously, these may cumulate and other legislation has increased the potential fine for each infraction (to $250,000 and $500,000). Courts uphold felony convictions of persons accused of violating the FDCA with criminal intent. See, e.g., United States v. Munoz, 430 F.3d 1357 (11th Cir.2005); United States v. Caputo, 456 F.Supp.2d 970 (N.D.Ill.2006) (ordering jail time for two officers of a small company that had violated numerous FDCA provisions in the course of selling a sterilizer for medical devices: 10 years for the CEO, and 6 years for the Chief Compliance Officer), aff'd in relevant part, 517 F.3d 935, 940–43 (7th Cir.2008); cf. United States v. Watkins, 278 F.3d 961 (9th Cir.2002) (holding that a felony conviction for intent to defraud requires knowledge that consumers might regard the false or misleading claims as material to their purchasing decisions); United States v. Mitcheltree, 940 F.2d 1329, 1345–52 (10th Cir.1991) (reversing conviction for lack of sufficient evidence of specific intent to defraud). See generally Brian Rubens, Comment, Common Law Versus Regulatory Fraud: Parsing the Intent Requirement of the Felony Penalty Provision of the Food, Drug, and Cosmetic Act, 72 U. Chi. L. Rev. 1501 (2005). In addition, persons who willfully violate an FDA injunction may face criminal contempt sanctions. See United States v. Themy–Kotronakis, 140 F.3d 858, 861–64 (10th Cir.1998). Federal prosecutors also may bring charges under general criminal statutes prohibiting false reports and conspiracies. See, e.g., United States v. Serian, 895 F.2d 432 (8th Cir.1990); United States v. Harkonen, 2010 WL 2985257, at *8–14 (N.D.Cal.2010) (rejecting post-trial motions of the CEO of InterMune, Inc., after he was convicted of wire fraud (but acquitted on a felony misbranding charge) for issuing a press release that offered a favorable interpretation (based on post-hoc subgroup analysis of a secondary endpoint) of an unsuccessful Phase III trial of Actimmune (interferon gamma–1b) in the treatment of pulmonary fibrosis, an off-label use), app. pending (9th Cir.); see also Ruben Castaneda, Firm to Pay $33 Million in Defrauding of FDA, Wash. Post, Oct. 20, 2001, at B3.

4. *Debarment.* In 1992, after a scandal involving bribes of FDA officials reviewing applications for the approval of generic drugs, Congress required that the agency permanently debar anyone convicted of a felony related to federal regulation of drug products from thereafter "providing services in any capacity to a person that has an approved or pending drug product application." 21 U.S.C. § 335a(a)(2); see also DiCola v. FDA, 77 F.3d 504 (D.C.Cir.1996) (rejecting constitutional challenges to a debarment order); Bae v. Shalala, 44 F.3d 489 (7th Cir.1995) (same); John R. Fleder, The History, Provisions, and Implementation of the Generic Drug Enforcement Act of 1992, 49 Food & Drug L.J. 89 (1994); Paula R. Katz, Protecting the Public's Health Through the Application Integrity Policy, 65 Food & Drug L.J. 539 (2010) (explaining that the FDA may, among other things, put a temporary hold on reviews of some or all of a drug company's pending applications if it discovers serious questions about the integrity of previously submitted data).

5. *Further commentary.* See John Braithwaite, Corporate Crime in the Pharmaceutical Industry (1984); John R. Fleder, The Role of the Department of Justice in Enforcement Matters Relating to the Food and Drug Administration, 46 Food Drug Cosm. L.J. 781 (1991); Nicholas Freitag, Federal Food and Drug Act Violations, 41 Am. Crim. L. Rev. 647 (2004); Dana H. Freyer, Corporate Compliance Programs for FDA–Regulated Companies: Incentives for Their Development and the Impact of the Federal Sentencing Guidelines for Organizations, 51 Food & Drug L.J. 225 (1996); Deborah F. Buckman, Annotation, Remedies Available for Violations of Federal Food, Drug, and Cosmetic Act, 25 A.L.R. Fed. 2d 431 (2008 & 2011 Supp.).

2. RULEMAKING

National Association of Pharmaceutical Mfrs. v. FDA

637 F.2d 877 (2d Cir.1981).

■ FRIENDLY, CIRCUIT JUDGE:

In 1962 Congress enacted various amendments to the Federal Food, Drug, and Cosmetic Act of 1938, to "strengthen and broaden existing laws in the drug field so as to bring about better, safer medicine and to establish a more effective system of enforcement of the drug laws." S. Rep. No. 1744, 87th Cong., 2d Sess. 8 (1962). Among the amendments was a section by which a drug is deemed adulterated if its packaging, processing, holding or manufacturing fail to conform to "current good manufacturing practice (CGMP) to assure that such drug meets the requirements of this chapter as to safety and has the identity and strength, and meets the quality and purity characteristics, which it purports or is represented to possess." 21 U.S.C. § 351(a)(2)(B). The Food and Drug Administration (FDA) issued its first regulations under this section in 1963. In February 1976, FDA announced a proposal to revise and update the then current CGMP regulations. * * *

The FDA received numerous comments both upon the substance of its requirements and upon its proposal that the new CGMP regulations should have the force of law. In an extensive preamble to the new regulations it set forth a legal analysis supporting its view that it had power to issue binding regulations and the reasons why it believed binding rather than merely interpretive regulations would be in the public interest. The regulations, now appearing at 21 C.F.R. Parts 210 and 211 (1980), were published on September 29, 1978, to be effective March 28, 1979. They cover a broad spectrum of affairs, including requirements for personnel practices, record keeping, building design, and procedures for the control of drug production, packaging and labeling. * * *

[T]he National Association of Pharmaceutical Manufacturers and the National Pharmaceutical Alliance, both trade associations, sought a declaration that FDA's attempt to give binding effect to the new CGMP regulations was beyond its authority. * * * Two different subsections of § 701 confer rulemaking authority upon the FDA. Section 701(a) provides:

> The authority to promulgate regulations for the efficient enforcement of this chapter, except as otherwise provided in this section, is vested in the Secretary [of Health and Human Services].

The effect of § 4 of the Administrative Procedure Act of 1946 (APA), now 5 U.S.C. § 553, is to require that rulemaking under § 701(a), with certain exceptions, including "interpretative rules," follow an informal notice and comment procedure, which was done here. Section 701(e) provides that "[a]ny action for the issuance, amendment, or repeal of any regulation" under various sections of the Act of which § 501(a)(2)(B) is not one, shall follow a complex procedure which has been read to include a trial-type hearing; § 701(f) provides that review of any order resulting from such rulemaking lies in a court of appeals. See Nat'l Nutritional Foods Ass'n v. FDA, 504 F.2d 761, 771–74 (2d Cir.1974). Admittedly § 701(e) procedures were not followed here and the FDA's authority to give binding effect to the CGMP regulations at issue must rest on § 701(a).

Reading the language of that subsection, which comes from the Act of 1938, with the eyes of 1980, one would have little difficulty in concluding that the words suffice to empower the Commissioner of the FDA, to whom the Secretary has delegated his powers, 21 C.F.R. § 5.1(a)(1) (1980), to issue regulations, substantive as well as procedural, having the force of law. The comprehensive opinion of Judge J. Skelly Wright in *National Petroleum Refiners Ass'n v. FTC*, 482 F.2d 672 (D.C.Cir.1973), catalogued the many instances in which general statutory provisions not differing essentially from § 701(a) have been held to endow agencies with power to issue binding rules and regulations. In the interest of historical accuracy, it should be noted that at one time it was widely understood that generalized grants of rulemaking authority conferred power only to make rules of a procedural or an interpretative nature, and not binding substantive regulations, for which a specific delegation was thought necessary. * * * In 1953, however, the Court decided *American Trucking Ass'ns v. United States*, 344

U.S. 298, * * * [and] this generous construction of agency rulemaking authority has become firmly entrenched.

Beyond this there is formidable authority to the effect that § 701(a) itself is a grant of power to issue binding regulations. * * * [T]his court, in *National Nutritional Foods Ass'n v. Weinberger*, 512 F.2d 688, 696 (2d Cir.1975), characterized the 1973 quartet of Supreme Court decisions as having dispelled "[w]hatever doubts might have been entertained regarding the FDA's power under § 701(a) to promulgate binding regulations." The court said: "[o]ur attention has not been directed to anything in the legislative history of §§ 701(a) and (e) that militates against these conclusions," and correctly stated that "over the last decade rule-making has been increasingly substituted for adjudication as a regulatory technique, with the support and encouragement of the courts, at least where the regulation involves specialized scientific knowledge." * * * In *United States v. Nova Scotia Food Products Corp.*, 568 F.2d 240, 246–48 (2d Cir.1977), we again read the 1938 Act as authorizing the issuance of binding substantive regulations under § 701(a). * * *

NOTES AND QUESTIONS

1. *Formal vs. informal rulemaking.* FDCA § 701(e) granted the agency the authority to issue regulations governing certain subjects, but it also required that interested parties be allowed to request a public hearing as part of the rulemaking process. See Pharmaceutical Mfrs. Ass'n v. Gardner, 381 F.2d 271, 278 (D.C.Cir.1967); Annotation, Necessity of Formal Hearing Prior to Issuance of Regulations Under § 701 of the Federal Food, Drug, and Cosmetic Act, 43 A.L.R. Fed. 320 (1979 & 2011 Supp.). For instance, until amended in 2007, the FDA's power to promulgate prescription drug advertising regulations was subject to this "formal" rulemaking procedure. See 21 U.S.C. § 352(n). These procedures became a source of frustrating delays for the agency. See Robert W. Hamilton, Rulemaking on a Record by the Food and Drug Administration, 50 Tex. L. Rev. 1132, 1142 (1972) ("[T]he FDA has conducted two major [formal rulemaking] proceedings that have been the subject of wide criticism. Both proceedings have taken (or will take) more than ten years from the formulation of the original proposal to the actual effective date of the regulation."). For that reason, when the courts decided that the residual rulemaking authority in FDCA § 701(a) empowered the FDA to issue binding regulations on matters not specifically covered by § 701(e), the agency began to utilize "notice-and-comment" procedures for the promulgation of rules. The courts also, however, allowed parties to bring "pre-enforcement" challenges to such rules in some cases. See Abbott Lab. v. Gardner, 387 U.S. 136 (1967) (holding that an FDA drug labeling regulation was ripe for judicial review). Although "informal" rulemaking avoids the cumbersome hearings required with formal rulemaking, searching judicial review on the merits and increasing procedural demands added by all three branches of government have made it increasingly difficult, so the FDA and other agencies have experimented with still further short-cuts for issuing regulations. See

Michael Kolber, Rulemaking Without Rules: An Empirical Study of Direct Final Rulemaking, 72 Alb. L. Rev. 79 (2009); Lars Noah, Doubts About Direct Final Rulemaking, 51 Admin. L. Rev. 401, 409–11 (1999) (describing the FDA's experience with one such technique, and arguing that it is unlawful); see also Syncor Int'l Corp. v. Shalala, 127 F.3d 90 (D.C.Cir.1997) (rejecting the FDA's claim that an interpretive rule was exempt from notice-and-comment requirements).

2. *Rulemaking vs. adjudication.* The FDA was one of the first federal agencies to make extensive use of its initially unclear rulemaking powers. In lieu of bringing enforcement actions under the open-ended provisions of the statute and generating adjudicatory precedent for future cases, the FDA began to promulgate more detailed rules to implement the statutory provisions. See Eric R. Claeys, The Food and Drug Administration and the Command-and-Control Model of Regulation, 49 St. Louis U. L.J. 105 (2004). Although infractions still required individual enforcement proceedings, the agency would simplify its burden of proof in those proceedings, which, coupled with the greater clarity of expectations, would help to promote improved compliance. The FDA implemented some of its misbranding authorities in this fashion. See Pharmaceutical Mfrs. Ass'n v. FDA, 634 F.2d 106, 108 (3d Cir.1980) (per curiam) (sustaining the FDA's power to issue a regulation requiring patient package inserts warning of the risk of cancer for estrogen-containing drug products). In addition, as mentioned earlier, the agency utilized its rulemaking power to facilitate implementation of the Drug Amendments of 1962, for instance by specifying what would qualify as "substantial evidence" of effectiveness and then granting itself summary judgment whenever a manufacturer was not able to provide the requisite data from clinical trials, or by issuing monographs specifying the circumstances under which nonprescription drugs would be considered GRASE. This provision does not, however, grant the agency carte blanche. See Association of Am. Physicians & Surgeons, Inc. v. FDA, 226 F.Supp.2d 204, 213 (D.D.C.2002) ("Section 371 does not constitute an independent grant of authority that permits FDA to issue *any* regulation the agency determines would advance the public health. Rather, § 371 permits the FDA to use rules as a means of administering authorities otherwise delegated to it by the Congress.").

3. *GMP regulations.* The implementation of the FDA's GMP authority illustrates some of the comparative advantages of rulemaking. In 1962, Congress amended the adulteration provision of the statute to impose a requirement that drug and device companies abide by good manufacturing practices. At first, the agency brought enforcement actions against firms thought to have violated this requirement, and it would have to persuade the court why a particular step in the production process failed to conform to GMPs. See United States v. Bel–Mar Lab., Inc., 284 F.Supp. 875, 882–84 (E.D.N.Y.1968). After some time, the FDA decided to issue a series of precise GMP requirements as binding regulations, which it first published as proposed rules and invited public comment. In addition to challenging the agency's statutory authority to issue any binding rules, an issue resolved in *NAPM v. FDA*, the drug industry attacked the GMP regulations on various other grounds. See National Ass'n of Pharm. Mfrs. v. HHS, 586 F.Supp. 740, 748–63 (S.D.N.Y.1984) (rejecting numerous substantive and procedural objections to these regulations); cf. Nutritional Health Alliance v. FDA, 318 F.3d 92, 98–101 (2d Cir.2003) (holding that the agency's authority to prevent adulteration (including through the issuance of GMPs) did not authorize the issuance of a rule—in response to incidents of acute iron poisoning in children—that required drug and dietary supplement manufacturers to distribute products containing 30 mg or more of iron per dosage unit in nonreusable unit-dose packages); id. at 101 ("We reject the FDA's construction because the risk that a product will be used or misused in an unintended manner is simply unrelated to 'adulteration' under any reasonable interpretation of that term.... With or without packaging, the iron-containing product is not subject to contamination, deterioration, or any other change that causes it to be unsafe.").

In subsequent enforcement actions, the courts would focus on questions of compliance with those precise requirements rather than on questions of whether the requirements amounted to GMPs under the statute (though some interpolation would remain necessary where the rules failed to address the precise issue in controversy):

> Current Good Manufacturing Practice (CGMP), explained in greater, but by no means sufficient, detail in regulations promulgated by the FDA, sets the minimum standards for drug manufacturers. Designed as a quality control measure to prevent super- and sub-potency, product mix-ups, contamination, and mislabeling, the CGMP regulations outline general rules for all aspects of drug manufacture including buildings and facilities, personnel, equipment, drug components and containers, production, packaging and labeling, and record-keeping. Failure to comply with CGMP regulations renders any resulting drug product "adulterated" and the drug product and its producer subject to regulatory action.

United States v. Barr Lab., Inc., 812 F.Supp. 458, 465 (D.N.J.1993); see also United States v. Utah Med. Prods., Inc., 404 F.Supp.2d 1315, 1323–24 (D.Utah 2005) (rejecting the FDA's arguments that a medical device component part supplier violated GMPs for failing to follow industry standards governing process validation, and complaining about "this extended and in some instances 'nitpicking' case ..., arising in part because of the general nature of the regulations themselves, which have the virtue of generality and the vice of imprecision"); Caitlin E. Fleming, Note, Overdosed and Contaminated: A Critical Examination of the FDA and Drug Industry's Role in Drug Safety in the Context of the Heparin Catastrophe, 13 Quinnipiac Health L.J. 117 (2009); Natasha Singer, Questions for Makers on Defects in Drugs, N.Y. Times, May 27, 2010, at B1 (discussing GMP problems affecting various OTC products). When the agency cites large companies for GMP violations, it may prompt compliance by delaying final approval of pending applications for any new drugs slated for manufacturing at the allegedly substandard facilities. See Melody Petersen, Faults Found at a Schering Plant, N.Y. Times, Mar. 2, 2001, at C3.

3. INFORMAL MECHANISMS

United States v. Bioclinical Systems, Inc.

666 F.Supp. 82 (D.Md.1987).

■ MOTZ, DISTRICT JUDGE:

The government has brought this action under the Federal Food, Drug and Cosmetic Act, 21 U.S.C. § 332(a), seeking to enjoin alleged violations of the Act by Bioclinical Systems, Inc. (a manufacturer of plated culture media) * * * * [T]he FDA's April inspection identified 29 violations of the FDA's Good Manufacturing Practices (GMPs). Although they are to some extent interrelated, these violations may for present purposes be divided into two categories: those relating to Bioclinical's failure to attain a sterility assurance level (SAL) of 0.1% and those not relating to that standard. * * *

The fundamental question which divides the parties is whether or not the Compliance Office of the Division of Compliance Programs of the FDA may properly insist upon manufacturers of plated culture media meeting an SAL of 0.1%. It may not do so. Congress has mandated that a full and deliberate public process, including the making of recommendations by a broad-based advisory committee and the opportunity for public hearing, be followed before the FDA may establish a GMP. The FDA has bypassed that process here. Instead, the Office of Compliance has been imposing an 0.1% SAL as a de facto requirement during the course of its inspections since March 1986 (when a draft set of Inspectional Guidelines incorporating the standard was issued by the FDA's Center for Devices and Radiological Health).

The government concedes that a GMP may not be properly established by adoption of a draft guideline. Rather, it argues that the 0.1% SAL constitutes a GMP independently of the draft guideline. This argument is conclusively rebutted by hard and concrete fact. A GMP must represent a "current good manufacturing process." See 21 U.S.C. § 360j(f)(1)(A). The evidence in this case is overwhelming that the in vitro diagnostic device industry (including manufacturers of plated culture media) does not attain an 0.1% SAL. * * *

At bottom, what the government is asserting here is that whatever the current industry practice may be, the SAL should be what the Office of Compliance dictates it to be. If the evidence demonstrated that the industry as a whole has been resisting in bad faith the adoption of a feasible good manufacturing practice in the face of a demonstrated hazard to the public health, there arguably would be merit in the government's position. However, the evidence does not so demonstrate. Ideally, of course, plated culture media should be manufactured under sterile conditions. It may also be assumed (although the government presented no evidence directly proving the fact) that technologically an 0.1% SAL could be met by the in vitro diagnostic device industry. However, the record does not establish that attainment of the 0.1% SAL is economically feasible. * * * More importantly, the record does not establish that the overriding interest of the public health requires the imposition of an 0.1% SAL. * * *

The question of whether or not an 0.1% SAL should be established as a GMP for the manufacture of plated culture media is not one which is within the expertise or the power of this court to resolve. However, it is equally not within the power of the FDA's Office of Compliance to impose the requirement unilaterally. Congress has specifically established the public review process which must be followed to resolve an issue of this magnitude, and it is through that process, not through enforcement actions, that the questions of public health and of technological and economic feasibility posed by the 0.1% SAL are to be decided.

Washington Legal Foundation v. Kessler

880 F.Supp. 26 (D.D.C.1995).

■ LAMBERTH, DISTRICT JUDGE:

* * * At issue in this case are activities of drug and medical device manufacturers which the FDA contends amount to improper labeling of medical products. Two practices in particular have attracted the attention of the FDA. The first involves the distribution by manufacturers to doctors of so-called "enduring materials" (such as medical journals, articles, and textbooks) which contain information regarding "off-label"[1] uses of the manufacturer's products. The distribution of enduring materials to health care professionals appears to be a common tool for manufacturers seeking to maintain good customer relations with those who purchase their products. The other practice with which the FDA has become concerned is manufacturer support of scientific or educational activities (such as medical symposia) at which off-label uses of the manufacturer's products are discussed or demonstrated. Again, sponsorship of medical symposia and the like is a common public relations practice for manufacturers of medical products.

According to WLF, the FDA has determined that each of these activities constitutes improper labeling and/or promotion when it involves the distribution of materials or sponsorship of activities in which off-label usage of one of the manufacturer's products is discussed. WLF further contends that this determination has taken the form of a specific agency policy which the FDA has been enforcing for several years against medical product manufacturers, and which it intends to continue to enforce in the future. * * * The FDA contends that so long as the agency has not released a formal policy statement or instituted an enforcement action against a

1. "Off-label" usage refers to the use of a drug or device in a manner not approved by the FDA and not set forth in the product's labeling materials. While manufacturers may not themselves promote such uses, it is not unlawful for doctors to employ or prescribe medical products for "unapproved" uses. Indeed, the FDA claims that it has "long recognized the important role that some unapproved uses may play in the practice of medicine."

manufacturer, there is no "final agency action" reviewable in this court. * * *

The FDA claims that it is in the process of revising its policies on industry-supported promotion of off-label uses of medical products. As part of this process, the FDA published a "Draft Policy Statement on Industry–Supported Scientific and Educational Activities." 57 Fed. Reg. 56,412 (1992). By its terms, this Draft Policy Statement represents a tentative agency position concerning how the FDA intends to distinguish between manufacturer-supported activities "that are otherwise independent from the promotional influence of the supporting company [and are therefore permissible] and those that are not [and therefore violate the Federal Food, Drug and Cosmetic Act]." Id. The Draft Policy Statement sets forth a number of criteria that the FDA considers useful in distinguishing between independent and impermissibly manufacturer-influenced activities. * * * The FDA maintains that the policies and procedures described in the Draft Policy Statement have not yet been adopted as official FDA policy, and that the agency is still in the process of formulating its final policy statement.

In October of 1993, plaintiff WLF filed a Citizen Petition with the FDA * * * request[ing] that the FDA formally withdraw its Draft Policy Statement * * * * At the heart of the motion to dismiss is defendants' contention that WLF's dispute is not yet ripe for judicial review. Specifically, FDA asserts that (1) because FDA is still considering how to respond to WLF's Citizen Petition, WLF's suit is "premature"; (2) this dispute is not ripe for review, inasmuch as FDA has not adopted an official policy concerning manufacturer-supported distribution of off-label usage information; and (3) resolution of the dispute in its present posture would improvidently require the court to step into the FDA's role as a formulator of public health policy. * * *

[W]ith regard to WLF's Citizen Petition, the FDA failed to follow the procedures set forth in its own regulations whereby the agency must respond to such petitions within 180 days of receiving them. FDA did not respond to WLF's petition for 270 days, and then only several weeks after the filing of the present lawsuit. At oral argument, counsel for the defendants explained that WLF's petition had "slipped through the cracks," and that the agency's failure to respond to the petition within the 180 day time period was wholly inadvertent. The court accepts this explanation, and also agrees with FDA that the agency's failure to respond timely to WLF's petition should not itself constitute a formal denial of the petition, for purposes of determining whether there has been final agency action. At the same time, however, the FDA's handling of WLF's Citizen Petition, as well as the statements in its filings and at oral argument, evidence a somewhat less vigilant concern for the doctors' First Amendment rights than this court would hope to see. * * *

[I]n light of the two and one-half year time period that FDA estimates will be required to resolve WLF's dispute, WLF's decision to seek judicial review cannot be described as an attempt to "flout" any "established administrative process." * * * [G]iven plaintiff's allegations that FDA has not only promulgated, but has also sought to enforce (albeit somewhat informally) a final agency policy, the court doubts very much that WLF is likely to "successfully vindicate [its] claims" in an administrative proceeding before the FDA. In light of these conclusions, the court finds that WLF is not barred by the exhaustion doctrine from maintaining the present suit. * * *

FDA maintains that it has not yet adopted an official policy concerning manufacturer-supported off-label usage information, and therefore an attempt by this court to resolve the dispute at this stage would be premature and would usurp the FDA's role as a formulator of administrative policy. The court is mindful of the serious prudential concerns raised by FDA's ripeness argument. * * *

Whether FDA has officially adopted a final policy, however, is not determinative. In the context of a ripeness inquiry, it is the effect of the agency's conduct which is most important in determining whether an agency has adopted a final policy. And this case illustrates why this must be so: If an agency's own characterization of the finality of its policy were determinative, that agency could effectively regulate industry without ever exposing itself to judicial review. A powerful agency such as FDA could achieve this result through the simple expedient of (1) never formally declaring the policy to be "final," and (2) threatening (but never actually initiating) enforcement procedures against companies which failed to comply with the agency's de facto policy. Indeed, this is precisely what plaintiff has alleged.

WLF's complaint alleges that the FDA has sought to enforce a final agency policy concerning manufacturer-supported dissemination of off-label usage information. With regard to manufacturers' distribution of "enduring materials" containing such information, WLF describes a number of different instances in which representatives of the FDA sent warning letters and followed up with telephone calls to manufacturers which had planned to distribute medical textbooks and other enduring materials to doctors. * * *

In addition to sending warning letters to individual companies, high-ranking officers of the FDA are alleged to have made general remarks which plaintiff contends reveal the existence of a definitive agency position concerning off-label usage information. The Commissioner of the FDA himself, defendant David Kessler, allegedly made the following statement in June of 1991: "I would urge all members of the pharmaceutical industry to take a long hard look at their promotional practices. I do not expect companies to wait until this guidance becomes final to put their advertising and promotional houses in order." More recently, David Adams, Director of the Policy Development and Coordination Staff in Commissioner Kessler's office is alleged to have written the following statement regarding the FDA's Draft Policy Statement:

> Although this document was published as a draft policy statement with an invitation to submit comments, it reflects actual agency policy. It tells you how the agency makes decisions from day to day in determin-

ing whether activities are subject to regulation and are potentially illegal under the Food, Drug and Cosmetic Act.

Other FDA officials are alleged to have made similar comments at various times.

FDA maintains that these letters and comments do not amount to "final agency action." According to FDA, the "regulatory letters" described above merely "reflect views of particular individuals, not the institutional decision of the agency." As such, defendants argue that this "informal advice given by specific employees of FDA" should not suggest the existence of any formal agency policy. Likewise, because neither the Draft Policy Statement nor the comments of Commissioner Kessler constitute "coercive imperatives" which the FDA is bound to adhere to, these are not evidence of a final policy either, according to FDA. Unfortunately, by focusing exclusively on the individual trees, FDA appears to have lost sight of the forest. The question here is not whether any single act on the part of the FDA signifies the existence of a final agency policy; rather, the aggregate effect of these acts must be analyzed to determine whether the agency by its conduct has objectively demonstrated the existence of such a policy. * * *

Although the FDA characterizes the "regulatory letters" and other statements of FDA officials as merely "advisory," the court must not be blind to the practical effects of these letters and other statements. As alleged in plaintiff's complaint, the collective effect of FDA's conduct has been to discourage manufacturers from disseminating information that they would otherwise have chosen to distribute. The result is that doctors, including WLF's member-doctors, have been prevented from receiving information which they claim to have an interest in receiving. Contrary to FDA's protestations, the plaintiff's allegations clearly set forth a causal connection between FDA's conduct and the decision of various companies to stop disseminating certain kinds of information and to stop supporting certain scientific and educational activities.

It may be true, as FDA argues, that a company which disagrees with the "advice" contained in FDA's regulatory correspondence may disregard this advice, go ahead with its planned activities, and then challenge the constitutionality of any adverse FDA action in an enforcement proceeding. However, the reality of the situation, as alleged by plaintiff, is that few if any companies are willing to directly challenge the FDA in this manner. In the first instance, the company must expose itself to the FDA's power to seize an entire product line if the FDA finds the products to be "misbranded." Although the company can then litigate the validity of the seizure (and therefore the policy pursuant to which the seizure was made), the prospect of lost sales and protracted litigation is understandably discouraging to these companies. In addition, the FDA wields enormous power over drug and medical device manufacturers through its power to grant or deny new product applications. It is evident that manufacturers are most reluctant to arouse the ire of such a powerful agency. The result, according to plaintiff, is that "FDA has been able to effectuate its policies without having to resort regularly to formal rulemaking." As evidence of this, the complaint describes a substantial reduction in the distribution of enduring materials to doctors and in the willingness of manufacturers to sponsor scientific and educational activities since the alleged implementation of FDA's off-label usage policy. * * *

Under such circumstances the presumption of reviewability attaches with particular force. The fact that this suit is being brought by doctors who have been prevented from receiving information rather than the manufacturers with whose conduct the FDA policy primarily interferes lends further credence to plaintiff's contention that the FDA's power over industry is such that it is able to implement de facto regulatory policies without formally adopting final agency positions. As a general proposition, the court finds the possibility of such a practice disturbing; in the context of the plaintiff's constitutional allegations, the court finds the possibility of such a practice intolerable. Thus, the court concludes that the allegations contained in the plaintiff's amended complaint clearly raise a question of fact as to whether the FDA has been enforcing a de facto policy concerning manufacturer-supported distribution of off-label usage information. * * *

NOTES AND QUESTIONS

1. *Round one in the WLF skirmish.* The federal courts' resolution of the merits of WLF's constitutional challenge is discussed at length in Chapter 4(C). Note, however, that most courts have declined to review the agency's regulatory letters for lack of ripeness or failure to exhaust administrative remedies. See Dietary Supplemental Coalition, Inc. v. Sullivan, 978 F.2d 560, 563 (9th Cir.1992); Professionals & Patients for Customized Care v. Shalala, 847 F.Supp. 1359, 1365 (S.D.Tex.1994), aff'd, 56 F.3d 592, 599 (5th Cir.1995); see also CareToLive v. von Eschenbach, 525 F.Supp.2d 938, 946–50 (S.D.Ohio 2007) (dismissing for lack of finality and ripeness a challenge brought by a patient advocacy group to the agency's issuance of a "complete response letter" that requested further information from a biotechnology company seeking approval of Provenge®), aff'd mem., 290 F.App'x 887 (6th Cir.2008).

2. *Guidance documents.* As informal rulemaking became increasingly cumbersome, the FDA shifted from promulgating binding rules to issuing nonbinding guidelines. First, as happened in *WLF*, these informal announcements may operate as de facto rules but escape normal procedural safeguards for their promulgation or review. See James Hunnicutt, Note, Another Reason to Reform the Federal Regulatory System: Agencies' Treating Nonlegislative Rules as Binding Law, 41 B.C. L. Rev. 153 (1999). Second, they allow the FDA to take positions that do not even constrain agency officials, which leaves regulated entities guessing about their rights and obligations. See Lars Noah, The FDA's New Policy on Guidelines: Having Your Cake and Eating It Too, 47 Cath. U. L. Rev. 113 (1997). Notwithstanding these concerns, in FDAMA Congress sanctioned (subject to certain limitations) the agency's shift to greater reliance on guidance documents. See 21 U.S.C. § 371(h); see also 75 Fed. Reg. 48,180 (2010) (providing a comprehensive list of FDA guidance documents). Indeed, rather than go to the trouble of amending its 25–year–old rules delineating "current" GMPs, the FDA has decided to issue guidance for the adoption of innovative quality control technologies by the pharmaceutical industry. See Leila Abboud & Scott Hensley, Factory Shift: New Prescription for Drug Makers, Wall St. J., Sept. 3, 2003, at A1.

Lars Noah, *Administrative Arm–Twisting in the Shadow of Congressional Delegations of Authority*

1997 WIS. L. REV. 873 (1997).

The typical subjects of administrative law scholarship, rulemaking and adjudication, represent only a small fraction of agency activity. This distortion in emphasis is not surprising given the well understood fact that most agency activity inevitably occurs behind the scenes and beyond the reach of the Administrative Procedure Act (APA). Exactly fifty years ago, the Attorney General's Manual on the APA recognized that agency "settlement of cases and issues by informal methods is nothing new," adding that "even where formal proceedings are fully available, informal procedures constitute the vast bulk of administrative adjudication and are truly the lifeblood of the administrative process." Half a century later, this observation continues to hold true, as does the seemingly intractable problem of controlling the exercise of such wide-ranging discretionary power.

Arm-twisting represents one broad and important category of informal agency activity. As used in this Article, administrative "arm-twisting" refers to a threat by an agency to impose a sanction or withhold a benefit in hopes of encouraging "voluntary" compliance with a request that the agency could not impose directly on a regulated entity. Although it provides agencies with significant flexibility, arm-twisting differs from many of the newfangled regulatory approaches that are designed primarily to benefit the targets of administrative control. Indeed, arm-twisting often saddles parties with more onerous regulatory burdens than Congress had authorized, accompanied by a diminished opportunity to pursue judicial challenges.

This phenomenon may be even more insidious than the frequently discussed tendency of agencies to develop informal but essentially binding policies without adhering to notice and comment rulemaking procedures. The use of informal mechanisms to evade increasingly burdensome procedural requirements and searching judicial scrutiny—the so-called "ossification" of the informal rulemaking process—has attracted significant attention in recent years. In contrast, the use of informal mechanisms to evade the substantive limitations on an agency's delegated authority has gone largely unnoticed. Although a few commentators have touched upon discrete aspects of this seemingly troublesome phenomenon, no one has evaluated arm-twisting as such. * * *

As suggested in the sections that follow, administrative agencies have numerous opportunities to pursue indirectly ends that they could not impose directly. Arm-twisting may occur during licensing, government contracting, and enforcement proceedings. It may reflect formally announced agency policy or instead result from informal, ad hoc bargaining. Agencies may threaten to deny licenses, refuse to enter into procurement agreements, disseminate adverse publicity, or impose other sanctions against uncooperative parties. Often such threats simply represent a more efficient method of achieving ends explicitly authorized by Congress, but in some cases they may allow agencies to pursue extrastatutory goals, seemingly in contravention of the limits on their delegated authority.

A. *Conditions Imposed During Licensing*

* * * In 1992, in response to complaints about excessive delays in approving drugs to treat AIDS and other life-threatening conditions, the [FDA] promulgated regulations to establish an accelerated approval procedure for new drugs and biologics intended to treat serious or life-threatening illnesses. Before approving a new drug, the FDA must find that it is both safe and effective, but, under the accelerated approval procedures, it will demand weaker evidence of effectiveness than it normally requires. The agency has succeeded in rapidly approving important new therapies during the last few years.

If a pharmaceutical company wishes to utilize this expedited licensing procedure, it must agree to several conditions on approval not explicitly authorized by Congress [prior to 1997]. For example, an applicant would have to accept any necessary postmarketing restrictions, including distribution only through certain medical facilities or by specially-trained physicians; distribution conditioned on the performance of specified medical procedures; and advance submission of all promotional materials for FDA review. The governing statute d[id] not, however, authorize the imposition of any of these conditions. Moreover, the FDA demands that the company waive its right to demand an evidentiary hearing in the event that the agency chooses to withdraw the approval. In response to industry complaints about such conditions, the agency explained that any "applicants objecting to these procedures may forego approval under these regulations and seek approval under the traditional approval process." However, with potentially millions of dollars in lost revenue for each additional month awaiting FDA approval, eligible drug companies cannot afford to forego these accelerated procedures, and so far the industry has opted not to challenge the rules in court. * * *

One may well ask how far an agency might go in conditioning licenses. In addition to postmarketing studies and the waiver of hearing rights, for example, could the FDA condition product approvals on agreements not to engage in broadcast advertising or not to raise drug prices faster than the rate of inflation? Could the agency demand waivers of patent rights or promises to contribute some percentage of profits to a public health agency (or perhaps the Republican National Committee)? * * *

B. *Government Contracting*

* * * In a few instances, threats to stop dealing with a firm accompany an allegation of some regulatory infraction. For example, "warning letters" issued by the FDA identify the supposed violation, provide the recipient with a limited period of time to take corrective action (coupled with a threat of formal enforcement proceedings), and, in the case of drugs and medical devices, explain that government purchasing entities have been advised to stop dealing with the company in the meantime. Again, because the federal government represents the single largest purchaser of prescription drugs in this country, few manufacturers would dare risk losing these contracts. If a company voluntarily corrects the alleged violations of federal law, it never gets an opportunity to challenge the legal basis for the FDA's objections. Should a company disagree with the agency's allegations and choose to pursue a judicial challenge rather than accede to its demands, the FDA invariably argues that the controversy is not yet ripe for review, and so far only a single court has held that a challenge was justiciable on the basis of such an interim procurement freeze.

C. *Voluntary Recalls and Adverse Publicity*

The [FDA] generally lacks the statutory authority to order a recall of potentially dangerous products subject to its regulatory jurisdiction. Although Congress has granted the agency such authority with regard to limited classes of products, and others have recommended providing it with broader recall powers, the FDA generally has resisted suggestions that the statute be amended to provide it with recall authority. Instead, the agency prefers encouraging voluntary recalls, and it has even promulgated detailed regulations setting forth its recall procedures and policies. * * *

This strategy has succeeded because firms know that a failure to cooperate with an agency's request risks more serious enforcement measures authorized by statute, such as product seizures, injunctions, and even criminal penalties. Because these measures require somewhat cumbersome judicial proceedings, however, the issuance of adverse publicity may be a more effective means of inducing prompt action. Companies often prefer a voluntary recall because it allows them to exercise greater control over the nature and extent of public notification regarding any hazards associated with their particular product.

The [FDCA] expressly authorizes the issuance of adverse publicity by the FDA, though only in limited circumstances. Even when Congress has delegated such power, however, some controversy surrounds the use of adverse publicity. In particular, targets of an information campaign often have no meaningful opportunity to respond to the charges or seek judicial review. In recognition of the risk of improper use, the FDA once proposed a policy to limit the issuance of such publicity. The agency never finalized this proposal, and it continues to rely on explicit or implicit threats of disseminating adverse publicity as a method of encouraging voluntary compliance with its various demands. * * *

D. *Consent Decrees in Enforcement Proceedings*

As is true with most civil lawsuits and criminal prosecutions, the vast majority of all administrative enforcement proceedings result in settlements. Although sometimes simply reflected in private agreements, these settlements often lead to the entry of judgment by a court in the form of a consent decree, which gives the court continuing jurisdiction over the dispute and the power to enforce the agreement by fashioning appropriate equitable remedies. In the course of settling enforcement actions, agencies sometimes manage to extract concessions from the companies suspected of violating statutory requirements, and they frequently include regulatory provisions in these administrative consent decrees that they could not impose directly on a regulated entity.

Again, the FDA provides some prime recent examples. In the early 1990s, the agency negotiated consent decrees with pharmaceutical companies that it had accused of unlawfully promoting certain prescription drug products. In one of these cases, a manufacturer agreed to undertake an extensive corrective advertising campaign and also to preclear all of its promotional materials with the FDA for a period of two years, even though the statute generally prohibits such mandatory preclearance of pharmaceutical advertising. In another case, a company agreed to establish an FDA-approved training program for its pharmaceutical sales representatives, even though the agency does not appear to have the power to regulate such communications. In these and other cases, explicit FDA threats of especially burdensome product seizures or injunctions prompted the drug companies to accept these unprecedented requirements. * * *

[*Discussion*:]

One may applaud some of these agency initiatives as refreshingly innovative alternatives to the typically inflexible and occasionally counterproductive regulations and enforcement policies of the federal government. Indeed, some of the approaches represent responses to past complaints by regulated firms about undue rigidity in administrative decisionmaking, and companies no doubt prefer negotiated outcomes (with strings attached) to the denial of a license, the rejection of a contract bid, or the imposition of a formal sanction. This same flexibility, however, carries with it opportunities for abuse. * * *

When private parties settle disputes, they bargain in the "shadow" of the law, with the prospect of judicial review serving to constrain the range of potential outcomes. When administrative agencies bargain with regulated entities, it is less clear that they operate in the shadow of the law, in particular the constraints on the power delegated by Congress. * * * Arm-twisting succeeds, and evades judicial or other scrutiny, in part because companies in pervasively regulated industries believe that they cannot afford to resist agency demands. For instance, some critics have accused the FDA of retaliating against firms that fail to cooperate. Whether or not such charges are accurate, the perception leads companies to accede to the agency's demands even though they may lack any basis in law or fact. * * *

Consider again the product approval examples discussed at the outset. Congress has authorized the FDA to impose certain conditions on * * * new drug approvals (e.g., warning requirements); it has not explicitly authorized other requirements (e.g., recalls or postmarketing surveillance); and it implicitly or explicitly forbade the imposition of still other requirements (e.g., preclearance of drug advertising). The latter category should be off limits, leaving parties at most to bargain over commitments about which Congress expressed no intent one way or another, though even that intermediate category could raise ultra vires concerns.

Perhaps the power to license implies a power to impose conditions on approval, but, to ameliorate the risk that regulators may impose ultra vires demands, one might insist that Congress explicitly authorize agencies to deviate from statutory directives. Congress has, for instance, invited the FDA to impose such other conditions on product approvals as it may deem necessary in certain limited circumstances. Beyond such situations, however, courts should hold agencies to the limits of their enabling statutes. * * *

Administrative arm-twisting hardly represents a new phenomenon, but it has received very little critical attention to date. Arm-twisting also is not a unitary, easily identified practice. Instead, federal officials have exerted their leverage across numerous regulatory programs and through a variety of mechanisms, including licensing, contracting, and enforcement monitoring. State and local officials also engage in forms of arm-twisting, in the context of land use planning and criminal plea bargaining, as have regulatory officials in Japan and elsewhere.

The one feature common to all of these examples is the use of negotiation and indirection by government officials eager to stretch the outer boundaries of their delegated powers. Even when agencies pursue laudable goals, such a practice poses serious concerns about sacrificing fairness and accountability. This Article has suggested a range of potential constraints on administrative arm-twisting to minimize the risks associated with this exercise of largely unchecked discretion, including heightened judicial supervision to ensure that Congress has explicitly authorized (or at least not prohibited) both the means used and the ends pursued by the agency, as well as greater openness by regulatory officials in describing what they regard as permissible subjects for negotiation. In addition, Congress must try to watch for and, where necessary, respond to administrative arm-twisting in order to prevent agencies from inappropriately aggrandizing their power. Although these are partial solutions at best, some effort must be made to push administrative bargaining out of complete darkness and, if not into the sunshine, at least into the shadow of the law.

E. OTHER ACTORS

1. FEDERAL AGENCIES

American Pharmaceutical Association v. Weinberger

377 F.Supp. 824 (D.D.C.1974), aff'd, 530 F.2d 1054 (D.C.Cir.1976).

■ PRATT, DISTRICT JUDGE:

This is an action for judicial review of a regulation of the Food and Drug Administration (FDA) which restricts the distribution of methadone to certain specified outlets as set forth in the regulation. In effect, it prohibits virtually all licensed pharmacies from dispensing this drug when lawfully prescribed by a physician, despite the fact that methadone was invented and was first used as a safe, useful and effective agent in the treatment of severe pain and for antitussive purposes. Decision is not made easier by the fact that in recent years methadone has become a widely known maintenance agent in the treatment of heroin addicts and there is evidence of serious abuses in the distribution of this drug. In their efforts to control improper distribution of methadone, there are strong public policy arguments on the side of defendants. At the same time, the popularity of methadone for use as a pain killer has declined because of the introduction of effective new drugs * * * *

Plaintiffs object to those parts of the regulations which purport to restrict the distribution of methadone to direct shipments from the manufacturer to (a) approved maintenance treatment programs, (b) approved hospital pharmacies, and (c) in cases where hospital pharmacies are unavailable in a particular area, to selected community pharmacies. * * * They argue that the restrictions imposed on the channels of distribution exceed the limits of FDA's authority, were promulgated on the basis of an inadequate record and, being discriminatory in several respects, violate the due process clause of the Fifth Amendment. * * * Since the court concludes that the regulation exceeds the limits of FDA's statutory authority insofar as it purports to restrict the channels of distribution for a drug which is not deemed solely investigational, the court need not address plaintiffs' latter two arguments.

The drug methadone, a synthetic substitute for morphine, is a "new" drug * * * first approved by FDA in the 1950s as safe for use as an analgesic and antitussive agent as well as for short-term detoxification of persons addicted to heroin. Subsequently, investigation of methadone for use in long-term maintenance of narcotic addicts (methadone maintenance) was approved by FDA pursuant to its authority under 21 U.S.C. § 355(i), the investigational new drug (IND) exemption. Section 355(i) of the Act empowers FDA to exempt from NDA approval requirements those new drugs "intended solely for investigational use by experts qualified by scientific training and experience to investigate the safety and effectiveness of drugs." Final guidelines for long-term maintenance programs were promulgated by FDA in 1971. A year later FDA determined that "retention of the drug (methadone) solely on an investigational status appears to be no longer warranted" and published a notice of proposed rulemaking which resulted, with certain modifications, in the regulations now in question.

The final regulation gave notice that pursuant to FDA's authority under 21 U.S.C. § 355(c), the Commissioner was withdrawing approval of all outstanding NDAs because of "a lack of substantial evidence that methadone is safe and effective for detoxification, analgesia, or antitussive use under the conditions of use that presently exist." 37 Fed. Reg. 26,794

(1972). Having withdrawn all approved NDAs, the [FDA]'s new regulatory scheme is presently the exclusive means of distribution for the drug methadone. The Commissioner has thereby created an admittedly unique classification for methadone since on the one hand he has determined that methadone should not be limited solely to investigational status while at the same time concluding that the drug is inappropriate for regular NDA approval. As statutory support for this novel solution to the methadone dilemma, defendants rely on an expansive interpretation of the Commissioner's NDA authority under § 355 of the Act. * * *

Congress apparently intended that the Secretary, or his delegate, FDA, be responsible for the adequacy of premarketing methods and controls inasmuch as the provision delineates the scope of the provision to the manufacturing, processing and packaging stage of a drug's genesis. The defendants point out, however, that § 355(d) also gives the Secretary the authority to refuse to approve an NDA where the reports of the investigations submitted do not include adequate tests showing whether the new drug is "safe for use under the conditions prescribed, recommended, or suggested in the proposed labeling thereof." Defendants argue that the term "safe" should be interpreted with reference not only to the inherent qualities of the drug under consideration but also in the sense of the drug's being secure from possible misuse. Such a broad interpretation would, according to defendants' theory, serve as the statutory foundation for FDA's exercise of authority in restricting methadone's channels of distribution because FDA's principal rationale for restricting distribution was "to help reduce the likelihood of diversion." 37 Fed. Reg. 26,790 (1972). * * *

[T]he context of the statute indicates that the term "safe" was intended to include only the inherent safety of the drug when used in the manner intended. Moreover, as also noted above, the subject of "controls" is specifically covered in provision (3) of the same subsection (d) wherein the term "safe" appears. Provision (3) extends the Secretary's authority to pass on the adequacy of methods, facilities and controls only with respect to manufacturing, processing and packaging. Under the doctrine of "expressio unius est exclusio alterius" any stage of the drug's genesis not specifically mentioned in provision (3) was presumably intended to be excluded from the Secretary's authority. Thus by examining the term "safe" in the context of those provisions of the Act in which it appears as well as in relationship to the provision of the Act which specifically deals with controls, the court concludes that the term "safe" was intended to refer to a determination of the inherent safety or lack thereof of the drug under consideration when used for its intended purpose.[9]

---

9. Even if the court were to agree with defendant's interpretation of the term "safe," this alone would not provide a statutory basis for the regulations challenged herein. At most such an interpretation would authorize FDA to deny or withdraw any methadone NDA based on a finding that the drug could not be "safely" distributed. As outlined in the court's opinion, FDA's discretion under the Act's NDA provisions is limited to either approving or denying NDAs and nowhere is FDA empowered to approve an NDA upon the condition that the drug be distributed only through specified channels.

Finally, the legislative history of the Act fully supports this conclusion. In enacting the Comprehensive Drug Abuse Prevention and Control Act of 1970, Congress was presented with a conscious decision as to how the lines of authority should be drawn with respect to the regulation of dangerous drugs. Congress decided to continue all control authority over the distribution of dangerous drugs in the Justice Department despite a recommendation of the Prettyman Commission that this function be transferred to HEW. The House Committee on Interstate and Foreign Commerce in their report on the Comprehensive Drug Abuse Prevention and Control Act of 1970 indicated that Title II of that Act, known as the Controlled Substances Act, was designed to "provide authority for the Department of Justice to keep track of all drugs subject to abuse manufactured or distributed in the United States in order to prevent diversion of these drugs from legitimate channels of commerce." Although it is nowhere specifically stated that Congress contemplated that the Justice Department would have exclusive authority to prevent diversion, this result would appear logically to follow from a comparison of the functions delegated to the Secretary of HEW with those assigned to the Attorney General.

In addition to being a "new" drug and thus within the jurisdiction of the FDA, methadone is a controlled substance within Schedule II of the Controlled Substances Act. Under this Act the Attorney General is made responsible for the registration of any person who manufactures, distributes or dispenses any controlled substance. An applicant may be refused registration if the Attorney General makes a determination that registering the applicant would be inconsistent with the public interest. Congress has also provided the specific means for revoking or suspending the authority of a registrant to distribute controlled substances. * * * In addition, Congress has specified the precise procedure to be followed by the Attorney General in attempting to revoke or suspend a registration.

The court concludes that Congress intended to create two complementary institutional checks on the production and marketing of new drugs. At the production or pre-marketing stage, the FDA is given the primary responsibility in determining which new drugs should be permitted to enter the flow of commerce. The Commissioner must approve or deny every NDA, or he may determine that a particular new drug qualifies for IND status in order to permit additional experimentation. When an IND exemption is approved, the Commissioner may, of course, severely restrict the distribution of the exempted drug to bona fide researchers and clinicians. But once a drug is cleared for marketing by way of a NDA-approval, for whatever uses the Commissioner deems appropriate, the question of permissible distribution of the drug, when that drug is a controlled substance, is one clearly within the jurisdiction of the Justice Department. The diversion of the particular drug to a use not approved by the Commissioner would be grounds for revocation of the offending distributor's registration. FDA attempts to accomplish peremptorily by way of its challenged regulation, that which could only be accomplished, according to the scheme of the Controlled Substances Act, by way of show-cause proceedings initiated by the Attorney General, i.e., revoking the authority of otherwise duly-registered distributors with respect to the drug methadone. To allow the challenged portions of the methadone regulations to stand, therefore, would be to abrogate the collective judgment of Congress with regard to the appropriate means of controlling unlawful drug diversion.

This is particularly true of the regulations' denial of authority to the plaintiffs at bar. Although the Attorney General generally has discretion to register applicants wishing to distribute or dispense controlled substances, in the case of "practitioners" the Attorney General must register them "if they are authorized to dispense under the law of the State in which they regularly conduct business." 21 U.S.C. § 823(f). Congress has thereby specifically sanctioned the registration of all State-licensed practitioners with the clear intent of permitting them to dispense controlled substances on an equal basis with all other approved distributors. In the face of such clear-cut congressional intent, it would be anomalous to suggest that an agency, by the mere issuance of a regulation, could modify these mandated channels of distribution. Accordingly, the court concludes that FDA has overstepped the bounds of its authority in purporting to limit the distribution of methadone in the manner contemplated by its regulations.

It is undoubtedly true that methadone poses unique problems of medical judgment, law enforcement and public policy but this fact alone cannot justify a federal agency of specifically delimited jurisdiction from implementing equally unique control solutions not authorized by Congress. The problem of unlawful diversion is one presently consigned by Congress to the Drug Enforcement Administration (DEA, formerly the Bureau of Narcotics and Dangerous Drugs) of the Department of Justice. FDA, on the other hand, has the responsibility of making the initial decision, based on all available medical and scientific data, as to whether a particular new drug is safe and effective for its intended use. While the functions of FDA and DEA are not entirely exclusive of one another,[16] a certain division of authority and responsibility was clearly intended by Congress and must be recognized by this court in order to preserve the integrity of the legislative scheme. Under these circumstances, the relative merits of FDA's plan to control the distribution of methadone, a controlled substance, must first be passed upon by Congress. * * *

NOTES AND QUESTIONS

1. *Role of the DEA.* The Controlled Substances Act establishes a "schedule" of narcotics. See 21 U.S.C. § 812. Schedule I includes drugs with a high potential for abuse that have no medically accepted use, such as heroin. Schedule II includes drugs with a high potential for abuse and

---

16. For example, the Attorney General, in exercising his authority under 21 U.S.C. § 811(a) to add or remove drugs from the schedules of controlled substances established by the Controlled Substances Act, must first call upon FDA for its recommendation. The recommendations of FDA, insofar as they concern "scientific and medical matters" relating to the "appropriate schedule, if any, under which such drug or substance should be listed" are binding on the Attorney General.

dependence that have a currently accepted medical use in treatment, such as opium. Schedule III includes drugs with a lower abuse potential that have a currently accepted medical use, such as anabolic steroids. Schedule IV includes drugs with a still lower abuse potential, such as phenobarbital. Schedule V includes drugs with the lowest abuse potential, such as limited concentrations of codeine, which are used in combination with non-narcotic active ingredients that have a separate medical use. In deciding whether a controlled substance has a currently accepted medical use, the DEA must consult with the FDA, and clinical trials of Schedule I drugs require the concurrence of both agencies. See Brian Vastag, Marijuana Study for Veterans with Trauma Faces Hurdle, Wash. Post, Oct. 2, 2011, at A8; see also Marc Kaufman, U.S. Is Working to Make Painkillers Harder to Obtain: Patients May Suffer as DEA Battles Abuse, Wash. Post, Feb. 15, 2004, at A3 (reporting that the DEA may shift hydrocodone from Schedule III to II); Andrew Pollack, A Drug Awaits a Nod from the D.E.A., N.Y. Times, June 22, 2006, at C3 (describing efforts to downclassify an amphetamine intended for use by ADHD patients by demonstrating a lower abuse potential).

In addition to making decisions about the appropriate scheduling for narcotics, the DEA supervises the manufacturing and distribution of legal narcotics. See, e.g., United States v. Global Distribs., Inc., 498 F.3d 613 (7th Cir.2007) (upholding a grant of summary judgment for the government on a complaint seeking civil penalties against a wholesaler for violating buyer identification and recordkeeping requirements in connection with sales of large quantities of cold medications containing pseudoephedrine to businesses that diverted them to produce methamphetamine, but remanding for reconsideration of the size of the fine imposed); see also John A. Gilbert, Jr., DEA Regulation of Controlled Substances and Listed Chemicals, 65 Food & Drug L.J. 623 (2010). The agency requires that manufacturers register their operations, and it assigns aggregate and individual production quotas for Schedule II drugs. See 21 U.S.C. §§ 823(a), 826; see also John Doe, Inc. v. DEA, 484 F.3d 561, 570–73 (D.C.Cir.2007) (upholding the denial of a manufacturer's request for a permit to import (for the purposes of conducting bioequivalency testing to support an application for approval of a generic version of the drug Marinol®) large quantities of dronabinol, the principle psychoactive component in marijuana and a Schedule I substance except when used as an active ingredient in an FDA-approved product). The agency once even tried to use this power to engage in a little arm-twisting. See Lars Noah, Challenges in the Federal Regulation of Pain Management Technologies, 31 J.L. Med. & Ethics 55, 63 (2003) (noting that, in trying to encourage the manufacturer of OxyContin® to restrict distribution to pain management specialists, the DEA Administrator "threatened to slash the company's annual production quota by approximately 95 percent"); see also id. at 55–56, 60–61, 64 (arguing that neither the FDA's clinical mindset nor the DEA's law enforcement mentality offered the broader public health perspective—or intermediate risk-management tools—necessary when trying to balance the needs of legitimate pain patients against the adverse societal consequences of abuse and diversion); Jessica G. Katz, Note, Heroin Maintenance Treatment: Its Effectiveness and the Legislative Changes Necessary to Implement It in the U.S., 26 J. Contemp. Health L. & Pol'y 300 (2010); Marc Kaufman, Drug Enforcement Agency Stripped of Role on New Painkillers, Wash. Post, Nov. 5, 2005, at A13; Anna W. Mathews & Gary Fields, Federal Agencies Seek to Curb Abuse of Potent Painkillers, Wall St. J., Dec. 3, 2003, at B1 (reporting that the FDA urges sponsors of new opioid analgesics to develop "abuse-management programs" but has rejected calls for distribution restrictions).

Finally, the DEA actively supervises the distribution of controlled substances by physicians and pharmacists. See Chein v. DEA, 533 F.3d 828 (D.C.Cir.2008) (upholding the revocation of a physician's DEA registration for numerous violations in connection with the dispensing of Schedule III–V substances, including the use of testosterone and phentermine (along with human growth hormone) in patients to enhance athletic performance or as anti-aging treatments); United States v. Bek, 493 F.3d 790, 798–99 (7th Cir.2007); Wedgewood Vill. Pharmacy v. DEA, 509 F.3d 541 (D.C.Cir. 2007) (vacating the revocation of a compounding pharmacy's registration); United States v. Hurwitz, 459 F.3d 463 (4th Cir.2006) (reversing the conviction of a physician who had prescribed very high doses of opioid analgesics); United States v. Nelson, 383 F.3d 1227 (10th Cir.2004) (upholding the conviction of a physician who issued thousands of prescriptions for hydrocodone over the Internet); Annotation, Federal Criminal Liability of Licensed Physician for Unlawfully Prescribing or Dispensing "Controlled Substance" or Drug in Violation of the Controlled Substances Act, 33 A.L.R. Fed. 220 (1977 & 2011 Supp.); see also United States v. Smith, 573 F.3d 639, 646–58 (8th Cir.2009) (online prescribing business); Barry Meier & Abby Goodnough, U.S. Seeks to Rein in Painkillers, N.Y. Times, Apr. 20, 2011, at B1 (reporting that the administration would seek amendments to the CSA to condition prescribing privileges for narcotic analgesics on physician training and that, in the meantime, the FDA issued a rule requiring that manufacturers offer voluntary training programs); cf. Natasha Singer, Agency Acts to Ease Delay of Pills for Elderly, N.Y. Times, Oct. 7, 2010, at A20 (reporting that the DEA had relaxed restrictions affecting use in nursing homes). See generally Christina Hardjasa, Note, Liberty or Death: Federalism, the DEA, and the War on Suffering, 6 Geo. J.L. & Pub. Pol'y 669 (2008); Dannielle M. Nunziato, Note, Preventing Prescription Drug Overdose in the Twenty-first Century: Is the Controlled Substances Act Enough?, 38 Hofstra L. Rev. 1261 (2010); Ashley B. Trehan, Note, Fear of Prescribing: How the DEA Is Infringing on Patients' Right to Palliative Care, 61 U. Miami. L. Rev. 961 (2007); Christian Davenport, Doctors Who Prescribe Oft–Abused Drugs Face Scrutiny, Wash. Post, Jan. 2, 2011, at A1; Marc Kaufman, DEA Revises Rule on Prescribing Painkillers, Wash. Post, Sept. 7, 2006, at A4.

2. *Other federal agencies.* Under the Clinical Laboratory Improvement Amendments of 1988 (CLIA), HHS exercises responsibility for overseeing clinical laboratories that provide diagnostic services. See 42 U.S.C. § 263a; see also 64 Fed. Reg. 73,561 (1999) (transferring certain functions to the FDA). Other component agencies within HHS that perform primarily research rather than regulatory functions—namely, the National Institutes of Health (NIH) and the Centers for Disease Control and Prevention (CDC)—often work in tandem with the FDA. The Consumer Product Safety Commission (CPSC) implements certain statutes that may apply to medical technologies. See Nutritional Health Alliance v. FDA, 318 F.3d 92, 102–04 (2d Cir.2003) (invalidating the FDA's iron supplement packaging rule, and adding that, even if some ambiguity existed about the reach of the adulteration provisions, the agency's interpretation was unreasonable because Congress had delegated such issues to the CPSC); see also Reynolds Holding, Federal Syringe Rule Takes Effect, Aiding Health Workers, S.F. Chron., Apr. 18, 2001, at A10 (reporting that OSHA mandated safety devices for "sharps" in order to prevent accidental needle sticks); cf. Chaps. 2(C) (DOD), 9(A) (CMS), 10(A) (PTO). Finally, Chapter 4(B) mentions the division of regulatory authority over the advertising of drugs and devices between the FDA and the Federal Trade Commission (FTC).

3. *Antibiotic resistance*. The overuse and misuse of antibiotics have created drug-resistant strains of many bacteria. These may contribute to 70,000 deaths each year in the United States. See Justin Gillis & Ceci Connolly, Emphasis on Cipro Worries Officials, Wash. Post, Oct. 19, 2001, at A17; see also Richard S. Saver, In Tepid Defense of Population Health: Physicians and Antibiotic Resistance, 34 Am. J.L. & Med. 431 (2008); David Brown, Drug–Resistant Cases of TB in U.S. Increase, Wash. Post, Mar. 24, 2006, at A10; Rob Stein, Drug–Resistant Staph Germ's Toll Is Higher Than Thought, Wash. Post, Oct. 17, 2007, at A1 (noting outbreaks of community-acquired methicillin-resistant staph aureus (MRSA)). Technological innovation in the field has begun to lag behind the pressing need for new weapons against resistant strains. See Maryn McKenna, The Enemy Within, Sci. Am., Apr. 2011, at 47, 53 ("Between 1998 and 2008 the FDA approved 13 new antibiotics. Only three had new mechanisms of action, something to which bacteria do not already possess resistance."); Roxanne Nelson, Few New Drugs: Dearth of New Antibiotics Threatens Public Health, Wash. Post, Mar. 30, 2004, at F1; Sabin Russell, Falling Behind: Medical Research Funding Drops as Deadly Mutations Are Increasingly Able to Beat Antibiotics, S.F. Chron., Jan. 20, 2008, at A1. In order to maximize the useful life of a new antibiotic, could the FDA approve it only for use by infectious disease specialists in hospitals (trusting them to save the drug for resistant pathogens), or might the agency persuade the DEA to place the drug in Schedule II? See Scott B. Markow, Note, Penetrating the Walls of Drug–Resistant Bacteria: A Statutory Prescription to Combat Antibiotic Misuse, 87 Geo. L.J. 531, 542–43 (1998) (doubting the legality of either one of these approaches); cf. Aaron S. Kesselheim & Kevin Outterson, Improving Antibiotic Markets for Long Term Sustainability, 11 Yale J. Health Pol'y L. & Ethics 101 (2011); William M. Sage & David A. Hyman, Combating Antimicrobial Resistance: Regulatory Strategies and Institutional Capacity, 84 Tul. L. Rev. 781 (2010); Laura Landro, The Informed Patient: Curbing Antibiotic Use in War on "Superbugs," Wall St. J., Sept. 3, 2008, at D1 (reporting that hospitals have begun to adopt, sometimes under pressure from public and private insurers, "antimicrobial stewardship programs," which involve teams of specialists monitoring antibiotic use to reduce the spread of resistant bacterial strains by, for example, urging physicians to resist the tendency to prescribe powerful antibiotics in favor of selecting the narrowest-spectrum drug available for treatment of a particular patient's infection).

4. *Distribution controls.* As explained in Chapter 4(A)(1), the FDA does have clear authority to specify prescription status, though it does so primarily through labeling (and allows state authorities to decide which health care providers enjoy prescribing and dispensing privileges). Such mechanisms may not go far enough.

> [T]o the extent that states have begun to liberalize their prescribing laws, the FDA might lose its longstanding confidence in the expert role played by licensed health care professionals in selecting appropriate therapeutic interventions . . . , and it has begun to consider intermediate risk management strategies in order to minimize the likelihood of patient injury. These efforts might include restricting distribution to certain specialists, patient informed consent requirements, structured postmarket surveillance, and mandatory concomitant therapy or monitoring. In addition, the agency might seek to prohibit certain off-label uses, perhaps in those situations where the labeling specifically contraindicates a use.
>
> Serious questions exist about the FDA's power to impose such restrictions under its current statutory authority, but the agency generally has managed to encourage drug manufacturers to accept such limitations as a condition of approval. In some cases, physicians must register with the manufacturer—attesting that they understand the risks and benefits of a particular drug—before they may prescribe it. For instance, when it approved Thalomid® (thalidomide) for the treatment of leprosy patients, the FDA conditioned approval on extremely strict marketing controls because of the serious risk of birth defects: distribution only through specially registered physicians and pharmacists, and tracking of patients who must agree to use two forms of contraception and undergo frequent pregnancy tests. The agency imposed comparable distribution restrictions in the course of approving Lotronex® (alosetron), Accutane® (isotretinoin), and Mifeprex® (mifepristone). Unless our current understandings of federalism would prevent such types of FDA interference with the practice of medicine, Congress could amend the statute in order to grant the agency explicit authority to impose such restrictions.
>
> One particularly controversial risk management strategy would allow only a limited group of medical specialists to prescribe certain especially hazardous drugs. After all, with the ever-expanding number and complexity of pharmaceutical treatments, general practitioners find it difficult to stay informed of appropriate interventions for different conditions, and they may find it even more difficult to resist the demands made by patients who have seen a product advertised for what ails them. The result may be indiscriminate prescribing of power-

ful therapeutic agents. Moreover, if states increasingly allow non-physicians to prescribe drugs, the FDA may have to rethink its broad deference to state licensing judgments and respond by imposing such special restrictions more frequently or even creating different classes of prescription drugs.

Lars Noah, Ambivalent Commitments to Federalism in Controlling the Practice of Medicine, 53 U. Kan. L. Rev. 149, 188–91 (2004); see also John Carreyrou, Narcotic "Lollipop" Becomes Big Seller Despite FDA Curbs, Wall St. J., Nov. 3, 2006, at A1 (reporting allegations that the manufacturer of Actiq® (fentanyl) has failed to abide by the terms of a risk-management program demanded by the agency to guard against off-label (non-cancer) use); Erik Eckholm & Olga Pierce, Methadone Rises as a Painkiller with Big Risks, N.Y. Times, Aug. 17, 2008, at A1 ("Methadone, once used mainly in addiction treatment centers to replace heroin, is today being given out by family doctors, osteopaths and nurse practitioners for throbbing backs ... and a host of other severe pains .... [The FDA] is now considering requiring doctors to take special classes on prescribing narcotics."); Gardiner Harris, F.D.A. Imposes Tougher Rules for Acne Drug, N.Y. Times, Aug. 13, 2005, at A1 ("The new program is the latest and by far most drastic of more than 40 efforts by the agency in the last 22 years to reduce harm from Accutane ... while allowing its continued use."); Marc Kaufman, Death After Abortion Pill Reignites Safety Debate, Wash. Post, Nov. 3, 2003, at A3 (reporting that the FDA has not enforced the restrictions that it had imposed on the distribution of mifepristone); Anna W. Mathews & Leila Abboud, FDA Approves Generic OxyContin, Wall St. J., Mar. 24, 2004, at A3 ("[T]he FDA has never limited any opioid to certain pharmacies, and agency officials say they don't have the authority to block certain physicians from prescribing a drug."); Aaron Zitner, Date–Rape Drug OK'd to Treat Sleep Disorder, L.A. Times, July 18, 2002, at A12 (reporting that the FDA approved GHB subject to stringent restrictions on patient access); cf. Ryan Cronin, Note, Bureaucrats vs. Physicians: Have Doctors Been Stripped of Their Power to Determine the Proper Use of Human Growth Hormone in Treating Adult Disease?, 27 Wash. U. J.L. & Pol'y 191 (2008).

As the FDA increasingly tried to encourage sponsors to adopt distribution controls, Congress in 2007 authorized the agency to impose "risk evaluation and mitigation strategy" (REMS) requirements. See FDAAA, Pub. L. No. 110–85, § 901(b), 121 Stat. 823, 930 (codified at 21 U.S.C. § 355–1(f)(3)(A)); Jennifer L. Bragg & Maya P. Florence, Life with a REMS: Challenges and Opportunities, 13 J. Health Care L. & Pol'y 269 (2010). Apart from questions of the scope of this statutory authority (or the lack of any such authority for previously creating similar controls), does the FDA cross a constitutional line when it purports to require that patients undergo periodic pregnancy testing and use contraceptives as a condition of access to a drug known to cause birth defects? See Lars Noah, Too High a Price for Some Drugs?: The FDA Burdens Reproductive Choice, 44 San Diego L. Rev. 231, 243–57 (2007); id. at 258 ("If anyone ever challenged this risk management strategy, a court would have to decide whether the policy grew out of state action, involved the exercise of a fundamental right, inappropriately conditioned access to a benefit on the waiver of one of these rights, and failed to serve a compelling governmental interest.''); see also Symposium, Conflicting Interests in Reproductive Autonomy and Their Impact on New Technologies, 76 Geo. Wash. L. Rev. 1457 (2008). If such conditions fail to reduce the number of birth defects, see Anti–Pregnancy Effort Fails, Wash. Post, July 31, 2007, at A10 (Accutane), could the agency go one step further and, at least in the case of teratogens indicated for chronic use, urge sellers to require that patients first undergo a sterilization procedure if they wish to use the drug?!

5. *Devices*. The FDA can designate medical devices as ''restricted'' in order to limit their distribution. See 21 U.S.C. § 360j(e). A few manufacturers of implanted devices offer training programs and will ''accredit'' surgeons to use the product only after they successfully have completed a certain number of procedures under the supervision of company personnel. See, e.g., Rita Rubin, Implantable Contraceptive Approved, USA Today, July 19, 2006, at 1D.

2. STATE REGULATORS

Rayford v. State

16 S.W.3d 203 (Tex.Ct.App.2000).

■ ROSENBEG, JUSTICE:

* * * Erma Rayford, individually, and Baby Images, Inc. (collectively, Rayford) appeal an injunction granted to the State of Texas under the Texas Food, Drug and Cosmetic Act (FDCA) and the Texas Deceptive Trade Practices Act (DTPA) preventing her from possessing and using a medical device, a fetal ultrasound scanner, for nondiagnostic use. * * *

In 1989, Rayford, a qualified ultrasound sonographer, purchased an RT–50 fetal ultrasound scanner from General Electric (GE) and went into business as Baby Images, Inc. She provided ultrasound scanning of unborn babies and videotapes of the scan and advertised the videos as keepsakes through brochures she mailed and distributed by hand. She performed ultrasound scanning for nondiagnostic purposes and did not require that consumers have a prescription from a licensed physician.

The Texas Department of Health inspected Rayford's facilities several times between 1994 and 1997. On each occasion, the inspector issued a Notice of Detention. The inspector found that Rayford's possession and use of the RT–50 adulterated and misbranded it. In 1996, the State brought an action seeking an injunction and penalties under the FDCA and DTPA. * * *

Rayford challenges the entry of partial summary judgment for the violation of section 431.021(b) of the FDCA, which prohibits the adulteration or misbranding of any medical device in commerce. Rayford asserts her use of the RT–50 ultrasound device for a nonmedical purpose does not make the device adulterated or misbranded in commerce. The State responds that the federal and state legislative schemes apply to the ultimate user of a device, not just the manufacturer, distributor, or seller of the device. The State argues Rayford's use of the ultrasound scanner for fetal imaging without a diagnostic purpose was a "new intended use," which gives the device a status as a class III device under the Federal Food Drug and Cosmetic Act (FFDCA), thereby making its use adulteration under the Texas Act. The State further argues the RT–50 was not properly labeled and Rayford's use without a prescription was misbranding in commerce. * * *

Because ultrasound devices are class II devices, for Rayford's RT–50 to be a class III device, it must not be substantially equivalent to the ultrasound devices already approved. First, GE submitted a premarket notification for the RT–50 as a device substantially equivalent to one previously marketed, as required for a class II device. The notification described the technical aspects of the device as well as its intended use, stating, "The RT–50 is intended to be used for abdominal, obstetric and gynecological ultrasound examinations in hospitals and clinics where ultrasound exams are routinely performed." The notification also indicated the RT–50's intended diagnostic use was fetal imaging. The FDA found the RT–50 to be substantially equivalent to other approved ultrasound devices. In the hands of GE, the RT–50 remained class II.

Next, because Rayford used the RT–50 for nondiagnostic uses, we examine whether Rayford's use destroyed the RT–50's substantial equivalence to the ultrasound devices by changing the intended use. Rayford used the RT–50 for fetal imaging, but not for approved medical or diagnostic purpose. Rayford's unapproved nondiagnostic use is not the intended use of the RT–50 as established by GE. This nondiagnostic use is a new use. Whether this nondiagnostic use is a new intended use is determined by the person responsible for labeling the RT–50. The person who is responsible for labeling is the person who engages in the manufacture, preparation, propagation, or processing of the device, including actions in furtherance of the distribution of the device from the original manufacturer to the person who makes final delivery or sale to the ultimate user. Rayford bought the RT–50. She is a user and possessor, not a manufacturer or distributor, of the RT–50. Further, she did not sell the RT–50, that is, she did not sell or distribute the RT–50 to the ultimate user. While Rayford was selling a service in using the machine, the federal statutory scheme does not include a seller of a device's service as a person responsible for labeling. Therefore, Rayford does not have labeling responsibility, and Rayford's nondiagnostic use of the RT–50 did not "substantially alter" it and is not a "new intended use." Accordingly, Rayford's RT–50 continued its class II designation.

Finally, the summary judgment affidavits of Byron Tart, Director of Promotion and Advertising Policy and Staff for the Compliance Office of the FDA, show the FDA was aware of nonmedical use of the ultrasound device. Nevertheless, the FDA did not codify the nonmedical use to class III as is provided for in the regulations. Because Rayford is not the person with labeling responsibility and the FDA did not classify the known use as class III, the RT–50 remains class II. Because we have concluded the device is not a class III device, the State did not prove Rayford had an adulterated device in commerce under the FDCA. * * *

[A] device is misbranded if it is a restricted device that is used in violation of section 360j(e) of the FFDCA. See Tex. Health & Safety Code Ann. § 431.112(r). The FFDCA provides that a restricted device is only to be used on written or oral authorization of a physician. A restricted or prescription device is a device that cannot have adequate directions for lay use. See 21 C.F.R. § 801.109 (1999). These devices are exempt from the requirement of directions because they are required to be in the possession of physicians or used only on order of physicians. See id. § 801.110.

The summary judgment evidence demonstrates the RT–50 is exempt from labeling for adequate directions for lay use. That exemption makes the RT–50 a prescription device. It is undisputed that Rayford used the device without the supervision or order of a licensed practitioner. Therefore, Rayford's use was a violation of section 431.112(r), making the RT–50 misbranded in commerce as a matter of law, and the trial court was correct in granting the summary judgment on this misbranding ground. * * *

Virtually all states have their own versions of the FDCA, including similarly broad prohibitions against the adulteration and misbranding of drugs and medical devices. See Uniform State Food, Drug, and Cosmetic Bill, Food Drug Cosm. L. Rep. (CCH) ¶ 10,100. California goes further and operates an approval system. See Cal. Health & Safety Code § 111550(b); see also Summit Tech. v. High–Line Med. Instruments, 922 F.Supp. 299, 317 (C.D.Cal.1996) (explaining that the "California FDCA is 'analogous' to the federal FDCA," and that both "statutes are comprehensive public health schemes administered by expert agencies"); James M. Gomez, Maker of HIV Test Kit Sues for State's O.K., L.A. Times, Sept. 28, 1993, at D2 (describing a dispute over an application filed with state regulators); cf. Rebecca Voelker, The Business of Baby Pictures, 293 JAMA 25, 26 (2005) (reporting that California now requires that pregnant women who undergo ultrasonography for the purpose of getting a "keepsake" fetal image sign a form explaining that the FDA opposes this procedure); A. Alexander, "Just Scanning Around" with Diagnostic Medical Ultrasound: Should States Regulate the Non–Diagnostic Uses of This Technology?, 16 Annals Health L. 1 (2007); Sam Lubell, The Womb as Photo Studio, N.Y. Times, Sept. 23, 2004, at E1. Recently, several states have become more aggressive in trying to regulate pharmaceutical marketing practices, see Chap. 4(B)(1), and drug pricing, see Chap. 9(C)(2), but, apart from an odd assortment of rules governing specific products (reflecting either peculiar local conditions or the special concerns of state lawmakers), other regulatory requirements are quite limited. When states or localities decide to regulate, questions arise about possible conflicts with federal requirements.

Dowhal v. SmithKline Beecham Consumer Healthcare

88 P.3d 1 (Cal.2004).

■ KENNARD, JUSTICE:

* * * On November 4, 1986, the voters of this state enacted Proposition 65 as an initiative measure. Proposition 65 added section 25249.6 to the Health and Safety Code: "No person in the course of doing business shall knowingly and intentionally expose any individual to a chemical known to the state to cause ... reproductive toxicity without first giving clear and reasonable warning to such individual ...." This provision does not apply, however, to "[a]n exposure for which federal law governs warning in a manner that preempts state authority."

The regulations adopted to implement Health and Safety Code section 25249.6 state that the required warning "must clearly communicate that the chemical in question is known to the state to cause ... birth defects or other reproductive harm." Cal. Code Regs., tit. 22, § 12601(a). The regulations also describe optional "safe harbor" warnings that are deemed to be clear and reasonable. One of the "safe harbor" warnings reads: "WARNING: This product contains a chemical known to the State of California to cause birth defects or other reproductive harm." The warning may be communicated through product labeling, point-of-sale signs, or public advertising. On April 1, 1990, the State of California listed nicotine as a chemical known to cause reproductive toxicity. * * *

The issue here is whether California's Proposition 65 requirements are preempted by the FDA regulation, or preserved by the savings clause, section 379r(d)(2), of the Food and Drug Administration Modernization Act of 1997. Section 379r(a) establishes the preemptive effective of federal regulation; it states in part: "[N]o State or political subdivision of a State may establish or continue in effect any requirement ... (2) that is different from or in addition to, or that is otherwise not identical with, a requirement under this chapter ...." The Modernization Act, however, contained a savings clause designed specifically to preserve Proposition 65. It provides: "This section shall not apply to a State requirement adopted by a State public initiative or referendum enacted prior to September 1, 1997." Proposition 65 is the only state enactment that falls within the savings clause.

Defendants here manufacture, market, and distribute products, such as gum and patches, that are designed to help people quit smoking through nicotine replacement therapy (NRT). Originally, the products were available only by prescription. In 1993, defendants sought FDA approval to sell them over the counter. Defendants' application presented a complex labeling issue because the products contain nicotine, a substance that if taken by a pregnant woman could cause harm to the fetus. On the other hand, the purpose of the products is to help individuals stop smoking, and smoking is even more dangerous to the fetus, because it may deliver more nicotine than the NRT products, and also exposes the smoker to carbon monoxide and other harmful chemicals. * * *

Partly in an effort to balance these competing concerns, the products underwent an unusually long approval process. As of 1996, the labels for the original Nicorette, Nicoderm, and Nicotrol prescription products carried a required warning: "Nicotine in any form may cause harm to your unborn baby." * * * But when the FDA approved over-the-counter sales in 1996, the FDA advised defendants that their products could carry the following pregnancy warning: "Nicotine can increase your baby's heart rate; . . . if you are pregnant or nursing a baby, seek the advice of a health professional before using this product." Failure to label the products "exactly as requested," the FDA warned producers, "may render the product mislabeled."

In January 1997, defendant McNeil asked the FDA for permission to change the label for its product Nicotrol to add the Proposition 65 "safe harbor" warning: "This product contains nicotine, a chemical known to the State of California to cause birth defects or other reproductive harm." The FDA denied the request, telling McNeil it "[m]ust use the labeling that was approved at the time of . . . approval." The California Attorney General, however, determined in a letter issued July 10, 1998, that the "increased heart rate" warning did not comply with Proposition 65, because it failed to warn that nicotine can "harm" the fetus, and suggested that nicotine only posed a narrow risk of an increased fetal heart rate "when the true risks appear to be significantly broader and more serious."

In August 1999, after the enactment of the Modernization Act, plaintiff Paul Dowhal, acting on behalf of the public, filed the complaint here. Plaintiff alleged defendants violated Health and Safety Code section 25249.6 because they placed products containing nicotine into the "stream of commerce" without the pregnancy warning required by Proposition 65. Plaintiff also alleged that by failing to provide an adequate warning, defendants committed an unfair business practice in violation of Business and Professions Code section 17200 et seq. He asked for an injunction barring defendants from offering their products for sale in California without providing an adequate Proposition 65 warning.

In November 1999, while this case was pending, the FDA granted permission to Novartis Consumer Health Care, Inc. to sell an NRT product called Habitrol. (Novartis is not a party to this case.) Although Habitrol is identical to some of defendants' products in nicotine content, indication for use, and method of administration, the FDA approved Novartis's warning to consumers: "Nicotine, whether from smoking or medication, can harm your baby." When defendant SmithKline learned about the Habitrol pregnancy warning, it asked the FDA whether it should change its warning. The FDA responded that it was "reviewing its position as it relates to the warnings of nicotine products concerning pregnancy and breast feeding." In May 2000, defendants SmithKline and McNeil each wrote to the FDA, again pointing out that Habitrol carried a different pregnancy warning than their products and that they faced litigation over the adequacy of their warning.

In June 2000, the FDA responded to SmithKline that while the FDA was reviewing its position on the pregnancy warning, SmithKline should continue to "use the current warning." On July 11, 2000, counsel for SmithKline wrote to the FDA seeking confirmation about the pregnancy warning that was required. The FDA responded by letter 10 days later, stating that the products "must" carry the pregnancy warning that had been specified when they were approved. In March 2001, the FDA sent a letter to SmithKline stating that even though Habitrol carried a different warning, the instructions concerning defendants' products remained unchanged: "The agency is currently reviewing its position regarding the pregnancy/nursing warning on OTC nicotine replacement products.... As we have stated previously, until the agency's review is complete, all sponsors of nicotine replacement products should continue to use the pregnancy/nursing warning that was approved by the agency as part of their NDA. Any additional or modified warning may render the product misbranded." * * *

While this appeal was pending, the FDA responded to a citizen's petition that plaintiff had filed with the agency on August 2, 2000. In a letter to plaintiff mailed August 17, 2001 the FDA reviewed the medical literature, and said it would "grant [plaintiff's] request for a consistent pregnancy warning for all OTC NRT drug products that clearly and reasonably communicates all of the known harm and conveys the relative reproductive harm of smoking, use of NRT drug products, and total abstinence from nicotine." The FDA denied plaintiff's request to require a warning on all NRT drug products similar to the "can harm your baby" warning on Habitrol. That warning, the FDA asserted, "overstates what is actually known about nicotine and its effect on the unborn child." It also rejected a proposal to use a label similar to that required for prescription drugs on the ground that the warning to doctors was "not easily translated into consumer friendly language." The FDA agreed that the "can increase your baby's heart rate" warning was insufficient, because it might lead consumers to believe that this was the only possible effect of nicotine. It proposed, instead, that all nicotine replacement products, including the products at issue and Habitrol, bear the uniform pregnancy warning quoted earlier in this opinion.[†] * * *

The United States Supreme Court has explained that federal preemption arises in three circumstances: "First, Congress can define explicitly the extent to which its enactments preempt state law. Preemption fundamentally is a question of congressional intent, and when Congress has made its intent known through explicit statutory language, the courts' task is an easy one. Second, in the absence of explicit statutory language, state law is preempted where it regulates conduct in a field that Congress intended the Federal Government to occupy exclusively. Such an intent may be inferred

---

† "If you are pregnant or breast-feeding, only use this medicine on the advice of your health care provider. Smoking can seriously harm your child. Try to stop smoking without using any nicotine replacement medicine. This medicine is believed to be safer than smoking. However, the risks to your child from this medicine are not fully known."

from a 'scheme of federal regulation ... so pervasive as to make reasonable the inference that Congress left no room for the States to supplement it,' or where an Act of Congress 'touch[es] a field in which the federal interest is so dominant that the federal system will be assumed to preclude enforcement of state laws on the same subject.' * * * Finally, state law is preempted to the extent that it actually conflicts with federal law. Thus, the Court has found preemption where it is impossible for a private party to comply with both state and federal requirements, or where state law 'stands as an obstacle to the accomplishment and execution of the full purposes and objectives of Congress.' "

The first and second forms of preemption are inapplicable here. The savings clause in the Modernization Act demonstrates both that Congress did not expressly preempt California law, and that it did not occupy the field of labeling of over-the-counter drugs. Thus the issue here concerns the third form of preemption, referred to as "conflict preemption." * * * The United States Supreme Court has never interpreted a savings clause so broadly as to permit a state enactment to conflict with a federal regulation scheme. The language of the Modernization Act's savings clause does not express an intention to preclude all conflict preemption. The legislative history suggests an intent to preclude conflict preemption in pursuit of national uniform labeling. * * * If the FDA's directive here prohibiting nonidentical labels is to be sustained, it must be on a basis relevant to consumer health, and not because the Proposition 65 label would frustrate the FDA's policy favoring national uniformity. * * *

Plaintiff argues that the FDA's August 17 letter did not establish a required federal warning, but merely "requested" defendants to submit supplements. But the term "requested" appears to be simply a matter of courtesy; it is apparent from the tenor of the letter that it imposes a duty on defendants. A company cannot use warnings the FDA considers misleading simply because it chooses not to comply with an FDA request to submit the forms required to change its warnings to the one adopted by the FDA. Plaintiff and his amici curiae point to language in the FDA's August 17 letter stating that "[a]ny other warnings proposed by the sponsor must be supported by data" as showing that defendants are not required to use warnings identical to the FDA warning. But this is standard language that appears, or is implied, in all FDA labeling decisions. A company is always free to change its label, after notifying the FDA, if it has new data showing the former warning was inappropriate. The possibility that new data may justify a change in the warning does not invalidate the approval of the existing warning; that warning continues to be binding until the new data emerge and a change is requested.

Plaintiff and his amici curiae point out that the FDA's August 17 letter has not been published in the *Federal Register*. There is no requirement, however, that it be so published to be effective. Congress was undoubtedly aware that one common means of FDA regulation is to publish rulings through letters to the parties requesting the rulings. * * * Finally, plaintiff and his amici curiae point out that Proposition 65 warnings need not appear on labels; warnings can also be conveyed through point-of-sale notices or public advertising. Because the FDA regulates only product labeling, they contend that a Proposition 65 warning conveyed through other means cannot be preempted.

The FDA's ruling, however, reflects the concern that Proposition 65 warnings on product labels might lead pregnant women to believe that NRT products were as dangerous as smoking, or nearly so, and thus discourage the women from stopping smoking. Warnings through point-of-sale posters or public advertising could have the same effect of frustrating the purpose of the federal policy. Conflict preemption does not require a direct contradiction between state and federal law; the state law is preempted if state law " 'stands as an obstacle to the accomplishment and execution of the full purposes and objectives of Congress.' " We conclude that the FDA's August 17, 2001, letter established a federal policy prohibiting defendants from giving consumers any warning other than the one approved by the FDA in that letter, and that the use of a Proposition 65 warning would conflict with that policy.

Plaintiff contends that his proposed warning advising pregnant women that defendants' products contain nicotine which "can harm your baby"—or words to that effect—is truthful. He argues that the enforcement authority of the FDA is limited to prohibiting "adulterated or misbranded" products, and that a truthful warning cannot render a product "misbranded." He points out that not only California, but also the United States Surgeon General and the Environmental Protection Agency (EPA) list nicotine as a chemical harmful to the fetus. Defendants dispute the point, arguing that the evidence is insufficient to show that nicotine can harm the fetus.

The FDA's August 17, 2001, letter sets out its views on the effect of nicotine on the fetus. Because of the FDA's scientific expertise and long administrative experience, these views are entitled to judicial deference. But a close reading of that letter shows that the FDA is aware that nicotine may endanger the fetus. * * * The FDA's objection to labels warning that nicotine "can" harm the baby is not that they are false, but that consumers may give too much weight to the warnings and decide to continue smoking instead of using an NRT product to stop smoking. But even though it is probably true that the nicotine in defendants' products can cause reproductive harm, the FDA has authority to prohibit truthful statements on a product label if they are "misleading," or if they are not stated in "such manner and form, as are necessary for the protection of users." * * * A truthful warning can be misleading or fail to communicate the facts necessary for the protection of users. * * *

[W]e do not know of any statute or constitutional provision that precludes the FDA from taking this ["paternalistic"] approach to regulation of nonprescription drugs. * * * Whether a label is potentially misleading or incomprehensible is essentially a judgment of how the consumer will respond to the language of the label. As we have noted, a truthful warning of an uncertain or remote danger may mislead the consumer into misjudging the dangers stemming from use of the product, and consequently making a medically unwise decision. The authority of the FDA, we conclude, extends to barring warnings that are misleading in this fashion. Although there is reason to believe that nicotine can cause reproductive harm, plaintiff has offered no qualitative assessment of this risk. The mere existence of the risk, however, is not necessarily enough to justify a warning; the risk of harm may be so remote that it is outweighed by the greater risk that a warning will scare consumers into foregoing use of a product that in most cases will be to their benefit. The FDA has so determined in this case, and we find no basis to question the FDA's expert determination. * * *

[I]n most cases FDA warnings and Proposition 65 warnings would serve the same purpose—informing the consumer of the risks involved in use of the product—and differences in wording would not call for federal preemption. Here, however, the FDA warning serves a nuanced goal—to inform pregnant women of the risks of NRT products, but in a way that will not lead some women, overly concerned about those risks, to continue smoking. This creates a conflict with the state's more single-minded goal of informing the consumer of the risks. That policy conflict justifies federal preemption here.

Committee of Dental Amalgam Mfrs. v. Stratton

92 F.3d 807 (9th Cir.1996).

■ PREGERSON, CIRCUIT JUDGE:

The defendants, Dr. James Stratton, Acting Director of the California Office of Health Hazard Assessment, and Dan Lungren, the Attorney General of the State of California (collectively the "State"), and the intervening party, Environmental Law Foundation (ELF), appeal the district court's grant of summary judgment in favor of the plaintiffs, Committee of Dental Amalgam Alloy Manufacturers and Distributors and Dentsply International, Inc. (collectively the "manufacturers"). The district court held that, as applied to dental amalgam, the Medical Device Amendments [of 1976] to the federal Food, Drug and Cosmetics Act (MDA) preempt California's Safe Drinking Water and Toxic Enforcement Act of 1986 ("Proposition 65"). * * *

[A]s a threshold matter, we must decide whether the district court was correct in holding that the MDA applied to dental amalgam. Congress defined the term "medical device" very broadly * * * * [W]e hold that dental amalgam does fall within the reach of the MDA. Dental amalgam is used in the treatment and prevention of tooth decay. Further, the FDA has already classified the component parts of dental amalgam [as medical devices]. * * *

Congress included an explicit preemption provision in the MDA. * * * In *Medtronic v. Lohr*, 518 U.S. 470 (1996), the Supreme Court rejected a broad construction of this preemption provision. * * * [I]n determining what kind of federal "requirement" and what kind of state "requirement" trigger preemption, the Supreme Court in *Medtronic* deferred to the FDA's regulation that narrowly construes the MDA's preemption clause. Section 808.1(d) provides, in relevant part:

> State or local requirements are preempted only when the Food and Drug Administration has established specific counterpart regulations or there are other specific requirements applicable to a particular device under the act, thereby making any existing divergent State or local requirements applicable to the device different from or in addition, the specific Food and Drug Administration requirement.

Based on this FDA regulation, a state or local "requirement" is preempted by the MDA only if specific counterpart requirements or regulations that are applicable to a particular device exist. * * * In addition, the Supreme Court in *Medtronic* specifically approved that part of the FDA regulation that provides that "[s]ection 521(a) does not preempt State and local requirements of general applicability where the purpose of the requirement relates either to other products in addition to devices . . . or to unfair trade practices in which the requirements are not limited to devices." * * *

The district court held that, even though the FDA has not established "specific" regulations relating to dental amalgam, the MDA still preempts Proposition 65. First, the district court held that 21 C.F.R. § 801.109, the FDA regulation describing the manufacturing and labeling requirements, is "specific" enough to trigger preemption. Second, the district court held that the FDA's alleged refusal to impose reproductive toxicity requirements on dental mercury is by itself preemptive.

The district court was wrong on both counts. In *Medtronic*, the Supreme Court held that the FDA's manufacturing and labeling requirements were not "specific" enough to preempt state law. * * * Further, Proposition 65 is a state law of general applicability which was not enacted "with respect to" medical devices. Proposition 65 applies to all products and services that pose a health risk to the public. Except for identifying chemicals known to pose a health risk, Proposition 65 is not directed at any product or industry. Nor has the State of California adopted any specific regulation or requirement that relates to dental amalgam. The State of California has listed mercury as a product which causes reproductive harm. As a result, consumer warnings for dental amalgam are now required.

Thus, we hold that the consumer warning requirement under California's Proposition 65 is not "specific" enough to trigger preemption because it is "not the kind[] of requirement[] that Congress and the FDA feared would impede the ability of federal regulators to implement and enforce specific federal requirements." * * *

We also reject the district court's holding that the FDA's failure to impose a warning requirement on dental amalgam is by itself preemptive. Inherent in the term "requirement" is the idea that there be a positive enactment from the FDA before preemption can be triggered. * * * To hold that inaction by the FDA is sufficient to trigger preemption would mean that manufacturers would be free to ignore state laws that are intended to protect consumers, during the period that the FDA is considering whether to issue specific regulations relating to particular products, or after the FDA, for whatever reason, has "decided," through inaction, not to regulate particular products. Such a holding would contradict Congress's stated intent of providing consumer protection from unsafe medical devices when it enacted the MDA. * * *

NOTES AND QUESTIONS

1. *Proposition 65.* California's warning requirements had the dual purpose of educating consumers and discouraging the continued sale of suspected toxins. Although the warnings have not had much of a direct impact on consumer behavior, they have persuaded several manufacturers to reformulate their products. See Michael Barsa, Note, California's Proposition 65 and the Limits of Information Economics, 49 Stan. L. Rev. 1223 (1997); see also Carl Cranor, Information Generation and Use Under Proposition 65: Model Provisions for Other Postmarket Laws?, 83 Ind. L.J. 609 (2008). Warnings are not required for exposures to listed chemicals shown to pose either "no significant risk" of cancer or, in the case of reproductive toxicants, "no observable effect" at an exposure 1,000 times higher than expected. "No significant risk" is defined as less than one excess cancer in a population of 100,000 exposed over a lifetime. See Baxter Healthcare Corp. v. Denton, 15 Cal.Rptr.3d 430, 453–57 (Ct.App.2004) (affirming a declaratory order exempting a manufacturer from the Proposition 65 warning requirement because it had proven that the plasticizer used in its medical devices posed no significant risk of cancer in humans even though the chemical was listed as an animal carcinogen). By state regulation, FDA-approved labeling for prescription drugs satisfies the warning requirement, but OTC products get no safe harbor. See Christopher Wanjek, Gee, Your Hair Smells Carcinogenic!, Wash. Post, Mar. 27, 2001, at T6 ("The [FDA] acknowledges that coal tar is carcinogenic but says that the over-the-counter coal-tar shampoos are safe .... But in California, where both hair and novel legal actions grow long and wild, ... [activists] are suing more than 20 manufacturers of coal-tar shampoos and ointments to require them to place warning labels on their products—and ultimately to sell them by prescription only."). How would the analysis in *Dowhal* have proceeded if the court had focused only on transdermal nicotine patches and if the FDA had decided to regulate these combination products as devices rather than as drugs?

2. *Dental amalgam update.* After using Prop. 65 against providers of dental care, see Consumer Cause, Inc. v. SmileCare, 110 Cal.Rptr.2d 627 (Ct.App.2001), activists turned their sights on the FDA. See Moms Against Mercury v. FDA, 483 F.3d 824 (D.C.Cir.2007) (dismissing for lack of subject matter jurisdiction a petition to review the agency's failure to take action on a form of dental amalgam because a device classification process remained pending). Although it continues to find no evidence of harm, the agency decided to elevate dental amalgam to Class II ("moderate risk") device status and urged dentists to discuss the issues with their patients. See Ashley Southall, F.D.A. Deems Mercury Level in Fillings Safe, N.Y. Times, July 29, 2009, at A13; see also Linda Shrieves, Ban Dental Mercury, Foes Again Urge FDA, Orlando Sent., May 6, 2011, at A1 (reporting that the agency held public meetings on the subject around the country).

3. *Specific state requirements.* See, e.g., Michelle K. Pulley, Comment, Government Tan Lines: Examining the Reach and Effectiveness of Federal and State Efforts to Protect Consumers from the Dangers of Indoor Tanning, 36 Pepp. L. Rev. 1161 (2009); Kevin M. Rodkey, Comment, Medical Technology Meets the Maryland General Assembly: A Case Study in Handling Advances in Automated External Defibrillator Technology, 12 J. Health Care L. & Pol'y 81 (2009). For one curious effort to employ the medical device preemption provision, see This That & the Other Gift & Tobacco, Inc. v. Cobb County, Ga., 285 F.3d 1319, 1322–23 (11th Cir.2002) (holding that the MDA did not preempt a state obscenity statute that barred the advertising of sexual devices). One early flashpoint involved state regulation of hearing aids. The courts rejected preemption arguments to the extent that the state requirements addressed subjects that differed from the labeling requirements imposed by the FDA. See Smith v. Pingree, 651 F.2d 1021, 1023–25 (5th Cir.1981); Kievlan v. Dahlberg Elecs., 144 Cal.Rptr. 585, 590 (Ct.App.1978); see also Massachusetts v. Hayes, 691 F.2d 57, 60–64 (1st Cir.1982) (rejecting one state's challenge to the FDA's denial of a request for an exemption from preemption for a hearing aid requirement). See generally Morgan Downey, Laboratories or Puppets? The Challenge of Federal Preemption of State Legislation, 34 Food Drug Cosm. L.J. 334 (1979).

4. *Implied federal preemption.* In contrast to medical devices and OTC drugs, Congress has not expressly preempted state regulation of prescription pharmaceuticals. On the contrary, when it enacted the Drug Amendments of 1962, Congress included a provision disavowing any intent to displace state control. See Pub. L. No. 87–781, § 202, 76 Stat. 780, 793 (1962) ("Nothing in the amendments made by this Act to the [FDCA] shall be construed as invalidating any provision of State law which would be valid in the absence of such amendments unless there is a direct and positive conflict between such amendments and such provision of State law."); see also 21 U.S.C. § 903 (Controlled Substances Act). In *Hillsborough County v. Automated Medical Laboratories, Inc.*, 471 U.S. 707 (1985), the Supreme Court held that FDA standards for the collection of blood plasma did not impliedly preempt a local ordinance that had imposed additional donor screening requirements: "Undoubtedly, overly restrictive local legislation could threaten the national plasma supply. Neither Congress nor the FDA, however, has struck a particular balance between safety and quantity; as we have noted, the regulations, which contemplated additional state and local requirements, merely establish minimum safety standards." Id. at 721. In another context, a court rejected the argument that federal law impliedly preempted a state statute requiring pharmacists to substitute generic drugs for prescribed brand-name drugs under certain circumstances. See Pharmaceutical Soc'y of N.Y. v. Lefkowitz, 586 F.2d 953, 958 (2d Cir.1978).

5. *Administrative preemption.* Even in the absence of express statutory preemption, an agency may issue regulations preempting state requirements. The FDA has done this in the case of three general OTC drug warnings. See 51 Fed. Reg. 8180, 8181 (1986) (Reye syndrome warning for drug products containing aspirin); 47 Fed. Reg. 54,750, 54,756–57 (1982) (general pregnancy warning for OTC products); 47 Fed. Reg. 50,442, 50,447–48 (1982) (tamper-resistant packaging and associated labeling requirements); see also 60 Fed. Reg. 16,962, 16,966 (1995) (protecting confidentiality in the reporting of adverse events). Courts may hold that agency requirements impliedly preempt inconsistent state laws, and agencies also can preempt state requirements for products that they have decided not to regulate. See Jack W. Campbell, IV, Regulatory Preemption in the Garcia/Chevron Era, 59 U. Pitt. L. Rev. 805 (1998); Amanda Frost, Judicial Review of FDA Preemption Determinations, 54 Food & Drug L.J. 367 (1999). More often, the FDA disclaims any intent to preempt, in compliance with an Executive Order requiring that all agencies assess the federalism impacts of their actions.

6. *Obstacle preemption.* Could a state prohibit the sale of a drug approved by the FDA? Some states had banned the diet drug fenfluramine before the FDA decided to withdraw approval, but this was done in response to the emerging safety concerns not known to the agency when it originally approved the drug. See Peggy Rogers, Florida Prohibits Diet Drug, Hous. Chron., Sept. 9, 1997, at A3 (adding that Tennessee also had done so previously); see also Boston Moves to Ban Mercury Thermometers, N.Y. Times, Nov. 16, 2000, at A25 (referring to "a nationwide push to remove [mercury thermometers] from American medicine cabinets as a threat to lakes and streams"). In addition, responding to concerns about the hazards of certain dietary supplements in the wake of DSHEA, some states have stepped into the regulatory vacuum: several jurisdictions banned gamma hydroxybutyrate (GHB), in some cases by classifying it as a Schedule I controlled substance, and the same happened with ephedra. See Iona N. Kaiser, Comment, Dietary Supplements: Can the Law Control the Hype?, 37 Hous. L. Rev. 1249, 1268–70 (2000). After the FDA approved mifepristone (Mifeprex®), some state legislatures considered imposing restrictions on its availability. To the extent that the Supreme Court has reinvigorated implied preemption in cases where state law stands as an "obstacle" to the achievement of federal purposes, would such state laws create an impermissible conflict? Note that the Clinton administration actively had encouraged the introduction of mifepristone in the U.S. market, and it took some unprecedented steps to facilitate approval. See Lars Noah, A Miscarriage in the Drug Approval Process?: Mifepristone Embroils the FDA in Abortion Politics, 36 Wake Forest L. Rev. 571 (2001); see also David Crary, Abortion Pill Remains Controversial, Wash. Post, Oct. 3, 2010, at A3 (reporting that almost 1.4 million women in the U.S. have taken mifepristone in the last decade, accounting for about 15% of all abortions); Marc Kaufman, Abortion Foes Want RU–486 Pill Pulled, Wash. Post, May 17, 2006, at A3 (reporting that opponents have lobbied Congress and petitioned the FDA to withdraw approval); Sandhya Somashekhar, Abortion Pills Prescribed via Net Targeted, Wash. Post, Dec. 31, 2010, at A2 ("State legislators in Iowa and Nebraska have announced their intention to try to ban telemedicine abortions . . . .").

7. *Other constraints on state regulation.* When the FDA first approved oral contraceptives in 1960, some states restricted their availability, but the Supreme Court held these laws unconstitutional. See Griswold v. Connecticut, 381 U.S. 479, 485–86 (1965); cf. Carey v. Population Servs. Int'l, 431 U.S. 678, 686–91 & n.9 (1977) (invalidating a state law that had allowed only licensed pharmacists to sell nonprescription contraceptives); Joshua A. Douglas, When Is a "Minor" Also an "Adult"?: An Adolescent's Liberty Interest in Accessing Contraceptives from Public School Distribution Programs, 43 Willamette L. Rev. 545 (2007). Any future state legislation preventing physicians from dispensing mifepristone may run afoul of the Court's abortion decisions. See Planned Parenthood v. Taft, 444 F.3d 502 (6th Cir.2006) (invalidating a state law that attempted to prevent the off-label use of mifepristone at lower dosages or later in pregnancy); Bradley E. Cunningham, Note, Implications of FDA Approval of RU–486: Regulating Mifepristone Within the Bounds of the Constitution, 90 Ky. L.J. 229 (2001–2002). Because mifepristone only works early in pregnancy (pre-viability), the constitutional test asks whether a state's restriction on the use of the drug would "unduly burden" a woman's right to choose an abortion. See Planned Parenthood v. Casey, 505 U.S. 833, 873–901, 877 (1992) (plurality). Although limitations on the types of physicians who are authorized to dispense the drug (e.g., only those licensed to perform surgical abortions) might pass muster, see Mazurek v. Armstrong, 520 U.S. 968, 972–75 (1997), it does not appear that states could entirely prohibit access to a method for terminating pregnancy approved by federal officials. The Supreme Court invalidated a state prohibition on one surgical method of abortion because, by leaving only an arguably riskier method available, the law created hazards to maternal health for which it failed to provide any exception. See Stenberg v. Carhart, 530 U.S. 914, 930–38 (2000); cf. Gonzales v. Carhart, 550 U.S. 124 (2007). To the extent that mifepristone still offers demonstrated advantages over surgical abortion procedures, see Michael F. Greene, Fatal Infections Associated with Mifepristone–Induced Abortion, 353 New Eng. J. Med. 2317 (2005), this would seem to prevent a state from prohibiting its use altogether. But what if the Supreme Court reverses course on abortion, and what about other therapeutic agents that do not raise the constitutional questions in connection with procreative choices? If a state entirely prohibited sales within its borders of an FDA-approved product, and it had done so without any apparent safety rationale, would the Constitution forbid such an exercise of a state's police power?

Whalen v. Roe

429 U.S. 589 (1977).

■ STEVENS, JUSTICE:

The constitutional question presented is whether the State of New York may record, in a centralized computer file, the names and addresses of all persons who have obtained, pursuant to a doctor's prescription, certain drugs for which there is both a lawful and an unlawful market. The district court enjoined enforcement of the portions of the New York State Controlled Substances Act of 1972 which require such recording on the ground that they violate appellees' constitutionally protected rights of privacy. * * *

Many drugs have both legitimate and illegitimate uses. In response to a concern that such drugs were being diverted into unlawful channels, in 1970 the New York Legislature created a special commission to evaluate the State's drug-control laws. The commission found the existing laws deficient in several respects. There was no effective way to prevent the use of stolen or revised prescriptions, to prevent unscrupulous pharmacists from repeatedly refilling prescriptions, to prevent users from obtaining prescriptions from more than one doctor, or to prevent doctors from over-prescribing, either by authorizing an excessive amount in one prescription or by giving one patient multiple prescriptions. In drafting new legislation to correct such defects, the commission consulted with enforcement officials in California and Illinois where central reporting systems were being used effectively.

The new New York statute classified potentially harmful drugs in five schedules.[7] Drugs, such as heroin, which are highly abused and have no recognized medical use, are in Schedule I; they cannot be prescribed. Schedules II through V include drugs which have a progressively lower potential for abuse but also have a recognized medical use. Our concern is limited to Schedule II which includes the most dangerous of the legitimate drugs. With an exception for emergencies, the Act requires that all prescriptions for Schedule II drugs be prepared by the physician in triplicate on an official form. The completed form identifies the prescribing physician; the dispensing pharmacy; the drug and dosage; and the name, address, and age of the patient. One copy of the form is retained by the physician, the second by the pharmacist, and the third is forwarded to the New York State Department of Health in Albany. A prescription made on an official form may not exceed a 30–day supply, and may not be refilled. * * *

A few days before the Act became effective, this litigation was commenced by a group of patients regularly receiving prescriptions for Schedule II drugs, by doctors who prescribe such drugs, and by two associations of physicians. * * * The district court found that the State had been unable to demonstrate the necessity for the patient-identification requirement on the basis of its experience during the first 20 months of administration of the new statute. There was a time when that alone would have provided a

7. These five schedules conform in all material aspects with the drug schedules in the Federal Comprehensive Drug Abuse Prevention and Control Act of 1970. 21 U.S.C. § 801 et seq. [For an update on state legislation in this area, see Richard L. Braun, Uniform Controlled Substances Act of 1990, 13 Campbell L. Rev. 365 (1991).]

basis for invalidating the statute. *Lochner v. New York*, 198 U.S. 45 (1905), involved legislation making it a crime for a baker to permit his employees to work more than 60 hours in a week. In an opinion no longer regarded as authoritative, the Court held the statute unconstitutional as "an unreasonable, unnecessary and arbitrary interference with the right of the individual to his personal liberty ...." The holding in *Lochner* has been implicitly rejected many times. State legislation which has some effect on individual liberty or privacy may not be held unconstitutional simply because a court finds it unnecessary, in whole or in part. For we have frequently recognized that individual States have broad latitude in experimenting with possible solutions to problems of vital local concern.

The New York statute challenged in this case represents a considered attempt to deal with such a problem. It is manifestly the product of an orderly and rational legislative decision. It was recommended by a specially appointed commission which held extensive hearings on the proposed legislation, and drew on experience with similar programs in other States. There surely was nothing unreasonable in the assumption that the patient-identification requirement might aid in the enforcement of laws designed to minimize the misuse of dangerous drugs. For the requirement could reasonably be expected to have a deterrent effect on potential violators as well as to aid in the detection or investigation of specific instances of apparent abuse. At the very least, it would seem clear that the State's vital interest in controlling the distribution of dangerous drugs would support a decision to experiment with new techniques for control. For if an experiment fails—if in this case experience teaches that the patient-identification requirement results in the foolish expenditure of funds to acquire a mountain of useless information—the legislative process remains available to terminate the unwise experiment. It follows that the legislature's enactment of the patient-identification requirement was a reasonable exercise of New York's broad police powers. * * *

Appellees contend that the statute invades a constitutionally protected "zone of privacy." The cases sometimes characterized as protecting "privacy" have in fact involved at least two different kinds of interests. One is the individual interest in avoiding disclosure of personal matters, and another is the interest in independence in making certain kinds of important decisions. Appellees argue that both of these interests are impaired by this statute. The mere existence in readily available form of the information about patients' use of Schedule II drugs creates a genuine concern that the information will become publicly known and that it will adversely affect their reputations. This concern makes some patients reluctant to use, and some doctors reluctant to prescribe, such drugs even when their use is medically indicated. It follows, they argue, that the making of decisions about matters vital to the care of their health is inevitably affected by the statute. Thus, the statute threatens to impair both their interest in the nondisclosure of private information and also their interest in making important decisions independently. We are persuaded, however, that the New York program does not, on its face, pose a sufficiently grievous threat to either interest to establish a constitutional violation. * * *

Even without public disclosure, it is, of course, true that private information must be disclosed to the authorized employees of the New York Department of Health. Such disclosures, however, are not significantly different from those that were required under the prior law. Nor are they meaningfully distinguishable from a host of other unpleasant invasions of privacy that are associated with many facets of health care. Unquestionably, some individuals' concern for their own privacy may lead them to avoid or to postpone needed medical attention. Nevertheless, disclosures of private medical information to doctors, to hospital personnel, to insurance companies, and to public health agencies are often an essential part of modern medical practice even when the disclosure may reflect unfavorably on the character of the patient. Requiring such disclosures to representatives of the State having responsibility for the health of the community does not automatically amount to an impermissible invasion of privacy.

Appellees also argue, however, that even if unwarranted disclosures do not actually occur, the knowledge that the information is readily available in a computerized file creates a genuine concern that causes some persons to decline needed medication. The record supports the conclusion that some use of Schedule II drugs has been discouraged by that concern; it also is clear, however, that about 100,000 prescriptions for such drugs were being filled each month prior to the entry of the district court's injunction. Clearly, therefore, the statute did not deprive the public of access to the drugs.

Nor can it be said that any individual has been deprived of the right to decide independently, with the advice of his physician, to acquire and to use needed medication. Although the State no doubt could prohibit entirely the use of particular Schedule II drugs, it has not done so. This case is therefore unlike those in which the Court held that a total prohibition of certain conduct was an impermissible deprivation of liberty. Nor does the State require access to these drugs to be conditioned on the consent of any state official or other third party. Within dosage limits which appellees do not challenge, the decision to prescribe, or to use, is left entirely to the physician and the patient. * * *

The appellee doctors argue separately that the statute impairs their right to practice medicine free of unwarranted state interference. If the doctors' claim has any reference to the impact of the 1972 statute on their own procedures, it is clearly frivolous. For even the prior statute required the doctor to prepare a written prescription identifying the name and address of the patient and the dosage of the prescribed drug. To the extent that their claim has reference to the possibility that the patients' concern about disclosure may induce them to refuse needed medication, the doctors' claim is derivative from, and therefore no stronger than, the patients'. Our rejection of their claim therefore disposes of the doctors' as well.

A final word about issues we have not decided. We are not unaware of the threat to privacy implicit in the accumulation of vast amounts of personal information in computerized data banks or other massive government files. The collection of taxes, the distribution of welfare and social security benefits, the supervision of public health, the direction of our Armed Forces, and the enforcement of the criminal laws all require the orderly preservation of great quantities of information, much of which is personal in character and potentially embarrassing or harmful if disclosed. The right to collect and use such data for public purposes is typically accompanied by a concomitant statutory or regulatory duty to avoid unwarranted disclosures. Recognizing that in some circumstances that duty arguably has its roots in the Constitution, nevertheless New York's statutory scheme, and its implementing administrative procedures, evidence a proper concern with, and protection of, the individual's interest in privacy. We therefore need not, and do not, decide any question which might be presented by the unwarranted disclosure of accumulated private data whether intentional or unintentional or by a system that did not contain comparable security provisions. We simply hold that this record does not establish an invasion of any right or liberty protected by the Fourteenth Amendment.

NOTES AND QUESTIONS

1. *Access*. The federal government has urged more states to adopt prescription monitoring programs. See Cynthia B. Gregorian, Addiction to Painkillers Is a Growing Problem: How to Kick It, Wash. Post, Dec. 5, 2010, at A13 ("Forty-three states have passed legislation to do just that, although only 33 states have money to fund them."); see also Ashley Dutko, Note, Florida's Fight Against Prescription Drug Abuse: Prescription Drug Monitoring Program, 34 Nova L. Rev. 739 (2010); Lizette Alvarez, Florida Shutting "Pill Mill" Clinics, N.Y. Times, Sept. 1, 2011, at A1. Doctors and drug companies continue, however, to oppose such efforts. See Melody Petersen & Barry Meier, Few States Track Prescriptions as Way to Prevent Overdoses, N.Y. Times, Dec. 21, 2001, at A1; cf. Stephanie Saul, Doctors Object as Drug Makers Learn Who's Prescribing What, N.Y. Times, May 4, 2006, at A1 (reporting that the industry has opposed state legislation prohibiting the collection and use of prescribing information for marketing efforts). The Court's opinion in *Whalen* suggests that, in exercising their traditional police powers, states may limit patients' access to products approved by the FDA. Nonetheless, the recognition that patients enjoy some constitutional right of access to therapeutic agents seems to mean that a state could not prohibit access altogether, at least not absent some genuine public health concern. As explained late in the next chapter, the courts generally have not read *Whalen* to protect any right of access to products not approved by the FDA.

2. *Medical records privacy*. The question at the heart of *Whalen* has, of course, become far more significant in the last few decades. See Barbara J. Evans, Congress' New Infrastructural Model of Medical Privacy, 84 Notre Dame L. Rev. 585 (2009); Mark A. Hall, Property, Privacy, and the Pursuit of Interconnected Electronic Medical Records, 95 Iowa L. Rev. 631 (2010); see also Douglas v. Dobbs, 419 F.3d 1097 (10th Cir.2005) (reviewing challenge to search of pharmacy records); Ellen Nakashima, Prescription

Data Used to Assess Consumers: Records Aid Insurers but Prompt Privacy Concerns, Wash. Post, Aug. 4, 2008, at A1. HHS issued sweeping new rules designed to protect medical records privacy. See 65 Fed. Reg. 82,462 (2000), modified, 67 Fed. Reg. 53,182 (2002) (codified as amended at 21 C.F.R. pts. 160–64); see also Rob Stein, Medical Privacy Law Nets No Fines: Lax Enforcement Puts Patients' Files at Risk, Critics Say, Wash. Post, June 5, 2006, at A1. New medical technologies promise to further complicate the issue in the future: the FDA has approved an implantable device with a scannable identification number that would allow health care providers to access an unconscious patient's medical records on the Internet. See Rob Stein, Use of Implanted Patient–Data Chips Stirs Debate on Medicine vs. Privacy, Wash. Post, Mar. 15, 2006, at A1 (discussing the uses and potential abuses of the VeriChip®); see also Crystal Spivey, Note, Breathing New Life into HIPAA's UHID—Is the FDA's Green Light to the Verichip the Prince Charming Sleeping Beauty Has Been Waiting For?, 9 DePaul J. Health Care L. 1317 (2006).

3. *Breakdowns in the pharmaceutical distribution system.* The large-scale diversion of drugs (especially though not exclusively prescription narcotics) by unauthorized wholesalers and pharmacy brokers (who may illicitly import, dilute, or improperly store their inventory), coupled with the ease of distribution through Internet sites that may not satisfy prescription requirements, has begun to endanger the public health. See Gilbert M. Gaul & Mary P. Flaherty, U.S. Prescription Drug System Under Attack: Multibillion–Dollar Shadow Market Is Growing Stronger (five-part series), Wash. Post, Oct. 19–23, 2003, at A1; see also Alec Klein, Used Medical Devices Being Sold on eBay: Refurbished Items Have Little Oversight, Wash. Post, Dec. 22, 2005, at D1; CNN, Jan. 24, 2006 (reporting that some individuals have begun offering to sell their unused prescription drugs (e.g., injectable fertility treatments) to other members of patient support groups on the Internet). The sale of counterfeit drugs also has become increasingly common. See Anna W. Mathews & Scott Hensley, FDA Targets an Upsurge in Fake Drugs, Wall St. J., Sept. 11, 2003, at B1; Ylan Q. Mui, Crackdown Targets Counterfeit Drugs: Raids Held Worldwide—Fake Medicines a Growing Enterprise, Wash. Post, Nov. 20, 2009, at A17; see also Adam Powell, Note, Benchmark Legislation: A Measured Approach in the Fight Against Counterfeit Pharmaceuticals, 61 Hastings L.J. 749 (2010). In 1988, Congress passed the Prescription Drug Marketing Act, which mandated that certain links in the chain of distribution maintain records tracing a particular product, 21 U.S.C. § 353(e), but it took the FDA almost two decades to implement this "pedigree" requirement because of opposition from wholesalers. See Barnaby J. Feder, F.D.A. Imposes Long–Delayed Rule to Require Tracking of Prescription Drugs, N.Y. Times, June 10, 2006, at C3 (reporting that embedded radio frequency identification (RFID) tags, which have been tried on shipments of OxyContin® and Viagra®, may facilitate such tracing); see also RxUSA Wholesale, Inc. v. HHS, 467 F.Supp.2d 285 (E.D.N.Y.2006) (granting a preliminary injunction against enforcement of part of this regulation), aff'd mem., 285 F.App'x 809 (2d Cir.2008); 73 Fed. Reg. 14,991 (2008) (FDA request for information regarding technologies used for the identification, validation, tracking, and authentication of prescription drugs in connection with its implementation of section 913 of the FDA Amendments Act of 2007); Suchira Ghosh, Note, The R.F.I.D. Act of 2006 and e-Pedigrees: Tackling the Problem of Counterfeit Drugs in the United States Wholesale Industry, 13 Mich. Telecomm. & Tech. L. Rev. 577 (2007); Jessica Maziarz, Comment, Radio Frequency Identification Technology: How Arizona Can Prevent the Sale of Counterfeit Prescription Drugs, 40 Ariz. St. L.J. 1085 (2008).

4. *Down the drain*. Apart from fears of diversion, the disposal of drugs and devices has become a growing environmental concern. See Christopher T. Nidel, Regulating the Fate of Pharmaceutical Drugs: A New Prescription for the Environment, 58 Food & Drug L.J. 81 (2003); Teirney Christenson, Comment, Fish on Morphine: Protecting Wisconsin's Natural Resources Through a Comprehensive Plan for Proper Disposal of Pharmaceuticals, 2008 Wis. L. Rev. 141; Chryssa V. Deliganis & Steve P. Calandrillo, Syringes in the Sea: Why Federal Regulation of Medical Waste Is Long Overdue, 41 Ga. L. Rev. 169 (2006); Gwendolyn McKee, Comment, Keeping Drugs out of the Toilet: The Need for Federal Action to Allow Consumer Drug Donation, 10 Quinnipiac Health L.J. 45 (2006); Martha Mendoza, Drugs Found in More Cities' Water, Orlando Sent., Sept. 12, 2008, at A12; Mike Stark, Programs Aim to Safely Dispose of Old Drugs: Potentially Dangerous Medications Are Being Collected by More States, Wash. Post, Jan. 31, 2010, at A2.

3. International Actors

Richard A. Merrill, *The Importance and Challenges of "Mutual Recognition"*

29 Seton Hall L. Rev. 736 (1998).

* * * In some ways we are, in 1998, at a stage of regulatory development comparable to that confronting Congress at the turn of the century. It was by then apparent that the production and marketing of food were no longer local activities. Meat packed in Chicago was being marketed in all of the nation's major cities. The same was increasingly true, but not so obvious, for the products of the fledgling pharmaceutical industry. Consumers could no longer rely exclusively, or indeed confidently, on local public health officials to protect their health and welfare. * * * [T]he inexorable growth of interstate trade had shifted primary regulatory responsibility to the federal level before World War II, particularly for medical products.

At the end of the twentieth century, comparable practical challenges face policy-makers in the United States and across the world. International commerce in food and medicines has exploded in the last generation. Many of the major pharmaceutical firms are genuine multi-nationals. Medical devices firms generally owe their allegiance to a single country, but their customers, in increasing numbers, are distributed around the world. * * *

The circumstances facing the United States and its trading partners today, however, differ in one obvious and important respect from those that confronted members of the United States Congress in 1906. If those turn-of-the-century Senators and Representatives were prepared, as a political matter, to create a cross-jurisdictional regulatory authority, they had a constitutional—that is, a legal—basis for doing so. By contrast, today the international legal order would not afford a firm anchor for a multinational regulatory authority even if there were support for one—which there surely is not. National regulatory requirements for medicines and foods—particularly foods—have long embodied diverse policies and served multiple goals. No country has been more determined to preserve its autonomy in setting and enforcing health protection standards than the United States. And no doubt many of our trading partners believe we have been as guilty as they of adopting standards whose real objective is to protect or advantage domestic producers.

Accordingly, there are formidable obstacles to international harmonization of regulatory requirements for food and medical products. At the same time, there are mounting pressures on both producer and consuming countries to reach agreement on product and production standards. Even where harmonization does not seem possible, there are pressures—internally generated in part—to reach work-sharing arrangements that permit trading partners to make use of, and rely upon, the production-site activities of a partner's regulatory authorities. These latter pressures may prove irresistible simply because the alternatives to trusting the work of officials in other countries are unworkable—either accepting products based on physical examination or refusing their entry.

The recent Mutual Recognition Agreement with the European Community (EU MRA) is one expression of this reality. It is a cautious attempt by United States and European Union (EU) policy-makers to work out terms of reciprocal trust in which our regulatory officials accept the work, and sometimes the results, of their officials. The success of the venture—not yet demonstrated—will have important implications not only for international trade but also for protection of U.S. consumers. * * * The United States enters into an agreement with a trading partner under the expectation that the trading partner will take steps to help FDA perform its primary function of applying domestic legal standards to products imported into the United States. The service contracted for may be the provision of information, such as sharing the report of an inspection, or it may be the evaluation of a medical device by a body recognized by the partner's regulatory authorities. In both cases, the assumption is that U.S. law provides the standards that ultimately determine the acceptability of an inspected facility or an imported product. In such an agreement, the role of the trading partner is not that of law maker but rather that of information source or service provider.

An agreement to harmonize standards, by contrast, * * * contemplates the establishment of a single common rule of conduct or single common measure of product compliance, i.e., establishment of a single standard that is observed in both countries. If we keep these descriptions in mind, we will have a clearer grasp of the requirements for domestic implementation of any agreement into which the United States enters and a better appreciation of the pace at which we are moving toward internationalization of regulation. * * *

[T]he Federal Food, Drug, and Cosmetic Act (FFDCA) now contains express legislative authorization for FDA to pursue certain types of international agreements. Indeed, Congress has sprinkled its authorization in a number of provisions, including two recently added by the FDA Modernization Act, passed in November 1997. * * * Assuring compliance with GMP requirements and facilitating inspections to verify compliance seem to be of particular concern to Congress. Other regulatory activities that might be the basis for international cooperation, and possible mutual recognition, are perhaps important but apparently less urgent.

The amended FFDCA adds an interesting geographic qualification to its instructions. FDA is specifically encouraged to reach mutual recognition agreements with the EU covering the regulation of all products within the agency's jurisdiction. Congress is thus on record as recognizing that there are some partners with whom we are more interested in cooperating than others. Maybe this is simply a reflection of the commercial importance of the trans-Atlantic trade. It may also demonstrate congressional acceptance of the proposition that the regulators in EU countries are as capable and vigorous as our own officials. * * *

United States FDA officials not only have a strong tradition of tough-minded regulation, but many share—though they do not often express—a conviction that they are more thorough and rigorous about regulation than their counterparts in other countries. They believe that U.S. standards are higher and, just as important, that their means of assuring compliance with those standards are more reliable and certainly less trusting. In their view, FDA regulation represents the "gold standard."

There is some evidence to support this self-assured view, but, whether or not it is fully justified, it is certainly genuine. This belief will almost certainly make harmonization more difficult and perhaps slow the drive toward mutual recognition. If United States regulatory officials start from the premise that FDA not only imposes the highest standards but also uses the most effective means for assuring compliance with those standards, "harmonization" appears to demand some relaxation of public health protection. At least it does so if other countries are not willing to adopt and enforce U.S. standards. This mindset may not ultimately impede FDA's willingness to enter into agreements of the mutual assistance variety, but it surely will be an impediment to efforts to achieve agreement on substantive standards. * * *

Another feature of the institutional culture at FDA is the widely-held conviction—or realization—that the agency is over-extended and under-resourced. The job that FDA has traditionally assumed is getting harder, not easier. * * * The realization that resources have not kept pace with workload, much less public expectations, helps explain the seriousness with which FDA officials seem prepared to entertain proposals for mutual recognition. If you can get other people to help you perform your functions—functions that you view as essential—this may help spread the cost of assuring compliance.

Another distinctive tradition has been reflected in the statute that FDA is responsible for administering. It can be described as paternalistic. Many U.S. officials—perhaps more in Congress than at FDA—have long contended that American firms regulated by FDA should not be able to market overseas products they cannot market in the United States. This conviction stems from language in the 1938 FFDCA, which FDA later interpreted as prohibiting the export of "new drugs" until they received FDA approval. FDA's policy made it impossible for a U.S. manufacturer to ship a drug overseas that FDA had not approved—even if the drug had not been rejected for approval here and would be or had been approved by foreign authorities. The same premise was later incorporated in the somewhat weaker controls imposed on the export of unapproved medical devices by the 1976 Medical Devices Amendments to the FFDCA.

Congress relaxed these restrictions on the export of unapproved products in 1996. But it would still be incorrect to say that, under U.S. law, it is lawful to export any product that a receiving country is prepared to accept. * * * In short, FDA has historically been viewed by Congress—and has come to view itself—as having responsibility to protect citizens of other countries as well as citizens of our own. This tradition, too, may impede harmonization efforts, particularly if they appear to contemplate any relaxation of U.S. standards. * * *

NOTES AND QUESTIONS

1. *Harmonization efforts.* In 1998, the FDA issued a final rule implementing the mutual recognition agreement with the EU. See 63 Fed. Reg. 60,122 (1998) (codified at 21 C.F.R. pt. 26). Previously, the agency had involved itself in various international harmonization efforts. See 63 Fed. Reg. 49,583 (1998) (statistical principles for clinical trials); 60 Fed. Reg. 11,260 (1995) (publishing five International Conference on Harmonization (ICH) guidelines related primarily to different aspects of study designs appropriate for the review of drug safety); see also Paul M. Booth, FDA Implementation of Standards Developed by the International Conference on Harmonization, 52 Food & Drug L.J. 203 (1997); Laura B. Faden & Christopher–Paul Milne, Pharmacovigilance Activities in the United States, European Union and Japan: Harmonic Convergence or Convergent Evolution?, 63 Food & Drug L.J. 683 (2008); Kai P. Purnhagen, The Challenge of Globalization in Pharmaceutical Law—Is an International Harmonization of Drug Approval Procedures Modeled After the European System Worth Considering?, 63 Food & Drug L.J. 623 (2008); Ann E. Ryan, Comment, Protecting the Rights of Pediatric Research Subjects in the International Conference on Harmonisation of Technical Requirements for Registration of Pharmaceuticals for Human Use, 23 Fordham Int'l L.J. 848 (2000). Difficulties may, however, arise with inspections of overseas facilities. See Gardiner Harris, Agency Head Outlines Difficulties and Risks of Food and Drug Imports, N.Y. Times, June 21, 2011, at B3 ("More than 80 percent of the active ingredients for drugs sold in the United States are made abroad—mostly in plants in China and India that are rarely inspected by the F.D.A. Half of all medical devices sold in the United States are made abroad."); Alicia Mundy, FDA Faulted in Heparin Case, Wall St. J., Apr. 30, 2010, at B7.

2. *Further commentary*. See Edward M. Basile et al., Export of Pharmaceuticals and Medical Devices Under the Federal Food, Drug & Cosmetic Act: FDA's Striking Change in Interpretation Post–Shelhigh, 64 Food & Drug L.J. 149 (2009); Michael J. Malinowski, Globalization of Biotechnology and the Public Health Challenges Accompanying It, 60 Alb. L. Rev. 119 (1996); Lars Noah, NAFTA's Impact on the Trade in Pharmaceuticals, 33 Hous. L. Rev. 1293 (1997); Brian L. Walser, Shared Technical Decisionmaking and the Disaggregation of Sovereignty: International Regulatory Policy, Expert Communities, and the Multinational Pharmaceutical Industry, 72 Tul. L. Rev. 1597 (1998); J. John Lee, Comment, What Is Past Is Prologue: The International Conference on Harmonization and Lessons Learned from European Drug Regulations Harmonization, 26 U. Pa. J. Int'l Econ. L. 151 (2005); Symposium, Globalization of Pharmaceuticals: International Regulatory Issues, 32 Am. J.L. & Med. 153 (2006).

CHAPTER 2

DEVELOPMENT AND TESTING OF EXPERIMENTAL THERAPIES

This chapter examines the regulatory mechanisms that govern the development and testing of new medical products. This process raises a variety of questions—such as what constitutes "research" triggering regulatory protections for human subjects; how to bridge the gap between the aspirations of the informed consent rules and the reality of their application; and what constraints exist on patient access to investigational medical technologies.

A. DRUG DISCOVERY AND TESTING

FDA, *From Test Tube to Patient*

<www.fda.gov/Drugs/ResourcesForYou/Consumers/ucm143455.htm> (4th ed. 2006).

* * * The drug research process is complicated, time-consuming, and costly; and the end result is never known at the outset. Literally hundreds, and sometimes thousands, of chemical compounds must be made and tested to find one that can achieve the desirable result without too serious side effects. Such a complicated process costs vast amounts of time and money. The FDA estimates that, on average, it takes eight-and-a-half years to study and test a new drug before the agency can approve it for the general public. That includes early laboratory and animal testing, as well as later clinical trials using human subjects. The role of the FDA in the early stages of drug research is small. * * *

New drug research starts by studying how the body functions, both normally and abnormally, at its most basic levels. * * * That, in turn, leads to a concept of how a drug might be used to prevent, cure, or treat a disease or medical condition. Once the concept has been developed, the researcher has a target. Sometimes, scientists find the right compound quickly. More often, hundreds or even thousands must be tested. In a series of test-tube experiments called assays, compounds are added one at a time to enzymes, cell cultures, or cellular substances grown in a laboratory. The goal is to find which additions show some chemical effect. Some may not work well, but may hint at ways of changing the compound's chemical structure to improve its performance. The latter process alone may require testing dozens or hundreds of compounds.

A more high tech approach is to use computers to simulate an enzyme or other drug target and to design chemical structures that might work against it. A computer can show scientists what the receptor site looks like and how one might tailor a compound to block an enzyme from attaching there. However, while computers give chemists clues to which compounds to make, they don't give any final answers. Compounds made based on a computer simulation still have to be put into a biological system to see whether they work.

A third approach involves testing compounds made naturally by microscopic organisms. Candidates include fungi, viruses, and molds, such as those that led to penicillin and other antibiotics. Scientists grow the microorganisms in what they call a fermentation broth, one type of organism per broth. Sometimes, 100,000 or more broths are tested to see whether any compound made by a microorganism has a desirable effect.

To this point, the search for a new drug has been confined to a laboratory test tube. Next, scientists have to test those compounds that have shown at least some desired effects in living animals. In animal testing, drug companies make every effort to use as few animals as possible and to ensure their humane and proper care. Two or more species are typically tested because a drug may affect one differently from another. Such tests show whether a potential drug has toxic side effects and what its safety is at different doses. The results point the way for human testing and, much later, product labeling.

So far, research has aimed at discovering what a drug does to the body. Now, it must also find out what the body does to the drug. So, in animal testing, scientists measure how much of a drug is absorbed into the blood, how it is broken down chemically in the body, the toxicity of its breakdown products (metabolites), and how quickly the drug and its metabolites are excreted from the body. Sometimes, such tests find a metabolite that is more effective than the drug originally picked for development.

More often than many scientists care to admit, researchers just have to give up when a drug is poorly absorbed, is unsafe, or simply doesn't work. The organization Pharmaceutical Research and Manufacturers of America estimates that only 5 in 5,000 compounds that enter preclinical testing make it to human testing, and only 1 of those 5 may be safe and effective enough to reach pharmacy shelves. Nevertheless, progress may yet be made. Occasionally, a stubborn scientist keeps looking and finds a usable compound after others had given up. In other cases, compounds may be put aside because they failed to work on one disease, only to be taken off the shelf years later and found to work on another. * * *

The path a drug travels from a lab to your medicine cabinet is usually long, and every drug takes a unique route. Often, a drug is developed to treat a specific disease. An important use of a drug may also be discovered by accident. For example, Retrovir (zidovudine, also known as AZT) was first studied as an anti-cancer drug in the 1960s with disappointing results. It wasn't until the 1980s that researchers discovered the drug could treat AIDS, and the Food and Drug Administration approved the drug, manufactured by GlaxoSmithKline, for that purpose in 1987. * * *

NOTES AND QUESTIONS

1. *Something old.* Researchers continue to look to nature for potential drug candidates. See Peter Landers, MS Drug's Epic Journey From Folklore to Lab—Drawing on Ancient Chinese Medicine, Research on Fungus and Insects Yields Potential Relief for Multiple Sclerosis, Wall St. J., June 22, 2010, at D2; Regina Nuzzo, Mark of the Vampire: The Saliva of a Bat Species Has an Enzyme That May Help Prevent Brain Damage in More Stroke Victims, L.A. Times, Oct. 30, 2006, at F3 ("Vampire bats aren't the only ghoulish creatures carrying around potential health treats. Now researchers are eyeing spider webs for a tricky new biomaterial that could be used in various medical applications."); Dennis O'Brien, Oceans of Medical Potential: Research on Marine Life Could Lead to Treatments for Cancer and Alzheimer's, Balt. Sun, Dec. 9, 2005, at 1D ("Since 1960, at least seven drugs based on compounds found in plants, soils and other terrestrial sources have been approved by the [FDA] .... [A]lmost two-thirds of anti-cancer agents investigated as drug treatment candidates between 1981 and 2002 were derived from natural products."). Venoms, for instance, have proven their potential as human pharmaceuticals. See Marc Kaufman, New Drug Is Approved to Treat Chronic Pain: Synthetic Snail Venom Is Considered a Last Resort, Wash. Post, Dec. 29, 2004, at A3; Rick Weiss, Venom as a Prelude to New Drug Treatments, Wash. Post, Mar. 7, 2005, at A8 (noting that the antihypertensive captopril was derived from green mamba toxin). In addition, of course, serendipity plays a role in drug development. See Thomas M. Burton, Flop Factor: By Learning from Failures, Lilly Keeps Drug Pipeline Full, Wall St. J., Apr. 21, 2004, at A1.

2. *Something new.* Researchers hope to replace the old brute force (and dumb luck) methods with more refined strategies for designing new pharmaceuticals. See Lars Noah, The Coming Pharmacogenomics Revolution: Tailoring Drugs to Fit Patients' Genetic Profiles, 43 Jurimetrics J. 1, 15–16 (2002) ("A number of companies are developing new drugs using information from gene databases to design products that target molecules associated with particular diseases. Others have begun to use biosimulators for virtual ('in silico') testing of investigational products, hoping to avoid the greater effort required for initial in vivo testing ...."); Robert D. Rosenberg, Redesigning Heparin, 344 New Eng. J. Med. 673 (2001) (describing the anticoagulant's history, including the synthesis of a related molecular version of the substance, and predicting future developments based on a better understanding of heparin's properties and function); Naomi Aoki, Inventing Designer Drugs, Boston Globe, Apr. 13, 2003, at D1. The rush to embrace "combinatorial chemistry and high-throughput screening" has not, however, panned out yet. See Peter Landers, Human Element: Drug Industry's Big Push into Technology Falls Short, Wall St. J., Feb. 24, 2004, at A1; see also Janet Woodcock & Raymond Woosley, The FDA Critical Path Initiative and Its Influence on New Drug Development, 59 Ann. Rev. Med. 1 (2008); John Markoff, Herculean Device for Molecular Mysteries, N.Y. Times, July 8, 2008, at F2 ("Experimentation in the use of supercomputers to model molecular interactions has been going on for more than a decade, but the field is still largely in its infancy."); Robert Weisman, Biotech Firms Want Drug Approval Hastened, Boston Globe, June 22, 2011, at C7 ("FDA spokeswoman Karen Riley ... said the agency approves 60 to 80 percent of submitted drug applications, but most experimental treatments never get that far—70 percent of drug candidates fail in mid-stage trials and 55 percent fail in late-stage trials ...."). Even if improved genetic information and enhanced computing power allow for greater initial precision in the identification of promising agents, testing in animals will have to continue for the foreseeable future. See Anna W. Mathews, Recent Cases Point to the Limitations of Animal Drug Tests, Wall St. J., Mar. 30, 2007, at B1 ("Before regulators approve a drug, it typically has been tested on hundreds of animals. The FDA requires initial testing in at least two species: one rodent, one nonrodent. By the end of the process, mice, pigs, rabbits, dogs, monkeys and other animals may have been used.").

International Primate Protection League v. Institute for Behavioral Research

799 F.2d 934 (4th Cir.1986).

■ WILKINSON, CIRCUIT JUDGE:

In this case we must decide whether a group of private individuals may challenge a medical researcher's compliance with federal standards for the care of laboratory animals. Because we find that the plaintiffs lack standing to bring such a lawsuit, we affirm the judgment of the district court in its dismissal of this action.

To imply a cause of action in these plaintiffs might entail serious consequences. It might open the use of animals in biomedical research to the hazards and vicissitudes of courtroom litigation. It may draw judges into the supervision and regulation of laboratory research. It might unleash a spate of private lawsuits that would impede advances made by medical science in the alleviation of human suffering. To risk consequences of this magnitude in the absence of clear direction from the Congress would be ill-advised. In fact, we are persuaded that Congress intended that the independence of medical research be respected and that administrative enforcement govern the Animal Welfare Act.

The principal complainant in this case, Alex Pacheco, first met the principal defendant, Dr. Edward Taub, in May 1981. Pacheco, an undergraduate student in the program of Environmental Studies at George Washington University in Washington, D.C., had worked frequently for the protection of animals * * * * He had founded the Ohio Animal Rights Committee and, in Washington, D.C., had founded People for the Ethical

Treatment of Animals, Inc. (PETA), on which he continued to serve as director. Taub, the chief of the Behavioral Biology Center of the Institute for Behavioral Research (IBR), was studying the capacity of monkeys to learn to use a limb after nerves had been severed. Funded by the National Institutes of Health (NIH), the project amplified Taub's earlier research in this area and attempted to discover benefits for the rehabilitation of human patients suffering from a serious neurological injury such as a stroke.

Pacheco offered to work as a volunteer for Taub on the neurological study at an IBR facility in Silver Spring, Maryland. Taub gave Pacheco the keys to the premises and permission to enter at any time, and Pacheco came regularly to the laboratory during the summer of 1981. He concluded from his observations that IBR did not provide the monkeys with sufficient food or water, a sanitary environment, or adequate veterinary care. On several nights during the week of August 27, 1981, Pacheco brought other researchers to IBR to confirm his impressions. * * * [T]he Assistant State's Attorney for Montgomery County filed criminal charges against Taub in the county district court, alleging seventeen violations of the animal cruelty statute.

On October 9 the Circuit Court for Montgomery County, without opposition from IBR, instructed Sgt. Swain and Dr. James Stunkard, a veterinarian, to supervise the transfer of the monkeys to an NIH facility in Poolesville, Maryland that Swain and Stunkard had chosen as the best place for temporary care and custody. * * * Dr. Taub stood trial in November 1981 in the District Court for Montgomery County, which on December 2 entered orders of conviction on six of the seventeen counts and acquittal on the other eleven counts. Fearing that the court order on custody of the monkeys would partially expire with the acquittals, PETA acted quickly to prevent the return of any animals to IBR. * * *

The plaintiffs in the former case, including PETA, hoped to require the Secretary of Agriculture to enforce against Taub and IBR the provisions of the Animal Welfare Act. The plaintiff in the latter case sought a more general declaration of the duties of Secretary Block and NIH to control the research treatment of animals and also requested an injunction to prevent the return of the seized monkeys to Taub and IBR. * * * The Court of Appeals of Maryland then granted a writ of certiorari and in August 1983 reversed the conviction, holding that Article 27, § 59 of the Maryland Code did not apply to an institution conducting medical research pursuant to a federal program. * * *

Not only do plaintiffs fail to allege cognizable injuries; they fail also to prove that the implicated federal statute authorizes their right to seek relief. The two shortcomings provide related, though alternative, bases for dismissal of this action.

The Animal Welfare Act is the federal statute on which plaintiffs rely in defining their allegations of mistreatment. The Act seeks to insure that "animals intended for use in research facilities ... are provided humane care and treatment." 7 U.S.C. § 2131(1). There is no indication, however, that Congress intended this goal to come at the expense of progress in medical research. To the contrary, both the language of the statute and the means chosen by Congress to enforce it preserve the hope that responsible primate research holds for the treatment and cure of humankind's most terrible afflictions. The statutory design is, in turn, inconsistent with the private right of action that plaintiffs assert.

The administrative enforcement that Congress envisioned for this statute is readily apparent.[1] The Act directs the Secretary of Agriculture to "promulgate standards to govern the humane handling, care, treatment, and transportation of animals," but cautions that "nothing in this chapter shall be construed as authorizing the Secretary to promulgate rules, regulations, or orders with regard to design, outlines, guidelines, or performance of actual research or experimentation by a research facility as determined by such research facility." 7 U.S.C. § 2143. * * * The Secretary may also remove an animal found to be suffering through the non-compliance of a laboratory—but only if the animal "is no longer required by the research facility to carry out the research, test, or experiment for which such animal has been utilized." Id. § 2146(a).

A review of the Act thus underscores two points. One is a commitment to administrative supervision of animal welfare. The other is the subordination of such supervision to the continued independence of research scientists. The Secretary's rulemaking authority does not extend to the design of experiments; the Secretary's enforcement authority does not extend to the confiscation of animals in use. In the words of Congress, "Under this bill the research scientist still holds the key to the laboratory door." H.R. Rep. No. 91–1651 (1966).

The amicus curiae brief of sixty-eight scientific and medical organizations reviews the history underlying these priorities. Research with primates helped to lead, for example, to the development of the polio vaccine, and other animal research has contributed to the discovery of insulin, the invention of transplantation techniques, and the improvement of cancer therapies. Amici predict that animal research will play some part in the prevention and treatment of such illnesses as multiple sclerosis, AIDS, and Alzheimer's disease. Recent amendments to the Animal Welfare Act have accordingly reaffirmed the congressional finding that "the use of animals is instrumental in certain research and education or for advancing knowledge of cures and treatments for diseases and injuries which afflict both humans and animals." H. Conf. Rep. No. 99–447 (1985).

Consistent with this purpose, Congress crafted a comprehensive plan for the regulation, inspection, and sanction of medical facilities that utilize animals in research. It is clear that the supervisory goals of the statute

1. Under the revised statute, enforcement by the Secretary of Agriculture will be supplemented by the requirement that each research facility appoint an Institutional Animal Committee, including at least one veterinarian and one person not affiliated with the facility, to monitor the treatment of animals. The committee will report uncorrected violations to the Department of Agriculture and to any federal agency that funds the research facility. 7 U.S.C. § 2143. This additional administrative system adopts for the Animal Welfare Act an approach that has been followed for many years by NIH.

were to be realized through a regime of administrative enforcement, with a right of judicial review for an aggrieved facility. It is equally clear that these goals were not to be realized through a succession of private lawsuits. * * *

The uniformity and specialization normally thought to accompany regulatory oversight, in this case that of the Secretary, would not inhere in enforcement of the statute through private rights of action. Judges and juries possess limited acquaintance with the problems and requirements of biomedical research. Their judgments and verdicts may fail to provide that modicum of consistency and predictability without which laboratory scientists would find it difficult to operate. To add extensive pre-trial discovery of a facility's practices to the administrative inspections already authorized by Congress would impose a gratuitous burden upon federally funded research. Finally, the prospect of damage awards in excess of the prescribed statutory penalties might discourage scientists from entering many lines of medical inquiry. * * * [W]e are convinced that Congress intended the administrative remedy to be the exclusive remedy. To accord plaintiffs standing to sue by virtue of a private cause of action would not conform to the aims of Congress in the Animal Welfare Act. * * *

NOTES AND QUESTIONS

1. *Other standing cases.* The Federal Laboratory Animal Welfare Act covers guinea pigs and hamsters, but not rats, mice, or birds. See Animal Legal Defense Fund, Inc. v. Espy, 23 F.3d 496 (D.C.Cir.1994) (concluding that the plaintiffs lacked standing to challenge the USDA's implementing regulation); see also Alternatives R & D Fdn. v. Glickman, 101 F.Supp.2d 7 (D.D.C.2000); cf. Animal Legal Defense Fund v. Shalala, 104 F.3d 424 (D.C.Cir.1997) (holding that the NAS committee responsible for revising the "Guide for the Care and Use of Laboratory Animals," which must be used by entities receiving NIH funding, was subject to the requirements of the Federal Advisory Committee Act); Progressive Animal Welfare Soc'y v. University of Wash., 790 P.2d 604 (Wash.1990). See generally Joshua E. Gardner, Note, At the Intersection of Constitutional Standing, Congressional Citizen–Suits, and the Humane Treatment of Animals: Proposals to Strengthen the Animal Welfare Act, 68 Geo. Wash. L. Rev. 330 (2000); D. Richard Joslyn, Annotation, Validity, Construction, and Application of Animal Welfare Act, 36 A.L.R. Fed. 627 (1978 & 2011 Supp.).

2. *No end in sight?* Efforts to find substitute testing methods have proceeded at a frustrating pace. See Gilbert M. Gaul, In U.S., Few Alternatives to Testing on Animals: Panel Has Produced 4 Options in 10 Years, Wash. Post, Apr. 12, 2008, at A1 (discussing widespread criticism of the work of the Interagency Coordinating Committee on the Validation of Alternative Methods). Indeed, animal testing may have to continue even after product approval. See id. ("[B]efore each batch is shipped, the manufacturer puts it through one of the oldest and most controversial animal tests available [i.e., LD_{50}]. To check the potency of its product under federal safety rules, Allergan Inc. injects mice with Botox until it finds a dose at which half of the animals die—a rough gauge of potential harm to humans."); see also Louis Jacobson, New Demands Spur Focus on Ancient Crab, Wash. Post, Mar. 17, 2003, at A9 (explaining that biomedical companies extract a chemical from the blood of horseshoe crabs for purposes of testing the safety of vaccines and implantable devices). The use of primates may, however, end soon. See Brian Vastag, Advances in Research May Help Spare Medical Chimps, Wash. Post, Aug. 14, 2011, at A1.

3. *Further commentary*. See Darian M. Ibrahim, Reduce, Refine, Replace: The Failure of the Three R's and the Future of Animal Experimentation, 2006 U. Chi. Legal Forum 195; Arthur B. LaFrance, Animal Experimentation: Lessons from Human Experimentation, 14 Animal L. 29 (2007); Martha C. Nussbaum, Animal Rights: The Need for a Theoretical Basis, 114 Harv. L. Rev. 1506 (2001) (book review); Shigehiko Ito, Comment, Beyond Standing: A Search for a New Solution in Animal Welfare, 46 Santa Clara L. Rev. 377 (2006); Lauren Magnotti, Note, Giving a Voice to Those Who Can't Speak for Themselves: Toward Greater Regulation of Animal Experimentation, 13 Buff. Envtl. L.J. 179 (2006).

The FDA has issued good laboratory practice (GLP) regulations that govern pre-clinical testing. See 21 C.F.R. pt. 58. If the results of such research are promising, then the sponsor may seek to test the investigational compound in humans. Because the FDCA prohibits the shipment of unapproved drugs in interstate commerce, pharmaceutical companies wishing to conduct tests of such items must seek an exemption under the investigational new drug (IND) provision of the Act:

> (1) The Secretary shall promulgate regulations for exempting from the operation of the foregoing subsections of this section drugs intended solely for investigational use by experts qualified by scientific training and experience to investigate the safety and effectiveness of drugs. Such regulations may, within the discretion of the Secretary, among other conditions relating to the public health, provide for conditioning such exemption upon—
>
> (A) the submission to the Secretary, before any clinical testing of a new drug is undertaken, of reports, by the manufacturer or the sponsor of the investigation of such drug, of preclinical tests (including tests on animals) of such drug adequate to justify the proposed clinical testing;
>
> (B) the manufacturer or the sponsor of the investigation of a new drug proposed to be distributed to investigators for clinical testing obtaining a signed agreement from each of such investigators that patients to whom the drug is administered will be under his personal supervision . . .; and

(C) the establishment and maintenance of such records, and the making of such reports to the Secretary, by the manufacturer or the sponsor of the investigation of such drug of data (including but not limited to analytical reports by investigators) obtained as the result of such investigational use of such drug ....

(4) ... Such regulations shall provide that such exemption shall be conditioned upon the manufacturer, or the sponsor of the investigation, requiring that experts using such drugs for investigational purposes certify to such manufacturer or sponsor that they will inform any human beings or their representatives that such drugs are being used for investigational purposes and will obtain the consent of such human beings or their representatives .... Nothing in the subsection shall be construed to require any clinical investigator to submit directly to the Secretary reports on the investigational use of drugs.

21 U.S.C. § 355(i). The FDA's implementing regulations cover issues such as control of the investigational drug, recordkeeping and investigator reports, and scrutiny by an institutional review board (IRB). See 21 C.F.R. pt. 312. "FDA's primary objectives in reviewing an IND are, in all phases of the investigation, to ensure the safety and rights of subjects, and in Phase 2 and 3, to help assure that the quality of the scientific evaluation of drugs is adequate to permit an evaluation of the drug's effectiveness and safety." Id. § 312.22(a). Unless the FDA raises an objection within 30 days of filing, the IND becomes effective.

The clinical investigation of a previously untested drug is divided into three phases. Although in general the phases are conducted sequentially, they may overlap. These three phases of an investigation are as follows:

(a) *Phase 1.*

(1) Phase 1 includes the initial introduction of an investigational new drug into humans. Phase 1 studies are typically closely monitored and may be conducted in patients or normal volunteer subjects. These studies are designed to determine the metabolism and pharmacologic actions of the drug in humans, the side effects associated with increasing doses, and, if possible, to gain early evidence on effectiveness. During Phase 1, sufficient information about the drug's pharmacokinetics and pharmacological effects should be obtained to permit the design of well-controlled, scientifically valid, Phase 2 studies. The total number of subjects and patients included in Phase 1 studies varies with the drug, but is generally in the range of 20 to 80.

(2) Phase 1 studies also include studies of drug metabolism, structure-activity relationships, and mechanism of action in humans, as well as studies in which investigational drugs are used as research tools to explore biological phenomena or disease processes.

(b) *Phase 2.* Phase 2 includes the controlled clinical studies conducted to evaluate the effectiveness of the drug for a particular indication or indications in patients with the disease or condition under study and to determine the common short-term side effects and risks associated

> with the drug. Phase 2 studies are typically well-controlled, closely monitored, and conducted in a relatively small number of patients, usually involving no more than several hundred subjects.
>
> (c) *Phase 3.* Phase 3 studies are expanded controlled and uncontrolled trials. They are performed after preliminary evidence suggesting effectiveness of the drug has been obtained, and are intended to gather the additional information about effectiveness and safety that is needed to evaluate the overall benefit-risk relationship of the drug and to provide an adequate basis for physician labeling. Phase 3 studies usually include from several hundred to several thousand subjects.

Id. § 312.21; see also Jürgen Drews, Drug Discovery: A Historical Perspective, 287 Science 1960 (2000); Richard J. Findlay, Originator Drug Development, 54 Food & Drug L.J. 227 (1999) (describing the drug development process, and providing estimates for the length of time typically required to complete each clinical trial phase); Justin A. Zivin, Understanding Clinical Trials, Sci. Am., Apr. 2000, at 69. The testing of experimental biological products must abide by the same regulatory requirements as other investigational drugs. See 21 C.F.R. § 601.25.

Phase I clinical trials occasionally cause serious injury to healthy volunteers. See, e.g., Elisabeth Rosenthal, British Rethinking Test Rules After Drug Trial Nearly Kills Six, N.Y. Times, Apr. 8, 2006, at A1 ("Although tests of [the monoclonal antibody] TGN1412 in monkeys showed no significant trouble, all six human subjects nearly died."). Conversely, because of their relatively short duration, narrow subject population, and small size, clinical trials of investigational drugs may fail to uncover rare or delayed adverse reactions. See Reporting Adverse Drug and Medical Device Events: Report of the AMA's Council on Ethical and Judicial Affairs, 49 Food & Drug L.J. 359, 360 (1994) (explaining that studies typically will detect only acute adverse reactions that occur at a rate of 1–in–1000 or higher). In addition, clinical trials historically have enrolled unrepresentative samples of patient populations. See Ken Getz & Doug Peddicord, Tuskegee, a Cloud Over Research: Minorities Are Not Participating Enough in Clinical Trials, Wash. Post, Sept. 30, 2008, at F5 ("African American, Latino and Asian populations account for about one-third of all Americans, but less than one-tenth of U.S. clinical trial participants come from these groups."); Roni C. Rabin, Aging: Trials Exclude Patients Who May Benefit, N.Y. Times, Feb. 15, 2011, at D6 (discussing elderly subjects). For instance, researchers traditionally excluded women of child-bearing age from studies of investigational drugs. See R. Alta Charo, Protecting Us to Death: Women, Pregnancy, and Clinical Research Trials, 38 St. Louis U. L.J. 135 (1993). The FDA has issued a series of guidelines to encourage the inclusion of so-called "special populations" in clinical trials in an effort to combat this problem.

In the future, advances in our understanding of genetics (coupled with more powerful information technologies) may help to streamline clinical trials. See Lars Noah, The Coming Pharmacogenomics Revolution: Tailoring Drugs to Fit Patients' Genetic Profiles, 43 Jurimetrics J. 1, 12 (2002)

("At present, when clinical trials produce equivocal results, sponsors may engage in statistical analyses designed to stratify the subject population in the hopes of identifying some subset in which the investigational product worked without causing unacceptable side effects. Pharmacogenetics could replace this brute force method with a more refined biological tool for making such cuts earlier in the process."); see also Barbara Binzak, How Pharmacogenomics Will Impact the Federal Regulation of Clinical Trials and the New Drug Approval Process, 58 Food & Drug L.J. 103 (2003); Janet Woodcock, FDA Policy on Pharmacogenomic Data in Drug Development, 66 La. L. Rev. 91 (2005); Christopher Rowland, Drug Makers Revamping Clinical–Trial System: New Test Strategies Focus on Weeding out Duds Sooner, Boston Globe, Dec. 21, 2004, at C1 (reporting that sponsors hope to identify biomarkers in order to gauge potential efficacy in Phase I trials). Apart from possible pharmacogenomic approaches, the agency has begun to show signs of greater flexibility in the allowable design of clinical trials. See Anna W. Mathews, FDA Signals It's Open to Drug Trials That Shift Midcourse, Wall St. J., July 10, 2006, at B1 (describing so-called "adaptive" trials); Guidelines to Help Drug Researchers, N.Y. Times, Jan. 13, 2006, at C4 (explaining that the FDA may allow what amount to pre-Phase I (exploratory) trials using microdoses in human subjects); see also Jamie L. Aldes, Note, The FDA Clinical Trial Process: Effectuating Change in the Regulatory Framework Governing Clinical Trials to Account for the Historical Shift from "Traditional" to "New" Phase I Trials, 18 Health Matrix 463 (2008).

United States v. Palazzo

558 F.3d 400 (5th Cir.2009).

■ STEWART, CIRCUIT JUDGE:

* * * Dr. [Maria Carmen] Palazzo was a duly licensed medical doctor specializing in psychiatry, with offices located in New Orleans * * * * [SmithKline Beecham hired her as an] investigator to carry out clinical studies to evaluate the efficacy and safety of Paxil in children and adolescents with obsessive-compulsive disorder. Dr. Palazzo received $5,410 for each subject who completed the study and agreed to review personally all case report forms regarding each study subject. * * * Dr. Palazzo did not comply with the criteria to provide satisfactory research records, and her contracts to participate in the drug studies were terminated. * * *

This appeal concerns the fifteen counts [of an indictment] for violating 21 U.S.C. § 355(i) and 21 C.F.R. § 312.62(b) for failure to properly prepare and maintain records with intent to defraud and mislead. Counts 41 through 52 include allegations of inaccuracies in Dr. Palazzo's psychiatric evaluations of subjects participating in the Paxil studies. These counts allege that Dr. Palazzo's psychiatric evaluations stated that subjects suffered from disorders when the subjects had not been diagnosed with the disorders. Counts 53 through 55 allege that Dr. Palazzo reported examining a subject, when in fact she did not personally examine the subject. The district court granted Dr. Palazzo's motion to dismiss counts 41 through 55 based on the nondelegation doctrine. * * *

[In *United States v. Smith,* 740 F.2d 734 (9th Cir.1984), the] court found that the statute placed the burden for record-keeping and reporting requirements on only manufacturers and sponsors. The court stated that the general authorization language contained in the statute to be "insufficient legislative guidance for the issuance of regulations which, if violated, would furnish the basis for criminal liability." Id. at 738. Ultimately, the court found § 355(i) to be ambiguous as applied to clinical investigators, invoked the rule of lenity,[2] and affirmed the district court's dismissal of the indictment against the defendant clinical investigator. * * *

[In *United States v. Garfinkel,* 29 F.3d 451 (8th Cir.1994), the court] analyzed § 355(i) and held the language of the statute to be ambiguous as it related to the FDA's authority over clinical investigators. Id. at 456. * * * [The] court reviewed § 355(i)'s legislative history and held that § 355(i) authorized the promulgation of clinical investigator record-keeping regulations. Id. at 457. * * * Ultimately, the court disagreed with what it characterized as the Ninth Circuit's determination [in *Smith*] that the statute violated the nondelegation doctrine and held that "the standards enunciated by the Act, along with judicial review and the procedural requirements dictated by the APA, impose[d] sufficient restraints upon FDA to satisfy the constitutional concerns underlying the nondelegation doctrine." Id. at 459. * * *

Dr. Palazzo concedes that the FDA has authority to impose record-keeping requirements on clinical investigators through regulations and properly did so through 21 C.F.R. § 312.62. If the parties questioned whether § 355(i) provided *sufficient guidance* for the FDA to promulgate regulations requiring clinical investigators to adhere to certain record-keeping requirements, the nondelegation doctrine would be an issue in this case. * * * The sole issue on appeal in the instant case, however, is whether 21 U.S.C. §§ 351(e) and 355(i) allow the imposition of criminal penalties on clinical investigators who violate the record-keeping requirements found in 21 C.F.R. § 312.62. This issue involves the scope of § 355(i), not the FDA's authority to promulgate regulations * * * *

Dr. Palazzo argues that § 355(i) only provides criminal sanctions for manufacturers and sponsors of clinical investigational studies. Therefore, she concludes that she cannot be held criminally liable for violating §§ 331(e) and 355(i) because she is not a manufacturer or sponsor of an investigational study. Dr. Palazzo maintains that the only permissible or lawful penalty for failure to adhere to these record-keeping requirements is disqualification from other investigational studies, a stated penalty within the FDA regulations. In addition, Dr. Palazzo argues that § 355(i) only gives the Secretary the authority to grant exemptions from criminal liabili-

---

2. "The rule of lenity provides that 'when a choice must be made between two readings of what conduct Congress has made a crime, it is appropriate, before choosing the harsher alternative, to require that Congress should have spoken in language that is clear and definite.' " United States v. Orellana, 405 F.3d 360, 370 (5th Cir.2005).

ty, not the authority to impose criminal liability on clinical investigators who violate the FDA's properly promulgated regulations. * * *

Based on the text of the statute, it is clear that § 355(i) addresses three separate issues regarding clinical drug testing. First, § 355(i) explicitly requires the Secretary of [HHS] to promulgate regulations providing exemptions of drugs for research from earlier subsections contained in 21 U.S.C. § 355, which regulate "new drugs." Second, § 355(i) allows the Secretary, in his/her discretion, to issue regulations regarding those exemptions in an effort to "protect[] the public health." Section 355(i) provides a non-exhaustive list of conditions upon which the Secretary may provide exemptions. Third, § 355(i) provides requirements for sponsors and manufacturers to make direct reports to the Secretary and explicitly states that clinical investigators are not required to submit reports directly to the Secretary.

On its face, § 355(i) does not provide criminal liability for sponsors and manufacturers of investigational drug studies or clinical investigators. Violations of § 355(i) are prohibited in 21 U.S.C. § 331(e), and criminal penalties for violating § 331(e) are found in 21 U.S.C. § 333(a). In addition, § 355(i) does not contain an explicit requirement governing the conduct of clinical investigators. The record-keeping and reporting requirements applicable to clinical investigators are contained in the regulations promulgated by the FDA in accordance with the authority given the FDA by Congress. Thus, we must turn to §§ 331(e) and 333 and the FDA's regulations concerning clinical investigators to determine whether clinical investigators are subject to criminal liability for failing to adhere to certain record-keeping and reporting requirements. * * *

[21 C.F.R. §] 312.62(b) provides requirements for clinical investigators, like Dr. Palazzo, "to prepare and maintain adequate and accurate case histories that record all observations and other data pertinent to the investigation on each individual administered the investigational drug." * * * [21 U.S.C.] § 331(e) prohibits a failure to establish or maintain *any* record, or make *any* report, required under § 355(i), but § 331(e) does not limit its prohibition only to reports required to be made directly to the Secretary. Section 355(i) allows the Secretary to establish reporting requirements, and the Secretary promulgated regulations specific to investigators in 21 C.F.R § 312.62(b). These are properly considered to be "required" reporting and record-keeping requirements under § 331(e), as § 355(i) allows the Secretary discretionary authority to issue regulations in an effort to protect the public health. The penalties for violating § 331(e) are found in 21 U.S.C. § 333, and specifically state that those violating § 331(e) "shall be imprisoned for not more than one year or fined not more than $1,000, or both." 21 U.S.C. § 333(a)(1). * * *

Thus, reviewing [21 C.F.R.] § 312.62(b) in conjunction with [21 U.S.C.] §§ 355(i), 331(e), and 333(a)(1) makes it apparent that the scope of the statute allows clinical investigators to be subjected to criminal liability. For the foregoing reasons, the district court's dismissal of counts 41 through 55 is reversed and remanded * * * *

NOTES AND QUESTIONS

1. *Keeping tabs on investigators*. For a critique of the court's analysis, see Megan S. Peterson, Casenote, Clinical Book–Cooking: United States v. Palazzo and the Dilemma of Attaching Criminal Liability to Experimental Drug Investigators for Faulty Record–Keeping, 56 Loy. L. Rev. 311, 329–36 (2010); id. at 332 ("Only after the court drew connections among multiple statutory provisions did the hazy lines of criminality begin to appear. If engaging in a particular course of action creates criminal liability, such a harsh penalty requires communication by express statutory language."); see also United States v. Keplinger, 776 F.2d 678 (7th Cir.1985) (prosecution for fraudulent animal testing of drugs). Are criminal proceedings against investigators the most appropriate response to failures to abide by FDA regulations? One alternative is to disqualify clinical investigators who have violated IND requirements. See 21 C.F.R. § 312.70. Can't the agency also accomplish its purpose by targeting the sponsor in cases of noncompliance by investigators? Cf. Gardiner Harris & Janet Roberts, After Sanctions, Doctors Get Drug Company Pay, N.Y. Times, June 3, 2007, § 1, at 1 (reporting that sponsors sometimes hire physicians with disciplinary problems as investigators). Doesn't the FDA otherwise risk unduly interfering in the practice of medicine? The agency attracted criticism for approving the antibiotic Ketek® partly on the strength of a clinical trial even after it had found instances of fraud that led to the successful prosecution of a researcher. See Marc Kaufman, Senator's HHS Trip for Antibiotic Data Yields Only Ire, Wash. Post, June 15, 2006, at A10.

2. *Constitutional rights of researchers*. Recall from Chapter 1(E)(2) the *Whalen* Court's rejection of the physicians' argument that New York's recordkeeping requirements violated their privacy-based right to practice medicine without interference. Commentators long have debated whether scientists enjoy First Amendment protection to engage in research free from governmental interference, and these issues resurfaced in the face of calls for greater governmental supervision of research that might have malevolent uses. See Rick Weiss, Terror Risk Screening of Bioresearch Urged, Wash. Post, Oct. 9, 2003, at A9. See generally Dana R. Irwin, Freedom of Thought: The First Amendment and the Scientific Method, 2005 Wis. L. Rev. 1479; Barry P. McDonald, Government Regulation or Other "Abridgements" of Scientific Research: The Proper Scope of Judicial Review Under the First Amendment, 54 Emory L.J. 979 (2005); Steve Keane, Note, The Case Against Blanket First Amendment Protection of Scientific Research: Articulating a More Limited Scope of Protection, 59 Stan. L. Rev. 505 (2006).

3. *Medical devices*. For investigational devices, a process roughly parallel to the IND approach described above governs how manufacturers may begin the testing process in humans. As explained in Chapter 3(B), different categories of medical devices require different levels of pre-market investigation. To the extent that human testing is required for an application to market a new device, the manufacturer must request an investigational device exemption (IDE) permitting limited distribution of the new device for use in clinical trials. See 21 U.S.C. § 360j(g); 21 C.F.R. pt. 812. (IDEs for devices that do not pose a significant risk need not be reviewed by the FDA—a sponsor need only secure IRB approval.)

> [I]nvestigational devices are ... subject to a ... set of complex and comprehensive regulations which set forth detailed procedures for determining whether investigational devices are safe and effective. To obtain approval of a device under the IDE, a manufacturer must submit an application to the FDA containing an abundance of information.... [T]he manufacturer must submit a detailed statement regarding the intended use of the device and the objectives and planned duration of the investigational study; a written protocol describing the methodology to be used and an analysis of the protocol demonstrating that the investigation is scientifically sound; an analysis of all risks involved; a description of each component, ingredient, property, and principle of operation of the device; a detailed description of the methods, facilities and controls used for manufacturing, processing, packing, storing and installing the device; sample agreements between the manufacturers and all proposed investigators; detailed information about the health care professionals and institutions participating in the investigation; proposed labeling; proposed informed consent forms; and a full set of written procedures for monitoring the investigation, including record and report maintenance. Pursuant to 21 C.F.R. § 812.27, the manufacturer must submit a bibliography of every publication relevant to the evaluation of the device and information from non-clinical testing. Based on the information submitted, the FDA will approve the device under the IDE unless "the risks to the subjects are not outweighed by the anticipated benefits to the subjects and the importance of the knowledge to be gained, or informed consent is inadequate, or the investigation is scientifically unsound, or there is reason to believe that the device as used is ineffective."

Martin v. Telectronics Pacing Sys., Inc., 105 F.3d 1090, 1095–96 (6th Cir. 1997). As revealed in the excerpts that follow, even this fairly precise regulatory process for the testing of experimental products poses some challenges for all parties concerned—manufacturers, prospective beneficiaries of the new products, regulatory agencies, and the courts.

Femrite v. Abbott Northwestern Hospital

568 N.W.2d 535 (Minn.Ct.App.1997).

■ HARTEN, JUSTICE:

Appellants Cary Femrite and Ruth Perkl underwent spinal fusion surgery that involved implantation with pedicle screw devices at respondent Abbott Northwestern Hospital. In December 1989, Femrite was implanted with a screw device known as the "VSP" or "Stefee" system manufactured by AcroMed. In February 1990, Perkl was implanted with a screw device known as the "Cotrel Dubousset" manufactured by Sofamor Danek. At the time of surgery, neither appellant was informed that the surgery was experimental or that implantation of the screw device in pedicles was investigational. Both appellants experienced complications and medical problems after receiving the implants. * * *

To enable a manufacturer to obtain necessary clinical data for FDA premarket approval, the FDA grants an Investigational Device Exemption (IDE), which permits a device (that would ordinarily require premarket approval) to be "shipped lawfully for the purpose of conducting investigations of that device." An "investigation" is defined as "a clinical investigation or research involving one or more subjects to determine the safety and effectiveness of a device." A hospital may not initiate investigational studies under an IDE without approval and oversight by a hospital's institutional review board (IRB). An IRB is a committee designed to review biomedical research involving patients. * * *

Appellants argue that the district court erred when it dismissed their claims based on Abbott's alleged negligence in performing its administrative functions. Appellants contend that Abbott allowed physicians to make spinal implantation of screw devices outside an approved IDE in violation of federal law, that Abbott violated state law by failing to obtain informed consent, and that Abbott failed to comply with its own internal case management policies. All of appellants' claims, however, depend on the single premise that it was unlawful for Abbott to allow physicians to use the screw devices in appellants' spinal surgeries. Thus, our determination hinges on whether federal law limited implantation of the screw device in spinal surgeries to investigational usage or simultaneously permitted it to be implanted into spinal pedicles as an "off-label" use. * * *

The district court determined that appellants failed to state a cause of action for negligence per se because appellants "were not participants in a clinical investigation or a research study." Appellants insist that the district court's disposition of this claim "begs the question" because they contend the screw device was an investigational device that could be used only within the context of a clinical investigation. * * * [T]he record is devoid of evidence to support appellants' assertion that in 1986 the FDA approved use of the screw devices for arms and legs, but specifically prohibited their use in spines.

Appellants also submit a 1995 FDA letter authorizing the use of the screw device * * * only for patients with severe spondylolisthesis. Appellants point out that the FDA letter authorizing use of the device for spondylolisthesis indicates that other uses of the device are considered investigational and could occur lawfully only pursuant to an approved IDE. Thus, appellants suggest that if spondylolisthesis is absent, the screw device may be implanted into spinal pedicles only within clinical investigations.

Abbott, on the other hand, argues that the use of the screw devices here was an "off-label" use because the FDA had already approved the device for use in long and flat bones. Abbott contends that implantation of the screw device in spinal fixation surgeries is an "off-label" use, and as such, involves medical discretion, which is beyond FDA regulation. * * *

To support their argument that "off-label" use of the screw devices was permitted, Abbott submitted an affidavit of James Benson, former Acting FDA Commissioner and Deputy Commissioner. Benson's affidavit states that "off-label" use is a "longstanding and common practice which has been acknowledged by the FDA." Benson's affidavit also states that use of screw devices in the pedicles of the spine did not violate FDA regulations or policy as of December 1992 (when he left the FDA).

Appellants nevertheless contend that it is anomalous to suggest that the screw device could be implanted in patients within the scope of clinical investigations—which were being conducted at Abbott at the time of appellants' surgeries—and at the same time lawfully be implanted into other patients who were not participating in the investigations. Appellants deny that physicians could consider "off-label" usage to be a standard of care in some cases and simultaneously investigational in others.

The record, however, demonstrates otherwise. In 1986, AcroMed received 510(k) approval to market bone screws or plates as a Class II device for use in long bones such as those in arms and legs. Given that approval, physicians could permissibly implant the screw device elsewhere in the body as an "off-label" use, albeit the approval was for use in arms and legs; nevertheless, manufacturers were not permitted to market the device for such usage because of the 1984 and 1985 FDA classification of the device as Class III investigational for pedicle spine usage. Manufacturers of the screws and plates for long, flat bones apparently sought authority to market these products for use as pedicle screw devices. To that end, the same manufacturers that received 510(k) approval to market their screw device for one purpose (long and flat bones) also requested FDA approval to conduct clinical investigations in their quest for eventual FDA approval to market the same screw device as a pedicle screw device. Therefore, a hospital could acquire the same device from a manufacturer either through routine commercial means for "off-label" use or as an investigational device under an IDE. * * * FDA "encourages surgeons using pedicle screw devices to enroll their patients in such approved clinical investigations." There is no evidence, however, that such enrollment is required. * * * [W]e conclude as a matter of law that the physicians' implantation of the screw devices in appellants' surgeries was a permissible "off-label" use not in violation of FDA regulations. Accordingly, we affirm summary judgment on appellants' FDA regulation negligence per se claims. * * *

NOTES AND QUESTIONS

1. *Informed consent at common law.* Might the conduct described in *Femrite* still amount to negligence even if not forbidden by the FDA? Although some courts require that physicians disclose to patients the fact that a treatment remains experimental, others have rejected informed consent claims premised on the failure to reveal a product's regulatory status. See, e.g., Southard v. Temple Univ. Hosp., 781 A.2d 101, 107–08 (Pa.2001); see also Lars Noah, Informed Consent and the Elusive Dichotomy Between Standard and Experimental Therapy, 28 Am. J.L. & Med. 361, 370–79 (2002) (summarizing tort doctrine applicable to the research setting). For a similar recent incident, see Deborah L. Shelton & Jason Grotto, Patients at Heart of Device Debate: Many Unaware of Potential Doctor Conflicts of Interest, Chi. Trib., May 23, 2011, at A1 (reporting that hundreds of patients undergoing heart valve repair at Northwestern hospital received annuloplasty rings invented by their cardiac surgeon unaware that the FDA had not yet cleared this device).

2. *The fine line between research and the practice of medicine*. Recall from Chapter 1(C) that the court in *Evers* rejected an FDA misbranding action against a physician who engaged in the off-label use of Calcium EDTA for the treatment of arteriosclerosis, while the court in *Retkwa* sustained a negligence per se claim in a medical malpractice case against a cosmetic surgeon for injecting liquid silicone, which had not yet received FDA approval for any use in patients. When does off-label use amount to experimentation? See Ancheff v. Hartford Hosp., 799 A.2d 1067, 1071–72, 1082 (Conn. 2002) (affirming a jury's conclusion that a hospital's protocol for off-label use of an antibiotic did not qualify as research); Sandra G. Boodman, Off Label, Off Base? Many Drug Uses Don't Rest on Strong Science, Wash. Post, May 23, 2006, at F1; Rita Rubin, More Studies Urged for Off–Label Drugs, USA Today, Nov. 25, 2008, at 7D; Bernadette Tansey, A Patient's Right to Know: How Much Should Doctors Disclose About Treatments Not Approved by the FDA?, S.F. Chron., May 1, 2005, at A1. In addition, recognize that no federal regulatory regime exists to control the introduction of novel medical procedures. See Anna C. Mastroianni, Liability, Regulation and Policy in Surgical Innovation: The Cutting Edge of Research and Therapy, 16 Health Matrix 351 (2006); Amer S. Ahmed, Note, The Last Twist of the Knife: Encouraging the Regulation of Innovative Surgical Procedures, 105 Colum. L. Rev. 1529 (2005). The FDA's IND regulations define "clinical investigation" as "any experiment in which a drug is administered or dispensed to, or used involving, one or more human subjects. For purposes of this part, an experiment is any use of a drug *except* for the use of a marketed drug in the course of medical practice." 21 C.F.R. § 312.3(b) (emphasis added). Should the existence of an IND or IDE for a new use of a previously approved product alter the FDA's usual policy of tolerating off-label uses? Why is an IND or IDE even required before undertaking clinical trials of a new use if the product already may lawfully move in interstate commerce? What if the agency had specifically rejected an application for an investigational exception for that use?

B. SUPERVISING RESEARCH

Institutional review boards function primarily as protectors of human subjects who participate in medical research of all sorts. At the same time, IRBs play an essential role in the approval process for new medical products. By overseeing research protocols to test the safety and effectiveness of experimental drugs and medical devices, IRBs enable clinical researchers to collect the data necessary for a thorough FDA assessment of new products. IRBs review and then supervise protocols involving the use of investigational drugs and medical devices, as well as other types of clinical research.

Several ethical codes provide guidance for clinical researchers. The Nuremberg Code, which emerged out of the trials of Nazi physicians after World War II, sets out a series of essential principles for permissible medical experiments. See 276 JAMA 1691 (1996); see also George J. Annas, The Legacy of the Nuremberg Doctors' Trial to American Bioethics and Human Rights, 10 Minn. J.L. Sci. & Tech. 19 (2009). In 1964, the World Medical Association adopted the Declaration of Helsinki, which provides additional guidance. See 277 JAMA 925 (1997). The American Medical Association also has issued guidelines on clinical research.

These codes and guidelines provided the underpinnings for the first formal regulations governing human research, which were originally issued in 1974 by the Department of Health, Education, and Welfare (the predecessor of HHS). See 30 Fed. Reg. 18,914 (1974) (codified as amended at 45 C.F.R. pt. 46). Seven years later, the FDA promulgated its regulations, which are excerpted below. See 46 Fed. Reg. 8942 (1981) (codified as amended at 21 C.F.R. pts. 50 & 56). Both the FDA and the NIH's Office of Human Research Protections (OHRP) have the authority to inspect and suspend research activities at institutions that receive federal funding. When inspectors suspend research activities at an institution, most projects in progress must cease immediately. See 21 C.F.R. § 56.121. Institutions that receive HHS funding must provide the Department with an "assurance" that all research conducted at the institution, regardless of the source of funding, will protect human subjects according to the principles in the regulations. See 45 C.F.R. § 46.103. The FDA's regulations apply to all studies of investigational drugs, medical devices, and biological products. The two sets of regulations are for the most part co-extensive, and, because most research institutions receive federal funding for at least some of the work being done under their roofs, IRBs generally hold all research protocols to the standards set out in these regulations. See Jesse A. Goldner, An Overview of Legal Controls on Human Experimentation and the Regulatory Implications of Taking Professor Katz Seriously, 38 St. Louis U. L.J. 63 (1993); see also Richard A. Epstein, The Erosion of Individual Autonomy in Medical Decisionmaking: Of the FDA and IRBs, 96 Geo. L.J. 559 (2008); Barbara J. Evans & Eric M. Meslin, Encouraging Translational Research Through Harmonization of FDA and Common Rule Informed Consent Requirements for Research with Banked Specimens, 27 J. Legal Med. 119 (2006); David Brown, Rule Update for Human–Subject Research, Wash. Post, July 24, 2011, at A6 (describing proposed revisions).

NOTES AND QUESTIONS

1. *IRB membership.* The regulations set out the minimum requirements for the composition of an IRB. See 21 C.F.R. § 56.107. The regulation requires that each IRB have at least five members, with varying backgrounds to promote complete review of research activities commonly conducted by the institution. In addition, it addresses issues of expertise and diversity, requiring that the IRB's membership reflect "consideration of race, gender, cultural backgrounds, and sensitivity to such issues as community attitudes, to promote respect for its advice and counsel in safeguarding the rights and welfare of human subjects." The regulation also refers to the need to include board members who are "able to ascertain the acceptability of proposed research in terms of institutional commitments and regulations, applicable law, and standards or professional conduct and practice" (lawyers, perhaps?). It requires the inclusion of persons knowledgeable about vulnerable categories of subjects, such as children, prisoners, pregnant women, or handicapped or mentally disabled persons, if the IRB will be reviewing research involving such subjects. Finally, IRBs must consist of members of more than one profession, must have members of both sexes, and must have at least one non-scientist member and one member who is not otherwise affiliated with the research institution. One member may, of course, fulfill several of these roles simultaneously on a small IRB.

2. *IRB autonomy and supervisory authority*. Once an IRB has approved a research protocol, the parent institution has the authority to subject the protocol to additional review, if desired, but an institution may not approve research that has already been rejected by the IRB. See 21 C.F.R. § 56.112. If clinical investigators fail to comply with requirements or deviate from an approved protocol, an IRB has the authority to suspend or terminate approval of the project. If the board suspends or terminates approval under these circumstances, it must report its actions immediately to the principal investigator, institution officials, and the FDA. See id. § 56.113.

3. *Reviewing the reviewers*. Surveys have found major deficiencies in IRB review and oversight at major research institutions. See Jon Cohen, Clinical Trial Monitoring: Hit or Miss?, 264 Science 1534, 1536 (1994) (explaining that, in over 3,000 IRB site inspections conducted between 1977 and 1994, the FDA found informed consent problems at over half of the inspected sites and deviations from approved study protocols at 29% of the sites); see also Hazel G. Beh, The Role of Institutional Review Boards in Protecting Human Subjects: Are We Really Ready to Fix a Broken System?, 26 Law & Psychol. Rev. 1 (2002); Ken Gatter, Fixing Cracks: A Discourse Norm to Repair the Crumbling Regulatory Structure Supporting Clinical Research and Protecting Human Subjects, 73 UMKC L. Rev. 581 (2005); Michael A. Morse et al., Monitoring and Ensuring Safety During Clinical Research, 285 JAMA 1201 (2001); FDA Announces New Initiative to Modernize the Regulation of Clinical Trials and Bioresearch Monitoring, Press Release P06–86, June 26, 2006. The FDA inspected and temporarily shut down a number of IRBs at well-regarded research institutions because of non-compliance with regulatory requirements governing human research. Don't forget that most IRBs are not federal government entities. Apart from the NIH's in-house IRBs, most of these boards are affiliated with state-run or private hospitals. Is it appropriate for the FDA to delegate quasi-regulatory functions to such entities? The inevitable ambiguities in the regulations result in potentially inconsistent and inexpert interpretations by IRBs.

4. *Putting IRBs in their place.* One commentator took the language appearing at the end of the immediately preceding note (unchanged from the first edition) to heart (and somewhat out of context) in the course of arguing that IRBs should strive to function more like judicial bodies, see Carl H. Coleman, Rationalizing Risk Assessment in Human Subject Research, 46 Ariz. L. Rev. 1 (2004), which prompted the following response:

Lars Noah, *Deputizing Institutional Review Boards to Police (Audit?) Biomedical Research*

25 J. LEGAL MED. 267 (2004).

In a provocative new article dealing with institutional review boards (IRBs), Professor Carl Coleman explains that these entities sometimes do an inadequate job of reviewing protocols for clinical trials, particularly in failing to make careful "risk assessments" when they approve proposed research involving human subjects. As I commented in a recent article on a related question:

> IRBs may become preoccupied with reviewing the niceties of the consent form and perhaps less concerned about their separate obligation to make independent risk-benefit assessments about the research protocol, confident that potential subjects can "vote with their feet" so long as the consent form contains all of the necessary information.

This is a terribly important point that other commentators have failed to emphasize.

In identifying the root causes of this problem, however, Coleman has misunderstood the intended role of IRBs, and his proposed solutions may do more harm than good. Recasting these boards as adjudicatory bodies may appeal to those with training in the law, but the scientists and physicians who staff IRBs will predictably—and I think appropriately—recoil at any such suggestion. These boards cannot function properly if asked to operate in the fashion of the judiciary.

Coleman devotes a good deal of his article to explaining the advantages of analogical reasoning (what bioethicists evidently like to call "casuistry"), and then proposes different ways to encourage IRBs to do more of it and less of what he suggests is now an essentially visceral—even arbitrary—review process. In the abstract, analogical reasoning has much to commend it, and members of IRBs probably do plenty of it already, though perhaps in a way that a lawyer would regard as unacceptably informal and insufficiently rigorous.

It is entirely unrealistic and unwise, however, to demand more structured analogical reasoning from IRBs using Coleman's suggestions for mandatory opinion writing, some form of appellate scrutiny, an obligation to abide by precedent, and the issuance of general guidelines after public hearings. * * * In fact, one might uncharitably argue that Coleman's article serves as an exemplar of the pitfalls associated with unsophisticated analogical reasoning—he contends that IRBs should act less like juries and more like appellate courts without ever once recognizing that these boards much more closely (and appropriately) resemble peer review mechanisms utilized by the scientific community.

This article does not focus on the details of IRB operations, a subject that has received ample attention from other commentators, some of whom have first-hand experience as members of such boards, and others (myself included) who have relied entirely on second-hand information. Coleman's recommendations for improving IRB functions probably will strike many commentators of the former stripe as wildly unrealistic, but this article instead emphasizes his failure to situate these boards correctly among the full range of decision making models. After clarifying the nature of risk-benefit assessment in protocol reviews and challenging suggested parallels to the role of juries in litigation, this article explains that efforts to promote consistency and transparency do not necessitate mimicking the judiciary. A better appreciation of how IRBs compare to a variety of related entities should lead to a more plausible set of suggestions for reform. * * *

IRBs do not * * * resemble juries except in the most superficial of ways. For the most part, these boards consist of individuals with expertise generally relevant to the questions under review, their members may become actively involved in the process of acquiring information relevant to their decisions, and they enjoy some measure of continuity over time. Their discussions and voting processes resemble jury deliberations no more closely than any number of other settings where groups meet to make decisions, ranging from condominium associations to faculty committees. Remarkably, Coleman goes so far as to suggest that the "jury system may do a better job than IRBs at weighing risks and benefits." For instance, he mentions the profound differences in expertise almost as an afterthought and then argues that this expertise may make IRBs worse than juries. * * * Although they may have valuable insights to offer about the clarity of informed consent documents, laypersons have absolutely no business making judgments about the merits of particular experimental designs or the characterization of uncertain risks and benefits to subjects. * * *

Coleman repeatedly refers to the lack of any appellate scrutiny as granting IRBs unreviewable discretion, but this intentional feature of the arrangement actually promotes the goal of human subject protection. Although academic and other institutions that house IRBs may choose to review board decisions (perhaps at the behest of a patient advocate even though no formal mechanism exists for challenging board decisions to approve a protocol), the regulations expressly prevent these institutions from overriding an IRB decision to reject a protocol. This asymmetry in granting unreviewable discretion may embolden boards by partially insulating them from the prospect of institutional pressures to placate disgruntled researchers or private sponsors. * * *

Coleman argues that IRB decisions should strive to emulate appellate decision making—a model that law professors in particular seem to favor because of its familiarity. Whether or not IRBs currently operate too much like juries, his suggestion for improved risk-benefit assessment in biomedical research seems seriously misguided for a number of reasons: it exaggerates the centrality of IRBs in existing systems of human subject protection, it incorrectly adopts a court-centered view of the processes used by other regulatory institutions, and it fails to appreciate some of the countervailing advantages of an underproceduralized decision making model. * * *

IRBs represent only one of several layers of protection against unethical and potentially dangerous research on human subjects. As Coleman concedes, many studies that reach an IRB grow out of federal grants, which have already undergone scrutiny by the National Institutes of Health (NIH) or other funding agency, but then he hastens to add that "privately funded research is often not subjected to any oversight other than the process of IRB review." Actually, most of the research that receives support from private industry requires initial clearance by the Food and Drug Administration (FDA), through an application for an investigational new drug (IND) or an investigational device exemption (IDE). * * *

Thus, one would hope that palpably foolish research would get nixed right from the start, even if unacceptably dangerous studies sometimes get past these initial efforts at screening. One also would hope that researchers at academic institutions have the sense to design clinical trials in ways that minimize the risk of injury to subjects and maximize the likely benefits to society, though here again the historical record—including some widely publicized recent mishaps—does not inspire confidence in relying entirely on an honor system. The FDA and the Department of Health and Human Services (HHS) occasionally do check up on IRBs, but not in the sense of reviewing particular decisions to approve protocols (at least not unless a scandal comes to light). Instead, the agencies spot-check IRBs for adherence to general procedural requirements, while sponsors of investigational products must select monitors to supervise clinical trials and notify the FDA of any problems that arise.

Checks exist at the back-end of the process as well, which may help to discourage lapses in the first place. The FDA retains the power to place a "clinical hold" on previously approved research if problems emerge. In addition, the agency will not review clinical trials in support of a licensing application if they failed to comply with human subject protection rules. For other types of studies, researchers presumably will hope to publish their results. The editors of prestigious biomedical journals have taken a more active role in trying to regulate the nature of research underlying the articles that they publish, which means that scientists eager for fame and fortune (or tenure) might take their responsibilities more seriously.

Finally, the threat of tort liability imposed on researchers or their institutions may encourage increased vigilance in the future. Coleman dismisses the deterrent potential of tort liability in this context by noting that subjects will have difficulty distinguishing any alleged injury from the sequelae of their underlying disease. By that logic, we also should dismiss any deterrent function for medical malpractice liability. Although good reasons exist to question this role for tort law in the context of either research or treatment, it has little or nothing to do with obstacles to proving causation. In short, IRBs operate within a larger context that both checks their decisions and provides alternative safeguards for human subjects.

Coleman explicitly "starts with the premise that IRBs are engaged in a process of *legal* decision-making, insofar as they are interpreting specific regulatory requirements pursuant to authority that has been delegated to them by administrative agencies." Although he quotes part of a sentence from my recently published casebook as support for this proposition, I must take issue with his premise. In fact, the clause in question comes from one of those thought questions that law students find so annoying: "Is it appropriate for the FDA to delegate quasi-regulatory functions to such entities?" Perhaps the term "quasi" should have been underscored to draw attention to the fact that the agency has not delegated full regulatory powers to IRBs.

Although they can attempt to suspend or terminate research in the event of failures to abide by any conditions imposed at the time of protocol approval, IRBs do not exercise any real power to sanction wayward investigators or provide definitive interpretations of federal law. Instead, the FDA and HHS have decided to add an extra layer of protection to the research enterprise, requiring that investigators jump through still another hoop before pursuing their work. If a researcher chooses to proceed without receiving the blessing of a local IRB, he or she answers to federal officials for this and any other transgressions. * * *

[T]he delegation of quasi-regulatory functions to entities such as IRBs is hardly unique. Governmental delegations of authority to private actors come in many other forms. * * * Although federal requirements for the creation and operation of IRBs may countenance the exercise of some delegated authority, the limited nature of this delegation counsels against recasting and proceduralizing boards as if they exercised the full panoply of powers vested in the FDA or HHS. Instead, the formal policy of relying on IRBs as front-line monitors adopted by these federal agencies in the 1970s represented an early version of what now goes under the banner of "audited self-regulation." This technique comes in many guises nowadays: companies of all types receive promises of prosecutorial leniency if they had corporate compliance programs in place, the Securities and Exchange Commission requires that publicly traded companies subject their financial statements to audits by independent accounting firms, hospitals participating in Medicare must establish peer review panels in order to monitor the quality of care delivered by physicians, and educational institutions receiving federal funds must undergo accreditation. These self-regulatory mechanisms do not involve the exercise of delegated governmental authority, and, notwithstanding their undoubted shortcomings as a substitute for the direct exercise of such authority, it would not make sense to propose reforms premised on an assumption that they acted in any such capacity.

Even if, for the sake of argument, we assume that IRBs act as deputized agents of federal regulators and play a central role in securing compliance with the law of human subject protection, it does not follow that these boards will function best only if they model themselves on their parent agencies. One administrative law scholar explained the general point as follows: "Complying with the bureaucratic requirements typically imposed on agencies—following detailed procedures, providing hearings, defending decisions to review boards and courts—could frustrate the benefits of private participation in governance by imposing significant burdens." IRBs do not—and should not even attempt to—emulate the judiciary in pursuit of more consistent and transparent decisions. Instead of converting these boards into adversarial dispute resolution bodies, we should work to bolster their essentially inquisitorial approach to decision making.

One of Coleman's central concerns grows out of the inconsistency evident in the decisions made by different IRBs, and he thinks that a court-like approach will help to produce a body of common law that might bring order to this chaos. First, this would do little in a landscape of dispersed, as opposed to hierarchical, decision making. Just as the courts in 50 different states have failed to hit upon (and choose to follow) the single "best" answer to questions that arise in all sorts of private disputes, a vision of the common law famously discredited by the legal realists and buried by the United States Supreme Court in *Erie Railroad Co. v. Tompkins*, demanding that IRBs more clearly communicate their rationales with one another will not measurably increase the odds of developing anything approaching a consensus. The really tough issues, after all, have multiple plausible answers (as reflected in the published literature debating contested questions about research ethics) or arise in highly idiosyncratic cases. Even on the more seemingly straightforward methodological questions concerning study design, profound and largely irreconcilable disagreements often exist.

Coleman argues that IRBs should act more like administrative law judges (ALJs), federal employees who must produce written opinions—including explanations when they deviate from agency precedent—and face a form of appellate review within the agency. He fails, however, to recognize that these systems have not worked particularly well. The federal disability benefits program run by the Social Security Administration, which uses more than 1,000 ALJs, offers a cautionary tale * * * * With as many as 5,000 IRBs of various sorts in operation around the country, a comparable effort to achieve consistency in the field of human subject protection could not possibly succeed.

The experience with utilization review in the Medicare and Medicaid programs may offer an even more pertinent lesson. In 1972, Congress delegated "medical necessity" determinations to more than 200 regional Professional Standards Review Organizations (PSROs). In the course of holding that PSROs did not have to abide by the Freedom of Information

Act, one federal appellate court defended the decision to delegate utilization review functions to these panels: " 'It is preferable and appropriate that organizations of professionals undertake review of members of their profession rather than for government to assume that role.... The purpose here is to assure that only doctors knowledgeable in the provision and practice of hospital care will review such care.' " The court added that, by rendering "conclusive" (unreviewable) decisions about coverage, "they do not and should not become part of a government organization .... [A]ny other arrangement would be impractical: if the Department undertook to review each of the hundreds of thousands of medical opinions submitted the result would be the creation of an unworkable bureaucratic monster."

PSROs could (and often did) sub-delegate their tasks to existing hospital utilization review committees. Although hospitals have relied on a peer review process in making credentialing and quality assurance decisions for at least the last half century, this approach suffers from many of the same limitations that critics say affect IRB operations, including conflicts of interest and a lack of rigor, consistency, and transparency. As with IRBs, however, hospital peer review represents just one of many imperfect quality control mechanisms used in medicine, and encumbering the process with additional procedures probably would make things worse rather than better. * * *

Informal exchanges of ideas would, of course, promote efficiency in the sense that each IRB would not have to reinvent the wheel when it first encounters a difficulty that has arisen elsewhere previously, but IRBs already have informal networks designed to accomplish this purpose. As a growing chorus of scholars have realized, norms develop through a variety of channels apart from legal institutions and processes, and this insight certainly holds true for the behavior of physicians and biomedical researchers. * * * The mandatory publication of formal opinions by IRBs would add little to this dialogue. * * *

The obligation to spell out on paper and then defend a decision to proceed with a particular experiment involving human subjects undoubtedly would promote reflection, as Coleman argues, but in placing this obligation on the IRB he has focused on the wrong actor. It may make more sense to view the PI as the source of the preliminary risk-benefit assessment and the IRB as the designated (and final) appellate body. In other contexts, courts sensibly have recognized that some official decisions are not justiciable, for instance where "action is committed to agency discretion." In the one reported case involving a disgruntled researcher's effort to challenge an IRB's decision, a federal court wisely declined to second guess the merits of that decision. * * *

Procedural changes made in the hopes of affording subjects improved safeguards could, however, ultimately backfire. If IRBs had to provide explanations and then anticipate appeals from the only party likely to press them (namely, a dissatisfied PI), then they may become paralyzed with the overwhelming workload, or else they might become more "gun shy" about ever rejecting protocols unless a patient advocate had the opportunity to challenge such approval decisions. The unintended consequences of the revolution in procedural due process initiated by the United States Supreme Court in the 1970s should inspire caution. * * * Judges naturally thought that imposing a duty to listen and then offer an explanation would help to prevent inaccurate and unfair decisions, but the profound flaws in this assumption quickly dawned on most members of the Court.

The same spirit that animated the procedural due process revolution infused the expanding judicial review of agency action. During the 1970s, the courts demanded that informal rulemaking produce a fuller record for review, confident that the use of such additional procedures would improve the quality of regulatory decisions, and then began scrutinizing those explanations more closely. In demanding better explanations that would make sense to persons trained as lawyers, however, courts imposed entirely unrealistic expectations of comprehensive rationality—what some scholars have referred to as a "synoptic" paradigm for decision making. Instead, regulatory officials operating in the face of uncertainty must muddle through in ways that reviewing courts later may find inexplicable. * * *

In fact, the risk assessment literature expresses a profound frustration with the way that judges have botched efforts to comprehend the underlying science and the inevitable uncertainties. Over the years, federal courts have made some remarkably silly mistakes as risk assessors. * * * The inclination to demand explanations that others will comprehend can have serious repercussions for decision makers who operate in areas largely devoid of single and demonstrably correct answers to tough questions. * * *

IRBs may do the most good by helping to educate researchers at an institution about the basics of federal law, as well as working to inculcate a commitment to ethical behavior. We want the PI to reflect carefully on what he or she plans to do; after all, a flawless protocol crafted with extensive collegial input by an IRB following guidance from institutions around the country and accompanied by a thorough written opinion means nothing if the researcher has not "bought into" the process. Ultimately, neither an IRB nor a federal agency can guard completely against intransigence by an uncooperative PI. Inevitably, some boards do a better job than others of persuading PIs to take their obligations seriously, and the increasing preoccupation with the details of consent forms may send the opposite signal—namely, that the game requires satisfying bureaucratic demands. Unlike judges and juries, however, and more like the licensing agencies that have given them a role to play, IRBs do their work before things go wrong.

In contrast to the generally all-or-nothing feedback received from courts, IRB decisions have an open and iterative quality. When members have questions or concerns, either before or after initially approving a protocol, this provides an occasion for a dialogue with the principal investigator. In many instances, the IRB returns a new protocol submission with a request for revisions designed to improve it. In a similar way, the editors of peer-reviewed journals often share some of the comments from referees with the author of a manuscript. At some point, of course, the board may reach an impasse with a recalcitrant PI (just as a journal editor may reject a manuscript as unsalvageable), and it will make a final decision adverse to the investigator, but, knowing that he or she cannot appeal the IRB's decision, the PI usually comes around or decides to pursue a different research project. In addition, IRBs must engage in continuing reviews of active studies and have the power to halt approved research in the event that the risk-benefit balance shifts mid-stream, which again differs from the judicial norm opposed to the reopening of final judgments. * * *

Institutional review boards unquestionably play an important role in protecting human research subjects, and they occupy a central though unusual position in this regulatory scheme. At times, these boards struggle with the weighty tasks assigned to them by governmental agencies, and various commentators have offered reform proposals in recent years. This article has provided an administrative law (and science) perspective on IRB operations as an alternative to a vision centered on the judiciary. In the end, it may not be possible to draw satisfying parallels to other types of decision makers in either of these broad domains, but that difficulty in no way diminishes the importance of searching for ways of improving the process of risk-benefit assessment and the supervision of research protocols.

In the area of human research subject protection, better guidance from the FDA, HHS, and NIH would have the dual benefit of minimizing inconsistency and relieving already overburdened IRBs. In contrast, Coleman's central proposals would not do much to reduce the former problem, and they might seriously worsen the latter difficulty. Undoubtedly this represents an overly idealized view of how IRBs operate in practice, but it does offer an ideal toward which they should strive. An appellate ideal, in contrast, would take boards in entirely the wrong direction.

NOTES AND QUESTIONS

1. *Still trying to put IRBs in their place.* For yet another suggested way of understanding how these peculiar entities operate, see Richard S. Saver, Medical Research Oversight from the Corporate Governance Perspective: Comparing Institutional Review Boards and Corporate Boards, 46 Wm. & Mary L. Rev. 619 (2004). What, if any, consequences follow from selecting among these different perspectives on the role of IRBs in protecting human research subjects? If these boards act under the color of state law, then might their activities raise First Amendment concerns (as a prior restraint on speech or an infringement on academic freedom)? See Symposium, Censorship and Institutional Review Boards, 101 Nw. U. L. Rev. 399 (2007).

2. *"Commercial" IRBs.* Many in-house IRBs at research institutions are now charging a fee for the initial and continuing review of research protocols in order to offset the significant costs associated with regulatory compliance. Such arrangements appear to present few if any ethical concerns. However, independent commercial IRBs also exist, with no affiliation to any research institution, and they charge substantial fees. See Paul T. Kefalides, Research on Humans Faces Scrutiny: New Policies Adopted, 132 Annals Internal Med. 513 (2000); Trudo Lemmens & Benjamin Freedman, Ethics Review for Sale? Conflict of Interest and Commercial Research Review Boards, 78 Milbank Q. 547 (2000); Barry Meier, An Overseer of Trials in Medicine Draws Fire, N.Y. Times, Mar. 27, 2009, at B3 (reporting that a sting operation by the GAO had caught a commercial IRB approving a plainly inadequate protocol for a fictitious investigational product submitted by a sham sponsor); Rick Weiss, Death Points to Risks in Research: One Woman's Experience in Gene Therapy Trial Highlights Weaknesses in the Patient Safety Net, Wash. Post, Aug. 6, 2007, at A1 (noting questions about a study protocol and consent forms approved by a commercial IRB). What ethical difficulties might such a system create?

3. *Pressures on academic medicine.* Financial connections between researchers and medical technology companies have generated increasing concern. See Michelle M. Mello et al., Academic Medical Centers' Standards for Clinical–Trial Agreements with Industry, 352 New Eng. J. Med. 2202 (2005); Kevin A. Schulman et al., A National Survey of Provisions in Clinical–Trial Agreements Between Medical Schools and Industry Sponsors, 347 New Eng. J. Med. 1335 (2002). The FDA now requires that sponsors disclose their investigators' financial interests in products that are the subject of research protocols. See 21 C.F.R. § 54.4; see also Jesse A. Goldner, Regulating Conflicts of Interest in Research: The Paper Tiger Needs Real Teeth, 53 St. Louis U. L.J. 1211 (2009); William M. Sage, Some Principles Require Principals: Why Banning "Conflicts of Interest" Won't Solve Incentive Problems in Biomedical Research, 85 Tex. L. Rev. 1413 (2007); Stephanie Saul & Jenny Anderson, Doctors' Links with Investors Raise Concerns, N.Y. Times, Aug. 16, 2005, at A1. Might greater government involvement in the funding and execution of research be preferable?

4. *Public disclosure.* The FDA requires researchers and sponsors to report adverse events associated with any research protocol, but it does not disclose the information to the public in order to avoid compromising manufacturers' interests. See Public Citizen Health Research Group v. FDA, 185 F.3d 898, 903–06 (D.C.Cir.1999). Some critics of the FDA's supervision of gene therapy trials argued that the agency should have disclosed serious adverse events associated with these trials in order to maximize the information on which participants might choose to continue or discontinue participation. Media coverage of these incidents (as well as a number of other factors) have made it increasingly difficult to recruit sufficient numbers of subjects for clinical trials. See Thomas Ginsberg, Please Stop Calling Them Drug "Trials," Phila. Inquirer, June 21, 2006, at C1; Linda Marsa, Clinical Trials Are Suffering: Suspicious of Medical Research, Volunteers Spurn Tests of Possibly Lifesaving Advances, L.A. Times, Dec. 2, 2002, § 6, at 1.

---

21 C.F.R. § 56.111. Criteria for IRB Approval of Research.

(a) In order to approve research covered by these regulations the IRB shall determine that all of the following requirements are satisfied:

(1) Risks to subjects are minimized: (i) by using procedures which are consistent with sound research design and which do not unnecessarily expose subjects to risk, and (ii) whenever appropriate, by using procedures already being performed on the subjects for diagnostic or treatment purposes.

(2) Risks to subjects are reasonable in relation to anticipated benefits, if any, to subjects, and the importance of the knowledge that may be expected to result. In evaluating risks and benefits, the IRB should consider only those risks and benefits that may result from the research (as distinguished from risks and benefits of therapies that subjects would receive even if not participating in the research). The IRB should not consider possible long-range effects of applying knowledge gained in the research (for example, the possible effects of the research on public policy) as among those research risks that fall within the purview of its responsibility.

(3) Selection of subjects is equitable. In making this assessment the IRB should take into account the purposes of the research and the setting in which the research will be conducted and should be particularly cognizant of the special problems of research involving vulnerable populations, such as children, prisoners, pregnant women, handicapped, or mentally disabled persons, or economically or educationally disadvantaged persons.

(4) Informed consent will be sought from each prospective subject or the subject's legally authorized representative, in accordance with and to the extent required by part 50.

(5) Informed consent will be appropriately documented, in accordance with and to the extent required by Sec. 50.27.

(6) Where appropriate, the research plan makes adequate provision for monitoring the data collected to ensure the safety of subjects.

(7) Where appropriate, there are adequate provisions to protect the privacy of subjects and to maintain the confidentiality of data.

(b) When some or all of the subjects, such as children, prisoners, pregnant women, handicapped, or mentally disabled persons, or economically or educationally disadvantaged persons, are likely to be vulnerable to coercion or undue influence additional safeguards have been included in the study to protect the rights and welfare of these subjects.

NOTES AND QUESTIONS

1. *Vulnerable populations.* What are the special problems with research involving such subjects? See, e.g., Rachel Wener, Comment, Not Situated to Exercise Free Power of Choice: Human Subject Research in Prison Settings, 26 Temp. J. Sci. Tech. & Envtl. L. 365 (2007); cf. Jerry Menikoff, The

Vulnerability of the Very Sick, 37 J.L. Med. & Ethics 51 (2009). With increased efforts at conducting drug research in pediatric populations, the need to protect the interests of children enrolled in clinical trials has attracted substantial attention. See Doriane L. Coleman, The Legal Ethics of Pediatric Research, 57 Duke L.J. 517 (2007); Paul Litton, Non–Beneficial Pediatric Research and the Best Interests Standard: A Legal and Ethical Reconciliation, 8 Yale J. Health Pol'y L. & Ethics 359 (2008); David Wendler et al., Quantifying the Federal Minimal Risk Standard: Implications for Pediatric Research Without a Prospect of Direct Benefit, 294 JAMA 826 (2005); John Solomon, Drug Testing on Foster Children: A Federal Probe Found AIDS Researchers Violated Rules, Phila. Inquirer, June 17, 2005, at A2; Sheryl G. Stolberg, Proposal to Test Smallpox Vaccine in Young Children Sets off Ethics Debate, N.Y. Times, Nov. 5, 2002, at A14. In one case addressing the issue, a court concluded that an IRB affiliated with Johns Hopkins University had "abdicated [its] responsibility" to review "the potential safety and health hazard impact of a research project," and it chastised the board for "instead suggesting to the researchers a way to miscast the characteristics of the study in order to avoid the responsibility inherent in nontherapeutic research involving children." Grimes v. Kennedy Krieger Inst., 782 A.2d 807, 813 (Md.2001) (discussing negligent oversight of a study to compare different methods of lead paint abatement in housing).

2. *Equipoise in clinical research.* When an investigator designs a protocol to test the relative safety and effectiveness of two different treatments for the same condition, the genuine uncertainty as to the relative merits of the two treatments is known as "equipoise." Commentators have noted that equipoise is an ethical necessity in order to justify such research. See Don Marquis, How to Resolve an Ethical Dilemma Concerning Randomized Clinical Trials, 341 New Eng. J. Med. 691 (1999); see also Stuart L. Nightingale, Challenges in Human Subject Protection, 50 Food & Drug L.J. 493 (1995). Consider some startling departures from this principle: a review of 33 trials conducted between 1959 and 1988 "determined that by the end of the eighth trial in 1973, the evidence was clear that heart attack patients who got streptokinase had 25 percent lower death rates than those who did not. That conclusion, and the percentage, did not budge while 34,542 more patients were enrolled in 25 more trials of streptokinase over the next 15 years." David Brown, Superfluous Medical Studies Called into Question, Wash. Post, Jan. 2, 2006, at A6 (describing an even more dramatic track-record for research with aprotinin, which is used to reduce bleeding during surgery: after a dozen trials had established the benefits of this drug, researchers conducted more than 50 additional trials over the next decade, publishing articles that failed to cite the vast majority of earlier studies); see also id. ("Nobody requires that medical scientists review previous research to make sure the question they are asking has not already been answered."); cf. Gardiner Harris, Heart Surgery Drug Pulled from Market, N.Y. Times, Nov. 6, 2007, at A25 (reporting that new research on aprotinin unearthed serious side effects, throwing into doubt its continued use given the availability of safer and cheaper alternatives). What's an IRB to do in such a situation? How about investigational products intended to prevent disease (e.g., vaccines)—can researchers justify enrolling healthy subjects in Phase III trials that may offer no direct benefit (even if efficacious) but pose some risk? See Rob Stein, Study of Breast Cancer Pill Raises Hopes and Concerns, Wash. Post, May 22, 2005, at A1 ("These kinds of questions are becoming increasingly common as researchers focus more and more on trying to prevent, rather than treat, disease—often testing powerful drugs on people who have theoretical risks based on nebulous attributes such as age and family history ...."); see also Jacqueline Fox, Reinvigorating the Concept of Benefit: The Failure of Drug Company–Sponsored Research on Human Subjects, 38 Seton Hall L. Rev. 605 (2008).

3. *Placebo-controlled clinical trials.* The use of placebos in clinical trials allows researchers to measure efficacy of the studied drug or treatment and to compare the placebo response. Indeed, from the FDA's perspective when it comes time to review a product approval application, placebo-controlled trials provide the clearest evidence of effectiveness. Most ethicists agree that such studies are appropriate when evaluating drugs to treat conditions for which there is no known effective treatment. However, when effective alternatives exist, even for treating a relatively mild medical condition, some ethicists argue that placebo-controlled designs are inappropriate. See C. Michael Stein & Theodore Pincus, Placebo–Controlled Studies in Rheumatoid Arthritis: Ethical Issues, 353 Lancet 400 (1999); Susan Okie, Health Officials Debate Ethics of Placebo Use, Wash. Post, Nov. 24, 2000, at A3 (noting that no one defends placebo controls where established therapies exist to treat serious and measurable conditions such as infections, diabetes and cancer); see also Sharona Hoffman, The Use of Placebos in Clinical Trials: Responsible Research or Unethical Practice?, 33 Conn. L. Rev. 449 (2001); Timothy S. Jost, The Globalization of Health Law: The Case of Permissibility of Placebo–Based Research, 26 Am. J.L. & Med. 175 (2000); Robert Temple & Susan S. Ellenberg, Placebo–Controlled Trials and Active–Control Trials in the Evaluation of New Treatments: Ethical and Scientific Issues, 133 Annals Internal Med. 455 (2000); cf. Anna W. Mathews, Ketek Sparks Calls to Stiffen Antibiotic Trials, Wall St. J., June 13, 2006, at B1 (reporting that the FDA is reconsidering its reliance on "noninferiority" rather than placebo-controlled trials for antimicrobial agents). Imagine a clinical trial with half of the patients randomized to the study medication, one-quarter to an approved medication for high blood pressure, and one-quarter to placebo; after a few months, the data safety monitoring board unblinds the preliminary results and suspects, based on the benefits and side-effects that the subjects experience, that the study medication works significantly more safely and effectively than the standard medication or placebo—should it halt the trial and offer the investigational drug to the subjects in the control groups who fared poorly? (Should the IRB have approved this study in the first place?)

4. *Definition of "research."* The FDA regulations describe circumstances in which IRB review is required in a somewhat circular manner: "Clinical investigation means any experiment that involves a test article and one or more human subjects, and that either must meet the requirements for prior submission to the [FDA] under section 505(i) or 520(g) of the Act [which govern investigational new drugs and medical devices respectively], or need not meet [these requirements] ... but the results of which are intended to be later submitted to ... the [FDA] as part of an application for a research or marketing permit." 21 C.F.R. § 56.102(c). With very limited exceptions, "any clinical investigation which must meet the requirements for prior submission ... to the [FDA] shall not be initiated unless that investigation has been reviewed and approved by, and remains subject to continuing review by, an IRB meeting the requirements of this part." Id. § 56.103(a); see also Albert R. Jonsen et al., Clinical Ethics 192 (4th ed. 1998) ("Clinical research is defined as any clinical intervention involving human subjects, patients or normal volunteers, performed in accord with a protocol designed to yield generalizable scientific knowledge."); Carl Elliott, Op–Ed., Useless Studies, Real Harm, N.Y. Times, July 29, 2011, at A27 (explaining that the purpose of so-called "seeding" trials "is not to advance research but to make doctors familiar with a new drug," adding that subjects may suffer serious injuries but IRBs "don't typically pass judgment on whether a study is being carried out merely to market a drug").

5. *Distinguishing between "research" and "treatment."* Not all experimental treatments constitute research requiring IRB approval. The distinction between therapy and research, and thus between "patients" and "subjects," has generated a good deal of commentary. See, e.g., Samuel Hellman & Deborah S. Hellman, Of Mice but Not Men: Problems of the Randomized Clinical Trial, 324 New Eng. J. Med. 1585 (1991) (discussing the tension in physicians' roles as caregivers and as scientists); see also David A. Lenrow, The Treating Physician as Researcher: Is Assuming This Dual Role a Violation of the Nuremberg Code?, 25 Temp. J. Sci. Tech. & Envtl. L. 15 (2006). More than three decades ago, the National Commission for the Protection of Human Subjects of Biomedical and Behavioral Research issued its well-known "Belmont Report." 44 Fed. Reg. 23,192 (1979). It offered the following guidance:

> It is important to distinguish between biomedical and behavioral research, on the one hand, and the practice of accepted therapy on the other, in order to know what activities ought to undergo review for the protection of human subjects of research. The distinction between research and practice is blurred partly because both often occur together (as in research designed to evaluate a therapy) and partly because notable departures from standard practice are often called "experimental" when the terms "experimental" and "research" are not carefully defined.... [T]he term "research" designates an activity designed to test a hypothesis, permit conclusions to be drawn, and thereby to develop or contribute to generalizable knowledge (expressed, for example, in theories, principles, and statements of relationships). Research is usually described in a formal protocol that sets forth an objective and a set of procedures designed to reach that objective. When a clinician departs in a significant way from standard or accepted practice, the innovation does not, in and of itself, constitute research. The fact that a procedure is "experimental," in the sense of new, untested

> or different, does not automatically place it in the category of research. Radically new procedures of this description should, however, be made the object of formal research at an early stage in order to determine whether they are safe and effective.... Research and practice may be carried on together when research is designed to evaluate the safety and efficacy of a therapy. This need not cause any confusion regarding whether or not the activity requires review; the general rule is that if there is any element of research in an activity, that activity should undergo review for the protection of human subjects.

Conversely, even the on-label use of FDA-approved products might have a research aspect to it insofar as physicians report unexpected adverse events in their patients that may lead to labeling revisions or product withdrawals by the FDA. See Lars Noah, Informed Consent and the Elusive Dichotomy Between Standard and Experimental Therapy, 28 Am. J.L. & Med. 361, 363 (2002) ("[P]roduct approval does not define the point at which an investigational intervention passes the threshold into standard therapy. Instead, the research phase continues after licensure, both in the sense that more safety data accumulates and insofar as physicians may improvise when using a product in ways not originally contemplated."); see also id. at 394–400 (elaborating); id. at 408 ("Whether we know it or not, and whether we like it or not, all patients are subjects in medical research."); Anna B. Laakmann, Collapsing the Distinction Between Experimentation and Treatment in the Regulation of New Drugs, 62 Ala. L. Rev. 305 (2011).

PROBLEM #3. *WHEN DOES TREATMENT BECOME RESEARCH?*

Frank Finagle, a plastic surgeon, chatted with a surgical colleague, Doris Dare, who told him about a different wound dressing material that she had been using with great success to speed the healing of large abdominal incisions. The FDA approved the wound dressing material for general surgical use, but only a few plastic surgeons have used it so far. Based on Dr. Dare's recommendation, Dr. Finagle decides to try the new wound dressing when he does tummy tucks and abdominal liposuction to see how he likes it. Hypothesizing that the material might work better than his usual choice, he decides to use it on his next couple of cases and to look for any higher or lower than usual incidence of wound healing problems. Does Dr. Finagle's plan require IRB approval? After liking the results in his initial surgical cases, Dr. Finagle decides to test the wound dressing in his next 20 patients to see whether their incisions heal well. He resolves to keep a tally of the results in his pocket planner (in addition to making the usual notations on his patients' charts) and to pen an article for a medical journal about his results if they seem promising. Does this plan require IRB approval?

Abdullahi v. Pfizer, Inc.

562 F.3d 163 (2d Cir.2009).

■ PARKER, CIRCUIT JUDGE:

* * * The central events at issue in these cases took place in 1996, during an epidemic of bacterial meningitis in northern Nigeria. The appel-

lants allege that at that time, Pfizer, the world's largest pharmaceutical corporation, sought to gain [FDA] approval for the use on children of its new antibiotic, trovafloxacin mesylate, marketed as Trovan. They contend that in April 1996, Pfizer dispatched three of its American physicians to work with four Nigerian doctors to experiment with Trovan on children who were patients in Nigeria's Infectious Disease Hospital (IDH) in Kano, Nigeria. Working in concert with Nigerian government officials, the team allegedly recruited two hundred sick children who sought treatment at the IDH and gave half of the children Trovan and the other half ceftriaxone, an FDA-approved antibiotic the safety and efficacy of which was well-established. Appellants contend that Pfizer knew that Trovan had never previously been tested on children in the form being used and that animal tests showed that Trovan had life-threatening side effects, including joint disease, abnormal cartilage growth, liver damage, and a degenerative bone condition. Pfizer purportedly gave the children who were in the ceftriaxone control group a deliberately low dose in order to misrepresent the effectiveness of Trovan in relation to ceftriaxone. After approximately two weeks, Pfizer allegedly concluded the experiment and left without administering follow-up care. According to the appellants, the tests caused the deaths of eleven children, five of whom had taken Trovan and six of whom had taken the lowered dose of ceftriaxone, and left many others blind, deaf, paralyzed, or brain-damaged.

Appellants claim that Pfizer, working in partnership with the Nigerian government, failed to secure the informed consent of either the children or their guardians and specifically failed to disclose or explain the experimental nature of the study or the serious risks involved. Although the treatment protocol required the researchers to offer or read the subjects documents requesting and facilitating their informed consent, this was allegedly not done in either English or the subjects' native language of Hausa. The appellants also contend that Pfizer deviated from its treatment protocol by not alerting the children or their guardians to the side effects of Trovan or other risks of the experiment, not providing them with the option of choosing alternative treatment, and not informing them that the non-governmental organization Médecins Sans Frontières (Doctors Without Borders) was providing a conventional and effective treatment for bacterial meningitis, free of charge, at the same site.

The appellants allege that, in an effort to rapidly secure FDA approval, Pfizer hastily assembled its test protocol * * * and received permission to proceed from the Nigerian government in March 1996. At the time, Pfizer also claimed to have secured approval from an IDH ethics committee. Appellants allege, however, that the March 1996 approval letter was backdated by Nigerian officials working at the government hospital well after the experiments had taken place and that at the time the letter was purportedly written, the IDH had no ethics committee. Appellants also contend that the experiments were condemned by doctors, including one on Pfizer's staff at the time of the Kano trial. In 1998, the FDA approved

Trovan for use on adult patients only. After reports of liver failure in patients who took Trovan, its use in America was eventually restricted to adult emergency care. In 1999, the European Union banned its use. * * *

In May 2007, the state of Kano brought criminal charges and civil claims against Pfizer, seeking over $2 billion in damages and restitution. Around the same time, the federal government of Nigeria sued Pfizer and several of its employees, seeking $7 billion in damages. None of these cases seek compensation for the subjects of the tests, who are the appellants before this court. * * *

The Alien Tort Statute (ATS), 28 U.S.C. § 1350, provides that "[t]he district courts shall have original jurisdiction of any civil action by an alien for a tort only, committed in violation of the law of nations or a treaty of the United States." Included in the Judiciary Act of 1789, the statute provided jurisdiction in just two cases during the first 191 years after its enactment. In the last thirty years, however, the ATS has functioned slightly more robustly, conferring jurisdiction over a limited category of claims. * * * [I]n *Sosa v. Alvarez–Machain*, 542 U.S. 692, 728–29 (2004), * * * [t]he Supreme Court confirmed that federal courts retain a limited power to "adapt[] the law of nations to private rights" by recognizing "a narrow class of international norms" to be judicially enforceable through our residual common law discretion to create causes of action. * * *

Appellants' ATS claims are premised on the existence of a norm of customary international law prohibiting medical experimentation on non-consenting human subjects. To determine whether this prohibition constitutes a universally accepted norm of customary international law, we examine the current state of international law by consulting the sources identified by Article 38 of the Statute of the International Court of Justice, to which the United States and all members of the United Nations are parties. * * *

The appellants ground their claims in four sources of international law that categorically forbid medical experimentation on non-consenting human subjects: (1) the Nuremberg Code, which states as its first principle that "[t]he voluntary consent of the human subject is absolutely essential"; (2) the World Medical Association's Declaration of Helsinki, which sets forth ethical principles to guide physicians world-wide and provides that human subjects should be volunteers and grant their informed consent to participate in research; (3) the guidelines authored by the Council for International Organizations of Medical Sciences (CIOMS), which require "the voluntary informed consent of [a] prospective subject"; and (4) Article 7 of the International Covenant on Civil and Political Rights (ICCPR), which provides that "no one shall be subjected without his free consent to medical or scientific experimentation." * * *

Agreements that are not self-executing or that have not been executed by federal legislation, including the ICCPR, are appropriately considered evidence of the current state of customary international law. A formal treaty, moreover, is not the lone primary source of customary international law. * * * [I]t was inappropriate for the district court to forego a more extensive examination of whether treaties, international agreements, or State practice have ripened the prohibition of nonconsensual medical experimentation on human subjects into a customary international law norm that is sufficiently (i) universal and obligatory, (ii) specific and definable, and (iii) of mutual concern, to permit courts to infer a cause of action under the ATS. * * *

The evolution of the prohibition into a norm of customary international law began with the war crimes trials at Nuremberg. * * * In August 1947, Military Tribunal 1, staffed by American judges and prosecutors and conducted under American procedural rules, promulgated the Nuremberg Code as part of the tribunal's final judgment against fifteen doctors who were found guilty of war crimes and crimes against humanity for conducting medical experiments without the subjects' consent. Among the nonconsensual experiments that the tribunal cited as a basis for their convictions were the testing of drugs for immunization against malaria, epidemic jaundice, typhus, smallpox and cholera. * * *

The American tribunal's conclusion that action that contravened the Code's first principle constituted a crime against humanity is a lucid indication of the international legal significance of the prohibition on nonconsensual medical experimentation. As Justices of the Supreme Court have recognized, "[t]he medical trials at Nuremberg in 1947 deeply impressed *upon the world* that experimentation with unknowing human subjects is morally and legally unacceptable." United States v. Stanley, 483 U.S. 669, 687 (1987) (Brennan, J., concurring in part and dissenting in part) (emphasis added). * * * [S]ince Nuremberg, states throughout the world have shown through international accords and domestic law-making that they consider the prohibition on nonconsensual medical experimentation identified at Nuremberg as a norm of customary international law. * * *

The international community's recognition in the ICCPR of its obligation to protect humans against nonconsensual medical experimentation, regardless of the source of the action, is powerful evidence of the prohibition's place in customary international law. * * * [T]he fact that the prohibition on medical experimentation on humans without consent has been consciously embedded by Congress in our law and reaffirmed on numerous occasions by the FDA demonstrates that the United States government views the norm as the source of a binding legal obligation even though the United States has not ratified the ICCPR in full.

In 1964, the World Medical Association adopted the Declaration of Helsinki, which enunciated standards for obtaining informed consent from human subjects. * * * [It] now provides that "subjects must be volunteers and informed participants in the research project." Art. 20. The Declaration also requires that "[i]n any research on human beings, each potential subject must be adequately informed of the aims, methods, . . . anticipated benefits and potential risks of the study, and the discomfort it may entail" and that researchers "obtain the subject's freely-given informed consent, preferably in writing." Art. 22. Although the Declaration itself is nonbinding, since the 1960s, it has spurred States to regulate human experimentation, often by incorporating its informed consent requirement into domestic laws or regulations. Currently, the laws and regulations of at least eighty-four countries, including the United States, require the informed consent of human subjects in medical research. * * *

Congress mandated patient-subject consent in drug research in 1962. In response, the FDA promulgated its first regulations requiring the informed consent of human subjects. Tellingly, the sources on which our government relied in outlawing non-consensual human medical experimentation were the Nuremberg Code and the Declaration of Helsinki, which suggests the government conceived of these sources' articulation of the norm as a binding legal obligation. * * *

The importance that the United States government attributes to this norm is demonstrated by its willingness to use domestic law to coerce compliance with the norm throughout the world. United States law requires that, as a predicate to FDA approval of any new drug, both American and foreign sponsors of drug research involving clinical trials, whether conducted here or abroad, procure informed consent from human subjects. Sponsors conducting research under an investigational new drug application (IND) are obligated to adhere to FDA regulations, which require informed consent. 21 C.F.R. § 312.20. Prior to April 2008, sponsors conducting research under non-IND guidelines were obligated to adhere to the ethical principles of the 1989 version of the Declaration of Helsinki or the host country's regulations, whichever offered greater protection to the human subject. * * * Foreign clinical studies not conducted under an IND must now comply with the Good Clinical Practice guidelines (GCP) promulgated by the International Conference on Harmonisation of Technical Requirements for Registration of Pharmaceuticals for Human Use, which require informed consent to medical experimentation. 21 C.F.R. § 312.120.

Additional international law sources support the norm's status as customary international law. The European Union embraced the norm prohibiting nonconsensual medical experimentation through a 2001 Directive passed by the European Parliament and the Council of the European Union. * * * Since 1997, thirty-four member States of the Council of Europe have also signed the Convention on Human Rights and Biomedicine, a binding convention and a source of customary international law. It provides that an "intervention in the health field may only be carried out after the person concerned has given free and informed consent to it" and that the informed consent of human subjects is required for their involvement in medical research. Art. 5. In 2005, the General Conference of the United Nations Educational, Scientific and Cultural Organization (UNESCO) adopted the Universal Declaration on Bioethics and Human Rights, which requires "the prior, free, express and informed consent of the person concerned" for research-oriented treatments.

This history illustrates that from its origins with the trial of the Nazi doctors at Nuremburg through its evolution in international conventions, agreements, declarations, and domestic laws and regulations, the norm prohibiting nonconsensual medical experimentation on human subjects has become firmly embedded and has secured universal acceptance in the community of nations. * * * The Nuremberg Code, Article 7 of the ICCPR, the Declaration of Helsinki, the Convention on Human Rights and Biomedicine, the Universal Declaration on Bioethics and Human Rights, the 2001 Clinical Trial Directive, and the domestic laws of at least eighty-four States all uniformly and unmistakably prohibit medical experiments on human beings without their consent, thereby providing concrete content for the norm. The appellants allege that Pfizer knowingly and purposefully conducted such experiments on a large scale. Whatever uncertainty may exist at the margin is irrelevant here because appellants allege a complete failure on the part of Pfizer and the Nigerian government to inform appellants of the existence of the Trovan experiments. These allegations, if true, implicate Pfizer and the Nigerian government in conduct that is at the core of any reasonable iteration of the prohibition against involuntary medical experimentation. While the prohibition in question applies to the testing of drugs without the consent of human subjects on the scale Pfizer allegedly conducted, we do not suggest that it would extend to instances of routine or isolated failures by medical professionals to obtain informed consent * * * *

The administration of drug trials without informed consent on the scale alleged in the complaints poses a real threat to international peace and security. Over the last two decades, pharmaceutical companies in industrialized countries have looked to poorer, developing countries as sites for the medical research essential to the development of new drugs. See James V. Lavery, Putting International Research Ethics Guidelines to Work for the Benefit of Developing Countries, 4 Yale J. Health Pol'y L. & Ethics 319, 320–21 (2004); HHS Office of Inspector Gen., The Globalization of Clinical Trials 5 (2001), http://www.oig.hhs.gov/oei/reports/oei–01–00–00190.pdf. Pharmaceutical companies recognize the potential benefits of drug trials to poor nations and have sought to promote access to medicines and health care in underserved populations through philanthropy and partnership with governments and NGOs. This trend offers the possibility of enormous health benefits for the world community. Life-saving drugs can potentially be developed more quickly and cheaply, and developing countries may be given access to cutting edge medicines and treatments to assist underresourced and understaffed public health systems, which grapple with life-threatening diseases afflicting their populations. * * *

The success of these efforts promises to play a major role in reducing the cross-border spread of contagious diseases, which is a significant threat to international peace and stability. The administration of drug trials without informed consent on the scale alleged in the complaints directly threatens these efforts because such conduct fosters distrust and resistance to international drug trials, cutting edge medical innovation, and critical international public health initiatives in which pharmaceutical companies play a key role. This case itself supplies an exceptionally good illustration of why this is so. The Associated Press reported that the Trovan trials in Kano apparently engendered such distrust in the local population that it was a factor contributing to an eleven month-long, local boycott of a polio vaccination campaign in 2004, which impeded international and national efforts to vaccinate the population against a polio outbreak with catastrophic results. According to the World Health Organization, polio originating in Nigeria triggered a major international outbreak of the disease between 2003 and 2006 * * * *

The administration of drug trials without informed consent also poses threats to national security by impairing our relations with other countries. Seven of the world's twelve largest pharmaceutical manufacturers—a group that includes Pfizer—are American companies. Consequently, American companies are likely to be sponsors of medical experiments on human subjects abroad. As this case illustrates, the failure to secure consent for human experimentation has the potential to generate substantial anti-American animus and hostility. Unsurprisingly, our government actively attempts to prevent this practice in foreign countries. For example, federal law requires that data generated from testing on human subjects abroad that is used to seek regulatory approval for a given drug must, at minimum, be the result of testing conducted consistent with the requirements of informed consent. Consequently, the U.S. government denies access to the U.S. market for any new drug unless the drug's research data is generated in a manner consistent with the customary international law norm prohibiting drug trials on human subjects without informed consent.

For these reasons, we hold that the appellants have pled facts sufficient to state a cause of action under the ATS for a violation of the norm of customary international law prohibiting medical experimentation on human subjects without their consent. In such an instance, ATS jurisdiction exists over plaintiffs' claims. * * *

Appellants have alleged that the Nigerian government was involved in all stages of the Kano test and participated in the conduct that violated international law. They allege that the Nigerian government provided a letter of request to the FDA to authorize the export of Trovan, arranged for Pfizer's accommodations in Kano, and facilitated the nonconsensual testing in Nigeria's IDH in Kano. Despite overcrowding due to concurrent epidemics, the Nigerian government extended the exclusive use of two hospital wards to Pfizer, providing Pfizer with control over scarce public resources and the use of the hospital's staff and facilities to conduct the Kano test, to the exclusion of MSF.

The unlawful conduct is alleged to have occurred in a Nigerian facility with the assistance of the Nigerian government and government officials and/or employees from the IDH and Aminu Kano Teaching Hospital. Pfizer's research team in Kano was comprised of three American physicians, Dr. Abdulhamid Isa Dutse (a physician in the Aminu Kano Teaching Hospital), and three other Nigerian doctors. The American and Nigerian members of Pfizer's team allegedly jointly administered the Kano test. Finally, in addition to assisting with the Kano test, Nigerian officials are alleged to have conspired to cover up the violations by silencing Nigerian physicians critical of the test and by back-dating an "approval letter" that the FDA and international protocol required to be provided prior to conducting the medical experiment. * * * At the pleading stage, these contentions meet the state action test because they adequately allege that the violations occurred as the result of concerted action between Pfizer and the Nigerian government. * * *

■ WESLEY, CIRCUIT JUDGE (dissenting):

* * * The majority relies on eight sources of customary international law to support its determination that a norm against non-consensual medical experimentation on humans by private actors is universal and obligatory. However, this evidence falls far short of the quantum necessary to establish the existence of such a norm: (1) the International Covenant on Civil and Political Rights has been described by the Supreme Court as a "well-known international agreement[] that despite [its] moral authority, ha[s] little utility," in defining international obligations, *Sosa,* 542 U.S. at 734, and moreover, it does not apply to private actors, such as the defendant in this action; (2) the Council of Europe's Convention on Human Rights and Biomedicine—a regional convention—was not ratified by the most influential nations in the region, such as France, Germany, Italy, the Netherlands, Russia and the United Kingdom, and it was promulgated on April 4, 1997, one year *after* the conduct at issue in this litigation; (3) the UNESCO Universal Declaration of Bioethics and Human Rights of 2005 and (4) the European Parliament Clinical Trial Directive of 2001 both also post-date the relevant time period by several years; (5) the Declaration of Helsinki issued by the World Medical Association, a private entity, and (6) the International Ethical Guidelines for Research Involving Human Subjects promulgated by CIOMS, another private entity, "express[] the sensibilities and the asserted aspirations and demands of some countries or organizations" but are not "statements of universally-recognized legal obligations," Flores v. Southern Peru Copper Corp., 414 F.3d 233, 262 (2d Cir.2003), (7) states' domestic laws, which, unsupported by express international accords, are not "significant or relevant for purposes of customary international law," id. at 249; and (8) the so-called Nuremberg Code, a statement of principles that accompanied a criminal verdict, possesses at best "subsidiary" value as a judicial decision. Taken together, this evidence falls short of charting the existence of a universal and obligatory international norm actionable against non-government actors under the ATS.

In support of its determination that non-consensual medical experimentation by private actors is a matter of mutual concern, the majority reasons that non-consensual medical experiments breed distrust of medical interventions and thereby accelerate the spread of infectious diseases across international borders. It is not enough, however, that tortious conduct could create some sort of international consequence. In order for conduct to be a matter of mutual concern, it must "threaten[] serious consequences in international affairs." *Sosa,* 542 U.S. at 715. Such is the case when an ambassador is assaulted, for example, because the assault "impinge[s] upon the sovereignty of the foreign nation and if not adequately redressed could rise to an issue of war." Id. Non-consensual medical experimentation by private actors simply does not present the same grave risk of serious consequences in international affairs and is therefore not a matter of mutual concern. For these reasons, I conclude that non-consensual medical experimentation by private actors, though deplorable, is not actionable under international law and would therefore affirm the district court's dismissal of plaintiffs' complaints. * * *

The majority centers its analysis around the Nuremberg Code, but, in the process, critically misstates its genesis and status in international law. Because the Code is a *sui generis* source of international law, its context is vital to understanding what it is—and what it is not. The Nuremberg trials are unquestionably one of this country's greatest and most enduring contributions to the field of international law. * * * However, the majority overlooks the fact that the Nuremberg Code dealt not with these general principles of law, but instead with the very specific issue of permissible medical experimentation. The ethical principles espoused in the Code had no forebears in either the London Charter or the judgment of the International Military Tribunal. They were developed exclusively in the Medical Case. * * * [T]he Code was developed by the United States military and announced by an American military court. Certainly, the Code is not a treaty and did not immediately bind any state. * * * The Code surely has evidentiary value in our inquiry, but there is nothing to indicate that the Code establishes a norm of international law prohibiting non-consensual medical experimentation or treatment by private actors, or compensates for the virtually non-existent evidentiary value of the other sources cited by the majority. * * *

The defendants in the Medical Case were not charged with conducting non-consensual medical tests per se. Rather, those tests, when conducted on prisoners of war and members of a discrete civilian population imprisoned in concentration camps, constituted "war crimes" and "crimes against humanity," offenses for which customary international law has imposed individual responsibility. Unlike the defendant in this action, the Nazi doctors convicted by the American military tribunal were not private actors. Each convicted defendant held a position of authority in either the medical services or the military of the Third Reich. Moreover, the atrocities for which they were convicted victimized state prisoners in state-administered concentration camps, according to the indictment, "for the benefit of the German Armed Forces." * * *

[E]ven assuming, for argument's sake, that international law prohibits states from conducting non-consensual medical tests, plaintiffs have not demonstrated that Pfizer acted under the color of law. * * * At most, plaintiffs' complaints alleged that the Nigerian government acquiesced to or approved the Trovan program in general without knowing its disturbing details. * * * ATS jurisdiction must be reserved only for acts that the nations of the world collectively determine interfere with their formal relations with one another—including those rare acts by private individuals that are so serious as to threaten the very fabric of peaceful international affairs. I cannot agree with my colleagues that Pfizer's alleged conduct poses the same threat or is so universally and internationally proscribed as to fit within that narrow class.

NOTES AND QUESTIONS

1. *Trovan's trials and tribulations*. Pfizer settled the lawsuit filed by the state of Kano in Nigeria, see Joe Stephens, Pfizer to Pay $75 Million to Settle Trovan–Testing Suit, Wash. Post, July 31, 2009, at A15, and, in early 2011, the company announced a global settlement agreement that resolved the private litigation in the United States. Among the trove of secret State Department files released by WikiLeaks, one document suggested that the company had tried to discredit the attorney general who initiated the federal litigation in Nigeria before settling that case for an undisclosed amount. See Duff Wilson, Secret Cable Discusses Pfizer's Actions in Nigeria Case, N.Y. Times, Dec. 11, 2010, at B2; see also Joe Stephens, Pfizer Seeks Dismissal of Lawsuit in Nigeria: Company Defends Tests on Children, Says Lives Saved in Epidemic, Wash. Post, Aug. 8, 2007, at D1.

2. *Outsourcing clinical trials*. For a variety of reasons (including the expenses associated with satisfying domestic regulatory requirements), pharmaceutical companies have moved more of their clinical trials offshore. See Gardiner Harris, Concern over Number of Foreign Clinical Trials for Drugs Sold in U.S., N.Y. Times, June 22, 2010, at A14 (summarizing a new report issued by the HHS Inspector General, which had found that 80% of drugs approved by the FDA in 2008 had undergone clinical trials overseas, 78% of subjects enrolled in such trials came from foreign study sites, ten drugs approved that year had not undergone a single domestic clinical trial, and the agency "was 16 times more likely to audit a domestic site than a foreign one"); Natasha Singer, A Study Faults Overseas Drug Trials, N.Y. Times, Feb. 19, 2009, at B7 (reporting concerns about the exploitation of vulnerable subjects and whether one can reliably extrapolate results to domestic patient populations). Apart from the regulations described in the excerpt from the *Abdullahi* opinion, how should the FDA respond to such developments? See Esther Chang, Note, Fitting a Square Peg into a Round Hole?: Imposing Informed Consent and Post–Trial Obligations on United States Sponsored Clinical Trials in Developing Countries, 11 S. Cal. Interdisc. L.J. 339 (2002); William Dubois, Note, New Drug Research, the Extraterritorial Application of FDA Regulations, and the Need for International Cooperation, 36 Vand. J. Transnat'l L. 161 (2003); see also Drew A. Harker & Chad E. Miller, The Foreign Corrupt Practices Act and Clinical Trials: A Trap for the Unwary, 63 Food & Drug L.J. 509 (2008); Gardiner Harris & Natasha Singer, U.S. Inquiry of Drug Makers Is Widened, N.Y. Times, Aug. 14, 2010, at B1.

3. *Further commentary*. See Adriana Petryna, When Experiments Travel: Clinical Trials and the Global Search for Human Subjects (2009); David P. Fidler, "Geographical Morality" Revisited: International Relations, International Law, and the Controversy over Placebo–Controlled HIV Clinical Trials in Developing Countries, 42 Harv. Int'l L.J. 299 (2001); Seth W.

Glickman et al., Ethical and Scientific Implications of the Globalization of Clinical Research, 360 New Eng. J. Med. 816 (2009); David Orentlicher, Universality and Its Limits: When Research Ethics Can Reflect Local Circumstances, 30 J.L. Med. & Ethics 403 (2002); David M. Carr, Note, Pfizer's Epidemic: A Need for International Regulation of Human Experimentation in Developing Countries, 35 Case W. Res. J. Int'l L. 15 (2003); James Cekola, Comment, Outsourcing Drug Investigations to India: A Comment on U.S., Indian, and International Regulation of Clinical Trials in Cross–Border Pharmaceutical Research, 28 Nw. J. Int'l L. & Bus. 125 (2007); Dennis M. Coyne, Note, International Pharmaceutical Mistrials: Existing Law for the Protection of Foreign Human Subjects and a Proposal for Reform, 29 B.U. Int'l L.J. 427 (2011); Adam H. Laughton, Note, Somewhere to Run, Somewhere to Hide?: International Regulation of Human Subject Experimentation, 18 Duke J. Comp. & Int'l L. 181 (2007); Yevgenia Shtilman, Comment, Pharmaceutical Drug Testing in the Former Soviet Union: Contract Research Organizations as Broker–Dealers in an Emerging Testing Ground for America's Big Pharma, 29 B.C. Third World L.J. 425 (2009).

C. SECURING INFORMED CONSENT

21 C.F.R. Part 50. Protection of Human Subjects.

§ 50.20 General Requirements for Informed Consent.

Except as provided in Sec. 50.23, no investigator may involve a human being as a subject in research covered by these regulations unless the investigator has obtained the legally effective informed consent of the subject or the subject's legally authorized representative. An investigator shall seek such consent only under circumstances that provide the prospective subject or the representative sufficient opportunity to consider whether or not to participate and that minimize the possibility of coercion or undue influence. The information that is given to the subject or the representative shall be in language understandable to the subject or the representative. * * *

§ 50.25 Elements of Informed Consent.

(a) *Basic elements of informed consent.* In seeking informed consent, the following information shall be provided to each subject:

(1) A statement that the study involves research, an explanation of the purposes of the research and the expected duration of the subject's participation, a description of the procedures to be followed, and identification of any procedures which are experimental.

(2) A description of any reasonably foreseeable risks or discomforts to the subject.

(3) A description of any benefits to the subject or to others which may reasonably be expected from the research.

(4) A disclosure of appropriate alternative procedures or courses of treatment, if any, that might be advantageous to the subject.

(5) A statement describing the extent, if any, to which confidentiality of records identifying the subject will be maintained and that notes the possibility that the [FDA] may inspect the records.

(6) For research involving more than minimal risk, an explanation as to whether any compensation and an explanation as to whether any medical treatments are available if injury occurs and, if so, what they consist of, or where further information may be obtained.

(7) An explanation of whom to contact for answers to pertinent questions about the research and research subjects' rights, and whom to contact in the event of a research-related injury to the subject.

(8) A statement that participation is voluntary, that refusal to participate will involve no penalty or loss of benefits to which the subject is otherwise entitled, and that the subject may discontinue participation at any time without penalty or loss of benefits to which the subject is otherwise entitled. * * *

NOTES AND QUESTIONS

1. *The patient/subject perspective.* Despite the fact that many IRBs have interpreted the "language understandable to the subject" clause in 21 C.F.R. § 50.20 to require informed consent forms to be written at an 8th grade reading level (what some have referred to as the Homer Simpson standard), comprehension problems persist. A 1995 survey of 371 subjects found that nearly 20% of respondents incorrectly believed that they had not participated in research. See Laura C. McBride & Mark R. Yessian, IRBs and Continuing Review: Regulatory Interference or Vital Safeguard?, Food Drug Cosm. & Med. Dev. L. Dig., Mar. 1999, at 13; see also James Flory & Ezekiel Emanuel, Intervention to Improve Research Participants' Understanding in Informed Consent for Research: A Systematic Review, 292 JAMA 1593 (2004); Michael K. Paasch–Orlow et al., Readability Standards for Informed–Consent Forms as Compared with Actual Readability, 348 New Eng. J. Med. 721 (2003); Jessica J. Flinn, Comment, Personalizing Informed Consent: The Challenge of Health Literacy, 2 St. Louis U. J. Health L. & Pol'y 379 (2009). Many patients apparently fail to understand that they have agreed to participate in a research protocol rather than or in addition to receiving standard therapy.

2. *Remuneration and other arguably coercive methods for enrolling subjects.* For many years, recruitment of research subjects has involved payment for participation, although most IRBs agree that this practice poses difficult ethical problems. More recently, some protocols to test drugs in pediatric populations have offered gift certificates to toy stores as well as cash. Federal guidelines offer little assistance in dealing with this thorny issue. The research community, patient advocates, and ethicists appear to agree that payments should compensate only for travel expenses and lost time at work. See Neal Dickert & Christine Grady, What's the Price of a Research Subject? Approaches to Payment for Research Participation, 341 New Eng. J. Med. 198 (1999) (discussing the relative merits of the market model, the wage-payment model, and the reimbursement model for compensating research subjects, and concluding that the wage-payment model most effectively reduces concerns about inappropriate inducement); see also Carl Elliott, Guinea–Pigging, New Yorker, Jan. 7, 2008, at 36 (describing people who try to make a living of it). Should participation in biomedical research be viewed as a civic duty akin to serving on a jury?! See Lars Noah, Coerced Participation in Clinical Trials: Conscripting Human Research Subjects, 62 Admin. L. Rev. 329, 362–66 (2010) (cautioning against a turn to "communitarian research ethics"); id. at 365–66 ("[I]n July 2009, a group of NIH bioethicists published a piece in *JAMA* arguing that all citizens have a civic—though not (yet) compulsory—obligation to participate in biomedical research. Their provocative article represents a natural extension of the justifications that they previously had offered in defense of [Medicare's 'coverage with study participation'] policy, and it comes perilously close to endorsing outright conscription.").

PROBLEM #4. *PATIENT PROTECTION AND PROTOCOL DESIGN*

Erik Smith, a cardiologist and clinical researcher at Empire University, submits a research protocol to his institution's IRB for review. The protocol, which is sponsored by Pharmarama, Inc., involves the testing of an investigational drug ("XK–99") to treat hypertension. The planned research will require that human subjects with hypertension discontinue all of their regular medications in order to participate. The study is a randomized, double-blind, placebo-controlled trial. In other words, half of the subjects enrolled will receive the investigational drug; the other half will receive a placebo. Patients will be enrolled in one or the other "arm" of the trial at random, and neither the patients nor their treating physicians will know whether they are receiving the active drug or placebo. Dr. Smith, as principal investigator (PI), requests permission to enroll 300 patients in order to generate statistically significant data about the effectiveness of the drug. Previous studies of the drug suggest that most of its side effects are minor and infrequent, with the exception of a small risk of blood clotting that can lead to embolism or stroke. The informed consent form provides:

> You have been invited to participate in a research protocol to test the effectiveness of a promising new anti-hypertension compound called XK–99. The principal investigator of the protocol is Dr. Erik Smith. If you have questions concerning the research at any time, you may leave a message for him at (999) 555–1000.
>
> If you participate in this research, you will be randomized into one of two groups. One group will receive the experimental hypertension drug XK–99. The other group will receive a placebo drug. You will receive XK–99 free of charge for the duration of the study. When the

research period has ended, you will have the opportunity to continue taking XK–99 if you wish.

Before you begin taking the research drugs, you must have several tests, including blood pressure tests and blood screening tests. A nurse will draw blood from you at the first research visit, and at each of the three follow-up visits during the study. You may also be asked to take an exercise stress test using a treadmill at the beginning of the study to determine how your blood pressure responds to exertion. If you experience a significant increase in blood pressure during the treadmill test, you will be asked to repeat the test at each of the three follow-up visits while you are taking the experimental drug.

Risks of participation: There are always some minor risks associated with the testing of any new medication. The risks of XK–99 include dizziness, fainting, and very rarely blood clotting. You should not operate a vehicle or heavy machinery until you know how you respond to XK–99. You should not drink alcohol while taking XK–99. The risks from having your blood drawn are very small—you may feel dizziness or faintness, and occasionally you may experience infection at the site of the needle jab. The risks of the treadmill tests are minimal for most people.

Benefits of participation: You will receive no compensation for taking part in this study, but you will receive free medication while in the study. You may find that the study drug helps to reduce your high blood pressure. You have the right to withdraw from this research protocol at any time and receive ordinary standard treatment instead. You will not be able to continue taking XK–99 if you withdraw from the research protocol before completion.

The IRB discusses the proposed protocol and declines to grant approval. What concerns might the IRB members have about the study design? About the informed consent form? The IRB reports its decision, with a detailed explanation of its concerns, to the PI, who expresses dismay and exasperation. The PI phones his friend and colleague Dr. Samantha Rendell, who is the Empire University Vice Provost for institutional research coordination. He complains that the IRB has rejected a "perfectly sound" research protocol and notes that, without IRB approval, the university cannot receive the half million dollar grant from Pharmarama to fund his research. What options, if any, are available to Dr. Smith and Dr. Rendell?

Kus v. Sherman Hospital

644 N.E.2d 1214 (Ill.App.Ct.1995).

■ McLAREN, JUDGE:

The plaintiff, Richard Kus, brought suit against the defendants, * * * alleging negligence and medical battery relating to the implantation of intraocular lenses [IOLs]. * * *

Prior to the plaintiff's intraocular lens implantations, pursuant to the medical staff bylaws of Sherman Hospital, an Institutional Review Board (IRB) was established at the hospital to protect the rights of patients who were human subjects of research. One of the functions of the IRB was to "require that a legally effective informed consent is obtained prior to conducting a research project." The bylaws of the IRB gave it "purview over all research or investigative activities" and reserved the right to "review the progress of all continuing studies ... for the purpose of safeguarding the rights of human subjects." Dr. Richard Fiedler chaired the Sherman IRB from 1978 to 1984 and testified that the purpose of the IRB was to make sure that the patient who was undergoing the procedure knew what he was getting into. Fiedler agreed that the IRB had the power to stop unsafe investigative practices. Specifically, Fiedler admitted that the IRB could stop a doctor from using consent forms which were not approved under the protocol for that specific research.

On March 5, 1980, Fiedler, on behalf of the IRB, issued a directive to all operating eye surgeons, including Dr. Vancil, which stated that "the original or a copy of the Informed Consent Form be on the chart of each patient undergoing an intraocular lens implant." On June 4, 1984, Fiedler issued a second directive to the same group of surgeons, which specified: "It is ... mandatory that prior to the insertion of one of these lenses that the hospital have a copy of the informed consent signed by the patient so that the lens can be implanted. Without the hospital's having the informed consent in its possession prior to the surgery, the surgery will not be allowed." The consent form referred to was the FDA-approved consent, detailed below.

The plaintiff's vision began to deteriorate in 1984, and he first went to see Dr. Vancil in January 1985. Vancil recommended cataract surgery and a lens implant, which, he allegedly told Kus, were "quite safe." Kus testified that Vancil never told him that the lens Vancil intended to implant was under investigation for safety and effectiveness. Indeed, Vancil gave Kus a booklet which described intraocular lens implant surgery as a "tried and true method" of vision correction after cataract surgery. Prior to surgery, in Vancil's office, Kus was presented with an informed consent document to read over and sign, which Kus did. The informed consent document which Kus signed had been modified from the FDA-approved and Sherman IRB-sanctioned consent form by the removal of a paragraph on "clinical investigation," which was meant to inform the patient that the lens was under investigation for safety and efficacy. The consent form which Kus signed was then placed in his chart at Sherman Hospital. Eye surgery proceeded on July 15, 1985. * * * Vancil implanted an intraocular lens manufactured by Americal into Kus' left eye. On that same day, July 15, 1985, a letter from Americal arrived in the office of the president of the hospital, John Graham. The letter was addressed to the IRB chairperson and indicated that, by order of July 3, 1985, the FDA had withdrawn Americal's investigational device exemption for a number of lenses, including the type implanted in Kus' left eye, and stated that, "FDA has ordered that further implantations of Americal's IOLs be stopped and returned to

Americal as soon as possible." There was no evidence presented as to the time the letter was actually received. * * *

When the plaintiff's vision deteriorated in his right eye, Vancil again recommended the implantation of an intraocular lens, this time one manufactured by Surgidev, which at that point had not been recalled. When Kus questioned Vancil as to why Vancil did not recommend the Americal lens for the right eye, Vancil responded that Americal "did not keep up with their paperwork." Surgery on the right eye commenced on January 15, 1986, with allegedly no consent form in Kus' hospital chart. Kus claimed he signed the consent form 2 to 10 days after the surgery, and the form then appeared in his hospital chart. Similar to the form for the surgery on Kus' left eye, the consent form for the right eye surgery was also modified, and the form made no reference to the fact that the lens was being evaluated for safety and effectiveness.

A receptionist for Dr. Vancil testified that the reason the informed consent forms were missing the section on "clinical investigation" was that Vancil directed the office staff to remove language from the consent form approved by Sherman Hospital's IRB because "he didn't want it on there." This removal was done for all of Vancil's 43 patients who underwent intraocular lens surgery at Sherman Hospital. A subpoena was issued for Dr. Vancil to testify, but it was returned not served.

The Medical Device Amendments of 1976 (MDA) to the Food, Drug and Cosmetic Act of 1938 authorize the Secretary of Health and Human Services to promulgate a regulatory scheme for the clinical investigation of experimental devices under an investigational device exemption. The purpose of such exemptions is:

> To encourage, to the extent consistent with the protection of the public health and safety and with ethical standards, the discovery and development of useful devices intended for human use and to that end to maintain optimum freedom for scientific investigators in their pursuit of that purpose.

In the year following the enactment of the MDA, the FDA issued regulations providing for "Investigational Exemptions for Intraocular Lenses." (21 C.F.R. § 813.1 et seq. (1993)). The regulations detail the application process by which intraocular lenses can be implanted into human subjects. Under the terms of the regulations, Sherman Hospital was an "institution," which is defined as a hospital which "engages in the conduct of research on human subjects." The IRB of an "institution" is charged with the responsibility to review and monitor all investigational studies of intraocular lenses. Specifically, the IRB: "Shall assure that the rights of human subjects are properly protected, that legally effective informed consent is obtained, and that the method of obtaining consent properly informs the human subject of the significant aspects of the study in accordance with Part 50 of this chapter."

Part 50, dealing with IRBs, requires that each subject be provided with basic information, including: "A statement that the study involves research, an explanation of the purposes of the research and the expected duration of the subject's participation, a description of the procedures to be followed, and identification of any procedures which are experimental." Part 50 also requires that informed consent be "documented by the use of a written consent form approved by the IRB and signed by the subject." The IRBs are also required to conduct "continuing review of research" on at least an annual basis, which includes the duty to review the informed consent process. In the case at bar, the defense's expert witness, Earnest Prentice, admitted that, if Sherman Hospital's IRB had audited any of Dr. Vancil's charts in the 1½ years before Kus' surgery, the IRB would have discovered Vancil's use of the modified consent form. Additionally, Prentice admitted that a choice existed at Sherman Hospital by September 1, 1983, between an FDA-approved lens and the experimental lenses which were implanted into Kus' eyes.

After the implants in Kus' eyes allegedly caused difficulty and permanent damage due to their design, Kus filed suit against Sherman Hospital, alleging, in part: (1) medical battery, (2) negligence under a lack of informed consent theory, and (3) negligence for failing to respond adequately to a product recall involving the lens manufactured by Americal. The trial court dismissed the medical battery and negligence involving the recall claims by directed verdict. The jury returned a verdict for the hospital on the negligence count for the lack of informed consent. * * *

In the case at bar, we determine that a hospital, as well as a physician, may be held liable for a patient's defective consent in a case involving experimental intraocular lenses, and thus the plaintiff's claim is therefore viable. * * * [T]he general rule [is] that, unlike the physician, "a hospital generally has no duty to obtain a like informed consent from the same patient." * * * The rationale underlying this rule is that the physician has the " 'technical knowledge and training necessary to advise each patient of the risks,' " and that " 'the hospital does not know the patient's medical history, nor the details of the particular surgery to be performed.' " * * *

While we agree that generally a hospital is not in the best position to inform a patient of risks, here it is clear that Sherman Hospital undertook the responsibility to inform the plaintiff of the experimental nature of his surgery. Moreover, a participating institution in the intraocular lens study is required to conduct "continued review of research" under the federal guidelines which includes the duty to review the informed consent process. Thus, Sherman Hospital also had the minimal duty here of checking to ensure that the form its IRB had promulgated was being used. * * * [T]he particular facts in the case before us require a determination that a hospital, as well as a physician, may be liable for claims arising from the lack of informed consent in this instance. * * *

Evidence in the record indicates that here the consent form approved by Sherman Hospital's IRB was modified by Dr. Vancil so that Kus allegedly did not know that he was participating in an experiment. Whether those modifications amounted to Kus' consent being "substantially at variance" with the treatment he actually received—that of an experimental nature—or whether Kus did or did not know of the experimental nature of the treatment are issues which necessarily belong before the jury. The evidence we glean from the record here clearly does not so overwhelmingly favor the hospital that a contrary verdict could [n]ever stand, and granting a directed verdict on the medical battery count was therefore prejudicial error. * * *

NOTES AND QUESTIONS

1. *More informed consent follies*. *Kus* illustrates the important role that IRBs play in supervising research, whether with investigational drugs or devices. In large institutions with many active research protocols, IRBs may find it difficult to monitor compliance at the level needed in *Kus*. A combination of deference to physicians and large workload may prevent boards from discovering significant deviations from informed consent or protocol requirements in a timely fashion. See Frances O. Kelsey, The FDA's Enforcement of IRBs and Patient Informed Consent, 44 Food Drug Cosm. L.J. 13 (1989).

2. *IOLs*. When it enacted the MDA in 1976, Congress included a special provision applicable only to intraocular lenses. The statute provided that the IDE requirements for IOLs should be "applicable in such a manner that the device shall be made reasonably available to physicians meeting appropriate qualifications." 21 U.S.C. § 360j(*l*)(3)(D)(iii); see also 41 Fed. Reg. 38,802, 38,803 (1976); American Soc'y of Cataract & Refractive Surgery v. Sullivan, 772 F.Supp. 666, 673 (D.D.C.1991) (explaining that the statute "evidences a clear congressional intent to assure patients access to the most advanced IOL devices"). This provision arguably granted IOLs a form of grandfathered status rather than genuinely subjecting them to clinical trials. The FDA later revoked its special IDE rules governing IOLs. See 62 Fed. Reg. 4164 (1997).

3. *IRB liability*. Does an IRB owe a duty of care to research participants, and what acts or omissions might establish a breach of any such common law duty? See Alice Dembner, Lawsuits Target Medical Research, Boston Globe, Aug. 12, 2002, at A1. Only a handful of courts have addressed such questions. See, e.g., Kernke v. Menninger Clinic, 172 F.Supp.2d 1347, 1352–53 (D.Kan.2001) (denying the defendants' motion for summary judgment on negligence claims brought by the estate of a subject in clinical trial of an investigational drug for schizophrenia); Friter v. Iolab Corp., 607 A.2d 1111, 1113 (Pa.Super.Ct.1992) ("[T]he hospital, as a participant in a clinical investigation . . . , specifically assumed a duty to ensure that informed consent was obtained by any patient participating in the [IOL] study."); see also Sharona Hoffman & Jessica W. Berg, The Suitability of IRB Liability, 67 U. Pitt. L. Rev. 365 (2005); E. Haavi Morreim, Litigation in Clinical Research: Malpractice Doctrines Versus Research Realities, 32 J.L. Med. & Ethics 474 (2004); David B. Resnik, Liability for Institutional Review Boards: From Regulation to Litigation, 25 J. Legal Med. 131 (2004); Richard S. Saver, Medical Research and Intangible Harm, 74 U. Cin. L.

Rev. 941 (2006); Roger L. Jansson, Comment, Researcher Liability for Negligence in Human Subject Research: Informed Consent and Researcher Malpractice Actions, 78 Wash. L. Rev. 229 (2003); Daniel J. Powell, Comment, Using the False Claims Act as a Basis for Institutional Review Board Liability, 69 U. Chi. L. Rev. 1399 (2002); Carla M. Stalcup, Note, Reviewing the Review Boards: Why Institutional Review Board Liability Does Not Make Good Business Sense, 82 Wash. U. L.Q. 1593 (2004); cf. Rob Stein, U.S. Compensation System Needed for Victims of Research, Panel Says, Wash. Post, Aug. 31, 2011, at A5.

Tivoli v. United States

1996 WL 1056005 (S.D.N.Y.1996).

■ FOX, DISTRICT JUDGE:

* * * In July 1991 Laura Tivoli was diagnosed as suffering from Cushings Syndrome, a disease of the endocrine system, and was referred by her treating physician to the NIH for evaluation and treatment. Cushings Syndrome is a condition in which the body overproduces cortisol. * * * There are four possible causes of Cushings Syndrome including a tumor on the pituitary gland, a condition which is called Cushings Disease and is treatable through surgical removal of the tumor. Plaintiff was referred to the NIH for evaluation for this surgical procedure. Every patient at the NIH Clinical Center is admitted pursuant to one or more protocols (studies) which are overseen by the Institutional Review Board (IRB) of the NIH.

On July 26, 1991, plaintiff underwent [an experimental] diagnostic procedure called an Inferior Petrosal Sinus Sampling (IPSS) to assist the physicians in confirming her diagnosis of Cushings Disease by confirming the location of a tumor on her pituitary gland which was causing the problem, and by lateralizing the tumor, i.e., determining in which lobe of the pituitary gland the tumor was located. The IPSS procedure involved the insertion of a catheter into the femoral vein in plaintiff's groin. The catheter was then manipulated through the body's venous system with the assistance of fluoroscopy to the base of the brain where, in the area close to the pituitary gland, a sampling of blood was to be taken. The analysis of that blood sample was expected to provide the sought after diagnostic information.

Unfortunately plaintiff suffered a cerebral hemorrhage during the IPSS procedure resulting in a severe brain stem stroke syndrome (a stroke) which left her crippled and disfigured. Plaintiff's IPSS (and those of other patients and volunteers) was performed pursuant to protocol 90–CH–194 on which Dr. Jack Yanovsky was the principal investigator. Physicians at the NIH recognized that the protocols limited and restricted their activities in dealing with and performing procedures on patients. This is further confirmed in the testimony of Dr. Gilman Grave, Chairman of the IRB at the NIH, who testified that the protocols which were approved by the IRB controlled the manner or means in which the sampling procedure was conducted, including the designation of the catheter used. The IRB also limited the performance of IPSS procedures to only two physicians, Dr. Donald Miller and Dr. John Doppman, who were required to comply with the terms of the protocol in performing the procedure. * * *

The IRB at the NIH had the function of reviewing all protocols presented to assess the risk benefit ratio of each protocol. The process was explained by Dr. George Chrouoss, the Chief of Pediatric Endocrinology at the NIH. The protocol itself is written by the principal investigator (PI). * * * The IRB can then approve the protocol, reject it, or add additional stipulations or requirements for its performance. * * *

[A] member of the IRB expressed concerns that the protocol which was being reviewed in July 1990 did not list all of the rare complications of venography. Drs. Miller and Doppman stated that the risk of serious complications or death in IPSS exists, but is, at most 0.9% based upon statistical analysis, as they set forth in their published article in the *Journal of Radiology* entitled "Petrosal Sinus Sampling: Technique and Rationale." * * * The IPSS is a specialized application of venography. While this application of venography was relatively new and still under study in 1991, and no incidents of stroke had been reported during an IPSS at that time, the technique of venography was not new, and the risks attendant to it, including that of stroke, were well known. * * *

The only physician who came to plaintiff's room to obtain any consent from her was Dr. Yanovsky, who was neither a radiologist nor, at that time, a Board Certified endocrinologist. He received her consent only to use some of the blood samples to be obtained during the IPSS for his protocol, and not for the performance of the IPSS procedure itself. It is particularly bizarre that this consent was obtained before Dr. Miller, the radiologist who was to perform the IPSS, had even met plaintiff, much less obtained her consent.

The [NIH] requirement that the consent be discussed with the patient, in the patient's own room, well in advance of the performance of the procedure, and by the radiologist who would actually be performing the procedure, is understandable and appropriate since Cushings patients often exhibit emotional and cognitive difficulties. A meeting with the physician in the patient's room well before the procedure was scheduled would allow both the time and the privacy necessary and conducive to a full and complete explanation of the procedure to be performed as well as a discussion of the attendant risks and alternatives. Plaintiff, who had been exhibiting nervousness and anxiety * * * had no such opportunity to meet and confer deliberatively with the physician who performed her IPSS. In the very execution of plaintiff's consent form the NIH deviated from its own procedures and policies. * * *

There was no discussion of the type of catheter to be used, or whether it was or was not the same catheter which had been used in all of the 400 or so prior IPSS procedures which had been mentioned to plaintiff as having been performed at NIH without serious mishap. In fact Yanovsky, the Principal Investigator on the protocol, did not even know that the

Mueller catheter, which had been used in most of the prior IPSS cases, had been discontinued by Dr. Miller who was then using the new and different Miller catheter to perform IPSS procedures. Since Yanovsky did not know about the change, and as PI it was his responsibility to keep the IRB advised, the IRB also did not know about the use of the Miller catheter until the catastrophic result of plaintiff's IPSS. Dr. Yanovsky further stated that if he had known of the use of the Miller catheter the change was significant enough to have warranted its inclusion in his study. IRB Chairman Dr. Grave confirmed that he too remained unaware of any difference between the catheters used by Drs. Miller and Doppman until the IRB meeting subsequent to plaintiff's IPSS. * * *

Dr. Yanovsky agreed that it is good medical practice to include and identify in the consent even remote risks of the procedure if of a life threatening nature. He further agreed that stroke or venous rupture is, and was at the time, a known complication of venography. Dr. Yanovsky conceded that the consent form itself does not contain the word stroke, or the phrase "like a stroke," and that the risk of stroke is a grave possibility as a complication of the IPSS.

The consent form contains no mention of a venous rupture or bleed as a possible complication of the IPSS. The only discussion of bleeding in the consent form is at the groin, the site of the incision which is hardly the same risk or complication as a stroke. [One expert] opined that the wording of the Yanovsky consent, including the use of the phrases "theoretical possibility" and "like a stroke" were not sufficient to convey in common medical terms to a patient the potential risks in the IPSS procedure for stroke and attendant disability and death.

The Yanovsky consent is signed by plaintiff and Yanovsky on page 7. On that same page the document lists and identifies several physicians to whom plaintiff could address questions or problems. It is noteworthy that the names of Drs. Miller and Doppman, the only two radiologists authorized to perform the IPSS procedure, are not among them, confirming Yanovsky's position that this consent form was not addressed to the IPSS procedure itself, but rather was limited to the use of plaintiff's blood samples obtained during the procedure in his study.

A consent to the performance of the IPSS procedure was obtained from plaintiff by Dr. Miller, the radiologist who performed the procedure. * * * As to risks and complications, the only information he provided to plaintiff which is at all significant here is "when you put a catheter in the vein at the base of the skull there is always a risk of clot forming in the cavernous sinus what we call cavernous sinus thrombosis, that's very serious, like a stroke.... That's never actually happened; we worry about it happening, but we've never seen it happen so it's theoretical." * * *

Plaintiff had no questions and signed the consent form which was witnessed by * * * a member of the team which was to perform the procedure. This too was a deviation from the normal practice and procedure at NIH as set forth on the very face of the NIH consent document which specifies that the execution of the consent should be witnessed by someone who was not a member of the operating team.

Plaintiff then made the previously mentioned remark which fixed her in Dr. Miller's memory. As she entered the procedure room she turned to Dr. Miller and said: "Nothing is going to happen, is it?" Miller responded: "Well you understand there aren't any guarantees, but as I told you, none of the Cushing patients have ever had any problems. The normal volunteers all went home okay. And they're fine. And that's really all I can tell you." * * *

Dr. Miller testified that there was nothing new about the catheter and that it contained no new material or device that had not received prior approval from the FDA. His testimony on that issue and the position taken by the government is patently absurd in the face of a medical journal article written by Dr. Miller, and submitted for publication to the *Journal of Radiology* on June 15, 1990. That article, entitled "Selective Catheterization of the Inferior Petrosal Sinuses: A New Catheter Design," is self explanatory as to Dr. Miller's position regarding the newness of the catheter design. The article goes on to describe in detail the draw backs of the previously used Mueller catheter, the reasons why "a new set of catheters was developed," and a brief description of the clinical trial in which IPSS procedures were performed on 22 patients in which "these new catheters" were used. Clearly Dr. Miller himself considered his new catheter to indeed be "new" when he submitted the article for publication in a professional journal, at least until plaintiff's tragic complication caused him to rethink his position.

Once a treatment, an instrument, or a drug has been approved, it may be utilized for other applications or purposes without the necessity for further FDA approval. That principle does not apply to IRB approvals, however, as evidenced by the IRB action in prohibiting the use of the Miller catheter after plaintiff's complication. * * *

Plaintiff was not told anything at all about the Miller catheter. She was not told that it was new or experimental or that it was different from the catheter which had been used in most of the 400 IPSS procedures which she was told had been performed without incident. She was also not told that the complications experienced by the two volunteer patients in January and February 1991 might plausibly have been catheter related neurologic episodes. She was not told of the risk of stroke in the IPSS procedure. * * *

Dr. Yanovsky mentioned nothing to plaintiff about alternatives to the IPSS procedure since his consent was only addressed to using blood samples to be taken during the IPSS. Dr. Miller mentioned alternatives such as CT and MRI scans and endocrine studies, but advised her that these were not nearly as accurate as the IPSS. While the IPSS had been found to be 100% accurate in the diagnosis of Cushings Disease and in the lateralization of the tumor (determining in which lobe of the pituitary gland the tumor is located) there were other tests available * * * which, in combination, would have diagnosed the presence of a pituitary tumor with an accuracy of between 95 and 97%. * * *

Plaintiff was at the time of her IPSS a social worker holding an MSW degree. She had experience in dealing with patients with various emotional and behavioral disorders but no medical background or experience. She specifically recalls that she was not advised of the risk of stroke in the IPSS because she did not at that time know exactly what a stroke was although she knew that it occurred "like in older people." She had read the NIH booklet provided to her entitled "Preparing for Petrosal Sinus Sampling" and had not seen the word stroke. If that word had been in the booklet she would have asked to have it explained. * * * She further stated that if she had been told that there had been prior complications with the use of Dr. Miller's catheter she "would have withdrawn from the petrosal sinus sampling." Her testimony is supported by the proof of the great number of questions which plaintiff had been asking of the physicians and nursing staff about her condition and the procedures, her previously noted anxiety, and most particularly by her hesitation and question to Dr. Miller as she entered the angio room for the IPSS procedure. * * *

Accordingly, since the physicians involved were government employees, the consent was inadequate as to the risk of stroke, the plaintiff suffered a stroke as a consequence of the IPSS procedure, and a reasonable patient in plaintiff's position would have considered the missing data significant and would not have consented to the procedure if the data had been provided, I find that the government is liable to the plaintiff for the injuries which she suffered during the IPSS procedure. * * *

NOTES AND QUESTIONS

1. Tivoli *transgressions*. The plaintiff in *Tivoli* sued the physicians who treated her under the umbrella of an NIH-supervised protocol; she did not sue the supervising IRB. The case does not involve a typical research protocol to evaluate the usefulness of an investigational device; instead, it is a protocol to evaluate an experimental procedure (which happened to involve the use of a device). Cf. Denise Grady, Riddled with Metal by Mistake in a Study, N.Y. Times, Mar. 22, 2011, at D5 (describing a device that fragmented during a study of a new radiation technique for treating breast cancer patients). The case is nonetheless useful as an illustration of how an individual physician-patient relationship can fail to conform to the ideals of the informed consent process in an experimental medical procedure. How many violations of the informed consent regulations or NIH policies can you identify in the *Tivoli* opinion? To what do you attribute these violations—carelessness, failure of the institution to educate its researchers properly about patient-protective policies, inadequate IRB oversight, or something else?

2. *IRB waivers of informed consent requirements*. The FDA's regulations exempt certain types of "minimal risk" studies from the informed consent requirements. See 21 C.F.R. § 56.110. Some commentators controversially proposed expanding these exempt categories, arguing that patients are often over-protected in the context of clinical trials that involve very little risk while paradoxically receiving little or no protection from physicians who wish to try experimental treatments as "therapeutic innovation." See Robert D. Truog et al., Is Informed Consent Always Necessary for Randomized, Controlled Trials?, 340 New Eng. J. Med. 804 (1999); see also Nancy M.P. King, The Line Between Clinical Innovation and Human Experimentation, 32 Seton Hall L. Rev. 573 (2002).

Doe v. Rumsfeld

297 F.Supp.2d 119 (D.D.C.2003).

■ SULLIVAN, DISTRICT JUDGE:

Plaintiffs, members of the active duty and selected National Guardsmen components of the Armed Forces as well as civilian contract employees of the Department of Defense (DOD) who have submitted or have been instructed to submit to anthrax vaccinations without their consent pursuant to the Anthrax Vaccine Immunization Program (AVIP), commenced this action * * * *

In 1970, the National Institutes of Health (NIH), the agency then charged with licensing biologic drugs, licensed AVA [Anthrax Vaccine Adsorbed] for use against anthrax. See 36 Fed. Reg. 8704, 8705 (1971). Two years later, authority to approve biologic drugs was delegated to the FDA. After the authority to license biologic drugs was delegated to the FDA, the agency initiated a review of the safety, effectiveness, and labeling of all licensed biologics. 21 C.F.R. § 601.25. * * * In that product review, the independent Biologics Review Panel recommended that the [anthrax] vaccine be classified as safe, effective, and not misbranded. In their recommendations the panel discussed the Brachman study and stated that the vaccine's "efficacy against inhalation anthrax is not well documented.... [N]o meaningful assessment of its value against inhalation anthrax is possible due to its low incidence." 50 Fed. Reg. 51,002 (1985). To date the AVA label does not specify which method of anthrax exposure it protects against. * * *

In September 1996, AVA's manufacturer submitted an IND application to the FDA in an attempt to get FDA approval for a modification of the AVA license to demonstrate the drug's effectiveness against inhalation anthrax. The IND application is still pending and, to date, there is no indication for inhalation anthrax on the label or in the product insert.

In 1997, * * * the Assistant Secretary of Defense (Health Affairs) wrote to the FDA's Lead Deputy Commissioner, stating that the "DOD has long interpreted the scope of the license to include inhalation exposure, including that which would occur in a biological warfare context" and inquiring "whether the FDA has any objection to our interpretation of the scope of the licensure for the anthrax vaccine." The Lead Deputy Commissioner responded "I believe your interpretation is not inconsistent with the current label." In a response to a citizen petition dated August 2002, the FDA's Associate Commissioner of Policy noted that the FDA still has yet to finalize the rule proposed in the December 13, 1985, *Federal Register*. But here, contradicting the panel's position regarding the Brachman study in the 1985 *Federal Register*, the FDA stated that the Brachman study included inhalation anthrax. Thus, the FDA concluded that "[t]he indication section of the labeling does not specify the route of exposure and thus includes both cutaneous and inhalation exposure."

The AVA product insert, which originally stated that the adverse reaction rate to the vaccine was 0.2 percent, was recently revised to reflect an adverse reaction rate between 5.0 percent and 35.0 percent. At least six deaths have been linked to the vaccine and the vaccine's pregnancy use risk has been upgraded from a Category C risk (risk cannot be ruled out) to a Category D risk (positive evidence of risk.)

In 1998, in response to concerns about the use of investigational new drugs during the 1991 Gulf War that may have led to unexplained illnesses among veterans, Congress signed into law 10 U.S.C. § 1107. This provision prohibits the administration of investigational new drugs, or drugs unapproved for their intended use, to service members without their informed consent. The consent requirement may be waived only by the President. In 1999, the President signed Executive Order 13139, pursuant to which the DOD must obtain informed consent from each individual member of the armed forces before administering investigational drugs and under which waivers of informed consent are granted only "when absolutely necessary." 64 Fed. Reg. 54,175 (1999). In August 2000, the DOD formally adopted these requirements in DOD Directive 6200.2.

In 1998, the DOD began a mass inoculation program using AVA as a preventative measure against inhalation anthrax for service members and civilian employees. The program was administered without informed consent or a presidential waiver. Plaintiffs contend that because AVA is not licensed for inhalation anthrax, its use by the DOD is not only investigational but it is also a drug unapproved for its intended use in violation of 10 U.S.C. § 1107, Executive Order 13139, and DOD Directive 6200.2. Defendants maintain that they are not in violation of any law because AVA is not an investigational new drug and it is licensed for inhalation anthrax. * * *

Courts have traditionally been hesitant to intervene in the conduct of military affairs. * * * While claims for damages are nonjusticiable, the circuits are divided with respect to the viability of claims for injunctive relief against the military. * * * [T]here is no bright line rule in the D.C. Circuit when it comes to establishing justiciability. What can be said with certainty is that this circuit has not ruled out the right of individuals to seek injunctive relief against the military in civilian courts in all cases. * * *

[P]laintiffs allege that the DOD acted arbitrarily and capriciously by failing to adhere to statutes and regulations governing its activities. Their claim is against the Secretary of Defense about a decision made in headquarters, not about a tactical decision military supervisors made in the field. Similarly, because plaintiffs are a diverse class and include civilian individuals who are not in the employ of the military, the danger of disrupting discipline and/or supervisory-subordinate relationships is minimal at best. * * *

Defendants maintain that Section 10 of the APA [Administrative Procedure Act] precludes judicial review. Specifically, they point to 5 U.S.C. § 701(b)(1)(G), which renders the APA's judicial review provisions inapplicable to acts of "military authority exercised in the field in time of war or in occupied territory." * * * As plaintiffs note, the AVIP was announced in December 1997, implemented initially in March 1998, and implemented force-wide in May of that year. Due to the vaccine shortages discussed above, few of the service members who fought in Afghanistan in 2001–2003 were vaccinated at all. The recommencement of the AVIP program was announced on June 29, 2002—a date which predated congressional authorization for the use of force in Iraq by four months and the recent hostilities by almost eighteen months. The plaintiffs in the instant case are not challenging military authority exercised in the field in a time of war or in occupied territory. In fact, according to plaintiffs, "[n]one of the plaintiffs are presently in the 'field' or in 'occupied territory.' " * * *

Having found that this claim is justiciable, the central question before the court is whether AVA is being used as an investigational new drug or as a drug unapproved for its intended use. At bottom, this inquiry turns on whether the FDA has made a final decision on the investigational status of AVA; and if not (1) whether the 1996 IND application establishes the vaccine's status as an investigational drug and (2) whether the DOD is using AVA in a manner inconsistent with its license and intended use.

[D]efendants' position is that 10 U.S.C. § 1107 is inapplicable because the AVA's license covers use against inhalation anthrax. They argue that the FDA has interpreted the lack of specificity concerning inhalation anthrax as permitting use of the vaccine against any route of exposure. * * * In addition, defendants point to a 1997 letter written by the Assistant Secretary of Defense stating that the IND application in no way suggests an official position that the DOD believed the approved label did not already encompass inhalation exposure. Defendants note that such interpretations by an agency within its area of expertise are entitled to substantial deference. * * *

While defendants' arguments concerning deference are correct, the dispute in this case has not focused on the language of a particular DOD statute. Rather, it is the FDA's term "investigational" that is at the heart of the dispute. Title 10 U.S.C. § 1107 and the attendant DOD regulation apply only if the FDA determines that AVA is an investigational drug or a drug unapproved for its present purpose. As plaintiffs note, the letters and declarations defendants cite are not "formal FDA opinion(s)." * * * [T]he personal opinions of FDA officials as expressed in a series of letters are not entitled to any particular deference. The apparent change in position from the December 1985 proposed rule and the cryptic use of a double negative (i.e. "it is not inconsistent"), fail to persuade this court that the view expressed in the 1997 letter is the FDA's formal opinion. * * *

In the case of AVA, the 1985 panel found insufficient data to license the drug for use against inhalation anthrax. To date, no additional studies have been performed and AVA's label does not specify use of the vaccine for this purpose. Moreover, the court is persuaded that the 1996 IND application remains pending today. The introduction to the application expressly states that one objective of the application is to obtain a specific indication for use of AVA against inhalation anthrax. While the government states that the inhalation anthrax aspect of the IND is no longer active, the documents submitted to this court under seal suggest otherwise. Finally, statements made by DOD officials suggest that the agency itself has, at some point at least, considered AVA experimental with respect to inhalation anthrax. Given all these factors, the court would be remiss to conclude that the original license included inhalation anthrax. Having reached that conclusion, the DOD's administration of the inoculation without consent of those vaccinated amounts to arbitrary action. * * *

Defendants base their public policy argument on the idea that requiring compliance with informed consent would render it infeasible to continue the AVIP for current military operations in Iraq or in conjunction with the war on terrorism. Essentially, defendants argue that the harm to the public interest would include disrupting the smooth functioning of the military, hampering military readiness, and reducing the military's ability to protect its service members. Should those individuals who have refused anthrax vaccinations be injured by anthrax, their injuries or deaths would have a detrimental effect on the military and its operation at large.

Plaintiffs counter by observing that if the risks of anthrax injuries were so manifestly present, the State Department, as well as the coalition forces of Britain and Australia, would have taken similar steps to protect their employees. Plaintiffs refute the government's argument concerning the cumbersome administrative results that could ensue from the granting of a preliminary injunction by stating that the DOD was able to comply with similar administrative proceedings in only three weeks between adoption of the predecessor of 10 U.S.C. § 1107 and the start of the Gulf War in 1991. * * *

The court is persuaded that the right to bodily integrity and the importance of complying with legal requirements, even in the face of requirements that may potentially be inconvenient or burdensome, are among the highest public policy concerns one could articulate. Moreover, the court is not convinced that requiring the DOD to obtain informed consent will interfere with the smooth functioning of the military. However, if obtaining informed consent were to significantly interfere with military function, defendants are free to seek a presidential waiver. If the Executive branch determines that this is truly an exigent situation, then obtaining a presidential waiver would be an expeditious end to this controversy. * * *

Defendants' position is that harm in the form of potential side effects is "hypothetical or, at best, unlikely to occur." Defendants refer to a de minimis risk of serious adverse reactions and report 105 serious adverse reactions from AVA in over 830,000 recipients. They stress that AVA has been used effectively in civilian industry for over 30 years. Having found that AVA is an investigational drug under 10 U.S.C. § 1107, the court is persuaded that requiring a person to submit to an inoculation without informed consent or the presidential waiver is an irreparable harm for which there is no monetary relief. * * *

Thus, because the plaintiffs are likely to prevail on the merits, defendants will not face substantial harm by the imposition of an injunction, the public interest is served, and plaintiffs face irreparable harm, the court finds that the plaintiffs meet the requirements for a preliminary injunction. The women and men of our armed forces put their lives on the line every day to preserve and safeguard the freedoms that all Americans cherish and enjoy. Absent an informed consent or presidential waiver, the United States cannot demand that members of the armed forces also serve as guinea pigs for experimental drugs.

NOTES AND QUESTIONS

1. *Subsequent history.* One week after the court's order (and 18 years after issuing its proposed rule), the FDA published a final rule that found AVA safe and effective for protection against inhalational anthrax. See 69 Fed. Reg. 255 (2004). After invalidating this rule on procedural grounds, the district court issued a permanent injunction against implementation of the AVIP. See Doe v. Rumsfeld, 341 F.Supp.2d 1 (D.D.C.2004). In response, the government invoked a newly enacted provision that authorized the use of unapproved drugs during an emergency. See Marc Kaufman, Pentagon Boosts Plan for Anthrax Inoculations: Emergency Provisions Invoked to Revive Use, Wash. Post, Feb. 2, 2005, at A3 (reporting that soldiers would have the right to refuse). When it authorized the use of unapproved medical products in the event of a declared national emergency (and without distinguishing between civilians and military personnel), Congress had included an informed consent requirement. See Project BioShield Act of 2004, Pub. L. No. 108–276, § 4(a), 118 Stat. 853 (codified at 21 U.S.C. § 360bbb–3(e)(1)(A)(ii)). Just as the six-month authorization for AVA expired, the FDA reissued its final order. See 70 Fed. Reg. 75,180, 75,183 (2005) (concluding that it was effective against inhalational anthrax); see also Doe v. Rumsfeld, 172 F.App'x 327 (D.C.Cir.2006) (rejecting the government's appeal as moot because the FDA's approval satisfied the district court's injunction). A substantive challenge to the FDA's decision to approve the vaccine failed. See Rempfer v. Sharfstein, 583 F.3d 860 (D.C.Cir.2009). When it comes to promoting the development of new biowarfare vaccines and treatments, the Pentagon has shown far less ingenuity. See Vernon Loeb, Biodefense Agency Urged for Safety of U.S. Troops, Wash. Post, Jan. 23, 2004, at A19; see also Kendra Marr, Biotechs Race for New Vaccine: Government Bid Calls for Improved Anthrax Shot,

Wash. Post, Oct. 6, 2008, at D1 ("[T]wo years ago, a revoked federal contract for a purportedly new and improved vaccine left a California biotech in ruins.").

2. *Soldiers vs. civilians.* Previously, the federal courts had rejected a challenge to the FDA's interim rule waiving (on grounds of infeasibility) informed consent requirements for the use of unapproved pretreatments for exposure to chemical and biological weapons on military personnel during Operation Desert Storm. See Doe v. Sullivan, 756 F.Supp. 12 (D.D.C.) (extending significant deference to both the DOD and the FDA, and concluding that special informed consent requirements did not apply because the unapproved drugs were intended for treatment rather than research), aff'd, 938 F.2d 1370 (D.C.Cir.1991). The military has a checkered history when it comes to human experimentation. During the height of the Cold War, the DOD sponsored experiments in which cancer patients and prisoners were exposed to total body radiation or were administered plutonium in order to test the body's response. The "Human Radiation Experiments" failed to use consent forms for the first five years; later, the consent forms greatly understated the risks involved. See In re Cincinnati Radiation Litig., 874 F.Supp. 796 (S.D.Ohio 1995); Advisory Cmte. on Human Radiation Experiments, Research Ethics and the Medical Profession, 276 JAMA 403 (1996); see also United States v. Stanley, 483 U.S. 669 (1987) (Army's secret LSD experiments); Catherine L. Annas & George J. Annas, Enhancing the Fighting Force: Medical Research on American Soldiers, 25 J. Contemp. Health L. & Pol'y 283 (2009). Does the uniqueness of the battlefield context justify the diminution of individual rights to refuse unwanted medical treatment? What if the DOD sought to vaccinate civilians in a combat zone without securing their informed consent? (In light of continuing fears of bioterrorism, of course, there is no longer a narrowly defined battlefield situated in a distant land. See Ryan R. Kemper, Note, Responding to Bioterrorism: An Analysis of Titles I and II of the Public Health Security and Bioterrorism Preparedness and Response Act of 2002, 83 Wash. U. L.Q. 385 (2005).) What if a public school board wanted to inoculate all of its students with an experimental drug without consent in order to prevent an outbreak of meningitis?

3. *Other exceptions to the informed consent requirement.* In various circumstances, individuals have had to submit to treatment without their informed consent, but these interventions generally are not experimental (and hence not governed by FDA or NIH regulations). For example, courts have ordered patients to remain hospitalized for lengthy periods of time to treat contagious diseases. See, e.g., City of New York v. Antoinette R., 630 N.Y.S.2d 1008 (Sup.Ct.1995) (ordering a woman with tuberculosis who refused to complete her course of treatment to remain in a hospital for up to seven months until she finished her antibiotics or demonstrated that she would comply with the medication regime outside of the hospital); see also Michelle A. Daubert, Comment, Pandemic Fears and Contemporary Quarantine: Protecting Liberty Through a Continuum of Due Process Rights, 54 Buff. L. Rev. 1299 (2007); Emily S. Huggins, Note, Assisted Outpatient Treatment: An Unconstitutional Invasion of Protected Rights or a Necessary Government Safeguard?, 30 J. Legis. 305 (2004) (discussing laws that mandate psychotropic medication for the mentally ill). Courts also have rejected challenges to public health laws that mandate inoculations. See, e.g., Jacobson v. Massachusetts, 197 U.S. 11 (1905) (upholding a city's smallpox vaccination requirement); see also Elizabeth R. Sheyn, An Accidental Violation: How Required Gardasil Vaccinations for Female Immigrants to the United States Contravene International Law, 88 Neb. L. Rev. 524 (2010); Sara Mahmoud–Davis, Note, Balancing Public Health and Individual Choice: A Proposal for a Federal Emergency Vaccination Law, 20 Health Matrix 219 (2010). Most state childhood vaccination laws allow parents to opt out. See Anthony Ciolli, Religious and Philosophical Exemptions to Mandatory School Vaccinations: Who Should Bear the Costs to Society?, 74 Mo. L. Rev. 287 (2009); Allan J. Jacobs, Needles and Notebooks: The Limits of Requiring Immunization for School Attendance, 33 Hamline L. Rev. 171 (2010); Sandra G. Boodman, Faith Lets Some Kids Skip Shots, Wash. Post, June 10, 2008, at F1; see also Margaret J. Kochuba, Comment, Public Health vs Patient Rights: Reconciling Informed Consent with HPV Vaccination, 58 Emory L.J. 761 (2009).

4. *The emergency research exception to general informed consent rules.* The FDA regulations recognize that, in some emergency situations, it may not be feasible to secure informed consent before using an experimental product:

> (a) The obtaining of informed consent shall be deemed feasible unless, before use of the test article (except as provided in paragraph (b) of this section), both the investigator and a physician who is not otherwise participating in the clinical investigation certify in writing all of the following:
>
> (1) The human subject is confronted by a life-threatening situation necessitating the use of the test article.
>
> (2) Informed consent cannot be obtained from the subject because of an inability to communicate with, or obtain legally effective consent from, the subject.
>
> (3) Time is not sufficient to obtain consent from the subject's legal representative.
>
> (4) There is available no alternative method of approved or generally recognized therapy that provides an equal or greater likelihood of saving the life of the subject.
>
> (b) If immediate use of the test article is, in the investigator's opinion, required to preserve the life of the subject, and time is not sufficient to obtain the independent determination required in paragraph (a) of this section in advance of using the test article, the determinations of the clinical investigator shall be made and, within 5 working days after the use of the article, be reviewed and evaluated in writing by a physician who is not participating in the clinical investigation....

21 C.F.R. § 50.23. In 2011, the FDA issued a final rule exempting from informed consent requirements experimental in vitro diagnostic devices intended for use in detecting biological, chemical or nuclear agents.

In some studies, researchers can predict the recurrence of this problem because the investigational products are designed to treat emergency medical conditions, such as heart attack, stroke, or trauma. It is often difficult or impossible to design traditional research protocols that will capture needed data because the relevant pool of potential subjects cannot consent to treatment in these situations. The applicable regulation provides, in part, as follows:

> (a) The IRB responsible for the review, approval, and continuing review of the clinical investigation described in this section may approve that investigation without requiring that informed consent of all research subjects be obtained if the IRB (with the concurrence of a licensed physician who is a member of or consultant to the IRB and who is not otherwise participating in the clinical investigation) finds and documents each of the following:
>
> (1) The human subjects are in a life-threatening situation, available treatments are unproven or unsatisfactory, and the collection of valid scientific evidence, which may include evidence obtained through randomized placebo-controlled investigations, is necessary to determine the safety and effectiveness of particular interventions.
>
> (2) Obtaining informed consent is not feasible because: (i) The subjects will not be able to give their informed consent as a result of their medical condition; (ii) The intervention under investigation must be administered before consent from the subjects' legally authorized representatives is feasible; and (iii) There is no reasonable way to identify prospectively the individuals likely to become eligible for participation in the clinical investigation.
>
> (3) Participation in the research holds out the prospect of direct benefit to the subjects because: (i) Subjects are facing a life-threatening situation that necessitates intervention; (ii) Appropriate animal and other preclinical studies have been conducted, and the information derived from those studies and related evidence support the potential for the intervention to provide a direct benefit to the individual subjects; and (iii) Risks associated with the investigation are reasonable in relation to what is known about the medical condition of the potential class of subjects, the risks and benefits of standard therapy, if any, and what is known about the risks and benefits of the proposed intervention or activity....
>
> (6) ... The IRB has reviewed and approved procedures and information to be used when providing an opportunity for a family member to object to a subject's participation in the clinical investigation....
>
> (7) Additional protections of the rights and welfare of the subjects will be provided, including, at least: (i) Consultation (including, where

> appropriate, consultation carried out by the IRB) with representatives of the communities in which the clinical investigation will be conducted and from which the subjects will be drawn; (ii) Public disclosure to the communities in which the clinical investigation will be conducted and from which the subjects will be drawn, prior to initiation of the clinical investigation, of plans for the investigation and its risks and expected benefits; (iii) Public disclosure of sufficient information following completion of the clinical investigation to apprise the community and researchers of the study, including the demographic characteristics of the research population, and its results; (iv) Establishment of an independent data monitoring committee to exercise oversight of the clinical investigation....

21 C.F.R. § 50.24(a); see also 76 Fed. Reg. 18,558 (2011) (announcing the availability of guidance); Gail E. Gillenwater, FDA's Emergency Research Rule: An Inch Given, a Yard Taken, 63 Food & Drug L.J. 217, 233–40 (2008) (cataloging completed, ongoing, and planned studies under this rule); id. at 232 ("During the first 10 years, emergency research studies were rare and relatively small ...."); id. at 218 ("Over the last few years, there has been a substantial increase in [its] use.... More than 36,000 nonconsenting patients with life-threatening conditions are scheduled to be enrolled in ongoing emergency research studies ...."); Richard S. Saver, Critical Care Research and Informed Consent, 75 N.C. L. Rev. 205 (1996). What concerns do the regulation leave unresolved? OHRP and others have criticized the FDA for relying on this rule in authorizing research on blood substitutes in severe trauma patients. See Thomas M. Burton, Blood–Substitute Study Is Criticized by US Agency, Wall St. J., Mar. 10, 2006, at A3; Rob Stein, FDA Faulted for Approving Studies of Artificial Blood, Wash. Post, Apr. 29, 2008, at A2; see also Andrew Pollack, For Stem Cells, a Role on the Battlefield, N.Y. Times, Sept. 9, 2008, at F5 (describing DARPA's interest in "blood pharming" to facilitate battlefield transfusions). See generally Douglas A. Grimm, Informed Consent for All! No Exceptions, 37 N.M. L. Rev. 39 (2007); Mark S. Stein & Julian Savulescu, Welfare Versus Autonomy in Human Subjects Research, 38 Fla. St. U. L. Rev. 303 (2011).

D. ACCESS TO UNAPPROVED PRODUCTS

Abigail Alliance for Better Access to Developmental Drugs v. von Eschenbach

495 F.3d 695 (D.C.Cir.2007) (en banc).

■ GRIFFITH, CIRCUIT JUDGE:

* * * The Abigail Alliance for Better Access to Developmental Drugs is an organization of terminally ill patients and their supporters that seeks expanded access to experimental drugs * * * * The Alliance's amended complaint alleges that this testing process [in pursuit of FDA approval] is

an extremely lengthy one, requiring nearly seven years for the average experimental drug. * * *

Terminally ill patients need not, however, always await the results of the clinical testing process. The FDA and Congress have created several programs designed to provide early access to promising experimental drugs when warranted. For example, under the "treatment IND" program, the FDA may approve use of an investigational drug by patients not part of the clinical trials for the treatment of "serious or immediately life-threatening disease[s]" if there exists "no comparable or satisfactory alternative drug or other therapy"; if "[t]he drug is under investigation in a controlled clinical trial"; and if the drug's sponsor "is actively pursuing marketing approval of the investigational drug with due diligence," 21 C.F.R. § 312.34(b)(1). The FDA reserves the right, however, to deny any treatment IND request if (1) the agency believes there is no "reasonable basis" to conclude that the drug is effective; or (2) granting the request "[w]ould ... expose the patient[] ... to an unreasonable and significant additional risk of illness or injury." Id. § 312.34(b)(3). Sponsors may not profit from any approved treatment IND program and may only "recover costs of manufacture, research, development, and handling of the investigational drug." Id. § 312.7(d)(3).

Concluding that the FDA's current process for early access to new drugs was inadequate to meet the needs of its terminally ill members, the Alliance submitted its own proposals to the FDA. Those proposals culminated in a "citizen petition" to the FDA, arguing that there is a "different risk-benefit tradeoff facing patients who are terminally ill and who have no other treatment options." Although the Alliance agreed that "[e]xtensive marshalling of evidence regarding drug interactions, dose optimization, and the like" is "appropriate for new drugs to treat patients with other alternatives ... [,] these steps may well entail a delay that is fatal" for terminally ill patients. * * * Accordingly, the Alliance requested that the FDA promulgate new regulations that would allow sponsors to market experimental drugs, under some circumstances, after the completion of Phase I trials.

The FDA never responded to the Alliance's citizen petition, but [it] did respond to the Alliance's earlier submissions. * * * Relying upon its experience exercising its scientific and medical judgment in creating its regulations for experimental drugs and, in certain circumstances, exceptions to those regulations for the terminally ill, the FDA noted that "a reasonably precise estimate of response rate" and "enough experience to detect serious adverse effects" are "critical" in determining when experimental drugs should be made available. For example, most experimental cancer drugs "have potentially lethal toxicity, with potentially large effects on a patient's remaining quality of life." Accordingly, "it does not serve patients well to make drugs too widely available before there is a reasonable assessment of such risks to guide patient decisions, and experience in managing them." The FDA concluded that accepting the Alliance's proposal "would upset the appropriate balance that [it is] seeking to maintain, by giving almost total weight to the goal of early availability and giving little recognition to the importance of marketing drugs with reasonable knowledge for patients and physicians of their likely clinical benefit and their toxicity."

Having thus been rejected by the FDA, the Alliance turned to the courts, arguing that the United States Constitution provides a right of access to experimental drugs for its members. In a complaint that mirrored much of its earlier submissions to the FDA, the Alliance argued that the FDA's lengthy clinical trials, combined with the "FDA's restrictions on pre-approval availability[,] amount to a death sentence for these [terminally ill] patients." Nor, the Alliance argues, are the FDA's exceptions to the clinical testing process sufficient to provide the terminally ill the access they need because they "are small, when they exist at all," and the ban on profits prevents many drug sponsors from participating. * * *

As framed by the Alliance, we now consider: "Whether the liberty protected by the Due Process Clause embraces the right of a terminally ill patient with no remaining approved treatment options to decide, in consultation with his or her own doctor, whether to seek access to investigational medications that the [FDA] concedes are safe and promising enough for substantial human testing."[5] That is, we must determine whether terminally ill patients have a fundamental right to experimental drugs that have passed Phase I clinical testing. If such a right exists, the Alliance argues that both 21 C.F.R. § 312.34(b)(3) (preventing access to experimental drugs for terminally ill patients where there is insufficient evidence of effectiveness or where there is an unreasonable risk of injury) and 21 C.F.R. § 312.7 (prohibiting drug manufacturers from profiting on the sale of experimental drugs) must be subjected to strict scrutiny because they interfere with a fundamental constitutional right. We do not address the broader question of whether access to medicine might ever implicate fundamental rights. * * *

We will assume *arguendo* that the Alliance's description of its asserted right would satisfy *Glucksberg*'s "careful description" requirement.[6] * * *

---

5. The dissent has recast the Alliance's proposed right away from the terms used in its briefs and oral argument—a right to access investigational new drugs—into a right "to try to save one's life" * * * * [W]e must examine the proposed right under *Glucksberg*, which specifically cautions against the type of broad generalization the dissent now employs. See Washington v. Glucksberg, 521 U.S. 702, 721 (1997). If the asserted right is so broad that it protects a person's efforts to save his life, it might subject to strict scrutiny any government action that would affect the means by which he sought to do so, no matter how remote the chance of success. * * *

6. We nonetheless have serious doubt about whether the Alliance's description of its proposed constitutional right could ever pass constitutional muster. The Alliance's claimed right depends on a regulatory determination that the drug is safe for testing, prompting an obvious question: How can a constitutional right be defined by an administrative regulation that is subject to change? Would an FDA decision requiring increased testing for safety and efficacy before the commencement of human clinical trials affect the Alliance's constitutional right? Moreover, we find it difficult to imagine how a right inextricably entangled with the details of shifting administrative regulations could be "deeply rooted in this Nation's history

The Alliance argues that its right can be found in our history and legal traditions because "the government never interfered with the judgment of individual doctors about the medical *efficacy* of particular drugs until 1962," i.e., when major amendments were made to the Food, Drug, and Cosmetic Act. The Alliance has little to say, however, about our Nation's history of regulating the *safety* of drugs. The Alliance's effort to focus on efficacy regulation ignores one simple fact: it is unlawful for the Alliance to procure experimental drugs not only because they have not been proven effective, but because they have not been proven safe. Although the Alliance contends that it only wants drugs that "are safe and promising enough for substantial human testing," i.e., drugs that have passed Phase I testing, current law bans access to an experimental drug on safety grounds until it has successfully completed all phases of testing. Thus, to succeed on its claim of a fundamental right of access for the terminally ill to experimental drugs, the Alliance must show not only that there is a tradition of access to drugs that have not yet been proven effective, but also a tradition of access to drugs that have not yet been proven safe. * * *

By 1870, at least twenty-five states or territories had statutes regulating adulteration (impure drugs), and a few others had laws addressing poisons. In the early history of our Nation, we observe not a tradition of protecting a right of access to drugs, but rather governments responding to the risks of new compounds as they become aware of and able to address those risks. Nor were the States the only regulators of access to drugs. * * * In 1848, the Import Drug Act banned "imported adulterated drugs" * * * * Congress acted again when it passed the Biologics Controls Act of 1902 in response to a series of deadly reactions to a tainted diphtheria vaccine that killed children in New Jersey and Missouri. * * * Congress followed with the Pure Food and Drugs Act of 1906, which prohibited the manufacture of any drug that was "adulterated or misbranded." The current regime of federal drug regulation began to take shape with the Food, Drug, and Cosmetic Act of 1938. The Act required that drug manufacturers provide proof that their products were safe before they could be marketed. * * *

Congress amended the FDCA in 1962 to explicitly require that the FDA only approve drugs deemed effective for public use. Thus, the Alliance argues that, prior to 1962, patients were free to make their own decisions whether a drug might be effective. But even assuming *arguendo* that efficacy regulation began in 1962, the Alliance's argument ignores our Nation's history of drug safety regulation described above. Nor can the Alliance override current FDA regulations simply by insisting that drugs which have completed Phase I testing are safe enough for terminally ill patients. Current law bars public access to drugs undergoing clinical testing on safety grounds. The fact that a drug has emerged from Phase I with a determination that it is safe for limited clinical testing in a controlled and closely-monitored environment after detailed scrutiny of each trial partici-

---

and tradition and implicit in the concept of ordered liberty." *Glucksberg*, 521 U.S. at 721 (quotation marks and citations omitted).

pant does not mean that a drug is safe for use beyond supervised trials. FDA regulation of post-Phase I drugs is entirely consistent with our historical tradition of prohibiting the sale of unsafe drugs.

But even setting the safety issue to one side, the Alliance's argument that effectiveness was not required before 1962 also fails under closer scrutiny. First, as a matter of history, at least some drug regulation prior to 1962 addressed efficacy. More importantly, an arguably limited history of efficacy regulation prior to 1962 does not establish a fundamental right of access to unproven drugs. The amendments made to the FDCA by Congress throughout the twentieth century demonstrate that Congress and the FDA have continually responded to new risks presented by an evolving technology. Recent government efficacy regulation has reflected Congress's exercise of its well-established power to regulate in response to scientific, mathematical, and medical advances.[12] * * *

The Alliance next turns to several common law doctrines, arguing that barring access to experimental drugs for terminally ill patients is "inconsistent with the way that our legal tradition treats persons in all other life-threatening situations." Specifically, the Alliance argues that three doctrines—(1) the doctrine of necessity; (2) the tort of intentional interference with rescue; and (3) the right to self-defense—each support the recognition of a right to self-preservation. Such a right to self-preservation, the Alliance believes, would permit "persons in mortal peril . . . to try to save their own lives, even if the chosen means would otherwise be illegal or involve enormous risks." Specifically, in this case, the Alliance believes that a right to self-preservation would give the terminally ill a constitutionally protected right of access to experimental drugs.

The Alliance offers, however, little detail about how necessity would apply to its case. (E.g., would terminally ill patients have a right to force drug companies to provide them with experimental drugs?) * * * The Alliance seeks access to drugs that are experimental and have not been shown to be safe, let alone effective at (or "necessary" for) prolonging life.[15]

---

12. * * * [W]e note a more plausible explanation for the limited efficacy regulation—the government was not previously able to systematically regulate effectively for efficacy * * * * It was not just advances in statistics and clinical trials, however, that improved governments' ability to regulate access to drugs. The ability of scientists to "detect, identify, and understand" the components of various drugs has contributed to "new regulatory approaches [that] would not have been feasible and could never have occurred" without these scientific advances. Peter Barton Hutt, The Importance of Analytical Chemistry to Food and Drug Regulation, 38 Vand. L. Rev. 479, 487 (1985). Further, the need for efficacy regulation became more pressing "[a]fter World War II [as] the number of drugs available, the range of diseases and conditions amenable to drug therapy, and the power of drugs all increased dramatically." Peter Temin, Taking Your Medicine: Drug Regulation in the United States 5 (1980).

15. The lynchpin of the dissent's argument that preventing access to experimental drugs implicates a right to preserve one's own life is that we have confused "what is necessary with what is sufficient." Because terminally ill patients have no other approved treatment options, so the argument goes, any drug having passed Phase I, no matter the remaining unexplored risk, is "necessary" for prolonging a patient's life. But the dissent ignores the fact that when these treatment decisions are being made, the safety and efficacy records of experimental drugs are not fully known. We thus cannot know until after the clinical testing process has

* * * It is difficult to see how a tort addressing interference with providing "necessary" aid would guarantee a constitutional right to override the collective judgment of the scientific and medical communities expressed through the FDA's clinical testing process. Thus, we cannot agree that the tort of intentional interference with rescue evidences a right of access to experimental drugs. * * * Because terminally ill patients cannot fairly be characterized as using reasonable force to defend themselves when they take unproven and possibly unsafe drugs, the Alliance's desire that the terminally ill be free to assume the risk of experimental drugs cannot draw support from the doctrine of self-defense.

Although it has not addressed the precise constitutional argument urged by the Alliance, we find it highly significant that the Supreme Court has rejected several similar challenges to the FDCA and related laws brought on statutory grounds. And other courts have rejected arguments that the Constitution provides an affirmative right of access to particular medical treatments reasonably prohibited by the government.[18] In keeping with those decisions, we conclude that the Alliance has not provided evidence of a right to procure and use experimental drugs that is deeply rooted in our Nation's history and traditions. To the contrary, our Nation's history evidences increasing regulation of drugs as both the ability of government to address these risks has increased and the risks associated with drugs have become apparent. Similarly, our legal traditions of allowing a necessity defense, prohibiting intentional interference with rescue, and recognizing a right of self-defense cannot justify creating a constitutional right to assume any level of risk without regard to the scientific and medical judgment expressed through the clinical testing process.[19] * * *

---

been completed that these drugs are in fact necessary. This argument also defies reality as the great majority of experimental drugs ultimately provide no benefit, and we fail to see how an ineffective and unsafe drug can be classified as necessary. * * *

18. No circuit court has acceded to an affirmative access claim. See, e.g., Mitchell v. Clayton, 995 F.2d 772, 775 (7th Cir.1993) ("most federal courts have held that a patient does not have a constitutional right to obtain a particular type of treatment or to obtain treatment from a particular provider if the government has reasonably prohibited that type of treatment or provider"); N.Y. State Ophthalmological Soc'y v. Bowen, 854 F.2d 1379, 1389 (D.C.Cir. 1988) ("We disagree that the constitutional right to privacy comprehensively protects all choices made by patients and their physicians or subjects to 'strict scrutiny' all government interference with choice of medical treatment. There is no basis under current privacy case law for extending such stringent protection to every decision bearing, however indirectly, on a person's health and physical well-being."); Carnohan v. United States, 616 F.2d 1120, 1122 (9th Cir.1980) ("Constitutional rights of privacy and personal liberty do not give individuals the right to obtain [the cancer drug] laetrile free of the lawful exercise of government police power."); Rutherford v. United States, 616 F.2d 455, 457 (10th Cir.1980) ("[T]he patient['s] ... selection of a particular treatment, or at least a medication, is within the area of governmental interest in protecting public health. The premarketing requirement of the [FDCA] is an exercise of Congressional authority to limit the patient's choice of medication. This is clear under the [Supreme Court's] decisions ...."); see also Sammon v. N.J. Bd. of Med. Exam'rs, 66 F.3d 639, 645 n.10 (3d Cir.1995); United States v. Burzynski Cancer Research Inst., 819 F.2d 1301, 1313–14 (5th Cir.1987).

19. * * * While we need not and do not address all of the Alliance's arguments regarding whether their proposed right is implicit in our Nation's system of ordered liberty,

Applying the rational basis standard to the Alliance's complaint, we cannot say that the government's interest does not bear a rational relation to a legitimate state interest. That conclusion is compelled by the Supreme Court's decision in *United States v. Rutherford*, 442 U.S. 544 (1979). In that case, terminally ill patients sought to prevent the FDA from prohibiting access to the drug laetrile, even though the drug had not been approved for public use. In rejecting a challenge by terminally ill patients claiming that the FDCA's safety requirement did not apply to them, the Supreme Court held that "[f]or the terminally ill, as for anyone else, a drug is unsafe if its potential for inflicting death or physical injury is not offset by the possibility of therapeutic benefit." Id. at 555–56; see also id. at 558 (noting that history has demonstrated that numerous "resourceful entrepreneurs" might try to take advantage of an unregulated market, which "suggest[s] why Congress could reasonably have determined to protect the terminally ill, no less than other patients, from the vast range of self-styled panaceas that inventive minds can devise"). * * *

[W]e must conclude that, prior to distribution of a drug outside of controlled studies, the government has a rational basis for ensuring that there is a scientifically and medically acceptable level of knowledge about the risks and benefits of such a drug. We therefore hold that the FDA's policy of limiting access to investigational drugs is rationally related to the legitimate state interest of protecting patients, including the terminally ill, from potentially unsafe drugs with unknown therapeutic effects. Although in the Alliance's view the FDA has unjustly erred on the side of safety in balancing the risks and benefits of experimental drugs, this is not to say that the FDA's balance can never be changed. The Alliance's arguments about morality, quality of life, and acceptable levels of medical risk are certainly ones that can be aired in the democratic branches, without injecting the courts into unknown questions of science and medicine. Our Nation's history and traditions have consistently demonstrated that the democratic branches are better suited to decide the proper balance between the uncertain risks and benefits of medical technology, and are entitled to deference in doing so. * * *

■ ROGERS, CIRCUIT JUDGE (dissenting):

* * * The court shifts the inquiry required by *Washington v. Glucksberg*, 521 U.S. 702 (1997), by changing the nature of the right, by conflating the right with the deprivation, and by prematurely advancing countervailing government interests. The court fails to come to grips with the Nation's history and traditions, which reflect deep respect and protection for the right to preserve life, a corollary to the right to life enshrined in the Constitution. The court confuses this liberty interest with the manner in which the Alliance alleges that the liberty has been deprived, namely by

we note a crucial difference between this case and one of the cases relied upon by the Alliance in making that argument, *Cruzan v. Director, Mo. Dep't of Health*, 497 U.S. 261 (1990). * * * [A] tradition protecting individual *freedom* from life-saving, but forced, medical treatment does not evidence a constitutional tradition of providing affirmative *access* to a potentially harmful, and even fatal, commercial good.

denying terminally ill patients access to investigational medications under the narrow conditions described by the Alliance. The court conflates the inquiry as to whether a fundamental right exists at all with whether the government has demonstrated a compelling interest, when strictly scrutinized, rendering its restrictive policy constitutional.

These missteps lead the court to rely upon how rights and liberties have been limited and restricted—addressing regulations to prevent fraud in the sale of misbranded and adulterated medications or safety restrictions applicable to all medicines for any palliative purpose—which says little about the historic importance of the underlying right of a person to save her own life. Likewise, in its treatment of the common law doctrines of necessity, interference with rescue, and self defense, the court points to evolved limitations on those doctrines while ignoring the core concerns that animate them, namely the special importance of life and attempts to preserve it. * * *

In the end, it is startling that the oft-limited rights to marry, to fornicate, to have children, to control the education and upbringing of children, to perform varied sexual acts in private, and to control one's own body even if it results in one's own death or the death of a fetus have all been deemed fundamental rights covered, although not always protected, by the Due Process Clause, but the right to try to save one's life is left out in the cold despite its textual anchor in the right to life. This alone is reason the court should pause about refusing to put the FDA to its proof when it denies terminal patients with no alternative therapy the only option they have left, regardless of whether that option may be a long-shot with high risks. * * *

The court commits a logical error of dramatic consequence by concluding that the investigational drugs are somehow not "necessary." While the potential cures may not prove *sufficient* to save the life of a terminally ill patient, they are surely *necessary* if there is to be any possibility of preserving her life. It bears outlining the history and common law basis for the Alliance's claim in order to demonstrate, once again, that the history and traditions of this Nation support the right of a terminal patient, and not the government, to make this fundamentally personal choice involving her own life. Because judicial precedents and the historical record require strict scrutiny before upsetting rights of this magnitude, the FDA must demonstrate a compelling governmental interest before its policy restricting access can survive. Accordingly, I would remand the case to the district court to make the initial determination * * * *

The Fifth Amendment of the Constitution proscribes the "depriv[ation] of life, liberty, or property." The Alliance claims a corollary to the right to life itself, namely the right to attempt to preserve it. As alleged by the Alliance, this right is deprived without due process of law when the FDA makes it practically impossible for Alliance members for whom conventional treatments have failed to access investigational new drugs that have been approved for substantial human testing. * * * The court fundamentally misunderstands the right claimed by the Alliance and trivially casts it as a function of the regulatory scheme. But the Alliance should not be penalized for anticipating a justification for infringing the right that might survive strict scrutiny. * * *

Under *Glucksberg*, the court's analysis should begin with an assessment of whether the right to attempt to preserve life can be found in the Nation's history and tradition. A review of this history demonstrates that this Nation has long entrusted in individuals those fundamentally personal medical decisions that lie at the core of personal autonomy, self-determination, and self-defense. * * * Although the concept of self-defense is most often thought of in terms of the response to an assault by another human being, its premise compels the same response in the face of other forms of aggression against life and limb, whether the aggressor be an animal or a diseased cell within one's body. There is, accordingly, no reason to think that the efforts of Alliance members to repel their terminal diseases do not implicate this concept. * * *

By interposing itself between a terminally ill patient and her only means of prolonging her life, the FDA's policy runs counter to the common law's historical prohibition on interfering with rescue. * * * No doubt the deceased members of the Alliance who were denied access to experimental drugs that were subsequently approved by the FDA would have been surprised to learn that these drugs, under the court's analysis, were unnecessary to the preservation of their lives. * * * The question presented in this case is not whether investigational drugs are necessary to a terminally ill patient who has exhausted conventional treatment options—they are—but who will make the subsequent decision about using these medications, the patient with her doctor or the government. * * *

[T]he court recognizes that common law rights are not unlimited but fails to acknowledge that the evolved limitations on hallowed rights do not undercut the core concerns that animate them—here, the special importance of life and attempts to preserve it. That the ultimate protection of such varying attempts to save life is cabined by precedents discussing "necessity" speaks not to the absence of an underlying right to attempt to protect life but rather to the recognition of competing governmental interests that in various circumstances justify the deprivation of or a limitation upon the right. Whether similar countervailing interests exist in this case is a question bearing on the resolution of strict scrutiny analysis, not on whether it should apply. * * *

Although the Supreme Court has not squarely addressed the right to use potentially life-saving *medications*, it has developed a sizable body of law regarding the right to a potentially life-saving medical *procedure* when the life or health of a pregnant woman is on the line. * * * In *Stenberg v. Carhart*, 530 U.S. 914 (2000), the Supreme Court squarely addressed whether a state may ban a particular medical procedure in cases where a patient's health or life is endangered. The Court held that "the governing standard requires an exception 'where it is necessary, in appropriate medical judgment for the preservation of the life or health of the mother.' " Id. at 931. * * * [F]or the court to conclude that the Supreme Court has not already decided that medical self-preservation is fundamental, the court is forced to conclude that when a patient's life is on the line, medical procedures like abortion are to be analyzed differently than medical treatments consisting of prescription medications. * * *

The court holds that because the Alliance seeks access only to "*potentially* life-saving drugs," the abortion cases are distinguishable. Nowhere in the Supreme Court's jurisprudence has it intimated that the government may ban procedures that represent a patient's only chance of survival because they might not be successful. The fundamental right does not accrue only upon a demonstration of surefire actualization; the trigger is the *necessity*, which is crucially different from the sufficiency to which the court repeatedly refers. Indeed, in *Stenberg*, the Supreme Court addressed the level of medical consensus needed for a procedure to become protected, holding that procedures supported by "substantial medical authority" could not be proscribed. See 530 U.S. at 938. The Court was careful not to require medical unanimity, see id. at 937, or even "general medical studies," see id. at 935, like those required for FDA approval of investigational new drugs for commercial marketing. Although *Gonzales v. Carhart*, 550 U.S. 124 (2007), clarifies that government may regulate to some extent "where there is uncertainty over whether the barred procedure is ever necessary to preserve ... health, given the availability of other ... procedures that are considered to be safe alternatives," id. at 166–67, *Stenberg* remains good law, and there are no alternatives to preserve life, let alone health, in this case. * * *

[T]he Alliance specifically alleges in attachments to its complaint that the FDA has denied terminally ill Alliance members access to investigational new drugs "reported to have great potential," and acknowledged by the "medical community" as "far and away ... superior to anything then available." At this stage of the proceedings, the court is required to accept the Alliance's allegations as true. Thus, there are situations where a terminally ill patient seeks access to a new medication that has not yet been approved by the FDA for commercial marketing but that has been recognized by the medical community as that patient's best chance to survive. In such instances, the Fifth Amendment guarantee of due process protects the terminally ill patient's pursuit of those medications. * * *

Against this substantial historical record demonstrating the deep roots of the right to preserve one's own life, it is no coincidence that neither the court nor the FDA can marshal evidence from the early history of the Nation demonstrating that the federal government or any state thought to restrain the terminally ill from accessing medical treatments and procedures that had not proven unsafe but were of unknown efficacy. * * * [T]he most fundamental rights are those that no government of the people would contemplate abridging * * * * The right to life, and the asserted corollary right to attempt to preserve life, is not a second derivative species of "liberty" whose protection by the Constitution should be approached with skepticism. Insofar as courts should be skeptical of interfering with the legislative debate and ongoing democratic discussions about fundamental issues of life and death, that skepticism is better applied to the latter portion of the strict scrutiny analysis—the evaluation of the competing government interests and the greater or lesser narrowness of the tailoring required in the face of scientific uncertainty and conflicting opinions. * * *

[I]n the alternative, the court shifts the target and looks to historical evidence of regulation for *safety*. The court claims that post-Phase I testing is designed not only to test a drug's efficacy but also to continue monitoring its safety. As support, the court lists instances in which drugs have been removed from the market after Phase I because of safety concerns. This inquiry confuses the right—to save one's life—with the alleged deprivation, which here occurs by means of an agency policy. Whether the FDA policy actually impermissibly infringes upon the asserted right is a factual question that is not properly resolved at the motion-to-dismiss stage when all reasonable inferences must be drawn to the plaintiff's benefit.[5] * * *

For more than half of this Nation's history, then, until the enactment of the 1906 Act, a person could obtain access to any new drug without any government interference whatsoever. Even after enactment of the FDCA in 1938, Congress imposed no limitation on the commercial marketing of new drugs based upon the drugs' efficacy. Rather, at that time, the FDA could interrupt the sale of new drugs only if it determined that the new drug was unsafe. Government regulation of such drugs premised on concern over a new drug's efficacy, as opposed to its safety, is of very recent origin. Even today, a patient may use a drug for unapproved purposes where the drug may be unsafe or ineffective for the off-label purpose. In short, encumbrances on the treatment decisions of a patient and her physician lack the historical pedigree of the rights that the Alliance seeks to vindicate.

Instead of confronting this history, the court relies on statutory restrictions that address misbranded or adulterated drugs, sales of poisons, and fraudulent curative claims, government restrictions that are not inconsistent with the right of a person to attempt to save her own life. None of the cited restrictions, focusing largely on the licensing of pharmacists, suggest a physician could not prescribe a new medication for a terminal patient. While Congress has imposed increased responsibilities on the drug industry and the FDA upon evidence of tragic consequences of some new drugs as a result of new technology, the FDA does not regulate physicians, and off-label prescription of medications is a long-standing practice that has not been outlawed. * * *

The common law traditions protecting necessity, forbidding interference with rescue, and supporting self-defense, and the Supreme Court's

---

5. Although the FDA does not stop examining drug safety after Phase I, nor does it stop after drugs receive full marketing approval. The FDA has pulled approved such drugs from the market, but it does not follow that the FDA can take any action abridging any right, related or not, on the basis of its legitimate interest in safety. At a certain point, the FDA determines that a drug is safe enough for widespread testing, and the Alliance alleges that this marker is Phase I approval, where the FDA authorizes expanded testing in up to "several hundred subjects." In fact, between 1997 and 2000, 5.34 percent of fully approved new drugs were pulled from the market. Since then, many more approved drugs have been withdrawn.

validation of the fundamental right of a pregnant woman to undergo a medical procedure to save her own life demonstrate that the protected liberty interest of the terminally ill to choose whether to pursue prescription medications that may save their lives is deeply rooted in this Nation's history. Nothing in the history of drug regulation demonstrates otherwise. * * * [T]he claimed right also falls squarely within the realm of rights implicit in ordered liberty. The core of liberty is autonomy. * * * It is difficult to imagine any context in which this liberty interest would be stronger than in trying to save one's own life. * * * Like the right claimed in *Cruzan*, the right claimed by the Alliance to be free of FDA imposition does not involve treatment by the government or a government subsidy. Rather, the Alliance seeks only to have the government step aside so as not to interfere with the individual right of self-determination. The Alliance claims that there is a protected right of terminally ill patients to choose to use potentially life-saving investigational new drugs that have been determined to be safe for substantial human testing. This reasoning tracks *Eisenstadt v. Baird*, 405 U.S. 438 (1972), where the Supreme Court noted that the right to be free from unwanted government intrusion into the fundamental decision whether to have children establishes a right of access to contraceptives. * * *

NOTES AND QUESTIONS

1. *Backstory*. In 1999, Abigail Burroughs, an undergraduate student at the University of Virginia, developed head and neck cancer. After traditional chemotherapy regimens failed, she unsuccessfully sought access to a pair of then investigational drugs: ImClone's Erbitux® and AstraZeneca's Iressa® (ImClone did not, however, have a compassionate use program at that time, and AstraZeneca's expanded access program, which eventually supplied Iressa to more than 20,000 lung cancer patients, did not allow persons with other types of cancer to participate). See Judy Foreman, A Push for Wider Use of Experimental Drugs, L.A. Times, Sept. 29, 2003, at F1; see also Andrew Pollack, Cancer Drug to Be Provided to Limited Number of Patients, N.Y. Times, Feb. 7, 2003, at C2 (reporting the creation of compassionate use programs for both Erbitux and Iressa). Shortly after Ms. Burroughs died in June 2001, her father established a non-profit advocacy group named in her memory. As recounted in the court's opinion, the Abigail Alliance had made no headway in petitioning the agency. In fact, the FDA repeatedly has rejected efforts by cancer patients seeking access to unapproved new drugs. See, e.g., Durovic v. Richardson, 479 F.2d 242 (7th Cir.1973); Tutoki v. Celebrezze, 375 F.2d 105 (7th Cir.1967) (affirming the dismissal of cancer patients' claim of access to the unapproved new drug Krebiozen); see also Garlic v. FDA, 783 F.Supp. 4 (D.D.C.1992) (dismissing challenge to the FDA's failure to approve tetrahydroaminoacrinine brought by patients with Alzheimer's disease); Duncan v. United States, 590 F.Supp. 39 (W.D.Okla.1984). The en banc decision reflected an 8–2 split on the court, and a petition for certiorari failed. See Robert Barnes, Supreme Court Lets Stand Experimental–Drug Ruling, Wash. Post, Jan. 15, 2008, at

A2 (adding that the Abigail Alliance would continue seeking a legislative solution); see also Ronald L. Trowbridge & Steven Walker, Op–Ed., The FDA's Deadly Track Record, Wall St. J., Aug. 14, 2007, at A17 (summarizing the Alliance's frustrating efforts to promote early access to a dozen promising cancer drugs). A couple of years later, the FDA revised its regulations to allow somewhat greater access to experimental drugs. See 74 Fed. Reg. 40,900 (2009) (codified at 21 C.F.R. pts. 312 & 316).

2. *Constitutional questions*. Does the recognition of a tort claim for interfering with rescue provide any basis for the constitutional right asserted in this case? (Even if, to make the issue more concrete, the FDA had seized an investigational drug shipped to a desperate patient by the manufacturer, the agency would enjoy immunity from these (and most other) types of tort claims. See Chap. 5(B)(3).) The dissent emphasized that the FDA could prevail if it demonstrated that its restrictions on access to investigational drugs (after Phase I and as applied to terminally ill patients who have run out of options) were narrowly tailored to serve a compelling interest, but do you think that the rules would survive strict scrutiny (and does the majority's analysis help the FDA on this score)? Does the agency have a compelling interest in ensuring that subjects remain under the closer supervision required in the research setting (and satisfy the precise criteria for enrollment in a clinical trial)? (In addition, does it have a broader interest in avoiding underenrollment in placebo-controlled trials?) Is there any non-medical value in permitting patients without other effective medical options to pursue a last hope for treatment, even without much evidence of safety or efficacy? Would the constitutional claim have greater force if asserted by a subject enrolled in the experimental arm of a Phase III trial after the FDA placed a clinical hold on further research of an investigational drug that had shown promise against advanced cancer? What if, after the completion of Phase III trials, the FDA refused to approve an investigational drug solely because of inadequate proof of effectiveness—would terminally ill patients who had exhausted their options have any better chance of persuading the majority that such a decision violated substantive due process? What if the FDA approved a drug for a narrow cancer indication and found a way to crack down on off-label use in other cancer patients (or, more plausibly, CMS refused to authorize Medicare reimbursement for such uses)?

3. *Practical questions*. Even if the Abigail Alliance or some other group prevailed in some forum to liberalize the rules of access, could patients force unwilling sponsors to supply them with still investigational drugs (and why might the manufacturers hesitate)? See, e.g., Geeta Anand, Saying No to Penelope—Father Seeks Experimental Cancer Drug, but a Biotech Firm Says Risk Is Too High, Wall St. J., May 1, 2007, at A1 (reporting that the FDA had not objected to allowing a young child with aggressive neuroblastoma that no longer responded to other treatments to try a new drug even though it had just begun Phase I trials in patients with small-cell lung cancer but, after considerable inquiry and notwithstanding intense lobbying, the company declined to do so for business reasons); see also Gunvalson v. PTC Therapeutics Inc., 303 F.App'x 128 (3d Cir.2008) (reversing district court's preliminary injunction that had ordered an IND sponsor to facilitate access for a teenage patient suffering from Duchenne muscular dystrophy but ineligible to enroll in clinical trials because the plaintiffs had little likelihood of success on the merits of their promissory estoppel claim where they failed to allege a sufficiently clear and definite promise or detrimental reliance); Amy Harmon, Fighting for a Last Chance at Life, N.Y. Times, May 17, 2009, at A1 (recounting the difficulties that A.L.S. patients encountered in convincing first the manufacturer and then the FDA to make the drug Iplex available on a compassionate use basis). What if a sponsor was willing to supply an investigational drug outside of a clinical trial but at an unaffordable price—if a group of desperate patients stole a supply from the sponsor, could they invoke a private necessity defense against a tort claim for conversion of property (or to criminal prosecution for theft)?

4. *Another flashpoint.* A few months before the court issued its decision in *Abigail Alliance*, the FDA delayed approval of Provenge® (sipuleucel-T), an active cellular immunotherapy for advanced prostate cancer, instead asking the sponsor Dendreon Corp. for more information, including an additional efficacy trial. Many disappointed patients (and investors) expressed outrage over this decision, see Rob Stein, FDA Delay in Cancer Therapy Is Attacked, Wash. Post, July 6, 2007, at A1, but their various pleas to the agency, courts, and Congress fared no better than the efforts mounted by the Abigail Alliance. See CareToLive v. von Eschenbach, 525 F.Supp.2d 952, 963–69 (S.D.Ohio 2007) (dismissing constitutional claims asserted by a patient advocacy group against two FDA employees involved in the review of Provenge); CareToLive v. von Eschenbach, 525 F.Supp.2d 938, 946–50 (S.D.Ohio 2007) (dismissing APA claims against the agency for lack of finality and ripeness) [excerpted in Chap. 11(B)], aff'd mem., 290 F.App'x 887 (6th Cir.2008); Shari Roan, Drug's Delay Mobilizes Prostate Patients to Activism, L.A. Times, Dec. 31, 2007, at F1. The FDA approved Provenge three years later, but initially it was unclear whether Medicare would cover this expensive drug. See Andrew Pollack, In Small Test, Experimental Prostate Drug Shows Promise, N.Y. Times, Nov. 18, 2010, at B4; see also id. ("An experimental drug is showing what some experts say is intriguing effectiveness .... Exelixis will now add many prostate cancer patients to the midstage clinical trial .... XL184 is believed to block the formation of blood vessels that feed tumors and also inhibits a protein called MET that helps spur tumor growth.").

5. *Further commentary.* See Richard A. Epstein, Against Permititis: Why Voluntary Organizations Should Regulate the Use of Cancer Drugs, 94 Minn. L. Rev. 1 (2009); Peter D. Jacobson & Wendy E. Parmet, A New Era of Unapproved Drugs: The Case of Abigail Alliance v. von Eschenbach, 297 JAMA 205 (2007); Jerry Menikoff, Beyond Abigail Alliance: The Reality Behind the Right to Get Experimental Drugs, 56 U. Kan. L. Rev. 1045 (2008); A. Seema Shah & Patricia Zettler, From a Constitutional Right to a Policy of Exceptions: Abigail Alliance and the Future of Access to Experimental Therapy, 10 Yale J. Health Pol'y L. & Ethics 135 (2010); Linda K. Leibfarth, Note, Giving the Terminally Ill Their Due (Process): A Case for

Expanded Access to Experimental Drugs Through the Political Process, 61 Vand. L. Rev. 1281 (2008); Daniel S. Morris, Note, The Death of "Life?" Due Process Doctrine After Abigail Alliance, 40 Rutgers L.J. 503 (2009); Ashley Ochs, Comment, A Study in Futility: Abigail Alliance for Better Access to Developmental Drugs Will Not Expand Access to Experimental Drugs for the Terminally Ill, 39 Seton Hall L. Rev. 559 (2009); James P. Sikora, Note, Providing Hope: Developing a Viable Regulatory Framework for Providing Terminally Ill Patients with Adequate Access to Investigational Drugs, 70 U. Pitt. L. Rev. 191 (2008); Judy Vale, Note, Expanding Expanded Access: How the Food and Drug Administration Can Achieve Better Access to Experimental Drugs for Seriously Ill Patients, 96 Geo. L.J. 2143 (2008).

6. *Laetrile in the states.* State courts also had considered the problems associated with physicians' and patients' assertions that the constitutional right of privacy protects the decision to obtain drugs (such as laetrile) not generally recognized as effective by the FDA. In *People v. Privitera*, 591 P.2d 919 (Cal.1979), the court concluded that a fundamental right of privacy, which ordinarily involves matters relating to marriage, procreation, contraception, family relationships and child rearing, was not implicated in decisions about medical treatment: "If the state has the power to ban a drug with a recognized medical use because of its potential for abuse, then—given a rational basis for doing so—the state clearly has the power to ban a drug not recognized as effective for its intended use." Id. at 923. The dissent in the case noted that "[t]he right to control one's own body is not restricted to the wise; it includes the 'foolish' refusal of medical treatment.... Without specific reference to a constitutional basis, the right to choose what may be a suicidal medical course has been upheld." Id. at 932 (Bird, J., dissenting) (referring to decisions permitting Jehovah's Witnesses to refuse life-saving blood transfusions). After the *Rutherford* litigation, approximately half of the states passed laws legalizing the use of laetrile for terminal cancer treatment. See, e.g., Alaska Stat. § 08.64.367; Ariz. Rev. Stat. § 36–2452; Colo. Rev. Stat. § 12–30–113; Del. Code Ann. § 4901.

7. *Importation of unapproved drugs for personal use.* FDA guidelines permit individuals to import up to a three-month supply of an unapproved new drug for personal use under two sets of circumstances: (1) the intended use is appropriately identified and is not for the treatment of a serious condition, and the product is not known to be a serious threat to health; or (2) the intended use is unapproved and for a serious condition for which treatment may not be available domestically, there is no known commercialization or promotion to persons residing in the U.S. by those involved in distribution of the product, the product does not represent an unreasonable risk, and the individual seeking to import the product provides the name of a doctor responsible for treatment in the U.S. or provides evidence that the product is for continuation of a treatment begun abroad. See Peter S. Reichertz & Melinda S. Friend, Hiding Behind Agency Discretion: The FDA's Personal Use Drug Importation Policy, 9 Cornell J.L. & Pub. Pol'y 493, 501–02 (2000); see also Sifre v. Robles, 917 F.Supp. 133 (D.P.R.1996) (holding that the plaintiff, an individual seeking to import "memory and intelligence enhancement drugs'' for personal use, did not meet the FDA's informal standards for such imports); Mary P. Flaherty & Gilbert M. Gaul, Millions of Americans Look Outside U.S. for Drugs, Wash. Post, Oct. 23, 2003, at A1 (reporting that the agency largely fails to enforce these limitations); Christopher Lee, U.S. to Stop Seizing Prescription Drugs Imported for Personal Use, Wash. Post, Oct. 5, 2006, at A16.

The FDA first adopted a more permissive version of this policy in 1988 so that patients suffering from AIDS and cancer could import limited quantities of unapproved drugs. The agency soon expanded the policy, but it specifically prohibited personal use importation of the French abortion pill RU–486, triggering a judicial challenge. See Benten v. Kessler, 799 F.Supp. 281, 289 (E.D.N.Y.1992) (granting a preliminary injunction because of the petitioner's likelihood of success on the merits of her claim that this limitation should have undergone notice-and-comment rulemaking procedures). The court of appeals stayed the preliminary injunction pending appeal, and the Supreme Court denied a petition to vacate that stay. See Benten v. Kessler, 505 U.S. 1084, 1085 (1992) (per curiam). In dissent, Justice Stevens argued that the FDA had impermissibly burdened the woman's liberty interest in selecting a method for terminating her pregnancy. See id. at 1086 (Stevens, J., dissenting); see also Elizabeth A. Silverberg, Note, Looking Beyond Judicial Deference to Agency Discretion: A Fundamental Right of Access to RU486?, 59 Brook. L. Rev. 1551 (1994).

8. *Medical marijuana.* Patient demands to use marijuana for medical purposes raise a similar set of issues. See, e.g., Pearson v. McCaffrey, 139 F.Supp.2d 113 (D.D.C.2001); Seeley v. State, 940 P.2d 604 (Wash.1997).

Raich v. Gonzales

500 F.3d 850 (9th Cir.2007).

■ PREGERSON, CIRCUIT JUDGE:

* * * Marijuana is a Schedule I controlled substance. For a substance to be designated a Schedule I controlled substance, it must be found: (1) that the substance "has a high potential for abuse"; (2) that the substance "has no currently accepted medical use in treatment in the United States"; and (3) that "[t]here is a lack of accepted safety for use of the drug or other substance under medical supervision." 21 U.S.C. § 812(b)(1). * * * [I]t is unlawful to knowingly or intentionally "manufacture, distribute, or dispense, or possess with intent to manufacture, distribute, or dispense, a controlled substance," except as otherwise provided in the statute. Id. § 841(a)(1). Possession of a controlled substance, except as authorized under the Controlled Substances Act, is also unlawful. See id. § 844(a).

California voters passed Proposition 215 in 1996, which is codified as the Compassionate Use Act of 1996. * * * [I]ts purpose is to

> ensure that seriously ill Californians have the right to obtain and use marijuana for medical purposes where that medical use is deemed appropriate and has been recommended by a physician who has deter-

> mined that the person's health would benefit from the use of marijuana in the treatment of cancer, anorexia, AIDS, chronic pain, spasticity, glaucoma, arthritis, migraine, or any other illness for which marijuana provides relief.

Cal. Health & Safety Code § 11362.5(b)(1)(A). * * * [T]he Compassionate Use Act exempts from liability under California's drug laws "a patient, or . . . a patient's primary caregiver, who possesses or cultivates marijuana for the personal medical purposes of the patient upon the written or oral recommendation or approval of a physician." Id. § 11362.5(d).

Appellant Angel McClary Raich is a Californian who uses marijuana for medical treatment. Raich has been diagnosed with more than ten serious medical conditions, including an inoperable brain tumor, a seizure disorder, life-threatening weight loss, nausea, and several chronic pain disorders. Raich's doctor, Dr. Frank Henry Lucido, testified that he had explored virtually every legal treatment alternative, and that all were either ineffective or resulted in intolerable side effects. Dr. Lucido provided a list of thirty-five medications that were unworkable because of their side effects. Marijuana, on the other hand, has proven to be of great medical value for Raich. Raich has been using marijuana as a medication for nearly eight years, every two waking hours of every day. * * * Raich is unable to cultivate marijuana for her own use. Instead, Raich's caregivers, John Doe Number One and John Doe Number Two, cultivate it for her. They provide marijuana to Raich free of charge. They have joined this action as plaintiffs anonymously in order to protect Raich's access to medical marijuana.

This action arose in response to a law enforcement raid on the home of another medical marijuana user, former plaintiff-appellant Diane Monson. On August 15, 2002, Butte County Sheriff's Department deputies, the Butte County District Attorney, and agents from the federal Drug Enforcement Administration (DEA) came to Monson's home. After DEA agents took control of Monson's six marijuana plants, a three-hour standoff between state and federal authorities ensued. The Butte County deputies and district attorney concluded that Monson's use of marijuana was legal under the Compassionate Use Act. The DEA agents, after conferring with the U.S. Attorney for the Eastern District of California, concluded that Monson possessed the plants in violation of federal law. The DEA agents seized and destroyed Monson's six marijuana plants.

Fearing raids in the future and the prospect of being deprived of their medicinal marijuana, Raich, Monson, and the John Doe plaintiffs * * * sought declaratory and injunctive relief. Specifically, plaintiffs-appellants argued: (1) that the Controlled Substances Act was unconstitutional as applied to them because the legislation exceeded Congress's Commerce Clause authority; (2) that through the Controlled Substances Act, Congress impermissibly exercised a police power that is reserved to the State of California under the Tenth Amendment; (3) that the Controlled Substances Act unconstitutionally infringed their fundamental rights protected by the Fifth and Ninth Amendments; and (4) that the Controlled Substances Act could not be enforced against them because their allegedly unlawful conduct was justified under the common law doctrine of necessity. * * * [T]he Supreme Court vacated our [earlier] opinion [reversing the district court's denial of plaintiffs' motion requesting a preliminary injunction] and held that Congress's Commerce Clause authority includes the power to prohibit purely intrastate cultivation and use of marijuana. See Gonzales v. Raich, 545 U.S. 1, 32–33 (2005). The Court remanded the case to us to address plaintiffs-appellants's remaining legal theories * * * *

Although Raich has not suffered any past injury, she is faced with the threat that the government will seize her medical marijuana and prosecute her for violations of federal drug law. The threat posed by deprivation of her medical treatment is serious and concrete: Raich's doctor testified that foregoing medical marijuana treatment might be fatal. The threat is not speculative or conjectural: DEA agents previously seized and destroyed the medical marijuana of former plaintiff-appellant Diane Monson. Monson's withdrawal from this action does not change the fact that DEA agents have—and may again—seize and destroy medical marijuana possessed by gravely ill Californians, including Raich. * * *

Raich first argues that she has a likelihood of success on the merits of her claim that the common law doctrine of necessity bars the federal government from enforcing the Controlled Substances Act against her medically-necessary use of marijuana. Raich avers that she is faced with a choice of evils: to either obey the Controlled Substances Act and endure excruciating pain and possibly death, or violate the terms of the Controlled Substances Act and obtain relief from her physical suffering. * * *[4] We do not believe that the *Oakland Cannabis* dicta abolishes more than a century of common law necessity jurisprudence. * * *

If Raich obeys the Controlled Substances Act she will have to endure intolerable pain including severe chronic pain in her face and jaw muscles due to temporomandibular joint dysfunction and bruxism, severe chronic pain and chronic burning from fibromyalgia that forces her to be flat on her back for days, excruciating pain from non-epileptic seizures, heavy bleeding and severely painful menstrual periods due to a uterine fibroid tumor, and acute weight loss resulting possibly in death due to a life-threatening wasting disorder. Alternatively, Raich can violate the Controlled Substances Act and avoid the bulk of those debilitating pains by using marijuana. * * * The government does not dispute the severity of

---

4. Dicta in a recent Supreme Court decision questioned the ongoing vitality of common law necessity defense. The majority in *United States v. Oakland Cannabis Buyers' Cooperative,* 532 U.S. 483, 490 (2001), stated that "it is an open question whether federal courts ever have authority to recognize a necessity defense not provided by statute." But the majority ultimately conceded that the "Court ha[d] discussed the possibility of a necessity defense without altogether rejecting it." Id. Three Justices filed a separate concurrence in *Oakland Cannabis,* noting that "the Court gratuitously casts doubt on 'whether necessity can ever be a defense' to *any* federal statute that does not explicitly provide for it, calling such a defense into question by a misleading reference to its existence as an 'open question.' " Id. at 501 (Stevens, J., concurring). "[O]ur precedent has expressed no doubt about the viability of the common-law defense, even in the context of federal criminal statutes that do not provide for it in so many words." Id.

her conditions or the likelihood that her pain would recur if she is deprived of marijuana. * * * Dr. Lucido's testimony makes clear that Raich had no legal alternatives: Raich "has tried essentially all other legal alternatives to cannabis and the alternatives have been ineffective or result in intolerable side effects." Raich's physician explained that the intolerable side effects included violent nausea, shakes, itching, rapid heart palpitations, and insomnia. We agree that Raich does not appear to have any legal alternative to marijuana use.

Although Raich appears to satisfy the factual predicate for a necessity defense, it is not clear whether the Supreme Court's decision in *United States v. Oakland Cannabis Buyers' Cooperative* forecloses a necessity defense to a prosecution of a seriously ill defendant under the Controlled Substances Act. 532 U.S. at 484 n.7. Similarly, whether the Controlled Substances Act encompasses a legislative "determination of values," id. at 491, that would preclude a necessity defense is also an unanswered question. These are difficult issues, and in light of our conclusion below that Raich's necessity claim is best resolved within the context of a specific prosecution under the Controlled Substances Act, where the issue would be fully joined, we do not attempt to answer them here. * * *

Though a necessity defense may be available in the context of a criminal prosecution, it does not follow that a court should prospectively enjoin enforcement of a statute. Raich's violation of the Controlled Substances Act is a legally recognized harm, but the necessity defense shields Raich from liability for criminal prosecution during such time as she satisfies the defense. Thus, if Raich were to make a miraculous recovery that obviated her need for medical marijuana, her necessity-based justification defense would no longer exist. Similarly, if Dr. Lucido found an alternative treatment that did not violate the law—a legal alternative to violating the Controlled Substances Act—Raich could no longer assert a necessity defense. That is to say, a necessity defense is best considered in the context of a concrete case where a statute is allegedly violated, and a specific prosecution results from the violation. Indeed, oversight and enforcement of a necessity defense-based injunction would prove impracticable: the ongoing vitality of the injunction could hinge on factors including Raich's medical condition or advances in lawful medical technology. Nothing in the common law or our cases suggests that the existence of a necessity defense empowers this court to enjoin the enforcement of the Controlled Substances Act as to one defendant. Because common law necessity prevents criminal liability, but does not permit us to enjoin prosecution for what remains a legally recognized harm, we hold that Raich has not shown a likelihood of success on the merits on her medical necessity claim for an injunction.[9] * * *

---

9. We cannot ignore that the unusual circumstances of this case raise the danger of acute preconviction harms. The arrest of Raich or her suppliers, or the confiscation of her medical marijuana would cause Raich severe physical trauma. Under the right circumstances, Raich might obtain relief from the courts for preconviction harm based on common law necessity.

The Supreme Court has a long history of recognizing unenumerated fundamental rights as protected by substantive due process * * * * But the Court has cautioned against the doctrine's expansion. * * * Raich asserts that she has a fundamental right to "mak[e] life-shaping medical decisions that are necessary to preserve the integrity of her body, avoid intolerable physical pain, and preserve her life." We note that Raich's carefully crafted interest comprises several fundamental rights that have been recognized at least in part by the Supreme Court. Yet, Raich's careful statement does not narrowly and accurately reflect the right that she seeks to vindicate. Conspicuously missing from Raich's asserted fundamental right is its centerpiece * * * * [T]he question becomes whether the liberty interest specially protected by the Due Process Clause embraces a right to make a life-shaping decision on a physician's advice to use medical marijuana to preserve bodily integrity, avoid intolerable pain, and preserve life, when all other prescribed medications and remedies have failed. We turn to whether the asserted right is "deeply rooted in this Nation's history and tradition," and "implicit in the concept of ordered liberty," such that "neither liberty nor justice would exist if they were sacrificed." Washington v. Glucksberg, 521 U.S. 702, 720–21 (1997).

It is beyond dispute that marijuana has a long history of use—medically and otherwise—in this country. Marijuana was not regulated under federal law until Congress passed the Marihuana Tax Act of 1937, Pub. L. No. 75–348, 50 Stat. 551 (repealed 1970), and marijuana was not prohibited under federal law until Congress passed the Controlled Substances Act in 1970. There is considerable evidence that efforts to regulate marijuana use in the early-twentieth century targeted recreational use, but permitted medical use. See Richard J. Bonnie & Charles H. Whitebread, The Forbidden Fruit and the Tree of Knowledge: An Inquiry into the Legal History of American Marijuana Prohibition, 56 Va. L. Rev. 971, 1010, 1027, 1167 (1970) (noting that all twenty-two states that had prohibited marijuana by the 1930s created exceptions for medical purposes). By 1965, although possession of marijuana was a crime in all fifty states, almost all states had created exceptions for "persons for whom the drug had been prescribed or to whom it had been given by an authorized medical person." Leary v. United States, 395 U.S. 6, 16–17 (1969).

The history of medical marijuana use in this country took an about-face with the passage of the Controlled Substances Act in 1970. Congress placed marijuana on Schedule I of the Controlled Substances Act, taking it outside of the realm of all uses, including medical, under federal law. As the Supreme Court noted in *Gonzales v. Raich,* 545 U.S. at 5, no state permitted medical marijuana usage until California's Compassionate Use Act of 1996. Thus, from 1970 to 1996, the possession or use of marijuana—medically or otherwise—was proscribed under state and federal law.

Raich argues that the last ten years have been characterized by an emerging awareness of marijuana's medical value. She contends that the rising number of states that have passed laws that permit medical use of marijuana or recognize its therapeutic value is additional evidence that the right is fundamental. * * * Since 1996, ten states other than California have passed laws decriminalizing in varying degrees the use, possession, manufacture, and distribution of marijuana for the seriously ill. See Alaska Stat. § 11.71.090; Colo. Rev. Stat. § 18–18–406.3; Haw. Rev. Stat. § 329–125; Me. Rev. Stat. Ann. tit. 22, § 2383–B; Mont. Code Ann. § 50–46–201; Nev. Rev. Stat. § 453A.200; Or. Rev. Stat. § 475.319; R.I. Gen. Laws § 21–28.6–4; Vt. Stat. Ann. tit. 18, § 4474b; Wash. Rev. Code § 69.51A.040. Other states have passed resolutions recognizing that marijuana may have therapeutic value, and yet others have permitted limited use through closely monitored experimental treatment programs.

We agree with Raich that medical and conventional wisdom that recognizes the use of marijuana for medical purposes is gaining traction in the law as well. But that legal recognition has not yet reached the point where a conclusion can be drawn that the right to use medical marijuana is "fundamental" and "implicit in the concept of ordered liberty." For the time being, this issue remains in "the arena of public debate and legislative action." * * * For now, federal law is blind to the wisdom of a future day when the right to use medical marijuana to alleviate excruciating pain may be deemed fundamental. Although that day has not yet dawned, considering that during the last ten years eleven states have legalized the use of medical marijuana, that day may be upon us sooner than expected. Until that day arrives, federal law does not recognize a fundamental right to use medical marijuana prescribed by a licensed physician to alleviate excruciating pain and human suffering.[16]

Third, Raich contends that the Controlled Substances Act infringes upon the sovereign powers of the State of California, most notably the police powers, as conferred by the Tenth Amendment. * * * The Compassionate Use Act, aimed at providing for the health of the state's citizens, appears to fall squarely within the general rubric of the state's police powers. Generally speaking, however, a power granted to Congress trumps a competing claim based on a state's police powers. * * * The Supreme Court held in *Gonzales v. Raich* that Congress acted within the bounds of its Commerce Clause authority when it criminalized the purely intrastate manufacture, distribution, or possession of marijuana in the Controlled Substances Act. * * * We hold that Raich failed to demonstrate a likelihood of success on her claim that the Controlled Substances Act violates the Tenth Amendment. Accordingly, the district court did not abuse its discretion in denying Raich's motion for preliminary injunction * * * *

---

16. Because we find no fundamental right here, we do not address whether any law that limits that right is narrowly drawn to serve a compelling state interest. We note, however, that, a recent Supreme Court case suggests that the Controlled Substances Act is not narrowly drawn when fundamental rights are concerned. See Gonzales v. O Centro Espirita Beneficente Uniao do Vegetal, 546 U.S. 418, 432–36 (2006) (observing that "mere invocation of the general characteristics of Schedule I substances, as set forth in the Controlled Substances Act, cannot carry the day," and that the government had presented no evidence that narrow [religious use] exceptions to the Schedule I prohibitions would undercut the government's ability to effectively enforce the [CSA]).

■ BEAM, SENIOR CIRCUIT JUDGE (concurring and dissenting):

* * * At oral argument, counsel for the parties conceded that there is not now pending nor has there ever been pending a prosecution or even a threatened prosecution of Raich for possession or use of personal amounts of medicinal marijuana. Indeed, counsel for Raich acknowledged at oral argument that, to his knowledge, there has never been a federal criminal prosecution for simple possession or use of medicinal marijuana against anyone anywhere in California. Counsel for the government likewise indicated a lack of knowledge of any such prosecution and stated that it would be "incredibly unlikely" that any such federal prosecution would ensue in the future. * * *

The doctrine of common law (medical) necessity is an affirmative defense assertable only in a criminal prosecution. After reference to several measures of potential injury and harm to Raich almost totally unrelated to a reasonably foreseeable criminal prosecution, the court ultimately recognizes the legal limitations of the defense, but only after issuing what amounts to a lengthy advisory opinion. Here we are engaged in the review of a civil proceeding seeking declaratory relief and injunction, not a criminal adjudication. * * *

NOTES AND QUESTIONS

1. *Nonprosecution policy*. Is it redundant or otherwise incoherent to pose the question about the existence of a fundamental constitutional right by asking whether Congress has recognized it? And does the court mean only the law-in-the-books (i.e., the statutory provision and regulation that place marijuana in Schedule I) or might it also take into account the law-in-action (i.e., the extent to which the Executive branch has chosen not to enforce it)? As it happens, the likelihood of federal prosecution further declined with the subsequent change of administrations. See Bob Egelko, New U.S. Pot Rule Unclear in State Cases, S.F. Chron., Apr. 11, 2009, at A1; Carrie Johnson, U.S. Eases Stance on Medical Marijuana: Attorney General Says Prosecuting Such Cases "Will Not Be a Priority," Wash. Post, Oct. 20, 2009, at A1 (reporting that the AG "directed federal prosecutors to back away from pursuing cases against medical marijuana patients"); see also Robert A. Mikos, A Critical Appraisal of the Department of Justice's New Approach to Medical Marijuana, 22 Stan. L. & Pol'y Rev. 633 (2011); Vijay Sekhon, Comment, Highly Uncertain Times: An Analysis of the Executive Branch's Decision to Not Investigate or Prosecute Individuals in Compliance with State Medical Marijuana Laws, 37 Hastings Const. L.Q. 553 (2010); cf. Zusha Elinson, Marijuana Dispensaries Are Facing New Scrutiny, N.Y. Times, Jan. 9, 2011, § 1, at 23A (reporting that, because California's state and local "laws are murky, dispensaries increasingly operate in the gray area between large-scale businesses and nonprofit health centers," adding that the IRS has become interested in scrutinizing these operations); Richard Perez–Pena, Marijuana for Patients Remains Off–Limits, N.Y. Times, July 18, 2011, at A13 (reporting that "mixed signals from the Obama administration have left [officials in several states] unsure whether their medical marijuana programs could draw federal prosecution of the people involved''); William Yardley, New Federal Crackdown Confounds States That Allow Medical Marijuana, N.Y. Times, May 8, 2011, at A13 (''[F]ederal prosecutors [differentiate between possession and distribution, and some] say states have simply let medical marijuana get out of hand.''). See generally Jay M. Zitter, Annotation, Construction and Application of Medical Marijuana Laws and Medical Necessity Defense to Marijuana Laws, 50 A.L.R.6th 353 (2009 & 2011 Supp.).

2. *A growing list of states.* See Troy E. Grandel, One Toke over the Line: The Proliferation of State Medical Marijuana Laws, 9 U.N.H. L. Rev. 135, 152 (2010) (''Fourteen states and the District of Columbia have already legalized medical marijuana, and seven other states either have bills in their legislatures or ballot measures pending that would do the same.''); see also Stephanie Simon, Colorado Gets Strict on Medical–Pot Rules, Wall St. J., Nov. 23, 2010, at A4 (''Many [states] have minimal regulations aimed at limiting the amount of marijuana that a patient can legally possess and cultivate. Other regulations tend to be a patchwork: Some states require patients to register, but some don't.''); Kristen Wyatt, Colorado Grapples with Effort to Create the First State Marijuana Regulations, Wash. Post, Nov. 27, 2010, at A5 (''[O]fficials are having a tough time writing regulations for a product that's never been scrutinized or safety-tested before.''). See generally Robert A. Mikos, On the Limits of Supremacy: Medical Marijuana and the States' Overlooked Power to Legalize Federal Crime, 62 Vand. L. Rev. 1421 (2009); Kevin D. Caton, Annotation, Preemption of State Regulation of Controlled Substances by Federal Controlled Substances Act, 60 A.L.R.6th 175 (2010). Simply exempting patients who use marijuana from state criminal laws does not necessarily ensure protection under other state laws. See Emerald Steel Fabricators, Inc. v. Bureau of Labor & Indus., 230 P.3d 518, 536 (Or.2010) (holding that, for purposes of applying a state's antidiscrimination law, the CSA preempted state medical marijuana law so that an employer had no obligation to accommodate an employee's disability).

3. *Marijuana's medical utility.* Prominent organizations and researchers have endorsed the use of marijuana in certain patients. See, e.g., Inst. of Med., Marijuana and Medicine: Assessing the Science Base 177 (1999) (''For patients such as those with AIDS or who are undergoing chemotherapy, and who suffer simultaneously from severe pain, nausea, and appetite loss, cannabinoid drugs might offer broad-spectrum relief not found in any other single medication.''); Lester Grinspoon & James B. Bakalar, Marihuana as Medicine: A Plea for Reconsideration, 273 JAMA 1875 (1995); Elizabeth M. Williamson & Fred J. Evans, Cannabinoids in Clinical Practice, 60 Drugs 1303, 1305–10 (2000); Rick Weiss, Research Supports Medicinal Marijuana: AIDS Patients in Controlled Study Had Significant Pain Relief, Wash. Post, Feb. 13, 2007, at A14. Congress, however, has not relented, reacting to the early initiatives in California and elsewhere by passing a resolution ''oppose[d] efforts to circumvent this [federal scheduling] process by legalizing marijuana, and other Schedule I drugs, for medicinal use without valid scientific evidence and the approval of the [FDA].'' Pub. L. No. 105–277, Div. F, 112 Stat. 2681–760, 2681–761 (1998).

The FDA also remains unmoved. See Gardiner Harris, F.D.A. Dismisses Medical Benefit from Marijuana, N.Y. Times, Apr. 21, 2006, at A1; see also Americans for Safe Access v. HHS, 399 F.App'x 314 (9th Cir.2010) (rejecting as premature a challenge to the agency's latest conclusion in connection with a pending DEA rescheduling petition that marijuana lacks medical utility).

4. *Rescheduling efforts.* Notwithstanding Congress' continuing judgment about the appropriate scheduling of marijuana, the DEA could downschedule the drug, but that agency repeatedly has denied rescheduling petitions, and reviewing courts have not distributed these decisions. See, e.g., Gettman v. DEA, 290 F.3d 430, 432 (D.C.Cir.2002) (dismissing for lack of standing); Alliance for Cannabis Therapeutics v. DEA, 15 F.3d 1131, 1133–34, 1137 (D.C.Cir.1994) (recounting the repeated challenges, and deferring on the merits); United States v. Greene, 892 F.2d 453, 455–56 (6th Cir.1989) (rejecting constitutional challenges). Furthermore, as the Supreme Court explained, moving marijuana to Schedule II would hardly bring federal law in line with permissive state laws:

> [E]ven if respondents are correct that marijuana does have accepted medical uses and thus should be redesignated as a lesser schedule drug, the CSA would still impose controls beyond what is required by California law. The CSA requires manufacturers, physicians, pharmacies, and other handlers of controlled substances to comply with statutory and regulatory provisions mandating registration with the DEA, compliance with specific production quotas, security controls to guard against diversion, recordkeeping and reporting obligations, and prescription requirements. Furthermore, the dispensing of new drugs, even when doctors approve their use, must await federal approval.

Gonzales v. Raich, 545 U.S. 1, 27–28 (2005).

5. *Further commentary.* See Randy E. Barnett, The Presumption of Liberty and the Public Interest: Medical Marijuana and Fundamental Rights, 22 Wash. U. J.L. & Pol'y 29 (2006); John D. Ingram, Medical Use of Marijuana, 33 Okla. City U. L. Rev. 589 (2008); Ruth C. Stern & J. Herbie DiFonzo, The End of the Red Queen's Race: Medical Marijuana in the New Century, 27 QLR 673 (2009); Note, Last Resorts and Fundamental Rights: The Substantive Due Process Implications of Prohibitions on Medical Marijuana, 118 Harv. L. Rev. 1985 (2005).

Suthers v. Amgen, Inc.

372 F.Supp.2d 416 (S.D.N.Y.2005).

■ CASTEL, DISTRICT JUDGE:

Plaintiffs Robert Suthers and Niwana Martin are courageous individuals who participated in a research trial for an experimental treatment for Parkinson's disease. The decision to participate in the trial was no small matter. It was accompanied by invasive surgery to implant a pump in the abdomen and catheters into the brain in order to deliver the treatment.

Each knew that there was a 50/50 chance of receiving nothing more than a placebo through the first six months of the trial.

Though plaintiffs did receive placebos for the first six months of the study, Mr. Suthers and Ms. Martin eventually received the experimental treatment as part of a second follow-on study, and viewed it as greatly relieving their symptoms. The medical researcher supervising their participation reports that Mr. Suther was able to walk up to two miles a day and Ms. Martin was able to walk and run and had an improved sense of smell and greater control over facial muscles. To their disappointment and, in their view, physical detriment, the experimental trials have been discontinued. They now bring suit seeking to compel the sponsor of the trial to resume the treatment. The sponsor, Amgen, Inc., maintains it had a legal right to terminate the experimental trials and, indeed, an ethical duty to do so because of data indicating that the treatment was neither safe nor effective.

By way of background, the experimental treatment at issue introduces into the brain a neurotrophic factor, specifically, glial-derived neurotrophic factor (GDNF). It holds the potential of stimulating the regeneration of the neurons that produce dopamine, a chemical that is present at diminished levels in those suffering from Parkinson's disease. Amgen selected New York University Medical Center (NYU) as one of the investigation centers that would conduct independent studies into the safety and efficacy of GDNF. In that role, NYU recruited Mr. Suthers and Ms. Martin, and determined them eligible to participate. Mr. Suthers and Ms. Martin underwent the implantation surgery. As noted, they initially received placebos in a double-blind study. Thereafter, they were permitted to participate in an open label (i.e., not blind) study in which they were treated with GDNF.

Amgen terminated the second study when it discovered that the GDNF treatment produced antibodies that potentially neutralized the human body's naturally produced GDNF and risked worsening a patient's condition. It also received test data indicating that administration of GDNF in primates caused neurotoxic responses, and in humans yielded no statistically significant results over a placebo. Plaintiffs, supported by several medical researchers, believe that Amgen needlessly overreacted to the data, and that GDNF is safe and beneficial to many with advanced Parkinson's disease, including themselves. * * *

Plaintiffs advance three legal theories to support their application for an injunction. First, they claim that GDNF is beneficial to them, and that Amgen contracted with them to supply GDNF so long as it proved to be beneficial. Second, they argue that Amgen made promises, which they relied upon to their detriment by having the surgery necessary in order to deliver GDNF to their brains; these promises, they argue, are enforceable under a theory of promissory estoppel. Third, they assert that Amgen owes them a fiduciary duty, and has breached that duty by unreasonably denying them access to GDNF. Amgen denies that it made any such enforceable promises to the plaintiffs and denies that it stands in the position of a fiduciary. * * *

Amgen labeled this second study with protocol number 20030160 ("the '160 Study"). The '160 consent document indicated that participants would receive GDNF [liatermin] for a finite period of 24 months, although it states that participants "may be able to receive liatermin for a longer time." It also disclosed that a study participant may be withdrawn from the study by the principal investigator, in the event of "termination or cancellation of the study by the sponsor." * * * While the '160 Study was underway, Amgen became increasingly concerned that GDNF was not a safe or efficacious method of treating Parkinson's. In June 2004, the '168 Study [Protocol #20020168], in which 17 patients received GDNF and 17 others received a saline-based placebo, was unblinded, and Amgen concluded that the data reflected no statistically significant clinical improvement for those patients receiving GDNF. * * * The findings that GDNF was causing cerebellar toxicity among primates, combined with concerns as to the low efficacy of GDNF treatment and the implications of neutralizing antibodies, prompted Amgen on August 26, 2004 to halt the human trials. Amgen notified the Food and Drug Administration (FDA) and its Canadian counterparts of its decision. Amgen notified principal investigators and participants of this decision on September 1, 2004.

Amgen's decision was met with opposition from participants in the clinical studies, and from some of the principal investigators who were administering GDNF to the study participants. In October 2004, Amgen representatives attended a conference on GDNF, where physicians, investigators, and advocacy groups expressed disagreement with the decision to halt clinical studies. One of the investigators who vigorously disagreed with Amgen's decision was Dr. [Michael] Hutchinson [the PI for the NYU site]. Hutchinson states that he observed improvements in the plaintiffs' conditions, and that he continues to believe that GDNF was a safe and beneficial treatment for Parkinson's disease. * * * Not all principal investigators participating in the '160 and '168 studies disagreed with Amgen's decision to halt GDNF treatment. The principal investigators at trials occurring at the University of Virginia, Oregon Health & Science University, the University of Toronto, and Duke University all have submitted affidavits stating their opinions that Amgen acted properly and prudently by discontinuing the supply of GDNF.

The disagreement over clinically administered GDNF's effectiveness prompted a January 11, 2005 meeting between GDNF investigators, Amgen representatives, and officials at the FDA. * * * The FDA stated that its role was to "facilitate discussion" and it noted that "[t]he decision to withdraw was, and remains, a decision made by Amgen." The [agency's] memorandum also summarized previous communications between Amgen and the FDA, noting that if data did not clearly direct whether to provide GDNF to patients already receiving it, "then it was the company's prerogative as to how to proceed." The FDA also noted "that in some prior situations with other drugs, when a drug has been discontinued, a company may have chosen to allow patients that are already receiving [the] drug to continue to do so for an extended period of time, and that the FDA has often permitted such proposals to go forth." Following the FDA meeting, Amgen announced that it would not provide GDNF to the plaintiffs on a "compassionate use" basis, contending that GDNF did not work. * * *

In support of their claim of an enforceable contractual promise, neither Mr. Suthers nor Ms. Martin points to any direct oral or written communications with Amgen. Rather, they rely upon a generalized understanding that they acquired from their conversations with a principal investigator, Dr. Hutchinson of NYU, and the language of the NYU consent documents that they executed. It is a basic principle of contract law that the unilateral understandings of one party, no matter how subjectively reasonable, are insufficient to form the basis of a contractual promise. * * *

Plaintiffs point to the language of the consent document in the '168 Study: "Participants who complete 6 months of treatment may be invited to participate in a separate extended treatment study, which guarantees, if you are eligible to be enrolled, that you will receive liatermin and not a placebo." Fairly read, this is nothing more than a promise that in the next phase of the study, no participant would receive placebo, and all would receive GDNF. It is not a restriction on Amgen's ability to terminate the study. Indeed, as previously noted, plaintiffs executed a second consent prior to being admitted to the '160 Study. This second consent document makes it plain that "Amgen, Inc. and/or Medtronic Inc. may decide to stop the study at any time." * * *

Indeed, none of the relevant documents could be fairly described as a contract between the plaintiffs and Amgen. The Study Protocol and the Clinical Trial Agreement were binding agreements between Amgen and NYU. The consent documents define the rights of the plaintiffs in their relationship to NYU. Plaintiffs have endeavored to characterize Dr. Hutchinson as the agent of Amgen with the authority to bind it. * * * The Clinical Trial Agreement between Amgen and NYU makes clear that Hutchinson and NYU performed as independent contractors, and not as agents of Amgen * * * * [A]ssuming arguendo that Dr. Hutchinson promised plaintiffs that they would receive GDNF indefinitely, the record at this stage does not contain evidence that would support a finding of sufficient showing of merits in their favor in establishing words or conduct on the part of Amgen that would reasonably give rise to an appearance and belief that Dr. Hutchinson acted as Amgen's agent.

Plaintiffs agreed to the trials—and the invasive surgery accompanying them—knowing that in the '168 Study, they might receive placebos. From the consent form, they knew that their participation in the '160 Study was not a matter of right. They also knew from the consent forms for both studies that Amgen could elect to terminate the studies. On the plaintiffs' part, their decisions to participate may have been an act of confidence in the prospects of GDNF, of selflessness in agreeing to participate in an important research project, of hopefulness borne of their frustration from the lack of success of other treatments, or some combination of these or other factors. It is not illogical for a participant to assume that a company that has invested hundreds of millions of dollars to acquire the rights to a therapeutic treatment, and then spent millions more to test it, would want to bring the treatment to market if safe and effective. But that is a far cry from establishing a contract by which Amgen bargained away the freedom to terminate the research trials in its sole discretion. * * * [The court rejected plaintiffs' promissory estoppel argument on similar grounds.]

Plaintiffs argue that Amgen owes them a fiduciary duty, and that duty has been breached. * * * At argument, plaintiffs' counsel acknowledged that no New York court has recognized a fiduciary relationship between the sponsor of a research trial and a participant in that trial. Plaintiffs urge that this court adopt the reasoning of the Maryland Supreme Court's decision in *Grimes v. Kennedy Krieger Inst. Inc.*, 782 A.2d 807 (2001). * * * *Grimes* concluded that there was a duty to the research subject independent of the consent, and that a consent form could not be utilized to immunize the researchers from liability. * * * In *Grimes*, the participants were in direct contact and privity with the party who was found to have owed them a duty. Here no claim is asserted against the principal investigator, Dr. Hutchinson, or NYU, with whom plaintiffs had their dealings. * * *

Could a hypothetical fiduciary, with a strong and acknowledged profit motive of its own, tolerate the administration of an unproven treatment or a placebo to the person to whom this duty of "undivided loyalty" is owed? The fiduciary duty envisioned by the plaintiffs would presumably mean that if it were in a study participant's best interests to continue a clinical study, then the sponsoring company would be without power to terminate it without risking a finding of breach. Such a standard provides no guidance on a host of issues, including how long the sponsor's fiduciary duty would extend, whether the research institution would also have a duty to continue treating the study participant indefinitely, and whether the fiduciary obligations of the study's sponsor would survive the decision of the patient to cease his or her relationship with the research institution.

Here, the trial was consciously structured to foster the independence and objectivity of the research institutions and principal investigators conducting the study. The independence ensures that the sponsoring company does not manipulate the study to the ultimate detriment of those who may someday use the treatment. Attempts by a sponsoring company to separately communicate with the participants in a trial once the trial is underway would likely undermine the trial's independence. In this case, there is no basis in fact or law to impose a fiduciary duty running from the sponsor of an independent study to participants who it does not select, has not met, and about whom it may not know the details of their medical conditions. The constraints upon the conduct of the sponsoring company include FDA regulations and the contractual commitments that it undertakes, as well as ethical constraints imposed internally and through the pressures of the marketplace. * * *

Because an insufficient showing of merits has been made, it is not necessary for me to resolve these hotly contested issues of whether plaintiffs would likely benefit, or needlessly face danger, from the resumption of treatments with GDNF. * * * The independent researcher in this case, Dr. Hutchinson, presented to plaintiffs consent documents that acknowledged Amgen's right to terminate the research trials. Plaintiffs signed these documents and do not presently claim that they were coerced or misled into doing so. At the preliminary injunction stage, plaintiffs have made an insufficient showing of merits on their claims that Amgen gave up the right to terminate the trials in its unfettered discretion. The plaintiffs' motion for a preliminary injunction is denied.

NOTES AND QUESTIONS

1. *Disappointing subjects' expectations.* For a similar decision involving other Parkinson's disease subjects who had participated in a GDNF trial, see Abney v. Amgen, Inc., 443 F.3d 540 (6th Cir.2006). Would the court have decided differently if Amgen had no basis for concerns over safety? What if the evidence of GDNF's efficacy looked more favorable but still underwhelming? What if Amgen had stopped the open-label trial simply because it had lost interest in pursuing FDA approval (perhaps because a competitor was about to corner the relevant market)? See Bruce M. Psaty & Drummond Rennie, Editorial, Stopping Medical Research to Save Money: A Broken Pact with Researchers and Patients, 289 JAMA 2128 (2003) (questioning the ethics of halting clinical trials solely for commercial reasons). Why did the plaintiffs not also try to assert a constitutional claim? The investigational drug Ampligen triggered similar litigation. One case closely paralleled the facts and holding in *Suthers*. See DeVito v. HEM, Inc., 705 F.Supp. 1076 (M.D.Pa.1988) (rejecting claims pressed by a subject with AIDS); see also Cacchillo v. Insmed, Inc., 638 F.3d 401, 406 (2d Cir.2011) (declining to issue a preliminary injunction ordering the sponsor of a completed (and unsuccessful) clinical trial of Iplex for muscular dystrophy to support a former subject's application to the FDA for a compassionate use exemption to continue taking the abandoned investigational drug). The court in a second case, however, found merit in a contract-based claim. A group of patients who were receiving Ampligen in a clinical trial to treat chronic fatigue syndrome sued the sponsor to enforce a provision in the informed consent form that promised an additional year of access to treatment with the drug in an open-label trial if they completed the placebo-controlled, double-blind trial. Although the drug caused some serious adverse reactions in the original study, the FDA had granted permission for the open-label study but denied the company's request for a treatment IND. Observing that "[s]omehow the category of unilateral contracts appears to have escaped HEM's notice," the court reminded the company that "the petitioners performed by submitting to the double-blind tests. They incurred the detriment of being tested upon for HEM's studies in exchange for the promise of a year's treatment of Ampligen. Upon completion of the ... tests, there was a binding contract." Dahl v. HEM

Pharm. Corp., 7 F.3d 1399, 1404–05 (9th Cir.1993) (affirming a preliminary injunction requiring the company to supply the drug).

2. *Treatment INDs*. The FDA has recognized that in certain situations where no satisfactory alternative treatment exists, physicians may wish to use an investigational new drug to treat an individual patient or small class of patients but not as part of a clinical trial. Recall from *Femrite* that they may do so as an off-label use when the product has already been approved for a different indication. If, however, a product has not received any prior approval, it will be available only pursuant to an IND. Regulations promulgated in 1987 allow a manufacturer to supply an investigational drug for treatment use in very ill patients. The criteria for treatment use include: (1) the drug is intended to treat a serious or immediately life-threatening disease; (2) there is no comparable or satisfactory alternative drug or other therapy available to treat that disease in the particular patient population; (3) the drug is being studied in a controlled clinical trial under an IND or clinical trials have been completed for the drug; and (4) the drug's sponsor is actively pursuing marketing approval. See 52 Fed. Reg. 19,466 (1987) (codified as amended at 21 C.F.R. § 312.34(b)(1)); see also AIDS Amendments of 1988, Pub. L. No. 100–607, § 201(4), 102 Stat. 3048, 3066–67 (codified as amended at 42 U.S.C. § 300cc–12) (endorsing the use of treatment INDs for investigational AIDS drugs). The regulations require that an IRB review the treatment IND protocol and that patients give informed consent under the usual consent criteria. A separate regulation allows for the use of investigational drugs in emergency situations where physicians may not have time to submit a request for a treatment IND. See 21 C.F.R. § 312.36; see also 57 Fed. Reg. 13,250 (1992) (announcing a "parallel track" policy to allow expanded availability protocols for patients who do not meet the enrollment criteria for on-going clinical trials); Dale L. Moore, An IRB Member's Perspective on Access to Innovative Therapy, 57 Alb. L. Rev. 559 (1994); Myron L. Marlin, Comment, Treatment INDs: A Faster Route to Drug Approval, 39 Am. U. L. Rev. 171 (1989). A similar mechanism exists for medical devices. See 21 U.S.C. § 360j(m) (humanitarian device exemption); Max Sherman et al., Humanitarian Use Devices, 57 Food & Drug L.J. 95 (2002); Jennifer C. Dooren, Medtronic Valve Wins FDA Approval, Wall St. J., Jan. 26, 2010, at D2 (explaining that "devices used to treat conditions affecting 4,000 or fewer U.S. patients a year" are eligible for this exemption from full approval requirements); see also Joseph J. Fins et al., Misuse of the FDA's Humanitarian Device Exemption in Deep Brain Stimulation for Obsessive–Compulsive Disorder, 30 Health Aff. 302 (2011); Gina Kolata, Study Is Ended as a Stent Fails to Stop Strokes, N.Y. Times, Sept. 8, 2011, at A1 (reporting that a brain stent approved by the FDA under this exemption failed miserably in a postapproval clinical trial).

3. *Patient demand for new therapies*. In the early 1990s, the spread of HIV triggered an outcry against the FDA's often painstakingly slow and seemingly rigid new drug approval process. AIDS activists (and those who lobby in favor of early access to experimental therapies for other life-threatening diseases) pointed out that people afflicted with diseases for which no effective treatment exists are often willing to tolerate higher degrees of risk in exchange for the chance at prolonging or improving the quality of life. See Mary T. Griffin, AIDS Drugs and the Pharmaceutical Industry: A Need for Reform, 17 Am. J.L. & Med. 363 (1991); Matthew C. Lovell, Second Thoughts: Do the FDA's Responses to a Fatal Drug Trial and the AIDS Community's Doubts About Early Access to Drugs Hint at a Shift in Basic FDA Policy?, 51 Food & Drug L.J. 273 (1996); Steven R. Salbu, Regulation of Drug Treatments for HIV and AIDS: A Contractarian Model of Access, 11 Yale J. on Reg. 401 (1994); Philip A. Leider, Comment, Domestic AIDS Vaccine Trials: Addressing the Potential for Social Harm to the Subjects of Human Experiments, 88 Cal. L. Rev. 1185 (2000); Lois K. Perrin, Note, The Catch–22 for Persons with AIDS: To Have or Not to Have Easy Access to Experimental Therapies and Early Approval for New Drugs, 69 S. Cal. L. Rev. 105 (1995); see also John J. Smith, Science, Politics, and Policy: The Tacrine Debate, 47 Food & Drug L.J. 511, 525 (1992) ("The potential impact of interest group advocacy goes far beyond HIV/AIDS and the Alzheimer's lobbies.").

4. *Finding clinical trials.* Many patients whose disease does not respond to standard therapy may want to participate in a clinical trial of an experimental product. Historically, patients would learn of such opportunities only if their regular physician happened to know of a potentially useful trial. Increasingly, investigators and sponsors advertise their clinical trials (sometimes on television), and Internet-savvy patients may locate clinical trials on their own. In 1997, Congress directed the NIH to create a database of information about clinical trials for drugs intended to treat serious or life-threatening diseases. See FDAMA, Pub. L. No. 105–115, § 113, 111 Stat. 2296 (1997). (One decade earlier Congress had directed the agency to establish a similar registry of investigational AIDS drugs trials. See 42 U.S.C. § 300cc–17.) In 2007, it expanded the scope of this database and, more importantly, converted it from simply providing a vehicle for access by interested subjects into a mechanism for guarding against the phenomenon of selective reporting by sponsors of completed trials. See FDAAA, Pub. L. No. 110–85, § 801, 121 Stat. 823, 904 (2007) (codified at 42 U.S.C. § 282(j)); see also Christine D. Galbraith, Dying to Know: A Demand for Genuine Public Access to Clinical Trial Results Data, 78 Miss. L.J. 705 (2009); Carolyne R. Hathaway et al., The Web of Clinical Trial Registration Obligations: Have Foreign Clinical Trials Been Caught?, 64 Food & Drug L.J. 261 (2009).

CHAPTER 3

PREMARKET APPROVAL AND POSTMARKET SURVEILLANCE

A. PHARMACEUTICAL PRODUCTS

1. NEW DRUG APPROVAL APPLICATIONS

Edison Pharmaceutical Co. v. FDA

600 F.2d 831 (D.C.Cir.1979).

■ TAMM, CIRCUIT JUDGE:

* * * In the 1950s, Dr. Murray Israel developed Cothyrobal, an injectable drug intended to treat hypercholesterolemia and hypothyroidism. Cothyrobal is a combination of the thyroid extract, sodium levothyroxine, and cyanocobalamin (vitamin B_{12}). Levothyroxine is a cholesterol lowering substance with some toxic side effects. Proponents of Cothyrobal claim that vitamin B_{12} inhibits the toxicity of levothyroxine while retaining its medicinal benefits.

In May 1969, Edison filed the NDA [new drug approval application] for Cothyrobal that is the subject of this appeal. The Commissioner found the information offered in support of the application deficient. * * * The basis for the Commissioner's decision was Edison's failure to submit double-blind controlled studies comparing the effects of Cothyrobal and levothyroxine which he determined were necessary to prove the efficacy of the drug. Edison appealed that ruling to this court, contending that the studies it had submitted were as scientifically sound as humanly possible. A panel of this court reversed and ordered the Commissioner to hold "a full evidentiary hearing" to determine whether double-blind testing comparing the effects of levothyroxine and Cothyrobal could be conducted safely and to determine "*all* relevant issues relating to the approvability of (Edison's) application."

The FDA held the required hearings in December 1975 and January 1976. The administrative law judge (ALJ) concluded that limited double-blind testing could be performed safely. He further found that the studies submitted with the NDA failed to demonstrate the safety and efficacy of Cothyrobal, as required by section 505(d) of the Act * * * * Accordingly, the ALJ refused approval of the NDA. That decision was affirmed by the Commissioner * * * *

Under section 505(d)(5) of the Act, an NDA must be denied if there is a lack of "substantial evidence that the drug will have the effect it purports or is represented to have under the conditions of use" contained in the proposed labeling. Substantial evidence is "evidence consisting of adequate and well-controlled investigations, including clinical investigations, by experts qualified by scientific training and experience to evaluate the effectiveness of the drug involved." 21 U.S.C. § 355(d). Uncontrolled studies or partially controlled studies alone are insufficient proof of a drug's efficacy. 21 C.F.R. § 314.111(a)(5)(ii)(*c*) (1978). "Isolated case reports, random experience, and reports lacking details which permit scientific evaluation will not be considered." Id. An "adequate and well-controlled investigation * * * [p]rovides a comparison of the results of treatment or diagnosis with a control in such a fashion as to permit quantitative evaluation."

Clinically controlled testing usually involves administration of treatment to two groups of comparable subjects afflicted with the same condition. The first group receives the test drug; the second group, the control group, receives either an inactive preparation known as a placebo or a known drug to which the test drug is being compared. The results of the two groups are then analyzed. Since human reaction to disease treatment may be influenced by a patient's expectations, and since observation of symptoms, particularly subjective symptoms, may be influenced by an observer's expectations, controlled investigations are usually conducted so neither subject nor observer knows which patient is part of the control group. This technique is called double-blinding. Double-blinding techniques are generally required to assure the formation of a scientifically valid judgment as to the therapeutic efficacy of a particular treatment. In certain circumstances, however, such as those involving diseases with high and predictable mortality rates, or signs and symptoms of predictable duration or severity, the regulations permit the use of historical controls. In an historically controlled study, the effects of the medication on a test population are compared with adequately documented accounts of the natural history of the disease instead of with control groups.

A double-blind controlled clinical investigation of Cothyrobal would require comparison of effects of Cothyrobal with those of levothyroxine. * * * [T]he Commissioner assumed arguendo that concurrent control group testing of Cothyrobal and levothyroxine was too dangerous to perform and examined each study submitted with the NDA to determine the approvability of the application. The Commissioner found these studies uniformly replete with inaccuracies and ambiguities, lacking protocol and statistical analysis. Specifically, the Commissioner set out in detail the substantive deficiencies of each. The Commissioner concluded, and we agree, that the studies were not "adequate and well-controlled" within the meaning of section 505(d) and did not establish the efficacy of Cothyrobal. On appeal, Edison does not dispute the specific inadequacies of the studies found by the Commissioner. * * *

Section 505(d)(1) of the Act requires that an NDA include "adequate tests by all methods reasonably applicable to show whether or not such drug is safe for use under the conditions prescribed, recommended, or suggested in the proposed labeling thereof." The Commissioner concluded that Edison failed to prove the safety of Cothyrobal. The Commissioner noted that Edison's own attempt to avoid the usual double-blind studies places the safety of the Cothyrobal in question. Because Edison argues that the toxic effects of levothyroxine make it humanly impossible to administer that drug in controlled testing, patients receiving Cothyrobal may be subject to the same risks as those receiving levothyroxine, absent a showing of the claimed ability of vitamin B_{12} to mitigate the antithyrotoxic effects of levothyroxine. * * *

Although the Commissioner recognized that studies showing the safety of a drug need not be adequate and well-controlled * * * he properly ruled that they "must be adequately constructed so that scientists can draw reasonable conclusions from them." The Commissioner, relying on testimony of three expert witnesses, concluded that both the animal studies and clinical testing offered by Edison were deficient and failed to demonstrate the safety of Cothyrobal. In addition, a number of witnesses, including some called by Edison, testified to adverse side effects, such as tachycardia and insomnia, which may have resulted from treatment with Cothyrobal. Edison failed to rebut this evidence. The Commissioner therefore concluded that Edison did not carry its burden of proving the safety of the drug. In view of the foregoing, we find the Commissioner's decision supported by substantial evidence. * * *

Edison next objects to the exclusion of testimonial evidence which it alleges demonstrates the efficacy of Cothyrobal. Edison argues that because the symptoms of hypothyroidism are difficult to recognize, efficacy can be assessed most accurately through the degree of relief experienced by the patients. Thus, according to Edison, the "best way" to prove that the drug works "is to bring the patients in themselves" and allow them to testify. Similarly, Edison contends that the most relevant expert testimony is that of doctors who have administered Cothyrobal and can relate their clinical impressions of the ability of the drug to relieve pain. Edison, therefore, characterizes the testimony of non-clinical FDA experts, despite their impressive credentials and scientific experience, as "meaningless," and suggests that the ALJ erred when he considered their criticisms of the studies submitted with the NDA.

Edison's attempt to replace evidence of "controlled" investigation with testimony relating personal experiences or clinical impressions is inconsistent with the Act, the accompanying regulations, and explicit Supreme Court precedent. Personal testimonials simply do not meet the exacting standards required by the Act and the regulations. [In *Weinberger v. Hynson, Westcott & Dunning, Inc.*, 412 U.S. 609 (1973), the Supreme] Court explained that the statutory and regulatory criteria

> express well-established principles of scientific investigation. Moreover, their strict and demanding standards, barring anecdotal evidence indicating that doctors "believe" in the efficacy of a drug, are amply justified by the legislative history. The hearings underlying the 1962 Act show a marked concern that impressions or beliefs of physicians, no matter how fervently held, are treacherous.

Id. at 619. Subjective evaluations by selected patients are even more suspect. We therefore conclude that the ALJ's rulings excluding personal testimonials accord with applicable law. We further find the admission of non-clinical FDA expert testimony entirely proper. * * *

SmithKline Corp. v. FDA

587 F.2d 1107 (D.C.Cir.1978).

■ Bazelon, Circuit Judge:

Smith, Kline & French Laboratories (SKF), a Division of SmithKline Corporation, has since 1950 produced and marketed Dexamyl, a prescription drug used as an anorectic in the treatment of obesity. Dexamyl is a combination drug containing Dexedrine (dextroamphetamine sulfate), an appetite suppressant, and amobarbital, a barbiturate designed to reduce the possible adverse side effects of Dexedrine. On August 24, 1976, the Acting Commissioner of Food and Drugs published an order denying SKF a hearing and refusing to approve the pending new drug applications (NDAs) for Dexamyl. 41 Fed. Reg. 35,741 (1976). SKF petitions this court to reverse the Acting Commissioner's summary judgment order and to remand to the Food and Drug Administration for an evidentiary hearing pursuant to 21 U.S.C. § 355(c). * * *

FDA has promulgated regulations implementing this statutory scheme. It has required that for a fixed combination prescription drug such as Dexamyl substantial evidence must be presented both that the drug is effective for its intended use and that each constituent component contributes to the claimed effects. In addition, FDA has specified criteria for the "adequate and well-controlled investigations" acceptable as substantial evidence of effectiveness. Although the Act appears to contemplate a hearing if FDA does not approve an NDA, FDA has developed summary judgment procedures in cases where an applicant has failed to submit substantial evidence of drug efficacy sufficient to meet regulatory standards. The Supreme Court has in principle approved such procedures, stating that, "(w)e cannot impute to Congress the design of requiring, nor does due process demand, a hearing when it appears conclusively from the applicant's 'pleadings' that the application cannot succeed." Weinberger v. Hynson, Westcott & Dunning, Inc., 412 U.S. 609, 621 (1973). * * *

On August 6, 1971, SKF submitted NDAs for Dexamyl * * * * FDA informed SKF by letter on January 15, 1973, that these NDAs were not approvable because "(t)he studies submitted fail to demonstrate the contribution of the sedative-tranquilizer constituent to the total effect of the drug." * * * On July 11, 1973, SKF submitted to FDA the results of five, new, double-blind, clinical trials testing the efficacy of Dexamyl (multi-investigator clinical trials). Two weeks later, on July 27, 1973, FDA informed SKF by letter that the record regarding Dexamyl was closed as of that date, and that no further data would be accepted from SKF.

Three years later, on August 24, 1976, FDA published an order denying a hearing and refusing to approve the pending NDAs for Dexamyl. * * * The Acting Commissioner based his holding on the fact that none of the evidence submitted by SKF met the regulatory standards for adequate and well-controlled clinical studies. * * * Prior to August 24, SKF had received no criticism from FDA of SKF's multi-investigator clinical trials. After reviewing FDA's August 24 order, SKF asked Herbert Solomon, Ph.D., Professor of Statistics at Stanford University, and William M. Wardell, M.D., Ph.D., Associate Professor of Pharmacology and Toxicology at the University of Rochester Medical Center, to review these studies. These two experts prepared affidavits averring that the studies were adequate and well-controlled clinical investigations under applicable scientific and regulatory standards. * * *

[T]he FDA regulations defining "well-controlled investigations" * * * for the most part express general norms of scientific research rather than exact rules of procedure. The task of a court of appeals reviewing an FDA grant of summary judgment thus becomes, at least in those cases which do not involve the violation of a manifestly "precise" regulation, the determination of whether the applicant's submission on its face is so conclusively deficient in light of these norms that no issue of fact remains whether "experts qualified by scientific training and experience" could "fairly and responsibly" conclude, on the basis of the submission, that "the drug will have the effect it purports or is represented to have under the conditions of use prescribed, recommended, or suggested in the labeling or proposed labeling thereof."

The difficulties besetting this enterprise are formidable. The issues entail complicated questions of scientific methodology, an area in which courts have little institutional competence. These questions must be confronted, moreover, in the absence of an evidentiary record. * * * Although courts will ordinarily exercise considerable deference to an "agency's technical expertise and experience," particularly with respect to questions involving " 'engineering and scientific' considerations," it is not clear how far that deference should extend when an agency has deliberately prevented the creation of a record by which its determinations can be probed for their underlying "basis in fact." * * * [W]hen a record is barren concerning an issue presented in a petition for review in this case the issue of whether an applicant's studies are methodologically adequate in light of the pertinent regulations we are asked to perform even this limited function on the basis of faith alone.

The instant case amply illustrates these difficulties. SKF strenuously urges that FDA's criticisms of its multi-investigator clinical trials are based upon "imprecise" regulations and are scientifically fallacious. Since FDA refused to consider these contentions, however, the record before us consists chiefly of SKF's NDA, together with its multi-investigator clinical trials, and FDA's August 24, 1976 order. We are thus confronted on one side by the arguments of lawyers, and on the other by the untested conclusions of FDA. To decide the scientific merit of these disputes, on the basis of the record now before us, would certainly be to risk the dangerous unreliability likely to occur when "technically illiterate judges" attempt substantively to review mathematical and scientific questions.

That risk may, in the end, prove inescapable, but it can perhaps be minimized if it is kept firmly in mind that we need not resolve the *scientific* question of the methodological adequacy of SKF's multi-investigator clinical trials, but the *legal* question of whether they are on their face conclusively inadequate in light of the pertinent regulations. The manner in which we resolve this latter question involves policy considerations: we must take account of both fairness to the petitioner and the public interest in effective drug regulation. Since FDA has precluded SKF from establishing on the record the factual predicates for its arguments that FDA's criticism of the multi-investigator clinical trials are scientifically inaccurate, rudimentary fairness requires that we at least give the factual claims underlying SKF's arguments the benefit of the doubt. * * *

SKF rests its claim to a hearing chiefly on its multi-investigator clinical trials. SKF argues that these trials establish both that Dexamyl is effective as an anorectic and that each of its components contributes to the effects claimed; i.e., that the Dexedrine in Dexamyl performs its weight-loss function undiminished by the presence of amobarbital, and that the amobarbital makes its own contribution by reducing adverse side effects experienced by patients who take Dexedrine alone. The trials tested Dexamyl tablets against Dexedrine. The studies were double-blind; neither investigators nor patients knew which of the two drugs had been prescribed to any particular patient. There were five investigators, scattered throughout the country; each was a physician who treated patients in his private medical practice for obesity. All followed the same protocol, under which 30 patients were selected for each study, 15 of whom were assigned randomly to one drug, and 15 to the other. The trials lasted eight weeks.

In its August 24, 1976 order, FDA noted numerous deficiencies which, it claimed, rendered the trials conclusively inadequate in light of the pertinent regulations. Before this court, however, FDA has chosen to press only six of these deficiencies. Should even a single one of these six deficiencies prove valid, we must sustain FDA's summary judgment order.

The subjects of the trials were selected from among patients between the ages of 18 and 60 who were at least 20 percent overweight, and who scored four or more on a prescribed Anxiety Manifestation Index. No patients were included if, among other things, they suffered from a number of specified diseases or had a history of drug abuse. The protocol also required that patients selected for a trial not have received any anorectic or tranquilizing medication for at least two weeks prior to their participation in the study, and tranquilizers, sedatives and other anorectic agents or measures for weight control were prohibited during the trial. Patients were placed on a 1200 calorie diet. * * *

Dexamyl's present labeling indicates use with obese patients, but the subjects of the trials were anxious, obese patients. Since anxiety was one of the side effects of Dexedrine that amobarbital was designed to remedy,

FDA argues that it is impossible to generalize the results obtained in the subpopulation of patients studied by the trials. Its point appears to be that the trials do not demonstrate whether Dexedrine produces in non-anxious obese patients side-effects that can be remedied by amobarbital. If no such side effects are produced, the prescription of amobarbital would be superfluous. FDA's contention is well grounded in its regulations. The trials provide no "assurance" that Dexedrine, in the amounts contained in Dexamyl, produces in non-anxious obese patients side effects capable of being remedied by amobarbital. This conclusion is not fatal to SKF, however, since it implies only that Dexamyl's labeling be altered to recommend Dexamyl for use with anxious, obese patients. SKF implies that it would accept such an alteration, and we must therefore examine the other deficiencies alleged by FDA to determine whether the trials are conclusively inadequate despite such an alteration in labeling.

The trials were conducted by physicians whose private medical practices included obese patients, and each physician-investigator was aware that the trials were testing the side-effect potential of the two drugs involved. The physicians were expected to use their normal but trained powers of observation, supplemented by specific inquiry where they deemed it appropriate. They completed forms recording extensive data for all patients. Particular attention was paid to adverse effects, which were detailed as to dates (onset and termination), severity, and relationship to the drug prescribed. The supervising physicians recorded whatever action they took as the result of such an adverse effect, including any reduction of dosage or outright discontinuance of the drug involved.

FDA regulations require a well-controlled study to explain its "methods of observation and recording of results, including the variables measured, quantitation, assessment of any subjects response, and steps taken to minimize bias on the part of the subject and observer." 21 C.F.R. § 314.111(a)(5)(ii)(*a*)(*3*). FDA contends that the trials are conclusively inadequate in light of this regulation since they nowhere describe what procedure (observation, general questions or specific inquiries) was actually used by each investigator to elicit adverse reaction data, whether specific inquiry was resorted to under the same circumstances or whether each of the investigators asked their subjects the same questions. * * *

We must ask, that is, whether the trials are so conclusively deficient in light of the norm of scientific research expressed by the regulation that no question of fact remains whether qualified experts could fairly and responsibly conclude from the trials whether Dexamyl was effective for its intended uses. SKF argues that such a question of fact exists. The trials were conducted in a double-blind fashion. Since neither investigators nor subjects knew which patients were receiving Dexamyl and which Dexedrine, SKF concludes that the possible irregularities in observation noted by FDA would not bias the trials' results. Whether the level of "explanation" offered by SKF was sufficient under the regulation thus involves a complex question of scientific methodology. We, of course, have neither the knowledge nor the competence to ourselves resolve this question. Giving petitioner's version of the facts the benefit of the doubt, however, we must agree that the question is presently unsettled. But we will not so abandon the public interest in the expeditious enforcement of the drug laws as to assume, in the absence of a more developed record, that SKF's contentions have truly raised a genuine issue of fact requiring an adjudicatory hearing.

The trials compared a "test" group of patients who received Dexamyl against a "control" group who received Dexedrine. FDA regulations require that a well-controlled study must include "(a) method of selection of the subjects that ... (iii) Assures comparability in test and control groups of pertinent variables." 21 C.F.R. § 314.111(a)(5)(ii)(*a*)(*2*). FDA argues that the trials are conclusively inadequate in light of this regulation because they fail to demonstrate the comparability of test and control subjects regarding the incidence and degree of anxiety. SKF vigorously contests this characterization of the trials, contending that they did indeed include a method of selection assuring comparability. The subjects were assigned to test and control groups on a random basis, and a statistical analysis of the Anxiety Manifestation Index for both groups indicated a random distribution of anxiety. FDA discounts this analysis, however, stating that the regulations require a check on the results of randomization at the conclusion as well as at the beginning of a study. In this FDA appears to be improperly elaborating on its own regulations, which require only that a study provide a "method of selection of the subjects" that would ensure comparability. * * *

FDA argues that the trials also failed to assure comparability between test and control groups with respect to the past use of amphetamines. This is important, FDA stresses, because "amphetamines as a class can produce both tolerance and dependence," and because "a subject's prior history of amphetamine use may affect ... the incidence of various side effects." 41 Fed. Reg. at 35,746. SKF contends, however, that these factors are irrelevant because no subject was included in the trials who had used amphetamines during the two weeks immediately prior to the commencement of the studies and because this two week "washout" period was sufficient to eliminate any interference that might be caused by a subject's prior history of amphetamine use. The issue of whether the two week washout period is sufficient to assure comparability in the selection of test and control groups appears to raise a question of fact. Whether this appearance is genuine, however, depends upon the state of opinion in the scientific community, a circumstance concerning which we are at present entirely ignorant. * * *

The trials analyzed data compiled by each of the five individual investigators. This data was then pooled or aggregated for further statistical analysis. FDA concluded that this pooling failed to provide the necessary assurance of comparability between test and control groups with respect to pertinent variables. SKF argues that FDA's conclusion overlooks the fact that all five investigators used the same experimental protocol, including the two week washout period for prior amphetamine use, the random assignment of subjects to test and control groups, and the double-blind administration of the trials. Thus, for example, if the washout period were effective in assuring comparability between test and control groups for a single investigator, it would also be so with respect to the aggregated data.

Since we have already concluded that the effectiveness of the washout period is an open question, we must also consider this aspect of the issue of pooling as unsettled. * * * The fact that different investigators used different techniques for soliciting or recording the data, for example, may present a bar to the statistical pooling of their results. But this is an intricate scientific question concerning which we cannot exercise independent judgment, and FDA has offered neither evidence nor explanation. Extending the benefit of the doubt to petitioner's general claim that the protocol was in fact sufficiently detailed to permit pooling, we must conclude that the question of whether a genuine issue of fact here exists remains open.

The trials compared Dexamyl to Dexedrine. FDA regulations state that a well-controlled study must provide "a comparison of the results of treatment or diagnosis with a control in such a fashion as to permit quantitative evaluation.... An effective regime of therapy may be used for comparison ...." 21 C.F.R. § 314.111(a)(5)(ii)(*a*)(*4*)(*iii*). FDA concluded that the trials were conclusively inadequate in light of this regulation "since the active control used, dextroamphetamine, does not permit a quantitative evaluation of the effects of Dexamyl."

> Because the anorectic effect of dextroamphetamine is only marginal to begin with (i.e., its advantage over placebo is small), and because its anorectic effect is highly variable, its effectiveness is not demonstrable in every study. * * * Accordingly, a finding of "no difference" between Dexamyl and dextroamphetamine in a particular study can mean either that both were effective or that neither was effective in that study.

41 Fed. Reg. at 35,750. * * *

SKF argues, if FDA recognizes Dexedrine as effective, the trials were not on their face deficient to use the drug as an active control. We agree with SKF in this matter. FDA's endorsement of Dexedrine as effective for the short term management of exogenous obesity provides at least prima facie support for SKF's view of the appropriateness of Dexedrine as an active control. Since, in contrast to other issues we have heretofore considered, SKF's position is supported by evidence, we conclude that there is a genuine issue of fact whether Dexedrine, although effective, is so unpredictable as to foreclose the possibility of quantitative evaluation. Such issues are not to be decided at summary judgment.

FDA requires that a well-controlled investigation explain "the methods used to minimize bias on the part of the observers and the analysts of the data." 21 C.F.R. § 314.111(a)(5)(ii)(*a*)(*4*). FDA concluded that the trials were conclusively deficient in light of this regulation. * * * SKF rejects this argument, noting that the steps taken in the trials to minimize analyst bias are stated in the protocol and final report. These include a multiple covariance quantitative analysis, a Chi–Square analysis of qualitative results, a report of the details and results of these analyses, and an analysis both of all subjects and of only those subjects who completed the entire eight week program.

Since it is impossible to determine, in the abstract, whether the information provided in the trials' protocol constitutes a sufficient "explanation" for purposes of the regulation, we must ask, once again, whether the trials are so conclusively deficient with respect to the norm of scientific research expressed by the regulation that no issue of fact remains whether qualified experts could fairly and responsibly conclude from the trials whether Dexamyl was effective for its intended uses. We have no way of answering this question in the absence of a more developed record. Giving the benefit of the doubt to petitioner, we conclude that the question remains open.

If Dexamyl's labeling were altered to recommend its use for anxious, obese patients, FDA's summary judgment order cannot be sustained. It remains an open question, however, whether the trials are conclusively deficient in light of FDA regulations requiring comparability of test and control groups, an explanation of the methods used to observe and record results, and an explanation of the methods used to minimize analyst bias. These issues cannot be resolved in the absence of an evidentiary record. * * * Since we cannot sustain FDA's summary judgment order and since, at the same time, we have no assurance that there is presently a genuine issue of fact to be aired at an adjudicatory hearing, this record should be remanded to FDA for a proceeding to determine whether such a genuine issue of fact exists. The extent of this proceeding should be as limited as its circumscribed purpose. Were this proceeding to become too lengthy or elaborate, it would create precisely the drain on FDA's resources [that] FDA's summary judgment regulations were designed to prevent. * * *

NOTES AND QUESTIONS

1. *Industry challenges to FDA decisionmaking*. Pharmaceutical manufacturers rarely pursue judicial challenges to the denial of an NDA, no doubt in recognition of the fact that courts show significant deference to the agency's expertise. See, e.g., Unimed, Inc. v. Richardson, 458 F.2d 787, 789 (D.C.Cir.1972) ("[W]e remind ourselves that our role in the congressional scheme is not to give an independent judgment of our own, but rather to determine whether the expert agency entrusted with regulatory responsibility has taken an irrational or arbitrary view of the evidence assembled before it."). The Cothyrobal NDA at issue in *Edison* had a checkered history. The inventor of the drug previously filed an antitrust lawsuit charging that a pair of his competitors had conspired with the FDA to block approval of Cothyrobal, a claim that the court remanded to the district court but not without first warning the agency to use an "unimpeachable review process." See Israel v. Baxter Lab., Inc., 466 F.2d 272, 283 (D.C.Cir. 1972). It took quite some time before the FDA got around to applying the same approval standards to levothyroxine sodium, a widely prescribed drug available since the 1950s. See 62 Fed. Reg. 43,535 (1997) (giving manufacturers three years to secure approval); see also 65 Fed. Reg. 24,488 (2000) (extending the deadline by one year). Although it approved an NDA in 2000 (for a product sold under the brand-name Unithroid®), the agency continued to defer taking action against unapproved products that remained on the market. See 66 Fed. Reg. 36,794 (2001) (effectively extending the original deadline by three years); Shari Roan, Longtime Drug's New Troubles: Synthroid, Taken by 8 Million People with Thyroid Problems, Is Under FDA Scrutiny, L.A. Times, July 23, 2001, at S1; see also Cody Labs., Inc. v. Sebelius, 2010 WL 3119279, at *7 (D.Wyo.2010) ("When a company obtains approval to market a drug that other companies have been marketing illegally, FDA may, in its discretion, allow a grace period before the initiation of any enforcement actions to permit manufacturers and consumers to adjust to the imminent removal of the unapproved products from the market."); id. at *16–17 (finding no merit in claims that the agency should have extended this limited grace period for manufacturers of a morphine sulfate solution); Natasha Singer, F.D.A. Says Millions Got Unapproved Heart Pills, N.Y. Times, Mar. 27, 2010, at B1 (describing a similar regulatory response to nitroglycerin tablets). Although the federal courts rejected a challenge to the policy of deferring action on unapproved levothyroxine products as an unreviewable exercise of enforcement discretion, the license-holder was allowed to press a claim that the FDA had acted inappropriately in releasing trade secret information to its competitors. See Jerome Stevens Pharm., Inc. v. FDA, 402 F.3d 1249, 1253–58 (D.C.Cir.2005).

2. *The shift from passive to active premarket review.* Since 1938, the FDA's governing statute has required that the agency review all new drugs for safety prior to marketing. See 21 U.S.C. § 355. Under the original provision, applications for approval automatically went into effect after 60 days, unless the agency extended the review period and notified the applicant. In 1962, Congress amended the FDCA to create a pre-approval system under which the NDA sponsor must demonstrate both safety and effectiveness for the new drug's intended use(s) and await FDA clearance for marketing. The agency also subjected drugs first marketed prior to 1962 to a complex retrospective review procedure as a prerequisite for continued marketing. In implementing the Drug Amendments of 1962, the FDA routinely disregarded testimonials as evidence of safety and effectiveness. See Upjohn Co. v. Finch, 422 F.2d 944, 951–52 (6th Cir.1970); see also Richard A. Merrill, The Architecture of Government Regulation of Medical Products, 82 Va. L. Rev. 1753, 1761–76 (1996) (providing a detailed discussion of how the current new drug approval process evolved from earlier approaches); Gardiner Harris, It Started More Than One Revolution, N.Y. Times, May 4, 2010, at D1 (explaining how challenges posed by the birth control pill—first approved by the FDA 50 years earlier—influenced the agency's evolving approach to drug regulation). The system remains passive, however, in the sense that the agency relies on applicants to submit full and accurate information. See Liora Sukhatme, Note, Deterring Fraud: Mandatory Disclosure and the FDA Drug Approval Process, 82 N.Y.U. L. Rev. 1210 (2007).

3. *Time and effort required for approval.* Pharmaceutical manufacturers expend tremendous resources in the preparation of applications for the approval of new drugs. The development process may take a dozen years on average, from early research and pre-clinical testing through the multi-stage clinical trials process and FDA review. As mentioned in Chapter 2(A), out of 5,000 initial candidates, only five typically enter clinical trials, and only one of those may reach the market. If one accounts for the numerous failures along the way and the cost of capital, controversial estimates place the average investment for an approved new drug at well over $1 billion. See Joseph A. DiMasi et al., The Price of Innovation: New Estimates of Drug Development Costs, 22 J. Health Econ. 151 (2003); Peter Landers, Cost of Developing a New Drug Increases to About $1.7 Billion, Wall St. J., Dec. 8, 2003, at B4; cf. Alex Berenson, Drug Makers Reap Benefits of Tax Break, N.Y. Times, May 8, 2005, § 1, at 1 (reporting that pharmaceutical manufacturers claim to generate most of their profits overseas, notwithstanding much higher prices and sales volume in the U.S., in order to minimize their domestic tax burdens). But see Roger Collier, Drug Development Cost Estimates Hard to Swallow, 180 Can. Med. Ass'n J. 279 (2009). In some respects, the motion picture industry reportedly operates in a similar fashion, with blockbuster movies dwarfed by flops, an overreliance on sequels to blockbusters and remakes of classics, and accounting practices that arguably inflate production expenditures.

4. *Drug lag.* For years, critics blamed the FDA's lengthy pre-approval process for creating a "drug lag" that delayed products already approved in Europe and elsewhere from reaching the U.S. market. See, e.g., Gen. Accounting Office, FDA Drug Approval—A Lengthy Process that Delays the Availability of New Drugs (1980); see also Peter Huber, Safety and the Second Best: The Hazards of Public Risk Management in the Courts, 85 Colum. L. Rev. 277 (1985) (explaining that delays in marketing risky but useful drugs may harm a greater number of patients); cf. Ariel Katz, Pharmaceutical Lemons: Innovation and Regulation in the Drug Industry, 14 Mich. Telecomm. & Tech. L. Rev. 1 (2007) (critiquing the drug lag literature). FDA review times improved substantially in the 1990s. See David A. Kessler et al., Approval of New Drugs in the United States: Comparison with the United Kingdom, Germany, and Japan, 276 JAMA 1826, 1829–31 (1996). Nonetheless, critics continue to complain about obstacles and undue delays in the process. See Chris Adams, Approval Time for New Drugs Increases Slightly, Wall St. J., Jan. 16, 2003, at D4 ("In 2002, the median approval time for standard drug applications was 15.3 months, up from . . . 12 months in 2000."); Scott Gottlieb, Op–Ed., The FDA Is Evading the Law, Wall St. J., Dec. 23, 2010, at A17 ("Europeans are now approving novel drugs an average of three months more rapidly than we do. Of 82 novel drugs that were submitted for approval in both the U.S. and Europe between 2006 to 2009, 11 were approved only in Europe."). But see Margaret A. Hamburg, Op–Ed., America's Innovation Agency: The FDA, Wall St. J., Aug. 1, 2011, at A13 (responding to the critics); Jonathan D. Rockoff & Ron Winslow, Drug Makers Refill Parched Pipelines, Wall St. J., July 11, 2011, at A1 ("Companies have won marketing approval so far this year for 20 innovative medicines .... There were just 21 such approvals all last year."). See generally Richard A. Epstein, Overdose: How Excessive Government Regulation Stifles Pharmaceutical Innovation (2006); Shelby D. Reed et al., How Changes in Drug–Safety Regulations Affect the Way Drug and Biotech Companies Invest in Innovation, 25 Health Aff. 1309 (2006).

5. *Accelerating drug approval.* Starting in the 1980s, in response to the previously mentioned demands from AIDS activists, the FDA developed mechanisms for accelerated approval. First, under expedited approval procedures, new drugs intended to treat life-threatening and seriously-debilitating illnesses (such as AIDS or cancer) could receive marketing approval with a weaker body of evidence demonstrating effectiveness than is normally required in the NDA process. Qualifying drugs might reach the market after two, instead of three, phases of human clinical trials, though the agency could then demand postapproval studies to discover additional information about the drug's safety and optimal use. See 21 C.F.R. §§ 312.80–.88. In 1992, the agency began to accept "surrogate marker" evidence in these cases—clinical indicators that can be used to predict the ultimate effectiveness of a given drug therapy for a targeted condition. See 21 C.F.R. §§ 314.510, 601.41; see also 57 Fed. Reg. 58,942 (1992); Sheila R. Shulman & Jeffrey S. Brown, The Food and Drug Administration's Early Access and Fast–Track Approval Initiatives: How Have They Worked?, 50 Food & Drug L.J. 503 (1995); Marc Kaufman, FDA Clears Once-a-Day AIDS Drug: Single–Pill Regimen Hailed as Milestone, Wash. Post, July 13, 2006, at A1 ("The FDA has approved 28 products in the U.S. to treat HIV infection—most of them as high-priority applications."). For example, in the case of new cancer treatments, tumor shrinkage might substitute for evidence of extended survival times. In 1997, Congress belatedly codified these "fast track" procedures. See 21 U.S.C. § 356; see also Mary K. Olson, Managing Delegation in the FDA: Reducing Delay in New–Drug Review, 29 J. Health Pol. Pol'y & L. 397 (2004); Deborah G. Parver, Comment, Expediting the Drug Approval Process: An Analysis of the FDA Modernization Act of 1997, 51 Admin. L. Rev. 1249 (1999).

The accelerated approval process has attracted some criticism. First, serious side effects sometimes emerge shortly after approval. See Anna W. Mathews, Are Too Many Unproven Drugs Receiving FDA Early Approval?, Wall St. J., Mar. 1, 2005, at B1. Second, sponsors have done a poor job of completing postapproval studies. See Jennifer C. Dooren, Drug Market Seen as Slow to Finish Postmarket Studies, Wall St. J., June 1, 2005, at D4. Third, such studies sometimes fail to find any benefit relative to the clinical end-point. See Rob Stein, Medication Under a Microscope: Studies Raise Questions About Drugs' Efficacy Against Disease, Wash. Post, Feb. 19, 2008, at A2; see also Rob Stein, Boosting "Good" Cholesterol Fails to Cut Heart, Stroke Risks, Wash. Post, May 27, 2011, at A3. For instance, the FDA approved Iressa® for lung cancer based on a fairly small clinical trial that showed tumor shrinkage in 10% of patients who had not responded to chemotherapy, but the agency rescinded its approval two years later after the sponsor submitted postapproval clinical trials that showed no improvement in survival. See Andrew Pollack, F.D.A. Restricts Access to Cancer Drug, Citing Ineffectiveness, N.Y. Times, June 18, 2005, at C2 (reporting that patients who had benefitted from the drug could continue to use it and that the sponsor could continue enrolling subjects in clinical trials, but noting that some criticized the decision for denying terminally-ill patients access to a potentially useful drug of last resort). A similar fate may befall Avastin® (bevacizumab) for use in breast cancer, though it would remain approved for use in the treatment of other cancers. See Rob Stein, FDA Advisers Reject Use of Avastin, Wash. Post, June 30, 2011, at A1. Finally, and somewhat controversially, the FDA has used its accelerated approval procedures with drugs that do not promise to treat desperately ill patients. See Lars Noah, A Miscarriage in the Drug Approval Process?: Mifepristone Embroils the FDA in Abortion Politics, 36 Wake Forest L. Rev. 571, 581–82 (2001); Christopher Rowland, FDA Chief Looks to Speed Diabetes, Obesity Drugs, Boston Globe, June 4, 2003, at A1.

6. *Altering the substantial evidence standard.* In 1997, Congress also relaxed the "substantial evidence" standard. If the FDA concludes that the data from one clinical trial are sufficient to establish substantial evidence of effectiveness, the statute now permits the agency to approve an NDA on this basis. The FDA retains the discretion, however, to require the traditional two adequate and well-controlled clinical trials. See 21 U.S.C. § 355(d); see also 62 Fed. Reg. 13,650 (1997); Jennifer Kulynych, Will FDA Relinquish the "Gold Standard" for New Drug Approval? Redefining "Substantial Evidence" in the FDA Modernization Act of 1997, 54 Food & Drug L.J. 127 (1999); Michael P. Van Huysen, Comment, Reform of the New Drug Approval Process, 49 Admin. L. Rev. 477 (1997); FDA Clarifies Guidelines for Approval of Drugs, Devices, Wash. Post, Jan. 31, 2003, at A12. Controversy also has arisen about the appropriate duration of clinical trials. See Anna W. Mathews, Are Long Trials Always Needed for New Drugs?, Wall St. J., Apr. 26, 2004, at B1; Shankar Vedantam, U.S. Alters Test Policy on Psychiatric Drugs: FDA Won't Require 6–Month Studies, Wash. Post, Oct. 26, 2005, at A3; see also Victor M. Montori et al., Randomized Trials Stopped Early for Benefit, 294 JAMA 2203 (2005). For a look at other countries' approaches to pharmaceutical regulation, see W. John Thomas, The Vioxx Story: Would It Have Ended Differently in the European Union?, 32 Am. J.L. & Med. 365 (2006); Nicholas R. Kennedy, Note, Taming the Perfect Poison: A Comparative Analysis of the EMEA's EPAR System and the FDA's Improved Warning Protocol, 33 B.C. Int'l & Comp. L. Rev. 323 (2010); Note, FDA Reform and the European Medicines Evaluation Agency, 108 Harv. L. Rev. 2009 (1995).

7. *User fees.* Under the Prescription Drug User Fee Act of 1992 (PDUFA), Pub. L. No. 102–571, 106 Stat. 4491 (codified at 21 U.S.C. §§ 379g–379h), sponsors of NDAs pay a substantial user fee (now over $1.5 million) to the agency for review of their applications. See 75 Fed. Reg. 46,952 (2010). In exchange for the authority to collect user fees, the agency agreed to spend the proceeds on hiring and training new personnel to participate in the

NDA review process, informally promising to reduce the NDA processing times significantly. See Bruce N. Kuhlik, Industry Funding of Improvements to the FDA's New Drug Approval Process: The Prescription Drug User Fee Act of 1992, 47 Food & Drug L.J. 483, 485–91 (1992); see also Merrill Goozner, Conflicts of Interest in the Drug Industry's Relationship with the Government, 35 Hofstra L. Rev. 737 (2006). Review times have fallen. See David Brown, Congress Seeks to Balance Drug Safety, Quick Approval, Wash. Post, July 5, 2007, at A4 ("From 1993 to 2003, the average approval time for standard drugs fell from 22 to 14 months. For fast-tracked 'priority' drugs it declined more steeply, from 13 months to six."); see also Mary K. Olson, PDUFA and Initial U.S. Drug Launches, 15 Mich. Telecomm. & Tech. L. Rev. 393 (2009); Leila Abboud, FDA Is Adjusting to Reduce Time to Get Drugs from Lab to Market, Wall St. J., June 23, 2003, at A2; Anna W. Mathews, Drug Firms Use Financial Clout to Push Industry Agenda at FDA, Wall St. J., Sept. 1, 2006, at A1 (reporting that in FY2004 the agency collected $232 million in user fees, which accounted for more than half of its budget for new drug reviews); cf. Daniel Carpenter et al., Early Entrant Protection in Approval Regulation: Theory and Evidence from FDA Drug Review, 26 J.L. Econ. & Org. 515 (2010) (finding longer review times for "me-too" products). Although the user fee amendments expired in October 1997, Congress has on three occasions extended the program for an additional five years. See Prescription Drug User Fee Amendments of 2007, Pub. L. No. 110–85, tit. I, 121 Stat. 825; Prescription Drug User Fee Amendments of 2002, Pub. L. No. 107–188, tit. V, 116 Stat. 687; FDAMA, Pub. L. No. 105–115, § 103, 111 Stat. 2296, 2299–304 (1997).

Notwithstanding the increased manpower, working under these deadlines reportedly has hurt morale among agency reviewers. See Chris Adams, FDA Looks to Cure Its High Attrition, Wall St. J., Aug. 19, 2002, at A4. The user fee program also may create pressures to approve products. See Gardiner Harris, Potentially Incompatible Goals at F.D.A., N.Y. Times, June 11, 2007, at A14; Marc Kaufman, Many FDA Scientists Had Drug Concerns, 2002 Survey Shows, Wash. Post, Dec. 16, 2004, at A1 (reporting that almost 20% of agency reviewers "said they had been pressured to recommend approval of a new drug despite reservations about its safety, effectiveness or quality"); Jonathan D. Rockoff, Criticism of FDA Resurfaces in Survey of Agency Scientists, Balt. Sun, July 21, 2006, at 2A; see also Henry Grabowski & Y. Richard Wang, Do Faster Food and Drug Administration Drug Reviews Adversely Affect Patient Safety? An Analysis of the 1992 Prescription Drug User Fee Act, 51 J.L. & Econ. 377 (2008); Mary K. Olson, The Risk We Bear: The Effects of Review Speed and Industry User Fees on New Drug Safety, 27 J. Health Econ. 175 (2008); James L. Zelenay, Jr., The Prescription Drug User Fee Act: Is a Faster Food and Drug Administration Always a Better Food and Drug Administration?, 60 Food & Drug L.J. 261 (2005); Amanda J. Dohrman, Note, Rethinking and Restructuring the FDA Drug Approval Process in Light of the Vioxx Recall, 31 J. Corp. L. 203 (2005).

E.R. Squibb & Sons, Inc. v. Bowen

870 F.2d 678 (D.C.Cir.1989).

■ GINSBURG, D.H., CIRCUIT JUDGE:

* * * During the 1950s, Squibb received FDA approval for, and began marketing, four oral combination drugs (referred to collectively as Mysteclin), each of which contained both the antibiotic tetracycline and one of two antifungal agents, nystatin or amphotericin B. Squibb included the antifungal agents on the theory that ingestion of tetracycline could lead to an overgrowth of the organism *Candida albicans*, a fungus that is commonly present in the human body but that can in some circumstances cause infection.

In 1962, Congress amended the FDCA to require proof that, in addition to being "safe for use," a drug is "effective in use." 21 U.S.C. § 355(b). * * * In accordance with the 1962 amendments, the FDA undertook a review of drugs that it had approved under the pre–1962 standard. In order to accomplish this task, it called upon the National Academy of Sciences–National Research Council (NRC) to perform preliminary evaluations of the effectiveness of pre–1962 drugs.

In 1969, the FDA announced that it would delete from the list of certifiable drugs in its regulations those drugs containing the combination of antibiotic and antifungal agents found in the various forms of Mysteclin, and that it would withdraw approval of all certifications granted pursuant to those regulations. The agency based this decision on the NRC's conclusion that "substantial evidence is lacking that each of these combination drugs will have the effect it purports or is represented to have." Squibb filed objections to this decision, which was then stayed pending the outcome of an evidentiary hearing in which manufacturers of the affected drugs were invited to demonstrate that their products met the statutory standards for effectiveness.

As of the time of the hearing, Squibb used two types of labeling for Mysteclin, depending upon the antifungal agent involved: for Mysteclin products containing amphotericin B, the labeling claimed effectiveness in preventing candidal disease attributable to antibiotic therapy; for products containing nystatin, the labeling claimed effectiveness only in suppressing candidal overgrowth. During the hearing, Squibb introduced several alternative forms of labeling for Mysteclin products containing amphotericin B, apparently in order to conform its labeling to what it hoped the evidence would show. The new labeling, like the labeling for the products containing nystatin, claimed effectiveness only against the possibility of candidal overgrowth in the intestinal tract. Although Squibb introduced evidence in support of both the disease and the suppression claims, it limits its current petition for review to the FDA's rejection of the suppression claim, and we tailor our discussion accordingly.

Following the hearing, the Administrative Law Judge held that Squibb had failed to show that Mysteclin is "effective in use" and ordered its certification withdrawn. Squibb appealed that decision to the Commissioner, who affirmed the ALJ in all relevant respects. Specifically, the Commissioner held that (1) in order to show that a drug is "effective in use," the manufacturer must demonstrate not only that it has the effect claimed on its label, but also that the claimed effect is of some medical significance; (2) Squibb had failed to establish "that suppression of gastrointestinal candida is itself a medically significant effect;" (3) the record evidence in fact showed that "candida overgrowth is not itself a disease" and that its suppression "is a pharmacologic, not necessarily a therapeutic, effect, i.e., it is a physiologic effect of no proven benefit to the patient;" and (4) in any event, the studies submitted by Squibb failed to establish that Mysteclin is effective in suppressing candidal overgrowth. The FDA then announced its final decision to withdraw approval for Mysteclin.

Squibb's primary contention is that the Commissioner erroneously required it to show that the suppression effect claimed for Mysteclin on its labeling is itself medically significant. As Squibb reads the 1962 amendments, a manufacturer, in order to satisfy the "effective in use" standard, need show only that a drug does what its label says it does, not that the claimed effect produces any particular medical benefit. Although no provision of the FDCA defines the term "effective in use," Squibb argues that both the plain language and the legislative history of the amendments evince a clear congressional intent compelling its interpretation, and that we must therefore reject the Commissioner's contrary reading. * * *

In support of its "plain language" argument, Squibb points to (1) the statutory provision for withdrawal of FDA approval if "there is a lack of substantial evidence that [a] drug will have the effect it purports or is represented to have under the conditions of use prescribed, recommended, or suggested in the labeling thereof," and (2) the definition of "substantial evidence" as "evidence . . . that the drug will have the effect it purports or is represented to have under the conditions of use prescribed, recommended, or suggested in the labeling . . . thereof." Squibb reads these provisions as clearly indicating that as long as the "effect" claimed for a drug in its labeling is not harmful (since, if it were, it would fail the Act's requirement that a drug be proven "safe for use") and as long as that claim is accurate, the Commissioner may not withdraw approval of the drug. In other words, Squibb interprets the Act as erecting, under the head of effectiveness, only a truth-in-labeling requirement.

The statutory language does not compel Squibb's reading, however. The cited provisions are directed primarily at the evidentiary standard that a manufacturer must meet in order to demonstrate that a drug is "effective in use;" they do not address the question whether any claimed "effect," however innocuous, is sufficient. * * *

Although the 1962 amendments are silent as to the precise meaning of "effective in use," the FDCA read as a whole would appear, if anything, to preclude the reading advanced by Squibb. The pre-marketing approval provisions here at issue apply, by their terms, only to "drugs," which the FDCA defines, insofar as relevant here, as "articles intended for use in the diagnosis, cure, mitigation, treatment, or prevention of disease in man," or "to affect the structure or any function of the body of man." The former provision plainly applies only to drugs whose intended effect is in some way related to disease. It would appear to foreclose Squibb's argument that Mysteclin is "effective in use" so long as it has only a safe use that is not disease-related. The latter provision, in contrast, appears to contemplate that a substance will be approved as a "drug" even though it has only a physiologic, rather than a therapeutic, effect. * * *

Squibb contends that because it has removed all therapeutic claims from its labeling for Mysteclin, the drug now falls solely within the "structure or ... function" definition, and thus must be approved if it is safe (which is not disputed) and it has the physiologic effect claimed for it. * * * In support of this view, Squibb notes that the FDA has approved several articles, most notably birth control pills and weight reduction remedies, as to which only physiologic claims are made and which have not been proven medically beneficial.

Whatever the merits of Squibb's argument with respect to drugs that are properly characterized as "structure or ... function" drugs, we do not think that Mysteclin is such a drug. First, it is questionable whether a drug that acts only upon non-human organisms that happen to reside within the human body can properly be understood as affecting the "body of man" (as opposed to the "prevention of disease in man") within the meaning of the definition. Second, assuming that such organisms could be understood as part of the human body, a drug that suppresses their growth does not affect the "structure" or "function" of the human body as the courts have construed those terms. * * *

[T]he "structure or ... function" definition, unlike the "disease in man" definition, is relatively narrow, and was not intended to encompass all articles that might have some remote physical effect upon the body. * * * Given Congress's intent, in adding the "structure or ... function" definition, specifically to bring "anti-fat" remedies within the regulatory framework, there is no doubt that articles intended to reduce weight, thus affecting the structure of the human body, fall within that definition. Similarly, articles intended to prevent pregnancy, thus affecting the reproductive function of the human body, fall within that definition. The suppression effect Squibb claims for Mysteclin, in contrast, would simply reduce the number of non-human organisms residing within the intestinal tract. Candida organisms are hardly part of the physical "structure" of the human body, nor does their suppression affect any "function" of the body in the sense that articles that induce sleep or inhibit digestion do.

Mysteclin's undisputed status as a drug, therefore, appears to depend upon its being an article "intended for use in the diagnosis, cure, mitigation, treatment, or prevention of disease in man." As such, the statutory mandate that it be shown "effective in use" would appear plainly to require a showing that, consistent with its identity as a "disease in man" drug, it has some disease-related effect. It is inconceivable that Congress meant for a drug to be approved without some showing of effectiveness in the intended use (i.e., relating to disease) that made it subject to regulation in the first place.

Nonetheless, we are reluctant for two reasons to rule, on the basis of the distinction between disease-related drugs and "structure or ... function" drugs, that the statute unambiguously precludes the reading advanced by Squibb. First, and most important, the FDA does not argue that anything turns on the definitional distinction discussed above. Rather, in response to Squibb's argument that Mysteclin is a drug only by virtue of the "structure or ... function" definition of drug (and as such need not be shown effective in any medically significant way), which it raised for the first time in its reply brief, the agency, at oral argument, offered only the broad rejoinder that some showing of therapeutic significance is required for all drugs—even those falling within the "structure or ... function" definition. Absent an explicit reference to "disease in man" in the latter definition, however, it is not clear to us that the statutory language compels the agency's broad reading. Moreover, in light of our conclusion that Mysteclin falls within the "disease in man" definition of drug, the agency's broad argument need not be decided in this case. * * *

As noted above, the FDA's reading of the 1962 amendments to require proof of some therapeutic effect finds strong support in the FDCA as a whole, at least for drugs falling within the "disease in man" definition. In this case, the Commissioner found that Squibb had failed to show that the suppression effect claimed for Mystesclin is of any therapeutic significance at all. Assuming for the moment the correctness of that finding for the purpose of evaluating the Commissioner's legal determination, we hold that the agency's reading of the statute as requiring it to withdraw approval for Mysteclin is a permissible interpretation of the statute. * * *

Squibb next challenges the Commissioner's conclusion that "the record contains no evidence to support Squibb's argument that suppression of gastrointestinal candida is itself a medically significant effect." Squibb asserts that it met its evidentiary burden on this point with the testimony of experts who stated that, in their view, suppression of candidal overgrowth is of some medical significance. One of the FDA's own witnesses, for example, testified that candidal overgrowth in the intestine is to be avoided because "the Candida can be an important cause of disease," including "Candida infections or disease, thrush, of the mouth or the esophagus or of the vagina or of the bowel, or of the skin." Squibb's witnesses testified to like effect, one also noting that in his opinion, "a drug with this [suppression] effect is of value in the practice of medicine."

According to Squibb, the Commissioner must defer to the opinions of these experts as long as their opinions are based upon substantial evidence. Squibb does not challenge, however, the Commissioner's conclusion that its studies failed to show that suppression of candidal overgrowth is of any disease-related significance. Squibb asserts that (1) both its studies and the testimony of its experts showed that Mysteclin does produce the claimed suppression effect; and (2) the Commissioner is required to defer to the experts on the medical significance of that effect. Because we reject Squibb's second argument, we need not address its first. * * *

In light of our holding that the Commissioner permissibly required Squibb to show some medical significance for its suppression claim, it follows that such a showing must meet the substantial evidence standard set forth in the 1962 amendments. Thus, Squibb was required to come forward with substantial evidence demonstrating not just that Mysteclin produces the claimed suppression effect, but also that effect is of some medical value. Since Squibb has adduced only anecdotal evidence to support its claim of medical efficacy—evidence that cannot constitute "substantial evidence" under either the statutory standard or the FDA's regulations—we find that the Commissioner's withdrawal of approval for Mysteclin is supported by the record. * * *

NOTES AND QUESTIONS

1. *Intended use and effectiveness.* After the court sustained the FDA's withdrawal of the NDAs for Mysteclin, can Squibb continue selling the product on the theory that it's not really a drug because the labeling only refers to non-therapeutic uses? Presumably it would continue making therapeutic claims for the tetracycline, but what if it sold the antifungal alone, claiming only to suppress candidal overgrowth? In fact, one company attempted to do just that, arguing that a veterinary product containing subtherapeutic levels of antibiotics and intended to reduce odors caused by bacteria in the digestive tract did not qualify as a "drug" because it served no therapeutic purpose and also did not directly affect the structure or function of the body. Nonetheless, the FDA succeeded in bringing an unapproved new drug charge against this product. See United States v. Undetermined Quantities of Bottles ... "Pets Smellfree," 22 F.3d 235, 240 (10th Cir.1994) (rejecting the claimant's reliance on the holding in *Squibb*). If, instead, it continued selling the combination, could Squibb make no claim for the antifungal (effectively recharacterizing it as an inactive ingredient)?

2. *Therapeutic benefit.* Other courts have sustained the FDA's demand that drugs serve a therapeutic purpose. See Warner–Lambert Co. v. Heckler, 787 F.2d 147, 154–56 (3d Cir.1986) (rejecting the plaintiff's claim that " 'effectiveness' as used in the Act means only that the drug will have the effect the manufacturer claims for it," and concluding that the demonstration of effectiveness must include evidence of a therapeutic level of action compared with placebo). Recall, however, the FDA's limited recent willingness to accept surrogate markers for clinical endpoints. Should the reduction of blood pressure (or cholesterol) qualify? Cf. Denise Grady, As Silent Killer Returns, Doctors Rethink Tactics to Lower Blood Pressure, N.Y. Times, July 14, 1998, at F1 (reporting that "it is not known whether all drugs that lower blood pressure also protect against heart attack and stroke"). If a drug serves a therapeutic purpose, though one that the FDA regards as inconsequential, how does the NDA fare? Cf. Laura Johannes &

Steve Stecklow, Dire Warnings About Obesity Rely on Slippery Statistic, Wall St. J., Feb. 9, 1998, at B1 ("[T]he FDA's bar for approving new drugs is lower for disease treatments than for other problems, such as baldness or skin wrinkles. The agency is less likely to approve a drug for a nondisease condition when it is shown to have serious side effects—such as those that diet drugs produce."); Jeannine Stein & Shari Roan, Diet Pill Dilemma: As Americans Keep Getting Fatter, Doctors Ask: Where Are the Drugs?, L.A. Times, Dec. 13, 2010, at E1 (reporting complaints "that the agency's standards for approving anti-obesity drugs are overly stringent and fail to recognize the health risks associated with carrying extra weight"); Stacie Stukin, Latisse Has Fans, Sure, but Risks Too: Sales of the Lash Growth Enhancer, Originally a Glaucoma Drug, Have Soared, L.A. Times, Dec. 7, 2009, at E1.

3. *Risk-benefit balancing*. The information derived from Phase III studies provides the data that the FDA reviewers use to evaluate the risk-benefit ratio for a drug. See 21 C.F.R. § 312.21. In performing this calculus, the agency recognizes that even effective drugs carry the risk of side effects for some patients, but that a small overall risk may be justified if the new drug promises significant potential benefits to the targeted class of patients. If Mysteclin serves no medically-significant purpose, won't its approval fail on lack of safety grounds (assuming that it's not completely benign)? Or is it better to view these as two separate inquiries with the final risk-benefit judgment left to the individual physician and patient? See Joshua T. Cohen & Peter J. Neumann, What's More Dangerous, Your Aspirin or Your Car? Thinking Rationally About Drug Risks (and Benefits), 26 Health Aff. 636 (2007). Consider this example:

> [L]idoflazine, an anti-anginal drug that is effective but has a tendency to cause potentially fatal heart rhythm abnormalities, was rejected [by the FDA] because it had not been shown to work in people unresponsive to other agents, so that there were no patients in whom the drug's excess risk was known to be worth taking. At almost the same time, however, another anti-anginal drug called bepridil, with risks similar to those of lidoflazine, *was* approved for people unresponsive to other agents when it was shown to be effective in such patients.

Robert M. Temple, Commentary on "The Architecture of Government Regulation of Medical Products," 82 Va. L. Rev. 1877, 1887 (1996). "For serious diseases, especially those poorly treated by available therapy, considerable toxicity is acceptable, and labeling is used to attempt to guide physicians in detecting and mitigating harm. In some cases, a relatively toxic drug will be identified as a 'second-line,' a drug to be used only in people who cannot tolerate, or do not respond to, safer agents." Id. at 1888; see also Chris Adams, Trial Judge: At FDA, Approving Cancer Treatments Can Be an Ordeal, Wall St. J., Dec. 11, 2002, at A1 (reporting that, after initially rejecting Eloxatin® as a "first line" therapy for colorectal cancer patients because the manufacturer had not shown extended survival, the FDA approved the drug as a "second line" treatment based on a trial demonstrating tumor shrinkage in 9% of patients who had not responded to chemotherapy); Gardiner Harris, Where Progress Is Rare, the Man Who Says No, N.Y. Times, Sept. 16, 2009, at A1 (profiling Dr. Richard Pazdur, the FDA's chief (and often vilified) reviewer of cancer drugs); Anna W. Mathews, Powerful Medicine: FDA Cancer Czar Stirs Debate on Agency's Role—Anemia–Drug Tussle Puts Pazdur on Spot, Wall St. J., Mar. 12, 2008, at A1; Andrew Pollack, After a Long Struggle, Cancer Drug Wins Approval, N.Y. Times, May 14, 2003, at C1 (reporting that the FDA approved Velcade® for multiple myeloma patients who have relapsed after trying at least two other treatments); Ron Winslow, What Makes a Drug Too Risky?, Wall St. J., Feb. 16, 2005, at B1.

Putting aside "second line" treatments (or "drugs of last resort") for patients with advanced cancer or another life-threatening disease, does it make sense for the FDA to approve new drugs that perform less well in clinical trials than products previously approved for the same indication? Cf. Lars Noah, The Coming Pharmacogenomics Revolution: Tailoring Drugs to Fit Patients' Genetic Profiles, 43 Jurimetrics J. 1, 4 (2002) ("The FDA's standards for safety and efficacy call for relative rather than absolute judgments about risks and benefits: an investigational new drug need only out perform a placebo, and not cause unacceptably severe or frequent adverse effects, to receive premarket clearance in this country. Thus, the agency sometimes approves drugs that appeared to work in substantially less than half of the subjects enrolled in the carefully controlled environment of a clinical trial and even though they may have caused some significant side effects."); Editorial, Comparing Prescription Drugs, N.Y. Times, Aug. 27, 2003, at A20 ("[T]he drugs used in this country are seldom tested against one another in head-to-head combat. Instead, each is tested separately against a placebo and then, if shown to be safe and effective, is approved for marketing."); see also Marc Kaufman, Painkiller Decision Suggests Shift in FDA's Risk–Benefit Equation, Wash. Post, Apr. 11, 2005, at A3 ("Certain drug risks that used to be acceptable to the agency have become unacceptable, and benefits that usually guaranteed approval of a new drug are no longer a sure bet—but whether that is good or bad depends on an observer's viewpoint.... That balance between the risks of a drug or medical device and its benefits is the central question before the FDA. Drug companies, public health advocates and financial analysts are looking for signals to suggest which way the agency is leaning, reading tea leaves that would show a slight tipping of the balance in favor of emphasizing drug risks or benefits. All drugs have both, and a billion-dollar drug approval (or withdrawal) can turn on which tendency is in ascendance.").

4. *Facilitating approval of treatments for biowarfare agents.* In addition to creating incentives to promote the development of vaccines and other treatments potentially useful against the threat of bioterrorism, see Pub. L. No. 109–417, title IV, 120 Stat. 2831 (2006), the government has relaxed the standards for approving such products. See 67 Fed. Reg. 37,988 (2002); see also Gail H. Javitt, Drugs and Vaccines for the Common Defense: Refining FDA Regulation to Promote the Availability of Products to Counter Biological Attacks, 19 J. Contemp. Health L. & Pol'y 37 (2002); Robert

Block, Antiterror Drugs May Be Stalled Without Funds, Wall St. J., May 3, 2004, at B1; John Mintz, Radiation Sickness Drug Developed, Wash. Post, May 19, 2003, at A2. See generally Heather Petruzzi, Note, The Missing Link: The Need for Patent Protection in the Development of Biodefense Vaccines, 37 Pub. Cont. L.J. 71 (2007); Symposium, Eliminating Legal, Regulatory, and Economic Barriers to Biodefense Vaccine Development, 8 J. Health Care L. & Pol'y 1 (2005).

5. *The role of politics in new drug approvals*. Usually, the FDA reviews whatever product applications happen to come in the door, but on occasion it will beat the bushes looking for a company willing to seek approval for a drug that the agency wants brought to the market. See, e.g., 40 Fed. Reg. 5351 (1975) (urging manufacturers to seek approval of DES for contraception), withdrawn, 54 Fed. Reg. 22,585 (1989); Ralph T. King, Jr., The Pill U.S. Drug Companies Dare Not Market, Wall St. J., June 26, 1998, at B1 ("In an unusual role reversal, the companies are resisting pressure from the FDA to market their birth-control pills as emergency contraception."); Katharine Q. Seelye, Accord Opens Way for Abortion Pill in U.S. in Two Years, N.Y. Times, May 17, 1994, at A1 (describing high-level pressure exerted by the Clinton administration on the French manufacturer of RU–486 to apply for FDA approval, and the manufacturer's decision to donate its rights to the Population Council to sponsor an NDA).

6. *Supplemental NDAs*. After a new drug has been approved, a sponsor wishing to add another indication to the labeling must submit an NDA supplement (frequently referred to as an "efficacy supplement") containing the results of additional clinical testing to demonstrate the drug's effectiveness for that new use. There are several reasons why companies frequently choose not to seek supplemental approval. See, e.g., David P. Hamilton, Do Statins Help Prevent Cancer? Few Tests Slated, Wall St. J., May 20, 2005, at B1. For instance, ethical constraints may complicate efforts to test approved drugs for unapproved but widely accepted medical uses. See David A. Kessler, Regulating the Prescribing of Human Drugs for Nonapproved Uses Under the Food, Drug, and Cosmetic Act, 15 Harv. J. Legis. 693, 730 (1978). Even if physicians could be found to supervise clinical investigations, companies must make trade-offs in allocating their limited research and development budgets, choosing between investigations of new chemical entities that might represent important therapeutic breakthroughs and conducting clinical trials to seek approval for secondary indications. See Martin D. Abeloff, Letter, Off–Label Uses of Anticancer Drugs, 267 JAMA 2473, 2474 (1992); Joseph A. DiMasi et al., New Indications for Already–Approved Drugs: An Analysis of Regulatory Review Times, 31 J. Clinical Pharmacol. 205 (1991). Nonetheless, some manufacturers choose to file such supplements for new uses of already approved drugs so that they can promote their products for these additional indications. See, e.g., Justin Gillis, Cancer Drug Gets New–Use Approval: Rituxan Can Treat Rheumatoid Arthritis, Wash. Post, Mar. 1, 2006, at D1; Scott Hensley, Pfizer's Lipitor Gets Marketing Tool: Expanded FDA Instructions Allow Company to Claim Drug Prevents Heart Attacks, Wall St. J., Aug. 2,

2004, at B3. As explained in Chapter 10(B), they also may receive an additional period of market exclusivity.

7. *Pediatric studies requirement.* The FDA has recognized that children may metabolize and excrete prescription drugs differently than adults. In order to maximize the potential benefit of therapeutic products for children, Congress included a requirement in FDAMA that the agency identify, publish, and annually update a list of approved drugs for which it might want additional information about safety and effectiveness in pediatric populations. See 21 U.S.C. § 355a(b). In 1998, the agency issued a rule to require that drug manufacturers engage in pediatric testing under certain circumstances, but a court invalidated the regulation as exceeding the FDA's delegated authority. See Association of Am. Physicians & Surgeons, Inc. v. FDA, 226 F.Supp.2d 204, 212–22 (D.D.C.2002). Rather than appeal this decision, the agency persuaded Congress to codify a substantially similar version of the rule. See Pediatric Research Equity Act of 2003, Pub. L. No. 108–155, 117 Stat. 1936 (codified at 21 U.S.C. § 355c); see also Francesca L. Kritz, Dose of Reality: As More Drugs Are Tested in Kids, Labels Are Changing, Wash. Post, Sept. 10, 2002, at F5; cf. Kate Greenwood, The Mysteries of Pregnancy: The Role of Law in Solving the Problem of Unknown but Knowable Maternal–Fetal Medication Risk, 79 U. Cin. L. Rev. 267 (2010) (favoring a similar response to the dearth of information about the use of drugs by pregnant women). Risks associated with certain medical devices suggest the potential value of pediatric studies for these technologies. See, e.g., John D. Miller, Images Suited for Kids, Wash. Post, Sept. 17, 2002, at F1 (reporting concerns that the use of CT scanners, especially in non-emergency cases and at adult power settings, unnecessarily may expose children to doses of radiation that can cause cancer). In response, Congress called on the FDA to issue guidance on devices intended for pediatric populations. See Medical Device User Fee and Modernization Act of 2002, Pub. L. No. 107–250, § 213, 116 Stat. 1588, 1614–15; see also Sujatha Vathyam, Note, No More "Hand–Me–Downs" Please!: Children Deserve Medical Devices Specifically Designed for and Tested on Children, 58 Rutgers L. Rev. 719 (2006); Steve Sternberg, Kids' Medical Devices Need More Scrutiny, USA Today, July 19, 2005, at 7D.

2. Generic Drugs and Bioequivalence Issues

Astellas Pharma US, Inc. v. FDA

642 F.Supp.2d 10 (D.D.C.2009).

■ Urbina, District Judge:

* * * Recognizing that the NDA process is costly and time-consuming, Congress amended the FDCA in 1984 pursuant to the "Hatch–Waxman Amendments." In an effort "to make available more low cost drugs," the amended FDCA permits the manufacturer of a generic version of a listed drug to obtain FDA approval through a far simpler, abbreviated new drug application (ANDA) containing a more limited set of information than that required for an NDA. 21 U.S.C. § 355(j). Rather than requiring the

applicant to make an independent showing that the proposed generic is itself safe and effective, the amended statute requires a showing that the proposed generic operates in the same manner as the pioneer drug on which it is based—its reference listed drug (RLD). Thus, the FDA's approval of a new generic drug relies on its prior determination that the RLD is safe and effective. * * *

[A] generic drug is considered to be "bioequivalent" to an RLD if "the rate and extent of absorption of the drug do not show a significant difference from the rate and extent of absorption of the listed drug when administered at the same molar dose of the therapeutic ingredient under similar experimental conditions in either a single dose or multiple doses." Id. § 355(j)(8)(B)(I). The applicable regulations identify several methodologies for testing bioequivalency, including comparative clinical trials, in vitro studies and "any other approach deemed adequate by FDA to measure bioavailability or establish bioequivalence." 21 C.F.R. § 320.24(b).

In April 1994, the FDA approved the plaintiff's NDA for the immunosuppressant tacrolimus, which it markets under the brand name Prograf. Prograf is indicated for the prophylaxis of organ rejection in patients receiving liver, kidney and heart transplants. Typically, the drug is administered orally. The plaintiff states that in fiscal year 2008, sales of Prograf constituted roughly half of the plaintiff's total U.S. revenues of $884 million. The plaintiff notes that tacrolimus is characterized as a narrow therapeutic index (NTI) drug, meaning that it is the type of drug for which "small changes in concentration in the body can lead to significant difference in pharmacodynamic and clinical response." The plaintiff also asserts that tacrolimus is a "critical dose" drug, meaning that "small changes in concentration in the body can lead to acute rejection, toxicities, or even death of the patient." As a result, "careful therapeutic monitoring of blood levels and clinical monitoring of each patient is necessary."

In 2006, the FDA published draft guidelines for establishing the bioequivalency of generic tacrolimus. The FDA recommended the following studies to establish bioequivalency: (1) a single-dose, two-treatment in vivo study of individuals in a fasting state and (2) a single-dose, two-treatment in vivo study of individuals in a fed state. The plaintiff states that over the past decade, the FDA has acknowledged the limitations of its existing bioequivalency guidelines for NTI drugs like tacrolimus. The plaintiff asserts that on multiple occasions, the FDA has considered amending its bioequivalency guidelines for NTI drugs but, inexplicably, has never implemented those changes.

In September 2007, the plaintiff submitted a "citizen petition" to the FDA. In the petition, the plaintiff requested that the FDA (1) require that bioequivalence studies be performed in transplant populations (rather than solely in healthy populations) for orally administered NTI immunosuppressants like tacrolimus and (2) revise labeling requirements for all orally administered NTI immunosuppressants to add warnings notifying physicians about the substitution of the generic for the name brand. In support of its petition, the plaintiff offered a letter authored by Dr. David C.

Cronin, a transplant surgeon and pharmacist, stating that due to the significant intrapatient variability in the pharmacokinetics of tacrolimus, the FDA's existing bioequivalency standards would not sufficiently predict the effects of the generic when administered to individual patients. Cronin also supported the plaintiff's petition for revising the label requirement, asserting that where tacrolimus formulations have been switched, physicians must be particularly vigilant in monitoring their patients to avoid serious adverse effects. The plaintiff also submitted a white paper from the National Kidney Foundation and a meeting report from the American Society of Transplantation, both of which expressed concerns about the general application of the FDA's current bioequivalence standards to special populations such as transplant recipients.

On August 10, 2009, the FDA denied the plaintiff's citizen petition in all relevant respects. The FDA concluded that additional bioequivalence studies conducted in transplant populations were not warranted:

> We note that single-dose bioequivalence studies are generally more sensitive at detecting formulation or other product-related characteristics that may affect bioequivalences to the RLD than multiple-dose (steady-state) bioequivalence studies. In addition, such multiple-dose studies are generally conducted in patients and hence may include sources of variability related to the disease state, which may confound bioequivalence outcomes. Moreover, with regard to tacrolimus, there is insufficient scientific evidence to suggest that the use of specific patient population(s) in bioequivalence studies would detect differences in formulation that might have clinical significance and that would not be detected by bioequivalence studies in healthy subjects. Therefore, additional bioequivalence studies conducted in transplant patients are not justified.

The FDA noted that the same bioequivalency testing framework was successfully employed in connection with generic versions of cyclosporine, another NTI immunosuppressant which, like tacrolimus, is a calcineurin inhibitor and which shares with tacrolimus a common mechanism of action.

In response to the plaintiff's assertion that tacrolimus can have varying effects on patients, which purportedly underscored the need for additional bioequivalency studies, the FDA stated that based on the current literature, this variability "[is] related to the active ingredient in the drug product." Because the generic version of tacrolimus "will contain the identical amount of the same active ingredient in the same form as Prograf," patient variability did not justify additional studies in transplant populations. Finally, the FDA addressed the various studies included by the plaintiff in support of its petition and concluded that they did not justify additional bioequivalency testing. The FDA also rejected the plaintiff's request for revised labeling requirements. The FDA concluded that, based upon its current knowledge and prior experience with similar drugs, additional warnings were unnecessary because "[t]he current review process for ANDAs is adequate to assure the interchangeability of generic versions of immunosuppressant drugs such as tacrolimus with their branded counterparts."

On August 10, 2009, the same day that it denied the plaintiff's citizen petition, the FDA approved the ANDA for a generic version of tacrolimus submitted by Sandoz, a leading manufacturer of generic drugs.[1] The next day, Sandoz announced the launch of its generic version of tacrolimus in the U.S. market. At the same time, the plaintiff filed the instant motion for a temporary restraining order and preliminary injunction. * * *

The plaintiff contends that it is likely to prevail on the merits because the FDA acted in an arbitrary and capricious manner in denying the plaintiff's citizen petition and approving Sandoz's ANDA without requiring additional bioequivalency studies. The plaintiff asserts that * * * the FDA cites no literature justifying its conclusion that variability among transplant patients is related to the active ingredient of tacrolimus. Indeed, the plaintiff contends that this conclusion is contradicted by several studies, cited by the plaintiff in its citizen petition, which suggest that variability may be associated with different formulations of an NTI immunosuppressant drug, such that a generic could produce different effects on patients despite having an identical amount of the same active ingredient. For instance, the plaintiff points to a study showing that Advagraf may have different effects on patients than Prograf despite the fact that the two drugs contain the same active ingredient. The plaintiff notes that, although the FDA's bioequivalence guidelines acknowledge that tacrolimus can have differing effects depending on whether the individual is fed or fasting when ingesting the drug, it cites no reason for singling out food effects. The FDA's recognition that food effects can have an effect on bioequivalency contradicts the FDA's assertion that variability among effects is related to the active ingredient of tacrolimus. In addition, the plaintiff asserts that in approving Sandoz's ANDA without requiring a bioequivalency study on a transplant population, the FDA ignored the unique vulnerability of transplant patients, who are often on multiple medications and face unique risks. The plaintiff also asserts that the FDA's reliance on its experience testing generic cyclosporine is inapposite, as the FDA has presented no evidence that cyclosporine and tacrolimus are similar chemical entities with similar properties. * * *

The defendants respond that the FDA considered the plaintiff's challenges regarding the adequacy of its bioequivalency testing guidelines and, applying its scientific and technical expertise, concluded that additional bioequivalency testing was not warranted. The defendants note that the reasoning underlying the FDA's determination was set forth in great detail in its response to the plaintiff's citizen petition. For instance, the FDA * * * reasoned that, while food effects are known to vary based on a drug's formulation, the plaintiff failed to explain how patient-specific factors, such as organ-type transplanted, current medications and the time elapsed after transplant, would lead to different effects based on different formulations.

1. Sandoz's ANDA had been pending for more than two years.

In short, the FDA concluded that the plaintiff's call for additional bioequivalency testing was based on nothing more than conjecture and was not supported by the scientific literature. * * *

[T]he FDA's "judgment as to what is required to ascertain the safety and efficacy of drugs falls squarely within the ambit of the FDA's expertise and merit deference" from the courts. A.L. Pharma, Inc. v. Shalala, 62 F.3d 1484, 1490 (D.C.Cir.1995). This high degree of deference has been applied to the FDA's determinations regarding which methodologies it determines are needed to test the bioequivalency of a given generic. See Serono Labs., Inc. v. Shalala, 158 F.3d 1313, 1325 (D.C.Cir.1998) (holding that an RLD manufacturer was unlikely to succeed on its challenge to the FDA's reliance on animal studies to establish the bioequivalency of a proposed generic because courts "are bound to show deference to the agency's fact-finding in this area of its technical expertise"); Bristol–Myers Squibb Co. v. Shalala, 923 F.Supp. 212, 217–18 (D.D.C.1996) (holding that the plaintiff demonstrated no likelihood of success in its challenge to the FDA's reliance on in vitro testing to establish bioequivalence because "there is nothing in the legislative history [to the Hatch–Waxman Amendments] to indicate that Congress intended to restrict FDA's historical discretion to decide how that requirement would be met"). * * *

In the instant case, the FDA produced a comprehensive response to the plaintiff's citizen petition, in which it specifically addressed the plaintiff's arguments and provided a detailed justification for its conclusion that additional bioequivalency testing was not needed. [It] indicates that the testing guidelines established for generic tacrolimus were based on the guidelines used to gauge the bioequivalency of generic cyclosporine, a similar NTI immunosuppressant which shares with tacrolimus a common mechanism of action. The FDA asserted—and the plaintiff has not disputed—that single-dose studies, like the ones called for in the bioequivalency guidelines at issue, are more sensitive than multi-dose, in-patient studies at predicting differences resulting from differences in formulation. The FDA asserted that the current scientific literature indicated that the effects of characteristics specific to transplant patients were related to the drug's active ingredient, and thus the FDA's conclusion that testing on transplant patients was not required appears to have been reasonable. Furthermore, the FDA specifically addressed the numerous studies relied on by the plaintiff and explained why each did not, in the FDA's view, justify additional bioequivalency testing.

The plaintiff has identified no studies or other evidence demonstrating that the FDA's conclusion was irrational, implausible or contrary to existing scientific consensus. The letter submitted by Cronin on behalf of the plaintiff reiterates that tacrolimus is an NTI, "critical dose" drug, but fails to explain why the FDA's bioequivalency guidelines for generic tacrolimus do not adequately address his concerns regarding patient variability. Furthermore, as the FDA points out, the comment filed by the American Society of Transplantation provided no new scientific or clinical data to support its position. In short, although the plaintiff provides ample support for the uncontroversial proposition that supplemental testing could reveal additional information pertinent to bioequivalency, it has made no showing that the testing guidelines established by the FDA were insufficient to meet its statutory obligation to ensure the safety and efficacy of new drugs. Given the high level of deference that must be afforded to the FDA in choosing which methodologies to employ to test bioequivalency for a given drug, the court concludes that the plaintiff has presented insufficient evidence to suggest that the FDA acted in an arbitrary and capricious manner in setting the bioequivalency guidelines for generic tacrolimus. Accordingly, the plaintiff has failed to demonstrate a likelihood of success on the merits with respect to its request for additional bioequivalency testing. * * *

The plaintiff contends that it will suffer irreparable harm without a temporary restraining order and preliminary injunction. * * * [A]lthough the plaintiff has indicated that sales of Prograf account for a sizable percentage of its U.S. revenues, it has failed to demonstrate how the introduction of generic tacrolimus would cause extreme hardship to the business or threaten its very existence. The plaintiff has not indicated to what extent it predicts its revenues will decline following the introduction of generic tacrolimus or how such a decline would affect its overall business operations. See Mead Johnson Pharm. Group v. Bowen, 655 F.Supp. 53, 56 (D.D.C.1986) (holding that a drug manufacturer failed to demonstrate irreparable harm because its "claim that it will suffer a loss of sales should an ANDA be approved and drug product marketed before this case is disposed of on the merits is pure speculation" as it had "failed to provide any proof of economic loss and merely states that it would probably lose 20 to 30 percent of its market during the first year"); see also Mylan Pharm., Inc. v. Shalala, 81 F.Supp.2d 30, 42–43 (D.D.C.2000) (holding that a drug manufacturer failed to establish irreparable harm because it "all but conceded" that its estimated lost revenues would not cause serious damage to the company). * * *

The plaintiff contends that the public interest would be served by restraining the FDA from approving any generic versions of tacrolimus without adequate testing. The plaintiff points out that there are enormous health risks associated with organ transplantation, and that organ rejection can result in the death of a transplant patient. Given these grave consequences, the plaintiff argues that the FDA should be required to withdraw its approval of any generic versions of tacrolimus until proper bioequivalency testing has been performed. The defendants contend that delaying the introduction of a safe generic on the market will merely result in higher prices for transplant patients seeking needed drugs. * * * [T]he plaintiff has failed to demonstrate that the FDA wrongfully approved Sandoz's ANDA for generic tacrolimus. Indeed, the evidence presented to the court strongly suggests that the interests of the public, and of transplant patients more specifically, will be served by permitting generic competition with the name brand version of tacrolimus. Accordingly, the court concludes that the public interest weighs in favor of denying the plaintiff's motion. * * *

Zeneca, Inc. v. Shalala

213 F.3d 161 (4th Cir.2000).

■ HAMILTON, SENIOR CIRCUIT JUDGE:

* * * In order to obtain approval of a generic drug, a manufacturer must provide information sufficient to establish that, among other things: (1) the generic drug is "bioequivalent" to the pioneer drug; (2) its active ingredients, route of administration, strength and dosage form are "the same as" those of the pioneer drug; and (3) the inactive ingredients are not "unsafe for use under the conditions prescribed, recommended, or suggested in the labeling proposed for the drug." With respect to the substitution of inactive ingredients in a parenteral [e.g., injectable] drug, the FDA's regulations require that most of the generic drug's inactive ingredients be the same as the inactive ingredients of the pioneer drug. Differences in inactive ingredients that are preservatives, buffers, or antioxidants are permitted as long as those differences do not affect the safety of the drug. Manufacturers of generic drugs are also required to show that "the labeling proposed for the new [generic] drug is the same as the labeling approved for the listed drug ... except for changes required ... because the new drug and the listed drug are produced or distributed by different manufacturers." * * *

Zeneca manufactures the pioneer drug Diprivan (a form of propofol), which the FDA approved in 1989 based on Zeneca's submission of an NDA. Diprivan is a parenteral drug used for inducing and maintaining anesthesia and for support of mechanical ventilation and sedation. Diprivan has a pH range of 7.0 to 8.5. Shortly after Zeneca introduced Diprivan in the United States, post-operative fevers and infections were documented and associated with its use. These post-operative fevers and infections were determined to be the result of microbial contamination caused by mishandling of the drug by medical personnel. With the FDA's encouragement, Zeneca decided to reformulate Diprivan by adding the preservative disodium edentate (EDTA) in order to prevent microbial contamination. Zeneca performed clinical studies on the safety of the reformulated Diprivan and, in return, was awarded three years of exclusivity for the reformulated Diprivan when it was approved in 1996.

In March 1997, Gensia submitted an ANDA to the FDA for approval of a generic propofol product with EDTA, the same composition as Diprivan. In July 1997, Gensia informed the FDA that it was evaluating the development of propofol using the preservative sodium metabisulfite (sulfite) instead of EDTA. In its July 1997 letter, Gensia provided preliminary data on a propofol product with sulfite that would have a pH range of 6.0 to 7.5. Gensia asked the FDA to review the preliminary data and consider, in particular, the proposed lower pH of Gensia's formulation and the safety of sulfite as a preservative. The Office of Generic Drugs (the OGD) undertook a review of the preliminary data. In addition, the FDA's Division of Anesthetic, Critical Care and Addiction Products, the division that reviewed and approved the NDA for Diprivan, provided consultation to the

OGD about the proposed propofol product containing sulfite. On January 16, 1998, Gensia withdrew its ANDA for propofol with EDTA and submitted an ANDA for propofol with sulfite with a new proposed pH range of 4.5 to 6.4.

On April 7, 1998, after learning that the FDA was considering an ANDA for generic propofol, Zeneca filed an administrative petition for a stay of action pursuant to 21 C.F.R. § 10.35 (1999). Zeneca's petition requested, among other things, that the FDA decline to approve any generic version of Diprivan that "contains an antimicrobial additive other than [EDTA], the safety of which is not supported by preclinical, clinical, or other scientific investigative studies." Zeneca contended that the substitution of sulfite for EDTA and the lower pH of Gensia's propofol with sulfite raised safety issues; specifically, issues of allergenicity, toxicity, antimicrobial effectiveness, and product stability. Further, Zeneca argued that the addition of a sulfite warning required by 21 C.F.R. § 201.22 to the label of Gensia's propofol with sulfite would violate the statutory "same labeling" requirement for generic drugs.

On January 4, 1999, the FDA approved Gensia's ANDA for propofol with sulfite. On the same day, the FDA denied Zeneca's petition. The FDA noted that it "did not require clinical studies to establish the safety of [Gensia's] drug product; instead, the Agency found that sufficient information was available both in the ANDA and before the Agency to address whether changing the preservative to sodium metabisulfite compromised the safety of the propofol injectable emulsion product." The FDA concluded that it "had substantial data to evaluate the possible effects of sodium metabisulfite in propofol because sodium or potassium metabisulfite is present in concentrations ranging from 0.1 mg/ml to 10 mg/ml in more than 50 approved drug products." Based on the information in the administrative record and its scientific expertise, the FDA determined that the presence of sulfite in Gensia's propofol did not affect the safety profile of the drug.

The FDA also concluded that Gensia's propofol with sulfite was safe and therapeutically equivalent to Diprivan. Of particular note, the FDA acknowledged that "patients with sulfite allergies should not be administered a formulation of propofol with [sulfite]. Appropriate labeling, however, is sufficient to protect against improper use of the product." Accordingly, the FDA required Gensia's propofol with sulfite product to include a "statement in the insert labeling informing practitioners of precautions related to the presence of sulfites," and to "highlight prominently on the container label that the product contains [sulfite]." The FDA concluded that these warnings "serve to alert practitioners of the potential for allergic reactions and are adequate to ensure safe use of the drug." Based on the addition of these warnings to the label of Gensia's propofol with sulfite, the FDA concluded that Gensia's propofol with sulfite was a safe generic drug when properly administered to the majority of the population, which has no allergic reaction to sulfites. * * *

Zeneca first argues that the FDA violated 21 C.F.R. §§ 314.94(a)(9)(iii) and 314.127(a)(8)(ii)(B) by approving Gensia's ANDA for propofol with sulfite without requiring Gensia to adequately show that the substitution of sulfite for EDTA as a preservative did not affect the safety of the drug formula based on Diprivan. Therefore, Zeneca argues, the FDA's approval was arbitrary and capricious. We conclude that Zeneca's argument is without merit.

Section 314.94(a)(9)(iii) permits substitution of preservatives in parenteral drugs "provided that the applicant identifies and characterizes the differences and provides information demonstrating that the differences do not affect the safety of the proposed drug product." Similarly, section 314.127(a)(8)(ii)(B) provides, in relevant part, that the FDA will not approve an ANDA for a generic drug product "unless it contains the same inactive ingredients, other than preservatives ... and, if it differs from the listed drug in a preservative ... the application contains sufficient information to demonstrate that the difference does not affect the safety of the drug product." Collectively, these regulatory sections establish that prior to approving an ANDA for a generic drug with a preservative that differs from the listed pioneer drug, the FDA must determine that the preservative does not affect the safety of the drug. In this case, the FDA concluded that the substitution of sulfite for EDTA as a preservative did not affect the safety of Gensia's propofol because warnings on the product's container and labeling would "serve to alert practitioners of the potential for allergic reactions and are adequate to ensure safe use of the drug."

As an initial matter, we note that the use of sulfites in prescription drugs is widespread. See Sulfiting Agents; Labeling in Drugs for Human Use; Warning Statement, 50 Fed. Reg. 47,558, 47,558 (1985) (proposed rule) (noting that, at that time, sulfites were present "in more than 1,100 oxygen-sensitive prescription drug products"). Moreover, the "FDA has not found evidence in the available information on sulfites in human drugs that demonstrates a significant health hazard to the general population." Id. at 47,560. Zeneca does not challenge this finding nor does it contest the FDA's determination that "sulfites serve a necessary public health function by maintaining the potency of certain medications." Sulfiting Agents; Labeling in Drugs for Human Use; Warning Statement, 51 Fed. Reg. 43,900, 43,903 (1986) (final rule). Accordingly, the issue before us is not whether sulfites, in and of themselves, are safe. They are. Rather, the issue is whether the substitution of sulfite for EDTA in Gensia's propofol with sulfite affects the safety of Gensia's propofol with sulfite. The FDA concluded that the substitution of sulfite for EDTA in Gensia's propofol with sulfite did not affect the safety of Gensia's propofol with sulfite because warning labels obviated any potential risks.

Zeneca argues that the FDA's reliance upon warnings on the product's container and labeling in making its decision as to whether Gensia's propofol with sulfite is safe for use is prohibited under the plain language of sections 314.94(a)(9)(iii) and 314.127(a)(8)(ii)(B). In other words, Zeneca argues, under the plain language of these two regulations, the FDA may not rely on an enhanced warning label to obviate the safety concerns associated with different preservatives.

In response, the FDA contends that Zeneca's argument is without merit, because it places an unreasonably narrow construction on the regulations at issue, regulations promulgated by the FDA. In support of its contention, the FDA points to the plain language of 21 U.S.C. § 355(j)(4)(H), the statute the two regulations at issue were promulgated to implement, which expressly provides that under the ANDA process, the FDA's consideration of the safety of inactive ingredients in generic drugs is dependent upon: (1) the "conditions prescribed, recommended, or suggested in the labeling"; and (2) the "type or quantity of inactive ingredients included or the manner in which the inactive ingredients are included."

Zeneca's argument challenges the FDA's interpretation of its own regulations, which interpretation "is entitled to 'substantial deference' and will be sustained unless it is plainly erroneous or inconsistent with the regulation[s]." We find the FDA's interpretation * * * to be consistent with the language of these regulations and not plainly erroneous. Specifically, the language of sections 314.94(a)(9)(iii) and 314.127(a)(8)(ii)(B) is broad enough to encompass the FDA's interpretation. Furthermore, the FDA's interpretation is completely faithful to the statute that these two regulations were promulgated to implement. * * *

Next we address Zeneca's argument that the FDA violated its own regulation requiring a generic drug's labeling to be the same as its pioneer counterpart. Section 355(j)(2)(A)(v) of the FFDCA allows labeling differences that are necessary "because the new [generic] drug and the listed [pioneer] drug are produced or distributed by different manufacturers." The FDA has interpreted § 355(j)(2)(A)(v) to permit changes in labeling because of "differences in expiration date, formulation, bioavailability, or pharmacokinetics, [or] labeling revisions made to comply with current FDA labeling guidelines or other guidance." In this case, the FDA interpreted 21 C.F.R. § 314.94(a)(8)(iv) to find that the sulfite warning for Gensia's propofol with sulfite fit squarely within the exceptions for (1) formulation differences and (2) differences required to comply with the labeling guidelines in the FDA's sulfite warning regulation. * * *

We find the FDA's interpretation of 21 C.F.R. § 314.94(a)(8)(iv) to be consistent with the language of the regulation and not plainly erroneous. The sulfite safety warning in Gensia's labeling is a direct result of the difference in formulation between Gensia's propofol with sulfite and Diprivan. Gensia was fully authorized to formulate its generic drug with a different preservative than is contained in Diprivan. Because a difference in preservative is a permitted variation in formulation, it is reasonable for the FDA to interpret its own regulation to allow corresponding differences in labeling to identify the preservative and provide any appropriate warnings.

In addition to permitting labeling changes based on differences in formulation, section 314.94(a)(8)(iv) permits changes in order "to comply with current FDA labeling guidelines and guidance." Section 201.22(b) of the FDA's regulations requires that prescription drugs containing sulfites

> shall bear the warning statement "Contains (insert the name of the sulfite, e.g., sodium metabisulfite), a sulfite that may cause allergic-type reactions . . . in certain susceptible people. The overall prevalence of sulfite sensitivity in the general population is unknown and probably low. Sulfite sensitivity is seen more frequently in asthmatic than in nonasthmatic people."

The FDA interpreted section 314.94(a)(8)(iv) to permit Gensia to include in its labeling the "warning statement" required by section 201.22, a current FDA labeling guideline. This interpretation is consistent with the language of section 314.94(a)(8)(iv). Furthermore, we see no merit to Zeneca's argument that the exception permitting revisions in labeling to comply with the FDA's current labeling guidelines only applies in situations in which the guidelines are issued after approval of the pioneer drug but before approval of the generic. * * *

NOTES AND QUESTIONS

1. *Establishing bioequivalence.* Subject to the patent and market exclusivity constraints discussed in Chapter 10, the FDA may approve an ANDA if the applicant demonstrates that its generic product is "bioequivalent" to (meaning that it has essentially the same rate and extent of absorption as) the innovator drug, a showing that substitutes for the much costlier clinical trials demanded as part of an NDA to demonstrate safety and effectiveness of the innovator drug. See, e.g., Somerset Pharm., Inc. v. Shalala, 973 F.Supp. 443, 453–54 (D.Del.1997) (deferring to the FDA's scientific judgment that metabolite testing could serve as an indicator of bioequivalence of generic versions of the drug selegiline hydrochloride indicated for the treatment of Parkinson's disease); see also Novartis Pharm. Corp. v. Leavitt, 435 F.3d 344 (D.C.Cir.2006); Warner–Lambert Co. v. Shalala, 202 F.3d 326 (D.C.Cir.2000) (rejecting a challenge brought by the manufacturer of a pioneer drug approved in a *capsule* dosage form against the FDA's decision to approve as "therapeutically equivalent" an ANDA for a capsule-shaped *tablet* version enclosed by a gelatin shell); Biovail Corp. v. FDA, 519 F.Supp.2d 39, 45–48 (D.D.C.2007) (denying a motion for a temporary restraining order brought by the manufacturer of Wellbutrin XL® (bupropion) after the agency approved a generic version of this extended-release antidepressant without also demanding proof of its bioequivalence to earlier versions of the drug even though that was claimed in the labeling); Linda A. Johnson, Wyeth Sues FDA to Block Generic Rival of Antibiotic Zosyn, Boston Globe, Sept. 24, 2009, at 10 (summarizing objections to the agency's approval of a generic version of an older formulation that the brand-name manufacturer had discontinued four years earlier after it added a pair of ingredients to guard against the possibility of a dangerous chemical reaction).

2. *Questioning bioequivalence.* Notwithstanding the FDA's reassurances, questions continue to arise about the equivalence of generic drugs. See Melinda Beck, Inexact Copies: How Generics Differ from Brand Names,

Wall St. J., Apr. 22, 2008, at D1 (reporting that an FDA review of 130 patient complaints about the generic version of Wellbutrin XL during its first year on the market found that the drug "reach[ed] its maximum blood concentration in two to three hours, compared to five to six hours for" the brand-name version but dismissed this difference as clinically insignificant); Thomas M. Burton, Doctors Raise Warnings About a Form of Clozapine, Wall St. J., Oct. 24, 2000, at B1; see also Evan H. Langdon, Comment, Switching to Generic: The Need for Physician and Patient Consent When Substituting Antiepileptic Medication, 25 J. Contemp. Health L. & Pol'y 166 (2008); cf. Susan Okie, Multinational Medicines—Ensuring Drug Quality in an Era of Global Manufacturing, 361 New Eng. J. Med. 737 (2009) (discussing reports of quality control problems with generic drugs); Natasha Singer, F.D.A. Again Warns the Generic Maker Apotex About the Conditions at Its Plants, N.Y. Times, Apr. 16, 2010, at B16 ("Concerns about the quality and effectiveness of generics have become prevalent enough among doctors and patients that the F.D.A. held a public advisory meeting this week to discuss the issue ...."). But cf. Aaron S. Kesselheim et al., Clinical Equivalence of Generic and Brand–Name Drugs Used in Cardiovascular Disease: A Systematic Review and Meta-analysis, 300 JAMA 2514, 2524 (2008) ("Even though there is little evidence of important clinical differences between generic and brand-name drugs in cardiovascular disease, many editorials expressed a negative view of generic drug interchangeability ...."). As noted in Chapter 9(C)(2), generic substitution laws generally allow pharmacists to dispense generic versions when filling a prescription for a brand-name drug. Imagine a transplant patient who has done well on Prograf for more than a year and then, unbeknownst to his physician, receives the new Sandoz version of tacrolimus instead (but is not monitored more closely by his physician to ensure a smooth transition to the cheaper drug)—does the *Astellas* court adequately address such concerns?

3. *Time and effort required for approval.* It may take up to five years and an initial investment of $1 million to secure FDA approval of an ANDA for a generic drug product. See Richard J. Findlay, Originator Drug Development, 54 Food & Drug L.J. 227, 229 (1999); see also In re Barr Lab., Inc., 930 F.2d 72 (D.C.Cir.1991) (reviewing a dispute over FDA delays); Gardiner Harris, Deal in Place for Inspecting Foreign Drugs, N.Y. Times, Aug. 13, 2011, at A1 (reporting that generic manufacturers had tentatively agreed to pay almost $300 million annually in FDA user fees); Natasha Singer, Generics Face Longer Wait for Approval, N.Y. Times, Feb. 20, 2010, at B3 (reporting that average approval times had increased from 16 months to almost 27 months over the last five years, with a current "backlog of nearly 2,000 pending generic applications"). See generally Richard G. Frank, The Ongoing Regulation of Generic Drugs, 357 New Eng. J. Med. 1993 (2007); Adam R. Young, Note, Generic Pharmaceutical Regulation in the United States with Comparison to Europe: Innovation and Competition, 8 Wash. U. Global Stud. L. Rev. 165 (2009).

4. *Battling generic competition.* NDA holders may raise bioequivalence objections in an effort to stall generic competition. In some instances, these are broad-based assaults on the standards used by the FDA. See, e.g., Schering Corp. v. Shalala, 995 F.2d 1103, 1104 (D.C.Cir.1993) (per curiam) (describing one company's efforts to challenge the FDA's bioequivalence criteria for non-systemic drugs); Graceway Pharms., Inc. v. Sebelius, 783 F.Supp.2d 104 (D.D.C.2011) (same); Sheryl G. Stolberg & Jeff Gerth, Keeping Down the Competition: How Companies Stall Generics and Keep Themselves Healthy, N.Y. Times, July 23, 2000, at A1. The most recent example of this conduct, as discussed in Chapter 11(A), involves drugs produced through biotechnology. In other cases, brand-name companies object to the agency's approval of a particular ANDA. See, e.g., Sanofi–Aventis U.S. LLC v. FDA, 733 F.Supp.2d 162 (D.D.C.2010) (rejecting brand-name manufacturer's request for a preliminary injunction after the agency approved a generic version of the anticoagulant Lovenox® (enoxaparin), a low molecular weight form of heparin); Leila Abboud, Raging Hormones: How Drug Giant Keeps a Monopoly on 60–Year–Old Pill, Wall St. J., Sept. 9, 2004, at A1 ("The Premarin saga shows the high stakes in the quest for drug knockoffs, and the lengths big companies go to protect their profits from attack by generic rivals."); see also Lars Noah, Sham Petitioning as a Threat to the Integrity of the Regulatory Process, 74 N.C. L. Rev. 1 (1995) [excerpted in Chap. 10(C)].

5. *Identical labeling*. In addition to containing the same active ingredient, a generic drug product must use the same labeling, subject to the exceptions discussed in *Zeneca*. This requirement can present obstacles to approval. See Melody Petersen, Label Issues Are Delaying Generic Drugs, N.Y. Times, Jan. 3, 2003, at C1. The FDA may, however, approve an ANDA even if its labeling includes only a subset of the indications approved for the pioneer drug. See Bristol–Myers Squibb Co. v. Shalala, 91 F.3d 1493, 1500 (D.C.Cir.1996). When the agency orders sellers of brand-name products to revise their labeling, it expects parallel changes for previously approved generic versions. See Julie Schmit, Updating Generic–Drug Labels Can Take Months, USA Today, Apr. 21, 2005, at 3B. These regulatory requirements have triggered some peculiar tort litigation, with courts occasionally holding brand-name manufacturers liable for inadequate warnings when patients suffer injuries while taking the generic versions. See, e.g., Conte v. Wyeth, Inc., 85 Cal.Rptr.3d 299 (Ct.App.2008) [excerpted in Chap. 7(A)(3)]; see also Lars Noah, Adding Insult to Injury: Paying for Harms Caused by a Competitor's Copycat Product, 45 Tort Trial & Ins. Prac. L.J. 673 (2010).

B. MEDICAL DEVICES

All new drugs must undergo premarket approval, prescription and OTC products alike (though recall that the FDA treats most nonprescription drugs as not new (GRASE) if they comply with the terms of an OTC monograph). The agency takes a somewhat different approach to medical devices. Although substantial equivalence to a pre–1976 device operates much like a GRASE determination, some post–1976 devices that are not substantially equivalent may remain exempt from premarket approval and some pre–1976 devices eventually may undergo premarket approval. It all depends on how the FDA classifies the device. In a tort preemption decision, the Supreme Court provided the following summary of the different routes to market.

Medtronic, Inc. v. Lohr

518 U.S. 470 (1996).

■ STEVENS, JUSTICE:

* * * While the FDCA provided for premarket approval of new drugs, it did not authorize any control over the introduction of new medical devices. As technologies advanced and medicine relied to an increasing degree on a vast array of medical equipment "[f]rom bedpans to brainscans," including kidney dialysis units, artificial heart valves, and heart pacemakers, policymakers and the public became concerned about the increasingly severe injuries that resulted from the failure of such devices. In 1970, for example, the Dalkon Shield, an intrauterine contraceptive device, was introduced to the American public and throughout the world. Touted as a safe and effective contraceptive, the Dalkon Shield resulted in a disturbingly high percentage of inadvertent pregnancies, serious infections, and even, in a few cases, death. * * *

In response to the mounting consumer and regulatory concern, Congress enacted the statute at issue here: the Medical Device Amendments of 1976 (MDA or Act). The Act classified medical devices in three categories based on the risk that they pose to the public. Devices that present no unreasonable risk of illness or injury are designated Class I and are subject only to minimal regulation by "general controls." Devices that are potentially more harmful are designated Class II; although they may be marketed without advance approval, manufacturers of such devices must comply with federal performance regulations known as "special controls." Finally, devices that either "present a potential unreasonable risk of illness or injury," or which are "purported or represented to be for a use in supporting or sustaining human life or for a use which is of substantial importance in preventing impairment of human health," are designated Class III. Pacemakers are Class III devices.

Before a new Class III device may be introduced to the market, the manufacturer must provide the FDA with a "reasonable assurance" that the device is both safe and effective. Despite its relatively innocuous phrasing, the process of establishing this "reasonable assurance," which is known as the "premarket approval" or "PMA" process, is a rigorous one. Manufacturers must submit detailed information regarding the safety and efficacy of their devices, which the FDA then reviews, spending an average of 1,200 hours on each submission.

Not all, or even most, Class III devices on the market today have received premarket approval because of two important exceptions to the

PMA requirement. First, Congress realized that existing medical devices could not be withdrawn from the market while the FDA completed its PMA analysis for those devices. The statute therefore includes a "grandfathering" provision which allows pre–1976 devices to remain on the market without FDA approval until such time as the FDA initiates and completes the requisite PMA. Second, to prevent manufacturers of grandfathered devices from monopolizing the market while new devices clear the PMA hurdle, and to ensure that improvements to existing devices can be rapidly introduced into the market, the Act also permits devices that are "substantially equivalent" to pre-existing devices to avoid the PMA process.

Although "substantially equivalent" Class III devices may be marketed without the rigorous PMA review, such new devices, as well as all new Class I and Class II devices, are subject to the requirements of § 360(k). That section imposes a limited form of review on every manufacturer intending to market a new device by requiring it to submit a "premarket notification" to the FDA (the process is also known as a "§ 510(k) process," after the number of the section in the original Act). If the FDA concludes on the basis of the § 510(k) notification that the device is "substantially equivalent" to a pre-existing device, it can be marketed without further regulatory analysis (at least until the FDA initiates the PMA process for the underlying pre–1976 device to which the new device is "substantially equivalent"). The § 510(k) notification process is by no means comparable to the PMA process; in contrast to the 1,200 hours necessary to complete a PMA review, the § 510(k) review is completed in an average of only 20 hours.

Congress anticipated that the FDA would complete the PMA process for Class III devices relatively swiftly. But because of the substantial investment of time and energy necessary for the resolution of each PMA application, the ever-increasing numbers of medical devices, and internal administrative and resource difficulties, the FDA simply could not keep up with the rigorous PMA process. As a result, the § 510(k) premarket notification process became the means by which most new medical devices–including Class III devices—were approved for market. In 1983, for instance, a House Report concluded that nearly 1,000 of the approximately 1,100 Class III devices that had been introduced to the market since 1976 were admitted as "substantial equivalents" and without any PMA review. This lopsidedness has apparently not evened out; despite an increasing effort by the FDA to consider the safety and efficacy of substantially equivalent devices, the House reported in 1990 that 80% of new Class III devices were being introduced to the market through the § 510(k) process and without PMA review. * * *

United States v. Caputo

517 F.3d 935 (7th Cir.2008).

■ EASTERBROOK, CHIEF JUDGE:

An autoclave sterilizes medical instruments quickly and cheaply. But some instruments can't stand the high temperatures and pressures of an autoclave, so there is a demand for sterilizers that use lower temperatures and non-aqueous sterilants. One system in widespread use relies on ethylene oxide gas as the sterilant. That gas is toxic and hard to handle, however, and Ross Caputo saw a business opportunity in these drawbacks. He designed a low-temperature system using a plasma of peracetic acid as the sterilant and in 1990 asked the Food and Drug Administration to approve this device, which his company AbTox Inc. called the Plazlyte.

Since 1976 it has been unlawful to sell a new medical device without the FDA's approval. The Medical Device Amendments to the [FDCA] have a grandfather clause covering devices that had been lawfully sold on or before May 28, 1976, or are "substantially equivalent" to them. 21 U.S.C. § 360c(f)(1)(A)(ii). AbTox asked the FDA to approve sales of a Plazlyte as "substantially equivalent" to units that employ ethylene oxide as the sterilant. We refer to "a" Plazlyte rather than "the" Plazlyte because AbTox made at least two models. The first had an interior volume of one cubic foot and used 10% peracetic acid made by mixing water with a solution of 30% peracetic acid. The water and the 30% solution were in separate bottles. This device used a two-cycle procedure, applying gas plasma twice to sterilize the instruments. The second model had an interior volume of approximately five cubic feet, used 5% peracetic acid from a single bottle (no dilution with water from a second bottle), and ran just one cycle, at a different pressure from the first model. We call the first model the small Plazlyte and the second model the large Plazlyte.

AbTox submitted the small Plazlyte for approval in 1990. It also submitted only those tests that favored the device's effectiveness; others, less helpful to AbTox, were concealed (or so a jury could conclude; we recount the evidence in the light most favorable to the verdict [against the defendants]). The agency's staff doubted whether the Plazlyte was equivalent to ethylene oxide systems and insisted on limiting the uses to which it could be put. When the FDA signed off on the small Plazlyte in 1994, it approved the device only for use with solid stainless-steel instruments. If AbTox wanted to sell the Plazlyte to sterilize instruments containing interior space that the gas plasma might not fully penetrate (such as those with hinges or lumens) or instruments made from materials that might react chemically with peracetic acid ($C_2H_4O_3$), an organic peroxide, it had to file an application for approval as a new device rather than one equivalent to a grandfathered device. Any medical instrument containing plastic, solder (usually made of lead, tin, or silver), or brass (an alloy of copper and zinc) was outside the scope of the FDA's approval.

A new and expensive machine (Plazlytes sold for about $100,000) for sterilizing solid instruments made of stainless steel had no prospect in the market. Autoclaves are cheaper and don't require the handling of acids. Caputo understood that AbTox would never be able to sell a single unit of the small Plazlyte for the limited use approved by the FDA. Caputo (and his assistant Robert Riley) did not try. Instead they immediately began promoting the large Plazlyte as a replacement for ethylene-oxide devices, and thus as suitable for general-purpose sterilization. It had begun selling the large Plazlyte outside the United States in 1993; thus, long before receiving the FDA's approval to sell the small Plazlyte, it knew that the small device would never be marketed and that the large Plazlyte would be promoted for use with many kinds of instruments—though it did not tell the FDA these things when negotiating the details of the limited use that would be allowed to the small Plazlyte.

Problems ensued when some hospitals used the Plazlyte to sterilize brass instruments employed for procedures in the eye. The Plazlyte left a blue-green residue on some of these instruments—and, although the instruments were sterile, the residue (copper and zinc acetate) was harmful to patients' eyes. Some patients experienced corneal decompensation, a severe condition that entails loss of vision.

In May 1995 the FDA found out what AbTox was telling customers and reminded it about the limitations on the scope of approval. This notice informed AbTox that the Plazlyte as promoted was "misbranded." AbTox then sought the FDA's approval to sell the large Plazlyte to sterilize a wider class of instruments; when the FDA rejected AbTox's request for expedited decision and told AbTox that it "may not market this device until you have received a letter from the FDA allowing you to do so," AbTox went on promoting the large Plazlyte as before. On September 27, 1996, the FDA sent AbTox another instruction to stop selling the large Plazlyte; AbTox failed to comply (though it did not tell the FDA so). The agency never authorized AbTox to sell the large Plazlyte for any use.

The Centers for Disease Control opened an investigation to discover what was causing the eye injuries. Meanwhile, in January 1998, the FDA inspected AbTox's facilities and discovered that it was still selling the large Plazlyte. The inspectors told AbTox to desist; it didn't. In April 1998 the FDA issued a warning to all hospitals, telling them that the large Plazlyte was not an approved device and at all events must not be used with any instruments containing solder, copper, or zinc, or for any ophthalmic instruments. The FDA directed AbTox to recall the devices; U.S. marshals seized its inventory; this criminal prosecution eventually followed. * * * A jury convicted them of these charges after an eight-week trial. Caputo has been sentenced to 120 months' imprisonment and Riley to 72 months. Both were ordered to make restitution of $17.2 million, the list price of all Plazlyte units ever sold [which this court remands for recalculation]. * * *

[T]he jury found, by its verdicts on both the fraud-on-the-United–States count and the misbranded-device counts, that the large Plazlyte could *not* lawfully be sold. The jury concluded not only that Caputo and Riley had lied to the agency when seeking approval of the small Plazlyte but also that the large Plazlyte differed enough from the small one that new approval was essential. For current purposes it is enough to concentrate on the latter conclusion. * * * Once the FDA certifies a medical device under the grandfather clause, the seller may make modifications to that device without obtaining fresh approval. The line between a "modification'' (no approval needed) and a new device (which must be submitted independently for approval) is drawn in 21 C.F.R. § 807.81. There are two principal inquiries: first, whether the changes ''significantly affect the safety or effectiveness of the device'' and, second, whether there is a ''major change or modification in the intended use of the device.'' 21 C.F.R. § 807.81(a)(3).

We doubt that the large Plazlyte could be described as a ''modification'' of the small one; recall that the large device had been placed on sale outside the United States in 1993, the year before the FDA approved the small device. ''Modification'' suggests a change in an approved device, not a different device that was already on sale before the approval. But suppose that this is wrong, and suppose further that the large Plazlyte was as safe as the small one notwithstanding the difference in the concentration and number of applications of the sterilant. There remains the rule that a ''major change or modification in the intended use of the device'' requires fresh approval. Promoting the large Plazlyte as suitable for use with all medical instruments is a major change in intended use, compared with using it for solid stainless-steel instruments alone. This expansion of use caused the copper and zinc acetates that injured patients. So the large Plazlyte, with its expanded ''intended use,'' was not covered by the FDA's approval of the small Plazlyte and could not lawfully be sold *at all*. * * *

Caputo and Riley try to avoid this conclusion by arguing that the Due Process Clause of the Fifth Amendment disabled the FDA from keeping the large Plazlyte off the market. The line between new and modified devices is too vague to be enforceable, the argument goes. We grant that phrases such as ''significantly affect'' and ''major change ... in the intended use'' are not self-defining. But then no legal phrase is. Think of ''material'' (as in ''material misrepresentations are forbidden''), a staple of legal discourse, or ''unreasonable'' * * * * The Supreme Court has rejected vagueness challenges to the antitrust laws, which must be an order of magnitude more ambulatory than § 807.81(a)(3), and has held that a rule cannot be deemed unconstitutionally vague if it suggests a metric for decision. Section 807.81(a)(3) tells us what dimensions of difference matter, even though it does not give an exact answer to the question ''how much is too much''? * * *

The uncertainty that is inevitable in legal standards (as opposed to numerical rules) often is offset by notice, so that people need not guess what is required of them. The FDA gave AbTox notice, and to spare. It published in March 1993 (before the small Plazlyte was approved) a ''Guidance'' stating that any change in the sterilant or chamber size of a sterilizer creates a new device that requires new approval. It sent letters, which AbTox ignored. (The letters not only called attention to the 1993 Guidance but also restated the FDA's view of AbTox's duties under the statute and regulation.) It sent an inspection team, whose directions AbTox spurned. * * *

To say that the FDA showered interpretations and advice on Caputo and Riley is not to say that the published ''Guidance'' has the effect of a regulation, let alone that AbTox was legally bound to comply with the letters. Only the statute, regulations, and formal directives of the agency (as opposed to its staff) have legal force. The agency did not issue its cease-and-desist and recall orders until April 1998. Until then Caputo and Riley were at liberty to chart their own course, as their own legal advisers counseled them. When they did this, however, they took a risk and could not then say "we didn't know" or "the regulation left us scratching our heads." The agency comprehensively alerted AbTox, Caputo, and Riley to its view of their legal obligations, and an agency's interpretation of its own regulations, no less than a judicial opinion, may disambiguate them. When Caputo and Riley chose to go their own way, the question on the table for the court became simply who is right about the meaning of the legal rules, not whether adequate notice was given.

Note that Caputo and Riley have not made an advice-of-counsel defense, though no one gets into a multi-million-dollar medical-device business without legal counsel. Perhaps they lied to their lawyers about what they were doing and thus cannot present a defense that depends on candor to counsel; or perhaps they decided to avoid asking for advice about § 807.81(a)(3) for fear of what the answer would be; finally, they may have asked and received a reply that they did not follow. The attorney-client privilege prevents us from knowing which. * * *

United States v. Snoring Relief Labs Inc.

210 F.3d 1081 (9th Cir.2000).

■ NELSON, CIRCUIT JUDGE:

* * * Snoring Relief tried to become the first company to market a self-fitting, anti-snoring mouthpiece without a prescription. SnorBan requires the patient to self-fit the device by placing it in boiling water, advancing her jaw forward, and inserting the device. The patient determines how far forward to advance her jaw, and then takes a dental impression. Advancing the jaw forward apparently improves the patient's airway and prevents snoring.

Snoring Relief did not seek pre-market approval or notification for SnorBan from FDA. On September 7, 1995, FDA notified Snoring Relief that it was violating the FDC Act by selling SnorBan without having submitted pre-market notification or receiving pre-market approval. On October 16, 1995, Snoring Relief submitted pre-market notification in the form of a letter from Snoring Relief's president; a journal article about anti-snoring mouthpieces; SnorBan fitting instructions; and a brochure written by Snoring Relief's president. Snoring Relief contended that its product was substantially equivalent to two other anti-snoring mouthpieces, both of which are available by prescription only. Snoring Relief wanted to make SnorBan available over-the-counter, and compared its self-fitting device to athletic mouth guards. Also, its application contended that there was not an increased risk of undiagnosed sleep apnea.

On April 1, 1996, FDA denied Snoring Relief's request to market SnorBan over-the-counter. FDA's Dental Devices Branch of the Office of Device Evaluation enlisted Dr. Susan Runner, a doctor of dental surgery and the Senior Regulatory Review Officer, to compare SnorBan to the prescription-only, anti-snoring mouthpieces. Dr. Runner concluded that marketing SnorBan without a prescription raised two new questions about safety and effectiveness: (1) It would require the patient to distinguish between simple snoring and obstructive sleep apnea, a potentially life-threatening condition; and (2) it would require the patient to determine if she has any temporomandibular joint (TMJ) disease that would not permit the use of an oral appliance. If the patient advances her jaw too far forward in fitting the device, she could suffer TMJ. Dr. Runner concluded that "selection of which patients are appropriate for oral appliance therapy should always be made by the health professional." Based on this evaluation, FDA denied SnorBan's request for an exemption and found that SnorBan is a Class III device requiring pre-market approval before it can be legally marketed.

Before and after FDA's final decision, Snoring Relief marketed SnorBan without pre-market approval. On February 22, 1996, FDA sent Snoring Relief a warning letter about this continued violation. On April 15, 1996, Snoring Relief responded not by asking to market SnorBan with a prescription, but by asking for a waiver from the pre-market notification requirement. Snoring Relief said its product was similar to the Stop Snore Collar, a pillow-like anti-snoring device that only required an apnea warning label. FDA disagreed, and in a May 9, 1996, letter distinguished mouthpieces from anti-snoring devices used externally such as pillows or nasal strips.

In a July 8, 1996, letter to FDA, Snoring Relief dismissed the distinction between intra-oral and extra-oral anti-snoring devices, and offered to provide a warning label about sleep apnea with its product. On July 23, 1996, FDA rejected Snoring Relief's continued attempts to market SnorBan without a prescription. FDA also warned against the illegal marketing of SnorBan. Snoring Relief continued to distribute its unapproved device without a prescription. On August 14, 1997, the government filed an in rem seizure action alleging that SnorBan is an adulterated, Class III device because it lacked pre-market approval * * * *

Snoring Relief did not contest that SnorBan was a "device" pursuant to the language of the FDC Act, nor did it petition for reclassification. * * * Snoring Relief claims to be exempt from FDA regulations (or be cleared for marketing) based on its pre-market notification to FDA that SnorBan is "substantially equivalent" to anti-snoring pillows, collars, and nasal strips. FDA repeatedly rejected these contentions. Initially, FDA compared SnorBan to other anti-snoring mouthpieces available by prescription only, concluding that a non-prescription anti-snoring mouthpiece presented new safety and effectiveness concerns about undiagnosed sleep apnea and TMJ. On two subsequent occasions, FDA rejected Snoring Relief's comparisons of SnorBan to anti-snoring pillows, collars, and nasal strips. These agency decisions should be narrowly reviewed under the APA's arbitrary and capricious standard. * * *

What Snoring Relief really wants is for the district court (and this court) to review FDA's decision de novo. But, as the government said, "the issue is an agency decision not to exercise its enforcement discretion to waive the pre-market notification requirement for SnorBan. FDA is entitled to decide how to exercise its discretion, and the court only reviews that decision under the arbitrary and capricious standard." We agree. * * *

The district court reviewed FDA's safety and effectiveness concerns about SnorBan regarding undiagnosed sleep apnea and potential TMJ, and concluded that Snoring Relief did not submit any new evidence to FDA suggesting that anti-snoring mouthpieces should be available without a prescription. The two articles that Snoring Relief submitted about anti-snoring mouthpieces both suggest that the mouthpieces should be fitted by medical personnel. Snoring Relief's two experts did not indicate whether they had any clinical experience with SnorBan. Furthermore, Snoring Relief submitted no medical studies suggesting that anti-snoring mouthpieces were safe for non-prescription use.

Snoring Relief argues that warning labels about sleep apnea and TMJ would have been sufficient, and that FDA allows such warnings with other anti-snoring products such as anti-snoring pillows, collars, and nasal strips. * * * FDA was not arbitrary and capricious in finding SnorBan was not substantially equivalent to these products—the agency consistently has found that extra-oral anti-snoring devices such as nasal strips present "no real safety concerns." Given the narrow arbitrary and capricious standard of review and the lack of contrary evidence presented by Snoring Relief, FDA's distinctions among these products were reasonable. * * *

Lawrence S. Makow, Note, *Medical Device Review at the Food and Drug Administration: Lessons from Magnetic Resonance Spectroscopy and Biliary Lithotripsy*

46 STAN. L. REV. 709 (1994).

* * * Renal lithotripsy—a dramatic nonsurgical solution for removing kidney stones—was first reported in 1980. Surgical removal of kidney stones had always been a risky operation because the injury to the body of the kidney can be significant, and kidney failure has major consequences. Treatment with extracorporeal shock wave lithotripsy [ESWL] therefore represented a significant breakthrough. Almost overnight, ESWL changed the face of kidney stone treatment: Operations to excise kidney stones rapidly dropped from 30 percent of all urological procedures to 2 percent. * * *

Lithotripsy is based on the principle that high pressure sonic energy can fragment rigid objects while leaving less rigid tissues virtually undisturbed. A lithotripter generates sound waves electrically by means of a spark plug or a metal plate. As the waves pass the speed of sound, they become shock waves, and an "acoustic lens" focuses the waves in the body at the point of the kidney stone. Because the stone is much more rigid than the surrounding body tissue, the focused shock waves destroy the stone without irreversibly damaging the surrounding environment. Repeated applications pulverize the stone into a sandy powder, which the patient can then pass through normal urination.

Common side effects of renal lithotripsy include transient injury to the renal parenchyma, subcutaneous bruising, short-lived pain, and in some cases an accumulation of stone dust in the ureter. Modern lithotripter technology, however, has reduced the occurrence of such problems. On balance, renal lithotripsy is widely considered a tremendous success.

The success of renal lithotripsy prompted investigators to examine applying the technology to gallstones. The incidence of symptomatic gallstones is far higher than that of kidney stones. Gallstone patients also suffer from serious and frequently debilitating pain. The standard treatment for gallstones has traditionally been severe—the complete removal of the gallbladder through an abdominal incision (cholecystectomy). The gallbladder is primarily a warehouse for bile, which the body needs to break down fatty foods; the gallbladder continuously stores and releases bile as needed into the intestines through the common bile duct.

As part of the adjustment to post-operative life without a gallbladder, cholecystectomy patients must follow low-fat diets for the balance of their lives. In addition, the operation itself can cause patients considerable trauma. Because the operation requires a large incision that dissects the abdominal muscles, patients are often incapacitated for several weeks following surgery and may be weak for much longer. And like most major surgery, traditional cholecystectomy involves the risks of general anesthesia.

Although a number of treatments for gallstones exist, cholecystectomy was the most common procedure until recently. Other methods include percutaneous transhepatic cholecystolitholysis (contact dissolution) with methyl tertbutyl ether (MTBE), and oral dissolution therapy, by ingesting salts of bile acids such as ursodeoxycholic acid (ursodiol). But serious limitations make these techniques less attractive than ESWL. Contact dissolution remains highly experimental and may cause necrosis of surrounding tissues. Oral dissolution techniques generally work slowly and do not give immediate symptomatic relief from the pain accompanying gallstones. Persistent pain forces many patients to seek cholecystectomies. Furthermore, the greater the mass of stone material in the gallbladder, the less effective dissolution techniques become. As a result, the FDA had approved ursodiol therapy only for patients who could not undergo surgery. For the majority of gallstone sufferers, there was no nonsurgical alternative.

While renal lithotripsy received rather expeditious approval by the FDA, biliary lithotripsy has been bogged down in the regulatory process. The discrepant treatment stems partially from the physiological differences between biliary and renal lithotripsy. The biliary treatment has been slightly less successful in completely fragmenting the stones. Although fragmentation rates routinely approach 95 percent for cholesterol gallstones, calcified stones are not as easily pulverized. The biggest concern about biliary lithotripsy, however, has been debris clearance—the patient's ability to get rid of the fragments once the stone is successfully crushed.

The clinical objective of renal lithotripsy is not merely relief from the symptoms of kidney stones, but complete stone clearance. The measure of success is the number of "stone-free" patients at the end of a given time period following therapy. Naturally, this same standard was applied to biliary lithotripsy, even though the gallbladder does not flush its contents as thoroughly as does the kidney. Designers of early clinical studies therefore expected stone clearance to be better achieved by using ESWL in conjunction with a dissolution agent, such as ursodiol. Unfortunately, ursodiol may also tend to inhibit stone clearance by further diminishing the gallbladder's ability to contract and squeeze out its contents. Thus, although lithotripsy can often reduce gallstones to a fine sludge, in some patients that sludge will not clear from the gallbladder for six to twelve months, or may persist indefinitely. In contrast, kidney stone fragments usually clear completely in a much shorter time.

When measured against the benchmark established by renal lithotripsy, the relatively modest stone clearance rates of biliary lithotripsy were initially disappointing. Still, biliary ESWL remains the only nonsurgical technique to provide rapid and ongoing symptomatic relief from the severe pain caused by gallstone disease. Although some physicians believe that any lingering sludge presents an unacceptable risk of stone recurrence, other physicians counter that recurrence is always possible in a gallstone patient because the factors that originally led to stone formation remain. If absolute certainty of nonrecurrence is the sine qua non for a therapy's success, no treatment that leaves the gallbladder in place would ever be acceptable despite eliminating symptoms.

A second factor that has reduced the perceived need for biliary ESWL has been the contemporaneous development of laparoscopic cholecystectomy—a new and less invasive surgical alternative. The laparoscope, a surgical device that allows physicians to peer inside the body with a tiny television camera, obviates the need for direct visual inspection through a large, open incision. Using the laparoscope, surgeons can remove the gallbladder without making a large incision. Instead, doctors manipulate surgical instruments in front of the fiber-optic camera and remove the gallbladder through a much smaller opening. The laparoscopic procedure has spread quickly and is now a standard technique. Although surgical treatment for gallstones still requires the removal of the gallbladder, such surgery is no longer nearly as debilitating as before. But laparoscopic cholecystectomy is still complex and involves serious risks, which have been exacerbated by surgeons who have rushed to learn the method in abbreviated seminars. Thus, the need for a more effective nonsurgical elimination of gallstones remains. * * *

In 1984, Dornier Medical Systems received premarket approval for a kidney ESWL system—a class III device. ESWL quickly became the favored technique for treating kidney stones. The success of renal ESWL prompted investigators to apply the technique to gallstones. In 1988, manufacturers initiated clinical trials intended to earn premarket approval for biliary lithotripsy. To optimize the study results, the applicants combined biliary ESWL with the adjuvant use of ursodiol based on the perceived synergy of the treatments: ESWL would cause stone fragmentation and create more stone surface area upon which the ursodiol could act, resulting in more rapid and complete clearance than either therapy alone. At an October 1989 hearing, an FDA panel considered the completed PMA applications of the biliary lithotripter manufacturers. The panel noted deficiencies in the applications and denied premarket approval.

A major reason for the failure of these initial applications was the study design. First, following the model of renal lithotripsy, researchers defined the therapeutic endpoint as a gallbladder free of all stones and debris. In retrospect, this objective probably created overly optimistic expectations. Although almost all patients undergoing gallstone lithotripsy enjoy immediate relief from pain, such symptomatic relief was overlooked in favor of complete stone clearance. Because of the gallbladder's physiological dissimilarity to the kidney, most patients in the original studies did not show stone-free gallbladders.

A second error was including patients with various stone types. After detailed examination of the clinical results, researchers found that ESWL was most effective (as measured by stone-free rates) for solitary stones of 20 millimeters in diameter or smaller and gradually less effective as the stone burden increased. Because ursodiol therapy alone was effective in treating these small solitary stones, the panel understandably doubted that the initial clinical studies demonstrated that ESWL added anything. Furthermore, the data lacked clarity in a number of areas, including how long the patients received treatment and how the manufacturers calculated certain statistical results. Based on these factors, the panel's recommendation against approval was clearly justified.

On August 2, 1990, the FDA issued "FDA Guidance to Firms on Biliary Lithotripsy Studies." The letter outlined the design of an acceptable study, requiring a separate control group of prospectively randomized patients who would be treated with ursodiol alone. This requirement essentially mandated that all clinical studies be redone. The FDA Guidance also announced that ursodiol had not been specifically approved for use with ESWL and that such use would require applicants to file a new drug approval supplement—adding an entirely new regulatory hurdle. The agency reasoned that ursodiol's efficacy had been shown only for intact stones, not stone fragments, but the FDA was probably more concerned with the uncertainty of ursodiol's safety in the postlithotripsy gallbladder.

The FDA's announcement hit the research community like a bombshell. For firms that had already submitted data or that were well into their clinical studies, the Guidance meant that those firms could not use the earlier studies unless CDRH [FDA's Center for Devices and Radiological Health] accepted their historical data. One firm left the industry within three months. The sheer expense of duplicating the studies was merely one of the problems facing manufacturers. Ursodiol therapy had been approved as an alternative treatment to open cholecystectomy for patients with light stone burdens, but the advent of the much less invasive laparoscopic cholecystectomy raised serious ethical questions about randomly assigning patients to an ursodiol-only experimental group. The surgical alternative was now open to a wider range of patients and caused fewer side effects. As a result, ursodiol monotherapy, with its marginal effectiveness, was widely considered obsolete. Yet the FDA Guidance required manufacturers seeking approval of biliary ESWL to conduct studies in which sick patients received much less effective treatment.

Although the panel's rejection of the original PMA applications was probably justified, the FDA's subsequent refusal to recognize the results of several well-designed studies remains unexplained. On September 16, 1992, a National Institutes of Health (NIH) panel issued a "consensus" statement on gallstone treatment. The panel cited ESWL-ursodiol stone-free rates of 95 percent in patients with solitary stones of less than 20 millimeters in diameter, and 80 percent in patients with up to three stones of 20 to 30 millimeters in diameter. Such results far exceed any claim for ursodiol monotherapy and should dispel any lingering doubt as to the superiority of ESWL and ursodiol combined.

Armed with the knowledge of biliary ESWL's clinical performance, which the NIH would later recognize, investigators remained convinced that combination therapy was more effective than ursodiol monotherapy, especially for solitary stones of 20 millimeters or smaller. To avoid what they considered a superfluous repetition of an entire clinical study, the investigators publicly confronted the FDA over its position. They objected to the agency changing the approval requirements midstream by requiring the ursodiol-only patient group and argued that historical controls should suffice to show the effectiveness of ursodiol alone. In response, the FDA defended its Guidance letter, arguing that despite the letter's late issuance, manufacturers had been on notice of its requirements for some time. The FDA further indicated that using historical controls would be "difficult, but we have not ruled out that possibility." The agency still has not granted PMA to any biliary lithotripter, despite receiving substantial data demonstrating biliary ESWL's superiority to the historical ursodiol monotherapy controls.

To gather historical data on ursodiol monotherapy, the remaining lithotripter manufacturers, together with physicians investigating the technology, pooled their ursodiol-only data. The FDA, however, responded by requesting more information. Specifically, the agency required the previously submitted new drug application (NDA) data about ursodiol from Ciba–Geigy, the only firm with an approved ursodiol formulation [Actigall®]. But Ciba–Geigy refused to provide the data to the lithotripter manufacturers or to the FDA. Understandably, the manufacturers are exasperated: "If

FDA maintains its current position, manufacturers are likely to drop their efforts to obtain approval of lithotripsy for biliary use." The FDA recently refused even to file the PMA applications of two biliary lithotripter manufacturers based on their lack of data from patients randomized prospectively to ursodiol-only treatment.

At the same time, a series of additional studies has demonstrated the superior effectiveness of combination therapy. Even surgeons, who would be economic competitors of biliary ESWL users, have recently recognized that the proper management of gallstones requires a flexible, interdisciplinary approach, with biliary ESWL as the favored therapy for certain patients. Nothing in the statute prevents the FDA from acknowledging this new data; in fact, the agency is explicitly empowered to do so.

Manufacturers have attempted to comply with the FDA's requirement of prospective randomized studies of ESWL-plus-ursodiol and ursodiol monotherapy. Given the serious ethical concerns about the drug monotherapy, researchers are apparently unwilling or unable to recruit patients for such studies. The situation appears deadlocked: The manufacturers cannot generate the required studies, and the FDA has not renounced its guidelines. Although most of the available data show biliary ESWL to be safe and effective for a readily identifiable segment of patients, the treatment remains frozen in an unapproved state. * * *

The atmosphere of uncertainty currently surrounding medical device approval creates real social costs. FDA approval is an absolute necessity to market medical devices in the United States, so any agency inconsistency makes manufacturers' product development plans more risky. This riskiness in turn increases the cost of capital that corporations allocate to device development, and therefore raises the profit threshold at which any project has a positive net present value. If the FDA's decisionmaking remains volatile, an increasing number of marginally profitable, yet socially desirable, technologies will not reach patients. * * *

The FDA should not require a new device to represent an improvement over existing treatments for all patients. Rather, the agency should only demand reasonable scientific evidence that the device does what its makers claim. The FDA may choose, through its power to approve labeling and restrict the scope of a device's use, to narrow the approval accordingly. But the agency should not completely block the commercial distribution of a proven safe device for which there is reasonable evidence of effectiveness. * * * If such a device meets the high safety standard, more of the efficacy judgment should be shifted from the agency to the medical community. * * *

The correlation between safety and efficacy varies among devices. Safety and efficacy are strongly linked where the device's failure would expose a patient to danger and weakly linked where the primary safety concerns are unrelated to how well the device accomplishes its intended effect. An example of a device exhibiting a strong linkage is a cardiac defibrillator. A primary safety concern is the reliability of the delivered shocks. A defibrillator is used exclusively in lifesaving situations. Thus, in reviewing the defibrillator, the FDA could not evaluate efficacy independently from safety concerns. To the extent that efficacy merges with safety, the rigorous standard for safety must also be applied to those aspects of efficacy.

The biliary lithotripter, in contrast, exemplifies weak linkage. The device's principal short-term safety concern—the effect of shock waves on tissue surrounding the treated area—is independent from whether the lithotripter is ultimately effective in breaking up stones. This major safety risk arises from a side effect of the system's operation. In cases of such weak linkage between safety and efficacy, the FDA should apply an asymmetric standard: While the manufacturer must still make a strong showing of the device's safety, the agency should approve the product even given only limited effectiveness in achieving its intended clinical outcome. Here, the FDA's role should primarily be to assure full disclosure of the device's efficacy data to the medical community.

In the case of biliary lithotripsy, such an "inform the market" approach would have two significant benefits. First, this approach would allow the FDA to recognize biliary ESWL studies that are not formally part of the data submitted by the manufacturers. Second, this approach would allow the FDA to approve biliary ESWL without conclusive proof that combination therapy of ESWL-plus-ursodiol is more effective than drug therapy alone. Given adequate assurances of safety, that decision would be left to the medical community. * * * By adhering to higher than threshold effectiveness standards, the FDA substitutes its decisions for the clinical choice of the physician. If a device is safe and sufficiently reliable data supports its effectiveness, the FDA has no reason to prohibit the device simply because the clinical role of the technology remains controversial.

Some analysts might argue that relaxing the standard for efficacy would flood the market with "snake oil" devices—products that, although safe, serve no real function and are essentially consumer scams. Despite this legitimate concern, a relaxed efficacy standard would not likely exacerbate the problem. First, even a highly effective device can easily be used on a patient who does not need it. In other words, a device's efficacy in any particular application will always ultimately depend on the clinical judgment of the patient's physician. Second, the makers of truly quack devices are not likely to seek FDA approval of their products. Rather, these manufacturers remain largely outside the regulatory system, and any additional stringency in the efficacy requirement would not deter such charlatans. Finally, several external restraints in the health care system limit the use of marginally effective technologies. These include the Medicare prospective payment system, which rewards efficient patient treatment, the separate requirement of approval of Medicare reimbursement by the Health Care Financing Administration (HCFA) [now CMS], utilization review by insurance companies, and the threat of medical malpractice liability. In particular, HCFA's separate review of a device's effectiveness in the actual practice setting may render the FDA's broad efficacy inquiry redundant.

Even if one could safely relegate the problem of fraudulent cures to a curiosity of a bygone era (and unfortunately that is not true), the problem of the subtlety and complexity of modern medical devices would remain. Practitioners may be unable to discern the effectiveness of a device prior to its use. Certainly, efficacy should remain an essential prong of the FDA's test for device approval. But the agency should only require reliable studies to establish the device's effectiveness in an identifiable group of patients. The FDA should not force manufacturers to prove that a device meets some substantive standard of efficacy relative to other therapeutic options. Once the threshold showing of efficacy has been made, and safety is clearly established, the medical community—not the FDA—should define the precise place of the technology in the existing array of treatment options.

The excessive involvement of the FDA presents several potential social costs. Overly stringent device review may deprive a physician of a diagnostic or therapeutic choice that may be optimal for a particular patient, thereby resulting in lower quality or more expensive care. Furthermore, excessive regulation discourages innovation and development; a prolonged battle with the FDA may deprive a manufacturer of the financial resources necessary to bring the technology to market. Nascent and incompletely proven technologies with the potential to blossom into medical staples may die prematurely. Even if the manufacturer has the financial resources to finish development, the potential for the device may be stunted. The FDA's denial of premarket approval—or an excessive delay in granting approval—broadcasts to the medical community that the technology is suspect, chilling the potential market. When safe and effective devices are squelched in this manner, society suffers a net loss. * * *

There is a final reason for extending PMA to safe devices when there is substantial, although vigorously debated, evidence of clinical efficacy. In the 1990 Act, Congress significantly enhanced the FDA's postmarket enforcement powers. The agency is therefore much more capable of correcting any error of mistaken approval. * * * In light of the FDA's power to monitor the use of devices and its authority to prohibit such use should problems emerge, the preemptive exclusion of a safe but controversially effective technology like biliary ESWL is even less justified. In such situations, no sound reason exists for the FDA to limit access to the device. * * *

NOTES AND QUESTIONS

1. *Latest on lithotripsy.* In 2000, the FDA finally approved a biliary lithotripter. Meanwhile, postapproval research found that renal lithotripsy significantly increased the risk of diabetes and hypertension. See Lawrence K. Altman, Blasting of Kidney Stones Has Risks, Study Reports, N.Y. Times, Apr. 10, 2006, at A18 ("The findings of the new study underscore the importance of following patients many years after they receive new therapies and how rarely studies do so because of costs and long-term research interest."); see also id. ("Stones in the kidneys and urinary tract system can be treated by a variety of other techniques that have improved during the 25 years that lithotripsy has been used [on an estimated one million U.S. patients].... [Conversely,] over the years, manufacturers have developed newer model machines that narrow the range of shock waves but that break up fewer stones."). The agency continues to face occasional criticism from device sponsors for changing approval requirements after initially signing off on proposed clinical trials. See, e.g., Jonathan D. Rockoff, J & J, FDA Clash over Device—Company Cries Foul After Agency, in Rejecting New Product, Requests More Data, Wall St. J., Feb. 18, 2011, at B2.

2. *Initial classifications*. A dozen years after Congress enacted the Medical Device Amendments of 1976, the FDA finished issuing rules classifying medical devices. Of the almost 2,000 types identified, approximately 30% were assigned to Class I (such as bandages), 60% to Class II (such as blood pressure monitoring devices), and 10% to Class III (such as artificial heart valves). In 1990, Congress further amended the statute by directing the FDA to consider down-classifying Class III devices marketed before 1976. See 21 U.S.C. § 360e(i). In practice, the difference in the degree of control over Class I and Class II devices (or for that matter Class III devices not yet subject to PMA requirements) is small. Class I devices need only comply with general controls applicable to all medical devices such as GMPs and labeling requirements. The FDA has exempted many low-risk Class I devices from PMN requirements. See 59 Fed. Reg. 63,005 (1994). In addition to general controls and premarket notification, Class II devices must also comply with special controls such as performance standards (though the FDA has yet to finalize any) or postmarket surveillance. Conversely, a decision to demand PMAs for long-used Class III devices (rather than downclassifying them) can threaten to eliminate an entire mode of treatment, which might, for instance, happen if the agency follows a recent advisory committee recommendation concerning electroconvulsive therapy (ECT). See David Brown, FDA Panel Seeks More Testing of "Shock–Therapy" Devices, Wash. Post, Jan. 29, 2011, at A3; Duff Wilson, F.D.A. Panel Is Split on Electroshock Risks, N.Y. Times, Jan. 29, 2011, at B7 (explaining that the agency might take more than a year to make a decision and that any call for PMAs would give sellers a couple of years to submit additional evidence of safety and effectiveness, not necessarily requiring clinical trials); see also Max Fink & Michael A. Taylor, Electroconvulsive Therapy: Evidence and Challenges, 298 JAMA 330 (2007).

3. *Comparing premarket clearance and premarket approval*. As the Supreme Court noted in *Medtronic*, the vast majority of new devices have been introduced after the filing of a premarket notification (PMN) under § 510(k) of the Act. A PMN must contain proposed labeling and an explanation of how the device is substantially equivalent in intended use and technological characteristics to a particular predicate device. In addition to having the same intended use, the device must have the same technological characteristics as the predicate device or, if it has different technological characteristics, must not raise different questions of safety and effectiveness than the predicate device. If a seller subsequently makes significant changes to the device, it must file either a supplement to the original PMN or a brand new PMN. See United States v. An Article of Device ... "Stryker," 607 F.Supp. 990, 996–97 (W.D.Mich.1985). In a recent report, the Institute of Medicine concluded that shortcomings in this system were beyond repair. See Inst. of Med., Medical Devices and the Public's Health: The FDA 510(k) Clearance Process at 35 Years (2011); see also 76 Fed. Reg. 45,825 (2011) (requesting comments on the report); Barry Meier, Fight over Medical Device Rules, Sight Unseen, N.Y. Times, July 28, 2011, at A1 (describing preemptive strikes by the industry in advance of the IOM report's release); Barry Meier, Group Faults the F.D.A. on Oversight of Devices, N.Y. Times, Apr. 13, 2011, at B10 (summarizing GAO criticisms). See generally James M. Flaherty, Jr., Defending Substantial Equivalence: An Argument for the Continuing Validity of the 510(k) Premarket Notification Process, 63 Food & Drug L.J. 901 (2008); Michael VanBuren, Note, Closing the Loopholes in the Regulation of Medical Devices: The Need for Congress to Reevaluate Medical Device Regulation, 17 Health Matrix 441 (2007).

Both pathways appear to have become more stringent in recent years. See Andrew Pollack, Medical Treatment, out of Reach, N.Y. Times, Feb. 10, 2011, at B1 ("The F.D.A. last year granted 19 premarket approvals ... down from 48 in 2000. The average time to win an approval through the less stringent 510(k) pathway, which is used for most devices, rose to 116 days in fiscal year 2008 from 97 days in fiscal year 2002. Agency figures show there have been increases in the proportion of applications sent back for questioning."); id. ("Acknowledging industry concerns, the F.D.A. [recently] proposed creating an 'innovation pathway' aimed at speeding regulatory reviews of a small number of groundbreaking devices ... and announced measures it said would make the regulatory process more predictable for the vast majority of devices."). Sponsors of devices subject to PMA requirements increasingly complain of a phenomenon like the so-called "drug lag" that used to affect their brethren in the pharmaceutical industry. See id. ("[N]umerous device executives and venture capitalists said the F.D.A. has tightened regulatory oversight in the last couple of years. Not only does it take longer to get approval but it can take months or years to even begin a clinical trial necessary to gain approval."); id. ("Device companies have been seeking early approval in Europe for years because it is easier. In Europe, a device must be shown to be safe, while in the United States it must also be shown to be effective in treating a disease or condition. And European approvals are handled by third parties, not a powerful central agency ...."); Matthew Perrone, FDA Approval Process Faulted at Hearings on Medical Devices, Wash. Post, Feb. 22, 2011, at A11 (reporting an industry claim that it "typically takes them two years longer to get devices approved in the United States than in Europe").

4. *Mammary prostheses*. First marketed in 1962, newer versions of breast implants introduced after 1976 had required only a showing of substantial equivalence. In 1992, however, after concerns arose about the safety of silicone-gel implants (particularly suspicions that leaking silicone could trigger autoimmune diseases such as scleroderma and lupus), the FDA placed a moratorium on their sale and called for the filing of PMAs (less flattering saline-filled implants remained available). Although epidemiological studies have discredited claims of an association with systemic disease, the agency remained concerned about the number of implants that rupture, which can cause a local inflammatory response and painful scarring. After the completion of clinical trials, the agency approved a pair of PMAs, though subject to a postapproval study requirement and other restrictions. See David Brown & Christopher Lee, FDA Ends Ban on Silicone Implants: Safety Concerns Led to '92 Moratorium, Wash. Post, Nov. 18, 2006, at A1; see also Rob Stein, Silicone Breast Implants Reasonably Safe, FDA Says, Wash. Post, June 23, 2011, at A2 ("Nearly 400,000 women received the devices in the United States last year."). How does the agency weigh the risks and benefits of a cosmetic device? Should it only ensure the provision of full risk information, leaving recipients and plastic surgeons to make the final choice? Are mastectomy patients undergoing reconstructive surgery situated differently than women seeking augmentation? How about other cosmetic implants? See, e.g., Natasha Singer, Questions on Using Fillers Near Eyes, N.Y. Times, Nov. 20, 2008, at E3 (noting that the FDA "has approved dermal fillers like Restylane and Juvederm for treatment of facial wrinkles and folds" but subsequently raised some questions about the safety of these devices).

5. *What's in your (hip) pocket?* In 2003, DePuy Orthopaedics, a unit of Johnson & Johnson, began foreign sales of the Articular Surface Replacement (ASR), a hip "resurfacing" implant that required less of a femoral anchor (essentially just a metal cap on the tip of the thigh bone) than traditional hip replacement systems and used a shallower metal rather than plastic "cup" for the hip socket. Because of the novelty of such devices, however, the FDA required the filing of a PMA, and it would take the company four years to submit the necessary clinical trial data to the agency. In the meantime, DePuy filed a PMN for a hip implant (the ASR XL Acetabular System) that paired a traditional femoral anchor with the ASR cup, pointing to its own slightly older though still relatively novel metal-on-metal hip implant as a predicate device. In 2005, after receiving clearance from the FDA, the company introduced this device in the United States. Just four years later, after it could no longer ignore accumulating reports of problems with the ASR cup (including the discovery of shed metallic debris that caused serious localized muscle and bone damage as well as findings of elevated blood levels of cobalt and chromium in patients), DePuy abandoned its pending PMA and began phasing out worldwide sales of these devices, finally undertaking a recall in 2010. Thousands of recipients have undergone revision surgery for an implant designed to last at least 15 years. For detailed accounts of this debacle, see Barry Meier, The Implants Loophole, N.Y. Times, Dec. 17, 2010, at B1 (adding that FDA also had allowed Zimmer "to sell a cup used in its unapproved hip resurfacing implant as part of a standard hip replacement"); Natasha Singer, Hip Implants Are Recalled by J. & J. Unit, N.Y. Times, Aug. 27, 2010, at B1; see also Barnaby J. Feder, F.D.A. Approves a Hip Resurfacing Implant, N.Y. Times, July 4, 2007, at C4 (reporting that the agency had granted PMAs filed by a couple of other manufacturers of such devices on the condition that surgeons first complete a training program offered by the companies); Barry Meier, Challenges Rise as Metallic Hips Fail at Fast Rate, N.Y. Times, Oct. 1, 2011, at A1; Jonathan D. Rockoff & Dionne Searcey, Hip Joints Set off New Rush to Court, Wall St. J., July 8, 2011, at B8 (reporting that about 1,000 lawsuits have been filed so far).

6. *Knee deep in another scandal?* In 2005, ReGen Biologics filed a § 510(k) notification for its Menaflex® Collagen Scaffold, a bovine-derived tissue implant used to repair a torn meniscus in the knee, claiming substantial equivalence to existing surgical meshes used to repair shoulders, hernias and bladders (apparently, just one year earlier, the company had begun work on a PMA but ran into various problems conducting a clinical trial). FDA staff repeatedly rejected the PMN and expressed concerns about the supporting data. Nonetheless, in 2008, after the Commissioner met with members of New Jersey's Democratic congressional delegation (all of whom had received sizeable campaign contributions from ReGen), the director of CDRH countermanded his subordinates and cleared the device. See Alicia Mundy, Political Lobbying Drove FDA Process, Wall St. J., Mar. 6, 2009, at A1. Less than one year later, after the change of administrations (and the resignations of the FDA Commissioner and CDRH director), the agency decided to reconsider the matter. See Lyndsey Layton, FDA Reports Political Pressure over Implant: Approved Knee Device Will Be Reviewed, Wash. Post, Sept. 25, 2009, at A21; Alicia Mundy, FDA Wrestles with Undoing Decision, Wall St. J., Mar. 22, 2010, at B1. Ultimately, the agency concluded that political pressure had so tainted its review process as to require revocation of the PMN. See Gardiner Harris, F.D.A. Vows to Revoke Approval of Device, N.Y. Times, Oct. 15, 2010, at A22 ("The F.D.A. had never before admitted that it approved a drug or device mistakenly, never rescinded such an approval without citing new information about the product, never admitted that a regulatory decision was influenced by politics, and never accused a former commissioner of questionable conduct."). In the spring of 2011, after declining to exercise its right to pursue an internal agency appeal, ReGen filed a judicial challenge in the federal district court in D.C., calling the FDA's decision arbitrary and capricious. Cf. Lars Noah, A Miscarriage in the Drug Approval Process?: Mifepristone Embroils the FDA in Abortion Politics, 36 Wake Forest L. Rev. 571, 592–93 (2001) ("An agency under new leadership cannot simply revoke a product approval as improvidently granted.... It would be most unusual for the FDA to propose withdrawing a recently approved drug on the basis of nothing more than a re-evaluation of the same evidence that it had previously reviewed, though it would not be entirely unprecedented.").

7. *Device reclassification.* The FDA requires that reclassification petitions provide:

> [E]vidence from well-controlled investigations, partially controlled studies, studies and objective trials without matched controls, well-documented case histories conducted by qualified experts, and reports

> of significant human experience with a marketed device, from which it can fairly and responsibly be concluded by qualified experts that there is reasonable assurance of the safety and effectiveness of a device under its conditions of use. The evidence required may vary according to the characteristics of the device, its conditions of use, the existence and adequacy of warnings and restrictions and the extent of experience with its use. Isolated case reports, random experience, reports lacking sufficient details to permit scientific evaluation, and unsubstantiated opinions are not regarded as valid scientific evidence to show safety and effectiveness.

21 C.F.R. § 860.7(c)(2). In 2001, for instance, the agency switched annuloplasty rings, which are used to repair heart valves, from Class III to Class II, but then serious adverse event reports for these implanted life-saving devices rose dramatically, raising questions about the wisdom of the FDA's decision. See Jason Grotto & Deborah L. Shelton, Heart Rings Get a Pass, Chi. Trib., May 22, 2011, at A1.

Contact Lens Manufacturers Association v. FDA

766 F.2d 592 (D.C.Cir.1985).

■ GINSBURG, RUTH BADER, CIRCUIT JUDGE:

* * * Congress itself was not positioned to determine the appropriate classification of every medical device then in existence or yet to be invented; nor could it describe the statutory categories with sufficient precision to ensure that each device would simply fall into the proper class of its own accord. The legislators therefore charged the FDA with the task of implementing the Amendments, and thus of essaying judgments appropriate to ensure safe and effective medical devices without stifling innovative technology.

Congress drew several initial bright lines, however, that significantly affected the classification process. * * * [U]nder provisions labeled "transitional," class III ranking automatically attached to "any device intended for human use ... which the [FDA] in a notice published in the *Federal Register* before the enactment date has declared to be a new drug." 21 U.S.C. § 360j(*l*)(1)(E). The FDA could later reclassify any device that, for whatever reason, had been "overclassified," but this remedy required a proffer of "new information," id. § 360c(e)—or, as the FDA formulated the standard, "valid scientific evidence" of safety and effectiveness. 21 C.F.R. §§ 860.7, 860.123(a)(6). The instant petition concerns the first attempt ever to reclassify a medical device committed to class III by the Amendments' "transitional provisions." Contact Lens Manufacturers Association (CLMA) challenges the FDA's withdrawal of the agency's own proposal to transfer certain rigid gas permeable (RGP) contact lenses from class III to class I. * * *

Contact lenses consisting almost entirely of polymethylmethacrylate (PMMA)—"hard" lenses—have been marketed in the United States since the early 1950s. Because the public's pre-Amendments experience with PMMA lenses was broad and substantially injury-free, these lenses will remain outside the Amendments' classification scheme until the FDA formally decides where to place them. That decision has not yet been made; three years ago, however, the FDA proposed to regulate PMMA lenses as class II devices. Hydroxyethylmethacrylate (HEMA) lenses—"soft" lenses—are a more recent development. The FDA first approved a HEMA lens in 1971. In September 1975, citing their relative novelty, the FDA announced that HEMA lenses—indeed all lenses "other than those consisting [almost wholly] of PMMA"—had been and would continue to be regarded as "new drugs" * * * *

The product at issue in this case is said to combine attractive features of both lens types described above. "RGP lenses" (like "PMMA lenses" or "HEMA lenses") is a generic term that indicates no single mix of polymers or manufacturing process; but all lenses properly called RGP share certain salient characteristics. The ideal RGP lens permits both the superior visual acuity attainable with a hard lens and the "direct transmission of oxygen to corneal tissue" that the hard lens regrettably prevents. Nearly a million people in the United States wore RGP lenses in 1982. As of 1975, however, RGP lenses, like soft lenses, were comparatively new and untested; since enactment of the Amendments the FDA has regarded RGP lenses as "transitional" class III devices by reason of the same September 1975 *Federal Register* announcement that resulted in placement of HEMA lenses in the class III category.

Consequently, before a manufacturer can market a particular RGP lens to the public, the manufacturer must demonstrate the safety and effectiveness of that lens convincingly enough to gain the FDA's pre-market approval. "In effect," the manufacturer must obtain "a license to market the device." (If RGP lenses were class I devices, the manufacturer would be required to make the showing CLMA regards as less burdensome that the lens was "substantially equivalent" to another RGP lens already on the market.) The expense of obtaining a class III device license—"estimated at $750,000–$1,000,000 (over and above development costs)," the bulk of which goes to clinical investigation—constitutes a significant barrier to entry. * * *

CLMA petitioned the FDA to reclassify RGP lenses from class III to class II. Pursuant to 21 U.S.C. § 360c(b) (1982), the FDA referred the petition to an expert advisory committee, the Ophthalmic Section of the Ophthalmic; Ear, Nose, and Throat; and Dental Devices Panel, which recommended the following month that the petition be granted on the condition that CLMA submit additional materials. * * * [T]he FDA announced that, although CLMA's upgraded submissions continued to be inadequate, "CLMA's objectives are meritorious," and therefore the FDA intended to adopt the reclassification proposal as the agency's own. * * *

[One] year after the FDA's initial indication of interest, the reclassification proposal emerged. "Based on a careful review of new, publicly available, valid scientific evidence," the proposal stated, "FDA has tentatively concluded that ... certain [RGP lenses] should be reclassified into class I." * * * The proposal extensively and favorably discussed the clinical data cited by reclassification proponents. Nevertheless, the FDA invited comment on a range of issues. * * * [After several extensions of the comment period and a public hearing,] CLMA's once high expectations for the RGP proposal ended: the FDA repudiated its "tentative conclusions" and withdrew its reclassification proposal altogether.

The FDA attributed its changed view to "comments and oral and written testimony that required it to reevaluate the evidence upon which it relied in the proposal, and to evaluate additional information." First, the agency explained, various commenters had demonstrated that the clinical studies cited as proof of the safety and effectiveness of CAB and polyacrylate-silicone lenses then on the market did not, after all, add up to "valid scientific evidence." Second, even if the studies did constitute such evidence, they were "insufficient to justify reclassification" because they "failed to establish the safety and effectiveness of [RGP] lenses as a generic type of device." Given the countless conceivable combinations of "polymer formulation and manufacturing processes," and the corresponding variations in lenses' "nontoxicity, biocompatibility, [and] light transmission," the FDA could not conclude that mere membership in the family of "RGP lenses" clinched any particular lens' safety and effectiveness.

The FDA thus determined that no reclassification of RGP lenses could provide reasonable assurance of safety and effectiveness: class I status was not feasible because the FDA could not determine whether a new lens was "substantially equivalent" to an already-marketed lens without securing a wealth of detailed information about both lenses' composition and manufacture; and class II status was not in order because, even if such information could be gathered for the purpose of establishing a "performance standard" and measuring new lenses against it, conformity with the standard would not guarantee that a lens would function safely and effectively in the human eye. "In short, FDA learned that at this stage in [RGP lens] development, there is no substitute for clinical trials [i.e., class III status] to provide reasonable assurance of the safety and effectiveness of these lenses."

CLMA complains, in petitioning for review, that the FDA has disregarded a medical consensus favoring reclassification and has rendered insensible the requirement of "valid scientific evidence." We recognize substantial merit in CLMA's argument that RGP lenses should not be locked within so tight a regulatory regime. Nonetheless, we cannot disturb the FDA's decision. The agency acted within an area of its expertise, it ruled in a manner at least arguably consistent with the statutory scheme, and it considered the matter in a detailed, adequately reasoned fashion. We therefore defer to the agency and affirm its judgment. * * *

The FDA has consistently maintained that proponents of reclassification assume the burden of demonstrating—through "publicly available, valid scientific evidence"—that the device's present classification is inappropriate and that the proposed classification will provide reasonable assurance of the device's safety and effectiveness. We cannot fault the FDA's assignment of the burden of proof to those seeking to change the status quo. Thus, CLMA's claim that maintenance of class III status for RGP lenses lacks record support, even if true, is off target. More to the point, CLMA asserts that the FDA in these proceedings has adopted an unreasonably strict view of what constitutes "valid scientific evidence." Though CLMA presses this argument with vigor, we are mindful that in such matters generalist courts see through a glass darkly and should be especially reluctant to upset an expert agency's judgment that a party has failed to adduce sufficient scientific proof of safety and effectiveness.

The FDA's rationale for withdrawing its reclassification proposal opens with the rather belated assertion that nothing in the record establishes the safety and effectiveness of RGP lenses now on the market. Facets of this position are unsettling. In justification of its current stance, the FDA disparaged the same studies it had once acclaimed, and retracted its earlier assertion that "the safety of the device also is shown by the absence of reports in the literature of serious, irreversible adverse effects on health presented by the device." But the reclassification proposal specifically asked for comment on whether "the data ... constitute sufficient 'valid scientific evidence.'" We would be denying the value of notice-and-comment rulemaking were we to condemn the FDA for altering its outlook on the basis of submissions it received.

Citing its regulation declaring that "isolated case reports, random experience, reports lacking sufficient details to permit scientific evaluation, and unsubstantiated opinions are not regarded as valid scientific evidence to show safety or effectiveness," the FDA discounted the praises sung by dozens of "contact lens professionals" who favored reclassification and who reported that none of their patients had ever experienced serious problems with RGP lenses. We find the FDA's categorical belittlement of these eyewitness comments somewhat numbing, but we cannot gainsay the FDA's judgment that although such testimonials may suffice to disprove safety and effectiveness, they fail to establish with scientific rigor the absence of danger.

The FDA's ultimate resistance to conceding the safety and effectiveness of lenses now on the market is perhaps most remarkable because these are the very lenses already granted premarket approval on the application of particular manufacturers. The agency's demand for compelling proof on matters presumably demonstrated to it convincingly by the licensed manufacturers, however, is a conundrum the statute itself sets up. Under the Amendments, trade secret information that a manufacturer submits to secure premarket approval may not be cited by the FDA or any third party in aid of reclassification proposals. Much as in patent law, Congress has determined that free riding is too high a price to pay for vigorous competition among medical device manufacturers; the FDA is not at liberty to disregard this determination. * * *

Of decisive importance, however, the FDA's refusal to reclassify RGP lenses does not stand or fall with the FDA's limited-purpose agnosticism about the safety and effectiveness of lenses currently on the market. Independently sufficient and far more persuasive is the FDA's determination that all reclassification proposals to date "inadequately characterize" the class of RGP lenses. That is, even if the available evidence demonstrates the safety and effectiveness of lenses already on the market, this evidence cannot be taken as proof that any RGP lens a manufacturer might create will meet the statutory requirements; thus, at least for the present, the premarket approval process is unavoidable. "The safety and effectiveness of a contact lens is a function of the complex interrelationship of material, design, and manufacture that results in a unique set of physical, chemical, mechanical, and optical characteristics." Alter any one of these variables, the FDA now maintains, and you have a unique new lens whose safety and effectiveness are unknown and, without thorough clinical testing, unknowable. * * * The inadequacy of generic characterization of RGP lenses thus emerges as a mainstay of the FDA's contention that nothing short of lens-by-lens clinical testing and premarket approval will ensure safety and effectiveness. * * *

We are cognizant of the ironies effected by the statute and the FDA's initially insecure administration of it. Considering the difficulty of the assignment Congress entrusted to the agency, and the respect we owe to the FDA's expert judgment, however, we cannot say that the action we have been asked to review is unlawful. * * * We hold simply and only that at this juncture, the FDA has not been shown to have proceeded without reason or regard for the statute in withdrawing its proposal to reclassify RGP lenses. The petition for review is accordingly dismissed and the challenged decision is affirmed.

Ethicon, Inc. v. FDA

762 F.Supp. 382 (D.D.C.1991).

■ GREEN, DISTRICT JUDGE:

* * * Plaintiff Ethicon, Inc. manufactures Vicryl poly(glycolide/L-lactide) absorbable surgical sutures ("poly (g/l) sutures"). Ethicon challenges the decision by defendants Food and Drug Administration (FDA) and Secretary of Health and Human Services Dr. Louis W. Sullivan to reclassify a generic class of poly (g/l) sutures from Class III to Class II under the Medical Device Amendments to the Federal Food, Drug, and Cosmetic Act. Ethicon seeks a judgment declaring the reclassification decision null and void for FDA's alleged failure to fulfill both substantive and procedural statutory requirements for the reclassification of medical devices. * * *

[D]efendant-intervenor United States Surgical Corporation (USSC) petitioned FDA to reclassify a generic class of poly (g/l) sutures from Class III to Class II. FDA referred the petition to its Administrative Panel on General and Plastic Surgery Devices, and a notice of the Panel's meeting was duly announced. The Panel received written testimony and held a hearing. * * * At the close of the hearing, the Panel unanimously recommended that poly (g/l) sutures be reclassified from Class III to Class II. * * *

FDA issued a letter ruling granting USSC's petition and reclassifying the generic class of poly (g/l) sutures. FDA found that sufficient publicly available scientific evidence existed to enable development of a performance standard for poly (g/l) sutures, the generic class of poly (g/l) sutures was well-characterized, and reclassification was warranted. It specifically commented that "a class III designation for absorbable poly (g/l) surgical sutures constitutes overregulation." FDA defined the generic class as including any "absorbable sterile, flexible strand as prepared and synthesized from homopolymers and copolymers made from glycolide and/or L-lactide." It thus determined that the generic class encompasses Vicryl and Dexon and any other poly (g/l) sutures that in the future could be shown to be substantially equivalent to either of them. * * *

Ethicon petitioned FDA to reconsider the reclassification decision and asked for a stay pending the decision on its petition. * * * FDA issued a letter ruling denying Ethicon's motion for a stay and petition for reconsideration. * * * Ethicon argues that FDA reached its reclassification decision improperly by failing to satisfy both the substantive and procedural statutory requirements for reclassification. * * *

Ethicon's first set of arguments centers on its contention that FDA's decision was grounded in an "inadequate characterization of the generic class" of poly (g/l) sutures. Ethicon faults FDA for wrongly generalizing from existing information, for assuming that all poly (g/l) sutures with the same glycolide-L-lactide ratios as the two on the market are "essentially identical." Ethicon alleges that by basing the reclassification on published evidence limited to Vicryl and Dexon, FDA contradicted the approach it followed in the *Contact Lens* case, where FDA denied reclassification because it determined that insufficient information existed to assure safety and effectiveness of certain contact lenses or to identify a generic class of such lenses for the purpose of reclassification. Finally, Ethicon claims that "the few paragraphs found in the publicly available literature that do discuss the manufacturing processes of poly (g/l) sutures are no substitute for the detailed description ... necessary to adequately understand the manufacturing variables and conditions that may affect the safety and effectiveness of any particular suture."

A review of the regulatory structure governing the determination of generic classes, briefly described above, and of *Contact Lens* reveals the lack of merit in Ethicon's arguments. First of all, there is no requirement that a device in a generic class be "essentially identical" to all others in its class. Rather, the device need only be "substantially equivalent." * * * The agency's characterization of a generic class or type of device is fact-specific, as is evident from the factors FDA's regulations require it to consider in making the determination that a device is safe and effective. The Panel must consider, inter alia, the persons for whose use the device is intended, the conditions and intended conditions of use of the device, the probable benefit to health from use weighed against probable injury or illness from use, and the reliability of the device. Inevitably the requisite evidence will vary, according to "the characteristics of the device, its conditions of use, the existence and adequacy of warnings and other restrictions, and the extent of experience with its use." * * *

[T]he instant controversy ultimately turns on a disagreement between the parties as to the interpretation of the statutory definition of a Class II device—in other words, what constitutes "sufficient information to establish a performance standard" that will "provide reasonable assurance of the safety and effectiveness of the device." In essence, Ethicon is disputing the quantity and quality of the evidence FDA considered—it is disagreeing with the conclusion that the evidence supports a finding of safety and effectiveness.

In FDA's view, "sufficient information" for evaluating a device requires that valid scientific evidence in the record correlates the control of performance parameters to safe and effective use of the device. Thus, the question is whether the administrative record contains sufficient information for the agency to understand the device and sufficient evidence to demonstrate that factors determining the device's safety and effectiveness are controllable. An examination of the two letter rulings and of the supporting administrative record make clear that FDA more than satisfied its mandate. * * *

After four years of study and after the unanimous recommendation of an independent panel composed of eminent physicians and researchers, FDA determined that poly (g/l) sutures posed no threat to the health or safety of the public that would prevent them from being more than adequately regulated as Class II devices under the Act. The court finds that "FDA has permissibly exercised its considerable discretion," and indeed reasonably acted, and therefore defers to the agency's decision. * * *

NOTES AND QUESTIONS

1. *Competition by other means.* Why would Ethicon resist an effort to partially deregulate a class of products that it sells? Should that in any way influence the court's analysis?

2. *Comparing devices to drugs.* Although the PMA process looks comparable to the NDA process, significant differences exist in the type of safety and effectiveness evidence required for approval. For instance, sponsors cannot conduct double-blind controlled trials of effectiveness in most cases because both the investigator and the patient will know whether or not the treatment uses the experimental device. Cf. Marlene Cimons, Fetal Cell Implants Improve Parkinson's Patients, L.A. Times, Feb. 1, 2001, at A16 (describing the controversial use of sham brain surgery including phony incisions to serve as a placebo control in a clinical trial). Moreover, unlike metabolized drugs whose mode of action may remain something of a mystery, medical devices have clear mechanical properties that one can assess without the same need for clinical trials. For instance, engineers usually can test the durability of materials by subjecting prototypes to simulated use in the lab, though failure analysis after actual use in patients may provide important additional information about questions such as biocompatibility. In addition, fundamental differences exist in the way drugs and devices are developed and used:

1. Medical devices are subject to frequent incremental innovations;

2. Devices generally are used by health professionals, while drugs are used primarily by patients;

3. New devices generally originate with physicians, whereas new drugs originate within industry;

4. The annual sales volume for a medical device is typically only a fraction of the sales volume for a drug, and often could not sustain the cost of a preapproval application;

5. Many devices are developed by small companies working with physicians. The viability of these companies depends on their ability to react promptly to advancements in technology and the changing needs of the physician. Complex or prolonged review would jeopardize their survival.

See Peter Barton Hutt et al., The Standard of Evidence Required for Premarket Approval Under the Medical Device Amendments of 1976, 47 Food & Drug L.J. 605, 612–13 (1992); see also id. at 625 ("[U]nlike drugs, many devices are not therapeutic in themselves, but instead are used as tools of a health professional. Therefore, their safety and effectiveness largely depends on the skill of the professional user."); Richard A. Merrill, The Architecture of Government Regulation of Medical Products, 82 Va. L. Rev. 1753, 1800 (1996) ("The Medical Device Amendments represented a conscious legislative attempt to avoid what some viewed as the innovation-stifling effects of FDA's drug approval system."); id. at 1808 ("[T]he Amendments were promoted as a new type of regulatory statute, one that would assure careful review of the few high risk technologies but permit less intrusive, less costly regulation of most devices.").

For these reasons, the FDCA provision governing PMAs, which by definition would be required only for the most innovative of medical devices, differs in important respects from the counterpart provision governing NDAs: it calls for something less than "substantial evidence" of effectiveness, and it explicitly provides for risk-benefit balancing when deciding whether a device is safe and effective. See 21 U.S.C. § 360c(a); see also David A. Kessler et al., The Federal Regulation of Medical Devices, 317 New Eng. J. Med. 357, 359 (1987) ("This statutory standard is less rigorous than the standard for the approval of new drugs.... For devices, data from well-controlled scientific studies are acceptable, but so is 'valid scientific evidence' from which experts can reasonably conclude that the device will be effective."). For a look at other countries' approaches to medical device regulation, see John Y. Chai, Medical Device Regulation in the United States and the European Union: A Comparative Study, 55 Food & Drug L.J. 57 (2000); Sharon Frank, An Assessment of the Regulations on Medical Devices in the European Union, 56 Food & Drug L.J. 99 (2001).

3. *Advisory committees and third party reviews.* Recall that the FDA sought assistance from the NAS when it undertook the "DESI" reviews of drugs approved before 1962. Even today, the agency maintains a large network of advisory committees composed of independent experts that will meet periodically to consider the merits of NDAs undergoing final review, and the FDA typically abides by the advice that it receives. Concerns have arisen about the independence of these outside experts. See Peter Lurie et al., Financial Conflict of Interest Disclosure and Voting Patterns at Food and Drug Administration Drug Advisory Committee Meetings, 295 JAMA 1921 (2006); Saurabh Anand, Note, Using Numerical Statutory Interpretation to Improve Conflict of Interest Waiver Procedures at the FDA, 83 S. Cal. L. Rev. 649 (2010); Ian J. Kellogg, Note, Prescription for a Cure: Does the FDA's Draft Guidance Adequately Manage Advisory Committee Members' Conflicts of Interest?, 19 Stan. L. & Pol'y Rev. 300 (2008). But see Thomas Stossel & David Shaywitz, Op–Ed., What's Wrong with Money in Science?, Wash. Post, July 2, 2006, at B3 (decrying "the witch hunt against supposed conflicts of interest in scientific and medical research," and lambasting *JAMA*'s publication of the study by Lurie et al.). In the case of medical devices, Congress mandated that similar advisory panels review PMAs as well as reclassification proposals. See 21 U.S.C. § 360c(b), (c), (f)(2)(B); see also Hutt et al., 47 Food & Drug L.J. at 618 n.69 ("In part, these provisions were an attempt to address medical practitioners' concerns that determinations of device safety and effectiveness, if left solely to the FDA, would be influenced by the FDA's institutional propensity to be too demanding of new technologies."). See generally Lars Noah, Scientific "Republicanism": Expert Peer Review and the Quest for Regulatory Deliberation, 49 Emory L.J. 1033, 1054–57 (2000). Critics of FDA delays in approving medical technologies have urged greater reliance on reviews conducted by non-governmental entities. See Charles J. Walsh & Alissa Pyrich, Rationalizing the Regulation of Prescription Drugs and Medical Devices: Perspectives on Private Certification and Tort Reform, 48 Rutgers L. Rev. 883, 987–1016 (1996). In FDAMA, Congress authorized a limited system of third party reviews for certain PMNs. See 21 U.S.C. § 360m; see also Karen M. Becker et al., Scientific Dispute Resolution: First Use of Provision 404 of the Food and Drug Administration Modernization Act of 1997, 58 Food & Drug L.J. 211 (2003).

4. *User fees.* Exactly one decade after Congress first authorized the FDA to charge user fees to review prescription drug applications, it granted the agency similar authority with regard to devices. See Medical Device User Fee and Modernization Act of 2002, Pub. L. No. 107–250, tit. I, 116 Stat. 1588 (codified at 21 U.S.C. §§ 379i–379j). Applicants must pay $220,000 for the agency to review a PMA (unless they qualify for a 75% discount as a small business), but it costs $4,000 for a PMN. See 76 Fed. Reg. 45,826 (2011); Medical Device Industry Fights FDA over Approval Speed, Fees, Chi. Trib., Sept. 22, 2006, at 6.

5. *Home test kits.* The FDA has approved several diagnostic devices for home use, including tests for pregnancy, blood sugar, and cholesterol. See Judy Mann, In the Privacy of Your Own Home, Wash. Post, Apr. 22, 1994, at E3. Approved tests for HIV and hepatitis C require a finger prick for blood that gets sent to a laboratory, which must then offer counseling when it reports the results back to the consumer. For almost two decades, however, the FDA resisted authorizing over-the-counter sale of in vitro diagnostic devices to test for HIV. See Gardiner Harris, F.D.A. to Weigh At–Home Testing for AIDS Virus, N.Y. Times, Oct. 13, 2005, at A1 ("A 1987 application for an at-home AIDS test kit led to years of controversy.... Federal regulators stalled the application for nine years, and at-home AIDS testing never caught on."); see also Steven R. Salbu, HIV Home Testing and the FDA: The Case for Regulatory Restraint, 46 Hastings L.J. 403, 454–55 (1995) ("[T]he FDA should not assess evidence that is not relevant to the evaluation of the primary safety and effectiveness of a medical device.... Accordingly, it is inappropriate for the FDA to consider ... whether [HIV] home testing reduces the likelihood that recipients of positive results will receive effective counseling."); cf. Denise Grady, Quick H.I.V. Test Is Giving Too Many False Positives, N.Y. Times, Dec. 10, 2005, at A16. What sorts of issues might have confronted the agency when it reviewed home test kits intended to screen children for illicit drug use? See Julie Davidow, Surge in Home Diagnostic Kits Provides Doctor in a Box, Seattle Post–Intel., Mar. 29, 2006, at A1 ("This month, the FDA approved the first at-home test for prescription drugs. The test detects methadone, oxycodone, anti-depressants, barbiturates and benzodiazepines, as well as a battery of illicit drugs in urine."); see also Chap. 11(C)(1) (discussing genetic tests).

C. POSTMARKET SURVEILLANCE AND RESPONSE

The FDA's premarket review process cannot possibly identify all of the risks associated with new medical technologies. See Gen. Accounting Office, FDA Drug Review: Post Approval Risks 3 (1990) (concluding that more than half of all drugs approved between 1976 and 1985 had serious risks that were discovered only after approval); Vanessa Eng, Note, Drug Safety: It's a Learning Process, 24 St. John's J. Legal Comment. 159 (2009); Bernadette Tansey, What FDA Approval Means, S.F. Chron., Mar. 3, 2005, at C1. In part this represents an unavoidable limitation in conducting clinical trials. It also poses important questions about the relative costs and benefits of a regulatory process that focuses most of its resources on premarket review. The agency's postmarket surveillance programs attempt to (1) detect previously unknown adverse reactions associated with a drug product; (2) evaluate in more detail the product's known risks; (3) uncover adverse reactions that arise from interactions with other products; and (4) uncover adverse reactions peculiar to particular segments of the patient population. See FDA, Managing the Risks from Medical Products Use: Creating a Risk Management Framework 52 (1999); see also Aaron S. Kesselheim et al., The Rise and Fall of Natrecor for Congestive Heart Failure: Implications for Drug Policy, 25 Health Aff. 1095 (2006); Symposium, Post–Marketing Surveillance: What FDA Really Wants, 62 Food & Drug L.J. no. 3 (2007).

For prescription drugs, the FDA has created a system of mandatory adverse drug experience (ADE) reporting by manufacturers, coupled with voluntary health care professional reporting, to monitor the safety of products after they enter the marketplace. The agency defines an ADE as "any adverse event associated with the use of a drug in humans, whether or not considered drug related." 21 C.F.R. § 314.80(a). Within 15 days of discovery, manufacturers must submit a report to the FDA of any ADE that is both "serious" and "unexpected," and they must "promptly investigate" such events. See id. § 314.80(c)(1). The agency demands such follow-up in part because raw ADE reports are little more than red-flags of potential safety problems. For instance, even if confirmed (and even if the treating physician has discounted all alternative explanations), patients may have experienced what amounts to a negative placebo effect. See Arthur J. Barsky et al., Nonspecific Medication Side Effects and the Nocebo Phenomenon, 287 JAMA 622 (2002).

For non-serious or expected ADEs, drug manufacturers need only submit periodic reports (quarterly for the first three years and annually thereafter), which must contain summaries of all 15–day reports, along with reports of other ADEs, and explanations of any action that the manufacturer has taken in response to the reported information. See 21 C.F.R. § 314.80(c)(2)(i)–(ii); cf. Marc Kaufman, Reports to FDA Were Late, Watchdog Says, Wash. Post, Aug. 4, 2004, at E2 (describing a consumer activist's allegations that the manufacturer of the statin drug Crestor® should have reported cases of rhabdomyolisis more quickly as "unexpected" ADEs even though already listed in labeling as a side effect at high doses, adding that the FDA rarely brings criminal charges against drug companies for violating these rules). When revising its rules governing the format and content of prescription drug labeling, the FDA decided to highlight the original approval date so that physicians could exercise greater caution when using newer products. See 71 Fed. Reg. 3922, 3936–37, 3973–74 (2006); cf. Mary K. Olson, Are Novel Drugs More Risky for Patients than Less Novel Drugs?, 23 J. Health Econ. 1135 (2004).

After a recent string of drug withdrawals and withering criticism over its handling of risk information discovered after approval, the agency promised to improve the way that it conducts postmarket surveillance. See Marc Kaufman & Brooke A. Masters, After Criticism, FDA Will Strengthen Drug Safety Checks, Wash. Post, Nov. 6, 2004, at A12; Shankar Vedantam, FDA Revamps Process for Safety of Drugs After Approval, Wash. Post, Jan. 31, 2007, at A6 (describing the agency's response to an IOM report). For instance, the agency announced the creation of a board to advise it on newly discovered safety concerns. See Gardiner Harris, F.D.A. to Create Advisory Panel to Warn Patients About Drugs, N.Y. Times, Feb. 16, 2005, at A1 (reporting, however, that this move failed to appease critics who have "call[ed] for a more muscular drug safety center with far more employees that would be independent of the F.D.A. or at least independent of its drug review division"); see also Curt D. Furberg et al., The FDA and Drug Safety: A Proposal for Sweeping Changes, 166 Archives Internal Med. 1938 (2006); Margaret Gilhooley, Vioxx's History and the Need for Better Procedures and Better Testing, 37 Seton Hall L. Rev. 941 (2007); Marc Kaufman, FDA Is Criticized over Drugs' Safety Problems, Wash. Post, Apr. 24, 2006, at A5 (summarizing a GAO report, which "concluded that the agency's entire system for reviewing the safety of drugs already on the market is too limited and broadly flawed"). The agency also proposed amending its rules in order to expand both the scope and the depth of safety reporting, including new requirements for the reporting of medication errors. See 68 Fed. Reg. 12,406 (2003) (explaining that this represented an on-going effort to harmonize its requirements with international standards, including the use of the term "suspected adverse drug reaction" (SADR) in lieu of ADE, as well as to improve the quality of submitted information); see also Grant H. Castle & Brian Kelly, Global Harmonization Is Not All That Global: Divergent Approaches in Drug Safety, 63 Food & Drug L.J. 601 (2008). Eight years later, this rulemaking proceeding remains pending.

In sweeping amendments passed in 2007, Congress gave the agency greater powers and duties with regard to postapproval risks. See Food and Drug Administration Amendments Act of 2007 (FDAAA), Pub. L. No. 110–85, tit. IX, 121 Stat. 823, 922 (amending 21 U.S.C. § 355). For instance, it ordered the FDA to disclose information about approved drugs undergoing postapproval review because of ADEs. See id. § 915, 121 Stat. at 958 (codified at 21 U.S.C. § 355(r)(2)(D)) (requiring that the agency maintain a web site to post preliminary risk information in advance of potential labeling revisions); David Brown, FDA to List Drugs Being Investigated: Complaints Will Be Posted Quarterly, Wash. Post, Sept. 6, 2008, at A2 ("FDA officials said they realize that the new policy . . . may unintentionally alarm some patients."); see also Francesca L. Kritz, Why All the Drug Alerts? Step-up Signals FDA Bid for Renewed Trust, Wash. Post, Feb. 26, 2008, at F1 ("[T]he agency has begun issuing three new types of advisories: an 'early communication' that indicates a recently reported problem with a drug; a 'public health advisory' that advises consumers to speak with their doctors because a drug may pose a serious risk; and a Q & A for physicians to help them answer patient questions."). Such disclosures must, however, take care to avoid overreactions that may cause more harm than good. See Lisa M. von Biela, A Disclosure Dilemma: What You Don't Know Can Kill You, but So Can What You Do Know, 65 Food & Drug L.J. 317 (2010) (discussing challenges faced by the FDA when deciding whether and how to disclose low probability but high consequence risks associated with therapeutic products); Scott M. Lassman, Transparency and Innuendo: An Alternative to Reactive Over–Disclosure, Law & Contemp. Probs., Sum. 2006, at 69; Lars Noah, The Imperative to Warn: Disentangling the "Right to Know" from the "Need to Know" About Consumer Product Hazards, 11 Yale J. on Reg. 293, 385–90, 394–97 (1994).

For medical devices, the FDA's somewhat more rigorous postmarket surveillance system appears designed to compensate for its more flexible premarket review system. Because few devices are subjected to a full premarket evaluation, the postmarketing surveillance process becomes more significant. In 1976, Congress required that all manufacturers submit medical device reports (MDRs) to the FDA whenever deaths, serious injuries, or dangerous malfunctions occurred in association with the use of a medical device. Initially, reporting rates for medical devices were disappointing. See Gen. Accounting Office, Medical Devices: Early Warning of Problems Is Hampered by Severe Underreporting 3 (1986) (finding that less than 1% of adverse events associated with the use of medical devices in hospitals were reported to the FDA and that more serious events were less likely to be reported). In 1990, Congress expanded MDR requirements to impose reporting obligations on distributors and user facilities, and it mandated more structured postmarket surveillance for many high risk devices, though it later watered down some of these provisions. See generally Edward M. Basile & Beverly H. Lorell, The FDA's Regulation of Risk Disclosure for Implantable Cardioverter Defibrillators: Has Technology Outpaced the Agency's Regulatory Framework?, 61 Food & Drug L.J. 251 (2006); William H. Maisel, Safety Issues Involving Medical Devices, 294 JAMA 955 (2005); Bonnie Scott, Oversight Overhaul: Eliminating the Premarket Review of Medical Devices and Implementing a Provider–Centered Postmarket Surveillance Strategy, 66 Food & Drug L.J. 377 (2011); Marc Kaufman, More Heart Devices Malfunction: As Sophistication Has Grown, So Have Failures, Wash. Post, Sept. 17, 2005, at A7.

Nelson v. American Home Products Corp.

92 F.Supp.2d 954 (W.D.Mo.2000).

■ Whipple, District Judge:

Rodger Nelson lost his eyesight while he was taking Cordarone, a prescription heart medication manufactured and sold by American Home Products Corporation and Wyeth–Ayerst Laboratories Company (collectively referred to as "defendants"). This products liability lawsuit followed. To recover damages from defendants, plaintiffs Rodger and Lou Nelson must prove, among other things, that defendants' drug caused Nelson's lost eyesight. Defendants have moved for summary judgment on grounds that the Nelsons have failed to generate any issues of material fact that would permit a reasonable inference in their favor on the issue of causation. Specifically, defendants argue that the Nelsons have failed to produce any admissible evidence that would entitle a reasonable trier of fact to infer that defendants' drug caused Nelson's lost eyesight. * * *

The requisite proof for causation must go beyond that which is required by the Food and Drug Administration for reporting adverse drug effects or re-labeling to warn of the potential for adverse drug effects. The FDA requires such reporting and re-labeling regardless of whether a causal connection has been proved. * * * [I]nformation that defendants are required to report without regard to proof of causation cannot be cited later as an admission of causation. * * *

Defendants' labeling changes and notification letters merely relayed information about a possible association between their drug and optic neuropathy. Spontaneous reporting by a pharmaceutical company should be encouraged; it serves "as a signaling system for adverse drug reactions that may not have been detected during pre-market testing." Haggerty v. Upjohn Co., 950 F. Supp. 1160, 1164 (S.D.Fla.1996). Such reporting does not, however, indicate causation. Id.; see also Adverse Drug Reaction Monitoring, 314 New Eng. J. Med. 1589, 1591 (1996) ("Despite their usefulness, one or even many reports of adverse reactions often do not provide sufficient information to confirm that a drug caused the reaction. A reaction may be caused by the suspect drug, another drug that a patient is taking, or the underlying diseases for which the drug was prescribed; it may also be entirely coincidental."). Evidence of an association may be sufficient for formulation of a hypothesis that can later be tested and confirmed, but it is not proof of causation in the courtroom or the scientific community.

In this respect, it is important to note that the literature on which the Nelsons' experts rely consists solely of anecdotal case reports. While such case reports may be relevant to the question of whether defendants had notice of the possible ocular side effects of Cordarone, they are not, without more, reliable evidence of causation. The case reports cited by the Nelsons' experts simply inform their readers about a noted temporal association between amiodarone and optic neuropathy and the authors' hypotheses about the methodology of causation. The reports are mere compilations of reported occurrences. The authors did not attempt to isolate and investigate the effects of alternative causative agents. The reports themselves do not contain a testable and systemic inquiry into the mechanism of causation. At most, these case reports relay a basis for scientific hypotheses; they do not demonstrate a causal link sufficient for admission to a finder of fact in court.

United States v. Laerdal Manufacturing Corp.

853 F.Supp. 1219 (D.Or.1994).

■ FRYE, DISTRICT JUDGE:

* * * Under the MDR regulations, the manufacturer of a medical device who receives information that reasonably suggests that the device may have caused or contributed to a death or serious injury is required to notify the FDA by telephone within five calendar days of receiving the information and is required to file a written report concerning the death or serious injury within fifteen working days of receipt of such information. The MDR regulations further provide that the manufacturer of a medical device is required to submit a written report to the FDA within fifteen working days of receipt of information that reasonably suggests that the device may have malfunctioned and that, if the malfunction was to recur, it is likely that the device may cause or contribute to a death or serious injury. 21 C.F.R. § 803.24.

The United States presented evidence at trial that during the summer of 1993 personnel of Laerdal Manufacturing became aware of the Grand Rapids incident which occurred on June 16, 1993 and became aware that the Grand Rapids incident involved a death. [The Grand Rapids fire department had responded to an emergency call in which the patient was experiencing cardiac difficulties. The Laerdal automated external defibrillator apparently failed to detect that the patient's heart was fibrillating, and therefore indicated that a shock to the heart was not warranted. Upon investigation, the tape of the patient's heart rhythm indicated fibrillation, according to experts; therefore, the device should have delivered a shock to the patient's heart.]

Laerdal Manufacturing contends that the United States did not show that it had violated the MDR regulations by not filing a report on the Grand Rapids incident because * * * the FDA investigator concluded during the inspection conducted in October and November of 1993 that the information regarding the death in the Grand Rapids incident was "indefinite." Laerdal Manufacturing asserts that it did not have information reasonably suggesting that its automated external defibrillator "caused or contributed to" the death. * * *

The regulation and the reporting procedure adopted by Laerdal Manufacturing do not require that the findings be more than "indefinite" when reported. The MDR regulations require Laerdal Manufacturing to submit an MDR report when any of the various company personnel are informed of events which "may have caused or contributed to a death." In the case of the Grand Rapids incident, the clinical investigator and the QA reliability engineer were informed in the summer of 1993 that a device manufactured by Laerdal Manufacturing was involved in treatment events in which a death occurred; that the device did not shock the patient during the incident; and that the device did commit to shock in five out of five replays into a quality assurance device after the incident. This information supports the conclusion that the device "may have caused or contributed to a death." An MDR report was not submitted until February 4, 1994, and then only to be cooperative with the FDA because the Director of Quality Assurance still felt that a report was not required.

There is testimony in the record that Laerdal Manufacturing has had other reported complaints of devices that have allegedly delivered shocks when they should not have and complaints where the device failed to detect and to treat ventricular fibrillation. * * * [The court enjoined the company from further noncompliance with MDR requirements.]

NOTES AND QUESTIONS

1. *Injunctions to secure compliance.* On appeal, the Ninth Circuit affirmed the ruling in *Laerdal*. Noting that 21 C.F.R. pt. 803 is a strict liability provision, the court concluded that the corporation's continued insistence that its violation of the reporting regulation was an unintentional, "good faith error" provided evidence of likely future violations:

> Laerdal cites as support for its failure to file a report "the ambiguous language of the regulation." ... At trial and on appeal, Laerdal has attempted to demonstrate the "foibles of the MDR system." It claims that "MDR reports languish for several months in a bureaucratic limbo" and that the consequences of its Grand Rapids violation were "merely trifling." ... Even if Laerdal had not intended to violate the regulation, its continued insistence on justifying its actions in committing the violation "is an important factor in deciding whether future violations are sufficiently likely to warrant an injunction." ... That Laerdal's self-justification extends to indicting the MDR system itself reflects "the sort of extraordinary intransigence and hostility" toward the FDA and the MDR regulations that support the inference of a likelihood to commit future violations.

United States v. Laerdal Mfg. Corp., 73 F.3d 852, 856 (9th Cir.1995); see also Jignesh S. Shah & William H. Maisel, Recalls and Safety Alerts Affecting Automated External Defibrillators, 296 JAMA 655 (2006) (finding that approximately 20% of AEDs had been subject to an FDA recall or alert and that 370 deaths were associated with confirmed malfunctions); David S. Hilzenrath, Firm Silent as Patients Died: Device Maker Pleads Guilty to Misleading FDA, Wash. Post, June 13, 2003, at A1 (reporting that the manufacturer of a fabric graft used to repair aortic aneurysms failed to notify the FDA of hundreds of serious malfunctions).

2. *The magnitude of underreporting of adverse events.* Even if manufacturers fully comply with mandatory adverse event reporting requirements, these reports represent only the proverbial tip of the iceberg because companies generally submit reports of adverse events based on what physicians and other health professionals send to them, and these reports comprise just a fraction of the total number of adverse drug reactions that occur. See Marc Kaufman, Drug Safety Panel Is Criticized, Wash. Post, June 8, 2005, at A5 ("The current voluntary system for reporting serious drug reactions is believed to capture only 10 percent of actual cases."); see also Sheila Weiss–Smith et al., The FDA Drug Safety Surveillance Program: Adverse Event Reporting Trends, 171 Archives Internal Med. 591 (2011) (noting that the FDA now receives approximately half a million ADE reports annually). Even when they report ADEs, some physicians have expressed frustration with the agency's response. See, e.g., Geeta Anand, Jaw Ailment Shows Industry Moves Slowly on Drug Warnings, Wall St. J., Dec. 8, 2004, at B1 (reporting that it took an oral surgeon more than two years to convince the FDA that a cancer drug might have caused dozens of cases of osteonecrosis); see also Gina Kolata, Drug for Bones Is Linked to Jaw Disease, N.Y. Times, June 2, 2006, at A17. When it enacted the Best Pharmaceuticals for Children Act, Congress included a separate requirement that the FDA promulgate a rule to require that drug labeling include a toll-free number for consumers to report adverse events to the agency. See Pub. L. No. 107–109, § 17(a), 115 Stat. 1408 (2002).

3. *Frequency of adverse events associated with a product.* Because the spontaneous reporting numerator represents only a tiny fraction of the actual number of ADEs, it remains difficult to estimate accurately the incidence of safety problems with many prescription drugs. To further complicate the drug safety picture, the FDA lacks useful data about the number of patients who take particular drugs as well as about the length and degree of exposure to these drugs. These data are necessary to determine the denominator for purposes of calculating the incidence of drug safety problems. Similar difficulties may arise with medical devices. See, e.g., Neal I. Muni & Thomas P. Gross, Problems with Drug–Eluting Coronary Stents: The FDA Perspective, 351 New Eng. J. Med. 1593 (2004); David Brown, Implantable Defibrillators Can Be Erratic, Studies Find, Wash. Post, Apr. 26, 2006, at A8. The agency could get around some of these limitations by tapping into the enormous databases now maintained by public and private insurers. See Natasha Singer, Public Database Is Urged to Monitor Drug Safety, N.Y. Times, Nov. 24, 2009, at B2; see also FDAAA, Pub. L. No. 110–85, § 905, 121 Stat. 823, 944 (2007) (codified at 21 U.S.C. § 355(k)(3)(C)(i)(III)(aa)) (directing the agency to make use of existing public databases such as that of the Medicare program); David Brown, Blood–Pressure Drugs Linked to Birth Defects, Wash. Post, June 8, 2006, at A12 (reporting that research funded by the FDA and using one state's Medicaid records discovered a significant increase in the risk of birth defects when pregnant women used ACE inhibitors during their first trimester).

4. *Sentinel systems.* In 1997, Congress directed the FDA to establish a "sentinel system" to facilitate efficient reporting by requiring that only a representative subset of user facilities file MDRs. See 21 U.S.C. § 360i(b)(1)(D)(5). This might allow for more targeted and thorough collection and investigation of adverse events (including near misses) involving medical devices (much in the same way that local public health departments responded to the spread of West Nile Virus by sampling the blood of sentinel chickens set out in designated locations rather than passively waiting for spontaneous citizen reports of dead crows). A pilot study of such a system generated dramatic increases in reporting rates over what one would have expected, and the agency has slowly expanded it. See Ross Kerber, FDA Halts Expansion of Network to Monitor Medical Device Safety, Boston Globe, July 14, 2005, at D1 ("The FDA had aimed to connect 500 of the nation's 5,000 eligible hospitals, but is stuck at 350 and won't fund further expansion for the next several years.... MedSun, whose full name is Medical Product Surveillance Network, was introduced in 2002 ...."). What obstacles prevent the expansion of a sentinel system, and might it function less well with pharmaceuticals? See Daniel S. Budnitz et al., National Surveillance of Emergency Department Visits for Outpatient Adverse Drug Events, 296 JAMA 1858 (2006). Congress directed the agency to undertake just such an effort for drugs. See FDAAA, Pub. L. No. 110–85, § 905(a), 121 Stat. 823, 944 (2007) (codified at 21 U.S.C. § 355(k)(3)); see also Bridget M. Kuehn, FDA Turns to Electronic "Sentinel" to Flag Prescription Drug Safety Problems, 300 JAMA 156 (2008); Richard Platt et al., The New Sentinel Network—Improving the Evidence of Medical–Product Safety, 361 New Eng. J. Med. 645 (2009); Rob Stein, Program Aims for Drug, Device Safety, Wash. Post, May 23, 2008, at A2.

5. *Postapproval study requirements.* The FDA long ago issued regulations that contemplated approving NDAs for certain types of drugs based on a commitment to conduct additional postmarket research. See 35 Fed. Reg. 14,784 (1970) (codified as amended at 21 C.F.R. § 310.303(a)). As noted previously, however, the agency enjoyed only limited statutory authority to require postapproval studies of new drugs. Pursuant to the fast-track regulations, which create an accelerated approval process for drug and biological products intended to treat serious or life-threatening illnesses, the FDA may require postapproval studies to establish a firmer connection between the initial efficacy data and the products' ultimate clinical benefits. See 21 C.F.R. §§ 314.510, 601.41 (noting that the applicant must carry out the studies "with due diligence"). In codifying these procedures, FDAMA required that sponsors make annual progress reports to the FDA on the status of their Phase IV studies, see 21 U.S.C. § 356b(a), and, ten years later, Congress granted the agency authority to order any NDA sponsor to undertake such trials. Whether the agency mandates Phase IV studies or persuades companies to undertake such research voluntarily, it may have difficulty ensuring that the additional work ever gets completed. See Gardiner Harris, Drug Makers Remain Years Behind on Testing Approved Medicines, Report Finds, N.Y. Times, Oct. 27, 2009, at A18; see also Charles Steenburg, The FDA's Use of Postmarketing (Phase IV) Study Requirements: Exception to the Rule?, 61 Food & Drug L.J. 295 (2006); Matthew Gordon, Note, Improving Post–Approval Risk Surveillance for Drugs: Active Post–Market Risk Identification, 15 Mich. Telecomm. & Tech. L. Rev. 297 (2008). Similarly, the agency sometimes asks manufacturers of devices subject to a PMA to conduct postapproval studies.

6. *Securities fraud litigation.* The failure to disclose information about reported adverse events may raise questions of securities fraud. See William O. Fisher, Key Disclosure Issues for Life Sciences Companies: FDA Product Approval, Clinical Test Results, and Government Inspections, 8 Mich. Telecomm. & Tech. L. Rev. 115 (2002). Some courts have required that plaintiffs establish the manufacturer's awareness of a statistically significant association between the drug and reported side effect during the time in question. See Oran v. Stafford, 226 F.3d 275, 284 (3d Cir.2000) ("Because the link between the two drugs [Pondimin® and Redux®] and heart-valve disorders was never definitively established during the relevant period even after the withheld [ADEs are] taken into account, AHP's failure to disclose this data cannot render its statements about the inconclusiveness of the relationship materially misleading."); San Leandro Emergency Med. Group v. Philip Morris Cos., 75 F.3d 801, 811 (2d Cir. 1996) (holding that drug companies need not disclose ADEs to investors until those reports provide statistically significant evidence of a causal link and are sufficiently serious to affect future earnings); see also N.J. Carpenters Pension & Annuity Funds v. Biogen Idec Inc., 537 F.3d 35, 47–58 (1st Cir.2008) (affirming dismissal for inadequate allegations of scienter (based on prior knowledge of risks) of a securities fraud class action lawsuit against the manufacturer of the MS drug Tysabri® (natalizumab) that was temporarily withdrawn shortly after FDA approval because two subjects in ongoing clinical trials developed progressive multifocal leukoencephalopathy (PML), a potentially fatal opportunistic infection); id. at 58 ("The company would have behaved irresponsibly (and possibly in violation of the securities laws) if it had made a public announcement which was possibly inaccurate because the situation of the PML incidences had not yet been adequately investigated."); cf. Yanek v. Staar Surgical Co., 388 F.Supp.2d 1110 (C.D.Cal.2005) (declining to dismiss shareholder lawsuit for securities fraud where manufacturer of implantable contact lens had forecast FDA approval); Scott Hensley & Betsy McKay, Lawsuit Alleges Irregularities with Vaccine, Wall St. J., Mar. 31, 2004, at B1 (describing an unusual whistleblower lawsuit filed under the Sarbanes–Oxley Act alleging fraud on shareholders for failing to disclose GMP violations).

In *Matrixx Initiatives, Inc. v. Siracusano*, 131 S.Ct. 1309 (2011), the manufacturer of Zicam Cold Remedy, an intranasal product that contained zinc gluconate, had received several adverse event reports linking the drug to anosmia (lost sense of smell) but failed to mention these to investors when making favorable forecasts about future sales and earnings. The Supreme Court unanimously rejected the manufacturer's argument that such ADEs could not amount to "material" information because they were only anecdotal reports and failed to demonstrate a statistically significant link between the product and the observed side effect: "Given that medical professionals and regulators act on the basis of evidence of causation that is not statistically significant, it stands to reason that in certain cases reasonable investors would as well." Id. at 1321; see also id. ("[A]ssessing the materiality of adverse event reports ... requires consideration of the source, content, and context of the reports. This is not to say that statistical significance (or the lack thereof) is irrelevant—only that it is not dispositive of every case."). The Court hastened to add that ADEs would not invariably have to get communicated to investors. See id. (explaining that this more flexible materiality "standard does not mean that pharmaceutical manufacturers must disclose all reports of adverse events"); id. ("[T]he mere existence of reports of adverse events—which says nothing in and of itself about whether the drug is causing the adverse events—will not satisfy this standard. Something more is needed, but that something more is not limited to statistical significance ....").

How exactly does this "contextual inquiry" operate in connection with ADEs? In *Matrixx*, the Court focused on the plaintiffs' allegations of, inter alia, prior published research (and not just in animals) linking other forms of zinc to anosmia, the manufacturer's lack of any prior testing on this question, a cluster of roughly a dozen ADEs (at least one of which claimed a close temporal association and another one ruled out the underlying cold as causing this side effect), and the fact that a couple of researchers took the reports seriously enough to present this information at a medical conference. See id. at 1322; see also id. at 1323 (adding that consumers likely would regard this risk as outweighing the benefit of symptomatic relief, especially given the availability of numerous alternative remedies, and that this line of Zicam products accounted for the bulk of the manufacturer's revenues). Note also that, as a homeopathic product, Zicam largely escaped premarket scrutiny by the FDA (at least in part because these products should be essentially inert), and that manufacturers of OTC drugs had no obligation at the time to report adverse events to the agency—do these features make any complaints received by the manufacturer more likely to be "material" to investors than in the case of powerful prescription drugs that have undergone clinical testing and the FDA's approval process? Cf. In re Carter–Wallace, Inc. Securities Litig., 220 F.3d 36, 40–42 (2d Cir.2000). In addition, although the early Zicam reports turned out to signal a real problem (additional reports soon followed and ultimately triggered a regulatory response, see Gardiner Harris, F.D.A. Warns Against Use of a Popular Cold Remedy, N.Y. Times, June 17, 2009, at A14), what about the more typical case where ADEs (even if they share some of the contextual features credited by the Court in *Matrixx*) ultimately prove to represent nothing more than background noise—would the failure to share these with investors also amount to material omissions (putting aside the fact that investors presumably would suffer no financial injury if the reports in fact remain uncorroborated and fail to trigger any adverse regulatory action)? Or might such ADEs nonetheless be deemed material insofar as reports of even spurious side effects may trigger overcautious regulatory responses or unfounded tort litigation?

Forsham v. Califano

442 F.Supp. 203 (D.D.C.1977).

■ CORCORON, DISTRICT JUDGE:

Plaintiffs are seven physicians who specialize in the treatment of diabetes and six diabetic patients taking phenformin hydrochloride prescribed by their physicians as part of their diabetic therapy. Phenformin is an orally administered drug designed to control blood sugar levels in patients with adult-onset diabetes who are not dependent on insulin and who cannot or will not reduce their daily caloric intake. Phenformin allows such diabetics to control their condition with fewer dietary restrictions and to delay the time when they must begin taking insulin.

The defendant is the Secretary of Health, Education and Welfare who, pursuant to Section 505(e) of the Federal Food, Drug and Cosmetic Act has suspended new drug applications for phenformin on grounds that the drug poses an "imminent hazard." The pertinent language of 21 U.S.C. § 355(e) states:

> That if the Secretary ... finds that there is an imminent hazard to the public health he may suspend the approval of such [new drug] application immediately and give the applicant prompt notice of his action and afford the applicant the opportunity for an expedited hearing under this subsection; but the authority conferred by this proviso to suspend the approval of an application shall not be delegated.

Plaintiffs seek to enjoin the Secretary from implementing his suspension order. * * *

While acknowledging the existence of "conflicting testimony" on the incidence of lactic acidosis among phenformin patients and the view expressed by the manufacturers that labeling changes made in January 1977 would reduce the incidence of phenformin-related lactic acidosis, the Secretary nonetheless deemed that the following factors necessitated his decision to suspend:

1. The discontinued marketing of phenformin in Norway and Canada based on the experience in those countries with phenformin-related lactic acidosis cases.

2. Adverse reports of phenformin-related lactic acidosis in Finland, Sweden, New Zealand, and Australia.

3. The discontinued use of phenformin by several diabetes clinics in major U.S. hospitals.

4. The unanimous October 1976 recommendation by the FDA Endocrinology and Metabolism Advisory Committee that phenformin be removed from the market.

5. The May 6, 1977, decision by the FDA's Bureau of Drugs to seek withdrawal of approval of NDAs for phenformin.

6. Calculations submitted by the FDA's Bureau of Drugs based on information it had received from phenformin manufacturers, research conducted in other countries, studies conducted in a group of university based medical centers and reports from individual hospitals. Those calculations indicated that * * * the estimated incidence of death due to lactic acidosis in phenformin users is between 0.125 and 2 deaths annually per 1,000 patients—a rate 5 to 80 times higher than that of other widely used drugs known to cause fatalities even when properly used * * * [and] that final administrative action on withdrawal of the NDAs for phenformin could take from six to twelve months during which time anywhere from 10 to 700 people could die from phenformin associated lactic acidosis.

Plaintiffs do not ask the court at this juncture to evaluate the relative merits of the conflicting medical views on the hazards posed by phenformin. Rather they assert (1) that the Secretary employed an improper standard in determining that phenformin posed an imminent hazard; (2) that the long standing availability of the data relied on by the Secretary and the chronology of events preceding his decision demonstrate a lack of the immediacy required to support such a determination; and (3) that the procedural mechanism employed by the Secretary in implementing his decision was arbitrary, capricious, and ultra vires. * * *

[W]e are not inclined to adopt plaintiff's "crisis" interpretation of imminent hazard. Rather we are more persuaded by defendant's suggested analogy to cases interpreting the imminent hazard provisions of the Federal Insecticide, Fungicide and Rodenticide Act which caution "against any approach to the term imminent hazard ... that restricts it to a concept of crisis" and adopt the view that "it is enough that there is substantial likelihood that serious harm will be experienced during ... any realistic projection of the administrative process."

We decide accordingly that the Secretary's criteria for evaluating the existence of an imminent hazard were not improper. There remains to be determined whether a rational connection exists between the facts on which he relied and his decision to suspend. Keeping in mind that "invocation of this emergency power is a matter which is peculiarly one of judgment," this court cannot say that the facts on which the Secretary relied, particularly the calculations provided by the Bureau of Drugs, do not adequately support his decision to suspend. * * * The mere fact that respectable scientific authority can be found on both sides of this question does not render the Secretary's decision arbitrary and capricious. Similarly, the fact that much of the raw data used by the Bureau in arriving at its conclusion had been available for some length of time does not preclude its use in finding an imminent hazard when, as the FDA alleged happened in this case, the magnitude of phenformin's risk was determined only after an extensive re-evaluation of the data following the May 13th hearing.

In view of the facts used by the Secretary to support his decision we are also not persuaded by plaintiffs' arguments that his decision was arbitrary because allegedly less drastic means such as the use of accepted labeling procedures might eventually result in reducing phenformin's hazards or that the decision was arbitrary because other drugs currently available might be equally as hazardous. Assuming, as we must at this juncture, the validity of the Bureau of Drug's projection of between four and 60 phenformin related deaths each month, we cannot find that the Secretary's conclusion that labeling changes "cannot be expected to achieve a needed reduction in the usage of phenformin within any reasonable time frame ... with so many lives at stake," was either arbitrary or unreasonable. Nor was it made so by his decision to act first on phenformin rather than some other drug which may pose a hazard of similar magnitude. * * *

NOTES AND QUESTIONS

1. *Imminent hazard and voluntary withdrawals.* This expedited withdrawal procedure raises procedural due process questions because it deprives the pharmaceutical manufacturer of a valuable property interest without affording a prior hearing, but the FDA never again invoked its imminent hazard authority. In connection with medical devices, the agency has used a comparable power to demand recalls. See, e.g., Kim A. Eagle, Safety Alerts Involving Device Therapy for Arrhythmias, 286 JAMA 843 (2001). The FDA more frequently obtains voluntary agreements from manufacturers to withdraw drugs when safety concerns emerge, though it maintains an official list of such products and prohibits pharmacists from compounding any of them. See 21 C.F.R. § 216. The agency also sometimes convinces companies to withdraw nonprescription drug products containing ingredients of questionable safety. For example, manufacturers of OTC cold remedies containing phenylpropanolamine (PPA) reformulated their products to remove the ingredient after studies demonstrated that it was associated with an increased risk of stroke in certain users. See Jeff Gerth & Sheryl G. Stolberg, Another Part of the Battle: Keeping a Drug in the Store, N.Y. Times, Dec. 13, 2000, at A1 (describing PPA's long marketing history and growing evidence of safety concerns); see also Douglas C. Chang et al., Multistate Outbreak of Fusarium Keratitis Associated with Use of a Contact Lens Solution, 296 JAMA 953 (2006); Barnaby J. Feder, From Asia to America, How Bausch's Crisis Grew, N.Y. Times, May 18, 2006, at C1 (detailing the events that ultimately led the manufacturer of the contact lens cleaning solution ReNu® to issue a global recall of its MoistureLoc line because the unanticipated interaction of its ingredients sometimes allowed *Fusarium* spores to survive, which could cause a serious eye infection).

2. *Troubling track record.* A 12–month period in the late 1990s witnessed the withdrawal of five drugs because of safety problems: the antihistamine terfenadine (Seldane®), the analgesic bromfenac (Duract®), the antihypertensive mibefradil (Posicor®), and the diet drugs fenfluramine (Pondimin®) and dexfenfluramine (Redux®). See Alastair J.J. Wood, The Safety of New Medicines: The Importance of Asking the Right Questions, 281 JAMA 1753, 1753 (1999) ("[A] staggering 19.8 million patients (almost 10% of the US population) were estimated to have been exposed to these 5 drugs before their removal."); see also Naomi Aoki, A Question of Speed and Safety, Boston Globe, Nov. 28, 2001, at G1 (noting "the growing number of drugs that have been recalled in the past three years—nearly a dozen implicated in more than 1,000 deaths"). Since then, a number of other drug withdrawals have occurred, including the acid reflux drug cisapride (Propulsid®), the diabetes treatment troglitazone (Rezulin®), a cholesterol-lowering statin (Baycol®), an antidepressant (Serzone®), a pair of antibiotics (Trovan® and Raxar®), an opioid analgesic (Palladone®), a dopamine agonist for Parkinson's disease (Permax®), an irritable bowel syndrome drug (Zelnorm®), a psoriasis drug (Raptiva®), an anti-bleeding agent (Trasylol®), and a leukemia drug (Mylotarg®). No doubt the most notable withdrawals occurred in 2004, after the announcement that long-term use of the prescription analgesic rofecoxib (Vioxx®) increased the risk of cardiovascular problems. See Alex Berenson et al., Despite Warnings, Drug Giant Took Long Path to Vioxx Recall, N.Y. Times, Nov. 14, 2004, § 1, at 1. Six months later, under pressure from the FDA, Pfizer "reluctantly" withdrew its similar drug. See Marc Kaufman, Another Pain Reliever Pulled, Wash. Post, Apr. 8, 2005, at A1 (reporting that the agency found that Bextra® also may cause a potentially fatal skin reaction); see also Rob Stein, In Long Quest for Diet Drug, Another Setback for Obese, Wash. Post, Oct. 9, 2010, at A1 (reporting the withdrawal of Meridia® (sibutramine) after 13 years on the market based on findings of serious cardiovascular risks and only modest efficacy). Celecoxib (Celebrex®), the only other selective COX–2 inhibitor (which were thought to relieve pain without the risk of gastrointestinal bleeding associated with aspirin and NSAIDs), remained on the market after the addition of a black box warning. See Alex Berenson, Celebrex Ads Are Back, Dire

Warnings and All, N.Y. Times, Apr. 29, 2006, at C1; see also FDA Rejects Merck's Successor to Vioxx, Wash. Post, Apr. 28, 2007, at A6 (Arcoxia®).

3. *Shaping up as a sequel to the Vioxx fiasco?* Although it has not had its NDA withdrawn (yet), the oral diabetes drug Avandia® (rosiglitazone) followed a trajectory eerily reminiscent of Vioxx. See Andrew J. Krentz, Editorial, Rosiglitazone: Trials, Tribulations and Termination, 71 Drugs 123 (2011). In 1999, the FDA approved the drug to help control blood sugar in patients with Type 2 diabetes. Millions of people took the drug, and, by 2006, GlaxoSmithKline (GSK) reported that global sales of rosiglitazone had surpassed $3 billion annually. In 2007, the FDA issued a safety advisory about cardiovascular risks based on a published meta-analysis of dozens of Avandia studies. See Stephanie Saul & Gardiner Harris, Years Ago, Agency Was Warned of a Drug's Risks, N.Y. Times, May 24, 2007, at C1. Later that same year, after an advisory committee narrowly voted to spare the drug, the FDA required the addition of a black box warning in the package insert. See Anna W. Mathews & Jeanne Whalen, Glaxo to Add Avandia Warning, Wall St. J., Nov. 15, 2007, at A5. Congressional hearings revealed various irregularities by the company and the agency, and further research confirmed the seriousness of the risk (with extrapolations suggesting that many tens of thousands of excess heart attacks and strokes occurred during Avandia's first decade on the market). See Alicia Mundy, Senators Say Glaxo Withheld Drug Data, Wall St. J., July 13, 2010, at B1; Rob Stein, New Data Point to Risks for Diabetes Drug, Wash. Post, June 29, 2010, at A2; see also David N. Juurlink, Editorial, Rosiglitazone and the Case for Safety over Certainty, 304 JAMA 469 (2010). In 2010, after another advisory committee meeting (and in tandem with an EU decision to suspend approval of the drug), the FDA decided to use its REMS authority to impose a variety of stringent distribution restrictions. See Janet Woodcock et al., Regulatory Action on Rosiglitazone by the U.S. Food and Drug Administration, 363 New Eng. J. Med. 1489 (2010); Gardiner Harris, F.D.A. to Restrict a Diabetes Drug, Citing Heart Risk, N.Y. Times, Sept. 24, 2010, at A1; Steve Sternberg, Avandia to Be Pulled from Retail Shelves, USA Today, May 19, 2011, at 3A ("[O]nly certified doctors will be allowed to prescribe the drug, and only to patients who've been informed of the risks and who will fill their prescriptions by mail order through specific pharmacies."). Meanwhile, entirely different safety questions have arisen with Actos® (pioglitazone), which belongs to the same class of drugs (one that had also included Rezulin before reports of liver failure prompted its withdrawal). See Jennifer C. Dooren, FDA Says Diabetes Drug Might Raise Cancer Risk, Wall St. J., June 16, 2011, at B9.

4. *SSRIs and suicide.* Selective serotonin reuptake inhibitors (SSRIs) have become heavily prescribed drugs for treating depression and similar conditions. After British regulators concluded in 2002 that these products increased the risk of suicide in teenagers, the FDA struggled to decide whether any risk existed (complicated by the fact that untreated depression causes suicide) and, if so, how best to respond given new questions about limited evidence of efficacy. After attracting heavy criticism for delaying its decision, the agency settled on enhanced warnings. See Shankar Vedantam,

Depression Drugs to Carry a Warning: FDA Orders Notice of Risks for Youths, Wash. Post, Oct. 16, 2004, at A1; see also David Healy, Did Regulators Fail over Selective Serotonin Reuptake Inhibitors?, 333 Brit. Med. J. 92 (2006); Sarah D. Gordon, Comment, Antidepressants and Teen Suicide: An Analysis of the FDA's Regulation of Pharmaceuticals for Use in Pediatric Patients, 57 Admin. L. Rev. 927 (2005); Benedict Carey, F.D.A. Expands Suicide Warning on Drugs, N.Y. Times, May 3, 2007, at A17 (reporting that the agency revised the black box warning to include young adults). Subsequent research suggested, however, that even this fairly moderate regulatory response, which resulted in reduced rates of prescribing, may have amounted to a dangerous overreaction. See Shankar Vedantam, Suicides Rose as Prescription Use Declined, Wash. Post, Sept. 6, 2007, at A1; see also Jeffrey A. Bridge et al., Clinical Response and Risk for Reported Suicidal Ideation and Suicide Attempts in Pediatric Antidepressant Treatment, 297 JAMA 1683 (2007). The agency recently has required other classes of drugs to carry similar warnings. See J. Taylor Hays & Jon O. Ebbert, Varenicline for Tobacco Dependence, 359 New Eng. J. Med. 2018, 2022 (2008) (Chantix®); Bernadette Tansey, Doctors Warned of Drugs' Danger: Anti–Epilepsy Medications Tied to Risk of Suicide, S.F. Chron., Feb. 1, 2008, at C1.

5. *Serendipity and spontaneity*. In some cases, spontaneous reporting fails to reveal serious risks associated with widely used drugs because the effects are either common in the population (e.g., heart attacks) and/or not acute (e.g., breast cancer). See David Brown, First, Do the Trials: Then, Do No Harm, Wash. Post, Aug. 4, 2002, at B1; Gina Kolata, When Drugs Cause Problems They Are Supposed to Prevent, N.Y. Times, Oct. 17, 2010, at A18. These side effects may come to light only after researchers conduct rigorous postapproval studies attempting to confirm efficacy for other uses, as happened with COX–2 inhibitors and hormone replacement therapy (HRT). In the case of HRTs, for example, which millions of women have taken to treat the symptoms of menopause (e.g., hot flashes), NIH sponsored a major trial to determine whether estrogen-containing products offered protection against heart disease and other conditions (as many physicians had come to believe), only to discover precisely the opposite of a protective effect. See Denise Grady, Breast Cancer Seen as Riskier with Hormone, N.Y. Times, Oct. 20, 2010, at A1; see also Rob Stein, Steroids for Head Injuries May Be Risky, Wash. Post, Oct. 9, 2004, at A8. In other cases, spontaneous reporting reveals peculiar side effects. See, e.g., Shankar Vedantam, Prescription for an Obsession? Gambling, Sex Manias Called Surprise Risks of Parkinson's Drugs, Wash. Post, Mar. 19, 2006, at A1 (reporting new evidence that dopamine agonists (e.g., Mirapex® and Requip®) may turn some patients into obsessive pleasure seekers, which prompted manufacturers to note such unconfirmed reports in labeling and patients to bring lawsuits for failure to warn); Sanofi Defends Safety of Its Sleeping Pill, Wall St. J., Mar. 22, 2006, at D4 (noting reports that Ambien® caused some users to drive or binge eat while asleep). Finally, some drug side effects (e.g., hirsutism noted with the antihypertensive minoxidil) suggest an entirely different use (e.g., topical minoxidil (Rogaine®) to treat baldness).

6. *"Black box" warnings and other intermediate responses.* Short of withdrawing a prescription drug, the FDA has several less draconian options for addressing newly discovered risks: require relabeling with stronger warnings and/or clearer directions for use, mandatory education programs for prescribers, or perhaps restrictions on distribution and use. As noted previously, the agency demanded black box warnings for the COX–2 inhibitor Celebrex, SSRIs, and HRTs. See Julie Bell, "Black Box" Leaves Patients in the Dark, Balt. Sun, June 30, 2003, at 7A (reporting that less than 1% of prescription drugs carry such warnings); see also Jennifer C. Dooren, FDA Requires Avandia, Actos to Have "Black Box" Warning, Wall St. J., Aug. 15, 2007, at D3 (risk of heart failure); Marc Kaufman, Study Cites Increased Death Risk from Asthma Drugs, Wash. Post, June 6, 2006, at A7 (Advair® and Serevent®); Donna Leinwand, Eczema Drug Labels to Warn of Potential Cancer Risk, USA Today, Jan. 20, 2006, at 3A (reporting that the FDA required black box warnings for Elidel® and Protopic® based on the results of high-dose animal studies and because of the prevalence of pediatric use); Karen Ravn, "Black Box" Warnings: Behind the FDA's Strictest Advisory, L.A. Times, Aug. 18, 2008, at F3 (fluoroquinolones (such as Cipro®) linked to tendon rupture).

Although black box warnings remain the exception, pharmaceutical manufacturers often make corrections to labeling after approval (particularly reductions in the recommended dose). See Duff Wilson, F.D.A. Puts New Limits on Cholesterol Drug, N.Y. Times, June 9, 2011, at B2 (reporting labeling revisions for Zocor® and other drugs containing simvastatin to recommend against use of the highest approved dose in new patients because of the risk of myopathy); Abigail Zuger, Caution: That Dose May Be Too High, N.Y. Times, Sept. 17, 2002, at F1; see also Thomas M. Burton, FDA to Require Diabetes Warning on Class of Schizophrenia Drugs, Wall St. J., Sept. 18, 2003, at D3 (explaining that the agency may demand revisions in the package insert simply to urge physicians to watch for suspected (but not yet confirmed) side effects); Marc Kaufman, Impotence Drugs Will Get Blindness Warning, Wash. Post, July 9, 2005, at A6 (same). The agency may decide to narrow the range of approved uses to the extent that the new adverse event information renders the risk-benefit ratio for just some of multiple indications unfavorable. See Kuhn v. Sandoz Pharm. Corp., 14 P.3d 1170, 1174–75 (Kan.2000) (summarizing FDA negotiations with the manufacturer of Parlodel® that led to the removal from the originally approved labeling of the indication for the suppression of lactation); David B. Ross, The FDA and the Case of Ketek, 356 New Eng. J. Med. 1601 (2007). Alternatively, companies confronted with new risk information may secure approval for lower-dose (and presumably safer) versions of a product. See, e.g., Suz Redfearn, Low–Dose Hormone Approved, Wash. Post, Mar. 25, 2003, at F1 (reporting that the manufacturer of Prempro® had done so, and noting a similar response many years earlier by sellers of oral contraceptives). The agency may try to limit the number of doses dispensed at a time. See, e.g., Andrew Schneider, Banned Pesticide

Allowed as Medicine: U.S. Bars Lindane, Except to Treat Lice, Balt. Sun, Aug. 14, 2006, at 1A. Finally, public education campaigns offer still another option for dealing with new risk information. See, e.g., Jennifer C. Dooren, FDA Warns of Possibly Lethal Drug Combination, Wall St. J., July 20, 2006, at D3; Marc Kaufman, FDA Offers Guidance on Hormone Replacement Therapy, Wash. Post, Sept. 10, 2003, at A3.

7. *Risk-benefit rebalancing?* The first half of this chapter discussed the risk-benefit calculus that FDA reviewers use to determine whether to grant marketing approval for a new drug or device. When it receives postmarket risk information, should the agency simply redo its original calculus under the approval criteria, or should different factors influence regulatory judgments at this stage? Cf. Gardiner Harris, Approval of Antibiotic Worried Safety Officials, N.Y. Times, July 19, 2006, at A15 (reporting that reports of serious ADEs coupled with lingering doubts about efficacy led some FDA employees to urge withdrawal of Ketek®). For instance, might Merck have acted too hastily in withdrawing Vioxx from the market (some physicians believe that the drug continued to make sense for patients without any pre-existing cardiac problems but at risk of developing an ulcer)? See Marc Kaufman, FDA Panel Opens Door for Return of Vioxx: Many Advisers Urge New Restrictions on Painkillers, Wash. Post, Feb. 19, 2005, at A1; see also Richard A. Epstein, Regulatory Paternalism in the Market for Drugs: Lessons from Vioxx and Celebrex, 5 Yale J. Health Pol'y L. & Ethics 741 (2005); Ralph F. Hall, The Risk of Risk Reduction: Can Postmarket Surveillance Pose More Risk Than Benefit?, 62 Food & Drug L.J. 473 (2007); Neil F. Hazaray, Note, Do the Benefits Outweigh the Risks? The Legal, Business, and Ethical Ramifications of Pulling a Blockbuster Drug off the Market, 4 Ind. Health L. Rev. 115 (2007). Some arthritis patients who had responded well to COX–2 inhibitors expressed frustration that they could no longer make the choice about whether to continue using Vioxx. See John Leland, Pain Pills Withdrawn, Many Renew Search for Relief, N.Y. Times, Mar. 6, 2005, § 1, at 30. Researchers also feared that the withdrawals would derail clinical trials of COX–2 inhibitors for other indications such as cancer and Alzheimer's disease. See Rob Stein, Studies on Painkillers in Jeopardy: Researchers Assess Risk–Benefit Ratio, Wash. Post, Dec. 26, 2004, at A1.

In 2000, the manufacturers of Lotronex® (alosetron), a drug used to treat irritable bowel syndrome (IBS), withdrew it from the market less than ten months after approval. Of the 300,000 patients who had taken the drug during that brief period, seventy developed severe constipation or ischemic colitis (a lack of blood flow to the colon); some cases required surgical intervention, and five people died. Those who favored withdrawing Lotronex argued that its risks were unacceptable because it only treated a non-life-threatening condition, but the majority of patients on the drug who had suffered no serious side effects protested the withdrawal because the drug had helped them to cope with a condition that significantly interfered with their daily life activities. See Denise Grady, FDA Pulls a Drug, and Patients Despair, N.Y. Times, Jan. 30, 2001, at F1. In an unprecedented move (and just two years after its withdrawal), the FDA allowed the drug back onto the market, though subject to some distribution restrictions that patients found frustrating. See Francesca L. Kritz, Still Irritable, Still Waiting: After Return to Market, Lotronex Can Be Hard to Get, Wash. Post, Feb. 11, 2003, at F1; see also Andrew Pollack, M.S. Drug Can Return, with Limits, N.Y. Times, June 6, 2006, at C1 (reporting that the FDA decided to allow Tysabri® to "return to the market, despite its risk of causing a fatal brain disease, under a program intended to closely monitor doctors who prescribe it and patients who use it"). Finally, to what extent should changes in the external environment (e.g., changing patterns of use and the advent of safer alternatives, including non-pharmaceutical treatment options) prompt the agency to revisit its approval decisions? See Erica Goode, Leading Drugs for Psychosis Come Under New Scrutiny, N.Y. Times, May 20, 2003, at A1 (reporting that the popularity of so-called "atypical" antipsychotics (e.g., Zyprexa® and Riperdal®) for treating schizophrenia and several other conditions has raised questions about their superiority over traditional antipsychotics (e.g., Haldol®) after factoring in the discovery of a possible link to diabetes and the ability to avoid some of the bothersome side effects of the older drugs by selecting lower doses); Parkinson's Drug Pulled off the Market, Wash. Post, Mar. 30, 2007, at A8 (reporting that the FDA requested the withdrawal of pergolide, a dopamine agonist, because it had been associated with heart valve damage since 2002 and "[t]here are other drugs in the same class that can be substituted").

Lars Noah, *Assisted Reproductive Technologies and the Pitfalls of Unregulated Biomedical Innovation*

55 FLA. L. REV. 603 (2003).

* * * Assisted reproductive technologies come in many forms and have gained fairly rapid acceptance in spite of the fact that most infertility patients must pay the costs out of pocket and that many of these treatments have arrived with little or no rigorous testing of their safety and effectiveness. Researchers have long recognized that some fertility treatments increased the odds of a multifetal pregnancy, which poses significant risks to maternal and fetal health, and newer studies have identified other safety concerns such as birth defects associated with particular ARTs. Notwithstanding a growing appreciation of such risks, however, doctors and patients seem unable or unwilling to take steps necessary to curb the overuse of ARTs or to reduce the likelihood of multiple births. * * *

Drugs that induce ovulation by first stimulating the follicles and then releasing the mature ova provide the cornerstone for all forms of ART. Such drugs may increase the odds of success with AI [artificial insemination], or they may be administered in preparation for IVF [in vitro fertilization]. The FDA has approved the use of the following pharmaceutical products for the treatment of infertility: clomiphene citrate (sold under the brand names Clomid® and Serophene®), human menopausal gonadotropins (hMG), also known as menotropins (sold under the brand names Pergonal® and Humegon®), urofollitropin (sold under the brand names

Fertinex® and Metrodin®), and human chorionic gonadotropin (hCG) (sold under the brand names Pregnyl® and A.P.L.®). These drugs first began to reach the market in the mid–1960s * * * *

In recent years, ARTs have become an increasingly popular medical intervention. In 1998, fertility clinics initiated more than 80,000 treatment cycles, which resulted in more than 20,000 deliveries, and more than one-third of those pregnancies resulted in multiple births. * * * ARTs are hardly innocuous medical interventions, and little doubt remains about their contribution to (or the negative consequences of) multifetal pregnancies. * * *

[T]he method used in ART has a direct link to the associated risks. The administration of drugs to induce ovulation or the transfer of numerous embryos after IVF predictably leads to multiple gestational pregnancies. Health care professionals can manage these risks of the procedures, but a variety of pressures may conspire against their success. In the use of IVF, a strong correlation exists between the number of embryos transferred and the rate of multiple gestational pregnancies. In order to protect against the associated risks, some researchers have recommended that physicians transfer only a single embryo. Others have urged transferring just two embryos. Several countries prohibit the transfer of more than three embryos. However, * * * with estimates that less than one-in-five transferred embryos successfully implant, patients and clinics anxious to improve the odds of a successful pregnancy will err on the high side. * * *

Fertility clinics do not absorb the additional costs incurred with multifetal pregnancies, which can be substantial, while they would lose business if their pregnancy success rates declined significantly. The advent of money-back guarantees only exacerbates the incentives of clinics to ensure success by transferring multiple embryos. Moreover, patients may discount these longer-term costs in favor of reducing the immediate out-of-pocket expenses and other costs associated with having to undergo repeated IVF procedures. * * *

As compared with IVF, fertility specialists will find it more difficult to reduce the chances of multiple gestational pregnancies that result from the use of drugs to induce ovulation because of their greater imprecision. Like other pharmaceutical agents, higher dosages increase effectiveness but also increase the risk of adverse effects. Normally, efficacy and safety operate independently of one another, though in some cases a therapeutic failure itself can present a serious risk to a patient. In the case of fertility drugs, however, the primary risk inheres in their very effectiveness.

If ultrasound monitoring detects an unusually high number of maturing follicles after the first round of hormones, physicians might recommend against the administration of hCG or attempts at insemination, but patients may resist the idea of deferring for another cycle and take their chances. The question is whether, under these circumstances, physicians who have fully informed such patients of the risks should proceed. Even if physicians have an ethical obligation to refuse to cater to their patients' unwise choices, in practice many of them may accede to the demands of clients seeking fertility treatments that offer the best chances of success with the lowest upfront expenditure of resources.

Although physicians might reduce the dosages of fertility drugs, researchers still have not identified optimal treatment protocols, and studies suggest that this strategy suffers from a lack of precision when compared to IVF followed by limited embryo transfer. Earlier recourse to IVF would give physicians a better opportunity to reduce the risks of triggering multifetal pregnancies, but ovarian stimulation alone remains the preferred first-line treatment for many types of infertility because of its relative cost-effectiveness.

Ultimately, because they either cannot or, for economic reasons, do not act to minimize the chance that numerous embryos will implant, physicians may have to recommend "selective reduction" after the fact in order to avoid the maternal and fetal risks associated with multiple gestational pregnancies. * * * [I]n connection with disclosing the risks of multifetal pregnancy before initiating therapy, physicians certainly should reveal the possible need for selective reduction. Many patients will, of course, decline to abide by such advice because they oppose anything akin to abortion or fear losing the entire pregnancy. If a physician knows ahead of time that their patient will reject such advice, the question again is whether he or she ethically can proceed with treatments that create a risk of a multifetal pregnancy.

In fact, many of the reported instances of high-order multifetal pregnancies, including recent cases of septuplets and octuplets, arose after the aggressive use of fertility drugs followed by the patient's refusal to undergo selective reduction. In one earlier case, a woman who had undergone Pergonal treatment and declined selective reduction of her septuplet pregnancy on religious grounds ended up delivering six very premature infants, three of whom died shortly after birth and the other three suffered long-term disabilities. The family decided to file a lawsuit against the fertility doctor and clinic, alleging malpractice for administering too high a dose of the drug and failing to detect by ultrasound an excessive number of maturing follicles. Over the doctor's vocal objections, his liability insurer settled the case for more than $6 million. * * *

The [FDA] enjoys clear authority to regulate fertility drugs, notwithstanding questions raised in other contexts as to whether infertility qualifies as a "disease" or whether ARTs "treat" rather than circumvent this condition. The approved labeling for some fertility drugs encourages physicians to advise their patients of the risks of multiple births. * * * The FDA certainly could strengthen the cautionary statements that accompany fertility drugs. Traditionally, however, the agency has tried to avoid the use of product labeling to communicate statements that have more to do with good professional practice than the intrinsic risks and benefits of a drug when used as intended. * * *

Although it usually relies on labeling to ensure safe use of drugs after approval, the FDA has begun to consider intermediate risk-management strategies. * * * [T]hese might include restricted distribution to certain specialists (e.g., reproductive endocrinologists), special patient informed consent requirements, structured postmarket surveillance, and mandatory concomitant therapy. As a last resort, the agency may revisit its risk-benefit judgments and withdraw approval of drugs if patterns of misuse pose an excessive hazard.

Apart from newly acquired risk information, several things have changed since the FDA first approved drugs for the treatment of infertility, and these developments may point in conflicting directions. The introduction and refinement of IVF techniques gave fertility drugs an additional application, but these techniques also now offer an alternative treatment that, if used responsibly, carries a reduced risk of multifetal pregnancy. Improvements in neonatology now allow infants to survive extreme prematurity but not without serious lasting consequences in many cases. These advances also may make patients and providers more willing to take their chances now that high-order multiples no longer doom the entire pregnancy. Moreover, the introduction of selective reduction offers an apparent fix for high-order multifetal pregnancies, which in turn may encourage patients and providers to gamble with more aggressive and risky interventions.

In short, the technological milieu has changed dramatically in the four decades since the first fertility drugs became available. In effect, a more primitive first-generation technology, though not rendered obsolete because it continues to facilitate use of the newer techniques, competes with more refined second-generation technologies (i.e., IVF and embryo transfer) and third-generation technologies (i.e., blastocyst culture and micromanipulation of gametes). The FDA needs to ask itself whether these developments have so altered its original risk-benefit calculus that some of its approved pharmaceutical treatments for infertility no longer satisfy statutory requirements for safety and effectiveness. Historically, the agency avoided making risk-benefit decisions about a product in this fashion, preferring to provide information so that health care professionals and patients could make comparative safety and effectiveness judgments. It has, however, begun taking a broader view of the sort suggested here, and the agency occasionally engages in retrospective evaluations of previously approved products.

If the FDA withdrew approval of fertility drugs, it would eliminate multifetal pregnancies caused directly by ovarian stimulation or indirectly by providing numerous oocytes for IVF and subsequent embryo transfer. Such a move would not entirely pull out the rug from under the fertility industry. Physicians could continue harvesting eggs, though only one or two at a time, and perform IVF. Indeed, IVF without ovarian stimulation may carry an offsetting benefit: the hormones that induce ovulation have a negative effect on the endometrium (the lining of the uterus), which reduces the chances of successful embryo implantation after transfer. Although it might require more cycles to achieve a pregnancy, eliminating fertility drugs will reduce some of the costs per cycle. Moreover, physicians and patients who remain concerned about reduced pregnancy rates without ovarian stimulation might opt for "embryo splitting" (blastomere separation) after fertilization to create a limited number of genetically identical embryos for transfer, assuming that this technique would not run afoul of any future prohibitions against human cloning.

In some infertile women, however, hormonal products may offer the only mechanism for triggering ovulation. The withdrawal of fertility drugs would deny them access to relatively safe and effective treatments for which no good substitutes exist at the present time. If the FDA chose to pursue this strategy, it might decide to retain one product—such as clomiphene citrate—as an option for anovulatory patients, though some women suffering from this condition may respond less well to clomiphene and benefit from having access to a wider range of pharmaceutical choices. For this reason, the FDA normally would allow the continued marketing of a product that benefits some class of patients even if misused by or for another class of individuals. Alternatively, the agency could try to restrict distribution of all fertility drugs for use only in anovulatory patients so that they would not be used as a routine adjunct or alternative to IVF. * * *

[C]onstitutional regard for procreative liberties should not stand as an obstacle to the withdrawal of fertility drugs if the FDA decides that they no longer represent safe and effective products, just as it would not prevent the agency from denying a marketing application for a new fertility drug that failed to satisfy normal criteria for approval. Insofar as multifetal pregnancies continue to occur—posing serious risks to both mothers and children—and more refined fertility treatments now exist that do not present such risks when undertaken without the use of fertility drugs, the agency should revisit its original decisions to approve these products for marketing. * * *

ARTs, like other medical technologies, do not exist in a vacuum, and legal institutions cannot assess their risks and benefits without reference to the ways that physicians and patients use these technologies in practice. The apparent rush to embrace the latest assisted reproductive technologies, and the countervailing preoccupation with the collateral challenges that they present, has left some fundamental questions about their safety underappreciated. As research continues to confirm older concerns about multifetal pregnancies and uncover other types of risks, and in light of the incentives shared by physicians and infertility patients, legal institutions need to reevaluate the appropriate uses of these technologies. Because neither industry self-regulation nor state legislation has responded fully to the problem, and because the prospect of tort liability alone will not encourage fertility specialists and clinics to exercise the necessary caution, a federal regulatory response seems to be in order. Although the FDA has begun to explore the idea of extending its jurisdiction to control certain medical procedures involving human reproductive tissues, an effort to further restrict or entirely prohibit the continued marketing of fertility drugs may offer a simpler and more effective (though no less controversial) approach to the problem of multifetal pregnancies.

NOTES AND QUESTIONS

1. *The "Octo-mom" strikes.* A recent octuplet pregnancy by an unemployed single mother (using IVF with donor sperm and evidently transferring a dozen embryos) garnered headlines. See Kimi Yoshino et al., It's All Just So Octo-licious: Nadya Suleman Can't Seem to Get Enough Kids, and Media Audiences Can't Seem to Get Enough of Her, L.A. Times, Feb. 28, 2009, at E1; see also Stephanie Saul, Birth of Octuplets Puts Focus on Fertility Industry and Risks, N.Y. Times, Feb. 12, 2009, at A1; Kimi Yoshino, Doctor Who Treated Octomom Is Ejected from Medical Association, L.A. Times, Oct. 20, 2009, at A4; Suleman Doctor's License Is Revoked, Boston Globe, June 2, 2011, at A2.

2. *Further commentary.* See Theresa Glennon, Choosing One: Resolving the Epidemic of Multiples in Assisted Reproduction, 55 Vill. L. Rev. 147 (2010); Richard J. Hawkins, Assisted Reproductive Technology and the Externality of Multiple Births, 2009 Mich. St. L. Rev. 719; Debora Spar & Anna M. Harrington, Building a Better Baby Business, 10 Minn. J.L. Sci. & Tech. 41 (2009); Catherine A. Clements, Note, What About the Children? A Call for Regulation of Assisted Reproductive Technology, 84 Ind. L.J. 331 (2009); Elyse W. Grant, Note, Assessing the Constitutionality of Reproductive Technologies Regulation: A Bioethical Approach, 61 Hastings L.J. 997 (2010); Stephanie N. Sivinski, Note, Putting Too Many (Fertilized) Eggs in One Basket: Methods of Reducing Multifetal Pregnancies in the United States, 88 Tex. L. Rev. 897 (2010); Alissa Stockage, Note, Regulating Multiple Birth Pregnancies: Comparing the United Kingdom's Comprehensive Regulatory Scheme with the United States' Progressive, Intimate Decision-making Approach, 18 Mich. St. J. Int'l L. 559 (2010); Ann B. Thomas, Note, Avoiding EMBRYOS "R" US: Toward a Regulated Fertility Industry, 27 Wash. U. J.L. & Pol'y 247 (2008).

D. THE PERILS OF BAD REGULATORY ADVICE

PROFESSIONAL RESPONSIBILITY EXERCISE*

Amy Taylor was a fourth year associate at Beckham, Caplin & Kramer (BCK), a small law firm in Washington, D.C., that specialized in food and drug law. Taylor enjoyed this specialty—it was both intellectually challenging and dealt with important public health issues.

One of the most interesting projects that Taylor had worked on thus far at BCK was on behalf of the Nonprescription Drug Manufacturers Alliance (NDMA), a trade association with more than 100 members. In 1988, the FDA had issued a final OTC monograph for nighttime sleep-aid

* Adapted from a fictional case study involving the FDA's regulation of caffeine as a food additive. See Philip B. Heyman & Lance Liebman, The Social Responsibilities of Lawyers 216–34 (Foundation Press 1988).

products, which allowed for the use of 50 mg of either diphenhydramine hydrochloride or doxylamine succinate as active ingredients. See 21 C.F.R. pt. 338. A few years later, the consumer advocacy group GadFly had filed a citizens petition asking the agency to remove doxylamine from the monograph. GadFly made a pair of arguments in contending that doxylamine was not generally recognized as safe and effective (GRASE): (1) newly completed animal studies with a chemical similar to doxylamine revealed a statistically significant increase in congenital abnormalities in the offspring; and (2) the clinical trials originally submitted by the manufacturers to demonstrate efficacy were conducted by a principal investigator later convicted of scientific fraud. After reviewing the material submitted with the petition, the FDA concluded that no grounds existed for concerns about the ingredient's safety, but it agreed that questions about the validity of the clinical trials cast doubt on its original finding that doxylamine qualified as GRASE and proposed to amend the monograph.

NDMA wanted to object to the proposed amendment, both on behalf of those member companies that used doxylamine and also on behalf of the entire industry insofar as this rule could set a dangerous precedent of revisiting previously concluded monograph proceedings. NDMA came to BCK for assistance, and the partner in charge of the account asked Taylor to draft comments in opposition to the FDA's proposal. A few manufacturers transmitted anecdotal evidence to confirm the ingredient's effectiveness, but it would take significant time and money to conduct new clinical trials. Because the notice of proposed rulemaking had not identified any safety concerns as the basis for withdrawing doxylamine, the comments argued that the FDA should postpone any final action until the industry had an opportunity to undertake the additional research.

A few months after completing the comments for NDMA, Taylor attended her tenth college reunion and struck up a conversation with Melanie Gruter, an old roommate who was finishing up a post-doc at the Harvard School of Public Health. In the course of comparing notes about their respective jobs, Taylor mentioned the NDMA project. Gruter replied that her lab had just completed an epidemiological study on the subject, which found an apparent increase in the rate of birth defects among women exposed to an average 100 mg of doxylamine a day during the first trimester of pregnancy. From her background research, Taylor knew that this study directly conflicted with prior work in the field. Although she lacked any real details about the research, much less the expertise to evaluate the study, Taylor trusted her old friend and began to wonder whether she had an ethical obligation to notify the FDA.

The following week, Paul Hadley, a senior partner at the firm, asked Taylor to join in a meeting with a new client that had just gotten underway in his office. When she arrived, Mr. Hadley introduced her to Steven Malone, director of regulatory affairs at Radford Drugs, Inc. The company produced a wide variety of OTC drug products in the U.S., and it wanted to introduce a new and powerful sleep-aid. Although they have no doubt that doxylamine works as claimed (and is more effective than 50 mg of diphenhydramine), the sudden uncertainty about the regulatory status of doxylamine led Radford's product development team to formulate a product containing 50 mg of diphenhydramine (as allowed by the monograph) along with 10 mg of doxylamine. Because the monograph would not allow such a combination in any event (even if the FDA relents on its proposal to withdraw doxylamine), the company wants to characterize doxylamine as an "inactive" ingredient. Mr. Malone wanted to know whether this strategy would allow the company to continue using doxylamine, even if the FDA decided to remove it from the monograph, but also avoid listing it on the label. Mr. Hadley asked Taylor to research the question and have a response by Monday morning.

A weekend spent with the applicable sections of the *Code of Federal Regulations* and a variety of *Federal Register* notices revealed the following: a regulation mandating that an OTC "product contains only suitable inactive ingredients which are safe in the amounts administered and do not interfere with the effectiveness of the preparation," 21 C.F.R. § 330.1(e); a regulation listing non-GRASE substances (to which doxylamine would be added if the FDA eventually finalizes its proposed withdrawal) and providing that "[a]ny OTC drug product ... containing any active ingredient(s) as specified in paragraph (a) of this section is regarded as a new drug," id. § 310.545(b); a regulation defining "active ingredient" for GMP purposes as "any component that is intended to furnish pharmacological activity or other direct [drug] effect," id. § 210.3(b)(7); and a boilerplate FDA comment that appeared in several final monographs for other OTC product categories recognizing that non-monograph active ingredients may still have legitimate uses as inactive ingredients, see, e.g., 56 Fed. Reg. 37,792 (1991); see also 42 Fed. Reg. 19,156, 19,157 (1977) ("[T]his proposal [which was never finalized] is intended to preclude the retention and redesignation of an active ingredient as an inactive ingredient unless it serves an acceptable function as an inactive ingredient.").

In addition, in the course of running an on-line search for commentary about the agency's definition of active ingredient, Taylor came across the following discussion in an opinion resolving private litigation under the Lanham Act for false or misleading advertising:

> Sandoz's counsel argued to the district court that "[i]f [the demulcents] relieve coughs they're active. That's true as a matter of common sense and normal English." Such an interpretation of FDA regulations, absent direct guidance from the promulgating agency, is not as simple as Sandoz proposes. The FDA has not found conclusively that demulcents must be labeled as active or inactive ingredients within the meaning of 21 C.F.R. § 210.3(b)(7). We decline to find and do not believe that the district court had to find, either "as a matter of common sense" or "normal English," that which the FDA, with all of its scientific expertise, has yet to determine. Because "agency decisions are frequently of a discretionary nature or frequently require expertise, the agency should be given the first chance to exercise that discretion or to apply that expertise." Thus, we are unable to conclude that

> Vicks's labeling of Pediatric 44's demulcents as inactive is literally false, even if Vicks concurrently claims that these ingredients enable its medicine to work the instant it is swallowed. Sandoz's position would require us to usurp administrative agencies' responsibility for interpreting and enforcing potentially ambiguous regulations.

Sandoz Pharm. Corp. v. Richardson–Vicks, Inc., 902 F.2d 222, 231 (3d Cir. 1990). Taylor also read an article recommending that the FDA revise its existing labeling rules to require the listing of all inactive ingredients. See Holly A. Brown, Comment, The Need for Regulation Mandating the Labeling of Inactive Ingredients in Pharmaceuticals, 8 Admin. L.J. 291 (1994).*

On Monday, Taylor was prepared to present her findings. She went through the possible legal arguments before concluding that Radford could not add doxylamine as an inactive ingredient because it did not serve a legitimate secondary (e.g., preservative or flavoring) function but instead had a pharmacological effect. She was somewhat taken aback, however, when Mr. Hadley quickly jumped in after she presented her conclusion: "Wait a minute, Amy," he said. "It's not so clear to me that Radford can't do so. I think that the company would have a solid basis in the law for going the inactive ingredient route." Taylor tried to disagree, but Malone broke in: "It sounds like we have a pretty good legal argument. Besides, what would the FDA do to me if the argument does not hold up? And how likely would it be that they would find out in the first place?"

Mr. Hadley explained that, if it was not listed on the label, the agency would indeed have difficulty in finding out whether doxylamine was, in fact, present in the product. Mr. Malone then asked what the FDA would do if it did decide to issue a final rule prohibiting the use of doxylamine as an active ingredient. "First of all," Mr. Hadley replied, "if it were able to put together some evidence that Radford had added doxylamine, the agency would send you a 'warning letter,' threatening to impose sanctions unless you immediately undertake some corrective action." "But how likely is it that the FDA would require us to recall the product?" Mr. Malone asked. "Based on my experience with the agency, not very likely," Mr. Hadley responded.

But Taylor did not agree with his assessment at all: "I'm not so sure that's true in this case. Given the recent public criticism over the need to withdraw several newly approved prescription drugs, the FDA might overreact and insist on a recall. In addition," she continued, "consumer groups might bring suit for fraud or make adverse public statements about the product. Recently, several consumer groups have been analyzing other FDA-regulated products and publicizing the results." She failed to mention the soon-to-be-published findings from the new epidemiological study.

* In 1997, a couple of years after the events described in this hypothetical case, Congress mandated such ingredient labeling. See FDAMA § 412(c) (codified at 21 U.S.C. § 352(e)(1)(A)(iii)). The FDA issued implementing regulations two years later. See 64 Fed. Reg. 13,254, 13,288 (1999) (codified at 21 C.F.R. § 201.66(c)(8)).

"But, Amy," Mr. Hadley countered, "there is a strong legal argument that low dose doxylamine serves a legitimate function as an inactive ingredient, and as such need not be included by name on the label." Before Taylor could respond, Mr. Malone broke in: "I agree with you, Paul. It sounds to me like we have a good legal basis for not including doxylamine on the label, and I'd like a letter from your firm on that for my files." "Sure, Steve," he responded, and turned toward Taylor. "Amy, I'll leave it to you to work something out with Steve. I suggest you put together a draft for him to look at sometime this week." Taylor went back to her office, but she did not feel comfortable about writing the letter.

DISCUSSION QUESTIONS

1. Before being assigned to work on the Radford problem, Amy Taylor prepared comments to the FDA arguing that it should not yet remove doxylamine from the OTC monograph. In one sense, Taylor's task presented no ethical dilemma. She was expressing the position of her client, the NDMA, and it is plainly a respectable argument under the law. But what if she knew that the industry only intended to stall and had never in fact planned to conduct any additional studies? Even if its commitment to undertake further research was entirely genuine, what if Taylor believes that some consumers might develop serious side effects, as the unpublished Harvard School of Public Health study seems to suggest? This would be a result of the delay she is advocating. (If an attorney knew that there had been a number of deaths during the early use of a new prescription drug in Europe but that there was no requirement that these be made known to the FDA, could she file the papers necessary for obtaining approval for use of the drug in the United States? Is this a different case?) What could Taylor do if she believed there was great danger in the actions her client proposed? Perhaps she could raise the issue directly with the client or urge the supervising partner to do this, but what factors would enter into a decision to take one of these steps?

2. In connection with the work for Radford, could (or must) Amy Taylor advise the FDA of her client's plan to hide doxylamine as an inactive ingredient? Is it any consolation that an existing FDA regulation mandates that the labels of all OTC drugs intended for systemic absorption caution pregnant or nursing women to "seek the advice of a health professional before using this product," 21 C.F.R. § 201.63(a)? Separately, is there any conflict of interest for the firm in representing these two clients?

3. An equally difficult question is what advice a lawyer should give to her client when she thinks what the client wants to do would, in all likelihood, be deemed unlawful by a regulatory agency or court, but there is room for doubt. Is there any obligation to go beyond informing the client of the attorney's view of the law and the attorney's prediction as to how the relevant tribunals would handle a dispute about the issue? If the client indicates that he intends to proceed despite advice that the proposed action is almost certainly illegal, does the lawyer have an obligation to remind the client of the impropriety of ignoring the law in that way or is it sufficient that the client is aware of the likely consequences? What if the lawyer will be expected to prepare documents or otherwise assist in the transaction? Is it at least proper for the lawyer to take these steps if she believes there is a "presentable" argument for the legality of what the client is proposing to do or should she impose a higher standard?

Even if any illegality is purely technical, i.e., it has no significant economic or health consequences, does Taylor have an obligation to try to persuade Malone that his company nonetheless should include doxylamine on the label? Would Taylor be wrong to continue to participate in and assist the transaction (e.g., by such further steps as negotiating to purchase product labels which she knew did not mention doxylamine) if she believed she was furthering a plain violation of the law? In particular, should Taylor draft the letter? Here, in contrast to negotiating with the seller of labels, there is the further issue that she is being asked to state as her own opinion legal views that she does not hold. And the very purpose of the opinion letter is to persuade private associates of Mr. Malone and regulatory officials that the company is acting in good faith. There are three types of letters that Taylor could write in this situation:

(a) An "Opinion Letter" stating that in her opinion the law does not require Radford to include doxylamine on the label. If she drafts such a letter she will be putting her (or Paul Hadley's) name and the name of the firm behind it.

(b) A letter specifying the legal risks of not including doxylamine on the label without stating whether she thinks the action is legal or not.

(c) A letter defending the client's failure to include doxylamine on the label. (This letter is a bit closer to the Opinion Letter, except that, as in option (b), an attorney need not say that she agrees with her client's position.)

Which type of letter would you draft if you were in Taylor's position? None of the letters would help Radford much in a court proceeding, but an Opinion Letter or a letter such as that listed above as option (c) might help the company in negotiations with the regulatory agency (as evidence of a good faith mistake) if the company tried to convince the FDA not to sanction it. What are the implications of preparing a draft to be worked out with the client (is this ever proper)?

4. Another troublesome issue raised by this case is what an attorney should do if she thinks that what her client wants to do is illegal but also thinks that the client is not likely to get caught. A particularly difficult variation of this issue is how candid an attorney should be when a client asks her concerning the likelihood of being discovered or the probability of various fines and penalties. Do you agree with the way Mr. Hadley handled the question? What else could he have done? How much does your response turn on the possible harmful consequences to others of the apparently proscribed conduct? If Malone had not come up with the idea of hiding doxylamine as an inactive ingredient, could Taylor (or Hadley) have suggested this gimmick to the client as long as accompanied by caveats about its questionable legality?

5. Obviously, Taylor doesn't agree with Mr. Hadley's response to Mr. Malone regarding the problem. As a junior attorney in a law firm, what are her options? What would you do in such a situation? How would your responses to the previous questions affect your decision (i.e., your perspective as to how harmful the consequences to consumers might be if doxylamine were not listed on the label, whether the act was illegal, how likely you think it is that the FDA would bring an enforcement action)?

Is it relevant that Taylor's law firm is known as a specialist in the food and drug law field? Does this give her an additional responsibility to avoid signing her name to views about FDA regulatory matters that she does not believe to be her best sense of correct law? Does she have a duty to her law firm to act so as to preserve their reputation as "wise" and "sound" lawyers in this field? If so, was she required to tell the client that this concern would influence her?

At what point would you refuse to work any longer on the case? What if you were a junior attorney in a government agency and disagreed with the way a senior attorney dealt with a matter? For example, suppose that you worked for the FDA and the Chief Counsel (your boss) advised the Commissioner to withdraw the proposed amendment without first considering the results of the just released Harvard School of Public Health study?

The following provisions of the *D.C. Rules of Professional Conduct* (2007) (patterned on the ABA's *Model Rules of Professional Conduct*) may offer some relevant guidance in considering these questions:

Rule 1.2(e): A lawyer shall not counsel a client to engage, or assist a client, in conduct that the lawyer knows is criminal or fraudulent, but a lawyer may discuss the legal consequences of any proposed course of conduct with a client and may counsel or assist a client to make a good-faith effort to determine the validity, scope, meaning, or application of the law.

comment 6: The fact that a client uses advice in a course of action that is criminal or fraudulent does not, of itself, make a lawyer a party to the course of action.... There is a critical distinction between presenting an analysis of legal aspects of questionable conduct and recommending the means by which a crime or fraud might be committed with impunity.

Rule 1.6(c): A lawyer may reveal client confidences and secrets, to the extent reasonably necessary: (1) to prevent a criminal act that the lawyer reasonably believes is likely to result in death or substantial bodily harm absent disclosure of the client's secrets or confidences by the lawyer....

comment 20: The lawyer's exercise of discretion in determining whether to make disclosures that are reasonably likely to prevent the death or substantial bodily injury of another requires consideration of such factors as the client's tendency to commit violent acts or, conversely, to make idle threats.... [T]he lawyer's decision not to disclose as permitted by the Rule does not violate Rule 1.6.

Rule 1.7(b): Except as permitted by paragraph (c), a lawyer shall not represent a client with respect to a matter if: (1) That matter involves a specific party or parties and a position to be taken by that client in that matter is adverse to a position taken or to be taken by another client in the same matter ....

Rule 2.1: In representing a client, a lawyer shall exercise independent professional judgment and render candid advice. In rendering advice, a lawyer may refer not only to law but to other considerations such as moral, economic, social, and political factors, that may be relevant to the client's situation.

Rule 5.2: (a) A lawyer is bound by the Rules of Professional Conduct notwithstanding that the lawyer acted at the direction of another person. (b) A subordinate lawyer does not violate the Rules of Professional Conduct if that lawyer acts in accordance with a supervisory lawyer's reasonable resolution of an arguable question of professional duty.

comment 2: When lawyers in a supervisor-subordinate relationship encounter a matter involving professional judgment as to ethical duty, the supervisor may assume responsibility for making the judgment. Otherwise a consistent course of action or position could not be taken.

Rule 8.3(a): A lawyer who knows that another lawyer has committed a violation of the Rules of Professional Conduct that raises a substantial question as to that lawyer's honesty, trustworthiness, or fitness as a lawyer in other respects, shall inform the appropriate professional authority.

In addition, consider comment 3 to Rule 1.13: "When constituents of the organization make decisions for it, the decisions ordinarily must be accepted by the lawyer even if their utility or prudence is doubtful.... [W]hen the lawyer knows that the organization is likely to be substantially injured by action of an officer or other constituent that violates a legal obligation to the organization or is in violation of law that might be imputed to the organization, the lawyer must proceed as reasonably necessary in the best interest of the organization." Elaborating on this idea, one scholar offered the following illustration: "A law violation, such as the illegal manufacture of a defective product, that threatens injury to nonclient third parties could still result in injury to the organization because of the threat of suits." Charles W. Wolfram, Modern Legal Ethics 744 (1986); see also id. at 692–710 (discussing the ethical problems that may arise in counseling clients and preparing opinion letters); Geoffrey C. Hazard, Jr., How Far May a Lawyer Go in Assisting a Client in Legally Wrongful Conduct?, 35 U. Miami L. Rev. 669, 682–83 (1981). Should a still broader perspective inform such choices? See Martin L. Hirsch, Side Effects of Corporate Greed: Pharmaceutical Companies Need a Dose of Corporate Social Responsibility, 9 Minn. J.L. Sci. & Tech. 607 (2008).

Finally, consider the following excerpt as it relates to questions about candor to the tribunal:

> Attorneys representing clients before agencies are subject to the same ethical obligations that govern their conduct before courts. In most jurisdictions, these include duties of candor to the tribunal, with correlative prohibitions against unnecessary delays or harassment of other parties. Rule 3.1 of the ABA's Model Rules of Professional Conduct directs that "a lawyer shall not bring or defend a proceeding, or assert or controvert an issue therein, unless there is a basis for doing so that is not frivolous." In addition, under the Model Code of Professional Responsibility "a lawyer shall not ... delay a trial ... when he knows or when it is obvious that such action would serve merely to harass or maliciously injure another." Although these rules are framed in terms of conduct during the course of litigation before courts, they have equal application to adjudicatory proceedings before agencies.
>
> Attorneys enjoy somewhat greater latitude in administrative proceedings that are not regarded as adjudicatory. Rule 3.9 of the Model Rules directs advocates in nonadjudicative proceedings before agencies to conform to the duties regarding candor to the tribunal, fairness to the opposing party and counsel, and the impartiality and decorum of the tribunal. Notably missing from Rule 3.9, however, are cross-references to Rules 3.1 and 3.2, which respectively proscribe frivolous claims and other conduct designed to delay or harass. Nonetheless, Rule 3.9 does not countenance conduct by lawyers in nonadjudicative proceedings that would be regarded as objectionable in adjudicative proceedings. As explained in the accompanying Comment, agencies "should be able to rely on the integrity of submissions made to it."
>
> Although the precise contours of these ethical duties may vary depending on whether the agency proceeding is considered adjudicative or legislative, an attorney generally is expected to act no differently than he or she would act when representing a client in court. In practice, however, these rules of professional responsibility may be viewed as somewhat less stringent in the administrative context than in the judicial .... In fact, some have suggested that Rule 3.9 might apply only to conduct during trial-type hearings in nonadjudicative proceedings before agencies, an interpretation that would leave a large class of regulatory submissions prepared by attorneys wholly exempt

> from the rules of professional responsibility. Other commentators have argued that conduct during informal, nonadjudicative proceedings should be governed by stricter rather than lesser ethical standards precisely because of the absence of any opportunity for testing through an adversarial presentation of evidence and arguments....
>
> Finally, it must be remembered that the rules of professional responsibility only set the outer boundaries for ethical behavior where transgressions may trigger severe disciplinary sanctions. In recognition of this limitation, courts have chosen to establish more demanding rules of conduct designed to preserve the integrity of the litigation process, most notably Rule 11. A similar approach may be necessary in the agency context.

Lars Noah, Sham Petitioning as a Threat to the Integrity of the Regulatory Process, 74 N.C. L. Rev. 1, 49–53 (1995). Citing this article, the FDA proposed revising its citizen petition procedures to, among other things, strengthen existing certification requirements. See 64 Fed. Reg. 66,822 (1999) (to be codified at 21 C.F.R. § 10.30(b)), withdrawn, 68 Fed. Reg. 16,461 (2003); see also Ubiotica Corp. v. FDA, 427 F.2d 376, 382 (6th Cir.1970) (stating that counsel was properly excluded from further participation in an agency hearing for conduct deemed "dilatory, recalcitrant, obstructive of orderly process, and contemptuous"); Christian D'Avignon–Aubut, Note, Certifying the Validity and Integrity of Reports on Clinical Studies Submitted to the FDA: A New Role for a New Breed of Lawyers, 20 Geo. J. Legal Ethics 499 (2007). Congress subsequently amended the statute to impose certification and other requirements on certain citizen petitions. See FDAAA, Pub. L. No. 110–85, § 914, 121 Stat. 823, 953 (2007) (codified at 21 U.S.C. § 355(q)).

Stanton v. Astra Pharmaceutical Products, Inc.

718 F.2d 553 (3d Cir.1983).

■ BECKER, CIRCUIT JUDGE:

* * * Pursuant to [21 U.S.C. § 355(j)(1), a provision that Congress added to the FDCA in 1962 authorizing the FDA to mandate the filing of certain reports], the Secretary promulgated regulations on May 28, 1964. These regulations require companies marketing registered drugs to submit to the FDA annual reports, 21 C.F.R. § 130.35(e) (1971), as well as immediate reports of all unexpected adverse reactions to those drugs, id. § 130.35(f).

Between May 28, 1964, and the end of 1970, Astra received 202 reports of adverse reactions allegedly related to Xylocaine. These reactions ranged from minor, temporary effects to death. Yet Astra forwarded none of these reports to the FDA, relying upon the advice of its counsel, Alan H. Kaplan, that Xylocaine was not a "new drug" and therefore was exempt from the reporting requirements embodied in 21 C.F.R. § 130.35(e) and (f). However, the company prepared the reports and made them a part of the

Establishment Inspection Reports seen by non-medical FDA inspectors who came to inspect Astra's facilities between 1964 and 1971.

In deciding not to file the reports ostensibly required by section 130.35, Astra also relied on a letter, dated October 2, 1963, from John F. Palmer, M.D., the Chief of the Department of Health, Education and Welfare's (HEW's) New Drug Status Branch, in which Dr. Palmer advised Astra that two-percent Xylocaine was "not now regarded" by the Division of Drugs as a "new drug" within the meaning of 21 U.S.C. § 321(p). On April 25, 1968, however, Arthur M. West, M.D., Acting Director of HEW's Division of Surgical Dental Drugs and Adjuncts, wrote to Astra and requested that the company file all reports prescribed in regulations promulgated pursuant to 21 U.S.C. § 355(j).

Upon receipt of this letter, Astra wrote back and reminded the FDA of both the 1963 letter from Dr. Palmer and the FDA's announcement on September 12, 1964, postponing the effective date of § 130.35(b)'s reporting requirements, see 29 Fed. Reg. 12,872 (1964). Dr. West responded in July 1969 by referring Astra to a statement published in the *Federal Register* on May 20, 1968, in which the FDA formally had revoked "all opinions previously given by the [FDA] to the effect that an article is 'not a new drug' or is 'no longer a new drug.' " Dr. West further informed Astra that, "since these drugs are presently under review by the National Academy of Sciences–National Research Council, we are deferring any final decision on the new drug status until the findings of the review are published." Thus, Astra knew, or should have known, by May 20, 1968, three and one-half years before [plaintiff] Harrikah Stanton's adverse reaction, that the FDA deemed Xylocaine to be a "new drug" for purposes of compliance with the reporting requirements of 21 U.S.C. § 355(j) and 21 C.F.R. § 130.35.

Despite the above exchanges between Astra and the FDA, Astra contends that 21 U.S.C. § 355(j) and 21 C.F.R. § 130.35(f) apply only to "new drugs" and not to "old drugs" or drugs that are generally recognized by experts as safe and effective; Astra further claims that Xylocaine had achieved such recognition by 1964. * * * [S]ection 130.35 does not admit of the exclusion urged by Astra. Section 130.35 applies to "[e]ach applicant for whom a new-drug application or supplement ... became effective or was approved *at any time* prior to June 20, 1963." 21 C.F.R. § 130.35(a), (b) (emphasis added). This language appears to encompass Xylocaine, which was approved by the FDA in 1948. Moreover, application of section 130.35 to a drug approved in 1948 would seem essential in light of the FDA's statutory obligation continually to monitor drugs already on the market in order to determine whether to withdraw FDA approval pursuant to 21 U.S.C. § 355(e).

Astra relies both on the 1963 letter from the FDA, in which the agency advised Astra that it did not consider Xylocaine to be a new drug, as well as on the FDA's 1964 suspension of the effectiveness of certain regulations pending the resolution of a court challenge. But neither the 1963 letter nor the 1964 suspension can avail Astra. While we concede that Astra initially was entitled to rely on the 1963 letter, the FDA effectively nullified the assertions contained in that letter when it announced in 1968, well before Harrikah Stanton's bone-marrow test in 1971, that "all opinions previously given by the [FDA] to the effect that an article is 'not a new drug' or is 'no longer a new drug' are hereby revoked," 33 Fed. Reg. 7758 (1968). And as for the 1964 suspension: that declaration stayed the enforcement of only 21 C.F.R. § 130.35(b), without any mention of subsections 130.35(e) and (f). * * * Thus, at least as of 1968, Astra knew, or should have known, that the FDA expected Astra to file the reports prescribed by section 130.35.

Second, the mere fact that Astra's attorneys interpreted section 130.35 incorrectly does not negate Astra's negligence in failing to comply with the regulations. Astra took a chance, and it is liable for the consequences of its acts. And even assuming that advice of counsel does constitute a legally cognizable excuse, that excuse could insulate Astra from liability only between the time that the FDA promulgated the regulations in 1964 and the time that the agency revoked all private letter-rulings as to new-drug status in 1968. Astra still had three and one-half years before the December 1971 tragedy to file the reports. * * *

Florida Breckenridge, Inc. v. Solvay Pharmaceuticals

174 F.3d 1227 (11th Cir.1999).*

■ Per curiam:

* * * In 1962, the FDCA was amended to require proof that the product was effective as well as safe. Congress made this new efficacy requirement retroactive to apply to all drugs that already had approved NDAs based on safety. The companies producing these drugs were given a two year window to submit revisions of their NDAs to prove their efficacy. In order to facilitate the efficacy evaluations of these drugs, the FDA set up the Drug Efficacy Study Implementation (DESI) program. Under this program, groups of drugs with approved NDAs were evaluated by an independent panel. If the panel found that the drugs met a certain standard for efficacy, the evidence was submitted to the FDA. If the FDA concurred with the DESI determination, a notice was published in the *Federal Register* and a supplemental NDA would be approved for these drugs. Under the FDCA, all drugs are new drugs and therefore require an approved NDA or ANDA before marketing unless they are generally recognized among experts as safe and effective for their labeled use (the "GRASE" exception) or are grandfathered.

By its terms, the DESI program applied only to drugs that already had approved NDAs as of 1962. In conjunction with the DESI program, the FDA developed a policy whereby drugs that were identical, similar or related ("ISR drugs") to an approved drug in the DESI review program could "piggy-back" off of the DESI review by submitting an ANDA after

* The opinion, which was published in the advance sheets of the *Federal Reporter*, was withdrawn from the bound volume at the request of the court.

the DESI review established the efficacy of the pioneer drug. For a time, FDA policy allowed a drug manufacturer to market an ISR drug after filing, but before approval of an ISR drug's ANDA. This policy was challenged in court and overturned in 1975. Hoffmann–LaRoche, Inc. v. Weinberger, 425 F.Supp. 890, 894 (D.D.C.1975) ("[T]he court holds that the FDA's policy of permitting new drugs to be marketed without an approved new drug application contravenes the clear statutory requirement of preclearance mandated by 21 U.S.C. § 355."). In response to this case, the FDA published a revision to its policy guidelines that "clarified" the agency's position. CPG 7132c.02, which Breckenridge submitted as an appendix to its brief, reads in part:

> The agency has decided to reaffirm that all products marketed as drugs under the DESI program are new drugs, and therefore, require an approved NDA or ANDA for marketing. In view of the reaffirmation of this policy, the agency must proceed to remove from the market all current DESI-effective prescription products that are not subjects of approved NDAs or ANDAs, and to prevent in the future the marketing of such unapproved products.

FDA Compliance Policy Guidelines § 440.100. This policy guideline document goes on to create priorities for the removal of unapproved drugs from the market. According to the FDA, there were so many unapproved drugs on the market that they needed to establish a triage system: "Considering the magnitude of the problem, the limitation on FDA's resources, and the resulting long time period before compliance can be fully attained, the agency has developed a strategy to handle unapproved products on a priority basis." Id. In stunning testament to the efficiency of the FDA's strategy, this policy is still in effect today because twenty-four years later, and thirty-six years after the 1962 amendments to the FDCA, there are still thousands of these unapproved drugs on the market. One of these drugs is Estratest, produced by Solvay.

Although the record contains conflicting dates, Solvay began marketing its Estratest drug in 1964 at the earliest. Estratest is a hormone supplement, consisting of esterified estrogens and methyltestosterone, that is widely prescribed to women who are suffering from the physical symptoms associated with menopause and who do not obtain relief from estrogen therapy alone. At the time of Estratest's entry into the marketplace, Solvay did not have, nor has it ever had over the past thirty-five years, an NDA or ANDA approved by the FDA. Obviously, Estratest could not have been directly subject to DESI review because it was not marketed, nor was it the subject of an approved NDA based on its safety, before the 1962 amendments to the FDCA became effective.

As part of the DESI process, a study evaluated the efficacy of a class of drugs that combined estrogens and androgens. The drugs under review all had approved NDAs from before 1962. None of these drugs contained Estratest's combination of esterified estrogens and methyltestosterone. The drugs were evaluated in a published notice, DESI 7661. On November 22, 1972, as noted in the correspondence log submitted by Solvay in their reply brief, Solvay's predecessor corporation contacted the FDA to determine whether Estratest could be considered ISR under the DESI 7661 notice. After an undescribed response from the FDA, there is a gap in the log until a letter from the FDA in July of 1979, which indicates that the FDA notified Solvay that Estratest was under legal review and that temporarily no action relating to the NDA requirement would be taken but that any continued marketing of Estratest was at Solvay's risk. Since that time and to this date, Solvay, while continuing to market Estratest, has been trying to get approval of NDAs for Estratest, but has gotten a series of not-approvable letters.

In the spring of 1997, Breckenridge introduced a drug, Menogen, into the marketplace. This drug contained esterified estrogens and methyltestosterone in the same dosages as Estratest and was marketed as the generic equivalent of Estratest. Breckenridge did not obtain approval of an NDA or ANDA before marketing Menogen, and has not obtained approval to this date. Breckenridge relies on Solvay's contention that Estratest is legally on the market without approval to extend also to Menogen. Shortly after Breckenridge began marketing Menogen, they received notification from Solvay that they believed Menogen infringed on Estratest's trade dress and that the generic equivalency claims constituted false advertising. In response, Breckenridge filed this suit for a declaratory judgment that their marketing of Menogen did not infringe the Estratest trade dress or constitute false advertising under the Lanham Act. Solvay counterclaimed, asserting claims for trade dress infringement and false advertising under the Lanham Act, the Florida Deceptive and Unfair Trade Practices Act and common law unfair competition law.

After discovery, both parties moved for summary judgment. The district court granted summary judgment for Breckenridge. On the trade dress infringement claim, the court held that no reasonable fact-finder could find a likelihood of confusion as to source between Estratest and Menogen. On the false advertising claim, the court held that because both parties were allowed on the market without FDA approval, the false advertising analysis was not governed by the FDA regulations regarding generic drugs and that in this world of non-regulated pharmaceuticals, a lower standard of equivalence was sufficient to render Breckenridge's claims literally true.

Solvay appealed the summary judgment to this court, arguing that the district court erred in its likelihood of confusion analysis and that drugs allowed on the market without FDA approval should still be subject to the FDA equivalency standards for advertised claims of generic equivalency. After Solvay filed its initial brief, the Department of Justice and the FDA filed an amicus curiae brief to address what they perceived as errors in the district court's opinion regarding the regulatory status of Estratest and Menogen and the resulting use of a different equivalency standard for generic drugs than is specified in the FDCA and FDA regulations. The government pointed out that the FDA's position is that neither drug is lawfully on the market because both require an approved NDA or ANDA before they may be legally sold, raising the point that unclean hands might bar either party from benefitting from trade law protection. The government did not explain why the FDA failed, for well over thirty years, to enforce the law and remove Estratest from the market. In response to the government's brief, both Solvay and Breckenridge harshly criticized the government for not reading the record, claiming that neither party ever told the court that they weren't subject to FDA regulation. Both parties continued to maintain, however, that although regulated they were not subject to FDA approval.

At oral argument, both parties continued to assert that they were lawfully on the market, although they could not articulate consistent or specific reasons why. They claimed to be surprised by the issue, claiming that it was never raised before the district court. At the end of oral argument, both parties agreed to submit supplemental briefs on the issue of whether protection was available under the Lanham Act for drugs sold in violation of the FDCA. Instead, two days before their supplemental brief was due, Solvay filed this motion to dismiss their appeal with prejudice. Breckenridge responded by requesting sanctions for a frivolous appeal pursuant to Fed. R. App. P. 38, and in the process executed a head-snapping reversal of position regarding Solvay's representations to the district court about Estratest's regulatory status. They did not, however, oppose Solvay's motion to dismiss.

It seems obvious to this court that this last-moment motion to dismiss, after the completion of oral arguments and without a settlement agreement, resulted from Solvay's realization that it was caught misrepresenting Estratest's regulatory status and wishes to avoid a published opinion that would alert the world to its misdeeds. This case comes right up to the line where the interests of justice would require us to deny Solvay's motion. Especially in light of the fact that the motion is unopposed, we will grant it. In our supervisory capacity, however, we feel that we must review the attorneys' conduct before this court and the district court and determine whether a disciplinary referral is appropriate.[2] Careful review of the record has uncovered a pattern of conduct by both parties' attorneys designed to mislead and confuse the court regarding the regulatory status of Estratest

---

2. Although this order focuses on the conduct of the attorneys for Solvay and Breckenridge, we note that the FDA is also due a share of criticism. It is incomprehensible that Estratest has been allowed on the market without approval for thirty-five years. It seems reasonable that most patients undergoing treatment for menopause fairly assume that any medication freely available and prescribed by their doctor has been proven safe and effective to the satisfaction of the FDA. They have a right to expect that the laws, as passed by Congress to protect them, are being enforced. To this date, Estratest has failed to satisfy the FDA that it is safe or effective as required by the FDCA, and yet the FDA has taken no action to remove the drug from the market. We are accustomed to hearing arguments in situations like this bemoaning scarce governmental resources and the like, but there can be no good excuse for allowing a company to violate the law for thirty-five years. If the drug is not safe or effective enough to be approved, thirty-five years seems like sufficient time to get around to taking some action. Certainly, Solvay was on notice that they were violating the law, and the FDA's inaction in no way excuses Solvay's conduct, but neither does Solvay's notice excuse the FDA's inaction.

and Menogen. Unfortunately, we must remind these attorneys that they are officers of the court. As such, they "owe duties of complete candor and primary loyalty to the court before which they practice." These duties are never subservient to a lawyer's duty to advocate zealously for his or her client. In this case, the attorneys for both parties have frustrated the system of justice, which depends on their candor and loyalty to the court, because they wanted to avoid an unpleasant truth about their clients' conduct. "In short, they have sold out to the client."

Normally, this sort of conduct is caught before it can do much harm by the adversarial nature of our system of justice. In this case, however, the adversarial parties both had an interest in hiding the fact that they needed FDA approval from the court. In Solvay's case, admitting that Estratest was not legally on the market would be fatal to their claims because the Lanham Act only protects parties engaged in lawful commerce. * * * Likewise, Breckenridge had an interest in hiding the FDCA violations from the court. Since this litigation began, the FDA has taken action against Breckenridge for, among other things, marketing Menogen without FDA approval.[4] Naturally, they would like to avoid making any admissions in this case. Furthermore, Breckenridge based its entire defense to the false advertising claim on the theory that there is a segment of the pharmaceutical market that is not subject to FDA approval, and that these drugs should be subject to a less stringent equivalency standard for the purposes of advertising generic equivalency. This theory is entirely dependent on misleading the court into believing that neither Estratest nor Menogen require FDA approval.

As discussed above, we believe that there is no magical exception that allows Solvay or Breckenridge to opt out of the FDA approval process. As the government's brief points out, both Estratest and Menogen are "new drugs" under the FDCA and require approved NDAs or ANDAs before they may be lawfully marketed. Because both parties had incentives to avoid addressing this threshold issue, the attorneys on both sides actively attempted to mislead and confuse the district court and this court regarding the regulatory status of both drugs. * * *

On several separate occasions, [District] Judge Ryskamp inquired about why neither drug needed FDA approval. When confronted with these questions, the attorneys either changed the subject without answering or gave a vague explanation claiming that for historical reasons the drugs were either not subject to FDA regulation or did not require FDA approval. * * * The attorneys effectively misled Judge Ryskamp into believing that Estratest's legal status had been established under a grandfather provision that caused them not to be regulated by the FDA. As previously discussed,

---

4. Once again, we are baffled as to why the FDA decided to go after the generic manufacturer, which had been marketing the drug for approximately one year, while ignoring Solvay's violations, which had been ongoing for thirty-five years. If we understand the government's argument, Breckenridge had violated other provisions of the FDCA, which made the enforcement action more urgent. Nonetheless, this seems insufficient to explain an enforcement differential of thirty-four years.

there is no possibly valid legal argument that would make this characterization true. Both parties admit that they are not subject to the grandfather provisions of the FDCA, and both drugs were introduced after the 1962 amendments. The judge clearly relied on the attorney's representations, and, in fact, based his decision on the false advertising claims on these misrepresentations.

In their briefs, the parties continued to make the general assertion that they were allowed on the market without approval. After the government filed its amicus brief, pointing out that both products were marketed unlawfully and that the attorneys had misrepresented the drugs' regulatory status, both parties responded by misrepresenting their own conduct at the trial level. Breckenridge accused the government of not reading any portion of the record below and of fabricating its charge, claiming that neither party ever represented to the court that the drugs were not subject to FDA regulation: "[N]either Solvay nor Breckenridge ever referred to Menogen or Estratest as 'unregulated.'" Solvay then jumped on the government-bashing bandwagon, claiming that "neither party made any such representation," and claiming to be "perplexed by the district court's statement that the drugs were not 'regulated' by the FDA." These assertions are outrageous. As quoted above, Mr. Jameson [counsel for Solvay] specifically told the court on two occasions that the drugs were "not subject to FDA regulation." Such mischaracterizations of the record are particularly egregious, considering that both attorneys made them while accusing the government of lying about the record.

At oral argument, the misconduct continued. Jameson first argued that Estratest was lawfully on the market as a direct result of the DESI review process. Jameson's statements give the impression that Estratest, itself, was subject to DESI review. It was not. As discussed above, Estratest was not even on the market in 1962, nor did it ever have an approved NDA. Further, his description of the purpose of DESI as being to examine drugs on the marketplace to see if they should remain on the marketplace is very misleading. The purpose was to examine drugs already approved as safe by the FDA, and to help drug companies provide the FDA with an evaluation of their efficacy. Estratest has never, to this date, been approved by the FDA as safe or effective. Jameson further misled the court by characterizing the DESI process as an "alternative to the 'formal' approval process." In fact, there are no alternatives to the "formal" approval process for DESI or ISR drugs. All DESI and ISR drugs are "new drugs" under the FDCA and require approval of an NDA or ANDA before lawful marketing. DESI never operates as an alternative to such approval. The falsity of this characterization is further proved by the fact that, subsequent to the publication of the DESI 7661 notice, Solvay filed an ANDA in an attempt to get approval and was warned by the FDA that marketing of the drug was at Solvay's risk. Jameson knew this—the information is all in papers that he appended to his reply brief as evidence that FDA knew that Estratest was on the market.

After realizing that this court would not be so easily bamboozled, Jameson attempted to refine his argument, arguing that the DESI review somehow operated as conclusive proof that Estratest falls under an exception under the FDCA known as the GRASE exception. Because we dismiss this appeal, we are precluded from ruling definitively on this claim. However, our review of the law, at this stage, points to the conclusion that it is wholly without merit. If a drug is generally recognized among qualified experts as safe and effective, it is not a new drug under the FDCA and therefore does not need an NDA. However, GRASE is a term of art, and the Supreme Court has explained that it really is not much of an exception because it requires at least the same exacting proof that NDA approval requires. Furthermore, GRASE cannot be construed to provide a way to evade the regulatory process by allowing a firm that has repeatedly failed to gain approval of an existing NDA to opt out of the approval process. Consequently, it would appear that Estratest cannot satisfy the GRASE exception.

Finally, Jameson argued that the FDA's failure to take action to remove them from the market proves that they are GRASE. Obviously, this is nonsense. Courts have already held that the FDA policy of deferring the removal of ISR drugs from the marketplace is not a defense, even to criminal prosecution for marketing a new drug without an approved NDA. In order to fall under the GRASE exception, a drug must meet requirements at least as stringent as those for NDA approval. Solvay has continually failed to obtain approval based on the evidence it has provided the FDA. They may not, then, circumvent the approval process merely by marketing their drug in defiance of the FDA for thirty-five years. Solvay has been attempting to get approval of its ANDA/NDA for 27 years, and has gotten a continual stream of not-approvable letters. The very fact that they are seeking approval indicates that they do not honestly believe that they fall under the GRASE exception. Furthermore, the exception cannot be used to succeed where the FDA screening process has specifically denied approval. This would pervert the statute, as the Supreme Court noted. Finally, even if Estratest could be said now, in 1999, to have gained GRASE status, that status would not retroactively render the past thirty-five years of illegal marketing lawful. * * *

During the course of this litigation, Mr. Jameson and Ms. Allison * * * engaged in a pattern of practice designed to mislead and confuse the court regarding the regulatory status of their clients' drugs. Although we grant the unopposed motion, we are referring this matter to the disciplinary committee of this court for further consideration.

NOTES AND QUESTIONS

1. *Questionable regulatory advice?* The *Solvay* court expressed outrage at the conduct of the lawyers during litigation. Do you think that they actually comprehended the byzantine FDA regulatory history? Did they have an obligation to seek counsel from lawyers who specialize in the area and better understand these complexities? Cf. Sacha Pfeiffer, Law Firms Push into Stem Cells: Specialty Practices Rise, Boston Globe, Nov. 7, 2006, at C1. And how would you interpret the fact that several years after the court's criticism of the agency for its inaction on Estratest the situation remained unchanged? See Chris Adams, Unapproved Drugs Linger on the Market: FDA Has Yet to Give OK to a Popular Hormone–Replacement Therapy Used Since 1964, Wall St. J., Mar. 20, 2003, at A4; Rita Rubin, The Case of One Unapproved Drug, USA Today, Sept. 18, 2006, at 2A. In contrast, the *Stanton* court dealt with a problem that arose from poor regulatory advice given to a company by a lawyer who specialized in FDA matters. Apart from the possibility that the company risked agency sanctions for its failure to comply (and also a negligence per se charge in a tort action), did that lawyer violate any ethical norms?

CHAPTER 4

DISSEMINATION OF PRODUCT INFORMATION

The FDA comprehensively regulates product composition as well as product information, and it controls the latter both directly—by imposing limitations on permissible labeling and advertising—and indirectly—by subjecting products to more stringent controls based on the intended uses reflected in the product information. It's hardly the only federal agency that regulates by controlling information (just think of the Securities and Exchange Commission), and it's hardly a recent development (the FDA's misbranding authority goes back a full century). This chapter discusses the reach of the agency's statutory power over the labeling and advertising of therapeutic products, directed to both physicians and patients, and then it considers the effect of constitutional limitations on the FDA's ability to exercise that authority.

A. LABELING

Kordel v. United States

335 U.S. 345 (1948).

■ DOUGLAS, JUSTICE:

* * * Kordel writes and lectures on health foods from information derived from studies in public and private libraries. Since 1941 he has been marketing his own health food products, which appear to be compounds of various vitamins, minerals and herbs. The alleged misbranding consists of statements in circulars or pamphlets distributed to consumers by the vendors of the products, relating to their efficacy. The petitioner supplies these pamphlets as well as the products to the vendors. Some of the literature was displayed in stores in which the petitioner's products were on sale. Some of it was given away with the sale of products; some sold independently of the drugs; and some mailed to customers by the vendors.

It is undisputed that petitioner shipped or caused to be shipped in interstate commerce both the drugs and the literature. Seven of the counts charged that the drugs and literature were shipped in the same cartons. The literature involved in the other counts was shipped separately from the drugs and at different times—both before and after the shipments of the drugs with which they were associated. The question whether the separate shipment of the literature saved the drugs from being misbranded within the meaning of the Act presents the main issue in the case.

Section 301(a) of the [FDCA] prohibits the introduction into interstate commerce of any drug that is adulterated or misbranded. It is misbranded according to § 502(a) if its "labeling is false or misleading in any particular" and unless the labeling bears "adequate directions for use." § 502(f). The term labeling is defined in § 201(m) to mean "all labels and other written, printed, or graphic matter (1) upon any article or any of its containers or wrappers, or (2) accompanying such article." Section 303 makes the violation of any of the provisions of § 301 a crime.

In this case the drugs and the literature had a common origin and a common destination. The literature was used in the sale of the drugs. It explained their uses. Nowhere else was the purchaser advised how to use them. It constituted an essential supplement to the label attached to the package. Thus the products and the literature were interdependent, as the court of appeals observed.

It would take an extremely narrow reading of the Act to hold that these drugs were not misbranded. A criminal law is not to be read expansively to include what is not plainly embraced within the language of the statute, since the purpose fairly to apprise men of the boundaries of the prohibited action would then be defeated. But there is no canon against using common sense in reading a criminal law, so that strained and technical constructions do not defeat its purpose by creating exceptions from or loopholes in it.

It would, indeed, create an obviously wide loophole to hold that these drugs would be misbranded if the literature had been shipped in the same container but not misbranded if the literature left in the next or in the preceding mail. The high purpose of the Act to protect consumers who under present conditions are largely unable to protect themselves in this field would then be easily defeated. The administrative agency charged with its enforcement has not given the Act any such restricted construction. The textual structure of the Act is not agreeable to it. Accordingly, we conclude that the phrase "accompanying such article" is not restricted to labels that are on or in the article or package that is transported.

The first clause of § 201(m)—all labels "upon any article or any of its containers or wrappers"—clearly embraces advertising or descriptive matter that goes with the package in which the articles are transported. The second clause—"accompanying such article"—has no specific reference to packages, containers or their contents as did a predecessor statute. It plainly includes what is contained within the package whether or not it is "upon" the article or its wrapper or container. But the second clause does not say "accompanying such article in the package or container," and we see no reason for reading the additional words into the text.

One article or thing is accompanied by another when it supplements or explains it, in the manner that a committee report of the Congress accompanies a bill. No physical attachment one to the other is necessary. It is the textual relationship that is significant. The analogy to the present case is obvious. We need not labor the point.

The false and misleading literature in the present case was designed for use in the distribution and sale of the drug, and it was so used. The fact that it went in a different mail was wholly irrelevant whether we judge the transaction by purpose or result. And to say that the prior or subsequent shipment of the literature disproves that it "is" misbranded when introduced into commerce within the meaning of § 301(a), is to overlook the integrated nature of the transactions established in this case. Moreover, the fact that some of the booklets carried a selling price is immaterial on the facts shown here. * * * [T]he booklets and drugs were nonetheless interdependent; they were parts of an integrated distribution program. The Act cannot be circumvented by the easy device of a "sale" of the advertising matter where the advertising performs the function of labeling.

Petitioner points out that in the evolution of the Act the ban on false advertising was eliminated, the control over it being transferred to the Federal Trade Commission. We have searched the legislative history in vain, however, to find any indication that Congress had the purpose to eliminate from the Act advertising which performs the function of labeling. Every labeling is in a sense an advertisement. The advertising which we have here performs the same function as it would if it were on the article or on the containers or wrappers. As we have said, physical attachment or contiguity is unnecessary under § 201(m)(2). * * *

United States v. Urbuteit

335 U.S. 355 (1948).

■ DOUGLAS, JUSTICE:

* * * Respondent Urbuteit terms himself a naturopathic physician and conducts the Sinuothermic Institute in Tampa, Florida. The machines against which the libel was filed are electrical devices allegedly aiding in the diagnosis and cure of various diseases and physical disorders such as cancer, diabetes, tuberculosis, arthritis, and paralysis. The alleged cures effected through its use are described in the allegedly false and misleading leaflet, "The Road to Health," published by Urbuteit and distributed for use with the machines.

Urbuteit shipped from Florida a number of these machines to one Kelsch, a former pupil of his who lives in Ohio. Kelsch used these machines in treating his patients and, though he did not receive them as a merchant, he sold some to patients. As part of this transaction Urbuteit contracted to furnish Kelsch with a supply of leaflets, which were sent from Florida to Ohio at a different time than when the machines were forwarded. Kelsch used the leaflets to explain the machines to his patients.

The leaflets seem to have followed the shipment of the machines. But as *Kordel v. United States* holds, that is immaterial where the advertising matter that was sent was designed to serve and did in fact serve the purposes of labeling. This machine bore only the words, U.S. Patent Sinuothermic Trade Mark. It was the leaflets that explained the usefulness of the device in the diagnosis, treatment, and cure of various diseases. Measured by functional standards, as § 201(m)(2) of the Act permits, these leaflets constituted one of the types of labeling which the Act condemns.

The power to condemn is contained in § 304(a) and is confined to articles "adulterated or misbranded when introduced into or while in interstate commerce." We do not, however, read that provision as requiring the advertising matter to travel with the machine. The reasons of policy which argue against that in the case of criminal prosecutions under § 303 are equally forcible when we come to libels under § 304(a). Moreover, the common sense of the matter is to view the interstate transaction in its entirety—the purpose of the advertising and its actual use. In this case it is plain to us that the movements of machines and leaflets in interstate commerce were a single interrelated activity, not separate or isolated ones. The Act is not concerned with the purification of the stream of commerce in the abstract. The problem is a practical one of consumer protection, not dialectics. The fact that the false literature leaves in a separate mail does not save the article from being misbranded. Where by functional standards the two transactions are integrated, the requirements of § 304(a) are satisfied, though the mailings or shipments are at different times. * * *

NOTES AND QUESTIONS

1. *Common origin.* The manufacturer need not also have authored the written material for it to qualify as labeling if used in connection with the sale of a product. See United States v. Diapulse Mfg. Corp., 389 F.2d 612 (2d Cir.1968) (holding that reprints of medical articles distributed with a device qualified as labeling); United States v. Lane Labs–USA, Inc., 324 F.Supp.2d 547 (D.N.J.2004) [excerpted in Chap. 1(B)(2)]; United States v. Vital Health Prods. Ltd., 786 F.Supp. 761 (E.D.Wis.1992) (same for newsletters published by third parties distributed with a product), aff'd mem., 985 F.2d 563 (7th Cir.1993). Where the written material is not so used, however, courts have rebuffed FDA claims that the mere placement at retail of a product near a book turns the latter into product labeling. See United States v. Articles of Drug for Veterinary Use, 50 F.3d 497 (8th Cir.1995); United States v. 24 Bottles "Sterling Vinegar & Honey," Etc., 338 F.2d 157 (2d Cir.1964).

2. *Prescription drugs.* Product information for prescription drugs rarely accompanies the product itself. Although physicians do not purchase prescription drugs for their patients, they do control the decision to use a particular drug. The physician acts as a proxy for the purchaser, and the FDA has classified any product-related literature given to physicians as labeling. See 21 C.F.R. § 202.1(*l*)(2). Doctors often receive only the "package insert" for prescription drugs. Patients often receive little more than a hodge-podge of cryptic warning stickers affixed to a container by the pharmacist. See Deborah Franklin, And Now, a Warning About Labels,

N.Y. Times, Oct. 25, 2005, at F1 ("[T]hey are not standardized, regulated or even reviewed by the F.D.A.").

3. *What's in a name?* The FDCA requires that labeling include the "established name" immediately after the brand name. See 21 U.S.C. § 352(e)(2); see also Abbott Lab. v. Gardner, 387 U.S. 136, 138 (1967) ("The underlying purpose of the 1962 amendment was to bring to the attention of doctors and patients the fact that many of the drugs sold under familiar trade names are actually identical to drugs sold under their 'established' or less familiar trade names at significantly lower prices."). Reacting to concerns about prescribing errors that result from confusingly similar brand names, the FDA now considers drug nomenclature issues when approving a new drug. See Anna W. Mathews, When a Drug Maker Launches New Baby, Uncle Sam Vets Name, Wall St. J., Mar. 17, 2006, at A1 (reporting that the agency rejected more than one-third of proposed names); see also Deidre A. Clarke, Comment, Proprietary Drug Name Approval: Taking the Duel out of Dual Agency Process, 12 Loy. J. Pub. Int. L. 433 (2011); Danielle A. Gentin, You Say Zantac, I Say Xanax: A Critique of Drug Trademark Approval and Proposals for Reform, 55 Food & Drug L.J. 255 (2000); Allison Connolly, Drug Makers Embrace Branding R & D—Companies Spend Heavily on Consultants to Develop Names for Medicines That Pass Regulatory Muster, Wall St. J., June 30, 2010, at B7. The agency also has required the use of bar codes on the labels of prescription drugs administered in hospital settings, though that alone will not reduce medication mix ups. See Marc Kaufman, Bar Codes Favored to Cut Hospitals' Drug Errors, Wash. Post, Feb. 26, 2004, at A3; see also Barnaby J. Feder, Universal ID Systems Urged for Medical Devices, N.Y. Times, Aug. 9, 2006, at C6.

4. *Misbranding authority*. As discussed in Chapter 1(C), the FDCA enumerates a series of conditions that could cause products to be misbranded. For example, a drug or medical device is deemed to be misbranded unless its labeling bears "such adequate warnings against use in those pathological conditions or by children where its use may be dangerous to health, or against unsafe dosage or methods or duration of administration or application, in such manner and form, as are necessary for the protection of users." 21 U.S.C. § 352(f)(2). One fundamental and sometimes contested question is whether the labeling must dictate prescription status for a drug.

1. DRAWING THE LINE BETWEEN RX AND OVER-THE-COUNTER

United States v. Article of Drug . . . Decholin

264 F.Supp. 473 (E.D.Mich.1967).

■ FREEMAN, DISTRICT JUDGE:

* * * The only substantive provision of concern is Federal Food, Drug and Cosmetic Act, § 503, as amended, 21 U.S.C. § 353, reading in pertinent part:

(b)(1) A drug intended for use by man which . . .

(B) because of its toxicity or other potentiality for harmful effect, or the method of its use, or the collateral measures necessary to its use, is not safe for use except under the supervision of a practitioner licensed by law to administer such drug . . .

(C) . . . shall be dispensed only (i) upon a written prescription of a practitioner licensed by law to administer such drug, or (ii) upon an oral prescription of such practitioner which is reduced promptly to writing and filed by the pharmacist, or (iii) by refilling any such written or oral prescription if such refilling is authorized by the prescriber either in the original prescription or by oral order which is reduced promptly to writing and filed by the pharmacist. . . .

(4) A drug which is subject to paragraph (1) of this subsection shall be deemed to be misbranded if at any time prior to dispensing its label fails to bear the statement "Caution: Federal law prohibits dispensing without prescription." A drug to which paragraph (1) of this subsection does not apply shall be deemed to be misbranded if at any time prior to dispensing its label bears the caution statement quoted in the preceding sentence.*

It is agreed that Decholin is a drug within the meaning of the Act and that the seized tablets had moved in interstate commerce. It is also undisputed that the labels on the libeled packages give no indication that Decholin may not lawfully be dispensed without prescription. The precise legal consideration raised by these motions is whether amended section 503 causes Decholin to be misbranded because its containers fail to carry such a precautionary statement. * * *

There is only one fundamental issue presented by these motions: is Decholin unsafe as a drug intended for human use without a prescription? Nevertheless, recognizing that in section 503(b)(1)(B) Congress listed a number of ostensibly different reasons why a drug may be unsafe for self-medication and attempting to deal with the parties' arguments in an organized fashion, the motions will be viewed as raising two issues. First, is the pharmacological effect of Decholin such that, unless it is taken pursuant to and in accordance with a physician's directions, reactions sufficient to cause the product to be unsafe may result from its ingestion? This will be called the "toxicity question." Second, does the fact that Decholin may be taken by a person who, although experiencing the indications set out on the label, has an ailment which Decholin cannot cure, coupled with the fact such an individual may postpone a visit to his physician in reliance upon the over-the-counter availability of Decholin, cause the drug to be unsafe? Because the gist of the government's argument on this issue is that an immediate professional diagnosis to detect the underlying cause of the symptoms in a particular case is a step which must precede or accompany use in order for the drug to be considered safe, this point will be called the "collateral measures question." Unfortunately, some of the subissues and

* In 1997, Congress amended this provision to replace the cautionary statement with a simple "Rx only" label designation. See 21 U.S.C. § 353(b)(4)(A).

contentions underlying each of these two topics are so similar that the effort to pinpoint two distinct inquiries will not be totally successful.

At the basis of both questions lies the fact that the indications mentioned on the Decholin container can stem from any one of what, for present purposes, will be considered as three types of causes: biliary tract obstruction, organic disease and various minor factors. These last include a host of elements ranging from pregnancy through dietary indiscretions, such as skipping meals, and on to old age. Claimant willingly agrees with the government that Decholin would not be prescribed by a physician to cure either a tract obstruction or an organic disease.

Toxicity Question

If the record showed clearly why a practitioner would not order Decholin for a person suffering from an obstruction or an organic disease, the toxicity question could be in a better posture for summary disposition. However, the affidavits of the experts suggest different reasons which may be grounded upon conflicting views on a factual issue, the pharmacological effect of the drug. The statements of claimant's authorities suggest that they would not prescribe Decholin in the presence of one of these major ailments primarily, if not exclusively, just because the drug would do no good for the patient. However, these experts are quick to point out that they have never heard of an instance in which a person with either an obstruction or an organic disease sustained any ill effect from self-medication with Decholin; and at least several of them doubt that harm would ever come to an individual who takes the drug under these circumstances. Therefore, Ames [the manufacturer appearing as the claimant] would consider Decholin safe for unrestricted distribution. * * *

There remain the opposing contentions why a practitioner would not recommend Decholin in some cases, and beneath these antagonistic positions lies another and more subtle conflict which has great significance with regard to the proper interpretation of section 503(b)(1)(B). Although this dispute is not formally expressed in the record, a critical study of the affidavits leaves little doubt that it is nonetheless real. Broadly speaking, it could be said to center around the issue whether a drug's potentiality for causing harm if taken without prescription should be considered from a theoretical or a practical viewpoint.

Even the government's most helpful spokesman, Dr. Sklar, did not mention that he knew or had heard of a case in which Decholin or any article of similar composition had done harm in any perceptible degree to a layman who had taken the preparation, without consulting a physician, upon experiencing the indications listed on the Decholin label. This is not surprising since the government admitted in answer to interrogatories that it knew of no actual cases of harm attributable to the product. On the other hand, statements made by three of claimant's experts leave the strong impression that the principal reason why they would consider Decholin safe for self-medication is the fact that their experiences have taught them that a person suffering from an organic disease or a biliary tract obstruction will feel so ill that, as a matter of course, he will seek professional help. Therefore, claimant's experts do not seem to be so much of the opinion that home treatment with Decholin cannot cause harm as they do of the view that it will not; whereas the government's affiants stress that Decholin could cause harm to the uninformed lay user, while the government itself all but concedes that if future unadvised laymen act as their predecessors have, the drug will not be responsible for any serious consequences. * * *

The legislative history of the 1951 amendment, which gave birth to section 503(b)(1)(B), shows that Congress did not desire to proscribe self-medication with a product just because under some set of circumstances—and especially hypothetical conditions—the drug may be harmful if taken without professional supervision. * * * In fact, throughout the entire House debate runs the theme that "common household remedies" were not meant to be taken off the over-the-counter market * * * articles which most physicians would consider perfectly harmless when taken in the normal course of events by a person with a modicum of common sense. Nevertheless, it is hard to imagine that under no circumstances could any of these drugs do serious harm to an individual who does not appreciate the nature of the cause which lies at the root of his symptoms. * * *

If, in attempting to evaluate a drug, a court were to consider every contingency and take account of the immaturity or stupidity of every potential user, it would not be paying heed to the [Senate] Committee's desire that it give to the word "safe" the ordinary meaning. Similarly, it seems that the government, in order to prevail in this case, must establish that Decholin has a potentiality for causing consequences for an unadvised layman which can actually be called harmful; for in common usage the term "safe" is not inapplicable to an article merely because the product may give rise to some effects which are uncomfortable or cause inconvenience. * * *

Without presuming to list all the factors which may merit consideration in a section 503(b)(1)(B) action, the following seem especially pertinent here. Probably the single most important element is the seriousness of the effect likely to result under the government's theory from unsupervised lay use of Decholin. The government's answers to interrogatories state that the possible aftermath of self-medication by a person suffering from a tract obstruction is jaundice or even death. If it can prove its contention in this regard, no one could maintain that the harm attributable to the drug is not serious. However, in order that the product's true danger can be understood—in order that its theoretical and practical potentials for causing injury can be more clearly distinguished—it would be necessary to know in much more detail the circumstances under which jaundice or death will follow the ingestion of Decholin. For instance, it would be at least helpful, if not actually essential, to understand whether a normal dosage or only a quantity which the reasonable layman is likely to realize constitutes an excessive amount of self-medication will produce these effects. Similarly, a decision would be easier to reach if the record indicated the immediacy of the harmful consequences. Will jaundice or worse result only if a person suffering from an obstruction prolongs his reliance upon Decholin past the point at which the typical individual in his condition would have become convinced of the futility of self-help and have sought professional diagnosis and treatment? If this is the case, what effect would the drug have on the average man? During the period in which he could be expected to take the tablets, would Decholin result in a worsening of his condition to any significant extent beyond the point to which it would have progressed during the time from the onset of the indications until he would probably have consulted a physician had the drug not been available without prescription? If so, would this deterioration actually represent a more serious threat to his life or simply require additional treatment? It would also seem significant if the effects allegedly produced by Decholin cause a noticeable change in a victim's condition with the result that he could be expected to appreciate that the drug is doing him no good and discontinue its use before real harm occurs.

Collateral Measures Question

In support of its position that it should be granted summary judgment on the basis of this issue regardless of the outcome of the toxicity question, the government relies upon the fact that both it and Ames agree that the Decholin indications may be caused by a disease or a disorder (e.g., biliary tract obstruction) which the drug cannot cure. The government argues that a person suffering from such an obstruction, for instance, is likely to go to the pharmacy, compare his symptoms with the Decholin label, purchase the drug, medicate himself and thereby postpone visiting a physician. Therefore, according to the government, Decholin is unsafe as a matter of law because the layman is unable to detect the true cause of his discomfort when a differential diagnosis is essential to his well-being, and because his easy access to Decholin is responsible for delaying recourse to the expert qualified to make this all-important determination. * * *

While Ames is probably correct in saying that the distribution of a drug was not intended by Congress to be restricted just because it will not serve as a cure in all instances in which it may be taken by a person following the manufacturer's recommendations, the fact that a particular product may be an ineffectual remedy under some circumstances could certainly be a substantial consideration in finding that it is unsafe for self-medication. Conversely, a showing that a drug has a tendency to cause laymen to delay seeking help in determining the natures of their illnesses is not per se sufficient to warrant removing it from the over-the-counter market.

Both of these observations find support in the legislative history surrounding the 1951 amendment. * * * [N]o Representative wished to prevent the free sale of common household remedies. Nevertheless, any of these articles—aspirin, seltzers and mouthwashes—have certainly been taken on countless occasions by people suffering from ailments which these products could not cure when the users' best interests would have been served by professional consultation in lieu of self-medication.[9] * * * If

---

9. During oral argument on these motions, government counsel was asked whether its view would not serve to make aspirin a prescription drug. His equivocal reply tended toward

merely establishing that the easy availability of a medicine has the tendency to postpone a differential diagnosis in a case in which the drug alone cannot provide a cure were enough to compel the removal of the product from a druggist's public shelves, there would be few drugs left on the over-the-counter market once the government saw fit to wage a full-scale assault on self-medication.

Assuming, therefore, that efficacy is not totally unrelated to the question of safety but that the simple fact that inefficacy will result in a postponement in seeking professional assistance is not sufficient to warrant a finding that a product is a prescription drug, the question remains regarding the circumstances in which ineffectiveness, coupled with the likelihood of delay, would serve as the basis for considering a remedy dangerous for unsupervised lay use. The first factor would be the seriousness of the effect that a delay might cause, with the government's case becoming stronger as its proof tends to show that the consequences of a postponed diagnosis do not merely border on inconvenience as opposed to actual harm. It also seems essential to know how much of a delay will be detrimental, for, in light of the legislative history, it is improper to view the 1951 enactment as a measure designed to protect the stubborn individual who continues to put his trust in self-medication long after the average person would have sought out a physician.

A third concern would certainly be the quality of the advice, invariably contained on a drug label, cautioning users to consult a practitioner if certain symptoms develop in addition to those for which the medicine has been recommended by its manufacturer. * * * [T]he pertinent question is not whether an individual is able to detect the cause of his ailment, but rather whether the symptoms described on the package as reasons for him to visit a physician are sufficient to alert him to the possibility that his illness may require professional attention. In other words, if a serious disease which Decholin cannot cure is the crux of the trouble, will nausea or severe abdominal pain appear along with excessive belching and constipation?

A fourth consideration is closely related to the third because an over-the-counter drug will probably carry, as Decholin does, a warning on its container to the effect that if the indications continue, a physician should be consulted. The issue is whether in a case where a particular drug will not alleviate the cause of an ailment it will, nevertheless, effect a disappearance of the indicative symptoms with the result that a user may have every reason to feel that he has been cured when, in fact, he has not been. * * *

PROBLEM #5. *FIGHTING AN OTC SWITCH TOOTH AND NAIL*

You represent a pharmaceutical company that sells an immensely successful prescription analgesic indicated for use by patients with arthri-

---

the negative, apparently because of his belief that Decholin, unlike aspirin, has the potential for being taken by a person who has a serious ailment that the drug cannot cure. This attempted distinction overlooks the fact that at the root of a headache may lie anything from nervous tension to a malignant brain tumor.

tis. Acting on a petition filed by a group of health insurers who provide prescription drug benefits but would prefer not having to pay for the use of this particular drug (not to mention the physician visits necessary to receive a prescription), the FDA has decided to switch this drug to nonprescription status because it has a relatively favorable safety profile and is intended only for symptomatic relief. Your client is outraged. Not only will it have to reduce the price of the drug dramatically or risk losing sales volume (because few health insurers reimburse patients for OTC products), but it also may face greater tort liability for any injuries that occur. Is there any basis for challenging the agency's decision in court? What other information would you need?

Lars Noah, *Treat Yourself: Is Self–Medication the Prescription for What Ails American Health Care?*

19 HARV. J.L. & TECH. 359 (2006).

* * * In recent years—whether a reaction to the tradition of physician paternalism, the realities of cost-containment pressures under managed care, or the need to put downward pressure on drug price inflation—demands have grown for expanded access to pharmaceuticals without first having to secure a prescription. * * * In 1998, WellPoint Health Networks—the parent company of Blue Cross and Blue Shield of California—petitioned the FDA to switch three popular nonsedating antihistamines from prescription (Rx) to over-the-counter (OTC) status. The insurer thereby hoped to save nearly $100 million annually for covered physician visits and prescription drug costs. The manufacturers of these drugs vehemently opposed the petition because they would have had to reduce their prices substantially once consumers absorbed the entire cost out of pocket.

The two sides, however, framed their arguments in terms of relative safety and effectiveness, with the manufacturers suggesting that more experience with prescription marketing would provide reassuring confirmation of the evident safety of these products, while the insurers emphasized that these second-generation antihistamines enjoyed an unmistakable safety advantage over the existing (and sedating) nonprescription substitutes. If causing drowsiness made the older antihistamines more dangerous, then perhaps WellPoint should have urged the FDA to move them to prescription status or withdraw them from the market altogether. (Of course it would not have wanted to petition only for the withdrawal of the existing OTC antihistamines because that might have increased its tab for the prescription products.) Even so, this aspect of the petition posed a difficult policy issue for the FDA—namely, what to do with older drugs when second-generation products offer distinct therapeutic benefits.

In 2001, a pair of advisory committees voted in favor of recommending the switch, but the FDA essentially disregarded the advice by failing to act on WellPoint's petition. Nonetheless, because an OTC switch becomes far more appealing once a prescription drug loses patent and market exclusivity protections (and faces the prospect of generic competition), the manufacturer of one of the antihistamines (Claritin) soon experienced a change of heart. Once this product reached the OTC marketplace, many health insurers limited coverage of the nonsedating antihistamines that remained in prescription status.

Two years after the advisory committee votes, and with two of the three antihistamines still restricted to prescription dispensing, the agency briefly showed renewed interest in the question of initiating an Rx-to-OTC switch over a manufacturer's objection. In fact, some observers wondered whether the newly created Medicare drug benefit had given the FDA's parent agency, the Department of Health and Human Services, the same financial incentive that had prompted WellPoint's petition. Indeed, the agency's proposed FY2004 budget suggested that it would "become more proactive" in this area because switches could "provide an expedient way to significantly reduce consumer health care costs." Although once again it failed to act on WellPoint's petition, the FDA confidently announced at the time that it had the power to order such a switch. In common with any number of other bold assertions emanating from this agency, the FDA's claim of authority may never be put to the test.

If the agency ever orders an Rx-to-OTC switch at the behest of payers rather sellers, it could inspire similar efforts for a range of popular and pricey prescription drugs. Even if the FDA leaves the initiative to the pharmaceutical industry, possible candidates for nonprescription marketing include various antihypertensives, cholesterol-lowering statins, weight-loss drugs, proton pump inhibitors for heartburn, and, more speculatively, treatments for urinary incontinence or erectile dysfunction. Whether such switches would serve or disserve the best interests of patients will depend on a variety of factors, but the agency should skeptically evaluate such petitions—whether initiated by insurers or manufacturers—whenever they appear to be motivated primarily by the prospect of financial gains to the petitioner. * * *

At least initially, virtually all new ingredients are available only by prescription while the FDA collects additional adverse event data. Thus, a product later switched OTC will have survived not only the agency's rigorous premarket review process for new chemical entities but also the test of time and a second round of FDA scrutiny. Even so, risks may not come to light until long after a switch occurs.

Although the statute and regulations provide some general criteria for differentiating between prescription and OTC products, ultimately that determination must be made on an ad hoc basis and without clear guidance. The 1951 amendments and the FDA's regulations mention toxicity, other harmful effects, methods of use, and the need for collateral measures, but they fail to indicate the point at which one or more of these factors will necessitate prescription-only availability. Toxicity concerns may relate to either acute or chronic effects, and this factor is often operationalized by reference to a product's "margin of safety" and the extent to which it needs to be carefully titrated for each patient. Other harmful effects may include the risk of interactions with food or other drug products and the potential for abuse. Methods of use and "collateral measures" may pose questions about the ability of laypersons to self-diagnose and self-administer as well as the need for periodic clinical monitoring. No one factor is determinative, however, as there are a number of approved OTC products that raise toxicity, drug interaction, self-diagnosis, and method of administration concerns.

Ultimately, the decision may turn on whether appropriate labeling can help to minimize these problems. FDA regulations provide that OTC drug product labeling must include directions and warnings "in such terms as to render them likely to be read and understood by the ordinary individual, including individuals of low comprehension, under customary conditions of purchase and use." In theory, therefore, the agency would not permit OTC marketing if overly complex labeling were necessary to ensure safe use. In practice, however, the FDA has required fairly detailed labeling in OTC monographs as a means of addressing toxicity concerns, serious drug interactions, fears about delaying medical intervention, and so forth.

For drugs that do not require the supervision of a physician, have a history of safe use, and present no abuse potential, the FDA has a pair of ways to authorize OTC marketing. First, a company may sell an OTC drug if it abides by the terms of the applicable "monograph," which specifies for a particular category of products the active ingredients and dosages that the agency has determined to be safe and effective, along with the precise labeling necessary to facilitate appropriate consumer use. As an illustration of this stringency, the FDA recently barred any references to "sinusitis" in the labeling of certain OTC cough-cold products. Any continued prescription marketing of active ingredients for indications recognized in an OTC monograph would constitute a misbranding violation under the FDCA. Nonmonograph ingredients, dosages, and indications could continue to be marketed as prescription products under an approved new drug application (NDA). The FDA has used the monograph process as a mechanism to switch dozens of prescription drugs.

The second route to OTC marketing requires that a company secure a supplemental NDA for a reformulation (including revised labeling and perhaps reduced dosage) of a product previously approved for prescription use. Manufacturers generally initiate switches of drugs that remain subject to NDAs, though they sometimes fail to persuade the FDA to take this action. The agency may require that the applicant conduct so-called actual use and label comprehension studies. Dual marketing of an ingredient for both a prescription and OTC use is possible under limited circumstances. For instance, the agency has approved the active ingredient ibuprofen at different dosages as a prescription and as an OTC analgesic. Of course, in the event of reduced dosage formulations, it did not take long for consumers to realize that they could self-medicate with prescription strength simply by exceeding the dose recommended in the OTC labeling.

Because analgesics relieve symptoms and do not purport to treat any underlying disease process, they would seem to represent natural candidates for OTC marketing. Nonetheless, even if most consumers would not need a physician's diagnostic skills in order to decide whether to select a particular pain reliever, the safety profile of such products may justify restrictions on access. Thus, the FDA requires prescription labeling when it first approves a new analgesic product, and many of these drugs never get switched OTC. * * *

OTC analgesics may pose significant risks, which the agency generally has tried to handle through revisions in labeling. For instance, researchers have linked prolonged use of NSAIDs [non-steroidal anti-inflammatory drugs] to sometimes fatal gastrointestinal bleeding. In the early 1980s, the FDA became aware of a link between Reye syndrome and the use of aspirin by children suffering from viral infections, and the labels of OTC drug products containing aspirin now must include a warning of this risk. Notably, the agency rejected suggestions urging "more drastic measures [such as] banning use of aspirin in products for individuals under 21 years of age or limiting such products to prescription use." More recently, after it received reports of an association between acetaminophen and liver toxicity, the FDA imposed special warning requirements. * * *

Recent switch efforts have raised questions that arguably range beyond the traditional factors considered by the FDA. For instance, notwithstanding favorable internal and advisory committee recommendations, the agency repeatedly has declined to act on petitions requesting OTC status for emergency contraceptives (the so-called "morning after pill"), though it considered the idea of an age restriction in response to fears expressed by social conservatives that readier access by teenagers would promote sexual promiscuity. In rejecting a switch application for lovastatin, a lower-dose version of the prescription cholesterol-lowering drug Mevacor, the agency responded in part to fears that patients might fail to make critical dietary and other lifestyle changes. Proponents of both of these switch candidates had argued that readier access would serve public health purposes—in preventing, respectively, unwanted pregnancies after contraceptive failures and in reducing the risk of cardiovascular disease. Nonetheless, the agency appeared to give these benefits short shrift relative to its more traditional focus on the potential detriments associated with OTC availability.

In the face of the FDA's intransigence over switching emergency contraceptives, state efforts to facilitate easier access to these products have included systems (referred to as collaborative practice arrangements) that allow pharmacists to dispense such drugs without first getting a physician's prescription for a particular patient. Conversely, recent concerns about methamphetamine have prompted legislators and retailers to place OTC cough-cold products containing the methamphetamine precursor pseudoephedrine behind the counter. Retailers also have begun to limit access to other OTC cough-cold products in response to problems with teenagers purchasing them for recreational purposes. Perhaps it would make sense to codify the notion of a pharmacist-controlled class of drugs to serve as a transitional step between prescription and OTC status when switching a new category of prescription pharmaceuticals. Other industrialized countries use just such an intermediate category of products, though the FDA emphatically has rejected proposals to create a "third class" of drugs.

Finally, when it considered the WellPoint petition to switch the nonsedating antihistamines, the agency repeatedly emphasized that it would disregard cost-savings (to insurers and patients). Nonetheless, responsiveness to anticipated changes in price will have a central impact on likely changes in patterns of use (for better or for worse), and the elasticity in demand should get factored into the equation. For instance, if consumers respond to their increased out-of-pocket costs by substituting the older (and cheaper) OTC antihistamines that cause sedation, then more traffic accidents might result; if, however, consumers respond by instead demanding newer (and more expensive but covered by insurance) prescription products for allergy relief, then they may encounter greater risks of side effects.

In short, the FDA should stop pretending that Rx-to-OTC switches turn solely on questions of a drug's intrinsic safety and efficacy. When the agency announced that it had ample authority to force an Rx-to-OTC switch over a manufacturer's objection, FDA officials pointed to their power to ensure drug safety. Although this authority would no doubt justify switching an erstwhile OTC drug to prescription status in light of newly discovered safety concerns, it is difficult to understand how switching from prescription to OTC status would ever promote the safe use of a drug. A switch may serve any number of other valuable ends, and such a move may not present any untoward risk to the public health, but, all other things being equal, is it not inherently (even if only marginally) safer to use a pharmaceutical under the supervision of a health care professional? Thus, in deciding whether to switch a drug, the FDA must openly confront a wide-range of factors while not losing sight of its primary obligation to promote the public health. * * *

In connection with the FDA's consideration of the WellPoint petition, observers repeatedly alluded to the "unprecedented" nature of the case. If understood to connote an objection to (rather than praise for) the agency's initiative, then this point can mean one of two things. First, a departure from settled FDA precedent may raise concerns about administrative procedure. Second, and more interestingly, a constitutional concern may underlie the objection to "unprecedented" agency action insofar as it raises a potential takings problem. * * *

Whatever its obligations to explain a departure from settled practice, an Rx-to-OTC switch initiated by the agency at the very least might trigger a statutory right to a hearing. Although the FDA may prevail on a sponsor to revise the labeling of a previously approved drug, especially to reflect newly discovered risk information, a demand to remove the prescription restriction looks more like the partial withdrawal of the license. In the case of new drugs, the FDA's enabling statute grants a sponsor the right to demand an evidentiary hearing before the agency withdraws an NDA. The statute also spells out the grounds that would justify such an action, typically the discovery of some new information casting doubt on the agency's original findings of safety and effectiveness. Although the agency clearly enjoys the authority to remove prescription restrictions unilaterally when that would serve the public health, a desire to improve consumer access and reduce prices (or at least reduce the expenses borne by health insurers) probably would not suffice. In short, a drug manufacturer facing an involuntary Rx-to-OTC switch may have valid objections—both procedural and substantive—if the FDA summarily alters this central aspect of the labeling that it had approved at the time of original licensure. * * *

It might promote clarity to understand such switches as a two-step process: the FDA revokes the NDA for the original drug, which carried prescription labeling, but offers to issue a new (though financially less desirable) license for an OTC version of the same drug as a substitute. It also could be understood as tantamount to revoking a license several months after approval because patients and health insurers (and their representatives in Congress) complained about exorbitant pricing, but offering to reissue the NDA if the sponsor promises to lower prices by 75%. Alternatively, imagine that the agency responds to such pressure by prematurely approving lower-priced generic copies of a newly licensed drug, ignoring any applicable patents and the market exclusivity period granted to the NDA sponsor by statute. In either case, the innovator pharmaceutical companies that had devoted tremendous resources in bringing the brand-name drugs to market would have reason to complain about unfair surprise and substantial interference in their reasonable investment-backed expectations. Any of these scenarios should raise constitutional hackles about a deprivation of property without due process of law or confiscatory government action without just compensation. * * *

An NDA does more than simply entitle a company to commercialize a new drug—it grants the recipient a period of market exclusivity against generic competition. Like patents, which clearly qualify as property, an NDA provides the sponsor with the right to exclude others and recoup its substantial investment in research and development. When proponents of Rx-to-OTC switches forecast substantial net savings to the health care system, those sums represent potential revenues lost to the license-holder, at least where the manufacturer did not initiate the requested switch. In short, aside from costs shifted from insurers to patients, aggregate savings realized in switching prescription drugs to nonprescription status represent financial losses suffered by the pharmaceutical industry. * * *

[W]hen the government grants a valuable privilege such as a license and then revokes it or renders it essentially valueless, and does so for reasons not previously announced as a basis for such action, courts may entertain a regulatory takings claim. In fact, even more clearly than claims about stranded investments in the utilities context, one might argue that a "deregulatory taking" occurs if the FDA grants a company the exclusive right to commercialize a therapeutic invention for a specified period of time but then unilaterally alters the terms of this monopoly in a fashion that substantially erodes the value of the investment. No taking would occur if Congress decided to deregulate the drug industry across the board by, for example, no longer requiring product licensure or physician intervention before dispensing prescription pharmaceuticals; when done on a case-by-case basis and against the backdrop of such longstanding regulatory barriers to entry, however, a manufacturer may well cry foul.

The choice between prescription and OTC distribution for a pharmaceutical product is nothing to sneeze at. Apart from the potentially enormous financial stakes for all involved—manufacturers, health insurers, and patients/consumers—the classification could have profound public health consequences, either positive or negative. Given changes in both technology and the marketplace, the FDA must grapple with an increasingly difficult balancing act when manufacturers or health insurers petition the agency for an Rx-to-OTC switch. Although scientific judgments about safety and effectiveness must remain the focal point, the FDA should not entirely blind itself to the larger economic forces at play, but it also must understand statutory and constitutional limitations on the extent to which it might begin to take cost into account. * * *

NOTES AND QUESTIONS

1. *Endorsing self-medication.* In the course of soliciting public input on its criteria for distinguishing prescription and nonprescription drugs, the FDA offered the following overview:

> Drugs found appropriate for OTC sale have an increasingly vital role in the U.S. health care system by providing consumers easy access to certain drugs that can be used safely for conditions that consumers can self-treat without the help of a health care practitioner. Consumers have access to more than 100,000 OTC drug products encompassing more than 800 active ingredients and covering more than 100 therapeutic categories or classes. In light of the continuously changing health care environment, including the growing self-care movement, the agency continues to examine its overall philosophy and approach to regulating OTC drug products.

65 Fed. Reg. 24,704 (2000); see also World Health Organization, Guideline for the Regulatory Assessment of Medicinal Products for Use in Self–Medication (2000); Eric P. Brass, Changing the Status of Drugs from Prescription to Over-the-Counter Availability, 345 New Eng. J. Med. 810 (2001); Robin E. Ferner & Keith Beard, Over the Counter Medicines: Proceed with Caution, 336 BMJ 694 (2008); Gina Kolata, There's a Blurry Line Between Rx and O.T.C., N.Y. Times, Dec. 21, 2003, § 4, at 3.

2. *Additional manufacturer disincentives.* In *Decholin*, the seller sought to defend OTC marketing, while nowadays one often finds the roles reversed, with the manufacturer wanting to retain prescription status. Pharmaceutical companies may resist OTC switches for reasons other than anticipated losses of revenue. As explained later in this chapter, regulatory jurisdiction over product advertising moves from the FDA to the Federal Trade Commission when a product goes OTC (although the Commission's standards offer somewhat greater flexibility, it also may impose more sweeping sanctions for regulatory infractions). More importantly, they would face increased exposure to tort liability, both because patterns of usage would change in ways that present heightened risks of inappropriate use and because of differences in the applicable tort doctrine. These are taken up where relevant in the chapters that follow.

3. *Other switch candidates.* In 2008, FDA rejected (for the third and final time) Merck's switch petition for Mevacor® (lovastatin). Cf. Peter Loftus, Pfizer Seeks New Life for Lipitor—As Generic Competition Looms, Drug Maker Explores Over-the-Counter Options for Blockbuster Pill, Wall St. J., Aug. 4, 2011, at B1. What other drugs would you consider moving to nonprescription status? See Stephanie Saul, F.D.A. Approves an Over-the-Counter Version of the Weight–Loss Drug Xenical, N.Y. Times, Feb. 8, 2007, at A16 (Alli®); cf. Catherine Saint Louis, Long Lashes Without Prescription, but with Risks, N.Y. Times, May 2, 2010, at A4 (discussing the ease of getting Latisse® notwithstanding Rx status). Why would the FDA probably never switch any of the old (and generally safe) antibiotics OTC? After switching several proton pump inhibitors (e.g., Prilosec®, Prevacid®, and Zegerid®), the agency discovered adverse effects from long-term use, including seizures and fractures, as well as a serious drug interaction (i.e., reducing the effectiveness of a popular anticoagulant). See Kay Lazar, Acid Reflux in Flux, Boston Globe, Apr. 4, 2011, at G12; Alicia Mundy, FDA Underscores Plavix Warning, Wall St. J., Oct. 20, 2010, at D2.

4. *Rx devices?* The statute lacks a comparable provision defining a class of medical devices that require a prescription, though the addition in 1976 of special authority over so-called "restricted" devices has served much the same purpose. See 21 U.S.C. § 360j(e); see also Lars Noah, Regulating Cigarettes: (Non)sense and Sensibility, 22 S. Ill. U. L.J. 677, 684 (1998) ("The available legislative history suggests that Congress viewed the term 'restricted' as largely synonymous with 'prescription.' . . . Initially, the FDA announced that all existing prescription devices would be regarded as restricted medical devices, but the courts invalidated this policy statement on procedural grounds. Two decades later the agency still has not promulgated general regulations to implement its authority over restricted medical devices."); cf. Veronica Knapp, FDA's Regulation of Tanning Beds: How Much Heat?, 66 Food & Drug L.J. 25, 40–46 (2011) (advocating that the agency use this authority to prohibit the use of tanning beds by minors). The agency also may use substantial equivalence determinations under § 510(k) to dictate Rx status. See United States v. Snoring Relief Labs Inc., 210 F.3d 1081 (9th Cir.2000) [excerpted in Chap. 3(B)]. Because ready access in the event of an emergency can save heart attack victims, laypersons now can purchase and use automated external defibrillators without professional supervision. See Barnaby J. Feder, Do It Yourself: The Home Heart Defibrillator, N.Y. Times, May 3, 2005, at C1; see also Lawrence Altman, Defibrillators for the Public Aid Survival, Study Says, N.Y. Times, Nov. 12, 2003, at A16 (noting that "the devices have become standard equipment in many airports, malls, convention centers and health clubs").

5. *Combatting the meth menace*. Federal law now requires "behind-the-counter" status for pseudoephedrine. See Pub. L. No. 109–177, tit. VII, § 711(b)(1), 120 Stat. 256 (2006) (codified at 21 U.S.C. § 830(e)); see also Patricia Stanley, Comment, The Combat Methamphetamine Epidemic Act: New Protection or New Intrusion?, 39 Tex. Tech L. Rev. 379 (2007); Note, Cooking up Solutions to a Cooked up Menace: Responses to Methamphetamine in a Federal System, 119 Harv. L. Rev. 2508 (2006). In the face of continuing abuse, some states have pursued stricter controls for products containing pseudoephedrine. See Abby Goodnough, States Battling Meth Makers Look to Limit Ingredients, N.Y. Times, Mar. 29, 2011, at A19 ("Faced with a surging methamphetamine problem, a number of states are weighing contentious bills this spring that would require a doctor's prescription for popular decongestants like Sudafed.... Two states, Mississippi and Oregon, already require prescriptions for pseudoephedrine; law enforcement officials there say meth lab seizures have plummeted since the laws were enacted."). That particular problem aside, does creating a more general "third class" of drugs make sense? See 72 Fed. Reg. 56,769 (2007) (seeking input about the merits of such an approach); Abram S. Barth, Is Three a Crowd or Company?: Behind-the-Counter Drugs, 63 Food & Drug L.J. 865 (2008) (expressing opposition); Daniel Healey, Plan BTC: The Case for a Third Class of Drugs in the United States, 63 Food & Drug L.J. 375 (2008).

6. *Emergency contraception*. Efforts to make the morning-after drug ("Plan B") available without a prescription continue to generate controversy. After lengthy delays and political jockeying (as recounted in the opinion excerpted below), the FDA approved a partial OTC switch. See Rob Stein, Plan B Use Surges, and So Does Controversy, Wash. Post, July 13, 2007, at A1. Before the agency's decision, states took an active role in either expanding or restricting the availability of this product. See Marc Kaufman, Plan B Battles Embroil States: Proposals Mirror Red–Blue Divide, Wash. Post, Feb. 27, 2006, at A1; Rita Rubin, FDA Faulted for Not Allowing OTC Emergency Contraception, USA Today, May 9, 2006, at 8D.

Tummino v. Torti

603 F.Supp.2d 519 (E.D.N.Y.2009).

■ KORMAN, DISTRICT JUDGE:

Plan B is an emergency contraceptive that can be used to reduce the risk of unwanted pregnancy after sexual intercourse. When used as directed, it can reduce the risk of pregnancy by up to 89 percent. Plan B acts mainly by stopping the release of an egg from an ovary. It may also prevent sperm from fertilizing an egg that has been released or, if fertilization has already occurred, block implantation of the resulting embryo in the uterus. Plan B does not have any known serious or long-term side effects, though it may have some mild and short-term side effects, such as nausea or abdominal pain, in some users. The approved dosage of Plan B is two pills taken 12 hours apart, each containing 0.75 mg of levonorgestrel, a synthetic hormone similar to the naturally occurring hormone progesterone. Because the drug works best when taken within 24 hours of sexual intercourse, it is commonly referred to as a "morning-after pill." Nevertheless, the drug is effective if the first dose is taken within 72 hours of sexual intercourse. Studies have shown that Plan B is equally effective if the two doses of levonorgestrel are taken less than 12 hours apart or at the same time.

Plan B was approved for prescription-only use in the United States in 1999 and is the only emergency contraceptive drug currently available in the United States. Plan B and other emergency contraceptives with the same active ingredient are available without a prescription or age restriction in much of the world, including virtually all major industrialized nations. Plaintiffs—individuals and organizations advocating wider distribution of and access to emergency contraceptives, as well as parents and their minor children seeking access to the same—brought this action challenging the denial of a citizen petition, which requested that the FDA make Plan B available without a prescription to women of all ages. The FDA considered the citizen petition in tandem with a number of proposals—referred to as supplemental new drug applications (SNDAs)—submitted by Women's Capital Corporation, the drug's original manufacturer. Women's Capital Corp. sold its right to market Plan B to Barr Pharmaceuticals, Inc. during the course of the proceedings * * * *

Many new drugs are initially approved for prescription-only status and then later considered for non-prescription status, i.e., an over-the-counter or OTC switch. A drug is suitable for OTC use when found to be safe and effective for self-administration and when its labeling clearly provides directions for safe use and warnings regarding unsafe use, side effects, and adverse reactions. See 21 C.F.R. § 330.10(a)(4). These regulations were promulgated following the adoption of the Durham–Humphrey Amendment to the FDCA in 1951. The amendment was intended, in part, "to relieve retail pharmacists and the public from burdensome and unnecessary restrictions on the dispensing of drugs that are safe for use without the supervision of a physician." S. Rep. No. 82–946 (1951). There are two means by which the FDA can switch a prescription-only drug to non-prescription status. First, it can promulgate a regulation changing the drug's status. See 21 U.S.C. § 353(b)(3). This rulemaking process may be initiated by the Commissioner, 21 C.F.R. § 310.200(b), or by any interested person who files a citizen petition, id. § 10.25(a). Within 180 days of receipt of the petition, the Commissioner must either approve or deny the petition or provide "a tentative response [to the petitioner], indicating why the agency has been unable to reach a decision on the petition." Id. § 10.30(e)(2)(iii). Alternatively, a drug sponsor may request an over-the-counter switch. Id. § 310.200(b). Unlike the first mechanism, this process does not require rulemaking. Nevertheless, only the drug sponsor can supplement its initial new drug application. Id. § 314.71(a). * * *

The Commissioner delegated authority over OTC switch applications to the FDA's Center for Drug Evaluation and Research (CDER). OTC switch applications are reviewed by two offices within CDER: the Office of Drug Evaluation (ODE) V, which reviews all OTC switch applications, and, in this case, the ODE III, which includes the Division of Reproductive and Urologic Drug Products. CDER may seek scientific advice from outside experts by empaneling an advisory committee to provide a recommendation on an application. After reviewing the OTC switch application and the advice of the advisory committee, the directors of the two ODEs make a decision. If the Director of CDER disagrees with that decision, the Director may change the decision.

On February 14, 2001, one of the named plaintiffs, the Association of Reproductive Health Professionals, and sixty-five other organizations filed a citizen petition, asking the FDA to switch Plan B, and all emergency contraceptives like it, from prescription-only to over-the-counter status without age or point-of-sale restrictions. The petition included affidavits from Dr. David Grimes, the chair of the World Health Organization task force that had conducted the largest and most definitive trials on Plan B to date, and Dr. Elizabeth Raymond, who conducted the label comprehension and actual use studies which the Plan B sponsor would ultimately submit in support of its SNDA. Numerous national organizations, including the American Medical Association, the American College of Obstetricians and Gynecologists, and the American Public Health Association, endorsed the petition. * * *

On September 6, 2001, the FDA advised the petitioners that it had not yet resolved the issues raised in the citizen petition, but that it would respond "as soon as we have reached a decision on your request." The FDA did not respond for nearly five more years, when it announced, on June 9, 2006, that it had denied the petition. During this period, however, the FDA communicated regularly with the Plan B sponsor about its anticipated SNDA. * * *

[W]hile the Plan B sponsor did not formally submit the SNDA until April 2003, the FDA was aware of and anticipated the application well in advance. Indeed, at an Office of the Commissioner's meeting in June 2002, FDA officials—including then-Deputy Commissioner Dr. Lester Crawford—and review staff discussed the "political sensitivity" of a potential switch to OTC status for Plan B. These discussions regarding the political implications of the switch applications were not limited to intra-agency meetings: On the very same day that the Plan B sponsor first formally requested OTC status, then-FDA Commissioner Dr. Mark McClellan discussed the pending application with Jay Lefkowitz, the Deputy Assistant to the President for Domestic Policy at the White House. Commissioner McClellan testified that he had provided several updates on the Plan B application to relevant policy staff at the White House.

Moreover, deposition testimony of several FDA senior staff members reveals that political and ideological factors played a determinative role in the nomination and selection process for membership on the Advisory Committee for Reproductive Health Drugs, which, along with the Advisory Committee for Non-prescription Drugs, was empaneled by the FDA to make recommendations as to how the FDA should respond to the OTC switch applications. See 68 Fed. Reg. 66,113 (2003). * * * The Deputy Director of the Office of New Drugs (OND), Dr. Sandra Kweder, who had been involved in the formation of many advisory committees, testified that * * * the Commissioner's office rejected many qualified nominees proposed by CDER in favor of individuals who shared a common ideological viewpoint. Specifically, "the backgrounds of many of the candidates that were forwarded [by the Commissioner's office] . . . had an ideological commonality. . . . They were . . . people who were very active in the Right to Life antiabortion world." * * *

In preparation for the advisory committee meeting, which would consider whether to recommend approval of the Plan B sponsor's switch applications, review staff met with and informed Commissioner McClellan that "[t]he results of the [actual use study] demonstrated that the frequency of unprotected sex did not increase, condom use did not decrease, and the overall use of effective contraception did not decrease [with use of Plan B]." Staff noted that while only 5 percent of subjects recruited for the actual use study were in the 16 and younger age group, the Plan B sponsor supplemented the actual use study data with reports and behavioral studies from the medical literature. These studies enrolled more than 1,000 subjects ages 16 and younger and lent further support to a finding that young adolescents can use Plan B safely in an OTC setting.

On December 16, 2003, the advisory committee voted 23 to 4 in favor of the recommendation to approve Plan B for over-the-counter status without age or point-of-sale restrictions; it voted unanimously that Plan B is safe for use in a non-prescription setting, and voted 27 to 1 that the actual use study data submitted by the Plan B sponsor could be generalized to the overall population of potential non-prescription users of Plan B, i.e., data from older age groups could be extrapolated to younger ones. Only a few panel members raised questions concerning the quality of the supporting data regarding young adolescent use and possible substitution of Plan B for other forms of contraception. And, significantly, at least two of those raising such concerns appear to have been appointed by the Commissioner's office to achieve ideological balance on the panel.

While the advisory committee does not have the final say regarding the OTC switch applications, the FDA has followed advisory committee recommendations in every OTC switch application in the last decade: Of the 23 OTC switch applications reviewed by advisory committees from 1994 to 2004, the Plan B over-the-counter switch application was the only one that was not approved after the joint committee voted to recommend its approval. A meeting in late December 2003 or early January 2004 sheds light on the reasons for this departure from the FDA's decision-making process. During that meeting, Dr. [Janet] Woodcock, Acting Deputy Commissioner, and Dr. Steven Galson, Acting [CDER] Director, told their subordinates, Drs. [John] Jenkins [OND Director] and Kweder, "that Plan B could not be approved on this round," and that the decision was to be made at the level of CDER Director or at the Commissioner's level. This was a departure from usual FDA procedures because under its "normal schema" a switch to OTC of a first in class drug, such as Plan B, would be handled at the Office Director level and would not require approval or sign off by the Commissioner's office. Moreover, they were told that the White House had been involved in the decision on Plan B. * * *

[T]he pressure coming from the White House appears to have been transmitted down by the Commissioner's office in such a way as to significantly affect Dr. Galson's position on the over-the-counter switch application. * * * Dr. Jenkins' testimony is corroborated by the deposition testimony of Dr. Susan Wood, then-Assistant Commissioner for Women's Health and Director of the FDA Office of Women's Health. Dr. Wood testified that Dr. Galson conveyed that "he felt that he would not be able to work with the leadership of the agency in an effective manner if [the not-approvable] letter . . . did not go through."

Nevertheless, FDA review staff continued their "first review cycle" for the OTC switch application submitted by the Plan B sponsor. On January 9, 2004, Dr. Curtis Rosebraugh, Deputy Director of the Division of OTC Drugs, recommended approval of the application submitted by the Plan B sponsor, concluding that Plan B has a "low misuse and abuse potential" and is "safe and effective." Moreover, he suggested that Plan B could decrease unwanted teen pregnancy by up to 70 percent and reduce teen abortions. On January 15, 2004, less than a week after Rosebraugh circulated his memorandum, and before other FDA offices had completed their respective reviews, Dr. Galson met with and informed members of the ODE III, ODE V and OND that the Commissioner's office had decided that the FDA would issue a not-approvable letter because of a lack of adequate data to support appropriate use of Plan B by adolescents under 16. There is evidence that Commissioner McClellan made this decision *before* FDA staff had completed their scientific reviews of that data. * * *

In mid-February, FDA staff attempted to address Commissioner McClellan's expressed concerns regarding the impact of non-prescription access to Plan B on young adolescents. They presented him with an analysis of additional data available on the OTC use of Plan B by adolescents. Staff concluded that "the benefits of timely access outweighed any risk for all women, including adolescents," and supported OTC availability without any age restriction. Commissioner McClellan, however, was "not convinced the studies had enough power to determine if there were behavioral differences between adults and adolescents" and directed CDER to work with the drug's sponsor on a marketing plan to restrict Plan B access to appropriate age groups. * * *

FDA scientific review staff uniformly and strongly supported approval of Plan B for OTC sales without age or point-of-sale restrictions. Numerous scientists submitted memoranda to this effect in March and April 2004. Significantly, the memoranda squarely addressed upper management concerns that there was insufficient data on young adolescent use. Reviewers analyzed the actual use data as well as data from five other studies that were submitted with the initial SNDA. * * * Dr. Rosebraugh concluded similarly:

> The data ... [are] quite compelling to dispel any potential concerns regarding adolescent use or changes in sexual[] behaviors associated with plan B use.... In terms of OTC switch applications, this drug has more information available to allow us to predict consumer behaviors than any drug the Divisions ha[ve] approved for switch in recent memory. If this is not enough data upon which to base a decision, it is unclear what would constitute enough data or even if that is an obtainable goal.

* * * Later in April 2004, Dr. Jenkins, Director of [OND], issued his review concurring with the recommendations of ODE III and ODE V. He concluded "that increased access for adolescents to emergency contraception did not result in inappropriate use of Plan B as a routine form of contraception, an increase in the number of sexual partners, an increase in the frequency of unprotected intercourse, or an increase in the frequency of sexually transmitted diseases." Responding directly to concerns that the label comprehension and actual use studies enrolled too few young adolescents, Dr. Jenkins noted: * * * "the agency has a long history of extrapolating findings from clinical trials in older patients to adolescents in both prescription and non-prescription approvals and this practice was recently incorporated into the Pediatric Research and Equity Act." See 21 U.S.C. § 355c(a)(2)(B)(ii) ("A study may not be needed in each pediatric age group if data from one age group can be extrapolated to another age group.").

Nevertheless, on May 6, 2004, Dr. Galson, Acting Director of [CDER], sent the Plan B sponsor a not-approvable letter on the initial SNDA. * * * [T]he Plan B sponsor submitted an amended SNDA in July 2004, formally proposing a dual marketing plan for Plan B that would allow non-prescription sales to persons age 16 and over who presented a valid identification to a pharmacist, and prescription-only sales to women 15 years and younger. The amended SNDA proposed that Plan B be kept behind-the-counter (BTC) at pharmacies so as to enforce the age restriction on non-prescription use. * * *

In January 2005, notwithstanding review staff's continued view that OTC access should be approved without age restriction, Dr. Galson * * * asked Dr. Jenkins to draft an approvable letter for the Plan B OTC switch application approving OTC status for women age 17 and over. Dr. Galson had concluded and informed Acting Commissioner Crawford that he was "comfortable with the science" and that OTC use of Plan B "should be approved over the counter for 17 and up." Acting Commissioner Crawford testified at his deposition that he concurred with Dr. Galson's recommendation. Nevertheless, in January or February 2005, before Dr. Galson could issue the letter he had instructed Dr. Jenkins to draft, Acting Commissioner Crawford removed Dr. Galson's authority to make a decision on the OTC switch application. This was the only time Dr. Galson had had his authority to make such a decision removed and the only time he is aware of it happening to any [CDER] Director.

Acting Commissioner Crawford's decision to remove Dr. Galson's authority effectively froze the review process for more than seven months * * * * Despite repeated inquiries from members of the Senate, Acting Commissioner Crawford failed to provide an answer as to when a decision on the Plan B switch application could be expected. This continued inaction moved Senators Patty Murray and Hillary Clinton to place a hold on his confirmation as Commissioner. To remove the hold, Michael Leavitt, the Secretary of Health and Human Services, sent a letter on July 13, 2005 to Senator Michael Enzi, Chairman of the Senate Committee on Health, Education, Labor and Pensions, assuring him that action would be taken on the Plan B application by September 1, 2005. On July 18, 2005, Crawford was confirmed by the Senate as FDA Commissioner.

Notwithstanding assurances that the FDA would act by September 1, 2005, Commissioner Crawford announced in late August 2005 that he would put off the decision yet again. In a letter dated August 26, 2005, Commissioner Crawford stated that, although the "scientific data are sufficient to support the safe use of Plan B as an OTC product . . . for women who are 17 years of age and older," the FDA is unable to reach a decision on the approvability of the application—even as to women 17 and older—because of "unresolved issues" related to the FDA's authority to approve the BTC regime of Plan B and the logistics of enforcing the age based and point-of-sale restrictions. That same day, the FDA announced its intention to issue an advance notice of a 60–day public comment period on whether rulemaking procedures were necessary to resolve and clarify these unresolved issues. See 70 Fed. Reg. 52,050 (2005). This decision presented a new obstacle to the Senate deadline of September 1, 2005 for a decision on Plan B, which had been a condition of the Senate's confirmation of Commissioner Crawford.

In August 2005, days after Commissioner Crawford's decision to further delay the decision-making on Plan B, Dr. Wood, Assistant Commissioner and Director of the FDA Office of Women's Health, resigned over the FDA's handling of the Plan B OTC switch application. In her resignation letter to Commissioner Crawford, Dr. Wood wrote:

> Sadly, your recent decision to not approve Plan B emergency contraception, overturning the clear scientific and clinical evidence, contradicts both the FDA mission and my commitment to women's health. The rationale offered is not convincing, and is in fact a denial of access to a product clearly established as safe and effective for all women who need it.

When Dr. Wood met with Dr. Woodcock to discuss her resignation, Dr. Woodcock expressed concern that the FDA's handling of Plan B could damage her own credibility. On October 7, 2005, Dr. Frank Davidoff, a member of the FDA's Non-prescription Drug Advisory Committee, also resigned because of the FDA's delayed action on the Plan B switch application.

The 60–day period for public comment on whether rulemaking procedures were necessary closed on November 1, 2005. The FDA received approximately 47,000 public comments and hired an outside company to review and summarize those comments. That review was completed six months later on May 19, 2006. After reviewing these materials, the FDA finally concluded—more than eleven months after halting its review of the OTC switch application to seek public comment—that it was not necessary after all to engage in agency rulemaking before deciding the Plan B sponsor's OTC switch application. Instead, on July 31, 2006, the FDA announced that "[n]on-prescription sales of [Plan B] could be approved for women 18 and older within weeks," although it requested more information regarding the Plan B sponsor's plan to enforce the age and point-of-sale restrictions, which required that Plan B be kept behind the pharmacy counter. By this point in time, Commissioner Crawford had resigned* and Dr. von Eschenbach had been made Acting Commissioner and nominated to replace him. * * *

In response to the FDA's request, the Plan B sponsor submitted yet another switch application in August 2006, this time asking the FDA to approve OTC use by women 18 and over instead of 16 and over. At the FDA's insistence, the sponsor agreed to take primary responsibility for enforcing compliance with the age restriction, to distribute the product only to licensed pharmacists, and to direct pharmacies to keep Plan B behind-the-counter. Moreover, the Plan B sponsor agreed to collect data and conduct postmarket research to determine the effectiveness of the Plan B dual marketing regime.

The Plan B sponsor's revised switch application conformed to the FDA's expressed willingness to entertain an application to make Plan B available without a prescription to women over the age of 18. Notwithstanding the conclusion of his immediate predecessor, Dr. Crawford, that the "scientific data are sufficient to support the safe use of Plan B as an OTC product . . . for women who are 17 years of age and older," Commissioner von Eschenbach had decided that 18, rather than age 17, is the "more appropriate cutoff point" for OTC use of Plan B because of "well-established state and private-sector infrastructures [which] restrict certain products to consumers 18 and older." He concluded "that to best protect and promote the public health," perceived regulatory efficiencies should outweigh the substantial health benefit 17 year old women would gain through OTC access to a drug product that—experts agreed—they could use safely and effectively. The following day, Dr. Galson issued a memorandum stating that "although [he had] previously concluded that OTC use would be restricted to women 17 or older, I have now determined that for the reasons Dr. von Eschenbach outlines," OTC use of Plan B should be restricted to women age 18 and over. Finally, on August 24, 2006, the FDA approved non-prescription use of Plan B for consumers 18 and older. * * *

* He did so for reasons apparently unrelated to his role in the review of the Plan B switch requests. See Stephanie Saul, Ex-F.D.A. Chief Is Charged with Conflict, N.Y. Times, Oct. 17, 2006, at A15 (reporting that Crawford had "resigned abruptly" after only two months in the post, subsequently pleading guilty to charges of conflict of interest and lying about holding stock in companies that the agency regulates).

At the request of members of Congress, * * * the Government Accountability Office (GAO) initiated an investigation * * * * The investigation was limited in scope to the FDA's actions leading up to the May 6, 2004 not-approvable letter for the initial SNDA and did not take into consideration the citizen petition or later SNDAs. Nevertheless, the findings of a congressional agency provide relevant background to this litigation and confirm conclusions that are compelled by the record here. See GAO, Food and Drug Administration: Decision Process to Deny Initial Application for Over-the-Counter Marketing of the Emergency Contraceptive Drug Plan B Was Unusual, Doc. No. GAO–06–109 (Nov. 2005). * * *

Plaintiffs have presented unrebutted evidence of the FDA's lack of good faith regarding its decisions on the Plan B switch applications. This lack of good faith is evidenced by, among other things, (1) repeated and unreasonable delays, pressure emanating from the White House, and the obvious connection between the confirmation process of two FDA Commissioners and the timing of the FDA's decisions; and (2) significant departures from the FDA's normal procedures and policies in the review of the Plan B switch applications as compared to the review of other switch applications in the past 10 years. * * *

[T]he advisory committee *and* FDA scientific review staff strongly recommended approving Plan B OTC without age restriction, finding that restricting access to young adolescents would present greater health risks that making Plan B freely available. * * * [D]espite this recommendation, the FDA refused to approve the citizen petition and first SNDA submitted by the Plan B sponsor. Instead, before the scientific reviews were complete, the Commissioner decided that unrestricted OTC access could not be approved, because of his concern about the inadequacy of data available for young adolescents. Plaintiffs have proffered evidence that the Commissioner did not make the decision on his own, but was pressured by the White House and "constituents who would be very unhappy with ... an over-the-counter Plan B." * * * Moreover, despite the overwhelming evidence that Plan B could be used safely and effectively by 17 year olds without a prescription, the FDA, citing fanciful and wholly unsubstantiated "enforcement" concerns, arbitrarily and capriciously limited that age group's access to Plan B.

Indeed, the evidence strongly suggests that even the decision to permit the OTC sale of Plan B to women over the age of 18 was made solely to facilitate the confirmation of Dr. von Eschenbach as Commissioner of the FDA. This change of policy came one day before Dr. von Eschenbach's confirmation hearing before a Senate committee. See Stephanie Saul, F.D.A. Shifts View on Next–Day Pill, N.Y. Times, Aug. 1, 2006, at A1. * * * Senators Hillary Clinton and Patty Murray had previously vowed to block any vote on Dr. von Eschenbach's nomination until the FDA decided whether to allow over-the-counter sales of Plan B. Id.; Gardiner Harris, Bush Picks F.D.A. Chief, but Vote Is Unlikely Soon, N.Y. Times, Mar. 16, 2006, at A18. Since the FDA had already reneged on its earlier promise to promptly reach a final decision on Plan B in order to obtain former-

Commissioner Crawford's confirmation, it must have been apparent to the FDA that a mere promise to decide would no longer suffice to secure Dr. von Eschenbach's confirmation. * * *

The evidence of lack of good faith is also confirmed by the manner in which the FDA departed from its normal procedures for evaluating OTC switch applications when it considered the Plan B applications. The most glaring procedural departure was the decision to act against the advisory committee's recommendation to approve the Plan B OTC switch application without age restriction. * * * The FDA's decision regarding Plan B departed from its general policies and practices in at least four other respects. The first is the placement of additional members on the Reproductive Health Drugs Advisory Committee for the purpose of achieving ideological balance. This goal of ideological diversity does not aid the FDA in its obligation to examine the safety and effectiveness of a drug's use in self-medication. The second departure was the unusual involvement of the White House in the Plan B decision-making process. Whether or not it was permissible for the FDA to discuss such questions with the White House, these discussions were not the norm for the FDA with respect to this type of decision.

The third departure concerns the timing of the decision to deny OTC use without age restriction. Plaintiffs presented evidence and the GAO made findings which indicate that the decision regarding the OTC status of Plan B may have been made before the scientific reviews of the OTC switch application were complete, and without consultation with FDA scientists. If the decision was made prior to the completion of the scientific reviews, this would certainly be evidence of a departure from the typical FDA decision-making process. Moreover, such a premature decision would lend further support to plaintiffs' theory that FDA upper management were pressured by the White House to deny young adolescents OTC access to Plan B regardless of whether the scientific evidence supported a finding that they could use Plan B safely and effectively.

The fourth departure was the FDA's refusal to extrapolate actual use study data from the older age group to the 16 and younger age group. There is evidence in the record that the FDA routinely extrapolated such data when reviewing the safety and effectiveness of various other contraceptives. Indeed, the draft minutes from an internal FDA meeting held in May 2004, contain the following comment regarding the decision not to extrapolate for Plan B:

> The inability to extrapolate adolescent safety and effectiveness for <14 year old females is not consistent with how CDER handles approval and distribution of prescription oral contraceptives, OTC male contraceptives such as condoms and spermacides or OTC female contraceptives such as gels and sponges. In addition, CDER routinely denies sponsors' requests to issue written requests for pediatric studies for oral contraceptives as the responses to these drugs are considered the same for all menstruating females and additional studies are not necessary.

This was contained in an initial draft of the minutes, although it was subsequently deleted for reasons which are unclear. Nevertheless, it accurately reflected the FDA's policy of extrapolating data from older to younger populations. * * *

Notwithstanding all of these departures, the FDA argues that there is no customary agency practice and "[e]very drug presents a unique collection of issues, and no two reviews will be identical." Plaintiffs do not argue, however, that the scientific review or risk benefit assessment of all proposed OTC drugs must be evaluated in the same manner. They question why the review of Plan B differed in so many significant ways from the review of other switch applications in the last 10 years. The FDA simply has not come forward with an adequate explanation, nor has it presented any evidence to rebut plaintiffs' showing that it acted in bad faith and in response to political pressure. Instead, the FDA has pursued a litigation strategy dependent on the assertion of the deliberative process privilege to prevent plaintiffs from obtaining conclusive evidence as to the merits of its claim. The FDA claims that it acted in good faith but has consistently sought to prevent plaintiffs from obtaining discovery to show otherwise. This claim of good faith fails in the face of the showing plaintiffs have made here. * * *

[R]emand to the FDA for it to reconsider its denial of the citizen petition is the appropriate remedy for two reasons. First, the circumstances have changed since these words were written. Commissioner von Eschenbach has resigned and his replacement, as well as a new Deputy Commissioner, has been nominated by the [new] President. This change in the leadership suggests that [the agency] can be "trusted to conduct a fair assessment of the scientific evidence." Second, a decision whether Plan B, a systemic hormonal contraceptive drug, may be used safely without a prescription by children as young as 11 or 12, is best left to the expertise of the FDA, to which Congress has entrusted this responsibility; it should not be made by a federal district court judge. A remand would serve no purpose with respect to one aspect of the FDA's decision—requiring that 17 year olds obtain a prescription for Plan B. The record is clear: the FDA's justification for the denial of OTC access to Plan B for women over the age of 17—rather than 18—"runs counter to the evidence" and "is so implausible that it could not be ascribed to a difference in view or the product of agency expertise." * * * The notion that those selling Plan B would not be able to determine whether an individual was 17, as opposed to 18, based on government issued identification is simply untenable. * * *

The denial of the citizen petition is vacated and the matter is remanded to the FDA to reconsider its decisions regarding the Plan B switch to OTC use. The FDA is also ordered to permit Barr Pharmaceuticals, Inc., the Plan B drug sponsor, to make Plan B available to 17 year olds without a prescription, under the same conditions as Plan B is now available to women over the age of 18. The latter order should be complied with within thirty days. Because of the foregoing, it is unnecessary to rule on plaintiffs various substantive challenges to the FDA's decisions regarding Plan B.

Similarly, it would be premature to reach the merits of plaintiffs' various constitutional challenges to the FDA's decisions regarding Plan B. * * *

NOTES AND QUESTIONS

1. *Playing political football.* Did Judge Korman regard the pressure emanating from the White House as more problematic than the congressional pressure (in this case exerted through a pair of threatened holds on the confirmation of nominees to lead the FDA), or did pressure from both of these branches so intrude on the agency's decisionmaking process that it failed substantive ("arbitrary [and] capricious") review under the APA? What if we reverse the roles, assuming that the FDA (under White House pressure) had pursued an OTC switch notwithstanding genuine public health concerns and Senators successfully placed holds on nominations in order to stall this agency action? See Gardiner Harris, F.D.A. Nominee Advances: Hurdles Linger, N.Y. Times, Sept. 21, 2006, at A27 (reporting that, immediately after the agency approved the partial OTC switch but with Dr. von Eschenbach's confirmation process still pending, two GOP Senators threatened to put a hold on the nomination); see also Lars Noah, A Miscarriage in the Drug Approval Process?: Mifepristone Embroils the FDA in Abortion Politics, 36 Wake Forest L. Rev. 571, 583 & n.56 (2001) (noting that Senate Republicans had placed a hold on Jane Henney, President Clinton's nominee to replace David Kessler as FDA Commissioner, in order to secure assurances that she would not actively pursue her predecessor's controversial initiatives to facilitate approval of an abortifacient drug and to regulate tobacco product advertising). In any event, the compromise regarding Plan B also had failed to mollify conservative public interest groups, though their earlier judicial challenge to the partial OTC switch failed on various justiciability grounds. See Association of Am. Physicians & Surgeons, Inc. v. FDA, 539 F.Supp.2d 4 (D.D.C.2008) (holding that the plaintiffs lacked standing and had failed to exhaust administrative remedies); see also id. at 11 (noting that they too alleged that the FDA had been "improperly influenced by political pressure"). See generally Alastair J.J. Wood et al., A Sad Day for Science at the FDA, 353 New Eng. J. Med. 1197 (2005); Susan F. Wood, The Role of Science in Health Policy Decisionmaking: The Case of Emergency Contraception, 17 Health Matrix 273 (2007); Anna P. Krishtul, Comment, The FDA's Recent About–Face: Plan B Age Restriction Is Unlawful Rulemaking and Violates Minors' Due Process Rights, 81 Temp. L. Rev. 303 (2008). Although the agency (now under still newer management) chose not to appeal Judge Korman's decision, it also has done essentially nothing to comply with his order. See April Hollis, FDA Named in Contempt Motion over Delays on Plan B Access, Wash. Drug Let., Nov. 22, 2010; see also Rob Stein, 17–Year-Olds to Gain Access to Plan B Pill: FDA Approves Nonprescription Sales, Wash. Post, Apr. 23, 2009, at A3 (reporting that, in order to comply with the court's order, the agency simply had advised Barr Pharmaceuticals that it would approve an age reduction of one year for OTC marketing if the company files an SNDA to make such a request). In the meantime, the FDA has approved a new

(Rx-only) emergency contraceptive, see Rob Stein, FDA Approves ella as 5–Day–After Emergency Contraceptive, Wash. Post, Aug. 14, 2010, at A1.

2. *Getting the inside scoop*. The second Bush administration tried to keep a tight lid on the FDA (and other agencies). See Gardiner Harris & William J. Broad, Scientists Welcome Administration's Words but Must Wait for Action, N.Y. Times, Jan. 22, 2009, at A23. Judge Korman's opinion—even as heavily abridged above—offers an unusually detailed (and disturbing) account of internal agency deliberations. Earlier in the litigation, the magistrate overseeing discovery had rejected the FDA's motion for a protective order. See Tummino v. von Eschenbach, 427 F.Supp.2d 212, 230–36 (E.D.N.Y.2006) (explaining that evidence of agency bad faith justified review beyond the bare administrative record and that the deliberative process privilege did not apply); see also In re Kessler, 100 F.3d 1015 (D.C.Cir.1996) (enforcing a subpoena of the Commissioner in litigation that challenged FDA action); United States v. Wood, 57 F.3d 733, 737–38 (9th Cir.1995) (holding that the FDA must disclose relevant internal records to a defendant when it brings a criminal prosecution). Litigants generally cannot, however, subpoena agency employees to testify. See 21 C.F.R. § 20.1. In this case, of course, the plaintiffs also had access to disgruntled former officials as well as published findings from the GAO's investigation.

The Freedom of Information Act (FOIA), 5 U.S.C. § 552, provides another avenue for trying to access relevant records held by the agency. The FDA receives roughly 10,000 such requests annually, and reviewing courts only require that the agency make a reasonable effort to locate requested documents. See CareToLive v. FDA, 631 F.3d 336 (6th Cir.2011) (granting the agency summary judgment on a challenge to the sufficiency of its response to a patient advocacy group's effort to unearth incriminating information in connection with the FDA's decision to delay approval of Provenge®); cf. Buc v. FDA, 762 F.Supp.2d 62, 67–73 (D.D.C.2011) (expressing little sympathy for the significant backlog of FOIA requests pending at CDER). The FDA and manufacturers may try to prevent disclosure by invoking one of FOIA's exemptions, especially the one protecting trade secrets and confidential commercial data. See Webb v. HHS, 696 F.2d 101 (D.C.Cir.1982); see also 21 U.S.C. § 331(j) (directing the FDA to protect trade secrets); 21 C.F.R. § 20.61; Public Citizen Health Research Group v. FDA, 185 F.3d 898 (D.C.Cir.1999); cf. Judicial Watch, Inc. v. FDA, 449 F.3d 141, 149 (D.C.Cir.2006) ("Applicants spend a great deal of resources to obtain data for an IND or NDA, and the FDA could not expect full and frank disclosure if it later released such proprietary information into the public domain. Exemption 4 does not categorically exempt all information in INDs and NDAs, however ...."); id. at 151 ("[D]ocuments dated after mifepristone's approval for abortion may still be predecisional and deliberative [under Exemption 5] with respect to other, nonfinal agency policies, including uses of the drug that the agency has not approved."); id. at 153 (affirming the agency's invocation of Exemption 6 (covering unwarranted invasions of personal privacy) where it "cited the danger of abortion-related violence to those who developed mifepristone, worked on its FDA approval, and continue to manufacture the drug ... for [withholding] both the names and addresses of persons and businesses associated with mifepristone"); Hoffmann–La Roche, Inc. v. Yoder, 950 F.Supp. 1348 (S.D.Ohio 1997) (rejecting one company's effort to use state trade secrets law to prevent a researcher from releasing data on Accutane). See generally Peter Lurie & Allison Zieve, Sometimes the Silence Can Be Like the Thunder: Access to Pharmaceutical Data at the FDA, Law & Contemp. Probs., Sum. 2006, at 85.

3. *Pharmacist refusals to dispense.* Plan B continues to require pharmacist involvement (even for those patients who can provide identification to prove that they exceed the age cut-off), and some members of the profession have refused to dispense the drug because they either regard it as an abortifacient or have religious qualms about all contraceptive drugs. See Brittany L. Grimes, Note, The Plan B for Plan B: The New Dual Over-the-Counter and Prescription Status of Plan B and Its Impact upon Pharmacists, Consumers, and Conscience Clauses, 41 Ga. L. Rev. 1395 (2007). Physicians occasionally also have refused to prescribe the drug to youngsters, and patterns of conscientious objection extend beyond Plan B to include other contraceptive products and genuine abortifacients (i.e., mifepristone). Some states acted to protect such decisions while others have attempted to prohibit this behavior. See Lars Noah, Too High a Price for Some Drugs?: The FDA Burdens Reproductive Choice, 44 San Diego L. Rev. 231, 251 & nn.76–77 (2007); Rob Stein, "Pro–Life" Drugstores Market Beliefs: No Contraceptives for Chantilly Shop, Wash. Post, June 16, 2008, at A1 ("California, New Jersey, Illinois and Washington state recently began requiring pharmacies to fill all prescriptions or help women fill them elsewhere, and at least another 10 states are considering such requirements.").

In one of its final acts, the Bush administration promulgated a rule creating a federal conscience clause. See 73 Fed. Reg. 78,072 (2008). A group of states and family planning organizations immediately challenged the regulation. See Rob Stein, Lawsuits Filed over Rule That Lets Health Workers Deny Care: Regulation to Protect "Conscience Rights" Called Too Broad, Wash. Post, Jan. 16, 2009, at A4. Shortly after his inauguration, the Obama administration proposed to rescind most of the rule, which it finally did two years later. See Rob Stein, Health "Conscience" Rule Replaced, Wash. Post, Feb. 19, 2011, at A3; see also Rob Stein, Under the New Health–Care Law, What Will Happen When Providers' Morals Conflict with Patients' Rights?, Wash. Post, May 11, 2010, at F1. Free exercise issues receive closer attention at the end of this chapter. For a sampling of the raft of commentary on this broader question, see Martha S. Swartz, "Conscience Clauses" or "Unconscionable Clauses": Personal Beliefs Versus Professional Responsibilities, 6 Yale J. Health Pol'y L. & Ethics 269 (2006); Catherine Grealis, Note, Religion in the Pharmacy: A Balanced Approach to Pharmacists' Right to Refuse to Provide Plan B, 97 Geo. L.J. 1715 (2009); Jeffrey P. Jarosch, Comment, Finding Space for Opposing Consciences: Rehabilitating the Moral Marketplace for the Emergency Contraception Debate, 103 Nw. U. L. Rev. 1461 (2009); Diana Snyder, Note, A Reasonable Time, Place and Manner Restriction: Medicare Reimbursement Law Should Require Pharmacists to Fill Prescriptions Regardless of Personal Belief, 36 Am. J.L. & Med. 652 (2010); Rachel White–Domain, Comment, Making Rules and Unmaking Choice: The Federal Conscience Clauses, the Provider Conscience Regulation, and the War on Reproductive Freedom, 59 DePaul L. Rev. 1249 (2010).

4. *Analogous debates over HPV vaccines?* A similar political dynamic—though at the state rather than the federal level (and in connection with public health recommendations for immunizing adolescent girls rather than requests for OTC availability)—threatened to interfere with the use of Gardasil®, a vaccine approved by the FDA to prevent the sexually transmitted disease human papillomavirus (HPV), which may cause cervical cancer. See Susan Levine, Parents Question HPV Vaccine: Push to Mandate Shots Rapidly Creates Backlash, Wash. Post, Mar. 4, 2007, at C1. See generally Kristin Cook, Note, Ethical and Legal Issues Accompanying Legislation Requiring HPV Vaccination of Girls, 18 Health Matrix 209 (2008); Tracy S. Dowling, Note, Mandating a Human Papillomavirus Vaccination for School Attendance: An Investigation into Whether Such Legislation Is Constitutional and Prudent, 34 Am. J.L. & Med. 65 (2008); Julie E. Gendel, Comment, Playing Games with Girls' Health: Why It Is Too Soon to Mandate the HPV Vaccine for Pre-teen Girls as a Prerequisite to School Entry, 39 Seton Hall L. Rev. 265 (2009); Lindsey Heinz, Comment, "Please, Don't Shot My Daughter!" Is There Legal Support for State–Compelled HPV Vaccination Laws? Why Ethical, Moral, and Religious Opposition to These Laws May Be Jumping the Gun, 56 U. Kan. L. Rev. 913 (2008); Jonathan T. Scott, Note, The Difficult Road to Compelling Vaccination for Sexually Transmitted Diseases—How Gardasil and Those Who Follow Will Change the Way That States Require Inoculation, 97 Ky. L.J. 697 (2008–2009); Katharine Southard, Note, One Step Forward, Two Steps Back: How Mandating the Human Papillomavirus Vaccine Will Increase the Use of Vaccine Exemptions and Negatively Impact Our Nation's Health, 28 J.L. & Pol'y 503 (2009).

5. *Prescribing privileges.* Traditionally, states regulated the practice of medicine and pharmacy, and they defined who could issue prescriptions. See Idaho Ass'n of Naturopathic Physicians, Inc. v. FDA, 582 F.2d 849 (4th Cir.1978); see also Lars Noah, Ambivalent Commitments to Federalism in Controlling the Practice of Medicine, 53 U. Kan. L. Rev. 149, 171 (2004) ("[F]ederal agencies normally designate which products require a prescription but then defer to state rules about who may issue such prescriptions."); id. at 176 ("For instance, a number of jurisdictions now allow advanced-practice nurses to exercise such authority without any physician supervision ...."); id. at 179–80 ("[A]s reflected by its approach to controlled substances, the federal government may further subdivide the category of prescription drugs and exert greater control over their use. Here again, however, it has decided to defer to state decisions concerning what classes of health care professionals may prescribe and dispense these pharmaceutical products."). For instance, a few states have considered granting limited prescribing privileges to psychologists. See James E. Long, Jr., Comment, Power to Prescribe: The Debate over Prescription Privileges for Psychologists and the Legal Issues Implicated, 29 Law & Psychol. Rev. 243 (2005); Shankar Vedantam, For Psychiatrists, a Bitter Pill in New Mexico, Wash. Post, July 1, 2002, at A1.

6. *Prescription restrictions in the new economy.* Although filling prescriptions by mail-order raised some eyebrows in the early 1990s, the FDA did not react. Cf. National Pharm., Inc. v. Feliciano-de-Melecio, 221 F.3d 235 (1st Cir.2000). With the advent of the Internet, however, concerns about dispensing have resurfaced. See United States v. Rx Depot, Inc., 290 F.Supp.2d 1238 (N.D.Okla.2003) (enjoining a business that arranged for Canadian pharmacies to fill prescriptions issued in the U.S. because this resulted in the importation of unapproved new drugs or the unauthorized reimportation of approved drugs); Christopher Rowland, US Steps up Seizures of Imported Drugs, Boston Globe, Mar. 26, 2006, at A1. More seriously, on-line prescribing has spread, blurring the distinction between Rx and OTC products and raising concerns that patients could receive hazardous pharmaceuticals without any meaningful supervision by physicians. Even so, the federal government has shown little interest in intruding on the prerogatives of state officials in this area. See Lisa Richardson & Charles Ornstein, State Chasing Web Medics Who Prescribe Sight Unseen, L.A. Times, Feb. 17, 2003, at A1; see also Linda C. Fentiman, Internet Pharmacies and the Need for a New Federalism: Protecting Consumers While Increasing Access to Prescription Drugs, 56 Rutgers L. Rev. 119 (2003) (advocating a federal regulatory response); Nicolas P. Terry, Prescriptions Sans Frontieres, 4 Yale J. Health Pol'y L. & Ethics 183 (2004); Phil Ayres, Comment, Prescribing a Cure for Online Pharmacies, 72 Tenn. L. Rev. 949 (2005); Laura Vanderstappen, Note, Internet Pharmacies and the Specter of the Dormant Commerce Clause, 22 Wash. U. J.L. & Pol'y 619 (2006); Jay M. Zitter, Annotation, State and Federal Regulation of Prescribing Medication over the Internet, 3 A.L.R.6th 1 (2005 & 2011 Supp.); cf. Robert Johnson, A Symbol of Confusion: Rx, Boston Globe, Oct. 19, 2003, at D1 ("[T]he Latin abbreviation Rx has been commandeered by a vast array of [online] marketers for use on consumer products from cleaning fluids to bottled tea. Government and industry watchdogs are cautioning consumers against trusting too much in Rx-labeled goods ....").

2. PROFESSIONAL LABELING

Prescription drugs are potent medications that unavoidably are associated with adverse effects, but the benefits of using such drugs outweigh the accompanying risks so long as the expert judgment of a trained professional is first applied in the decision to use a drug for a particular patient. The labeling for prescription drugs provides comprehensive information to help physicians in making therapeutic risk-benefit decisions in individual cases. As one would expect, physician labeling contains far more detailed risk information than is generally possible in the labeling of most consumer products.

In the labeling for any prescription drug, the FDA demands that cautionary information be categorized according to the relative severity of the hazard and the degree to which the risk has been substantiated. Topic headings in prescription drug labeling include: Clinical Pharmacology, Indications and Usage, Contraindications, Warnings, Precautions, and Adverse Reactions. The placement of risk information into one of the latter several categories depends on the relative severity of a hazard, ranging from situations where risks "clearly outweigh any possible benefit" (to be noted as contraindications), to non-serious side effects that occur with a frequency of less than one in a thousand (to be noted as "rare" adverse reactions). The Warnings section of the package insert is reserved for risks that are more serious than adverse reactions but are not so serious as to clearly outweigh possible benefits of a drug, and particularly serious risks may have to be highlighted as a "boxed warning." This hierarchy stands in marked contrast to the agency's largely undifferentiated approach for OTC drug labeling.

Whatever category is appropriate for the disclosure of hazard information in the package insert, the FDA demands that the risk be substantiated. The regulations provide, for instance, that only "[k]nown hazards and not theoretical possibilities shall be listed" as contraindications. See 21 C.F.R. § 201.80(d). The agency explained in the preamble to this rule that "including theoretical hazards as contraindications in drug labeling would cause that very important section of the labeling to lose its significance." 44 Fed. Reg. 37,434, 37,447 (1979). A statement in the Warnings section is only appropriate after "reasonable evidence of an association of a serious hazard with a drug" is found, though "a causal relationship need not have been proved." 21 C.F.R. § 201.80(e). Evidence from long-term animal studies normally should be included in the Precautions section, together with an explanation of species and bioassay results, though in some cases "serious animal toxicity data may require warnings in drug labeling." Id. § 201.80(e), (f)(5). The FDA even requires that the Adverse Reactions section, which contains some of the least serious risk information in the package insert, only include those side effects that are "reasonably associated" with use of the drug. See id. § 201.80(g); see also 71 Fed. Reg. 3922, 3949 (2006) (explaining revisions to these rules).

The FDA's rules governing the disclosure of potential risks of use by pregnant women illustrate the interplay between categorization and substantiation. A "Pregnancy category" designation, accompanied by a specified explanation and any additional information concerning the risk of birth defects, must appear in the Precautions section of most package inserts, depending on the available evidence of a drug's potential teratogenicity. See 21 C.F.R. § 201.80(f)(6)(i); see also 73 Fed. Reg. 30,831 (2008) (proposing to revise this rule). If adequate and well-controlled clinical studies have failed to demonstrate any risk to the fetus, the drug is to be designated as Pregnancy category A. Pregnancy category B is appropriate in cases where clinical studies have not been performed in pregnant women but the data from animal testing fail to demonstrate a risk to the fetus, and Pregnancy category C should be used if the animal test results were unfavorable but the benefits of use outweigh the possible risk of birth defects. In the event that there is positive human evidence of a risk to the fetus, but the potential benefits from use of the drug by pregnant women may be acceptable, Pregnancy category D should appear in the Precautions section of the package insert along with a cross-reference to the Warnings section which must include a specified hazard statement. Finally, if evidence from use in humans or animals discloses a risk of birth defects which clearly outweighs any possible benefit of using the drug during pregnancy, Pregnancy category X is appropriate, along with a cross-reference to the Contraindications section. Although the use of different letters for each category is unique, the scheme used for teratogenic risk information reflects the FDA's general categorization and substantiation requirements applicable to other prescription drug hazards.

More than a decade ago, in recognition of the problems with excessive detail and physician inattention, the FDA announced plans to revise prescription drug labeling in order to highlight the most significant information. See 65 Fed. Reg. 38,563, 38,564 (2000) (explaining that the agency has "engaged in several initiatives to make prescription drug labeling a better information source for health care practitioners—clearer, more informative, more accessible, and more consistent"); Sarah Lueck, FDA Frames Plan to Revamp Rules for Drug Labeling, Wall St. J., June 26, 2000, at B12 ("The agency envisions drug labels resembling nutrition labels found on packaged foods, which look similar and contain the same types of data across product categories."). Six years later, the preamble accompanying the final rule began by explaining that recently "there has been an increase in the length, detail, and complexity of prescription drug labeling information, making it harder for health care practitioners to find specific information and to discern the most critical information." 71 Fed. Reg. 3922 (2006). In an effort to help physicians cope with these changes, the FDA mandated significant modifications to the package insert. See id. at 3931, 3972–73 (codified at 21 C.F.R. pt. 201). First, it added a relatively short "highlights" section at the outset. Second, the agency included a table of contents before the comprehensive prescribing information. Third, it reordered the required sections in the package insert to move the most important and frequently referenced information closer to the beginning. Fourth, the FDA called for changes in type face, such as requiring bold type in order to highlight subheadings and a minimum font size in order to improve readability. An exemplar of a reformatted package insert as originally proposed appears as an appendix to this chapter (the final rule differs in minor respects). An initial review of the new rule's impact on the volume of risk information painted a discouraging picture. See Jon Duke et al., A Quantitative Analysis of Adverse Events and "Overwarning" in Drug Labeling, 171 Archives Internal Med. 944, 945–46 (2011) (finding an average of 70 ADEs listed in current package inserts, and concluding that this "may induce information overload and reduce physician comprehension of important safety warnings").

New information may require multiple avenues of dissemination and the passage of time before it sinks in and alters prescribing behavior. See

Lars Noah, Medicine's Epistemology: Mapping the Haphazard Diffusion of Knowledge in the Biomedical Community, 44 Ariz. L. Rev. 373 (2002). One study sponsored in part by the FDA found that labeling revisions and other efforts to communicate new risk information to physicians have essentially no effect on prescribing behavior. Two years after the heartburn remedy Propulsid® (cisapride) entered the market, the FDA revised the labeling in response to reports of serious cardiac side effects, but this had no apparent effect on its use. Three years later, in the face of accumulating adverse event information, the FDA again revised the labeling to strengthen the black box warning, and it ordered the manufacturer to send 800,000 copies of a letter designed to draw attention to this information. The study attempted to quantify to what extent the second effort to disseminate clinically-relevant information altered prescribing behavior in the first year after publication, and it found "no material reduction" in the contraindicated uses of the drug. See Walter Smalley et al., Contraindicated Use of Cisapride: Impact of Food and Drug Administration Regulatory Action, 284 JAMA 3036, 3039 (2000) (concluding that "[t]he exposure of [hundreds of thousands of] patients to inappropriate cisapride use, despite the prominent publication of case reports, label changes, and Dear Health Care Professional letters, highlights the need to develop more effective methods for modifying practice to reflect new information about a drug's risks and benefits"); see also Karen E. Lasser et al., Adherence to Black Box Warnings for Prescription Medications in Outpatients, 166 Archives Internal Med. 338 (2006); Nilay D. Shah et al., Responding to an FDA Warning—Geographic Variation in the Use of Rosiglitazone, 363 New Eng. J. Med. 2081 (2010); Rita Rubin, Drug Warnings Outline Danger, USA Today, Apr. 26, 2005, at 1D.

A commentary accompanying this study decried the loss of safe and effective drugs prompted by such prescribing mistakes, and it blamed these sorts of errors on "the overwhelming amount of information on drugs." Raymond L. Woosley, Drug Labeling Revisions—Guaranteed to Fail?, 284 JAMA 3047, 3047 (2000); see also id. at 3048 ("In the last 25 years, the package inserts for new drugs have increased in length more than 5-fold. For example, the 2-page package insert for cisapride, when printed in 12-point font on 8.5 x 11 paper, is more than 10 pages long and contains more than 470 facts about the drug. Practicing physicians would have difficulty mastering all of this information for even one drug, much less the 40 to 100 medications that they regularly prescribe."); Andrea Petersen, How Drug Alerts Trickle Down to Your Doctor: Amid Flurry of Red Flags About Serious Side Effects, Prescribing Turns Trickier, Wall St. J., Sept. 15, 2004, at D4 ("[R]esearch underscores how difficult it is for doctors to stay on top of the mass of drug information, and decide how or whether to act. The number of drugs has exploded in recent years, so there are simply more side effects and potential drug-to-drug interactions to keep track of."); Jonathan D. Rockoff, Doctors Buried by Drug Data, Balt. Sun, Apr. 7, 2006, at 1D. The inexplicable prescribing patterns for Propulsid, particularly its continued use in pediatric patients, also may reflect the manufacturer's success in negotiating milder revisions to labeling and in managing to promote this off-label use indirectly. See Gardiner Harris & Eric Koli, Lucrative Drug, Danger Signals and the F.D.A., N.Y. Times, June 10, 2005, at A1; Stephanie Saul, Senators Ask Drug Giant to Explain Grants to Doctors, N.Y. Times, July 6, 2005, at C3.

The FDA has recognized that a problem exists—agency officials openly chastised physicians for disregarding instructions in the labeling for newly approved drugs, and they warned that the FDA might have to become more cautious in approving medical technologies because physicians seem incapable of following directions. See Peter Honig et al., Letter, How Many Deaths Are Due to Medical Errors?, 284 JAMA 2187, 2188 (2000); see also Karen E. Lasser et al., Timing of New Black Box Warnings and Withdrawals for Prescription Medications, 287 JAMA 2215 (2002) (explaining that the use of such warnings may not save a drug from eventual withdrawal); Gardiner Harris, F.D.A. Imposes Tougher Rules for Acne Drug, N.Y. Times, Aug. 13, 2005, at A1 ("Health officials say the new plan is the latest sign the F.D.A. is losing faith that the nation's doctors and pharmacists can adequately safeguard the health of patients.... [T]ime after time over the last decade, medical professionals have ignored the advice [in labeling], providing drugs to patients at risk of severe complications.... [I]nstead [of withdrawing effective drugs], the agency has begun fashioning restricted distribution programs ... to ensure that health professionals follow its guidelines."); Gardiner Harris, F.D.A. to Restrict a Diabetes Drug, Citing Heart Risk, N.Y. Times, Sept. 24, 2010, at A1 ("In explaining why the F.D.A. decided against only adding more warnings to Avandia's label, ... [CDER's director] said, 'We know that labels are often not read.' It was an extraordinary acknowledgment from a veteran of an agency that for decades relied almost exclusively on label warnings to control drug use.").

In some cases, of course, widespread publicity about newly discovered risks may have dramatic impacts on prescribing patterns (at least when coupled with a decline in promotional efforts). See Sumit R. Majumdar et al., Promotion and Prescribing of Hormone Therapy After Report of Harm by the Women's Health Initiative, 292 JAMA 1983, 1987 (2004) ("A year and a half after these results were published, there had been a 43% decrease in the prescription of hormone therapy in the United States."). Physicians may, however, overreact to newly publicized research and fail to appreciate its limitations. After a clinical trial demonstrated that spironolactone effectively treated patients with congestive heart failure, prescribing rates for this underutilized old drug increased dramatically, but so did the rates of a serious side effect (hyperkalemia) known to be associated with the drug—in their enthusiasm, physicians had gone beyond the narrow inclusion criteria for subjects enrolled in the clinical trial (and who had enjoyed a favorable balance between risks and benefits) to use the drug in high-risk patients, at higher (and riskier) dosages, or in combination with other drugs. See John J.V. McMurray & Eileen O'Meara, Treatment of Heart Failure with Spironolactone: Trial and Tribulations, 351 New Eng. J. Med. 526 (2004); Ron Winslow, Heralded Heart Drug Has Unexpected Risks: Hospitalizations, Deaths Highlight Hazards of Applying Study Results to Individual Patients, Wall St. J., Aug. 5, 2004, at D1 (reporting that an extrapolation of these findings to the United States would mean an additional 4,200 deaths annually).

Bradley v. Weinberger

483 F.2d 410 (1st Cir.1973).

■ COFFIN, CHIEF JUDGE:

Plaintiffs, 178 physicians who treat diabetes and one diabetes patient who uses oral hypoglycemic agents to control the disease by lowering the blood sugar level, brought suit to enjoin the defendants Secretary of Health, Education and Welfare and the Commissioner of the Food and Drug Administration (FDA) from enforcing and the defendant drug companies from complying with the FDA's proposal for altering the labeling of those drugs. The district court granted a preliminary injunction, being persuaded that there was a reasonable likelihood of success in showing that the FDA had failed to comply with the statutes and its own regulation requiring that under some circumstances labeling make reference to the existence of a serious medical controversy. We vacate the injunction for reasons important to the proper judicial role in reviewing administrative actions.

This controversy revolves around a long-term, federally funded study undertaken by the University Group Diabetes Program (hereafter the UGDP study) to determine the effects of oral hypoglycemic agents on vascular complications in patients with adult-onset diabetes. The study, involving twelve clinics and 1200 patients, consisted of four treatment groups: diet alone, diet plus regular insulin doses, diet plus varying insulin doses, and diet plus fixed doses of either tolbutamide or phenformin (two hypoglycemic agents). After monitoring the patients for from five to eight years, the study concluded that the combination of diet and either tolbutamide or phenformin was no more effective than diet alone in prolonging life but that those oral agents might be more hazardous than diet or diet plus insulin insofar as cardiovascular mortality was concerned. The latter conclusion, which led the investigators to discontinue use of the agents in the study as an unethical risk, was based on findings that patients treated with the two agents used in the study suffered more than twice as many cardiovascular deaths than patients receiving the other treatments.

After the study received much publicity and criticism, the FDA convened an ad hoc committee of experts on May 21, 1970, to evaluate the study's findings and the following day issued a press release agreeing with the UGDP study's conclusions and indicating that the agency would require labeling changes to reflect those views. After more extensive evaluation, the FDA concluded that protection of the public required a strong warning to physicians recommending use of an oral agent only if other treatments were inadvisable and noting the UGDP's findings regarding the apparently increased danger of cardiovascular mortality. This evaluation and proposed labeling change was first formally published in the FDA *Drug Bulletin* of June, 1971.

On October 7, 1971, the Committee on the Care of the Diabetic, consisting of eminent doctors and experts in the field including some of the plaintiff doctors, submitted through its counsel a petition to the FDA. It asked the FDA to rescind its labeling recommendation, insure that all future FDA comments on the UGDP study include references to its alleged deficiencies and controversial nature, provide petitioners with the complete raw data of the study, and, "in accord with its policy of fair balance," disseminate with equal emphasis and frequency studies and individual expert opinions differing with the study. The petition was accompanied by a detailed scientific critique of the UGDP study and some 250 pages of scientific studies, papers and comments illustrating the nature and extent of the opposition viewpoint. The study was primarily criticized for inadequate patient selection controls and use of fixed, rather than variable, doses of the drugs, contrary to allegedly accepted medical practice. The FDA proposal was attacked for extending the study's findings to all oral agents and patients despite the study's own warning that such extrapolation could not be made on a statistical basis. The petition also referred to two smaller studies which indicated no cardiovascular complications from oral agents. It was supplemented in January, 1972, by another 220 pages of scientific materials.

In the May, 1972, *Drug Bulletin*, the FDA published the "Final Labeling Approved for Oral Hypoglycemic Drugs," which proposed changes in the "indications" section of the label and the addition of a "special warning" section. The proposal speaks of "the increased cardiovascular hazard which appears to be associated with oral hypoglycemic agents," notes that the UGDP study was the basis for the change, recites its findings, states that these conclusions apply to all oral agents, not just those employed in the study, and ends with the comment that "further studies are being undertaken to shed additional light on the role" of the oral agents. On June 5, 1972, the Commissioner formally replied to the Committee's petition with an eleven-page, single-space letter addressing generally the legal and medical issues and with a 100 page appendix dealing specifically with the scientific criticisms of the study, criticizing the two contrary studies referred to by the petition, and appending the comments of major medical groups and various scientific papers supportive of the FDA's position. * * *

[T]here appears to be no prior case in which an FDA drug labeling decision was challenged not by the producer but by concerned medical practitioners, and no case in which the misbranding statutes and regulations were sought to be applied not to the manufacturer's label but to the FDA's proposal for alteration of the label in light of new information. * * *

The definitional statute (21 U.S.C. § 321(n)) provides: "If an article is alleged to be misbranded because the labeling is misleading, then in determining whether the labeling is misleading there shall be taken into account (among other things) not only representations made or suggested . . . but also the extent to which the labeling fails to reveal facts material in light of such representations or material with respect to consequences which may result from the use of the article to which the labeling relates." Implementing the latter definition is regulation 1.3:

> The existence of a difference of opinion, among experts qualified by scientific training and experience, as to the truth of a representation made or suggested in the labeling is a fact (among other facts) the failure to reveal which may render the labeling misleading, if there is a material weight of opinion contrary to such representation.

One reading of this regulation would suggest that unsubstantiated individual clinical opinions of qualified experts, which are insufficient under the "substantial evidence" test enacted in the effectiveness section, might be sufficient to create a fact omission of which might render the labeling misleading.

The Commissioner never considered the meaning of this regulation, its relationship to the substantial evidence test, the intersection of the safety, effectiveness, and misbranding requirements, or the applicability of the misbranding requirements, both statutory and regulatory, to an FDA proposal for re-labeling, for the simple reason that the issue was not presented to him. Arguably these are simply issues of law which we are fully capable of resolving without administrative assistance. But as the Supreme Court has very recently noted in similarly resolving a closely analogous case, the interpretation of even definitional sections in the drug law will often involve expert knowledge and the ability to evaluate the scientific evidence that becomes relevant. * * *

Because the plaintiffs failed to exhaust their administrative remedies regarding the issues they now present and, consequently, the district court reviewed the agency decision on something other than the administrative record, we must vacate the injunction.

NOTES AND QUESTIONS

1. *Making a federal case out of it.* The dispute over the UGDP study continued, including a FOIA request appealed to the Supreme Court. See Forsham v. Harris, 445 U.S. 169 (1980) (sustaining the government's refusal to provide original study records over which it had no custody); see also Gina Kolata, Controversy over Study of Diabetes Drugs Continues for Nearly a Decade, 203 Science 986 (1979). After some further skirmishing, the FDA issued a warning requirement based on the disputed study. See 49 Fed. Reg. 14,303 (1984) (codified at 21 C.F.R. § 310.517). Given the well-accepted practice of off-label prescribing, why did the group of physicians go to such lengths in challenging the FDA's new labeling requirements? In 2000, Congress enacted the Data Quality Act, which some groups have tried to use in challenging the scientific basis for agency pronouncements. See Rick Weiss, New Initiative Planned to Get Marijuana Curbs Eased, Wash. Post, Oct. 4, 2004, at A2. In 2007, Congress mandated that the FDA post internal differences of opinion concerning an approval decision on its web site. See FDAAA, Pub. L. No. 110–85, § 916, 121 Stat. 823, 959 (2007) (codified at 21 U.S.C. § 355(*l*)(2)(C)(iv)); see also Karen Baswell, Note,

Time for a Change: Why the FDA Should Require Greater Disclosure of Differences of Opinion on the Safety and Efficacy of Approved Drugs, 35 Hofstra L. Rev. 1799 (2007); Gardiner Harris, New F.D.A.: Transparence and Flexibility, N.Y. Times, Sept. 25, 2010, at A9; Anna W. Mathews, Side Effects: An FDA Reviewer Battles the Drug His Boss Approved, Wall St. J., Oct. 26, 2005, at A1 (documenting internal disagreement over the diabetes drug Symlin®); cf. Kenneth Chang, White House Issues Long–Delayed Science Guidelines, N.Y. Times, Dec. 18, 2010, at A13.

2. *Daring to disagree with the FDA.* The agency revised its regulation in the wake of the *Bradley* decision to clarify that it does not allow any "statement of differences of opinion with respect to warnings (including contraindications, precautions, adverse reactions, and other information relating to product hazards) required in labeling." 21 C.F.R. § 1.21(c)(1). In the course of rejecting suggestions that labels communicate dissenting opinions, the agency emphasized that "labeling is not intended to be a dispositive treatise of all possible medical opinion .... The opinions of individual physicians on such matters can be, and are, thoroughly and adequately discussed through medical journals, treatises, meetings of professional associations, and other similar events." 40 Fed. Reg. 28,582, 28,583 (1975). As explained in the preamble to the proposed regulation, the agency feared that including disclamatory opinions in warnings would "be confusing and misleading." 39 Fed. Reg. 33,229, 33,231–32 (1974) (adding that "disagreement is properly the subject of scientific discussion in professional journals and symposia, but not in drug labeling").

3. *Influencing the practice of medicine.* The FDA has recognized that labeling should not provide the sole source of information relevant to prescribing decisions. In issuing a rule governing the format of package inserts, the FDA rejected suggestions calling for the inclusion of general statements about good professional practice: "There are potentially many such statements, which, if all are included in drug labeling, would transform labeling into small textbooks of medicine." 44 Fed. Reg. 37,434, 37,436 (1979) ("Physicians are always in a position to pursue additional information through normal educational sources, such as treatises and medical journals."). As explained in the preamble to the proposed regulation, the agency hoped to improve package inserts in part by "eliminating extraneous information which can best be obtained from the published literature." 40 Fed. Reg. 15,392, 15,392 (1975). Even so, the FDA has mandated a best practices statement in the labeling of antibiotics, reminding physicians against overprescribing them because of the public health consequences associated with growing drug-resistance. See 68 Fed. Reg. 6062 (2003). In part, the agency's concession that package inserts should not provide the sole source of prescribing information grows from the inevitable obsolescence of the labeling as well as the variable appropriate uses to which physicians may put approved products. The FDA also uses other avenues to communicate with health care providers, including regular columns in prominent medical journals. In addition to publicizing new risk information, it may use these fora to influence best practices. See, e.g., Cochlear–Implant Children Run Higher Risk of Meningitis, Wall St. J., July

31, 2003, at D3 (reporting that the FDA and CDC had published an article about this new risk information in the *New England Journal of Medicine*); cf. Anna W. Mathews & Thomas M. Burton, After Medtronic Lobbying Push, the FDA Had a Change of Heart: Agency Squelches an Article Raising Doubts on Safety of Device to Repair Artery, Wall St. J., July 9, 2004, at A1 (describing stent graft manufacturer's success in blocking a paper written by agency scientists that had recommended surgery for most aortic aneurysm patients).

4. *Avenues for airing differences of opinion.* Just before the controversial abortion drug Mifeprex® (mifepristone) reached the U.S. market, pro-choice groups sent letters to physicians recommending a less cumbersome treatment regimen in an effort to expand use, see Sarah Lueck, Groups Offer Abortion–Drug Variations, Wall St. J., Oct. 30, 2000, at B2, while pro-life groups sent letters to physicians providing more dramatic risk information in an effort to discourage use. See Rachel Zimmerman, Wrangling over Abortion Intensifies as RU486 Pill Nears the Market, Wall St. J., Nov. 14, 2000, at B1 (reporting that one group "sent 150,000 letters to obstetrician/gynecologists and family-practice physicians warning of possible adverse effects"). In addition, just prior to that approval, the manufacturer of the ulcer drug Cytotec® (misoprostol), which doctors widely prescribe for off-label use to induce labor and is specifically identified in the labeling for Mifeprex as needed to complete the abortion, sent a letter to health care providers warning that its drug should never be administered to pregnant women, a position that the company clarified a few months later under pressure from the FDA. See Ralph W. Hale & Stanley Zinberg, Editorial, Use of Misoprostol in Pregnancy, 344 New Eng. J. Med. 59, 60 (2001) ("The timing of the letter, just weeks before the FDA announced its approval of mifepristone, left many people wondering whether there were other motivations for Searle's actions."). It seems unlikely that any other drug will generate similar efforts to influence prescribing behavior, but this episode demonstrates that physicians may receive conflicting off-label drug information from a variety of sources.

5. *Mandating misleading risk information.* Some warnings are designed to serve a collateral purpose. For instance, the FDA once required that products containing CFC propellants include the following warning on their label: "Contains a chlorofluorocarbon that may harm the public health and environment by reducing ozone in the upper atmosphere." 21 C.F.R. § 369.21 (OTC drugs); id. § 801.425(a) (medical devices). The warning was designed to promote environmentally conscious purchasing decisions rather than convey information about risks to the user. See Lars Noah, The Imperative to Warn: Disentangling the "Right to Know" from the "Need to Know" About Consumer Product Hazards, 11 Yale J. on Reg. 293, 313–14, 398 (1994) (criticizing this approach); see also Andrew Pollack, Expected Ban on Primatene Mist Raises Some Concerns, N.Y. Times, May 12, 2006, at C6 (reporting that this product—the only OTC inhaler available to asthmatics—soon could be removed from the market because it uses a CFC propellant).

6. *Professional labeling for devices.* Prescription medical devices must bear information concerning "any relevant hazards, contraindications, side effects, and precautions." 21 C.F.R. § 801.109(c). Although these elements are not spelled out in the same detail contained in the regulations governing package inserts for drugs, the FDA's guidelines set forth identical categorization and substantiation requirements for device labeling. Class labeling requirements for certain products such as intrauterine devices (IUDs) contemplate the same level of detail as found in prescription drug package inserts. See id. § 801.427(b)(1). In addition, through premarket approval of Class III devices, the FDA establishes detailed requirements regarding the labeling of a device in advance of sale. Most Class I devices and Class II devices, as well as some Class III devices for which premarket approval has not yet been required, are subject to premarket notification requirements, and the FDA does review labeling when deciding whether a device is "substantially equivalent" to a previously marketed device. See 21 U.S.C. § 360(k); 21 C.F.R. §§ 807.81–.97; see also Chap. 3(B).

3. PATIENT LABELING

Prescription drug warning requirements have not been confined to physician labeling. Over the last several decades, the FDA has proposed requiring that information be given directly to patients. In 1970, the agency mandated that sellers of oral contraceptives supply a "patient package insert" (PPI). The insert included the following cautionary information: "Do Not Take This Drug Without Your Doctor's Continued Supervision. The oral contraceptives are powerful and effective drugs which can cause side effects in some users and should not be used at all by some women. The most serious known side effect is abnormal blood clotting which can be fatal." 21 C.F.R. § 130.45(d)(1) (1970). The FDA revised this requirement several times since then to include far more detailed warnings. In addition, the agency has required PPIs on a case-by-case basis as a condition of NDA approval.

Pharmaceutical Manufacturers Association v. FDA

484 F.Supp. 1179 (D.Del.), aff'd, 634 F.2d 106 (3d Cir.1980).

■ STAPLETON, DISTRICT JUDGE:

In this case, plaintiffs * * * challenge the validity of a regulation promulgated by the Food and Drug Administration which requires certain information to be provided to patients for whom drugs containing estrogens are prescribed. * * * The regulation in question, codified in 21 C.F.R. § 310.515, is one of only four regulations which require patient labeling to be dispensed with a prescription drug.[1] The regulation was proposed on

1. The others apply to oral contraceptives, 21 C.F.R. § 310.501, to progestational drug products, id. § 310.516, and to isoproterenol inhalation preparations, id. § 201.304. The agency's authority to require patient labeling on prescription drugs has never been subject to a court challenge.

September 29, 1976, with a notice of proposed rulemaking published in the *Federal Register* (41 Fed. Reg. 43,108) permitting sixty days for comments. The regulation as proposed and as promulgated outlined several categories of information which must be included in a patient package insert, and required that such an insert be provided to a patient every time the drug was dispensed or administered (i.e., injected). Thus, physicians as well as pharmacists are required to provide the labeling when they act as dispensers of the medication.

The agency's action came as a result of several studies published in 1975 which indicated an association between the use of conjugated estrogens and an increased risk of endometrial cancer in women. The FDA convened its Obstetrics and Gynecology Advisory Committee to review the studies, and that Committee proposed changes in the physician labeling provided by manufacturers of estrogen. * * * The final rule, published July 22, 1977, was accompanied by a lengthy preamble which attempted to deal with the comments the agency had received and to explain the purpose and effect of the rule. * * *

Plaintiffs and plaintiff-intervenors raise a number of challenges to the regulation. First, they contend that the FDA lacks statutory authority to require patient packaging inserts for prescription drugs. They next assert that such a requirement is an unconstitutional interference with the practice of medicine. Finally, they challenge the adequacy of the FDA's findings and conclusions embodied in the preamble to the regulation and argue that, based on the administrative record, the regulation is "arbitrary, capricious, an abuse of discretion, or otherwise not in accordance with law." 5 U.S.C. § 706(2)(A). * * *

The primary objective of the Federal Food, Drug and Cosmetic Act is the protection of the public health. As such, its rulemaking authority under Section 701(a) has been broadly construed to uphold a wide variety of assertions of regulatory power. * * * At the same time, the broad language of Section 701(a) does not give the FDA unlimited regulatory powers; regulations issued under that section must effectuate a congressional objective expressed elsewhere in the Act. In the instant case, the agency maintains that it has promulgated the challenged regulation pursuant to Section 701(a) in order to effectuate the objectives reflected in Sections 502(a) and 505(d) of the Act. * * *

These statutory provisions, combined with Section 701(a), provide direct support for the challenged regulation. Among other things they reflect a clear congressional objective that the users of drugs, whether prescription or non-prescription, shall receive facts "material ... with respect to consequences which may result from the use of the ... (drug) under the conditions of use prescribed in the labeling thereof or under such conditions of use as are customary or usual." 21 U.S.C. § 321(n). The Commissioner, in furtherance of this objective, has seen fit in the challenged regulation to require that information concerning consequences which may result from the use of estrogen drugs be provided to the users thereof on their labeling. I think it clear that Section 701(a) authorizes him to do so.

The plaintiffs acknowledge that Sections 201 and 502 may be read in this manner, but maintain that this reading is contrary to the legislative history of the 1938 Act and is specifically precluded by the enactment of the Durham–Humphrey amendments to the Act in 1951.

Relying on the legislative history of the 1938 Act, the plaintiffs assert that Section 502(a) was never intended to apply to drugs dispensed on prescription. I find nothing in that legislative history to support this position. Indeed, all the evidence persuades me that the opposite is true. Despite a number of requests from representatives of the medical profession that prescription drugs be exempted from all labeling requirements, the final version of the Act provided an exemption only with respect to certain identified requirements. Section 503(b) exempted any drug dispensed on a written prescription from the labeling requirements of Section 502(b) (relating to quantity of contents) and 502(e) (relating to common names), and exempted prescription narcotics from the requirement that the label carry a warning that the drug may be habit forming, so long as the prescription was not refillable. It did not, however, exempt prescription drugs from the requirements of either 502(a) or 502(f), and both were understood to apply fully to all drug preparations.[9] * * *

Finally, plaintiffs argue that any authority which the FDA may have had under the 1938 Act with respect to patient labeling of prescription drugs was withdrawn by Congress in 1951. One of the amendments adopted in that year exempted prescription drugs from the "warnings against misuse" requirement and the "adequate directions for use" requirement of Section 502(f) in those situations where the label contains certain specified information, including whatever warnings or directions for use are specified by the physician in the prescription. According to plaintiffs, the adoption of this exemption as Section 503(b)(2) of the Act was intended by Congress to deprive the Secretary of authority to require that patient labeling for prescription drugs contain information regarding possible undesirable effects of the prescribed use. * * *

[W]hile plaintiffs are correct in pointing out that the effect of the Section 503(b)(2) exemption as enacted in 1951 was to make the prescribing physician the primary source of information available to a consumer of a prescription drug, this does not mean that Congress intended to leave this matter to the unregulated discretion of the prescribing physician. The retention of Section 502(a) as a regulatory provision applicable to prescription drugs precludes one from attributing that intention to Congress. * * * [W]hen the Commissioner determines that the possible side effects of a

---

9. Section 502(f) authorized the Secretary to exempt any drug from the "adequate directions for use" requirement if such directions are not necessary for the protection of the public health, but did not authorize an exemption from the warnings requirement of that subsection. After the passage of the 1938 Act, the Administrator did exempt drugs dispensed by prescription from the directions for use requirement. 21 C.F.R. § 1.106, 3 Fed. Reg. 3168 (1938).

drug when used as customarily prescribed are sufficiently serious as to be material to the patient's decision on use of the drug, he or she may require disclosure of those side effects on the labeling pursuant to Section 701(a). * * *

I next turn to the question of whether requiring patient package inserts to be dispensed with prescription drugs interferes with any constitutionally protected right of physicians. Plaintiffs argue that the mandatory nature of the regulation interferes with the doctor-patient relationship, and thus with the practice of medicine, by requiring the physician to communicate information emanating from Washington without regard to his or her professional judgment concerning the accuracy of the advice or the desirability of the patient being exposed to it.

The plaintiffs' argument is founded in part on their conception of the appropriate distribution of regulatory authority between the states and the federal government and in part on their view that a licensed physician's professional judgment may not be subjected to prior restraint and that society's interest in regulating the practice of medicine can be satisfactorily served by review of physician conduct in the context of malpractice or professional censure proceedings.

To the extent that the plaintiffs' claim of unconstitutional interference with the right to practice medicine is founded on a notion of federalism which reserves all rights over such regulation to the states, it is without merit. It is undisputed that the practice of medicine is subject to the exercise of state police power where such regulation furthers a legitimate state interest. But that assumption does not imply an absence of federal jurisdiction over the same area, where the federal regulation constitutes a reasonable exercise of a power vested in Congress under the Constitution. * * * The fact that the practice of medicine is an area traditionally regulated by the states does not invalidate those provisions of the Act which may at times impinge on some aspect of a doctor's practice.

Turning to plaintiff's view of a physician's right to exercise professional judgment, it is important to focus on what the challenged regulation does not do. The regulation at issue here does not forbid a physician from prescribing conjugated estrogen drugs, or limit the physician's exercise of professional judgment in that regard. Nor does it limit the information the physician may impart to his or her patients concerning estrogens. If the physician disagrees with a perceived "slant" of the labeling provided by the manufacturer, or with the facts stated therein, he or she is free to discuss the matter fully with the patient, noting his own disagreement and views. The sample labeling encourages the patient to have this kind of open discussion with her doctor.

When these limitations on the effect of the challenged regulation are considered, it becomes apparent that the plaintiffs urge recognition not of a right to exercise judgment in prescribing treatment, but rather of a right to control patient access to information. * * * [L]abeling is only one of many sources from which patients receive information about drugs and the control which the plaintiffs claim to have possessed prior to the challenged regulation is largely illusory. But there is a more fundamental problem with their position. There simply is no constitutional basis for recognition of a right on the part of physicians to control patient access to information concerning the possible side effects of prescription drugs. The cases cited by plaintiffs do contain language referring to a doctor's right to practice medicine, but the rights there recognized were only those necessary to facilitate the exercise of a right which patients were found to possess. The physician rights discussed are thus derivative of patient rights and do not exist independent of those rights. * * *

The patient rights recognized in the line of cases relied upon by plaintiffs flow from a constitutionally protected right of privacy. * * * To the extent these cases have any bearing on the present issue, then, their rationale would appear to support the challenged regulation. The objective of that regulation is to provide the patient with the facts relevant to a choice about the use, and manner of use, of estrogen drugs. The asserted right to limit patient access to such information can hardly be said to facilitate the patient's "interest in independence" in decision making.

By holding that physicians do not possess the constitutional right which plaintiffs claim, I do not overlook the affidavits of numerous experienced physicians who foresee patient anxiety and ruptured physician-patient relationships as a result of the implementation of the regulation. These matters are clearly relevant to an evaluation of the wisdom of the regulation. They do not, however, render it constitutionally infirm. * * *

The preamble to the challenged regulation provides a concise general statement of its basis and purpose. The evidence supporting the decision to require patient labeling is reviewed and the major concerns addressed in the comments are noted and responded to. In particular, the Commissioner notes that he had considered whether to allow the prescribing physician to determine that the labeling should not be given to a particular patient, but that "such (an) option is not provided in this regulation." 42 Fed. Reg. 37,636, 37,639–40 (1977).

The reasons for the denial of such an option are also sufficiently articulated to permit a determination that it has a rational basis. Given the purposes of the Act and its mislabeling provisions, the touchstone of any decision of the Commissioner is the safety and health of the patient. With this touchstone in mind, the primary factors to be weighed in deciding to grant or deny the option for which plaintiffs press are (1) the extent and character of the risk involved in using estrogen drugs, (2) the efficacy of, or the benefit to be derived from, providing patients with information concerning that risk, and (3) the extent and character of any risk involved in exposing all patients to that information. The Commissioner explains his views in each of these areas. First, it is apparent that he considers the risk associated with the use of estrogen drugs to be great, in terms of both the number of users and the gravity of the consequences to those who are adversely affected. Second, he explains that he finds this to be an area where patients are capable of understanding the advantages and risk of use and where most patients, because of the nature of the condition for which the drug is prescribed, have a real option to use or not to use it. And, finally, on the other side of the balance, the Commissioner states that, unlike the situation with respect to some other drugs, he finds no likelihood of a substantial adverse effect on patients from exposure to the information provided by the labeling. Based on these considerations, the decision was made against affording the option.

I do not understand plaintiffs to contend that a reasonable person could not have assessed the risk of use and the efficacy of providing information to patients in the way the Commissioner did. They vigorously dispute his finding, however, with respect to the absence of substantial adverse effect from use of the labeling. Specifically, they point to affidavits filed in this case in which experienced physicians note their concerns that for some patients exposure to the labeling information will result in unnecessary anxiety, failure to follow prescribed treatment, ruptured doctor-patient relationships, self-diagnosis, and symptoms by suggestion.

The question before the court, however, is not whether evidence exists which would tend to support an approach different from that taken by the Commissioner; the question is whether the record affirmatively demonstrates that the Commissioner's action had a rational basis. As earlier noted, I conclude that the preamble provides such assurance. In addition to the material already described, the preamble expressly addresses and evaluates the possibility of discontinued treatments, suggestion-induced symptoms, self-diagnosis, and strained doctor-patient relations. With respect to the patient compliance with prescribed dosage regimen and suggestion-induced side effects, for example, the Commissioner commented:

> The factors behind patient adherence to agreed medication regimens are complex. With the present state of knowledge it is impossible to predict accurately the influence that patient labeling will have on adherence to agreed medication regimens. Experience with oral contraceptive patient labeling suggests, however, that patient experience with drug therapy, rather than written information, primarily determines discontinuation of drug therapy. Furthermore, in the case of estrogens, the Commissioner firmly believes patients should take these drugs for as brief a period as possible and that women should be appraised of the reasons why this is the case. In the suggested wording of the patient labeling, patients are consistently referred to their physician so that decisions can be made in the context of appropriate medical advice. If a patient decides to follow the instruction of her physician, the Commissioner does not believe that patient labeling will significantly increase the incidence of suggestion-induced side effects. Suggestion effects, moreover, seem to play a minimal role in determining serious adverse reactions. It is, in any event, possible to hypothesize beneficial as well as negative effects of suggestion. Clear expectations about the effects of drug therapy, reinforced by patient labeling, may make patients more sensitive and aware of certain physical or psychological reactions. Effects which might otherwise go unnoticed may be identified as drug related. Although this may have the effect of nominally increasing the

> reported incidence of less serious adverse reaction it also may have beneficial results. Patients may be more sensitive to "warning signals" of serious adverse effect.... It is the Commissioner's opinion that the possible positive effects of supplying accurate side-effect information outweigh the possible negative effects.

While reasonable minds might reach different conclusions, this explication of the Commissioner's reasoning is sufficient to demonstrate that the challenged regulation is the product of a rational process.

Plaintiffs complain, however, that, even if the Commissioner has provided a sufficient explanation of his reasoning and analysis, the absence from the administrative record of a factual basis for that reasoning and analysis renders his action arbitrary and capricious. They point specifically to the absence of any clinical or expert opinion evidence to support the Commissioner's view that no substantial adverse consequence can be expected to flow from the receipt by patients of the labeling information.

To be rational, informal agency decisionmaking must have a factual basis. This does not mean, however, that the administrative record must contain evidence to support each step in the agency's reasoning process. A determination of whether an agency action is rendered arbitrary and capricious by the absence of record evidence in a particular area necessarily depends on the circumstances, including such things as the character of the finding or conclusion said to be lacking in support, its importance in the deliberative process, whether it is a matter with which the agency has regular experience and expertise, the availability of competent evidence on the issue, and the character of any contrary evidence offered by commentors.

Here, in order to pass upon the contention that a physician option should be provided, the Commissioner was called upon to forecast possible patient reaction to the labeling information. This was a matter with respect to which the agency had had some relevant prior experience. At the same time, patient labeling was a relatively new phenomenon, and the record suggests that clinical data on its effect was not yet available. Moreover, the issue was one as to which a rational judgment could be made based on the Commissioner's specific knowledge of the information to be conveyed and his general knowledge of human nature, at least in the absence of any evidence suggesting that patterns of common experience were likely to be misleading. In this context, I believe the Commissioner was entitled to make a forecast without supporting clinical data or expert opinion. The challenged regulation is not arbitrary, capricious, or otherwise contrary to law and defendants' motion for summary judgment will be granted.

Henley v. FDA

77 F.3d 616 (2d Cir.1996).

■ McLaughlin, Circuit Judge:

* * * The FDA regulates the labeling of oral contraceptives, including the package inserts. Before 1989, the FDA's oral contraceptive labeling

regulations required a specific warning in the package insert that estrogen, a component of oral contraceptives, has "been shown to cause cancer in animals, which showing justifies the inference that estrogens may cause cancer in humans." 21 C.F.R. § 310.501 (1989).

In 1989, after notice and comment proceedings, the FDA revised the requirements for patient package inserts for oral contraceptives (the "1989 Ruling"). See 54 Fed. Reg. 22,585 (1989). The new regulations required the inclusion of general categories of information—e.g., the effectiveness of the drug, its side effects, risks associated with cigarette smoking, potential adverse reactions, etc. Significantly, the FDA no longer mandated the use of any specific wording, including the animal carcinogen warning. The change from a specific warning to a general description was purportedly made so that information on the risks and benefits of the drug could thereafter be updated on a more timely basis without having to engage in protracted notice and comment rule-making procedures.

Elizabeth Henley, on behalf of * * * a women's health organization, filed a citizen petition with the FDA, requesting the FDA to amend the warning label requirements for oral contraceptives. * * * Henley asserted that many women do not want to rely solely on early detection, but, rather, on early prevention, i.e., eliminating or reducing their exposure to animal or human carcinogens. * * * Henley's petition further listed thirteen human studies that allegedly established a correlation between long-term oral contraceptive use and breast cancer. Thus, Henley argued, "[w]omen have the right to all the information necessary to make their own choice as to whether or not the benefits of using the pill outweigh the risk."

The FDA denied Henley's petition. It maintained that recent scientific studies involving women and oral contraceptives indicated no increased risk of cancer in humans. * * * In addition, the FDA explained that it continually monitors scientific information pertaining to the use of oral contraceptives, and updates, when appropriate, the guidance texts that it provides to drug companies. It further claimed that the 1989 Ruling made it possible to update package inserts more promptly because revisions would not be subject to notice and comment rule-making. * * *

The Administrative Procedure Act (APA) provides that a district court may set aside an agency's findings, conclusions or actions only if they are "arbitrary, capricious, an abuse of discretion, or otherwise not in accordance with law." 5 U.S.C. § 706(2)(A). * * * An agency rule may be deemed arbitrary, capricious or an abuse of discretion "if the agency has relied on factors which Congress has not intended it to consider, entirely failed to consider an important aspect of the problem, offered an explanation for its decision that runs counter to the evidence before the agency, or is so implausible that it could not be ascribed to a difference in view or the product of agency expertise." Motor Vehicle Mfrs. Ass'n v. State Farm Mut. Auto. Ins. Co., 463 U.S. 29, 43 (1983).

Although the scope of judicial review under this standard is narrow and deferential, "a reviewing court must be certain that an agency has considered all the important aspects of the issue and articulated a satisfactory explanation for its action, including a rational connection between the facts found and the choice made." But, a reviewing court cannot "substitute its judgment for that of the agency," Citizens to Preserve Overton Park, Inc. v. Volpe, 401 U.S. 402, 416 (1971), particularly when that determination is propelled by the agency's scientific expertise, see Baltimore Gas & Elec. Co. v. Natural Resources Defense Council, Inc., 462 U.S. 87, 103 (1983).

Obviously, as [the district court] noted, "the FDA's determination of what labeling best reflects current scientific information regarding the risks and benefits of oral contraceptives involves a high degree of expert scientific analysis." The regulations prior to the 1989 Ruling were based on research from 1978. According to the FDA, studies performed on women after 1978 have failed to establish an increase in the risk of cancer for women taking the oral contraceptive formulations that are currently in use. Although acknowledging that animal studies indicate a link between estrogen and cancer, the FDA maintains that those results are simply not as probative as the results of recent human studies. Specifically, the FDA noted that animal studies employed higher doses of estrogen than those currently contained in oral contraceptives, and that data from human studies are more directly applicable to women than data from animal studies.

Based on the information and studies cited by the FDA and the reasons proffered for its determination, we cannot say that its labeling decision was irrational, unsupported by relevant factors, counter to the evidence, or "so implausible that it could not be ascribed to a difference in view or the product of agency expertise." Certainly, neither the outside of a drug package nor its insert can contain the entire body of scientific research, and the average consumer cannot be expected to analyze and weigh each conflicting study. The FDA possesses the requisite know-how to conduct such analyses, by sifting through the scientific evidence to determine the most accurate and up-to-date information regarding a particular drug, and how those data affect human usage. We therefore defer to its reasonable findings in this case. See, e.g., Schering Corp. v. FDA, 51 F.3d 390, 399 (3d Cir.1995) (finding that FDA's "judgments as to what is required to ascertain the safety and efficacy of drugs fall squarely within the ambit of the FDA's expertise and merit deference from us").

Henley also argues that the FDA's approved labeling is "misleading," because its content does not disclose that animal studies reveal a relationship between estrogen use and cancer. Consequently, she contends that the FDA's decision is contrary to law. We disagree. * * * As discussed above, the FDA has rationally concluded, based on its expertise, that the inclusion of an animal carcinogen warning is not warranted in light of current scientific studies performed on humans. The pertinent animal studies in this case—showing a connection between estrogen and cancer—are not necessarily applicable to humans, particularly where the animal studies used relatively higher dosages than would normally be ingested by humans. We therefore find that the FDA did not fail to reveal facts material to the use of the drug, see 21 U.S.C. § 321(n), and conclude that its labeling decision was not misleading. * * *

Henley has presented sound and cogent arguments for the inclusion of cautionary information, and we might not have chosen the FDA's course had it been ours to chart. But that is hardly the point. Where, as here, an agency's determination cannot be characterized as arbitrary, capricious, an abuse of discretion, or contrary to law, the APA precludes us from substituting our judgment for that of the agency.

NOTES AND QUESTIONS

1. *Practice of medicine objections.* The concern about patient overreaction to risk information is not just theoretical. See Amy D. Marcus, The Real Drug Problem: Forgetting to Take Them, Wall St. J., Oct. 21, 2003, at D1 ("[T]he major reason [for non-adherence] appears to be a fear of side effects."); see also Andrew Pollack, Drug Makers Nag Patients to Stay the Course, N.Y. Times, Mar. 11, 2006, at C1. In the PMA's challenge, what exactly was the basis for the industry's claim of an unconstitutional interference with the practice of medicine? Apart from the federalism issue, did it suggest that physicians enjoyed a First Amendment right to communicate freely with patients? Imagine that a PPI advocated that the patient undergo an abortion if she became pregnant while taking a drug known to cause birth defects—could the FDA force a health care provider morally opposed to abortion to hand out this leaflet (especially in one of the many states that protects so-called "conscientious objectors," as noted toward the end of this chapter), or does the patient's right to receive such information trump the physician's right? Cf. Planned Parenthood v. Casey, 505 U.S. 833, 884 (1992) (plurality) ("All that is left of petitioners' argument is an asserted First Amendment right of a physician not to provide information about the risks of abortion, and childbirth, in a manner mandated by the state. To be sure, the physician's First Amendment rights not to speak are implicated, but only as part of the practice of medicine, subject to reasonable licensing and regulation by the state. We see no constitutional infirmity in the requirement that the physician provide the information mandated by the state here."); Paula Berg, Toward a First Amendment Theory of Doctor–Patient Discourse and the Right to Receive Unbiased Medical Advice, 74 B.U. L. Rev. 201 (1994).

2. *PPIs for everyone?* In 1979, based on studies indicating the usefulness of supplying written information directly to patients, the FDA proposed regulations that would have required PPIs for most prescription drug products. See 44 Fed. Reg. 40,016, 40,020–21 (1979). Although the agency recognized that consumers may have difficulties understanding some of the concepts and information described in professional labeling, the proposed PPIs would have differentiated between Contraindications, Warnings, Precautions, and Adverse Reactions in much the same way as the package insert directed to physicians. After receiving various complaints about the costs of such an undertaking, the FDA instead established a three-year pilot program mandating the distribution of PPIs for ten classes of drugs. See 45 Fed. Reg. 60,754, 60,773 (1980). Even this scaled-down program was stayed by the agency in 1981, and it was revoked the following year. See 46 Fed. Reg. 23,739, 23,815 (1981); 47 Fed. Reg. 39,147 (1982); see also Public Citizen v. HHS, 671 F.2d 518 (D.C.Cir.1981) (reviewing a procedural challenge to the stay); Rosalind M. Kendellen, The Food and Drug Administration Retreats from Patient Package Inserts for Prescription Drugs, 40 Food Drug Cosm. L.J. 172 (1985).

3. *Voluntary PPIs*. In the early 1990s, as part of its "MedGuide" initiative, the FDA proposed guidelines for the development of PPIs for all prescription drug products. See 60 Fed. Reg. 44,182 (1995); see also Howard M. Rowe, Patient Package Inserts: The Proper Prescription?, 50 Food & Drug L.J. 95 (1995). Congress intervened, however, by placing a temporary moratorium on finalization of this proposal in order to allow the industry to develop its own voluntary program to replace the agency's initiative. See Pub. L. No. 104–180, § 601, 110 Stat. 1569, 1593 (1996); see also Julie Bell, "Black Box" Leaves Patients in the Dark, Balt. Sun, June 30, 2003, at 7A (reporting that black box warnings do not appear in PPIs); Francesca L. Kritz, Not–So–Fine Print: Patient Drug Leaflets Omit Key Warnings, Other Information, Wash. Post, Aug. 13, 2002, at F1 (describing problems in the implementation of the voluntary PPI program). Nowadays, pharmacists often supply computer-generated information sheets to accompany prescriptions, sometimes but not always with assistance from pharmaceutical manufacturers or medical associations. See 60 Fed. Reg. at 44,193–95; William H. Shrank & Jerry Avorn, Educating Patients About Their Medications: The Potential and Limitations of Written Drug Information, 26 Health Aff. 731 (2007); Jonathan D. Rockoff, Prescription Leaflets Lack Key Safety Data, Wall St. J., Dec. 17, 2008, at D3. For the most part, however, prescription drug labeling still remains geared toward providing physicians with the information that may be relevant in deciding whether to prescribe a medication for a particular patient. Contrast the FDA's requirements, discussed in Chapter 2(C), for the documentation of informed consent from patients when they serve as subjects in clinical trials.

4. *OTC labeling*. For nonprescription products, the FDA has demanded detailed warning statements for acute risks, with an emphasis on providing directions for safe use or highlighting the consequences of misuse. The whole premise of making drugs available to consumers without a prescription is that self-diagnosis of certain conditions and self-treatment with these medications does not create safety concerns. Because few drugs are entirely risk free, OTC drug products can be marketed only if consumers are given information adequate to minimize the danger of any side effects. In 1999, the FDA substantially reformatted the labeling of nonprescription drugs in order to enhance the readability of the required information. See 64 Fed. Reg. 13,254, 13,286 (1999) (codified at 21 C.F.R. § 201.66).

In addition to risk labeling requirements for particular drugs, general warnings mandated for all OTC drug products include "Keep this and all drugs out of the reach of children," and "In case of accidental overdose seek professional assistance or contact a poison control center immediately." 21 C.F.R. § 330.1(g). Another general warning required for OTC drug products intended for systemic absorption cautions pregnant and nursing women to "seek the advice of a health professional before using this product." Id. § 201.63(a). A few nonprescription medical devices are subject to specific FDA risk labeling requirements. For example, every tampon package must at a minimum include the following statement: "Tampons are associated with Toxic Shock Syndrome (TSS). TSS is a rare but serious disease that may cause death. Read and save the enclosed information." 21 C.F.R. § 801.430(c). The accompanying package insert must include a number of detailed statements describing the precise risks of TSS and instructions for minimizing the risk.

B. ADVERTISING

As mentioned in *Kordel*, Congress initially lodged authority over advertising in the Federal Trade Commission (FTC). Subsequent amendments to the FDCA gave the FDA limited power to regulate the advertising of prescription drugs and so-called "restricted" medical devices. See 21 U.S.C. § 352(n), (q) & (r). The FTC retains authority over the advertising for other FDA-regulated products, including OTC drugs and dietary supplements. See Novartis Corp. v. FTC, 223 F.3d 783 (D.C.Cir.2000) (rejecting a challenge to a corrective advertising order for a nonprescription analgesic product); FTC v. Pantron I Corp., 33 F.3d 1088 (9th Cir.1994) (sustaining an enforcement action for false advertising against the seller of a baldness remedy); Thompson Med. Co. v. FTC, 791 F.2d 189, 192–93 (D.C.Cir.1986) (holding that the FDA's review of labeling claims for OTC drugs did not prevent an FTC enforcement action against OTC drug product advertising); see also Anne V. Maher & Lesley Fair, The FTC's Regulation of Advertising, 65 Food & Drug L.J. 589 (2010).

The statute provides that a prescription drug shall be deemed misbranded "unless the manufacturer, packer, or distributor thereof includes in all advertisements . . . such other information in brief summary relating to side effects, contraindications, and effectiveness as shall be required in regulations." 21 U.S.C. § 352(n). The FDA does not, however, enjoy unlimited power to regulate prescription drug advertising. For instance, it can neither entirely prohibit nor routinely demand preclearance of proposed promotional campaigns.

Under the FDA's implementing regulations, advertising causes a prescription drug to be misbranded if it is false or misleading, fails to reveal material facts, or fails to present a fair balance of information. See 21 C.F.R. § 202.1(e)(5). Advertising claims concerning safety, effectiveness, and indications are limited to those appearing in FDA-approved labeling. See id. § 202.1(e)(4), (6). The agency interprets the statutory provision broadly to "include advertisements in published journals, magazines, other periodicals, and newspapers, and advertisements broadcast through media such as radio, television, and telephone communication systems." Id. § 202.1(*l*)(1). After originally promulgating its advertising regulations in the 1960s, the agency has preferred to issue technically nonbinding policy statements and guidelines, pursue individualized enforcement actions in this area, or recharacterize certain advertisements as promotional labeling. See, e.g., 62 Fed. Reg. 14,912, 14,913–16 (1997) (listing numerous FDA guidance documents concerning prescription drug advertising); Thomas A. Hayes, Drug Labeling and Promotion: Evolution and Application of Regulatory Policy, 51 Food & Drug L.J. 57 (1996).

The FDA's authority to regulate restricted medical device advertising remained essentially dormant until it decided to assert control over tobacco products in order to limit their marketing. See 61 Fed. Reg. 44,396 (1996) (codified at 21 C.F.R. pt. 897 (1997)). Although eventually invalidated on other grounds, see FDA v. Brown & Williamson Tobacco Corp., 529 U.S. 120 (2000), the agency's effort to invoke this statutory authority seemed far-fetched, especially because the legislative history and contemporaneous FDA interpretation of the term "restricted" equated it with the term "prescription." See Lars Noah, Nicotine Withdrawal: Assessing the FDA's Effort to Regulate Tobacco Products, 48 Ala. L. Rev. 1, 27–33 (1996). For further commentary on the scope of the agency's power to regulate the advertising of medical devices, see Edward M. Basile et al., Medical Device Labeling and Advertising: An Overview, 54 Food & Drug L.J. 519 (1999); Sandra J.P. Dennis, Promotion of Devices: An Extension of FDA Drug Regulation or a New Frontier?, 48 Food & Drug L.J. 87 (1993).

1. DETAILING AND CONTINUING MEDICAL EDUCATION PROGRAMS

Yarrow v. Sterling Drug, Inc.

263 F.Supp. 159 (D.S.D.1967).

■ NICHOL, CHIEF JUDGE:

* * * Sterling, as do others in the drug manufacturing industry, places its product information before the doctor by use of listings in a reference work, known as the *Physicians' Desk Reference* (PDR); by use of product cards mailed to the physician; by use of special letters mailed to the physician; and by use of "detail men," who call personally on the physician, orally give him information on new drugs being introduced, and who leave literature on such new drugs and samples thereof with the doctor.

The warnings published in the PDR on the side effects of the drug Aralen, from 1958 until 1961, refer to "visual disturbances." There was no listing of Aralen in the PDR in 1962. In 1963, the warning included blurring of vision, corneal changes, and retinal changes reported to be rare and largely irreversible. In 1964, the warning was largely the same, containing more specifics regarding retinal change, reported rare and irreversible.

The product card on Aralen, in 1957, included blurring of vision on the side effects. In 1959, the product card warned of temporary blurring of vision, corneal changes, and advised periodic eye examinations; in 1960, it warned of temporary blurring of vision, retinal vascular response, macular lesions, evidently irreversible, and advised periodic eye examinations. The same warning was given in 1961. In 1962, the Aralen product card warns of temporary blurring of vision, corneal changes and retinal changes. It suggests trimonthly examinations. A letter mailed in 1963 advised doctors that "certain ocular complications have sometimes been reported during prolonged daily administration of chloroquine." It suggested trimonthly examinations, and asked that vision impairment and retinal change be reported.

The most significant and efficient means of presenting drug information to the doctor entails the use of detail men who make periodic personal calls on the individual doctor. In this case, Sterling's detail man introduced Mrs. Yarrow's doctor to Aralen, explained its uses and that it was the trade name for chloroquine phosphate. This was late in 1957, or early in 1958. From that time on, although the Sterling detail man called on the doctor at four to six week intervals, the detail man did not bring the side effects of Aralen to his attention.

The record shows that the detail men receive special training as to the various drugs, and that for the most part, they were pharmacists, chemists, or had a medical background. The detail men are kept up to date on the latest developments in drugs. The doctor testified that he received great amounts of literature on the various drugs he was using; that it was impossible to read all of it; that he relied on detail men, medical conventions, various articles in medical journals, and conversations with other doctors for information on the drugs he was prescribing. * * *

Where the doctor is inundated with the literature and product cards of the various drug manufacturers, as shown here by the facts, a change in the literature or an additional letter intended to present new information on drugs to the doctor is insufficient. The most effective method employed by the drug company in the promotion of new drugs is shown to be the use of detail men; thus, the court feels that this would also present the most effective method of warning the doctor about recent developments in drugs already employed by the doctor, at no great additional expense. The detail men visit the doctors at frequent intervals and could make an effective oral warning, accompanied by literature on the development, that would affirmatively notify the doctor of side effects such as shown in the facts in this case. * * *

NOTES AND QUESTIONS

1. *Detailing in the courts.* The appellate court affirmed. See Sterling Drug, Inc. v. Yarrow, 408 F.2d 978, 992 (8th Cir.1969) ("This does not mean that every physician in the United States must have been given an immediate warning by a personal messenger. But it does mean that the trial court was justified in finding that it was unreasonable to fail to instruct the detail men, at least, to warn the physicians on whom they regularly called ....''); see also Stevens v. Parke, Davis & Co., 507 P.2d 653, 663 (Cal.1973); Mahr v. G.D. Searle & Co., 390 N.E.2d 1214, 1232 (Ill.App.Ct.1979). Sales reps are, however, more apt to share with physicians the latest risk information about a competitor's product. Questions surrounding tort liability for failure-to-warn claims will be addressed at greater length in Chapter 7.

2. *Detailing today.* Pharmaceutical detailing goes back to 1850, and, even with the expansion in outlets for advertising, it remains an important and controversial promotional mechanism. See Stephanie Saul, Gimme an Rx! Cheerleaders Pep up Drug Sales, N.Y. Times, Nov. 28, 2005, at A1; Cyril T. Zaneski, Medical Sales Reps Arrive Bearing Gifts, Balt. Sun, June 17, 2004, at 1A (''The number ... has doubled during the past decade to more than 90,000—or a rep for every nine physicians.''); see also Jaime Reidy, Hard Sell: The Evolution of a Viagra Salesman (2005). Under an industry code adopted in 2002, most companies have stopped offering doctors pricey gifts, lavish dinners, and junkets to vacation spots. See Scott Hensley, Sorry, Doc, No Dinners-to-Go, Wall St. J., Apr. 23, 2002, at D4; see also Howard L. Dorfman, The 2009 Revision to the PhRMA Code on Interactions with Healthcare Professionals: Challenges and Opportunities for the Pharmaceutical Industry in the Age of Compliance, 31 Campbell L. Rev. 361 (2009); Natasha Singer, No Lipitor Mug? Drug Makers Cut out Goodies for Doctors, N.Y. Times, Dec. 31, 2008, at A1; cf. Christopher Lee, Drugmakers, Doctors Get Cozier: Gifts Continue, Contacts Increase Despite Guidelines, Wash. Post, Apr. 29, 2007, at A3. In addition, payola-style abuses of earlier decades have largely vanished. Cf. Gardiner Harris, As Doctor Writes Prescription, Drug Company Writes a Check, N.Y. Times, June 27, 2004, § 1, at 1 (reporting that one manufacturer paid loyal physicians ''consulting fees'' and a bonus per patient purportedly enrolled in a clinical trial of its expensive new treatment for hepatitis C); Barry Meier, Implant Program for Heart Device Was a Sales Spur, N.Y. Times, Sept. 27, 2005, at A1; Barry Meier & Stephanie Saul, Marketing of Vioxx, N.Y. Times, Feb. 11, 2005, at A1; Gregory Zuckerman, Biovail Is Paying Doctors Prescribing New Heart Drug, Wall St. J., July 21, 2003, at C1.

3. *Detailing works.* Manufacturers spend big bucks on sales calls and other forms of advertising because it pays dividends. See Melody Petersen, Less Return in Marketing of Medicines, a Study Says, N.Y. Times, Dec. 12, 2002, at C5 (reporting that ''the top drug companies generated $17 in sales from each dollar spent on marketing,'' though that represents a decline from a ratio of better than 22:1 just three years earlier); Natasha Singer, A Fight over How Drugs Are Pitched, N.Y. Times, Apr. 25, 2011, at B1 (''Drug makers spent about $6.3 billion on marketing visits to doctors in 2009 ....''). One review of studies about promotional interactions between physicians and the pharmaceutical industry reached the following sobering conclusion:

> [M]ost studies found negative outcomes associated with the interaction. These included an impact on knowledge (inability to identify

> wrong claims about medication), attitude (positive attitude toward pharmaceutical representatives; awareness, preference, and rapid prescription of a new drug), and behavior (making formulary requests for medications that rarely held important advantages over existing ones; nonrational prescribing behavior; increasing prescription rate; prescribing fewer generic but more expensive, newer medications at no demonstrated advantage).

Ashley Wazana, Physicians and the Pharmaceutical Industry: Is a Gift Ever Just a Gift?, 283 JAMA 373, 378 (2000); see also Jason Dana & George Loewenstein, A Social Science Perspective on Gifts to Physicians from Industry, 290 JAMA 252 (2003); Thomas L. Hafemeister & Sarah P. Bryan, Beware Those Bearing Gifts: Physicians' Fiduciary Duty to Avoid Pharmaceutical Marketing, 57 U. Kan. L. Rev. 491 (2009); Puneet Manchanda & Elisabeth Honka, The Effects and Role of Direct-to-Physician Marketing in the Pharmaceutical Industry: An Integrative Review, 5 Yale J. Health Pol'y L. & Ethics 785 (2005); Lars Noah, Medicine's Epistemology: Mapping the Haphazard Diffusion of Knowledge in the Biomedical Community, 44 Ariz. L. Rev. 373, 430–34 (2002) (discussing the nature and impact of industry advertising); Roni C. Rabin, Free Drug Samples? Bad Idea, Some Say, N.Y. Times, May 1, 2007, at F5; cf. Scott Hensley, Side Effects: As Drug–Sales Teams Multiply, Doctors Start to Tune Them Out, Wall St. J., June 13, 2003, at A1.

4. *FDA's authority*. The agency has only limited power to control detailing. The FDA has taken action against companies when it discovers that their sales representatives have made misleading claims. See Chris Adams, FDA Cites Firms for Improper Statements, Wall St. J., July 30, 2001, at B6 ("In at least nine recent cases, the [FDA] cited companies for improper statements or other presentations allegedly made by company representatives working the booths at medical conferences."); Bernadette Tansey, FDA Slaps Drugmakers for Misleading Claims, S.F. Chron., Aug. 9, 2003, at B1 ("The FDA warned Gilead for the second time in just over a year that its sales representatives were downplaying the risks and exaggerating the benefits of its HIV drug, Viread."). Verbal statements do not, however, appear to qualify as "labeling" or "advertising" under the FDCA, though they may provide the basis for concluding that a product has a broader intended use than revealed in its labeling. See Lars Noah, Death of a Salesman: To What Extent Can the FDA Regulate the Promotional Statements of Pharmaceutical Sales Representatives?, 47 Food & Drug L.J. 309 (1992).

5. *Stepping into the breach*. Aside from the FDA's limited authority, other actors have become more involved in trying to supervise detailing. HHS's Office of the Inspector General (OIG), acting under its authority to investigate fraud and abuse involving the Medicare and Medicaid programs, has issued guidelines designed to restrict marketing practices. See Robert Pear, Drug Industry Is Told to Stop Gifts to Doctors, N.Y. Times, Oct. 1, 2002, at A1. In addition, several states have enacted laws regulating industry gifts to physicians. See, e.g., Cal. Health & Safety Code § 119402 (requiring the adoption of compliance programs that satisfy the OIG and PhRMA marketing guidelines); Minn. Stat. § 151.461 (prohibiting significant gifts); Vt. Stat. § 33–2005 (requiring annual reports); see also Troyen A. Brennan & Michelle M. Mello, Editorial, Sunshine Laws and the Pharmaceutical Industry, 297 JAMA 1255 (2007); Timothy S. Jost, Oversight of Marketing Relationships Between Physicians and the Drug and Device Industry: A Comparative Study, 36 Am. J.L. & Med. 326 (2010); Joshua A. Weiss, Note, Medical Marketing in the United States: A Prescription for Reform, 79 Geo. Wash. L. Rev. 260 (2010). A little-noticed provision in the health reform legislation created a federal gift disclosure requirement. See Patient Protection and Affordable Care Act, Pub. L. No. 111–148, § 6002, 124 Stat. 804 (2010) (codified at 42 U.S.C. § 1128G); Tricia Bishop, Laws on Incentives to Use Firm's Product Called Weak, Balt. Sun, Dec. 7, 2010, at 1A ("Beginning in 2012, drug and medical-device makers must record the payments they make to doctors, and they'll have to publicize them in a database by 2013 .... But there aren't yet uniform reporting requirements or the means to check the accuracy of disclosures ...."); see also id. ("Laws went into effect last year in Massachusetts, which now requires the disclosure of gifts over $50, and in Vermont, which actually bans some gifts to health care providers within the state.... [S]ome trade organizations have recently revamped their ethical guidelines, tightening rules regarding payments to health care providers.").

6. *Fighting fire with fire.* Some governmental agencies and insurers engage in "counter detailing" to counterbalance the influence of industry advertising. See Scott Hensley, As Drug Bill Soars, Some Doctors Get an "Unsales" Pitch, Wall St. J., Mar. 13, 2006, at A1 (describing a program in Pennsylvania to encourage prescribing of cheaper generic drugs); Marc Kaufman, Doctors Hear Alternatives to Drug–Firm Sales Pitches, Wash. Post, Aug. 5, 2002, at A1; Betsy McKay, Caution Is Prescribed for Antibiotics: U.S. Agency Moves to Urge Doctors and Patients to Use Treatments in Moderation, Wall St. J., Sept. 17, 2003, at D11; see also Michael A. Fischer & Jerry Avorn, Economic Implications of Evidence–Based Prescribing for Hypertension: Can Better Care Cost Less?, 291 JAMA 1850, 1854 (2004) ("There are many possible reasons for this large divergence between routine practice on the one hand and clinical trial data and evidence-based recommendations on the other. Foremost among these is the vigorous marketing of newer, more costly agents compared with virtually no marketing for older, off-patent drugs."). Not wanting to be outdone (or undercut), some manufacturers have offered discounts to entities on the condition that they make no disparaging remarks about the brand-name drug. See Sarah Rubenstein, How Lilly Influences What Prescribers Say About Cymbalta, Wall St. J., Aug. 5, 2005, at B1.

Once a new drug has received FDA approval, physicians may prescribe it for any therapeutic use that they like, whether or not that indication appears in the labeling approved by the agency. See 59 Fed. Reg. 59,820,

59,821 (1994); James M. Beck & Elizabeth D. Azari, FDA, Off–Label Use, and Informed Consent, 53 Food & Drug L.J. 71 (1998); Christopher R. Page, Comment, These Statements Have Not Been Approved by the FDA: Improving the Postapproval Regulation of Prescription Drugs, 88 Or. L. Rev. 1189 (2009). Until recently, however, companies could not promote their products for any uses not appearing in this approved labeling. See 21 C.F.R. §§ 201.100(c)(1), 202.1(e)(6)(i) & (xi); see also Lars Noah, Constraints on the Off–Label Uses of Prescription Drug Products, 16 J. Prods. & Toxics Liab. 139, 143–46 (1994); John E. Osborn, Can I Tell You the Truth? A Comparative Perspective on Regulating Off–Label Scientific and Medical Information, 10 Yale J. Health Pol'y L. & Ethics 299 (2010); Michael J. Andersen, Note, Bound Guidance: FDA Rulemaking for Off–Label Pharmaceutical Drug Marketing, 60 Case W. Res. L. Rev. 531 (2010).

In the early 1990s, the FDA became concerned that some manufacturers were indirectly promoting off-label uses, for instance by sponsoring continuing medical education (CME) programs and scientific symposia featuring discussions about such uses of their products and by providing health care professionals with enduring materials (namely, textbooks or article reprints) mentioning such uses. In addition to bringing enforcement actions against particular companies, the FDA published what it characterized as a "Draft Policy Statement" to respond to industry-supported scientific and educational activities concerning drugs and medical devices. See 57 Fed. Reg. 56,412 (1992); David G. Adams, FDA Policy on Industry–Supported Scientific and Educational Activities: Current Developments, 47 Food & Drug L.J. 629 (1992); see also WLF v. Kessler, 880 F.Supp. 26 (D.D.C.1995) [excerpted in Chap. 1(D)(3)] (finding constitutional challenge to this policy ripe for review). This document cautioned that CME programs funded by the pharmaceutical and medical device industries would be subject to regulation as promotional labeling or advertising for any products discussed during these programs except in limited circumstances where the sponsoring companies ensure that the program will be independent and objective.

FDA officials repeatedly have suggested that many industry-sponsored CME events are merely elaborate advertising opportunities. See David G. Adams, FDA Regulation of Communications on Pharmaceutical Products, 24 Seton Hall L. Rev. 1399 (1994); see also Scott H. Podolsky & Jeremy A. Greene, A Historical Perspective of Pharmaceutical Promotion and Physician Education, 300 JAMA 831 (2008); Marc A. Rodwin, Drug Advertising, Continuing Medical Education, and Physician Prescribing: A Historical Review and Reform Proposal, 38 J.L. Med. & Ethics 807 (2010); Robert M. Tenery, Jr., Interactions Between Physicians and the Health Care Technology Industry, 283 JAMA 391, 392 (2000) ("Unfortunately, while the need for CME for physicians has increased with rapidly expanding technology, the funding from independent sources has decreased proportionately."); Scott Hensley, Remedial Lessons: When Doctors Go to Class, Industry Often Foots the Bill, Wall St. J., Dec. 4, 2002, at A1 ("Many physicians view industry-sponsored courses—even those that follow all the rules—as verging on infomercials."); Shankar Vedantam, Industry Role in Medical

Meeting Decried: Symposiums Sponsored by Pharmaceutical Companies Trouble Some Psychiatrists, Wash. Post, May 26, 2002, at A10; Elizabeth Williamson & Christopher Lee, Conflict Alleged in Drug Firms' Education Role, Wash. Post, June 27, 2007, at A3 ("Overall, commercial sponsors pick up about half of the $2.25 billion annual cost of the courses doctors must attend to keep their licenses.").

In 1997, Congress authorized manufacturers to disseminate enduring materials that discussed off-label uses of approved drugs, devices, and biologic products under certain circumstances. See FDAMA, Pub. L. No. 105–115, § 401(a), 111 Stat. 2296, 2356–64 (1997) (codified at 21 U.S.C. § 360aaa); see also 63 Fed. Reg. 64,556 (1998) (codified at 21 C.F.R. pt. 99). FDAMA did not address CME programs, and the agency published its final guidance on that subject just one month after enactment of the legislation. See 62 Fed. Reg. 64,074 (1997); see also New Rule Limits What Physicians Say in Classes, Wall St. J., Sept. 29, 2004, at D4 (reporting that the Accreditation Council for CME adopted stricter standards for commercial support). As explained later, these different restrictions were challenged on First Amendment grounds. After the FDAMA provision sunset in 2006, the agency issued a new guidance document to replace the inoperative regulations governing the dissemination of enduring materials, which basically allows manufacturers to mail physicians unadorned reprints of original research articles appearing in genuinely peer-reviewed journals discussing clinical trials meeting the FDA's rigorous standards but only if accompanied by any relevant negative information and a prominent disclaimer is affixed. See 74 Fed. Reg. 1694 (2009); Michelle M. Mello et al., Shifting Terrain in the Regulation of Off–Label Promotion of Pharmaceuticals, 360 New Eng. J. Med. 1557, 1559–61 (2009); Santosh V. Coutinho, Comment, License to Promote, or Just What the Doctor Ordered? The New FDA Guidance on Dissemination of Off-label Reprints by Pharmaceutical Companies, 28 Temp. J. Sci. Tech. & Envtl. L. 279 (2009).

Some companies continue to run afoul of the FDA's restrictions on off-label promotion. See, e.g., Michael A. Steinman et al., The Promotion of Gabapentin: An Analysis of Internal Industry Documents, 145 Annals Internal Med. 284 (2006); Melody Petersen, Court Papers Suggest Scale of Drug's Use, N.Y. Times, May 30, 2003, at C1 ("Warner–Lambert paid dozens of doctors tens of thousands of dollars each to speak to other physicians about how Neurontin, an epilepsy drug, could be prescribed for more than a dozen other medical uses that had not been approved by the [FDA]."); see also Gov't Accountability Office, Prescription Drugs: FDA's Oversight of the Promotion of Drugs for Off-label Uses, GAO–08–835 (2008); Alex Berenson, Indictment of Doctor Tests Drug Marketing Rules, N.Y. Times, July 22, 2006, at A1 (reporting the arrest of a psychiatrist accused of conspiring with the manufacturer of Xyrem® (gamma hydroxybutyrate) to publicize off-label uses of this narcolepsy drug at CME events); Andrew Pollack, Talking up a Drug for This (and That), N.Y. Times, Apr. 27, 2003, § 3, at 1; Natasha Singer, Maker of Botox Settles Inquiry on Off–Label Use, N.Y. Times, Sept. 2, 2010, at A1 (reporting that Allergan agreed to pay $600 million in fines, and adding that three other drug manufacturers charged with off-label promotion recently entered into settlements for $520 million, $1.41 billion, and $2.3 billion).

United States v. American College of Physicians

475 U.S. 834 (1986).

■ MARSHALL, JUSTICE:

A tax-exempt organization must pay tax on income that it earns by carrying on a business not "substantially related" to the purposes for which the organization has received its exemption from federal taxation. The question before this Court is whether respondent, a tax-exempt organization, must pay tax on the profits it earns by selling commercial advertising space in its professional journal * * * *

[T]he American College of Physicians is an organization exempt from taxation under § 501(c)(3) of the Internal Revenue Code. The purposes of the College, as stated in its articles of incorporation, are to maintain high standards in medical education and medical practice; to encourage research, especially in clinical medicine; and to foster measures for the prevention of disease and for the improvement of public health. * * * In furtherance of its exempt purposes, respondent publishes *The Annals of Internal Medicine*, a highly regarded monthly medical journal containing scholarly articles relevant to the practice of internal medicine. Each issue of *Annals* contains advertisements for pharmaceuticals, medical supplies, and equipment useful in the practice of internal medicine, as well as notices of positions available in that field. Respondent has a longstanding policy of accepting only advertisements containing information about the use of medical products, and screens proffered advertisements for accuracy and relevance to internal medicine. * * *

Respondent has maintained throughout this litigation that the advertising in *Annals* performs an educational function supplemental to that of the journal's editorial content. Testimony of respondent's witnesses at trial tended to show that drug advertising performs a valuable function for doctors by disseminating information on recent developments in drug manufacture and use. In addition, respondent has contended that the role played by the Food and Drug Administration, in regulating much of the form and content of prescription-drug advertisements, enhances the contribution that such advertisements make to the readers' education. All of these factors, respondent argues, distinguish the advertising in *Annals* from standard commercial advertising. Respondent approaches the question of substantial relation from the perspective of the journal's subscribers; it points to the benefit that they may glean from reading the advertisements and concludes that that benefit is substantial enough to satisfy the statutory test for tax exemption. The court of appeals took the same approach. It concluded that the advertisements performed various "essential" functions for physicians and found a substantial relation based entirely upon the medically related content of the advertisements as a group.

The government, on the other hand, looks to the conduct of the tax-exempt organization itself, inquiring whether the publishers of *Annals* have performed the advertising services in a manner that evinces an intention to use the advertisements for the purpose of contributing to the educational value of the journal. Also approaching the question from the vantage point of the College, the Claims Court emphasized the lack of a comprehensive presentation of the material contained in the advertisements. * * *

We believe that the Claims Court was correct to concentrate its scrutiny upon the conduct of the College rather than upon the educational quality of the advertisements. For all advertisements contain some information, and if a modicum of informative content were enough to supply the important contribution necessary to achieve tax exemption for commercial advertising, it would be the rare advertisement indeed that would fail to meet the test. * * *

[T]he advertising in *Annals* does not contribute importantly to the journal's educational purposes. This is not to say that the College could not control its publication of advertisements in such a way as to reflect an intention to contribute importantly to its educational functions. By coordinating the content of the advertisements with the editorial content of the issue, or by publishing only advertisements reflecting new developments in the pharmaceutical market, for example, perhaps the College could satisfy the stringent standards erected by Congress and the Treasury. * * *

■ BURGER, CHIEF JUSTICE (concurring):

Most medical journals are not comparable to magazines and newspapers published for profit. Their purpose is to assemble and disseminate to the profession relevant information bearing on patient care. The enormous expansion of medical knowledge makes it difficult for a general practitioner—or even a specialist—to keep fully current with the latest developments without such aids. In a sense these journals provide continuing education for physicians—a "correspondence course" not sponsored for profit but public health.

There is a public value in the widest possible circulation of such data, and advertising surely tends to reduce the cost of publication and hence the cost to each subscriber, thereby enhancing the prospect of wider circulation. Plainly a regulation recognizing these realities would be appropriate. Such regulations, of course, are for the Executive Branch and the Congress, not the courts. I join the opinion because it reflects a permissible reading of the present Treasury regulations.

NOTES AND QUESTIONS

1. *Editorial conflicts of interest.* Notwithstanding the Court's decision, most biomedical journals continue to refuse advertisements from sellers of non-health care products or services on the view that advertisements can serve an educational function. See Robert H. Fletcher & Suzanne W. Fletcher, Editorial, Pharmaceutical Advertisements in Medical Journals,

116 Annals Internal Med. 951 (1992). Given the substantial advertising revenues that they receive from drug and device manufacturers, editors of biomedical journals may have a pro-industry bias. See Shankar Vedantam, Business, Science Clash at Medical Journal, Wash. Post, Feb. 7, 2004, at A2; see also Richard A. Deyo et al., The Messenger Under Attack: Intimidation of Researchers by Special–Interest Groups, 336 New Eng. J. Med. 1176, 1179 (1997) (suggesting that journals may "need to set up defenses against potential threats of withholding advertising," adding that "[r]esearch on efficacy, safety, and cost effectiveness in the trillion-dollar health care industry frequently has important financial consequences"); David Armstrong, Bitter Pill: How the New England Journal Missed Warning Signs on Vioxx, Wall St. J., May 15, 2006, at A1 (reporting that Merck purchased the bulk of more than 900,000 reprints of a favorable article on Vioxx produced by one of the leading medical journals, earning the publisher approximately $750,000). Editors strenuously deny that their judgments are affected, but they have recognized the need to guard against such influence. Some commentators have proposed that, in order to reduce real or perceived conflicts of interest, biomedical journals should adopt precisely the opposite of their current policy—namely, to accept advertising from sellers of health care products only as a last resort. See David Orentlicher & Michael K. Hehir, II, Advertising Policies of Medical Journals: Conflicts of Interest for Journal Editors and Professional Societies, 27 J.L. Med. & Ethics 113, 113–16, 118 (1999). Their proposal has fallen on deaf ears. In fact, responding to the loss of advertising revenue that resulted when drug companies shifted promotional campaigns to television, a group of biomedical journals touted the results of a study finding that print ads directed to health care professionals provide companies with the most cost-effective promotional outlet. See Vanessa O'Connell, Medical Journals Chase Drug–Ad Dollars, Wall St. J., May 22, 2001, at B8; cf. Deborah Korenstein et al., Adherence of Pharmaceutical Advertisements in Medical Journals to FDA Guidelines and Content for Safe Prescribing, 6 PLoS ONE e23336 (2011) (finding problems with most ads).

2. *Garbage in, garbage out.* For a skeptical assessment of the quality of some of the information appearing in the biomedical literature, see Lars Noah, Sanctifying Scientific Peer Review: Publication as a Proxy for Regulatory Decisionmaking, 59 U. Pitt. L. Rev. 677, 696–709 (1998); see also John P.A. Ioannidis, Contradicted and Initially Stronger Effects in Highly Cited Clinical Research, 294 JAMA 218 (2005); Jenny White & Lisa A. Bero, Corporate Manipulation of Research: Strategies Are Similar Across Five Industries, 21 Stan. L. & Pol'y Rev. 105 (2010); Lawrence K. Altman, For Science's Gatekeepers, a Credibility Gap, N.Y. Times, May 2, 2006, at F1 (noting "a widespread misimpression that passing peer review is the scientific equivalent of the Good Housekeeping seal of approval"); id. ("Journals have devolved into information-laundering operations for the pharmaceutical industry, say Dr. Richard Smith, the former editor of the British Medical Journal, and Dr. Richard Horton, the editor of the Lancet . . . ."); Michael Kranish, Flaws Are Found in Validating Medical Studies: Many See Need to Overhaul Standards for Peer Review, Boston Globe, Aug.

15, 2005, at A1. For instance, published articles often fail to provide information about toxicity identified during clinical trials investigating a therapy's effectiveness. See John P.A. Ioannidis & Joseph Lau, Completeness of Safety Reporting in Randomized Trials, 285 JAMA 437, 442 (2001); Klim McPherson & Elina Hemminki, Synthesizing Licensing Data to Assess Drug Safety, 328 Brit. Med. J. 518 (2004); Anna W. Mathews, Worrisome Ailment in Medicine: Misleading Journal Articles, Wall St. J., May 10, 2005, at A1.

3. *Authorial conflicts of interest.* Potential conflicts of interest have become endemic among biomedical researchers. See Justin E. Bekelman et al., Scope and Impact of Financial Conflicts of Interest in Biomedical Research, 289 JAMA 454, 456 (2003) ("Approximately one third of investigators at academic institutions have personal financial ties with industry sponsors."); Eric G. Campbell et al., Institutional Academic–Industry Relationships, 298 JAMA 1779 (2007); Symposium, Dangerous Liaisons? Industry Relations with Health Professionals, 37 J.L. Med. & Ethics 398 (2009); Abigail Zuger, How Tightly Do Ties Between Doctor and Drug Company Bind?, N.Y. Times, July 27, 2004, at F5. Biases may affect the outcome of industry-financed studies. See Lars Noah, Medicine's Epistemology: Mapping the Haphazard Diffusion of Knowledge in the Biomedical Community, 44 Ariz. L. Rev. 373, 407 (2002) ("Numerous surveys have found that research on new drugs is more likely to turn out favorably when sponsored by the manufacturer."); see also id. at 406–12, 415, 422–24 (describing the pervasive nature of conflicts of interest in the production and dissemination of biomedical research); id. at 408–09 (explaining the shortcomings in requirements for the disclosure of potential conflicts); Paul M. Ridker & Jose Torres, Reported Outcomes in Major Cardiovascular Clinical Trials Funded by For–Profit and Not-for-Profit Organizations: 2000–2005, 295 JAMA 2270 (2006); Nicholas Bakalar, Study Sees a Slant in Articles on Drug, N.Y. Times, Apr. 13, 2010, at D5 (Avandia®); Shirley S. Wang, Simply Disclosing Funds Behind Studies May Not Erase Bias, Wall St. J., Aug. 4, 2006, at A11; cf. David Armstrong, Aspirin Dispute Is Fueled by Funds of Industry Rivals, Wall St. J., Apr. 24, 2006, at A1 (reporting that some authors have financial stakes in drugs that lead them to disparage competitors); Daniel Carlat, Op–Ed., Generic Smear Campaign, N.Y. Times, May 9, 2006, at A27 (same, focusing on sleep aids).

Most journals require that authors disclose any potential conflicts of interest, and some of these disclosures reveal remarkable linkages between researchers and drug companies. See Cynthia Crossen, A Medical Researcher Pays for Challenging Drug–Industry Funding, Wall St. J., Jan. 3, 2001, at A1 ("Since the early 1980s, connections in biomedicine between academics and drug companies have become so pervasive that a recent footnote to an article on antidepressants in the *New England Journal of Medicine* disclosed more than 350 financial ties between the authors of the article and pharmaceutical companies that sell antidepressants."). These disclosure policies do not always work. See Carey Goldberg, Some Seek to Lift Veil on Research Funding, Boston Globe, Aug. 8, 2006, at B1; Robert Tomsho, Research Conflicts Go Undisclosed: Study Says Medical Journals

Don't Effectively Monitor Financial Ties of Authors, Wall St. J., July 13, 2004, at D3. It should be noted that conflicts of interest are not limited to industry-funded research. See Liz Szabo, '98 Study Linking Vaccines to Autism "An Elaborate Fraud," USA Today, Jan. 6, 2011, at 9A (noting that Dr. Andrew Wakefield "was paid more than $675,000 by a lawyer hoping to sue vaccine makers"); Rick Weiss, Results Retracted on Ecstasy Study, Wash. Post, Sept. 6, 2003, at A3 ("The error has renewed charges that government-funded scientists ... have been biased in their assessment of ecstasy's risks and potential benefits.").

4. *Getting the full picture.* Studies that fail to yield favorable results may never see the light of day. See Robert Steinbrook, Gag Clauses in Clinical–Trial Agreements, 352 New Eng. J. Med. 2160 (2005); see also An–Wen Chan et al., Empirical Evidence for Selective Reporting of Outcomes in Randomized Trials: Comparison of Protocols to Published Articles, 291 JAMA 2457 (2004); Susan Haack, Scientific Secrecy and "Spin": The Sad, Sleazy Saga of the Trials of Remune, Law & Contemp. Probs., Sum. 2006, at 47, 54–66; Shankar Vedantam, A Silenced Drug Study Creates an Uproar, Wash. Post, Mar. 18, 2009, at A1 (discussing an early study of the atypical antipsychotic Seroquel® that AstraZeneca decided to bury); Dan Vergano, Drug Companies Send Unfavorable Research to the Nether Regions, USA Today, May 17, 2001, at 8D (reporting that federal guidelines for the use of nicotine inhalers may have been skewed insofar as manufacturers prevented the publication of negative results, which researchers refer to as the "file drawer effect"). In response to this "publication bias," efforts have been made to ensure that we get a more complete picture of drug research. See Scott Hensley, Drug Makers Urged to Publish Data: Industry Guidelines Aim to Quell Any Suspicions About Negative Findings, Wall St. J., June 30, 2004, at D7; Shankar Vedantam, Journals Insist Drug Manufacturers Register All Trials, Wash. Post, Sept. 9, 2004, at A2 (reporting that editors from a group of prestigious medical journals adopted a policy of publishing drug research only if registered at the inception of a clinical trial); see also Lisa M. Schwartz & Steven Woloshin, Lost in Transmission—FDA Drug Information That Never Reaches Clinicians, 361 New Eng. J. Med. 1717 (2009); Barry Meier, For Drug Makers, a Downside to Full Disclosure, N.Y. Times, May 23, 2007, at C1 (reporting that an independent researcher found increased cardiovascular risks after conducting a meta-analysis of posted studies on Avandia).

5. *Vanity press.* Industry unmistakably influences editorial choices when companies sponsor symposia or special issues of a medical journal. See Paula A. Rochon et al., Evaluating the Quality of Articles Published in Journal Supplements Compared with the Quality of Those Published in the Parent Journal, 272 JAMA 108, 111–12 (1994) (finding that supplements contained articles of inferior quality due to the lack of regular peer review). One study of the phenomenon found that "industry-sponsored symposiums are promotional in nature and that journals often abandon the peer-review process when they publish symposiums." Lisa A. Bero et al., The Publication of Sponsored Symposiums in Medical Journals, 327 New Eng. J. Med. 1135, 1137 (1992) ("Financial pressures on journals appear to contribute to the increasing publication of symposiums."). Companies sometimes also ghost-write manuscripts. See Melody Petersen, Madison Ave. Has Growing Role in the Business of Drug Research, N.Y. Times, Nov. 22, 2002, at A1 (adding that subsidiaries of advertising agencies occasionally even conduct the underlying research); Natasha Singer, Report Urges More Curbs on Medical Ghostwriting, N.Y. Times, June 25, 2010, at B4.

2. DIRECT-TO-CONSUMER ADVERTISING

Twenty five years ago, pharmaceutical companies engaged in essentially no prescription drug advertising to lay consumers. By the early 1990s, drug advertisements became a common feature of weekly magazines and occasionally were broadcast on specialty cable television stations. Prescription drug advertisements now regularly also appear in newspapers and on the major television networks. Given the rapid growth of direct-to-consumer advertising (DTCA) and the shortcomings of rules designed to control advertising directed to physicians, the FDA began to rethink its regulatory approach. See Lars Noah, Advertising Prescription Drugs to Consumers: Assessing the Regulatory and Liability Issues, 32 Ga. L. Rev. 141 (1997). In contrast, the European Union has prohibited the advertising of prescription drugs to the general public. See Council Directive 92/28, 1992 O.J. (L113), art. 3. (Indeed, only New Zealand allows such advertising, though Canada had considered it, and the EU once proposed relaxing some of its rules.)

The most significant limitation on DTCA under the existing regulations, requiring that manufacturers include a "brief summary" of all side effects and contraindications so as to provide fair balance for promotional claims, see 21 C.F.R. § 202.1(e)(4), (5), also seems to be the least meaningful restriction in the lay consumer context. This inaptly named brief summary has come to mean appending much of the package insert with the advertisement, often in small font sizes and on the back of the page. Although physicians may have sufficient interest and expertise to read the brief summary, it seems implausible that most laypersons even try to make sense of this detailed information. The brief summary requirement previously had made non-print advertising nearly impossible, until the FDA announced guidelines in August 1997 that eased some of the restrictions on broadcast promotions. So-called "reminder" and "help seeking" advertisements do not even have to satisfy these requirements. See Alicia Mundy, Making a Name for Drugs Without Using Their Names: Some Ads Highlight Only Web Addresses So Side Effects Don't Have to Be Listed, Wall St. J., Aug. 29, 2008, at B1.

The FDA summarized the competing arguments concerning direct-to-consumer prescription drug advertising as follows:

> Proponents argue that direct-to-consumer promotion is of educational value and will improve the physician-patient relationship, increase patient compliance with drug therapy and physician visits, and lower drug prices. Opponents contend that consumers do not have the expertise to accurately evaluate and comprehend prescription drug advertising. Opponents also argue that such promotion is misleading

> by failing to adequately communicate risk information, and that such promotion will damage the physician-patient relationship, increase drug prices, increase liability actions, and lead to over-medication and drug abuse.

60 Fed. Reg. 42,581, 42,582 (1995); see also id. at 42,583–84 (also noting questions about lay comprehension of the technical information currently used in the brief summary and in disclosure statements used with broadcast advertisements); 61 Fed. Reg. 24,314 (1996) (requesting additional comments, particularly about suggestions that it simplify the brief summary requirement to demand that companies communicate information only about major risks but in non-technical language, provide only a generic disclosure statement that all prescription drugs entail significant risks, or vary the level of detail depending on the medium used); Mike Mitka, Researchers Critical of TV Drug Ads, 297 JAMA 939 (2007). For instance, it appears that the aggressive marketing of COX–2 inhibitors led to the dangerous overprescribing of these drugs. See Marc Kaufman, New Study Criticizes Painkiller Marketing: Arthritis Drug Ads a Factor in Overuse, Wash. Post, Jan. 25, 2005, at A1.

In 1999, the FDA finalized its guideline governing broadcast advertising of prescription drugs. See 64 Fed. Reg. 43,197 (1999). In relevant part, it provides:

> The prescription drug advertising regulations distinguish between print and broadcast advertisements. Print advertisements must include the brief summary, which generally contains each of the risk concepts from the product's approved package labeling. Advertisements broadcast through media such as television, radio, or telephone communications systems must disclose the product's major risks in either the audio or audio and visual parts of the presentation; this is sometimes called the major statement. This guidance does not address the major statement requirement. Sponsors of broadcast advertisements are also required to present a brief summary or, alternatively, may make "adequate provision . . . for dissemination of the approved or permitted package labeling in connection with the broadcast presentation" (21 CFR 202.1(e)(1)). This is referred to as the adequate provision requirement. The regulations thus specify that the major statement, together with adequate provision for dissemination of the product's approved labeling, can provide the information disclosure required for broadcast advertisements. The purpose of this guidance is to describe an approach that FDA believes can fulfill the requirement for adequate provision in connection with consumer-directed broadcast advertisements for prescription drug and biological products [but it does not cover restricted medical devices]. The approach presumes that such advertisements:
>
> - Are not false or misleading in any respect. For a prescription drug, this would include communicating that the advertised product is available only by prescription and that only a prescribing healthcare

professional can decide whether the product is appropriate for a patient.

- Present a fair balance between information about effectiveness and information about risk.
- Include a thorough major statement conveying all of the product's most important risk information in consumer-friendly language.
- Communicate all information relevant to the product's indication (including limitations to use) in consumer-friendly language.

A sponsor wishing to use consumer-directed broadcast advertisements may meet the adequate provision requirement through an approach that will allow most of a potentially diverse audience to have reasonably convenient access to the advertised product's approved labeling. This audience will include many persons with limited access to technologically sophisticated outlets (e.g., the Internet) and persons who are uncomfortable actively requesting additional product information or are concerned about being personally identified in their search for product information. One acceptable approach to disseminating the product's approved labeling is described below. This approach includes the following components:

A. Disclosure in the advertisement of an operating toll-free telephone number for consumers to call for the approved package labeling. Upon calling, consumers should be given the choice of:

- Having the labeling mailed to them in a timely manner (e.g., within 2 business days for receipt generally within 4–6 days); or
- Having the labeling read to them over the phone (e.g., by offering consumers a selection of prerecorded labeling topics).

B. Reference in the advertisement to a mechanism to provide package labeling to consumers .... One acceptable mechanism would be to provide the additional product information in the form of print advertisements appearing concurrently in publications that reach the exposed audience. The location of at least one of these advertisements would be referenced in the broadcast advertisement. If a print advertisement is part of an adequate provision procedure, it should supply a toll-free telephone number and an address for further consumer access to full package labeling....

C. Disclosure in the advertisement of an Internet web page (URL) address that provides access to the package labeling.

D. Disclosure in the advertisement that pharmacists, physicians (or other healthcare providers), or veterinarians (in the case of animal drugs) may provide additional product information to consumers. This statement should communicate clearly that the referenced professional is a source of additional product information....

When a broadcast advertisement is presented in a foreign language, the information sources that are part of the advertisement's "adequate

> provision'' mechanism (i.e., print advertisements or brochures, web sites, toll-free telephone number recorded messages or operators) should be in the language of the broadcast ad. Regardless of the language used for the advertisement, current broadcast advertising regulations require the dissemination of approved product labeling, which, in most cases, must be in English, and is generally written in language directed to healthcare professionals. The agency strongly encourages sponsors to consider the benefits of also providing consumers with nonpromotional, consumer-friendly product information in the language of the broadcast ad (e.g., FDA-approved patient labeling or accurate, consumer-friendly translations of product labeling information).

Five years later, the agency issued a substantially similar guidance for consumer advertising of restricted devices. See 69 Fed. Reg. 6308, 6309 (2004); Bruce Patsner, Problems Associated with Direct-to-Consumer Advertising (DTCA) of Restricted, Implantable Medical Devices: Should the Current Regulatory Approach Be Changed?, 64 Food & Drug L.J. 1 (2009); see also 75 Fed. Reg. 15,376 (2010) (proposed rule governing the "major statement" requirement in broadcast ads); 74 Fed. Reg. 25,245 (2009) (draft guidance on presenting risk information in promotions); Lisa M. Schwartz et al., Using a Drug Facts Box to Communicate Drug Benefits and Harms: Two Randomized Trials, 150 Annals Internal Med. 516 (2009); Dan Neil, Warning: New Drug Commercials May Cause Drowsiness, L.A. Times, July 14, 2009, at B1.

Evidently, these guidelines have not cut down on problems of industry failures to comply with the advertising rules, and the agency sometimes has issued multiple letters raising objections to the consumer marketing campaigns for particular drugs. See Gen. Accounting Office, Prescription Drugs: FDA Oversight of Direct-to-Consumer Advertising Has Limitations, GAO–03–177 (2002); Chris Adams, Xenical Ads Avoid Listing Unpleasant Side Effects, Wall St. J., Apr. 3, 2001, at B1 (describing one company's creative effort to circumvent the rules); Robert Pear, Investigators Find Repeated Deception in Ads for Drugs, N.Y. Times, Dec. 4, 2002, at A22 (reporting that, over a five year period, the FDA issued 88 enforcement letters for advertising violations); Melody Petersen, Who's Minding the Drugstore?, N.Y. Times, June 29, 2003, § 3, at 1 (noting complaints that the agency has become less vigilant); Julie Schmit, A Winded FDA Races to Keep up with Drug Ads That Go Too Far, USA Today, May 31, 2005, at 1A (reporting that the agency has ordered more corrective advertising). Apart from traditional print and television advertising, drug companies have come up with other methods for promoting their wares directly to consumers. See, e.g., Gardiner Harris, Pushing Pills: Drug Makers Offer Coupons for Free Prescriptions, Wall St. J., Mar. 13, 2002, at B1; Rhonda L. Rundle, A New Wrinkle in Rewards Programs, Wall St. J., Mar. 2, 2005, at D3 (describing incentives similar to frequent flyer programs); see also Louis Boyarsky, Comment, Stealth Celebrity Testimonials of Prescription Drugs: Placing the Consumer in Harm's Way and How the FDA Has Dropped the Ball, 28 Loy. L.A. Ent. L. Rev. 101 (2007–2008); Stephanie Saul, More

Celebrities Finding Roles as Antidepressant Advocates, N.Y. Times, Mar. 21, 2005, at C8.

Advertising directed to consumers has succeeded in dramatically increasing drug sales. See Julie Appleby, Prescriptions Increase as Drugmakers Spend More on Ads, USA Today, Feb. 21, 2001, at 6B (reporting that companies spent more than $2 billion advertising prescription drugs directly consumers in 2000, and that sales increased to $145 billion); Steven Pearlstein, Drug Firms Take a Dose of Responsibility for Ads, Wash. Post, Aug. 3, 2005, at D1 ("A study by the Kaiser Family Foundation found that each $1 invested in advertising yields an extra $4.20 in sales."); see also John E. Calfee et al., Direct-to-Consumer Advertising and the Demand for Cholesterol–Reducing Drugs, 45 J.L. & Econ. 673 (2002); Meredith B. Rosenthal et al., Promotion of Prescription Drugs to Consumers, 346 New Eng. J. Med. 498 (2002); Keith J. Winstein & Suzanne Vranica, Drug Firms' Spending on Consumer Ads Fell 8% in '08, a Rare Marketing Pullback, Wall St. J., Apr. 16, 2009, at B2 ("U.S. spending on such drug ads hit a peak of $4.8 billion in 2007 ...."); FDA Survey Finds Drug Ads Influence Requests by Patients, Wall St. J., Jan. 14, 2003, at D5. In 2005, the FDA announced yet another public meeting to consider a number of broad questions related to DTCA. See 70 Fed. Reg. 54,054 (2005) (summarizing milestones in the agency's supervision of the practice); see also Thomas Ginsberg, Drug Ads Pour in for Review: The FDA Said It Had Seen "A Huge Increase" in Advertising Submitted for Scrutiny Under a Voluntary Industry Program, Phila. Inquirer, Feb. 23, 2006, at C1; Margaret W. Pressler, Drug Firms Seek Ad Remedy: Industry Hopes Self–Policing Cures Marketing Complaints, Wash. Post, Aug. 3, 2005, at D2; Tony Pugh, Deluge of Drug Ads Has FDA Struggling to Stop the Hype, Phila. Inquirer, Jan. 30, 2004, at C1 (reporting that companies had submitted approximately 37,000 promotional items to the agency in the previous year). Stay tuned for further developments in this area.

NOTES AND QUESTIONS

1. *Internet promotion.* It remains unclear whether the FDA will choose to address Internet promotional issues separately from the other forms of direct consumer advertising. How should a pharmaceutical company append a brief summary to any product-specific promotions included on its home page; can this site include hypertext links to other sites on the Internet not sponsored by the company but that discuss the product or disease condition; must a company sponsoring promotional Web sites in foreign countries abide by FDA restrictions simply because the same drug product received narrower approval in the United States? See 61 Fed. Reg. 48,707 (1996) (announcing a public meeting to discuss such questions); see also Emilé L. Loza, FDA Regulation of Internet Pharmaceutical Communications, 55 Food & Drug L.J. 269 (2000); Nancy K. Plant, Prescription Drug Promotion on the Internet: Tool for the Inquisitive or Trap for the Unwary?, 42 St. Louis U. L.J. 89 (1998); Francesca L. Kritz, Drug Firms Jockey for Space Online, Wash. Post, June 16, 2009, at F1; Christian

Torres, Citing Risks, Drug Firms Going Offline, Wash. Post, Aug. 14, 2011, at A3 (reporting regulatory concerns associated with manufacturers' use of social media and delays in the FDA's issuance of guidelines).

2. *Further commentary*. See Marshall H. Chin, The Patient's Role in Choice of Medications: Direct-to-Consumer Advertising and Patient Decision Aids, 5 Yale J. Health Pol'y L. & Ethics 771 (2005); Julie M. Donohue et al., A Decade of Direct-to-Consumer Advertising of Prescription Drugs, 357 New Eng. J. Med. 673 (2007); Ronald M. Green, Direct-to-Consumer Advertising and Pharmaceutical Ethics: The Case of Vioxx, 35 Hofstra L. Rev. 749 (2006); Matthew F. Hollon, Editorial, Direct-to-Consumer Advertising: A Haphazard Approach to Health Promotion, 293 JAMA 2030 (2005); Davina C. Ling et al., Deregulating Direct-to-Consumer Marketing of Prescription Drugs: Effects on Prescription and Over-the-Counter Product Sales, 45 J.L. & Econ. 691 (2002); Amanda L. Connors, Comment, Big Bad Pharma: An Ethical Analysis of Physician–Directed and Consumer–Directed Marketing Tactics, 73 Alb. L. Rev. 243 (2009).

Bober v. Glaxo Wellcome PLC

246 F.3d 934 (7th Cir.2001).

■ WILLIAMS, CIRCUIT JUDGE:

Mortimer Bober brought a class action lawsuit against the firms that manufacture and market Zantac 75 and Zantac 150, the over-the-counter and prescription strength forms of the stomach acid reliever ranitidine, on the ground that the firms provide consumers with false and misleading information about the substitutability of the two drugs, in violation of Illinois law. * * *

Zantac 150 is manufactured and sold by British drug company Glaxo Wellcome PLC and its American subsidiary Glaxo Wellcome, Inc. The Food and Drug Administration has approved it for use in the treatment of various digestive tract conditions, including certain kinds of ulcers and certain esophageal conditions. As its name suggests, it contains 150 milligrams of ranitidine, and it is available only with a prescription. Zantac 75 is manufactured by Glaxo Wellcome, Inc. and is sold by Warner–Lambert Consumer Healthcare, a joint venture formed by Glaxo Wellcome, Inc. and Warner–Lambert Company, another American drug company. According to its FDA-approved packaging, it is to be used for the relief and prevention of heartburn associated with acid indigestion and sour stomach. As its name too suggests, it contains 75 milligrams of ranitidine, but it may be purchased without a prescription.

Bober's complaint alleges that Glaxo Wellcome PLC and the other three defendants provide false and misleading information regarding whether Zantac 75 can be substituted for Zantac 150. The answer to that question was important to Bober because, at the time he filed this lawsuit, he was paying $1.47 per tablet for the Zantac 150 his doctor had prescribed for him, while an equivalent dose of Zantac 75 (two tablets) cost $.80. In an effort to obtain information on the substitutability of Zantac 75 and Zantac 150, Bober twice called a consumer hotline for Zantac 75 users set up by Warner–Lambert. When Bober first called the Zantac 75 consumer hotline, the hotline operator "told Mr. Bober that Zantac 75 and Zantac 150 were not the same medications, and that Mr. Bober could not substitute two Zantac 75 tablets for one Zantac 150 tablet." When Bober called the hotline a second time, a recorded message advised Bober, "If your doctor has directed you to take prescription Zantac, you should not substitute Zantac 75 for your prescription."

Bober's complaint also notes that Warner Lambert maintains a web site providing information about Zantac 75, although the complaint does not say whether Bober ever visited the web site. At the time Bober filed his complaint, a page on that web site answering frequently asked questions about Zantac 75 responded to a question about whether Zantac 75 could be substituted for Zantac 150 by informing visitors, "If your physician has prescribed a medicine, you should not substitute any other medicine for your prescription. You should always ask your physician any questions you may have about changing your medication."

In his complaint, Bober claims that the three quoted statements are false and misleading because, contrary to what the three statements imply, Zantac 75 and Zantac 150 contain the same medicine (ranitidine) and are therefore readily substitutable. On that basis, Bober's complaint alleges that the three statements violate the Illinois Consumer Fraud and Deceptive Business Practices Act ("CFA") and the similar laws of other states. * * * To establish a violation of the CFA's prohibition on deceptive acts or practices, a plaintiff must prove that: (1) the defendant engaged in a deceptive act or practice; (2) the defendant intended that the plaintiff rely on the act or practice; and (3) the act or practice occurred in the course of conduct involving a trade or commerce. Only the first of these requirements is at issue here. * * *

Bober's estate contends that the three statements at issue are deceptive in essentially three ways. First, Bober's estate asserts that the statements falsely claim that Zantac 75 and Zantac 150 do not contain the same medicine. None of the statements, however, expressly makes such a claim. The statements do claim that the two drugs are different medications, but that claim is completely true. The drugs are approved for very different maladies, went through different approval processes, and are sold in different ways. Moreover, to the extent that anyone could imply from the statements at issue that the drugs contain different medicine, information available to Zantac users, and in Bober's possession, would dispel any such implication. The web page that answers frequently asked questions about Zantac 75 (a printout of which is attached to Bober's complaint) expressly states that Zantac 75 and Zantac 150 contain the same medicine. Likewise, the packaging information for Zantac 75 (which is also attached to Bober's complaint) strongly suggests the same fact when it explains that the active ingredient in Zantac 75 is ranitidine and promotes Zantac 75's safety by noting that prescription strength Zantac has an excellent safety record. Put simply, none of the three statements at issue can reasonably be read as falsely claiming or implying that Zantac 75 and Zantac 150 do not contain the same medicine.

Second, Bober's estate asserts that, in describing Zantac 75 and Zantac 150 as different medications and discouraging substitution of the former for the latter, the three statements at issue misrepresent the therapeutic equivalence of equal doses of the two drugs (an equivalence we assume exists in reviewing the sufficiency of Bober's complaint) by implying that Zantac 150 is more effective than Zantac 75 in treating the conditions for which Zantac 150 is prescribed. While it is clear that the statements at issue go out of their way to avoid any implication that equal doses of the drugs are therapeutically equivalent, we think that the statements also avoid any implication that the drugs are not therapeutically equivalent. In the context of all the information available to Bober and other Zantac users, including the three statements at issue, the packaging information for Zantac 75, and the Zantac 75 frequently asked question web page, it should have been clear to Bober and other Zantac users both that Zantac 75 and Zantac 150 contain the same active ingredient and that inquiries about substituting the former for the latter are properly directed to a user's treating physician. The available information, in our view, dispels any tendency to deceive that the statements at issue might otherwise have had. Accordingly, none of the three statements at issue can reasonably be read as misrepresenting the therapeutic equivalence of equal doses of Zantac 150 and Zantac 75.

Finally, Bober's estate asserts that the statements at issue both claim and imply that Zantac 75 simply cannot be substituted for Zantac 150, despite the fact that it would be perfectly appropriate for a doctor to recommend such a substitution. Again, the problem for Bober's estate is that examining the statements at issue, together and in the context of the other information available to Zantac users, eliminates any possibility of deception with regard to substitutability. From such a perspective, the statements discouraging substitution can only be read to discourage users from making a substitution without consulting their physicians. So read, the statements do not falsely claim or imply that Zantac 75 cannot be substituted for Zantac 150. As a matter of law, none of the three statements on which Bober based his CFA claims is deceptive.

Alternatively, Glaxo argues that all three of the statements are protected by section 10b(1) of the CFA, which excludes from liability "actions . . . specifically authorized by laws administered by any regulatory body or offices acting under statutory authority of this State or the United States." 815 Ill. Comp. Stat. 505/10b(1). It also argues that the statements were "labeling" specifically authorized by the FDA. The case law interpreting the relevant portion of the CFA's exemption provision is not entirely clear on the question of what is meant by "specifically authorized." * * * Taken together, the cases stand for the proposition that the state CFA will not impose higher disclosure requirements on parties than those that are sufficient to satisfy federal regulations. If the parties are doing something specifically authorized by federal law, section 10b(1) will protect them from liability under the CFA. On the other hand, the CFA exemption is not available for statements that manage to be in technical compliance with federal regulations, but which are so misleading or deceptive in context that federal law itself might not regard them as adequate.

The question is thus whether the statements Bober complains of are sufficiently within what is authorized by federal law that Glaxo is entitled to section 10b(1) protection. On this question, we limit our examination to the operator's statement—the only one that is even potentially misleading. The regulations implementing the FDCA are extensive and extremely detailed. Of particular relevance to the "different medications" part of the operator's statement are the regulations defining what constitutes a "new drug." A drug may be considered new based on "[t]he newness of use of such drug in diagnosing, curing, mitigating, treating, or preventing a disease . . . even though such drug is not a new drug when used in another disease or to affect another structure or function of the body." 21 C.F.R. § 310.3(h)(4). Before any "new drug" can be marketed, the manufacturer has to file a "new drug application" and meet the various testing, production, and labeling requirements set out in the Code. There is no dispute that Zantac 75 satisfies this definition of new drug. Even if we assume that in all other relevant respects it is identical to Zantac 150, Zantac 75 is marketed as a nonprescription treatment for acid indigestion, while Zantac 150 is a prescription drug treatment for duodenal and gastric ulcers (among other things). Indeed, Glaxo submitted a new drug application prior to marketing Zantac 75. * * * Given that for federal regulatory purposes Zantac 75 and Zantac 150 were indeed different "drugs," the express terms of the regulations taken as a whole specifically authorized Glaxo to say that they were different "medications," even if the statement may have led Mr. Bober as a layperson to misunderstand what was being said.

The second half of the operator statement is not so easily dealt with, but ultimately we believe that the Illinois courts would find that it too was specifically authorized. The situation here is not a common one. When Mr. Bober asked whether he could substitute Zantac 75 for Zantac 150, the operator said he "could not." In assessing whether this was a specifically authorized response, it is significant that the federal regulations governing drug labeling and advertising imposed competing constraints on Glaxo, such that Mr. Bober's question was particularly tricky to answer. The manufacturer of a drug may not recommend or even suggest uses for a drug that are not approved by the FDA or supported by sufficient medical evidence. 21 C.F.R. § 330.1(d) (OTC advertising); id. § 202.1(e)(6) (prescription advertising). There is no dispute that Zantac 75 had not been tested for the use to which Mr. Bober sought to put it, which means that Glaxo was prohibited from even suggesting that substitution would be appropriate. A drug is considered to be misbranded if its labeling or advertising makes any "statements comparing the safety or effectiveness, either greater or less of the drug with other agents for the same indication" if that statement is not supported by "adequate and well controlled studies." 21 C.F.R. § 201.57(c)(3)(v) (prescription labeling); 21 C.F.R. § 201.6(a) (general labeling). Glaxo concedes that it had not conducted any studies that would have allowed it to say that two Zantac 75 tablets would be less (or more) effective than one Zantac 150 tablet for treatment of Mr. Bober's illness. Glaxo's position was thus precarious. It had to answer Mr. Bober's question in a way that did not suggest he could use Zantac 75 for an "off-label" purpose, while at the same time it had to avoid the unsubstantiated suggestion that Zantac 150 would be superior to Zantac 75. * * *

Glaxo chose to reconcile its competing obligations by answering Bober's question with the statement "you cannot substitute" Zantac 75 for Zantac 150. This statement was technically accurate, because only Bober's doctor could approve an "off-label" use for Zantac 75 and the substitution of one drug for the other. The statement was also consistent with those federal regulations requiring Glaxo to refrain from suggesting "off-label" uses for Zantac 75. In protecting itself on that side, however, Glaxo predictably opened itself up to the claim Mr. Bober is now making, namely that the statement improperly suggested that Zantac 150 was superior to Zantac 75. While Glaxo could have added "ask your doctor" without being accused of suggesting an "off-label" use and thus perhaps struck a more perfect balance between its competing regulatory obligations, under the circumstances what it chose to say and not to say was a sufficiently careful compromise to fall within what is specifically authorized by federal law.

The pharmaceutical industry is highly regulated, both at the federal level and internationally. Technical requirements abound, and it is not only possible but likely that ordinary consumers will find some of them confusing, or possibly misleading as the term is used in statutes like Illinois's CFA. But, recognizing the primacy of federal law in this field, the Illinois statute itself protects companies from liability if their actions are authorized by federal law. * * *

■ WOOD, CIRCUIT JUDGE (concurring):

* * * Although the majority acknowledges that these were three representations made at three different times, it analyzes the Bober claim as if he either heard everything at once or as if no individual statement could be deceptive for CFA purposes if the aggregate of everything the defendants said about Zantac would ultimately have given an accurate picture. * * * Even if we can assume that consumers will assimilate all the information they are given on a given occasion, I find no Illinois case holding that a company can avoid potential liability for deceptive statements if it has buried further explanatory material on a web site or in a brochure that some consumers may never see. It is even worse if, as here, the absent information would only potentially save an otherwise misleading statement. I am quite troubled by the implication one could draw from the majority's opinion that consumers have such an unbounded duty of inquiry. Such a holding would be inconsistent with Illinois's understanding of its own law, which requires that the statute be interpreted in a way consistent with its strong consumer protection purpose. What if Mr. Bober had stopped with the first telephone call, and never heard the recorded message? What if he had no access to a computer, or was not comfortable using one, and thus never visited the web site? The only answer that I can give to

these questions is that Illinois law recognizes these risks and that is why it requires each separate statement to be assessed on its own. * * *

Looking at each of the statements individually, I agree with the majority that the recorded statement and the web site statement were not misleading. * * * Even if we approach this case as one in which two Zantac 75 tablets and one Zantac 150 tablet both deliver the same amount of ranitidine in the same way (which is a contested fact at this point), it remains true that prescription strength medication and non-prescription medication differ in important respects not related to the active ingredient. As the majority points out, there are different testing and approval procedures necessary for the different dosage levels of the identical medication. Perhaps more importantly, prescription medications as a practical matter give the patient a package of product and service: the product is the 150 mg. of ranitidine, and the service is a combination of the pharmacist's monitoring of dosage quality, amounts, potential interactions with other prescription drugs known to the pharmacy, and advice, and the doctor's ability to conduct similar medical monitoring, to the extent the patient needs to report back for prescription refills from time to time. Those kinds of services from the pharmacist cost money, just as any other retail-level service does. It is therefore not surprising that the version of the product that comes securely tied to a high level of service costs more than the "discount" version. A simple recorded message that tells the patient not to substitute until he or she finds out why the doctor made a particular choice is not misleading. * * *

The operator, however, gave Mr. Bober a different message. That message had two parts, both of which I find problematic. First, the operator said that Zantac 75 and Zantac 150 were not the "same medications"; second, he or she said that Mr. Bober "could not" substitute one for the other. From the layperson's point of view, which Illinois law requires us to use, both of these representations might be shown to be misleading. Even if someone who had spent a career in the pharmaceutical industry would recognize that as a matter of federal regulation the two forms of Zantac are different "medications," a trier of fact might well conclude that an average consumer, asking whether she could substitute the products, would be misled by the statement "they are different medications" into believing that Zantac 75 could in no circumstances be used to treat the illness for which she was taking Zantac 150. * * * The average consumer could also be misled by the flat statement that one "could not" substitute Zantac 75 for Zantac 150. Understood literally, this is simply not true. With the doctor's authorization, substitution certainly is possible, as both the recorded message and the web site conceded. But that qualification was not given by the operator. A more trusting caller might simply give up the quest and never even think to raise the subject with her doctor. * * *

Vess v. Ciba–Geigy Corp. USA

317 F.3d 1097 (9th Cir.2003).

■ FLETCHER, CIRCUIT JUDGE:

* * * Ritalin, a Schedule II controlled substance, is commonly prescribed for Attention Deficit Disorder/Attention Deficit Hyperactivity Disor-

der (ADD/ADHD). Vess alleges that he "was prescribed, and purchased, and ingested" Ritalin when he was nine years old. Defendants-appellees are: Novartis Pharmaceuticals (the successor in interest to named defendant Ciba–Geigy Corp.), the primary or exclusive manufacturer of Ritalin in the United States since 1955; the American Psychiatric Association (APA), publisher of the *Diagnostic and Statistical Manual of Mental Disorders* (*DSM*), commonly used by medical professionals to diagnose ADD/ADHD; and the nonprofit advocacy group Children and Adults with Attention Deficit/Hyperactivity Disorder (CHADD).

Vess's first amended complaint alleges that the three defendants have acted illegally to increase sales of Ritalin. The complaint alleges an illegal conspiracy involving all three defendants, and illegal individual actions (and inactions) by defendant Novartis. * * * Vess asserts the same three causes of action against all of the defendants. Vess's first cause of action asserts a violation of Cal. Civ. Code § 1770, which prohibits "unfair methods of competition and unfair or deceptive acts or practices undertaken by any person in a transaction intended to result or which results in the sale ... of goods or services to any consumer." Vess's second cause of action asserts a violation of Cal. Bus. & Prof. Code § 17200, which prohibits "unlawful, unfair or fraudulent business act[s] or practice[s]" and "unfair, deceptive, untrue or misleading advertising." Vess's third cause of action asserts a violation of Cal. Bus. & Prof. Code § 17500, which prohibits "any statement" that is "untrue or misleading" and made with the "intent directly or indirectly to dispose of" property or services. * * *

Novartis moved to dismiss Vess's first amended complaint for failure to plead with particularity under [FRCP] Rule 9(b) * * * * In some of his non-conspiracy allegations against Novartis, Vess neither mentions the word "fraud," nor alleges facts that would necessarily constitute fraud. For example, Vess alleges that Novartis: (1) "negligently" failed to disclose its financial relationship with the APA and CHADD, knowing that the information would be important to those diagnosed with ADD/ADHD and to those who were subsequently prescribed Ritalin; (2) took steps to increase the sales of Ritalin in various ways; (3) failed to warn consumers that the full range of Ritalin's side effects has not yet been adequately studied; (4) failed to disclose the limited effectiveness of its product; and (5) failed to disclose that the clinical literature on ADD/ADHD referred to in the *DSM* is of poor quality. * * * Novartis did not move in the district court to dismiss under Rule 12(b)(6) for failure to state a claim. On remand, it will be free to make such a motion to test the legal sufficiency of Vess's surviving non-fraud allegations. We intimate no view on the likely success of such a motion. * * *

Vess alleges a fraudulent conspiracy between the APA and the other defendants, but he does not provide the particulars of when, where, or how the alleged conspiracy occurred. He alleges that the APA received financial contributions from Novartis, but he offers scant specifics as to when or between whom the money changed hands. He further alleges that the APA fraudulently included ADD in the *DSM* even though ADD failed to meet the manual's own diagnostic criteria, but he fails to indicate which criteria it failed to satisfy and how it failed to satisfy them. He charges that the APA sought to conceal its fraud by improperly clustering testing data for ADD with testing data for other conditions, but the allegation is unsupported by details, such as the names of those conditions. Vess also fails to point to the specific scientific literature that the APA failed to "fully address or actually obscured." Finally, he alleges that the APA misrepresented its connection to Novartis, but he does not identify any specific misrepresentations or specify when and where they occurred. These allegations are not particular enough to satisfy Rule 9(b). * * *

When the APA initially moved to dismiss Vess's complaint for failure to satisfy the heightened pleading requirements of Rule 9(b), the district court did not rule on the motion and allowed Vess to amend his complaint. When the APA renewed its motion as to Vess's first amended complaint, the district court granted the motion without prejudice and with leave to amend. Only after Vess declined to amend his complaint again did the district court dismiss with prejudice under Rule 9(b) for failure to plead with particularity and under Rule 12(b)(6) for failure to state a claim. Given that the claims against the APA in Vess's first amended complaint are grounded in fraud, that Vess has failed to comply with Rule 9(b), and that Vess declined to amend further, we affirm the district court's dismissal with prejudice as to the APA under both Rule 9(b) and Rule 12(b)(6). * * *

Vess's allegations against CHADD fall far short of satisfying Rule 9(b). Vess does allege that CHADD received $748,000 from Novartis between 1991 and 1994, but that is where the detail both begins and ends. Vess does not explain how CHADD "deliberately attempted to increase the sales of Ritalin," and he identifies no specific "misinformation" distributed by CHADD. * * * Because Vess declined to amend his complaint further when given the opportunity, we affirm the district court's dismissal of the claims against CHADD with prejudice under both Rule 9(b) and Rule 12(b)(6).

Vess also appeals the district court's determination that his suit constitutes a "Strategic Lawsuit Against Public Participation" (SLAPP) suit within the meaning of the California statute, Cal. Civ. Proc. Code § 425.16. A SLAPP suit is one in which the plaintiff's alleged injury results from petitioning or free speech activities by a defendant that are protected by the federal or state constitutions. California's anti-SLAPP statute was "enacted to allow early dismissal of meritless * * * cases aimed at chilling expression through costly, time-consuming litigation." * * *

Vess argues that his suit does not come within the paradigm of the SLAPP statute. He states that he is not a large private company seeking to deter private individuals from engaging in political debate, but rather a "little guy" seeking to vindicate his rights under California's consumer protection statutes. While Vess may be right that his is not a paradigmatic example of a SLAPP suit, he is wrong that it does not come within the statute. * * * California and federal courts have repeatedly permitted defendants to move to strike under the anti-SLAPP statute despite the fact that they were neither small nor championing individual interests. See, e.g., DuPont Merck Pharm. Co. v. Superior Court, 92 Cal.Rptr.2d 755 (Ct.App.2000) (permitting defendant DuPont Merck to invoke anti-SLAPP statute against prospective class action plaintiffs seeking relief under the same statutes on which Vess relies). * * *

A court considering a motion to strike under the anti-SLAPP statute must engage in a two-part inquiry. First, a defendant "must make an initial prima facie showing that the plaintiff's suit arises from an act in furtherance of the defendant's rights of petition or free speech." The defendant need not show that the plaintiff's suit was brought with the intention to chill the defendant's speech; the plaintiff's "intentions are ultimately beside the point." Similarly, the defendant bringing a motion to strike need not show that any speech was actually chilled. Second, once the defendant has made a prima facie showing, "the burden shifts to the plaintiff to demonstrate a probability of prevailing on the challenged claims." * * *

The APA and CHADD have made a sufficient showing under the first part of the inquiry. A protected act of free speech includes "any written or oral statement or writing made in a place open to the public or a public forum in connection with an issue of public interest," and "any other conduct in furtherance of the exercise of the constitutional right of petition or the constitutional right of free speech in connection with a public issue or an issue of public interest." The APA's protected speech, within the meaning of the statute, consists of the publication of the *DSM*. CHADD's protected speech consists of its public advocacy activities in connection with the use of Ritalin.

As to the APA and CHADD, Vess cannot make a proper showing under the second part of the inquiry. The district court dismissed Vess's complaint against the APA and CHADD with prejudice under Rules 9(b) and 12(b)(6), and we have affirmed that dismissal. Thus, Vess cannot demonstrate a "probability that [he] will prevail on [his] claim." We therefore affirm the district court's grant of the APA and CHADD's motion to strike under the anti-SLAPP statute. As to Novartis, however, we reverse * * * [b]ecause we reverse the district court's dismissal of Vess's complaint against Novartis insofar as it alleges non-fraudulent conduct * * * * The district court awarded attorneys' fees to all three defendants under the anti-SLAPP statute. We affirm that award as to the APA and CHADD, who prevailed in their motions to strike. * * *

NOTES AND QUESTIONS

1. *Ragging on Ritalin.* The diagnosis of attention deficit hyperactivity disorder (ADHD), and the use of Ritalin® (methylphenidate hydrochloride) and other psychoactive drugs in its treatment, has long generated controversy. See Connie Lenz, Prescribing a Legislative Response: Educators, Physicians, and Psychotropic Medication for Children, 22 J. Contemp.

Health L. & Pol'y 72 (2005); Emily Berntsen, Note, The Child Medication Safety Act: Special Treatment for the Parents of Children with ADHD?, 83 Wash. U. L.Q. 1567 (2005); Gardiner Harris, F.D.A. Strengthens Warnings on Stimulants' Risks, N.Y. Times, Aug. 22, 2006, at A14; Shankar Vedantam, Debate over Drugs for ADHD Reignites, Wash. Post, Mar. 27, 2009, at A1 (reporting that prescriptions for ADHD drugs have reached almost 40 million annually); see also Gardiner Harris, Use of Antipsychotics in Children Is Criticized, N.Y. Times, Nov. 19, 2008, at A20. The *Vess* lawsuit represented part of the latest wave of Ritalin litigation. See Hernandez v. Ciba–Geigy Corp., 200 F.R.D. 285 (S.D.Tex.2001) (dismissing a similar complaint); Dawson v. Ciba–Geigy Corp., 145 F.Supp.2d 565 (D.N.J.2001) (rejecting a removal petition); Ann Chiumino, Comment, Class Action Suits Prompt Governmental Action to Examine Ritalin Use and Regulation, 13 Loy. Consumer L. Rev. 380 (2001); cf. D.A.B. v. Brown, 570 N.W.2d 168 (Minn.Ct.App.1997) (rejecting for lack of injury a complaint under state's consumer fraud statute brought on behalf of a group of pediatric patients after the conviction of their treating physician for accepting kickbacks from the manufacturer of hGH).

2. *Atypical advertising.* Even if not actionable, the allegations that the manufacturer of Ritalin influenced an organization of medical professionals or sponsored a patient advocacy group may have some foundation and are hardly unique to this particular drug. See Lars Noah, Pigeonholing Illness: Medical Diagnosis as a Legal Construct, 50 Hastings L.J. 241, 290–94 (1999) [excerpted in Chap. 11(D)(3)]; Thomas Ginsberg, Donations Tie Drug Firms and Nonprofits, Phila. Inquirer, May 28, 2006, at A1 ("[M]any patient groups and drug companies maintain close, multimillion-dollar relationships while disclosing limited or no details about the ties.... For drug companies, patient groups [including CHADD] carry credibility that the industry sometimes lacks to target patients and 'opinion leaders' who drive prescriptions, and hence, sales. Nonprofits also help patients stay on the medicine and push insurers to pay for it."). Similar allegations have arisen concerning efforts to have the APA recognize premenstrual dysphoric disorder (PMDD) as distinct from premenstrual syndrome. Although the latest edition of the *DSM* left that question unresolved, Eli Lilly received approval from the FDA to market a version of Prozac® for the treatment of PMDD and then engaged in an aggressive advertising campaign. See Tara Parker–Pope, Drug Companies Push Use of Antidepressants to Treat Severe PMS, Wall St. J., Feb. 23. 2001, at B1; Shankar Vedantam, Renamed Prozac Fuels Women's Health Debate, Wash. Post, Apr. 29, 2001, at A1. Questions continue to arise about industry ties with the APA. See Thomas R. Insel, Psychiatrists' Relationships with Pharmaceutical Companies: Part of the Problem or Part of the Solution?, 303 JAMA 1192 (2010); Benedict Carey & Gardiner Harris, Psychiatric Association Faces Senate Scrutiny over Drug Industry Ties, N.Y. Times, July 12, 2008, at A13; Rob Stein, The Next Generation of Mental Disorders?, Wash. Post, Feb. 10, 2010, at A1; Shankar Vedantam, Experts Defining Mental Disorders Are Linked to Drug Firms, Wash. Post, Apr. 20, 2006, at A7 ("Every psychiatric expert involved in writing the standard diagnostic criteria for disorders such as depression and schizophrenia has had financial ties to drug companies that sell medications for those illnesses, a new analysis has found.'').

3. *Full court press for HPV vaccine.* Could one lodge similar objections to Merck's aggressive lobbying of states to require the use of its new vaccine Gardasil® (designed to prevent a sexually transmitted disease, human papillomavirus (HPV), that is linked to cervical cancer)? See Amy Gardner, Drugmaker Assists in Pushing for Mandate for HPV Vaccination, Wash. Post, Feb. 11, 2007, at C5; see also Sheila M. Rothman & David J. Rothman, Marketing HPV Vaccine: Implications for Adolescent Health and Medical Professionalism, 302 JAMA 781, 785 (2009) (criticizing the manufacturer's grants to professional medical associations, which were designed to spread the word); Rob Stein, A Vaccine Debate Once Focused on Sex Shifts as Boys Join the Target Market, Wash. Post, Mar. 26, 2009, at A1 (reporting that "the company eventually abandoned the strategy in the face of an intense backlash from critics''); cf. Sylvia Law, Human Papillomavirus Vaccination, Private Choice, and Public Health, 41 U.C. Davis L. Rev. 1731, 1758–60 (2008) (responding to criticisms of Merck's lobbying efforts).

4. *Consumer fraud litigation blossoms.* Patients (and private insurers) have brought claims under state consumer protection statutes, though usually focusing on allegedly misleading manufacturer communications to physicians rather than direct advertising to consumers. See, e.g., In re Celexa & Lexapro Mktg. & Sales Practices Litig., 751 F.Supp.2d 277 (D.Mass.2010) (antidepressants allegedly marketed for off-label use in pediatric patients); In re Bayer Corp. Combination Aspirin Prods. Mktg. & Sales Practices Litig., 701 F.Supp.2d 356 (E.D.N.Y.2010); In re Epogen & Aranesp Off–Label Mktg. & Sales Practices Litig., 590 F.Supp.2d 1282 (C.D.Cal.2008); Prohias v. Pfizer, Inc., 490 F.Supp.2d 1228 (S.D.Fla.2007) (declining to dismiss consumer fraud and negligent misrepresentation claims against the manufacturer of Lipitor® (atorvastatin) for purchasers' economic injuries allegedly resulting from advertisements that implied the cholesterol-lowering drug's usefulness in reducing the risk of heart disease before the FDA had approved such additional claims in labeling); New Jersey Citizen Action v. Schering–Plough Corp., 842 A.2d 174, 177–78 (N.J.App.Div.2003) (dismissing claims based on DTCA for Claritin® (loratadine)); see also Joseph J. Leghorn et al., Defending an Emerging Threat: Consumer Fraud Class Action Suits in Pharmaceutical and Medical Device Products–Based Litigation, 61 Food & Drug L.J. 519 (2006); cf. State v. Johnson & Johnson, 704 S.E.2d 677 (W.Va.2010) (holding that FDA warning letters, which triggered corrective action by a drug manufacturer, would not collaterally estop the company from defending against subsequent state charges that its mailings to physicians had contained false and misleading representations, reversing a fine of almost $5 million under the state's consumer protection statute against the manufacturer of the atypical antipsychotic Risperdal® (risperidone) and narcotic pain patch Duragesic® (fentanyl)); Peter Loftus, Drug Maker Is Ordered to Pay $327 Million, Wall St. J., June 6, 2011, at B3 (reporting that South Carolina had secured a sizeable civil penalties in connection with the marketing of Risperdal).

5. *Conspiracy theories abound.* Plaintiffs in these consumer fraud cases sometimes also include (though generally without success so far) claims under the federal Racketeer Influenced and Corrupt Organizations (RICO) Act, alleging instances of mail or wire fraud as predicate acts. See, e.g., Ironworkers Local Union 68 v. AstraZeneca Pharms., LP, 634 F.3d 1352 (11th Cir.2011) (off-label marketing of Seroquel® (quetiapine fumarate)); UFCW Local 1776 v. Eli Lilly & Co., 620 F.3d 121 (2d Cir.2010) (rejecting such claims against manufacturer for allegedly misrepresenting to physicians the safety and effectiveness of Zyprexa® (olanzapine)); In re Neurontin Mktg., Sales Practices & Prods. Liab. Litig., 677 F.Supp.2d 479 (D.Mass. 2010) (off-label marketing of gabapentin); see also J. Gordon Cooney, Jr. et al., Back to the Future: Civil RICO in Off–Label Promotion Litigation, 77 Def. Couns. J. 168 (2010).

C. FIRST AMENDMENT CONSTRAINTS

Thompson v. Western States Medical Center

535 U.S. 357 (2002).

■ O'CONNOR, JUSTICE:

Section 127(a) of the Food and Drug Administration Modernization Act of 1997, 111 Stat. 2328, 21 U.S.C. § 353a, exempts "compounded drugs" from the Food and Drug Administration's standard drug approval requirements as long as the providers of those drugs abide by several restrictions, including that they refrain from advertising or promoting particular compounded drugs. Respondents, a group of licensed pharmacies that specialize in compounding drugs, sought to enjoin enforcement of the subsections of the Act dealing with advertising and solicitation, arguing that those provisions violate the First Amendment's free speech guarantee. * * *

In *Central Hudson Gas & Elec. Corp. v. Public Serv. Comm'n of N.Y.*, 447 U.S. 557 (1980), we articulated a test for determining whether a particular commercial speech regulation is constitutionally permissible. Under that test we ask as a threshold matter whether the commercial speech concerns unlawful activity or is misleading. If so, then the speech is not protected by the First Amendment. If the speech concerns lawful activity and is not misleading, however, we next ask "whether the asserted governmental interest is substantial." If it is, then we "determine whether the regulation directly advances the governmental interest asserted," and, finally, "whether it is not more extensive than is necessary to serve that interest." Each of these latter three inquiries must be answered in the affirmative for the regulation to be found constitutional. * * *

The government does not attempt to defend the FDAMA's speech-related provisions under the first prong of the *Central Hudson* test; i.e., it does not argue that the prohibited advertisements would be about unlawful activity or would be misleading. Instead, the government argues that the FDAMA satisfies the remaining three prongs of the *Central Hudson* test.

The government asserts that three substantial interests underlie the FDAMA. The first is an interest in "preserv[ing] the effectiveness and integrity of the FDCA's new drug approval process and the protection of the public health that it provides." The second is an interest in "preserv[ing] the availability of compounded drugs for those individual patients who, for particularized medical reasons, cannot use commercially available products that have been approved by the FDA." Finally, the government argues that "[a]chieving the proper balance between those two independently compelling but competing interests is itself a substantial governmental interest."

Explaining these interests, the government argues that the FDCA's new drug approval requirements are critical to the public health and safety. It claims that the FDA's experience with drug regulation demonstrates that proof of the safety and effectiveness of a new drug needs to be established by rigorous, scientifically valid clinical studies because impressions of individual doctors, who cannot themselves compile sufficient safety data, cannot be relied upon. The government also argues that a premarket approval process, under which manufacturers are required to put their proposed drugs through tests of safety and effectiveness in order to obtain FDA approval to market the drugs, is the best way to guarantee drug safety and effectiveness. * * *

Preserving the effectiveness and integrity of the FDCA's new drug approval process is clearly an important governmental interest, and the government has every reason to want as many drugs as possible to be subject to that approval process. The government also has an important interest, however, in permitting the continuation of the practice of compounding so that patients with particular needs may obtain medications suited to those needs. And it would not make sense to require compounded drugs created to meet the unique needs of individual patients to undergo the testing required for the new drug approval process. Pharmacists do not make enough money from small-scale compounding to make safety and efficacy testing of their compounded drugs economically feasible, so requiring such testing would force pharmacists to stop providing compounded drugs. Given this, the government needs to be able to draw a line between small-scale compounding and large-scale drug manufacturing. That line must distinguish compounded drugs produced on such a small scale that they could not undergo safety and efficacy testing from drugs produced and sold on a large enough scale that they could undergo such testing and therefore must do so.

The government argues that the FDAMA's speech-related provisions provide just such a line * * * * The government argues that advertising particular products is useful in a broad market but is not useful when particular products are designed in response to an individual's "often unique need[s]." The government contends that, because of this, advertising is not typically associated with compounding for particular individuals. In contrast it is typically associated, the government claims, with large-scale production of a drug for a substantial market. The government argues that advertising, therefore, is "a fair proxy for actual or intended large-scale manufacturing," and that Congress' decision to limit the FDAMA's compounding exemption to pharmacies that do not engage in promotional activity was "rationally calculated" to avoid creating " 'a loophole that would allow unregulated drug manufacturing to occur under the guise of pharmacy compounding.' "

The government seems to believe that without advertising it would not be possible to market a drug on a large enough scale to make safety and efficacy testing economically feasible. The government thus believes that conditioning an exemption from the FDA approval process on refraining from advertising is an ideal way to permit compounding and yet also guarantee that compounding is not conducted on such a scale as to undermine the FDA approval process. Assuming it is true that drugs cannot be marketed on a large scale without advertising, the FDAMA's prohibition on advertising compounded drugs might indeed "directly advanc[e]" the government's interests. Even assuming that it does, however, the government has failed to demonstrate that the speech restrictions are "not more extensive than is necessary to serve [those] interest[s]." In previous cases addressing this final prong of the *Central Hudson* test, we have made clear that if the government could achieve its interests in a manner that does not restrict speech, or that restricts less speech, the government must do so. * * *

Several non-speech-related means of drawing a line between compounding and large-scale manufacturing might be possible here. First, it seems that the government could use the very factors the FDA relied on to distinguish compounding from manufacturing in its 1992 [Compliance Policy] Guide. For example, the government could ban the use of "commercial scale manufacturing or testing equipment for compounding drug products." It could prohibit pharmacists from compounding more drugs in anticipation of receiving prescriptions than in response to prescriptions already received. It could prohibit pharmacists from "[o]ffering compounded drug products at wholesale to other state licensed persons or commercial entities for resale." Alternately, it could limit the amount of compounded drugs, either by volume or by numbers of prescriptions, that a given pharmacist or pharmacy sells out of state. Another possibility not suggested by the Guide would be capping the amount of any particular compounded drug, either by drug volume, number of prescriptions, gross revenue, or profit that a pharmacist or pharmacy may make or sell in a given period of time. It might even be sufficient to rely solely on the non-speech-related provisions of the FDAMA, such as the requirement that compounding only be conducted in response to a prescription or a history of receiving a prescription, 21 U.S.C. § 353a(a), and the limitation on the percentage of a pharmacy's total sales that out-of-state sales of compounded drugs may represent, § 353a(b)(3)(B).

The government has not offered any reason why these possibilities, alone or in combination, would be insufficient to prevent compounding from occurring on such a scale as to undermine the new drug approval process. Indeed, there is no hint that the government even considered these or any other alternatives. Nowhere in the legislative history of the FDAMA or petitioners' briefs is there any explanation of why the government believed forbidding advertising was a necessary as opposed to merely convenient means of achieving its interests. * * * If the First Amendment means anything, it means that regulating speech must be a last—not first—resort. Yet here it seems to have been the first strategy the government thought to try.

The dissent describes another governmental interest—an interest in prohibiting the sale of compounded drugs to "patients who may not clearly need them"—and argues that "Congress could ... conclude that the advertising restrictions 'directly advance' " that interest. Nowhere in its briefs, however, does the government argue that this interest motivated the advertising ban. * * * The *Central Hudson* test is significantly stricter than the rational basis test, however, requiring the government not only to identify specifically "a substantial interest to be achieved by [the] restrictio[n] on commercial speech," but also to prove that the regulation "directly advances" that interest and is "not more extensive than is necessary to serve that interest." The government has not met any of these requirements with regard to the interest the dissent describes.

Even if the government had argued that the FDAMA's speech-related restrictions were motivated by a fear that advertising compounded drugs would put people who do not need such drugs at risk by causing them to convince their doctors to prescribe the drugs anyway, that fear would fail to justify the restrictions. Aside from the fact that this concern rests on the questionable assumption that doctors would prescribe unnecessary medications (an assumption the dissent is willing to make based on one magazine article and one survey, neither of which was relied upon by the government), this concern amounts to a fear that people would make bad decisions if given truthful information about compounded drugs. We have previously rejected the notion that the government has an interest in preventing the dissemination of truthful commercial information in order to prevent members of the public from making bad decisions with the information. * * *

Even if the government had asserted an interest in preventing people who do not need compounded drugs from obtaining those drugs, the statute does not directly advance that interest. The dissent claims that the government "must exclude from the area of permitted drug sales ... those compounded drugs sought by patients who may not clearly need them." Yet the statute does not directly forbid such sales. It instead restricts advertising, of course not just to those who do not need compounded drugs, but also to individuals who do need compounded drugs and their doctors. Although the advertising ban may reduce the demand for compounded drugs from those who do not need the drugs, it does nothing to prevent such individuals from obtaining compounded drugs other than requiring prescriptions. But if it is appropriate for the statute to rely on doctors to refrain from prescribing compounded drugs to patients who do not need them, it is not clear why it would not also be appropriate to rely on doctors to refrain from prescribing compounded drugs to patients who do not need them in a world where advertising was permitted.

The dissent may also be suggesting that the government has an interest in banning the advertising of compounded drugs because patients who see such advertisements will be confused about the drugs' risks. This argument is precluded, however, by the fact that the government does not argue that the advertisements are misleading. Even if the government did argue that it had an interest in preventing misleading advertisements, this interest could be satisfied by the far less restrictive alternative of requiring each compounded drug to be labeled with a warning that the drug had not undergone FDA testing and that its risks were unknown.

If the government's failure to justify its decision to regulate speech were not enough to convince us that the FDAMA's advertising provisions were unconstitutional, the amount of beneficial speech prohibited by the FDAMA would be. Forbidding the advertisement of compounded drugs would affect pharmacists other than those interested in producing drugs on a large scale. It would prevent pharmacists with no interest in mass-producing medications, but who serve clienteles with special medical needs, from telling the doctors treating those clients about the alternative drugs available through compounding. For example, a pharmacist serving a children's hospital where many patients are unable to swallow pills would be prevented from telling the children's doctors about a new development in compounding that allowed a drug that was previously available only in pill form to be administered another way. Forbidding advertising of particular compounded drugs would also prohibit a pharmacist from posting a notice informing customers that if their children refuse to take medications because of the taste, the pharmacist could change the flavor, and giving examples of medications where flavoring is possible. The fact that the FDAMA would prohibit such seemingly useful speech even though doing so does not appear to directly further any asserted governmental objective confirms our belief that the prohibition is unconstitutional. * * *

■ Breyer, Justice (dissenting):

* * * [T]he advertising restriction "directly advances" the statute's important safety objective. That objective, as the Court concedes, is to confine the sale of untested, compounded, drugs to where they are medically needed. But to do so the statute must exclude from the area of permitted drug sales both (1) those drugs that traditional drug manufacturers might supply after testing—typically drugs capable of being produced in large amounts, and (2) those compounded drugs sought by patients who may not clearly need them—including compounded drugs produced in small amounts. The majority's discussion focuses upon the first exclusionary need, but it virtually ignores the second. * * *

This description overlooks the need for a second line—a line that will distinguish (1) sales of compounded drugs to those who clearly need them from (2) sales of compounded drugs to those for whom a specially tailored but untested drug is a convenience but not a medical necessity. That is to say, the statute, in seeking to confine distribution of untested tailored drugs, must look both at the amount supplied (to help decide whether ordinary manufacturers might provide a tested alternative) and at the nature of demand (to help separate genuine need from simple convenience).

This second intermediate objective is logically related to Congress' primary end—the minimizing of safety risks. The statute's basic exemption from testing requirements inherently creates risks simply by placing untested drugs in the hands of the consumer. Where an individual has a specific medical need for a specially tailored drug those risks are likely offset. But where an untested drug is a convenience, not a necessity, that offset is unlikely to be present. That presumably is why neither the Food and Drug Administration (FDA) nor Congress anywhere suggests that all that matters is the total amount of a particular drug's sales. That is why the statute's history suggests that the amount supplied is not the whole story. That is why the statute itself, as well as the FDA policy that the statute reflects, lists several distinguishing factors, of which advertising is one. And that is likely why, when faced with the possibility of severing the advertising restriction from the rest of the statute, the government argued that the "other conditions in section 353a alone are inadequate to achieve Congress's desired balance among competing interests."

Ensuring that the risks associated with compounded drug prescriptions are offset by the benefits is also why public health authorities, testifying in Congress, insisted that the doctor's prescription represent an individualized determination of need. And that, in part, is why federal and state authorities have long permitted pharmacists to advertise the fact that they compound drugs, while forbidding the advertisement of individual compounds. * * * These policies and statutory provisions reflect the view that individualized consideration is more likely present, and convenience alone is more likely absent, when demand for a compounding prescription originates with a doctor, not an advertisement. The restrictions try to assure that demand is generated doctor-to-patient-to-pharmacist, not pharmacist-to-advertisement-to-patient-to-doctor. And they do so in order to diminish the likelihood that those who do not genuinely need untested compounded drugs will not receive them.

There is considerable evidence that the relevant means—the advertising restrictions—directly advance this statutory objective. No one denies that the FDA's complex testing system for new drugs—a system that typically relies upon double-blind or other scientific studies—is more likely to find, and to assess, small safety risks than are physicians or pharmacists relying upon impressions and anecdotes. Nor can anyone deny that compounded drugs carry with them special risks. After all, compounding is not necessarily a matter of changing a drug's flavor, but rather it is a matter of combining different ingredients in new, untested ways, say, adding a pain medication to an antihistamine to counteract allergies or increasing the ratio of approved ingredients in a salve to help the body absorb it at a faster rate. And the risks associated with the untested combination of ingredients or the quicker absorption rate or the working conditions necessary to change an old drug into its new form can, for some patients, mean infection, serious side effects, or even death.

There is considerable evidence that consumer oriented advertising will create strong consumer-driven demand for a particular drug. And there is strong evidence that doctors will often respond affirmatively to a patient's request for a specific drug that the patient has seen advertised. In these circumstances, Congress could reasonably conclude that doctors will respond affirmatively to a patient's request for a compounded drug even if the doctor would not normally prescribe it. When a parent learns that a child's pill can be administered in liquid form, when a patient learns that a compounded skin cream has an enhanced penetration rate, or when an allergy sufferer learns that a compounded antiinflammatory/allergy medication can alleviate a sinus headache without the sedative effects of antihistamines, that parent or patient may well ask for the desired prescription. And the doctor may well write the prescription even in the absence of special need—at least if any risk likely to arise from lack of testing is so small that only scientific testing, not anecdote or experience, would reveal it. * * *

I do not believe that Congress could have achieved its safety objectives in significantly less restrictive ways. Consider the several alternatives the Court suggests. First, it says that "the government could ban the use of 'commercial scale manufacturing or testing equipment for compounding drug products.'" This alternative simply restricts compounding to drugs produced in small batches. It would neither limit the total quantity of compounded drugs produced, nor help in any way to assure the kind of individualized doctor-patient need determination that the statute's advertising restriction are designed to help achieve. * * * [T]he Court says that the government could "ca[p] the amount of any particular compounded drug, either by drug volume, number of prescriptions, gross revenue, or profit." This alternative, like the others, ignores the patient-need problem, while simultaneously threatening to prevent compounded drugs from reaching those who genuinely need them, say, a patient whose prescription represents one beyond the arbitrarily imposed quantitative limit. * * *

The Court adds that "[t]he government has not offered any reason why these possibilities, alone or in combination, would be insufficient." The government's failure to do so may reflect the fact that only the Court, not any of the respondents, has here suggested that these "alternatives," alone or in combination, would prove sufficient. In fact, the FDA's Compliance Policy Guide, from which the Court draws its first four alternatives, specifically warned that these alternatives alone were insufficient to successfully distinguish traditional compounding from unacceptable manufacturing. * * *

[T]he government fears the safety consequences of multiple compound-drug prescription decisions initiated not by doctors but by pharmacist-to-patient advertising. Those consequences flow from the adverse cumulative effects of multiple individual decisions each of which may seem perfectly reasonable considered on its own. The government fears that, taken together, these apparently rational individual decisions will undermine the safety testing system, thereby producing overall a net balance of harm. Consequently, the government leaves pharmacists free to explain through advertisements what compounding is, to advertise that they engage in compounding, and to advise patients to discuss the matter with their physicians. And it forbids advertising the specific drug in question, not because it fears the "information" the advertisement provides, but because it fears the systematic effect, insofar as advertisements solicit business, of advertisements that will not fully explain the complicated risks at issue. And this latter fear is more than plausible.

I do not deny that the statute restricts the circulation of some truthful information. It prevents a pharmacist from including in an advertisement the information that "this pharmacy will compound Drug X." Nonetheless, this Court has not previously held that commercial advertising restrictions automatically violate the First Amendment. Rather, the Court has applied a more flexible test. It has examined the restriction's proportionality, the relation between restriction and objective, the fit between ends and means. * * * It has done so because it has concluded that, from a constitutional perspective, commercial speech does not warrant application of the Court's strictest speech-protective tests. And it has reached this conclusion in part because restrictions on commercial speech do not often repress individual self-expression; they rarely interfere with the functioning of democratic political processes; and they often reflect a democratically determined governmental decision to regulate a commercial venture in order to protect, for example, the consumer, the public health, individual safety, or the environment. * * *

The Court, in my view, gives insufficient weight to the government's regulatory rationale, and too readily assumes the existence of practical alternatives. It thereby applies the commercial speech doctrine too strictly. In my view, the Constitution demands a more lenient application, an application that reflects the need for distinctions among contexts, forms of regulation, and forms of speech, and which, in particular, clearly distinguishes between "commercial speech" and other forms of speech demanding stricter constitutional protection. Otherwise, an overly rigid "commercial speech" doctrine will transform what ought to be a legislative or regulatory decision about the best way to protect the health and safety of the American public into a constitutional decision prohibiting the legislature from enacting necessary protections. * * *

Finally, the majority would hold the statute unconstitutional because it prohibits pharmacists from advertising compounded drugs to doctors. Doctors, however, obtain information about individual drugs through many other channels. And there is no indication that restrictions on commercial advertising have had any negative effect on the flow of this information. Nor, with one exception, have doctors or groups of doctors complained that the statute will interfere with that flow of information in the future. Regardless, we here consider a facial attack on the statute. The respondents here focus their attack almost entirely upon consumer-directed advertising. They have not fully addressed separate questions involving the effect of advertising restrictions on information received by physicians. I would consequently leave these questions in abeyance. * * *

Lars Noah, *Truth or Consequences?: Commercial Free Speech vs. Public Health Promotion (at the FDA)*

21 Health Matrix 31 (2011).

It takes little insight to recognize fundamental tensions between constitutional protections of commercial speech and efforts to safeguard the public's health. The First Amendment values autonomy, while public health promotion often reflects paternalistic impulses, not trusting citizens to make sensible lifestyle choices. Some public health measures aim, of course, to facilitate autonomous decisionmaking by attempting to ensure fuller access to useful information, whether by guarding against deceptive advertising or mandating the provision of otherwise undersupplied information. Because such approaches do not, however, work well at moving individuals' behavior in directions desired by the government, public health officials may attempt to control choice more directly. Although direct controls would not run into free speech obstacles, other constitutional rights might stand in the way, to say nothing of political resistance and implementation difficulties.

Given the intrinsic shortcomings encountered with these two options, a potentially appealing intermediate course exists: limit access to the information that encourages undesirable choices. This option does not, of course, seem "intermediate" when viewed from a First Amendment perspective. Although less intrusive and more politically palatable than direct control of behavior, and also much more likely to work than risk disclosure requirements or public education campaigns, suppressing information simply because it tends to result in suboptimal consumer choices reflects a decidedly paternalistic approach anathema to the First Amendment. In other domains where constitutional rights may conflict with public health efforts, the Supreme Court has shown a degree of flexibility. In commercial speech cases, however, it has become increasingly unwilling to find a middle ground; in recent years, for instance, the Court has invalidated restrictions on the advertising of alcohol and tobacco products notwithstanding the serious threats that these pose to the public health. * * *

[In *Thompson v. Western States Medical Center*,] the Court never directly confronted the hybrid nature of the case—namely, did the speech restriction relate to product sales or professional services? The sales-service distinction, familiar in tort doctrine, also appears to have made some difference in the how the Court heretofore had resolved commercial speech cases. Although FDAMA's advertising restriction straddled the line, the statute appeared to operate primarily on the sale of a product rather than the rendition of a service. It lacked, however, the "vice" aspect of prior cases involving government efforts to protect citizens from harms associated with gambling or the consumption of alcohol and tobacco products.

The Court also failed to appreciate the nature of the unconstitutional conditions problem before it. The majority treated the case as involving a *prohibition* on a particular type of speech, noting for instance that the respondents "[f]ear[ed] that they would be prosecuted under the FDAMA if they continued to distribute" promotional materials about specific compounded drugs. Violations of section 127(a) would not, however, have led to prosecution—instead, deviations from that provision would have removed FDAMA's special exception to new drug approval requirements, and pharmacists then would face the threat of prosecution only if they distributed drugs in violation of section 505(a) of the FDCA.[110] To put it another way, pharmacists were as free as anyone else to advertise the availability of particular drugs so long as they first satisfied product licensing requirements, and it is the failure to do the latter rather than the desire to do the former that would have triggered the risk of federal prosecution. These are subtle but potentially important differences—perhaps not likely to alter the Court's ultimate judgment in the case, but critical to appreciating the potentially radical consequences of its decision.[112]

Preliminarily, the majority pointed out that the government made no argument under *Central Hudson*'s first prong that the prohibited speech related to unlawful activity or was misleading. This threshold concession seems at least mildly curious. It violates federal law to sell an unapproved new drug. Before FDAMA carved out a limited exception for drugs compounded under certain circumstances, and notwithstanding the FDA's prior policy of turning a blind eye to the practice, pharmacists who sold unapproved new drugs technically violated federal law. After the Court struck down section 127(a) (advertising restriction and all), it again became a violation of federal law. In short, the underlying conduct (sale of an unapproved new drug, including one compounded in contravention of FDAMA's narrow safe harbor) represented an unlawful activity, so the government could freely prohibit any advertising about that activity. At most, section 127(a) posed an unconstitutional conditions problem insofar as it had predicated the availability of an exception to an existing legal requirement on the waiver of First Amendment rights. Without getting

---

110. Thus, if a pharmacy advertised that it would soon begin compounding a particular drug but subsequently decided not to bother, then it has violated no federal law. If it did compound the previously advertised product, then the pharmacy might face charges under the FDCA for selling an unapproved new drug, and the act of advertising would deprive it of an otherwise available defense under FDAMA § 127(a).

112. * * * [T]he FDA enforces its new drug approval requirements based on manufacturers' claims (including claims made in advertising) about the uses of their products, so the sale of a drug approved for one use but advertised for other uses would violate federal law. More generally, deciding whether a product qualifies as a "drug" as opposed to a less closely regulated product—i.e., device, food additive, food, dietary supplement, tobacco product, cosmetic, or entirely beyond the FDA's jurisdiction—depends on its "intended use" based primarily on the information communicated by the seller. If the FDA could no longer indirectly penalize commercial speech by subjecting the products described by such speech to more rigorous regulatory controls, then most erstwhile therapeutic products could escape agency licensure requirements altogether and face only the general prohibitions on misbranding that apply to all FDA-regulated products.

into that muddle, other than to point out that this doctrine seems out of place in commercial speech cases, one wonders why the government did not at least make this argument.

Instead, the government used existing requirements for product licensure—premised on a thorough evaluation of safety and effectiveness—as the basis for asserting that it had a substantial interest in limiting advertising about compounded drugs that had not undergone licensing. It then apparently made a tactical blunder, however, in offering another substantial government interest (at least as the majority explained it)—namely, that Congress wanted to ensure that patients with special needs could access compounded drugs. The problem, of course, is that this interest explained FDAMA's safe harbor rather than the advertising restriction in particular (indeed, it ran directly counter to the advertising restriction). This quandary forced the government to invoke a third substantial interest in finding a balance between its pair of competing interests, which the majority then could dismiss as a simple exercise in expediency and one readily accomplished by any number of less restrictive alternatives. If nothing else, the Court's evident confusion about the various interests asserted by the government indicates the importance of carefully delineating the nature and relative weightiness of the ends sought before judging the fit between those ends and the selected means of accomplishment.

Even accepting at face value the seemingly contrived—or unusually candid—account of the conflicting interests at stake, the majority's application of *Central Hudson*'s nexus prongs fares little better. It quibbled with the government's apparent assumption that advertising roughly coincided with the scale of operations and that advertised compounding of particular drugs would indicate activity on a large enough scale that testing for safety and effectiveness as a prelude to FDA licensure would not prove to be cost prohibitive. The agency does not, however, impose licensing requirements based on ability to pay. The FDA has prevented individual researchers (and patients in dire straits) from using investigational products even though they obviously lacked the financial wherewithal (and time) to secure approval. In addition, because even large pharmaceutical firms will have little incentive to develop products intended to treat rare conditions, Congress has crafted a number of incentives for so-called "orphan" drugs, but it has not waived normal NDA requirements in such situations.

Instead, as the FDA's earlier CPG on the subject had reflected, advertising of compounded products would provide one of several indicia that a pharmacist had crossed the line from professional service provider (engaged in extemporaneous customization to serve the genuine needs of a particular patient) to a commercial supplier no different from any other manufacturer (large or small) of pharmaceutical products who wanted to avoid the hassles associated with getting FDA permission. In short, it hardly seems crazy to take the position that the advertising restriction directly advanced the government's interest in ensuring that this narrow exception from federal licensure requirements did not swallow the rule (and the far weightier public health interests served by that rule relative to the arguably then attenuated countervailing interest in assisting patients with special needs who now would have greater access to compounded drugs even though unadvertised).

After expressing doubts under the third prong, the majority assumed for the sake of argument that the advertising restriction directly advanced the government's substantial interest(s). It then suggested that any number of non-speech-restrictive alternatives would serve those interests equally well. "First, it seems that the Government could use the very factors the FDA relied on to distinguish compounding from manufacturing in its 1992 Guide," presumably except for the first (advertising) factor. Congress, however, obviously must have felt that these factors did not quite do the trick. "It might even be sufficient to rely solely on the non-speech-related provisions of the FDAMA ...." Again, however, Congress evidently viewed the advertising restriction as a necessary additional limitation on the exception; indeed, the unappealed inseverability holding reinforces the notion that Congress regarded these various restrictions as an essential package. * * * The majority showed little evident appreciation of the practical limitations associated with its preferred regulatory options. Although mere ease of enforcement obviously would fail to justify an overbroad restriction on commercial speech, a carefully tailored restriction that facilitated compliance monitoring should not fail simply because harder to enforce non-speech alternatives might partly serve the government's purposes. * * *

As an exercise in constitutional jurisprudence, *Western States* hardly broke new ground, at least not superficially. The members of the Court evaluated the case using a well-worn form of intermediate scrutiny, differing in their respective assessments of whether the government had demonstrated a sufficient nexus between the means selected and its asserted interest in preventing the risks associated with the commercialization of unapproved new drugs under the guise of pharmacy compounding. The decision did stand out as the first time that the Supreme Court invalidated a recently enacted congressional restriction on advertising, thereby showing little deference to the judgments of a coordinate branch of government. It certainly solidified a trend evident during the previous decade of taking seriously the constitutional rights of entities wishing to engage in commercial speech, especially insofar as the Court *sub silentio* applied the unconstitutional conditions doctrine.

In some ways, the FDA's reaction to the Court's decision in *Western States* represented the most startling aspect of this litigation. Instead of a grudging response, the agency took it as an occasion to reconsider its entire approach to regulation. Less than three weeks after the Court announced its decision, the FDA published a notice inviting public comments on a series of questions that implied it might welcome suggestions favoring the deregulation of labeling and advertising. This represented a dramatic about-face for an agency that previously had taken the position that it need not concern itself with the First Amendment. Although perhaps an admirable act of self-examination, nothing ever came of the FDA's remarkable proposal to get out of the business of controlling the dissemination of information.

Western States has received scant attention from commentators. Only after cutting through the majority's simplistic description of (or perhaps failure to comprehend) the complex regulatory regime can one appreciate the potentially far-reaching consequences of the decision. Although the FDA's initial reaction to *Western States* came across as little more than a cynical political exercise, and the agency's subsequent inattention to the Supreme Court's broader command seemed entirely predictable, the robust version of commercial free speech doctrine that seems to prevail today could profoundly impinge upon the FDA's (and other agencies') preferred methods for promoting the public's health.

Medical technologies pose distinctive problems under the First Amendment. In contrast to vice products (such as alcohol, tobacco, and junk foods) that often attract the attention of courts and commentators, sellers of prescription drugs and devices do not direct their pitches to children (where one would expect a paternalistic response) or rely primarily on image advertising (or cartoon characters) to convey their messages. Although hardly dull, print and broadcast ads for this class of products communicate far more in the way of information than one finds in efforts to promote beer or fast food. Prescription restrictions also mean that laypersons cannot thoughtlessly act upon advertisements for the latest pharmaceutical product, and marketing geared toward the physician intermediaries who must authorize patient access confronts a far more sophisticated audience. In short, by dint of the nature of medical technologies, the mechanisms for accessing them, and the extensive regulations that currently govern their marketing, commercial speech in this area tends to be more information-laden than typical of other industries. * * *

Western States leaves outright prohibitions designed to dampen demand (or to serve other collateral purposes) vulnerable to constitutional invalidation, while more limited restrictions or disclosure requirements designed to guard against potentially misleading promotional messages would seem to survive. As the Court has made abundantly clear, however, "misleading" does not have a capacious meaning—if the concept encompassed fears that truthful information might "lead persons astray," then demand dampening to promote the public health would seem to pass muster. Instead, because "mislead" connotes a more limited concern about the potential for information to "deceive," the First Amendment allows the government to guard against the dissemination of false or deceptive commercial speech but not much else. * * *

The fundamental tension between the First Amendment and public health, already evident in other domains, seems to be even more pronounced in connection with the marketing of medical technologies. Perhaps this illuminates a central flaw in the Supreme Court's current approach to commercial speech cases insofar as its increasingly stringent application of *Central Hudson*'s nexus prongs has effectively narrowed the range of substantial government interests that can pass muster. Conversely, it might suggest that public health regulatory agencies have gone about their business in entirely the wrong way insofar as they prefer to manipulate the flow of information instead of directly tackling hazardous behaviors. Whatever the case, the tension between the First Amendment and efforts at public health promotion highlights the mistakes that might arise from importing either constitutional doctrine or regulatory policy designed for vice products when examining issues related to prescription pharmaceuticals and devices. Otherwise, we stand little chance of sensibly balancing public health promotion with the guarantees of free speech.

NOTES AND QUESTIONS

1. *Origins of the commercial speech doctrine.* Until the mid–1970s, commercial speech received no constitutional protection. As it happens, the first decision extending the First Amendment to such speech arose in a prescription drug advertising case. In *Virginia State Board of Pharmacy v. Virginia Citizens Consumer Council*, 425 U.S. 748 (1976), the Court struck down a state prohibition against the advertising of prescription drug prices because even such purely commercial speech, bereft of all the other qualities typically associated with protected speech, still deserved some constitutional protection. The Court noted that the public's interest in the free flow of commercial information might be "as keen, if not keener by far" than its interest in political debate, and it added that the information at issue could have a profound impact on the consumer's quality of life. See id. at 763–64 ("When drug prices vary as strikingly as they do, information as to who is charging what becomes more than a convenience. It could mean the alleviation of physical pain or the enjoyment of basic necessities."). In *Bolger v. Youngs Drug Products Corp.*, 463 U.S. 60 (1983), another early commercial speech decision, the Court held that a federal law prohibiting unsolicited mailings was unconstitutional when applied to a pharmaceutical company distributing informational pamphlets that encouraged the use of contraceptives, emphasizing that such materials—containing information related to public health matters—deserved a high degree of protection under the Constitution. See id. at 69. See generally Lars Noah, Liberating Commercial Speech: Product Labeling Controls and the First Amendment, 47 Fla. L. Rev. 63 (1995).

2. *Other unconstitutional conditions?* Another exception to the general prohibition against selling unapproved drugs allows the movement of an investigational new drug (IND) in interstate commerce so that the sponsor may conduct clinical trials necessary to secure approval. See 21 U.S.C. § 355(i). The exception forbids any advertising by IND sponsors. See 21 C.F.R. § 312.7(a) (2010); see also Natasha Singer, F.D.A. Aims at Doctors' Drug Pitches, N.Y. Times, Feb. 1, 2010, at B1 (reporting that, for the first time, the agency had sent a warning letter to a prominent dermatologist serving as an investigator of such a trial for running afoul of this restriction); cf. United States v. Endotec, Inc., 563 F.3d 1187, 1198–200 (11th Cir.2009) (explaining that the statutory "custom device" exemption from premarket approval requirements becomes inapplicable if the supplier advertises the availability of the unapproved medical device). Does *Western States* jeopardize this longstanding condition (even if it could not impose the restriction directly, can't the government extract such a restriction as a concession so long as it is germane to an interest that the government could pursue)? Cf. United States v. Caputo, 517 F.3d 935, 939 (7th Cir.2008) (calling it "a difficult question" where a product manufacturer "struck a bargain with the FDA in the approval process by promising to limit its promotion").

3. *Dampening consumer demand.* How would the now-defunct policy against any advertising of Schedule II drugs to consumers have fared under the Court's test? See Matthew N. Strawn, Comment, Recent Developments in Direct Consumer Advertising of Attention Disorder Stimulants and Creating Limits to Withstand Constitutional Scrutiny, 19 J. Contemp. Health L. & Pol'y 495, 500–03 (2003) (explaining that, until 2001, a "gentlemen's agreement" between the federal government and the pharmaceutical industry, based on a provision in an international convention that the U.S. had signed, prohibited DTCA of these controlled substances); id. at 512–20 (arguing that the government could craft legislation restricting such advertising without running afoul of the First Amendment, though not taking into account the Supreme Court's decision in *Western States*). How about the rule against disseminating so-called "reminder ads" in print if the FDA has mandated a "black box" warning for a product, 21 C.F.R. § 202.1(e)(2)(i)? In 2007, Congress considered bills that would have given the agency the power to impose a moratorium on consumer advertising of certain new Rx drugs during their first couple of years on the market—would that have survived a First Amendment challenge (would Justice Breyer's dissent for four members of the Court in *Western States* clearly sustain such a restriction; does the majority's rejection of his analysis necessarily forecast its invalidity)? See Noah, supra, 21 Health Matrix at 85–89; see also David C. Vladeck, The Difficult Case of Direct-to-Consumer Drug Advertising, 41 Loy. L.A. L. Rev. 259 (2007); cf. Margaret Gilhooley, Drug Safety and Commercial Speech: Television Advertisements and Reprints on Off-Label Uses, 47 San Diego L. Rev. 845 (2010).

4. *Drug advertising by attorneys.* What about personal injury lawyers who, in the course of searching for clients, make claims to laypersons about the dangers associated with therapeutic products. See Lars Noah, Platitudes About "Product Stewardship" in Torts: Continuing Drug Research and Education, 15 Mich. Telecomm. & Tech. L. Rev. 359, 377 & n.75 (2009) ("[P]laintiffs' lawyers do their share of tacky (and potentially hazardous) direct advertising to users of such products, though they would not have to fear tort claims brought by patients who discontinued a prescribed (and still net beneficial) course of treatment ... in response to exaggerated risk information appearing in ads trolling for clients."). Imagine that a state disciplinary board issued a rule to guard against the adverse public health consequences of attorneys exaggerating the risks associated with still-marketed prescription drugs, perhaps demanding that such ads include the following statement (as some already do voluntarily): "Never stop taking any medication before asking your doctor." Is that constitutional? Unlike pharmacists who want to advertise compounded drugs, lawyers who engage in drug-related advertising do not contemplate any sale of a product, which means that the case law governing professional speech (or product disparagement) would govern the analysis.

5. *State and local interference with commercial speech.* San Francisco once considered prohibiting any print advertisements in bus shelters of drugs for the treatment of AIDS because of concerns that they conveyed an overly optimistic message about their safety and effectiveness and may undermine efforts to encourage safer sex. See John Ritter, Ads Linked to Rise in Rate of HIV Infections: City Considers Ban on Drug Billboards, USA Today, Apr. 6, 2001, at 4A; see also Sabin Russell, Deceptive AIDS Ads Must Stop, FDA Says, S.F. Chron., Apr. 28, 2001, at A1 (reporting that the agency sent warning letters to companies). Florida recently banned all advertising of controlled substances by pain clinics as part of a new law already challenged on constitutional grounds. See Bob LaMendola, Crackdown Leaves Pain Clinics Hurting, Ft. Laud. Sun Sent., Oct. 2, 2010, at 1D. How would such restrictions fare under the First Amendment?

6. *Data mining.* A handful of states have attempted to prohibit prescription data mining by drug companies seeking to better target advertising to physicians. See David Orentlicher, Prescription Data Mining and the Protection of Patients' Interests, 38 J.L. Med. & Ethics 74 (2010); Michael Heesters, Comment, An Assault on the Business of Pharmaceutical Data Mining, 11 U. Pa. J. Bus. L. 789 (2009); Christopher Lee, Doctors, Legislators Resist Drugmakers' Prying Eyes, Wash. Post, May 22, 2007, at A1; cf. Duff Wilson, Drug App Comes Free, Ads Included, N.Y. Times, July 29, 2011, at B1 (discussing Epocrates, a popular smartphone app that provides medical professionals with searchable drug information alongside targeted promotional messages). The industry mounted First Amendment challenges to these laws. See Alexander D. Baxter, Note, IMS Health v. Ayotte: A New Direction on Commercial Speech Cases, 25 Berkeley Tech. L.J. 649 (2010); Jennifer L. Klocke, Comment, Prescription Records for Sale: Privacy and Free Speech Issues Arising from the Sale of De-identified Medical Data, 44 Idaho L. Rev. 511 (2008); cf. Brienne T. Greiner, Note, A Tough Pill to Swallow: Does the First Amendment Prohibit WV from Regulating Pharmaceutical Companies' Advertising Expenses to Lower the Cost of Prescription Drugs?, 109 W. Va. L. Rev. 107 (2006). Note that these states had not restricted detailing but only sought to make it harder for company sales reps to tailor their pitches based on knowledge about any particular physician's prescribing behavior.

In *Sorrell v. IMS Health Inc.*, 131 S.Ct. 2653 (2011), the Court invalidated Vermont's law on First Amendment grounds, emphasizing that the state had imposed a restriction on the creation and dissemination of information based on its content and speaker without adequate justification: "Vermont may be displeased that detailers who use prescriber-identifying information are effective in promoting [more expensive and allegedly less safe] brand-name drugs.... The State may not burden the speech of others in order to tilt public debate in a preferred direction." Id. at 2671. The three dissenters objected to the majority's use of heightened scrutiny to assess legislation that only indirectly affected commercial speech, noting that the FDA and other agencies routinely impose content- and speaker-based restrictions. See id. at 2677–78 (Breyer, J., dissenting) ("If the Court means to create constitutional barriers to regulatory rules that might affect the content of a commercial message, it has embarked upon an unprecedented task—a task that threatens significant judicial interference with widely accepted regulatory activity."); id. at 2682–83 ("Vermont's attempts to ensure a 'fair balance' of information is no different from the FDA's similar requirement .... No one has yet suggested that substantial portions of federal drug [advertising] regulation are unconstitutional."); see also id. at 2679 ("By inviting courts to scrutinize whether a state's legitimate regulatory interests can be achieved in less restrictive ways whenever they touch (even indirectly) upon commercial speech, today's majority risks repeating the mistakes of the past ...."); id. at 2685 (fearing that the majority "reawakens *Lochner*'s pre-New Deal threat of substituting judicial for democratic decisionmaking where ordinary economic regulation is at issue"). After this decision, how might state laws limiting the value of drug company gifts to physicians fare? Are FDA restrictions on prescription drug advertising (apart from those designed to guard against potentially false and misleading messages) now vulnerable under the First Amendment? In *Western States*, the Court had focused on the constitutionality of prohibitions against promotional efforts directed toward laypersons; in *Sorrell*, the Court addressed the constitutionality of restrictions on industry advertising directed to physicians only obliquely. More than a decade earlier, however, lower federal courts had struggled with those very questions.

Washington Legal Foundation v. Friedman

13 F.Supp.2d 51 (D.D.C.1998).

■ Lamberth, District Judge:

Plaintiff Washington Legal Foundation (WLF) is a non-profit public interest law and policy center that defends "the rights of individuals and businesses to go about their affairs without undue influence from government regulators." In this action, WLF seeks to enjoin the Food and Drug Administration (FDA) and the Department of Health and Human Services (HHS) from enforcing policies restricting certain forms of manufacturer promotion of off-label uses for FDA-approved drugs and devices. The policies at issue—expressed through Guidance Documents—concern manufacturer distribution of reprints of medical textbooks and peer-reviewed journal articles ("enduring materials"), and manufacturer involvement in continuing medical education seminars and symposia ("CME"). * * *

FDA's first contention—that the Guidance Documents are a restraint upon conduct and not upon speech—may be addressed quickly. There is little question that the relevant "conduct" is the off-label prescription of drugs by physicians. The distribution of enduring materials and sponsorship of CME seminars addressing and encouraging that conduct is speech. * * * [T]he activities at issue in this case are only "conduct" to the extent that moving one's lips is "conduct," or to the extent that affixing a stamp and distributing information through the mails is "conduct." * * * This court is hard pressed to believe that the agency is seriously contending that "promotion" of an activity is conduct and not speech, or that "promotion" is entitled to no First Amendment protection. There may certainly be a "line" between education and promotion as regards a drug manufacturer's marketing activities, but that is the line between pure speech and commercial speech, not between speech and conduct. * * *

The FDA next asserts that the speech regulated by the Guidance Documents falls outside of the ambit of the First Amendment because of the federal government's extensive power to regulate the pharmaceutical industry * * * * First, the argument that a certain subset of speech may be considered completely outside of the First Amendment framework because the speech occurs in an area of extensive government regulation is a proposition whose continuing validity is at best questionable in light of the Supreme Court's most recent commercial speech cases. See Central Hudson Gas & Elec. Corp. v. Public Serv. Comm'n of New York, 447 U.S. 557 (1980). * * * Any lingering doubt as to whether the government may impose restrictions upon speech without offending the First Amendment merely because it has the authority to regulate the underlying activity was resolved in *44 Liquormart, Inc. v. Rhode Island*, 517 U.S. 484 (1996). In that case, the Supreme Court expressly rejected the concept embodied in *Posadas de Puerto Rico Assoc. v. Tourism Co. of Puerto Rico*, 478 U.S. 328 (1986), that because the government had the power to extensively regulate in a certain area (casino gambling) it also had the authority to regulate speech without raising First Amendment concerns. * * *

Having concluded that manufacturer distribution of enduring materials and suggesting content or speakers for CME seminars in which the focus is on the sponsor's product is properly classified as commercial speech, this court will now analyze the constitutionality of the Guidance Documents under *Central Hudson*'s four-prong test.

1. The Speech Is Neither Unlawful Nor Inherently Misleading.

* * * In claiming that the speech at issue involves "illegal activities," the FDA does not seriously press any argument that off-label prescriptions are illegal. Rather, the agency directs attention to the statutory basis for the Guidance Documents and asserts that the speech cannot survive the first prong of the *Central Hudson* test because a drug or device is considered to be misbranded as a matter of law if it is promoted by the manufacturer for an off-label use. Therefore, when a manufacturer disseminates information about a drug product that diverges from the treatments included on the label, that manufacturer may be engaged in misbranding, which is illegal. However, the tautological nature of this argument exposes its shortcomings. * * *

It is clear that when the Supreme Court declares that the First Amendment does not protect illegal activity, it is referring to the conduct that the speech is promoting (e.g., prostitution, counterfeiting, narcotic use, and the like), and not the speech subject to the restriction. Therefore, only at such time as off-label prescriptions are proscribed by law could the FDA legitimately claim that speech at issue addresses "illegal activities."

Whether the speech subject to the restrictions in the Guidance Documents is truthful and non-misleading presents a somewhat closer question. Notably, speech that is merely "potentially misleading" does not render it able to be proscribed under the commercial speech test without further analysis. * * * In order to end the *Central Hudson* analysis on the first prong, the speech must be "inherently misleading" * * * *

In asserting that any and all scientific claims about the safety, effectiveness, contraindications, side effects, and the like regarding prescription drugs are presumptively untruthful or misleading until the FDA has had the opportunity to evaluate them, FDA exaggerates its overall place in the universe. It is certainly the case that by statute, no drug may be introduced or delivered into interstate commerce without FDA approval, and that the claims that a manufacturer may make about a drug through labeling, advertising and other forms of promotion are subject to FDA regulatory authority. However, the conclusions reached by a laboratory scientist or university academic and presented in a peer-reviewed journal or textbook, or the findings presented by a physician at a CME seminar are not "untruthful" or "inherently misleading" merely because the FDA has not yet had the opportunity to evaluate the claim. * * *

To categorize the speech at issue here as "inherently misleading" is particularly unsupportable when one considers all the controls available to FDA to ensure that the information manufacturers wish to distribute is scientifically reliable * * * * These controls would greatly circumscribe the possibility that untruthful or misleading information would be disseminated by manufacturers. This court finds that the Guidance Documents address speech that is directed toward lawful activity and that is not misleading. Therefore, the first prong of the *Central Hudson* test is satisfied.

2. The Government's Interest Is Substantial.

Under *Central Hudson*, the second inquiry is whether the interest asserted by the government is substantial. The Supreme Court has consistently held that the government has a substantial interest in protecting the health and safety of its citizens. There are few, if any, more important functions performed by any regulatory agency than the function this case concerns—ensuring that when a citizen takes a prescription drug, that individual has absolute assurance that the product is safe and effective for the condition for which his physician has prescribed it. Any claim that the government's general interest is insufficient under *Central Hudson* is frivolous.

Within the general category of promoting health and safety, the government describes two more specific interests: 1) ensuring that physicians receive accurate and unbiased information so that they may make informed prescription choices, and 2) providing manufacturers with ample incentive to get previously unapproved uses on label. As one of these interests is legitimate and the other is not, they will be considered separately.

a. The Government Cannot Justify the Guidances out of the Fear that Information Will Be Misused by Physicians.

* * * The agency claims that "most physicians, well-educated and experienced though they may be, do not have the resources, experience, or education to critically evaluate evidence concerning off-label uses. While physicians may believe that they are in a better position than FDA to evaluate off-label claims, both the evidence and the law say otherwise." To the extent that the FDA is endeavoring to keep information from physicians out of concern that they will misuse that information, the regulation is wholly and completely unsupportable.

If there is one fixed principle in the commercial speech arena, it is that "a State's paternalistic assumption that the public will use truthful, nonmisleading commercial information unwisely cannot justify a decision to suppress it." *44 Liquormart*, 517 U.S. at 497; see also id. at 503 ("The First Amendment directs us to be especially skeptical of regulations that seek to keep people in the dark for what the government perceives to be their own good"). To endeavor to support a restriction upon speech by alleging that the recipient needs to be shielded from that speech for his or her own protection, which is the gravamen of FDA's claim here, is practically an engraved invitation to have the restriction struck.

In this instance, the government's notion that the scientific research product which the manufacturers seek to distribute needs to be withheld for the "good of the recipient" is even more unsupportable than usual. First, it must be noted that the manufacturers are not seeking to distribute this information to the general consumer public, who likely lack the knowledge or sophistication necessary to make informed choices on the efficacy of prescription drugs. Rather, they seek to disseminate this information exclusively to physicians. A physician's livelihood depends upon the ability to make accurate, life-and-death decisions based upon the scientific evidence before them. They are certainly capable of critically evaluating journal articles or textbook reprints that are mailed to them, or the findings presented at CME seminars. Furthermore, the FDA does not question a physician's evaluative skills when an article about an off-label use appears among a group of articles in the *New England Journal of Medicine*, or when one physician refers a peer physician to a published article he recently perused, or even when a physician requests a reprint from a manufacturer. Why the ability of a doctor to critically evaluate scientific findings depends upon how the article got into the physician's hands, or whether a manufacturer suggests speakers or content for a CME seminar, is unclear to this court.

In light of the fact that the Supreme Court has repeatedly rejected governmental attempts to equate less information with better decision-making, and in light of the fact that the FDA does not question a physician's evaluative skills when the information comes from a source other than a drug manufacturer, concerns about a physician's ability to critically evaluate materials presented to him is not a "substantial interest."

b. The Government Does Have a Substantial Interest in Compelling Manufacturers to Get Off–Label Treatments On–Label.

The other substantial interest that the regulations purportedly advance is that they provide an incentive for manufacturers to go through the strict FDA preclinical and clinical trial process to get off-label uses on-label. As explained previously, defendants have proved to this court's satisfaction that dissemination of scientific information on off-label uses is an effective means of influencing physicians to prescribe a drug for a given condition. Consequently, the dissemination of information demonstrating that a drug is effective has a positive effect upon sales of the drug. But, if the manufacturer's ability to disseminate any information on a new use for a previously approved drug is made wholly contingent upon FDA approval of that use, the manufacturer will be encouraged, if not compelled, to obtain FDA approval.

Plaintiff appears to take issue with the idea that the government has a substantial interest in requiring manufacturers to get new uses for previously approved drugs on-label. They assert that off-label uses are on the whole beneficial to the public health, contending that "the ability to prescribe off-label is essential to saving patients' lives." They cite the large number of off-label prescriptions written by physicians every year, and again state that, even by FDA's own admissions, off-label treatments may constitute the standard of care for some conditions. In sum, plaintiff argues that "the fact that a use is off-label rather than on-label has no necessary correlation to the benefits of that use." * * *

However, whether compelling manufacturers to get new uses on-label is wise government policy when considered against the backdrop of present day medical realities, financial constraints and procedural burdens is a policy question that must be addressed to Congress, not to this court. Congress has concluded that it benefits the public health to require manufacturers to get all uses approved by the FDA. The Supreme Court has held that the approval requirement is not subject to exceptions based upon the difficulty of obtaining approval, the cost, or even the conceded benefits of the unapproved use. In light of the fact that Congress has declared that all uses for a drug must be proven safe and effective by the FDA, and has recently reaffirmed that position through the 1997 Food and Drug Amendments, this court finds that this interest—that off-label uses of previously approved drugs are subjected to the FDA's evaluation process—is of sufficient importance so as to constitute a "substantial government interest" as contemplated by *Central Hudson*.

3. The Guidance Documents Directly Advance a Substantial Government Interest in Requiring Manufacturers to Submit Supplemental Applications to Obtain Approval for New Uses.

Under the *Central Hudson* test, commercial speech restrictions must advance the government's interest in "a direct and material way." * * * It is clear that manufacturers have incentives to circumvent subsequent approval requirements, but one wonders what incentives they have to obtain them? For a brand-new drug, the incentive is simple: the pharmaceutical company cannot manufacture or introduce the drug into interstate commerce without FDA approval. However, the drugs subject to off-label prescriptions are already in interstate commerce, so the obvious restriction on conduct is unavailable.

Therefore, one of the few mechanisms available to FDA to compel manufacturer behavior is to constrain their marketing options; i.e. control the labeling, advertising and marketing. If a manufacturer is proscribed from distributing enduring materials and/or sponsoring CME seminars that address that manufacturer's product absent FDA approval of that use, that proscription provides a strong incentive to get the use on-label, in light of the connection between marketing and sales. Because the restrictions on the distribution of enduring materials and involvement with CME do provide an incentive for manufacturers to have previously approved drugs evaluated by the FDA for safety and effectiveness for an off-label use, this court finds that the restrictions in the Guidance Documents directly advance a substantial interest.

4. The Guidance Documents Are Unconstitutional Because They Are More Extensive than Necessary.

While commercial speech jurisprudence does not require the government to employ the least restrictive means of advancing an interest, the regulating body must make an effort to reasonably fit its means to its end sought. A commercial speech restriction will fail if it burdens "substantially more speech than necessary." United States v. Edge Broad. Co., 509 U.S. 418, 430 (1993). The court finds that the restrictions in the Guidance Documents are considerably more extensive than necessary to further the substantial government interest in encouraging manufacturers to get new uses on-label.

This determination is based in large part upon the fact that there exist less-burdensome alternatives to this restriction on commercial speech. The most obvious alternative is full, complete, and unambiguous disclosure by the manufacturer. Full disclosure not only addresses all of the concerns advanced by the FDA, but addresses them more effectively. It is less restrictive on speech, while at the same time deals more precisely with the concerns of the FDA and Congress.

First, it assuages concerns that the message communicated is inherently or potentially misleading, or that a physician would be deceived or misled by the speech. That the use discussed therein had not been approved by the FDA would be readily apparent. A physician would be immediately alerted to the fact that the "substantial evidence standard" had not been satisfied, and would evaluate the communicated message accordingly. And, the failure to provide such disclosure would render the communication subject to the full battery of FDA enforcement options, because not including such disclosure when required would clearly render the materials "inherently misleading."

Second, permitting this limited form of manufacturer communication still leaves more than adequate incentives compelling drug manufacturers to get new uses approved by the FDA. As plaintiffs noted at oral argument, it is a very narrow form of manufacturer communication upon which this court is ruling in enjoining enforcement of the Guidance Documents. There still are enormous differences between the permitted marketing of on-label as opposed to off-label uses. Manufacturers still are proscribed from producing and distributing any internally-produced marketing materials to physicians concerning off-label uses, or from involvement with seminars not conducted by an "independent program provider." Nor may the drug companies initiate person-to-person contact with a physician about an off-label use. Nor may they advertise off-label uses for previously approved drugs directly to the consumer. If a manufacturer wishes to engage in any of these or other marketing techniques, it cannot do so without first obtaining FDA approval of the off-label use. The fact that these adequate incentives still exist to get off-label treatments on-label is central to this court's finding that the First Amendment is violated by the Guidance Documents. Were manufacturers permitted to engage in all forms of marketing of off-label treatments, a different result might be compelled.

Third, to the extent that physicians look to FDA approval as an important (or the exclusive) indication of safety and effectiveness, and either will not prescribe or are reluctant to prescribe absent such approval, manufacturers will seek to obtain FDA approval to make their products more appealing to that market. And, to the extent that the tort regime looks to FDA approval as the definition of the "standard of care," the call to get new uses on-label will come from sources other than the FDA.

Fourth, the court must again note that off-label prescriptions, presently legal, do constitute the most effective treatment available for some conditions. Through the government's well-intentioned efforts to prevent misleading information from being communicated, a great deal of truthful information will also be embargoed. In this case, the truthful information may be life saving information, or information that makes a life with a debilitating condition more comfortable. Finally, this alternative comports with the Supreme Court's preference for combating potentially problematic speech with more speech. * * *

NOTES AND QUESTIONS

1. *Rulemaking vs. adjudication*. Before commercial speech enjoyed constitutional status, lower courts had rejected First Amendment objections to FDA *enforcement* actions seizing books that were used as product labeling.

See United States v. Articles of Drug * * * Century Food Co., 32 F.R.D. 32 (S.D.Ill.1963); United States v. 8 Cartons * * * Molasses, 103 F.Supp. 626, 627 (W.D.N.Y.1951). Then, just as the Supreme Court began to extend protections to commercial speech, the FDA started to utilize its authority to issue rules of general application as a more efficient means for exercising control than engaging in case-by-case enforcement of the broad substantive restrictions on product marketing set forth in the statute. The confluence of these two developments raised significant questions about the constitutionality of the FDA's promulgation of broad-based, prophylactic rules designed to reduce the potential for the dissemination of misleading information to consumers and health care professionals. See John Kamp et al., FDA Marketing v. First Amendment: Washington Legal Foundation Legal Challenges to Off–Label Policies May Force Unprecedented Changes at FDA, 54 Food & Drug L.J. 555 (1999).

This question was first broached in the early 1990s, in connection with the FDA's sweeping new rules governing the labeling of food and dietary supplements, especially restrictions on the use of health claims. In *Pearson v. Shalala*, 164 F.3d 650 (D.C.Cir.1999), the court invalidated some of these on First Amendment grounds because the FDA had declined to allow the use of disclaimers as a more tailored response to the potential for misleading consumers than the outright suppression of any unapproved health claims. See id. at 655–59; see also Alliance for Natural Health U.S. v. Sebelius, 714 F.Supp.2d 48 (D.D.C.2010) (ordering the FDA to allow, with appropriate disclaimers, various anti-cancer claims for dietary supplements containing selenium). The appellate court in *Pearson* also suggested, as had Judge Lamberth in his *WLF* opinion, that adjudication may be more apt a procedure than rulemaking for dealing with these issues. Although case-by-case, after-the-fact enforcement—as done, for instance, by the FTC—is typically less efficient than broad-based, prospective rulemaking, the First Amendment may demand such a more particularized regulatory approach, especially given the risk of obsolescence where rules are predicated on evolving scientific information about dietary practices or therapeutic interventions. After *WLF*, when raised in the context of agency enforcement actions against off-label promotion, lower courts have rejected First Amendment defenses. See United States v. Caronia, 576 F.Supp.2d 385, 393–402 (E.D.N.Y.2008); United States v. Caputo, 288 F.Supp.2d 912, 920–22 (N.D.Ill.2003), aff'd on other grounds, 517 F.3d 935, 939–40 (7th Cir. 2008) (suggesting possible merit to the avoided constitutional objections).

2. *Commercial vs. scientific speech.* Some commentators have argued that therapeutic information disseminated by drug and device manufacturers deserves more constitutional protection than simple product advertising. See Martin H. Redish, Product Health Claims and the First Amendment: Scientific Expression and the Twilight Zone of Commercial Speech, 43 Vand. L. Rev. 1433 (1990); Glenn C. Smith, Avoiding Awkward Alchemy in the Off–Label Drug Context and Beyond: Fully–Protected Independent Research Should Not Transmogrify into Mere Commercial Speech Just Because Product Manufacturers Distribute It, 34 Wake Forest L. Rev. 963 (1999). Judge Lamberth rejected this argument as follows:

> Typical "commercial speech" is authored and/or uttered directly by the commercial entity that wishes to financially benefit from the message. A purveyor of goods or services makes claims about his products in order to induce a purchase. In this instance, by contrast, the speech that the manufacturers wish to "communicate" is the speech of others—the work product of scientists, physicians and other academics. It is beyond dispute that when considered outside of the context of manufacturer promotion of their drug products, CME seminars, peer-reviewed medical journal articles and commercially-available medical textbooks merit the highest degree of constitutional protection. Scientific and academic speech reside at the core of the First Amendment. Plaintiff claims that because this speech merits full protection when uttered by a scientist or academic, the level of constitutional scrutiny should not change merely because a corporation wishes to enhance the distribution of that message.... Through distributing enduring materials and sponsoring CME seminars, drug manufacturers call a physician's attention to the subject drug product, showing that the drug effectively treats a certain condition (emphasize a desirable quality) in the hopes that the physician will prescribe (buy or patronize) the drug. The fact that an effective means for accomplishing that goal is through providing the academic research results generated by others does not mean that the activity is not an "advertisement." ... Were pharmaceutical manufacturers attempting to provide free yearly subscriptions to the Journal of American Medicine, or seeking to support CME regardless of whether their products would ultimately be addressed, a different conclusion might be compelled, as the speech would be closer to a public service. But, as long as the manufacturer seeks to disseminate information centered upon its product, this prong of the test is satisfied.

WLF v. Friedman, 13 F.Supp.2d at 62–64. Shouldn't it make a difference that this challenge nominally had been mounted by the intended recipients (i.e., physicians) rather than the suppliers (i.e., product manufacturers) of the information?

What if the FDA had decided instead to treat as promotional labeling or advertising any articles published in peer-reviewed journals and authored by academic scientists when they endorse an off-label use of a product manufactured by the company that had sponsored the research (but did nothing further to disseminate it)? See J. Howard Beales, III, Economic Analysis and the Regulation of Pharmaceutical Advertising, 24 Seton Hall L. Rev. 1370, 1395 n.111 (1994) ("[I]f financial support from a pharmaceutical manufacturer converts speech at scientific meetings into promotional pieces, it would appear to suffice to make journal articles by those same people promotional pieces as well."); David A. Kessler & Wayne L. Pines, The Federal Regulation of Prescription Drug Advertising and Promotion, 264 JAMA 2409, 2409–10 (1990) (explaining that the FDA "has defined its authority in this area to cover virtually any material issued by or sponsored by a drug manufacturer," but adding that "[a] person with no ties to a drug manufacturer can say anything he or she wants about a drug"); see also Barry Meier & Duff Wilson, Spine Experts Repudiate Medtronic Studies, N.Y. Times, June 29, 2011, at B1 (reporting controversy over studies published by researchers with financial ties to the manufacturer of Infuse® (a bioengineered bone growth product approved by the FDA for certain types of spinal fusion) that allegedly understated its risks and advocated off-label uses); cf. FDA, Compliance Policy Guide No. 7132b.17 (Aug. 15, 1989) (declining to treat independently-authored articles as drug labeling or advertising). Isn't that essentially how the FDA's policy on sponsored CME operates? Would it violate the First Amendment for the agency to take enforcement action against drugs or devices misleadingly described in published articles based on research underwritten by the manufacturer? For a skeptical analysis of the constitutionality of the FDA's restrictions on direct and indirect promotion of off-label uses to physicians in the wake of *Western States*, see Lars Noah, Truth or Consequences?: Commercial Free Speech vs. Public Health Promotion (at the FDA), 21 Health Matrix 31, 68–84 (2011). Chapter 7(B)(3) revisits some of these issues in connection with the imposition of tort liability for failure to warn.

3. *Continuation of the WLF litigation.* As mentioned earlier, FDAMA included a provision giving drug and device companies greater (though still limited) freedom to distribute enduring materials. After further briefing, Judge Lamberth held that this part of the statute also violated the First Amendment. See WLF v. Henney, 56 F.Supp.2d 81 (D.D.C.1999). The district court's analysis suffered from serious flaws. For instance, Judge Lamberth's earlier conclusion that the government lacked a substantial interest in protecting health care providers from misleading information makes little sense. See, e.g., David C. Radley et al., Off-label Prescribing Among Office–Based Physicians, 166 Archives Internal Med. 1021, 1025 (2006) (finding "that about 21% of all estimated uses for commonly prescribed medications were off-label, and that 15% of all estimated uses lacked scientific evidence of therapeutic efficacy"); see also Mitchell Oates, Note, Facilitating Informed Medical Treatment Through Production and Disclosure of Research into Off-label Uses of Pharmaceuticals, 80 N.Y.U. L. Rev. 1272 (2005). Instead, because physicians are a sophisticated audience, measures short of broadly prohibiting such communications rendered the FDA's original policies vulnerable under the final (nexus) prong of the commercial speech test (as Judge Lamberth noted in discussing disclaimers), but FDAMA's more carefully drawn limitations might have survived on that score.

Nonetheless, the Justice Department lawyer (and former Deputy FDA Commissioner) who argued the case on appeal offered a fanciful interpretation of the relevant FDAMA provision as creating no directly enforceable restrictions but instead a "safe harbor," suggesting that a company not moored in this safe harbor might still not run afoul of the pre-existing limitations on off-label promotion. Somewhat remarkably the court took the bait when it decided to dismiss the appeal and lift most of the injunction. See WLF v. Henney, 202 F.3d 331 (D.C.Cir.2000); see also WLF v. Henney, 128 F.Supp.2d 11, 15 (D.D.C.2000) (concluding that nothing remained of the injunction). Although perhaps a plausible characterization of the agency's earlier guidance documents, this reading seemingly ignored the effect of FDAMA's provision making violations a distinct "prohibited act" under the statute that could trigger the imposition of sanctions (in stark contrast, as noted earlier, to FDAMA's restriction on advertising by pharmacies that engaged in compounding), and it also disregarded the practical consequences of any such safe harbor. Judge Lamberth understood those realities when, in the first phase of the litigation, he had rejected the FDA's claim that the challenge to the draft policy statement wasn't ripe for judicial review (recall from Chapter 1(D)(3) that he had speculated that the FDA would "threaten[] (but never actually initiat[e]) enforcement procedures against companies which failed to comply with the agency's *de facto* policy"). Such a scenario would render hollow the D.C. Circuit's assurance that companies would remain free to raise their constitutional objections in subsequent enforcement actions. See 202 F.3d at 336 n.6.

4. *Further commentary*. See Margaret Gilhooley, Constitutionalizing Food and Drug Law, 74 Tul. L. Rev. 815 (2000); Lars Noah, What's Wrong with "Constitutionalizing Food and Drug Law"?, 75 Tul. L. Rev. 137 (2000); Edmund Polubinski, III, Note, Closing the Channels of Communication: A First Amendment Analysis of the FDA's Policy on Manufacturer Promotion of "Off–Label" Use, 83 Va. L. Rev. 991 (1997); Symposium, The First Amendment in Food and Drug Law, 58 Food & Drug L.J. 299 (2003); Symposium, Marketing Health: The Growing Role of Commercial Speech Doctrine in FDA Regulation, 37 Am. J.L. & Med. 203 (2011).

PROBLEM #6. *STRETCHING THE FIRST AMENDMENT*

Emboldened by the recent decisions striking down statutory provisions and agency rules limiting the dissemination of therapeutic product information, the Nonprescription Drug Manufacturers Alliance (NDMA) has asked you about challenging the FDA's OTC drug labeling restrictions on First Amendment grounds. In particular, your client objects to the agency's prohibition against making any therapeutic claims that have not yet been approved in the applicable monograph or in a separate NDA. See 21 C.F.R. § 330.1(c)(2). For instance, when information about the advantages of using aspirin to reduce the risk of heart attacks first came to light in the 1980s, manufacturers could not make any cardio-protective claims in their labeling without running afoul of the FDA's rules. Only when the agency issued part of its monograph for internal analgesics a decade later could manufacturers provide "professional labeling" (essentially a package insert for physicians) that mentioned this use. See 63 Fed. Reg. 56,802, 56,814–15 (1998) (codified at 21 C.F.R. § 343.80) (allowing references to the use of aspirin in reducing the risk of stroke in patients who have had transient ischemia of the brain due to fibrin platelet emboli, and for reducing the risk of death and/or nonfatal myocardial infarction (MI) in patients with a previous infarction or unstable angina pectoris or a suspected acute MI). The FDA does not, however, allow any such labeling claims directed to consumers, see id. at 56,808–09, and it has proposed requiring a label warning that consumers should check with their physicians before using aspirin-containing OTC products for such a purpose. See 58 Fed. Reg. 54,224 (1993) (to be codified at 21 C.F.R. § 201.314(i)). What are your prospects for success in mounting such a constitutional challenge?

United States v. An Article ... "Hubbard Electrometer"

333 F.Supp. 357 (D.D.C.1971).

■ GESELL, DISTRICT JUDGE:

This is an action by the United States seeking nationwide condemnation of a gadget known as an E-meter and related writings * * * * This suit was originally tried to a jury before another judge of this court and the conviction there obtained was reversed on appeal after a long trial because of certain First Amendment problems suggested by the instructions and evidentiary rulings. See Founding Church of Scientology v. United States, 409 F.2d 1146 (D.C.Cir.1969). The present trial was conducted to the court without a jury * * * *

The E-meter is essentially a simple galvanometer using two tin cans as electrodes. It is crude, battery-powered, and designed to measure electrical skin resistance. It is completely harmless and ineffective in itself. A person using the meter for treatment holds the tin cans in his hands during an interview with the operator who is known as an auditor and who purports to read indicators from the galvanometer needle as it notes reactions to questions. * * *

L. Ron Hubbard, writing in a science fiction magazine in the 1940s, first advanced the extravagant false claims that various physical and mental illnesses could be cured by auditing. He played a major part in developing Scientology. Thereafter, commencing in the early 1950s, numerous Scientology books and pamphlets were written explaining how various illnesses can be and had been cured through auditing. These materials were widely distributed. Hubbard, who wrote much of the material, is a facile, prolific author and his quackery flourished throughout the United States and in various parts of the world. He was supported by other pamphleteers and adherents who also promoted the practice of Scientology and touted its alleged benefits.

Hubbard and his fellow Scientologists developed the notion of using an E-meter to aid auditing. Substantial fees were charged for the meter and for auditing sessions using the meter. They repeatedly and explicitly represented that such auditing effectuated cures of many physical and mental illnesses. An individual processed with the aid of the E-meter was said to reach the intended goal of "clear" and was led to believe there was reliable scientific proof that once cleared many, indeed most illnesses would automatically be cured. Auditing was guaranteed to be successful. All this was and is false—in short, a fraud. Contrary to representations made, there is absolutely no scientific or medical basis in fact for the claimed cures attributed to E-meter auditing.

Unfortunately the government did not move to stop the practice of Scientology and a related "science" known as Dianetics when these activities first appeared and were gaining public acceptance. Had it done so, this tedious litigation would not have been necessary. The government did not sue to condemn the E-meter until the early 1960s, by which time a religious cult known as the Founding Church of Scientology had appeared. This religion, formally organized in 1955, existed side-by-side with the secular practice of Scientology. Its adherents embrace many of Hubbard's teachings and widely disseminate his writings. The Church purports to believe that many illnesses may be cured through E-meter auditing by its trained ministers through an appeal to the spirit or soul of a man. As a matter of formal doctrine, the Church professes to have abandoned any contention that there is a scientific basis for claiming cures resulting from E-meter use. The Church, however, continued widely to circulate Scientology literature * * * , which hold[s] out false scientific and medical promises of certain cure for many types of illnesses.

In 1962, when the government seized the E-meters involved in the present controversy, it took them from the premises of the Church, confiscating some E-meters which were actually then being used primarily by ministers of the Church to audit adherents or to train auditors for subsequent church activity. Thus the government put itself in the delicate position of moving against not only secular uses of the E-meter but other uses purporting to be religious, and the court accordingly confronts the necessity of reconciling the requirements of the [FDCA] prohibiting misbranding and the requirements of the First Amendment protecting religious institutions and religious beliefs from governmental interference under the First Amendment.

The court of appeals has ruled that the evidence at the prior trial and reintroduced at this trial established prima facie that the Founding Church of Scientology, the principal claimant here, is a bona fide religion and that the auditing practice of Scientology and accounts of it are religious doctrine. No evidence to the contrary was offered by the government on the second trial. Accordingly, for purposes of this particular case only, claimant must be deemed to have met its burden of establishing First Amendment standing for whatever significance the religious practice of Scientology may have on the outcome of this particular litigation. * * *

[I]t must first be determined whether the E-meter is a device within the meaning of the Act. It obviously meets the statutory definition of an apparatus or contrivance intended for use in the diagnosis, cure, mitigation or treatment of disease. Moreover, it is held out as such in the constant promotion of E-meter auditing, a process designed to effectuate cures of mental and physical illnesses. Claimants contend that the E-meter is harmless in itself, cures nothing by itself, and therefore cannot be a device since those who use it appreciate its ineffectiveness and cannot therefore have the requisite intent. This begs the question. The device plays a key part in both the secular and religious auditing process which is used and intended to be used in the cure, mitigation or treatment of disease. It need not be the only agent in an allegedly curative process to be a device within the definition. The E-meter is a device within the meaning of the Act.

Over 100 E-meters were seized. At the same time the government seized some 200 separate pieces of literature containing approximately 20,000 pages, much of which it now contends demonstrates misbranding of the device by misrepresentation and lack of adequate directions for use under 21 U.S.C. §§ 334 and 352. The writings seized were located in a bookstore, or "Distribution Center," separately incorporated but owned by the Church, with offices in the basement of the Church premises. The Center advertised and sold for profit a long list of Scientology, Dianetics and other writings concerned with auditing in book, pamphlet, newsletter and other forms.

A few of these writings are primarily religious in nature. Others contain medical or scientific claims in a partially religious context. Most of the material, however, explains aspects of Scientology and Dianetics in purely matter-of-fact medical and scientific terms without any apparent religious reference. While the court of appeals concluded that literature setting forth the theory of auditing, including the claims for curative efficacy contained therein, is religious doctrine and hence as a matter of law not labeling, it recognized this was so only if the person charged with misrepresentation explicitly held himself out as making religious as opposed to medical, scientific or otherwise secular claims. The bulk of the material is replete with false medical and scientific claims devoid of any religious overlay or reference. * * * Thus the literature has all the necessary elements of labeling specified in 21 U.S.C. § 321(m) since it "accompanied" the device within the meaning of the Act. * * *

A single false scientific non-religious label claim is sufficient to support condemnation, and in fact there are many. Moreover, differentiation of individual documents as a practical matter is of little value when it comes to an overall resolution of the controversy. Realistically, the writings cannot only be viewed separately. They are available and distributed in infinite combinations. Whole books are involved which often ramble, contradict and are constructed to make diversified appeals that are basically secular and directed to varying temperaments, ages and attitudes of potential readers. Much of the material is skillful propaganda designed to make Scientology and E-meter auditing attractive in many varied, often inconsistent wrappings.

The food and drug laws are designed to protect the public. The literature disseminated by various Scientology groups is written for popular lay consumption. The words and thrust of the writings must accordingly be so considered. Claims as to the efficacy of the E-meter must be read to mean what they clearly purport to say to ordinary lay readers. The court notes that the task of determining whether a claim or representation is religious or non-religious, or whether a religious claim is genuine or merely "tacked on" to basically pseudo-scientific claims, is hardly less troublesome than the task of determining whether a religious claim is true or false. The court has attempted to resolve the difficulty thus presented by the court of appeals by refusing to consider the truth or falsity of any claim which, in the understanding of the average reader, could be construed as resting on religious faith. All doubts on this issue have been resolved in favor of the claimants. But the overall effect of the many separate writings and the writings as a whole cannot be seriously questioned. Whether the documents are viewed singly or as a whole, the proof showed that many false scientific claims permeate the writings and that these are not even inferentially held out as religious, either in their sponsorship or context.

It should be kept in mind at all times that the Church is but one of several groups engaged in the promotion of Scientology; others include the Hubbard Guidance Center, that offers non-religious processing and auditing to the public for a fee; Hubbard Association of Scientologists International (HASI), a world-wide organization promoting Scientology among members of the organization who receive a monthly magazine ("Ability") and other benefits; and the Distribution Center, Inc., already mentioned. The combined effort of all these activities is to persuade the public to come forward for auditing with an E-meter for a fee, and while some may be motivated or attracted by religious considerations, others who audit or are audited are not.

An individual was not required to be either a Church member or a Scientologist to be audited at cost of $500 for 25 hours, with state of "clear" guaranteed for $5,000. The E-meter was available for sale to the public for a fee of $125. The benefits of auditing were extravagantly advertised. At the time this action was commenced, E-meters—perhaps as many as one-third the total supply—were being used by members of the public without any religious control or supervision. The writings were distributed to accompany the E-meter and intended to promote its use by members of the public; they were used by laymen for secular purposes; individually a great many contain false unqualified scientific claims without even a religious overlay or suggestion. Viewed as a whole the thrust of the writings is secular, not religious. The writings are labeling within the meaning of the Act. Thus, the E-meter is misbranded and its secular use must be condemned along with secular use of the offensive literature as labeling. The misbranding results not only from misrepresentation by reason of 21 U.S.C. § 352(a) but because the labeling failed to bear adequate directions for use required by 21 U.S.C. § 352(f)(1).

On the basis of these findings, the government is entitled to some relief. It is only when the court confronts the question of appropriate remedy that serious difficulties arise. * * * A law designed to afford protection to the public against genuine evils may be used to regulate the activities of religion only if the regulation involved is the narrowest possible remedy to achieve the legitimate non-religious end, which in this case is only to protect the public against misrepresentation since the E-meter is harmless in itself. * * *

The literature held to make false representations, while in itself non-religious, nevertheless comprises for some, part of the writings, teachings, and history of a religion. Those who belong to the Church and accept its beliefs assert that many illnesses may be alleviated by religious counseling designed to free the spirit of encumbrances. They find in the rationale and procedures of Scientology satisfactory early explanations and techniques to implement what is essentially faith healing by use of the E-meter. Thus they purport to read the purely secular writings of Scientology with semantic interpretations fostered by their evolving religious doctrine. Purely scientific statements are given a theological slant by the initiated and the occasional theological indications in the writings are given enthusiastic exaggeration. What the layman reads as straight science fiction becomes to the believer a bit of early imperfect scripture. The result of all this is that what may appear to the layman as a factual scientific representation (clearly false) is not necessarily this at all when read by one who has embraced the doctrine of the Church.

Accordingly, the government's protestations that it is not interfering with religious practice when it seeks to condemn the E-meter and related literature must be qualified. The Church is a religious institution protected by the First Amendment. The E-meter is used by its ministers as part of the ritual and practice of the Church. Serious interference indeed results if the Church is entirely prohibited from using the E-meter by condemnation or if the court orders the Food and Drug Administration to oversee a general rewriting of all the writings the Church purveys. Where there is a belief in a scientific fraud there is nonetheless an interference with the religion that entertains that belief if its writings are censored or suppressed. Similarly, if a church uses a machine harmless in itself to aid its ministers in communicating with adherents, the destruction of that machine intrudes on religion. The dilemma cannot be resolved by attempting to isolate purely false scientific claims from claims that have sufficient religious content to be outside the food and drug laws. There is a religious substance to everything when seen with the eyes of the believer.

For these reasons, the Church may not be wholly prevented from practicing its faith or from seeking new adherents. A decree of condemnation which ordered destruction of the device, with its necessary res judicata effect as to all E-meters in the country, would achieve this effect. On the other hand, a condemnation decree which allowed the FDA to reform the writings as is done in the usual commercial drug misbranding case would give a government agency excessive power to interfere with the exercise of religion, fostering that government "entanglement" with religion which has been recently condemned by the Supreme Court. Neither of these possible remedies is acceptable to the court.

Had the government proceeded in equity to enjoin specific non-religious practices or representations which it believed to violate the Act, the court could have curtailed the purely commercial use of the E-meter while leaving the Church free to practice its belief under limited circumstances. An action in rem, however, acts only upon the device, and the court cannot fashion a remedy in libel which distinguishes with particularity between religious and non-religious uses. An equity proceeding is clearly the most satisfactory remedy in this and any similar future cases, and may in some instances be the only remedy which the government may seek consistent with the First Amendment.

Dismissal of this libel after eight years of legal proceedings is not justified on the grounds that the government has not used the most appropriate remedy. A decree of condemnation will therefore be entered, but the Church and others who base their use upon religious belief will be allowed to continue auditing practices upon specified conditions which allow the Food and Drug Administration as little discretion as possible to interfere in future activities of the religion. Pursuant to 21 U.S.C. § 334(d), upon the findings and conclusions contained in this Memorandum Opinion, relief in the following form shall be set out in an implementing order: * * *

The device may be used or sold or distributed only for use in bona fide religious counseling. No user, purchaser or distributee (other than the Founding Church of Scientology or an ordained practicing minister of the Church) shall be considered engaged in bona fide religious counseling unless and until such user, purchaser or distributee has filed an affidavit with the Secretary of the Food and Drug Administration stating the basis on which a claim of bona fide religious counseling is made, together with an undertaking to comply with all conditions of the judgment so long as the E-meter is used.

The device should bear a prominent, clearly visible notice warning that any person using it for auditing or counseling of any kind is forbidden by law to represent that there is any medical or scientific basis for believing or asserting that the device is useful in the diagnosis, treatment or prevention of any disease. It should be noted in the warning that the device has been condemned by a United States District Court for misrepresentation and misbranding under the food and drug laws, that use is permitted only as part of religious activity, and that the E-meter is not medically or scientifically capable of improving the health or bodily functions of anyone. Each user, purchaser, and distributee of the E-meter shall sign a written statement that he has read such warning and understands its contents and such statements shall be preserved.

Any and all literature which refers to the E-meter or to auditing, including advertisements, distributed directly or indirectly by the seller or distributor of the E-meter or by anyone utilizing or promoting the use of the E-meter, should bear a prominent notice printed in or permanently affixed to each item or such literature, stating that the device known as a Hubbard Electrometer, or E-meter, used in auditing, has been condemned by a United States District Court on the grounds that the literature of Dianetics and Scientology contains false and misleading claims of a medical or scientific nature and that the E-meter has no proven usefulness in the diagnosis, treatment or prevention of any disease, nor is it medically or scientifically capable of improving any bodily function. Where the notice is printed in or affixed to literature, it should appear either on the outside front cover or on the title page in letters no smaller than 11–point type. * * *

NOTES AND QUESTIONS

1. *Free exercise.* The appellate court had reversed the original judgment in this case because it thought that the Supreme Court's free exercise decisions dictated a narrow interpretation of the term "labeling" when it related to the practice of religion:

> [T]he E-meter has been condemned, not because it is itself harmful, but because the representations made concerning it are "false or misleading." And the largest part of those representations is contained in the literature of Scientology describing the process of auditing which appellants have claimed, without contest from the government, is part of the doctrine of their religion and central to its exercise. Thus if their claims to religious status are accepted, a finding that the seized literature misrepresents the benefits from auditing is a finding that their religious doctrines are false. To construe the Food, Drug and Cosmetic Act to permit such a finding would, in the light of *United States v. Ballard*, 322 U.S. 78 (1944), present the gravest constitutional difficulties.... Were the literature here introduced clearly secular, we might well conclude that under existing law it constituted "labeling" for purposes of the Act. Such a conclusion might be justified by a broad reading of the statute, consistent with its high purpose of protecting the public health and pocketbook against health frauds. However, such broad readings are not favored when they impinge upon constitutionally sensitive areas, especially in the absence of a showing of legislative intent to regulate these areas. Nothing in the history or interpretation of the Act indicates that it was meant to deal with the special problem of religious healing, a problem often given legislative treatment separate from that imposed upon the general area of public health and medical practice. In light of these considerations, highlighted by the explicit holding of *Ballard*, we interpret the Act as not including within its concept of "labeling" the literature developing the doctrines of a religion.

Founding Church of Scientology v. United States, 409 F.2d 1146, 1156–57, 1159–60 (D.C.Cir.1969); see also Sheldon R. Shapiro, Annotation, Regulation Under Federal Food, Drug, and Cosmetic Act as Affected by Religious Guarantees of First Amendment, 13 A.L.R. Fed. 747 (1972).

Note, however, that subsequent decisions of the Supreme Court eroded the protections afforded the free exercise of religion in holding that the clause does not require that laws of general application provide special exceptions. See Employment Div. v. Smith, 494 U.S. 872, 879 (1990) (rejecting free exercise claim by Native American employee fired after ingesting peyote, a Schedule I hallucinogenic substance); see also Olsen v. DEA, 878 F.2d 1458 (D.C.Cir.1989) (sustaining the agency's refusal to exempt from the Controlled Substances Act the religious use of marijuana by members of the Ethiopian Zion Coptic Church). Would the Church have more success today by asserting a free speech claim instead? Or could it use the Religious Freedom Restoration Act, which Congress enacted in an effort to resurrect the strict scrutiny previously recognized under free exercise clause? See, e.g., Gonzales v. O Centro Espírita Beneficente União do Vegetal, 546 U.S. 418 (2006) (holding that the government had failed to demonstrate that its asserted interest in the uniform application of the CSA was sufficiently compelling to justify a prohibition on the sacramental use of hoasca, a tea containing the Schedule I hallucinogen dimethyltryptamine, in part because the federal government has long made an exception for the use of peyote by Native Americans).

2. *The tax man cometh.* A different federal agency became a thorn in the side of the Church, rejecting its claims for tax-exempt status, as well as tax deductions claimed by persons who spent money on auditing, because the IRS viewed these as primarily commercial rather than religious activities. The courts upheld these determinations. See Hernandez v. Commissioner, 490 U.S. 680 (1989); Church of Scientology of California v. Commissioner, 823 F.2d 1310 (9th Cir.1987). See generally Janet Reitman, Inside Scientology: The Story of America's Most Secretive Religion (2011); Paul Horwitz, Scientology in Court: A Comparative Analysis and Some Thoughts on Selected Issues in Law and Religion, 47 DePaul L. Rev. 85 (1997); Mark Oppenheimer, Weird, Sure. A Cult, No, Wash. Post, Aug. 5, 2007, at B2.

3. *Conscientious objectors.* "More than a dozen states are considering new laws to protect health workers who do not want to provide care that conflicts with their personal beliefs, a surge of legislation that reflects the intensifying tension between asserting individual religious values and defending patients' rights." Rob Stein, Health Workers' Choice Debated: Proposals Back Right Not to Treat, Wash. Post, Jan. 30, 2006, at A1 (adding that "[m]ost states have long had laws to protect doctors and nurses who do not want to perform abortions from being fired, disciplined or sued"). One bioethicist speculated that, under at least some of these broad proposals, physicians "could refuse to notify parents that their child was due for a chicken pox inoculation because the vaccine was originally produced using fetal tissue cell cultures." Id. More concretely, as previously noted in connection with the controversy over the OTC switch of Plan B (Chap. 4(A)(1)), pharmacists have refused to fill prescriptions for contraceptive products, and several states enacted laws to combat this behavior. Would such state legislation present any constitutional concerns? See Stormans, Inc. v. Selecky, 586 F.3d 1109, 1127–42 (9th Cir.2009) (vacating a preliminary injunction after finding little merit in a free exercise challenge to a new state rule, promulgated in response to reports of individual pharmacists' refusals to dispense Plan B on moral or religious grounds, that required pharmacies to dispense FDA-approved drugs without discriminating among patients); Noel E. Horton, Comment, Article I, Section 11: A Poor "Plan B" for Washington's Religious Pharmacists, 85 Wash. L. Rev. 739 (2010). How do the issues differ when pharmacies refuse to stock other types of drugs on other grounds? Cf. Marc Kaufman, Painkillers Understocked in Minority Areas, Wash. Post, Oct. 14, 2005, at A4.

4. *Free speech redux.* Wholly apart from the free exercise concerns, does the district court's order present free speech problems (and is the speech that the order interferes with just commercial)? Is it in fact accurate to say that "the E-meter is not ... capable of improving the health or bodily functions of anyone"? Does such a definitive conclusion, to borrow Judge Lamberth's wonderfully sarcastic phrase, exaggerate the FDA's "overall place in the universe"? In *Bradley v. Weinberger* (Chap. 4(A)(2)), could the sellers have argued that the agency's requirement for an unqualified warning in the labeling of all oral hypoglycemic drugs amounted to coerced speech in violation of the First Amendment? Many years later, the Church of Scientology exercised its rights to free speech when it mounted publicity campaigns attacking psychotropic drugs. See Thomas M. Burton, Medical Flap: Anti–Depression Drug of Eli Lilly Loses Sales After Attack by Sect, Wall St. J., Apr. 19, 1991, at A1; Michael Tackett, Scientologist Campaign Shakes Drug Firm, Advertising Industry, Chi. Trib., June 30, 1991, at 17.

Conant v. Walters

309 F.3d 629 (9th Cir.2002).

■ SCHROEDER, CHIEF JUDGE:

* * * The federal government promulgated its policy in 1996 in response to initiatives passed in both Arizona and California decriminalizing the use of marijuana for limited medical purposes and immunizing physicians from prosecution under state law for the "recommendation or approval" of using marijuana for medical purposes. See Cal. Health & Safety Code § 11362.5. The federal policy declared that a doctor's "action of recommending or prescribing Schedule I controlled substances is not consistent with the 'public interest' (as that phrase is used in the federal Controlled Substances Act)" and that such action would lead to revocation of the physician's registration to prescribe controlled substances. * * * The policy also said that the DOJ and the HHS would send a letter to practitioner associations and licensing boards informing those groups of the policy. The federal agencies sent a letter two months later to national, state, and local practitioner associations outlining the Administration's position ("Medical Leader Letter"). The Medical Leader Letter cautioned that physicians who "intentionally provide their patients with oral or written statements in order to enable them to obtain controlled substances in violation of federal law ... risk revocation of their DEA prescription authority." * * *

[T]here was substantial agreement between the parties as to what doctors could and could not do under the federal law. The government agreed with plaintiffs that revocation of a license was not authorized where a doctor merely discussed the pros and cons of marijuana use. The [district] court went on to observe that the plaintiffs agreed with the government that a doctor who actually prescribes or dispenses marijuana violates federal law. The fundamental disagreement between the parties concerned the extent to which the federal government could regulate doctor-patient communications without interfering with First Amendment interests. * * *

The dispute in the district court in this case focused on the government's policy of investigating doctors or initiating proceedings against doctors only because they "recommend" the use of marijuana. While the government urged that such recommendations lead to illegal use, the district court concluded that there are many legitimate responses to a recommendation of marijuana by a doctor to a patient. * * * For example, the doctor could seek to place the patient in a federally approved, experimental marijuana-therapy program. Alternatively, the patient upon receiving the recommendation could petition the government to change the law. By chilling doctors' ability to recommend marijuana to a patient, the district court held that the prohibition compromises a patient's meaningful participation in public discourse. * * *

On appeal, the government first argues that the "recommendation" that the injunction may protect is analogous to a "prescription" of a controlled substance, which federal law clearly bars. We believe this characterizes the injunction as sweeping more broadly than it was intended or than as properly interpreted. If, in making the recommendation, the physician intends for the patient to use it as the means for obtaining marijuana, as a prescription is used as a means for a patient to obtain a controlled substance, then a physician would be guilty of aiding and abetting the violation of federal law. * * *

A doctor's anticipation of patient conduct, however, does not translate into aiding and abetting, or conspiracy. A doctor would aid and abet by acting with the specific intent to provide a patient with the means to acquire marijuana. Similarly, a conspiracy would require that a doctor have knowledge that a patient intends to acquire marijuana, agree to help the patient acquire marijuana, and intend to help the patient acquire marijuana. Holding doctors responsible for whatever conduct the doctor could anticipate a patient might engage in after leaving the doctor's office is simply beyond the scope of either conspiracy or aiding and abetting. * * *

The government policy does, however, strike at core First Amendment interests of doctors and patients. An integral component of the practice of medicine is the communication between a doctor and a patient. Physicians must be able to speak frankly and openly to patients. That need has been recognized by the courts through the application of the common law doctor-patient privilege. See Fed.R.Evid. 501.

The doctor-patient privilege reflects "the imperative need for confidence and trust" inherent in the doctor-patient relationship and recognizes that "a physician must know all that a patient can articulate in order to identify and to treat disease; barriers to full disclosure would impair diagnosis and treatment." Trammel v. United States, 445 U.S. 40, 51 (1980). The Supreme Court has recognized that physician speech is entitled to First Amendment protection because of the significance of the doctor-patient relationship. See Planned Parenthood of S.E. Pa. v. Casey, 505 U.S. 833, 884 (1992) (plurality) (recognizing physician's First Amendment right not to speak); Rust v. Sullivan, 500 U.S. 173, 200 (1991) (noting that regulations on physician speech may "impinge upon the doctor-patient relationship"). * * * Being a member of a regulated profession does not, as the government suggests, result in a surrender of First Amendment rights. To the contrary, professional speech may be entitled to "the strongest protection our Constitution has to offer." Florida Bar v. Went For It, Inc., 515 U.S. 618, 634 (1995). * * *

The government's policy in this case seeks to punish physicians on the basis of the content of doctor-patient communications. Only doctor-patient conversations that include discussions of the medical use of marijuana trigger the policy. Moreover, the policy does not merely prohibit the discussion of marijuana; it condemns expression of a particular viewpoint, i.e., that medical marijuana would likely help a specific patient. Such condemnation of particular views is especially troubling in the First Amendment context. "When the government targets not subject matter but particular views taken by speakers on a subject, the violation of the First Amendment is all the more blatant." Rosenberger v. Rector, 515 U.S. 819, 829 (1995). Indeed, even content-based restrictions on speech are "presumptively invalid." R.A.V. v. St. Paul, 505 U.S. 377, 382 (1992). * * *

The government relies upon *Rust* and *Casey* to support its position in this case. However, those cases did not uphold restrictions on speech itself. *Rust* upheld restrictions on federal funding for certain types of activity, including abortion counseling, referral, or advocacy. In *Casey*, a plurality of the Court upheld Pennsylvania's requirement that physicians' advice to patients include information about the health risks associated with an abortion and that physicians provide information about alternatives to abortion. The plurality noted that physicians did not have to comply if they had a reasonable belief that the information would have a "severely adverse effect on the physical or mental health of the patient," and thus the statute did not "prevent the physician from exercising his or her medical judgment." The government's policy in this case does precisely that. * * *

In this case, the record is replete with examples of doctors who claim a right to explain the medical benefits of marijuana to patients and whose exercise of that right has been chilled by the threat of federal investigation. The government even stipulated in the district court that a "reasonable physician would have a genuine fear of losing his or her DEA registration to dispense controlled substances if that physician were to recommend marijuana to his or her patients." * * * Throughout this litigation, the government has been unable to articulate exactly what speech is proscribed, describing it only in terms of speech the patient believes to be a recommendation of marijuana. Thus, whether a doctor-patient discussion of medical marijuana constitutes a "recommendation" depends largely on the meaning the patient attributes to the doctor's words. This is not permissible under the First Amendment. * * *

■ KOZINSKI, CIRCUIT JUDGE (concurring):

* * * [F]or me the fulcrum of this dispute is not the First Amendment right of the doctors. That right certainly exists and its impairment justifies the district court's injunction for the reasons well explained by Chief Judge Schroeder. But the doctors' interest in giving advice about the medical use of marijuana is somewhat remote and impersonal; they will derive no direct benefit from giving this advice, other than the satisfaction of doing their

jobs well. At the same time, the burden of the federal policy the district court enjoined falls directly and personally on the doctors: By speaking candidly to their patients about the potential benefits of medical marijuana, they risk losing their license to write prescriptions, which would prevent them from functioning as doctors. In other words, they may destroy their careers and lose their livelihoods.

This disparity between benefits and burdens matters because it makes doctors peculiarly vulnerable to intimidation; with little to gain and much to lose, only the most foolish or committed of doctors will defy the federal government's policy and continue to give patients candid advice about the medical uses of marijuana. Those immediately and directly affected by the federal government's policy are the patients, who will be denied information crucial to their well-being, and the State of California, whose policy of exempting certain patients from the sweep of its drug laws will be thwarted. In my view, it is the vindication of these latter interests—those of the patients and of the state—that primarily justifies the district court's highly unusual exercise of discretion in enjoining the federal defendants from even investigating possible violations of the federal criminal laws.

In 1996, the people of California, acting by direct initiative, adopted a narrow exemption from their laws prohibiting the cultivation, sale and use of marijuana. The exemption applies only to patients whose physicians recommend or prescribe the drug for medical purposes. To those unfamiliar with the issue, it may seem faddish or foolish for a doctor to recommend a drug that the federal government finds has "no currently accepted medical use in treatment in the United States," 21 U.S.C. § 812(b)(1)(B). But the record in this case, as well as the public record, reflect a legitimate and growing division of informed opinion on this issue. A surprising number of health care professionals and organizations have concluded that the use of marijuana may be appropriate for a small class of patients who do not respond well to, or do not tolerate, available prescription drugs. * * *

At about the time the IOM [Institute of Medicine] study got underway, the British House of Lords—a body not known for its wild and crazy views—opened public hearings on the medical benefits and drawbacks of cannabis. Like the IOM, the Lords concluded that "cannabis almost certainly does have genuine medical applications, especially in treating the painful muscular spasms and other symptoms of MS and in the control of other forms of pain." * * * In June 2001, Canada promulgated its Marihuana Medical Access Regulations after an extensive study of the available evidence. The new regulations allow certain persons to cultivate and possess marijuana for medical use, and authorize doctors to recommend and prescribe marijuana to patients who are suffering from severe pain, muscle spasms, anorexia, weight loss or nausea, and who have not found relief from conventional therapies. Numerous other studies and surveys support the use of medical marijuana in certain limited circumstances. * * *

The total number of states that have approved marijuana for medical purposes now stands at nine. The evidence supporting the medical use of marijuana does not prove that it is, in fact, beneficial. There is also much evidence to the contrary, and the federal defendants may well be right that marijuana provides no additional benefit over approved prescription drugs, while carrying a wide variety of serious risks. What matters, however, is that there is a genuine difference of expert opinion on the subject, with significant scientific and anecdotal evidence supporting both points of view. For the great majority of us who do not suffer from debilitating pain, or who have not watched a loved one waste away as a result of AIDS-induced anorexia, it doesn't much matter who has the better of this debate. But for patients suffering from MS, cancer, AIDS or one of the other afflictions listed in the IOM report, and their loved ones, obtaining candid and reliable information about a possible avenue of relief is of vital importance.

It is well established that the right to hear—the right to receive information—is no less protected by the First Amendment than the right to speak. Indeed, the right to hear and the right to speak are flip sides of the same coin. As Justice Brennan put it pithily, "It would be a barren marketplace of ideas that had only sellers and no buyers." This does not mean, however, that the right to speak and the right to listen always carry the same weight when a court exercises its equitable discretion. In this case, for instance, it is perfectly clear that the harm to patients from being denied the right to receive candid medical advice is far greater than the harm to doctors from being unable to deliver such advice. While denial of the right to speak is never trivial, the simple fact is that if the injunction were denied, the doctors would be able to continue practicing medicine and go on with their lives more or less as before. It is far different for patients who suffer from horrible disabilities * * * * Enforcement of the federal policy will cut such patients off from competent medical advice and leave them to decide on their own whether to use marijuana to alleviate excruciating pain, nausea, anorexia or similar symptoms. But word-of-mouth and the Internet are poor substitutes for a medical doctor; information obtained from chat rooms and tabloids cannot make up for the loss of individualized advice from a physician with many years of training and experience.

A few patients may be deterred by the lack of a doctor's recommendation from using marijuana for medical purposes, but I suspect it would be very few indeed, because the penalties under state law for possession of small amounts of the drug are trivial. A far more likely consequence is that, in the absence of sound medical advice, many patients desperate for relief from debilitating pain or nausea would self-medicate, and wind up administering the wrong dose or frequency, or use the drug where a physician would advise against it. Whatever else the parties may disagree about, they agree that marijuana is a powerful and complex drug, the kind of drug patients should not use without careful professional supervision. The unintended consequence of the federal government's policy—a policy no doubt adopted for laudable reasons—will be to dry up the only reliable source of advice and supervision critically ill patients have, and drive them to use this powerful and dangerous drug on their own.

Which points to the second important interest impaired by the federal government's policy: California's interest in legalizing the use of marijuana in certain limited circumstances, so that critically ill patients may use it if and only if it is medically advisable for them to do so. The state relies on the recommendation of a state-licensed physician to define the line between legal and illegal marijuana use. The federal government's policy deliberately undermines the state by incapacitating the mechanism the state has chosen for separating what is legal from what is illegal under state law. * * *

Nor does the state have another mechanism available to distinguish lawful from unlawful conduct. The state law in question does not legalize use of marijuana by anyone who believes he has a medical need for it. Rather, state law is closely calibrated to exempt from regulation only patients who have consulted a physician. And the physician may only recommend marijuana when he has made an individualized and bona fide determination that the patient is within the small group that may benefit from its use. If medical doctors are unable or unwilling to make this determination because they fear losing their DEA registration, there is no one who can take their place. Nurses and paramedics aren't qualified to do it, which is why they don't have authority to write prescriptions in the first place. Lawyers, judges and police can't do it, except by asking the advice of physicians. State administrators can't do it. If doctors are taken out of the picture—as the federal policy clearly aims to do—the state's effort to withdraw its criminal sanctions from marijuana use by the small group of patients who could benefit from such use is bound to be frustrated. * * *

If a doctor abuses this privilege by recommending marijuana without examining the patient, without conducting tests, without considering the patient's medical history or without otherwise following standard medical procedures, he will run afoul of state as well as federal law. But doctors who recommend medical marijuana to patients after complying with accepted medical procedures are not acting as drug dealers; they are acting in their professional role in conformity with the standards of the state where they are licensed to practice medicine. The doctor-patient relationship is an area that falls squarely within the states' traditional police powers. The federal government may not force the states to regulate that relationship to advance federal policy. * * *

It may well be, as our opinion holds, that interference with the rights of doctors to speak is sufficient to support the district court's injunction. Nevertheless, it remains a significant step for a court to enjoin the prosecution and even investigation of what federal officials believe may be a violation of federal law. In affirming the district court, I therefore find comfort in knowing that the interests of the patients, and those of the state, provide significant additional support for the district court's exercise of discretion.

NOTES AND QUESTIONS

1. *Semantics*. Why had the plaintiffs conceded that state law could not authorize a physician to prescribe a drug that the federal government classifies as Schedule I—does the act of providing a patient with a prescription not qualify as speech? And doesn't the concurring opinion convincingly demonstrate that the California law uses the term "recommendation" as a synonym for "prescription" rather than its more usual connotation (e.g., a suggestion)? Cf. United States v. Nazir, 211 F.Supp.2d 1372, 1375 (S.D.Fla. 2002) ("[T]he word prescription in [21 U.S.C.] § 353(b)(1), in common parlance, means only a bona fide order—i.e., directions for the preparation and administration of a medicine, remedy, or drug for a real patient who actually needs it after some sort of examination or consultation by a licensed doctor—and does not include pieces of paper by which physicians are directing the issuance of a medicine, remedy, or drug to patients who do not need it, persons they have never met, or individuals who do not exist."). Does the concurring opinion persuade you that the federal policy threatens to intrude on states' rights to regulate the practice of medicine? For more on issues of physician speech, see Robert Post, Informed Consent to Abortion: A First Amendment Analysis of Compelled Physician Speech, 2007 U. Ill. L. Rev. 939; Whitney D. Pile, Note, The Right to Remain Silent: A First Amendment Analysis of Abortion Informed Consent Laws, 73 Mo. L. Rev. 243 (2008); Lauren R. Robbins, Comment, Open Your Mouth and Say "Ideology": Physicians and the First Amendment, 12 U. Pa. J. Const. L. 155 (2009).

2. *Physician prescribing of Schedule II controlled substances*. The DEA has threatened to revoke registrations of physicians who engage in off-label uses of certain Schedule II drugs. First, when it down-scheduled synthetic tetrahydrocannabinol (THC), the principal psychoactive component in marijuana, the agency prohibited any use beyond the FDA's approved labeling for the treatment of nausea in cancer patients. See 51 Fed. Reg. 17,476, 17,477 (1986). More recently, as part of an effort to undercut Oregon's Death with Dignity Act, the DEA threatened to sanction physicians who assist in the suicide of terminally-ill patients using Schedule II drugs approved by the FDA for other purposes. See Robert Steinbrook, Physician–Assisted Suicide in Oregon: An Uncertain Future, 346 New Eng. J. Med. 460 (2002); see also Lars Noah, Challenges in the Federal Regulation of Pain Management Technologies, 31 J.L. Med. & Ethics 55, 61 (2003) (pointing out that the DEA seemed more willing than the FDA to prevent off-label prescribing). The Supreme Court invalidated this policy as exceeding the bounds of the authority delegated to the Attorney General. See Gonzales v. Oregon, 546 U.S. 243 (2006); id. at 270 ("[The CSA] manifests no intent to regulate the practice of medicine generally. The silence is understandable given the structure and limitations of federalism .... The structure and operation of the CSA presume and rely upon a functioning medical profession regulated under the states' police powers."); id. at 275 ("The government, in the end, maintains that the prescription requirement delegates to a single Executive officer the power to effect a radical shift of authority from the states to the federal government to define general standards of medical practice in every locality.... Congress did not have this far-reaching intent to alter the federal-state balance ...."); see also Ronald A. Lindsay et al., Hastened Death and the Regulation of the

Practice of Medicine, 22 Wash. U. J.L. & Pol'y 1 (2006); Marc Kaufman, Assisted–Suicide Ruling May Affect Painkiller Cases, Wash. Post, Jan. 22, 2006, at A4. See generally Herbert Hendin & Kathleen Foley, Physician–Assisted Suicide in Oregon: A Medical Perspective, 106 Mich. L. Rev. 1613 (2008); Emily P. Hughes, Note, The Oregon Death with Dignity Act: Relief of Suffering at the End of Medicine's Ability to Heal, 95 Geo. L.J. 207 (2006).

3. *Consequences for FDA restrictions on medical practice.* Do these recent controversies over direct federal interference with physicians suggest that constitutional precepts might imperil FDA rules that indirectly constrain physician authority?

> The conventional wisdom holds that the federal government has absolutely no business regulating medical professionals. As a descriptive claim, such a view coincides with the historical record fairly well: states have taken the lead in supervising health care professionals, and the federal government generally has seen little need to meddle in the field and risk antagonizing organized medicine. As a constitutional matter, however, such a view misses the mark. Although the Supreme Court has made it clear that states enjoy broad authority to regulate health care professionals, the states do not enjoy the exclusive jurisdiction to do so. The repeated federal expressions of deference to professional medical autonomy are rooted in politics rather than constitutional law. Notwithstanding the recent federalism revival, modern medicine has become big business, with interstate aspects that fit within even the narrower interpretation of the Commerce Clause. Finally, as a normative matter, the conventional wisdom sweeps too broadly. Although recent federal intrusions into the practice of medicine look questionable as a matter of policy, regulatory initiatives that interfere with the freedom of physicians in other less politically charged settings may have a great deal to commend themselves as a matter of policy. For instance, efforts to protect patients by limiting the distribution of hazardous prescription drugs should not founder on an exaggerated preoccupation with the rights of either states or physicians.

Lars Noah, Ambivalent Commitments to Federalism in Controlling the Practice of Medicine, 53 U. Kan. L. Rev. 149, 192–93 (2004).

Federal Register / Vol. 65, No. 247 / Friday, December 22, 2000 / Proposed Rules 81125

HIGHLIGHTS OF PRESCRIBING INFORMATION

CAPOTEN® TABLETS ▼℞
(captopril tablets)

> **WARNING: USE IN PREGNANCY**
> **When used in pregnancy during the second and third trimesters, ACE inhibitors can cause injury and even death to the developing fetus.** When pregnancy is detected, CAPOTEN should be discontinued as soon as possible. See WARNINGS/PRECAUTIONS: Fetal/Neonatal Morbidity and Mortality (5.5).

RECENT LABELING CHANGES

Indications (1.x)
Warnings/Precautions (5.x, 5.y, 5.z)
Adverse Reactions (8.x)

INDICATIONS AND USAGE

- **Hypertension** (caution in renally-impaired patients), alone or in combination with other anti-hypertensives (1.1)
- **Congestive Heart Failure**, usually in combination with diuretics and digitalis (1.2)
- **Left Ventricular (LV) Dysfunction after Myocardial Infarction** to improve survival and reduce morbidity in clinically stable patients with LV ejection fraction ≤ 40% (1.3)
- **Diabetic Nephropathy** (Type I IDD with proteinuria > 500 mg/day and retinopathy) (1.4)

DOSAGE AND ADMINISTRATION

General: Take 1 hour before meals. Individualize dosage.

Indication	Initiation of Therapy	Usual Daily Dose	Do Not Exceed
Hypertension	25 mg bid or tid	25-150 mg bid or tid*	**450 mg/day**
Heart Failure	25 mg tid	50-100 mg tid	**450 mg/day**
LV Dysfunction after MI	12.5 mg tid†	50 mg tid	
Diabetic Nephropathy		25 mg tid	

* Usual daily dosing does not exceed 50 mg BID or TID. Consider adding a thiazide-type diuretic. (2.2)
† A single dose of 6.25 mg should precede initiation of 12.5 mg therapy. (2.4)

Adjust dose in renal impairment (2.6, 5.7)

HOW SUPPLIED

Tablets: 12.5, 25, 50, 100 mg; scored (3)

CONTRAINDICATIONS

Known hypersensitivity (e.g., angioedema) to any ACE inhibitor.

WARNINGS/PRECAUTIONS

- Angioedema with possibility of airway obstruction (5.1)
- Neutropenia (<1000/mm^3) with myeloid hypoplasia (5.2)
- Excessive hypotension (5.4)
- Fetal/Neonatal Morbidity and Mortality (5.5)
- Hepatic failure (5.6)
- Use with caution in renal impairment. (2.6, 5.7)
- Hyperkalemia (5.8)
- Cough (5.9)

Most Common Adverse Reactions (≥ n/100) (8)

- rash (sometimes with arthralgia and eosinophilia), taste impairment (diminution or loss), cough, pruritus, chest pain, palpitations, tachycardia, proteinuria

To report SUSPECTED SERIOUS ADRs, call (manufacturer) at (phone #) or FDA's MedWatch at 1-800-FDA-1088

DRUG INTERACTIONS

- Diuretics (6.1)
- Other vasodilators (6.2)
- Agents Causing Renin Release (6.3)
- Beta-Blockers (6.4)
- Agents Increasing Serum Potassium (6.5)
- Lithium (6.7)

USE IN SPECIFIC POPULATIONS

- Pregnancy: Fetal/Neonatal Morbidity and Mortality (5.5)
- Lactating Women: Potential for serious adverse reactions in nursing infants. (7.3)
- Pediatric Use: Safety and effectiveness not established. Use only if other measures ineffective. (7.4)
- Renal-impairment: Use with caution. (2.6, 5.7)

See P for PATIENT COUNSELING INFORMATION

These highlights do not include all the information needed to prescribe Capoten safely and effectively. See Capoten's comprehensive prescribing information provided below.

m/yy

COMPREHENSIVE PRESCRIBING INFORMATION: INDEX

! **WARNING REGARDING USE IN PREGNANCY**
1 **INDICATIONS AND USAGE**
1.1 Hypertension
1.2 Heart Failure
1.3 Left Ventricular Dysfunction after Myocardial Infarction
1.4 Diabetic Nephropathy
2 **DOSAGE AND ADMINISTRATION**
2.1 General
2.2 Hypertension
2.3 Heart Failure
2.4 LVF after MI
2.5 Diabetic Nephropathy
2.6 Dosage Adjustment in Renal Impairment
3 **HOW SUPPLIED/STORAGE AND HANDLING**
4 **CONTRAINDICATIONS**
5 **WARNINGS/PRECAUTIONS**
5.1 Angioedema
5.2 Neutropenia/Agranulocytosis
5.3 Proteinuria
5.4 Hypotension in salt/volume depletion
5.5 Fetal/Neonatal Morbidity/Mortality
5.6 Hepatic Failure
5.7 Impaired Renal Function
5.8 Hyperkalemia
5.9 Cough
5.10 Valvular Stenosis
5.11 Surgery/Anesthesia
5.12 Hemodialysis
6 **DRUG INTERACTIONS**
6.1 Hypotension--Patients on DiureticTherapy
6.2 Agents Having Vasodilator Activity
6.3 Agents Causing Renin Release
6.4 Agents With Sympathetic Activity
6.5 Agents Increasing Serum Potassium
6.6 Inhibitors of Endogenous Prostaglandin Synthesis
6.7 Lithium
6.8 Drug/Laboratory Test Interaction (Acetone)
7 **USE IN SPECIFIC POPULATIONS**
7.1 Pregnancy
7.2 Labor and Delivery
7.3 Lactating Women
7.4 Pediatric Use
7.5 Geriatric Use
8 **ADVERSE REACTIONS**
8.1 Altered Laboratory Findings
10 **OVERDOSAGE**
11 **DESCRIPTION**
12 **CLINICAL PHARMACOLOGY**
12.1 Mechanism of Action
12.2 Pharmacodynamics
12.3 Pharmacokinetics
13 **NONCLINICAL TOXICOLOGY**
13.1 Carcinogenesis, Mutagenesis, Impairment of Fertility
13.2 Animal Toxicology
14 **CLINICAL STUDIES**
P **PATIENT COUNSELING INFORMATION**

81126 Federal Register / Vol. 65, No. 247 / Friday, December 22, 2000 / Proposed Rules

COMPREHENSIVE PRESCRIBING INFORMATION

! WARNING: USE IN PREGNANCY
When used in pregnancy during the second and third trimesters, ACE inhibitors can cause injury and even death to the developing fetus. When pregnancy is detected, CAPOTEN should be discontinued as soon as possible. See WARNINGS/PRECAUTIONS: Fetal/Neonatal Morbidity and Mortality (5.5).

1 INDICATIONS AND USAGE

1.1 **Hypertension:** CAPOTEN is indicated for the treatment of hypertension.

In using CAPOTEN, consideration should be given to the risk of neutropenia/agranulocytosis (see WARNINGS/PRECAUTIONS).

CAPOTEN (captopril) may be used as initial therapy for patients with normal renal function, in whom the risk is relatively low. In patients with impaired renal function, particularly those with collagen vascular disease, captopril should be reserved for hypertensives who have either developed unacceptable side effects on other drugs, or have failed to respond satisfactorily to drug combinations.

CAPOTEN is effective alone and in combination with other antihypertensive agents, especially thiazide-type diuretics. The blood pressure lowering effects of captopril and thiazides are approximately additive.

1.2 **Heart Failure:** CAPOTEN is indicated in the treatment of congestive heart failure usually in combination with diuretics and digitalis. The beneficial effect of captopril in heart failure does not require the presence of digitalis, however, most controlled clinical trial experience with captopril has been in patients receiving digitalis, as well as diuretic treatment.

1.3 **Left Ventricular Dysfunction After Myocardial Infarction:** CAPOTEN is indicated to improve survival following myocardial infarction in clinically stable patients with left ventricular dysfunction manifested as an ejection fraction ≤ 40% and to reduce the incidence of overt heart failure and subsequent hospitalizations for congestive heart failure in these patients.

1.4 **Diabetic Nephropathy:** CAPOTEN is indicated for the treatment of diabetic nephropathy (proteinuria >500 mg/day) in patients with type I insulin-dependent diabetes mellitus and retinopathy. CAPOTEN decreases the rate of progression of renal insufficiency and development of serious adverse clinical outcomes (death or need for renal transplantation or dialysis).

2 DOSAGE AND ADMINISTRATION

2.1 CAPOTEN (captopril) should be taken one hour before meals. Dosage must be individualized.

2.2 **Hypertension:** Initiation of therapy requires consideration of recent antihypertensive drug treatment, the extent of blood pressure elevation, salt restriction, and other clinical circumstances. If possible, discontinue the patient's previous antihypertensive drug regimen for one week before starting CAPOTEN.

The initial dose of CAPOTEN is 25 mg bid or tid. If satisfactory reduction of blood pressure has not been achieved after one or two weeks, the dose may be increased to 50 mg bid or tid. Concomitant sodium restriction may be beneficial when CAPOTEN (captopril) is used alone.

The dose of CAPOTEN in hypertension usually does not exceed 50 mg tid. Therefore, if the blood pressure has not been satisfactorily controlled after one to two weeks at this dose, (and the patient is not already receiving a diuretic), a modest dose of a thiazide-type diuretic (e.g., hydrochlorothiazide, 25 mg daily), should be added. The diuretic dose may be increased at one- to two-week intervals until its highest usual antihypertensive dose is reached.

If CAPOTEN is being started in a patient already receiving a diuretic, CAPOTEN therapy should be initiated under close medical supervision (see DRUG INTERACTIONS regarding hypotension (6.1)), with dosage and titration of CAPOTEN as noted above.

If further blood pressure reduction is required, the dose of CAPOTEN may be increased to 100 mg bid or tid and then, if necessary, to 150 mg bid or tid (while continuing the diuretic).

The usual dose range is 25 to 150 mg bid or tid. A maximum daily dose of 450 mg CAPOTEN should not be exceeded.

For patients with severe hypertension (e.g., accelerated or malignant hypertension), when temporary discontinuation of current antihypertensive therapy is not practical or desirable, or when prompt titration to more normotensive blood pressure levels is indicated, diuretic should be continued but other current antihypertensive medication stopped and CAPOTEN dosage promptly initiated at 25 mg bid or tid, under close medical supervision.

When necessitated by the patient's clinical condition, the daily dose of CAPOTEN may be increased every 24 hours or less under continuous medical supervision until a satisfactory blood pressure response is obtained or the maximum dose of CAPOTEN is reached. In this regimen, addition of a more potent diuretic, e.g., furosemide, may also be indicated.

Beta-blockers may also be used in conjunction with CAPOTEN therapy (see DRUG INTERACTIONS (6.4)), but the effects of the two drugs are less than additive.

2.3 **Heart Failure:** Initiation of therapy requires consideration of recent diuretic therapy and the possibility of severe salt/volume depletion. In patients with either normal or low blood pressure, who have been vigorously treated with diuretics and who may be hyponatremic and/or hypovolemic, a starting dose of 6.25 or 12.5 mg tid may minimize the magnitude or duration of the hypotensive effect (see WARNINGS/PRECAUTIONS: Hypotension (5.4)); for these patients, titration to the usual daily dosage can then occur within the next several days.

For most patients the usual initial daily dosage is 25 mg tid. After a dose of 50 mg tid is reached, further increases in dosage should be delayed, where possible, for at least two weeks to determine if a satisfactory response occurs. Most patients studied have had a satisfactory clinical improvement at 50 or 100 mg tid. A maximum daily dose of 450 mg of CAPOTEN should not be exceeded.

CAPOTEN should generally be used in conjunction with a diuretic and digitalis. CAPOTEN therapy must be initiated under very close medical supervision.

2.4 **Left Ventricular Dysfunction After Myocardial Infarction:** The recommended dose for long-term use in patients following a myocardial infarction is a target maintenance dose of 50 mg tid.

Therapy may be initiated as early as three days following a myocardial infarction. After a single dose of 6.25 mg, CAPOTEN therapy should be initiated at 12.5 mg tid. CAPOTEN should then be increased to 25 mg tid during the next several days and to a target dose of 50 mg tid over the next several weeks as tolerated (see CLINICAL PHARMACOLOGY (12.2)) .

CAPOTEN may be used in patients treated with other post-myocardial infarction therapies, e.g., thrombolytics, aspirin, beta blockers.

2.5 **Diabetic Nephropathy:** The recommended dose of CAPOTEN for long term use to treat diabetic nephropathy is 25 mg tid.

Other antihypertensives such as diuretics, beta blockers, centrally acting agents or vasodilators may be used in conjunction with CAPOTEN if additional therapy is required to further lower blood pressure.

2.6 **Dosage Adjustment in Renal Impairment:** Because CAPOTEN is excreted primarily by the kidneys, excretion rates are reduced in patients with impaired renal function. These patients will take longer to reach steady-state captopril levels and will reach higher steady-state levels for a given daily dose than patients with normal renal function. Therefore, these patients may respond to smaller or less frequent doses.

Accordingly, for patients with significant renal impairment, initial daily dosage of CAPOTEN should be reduced, and smaller increments utilized for titration, which should be quite slow (one- to two-week intervals). After the desired therapeutic effect has been achieved, the dose should be slowly back-titrated to determine the minimal effective dose. When concomitant diuretic therapy is required, a loop diuretic (e.g., furosemide), rather than a thiazide diuretic, is preferred in patients with severe renal impairment. (See also WARNINGS/PRECAUTIONS: Hemodialysis (5.12))

3 HOW SUPPLIED

12.5 mg tablets in bottles of 100 and 1000, 25 mg tablets in bottles of 100 and 1000, 50 mg tablets in bottles of 100 and 1000, and 100 mg tablets in bottles of 100. Bottles contain a desiccant-charcoal canister.

Unimatic unit-dose packs containing 100 tablets are also available for each potency: 12.5 mg, 25 mg, 50 mg, and 100 mg.

The 12.5 mg tablet is a biconvex oval with a partial bisect bar; the 25 mg tablet is a biconvex rounded square with a quadrisect bar; the 50 and 100 mg tablets are biconvex ovals with a bisect bar. All captopril tablets are white and may exhibit a slight sulfurous odor.

Storage: Do not store above 86° F. Keep bottles tightly closed (protect from moisture).

4 CONTRAINDICATIONS

CAPOTEN (captopril) is contraindicated in patients who are hypersensitive to this product or any other angiotensin-converting enzyme inhibitor (e.g., a patient who has experienced angioedema during therapy with any other ACE inhibitor).

5 WARNINGS/PRECAUTIONS

To report SUSPECTED SERIOUS ADRs, call (manufacturer) at (phone #) or FDA's MedWatch at 1-800-FDA-1088

5.1 Angioedema

Angioedema involving the extremities, face, lips, mucous membranes, tongue, glottis or larynx has been seen in patients treated with ACE inhibitors, including captopril. If angioedema involves the tongue, glottis or larynx, airway obstruction may occur and be fatal. Emergency therapy, including but not necessarily limited to, subcutaneous administration of a 1:1000 solution of epinephrine should be promptly instituted.

Swelling confined to the face, mucous membranes of the mouth, lips and extremities has usually resolved with discontinuation of captopril; some cases required medical therapy. (See PATIENT COUNSELING INFORMATION (P) and ADVERSE REACTIONS (8).)

5.2 Neutropenia/Agranulocytosis

Neutropenia (<1000/mm³) with myeloid hypoplasia has resulted from use of captopril. About half of the neutropenic patients developed systemic or oral cavity infections or other features of the syndrome of agranulocytosis.

The risk of neutropenia is dependent on the clinical status of the patient:

In clinical trials in patients with hypertension who have normal renal function (serum creatinine less than 1.6 mg/dL and no collagen vascular disease), neutropenia has been seen in one patient out of over 8,600 exposed.

In patients with some degree of renal failure (serum creatinine at least 1.6 mg/dL) but no collagen vascular disease, the risk of neutropenia in clinical trials was about 1 per 500, a frequency over 15 times that for uncomplicated hypertension. Daily doses of captopril were relatively high in these patients, particularly in view of their diminished renal function. In foreign marketing experience in patients with renal failure, use of allopurinol concomitantly with captopril has been associated with neutropenia but this association has not appeared in U.S. reports.

In patients with collagen vascular diseases (e.g., systemic lupus erythematosus, scleroderma) and impaired renal function, neutropenia occurred in 3.7 percent of patients in clinical trials. While none of the over 750 patients in formal clinical trials of heart failure developed neutropenia, it has occurred during the subsequent clinical experience. About half of the reported cases had serum creatinine ≥ 1.6 mg/dL and more than 75 percent were in patients also receiving procainamide. In heart failure, it appears that the same risk factors for neutropenia are present.

The neutropenia has usually been detected within three months after captopril was started. Bone marrow examinations in patients with neutropenia consistently showed myeloid hypoplasia, frequently accompanied by erythroid hypoplasia and decreased numbers of megakaryocytes (e.g., hypoplastic bone marrow and pancytopenia); anemia and thrombocytopenia were sometimes seen.

In general, neutrophils returned to normal in about two weeks after captopril was discontinued, and serious infections were limited to clinically complex patients. About 13 percent of the cases of neutropenia have ended fatally, but almost all fatalities were in patients with serious illness, having collagen vascular disease, renal failure, heart failure or immunosuppressant therapy, or a combination of these complicating factors.

Evaluation of the hypertensive or heart failure patient should always include assessment of renal function.

If captopril is used in patients with impaired renal function, white blood cell and differential counts should be evaluated prior to starting treatment and at approximately two-week intervals for about three months, then periodically.

In patients with collagen vascular disease or who are exposed to other drugs known to affect the white cells or immune response, particularly when there is impaired renal function, captopril should be used only after an assessment of benefit and risk, and then with caution.

All patients treated with captopril should be told to report any signs of infection (e.g., sore throat, fever). If infection is suspected, white cell counts should be performed without delay.

Since discontinuation of captopril and other drugs has generally led to prompt return of the white count to normal, upon confirmation of neutropenia (neutrophil count <1000/mm³) the physician should withdraw captopril and closely follow the patient's course.

5.3 Proteinuria

Total urinary proteins greater than 1 g per day were seen in about 0.7 percent of patients receiving captopril. About 90 percent of affected patients had evidence of prior renal disease or received relatively high doses of captopril (in excess of 150 mg/day), or both. The nephrotic syndrome occurred in about one-fifth of proteinuric patients. In most cases, proteinuria subsided or cleared within six months whether or not captopril was continued. Parameters of renal function, such as BUN and creatinine, were seldom altered in the patients with proteinuria.

5.4 Hypotension

Excessive hypotension was rarely seen in hypertensive patients but is a possible consequence of captopril use in salt/volume depleted persons (such as those treated vigorously with diuretics), patients with heart failure or those patients undergoing renal dialysis. (See DRUG INTERACTIONS (6.1).)

In heart failure, where the blood pressure was either normal or low, transient decreases in mean blood pressure greater than 20 percent were recorded in about half of the patients. This transient hypotension is more likely to occur after any of the first several doses and is usually well tolerated, producing either no symptoms or brief mild lightheadedness, although in rare instances it has been associated with arrhythmia or conduction defects. Hypotension was the reason for discontinuation of drug in 3.6 percent of patients with heart failure.

BECAUSE OF THE POTENTIAL FALL IN BLOOD PRESSURE IN THESE PATIENTS, THERAPY SHOULD BE STARTED UNDER VERY CLOSE MEDICAL SUPERVISION. A starting dose of 6.25 or 12.5 mg tid may minimize the hypotensive effect. Patients should be followed closely for the first two weeks of treatment and whenever the dose of captopril and/or diuretic is increased. In patients with heart failure, reducing the dose of diuretic, if feasible, may minimize the fall in blood pressure.

Hypotension is not *per se* a reason to discontinue captopril. Some decrease of systemic blood pressure is a common and desirable observation upon initiation of CAPOTEN (captopril) treatment in heart failure. The magnitude of the decrease is greatest early in the course of treatment; this effect stabilizes within a week or two, and generally returns to pretreatment levels, without a decrease in therapeutic efficacy, within two months.

5.5 Fetal/Neonatal Morbidity and Mortality

ACE inhibitors can cause fetal and neonatal morbidity and death when administered to pregnant women. Several dozen cases have been reported in the world literature. When pregnancy is detected, ACE inhibitors should be discontinued as soon as possible.

The use of ACE inhibitors during the second and third trimesters of pregnancy has been associated with fetal and neonatal injury, including hypotension, neonatal skull hypoplasia, anuria, reversible or irreversible renal failure, and death. Oligohydramnios has also been reported, presumably resulting from decreased fetal renal function; oligohydramnios in this setting has been associated with fetal limb contractures, craniofacial deformation, and hypoplastic lung development. Prematurity, intrauterine growth retardation, and patent ductus arteriosus have also been reported, although it is not clear whether these occurrences were due to the ACE inhibitor exposure.

These adverse effects do not appear to have resulted from intrauterine ACE inhibitor exposure that has been limited to the first trimester. Mothers whose embryos and fetuses are exposed to ACE inhibitors only during the first trimester should be so informed. Nonetheless, when patients become pregnant, physicians should make every effort to discontinue the use of captopril as soon as possible.

Rarely (probably less often than once in every thousand pregnancies), no alternative to ACE inhibitors will be found. In these rare cases, the mothers should be apprised of the potential hazards to their fetuses, and serial ultrasound examinations should be performed to assess the intraamniotic environment.

If oligohydramnios is observed, captopril should be discontinued unless it is considered life-saving for the mother. Contraction stress testing (CST), a non-stress test (NST), or biophysical profiling (BPP) may be appropriate, depending upon the week of pregnancy. Patients and physicians should be aware, however, that oligohydramnios may not appear until after the fetus has sustained irreversible injury.

Infants with histories of in utero exposure to ACE inhibitors should be closely observed for hypotension, oliguria, and hyperkalemia. If oliguria occurs, attention should be directed toward support of blood pressure and renal perfusion. Exchange transfusion or dialysis may be required as a means of reversing hypotension and/or substituting for disordered renal function. While captopril may be removed from the adult circulation by hemodialysis, there is inadequate data concerning the effectiveness of hemodialysis for removing it from the circulation of neonates or children. Peritoneal dialysis is not effective for removing captopril; there is no information concerning exchange transfusion for removing captopril from the general circulation.

When captopril was given to rabbits at doses about 0.8 to 70 times (on a mg/kg basis) the maximum recommended human dose, low incidences of craniofacial malformations were seen. No teratogenic effects of captopril were seen in studies of pregnant rats and hamsters. On a mg/kg basis, the doses used were up to 150 times (in hamsters) and 625 times (in rats) the maximum recommended human dose.

5.6 Hepatic Failure

Rarely, ACE inhibitors have been associated with a syndrome that starts with cholestatic jaundice and progresses to fulminant hepatic necrosis and (sometimes) death. The mechanism of this syndrome is not understood. Patients receiving ACE inhibitors who develop jaundice or marked elevations of hepatic enzymes should discontinue the ACE inhibitor and receive appropriate medical follow-up.

5.7 Impaired Renal Function

Hypertension--Some patients with renal disease, particularly those with severe renal artery stenosis, have developed increases in BUN and serum creatinine after reduction of blood pressure with captopril. Captopril dosage reduction and/or discontinuation of diuretic may be required. For some of these patients, it may not be possible to normalize blood pressure and maintain adequate renal perfusion.

Heart Failure--About 20 percent of patients develop stable elevations of BUN and serum creatinine greater than 20 percent above normal or baseline upon long-term treatment with captopril. Less than 5 percent of patients, generally those with severe preexisting renal disease, required discontinuation of treatment due to progressively increasing creatinine; subsequent improvement probably depends upon the severity of the underlying renal disease.

See CLINICAL PHARMACOLOGY (12), DOSAGE AND ADMINISTRATION (2.6), ADVERSE REACTIONS: Altered Laboratory Findings (8.1).

5.8 Hyperkalemia

Elevations in serum potassium have been observed in some patients treated with ACE inhibitors, including captopril. When treated with ACE inhibitors, patients at risk for the development of hyperkalemia include those with: renal insufficiency; diabetes mellitus; and those using concomitant potassium-sparing diuretics, potassium supplements or potassium-containing salt substitutes; or other drugs associated with increases in serum potassium. In a trial of type I diabetic patients with proteinuria, the incidence of withdrawal of treatment with captopril for hyperkalemia was 2% (4/207). In two trials of normotensive type I diabetic patients with microalbuminuria, no captopril group subjects had hyperkalemia (0/116). (See PATIENT COUNSELING INFORMATION (P); DRUG INTERACTIONS (6.5); ADVERSE REACTIONS: Altered Laboratory Findings (8.1).)

5.9 Cough

Cough has been reported with the use of ACE inhibitors. Characteristically, the cough is nonproductive, persistent and resolves after discontinuation of therapy. ACE inhibitor-induced cough should be considered as part of the differential diagnosis of cough.

5.10 Valvular Stenosis

There is concern, on theoretical grounds, that patients with aortic stenosis might be at particular risk of decreased coronary perfusion when treated with vasodilators because they do not develop as much afterload reduction as others.

5.11 Surgery/Anesthesia

In patients undergoing major surgery or during anesthesia with agents that produce hypotension, captopril will block angiotensin II formation secondary to compensatory renin release. If hypotension occurs and is considered to be due to this mechanism, it can be corrected by volume expansion.

5.12 Hemodialysis

Recent clinical observations have shown an association of hypersensitivity-like (anaphylactoid) reactions during hemodialysis with high-flux dialysis membranes (e.g., AN69) in patients receiving ACE inhibitors. In these patients, consideration should be given to using a different type of dialysis membrane or a different class of medication.

6 DRUG INTERACTIONS

6.1 Hypotension--Patients on Diuretic Therapy

Patients on diuretics and especially those in whom diuretic therapy was recently instituted, as well as those on severe dietary salt restriction or dialysis, may occasionally experience a precipitous reduction of blood pressure usually within the first hour after receiving the initial dose of captopril.

The possibility of hypotensive effects with captopril can be minimized by either discontinuing the diuretic or increasing the salt intake approximately one week prior to initiation of treatment with CAPOTEN or initiating therapy with small doses (6.25 or 12.5 mg). Alternatively, provide medical supervision for at least one hour after the initial dose. If hypotension occurs, the patient should be placed in a supine position and, if necessary, receive an intravenous infusion of normal saline. This transient hypotensive response is not a contraindication to further doses which can be given without difficulty once the blood pressure has increased after volume expansion.

6.2 Agents Having Vasodilator Activity

Data on the effect of concomitant use of other vasodilators in patients receiving CAPOTEN for heart failure are not available; therefore, nitroglycerin or other nitrates (as used for management of angina) or other drugs having vasodilator activity should, if possible, be discontinued before starting CAPOTEN. If resumed during CAPOTEN therapy, such agents should be administered cautiously, and perhaps at lower dosage.

6.3 Agents Causing Renin Release

Captopril's effect will be augmented by antihypertensive agents that cause renin release. For example, diuretics (e.g., thiazides) may activate the renin-angiotensin-aldosterone system.

6.4 Agents Affecting Sympathetic Activity

The sympathetic nervous system may be especially important in supporting blood pressure in patients receiving captopril alone or with diuretics. Therefore, agents affecting sympathetic activity (e.g., ganglionic blocking agents or adrenergic neuron blocking agents) should be used with caution. Beta-adrenergic blocking drugs add some further antihypertensive effect to captopril, but the overall response is less than additive.

6.5 **Agents Increasing Serum Potassium**

Since captopril decreases aldosterone production, elevation of serum potassium may occur. Potassium-sparing diuretics such as spironolactone, triamterene, or amiloride, or potassium supplements should be given only for documented hypokalemia, and then with caution, since they may lead to a significant increase of serum potassium. Salt substitutes containing potassium should also be used with caution.

6.6 **Inhibitors Of Endogenous Prostaglandin Synthesis**

It has been reported that indomethacin may reduce the antihypertensive effect of captopril, especially in cases of low renin hypertension. Other nonsteroidal anti-inflammatory agents (e.g., aspirin) may also have this effect.

6.7 **Lithium**

Increased serum lithium levels and symptoms of lithium toxicity have been reported in patients receiving concomitant lithium and ACE inhibitor therapy. These drugs should be coadministered with caution and frequent monitoring of serum lithium levels is recommended. If a diuretic is also used, it may increase the risk of lithium toxicity.

6.8 **Drug/Laboratory Test Interaction**

Captopril may cause a false-positive urine test for acetone.

7 USE IN SPECIFIC POPULATIONS

7.1 **Pregnancy Categories C (first trimester) and D (second and third trimesters) See WARNINGS/PRECAUTIONS: Fetal/Neonatal Morbidity and Mortality (5.5).**

7.3 **Lactating Women**

Concentrations of captopril in human milk are approximately one percent of those in maternal blood. Because of the potential for serious adverse reactions in nursing infants from captopril, a decision should be made whether to discontinue nursing or to discontinue the drug, taking into account the importance of CAPOTEN (captopril) to the mother. (See USE IN SPECIFIC POPULATIONS: Pediatric Use (7.4).)

7.4 **Pediatric Use**

Safety and effectiveness in children have not been established. There is limited experience reported in the literature with the use of captopril in the pediatric population; dosage, on a weight basis, was generally reported to be comparable to or less than that used in adults.

Infants, especially newborns, may be more susceptible to the adverse hemodynamic effects of captopril. Excessive, prolonged and unpredictable decreases in blood pressure and associated complications, including oliguria and seizures, have been reported.

CAPOTEN (captopril) should be used in children only if other measures for controlling blood pressure have not been effective.

8 ADVERSE REACTIONS

Reported incidences are based on clinical trials involving approximately 7000 patients.

Renal: About one of 100 patients developed proteinuria (see WARNINGS/PRECAUTIONS (5.3)).

Each of the following has been reported in approximately 1 to 2 of 1000 patients and are of uncertain relationship to drug use: renal insufficiency, renal failure, nephrotic syndrome, polyuria, oliguria, and urinary frequency.

Hematologic: Neutropenia/agranulocytosis has occurred (see WARNINGS/PRECAUTIONS (5.2)). Cases of anemia, thrombocytopenia, and pancytopenia have been reported.

Dermatologic: Rash, often with pruritus, and sometimes with fever, arthralgia, and eosinophilia, occurred in about 4 to 7 (depending on renal status and dose) of 100 patients, usually during the first four weeks of therapy. It is usually maculopapular, and rarely urticarial. The rash is usually mild and disappears within a few days of dosage reduction, short-term treatment with an antihistaminic agent, and/or discontinuing therapy; remission may occur even if captopril is continued. Pruritus, without rash, occurs in about 2 of 100 patients. Between 7 and 10 percent of patients with skin rash have shown an eosinophilia and/or positive ANA titers. A reversible associated pemphigoid-like lesion, and photo sensitivity, have also been reported.

Flushing or pallor has been reported in 2 to 5 of 1000 patients.

Cardiovascular: Hypotension may occur; see DRUG INTERACTIONS (6.1) for discussion of hypotension with captopril therapy.

Tachycardia, chest pain, and palpitations have each been observed in approximately 1 of 100 patients.

Angina pectoris, myocardial infarction, Raynaud's syndrome, and congestive heart failure have each occurred in 2 to 3 of 1000 patients.

Dysgeusia: Approximately 2 to 4 (depending on renal status and dose) of 100 patients developed a diminution or loss of taste perception. Taste impairment is reversible and usually self-limited (2 to 3 months) even with continued drug administration. Weight loss may be associated with the loss of taste.

Angioedema: Angioedema involving the extremities, face, lips, mucous membranes, tongue, glottis or larynx has been reported in approximately one in 1000 patients. Angioedema involving the upper airways has caused fatal airway obstruction. (See PATIENT COUNSELING INFORMATION (P).)

Cough: Cough has been reported in 0.5-2% of patients treated with captopril in clinical trials. (See WARNINGS/PRECAUTIONS: Cough (5.9).)

The following have been reported in about 0.5 to 2 percent of patients but did not appear at increased frequency compared to placebo or other treatments used in controlled trials: gastric irritation, abdominal pain, nausea, vomiting, diarrhea, anorexia, constipation, aphthous ulcers, peptic ulcer, dizziness, headache, malaise, fatigue, insomnia, dry mouth, dyspnea, alopecia, paresthesias.

Other clinical adverse effects reported since the drug was marketed are listed below by body system. In this setting, an incidence or causal relationship cannot be accurately determined.

Body as a whole: Anaphylactoid reactions (see WARNINGS/PRECAUTIONS: Hemodialysis (5.12)).

General: Asthenia, gynecomastia.

Cardiovascular: Cardiac arrest, cerebrovascular accident/insufficiency, rhythm disturbances, orthostatic hypotension, syncope.

Dermatologic: Bullous pemphigus, erythema multiforme (including Stevens-Johnson syndrome), exfoliative dermatitis.

Gastrointestinal: Pancreatitis, glossitis, dyspepsia.

Hematologic: Anemia, including aplastic and hemolytic.

Hepatobiliary: Jaundice, hepatitis, including rare cases of necrosis, cholestasis.

Metabolic: Symptomatic hyponatremia.

Musculoskeletal: Myalgia, myasthenia.

Nervous/Psychiatric: Ataxia, confusion, depression, nervousness, somnolence.

Respiratory: Bronchospasm, eosinophilic pneumonitis, rhinitis.

Special Senses: Blurred vision.

Urogenital: Impotence.

As with other ACE inhibitors, a syndrome has been reported which may include: fever, myalgia, arthralgia, interstitial nephritis, vasculitis, rash or other dermatologic manifestations, eosinophilia and an elevated ESR.

Fetal/Neonatal Morbidity and Mortality

See WARNINGS/PRECAUTIONS: Fetal/Neonatal Morbidity and Mortality.

8.1 **Altered Laboratory Findings**

Serum Electrolytes: Hyperkalemia: small increases in serum potassium, especially in patients with renal impairment (see WARNINGS/PRECAUTIONS (5.8)).

Hyponatremia: particularly in patients receiving a low sodium diet or concomitant diuretics.

BUN/Serum Creatinine: Transient elevations of BUN or serum creatinine especially in volume or salt depleted patients or those with renovascular hypertension may occur. Rapid reduction of longstanding or markedly elevated blood pressure can result in decreases in the glomerular filtration rate and, in turn, lead to increases in BUN or serum creatinine.

Hematologic: A positive ANA has been reported.

Liver Function Tests: Elevations of liver transaminases, alkaline phosphatase, and serum bilirubin have occurred.

81130 Federal Register / Vol. 65, No. 247 / Friday, December 22, 2000 / Proposed Rules

10 OVERDOSAGE

Correction of hypotension would be of primary concern. Volume expansion with an intravenous infusion of normal saline is the treatment of choice for restoration of blood pressure.

While captopril may be removed from the adult circulation by hemodialysis, there is inadequate data concerning the effectiveness of hemodialysis for removing it from the circulation of neonates or children. Peritoneal dialysis is not effective for removing captopril; there is no information concerning exchange transfusion for removing captopril from the general circulation.

11 DESCRIPTION

CAPOTEN (captopril) is a specific competitive inhibitor of angiotensin I-converting enzyme (ACE), the enzyme responsible for the conversion of angiotensin I to angiotensin II.

CAPOTEN is designated chemically as 1-[(2S)-3-mercapto-2-methylpropionyl]-L-proline [MW 217.29].

Captopril is a white to off-white crystalline powder that may have a slight sulfurous odor; it is soluble in water (approx. 160 mg/mL), methanol, and ethanol and sparingly soluble in chloroform and ethyl acetate.

CAPOTEN is available in potencies of 12.5 mg, 25 mg, 50 mg, and 100 mg as scored tablets for oral administration. Inactive ingredients: microcrystalline cellulose, corn starch, lactose, and stearic acid.

12 CLINICAL PHARMACOLOGY

12.1 Mechanism of Action

The mechanism of action of CAPOTEN has not yet been fully elucidated. Its beneficial effects in hypertension and heart failure appear to result primarily from suppression of the renin-angiotensin-aldosterone system. However, there is no consistent correlation between renin levels and response to the drug. Renin, an enzyme synthesized by the kidneys, is released into the circulation where it acts on a plasma globulin substrate to produce angiotensin I, a relatively inactive decapeptide. Angiotensin I is then converted by angiotensin converting enzyme (ACE) to angiotensin II, a potent endogenous vasoconstrictor substance. Angiotensin II also stimulates aldosterone secretion from the adrenal cortex, thereby contributing to sodium and fluid retention.

CAPOTEN prevents the conversion of angiotensin I to angiotensin II by inhibition of ACE, a peptidyldipeptide carboxy hydrolase. This inhibition has been demonstrated in both healthy human subjects and in animals by showing that the elevation of blood pressure caused by exogenously administered angiotensin I was attenuated or abolished by captopril. In animal studies, captopril did not alter the pressor responses to a number of other agents, including angiotensin II and norepinephrine, indicating specificity of action.

ACE is identical to "bradykininase," and CAPOTEN may also interfere with the degradation of the vasodepressor peptide, bradykinin. Increased concentrations of bradykinin or prostaglandin E^2 may also have a role in the therapeutic effect of CAPOTEN.

Inhibition of ACE results in decreased plasma angiotensin II and increased plasma renin activity (PRA), the latter resulting from loss of negative feedback on renin release caused by reduction in angiotensin II. The reduction of angiotensin II leads to decreased aldosterone secretion, and, as a result, small increases in serum potassium may occur along with sodium and fluid loss.

The antihypertensive effects persist for a longer period of time than does demonstrable inhibition of circulating ACE. It is not known whether the ACE present in vascular endothelium is inhibited longer than the ACE in circulating blood.

12.2 Pharmacodynamics

Administration of CAPOTEN results in a reduction of peripheral arterial resistance in hypertensive patients with either no change, or an increase, in cardiac output. There is an increase in renal blood flow following administration of CAPOTEN and glomerular filtration rate is usually unchanged.

Reductions of blood pressure are usually maximal 60 to 90 minutes after oral administration of an individual dose of CAPOTEN. The duration of effect is dose related. The reduction in blood pressure may be progressive, so to achieve maximal therapeutic effects, several weeks of therapy may be required. The blood pressure lowering effects of captopril and thiazide-type diuretics are additive. In contrast, captopril and beta-blockers have a less than additive effect.

Blood pressure is lowered to about the same extent in both standing and supine positions. Orthostatic effects and tachycardia are infrequent but may occur in volume depleted patients. Abrupt withdrawal of CAPOTEN has not been associated with a rapid increase in blood pressure.

12.3 Pharmacokinetics

After oral administration of therapeutic doses of CAPOTEN, rapid absorption occurs with peak blood levels at about one hour. The presence of food in the gastrointestinal tract reduces absorption by about 30 to 40 percent; captopril therefore should be given one hour before meals. Based on carbon-14 labeling, average minimal absorption is approximately 75 percent. In a 24-hour period, over 95 percent of the absorbed dose is eliminated in the urine; 40 to 50 percent is unchanged drug; most of the remainder is the disulfide dimer of captopril and captopril-cysteine disulfide.

Approximately 25 to 30 percent of the circulating drug is bound to plasma proteins. The apparent elimination half-life for total radioactivity in blood is probably less than 3 hours. An accurate determination of half-life of unchanged captopril is not, at present, possible, but it is probably less than 2 hours. In patients with renal impairment, however, retention of captopril occurs (see DOSAGE AND ADMINISTRATION (2.6)).

Studies in rats and cats indicate that CAPOTEN does not cross the blood-brain barrier to any significant extent.

13 NONCLINICAL TOXICOLOGY

13.1 Carcinogenesis, Mutagenesis and Impairment of Fertility

Two-year studies with doses of 50 to 1350 mg/kg/day in mice and rats failed to show any evidence of carcinogenic potential. The high dose in these studies is 150 times the maximum recommended human dose of 450 mg, assuming a 50-kg subject. On a body-surface-area basis, the high doses for mice and rats are 13 and 26 times the maximum recommended human dose, respectively.

Studies in rats have revealed no impairment of fertility.

13.2 Animal Toxicology

Chronic oral toxicity studies were conducted in rats (2 years), dogs (47 weeks; 1 year), mice (2 years), and monkeys (1 year). Significant drug-related toxicity included effects on hematopoiesis, renal toxicity, erosion/ulceration of the stomach, and variation of retinal blood vessels.

Reductions in hemoglobin and/or hematocrit values were seen in mice, rats, and monkeys at doses 50 to 150 times the maximum recommended human dose (MRHD) of 450 mg, assuming a 50-mg subject. On a body-surface-area, these doses are 5 to 25 times maximum recommended human dose (MRHD). Anemia, leukopenia, thrombocytopenia, and bone marrow suppression occurred in dogs at doses 8 to 30 times MRHD on a body-weight basis (4 to 15 times MRHD on a surface-area basis). The reductions in hemoglobin and hematocrit values in rats and mice were only significant at 1 year and returned to normal with continued dosing by the end of the study. Marked anemia was seen at all dose levels (8 to 30 times MRHD) in dogs, whereas moderate to marked leukopenia was noted only at 15 and 30 times MRHD and thrombocytopenia at 30 times MRHD. The anemia could be reversed upon discontinuation of dosing. Bone marrow suppression occurred to a varying degree, being associated only with dogs that died or were sacrificed in a moribund condition in the 1 year study. However, in the 47-week study at a dose 30 times MRHD, bone marrow suppression was found to be reversible upon continued drug administration.

Captopril caused hyperplasia of the juxtaglomerular apparatus of the kidneys in mice and rats at doses 7 to 200 times MRHD on a body-weight basis (0.6 to 35 times MRHD on a surface-area basis); in monkeys at 20 to 60 times MRHD on a body-weight basis (7 to 20 times MRHD on a surface-area

Federal Register / Vol. 65, No. 247 / Friday, December 22, 2000 / Proposed Rules 81131

basis); and in dogs at 30 times MRHD on a body-weight basis (15 times MRHD on a surface-area basis).

Gastric erosions/ulcerations were increased in incidence in male rats at 20 to 200 times MRHD on a body-weight basis (3.5 and 35 times MRHD on a surface-area basis); in dogs at 30 times MRHD on a body-weight basis (15 times on MRHD on a surface-area basis); and in monkeys at 65 times MRHD on a body-weight basis (20 times MRHD on a surface-area basis). Rabbits developed gastric and intestinal ulcers when given oral doses approximately 30 times MRHD on a body-weight basis (10 times MRHD on a surface-area basis) for only 5 to 7 days.

In the two-year rat study, irreversible and progressive variations in the caliber of retinal vessels (focal sacculations and constrictions) occurred at all dose levels (7 to 200 times MRHD) on a body-weight basis; 1 to 35 times MRHD on a surface-area basis in a dose-related fashion. The effect was first observed in the 88th week of dosing, with a progressively increased incidence thereafter, even after cessation of dosing.

14 CLINICAL STUDIES

Congestive Heart Failure: In patients with heart failure, significantly decreased peripheral (systemic vascular) resistance and blood pressure (afterload), reduced pulmonary capillary wedge pressure (preload) and pulmonary vascular resistance, increased cardiac output, and increased exercise tolerance time (ETT) have been demonstrated. These hemodynamic and clinical effects occur after the first dose and appear to persist for the duration of therapy. Placebo controlled studies of 12 weeks duration in patients who did not respond adequately to diuretics and digitalis show no tolerance to beneficial effects on ETT; open studies, with exposure up to 18 months in some cases, also indicate that ETT benefit is maintained. Clinical improvement has been observed in some patients where acute hemodynamic effects were minimal.

Left Ventricular Dysfunction After Myocardial Infarction: The Survival and Ventricular Enlargement (SAVE) study was a multicenter, randomized, double-blind, placebo-controlled trial conducted in 2,231 patients (age 21-79 years) who survived the acute phase of a myocardial infarction and did not have active ischemia. Patients had left ventricular dysfunction (LVD), defined as a resting left ventricular ejection fraction ≤ 40%, but at the time of randomization were not sufficiently symptomatic to require ACE inhibitor therapy for heart failure. About half of the patients had had symptoms of heart failure in the past. Patients were given a test dose of 6.25 mg oral CAPOTEN (captopril) and were randomized within 3-16 days post-infarction to receive either CAPOTEN or placebo in addition to conventional therapy. CAPOTEN was initiated at 6.25 mg or 12.5 mg tid and after two weeks titrated to a target maintenance dose of 50 mg tid. About 80% of patients were receiving the target dose at the end of the study. Patients were followed for a minimum of two years and for up to five years, with an average follow-up of 3.5 years.

Baseline blood pressure was 113/70 mm Hg and 112/70 mm Hg for the placebo and CAPOTEN groups, respectively. Blood pressure increased slightly in both treatment groups during the study and was somewhat lower in the CAPOTEN group (119/74 vs. 125/77 mm Hg at 1 yr).

Therapy with CAPOTEN improved long-term survival and clinical outcomes compared to placebo. The risk reduction for all cause mortality was 19% (P = 0.02) and for cardiovascular death was 21% (P = 0.014). Captopril treated subjects had 22% (P = 0.034) fewer first hospitalizations for heart failure. Compared to placebo, 22% fewer patients receiving captopril developed symptoms of overt heart failure. There was no significant difference between groups in total hospitalizations for all cause (2056 placebo; 2036 captopril).

CAPOTEN was well tolerated in the presence of other therapies such as aspirin, beta blockers, nitrates, vasodilators, calcium antagonists and diuretics.

Diabetic Nephropathy: In a multicenter, double-blind, placebo controlled trial, 409 patients, age 18-49 of either gender, with or without hypertension, with type I (juvenile type, onset before age 30) insulin-dependent diabetes mellitus, retinopathy, proteinuria ≥ 500 mg per day and serum creatinine ≤ 2.5 mg/dL, were randomized to placebo or CAPOTEN (25 mg tid) and followed for up to 4.8 years (median 3 years). To achieve blood pressure control, additional antihypertensive agents (diuretics, beta blockers, centrally acting agents or vasodilators) were added as needed for patients in both groups.

The CAPOTEN group had a 51% reduction in risk of doubling of serum creatinine (P < 0.01) and a 51% reduction in risk for the combined endpoint of end-stage renal disease (dialysis or transplantation) or death (P < 0.01). CAPOTEN treatment resulted in a 30% reduction in urine protein excretion within the first 3 months (P < 0.05), which was maintained throughout the trial. The CAPOTEN group had somewhat better blood pressure control than the placebo group, but the effects of CAPOTEN on renal function were greater than would be expected from the group differences in blood pressure reduction alone. CAPOTEN was well-tolerated in this patient population.

In two multicenter, double-blind, placebo controlled studies, a total of 235 normotensive patients with insulin-dependent diabetes mellitus, retinopathy and microalbuminuria (20-200 µg/min) were randomized to placebo or CAPOTEN (50 mg bid) and followed for up to 2 years. CAPOTEN delayed the progression to overt nephropathy (proteinuria ≥ 500 mg/day) in both studies (risk reduction 67% to 76%; P < 0.05). CAPOTEN also reduced the albumin excretion rate. However, the long term clinical benefit of reducing the progression from microalbuminuria to proteinuria has not been established

P PATIENT COUNSELING INFORMATION

Patients should be advised to immediately report to their physician any signs or symptoms suggesting angioedema (e.g., swelling of face, eyes, lips, tongue, larynx and extremities; difficulty in swallowing or breathing; hoarseness) and to discontinue therapy. (See WARNINGS/PRECAUTIONS (5.1).)

Patients should be told to report promptly any indication of infection (e.g., sore throat, fever), which may be a sign of neutropenia, or of progressive edema which might be related to proteinuria and nephrotic syndrome.

All patients should be cautioned that excessive perspiration and dehydration may lead to an excessive fall in blood pressure because of reduction in fluid volume. Other causes of volume depletion such as vomiting or diarrhea may also lead to a fall in blood pressure; patients should be advised to consult with the physician.

Patients should be advised not to use potassium-sparing diuretics, potassium supplements or potassium-containing salt substitutes without consulting their physician. (See WARNINGS/PRECAUTIONS (5.8); DRUG INTERACTIONS (6.5); ADVERSE REACTIONS (8).)

Patients should be warned against interruption or discontinuation of medication unless instructed by the physician.

Heart failure patients on captopril therapy should be cautioned against rapid increases in physical activity.

Patients should be informed that CAPOTEN (captopril) should be taken one hour before meals (see DOSAGE AND ADMINISTRATION (2.1)).

Pregnancy. Female patients of childbearing age should be told about the consequences of second- and third-trimester exposure to ACE inhibitors, and they should also be told that these consequences do not appear to have resulted from intrauterine ACE-inhibitor exposure that has been limited to the first trimester. These patients should be asked to report pregnancies to their physicians as soon as possible.

[FR Doc. 00–32375 Filed 12–21–00; 8:45 am]

BILLING CODE 4160–01–C

PART II

TORT LIABILITY

CHAPTER 5

PRODUCTS LIABILITY: PRELIMINARIES

To this point, we have focused on federal regulation of medical technologies. Although important, the FDA does not have a monopoly over the control of drugs and medical devices. Tort litigation under state law generates significant, even if less direct, regulatory pressures on suppliers of such products. This chapter introduces several general features of products liability doctrine as it applies to medical technologies, focusing in particular on the points of overlap between public and private law. The chapters that follow provide more detailed coverage of the different categories of tort liability applicable to the sale and use of allegedly defective medical products.

A. STRICT LIABILITY AND UNAVOIDABLY UNSAFE PRODUCTS

Products liability law, whether framed in terms of strict liability or negligence (or, for that matter, as a breach of implied warranty), allows consumers to recover damages caused by "defective" products sold by the defendant. Product manufacturers and others in the chain of distribution may face tort liability for (1) manufacturing defects (i.e., when a product comes off the assembly line out of specifications); (2) design defects (i.e., when the specifications themselves are deemed unreasonably unsafe because the risks associated with the design outweigh its utility when compared with reasonable alternative designs); or (3) inadequate warnings about inherent risks in the design that the defendant knew or should have known about but that consumers were unlikely to recognize. As explained in Chapter 6, the test for design defect used to (and in a few jurisdictions continues to) ask instead whether the product's performance disappointed the expectations of a reasonable consumer.

The earliest cases arose from such things as exploding glass bottles and defective automobiles, and then came the mammoth asbestos litigation. Although claims involving such products continue to occupy the courts, lawsuits against the manufacturers of drugs and medical devices have become increasingly important in the last few decades, both in their volume and in the conceptual challenges that they pose. See Alex Berenson, Drug Industry Braces for New Suits over Even More of Its Products, N.Y. Times, Apr. 22, 2006, at C1 ("As Merck reels from 11,500 suits over Vioxx, its arthritis drug, the rest of the industry is girding for challenges over another half a dozen widely used medications that plaintiffs' lawyers say have hidden and severe side effects or were improperly marketed. Unlike Vioxx, which Merck stopped selling in 2004, the other drugs [Seroquel, Ortho–Evra, Prempro, and Fosamax] remain on the market.''); id. (''To gain leverage against the companies, trial lawyers aim to build 'inventories' of hundreds or thousands of plaintiffs that they can settle simultaneously for hundreds of millions of dollars.... Wyeth has spent $15 billion since 1998 to resolve lawsuits over its fen-phen diet-drug combination.''); Lisa Girion, State Vioxx Trial Is Set as Drug Suits Boom, L.A. Times, June 27, 2006, at C1 (calling ''the pharmaceutical industry the nation's No. 1 target of product liability lawsuits,'' adding that ''[m]ore than 71,000 drug lawsuits have been filed in federal courts since 2001 and ... now account for more than a third of all product liability filings''); Duff Wilson, AstraZeneca Has Settled Most of Its Seroquel Suits, N.Y. Times, July 29, 2011, at B6 (reporting that the company spent more than $1 billion to defend and settle in excess of 28,000 cases alleging a failure to warn about the risk of weight gain and diabetes associated with the use of its antipsychotic drug, adding that it had cost Eli Lilly still more to settle similar litigation); see also Frank M. McClellan, The Vioxx Litigation: A Critical Look at Trial Tactics, the Tort System, and the Roles of Lawyers in Mass Tort Litigation, 57 DePaul L. Rev. 509 (2008); Jane Stapleton, Liability for Drugs in the U.S. and EU: Rhetoric and Reality, 26 Rev. Litig. 991 (2007). As a result, courts have created a variety of special rules to accommodate products liability litigation against the sellers and users of medical technologies.

Restatement (Second) of the Law of Torts (American Law Inst. 1965):

§ 402A. Special Liability of Seller of Product for Physical Harm to User or Consumer

> Comment k: *Unavoidably unsafe products.* There are some products which, in the present state of human knowledge, are quite incapable of being made safe for their intended and ordinary use. These are especially common in the field of drugs. An outstanding example is the vaccine for the Pasteur treatment of rabies, which not uncommonly leads to very serious and damaging consequences when it is injected. Since the disease itself invariably leads to a dreadful death, both the marketing and use of the vaccine are fully justified, notwithstanding the unavoidable high degree of risk which they involve. Such a product, properly prepared, and accompanied by proper directions and warning, is not defective, nor is it unreasonably dangerous. The same is true of many other drugs, vaccines, and the like, many of which for this very reason cannot legally be sold except to physicians, or under the prescription of a physician. It is also true in particular of many new or experimental drugs as to which, because of lack of time and opportunity for sufficient medical experience, there can be no assurance of safety, or perhaps even of purity of ingredients, but such experience as there is justifies the marketing and use of the drug notwithstanding a medically recognizable risk. The seller of such products, again with the qualification that they are properly prepared and marketed, and proper

warning is given, where the situation calls for it, is not to be held to strict liability for unfortunate consequences attending their use, merely because he has undertaken to supply the public with an apparently useful and desirable product, attended with a known but apparently reasonable risk.

Brown v. Superior Court (Abbott Laboratories)

751 P.2d 470 (Cal.1988).

■ MOSK, JUSTICE:

* * * The doctrine of strict liability had its genesis in a concurring opinion by Justice Roger Traynor in *Escola v. Coca Cola Bottling Co.*, 150 P.2d 436 (Cal.1944). He suggested that a manufacturer should be absolutely liable if, in placing a product on the market, it knew the product was to be used without inspection, and it proved to have a defect that caused injury. The policy considerations underlying this suggestion were that the manufacturer, unlike the public, can anticipate or guard against the recurrence of hazards, that the cost of injury may be an overwhelming misfortune to the person injured whereas the manufacturer can insure against the risk and distribute the cost among the consuming public, and that it is in the public interest to discourage the marketing of defective products. This court unanimously adopted Justice Traynor's concept in *Greenman v. Yuba Power Products, Inc.*, 377 P.2d 897 (Cal.1963), holding a manufacturer strictly liable in tort and using the formulation of the doctrine set forth in *Escola*.

Strict liability differs from negligence in that it eliminates the necessity for the injured party to prove that the manufacturer of the product which caused injury was negligent. It focuses not on the conduct of the manufacturer but on the product itself, and holds the manufacturer liable if the product was defective. In 1965, soon after our decision in *Greenman*, the *Restatement Second of Torts* published section 402A, which set forth the strict liability doctrine. Almost all states have adopted some form of strict liability since that time. * * *

Even before *Greenman* was decided, the members of the American Law Institute, in considering whether to adopt a rule of strict liability, pondered whether the manufacturer of a prescription drug should be subject to the doctrine. During a rather confusing discussion of a draft of what was to become section 402A, a member of the Institute proposed that drugs should be exempted from strict liability on the ground that it would be "against the public interest" to apply the doctrine to such products because of "the very serious tendency to stifle medical research and testing." Dean Prosser, who was the reporter for the *Restatement Second of Torts*, responded that the problem was a real one, and that he had it in mind in drafting section 402A. A motion to exempt prescription drugs from the section was defeated on the suggestion of Dean Prosser that the problem could be dealt with in the comments to the section. However, a motion to state the exemption in a comment was also defeated. At the next meeting of the Institute in 1962, section 402A was approved together with comment k thereto.

The comment provides that the producer of a properly manufactured prescription drug may be held liable for injuries caused by the product only if it was not accompanied by a warning of dangers that the manufacturer knew or should have known about. * * * Comment k has been analyzed and criticized by numerous commentators. While there is some disagreement as to its scope and meaning, there is a general consensus that, although it purports to explain the strict liability doctrine, in fact the principle it states is based on negligence. * * * Comment k has been adopted in the overwhelming majority of jurisdictions that have considered the matter. * * *

[T]he fact that a drug with dangerous side effects may be characterized as containing a defect in design does not necessarily mean that its producer is to be held strictly liable for the defect. The determination of that issue depends on whether the public interest would be served by the imposition of such liability. As we have seen, the fundamental reasons underlying the imposition of strict liability are to deter manufacturers from marketing products that are unsafe, and to spread the cost of injury from the plaintiff to the consuming public, which will pay a higher price for the product to reflect the increased expense of insurance to the manufacturer resulting from its greater exposure to liability.

These reasons could justify application of the doctrine to the manufacturers of prescription drugs. It is indisputable, as plaintiff contends, that the risk of injury from such drugs is unavoidable, that a consumer may be helpless to protect himself from serious harm caused by them, and that, like other products, the cost of insuring against strict liability can be passed on by the producer to the consumer who buys the item. Moreover, as we observe below, in some cases additional testing of drugs before they are marketed might reveal dangerous side effects, resulting in a safer product.

But there is an important distinction between prescription drugs and other products such as construction machinery, a lawnmower, or perfume, the producers of which were held strictly liable. In the latter cases, the product is used to make work easier or to provide pleasure, while in the former it may be necessary to alleviate pain and suffering or to sustain life. Moreover, unlike other important medical products (wheelchairs, for example), harm to some users from prescription drugs is unavoidable. Because of these distinctions, the broader public interest in the availability of drugs at an affordable price must be considered in deciding the appropriate standard of liability for injuries resulting from their use.

Perhaps a drug might be made safer if it was withheld from the market until scientific skill and knowledge advanced to the point at which additional dangerous side effects would be revealed. But in most cases such a delay in marketing new drugs—added to the delay required to obtain approval for release of the product from the Food and Drug Administration—would not serve the public welfare. Public policy favors the development and marketing of beneficial new drugs, even though some risks, perhaps serious ones, might accompany their introduction, because drugs can save lives and reduce pain and suffering.

If drug manufacturers were subject to strict liability, they might be reluctant to undertake research programs to develop some pharmaceuticals that would prove beneficial or to distribute others that are available to be marketed, because of the fear of large adverse monetary judgments. Further, the additional expense of insuring against such liability—assuming insurance would be available—and of research programs to reveal possible dangers not detectable by available scientific methods could place the cost of medication beyond the reach of those who need it most.

Dean Prosser summed up the justification for exempting prescription drugs from strict liability as follows: "The argument that industries producing potentially dangerous products should make good the harm, distribute it by liability insurance, and add the cost to the price of the product, encounters reason for pause, when we consider that two of the greatest medical boons to the human race, penicillin and cortisone, both have their dangerous side effects, and that drug companies might well have been deterred from producing and selling them. Thus far the courts have tended to hold the manufacturer to a high standard of care in preparing and testing drugs of unknown potentiality and in giving warning; but in the absence of evidence that this standard has not been met, they have refused to hold the maker liable for unforeseeable harm."

The possibility that the cost of insurance and of defending against lawsuits will diminish the availability and increase the price of pharmaceuticals is far from theoretical. Defendants cite a host of examples of products which have greatly increased in price or have been withdrawn or withheld from the market because of the fear that their producers would be held liable for large judgments. For example, according to defendant E.R. Squibb & Sons, Inc., Bendectin, the only antinauseant drug available for pregnant women, was withdrawn from sale in 1983 because the cost of insurance almost equalled the entire income from sale of the drug. Before it was withdrawn, the price of Bendectin increased by over 300 percent.*

Drug manufacturers refused to supply a newly discovered vaccine for influenza on the ground that mass inoculation would subject them to enormous liability. The government therefore assumed the risk of lawsuits resulting from injuries caused by the [1976 swine flu] vaccine. One producer of diphtheria-tetanus-pertussis vaccine withdrew from the market, giving as its reason "extreme liability exposure, cost of litigation and the difficulty of continuing to obtain adequate insurance." There are only two manufacturers of the vaccine remaining in the market, and the cost of each dose rose a hundred-fold from 11 cents in 1982 to $11.40 in 1986, $8 of which was for an insurance reserve. The price increase roughly paralleled an increase in the number of lawsuits from one in 1978 to 219 in 1985.

* More recently, in the face of lawsuits and plummeting demand triggered by the resulting adverse publicity, the manufacturer of a vaccine against Lyme disease decided to withdraw its FDA-approved product from the market. See Sole Lyme Vaccine Is Pulled off Market, N.Y. Times, Feb. 28, 2002, at C5.

Finally, a manufacturer was unable to market a new drug for the treatment of vision problems because it could not obtain adequate liability insurance at a reasonable cost.

There is no doubt that, from the public's standpoint, these are unfortunate consequences. And they occurred even though almost all jurisdictions follow the negligence standard of comment k. It is not unreasonable to conclude in these circumstances that the imposition of a harsher test for liability would not further the public interest in the development and availability of these important products. Our purpose is to demonstrate that there is a rational connection between the cost and availability of pharmaceuticals and the liability imposed on their manufacturers for injuries resulting from their use. We decline to hold, therefore, that a drug manufacturer's liability for injuries caused by the defective design of a prescription drug should be measured by the standard [of strict liability] * * * *

One further question remains in this aspect of the case. Comment k, as we have seen, provides that the maker of an "unavoidably unsafe" product is not liable for injuries resulting from its use if the product is "properly prepared, and accompanied by proper directions and warning." With the few exceptions noted above, the courts which have adopted comment k have viewed all prescription drugs as coming within its scope. * * *

It seems unjust to grant the same protection from liability to those who gave us thalidomide as to the producers of penicillin.† If some method could be devised to confine the benefit of the comment k negligence standard to those drugs that have proved useful to mankind while denying the privilege to those that are clearly harmful, it would deserve serious consideration. But we know of no means by which this can be accomplished without substantially impairing the public interest in the development and marketing of new drugs, because the harm to this interest arises in the very process of attempting to make the distinction. * * * [T]he question of the superiority of one drug over another would have to be decided not in the abstract but in reference to the plaintiff, since the advantages of a drug cannot be isolated from the condition of a particular patient. Thus, in one case the drug that injured the plaintiff might be the better choice, while this would not be true as to another user. * * *

[T]he eligibility of each drug for favorable treatment must be tested at a trial, with its attendant litigation costs, and the drug must survive two risk/benefit challenges, first by the judge and then by the jury. In order to vindicate the public's interest in the availability and affordability of prescription drugs, a manufacturer must have a greater assurance that his products will not be measured by a strict liability standard * * * *[11]

† Ironically, one decade later, the FDA approved thalidomide for the treatment of Hansen's disease, though it conditioned approval on extremely strict distribution controls given the serious risk of birth defects. See Sheryl G. Stolberg, Thalidomide Approved to Treat Leprosy, with Other Uses Seen, N.Y. Times, July 17, 1998, at A1.

11. * * * We concede that the language of the comment is unclear in this respect. Some portions suggest that it is to apply to all prescriptions drugs (the comment describes the

In conclusion, and in accord with almost all our sister states that have considered the issue, we hold that a manufacturer is not strictly liable for injuries caused by a prescription drug so long as the drug was properly prepared and accompanied by warnings of its dangerous propensities that were either known or reasonably scientifically knowable at the time of distribution.[12]

Grundberg v. Upjohn Co.

813 P.2d 89 (Utah 1991).

■ DURHAM, JUSTICE:

* * * Plaintiffs allege that Grundberg took a 0.5 milligram dose of Halcion the day she [fatally] shot her mother. They allege that this dose was recommended by her physician and was consistent with Upjohn's recommended dosage. Plaintiffs assert that Grundberg shot her mother while in a state of Halcion-induced intoxication, which allegedly included side effects such as depression, psychosis, depersonalization, aggressive assaultive behavior, and homicidal compulsion.

Plaintiffs' complaint states several causes of action, including common law negligence and strict liability. Plaintiffs claim that Upjohn failed to adequately warn about certain adverse side effects of Halcion and that Halcion was defectively designed. The failure-to-warn claim is scheduled for trial. The strict liability claim based on design defect is the subject of Upjohn's pending summary judgment motion, the outcome of which depends on this court's resolution of the certified question.

The parties agree that the *Restatement (Second) of Torts* section 402A, comment k (1965) and the principles it embodies provide an exemption from strict liability for a claimed design defect in the case of products that are "unavoidably unsafe." In moving for partial summary judgment, Upjohn argued that public policy supporting the research and development of

---

products to which it applies as those which "in the present state of human knowledge, are quite incapable of being made safe for their intended and ordinary use"). Other passages distinguish among drugs ("many ... drugs, vaccines and the like" are not "unreasonably dangerous" if they are "properly prepared, and are accompanied by appropriate warnings"). Nevertheless, we are of the view that the comment was intended to and should apply to all prescription drugs. As we note above, almost all jurisdictions that have adopted the rule stated in the comment view its provisions as granting immunity from strict liability to all such drugs. In addition, * * * the benefit of the negligence standard stated in the comment would be greatly diminished if all drugs were required to run the gauntlet of a risk/benefit analysis in order to qualify for application of the standard.

12. Our conclusion does not mean, of course, that drug manufacturers are free of all liability for defective drugs. They are subject to liability for manufacturing defects, as well as under general principles of negligence, and for failure to warn of known or reasonably knowable side effects. It should also be noted that the consumers of prescription drugs are afforded greater protection against defects than consumers of other products, since "the drug industry is closely regulated by the Food and Drug Administration, which actively controls the testing and manufacture of drugs and the method by which they are marketed, including the contents of warning labels."

new drugs requires a holding that *all* FDA-approved prescription medications are "unavoidably unsafe" products under comment k and, as such, manufacturers of those drugs would not be liable for a claim based on defective design. Plaintiffs argue that whether a drug is "unavoidably unsafe" must be determined on a case-by-case basis, with a determination in each case of whether the specific drug's benefit exceeded its risk at the time it was distributed. The [federal] district court found this to be a controlling question of law and certified it to this court. * * *

We agree with comment k's basic proposition—that there are some products that have dangers associated with their use even though they are used as intended. We also agree that the seller of such products, when the products are properly prepared and marketed and distributed with appropriate warnings, should not be held strictly liable for the "unfortunate consequences" attending their use. Thus, we adopt comment k's basic policy as the law to be applied in this state and must now turn to the issue of how to apply that policy. * * *

By its terms, comment k excepts unavoidably unsafe products from strict liability only to the extent that the plaintiff alleges a design defect; comment k's immunity from strict liability does not extend to strict liability claims based on a manufacturing flaw or an inadequate warning. The purpose of comment k is to protect from strict liability products that cannot be designed more safely. If, however, such products are mismanufactured or unaccompanied by adequate warnings, the seller may be liable even if the plaintiff cannot establish the seller's negligence. * * * Both parties agree in this case that the prerequisite to a comment k exemption—that the drug was properly prepared and accompanied by warnings of its dangerous propensities—must be established on a case-by-case basis. This limitation on the scope of comment k immunity is universally recognized. * * *

In reviewing the approaches of other jurisdictions toward strict products liability for design defects in drug products, we are troubled by the lack of uniformity and certainty inherent in the case-by-case approach and fear the resulting disincentive for pharmaceutical manufacturers to develop new products. * * * We find the *Brown* result more in line with the public policy considerations in the important area of pharmaceutical product design. We do not agree, however, with the *Brown* court's apparent attempt to use the plain language of comment k as the vehicle for exempting all prescription drugs from strict liability rather than relying on the policies underlying that comment.

The American Law Institute's Restatements are drafted by legal scholars who attempt to summarize the state of the law in a given area, predict how the law is changing, and suggest the direction the law should take. The Restatement serves an appropriate advisory role to courts in approaching unsettled areas of law. We emphasize, however, that section 402A of the *Restatement (Second) of Torts*, as drafted in 1965, is not binding on our decision in this case except insofar as we explicitly adopt its various doctrinal principles. We agree with the principle comment k embodies, that manufacturers of unavoidably dangerous products should not be liable for a claim of design defect. We are persuaded that all prescription drugs should be classified as unavoidably dangerous in design because of their unique nature and value, the elaborate regulatory system overseen by the FDA, the difficulties of relying on individual lawsuits as a forum in which to review a prescription drug's design, and the significant public policy considerations noted in *Brown*. * * *

Because prescription drugs are chemical compounds designed to interact with the chemical and physiological processes of the human body, they will almost always pose some risk of side effects in certain individuals. Despite these risks, new drugs are continually approved by the FDA because of their social benefit in saving lives and alleviating human suffering. The health care system and general standard of living in this country, for example, would be seriously impaired without such essential drug products as antibiotics that allow quick recovery from ailments that were once debilitating or even fatal. * * *

Despite inherent risks, *and in contrast to any other product*, society has determined that prescription medications provide a unique benefit and so should be available to physicians with appropriate warnings and guidance as to use. The federal government has established an elaborate regulatory system, overseen by the FDA, to control the approval and distribution of these drugs. No other class of products is subject to such special restrictions or protections in our society. * * *

We find this extensive regulatory scheme capable of and appropriate for making the preliminary determination regarding whether a prescription drug's benefits outweigh its risks. The structured follow-up program imposed by law ensures that drugs are not placed on the market without continued monitoring for adverse consequences that would render the FDA's initial risk/benefit analysis invalid. Allowing individual courts and/or juries to continually reevaluate a drug's risks and benefits ignores the processes of this expert regulatory body and the other avenues of recovery available to plaintiffs. * * *

Finally, we do not believe that a trial court in the context of a products liability action is the proper forum to determine whether, as a whole, a particular prescription drug's benefits outweighed its risks at the time of distribution. In a case-by-case analysis, one court or jury's determination that a particular drug is or is not defectively designed has no bearing on any future case. As a result, differences of opinion among courts in differing jurisdictions leaves unsettled a drug manufacturer's liability for any given drug. Although the FDA may have internal differences of opinion regarding whether a particular new drug application should be approved, the individuals making the ultimate judgment will have the benefit of years of experience in reviewing such products, scientific expertise in the area, and access to the volumes of data they can compel manufacturers to produce. Nor is the FDA subject to the inherent limitations of the trial process, such as the rules of evidence, restrictions on expert testimony, and scheduling demands.[9] * * *

Although we do not accept the notion that courts are unsuited to address design defect claims in any products liability action, we do agree that prescription drug design presents precisely this type of "polycentric" problem. A drug is designed to be effectively administered to specific individuals for one or a number of indications. To determine whether a drug's benefit outweighs its risk is inherently complex because of the manufacturer's conscious design choices regarding the numerous chemical properties of the product and their relationship to the vast physiologic idiosyncracies of each consumer for whom the drug is designed. Society has recognized this complexity and in response has reposed regulatory authority in the FDA. Relying on the FDA's screening and surveillance standards enables courts to find liability under circumstances of inadequate warning, mismanufacture, improper marketing, or misinforming the FDA—avenues for which courts are better suited. Although this approach denies plaintiffs one potential theory on which to rely in a drug products liability action, the benefits to society in promoting the development, availability, and reasonable price of drugs justifies this conclusion.

In light of the strong public interest in the availability and affordability of prescription medications, the extensive regulatory system of the FDA, and the avenues of recovery still available to plaintiffs by claiming inadequate warning, mismanufacture, improper marketing, or misrepresenting information to the FDA, we conclude that a broad grant of immunity from strict liability claims based on design defects should be extended to FDA-approved prescription drugs in Utah. * * *

■ STEWART, JUSTICE (dissenting):

The majority holds that a drug that is avoidably unsafe to human life or health is exempt from strict liability for design defects if approved by the FDA, even though alternative drugs can provide the same, or even better, therapy, with less risk to life or health. Thus, such FDA-approved drugs as various decongestants, expectorants, deodorants, hair growth stimulants, skin moisturizers, and cough and cold remedies, for example, have the same immunity as rabies or polio vaccines or medications essential in the treatment of cancer, heart disease, or AIDS. I see no basis for according drugs used to treat comparatively minor ailments a blanket immunity from strict liability for design defects if they are unreasonably dangerous to those who use them.

---

9. There is also a certain moral question to be addressed when determining whether a product's benefit outweighs its risk when faced with the reality of an injured plaintiff. For example, in the case of a vaccine, certain benefits of the drug's availability will accrue to group A, the individuals who are prevented from contracting the disease. A smaller number of individuals, however, may contract the disease and react violently to a component of the drug or, as some other result of the drug's properties, suffer terribly. Under a case-by-case approach, courts or juries must ask which is a more significant interest: efficacy with respect to group A versus harm to group B? The FDA must ask the same question: Does the benefit of this product outweigh its risk? The distinction is that the FDA is in a more objective and informed posture to make that determination.

The limited immunity conferred by comment k on a few drugs was given only after thorough consideration by the American Law Institute. However, this court gives blanket immunity for design defects to all FDA-approved drugs on the basis of blind reliance upon the efficacy and integrity of FDA procedures, about which the majority knows almost nothing. * * * In truth, FDA safety procedures do not justify abdication of judicial responsibility. For example, the FDA does not require existing drugs to undergo newly developed tests which would increase the likelihood that a product is in fact safe. * * *

Numerous congressional investigations have demonstrated that the FDA has often approved drugs in complete ignorance of critical information relating to the hazards of such drugs which was contained either in its own files or in the published medical literature, or both. For example, the FDA approved Oraflex on April 19, 1982, for the treatment of arthritis. The manufacturer withdrew the drug from the market on August 4, 1982, because eleven deaths were reported to be associated with the drug's use in the United States and sixty-one deaths were reported in the United Kingdom. Of principal concern were reports of serious and sometimes fatal Oraflex-associated liver and kidney disease. * * * The FDA approved Merital for the treatment of depression on December 31, 1984. Merital was withdrawn from the market in January 1986 because of a large number of reports of serious immune-allergic or hypersensitivity reactions, including several fatalities, associated with its use. * * * The FDA approved Zomax on October 28, 1980, for the relief of mild to moderately severe pain. On March 4, 1983, marketing of the drug was halted by its manufacturer due to a large number of allergic reactions, including deaths, associated with its use. Eventually, more than 2,100 reactions were reported to the FDA. * * *

Although the FDA has a mechanism for the withdrawal of pharmaceutical agents which are found to be dangerous, the mechanism is slow and sometimes unreliable. For example, several studies were published in the early 1950s which should have put diethylstilbestrol (DES) manufacturers on notice that DES injured the reproductive systems of female fetuses whose mothers were exposed to the drug. However, it was not until 1971, nearly twenty years later, that the FDA finally banned the use of DES to prevent miscarriages, the most common use of the drug. * * * In relying on the efficacy of FDA approval procedures as the basis for dispensing with the judicial remedy of product liability, the majority simply ignores FDA failures to protect the public against unnecessary and unacceptable risks. * * *

Furthermore, not a shred of evidence has been presented to this court that indicates that liability under the tort system has deterred pharmaceutical companies from introducing new drugs. Even if that were the case, the question that must be answered, given the majority's holding, is why comment k does not provide a proper accommodation of all the competing policy interests involved in the issue before the court. Why should those who are seriously injured or suffer because of the death of another have to stand the expense of such losses to support the high profit margins in the drug industry? * * *

Certain drugs clearly qualify for comment k exemption, even though the drugs' risk may be comparatively great. A drug's social utility may be so great, for example, a chemotherapeutic agent used for treatment of cancer, that it would obviously qualify for comment k exemption. Other drugs, such as sleeping compounds or dandruff cures, whose social utility may not be of such a high order, would not automatically qualify. * * * The majority opinion states that a case-by-case analysis would leave drug companies uncertain regarding questions of immunity and would result in patchwork verdicts when a drug may be found to be subject to comment k exemption in one case but not subject to the exemption in another case. That consideration has little merit, in my view. We tolerate nonuniformity of result in negligence cases all the time. Nothing this court does can bring about uniformity of result with respect to drugs. The states are already divided on the issue of whether FDA approval of a drug should confer immunity from design defects, although it appears that no state has gone as far as Utah now does. Suffice to say, a number of courts apply comment k on a case-by-case basis—a task that cannot be avoided even under the majority's position if a strict liability claim is coupled with a negligence claim, as is usually the case.

Significantly, Congress has not shared this court's professed concern for uniformity. Whatever lack of uniformity there has been in drug cases has been insufficient to justify uniform national products liability legislation. Furthermore, the Legislature of this State thought that a presumption was sufficient protection for manufacturers rather than outright immunity. It is indeed ironic that the policy of uniformity weighs more heavily in this court than in the United States Congress or the Utah Legislature. We can only deal with the law in Utah, and the possibility of patchwork verdicts on a nationwide basis is simply beyond our power to affect. * * *

In this case, * * * [t]he majority ignores the fact that the FDA found Halcion to be neither unique nor particularly essential and presented no advancement over existing therapeutic alternatives. Perhaps not all would have been appropriate medications, but with so many possible alternatives, it is doubtful that Halcion should be immune from strict liability.

NOTES AND QUESTIONS

1. *Making sense of comment k.* A few other jurisdictions apply comment k in a blanket fashion. See, e.g., Hackett v. G.D. Searle & Co., 246 F.Supp.2d 591, 595 (W.D.Tex.2002); Young v. Key Pharm., 922 P.2d 59 (Wash.1996). A handful of courts apply comment k on a case-by-case basis. See, e.g., Savina v. Sterling Drug, Inc., 795 P.2d 915 (Kan.1990); Castrignano v. E.R. Squibb & Sons, Inc., 546 A.2d 775 (R.I.1988). A few courts reject comment k altogether. See Shanks v. Upjohn Co., 835 P.2d 1189, 1196–98 (Alaska 1992); Allison v. Merck & Co., 878 P.2d 948, 953–56 (Nev.1994). See generally Richard C. Ausness, Unavoidably Unsafe Products and Strict

Products Liability: What Liability Rule Should Be Applied to the Sellers of Pharmaceutical Products?, 78 Ky. L.J. 705 (1989–1990); Joanne R. Galbreath, Annotation, Products Liability: What Is an "Unavoidably Unsafe" Product, 70 A.L.R.4th 16 (1989 & 2011 Supp.). Another ambiguity concerns its application to investigational drugs. Comment k embraces experimental products, but would the *Grundberg* court exempt such products from design defect scrutiny even though the FDA has not yet approved them?

2. *Medical devices*. Although comment k referred only to prescription drugs and vaccines, several courts have applied it to comparable medical devices. See Parkinson v. Guidant Corp., 315 F.Supp.2d 741, 747 (W.D.Pa. 2004); Breen v. Synthes–Stratec, Inc., 947 A.2d 383, 387–88 & n.5 (Conn. App.Ct.2008); Tansy v. Dacomed Corp., 890 P.2d 881, 885 (Okla.1994) ("Most courts which have considered the question have found that comment k applies to medical devices, especially those which are implanted in the human body."). Is it really accurate to characterize implantable or other devices as "unavoidably unsafe"? Chapter 6(B)(1) revisits this question.

3. *Nonprescription products*. By its terms, comment k does not apply exclusively to *prescription* drugs, though courts routinely have read it in that fashion. See, e.g., Lofton v. McNeil Consumer & Specialty Pharms., 682 F.Supp.2d 662, 679 (N.D.Tex.2010) ("The court will not ... apply this exception to an over-the-counter drug, even if at one time ibuprofen was a prescription drug."). Indeed, most of the examples of trivial products referred to by the dissent in *Grundberg* were nonprescription drugs, but consider the following:

> In an earlier era, when OTC drugs offered marginal symptomatic relief and generally posed only trivial risks, it made sense to apply the same [design defect] standard used for cosmetics, appliances, and other consumer goods. Now that OTC drugs may offer some genuine clinical utility accompanied by non-trivial risks, courts may conclude that these products qualify as "unavoidably unsafe" and deserve some protection from strict liability claims. After all, the movement of a product from prescription to nonprescription status does not alter its intrinsic character so much as the means of access and the method of marketing.

Lars Noah, Treat Yourself: Is Self–Medication the Prescription for What Ails American Health Care?, 19 Harv. J.L. & Tech. 359, 380 (2006). The *Restatement (Third) of Torts: Products Liability*, however, treats nonprescription drugs (and medical devices) as subject to the general provisions applicable to all other consumer products. See Rest. (3d) § 2 cmt. k.

4. *Blood and tissue products*. Essentially all states exempt blood from strict products liability. See Michael J. Miller, Note, Strict Liability, Negligence and the Standard of Care for Transfusion–Transmitted Disease, 36 Ariz. L. Rev. 473, 488–90 (1994). These "blood shield" statutes also protect commercial suppliers of blood-derived products from strict liability claims. See McKee v. Cutter Lab., 866 F.2d 219, 221–22 (6th Cir.1989); Rogers v. Miles Lab., 802 P.2d 1346, 1350–52 (Wash.1991). But see JKB, Sr. v.

Armour Pharm. Co., 660 N.E.2d 602, 605–06 (Ind.Ct.App.1996) (holding that state statute did not protect manufacturers). Does the extension to manufacturers of derivative products make sense? The statutes also cover other types of human tissue products. See Condos v. Musculoskeletal Transplant Found., 208 F.Supp.2d 1226 (D.Utah 2002); Cryolife v. Superior Ct., 2 Cal.Rptr.3d 396 (Ct.App.2003); see also Rest. (3d) § 19(c) ("Human blood and human tissue, even when provided commercially, are not subject to the rules of this Restatement."); Jason L. Williams, Note, Patient Safety or Profit: What Incentives Are Blood Shield Laws and FDA Regulations Creating for the Tissue Banking Industry?, 2 Ind. Health L. Rev. 295 (2005). Blood and tissue suppliers remain subject to tort liability in cases of negligence, though many courts define the standard of care as the relevant custom in the industry, which makes it difficult for plaintiffs to recover. See, e.g., Ward v. Lutheran Hosp. & Homes Soc'y of Am., Inc., 963 P.2d 1031, 1036–37 (Alaska 1998); Brown v. United Blood Servs., 858 P.2d 391, 395–99 (Nev.1993). But see Doe v. Cutter Biological, Inc., 971 F.2d 375, 382–84 (9th Cir.1992) (denying the defendant's motion for summary judgment); Advincula v. United Blood Servs., 678 N.E.2d 1009, 1027–28 (Ill. 1996). See generally Steven R. Salbu, AIDS and the Blood Supply: An Analysis of Law, Regulation, and Public Policy, 74 Wash. U. L.Q. 913 (1996); Jay M. Zitter, Annotation, Liability of Blood Supplier or Donor for Injury or Death Resulting from Blood Transfusion, 24 A.L.R.4th 508 (1982 & 2011 Supp.).

5. *Legislative responses.* In one instance, Congress decided to protect the manufacturers of especially valuable pharmaceutical products from the threat of tort liability. In 1986, in response to fears of critical vaccine shortages and the dramatic price increases mentioned by the *Brown* court, Congress enacted the National Childhood Vaccine Injury Act. See 42 U.S.C. § 300aa–1 et seq. Manufacturers of listed vaccines must pay an excise tax (75¢/dose at present) in order to fund an administrative compensation system, and the legislation adds procedural and substantive barriers that are designed to discourage the filing of tort claims. The Supreme Court described the basic contours of this mechanism, which loosely resembles workers' compensation systems, as follows:

> For injuries and deaths traceable to vaccinations, the Act establishes a scheme of recovery designed to work faster and with greater ease than the civil tort system. Special masters in the Court of Federal Claims hear vaccine-related complaints, which they adjudicate informally, within strict time limits, subject to similarly expeditious review. A claimant alleging that more than $1,000 in damages resulted from a vaccination after the Act's effective date in 1988 must exhaust the Act's procedures and refuse to accept the resulting judgment before filing any de novo civil action in state or federal court. The streamlining does not stop with the mechanics of litigation, but goes even to substantive standards of proof. While a claimant may establish prima facie entitlement to compensation by introducing proof of actual causation, she can reach the same result by meeting the requirements of what the Act calls the Vaccine Injury Table. The table lists the

> vaccines covered under the Act, together with particular injuries or conditions associated with each one. A claimant who meets certain other conditions not relevant here makes out a prima facie case by showing that she (or someone for whom she brings a claim) "sustained, or had significantly aggravated, any illness, disability, injury, or condition set forth in the Vaccine Injury Table in association with [a] vaccine ... or died from the administration of such vaccine, and the first symptom or manifestation of the onset or of the significant aggravation of any such illness, disability, injury, or condition or the death occurred within the time period after vaccine administration set forth in the Vaccine Injury Table." Thus, the rule of prima facie proof turns the old maxim on its head by providing that if the post hoc event happens fast, *ergo propter hoc*. The Secretary of Health and Human Services may rebut a prima facie case by proving that the injury or death was in fact caused by "factors unrelated to the administration of the vaccine." If the Secretary fails to rebut, the claimant is entitled to compensation.

Shalala v. Whitecotton, 514 U.S. 268, 269–71 (1995). See generally Joanna B. Apolinsky & Jeffrey A. Van Detta, Rethinking Liability for Vaccine Injury, 19 Cornell J.L. & Pub. Pol'y 537 (2010); Lainie Rutkow et al., Balancing Consumer and Industry Interests in Public Health: The National Vaccine Injury Compensation Program and Its Influence During the Last Two Decades, 111 Penn St. L. Rev. 681 (2007); Rob Henson, Comment, Inoculated Against Recovery: A Comparative Analysis of Vaccine Injury Compensation in the United States and Great Britain, 15 Tulsa J. Comp. & Int'l L. 61 (2007); Russell G. Donaldson, Annotation, Construction and Application of the National Childhood Vaccine Injury Act, 129 A.L.R. Fed. 1 (1996 & 2011 Supp.); Robert Barnes, Supreme Court Rules Vaccine Makers Protected from Lawsuits, Wash. Post, Feb. 23, 2011, at A2 ("The program has awarded nearly $2 billion for vaccine-injury claims in nearly 2,500 cases since 1989."). Congress subsequently extended coverage to vaccines against influenza and hepatitis A. See Pub. L. No. 108–357, §§ 889–890, 118 Stat. 1418, 1643–44 (2004). Congress went even further when it immunized manufacturers of countermeasures to chemical, biological, radiological, nuclear, and epidemic threats from tort claims under certain circumstances. See Public Readiness and Emergency Preparedness Act, Pub. L. No. 109–148, Div. C, 119 Stat. 2818 (2005) (codified at 42 U.S.C. § 247d–6d & –6e) (authorizing lawsuits only in the case of "willful misconduct"); Lincoln Mayer, Note, Immunity for Immunizations: Tort Liability, Biodefense, and Bioshield II, 59 Stan. L. Rev. 1753 (2007).

Manufacturers have faced allegations that the mercury-based preservative thimerosal (used to extend the shelf life of multiple-dose vials) caused autism in children. See Bernard Wysocki, Jr., Fearing Avian Flu, Bioterror, U.S. Scrambles to Fill Drug Gap, Wall St. J., Nov. 9, 2005, at A1 ("Vaccine makers point to the heavy costs of litigating suits alleging a link between vaccines and autism. Despite scholarly studies that have found no link, some 350 lawsuits have been filed, costing $200 million, industry executives say. None has yet gone to trial."). Most courts have held that the NCVIA encompasses such claims. See Troxclair v. Aventis Pasteur, Inc., 864 A.2d 1147, 1151–54 (N.J.App.Div.2005); cf. Moss v. Merck & Co., 381 F.3d 501 (5th Cir.2004) (holding that claims brought against the manufacturer of thimerosal used in vaccines and derivative claims brought by parents were not covered); Doe 2 v. Ortho–Clinical Diagnostics, Inc., 335 F.Supp.2d 614, 621–25 (M.D.N.C.2004) (holding that claims related to thimerosal used in RhoGAM, a drug administered during pregnancy, were not covered even if subsequent vaccinations allegedly aggravated the child's autism); Blackmon v. American Home Prods. Corp., 267 F.Supp.2d 667, 678 (S.D.Tex.2002) (claims against chemical manufacturers that sold the preservative to vaccine companies were not covered). As noted below, see Chap. 5(C)(1), most of these claims have stumbled on causation grounds.

Restatement (Third) of the Law of Torts: Products Liability

(American Law Inst. 1998):

§ 6. Liability of Commercial Seller or Distributor for Harm Caused by Defective Prescription Drugs and Medical Devices

(a) A manufacturer of a prescription drug or medical device who sells or otherwise distributes a defective drug or medical device is subject to liability for harm to persons caused by the defect. A prescription drug or medical device is one that may be legally sold or otherwise distributed only pursuant to a health-care provider's prescription.

(b) For purposes of liability under Subsection (a), a prescription drug or medical device is defective if at the time of sale or other distribution the drug or medical device:

(1) contains a manufacturing defect as defined in § 2(a) [i.e., when the product departs from its intended design even though all possible care was exercised in the preparation and marketing of the product]; or

(2) is not reasonably safe due to defective design as defined in Subsection (c); or

(3) is not reasonably safe due to inadequate instructions or warnings as defined in Subsection (d).

(c) A prescription drug or medical device is not reasonably safe due to defective design if the foreseeable risks of harm posed by the drug or medical device are sufficiently great in relation to its foreseeable therapeutic benefits that reasonable health-care providers, knowing of such foreseeable risks and therapeutic benefits, would not prescribe the drug or medical device for any class of patients.

(d) A prescription drug or medical device is not reasonably safe due to inadequate instructions or warnings if reasonable instructions or warnings regarding foreseeable risks of harm are not provided to:

(1) prescribing and other health-care providers who are in a position to reduce the risks of harm in accordance with the instructions or warnings; or

(2) the patient when the manufacturer knows or has reason to know that health-care providers will not be in a position to reduce the risks of harm in accordance with the instructions or warnings.

(e) A retail seller or other distributor of a prescription drug or medical device is subject to liability for harm caused by the drug or device if:

(1) at the time of sale or other distribution the drug or medical device contains a manufacturing defect as defined in § 2(a); or

(2) at or before the time of sale or other distribution of the drug or medical device the retail seller or other distributor fails to exercise reasonable care and such failure causes harm to persons.

Subsequent chapters will address each of these categories of defect in greater detail. For present purposes just note that, instead of comment k immunity for design defect claims, the drafters chose to create a seemingly more manufacturer-protective standard for reviewing the design of prescription drugs and medical devices than applied to other types of products, where the test is risk-utility balancing that allows a finding of design defect if the plaintiff proves that a reasonable alternative design exists. See James A. Henderson, Jr. & Aaron D. Twerski, Drug Designs Are Different, 111 Yale L.J. 151 (2001). The standard for inadequate warnings also differs from that applied to other products insofar as this provision adheres to the "learned intermediary" rule, which generally requires warnings directed only to physicians. Only the manufacturing defect test is identical to that applied to other products.

For a comprehensive assessment of section 6, published as part of a symposium celebrating the tenth anniversary of the completion of the ALI's project, see Lars Noah, This Is Your Products Liability Restatement on Drugs, 74 Brook. L. Rev. 839 (2009). As explained in the conclusion:

> At least the medical technology industry got its own blackletter rules this time around. In contrast to some of the other special provisions in the *Products Liability Restatement* (e.g., food), section 6 has attracted substantial attention. Given the expansion in litigation concerning drugs and medical devices, it has the potential to have a substantial practical impact; it also raises intriguing doctrinal questions and provides some interesting contrasts with the core of products liability. Unfortunately (whether from a failure to appreciate some of the tricky regulatory or medical practice issues, a narrow focus on only one of the subsections, or a preoccupation with taking sides), much of the published literature has done a poor job of grappling with the genuinely difficult questions presented by section 6 . . . [or] the interrelationships between different facets of this special provision.

Id. at 925–26; see also id. at 840 ("[S]o far the special provisions of the *Products Liability Restatement* applicable to prescription drugs and devices have had little discernable impact. These provisions have, however, provoked a great deal of scholarly commentary, and the few courts to consider the issue have uncritically relied upon the published critiques."); id. ("I find little merit in most of these negative assessments, though I point out a number of flaws, ambiguities, and arguable inconsistencies in the new *Restatement*'s special provisions that seemingly no one else has identified."). Portions of this piece are excerpted or cited as relevant in subsequent chapters.

B. THE RELATIONSHIP TO REGULATORY STANDARDS

Restatement (Third) of the Law of Torts: Products Liability

(American Law Inst. 1998):

§ 4. Noncompliance and Compliance with Product Safety Statutes or Regulations

In connection with liability for defective design or inadequate instructions or warnings:

(a) a product's noncompliance with an applicable product safety statute or administrative regulation renders the product defective with respect to the risks sought to be reduced by the statute or regulation; and

(b) a product's compliance with an applicable product safety statute or administrative regulation is properly considered in determining whether the product is defective with respect to the risks sought to be reduced by the statute or regulation, but such compliance does not preclude as a matter of law a finding of product defect.

This asymmetrical treatment of noncompliance and compliance for all types of tort cases goes way back and certainly is reflected in litigation involving FDA-regulated products. See Jeffrey N. Gibbs & Bruce F. Mackler, Food and Drug Administration Regulation and Products Liability: Strong Sword, Weak Shield, 22 Tort & Ins. L.J. 194 (1987); Richard A. Merrill, FDA Regulatory Requirements as Tort Standards, 12 J.L. & Pol'y 549 (2004).

1. THE CONSEQUENCES OF NONCOMPLIANCE

Stanton v. Astra Pharmaceutical Products, Inc.

718 F.2d 553 (3d Cir.1983).

■ BECKER, CIRCUIT JUDGE:

* * * Harrikah Stanton was an eight-month-old infant on December 2, 1971, when she entered Harrisburg Hospital and submitted to a bone-

marrow test to determine the cause of the hemolytic anemia from which she had suffered since birth. In performing the test, the hematologist, Dr. Herbert S. Bowman, injected a two-percent solution of Xylocaine into Harrikah's right posterior iliac crest to anesthetize the area from which he would aspirate bone marrow. The Xylocaine, known generically as lidocaine hydrochloride, was a local anesthetic manufactured by Astra.

Shortly after the procedure, Harrikah began convulsing and experienced cardiac and respiratory arrest. Dr. Marita Fabian, a senior resident at the hospital, and other hospital employees attempted to resuscitate her, but to little avail. The cardiac arrest resulted in severe and irreversible brain damage. Harrikah cannot walk, talk, or stand; her development has not progressed beyond that of a three- to four-month old child. She will require constant care for the rest of her life.

On October 24, 1973, plaintiffs commenced this negligence and product-liability action against Astra * * * * In response to the "special questions," the jury found that Harrikah had suffered an adverse reaction to Xylocaine; that Astra had acted negligently in failing to file the annual and adverse-reaction reports required by subsections 130.35(e) and (f); that the failure to file these reports rendered Xylocaine a defective product; and that Astra's negligence and the product's defective nature were substantial factors in causing Harrikah's injury. * * *

We first will consider the question of the applicability of section 130.35; in the course of our discussion, we will outline the rather complex statutory and regulatory schema governing marketed drugs. Because we conclude that Astra had a duty to file the reports required by section 130.35, we then will proceed to the consequences of noncompliance. The jury determined that noncompliance with the FDA's regulations engendered liability based on negligence as well as strict liability under *Restatement (Second) of Torts* § 402A (1965). We will discuss separately each basis of liability. We conclude that the jury had sufficient evidence to find that Astra's conduct was negligent per se and that such conduct proximately caused Harrikah's injuries; we further conclude that the jury could find that Xylocaine was a defective product within the meaning of section 402A and that the defective product also was a proximate cause of the harm. * * *

Between May 28, 1964, and the end of 1970, Astra received 202 reports of adverse reactions allegedly related to Xylocaine. These reactions ranged from minor, temporary effects to death. Yet Astra forwarded none of these reports to the FDA, relying upon the advice of its counsel [as discussed in the excerpt of the court's opinion appearing in Chapter 3(D).] * * * Astra cannot seriously dispute that section 130.35 was promulgated to protect individuals such as Harrikah Stanton from precisely the type of harm that here occurred—an unexpected adverse reaction to Xylocaine. It thus would appear that Astra's failure to file the reports constituted negligence per se.

Astra points out, however, that noncompliance with safety regulations does not result inexorably in a finding of negligence because Pennsylvania law appears to follow the *Restatement (Second) of Torts* in recognizing a class of "excused violations." In particular, Astra argues that its failure to comply with the applicable statutes and regulations is excused by three circumstances: (1) Astra neither knew nor should have known of the need to comply; (2) Astra's counsel advised the company that there was no need to file the reports with the FDA; and (3) the reports actually had been prepared and were available to FDA plant inspectors. We agree that Pennsylvania law allows a defendant to offer excuses for a statutory or regulatory violation; however, the record permitted the jury to reject each of the excuses proffered by Astra.

First, even assuming that Astra at one time had reason to believe that 21 C.F.R. § 130.35 did not apply to Xylocaine, the FDA formally revoked in 1968 all previous opinions as to new-drug status and expressly informed Astra in 1969 that the FDA expected compliance with section 130.35. Thus, at least as of 1968, Astra knew, or should have known, that the FDA expected Astra to file the reports prescribed by section 130.35.

Second, the mere fact that Astra's attorneys interpreted section 130.35 incorrectly does not negate Astra's negligence in failing to comply with the regulations. Astra took a chance, and it is liable for the consequences of its acts. And even assuming that advice of counsel does constitute a legally cognizable excuse, that excuse could insulate Astra from liability only between the time that the FDA promulgated the regulations in 1964 and the time that the agency revoked all private letter-rulings as to new-drug status in 1968. Astra still had three and one-half years before the December 1971 tragedy to file the reports. Nor can we accept the availability of the reports to plant inspectors as an excuse for Astra's conduct. Plant inspectors are not physicians and do not possess the expertise necessary to facilitate a full evaluation of the reports. * * *

That Astra was negligent in failing to file the reports is not in itself sufficient to sustain the finding that Astra was liable. The negligence must also have been a proximate cause of Harrikah Stanton's injury. * * * [P]laintiffs attempted to establish causation by introducing evidence tending to show that the information withheld from the FDA was of great importance and that the agency could not properly perform its regulatory and supervisory roles without access to the unreported data, and that the FDA would have taken action had it been aware of Xylocaine's propensity to cause adverse reactions despite low dosage. Moreover, it was clear that Xylocaine had caused Harrikah's injuries: the jury found that Harrikah Stanton had experienced an adverse reaction, and Astra has never seriously argued that Xylocaine was not a "substantial factor" in causing that reaction.

Astra contends, however, as it did before the district court, that the evidence adduced by plaintiffs cannot support the jury's conclusion that the failure to file the reports was a substantial factor in causing Harrikah's injury because no witness stated expressly that, had those reports been filed, the FDA would have taken some action that would have saved this particular child from harm. It is true that the record does not contain such a statement, and that plaintiffs' evidence of causation is not very strong. On this point, the case thus is an extremely close one. * * *

The jury heard the testimony of four well qualified expert witnesses. They heard from these witnesses an analysis of the numerous adverse-reaction reports received by Astra, some of which described incidents of cardiac and respiratory arrest. They heard express testimony from these witnesses that Astra's conduct deprived the FDA and the medical community of important information, the lack of which would bias an evaluation of the safety of Xylocaine, and they heard testimony from which they could infer, keeping in mind the FDA's statutory duty continually to monitor marketed drugs for safety and effectiveness: (1) that had the FDA had these reports, it would have required notice to the medical community (through the package insert or PDR) of the critical information contained in the more than 200 adverse-reaction reports of the incidence of cardiac and respiratory arrest, notwithstanding low dosage of Xylocaine; and (2) that physicians receiving this information would have considered it in deciding how—and whether—to administer Xylocaine to their patients. Resolving every inference in plaintiffs' favor, we cannot conclude that the record was devoid of the requisite minimum quantum of evidence supporting the verdict. * * *

Plaintiffs' theory of strict liability is that the federal regulatory scheme creates an expectation on the part of the ordinary user of Xylocaine that the FDA would allow the continued marketing of the drug only after evaluating the information contained in reports required by regulations such as 21 C.F.R. § 130.35. By failing to file those reports, plaintiffs assert, Astra deprived the FDA and Harrikah Stanton's doctors of important information that people such as plaintiffs would have expected the agency and the physicians to have received and considered. * * *

In *Toole v. Richardson–Merrell Inc.*, 60 Cal.Rptr. 398 (Ct.App.1967), the California Court of Appeal confronted a section 402A claim similar to the one now before us and upheld a jury verdict holding a drug company strictly liable for injuries sustained by a plaintiff where the company had violated reporting provisions of the [FDCA]. Plaintiff had used the drug Triparanol (designed to treat arteriosclerosis), sold under the trade name "MER/29," and had developed cataracts in both eyes; Richardson Merrell's new-drug application had not disclosed the full extent of the company's knowledge regarding similar effects. Finding that the statutory violations rendered Triparanol a defective product because improperly prepared and marketed, the court declared:

> In light of the non-disclosure of significant facts which, if known to the FDA, would have enabled its scientists to make a more critical analysis of [the drug], it can hardly be said that the FDA's permission to market the drug was an informed judgment, based on all the known facts, or that it was uninfluenced by [defendant's] non-disclosure. * * *

We conclude that a Pennsylvania court applying Pennsylvania law would allow a jury to determine on the facts of this case that Xylocaine was a defective product within the meaning of section 402A. First, plaintiffs adduced evidence that, by failing to comply with 21 C.F.R. § 130.35, Astra deprived the FDA and, derivatively, the medical community at large of important information relating to the dangerousness of Xylocaine and that, without such information, the FDA could not make the professional and medical judgments that reasonable consumers rightfully expected it to make as a precondition of permitting the continued marketing of Xylocaine. Second, although plaintiffs' evidence was not particularly strong, we believe that plaintiffs presented sufficient evidence that the FDA would have acted had it received the unreported information. * * *

NOTES AND QUESTIONS

1. *Negligence (defectiveness) per se.* For a comparable decision, see Lukaszewicz v. Ortho Pharm. Corp., 510 F.Supp. 961, 964–65 (E.D.Wis.1981); see also Benedi v. McNeil–P.P.C., Inc., 66 F.3d 1378, 1387–89 (4th Cir. 1995) (sustaining negligence claim and punitive damage award where manufacturer had delayed submitting adverse reaction reports to the FDA during an OTC drug monograph rulemaking). But see Talley v. Danek Med., Inc., 179 F.3d 154, 161 (4th Cir.1999) (holding that an alleged failure to secure agency approval of a medical device would not support a negligence per se claim because the requirement was administrative rather than substantive in setting a standard of care); Iacangelo v. Georgetown Univ., 595 F.Supp.2d 87, 92–93 (D.D.C.2009) (same). See generally Andrew E. Costa, Negligence Per Se Theories in Pharmaceutical and Medical Device Litigation, 57 Me. L. Rev. 51 (2005). Questions have arisen about failures to disclose ADEs with drugs that the FDA subsequently withdrew from the market, which in any resulting tort litigation alleging negligence per se would simplify the causation difficulty discussed in *Stanton*. See Laura Johannes, Heart–Valve Problem That Felled Diet Pills Has Arisen Previously, Wall St. J., Dec. 11, 1997, at A1; David Willman, Risk Was Known as FDA OK'd Fatal Drug, L.A. Times, Mar. 11, 2001, at A1.

2. *Excuses, excuses.* The *Rest. (3d)* § 4 would recognize no excuses for noncompliance. See id. cmt. d. Is that position unduly restrictive? What if the FDA informally waived an obligation to comply in order to deal with unusual circumstances (e.g., a bioterrorist attack)? Or what if the agency's longstanding exercise of its prosecutorial discretion against demanding literal compliance with a particular requirement amounted to the de facto revocation of an obligation to comply? How would judges and juries presented with ambiguous regulations come to understand their application in practice? Cf. McNeil Pharm. v. Hawkins, 686 A.2d 567, 582–86 (D.C. 1996) (requiring plaintiffs to introduce expert testimony about the application of the statute and FDA regulations in order to support a negligence per se claim); Northern Trust Co. v. Upjohn Co., 572 N.E.2d 1030, 1040 (Ill.App.Ct.1991) (same).

3. *Private rights of action.* Courts have rejected suggestions that the FDCA creates an implied private right of action, which would allow litigants to recover damages directly from other parties in case they have violated the statute. See, e.g., Bailey v. Johnson, 48 F.3d 965, 967–68 (6th Cir.1995); see also James M. Beck & John A. Valentine, Challenging the Viability of FDCA–Based Causes of Action in the Tort Context: The Orthopedic Bone Screw Experience, 55 Food & Drug L.J. 389 (2000). How might a private right of action under federal law differ from a negligence per se claim under state tort law premised on a violation of federal law? Cf. Wheeler v. DePuy Spine, Inc., 706 F.Supp.2d 1264, 1268–70 (S.D.Fla.2010) (rejecting a claim for alleged violations of FDA requirements because, absent a private right of action, state law did not authorize negligence per se claims). Even if plaintiffs allege noncompliance with federal regulatory requirements, such claims would not provide the basis for exercising federal question jurisdiction. See Mohr v. Targeted Genetics, Inc., 690 F.Supp.2d 711, 730 (C.D.Ill.2010) (rejecting an effort to remove a case lacking complete diversity to a federal court on this basis); Guckin v. Nagle, 259 F.Supp.2d 406 (E.D.Pa.2003) (rejecting a manufacturer's petition to remove (on the basis of federal question jurisdiction) tort claims filed against multiple parties in state court by a subject injured during a clinical trial of a device under an IDE); see also Jamison v. Purdue Pharma Co., 251 F.Supp.2d 1315, 1326–27 (S.D.Miss.2003) (rejecting drug manufacturers' effort to remove tort claims to federal court on the theory that they acted under the direction of federal officers); id. at 1326 ("[D]efendants have established only that they are participants in a highly regulated industry.... [T]hey are for-profit corporations that do not derive their primary income from federal funding. They are not government contractors, delivering either a product or a service to the United States, or to beneficiaries designated by the government. Finally, the defendants do not operate as a public utility under the direct control of the federal government.").

2. Compliance and Federal Preemption

Recall that *Restatement (Third)* § 4(b) makes compliance with safety standards relevant to (but not dispositive of) questions about product defectiveness. This blackletter formulation accurately reflects case law involving drugs and medical devices. For instance, some courts have allowed juries to find that the specific warnings provided to patients by manufacturers of oral contraceptives were inadequate even though the labeling fully complied with the FDA's PPI regulation. See, e.g., Gurski v. Wyeth–Ayerst, 953 F.Supp. 412, 416–17 (D.Mass.1997); see also O'Gilvie v. International Playtex, Inc., 821 F.2d 1438, 1442–43 (10th Cir.1987) (same, for compliance with tampon warning label requirement). But see MacPherson v. Searle & Co., 775 F.Supp. 417, 420, 425 (D.D.C.1991) (granting summary judgment to the manufacturer because the required PPI adequately warned of the risk of injury suffered by the plaintiff); West v. G.D. Searle & Co., 879 S.W.2d 412, 414 (Ark.1994) (affirming same); see also Haddix v. Playtex Family Prods. Corp., 964 F.Supp. 1242, 1246 (C.D.Ill. 1997) (same, for FDA-mandated warnings of toxic shock syndrome on tampon labels).

In the course of deciding that comment k should protect all prescription drugs from the threat of strict products liability for design defect, the *Brown* and *Grundberg* courts offered a series of policy arguments that might justify giving compliance with FDA requirements greater weight. A few courts have taken this additional step, though somewhat tentatively. See, e.g., Ramirez v. Plough, Inc., 863 P.2d 167, 172 (Cal.1993) [excerpted in Chap. 7(C)(2)] (rejecting an inadequate warning claim against the seller of an OTC drug labeled in conformity with FDA requirements); see also Peter H. Schuck, Multi–Culturalism Redux: Science, Law, and Politics, 11 Yale L. & Pol'y Rev. 1, 39 (1993) ("For better or for worse, the FDA is the agency that the public has empowered to make authoritative judgments of this kind on its behalf."). Such expressions of deference to administrative judgments about relative product safety remain rare, however.

Restatement (Third) of the Law of Torts: Products Liability

(American Law Inst. 1998):

§ 4. Noncompliance and Compliance with Product Safety Statutes or Regulations

> Comment e. Occasionally, after reviewing relevant circumstances, a court may properly conclude that a particular product safety standard set by statute or regulation adequately serves the objectives of tort law and therefore that the product that complies with the standard is not defective as a matter of law. Such a conclusion may be appropriate when the safety statute or regulation was promulgated recently, thus supplying currency to the standard therein established; when the specific standard addresses the very issue of product design or warning presented in the case before the court; and when the court is confident that the deliberative process by which the safety standard was established was full, fair, and thorough and reflected substantial expertise. Conversely, when the deliberative process that led to the safety standard with which the defendant's product complies was tainted by the supplying of false information to, or the withholding of necessary and valid information from, the agency that promulgated the standard or certified or approved the product, compliance with regulation is entitled to little or no weight.

Lars Noah, *Rewarding Regulatory Compliance: The Pursuit of Symmetry in Products Liability*

88 GEO. L.J. 2147 (2000).

* * * Only after developing a proper appreciation of the rigors of the regulatory process of a particular agency can one decide whether an inevitably qualified government standards defense makes any sense. In addition to starting at the beginning (and not becoming distracted by

highly visible regulatory failures such as breast implants or fenfluramine, which would not benefit from a compliance defense to tort claims in any event), I will emphasize regulatory standards that emerge from a structured and public rulemaking process. Such an emphasis differs from the individualized product licensing decisions that normally frame this debate * * * *

I. *Contrasting Administrative and Judicial Regulation of Drug Labeling*

Imagine the following situation. The FDA promulgates a regulation specifying the risk information that must appear in the labeling of all prescription drugs of a certain therapeutic class. In order to promote labeling clarity and uniformity, the FDA also explicitly prohibits the inclusion of any additional warnings about this particular hazard. As happens with many regulatory initiatives, years elapse between the initial formulation of this proposal and its publication as a final rule. Under the Administrative Procedure Act (APA), agencies must, at a minimum, publish a notice of their proposed action, provide an opportunity for public comment, and issue an explanatory preamble to accompany the final text of the regulation. The issuance of a regulation represents the commitment of significant resources and reflects input by dozens of agency personnel from various disciplines.

Moreover, as observers of the administrative process know all too well, publication of a regulation in the *Federal Register* does not settle matters. Nowadays, agencies must transmit their rules to Congress for fast-track consideration and a possible override resolution, and, more plausibly, agencies fear judicial scrutiny followed by a remand. For purposes of this hypothetical, assume that a public interest group files a petition to review the regulation in the U.S. Court of Appeals for the D.C. Circuit, claiming that the FDA's mandatory labeling statement is not sufficiently alarming given the nature of the hazard revealed by the administrative record, and that the prohibition on additional warnings of this particular risk amounted to arbitrary and capricious decisionmaking in light of the public health mandate underlying the agency's enabling statute. After considering these arguments and concluding that agency officials had taken the requisite hard look at the relevant comments and other information in the rulemaking record, the court denies the petition for review.

Even after running the gauntlet of these legislative and judicial checks, agencies cannot rest on their laurels. Often agencies must interpret and clarify the meaning of their regulations in the course of enforcement actions or through the issuance of guidelines. In addition, agencies may have to revisit regulations in light of changed circumstances, and they must respond to petitions urging the amendment or repeal of an existing rule, which then may trigger another round of judicial review. For example, the same group that unsuccessfully challenged the original rule in federal court may resurrect its objections by filing a citizen petition with the FDA requesting an amendment to the rule and then seeking judicial review of any agency decision to deny that request. As a number of administrative law scholars have noted in recent years, these numerous obstacles tend to discourage rulemaking altogether. When agencies do go to all of that trouble, however, their handiwork deserves more than the casual acknowledgment that the courts typically give it when resolving products liability litigation.

Now let us leave the comforting confines of the Beltway to discover how drug labeling is regulated in the heartland. Consider the fate of three pharmaceutical companies selling essentially identical products, but with differences in their labeling, which face tort litigation brought by patients who suffered precisely the side effect that the FDA's final rule sought to address. Company *A* blatantly failed to comply with the labeling regulation, and, among other things, the plaintiff pursues a negligence per se claim premised on the violation of this relevant safety requirement. Company *B* scrupulously complied with the labeling regulation; consequently, the company, emphasizing that it could not have provided additional risk information without running afoul of the FDA's rule, moves for summary judgment on the plaintiff's failure-to-warn claims. Company *C*, in a justified fit of paranoia, included both the FDA-mandated cautionary statement as well as additional language crafted by its legal staff and designed to make this—and all of the other hazard information—as alarming as possible; however, the plaintiff still pursues a failure-to-warn action premised on a theory of dilution by "overwarning" and, among other things, pursues a negligence per se claim for violating the agency's prohibition on additional risk information.

Under prevailing tort doctrines, all three plaintiffs will reach the jury, in two cases with the benefit of negligence per se instructions, and, in the suit against Company *B*, the trial judge will reject any suggestion that regulatory compliance conclusively establishes the absence of negligence or product defectiveness. As a consequence, often unsophisticated jurors in different parts of the country will make their own judgments about appropriate prescription drug labeling, effectively second-guessing the FDA's far more expert, accountable, and uniform determination that, in this hypothetical, has been affirmed by a federal court after reviewing the wealth of information compiled during the agency's rulemaking proceeding.

What accounts for this puzzling state of affairs? In most jurisdictions, the unexcused violation of a relevant safety statute or regulation constitutes negligence (or defectiveness) as a matter of law. In contrast, most jurisdictions consider proof of compliance with an applicable government safety standard at best as some relevant evidence when assessing allegations that a product is defective or that the defendant's conduct was negligent. Courts routinely note that government standards establish only "minimum" requirements, which a jury can decide a reasonable person should have exceeded under the circumstances. The statutory safety standards at issue in many of the earliest compliance cases were, however, quite limited in scope, often lacked any direct enforcement mechanism, and sometimes expressly preserved common-law tort remedies. In addition, the courts in these early cases emphasized that standards of this sort could not possibly have specified the safeguards appropriate for highly variable settings such as railroad crossings of differing types spread throughout the country.

In the century since the development of the common-law rule against recognizing a regulatory compliance defense, the focus of tort litigation has shifted from heavily context-dependent collision cases to recurring situations such as defects in mass-produced consumer goods, which are more readily subject to nationally uniform requirements for safeguards that should perform equally well anywhere in the land. At the same time, the sources and complexity of government safety regulations have changed dramatically—from vague commands issued by generalist legislatures to precise requirements formulated by specialist administrators. Modern regulatory systems typically represent legislative or administrative efforts to set optimal—not minimal—safety standards * * * *

Nonetheless, rejection of the government standards defense remains the prevailing rule by far. Courts continue to give little or no weight to compliance with today's far more intricate regulatory regimes, frequently dismissing the defense out of hand with the oft-repeated and largely unexamined premise that government safety standards are nothing more than minimum requirements. Although not formally obligated to adopt relevant federal regulations as particularizing the standard of care in tort litigation, at least absent preemption, courts should take them more seriously than they do at present.

II. *Accountable Regulation: Myths About Jury Competence and Agency Capture*

Wholly apart from the suggestion that government standards represent only minimum safety requirements, critics of the compliance defense denigrate the institutions that generate these requirements and applaud the independence and common sense of jurors in making judgments about appropriate levels of safety. But such a "grass roots" approach lodges profoundly important choices affecting society in our least representative, expert, or accountable institutions.

As the decisionmakers empowered by the citizenry to set safety standards, legislatures and regulatory agencies select the levels of product risk that they deem appropriate based on scientific, economic, and—yes—political considerations. When courts treat these standards as presumptively sub-optimal, they basically arrogate such important decisions for themselves and, in particular, juries. At some level, the longstanding rejection of a compliance defense appears to reflect a populist faith in laypersons and an accompanying distrust of distant federal bureaucracies.

Commentators who object to a regulatory compliance defense have identified various flaws in the administrative process, including claims that regulated entities have "captured" the agencies that oversee their activities. But, just as opponents of tort reform legitimately decry the lack of empirical evidence of a litigation crisis, proponents of the government standards defense should object to the agency capture thesis as supported by little more than anecdote and suspicion. To the extent that this turns on impressionistic assessments, let me suggest that health and safety agencies like the FDA have become more beholden to groups that purport to represent the public interest.

Although the dynamic surely differed in previous decades, and no one disputes the tremendous resources that industry can deploy to influence the legislative and regulatory processes even today, regulated entities operate at the mercy of powerful agencies such as the FDA, while consumer groups have nothing to lose by aggressively pursuing their agenda and vocally criticizing the agency when they fail to prevail. Indeed, without the persistent efforts of consumer interest organizations, a pair of important FDA warning regulations mentioned herein might never have seen the light of day because of industry resistance. When their arguments fail to move agency experts or otherwise lose out in the political process, however, should consumer activists get to keep waging what they regard as the good fight in the more congenial arena of tort litigation, addressing their gripes to receptive panels of jurors accountable to no one for decisions that have undoubted regulatory effects? Unless something indicates a profound failure of the regulatory process in a particular situation, I think not. * * *

III. *Distinguishing an FDA Compliance Defense from Preemption*

On rare occasions, courts have deferred to FDA determinations. For instance, in a 1993 decision involving an inadequate warning claim against the manufacturer of a nonprescription drug product, the California Supreme Court concluded that "there is some room in tort law for a defense of statutory compliance," in part because courts lack "the procedure and resources to conduct the relevant inquiries." Occasionally, legislatures adopt an FDA compliance defense, as Congress did for childhood vaccines in 1986, and as New Jersey did for all FDA-regulated products in 1987. Notwithstanding these limited pockets of protection, the recognition of an FDA compliance defense remains the exception. Courts still routinely ignore the agency's regulations and approval decisions in products liability litigation.

The primary rationale for disregarding the FDA's drug labeling decisions is that the agency has imposed only "minimum" standards open to supplementation by a lay jury's verdict enforcing a manufacturer's common-law duty to warn. As one former agency official commented several years ago, however, the "FDA surely does not regard its own prescription drug labeling decisions as merely establishing a floor." Nonetheless, the agency's formal pronouncements on the subject have contributed to the courts' confusion by disavowing any intent to influence tort litigation through its regulatory decisions. The FDA's apparent lack of opposition to judicial second-guessing in this context is difficult to fathom, though one commentator has suggested that public health agencies may not mind having the tort system serve as a "safety valve" for deflecting adverse publicity from themselves when hazards with a product subsequently come to light.

Preemption offers a blunter tool for securing judicial respect for federal standards. Under the rubric of federal preemption, Congress and the FDA may announce that their labeling or other requirements displace state authority to regulate. Over the course of the last decade, an increasing number of courts have interpreted such provisions as displacing state tort actions as well, primarily in medical device cases, and sometimes even in the absence of compliance with any particular federal safety standard. Because no statutory preemption clause applies in the case of drug regulation and implied preemption arguments rarely succeed in this context, pharmaceutical manufacturers can find little solace in these decisions.

Nonetheless, when the Supreme Court decided that provisions in other statutes displacing state authority to regulate also expressly preempted tort claims, it made a critical concession that should influence any debate about the advisability of adopting a government standards defense[:] * * * damage awards predicated on a manufacturer's departure from the common-law standard of reasonable care potentially have as much of a regulatory effect as positive law requirements reflected in state statutes or rules. Critics of the regulatory compliance defense respond that a tort judgment does not dictate any alteration of primary conduct, but in the next breath they emphasize the need to retain the threat of liability to serve a deterrent function given the often inconsequential administrative sanctions. They can't have it both ways. Although I agree that the regulatory impact of tort judgments does not necessarily establish an intent by Congress to preempt tort claims to the same extent as requirements imposed directly by state officials, juries indirectly—and inconsistently—but unmistakably do set product safety standards in this country. Once we accept the notion that jurors effectively regulate with their verdicts, one may ask whether this arrangement makes sense.

IV. *Blending Administrative and Judicial Regulation*

Professor Rabin emphasizes two comparative advantages enjoyed by the tort system: a superior capacity for ferreting out information about unscrupulous corporate behavior and attention to compensatory aims not taken into account by administrative agencies. Before evaluating these arguments separately, one must remember that manufacturers would continue to face the prospect of liability in most cases. Although a sweeping federal preemption defense would sacrifice the supposed virtues of the tort system, a regulatory compliance defense should have only a modest impact. Tort liability would remain in place to compensate plaintiffs and deter defendants insofar as genuinely defective products cause injuries. The government standards defense only goes to questions of breach and, in appropriate cases, provides a basis for concluding that a product manufactured, designed, and labeled in accordance with federal safety requirements was not in fact defective.

A. *Generating Information*

Professor Rabin's information-based argument does not seem terribly compelling. Although individual product approvals may depend upon licensing applicants for full disclosure, broad-based rulemaking initiatives give agencies access to a wealth of information, far more than typical in tort litigation. Where regulations dictate appropriate risk labeling for a range of similar products, much of this information will appear in refereed scientific journals, and the FDA can call on other health protection agencies, such as the Centers for Disease Control and Prevention, or prestigious scientific organizations, such as the National Academy of Sciences (NAS) and the Federation of American Societies for Experimental Biology (FASEB), to assist with compiling and reviewing the available research. The ad hoc panels of court-appointed experts that Professor Rabin describes, even in the highly unlikely event that they ever became widespread, could not possibly match the FDA's capacity for gathering and evaluating relevant risk information. Indeed, his use of tobacco as an illustration of the tort system's capacity for uncovering corporate misconduct is particularly inapt; the FDA first broke the story concerning the internal tobacco industry records and witnesses as a prelude to its rulemaking effort in this area. The lawyers who later capitalized on these disclosures might never have uncovered the documents or whistleblowers without the agency's initiative.

Ultimately, however, a regulatory compliance defense should not diminish whatever additional information that the tort system can supply. Plaintiffs will not have reduced incentives to discover fraud on an agency just because defendants get to assert a compliance defense, for which defendants would shoulder the burden of proof. On the contrary, plaintiffs may search more actively for evidence of corporate misconduct. If they do not already have an incentive to assert claims of negligence per se based on violations of relevant safety standards, plaintiffs will have every reason to find evidence of noncompliance, nondisclosure, or fraud in order to defeat the defense.

B. *Compensating Injured Victims*

Professor Rabin's compensatory argument also misses the mark. In effect, he suggests that some states have adopted a form of strict products liability that takes questions about defectiveness out of the equation. If true, then the compliance defense has nothing to say. In these jurisdictions, enterprises would know that they must pay for any product-related injuries to consumers, no matter the state-of-the-art, the clarity of risk information, or the social disutilities of the price increases that would have to accompany such a regime of compulsory insurance. The compliance defense would, however, remain of interest in those far more numerous jurisdictions that continue to inquire about defectiveness before spreading the costs of product-related injuries by imposing strict liability. Indeed, even in California, which Professor Rabin identifies as following a particularly strict version of products liability on the strength of yet another automobile case, the compliance defense would make a difference in prescription drug and medical device litigation because proof of some genuine product defect remains essential in that and most other jurisdictions so as not to deter the marketing of unavoidably unsafe therapeutic products.

As a related point, Professor Rabin explains that agencies set safety standards based on a comparison of risks and benefits but without any view toward the compensation of injuries. That might, however, actually argue in favor of borrowing such standards. Unlike jurors who may become fixated on awarding compensation to the needy plaintiff put before them, sometimes without any apparent regard to issues of defect or causation (or, indeed, aggregate compensatory questions), agency determinations appropriately focus on safety questions and have the advantage of taking a broader view of the inevitable tradeoffs involved in specifying appropriate product designs and disclosures of risk information. Moreover, it is not clear how agencies would react if they took compensatory issues into account when setting product safety standards. Professor Rabin implies that the range of covered injuries would expand, but that is hardly obvious.

One could offer a similar response to critics of the government standards defense who worry about regulatory obsolescence and administrative inertia. They assume uni-directionality, but this ignores the possibility that new scientific information may reveal excessive protectiveness in earlier standards formulated in the face of greater uncertainty. Indeed, obsolescence of this sort has not deterred courts from using *violations* of federal safety standards to assist plaintiffs in making negligence per se claims, and the often asserted difficulties in gauging compliance generally have not done so either. If federal product safety requirements appropriately set the standard of care when it helps plaintiffs, notwithstanding concerns that agencies may have set the requirements without considering compensatory issues or may have failed to keep them up-to-date, then compliance with those same requirements should satisfy the standard of care in products liability cases even though it happens to help defendants.

C. *Influencing Administrative Regulation*

In the highly unlikely event that an FDA compliance defense ever catches on with the courts, one should inquire whether this might filter back to alter the agency's standard-setting process in any way. To the extent that plaintiffs' lawyers and their close allies in the public interest community have not already become heavily involved in product safety rulemaking proceedings, they may have enhanced incentives to submit comments and provide any possibly relevant data to the FDA in the future. Although industry representatives will understand that the stakes have increased, they may, at the same time, prefer a more expeditious conclusion to the agency's rulemaking proceedings than in the past, when efforts to delay or derail finalization of rules typically worked to the industry's advantage (at least in a regime where a standard only serves to punish, whether in public or private litigation). The agency may proceed somewhat more deliberately, but the defense would not come into play in the absence of a final regulation. Moreover, after the promulgation of a rule, products liability defectiveness per se claims will remain available in cases of agency underenforcement, which will continue to promote industry compliance with FDA regulations notwithstanding scarce resources.

In short, the regulatory compliance defense might improve FDA standard-setting as much as it can help rationalize products liability litigation. Even if that assessment seems unduly optimistic, increased judicial deference to government standards in tort suits would not impede the administrative process. In any event, the debate about this question too frequently focuses on the private law half of the equation and underemphasizes or misunderstands the public law half. The regulatory dimension deserves at least as much attention as the perspective rooted in tort law.

Just as they malign proponents of the government standards defense for idealizing agencies and caricaturing the courts as inept, opponents of the defense inappropriately idealize the judiciary and caricature the regulatory process as corrupt. Both public and private law approaches to product risks suffer from imperfections, but that does not mean that each system somehow makes up for the other's limitations simply by operating in parallel, oblivious to their own weaknesses and the corresponding strengths of the other system of risk regulation. The FDA regulatory compliance defense does not put us to the stark all-or-nothing choice associated with federal preemption; instead, it appropriately attempts to blend the two systems in a manner that maximizes the strengths of each. Standards adopted by the FDA through rulemaking procedures provide the strongest case for the recognition of such a defense, and the courts should at least embrace the limited concession to this effect in the new *Restatement*, even if they remain doubtful about a broader compliance defense. * * *

NOTES AND QUESTIONS

1. *Another proposal*. For an intriguing though somewhat cumbersome (and largely unrealistic) "hybrid adjudication" scheme designed to better integrate these two approaches, see Catherine T. Struve, The FDA and the Tort System: Postmarketing Surveillance, Compensation, and the Role of Litigation, 5 Yale J. Health Pol'y L. & Ethics 587, 616–29, 646–69 (2005) (proposing the creation of an alternative track, which companies could opt into at the time of applying for product approval, that would use qui tam actions brought on behalf of the United States in its capacity as parens patriae, referring safety and causation questions back to the FDA to exercise its primary jurisdiction, and calculating any compensatory damages in federal bench trials).

2. *Precursors*. An earlier study initiated by the American Law Institute had recommended the recognition of a regulatory compliance defense, especially for prescription drugs. See 2 ALI, Reporters' Study, Enterprise Responsibility for Personal Injury: Approaches to Legal and Institutional Change 95–110 (1991). In an article published at the same time, the future reporters for the *Restatement (Third)* seemed dubious about the tendency to disregard compliance with FDA requirements. See James A. Henderson, Jr. & Aaron D. Twerski, Doctrinal Collapse in Products Liability: The Empty Shell of Failure to Warn, 65 N.Y.U. L. Rev. 265, 320 (1990) ("[F]or reasons that we find difficult to understand, courts have not deferred to the determinations of product safety agencies such as the [FDA] .... The analysis usually begins and ends with the statement that agency standards are minimum, not maximum, standards and that courts are therefore free to disregard them."). Although the new *Restatement* in comment e to § 4 provides an opening for the recognition of a regulatory compliance defense as a general matter, elsewhere it expresses only limited confidence in the FDA. See Rest. (3d) § 6 cmt. b, at 146 ("[U]nqualified deference to these regulatory mechanisms is considered by a growing number of courts to be unjustified. An approved prescription drug or medical device can present significant risks without corresponding advantages.").

3. *Standards vs. approvals*. One might distinguish compliance with generally applicable standards and individualized product approval decisions, in part because rulemaking is a more open and accountable decisionmaking process than licensing decisions that often occur behind the scenes and depend on the sponsor to provide all relevant information to the agency. Conversely, one might regard licensing decisions as more significant because they represent a more focused and tailored risk-benefit judgment about a particular product than rulemaking that generates broad and perhaps ambiguous regulations. Comment e is unclear on this score, though it seems to express a preference for safety standards embodied in agency regulations. In some instances, courts have noted their frustration when asked to untangle the meaning and application of FDA regulations in private litigation where the agency itself has not concluded that a manufacturer has either violated or complied with those requirements. See, e.g., National Bank of Commerce v. Kimberly–Clark Corp., 38 F.3d 988, 996 (8th Cir.1994). In a lengthy section of the *Stanton* opinion excluded from the previous excerpt, the court undertook a detailed analysis of how the FDA's evolving rules for the reporting of adverse drug events applied to Astra during the time period in question.

4. *Minimum standards vs. optimal standards*. The primary rationale for disregarding the FDA's drug and medical device risk-benefit decisions is that the agency has imposed only "minimum" standards open to supplementation by a lay jury's verdict enforcing a manufacturer's common law tort duty. See, e.g., Wells v. Ortho Pharm. Corp., 788 F.2d 741, 746 (11th Cir.1986); Plenger v. Alza Corp., 13 Cal.Rptr.2d 811, 819 n.7 (Ct.App.1992); Savina v. Sterling Drug, 795 P.2d 915, 931 (Kan.1990); Feldman v. Lederle Lab., 625 A.2d 1066, 1070 (N.J.1993); Washington State Physicians Ins. Exch. & Ass'n v. Fisons Corp., 858 P.2d 1054, 1069 (Wash.1993). Even if not conclusive, most courts will allow a manufacturer to introduce evidence of compliance with FDA requirements at trial. See, e.g., O'Gilvie v. International Playtex, Inc., 821 F.2d 1438 (10th Cir.1987); Foyle v. Lederle Lab., 674 F.Supp. 530, 533 (E.D.N.C.1987); see also N.C. Gen. Stat. § 99B–6(b)(4) (requiring that courts take into account FDA approval of labeling when resolving design defect claims).

5. *Tort reform statutes*. In the National Childhood Vaccine Injury Act, Congress included an FDA compliance defense against tort liability for inadequate warnings and for punitive damages. See 42 U.S.C. §§ 300aa–

22(b), 300aa–23(d); see also Blackmon v. American Home Prods. Corp., 328 F.Supp.2d 659, 664–67 (S.D.Tex.2004) (holding that the NCVIA bars all design defect claims but that manufacturers must prove compliance with FDA requirements in order to enjoy the presumption that their warnings to health care professionals were adequate). A few states have codified an FDA compliance defense. See Mich. Comp. Laws Ann. § 600.2946(5) (treating FDA drug approval as a conclusive defense absent evidence of fraud); Tex. Civ. Prac. Code § 8, 2007 (creating a rebuttable presumption of adequate warning). Courts rejected constitutional challenges to the Michigan statute. See Garcia v. Wyeth–Ayerst Lab., 385 F.3d 961 (6th Cir.2004) (rejecting Fifth and Seventh Amendment objections, though first deciding to sever its exceptions for fraud on or bribery of FDA officials as preempted); Taylor v. Smithkline Beecham Corp., 658 N.W.2d 127 (Mich.2003) (rejecting argument that the law impermissibly delegated state legislative authority to the FDA). See generally Jason Murdey, Preemption of the "Fraud on the FDA" Exception to Michigan's Tort Immunity Statute for Drug Manufacturers: Reconsidering Garcia and Desiano After Levine, 66 Food & Drug L.J. 85 (2011); Jason C. Miller, Note, When and How to Defer to the FDA: Learning from Michigan's Regulatory Compliance Defense, 15 Mich. Telecomm. & Tech. L. Rev. 565 (2009). A few other states provide an FDA compliance defense against only punitive damage claims. See Ariz. Rev. Stat. Ann. § 12–701(A); Ohio Rev. Code Ann. § 2307.801(C); Or. Rev. Stat. § 30.927 (1); Utah Code Ann. § 78–18–2(1); see also Elissa Levy, Note, The HEALTH Act's FDA Defense to Punitive Damages: A Gift to Drug Makers or to the Public?, 74 Fordham L. Rev. 2425 (2006); Joan E. Shreffler, Comment, Bad Medicine: Good–Faith FDA Approval as a Recommended Bar to Punitive Damages in Pharmaceutical Products Liability Cases, 84 N.C. L. Rev. 737 (2006).

6. *Further commentary*. See Michael D. Green, Statutory Compliance and Tort Liability: Examining the Strongest Case, 30 U. Mich. J.L. Reform 461 (1997); Richard L. Manning, Products Liability and Prescription Drug Prices in Canada and the United States, 40 J.L. & Econ. 203 (1997); Lars Noah, Civil Jury Nullification, 86 Iowa L. Rev. 1601 (2001); W. Kip Viscusi et al., Deterring Inefficient Pharmaceutical Litigation: An Economic Rationale for the FDA Regulatory Compliance Defense, 24 Seton Hall L. Rev. 1437 (1994); Scott S. Evans, Note, Dynamic Incentives: Improving the Safety, Effectivity, and Availability of Medical Products Through Progressively Increasing Damage Caps for Manufacturers, 2007 U. Ill. L. Rev. 1069; Alec Johnson, Note, Vioxx and Consumer Product Pain Relief: The Policy Implications of Limiting Courts' Regulatory Influence over Mass Consumer Product Claims, 41 Loy. L.A. L. Rev. 1039 (2008).

Even if courts refuse to credit compliance as a matter of common law, they might feel compelled to do so by the operation of federal preemption. Pharmaceutical manufacturers have argued that sweeping FDA regulation impliedly preempts tort claims against them. For the most part, this argument has met with little success. See David R. Geiger & Mark D. Rosen, Rationalizing Product Liability for Prescription Drugs: Implied Preemption, Federal Common Law, and Other Paths to Uniform Pharmaceutical Safety Standards, 45 DePaul L. Rev. 395 (1996); Jonathan V. O'Steen & Van O'Steen, The FDA Defense: Vioxx and the Argument Against Federal Preemption of State Claims for Injuries Resulting from Defective Drugs, 48 Ariz. L. Rev. 67 (2006); Beverly L. Jacklin, Annotation, Federal Preemption of State Common–Law Products Liability Claims Pertaining to Drugs, Medical Devices and Other Health–Related Items, 98 A.L.R. Fed. 124 (1990 & 2011 Supp.); see also Jennifer A. Surprenant, Note, Should Preemption Apply in a Pharmaceutical Context? An Analysis of the Preemption Debate and What Regulatory Compliance Statutes Contribute to the Discussion, 77 Fordham L. Rev. 327 (2008); Gardiner Harris & Alex Berenson, Drug Makers Near Old Goal: A Legal Shield, N.Y. Times, Apr. 6, 2008, at A1 ("After decades of being dismissed by courts, the [preemption] tactic now appears to be on the verge of success ...."). In *Wyeth v. Levine*, 555 U.S. 555 (2009) [excerpted below], the Supreme Court addressed this question without entirely settling it.

A few of the federal statutes implemented by the FDA include preemption clauses, most notably the medical device provisions of the FDCA:

> (a) General rule. Except as provided in subsection (b) of this section, no State or political subdivision of a State may establish or continue in effect with respect to a device intended for human use any requirement—
>
> (1) which is different from, or in addition to, any requirement applicable under this chapter to the device, and
>
> (2) which relates to the safety or effectiveness of the device or to any other matter included in a requirement applicable to the device under this chapter.
>
> (b) Exempt requirements. Upon application of a State or a political subdivision thereof, the Secretary may, by regulation promulgated after notice and opportunity for an oral hearing, exempt from subsection (a) of this section, under such conditions as may be prescribed in such regulation, a requirement of such State or political subdivision applicable to a device intended for human use if—
>
> (1) the requirement is more stringent than a requirement under this chapter which would be applicable to the device if an exemption were not in effect under this subsection; or
>
> (2) the requirement—(A) is required by compelling local conditions, and (B) compliance with the requirement would not cause the device to be in violation of any applicable requirement under this chapter.

21 U.S.C. § 360k. This avenue for protection from tort liability has worked far better, especially after 1992 when the United States Supreme Court decided for the first time that federal statutes displacing nonidentical requirements expressly preempted state common law as well as positive

law. See Cipollone v. Liggett Group, Inc., 505 U.S. 504, 518–30 (1992) (plurality opinion); see also Robert S. Adler & Richard A. Mann, Preemption and Medical Devices: The Courts Run Amok, 59 Mo. L. Rev. 895 (1994); Roger W. Bivans, Note, Substantially Equivalent? Federal Preemption of State Common–Law Claims Involving Medical Devices, 74 Tex. L. Rev. 1087 (1996). Indeed, by the mid–1990s, the courts had become so receptive to preemption arguments that an officer from one pacemaker company testified in opposition to a products liability bill then before Congress, brashly announcing his belief "that tort reform has already arrived for medical device manufacturers," and worrying that the proposed legislation might weaken the industry's existing defense to liability! See Products Liability Standards: Hearings Before a Subcomm. of the House Comm. on Energy & Commerce, 103d Cong. 196 (1994) (statement of William Nealon, Vice Pres. & Gen. Counsel, Telectronics Pacing Sys.). The Supreme Court threw some cold water on that idea just a couple of years later in *Medtronic, Inc. v. Lohr*, 518 U.S. 470 (1996) (plurality), a fractured opinion rejecting use of the preemption defense in a pacemaker case and questioning whether it would ever be available. Indeed, some commentators read *Lohr* as signalling the demise of the preemption defense in medical device tort litigation. See Robert B. Leflar & Richard A. Mann, The Preemption Pentad: Federal Preemption of Products Liability Claims After Medtronic, 64 Tenn. L. Rev. 691 (1997). But see Lars Noah, The Preemption Morass, Legal Times, July 29, 1996, at S37 (disagreeing with this prediction). The Court's latest foray into this area offered far greater clarity about the reach of express preemption as a defense in tort litigation against manufacturers of medical devices.

Riegel v. Medtronic, Inc.

552 U.S. 312 (2008).

■ SCALIA, JUSTICE:

* * * The FDA spends an average of 1,200 hours reviewing each [PMA] application and grants premarket approval only if it finds there is a "reasonable assurance" of the device's "safety and effectiveness." 21 U.S.C. § 360e(d). * * * Once a device has received premarket approval, the MDA forbids the manufacturer to make, without FDA permission, changes in design specifications, manufacturing processes, labeling, or any other attribute, that would affect safety or effectiveness. Id. § 360e(d)(6)(A)(i). If the applicant wishes to make such a change, it must submit, and the FDA must approve, an application for supplemental premarket approval, to be evaluated under largely the same criteria as an initial application. After premarket approval, the devices are subject to reporting requirements. Id. § 360i. * * * The FDA has the power to withdraw premarket approval based on newly reported data or existing information and must withdraw approval if it determines that a device is unsafe or ineffective under the conditions in its labeling. Id. § 360e(e)(1). * * *

The device at issue is an Evergreen Balloon Catheter marketed by defendant-respondent Medtronic, Inc. It is a Class III device that received premarket approval from the FDA in 1994; changes to its label received supplemental approvals in 1995 and 1996. Charles Riegel underwent coronary angioplasty in 1996, shortly after suffering a myocardial infarction. His right coronary artery was diffusely diseased and heavily calcified. Riegel's doctor inserted the Evergreen Balloon Catheter into his patient's coronary artery in an attempt to dilate the artery, although the device's labeling stated that use was contraindicated for patients with diffuse or calcified stenoses. The label also warned that the catheter should not be inflated beyond its rated burst pressure of eight atmospheres. Riegel's doctor inflated the catheter five times, to a pressure of 10 atmospheres; on its fifth inflation, the catheter ruptured. Riegel developed a heart block, was placed on life support, and underwent emergency coronary bypass surgery. * * *

[Plaintiffs'] complaint alleged that Medtronic's catheter was designed, labeled, and manufactured in a manner that violated New York common law, and that these defects caused Riegel to suffer severe and permanent injuries. * * * [The federal district court dismissed most of these claims as preempted, and the appellate court affirmed.] Since the MDA expressly preempts only state requirements "different from, or in addition to, any requirement applicable ... to the device" under federal law, id. § 360k(a)(1), we must determine whether the federal government has established requirements applicable to Medtronic's catheter. * * *

[S]tate requirements are preempted "only when the Food and Drug Administration has established specific counterpart regulations or there are other specific requirements applicable to a particular device." 21 C.F.R. § 808.1(d). Informed by the regulation, we [previously] concluded that federal manufacturing and labeling requirements applicable across the board to almost all medical devices did not preempt the common-law claims of negligence and strict liability at issue in *Medtronic, Inc. v. Lohr*, 518 U.S. 470 (1996). The federal requirements, we said, were not requirements specific to the device in question—they reflected "entirely generic concerns about device regulation generally." Id. at 501. While we disclaimed a conclusion that general federal requirements could never preempt, or general state duties never be preempted, we held that no preemption occurred in the case at hand based on a careful comparison between the state and federal duties at issue.

Even though substantial-equivalence review under § 510(k) is device specific, *Lohr* also rejected the manufacturer's contention that § 510(k) approval imposed device-specific "requirements." * * * Unlike general labeling duties, premarket approval is specific to individual devices. And it is in no sense an exemption from federal safety review—it *is* federal safety review. Thus, the attributes that *Lohr* found lacking in § 510(k) review are present here. While § 510(k) is "focused on *equivalence*, not safety," id. at 493, premarket approval is focused on safety, not equivalence. While devices that enter the market through § 510(k) have "never been formally reviewed under the MDA for safety or efficacy," the FDA may grant premarket approval only after it determines that a device offers a reasonable assurance of safety and effectiveness. And while the FDA does not "require" that a device allowed to enter the market as a substantial equivalent "take any particular form for any particular reason," the FDA requires a device that has received premarket approval to be made with almost no deviations from the specifications in its approval application, for the reason that the FDA has determined that the approved form provides a reasonable assurance of safety and effectiveness.

We turn, then, to the second question: whether the Riegels' common-law claims rely upon "any requirement" of New York law applicable to the catheter that is "different from, or in addition to" federal requirements and that "relates to the safety or effectiveness of the device or to any other matter included in a requirement applicable to the device." 21 U.S.C. § 360k(a). Safety and effectiveness are the very subjects of the Riegels' common-law claims, so the critical issue is whether New York's tort duties constitute "requirements" under the MDA.

In *Lohr*, five Justices concluded that common-law causes of action for negligence and strict liability do impose "requirement[s]" and would be preempted by federal requirements specific to a medical device. See 518 U.S. at 512 (opinion of O'Connor, J., joined by Rehnquist, C.J., and Scalia and Thomas, JJ.); id. at 503–05 (opinion of Breyer, J.). We adhere to that view. In interpreting two other statutes we have likewise held that a provision preempting state "requirements" preempted common-law duties. * * * Congress is entitled to know what meaning this Court will assign to terms regularly used in its enactments. Absent other indication, reference to a state's "requirements" includes its common-law duties. * * *

In the present case, there is nothing to contradict this normal meaning. To the contrary, in the context of this legislation excluding common-law duties from the scope of preemption would make little sense. State tort law that requires a manufacturer's catheters to be safer, but hence less effective, than the model the FDA has approved disrupts the federal scheme no less than state regulatory law to the same effect. Indeed, one would think that tort law, applied by juries under a negligence or strict-liability standard, is less deserving of preservation. A state statute, or a regulation adopted by a state agency, could at least be expected to apply cost-benefit analysis similar to that applied by the experts at the FDA: How many more lives will be saved by a device which, along with its greater effectiveness, brings a greater risk of harm? A jury, on the other hand, sees only the cost of a more dangerous design, and is not concerned with its benefits; the patients who reaped those benefits are not represented in court. As Justice Breyer explained in *Lohr*, it is implausible that the MDA was meant to "grant greater power (to set state standards 'different from, or in addition to' federal standards) to a single state jury than to state officials acting through state administrative or legislative lawmaking processes." 518 U.S. at 504. * * *

The dissent would narrow the preemptive scope of the term "requirement" on the grounds that it is "difficult to believe that Congress would, without comment, remove all means of judicial recourse" for consumers injured by FDA-approved devices. But, as we have explained, this is exactly what a preemption clause for medical devices does by its terms. The operation of a law enacted by Congress need not be seconded by a committee report on pain of judicial nullification. It is not our job to speculate upon congressional motives. If we were to do so, however, the only indication available—the text of the statute—suggests that the solicitude for those injured by FDA-approved devices, which the dissent finds controlling, was overcome in Congress's estimation by solicitude for those who would suffer without new medical devices if juries were allowed to apply the tort law of 50 states to all innovations.

In the case before us, the FDA has supported the position taken by our opinion with regard to the meaning of the statute. We have found it unnecessary to rely upon that agency view because we think the statute itself speaks clearly to the point at issue. If, however, we had found the statute ambiguous and had accorded the agency's current position deference, the dissent is correct that * * * the degree of deference might be reduced by the fact that the agency's earlier position was different. But of course the agency's earlier position (which the dissent describes at some length and finds preferable) is even more compromised, indeed deprived of all claim to deference, by the fact that it is no longer the agency's position. * * *

The Riegels contend that the duties underlying negligence, strict-liability, and implied-warranty claims are not preempted even if they impose "requirements," because general common-law duties are not requirements maintained "with respect to devices." Again, a majority of this Court suggested otherwise in *Lohr*. See 518 U.S. at 504–05 (opinion of Breyer, J.); id. at 514 (opinion of O'Connor, J., joined by Rehnquist, C.J., and Scalia and Thomas, JJ.). And with good reason. The language of the statute does not bear the Riegels' reading. The MDA provides that no state "may establish or continue in effect *with respect to a device* . . . *any requirement*" relating to safety or effectiveness that is different from, or in addition to, federal requirements. 21 U.S.C. § 360k(a) (emphasis added). The Riegels' suit depends upon New York's "continu[ing] in effect" general tort duties "with respect to" Medtronic's catheter. Nothing in the statutory text suggests that the preempted state requirement must apply *only* to the relevant device, or only to medical devices and not to all products and all actions in general.

The Riegels' argument to the contrary rests on the text of an FDA regulation which states that the MDA's preemption clause does not extend to certain duties, including "[s]tate or local requirements of general applicability where the purpose of the requirement relates either to other products in addition to devices (e.g., requirements such as general electrical codes, and the Uniform Commercial Code (warranty of fitness)), or to unfair trade practices in which the requirements are not limited to devices." 21 C.F.R. § 808.1(d)(1). Even assuming that this regulation could play a role in defining the MDA's preemptive scope, it does not provide unambiguous support for the Riegels' position. The agency's reading of its own rule is entitled to substantial deference, and the FDA's view put forward in this case is that the regulation does not refer to general tort duties of care * * * * [Moreover, the regulation] states that the MDA sets forth a "general rule" preempting state duties "having the force and effect of law (whether established by statute, ordinance, regulation, *or court decision*)." Id. § 808.1(b) (emphasis added). This sentence is far more comprehensible under the FDA's view that § 808.1(d)(1) has no application here than under the Riegels' view. We are aware of no duties established by court decision other than common-law duties, and we are aware of no common-law duties that relate solely to medical devices.

The Riegels' reading is also in tension with the regulation's statement that adulteration and misbranding claims are preempted when they "ha[ve] the effect of establishing a substantive requirement for a specific device, e.g., a specific labeling requirement" that is "different from, or in addition to" a federal requirement. Id. § 808.1(d)(6)(ii). Surely this means that the MDA would preempt a jury determination that the FDA-approved labeling for a pacemaker violated a state common-law requirement for additional warnings. The Riegels' reading of § 808.1(d)(1), however, would allow a claim for tortious mislabeling to escape preemption so long as such a claim could also be brought against objects other than medical devices. All in all, we think that § 808.1(d)(1) can add nothing to our analysis but confusion. Neither accepting nor rejecting the proposition that this regulation can properly be consulted to determine the statute's meaning; and neither accepting nor rejecting the FDA's distinction between general requirements that directly regulate and those that regulate only incidentally; the regulation fails to alter our interpretation of the text insofar as the outcome of this case is concerned.

State requirements are preempted under the MDA only to the extent that they are "different from, or in addition to" the requirements imposed by federal law. Thus, § 360k does not prevent a state from providing a damages remedy for claims premised on a violation of FDA regulations; the state duties in such a case "parallel," rather than add to, federal requirements. *Lohr*, 518 U.S. at 495; see also id. at 513 (O'Connor, J., concurring in part and dissenting in part). The district court in this case recognized that parallel claims would not be preempted, but it interpreted the claims here to assert that Medtronic's device violated state tort law notwithstanding compliance with the relevant federal requirements. * * *

■ STEVENS, JUSTICE (concurring in part and concurring in the judgment):

The significance of the preemption provision in the [MDA] was not fully appreciated until many years after it was enacted. It is an example of a statute whose text and general objective cover territory not actually envisioned by its authors. * * * There is nothing in the preenactment history of the MDA suggesting that Congress thought state tort remedies had impeded the development of medical devices. * * * [T]he overriding purpose of the legislation was to provide additional protection to consumers, not to withdraw existing protections. It was the then-recent development of state premarket regulatory regimes that explained the need for a provision preempting conflicting administrative rules. But the language of the provision reaches beyond such regulatory regimes to encompass other types of "requirements." Because common-law rules administered by judges, like statutes and regulations, create and define legal obligations, some of them unquestionably qualify as "requirements."[1] * * *

■ GINSBURG, JUSTICE (dissenting):

The Medical Device Amendments of 1976, as construed by the Court, cut deeply into a domain historically occupied by state law. The MDA's preemption clause, the Court holds, spares medical device manufacturers from personal injury claims alleging flaws in a design or label once the application for the design or label has gained premarket approval from the [FDA] * * * *[1] I dissent from today's constriction of state authority. Congress, in my view, did not intend § 360k(a) to effect a radical curtailment of state common-law suits seeking compensation for injuries caused by defectively designed or labeled medical devices. * * *

Federal laws containing a preemption clause do not automatically escape the presumption against preemption. A preemption clause tells us that Congress intended to supersede or modify state law to some extent. In the absence of legislative precision, however, courts may face the task of determining the substance and scope of Congress' displacement of state law. Where the text of a preemption clause is open to more than one plausible reading, courts ordinarily "accept the reading that disfavors preemption." * * *

A series of high-profile medical device failures that caused extensive injuries and loss of life propelled adoption of the MDA. Conspicuous among these failures was the Dalkon Shield intrauterine device, used by approximately 2.2 million women in the United States between 1970 and 1974. Aggressively promoted as a safe and effective form of birth control, the Dalkon Shield had been linked to 16 deaths and 25 miscarriages by the middle of 1975. By early 1976, "more than 500 lawsuits seeking compensatory and punitive damages totaling more than $400 million" had been filed. Given the publicity attending the Dalkon Shield litigation and Congress' awareness of the suits at the time the MDA was under consideration, I find

---

1. The verdicts of juries who obey those rules, however, are not "requirements" of that kind. Juries apply rules, but do not make them. And while a jury's finding of liability may induce a defendant to alter its device or its label, this does not render the finding a "requirement" within the meaning of the MDA. "A requirement is a rule of law that must be obeyed; an event, such as a jury verdict, that merely motivates an optional decision is not a requirement." Bates v. Dow Agrosciences LLC, 544 U.S. 431, 445 (2005). It is for that reason that the MDA does not grant "a single state jury" any power whatsoever to set any standard that either conforms with or differs from a relevant federal standard. * * *

1. The Court's holding does not reach an important issue outside the bounds of this case: the preemptive effect of § 360k(a) where evidence of a medical device's defect comes to light only *after* the device receives premarket approval.

informative the absence of any sign of a legislative design to preempt state common-law tort actions. * * *

Congress enacted the MDA after decades of regulating drugs and food and color additives * * * * The FDCA contains no preemption clause, and thus the Court's interpretation of § 360k(a) has no bearing on tort suits involving drugs and additives. But § 360k(a)'s confinement to medical devices hardly renders irrelevant to the proper construction of the MDA's preemption provision the long history of federal and state controls over drugs and additives in the interest of public health and welfare. Congress' experience regulating drugs and additives informed, and in part provided the model for, its regulation of medical devices. * * *

Between 1938 and 1976, Congress enacted a series of premarket approval requirements, first for drugs, then for additives. * * * The measures just listed, like the MDA, were all enacted with common-law personal injury litigation over defective products a prominent part of the legal landscape. At the time of each enactment, no state regulations required premarket approval of the drugs or additives in question, so no preemption clause was needed as a check against potentially conflicting state regulatory regimes. A different situation existed as to medical devices when Congress developed and passed the MDA. * * *

Congress' experience regulating drugs also casts doubt on Medtronic's policy arguments for reading § 360k(a) to preempt state tort claims. Section 360k(a) must preempt state common-law suits, Medtronic contends, because Congress would not have wanted state juries to second-guess the FDA's finding that a medical device is safe and effective when used as directed. * * * But the process for approving new drugs is at least as rigorous as the premarket approval process for medical devices. Courts that have considered the question have overwhelmingly held that FDA approval of a new drug application does not preempt state tort suits. Decades of drug regulation thus indicate, contrary to Medtronic's argument, that Congress did not regard FDA regulation and state tort claims as mutually exclusive.

Refusing to read § 360k(a) as an automatic bar to state common-law tort claims would hardly render the FDA's premarket approval of Medtronic's medical device application irrelevant to the instant suit. First, a "preemption provision, by itself, does not foreclose (through negative implication) any possibility of implied conflict preemption." Accordingly, a medical device manufacturer may have a dispositive defense if it can identify an actual conflict between the plaintiff's theory of the case and the FDA's premarket approval of the device in question. * * * Second, a medical device manufacturer may be entitled to interpose a regulatory compliance defense based on the FDA's approval of the premarket application. Most states do not treat regulatory compliance as dispositive, but regard it as one factor to be taken into account by the jury. In those states, a manufacturer could present the FDA's approval of its medical device as evidence that it used due care in the design and labeling of the product. The Court's broad reading of § 360k(a) saves the manufacturer from any need to urge these defenses. * * *

NOTES AND QUESTIONS

1. *Doctrinal questions affecting the preemption analysis.* Why does the majority assume that a safer catheter design would require a trade-off, resulting in reduced effectiveness? New York products liability doctrine (like that used in many other jurisdictions) required that plaintiffs demonstrate the existence of a reasonable alternative design (i.e., one that is safer but generally no less effective or dramatically more expensive, etc.) before concluding that the defendant's design suffers from a defect, and the *Products Liability Restatement* standard for prescription products offers device manufacturers still greater protection. Moreover, in what sense might revised labeling to promote safer use reduce effectiveness or necessitate any other trade-offs? No doubt Justice Scalia would respond that, even if one can quibble with the applicability of these presumed concerns in any particular case, Congress enjoys the prerogative to make such broad policy judgments. Conversely, the dissent repeatedly objected to insulating manufacturers of "defectively designed and labeled" devices from liability, but doesn't that beg the central question? In what sense can a device approved by the FDA be called "defective" (after all, as suggested by Justice Ginsburg's first footnote, the agency had not belatedly discovered any flaw in this catheter)? Perhaps a jury presented with Mr. Riegel's case would so conclude (notwithstanding the fact that his injury seems to have resulted from medical malpractice rather than any product defect), but on what basis would it reach a conclusion of defectiveness in the face of the FDA's contrary view (and isn't that precisely what justifies recognizing a preemption defense, or would simply letting the manufacturer introduce it as some evidence, as Justice Ginsburg preferred, suffice)? And if Medtronic proposed to redesign its catheter to satisfy this jury's sense of appropriate design (not under compulsion, as explained by Justice Stevens' first footnote, but to guard against the risk of similar verdicts in the future), how would the company proceed in the event that the FDA rejected a PMA supplement (would Justice Ginsburg treat that as an instance of implied preemption by virtue of an actual conflict between federal and state law in the event of a subsequent suit challenging the failure to adopt the rejected redesign)?

2. *Reactions to* Riegel. Federal legislators expressed dismay over the Court's decision but so far have not managed to enact a bill to override it. See Linda Greenhouse, Justices Shield Medical Devices from Lawsuits, N.Y. Times, Feb. 21, 2008, at A1 (reporting that two members of Congress who played significant roles in passage of the MDA, Ted Kennedy and Henry Waxman, explained that they never had intended to displace tort litigation); Barry Meier & Natasha Singer, Drug Ruling Puts Devices in Spotlight, N.Y. Times, Mar. 5, 2009, at B1 (reporting that "influential members of Congress plan to introduce a bill [S.540/H.R.1346] that would supersede last year's Supreme Court device ruling," though noting that the legislature previously had failed to act on the proposed "Medical Device Safety Act of 2008"); see also Malika Kanodia, Comment, The Fate of the Injured Patient in the Wake of Riegel v. Medtronic: Should Congress Interject?, 32

Hamline L. Rev. 791 (2009). Lower courts quickly got the message. See In re Medtronic, Inc. Sprint Fidelis Leads Prods. Liab. Litig., 592 F.Supp. 2d 1147, 1152 (D.Minn.2009) ("In the ten months following *Riegel*, courts across the country have applied Section 360(k) broadly, preempting all manner of claims ...."), aff'd, 623 F.3d 1200, 1205–08 (8th Cir.2010). See generally Bruce Patsner, Riegel v. Medtronic, Inc.: Revisiting Preemption for Medical Devices, 37 J.L. Med. & Ethics 305 (2009); Catherine M. Sharkey, What Riegel Portends for FDA Preemption of State Law Products Liability Claims, 103 Nw. U. L. Rev. 437 (2009); Daniel W. Whitney, Guide to Preemption of State-law Claims Against Class III PMA Medical Devices, 65 Food & Drug L.J. 113 (2010); Jenea M. Reed, Note, In the Shadows of Lohr: The Disconnect Within the Supreme Court's Preemption Jurisprudence in Medical Device Liability Cases, 64 U. Miami L. Rev. 305 (2009).

3. *The FDA's position*. As noted in *Riegel*, the FDA's position on the desirability of preempting tort claims has flip-flopped. During the 1990s, the FDA filed amicus briefs in some of the cases, arguing that the MDA did not preempt any tort claims. See, e.g., Duvall v. Bristol–Myers–Squibb Co., 65 F.3d 392, 401 n.9 (4th Cir.1995), vacated, 518 U.S. 1030 (1996); see also Margaret J. Porter, The Lohr Decision: FDA Perspective and Position, 52 Food & Drug L.J. 7 (1997). Frustrated by its inability to persuade the courts in this way, the agency published a proposal to disclaim any intent to preempt tort claims against manufacturers of medical devices, see 62 Fed. Reg. 65,384 (1997), but it withdrew this notice after questions arose about the propriety of the FDA's decision to share a prepublication draft of the proposal with public interest groups closely aligned with plaintiffs' lawyers. See 63 Fed. Reg. 39,789 (1998). After 2000, however (with the transition from the Clinton to the Bush administration), the FDA began to press for preemption in tort litigation (and not solely in medical device cases). See Alicia Mundy, Bush Rule Changes Could Block Product–Safety Suits, Wall St. J., Oct. 15, 2008, at A11; see also Richard C. Ausness, "After You, My Dear Alphonse!": Should the Courts Defer to the FDA's New Interpretation of § 360k(a) of the Medical Device Amendments?, 80 Tul. L. Rev. 727 (2006).

4. *Distinguishing preemption from a compliance defense*. The *Products Liability Restatement* drew a sharp distinction between a regulatory compliance defense and federal preemption:

> When a court concludes that a defendant is not liable by reason of having complied with a safety design or warnings statute or regulation, it is deciding that the product in question is not defective as a matter of the law of that state. The safety statute or regulation may be a federal provision, but the decision to give it determinative effect is a state-law determination. In contrast, in federal preemption, the court decides as a matter of federal law that the relevant federal statute or regulation reflects, expressly or impliedly, the intent of Congress to displace state law, including state tort law, with the federal statute or regulation. The question of preemption is thus a question of federal law, and a determination that there is preemption nullifies otherwise

> operational state law. The complex set of rules and standards for resolving questions of federal preemption are beyond the scope of this Restatement. However, when federal preemption is found, the legal effect is clear. Judicial deference to federal product safety statutes or regulations occurs not because the court concludes that compliance with the statute or regulation shows the product to be nondefective; the issue of defectiveness under state law is never reached. Rather, the court defers because, when a federal statute or regulation is preemptive, the Constitution mandates federal supremacy.

Rest. (3d) § 4 cmt. e. In the early years, some lower courts had dismissed tort claims as preempted even in cases of failures to comply with FDA requirements. For instance, in *Talbott v. C.R. Bard, Inc.*, 865 F.Supp. 37 (D.Mass.1994), aff'd, 63 F.3d 25 (1st Cir.1995), a manufacturer of cardiac catheters successfully invoked the preemption defense in a wrongful death action even though it had already pled guilty to numerous charges of filing false statements with the FDA and other statutory violations, infractions for which the company was ordered to pay $61 million in civil and criminal penalties. In *Riegel*, however, the Court concluded that the statute would not preempt tort claims in cases of noncompliance with federal safety standards. See Bausch v. Stryker Corp., 630 F.3d 546, 549–58 (7th Cir. 2010) (ceramic hip implant deemed adulterated by the FDA and later recalled); Purcel v. Advanced Bionics Corp., 2010 WL 2679988, at *2–7 (N.D.Tex.2010) (allowing tort claims against the manufacturer of a cochlear implant that had settled FDA adulteration charges); Mark Herrmann et al., The Meaning of the Parallel Requirements Exception Under Lohr and Riegel, 65 N.Y.U. Ann. Surv. Am. L. 545 (2010); see also Catherine M. Sharkey, The Fraud Caveat to Agency Preemption, 102 Nw. U. L. Rev. 841 (2008). Arguably, then, federal preemption is nothing more than a regulatory compliance defense that courts have read into federal statutes that expressly displace state law. See Lars Noah, Reconceptualizing Federal Preemption of Tort Claims as the Government Standards Defense, 37 Wm. & Mary L. Rev. 903 (1996). This is not just a semantic distinction—if preemption is really just a compliance defense, then it may, among other things, affect who has the burden of proof.

5. *Is preemption reserved only for PMA'd devices?* The majority in *Riegel* emphasized the difference between premarket notification and premarket approval, but might express preemption still operate to prevent at least some tort claims against devices cleared under § 510(k)? See Lars Noah, Amplification of Federal Preemption in Medical Device Cases, 49 Food & Drug L.J. 183, 206–11 (1994). For instance, devices that need not go through the PMA process but must abide by specific labeling requirements may escape failure-to-warn claims. See Papike v. Tambrands Inc., 107 F.3d 737, 740–42 (9th Cir.1997) (tampons and toxic shock syndrome); Murphy v. Playtex Fam. Prods. Corp., 176 F.Supp.2d 473, 482–83 (D.Md.2001) (same), aff'd mem., 69 F.App'x 140 (4th Cir.2003); see also Whitson v. Safeskin Corp., 313 F.Supp.2d 473, 477–79 (M.D.Pa.2004) (holding that the FDA's allergy labeling requirements for latex gloves, which it had announced in a manual used to evaluate premarket notification filings, preempted breach of implied warranty claims); Betterton v. Evans, 351 F.Supp.2d 529 (N.D.Miss.2004) (device marketed under a product development protocol). In addition, an IDE may trigger preemption. See Robinson v. Endovascular Technologies, Inc., 119 Cal.Rptr.3d 158, 164–65 (Ct.App.2010). Conversely, some tort claims might remain available even against PMA'd devices. See, e.g., Davenport v. Medtronic, Inc., 302 F.Supp.2d 419, 433, 439–40 (E.D.Pa. 2004) (holding that approval does not preempt negligent marketing claim for an off-label use, but granting manufacturer's motion for summary judgment); Steele v. Depuy Orthopaedics, Inc., 295 F.Supp.2d 439 (D.N.J. 2003) (rejecting preemption defense where PMA supplement failed to address the particular risk). But cf. Cupek v. Medtronic, Inc., 405 F.3d 421, 424–25 (6th Cir.2005) (preempting claims asserting a post-sale duty to warn or recall); McMullen v. Medtronic, Inc., 421 F.3d 482, 488–90 (7th Cir.2005) (same).

PROBLEM #7. *PREEMPTION AND PREMARKET NOTIFICATION*

You represent Cardiotronics, Inc., the manufacturer of a pulse generator incorporating a new power source. After filing a premarket notification with the FDA in 2005, an agency reviewer demands that Cardiotronics provide additional information about the long-term reliability of this new power source as compared with traditional battery packs. Your client promptly submits the requested data. After further review, the FDA concludes that the pacemaker is substantially equivalent to a predicate device, but it insists that the pacemaker's labeling be revised to convey information about the possible risks of sudden failure associated with this new power source. In 2009, one unit inexplicably fails, causing serious injury to the user. Thereupon the patient sues Cardiotronics, asserting claims of design defect and inadequate warning. Assume that you are in a jurisdiction that requires plaintiffs in all design defect cases to prove that a "reasonable alternative design" existed. You file a motion for summary judgment, arguing that these claims are preempted. Will it work?

Buckman v. Plaintiffs' Legal Committee

531 U.S. 341 (2001).

■ REHNQUIST, CHIEF JUSTICE:

Respondent represents plaintiffs who claim injuries resulting from the use of orthopedic bone screws in the pedicles of their spines. Petitioner is a consulting company that assisted the screws' manufacturer, AcroMed Corporation, in navigating the federal regulatory process for these devices. Plaintiffs say petitioner made fraudulent representations to the Food and Drug Administration in the course of obtaining approval to market the screws. Plaintiffs further claim that such representations were at least a "but for" cause of injuries that plaintiffs sustained from the implantation of these devices: Had the representations not been made, the FDA would not have approved the devices, and plaintiffs would not have been injured. Plaintiffs sought damages from petitioner under state tort law. * * *

It is not disputed that the bone screws manufactured by AcroMed are Class III devices. Class III devices must complete a thorough review process with the FDA before they may be marketed. * * * An exception to the PMA requirement exists for devices that were already on the market prior to the MDA's enactment in 1976. The MDA allows these "predicate" devices to remain available until the FDA initiates and completes the PMA process. * * * Demonstrating that a device qualifies for this exception is known as the "§ 510(k) process" * * * *

In 1984, AcroMed sought § 510(k) approval for its bone screw device, indicating it for use in spinal surgery. See In re Orthopedic Bone Screw Prods. Liab. Litig., 159 F.3d 817, 820 (3d Cir.1998). The FDA denied approval on the grounds that the Class III device lacked substantial equivalence to a predicate device. In September 1985, with the assistance of petitioner, AcroMed filed another § 510(k) application. "The application provided additional information about the ... device and again indicated its use in spinal surgery. The FDA again rejected the application, determining that the device was not substantially equivalent to a predicate device and that it posed potential risks not exhibited by other spinal-fixation systems." Id. In December 1985, AcroMed and petitioner filed a third § 510(k) application. "AcroMed and [petitioner] split the ... device into its component parts, renamed them 'nested bone plates' and '[cancellous] bone screws' and filed a separate § 510(k) application for each component. In both applications, a new intended use was specified: rather than seeking clearance for spinal applications, they sought clearance to market the plates and screws for use in the long bones of the arms and legs. AcroMed and Buckman claimed that the two components were substantially equivalent to predicate devices used in long bone surgery. The FDA approved the devices for this purpose in February 1986." Id. * * *

[T]he District Court for the Eastern District of Pennsylvania has been the recipient of some 2,300 civil actions related to these medical devices. Many of these actions include state-law causes of action claiming that petitioner and AcroMed made fraudulent representations to the FDA as to the intended use of the bone screws and that, as a result, the devices were improperly given market clearance and were subsequently used to the plaintiffs' detriment. The district court dismissed these "fraud-on-the-FDA" claims, first on the ground that they were expressly preempted by the MDA, and then, after our decision in *Medtronic*, on the ground that these claims amounted to an improper assertion of a private right of action under the MDA. * * *

[T]he relationship between a federal agency and the entity it regulates is inherently federal in character because the relationship originates from, is governed by, and terminates according to federal law. Cf. Boyle v. United Technologies Corp., 487 U.S. 500, 504–05 (1988) (allowing preemption of state law by federal common law where the interests at stake are "uniquely federal" in nature). Here, petitioner's dealings with the FDA were prompted by the MDA, and the very subject matter of petitioner's statements were dictated by that statute's provisions. Accordingly—and in contrast to situations implicating "federalism concerns and the historic primacy of state regulation of matters of health and safety," *Medtronic*, 518 U.S. at 485—no presumption against preemption obtains in this case.

Given this analytical framework, we hold that the plaintiffs' state-law fraud-on-the-FDA claims conflict with, and are therefore impliedly preempted by federal law.[2] The conflict stems from the fact that the federal statutory scheme amply empowers the FDA to punish and deter fraud against the agency, and that this authority is used by the agency to achieve a somewhat delicate balance of statutory objectives. The balance sought by the agency can be skewed by allowing fraud-on-the-FDA claims under state tort law.

As described in greater detail above, the § 510(k) process sets forth a comprehensive scheme for determining whether an applicant has demonstrated that a product is substantially equivalent to a predicate device. * * * Admittedly, the § 510(k) process lacks the PMA review's rigor: The former requires only a showing of substantial equivalence to a predicate device, while the latter involves a time-consuming inquiry into the risks and efficacy of each device. Nevertheless, to achieve its limited purpose, the § 510(k) process imposes upon applicants a variety of requirements that are designed to enable the FDA to make its statutorily required judgment as to whether the device qualifies under this exception.

Accompanying these disclosure requirements are various provisions aimed at detecting, deterring, and punishing false statements made during this and related approval processes. The FDA * * * has at its disposal a variety of enforcement options that allow it to make a measured response to suspected fraud upon the agency.[4]

This flexibility is a critical component of the statutory and regulatory framework under which the FDA pursues difficult (and often competing) objectives. For example, with respect to Class III devices, the FDA simultaneously maintains the exhaustive PMA and the more limited § 510(k) processes in order to ensure both that medical devices are reasonably safe and effective and that, if the device qualifies under the § 510(k) exception, it is on the market within a relatively short period of time. Similarly, "off-label" usage of medical devices (use of a device for some other purpose than that for which it has been approved by the FDA) is an accepted and necessary corollary of the FDA's mission to regulate in this area without directly interfering with the practice of medicine. Indeed, a recent amendment to the FDCA expressly states in part that "[n]othing in this chapter shall be construed to limit or interfere with the authority of a health care

2. In light of this conclusion, we express no view on whether these claims are subject to express preemption under 21 U.S.C. § 360k.

4. The FDCA leaves no doubt that it is the federal government rather than private litigants who are authorized to file suit for noncompliance with the medical device provisions: "[A]ll such proceedings for the enforcement, or to restrain violations, of this chapter shall be by and in the name of the United States." 21 U.S.C. § 337(a).

practitioner to prescribe or administer any legally marketed device to a patient for any condition or disease within a legitimate health care practitioner-patient relationship." 21 U.S.C. § 396. Thus, the FDA is charged with the difficult task of regulating the marketing and distribution of medical devices without intruding upon decisions statutorily committed to the discretion of health care professionals.

State-law fraud-on-the-FDA claims inevitably conflict with the FDA's responsibility to police fraud consistently with the agency's judgment and objectives. As a practical matter, complying with the FDA's detailed regulatory regime in the shadow of 50 States' tort regimes will dramatically increase the burdens facing potential applicants—burdens not contemplated by Congress in enacting the FDCA and the MDA. Would-be applicants may be discouraged from seeking § 510(k) approval of devices with potentially beneficial off-label uses for fear that such use might expose the manufacturer or its associates (such as petitioner) to unpredictable civil liability. In effect, then, fraud-on-the-FDA claims could cause the agency's reporting requirements to deter off-label use despite the fact that the FDCA expressly disclaims any intent to directly regulate the practice of medicine, and even though off-label use is generally accepted.

Conversely, fraud-on-the-FDA claims would also cause applicants to fear that their disclosures to the FDA, although deemed appropriate by the agency, will later be judged insufficient in state court. Applicants would then have an incentive to submit a deluge of information that the agency neither wants nor needs, resulting in additional burdens on the FDA's evaluation of an application. As a result, the comparatively speedy § 510(k) process could encounter delays, which would, in turn, impede competition among predicate devices and delay health care professionals' ability to prescribe appropriate off-label uses. * * *

Respondent also suggests that we should be reluctant to find a preemptive conflict here because Congress included an express preemption provision in the MDA. To the extent respondent posits that anything other than our ordinary preemption principles apply under these circumstances, that contention must fail * * * *

We must also reject respondent's attempt to characterize both the claims at issue in *Medtronic* (common-law negligence action against the manufacturer of an allegedly defective pacemaker lead) and the fraud claims here as "claims arising from violations of FDCA requirements." Notwithstanding the fact that *Medtronic* did not squarely address the question of implied preemption, it is clear that the *Medtronic* claims arose from the manufacturer's alleged failure to use reasonable care in the production of the product, not solely from the violation of FDCA requirements. In the present case, however, the fraud claims exist solely by virtue of the FDCA disclosure requirements. Thus, although *Medtronic* can be read to allow certain state-law causes of actions that parallel federal safety requirements, it does not and cannot stand for the proposition that any violation of the FDCA will support a state-law claim.

In sum, were plaintiffs to maintain their fraud-on-the-agency claims here, they would not be relying on traditional state tort law which had predated the federal enactments in questions. On the contrary, the existence of these federal enactments is a critical element in their case. For the reasons stated above, we think this sort of litigation would exert an extraneous pull on the scheme established by Congress, and it is therefore preempted by that scheme. * * *

■ STEVENS, JUSTICE (concurring):

As the Court points out, an essential link in the chain of causation that respondent must prove in order to prevail is that, but for petitioner's fraud, the allegedly defective orthopedic bone screws would not have reached the market. The fact that the Food and Drug Administration (FDA) has done nothing to remove the devices from the market, even though it is aware of the basis for the fraud allegations, convinces me that this essential element of the claim cannot be proved. I therefore agree that the case should not proceed.[1]

This would be a different case if, prior to the instant litigation, the FDA had determined that petitioner had committed fraud during the § 510(k) process and had then taken the necessary steps to remove the harm-causing product from the market. Under those circumstances, respondent's state-law fraud claim would not depend upon speculation as to the FDA's behavior in a counterfactual situation but would be grounded in the agency's explicit actions. In such a case, a plaintiff would be able to establish causation without second-guessing the FDA's decisionmaking or overburdening its personnel, thereby alleviating the government's central concerns regarding fraud-on-the-agency claims.

If the FDA determines both that fraud has occurred and that such fraud requires the removal of a product from the market, state damages remedies would not encroach upon, but rather would supplement and facilitate, the federal enforcement scheme. Cf. Medtronic, Inc. v. Lohr, 518 U.S. 470, 495 (1996) (holding that the presence of a state-law damages remedy for violations of FDA requirements does not impose an additional requirement upon medical device manufacturers but "merely provides another reason for manufacturers to comply with ... federal law"); id. at 513 (O'Connor, J., concurring in part and dissenting in part) (same).

Under the preemption analysis the Court offers today, however, parties injured by fraudulent representations to federal agencies would have no remedy even if recognizing such a remedy would have no adverse consequences upon the operation or integrity of the regulatory process. I do not believe the reasons advanced in the Court's opinion support the conclusion that Congress intended such a harsh result. Cf. Silkwood v. Kerr–McGee

1. Though my analysis focuses on the failure of the plaintiffs to establish a necessary element of their claim, that failure is grounded not in the minutiae of state law but in the details of the federal regulatory system for medical devices. Therefore, while this case does not fit neatly into our pre-existing preemption jurisprudence, it is accurate, in a sense, to say that federal law "preempts" this state-law fraud-on-the-FDA claim because the FDA has not acknowledged such a fraud and taken steps to remove the device from the market.

Corp., 464 U.S. 238, 251 (1984) (declining to infer that a federal statutory scheme that affords no alternative means of seeking redress preempted traditional state-law remedies). For that reason, although I concur in the Court's disposition of this case, I do not join its opinion.

NOTES AND QUESTIONS

1. *Trying to make sense of* Buckman. Apart from the Court's willingness to engage in implied preemption analysis without seeming to pay any attention to an express preemption provision (and in a case involving a device that came to market under § 510(k)), is it suggesting that defectiveness per se claims might no longer exist (at least absent a specific FDA finding of noncompliance)? Consider the following initial reaction to *Buckman*:

> First, the decision will not be confined just to medical device firms. Rehnquist's opinion for the majority emphasized that Congress clearly wanted the Medical Device Amendments of 1976 enforced exclusively by the FDA, but the statutory provision that he cited for this proposition pre-dated those amendments by almost four decades, and it applies equally to all of the products regulated by this agency. Now that the Supreme Court has fully embraced a concept thought outrageous just ten years earlier—namely, that jury verdicts can have the same regulatory effect as positive state law—and broadened the application of implied preemption analysis where state tort law may create an obstacle to federal purposes (without really bothering to ask whether and how Congress may have expressed any such a concern with a preemption clause), pharmaceutical manufacturers may get to share in the bounty enjoyed to varying extents by their counterparts in the medical device industry during the last decade.
>
> Second, even if not extended beyond medical device litigation, *Buckman* might signal the demise of tort claims premised on other alleged violations of federal safety rules. Contrary to the majority's suggestion, courts that recognize a fraud-on-the-FDA claim have chosen to do so as a matter of state common law. Although the FDA's regulatory activities provide an essential predicate for such an action for fraud, this feature in no way distinguishes it from a negligence per se claim premised on alleged violations of the agency's labeling, manufacturing, or product approval requirements. Indeed, in the case of failures to comply with FDA requirements for the reporting of serious adverse events, is there any meaningful distinction between fraud-on-the-agency and negligence per se claims? Moreover, the rationales invoked by the majority would apply equally well: preemption of negligence per se claims would minimize the burden created by the possibility of inconsistent interpretations of FDA standards, and it would account for the possibility that, in exercising its delegated enforcement discretion, the agency might decide against demanding 100% compliance with its requirements in order to promote other

policies. (For instance, the agency has explained that it prefers selectivity in the reporting of side effects so that it can better process the reports.)

Five years ago, in *Medtronic v. Lohr*, a plurality of the Court decided that compliance with federal safety requirements would rarely if ever insulate a medical device manufacturer from tort claims under principles of express preemption; last Term, in *Buckman*, however, a clear majority decided that noncompliance with those same requirements would insulate a company from certain tort claims under principles of implied preemption. Hasn't the Court gotten it exactly backwards?! Isn't it more likely that the threat of liability for conduct that fully complies with federal safety requirements creates a greater obstacle to the achievement of the FDA's public health purposes? Instead of using this occasion to bury a defense to tort claims that appeared to be so shaky after *Lohr*, the Supreme Court in *Buckman* seemingly has reinforced (and clearly it has further confused) the use of preemption to insulate suppliers of medical devices and perhaps also other medical technologies from products liability.

Lars Noah, Inverting the Products Liability Preemption Defense, Health L. News, Sept. 2001, at 6. But cf. Thomas O. McGarity, Beyond Buckman: Wrongful Manipulation of the Regulatory Process in the Law of Torts, 41 Washburn L.J. 549 (2002) (criticizing the decision, and urging that it be narrowly construed). Although none of the Justices in *Riegel* cited *Buckman*, did the Court's conclusion that only claims of noncompliance would escape express preemption throw any doubt on *Buckman*'s continued vitality? See Hughes v. Boston Scientific Corp., 631 F.3d 762, 767–76 (5th Cir.2011); In re Medtronic, Inc., Sprint Fidelis Leads Prods. Liab. Litig., 623 F.3d 1200, 1204–07 (8th Cir.2010) (trying to reconcile this incongruity in multidistrict litigation over fractures in ICD leads approved by the FDA but later recalled by the manufacturer). For a sampling of *Buckman*'s uneven impact on cases involving medical devices, see Webster v. Pacesetter, Inc., 259 F.Supp.2d 27, 36–37, 39 (D.D.C.2003) (adhering to decision); Woods v. Gliatech, Inc., 218 F.Supp.2d 802 (W.D.Va.2002) (distinguishing other types of fraud claims); Behrens v. United Vaccines, Inc., 189 F.Supp.2d 945 (D.Minn.2002). A few lower courts have applied *Buckman* to preempt certain claims against drug manufacturers. See Bouchard v. American Home Prods. Corp., 213 F.Supp.2d 802 (N.D.Ohio 2002); Flynn v. American Home Prods. Corp., 627 N.W.2d 342 (Minn.Ct.App.2001). But see Caraker v. Sandoz Pharm. Corp., 172 F.Supp.2d 1018, 1040–44 (S.D.Ill. 2001); Bryant v. Hoffmann–LaRoche, Inc., 585 S.E.2d 723 (Ga.Ct.App. 2003).

Wyeth v. Levine

555 U.S. 555 (2009).

■ STEVENS, JUSTICE:

* * * Phenergan is Wyeth's brand name for promethazine hydrochloride, an antihistamine used to treat nausea. The injectable form of Phener-

gan can be administered intramuscularly or intravenously, and it can be administered intravenously through either the "IV-push" method, whereby the drug is injected directly into a patient's vein, or the "IV-drip" method, whereby the drug is introduced into a saline solution in a hanging intravenous bag and slowly descends through a catheter inserted in a patient's vein. The drug is corrosive and causes irreversible gangrene if it enters a patient's artery.

[Diana] Levine's injury resulted from an IV-push injection of Phenergan. On April 7, 2000, as on previous visits to her local clinic for treatment of a migraine headache, she received an intramuscular injection of Demerol for her headache and Phenergan for her nausea. Because the combination did not provide relief, she returned later that day and received a second injection of both drugs. This time, the physician assistant administered the drugs by the IV-push method, and Phenergan entered Levine's artery, either because the needle penetrated an artery directly or because the drug escaped from the vein into surrounding tissue (a phenomenon called "perivascular extravasation") where it came in contact with arterial blood. As a result, Levine developed gangrene, and doctors amputated first her right hand and then her entire forearm. In addition to her pain and suffering, Levine incurred substantial medical expenses and the loss of her livelihood as a professional musician.

After settling claims against the health center and clinician, Levine brought an action for damages against Wyeth, relying on common-law negligence and strict-liability theories. Although Phenergan's labeling warned of the danger of gangrene and amputation following inadvertent intra-arterial injection,[1] Levine alleged that the labeling was defective because it failed to instruct clinicians to use the IV-drip method of intravenous administration instead of the higher risk IV-push method. More broadly, she alleged that Phenergan is not reasonably safe for intravenous

---

1. The warning for "Inadvertent Intra-arterial Injection" stated: "Due to the close proximity of arteries and veins in the areas most commonly used for intravenous injection, extreme care should be exercised to avoid perivascular extravasation or inadvertent intra-arterial injection. Reports compatible with inadvertent intra-arterial injection of Phenergan Injection, usually in conjunction with other drugs intended for intravenous use, suggest that pain, severe chemical irritation, severe spasm of distal vessels, and resultant gangrene requiring amputation are likely under such circumstances. Intravenous injection was intended in all the cases reported but perivascular extravasation or arterial placement of the needle is now suspect. There is no proven successful management of this condition after it occurs.... Aspiration of dark blood does not preclude intra-arterial needle placement, because blood is discolored upon contact with Phenergan Injection. Use of syringes with rigid plungers or of small bore needles might obscure typical arterial backflow if this is relied upon alone. When used intravenously, Phenergan Injection should be given in a concentration no greater than 25 mg per mL and at a rate not to exceed 25 mg per minute. When administering any irritant drug intravenously, it is usually preferable to inject it through the tubing of an intravenous infusion set that is known to be functioning satisfactorily. In the event that a patient complains of pain during intended intravenous injection of Phenergan Injection, the injection should be stopped immediately to provide for evaluation of possible arterial placement or perivascular extravasation."

administration because the foreseeable risks of gangrene and loss of limb are great in relation to the drug's therapeutic benefits.

Wyeth filed a motion for summary judgment, arguing that Levine's failure-to-warn claims were preempted by federal law. The * * * [trial] court reviewed the sparse correspondence between Wyeth and the FDA about Phenergan's labeling and found no evidence that Wyeth had "earnestly attempted" to strengthen the intra-arterial injection warning or that the FDA had "specifically disallowed" stronger language. The record, as then developed, "lack[ed] any evidence that the FDA set a ceiling on this matter."

The evidence presented during the 5–day jury trial showed that the risk of intra-arterial injection or perivascular extravasation can be almost entirely eliminated through the use of IV-drip, rather than IV-push, administration. An IV drip is started with saline, which will not flow properly if the catheter is not in the vein and fluid is entering an artery or surrounding tissue. By contrast, even a careful and experienced clinician using the IV-push method will occasionally expose an artery to Phenergan. While Phenergan's labeling warned against intra-arterial injection and perivascular extravasation and advised that "[w]hen administering any irritant drug intravenously it is usually preferable to inject it through the tubing of an intravenous infusion set that is known to be functioning satisfactorily," the labeling did not contain a specific warning about the risks of IV-push administration.

The trial record also contains correspondence between Wyeth and the FDA discussing Phenergan's label. The FDA first approved injectable Phenergan in 1955. In 1973 and 1976, Wyeth submitted supplemental new drug applications, which the agency approved after proposing labeling changes. Wyeth submitted a third supplemental application in 1981 in response to a new FDA rule governing drug labels. Over the next 17 years, Wyeth and the FDA intermittently corresponded about Phenergan's label. The most notable activity occurred in 1987, when the FDA suggested different warnings about the risk of arterial exposure, and in 1988, when Wyeth submitted revised labeling incorporating the proposed changes. The FDA did not respond. Instead, in 1996, it requested from Wyeth the labeling then in use and, without addressing Wyeth's 1988 submission, instructed it to "[r]etain verbiage in current label" regarding intra-arterial injection.* After a few further changes to the labeling not related to intra-arterial injection, the FDA approved Wyeth's 1981 application in 1998, instructing that Phenergan's final printed label "must be identical" to the approved package insert.

Based on this regulatory history, the trial judge instructed the jury that it could consider evidence of Wyeth's compliance with FDA requirements but that such compliance did not establish that the warnings were

* In a subsequent footnote not retained with this excerpt, the majority explained that, in its amicus brief, "the United States concedes that the FDA did not regard the proposed warning as substantively different: '[I]t appears the FDA viewed the change as non-substantive and rejected it for formatting reasons.' "

adequate. * * * [T]he jury found that Wyeth was negligent, that Phenergan was a defective product as a result of inadequate warnings and instructions, and that no intervening cause had broken the causal connection between the product defects and the plaintiff's injury. It awarded total damages of $7,400,000, which the court reduced [by $626,000] to account for Levine's earlier settlement with the health center and clinician. * * *

The trial court proceedings established that Levine's injury would not have occurred if Phenergan's label had included an adequate warning about the risks of the IV-push method of administering the drug. The record contains evidence that the physician assistant administered a greater dose than the label prescribed, that she may have inadvertently injected the drug into an artery rather than a vein, and that she continued to inject the drug after Levine complained of pain. Nevertheless, the jury rejected Wyeth's argument that the clinician's conduct was an intervening cause that absolved it of liability. * * * That the inadequate label was both a but-for and proximate cause of Levine's injury is supported by the record and no longer challenged by Wyeth.[2]

The trial court proceedings further established that the critical defect in Phenergan's label was the lack of an adequate warning about the risks of IV-push administration. Levine also offered evidence that the IV-push method should be contraindicated and that Phenergan should never be administered intravenously, even by the IV-drip method. Perhaps for this reason, the dissent incorrectly assumes that the state-law duty at issue is the duty to contraindicate the IV-push method. But, as the Vermont Supreme Court explained, the jury verdict established only that Phenergan's warning was insufficient. It did not mandate a particular replacement warning, nor did it require contraindicating IV-push administration: "There may have been any number of ways for [Wyeth] to strengthen the Phenergan warning without completely eliminating IV-push administration." 944 A.2d 179, 189 n.2 (Vt.2006). We therefore need not decide whether a state rule proscribing intravenous administration would be preempted. * * *

As it enlarged the FDA's powers to "protect the public health" and "assure the safety, effectiveness, and reliability of drugs," Congress took care to preserve state law. The 1962 amendments added a saving clause, indicating that a provision of state law would only be invalidated upon a "direct and positive conflict" with the FDCA. § 202, 76 Stat. 781, 793. * * * And when Congress enacted an express preemption provision for medical devices in 1976, it declined to enact such a provision for prescription drugs.

In 2007, after Levine's injury and lawsuit, Congress again amended the FDCA. 121 Stat. 823. For the first time, it granted the FDA statutory authority to require a manufacturer to change its drug label based on

---

2. The dissent nonetheless suggests that physician malpractice was the exclusive cause of Levine's injury. The dissent's frustration with the jury's verdict does not put the merits of Levine's tort claim before us, nor does it change the question we must decide—whether federal law preempts Levine's state-law claims.

safety information that becomes available after a drug's initial approval. FDCA § 901(a). In doing so, however, Congress did not enact a provision in the Senate bill that would have required the FDA to preapprove all changes to drug labels. See S. 1082, 110th Cong., 1st Sess., § 208, pp.107–14 (2007) (as passed) (proposing new § 506D). Instead, it adopted a rule of construction to make it clear that manufacturers remain responsible for updating their labels. See 121 Stat. at 925–26.

Wyeth first argues that Levine's state-law claims are preempted because it is impossible for it to comply with both the state-law duties underlying those claims and its federal labeling duties. The FDA's premarket approval of a new drug application includes the approval of the exact text in the proposed label. Generally speaking, a manufacturer may only change a drug label after the FDA approves a supplemental application. There is, however, an FDA regulation that permits a manufacturer to make certain changes to its label before receiving the agency's approval. Among other things, this "changes being effected" (CBE) regulation provides that if a manufacturer is changing a label to "add or strengthen a contraindication, warning, precaution, or adverse reaction" or to "add or strengthen an instruction about dosage and administration that is intended to increase the safe use of the drug product," it may make the labeling change upon filing its supplemental application with the FDA; it need not wait for FDA approval. 21 C.F.R. § 314.70(c)(6)(iii)(A), (C) (2008).

Wyeth argues that the CBE regulation is not implicated in this case because a 2008 amendment provides that a manufacturer may only change its label "to reflect newly acquired information." 73 Fed. Reg. 49,603, 49,609 (2008). Resting on this language (which Wyeth argues simply reaffirmed the interpretation of the regulation in effect when this case was tried), Wyeth contends that it could have changed Phenergan's label only in response to new information that the FDA had not considered. And it maintains that Levine has not pointed to any such information concerning the risks of IV-push administration. Thus, Wyeth insists, it was impossible for it to discharge its state-law obligation to provide a stronger warning about IV-push administration without violating federal law. Wyeth's argument misapprehends both the federal drug regulatory scheme and its burden in establishing a preemption defense.

We need not decide whether the 2008 CBE regulation is consistent with the FDCA and the previous version of the regulation, as Wyeth and the United States urge, because Wyeth could have revised Phenergan's label even in accordance with the amended regulation. As the FDA explained in its notice of the final rule, " 'newly acquired information' " is not limited to new data, but also encompasses "new analyses of previously submitted data." Id. at 49,604. The rule accounts for the fact that risk information accumulates over time and that the same data may take on a different meaning in light of subsequent developments: "[I]f the sponsor submits adverse event information to FDA, and then later conducts a new analysis of data showing risks of a different type or of greater severity or frequency than did reports previously submitted to FDA, the sponsor meets the requirement for 'newly acquired information.' " Id. at 49,607.

The record is limited concerning what newly acquired information Wyeth had or should have had about the risks of IV-push administration of Phenergan because Wyeth did not argue before the trial court that such information was required for a CBE labeling change. Levine did, however, present evidence of at least 20 incidents prior to her injury in which a Phenergan injection resulted in gangrene and an amputation.[4] After the first such incident came to Wyeth's attention in 1967, it notified the FDA and worked with the agency to change Phenergan's label. In later years, as amputations continued to occur, Wyeth could have analyzed the accumulating data and added a stronger warning about IV-push administration of the drug.

Wyeth argues that if it had unilaterally added such a warning, it would have violated federal law governing unauthorized distribution and misbranding. * * * [S]trengthening the warning about IV-push administration would not have made Phenergan a new drug. Nor would this warning have rendered Phenergan misbranded. The FDCA does not provide that a drug is misbranded simply because the manufacturer has altered an FDA-approved label; instead, the misbranding provision focuses on the substance of the label and, among other things, proscribes labels that fail to include "adequate warnings." 21 U.S.C. § 352(f). Moreover, * * * the very idea that the FDA would bring an enforcement action against a manufacturer for strengthening a warning pursuant to the CBE regulation is difficult to accept—neither Wyeth nor the United States has identified a case in which the FDA has done so.

Wyeth's cramped reading of the CBE regulation and its broad reading of the FDCA's misbranding and unauthorized distribution provisions are premised on a more fundamental misunderstanding. Wyeth suggests that the FDA, rather than the manufacturer, bears primary responsibility for drug labeling. Yet through many amendments to the FDCA and to FDA regulations, it has remained a central premise of federal drug regulation that the manufacturer bears responsibility for the content of its label at all times. It is charged both with crafting an adequate label and with ensuring that its warnings remain adequate as long as the drug is on the market. * * * Thus, when the risk of gangrene from IV-push injection of Phenergan became apparent, Wyeth had a duty to provide a warning that adequately described that risk, and the CBE regulation permitted it to provide such a warning before receiving the FDA's approval.

Of course, the FDA retains authority to reject labeling changes made pursuant to the CBE regulation in its review of the manufacturer's supplemental application, just as it retains such authority in reviewing all supplemental applications. But absent clear evidence that the FDA would

4. Levine also introduced evidence that Pfizer had withdrawn Vistaril, another antinausea drug, from intravenous use several decades earlier because its intravenous injection had resulted in gangrene and amputations.

not have approved a change to Phenergan's label, we will not conclude that it was impossible for Wyeth to comply with both federal and state requirements. Wyeth has offered no such evidence. It does not argue that it attempted to give the kind of warning required by the Vermont jury but was prohibited from doing so by the FDA. And while it does suggest that the FDA intended to prohibit it from strengthening the warning about IV-push administration because the agency deemed such a warning inappropriate in reviewing Phenergan's drug applications, both the trial court and the Vermont Supreme Court rejected this account as a matter of fact.

In its decision on Wyeth's motion for judgment as a matter of law, the trial court found "no evidence in this record that either the FDA or the manufacturer gave more than passing attention to the issue of" IV-push versus IV-drip administration. The Vermont Supreme Court likewise concluded that the FDA had not made an affirmative decision to preserve the IV-push method or intended to prohibit Wyeth from strengthening its warning about IV-push administration. 944 A.2d at 188–89. Moreover, Wyeth does not argue that it supplied the FDA with an evaluation or analysis concerning the specific dangers posed by the IV-push method. We accordingly cannot credit Wyeth's contention that the FDA would have prevented it from adding a stronger warning about the IV-push method of intravenous administration.

Impossibility preemption is a demanding defense. On the record before us, Wyeth has failed to demonstrate that it was impossible for it to comply with both federal and state requirements. The CBE regulation permitted Wyeth to unilaterally strengthen its warning, and the mere fact that the FDA approved Phenergan's label does not establish that it would have prohibited such a change.

Wyeth also argues that requiring it to comply with a state-law duty to provide a stronger warning about IV-push administration would obstruct the purposes and objectives of federal drug labeling regulation. Levine's tort claims, it maintains, are preempted because they interfere with "Congress's purpose to entrust an expert agency to make drug labeling decisions that strike a balance between competing objectives." * * * The most glaring problem with this argument is that all evidence of Congress' purposes is to the contrary. Building on its 1906 Act, Congress enacted the FDCA to bolster consumer protection against harmful products. Congress did not provide a federal remedy for consumers harmed by unsafe or ineffective drugs in the 1938 statute or in any subsequent amendment. Evidently, it determined that widely available state rights of action provided appropriate relief for injured consumers. It may also have recognized that state-law remedies further consumer protection by motivating manufacturers to produce safe and effective drugs and to give adequate warnings.

If Congress thought state-law suits posed an obstacle to its objectives, it surely would have enacted an express preemption provision at some point during the FDCA's 70–year history. * * * Its silence on the issue, coupled with its certain awareness of the prevalence of state tort litigation, is powerful evidence that Congress did not intend FDA oversight to be the exclusive means of ensuring drug safety and effectiveness. * * *

Wyeth relies not on any statement by Congress, but instead on the preamble to a 2006 FDA regulation governing the content and format of prescription drug labels. In that preamble, the FDA declared that the FDCA establishes "both a 'floor' and a 'ceiling,' " so that "FDA approval of labeling . . . preempts conflicting or contrary State law." 71 Fed. Reg. 3922, 3934–35 (2006). It further stated that certain state-law actions, such as those involving failure-to-warn claims, "threaten FDA's statutorily prescribed role as the expert Federal agency responsible for evaluating and regulating drugs." Id. at 3935.

This Court has recognized that an agency regulation with the force of law can preempt conflicting state requirements. In such cases, the Court has performed its own conflict determination, relying on the substance of state and federal law and not on agency proclamations of preemption. We are faced with no such regulation in this case, but rather with an agency's mere assertion that state law is an obstacle to achieving its statutory objectives. Because Congress has not authorized the FDA to preempt state law directly, the question is what weight we should accord the FDA's opinion. * * *

[T]he FDA's 2006 preamble does not merit deference. When the FDA issued its notice of proposed rulemaking in December 2000, it explained that the rule would "not contain policies that have federalism implications or that preempt State law." 65 Fed. Reg. 81,103 (2000). In 2006, the agency finalized the rule and, without offering states or other interested parties notice or opportunity for comment, articulated a sweeping position on the FDCA's preemptive effect in the regulatory preamble. The agency's views on state law are inherently suspect in light of this procedural failure.

Further, the preamble is at odds with what evidence we have of Congress' purposes, and it reverses the FDA's own longstanding position without providing a reasoned explanation, including any discussion of how state law has interfered with the FDA's regulation of drug labeling during decades of coexistence. The FDA's 2006 position plainly does not reflect the agency's own view at all times relevant to this litigation. Not once prior to Levine's injury did the FDA suggest that state tort law stood as an obstacle to its statutory mission. To the contrary, it cast federal labeling standards as a floor upon which states could build and repeatedly disclaimed any attempt to preempt failure-to-warn claims. For instance, in 1998, the FDA stated that it did "not believe that the evolution of state tort law [would] cause the development of standards that would be at odds with the agency's regulations." 63 Fed. Reg. 66,378, 66,384 (1998). It further noted that, in establishing "minimal standards" for drug labels, it did not intend "to preclude the states from imposing additional labeling requirements."

In keeping with Congress' decision not to preempt common-law tort suits, it appears that the FDA traditionally regarded state law as a complementary form of drug regulation. The FDA has limited resources to monitor the 11,000 drugs on the market, and manufacturers have superior access to information about their drugs, especially in the postmarketing phase as new risks emerge. State tort suits uncover unknown drug hazards and provide incentives for drug manufacturers to disclose safety risks promptly. They also serve a distinct compensatory function that may motivate injured persons to come forward with information. Failure-to-warn actions, in particular, lend force to the FDCA's premise that manufacturers, not the FDA, bear primary responsibility for their drug labeling at all times. Thus, the FDA long maintained that state law offers an additional, and important, layer of consumer protection that complements FDA regulation. The agency's 2006 preamble represents a dramatic change in position. * * *

In short, Wyeth has not persuaded us that failure-to-warn claims like Levine's obstruct the federal regulation of drug labeling. Congress has repeatedly declined to preempt state law, and the FDA's recently adopted position that state tort suits interfere with its statutory mandate is entitled to no weight. Although we recognize that some state-law claims might well frustrate the achievement of congressional objectives, this is not such a case. * * *

■ BREYER, JUSTICE (concurring):

I write separately to emphasize the Court's statement that "we have no occasion in this case to consider the preemptive effect of a specific agency regulation bearing the force of law." * * * The FDA may seek to determine whether and when state tort law acts as a help or a hindrance to achieving the safe drug-related medical care that Congress sought. It may seek to embody those determinations in lawful specific regulations describing, for example, when labeling requirements serve as a ceiling as well as a floor. And it is possible that such determinations would have preemptive effect. I agree with the Court, however, that such a regulation is not at issue in this case.

■ THOMAS, JUSTICE (concurring in the judgment):

* * * I have become increasingly skeptical of this Court's "purposes and objectives" preemption jurisprudence. Under this approach, the Court routinely invalidates state laws based on perceived conflicts with broad federal policy objectives, legislative history, or generalized notions of congressional purposes that are not embodied within the text of federal law. Because implied preemption doctrines that wander far from the statutory text are inconsistent with the Constitution, I concur only in the judgment. * * *

[I]n order to protect the delicate balance of power mandated by the Constitution, the Supremacy Clause must operate only in accordance with its terms. The clause provides: "This Constitution, and the Laws of the United States which shall be made in Pursuance thereof; and all Treaties made, or which shall be made, under the Authority of the United States, shall be the supreme Law of the Land; and the Judges in every State shall be bound thereby, any Thing in the Constitution or Laws of any state to the Contrary notwithstanding." Art. VI, cl. 2. * * * The Supremacy Clause thus requires that preemptive effect be given only those to federal standards and policies that are set forth in, or necessarily follow from, the statutory text that was produced through the constitutionally required bicameral and presentment procedures. * * * Congressional and agency musings, however, do not satisfy the Art. I, § 7 requirements for enactment of federal law and, therefore, do not preempt state law under the Supremacy Clause. * * *

The Court has generally articulated a very narrow "impossibility standard"—in part because the overly broad sweep of the Court's "purposes and objectives" approach has rendered it unnecessary for the Court to rely on "impossibility" preemption. The Court, in fact, has not explained why a narrow "physical impossibility" standard is the best proxy for determining when state and federal laws "directly conflict" for purposes of the Supremacy Clause. There could be instances where it is not "physically impossible" to comply with both state and federal law, even when the state and federal laws give directly conflicting commands. For example, if federal law gives an individual the right to engage in certain behavior that state law prohibits, the laws would give contradictory commands notwithstanding the fact that an individual could comply with both by electing to refrain from the covered behavior. Therefore, "physical impossibility" may not be the most appropriate standard for determining whether the text of state and federal laws directly conflict. * * *

[I]t was physically possible for Wyeth to comply with a state-law requirement to provide stronger warnings on Phenergan about the risks of the IV-push administration method while continuing to market Phenergan in compliance with federal law. * * * To say, as the statute does, that Wyeth may not market a drug without federal approval (i.e., without an FDA-approved label) is not to say that federal approval gives Wyeth the unfettered right, for all time, to market its drug with the specific label that was federally approved. Initial approval of a label amounts to a finding by the FDA that the label is safe for purposes of gaining federal approval to market the drug. It does not represent a finding that the drug, as labeled, can never be deemed unsafe by later federal action, or as in this case, the application of state law. * * *

The majority, while reaching the right conclusion in this case, demonstrates once again how application of "purposes and objectives" preemption requires inquiry into matters beyond the scope of proper judicial review. * * * Certainly, the absence of a statutory provision preempting all state tort suits related to approved federal drug labels is pertinent to a finding that such lawsuits are not preempted. But the relevance is in the fact that no statute explicitly preempts the lawsuits, and not in any inferences that the Court may draw from congressional silence about the motivations or policies underlying Congress' failure to act. * * *

■ ALITO, JUSTICE (dissenting):

* * * The Court frames the question presented as a "narro[w]" one—namely, whether Wyeth has a duty to provide "an adequate warning about using the IV-push method" to administer Phenergan. But that ignores the

antecedent question of who—the FDA or a jury in Vermont—has the authority and responsibility for determining the "adequacy" of Phenergan's warnings. Moreover, it is unclear how a "stronger" warning could have helped respondent; after all, the physician's assistant who treated her disregarded at least six separate warnings that are already on Phenergan's labeling, so respondent would be hard pressed to prove that a seventh would have made a difference.

More to the point, the question presented by this case is not a "narrow" one, and it does not concern whether Phenergan's label should bear a "stronger" warning. Rather, the real issue is whether a state tort jury can countermand the FDA's considered judgment that Phenergan's FDA-mandated warning label renders its intravenous (IV) use "safe." Indeed, respondent's amended complaint alleged that Phenergan is "not reasonably safe for intravenous administration," respondent's attorney told the jury that Phenergan's label should say, " 'Do not use this drug intravenously,' " [and] respondent's expert told the jury, "I think the drug should be labeled 'Not for IV use' " * * * *

Federal law, however, *does* rely on the FDA to make safety determinations like the one it made here. The FDA has long known about the risks associated with IV push in general and its use to administer Phenergan in particular. Whether wisely or not, the FDA has concluded—over the course of extensive, 54–year-long regulatory proceedings—that the drug is "safe" and "effective" when used in accordance with its FDA-mandated labeling. The unfortunate fact that respondent's healthcare providers ignored Phenergan's labeling may make this an ideal medical-malpractice case. But turning a common-law tort suit into a "frontal assault" on the FDA's regulatory regime for drug labeling upsets the well-settled meaning of the Supremacy Clause and our conflict preemption jurisprudence. * * *

[A] drug's warning label "serves as the standard under which the FDA determines whether a product is safe and effective." 50 Fed. Reg. 7470 (1985). Labeling is "[t]he centerpiece of risk management," as it "communicates to health care practitioners the agency's formal, authoritative conclusions regarding the conditions under which the product can be used safely and effectively." 71 Fed. Reg. 3922, 3934 (2006). The FDA has underscored the importance it places on drug labels by promulgating comprehensive regulations—spanning an entire part of the Code of Federal Regulations, see 21 C.F.R. pt. 201, with seven subparts and 70 separate sections—that set forth drug manufacturers' labeling obligations. * * *

Where the FDA determines, in accordance with its statutory mandate, that a drug is on balance "safe," our conflict preemption cases prohibit any state from countermanding that determination. Thus, as the Court itself recognizes, it is irrelevant in conflict preemption cases whether Congress "enacted an express preemption provision at some point during the FDCA's 70–year history." Rather, the ordinary principles of conflict preemption turn solely on whether a state has upset the regulatory balance struck by the federal agency. * * * Through Phenergan's label, the FDA offered medical professionals a menu of federally approved, "safe" and "effective" alternatives—including IV push—for administering the drug. Through a state tort suit, respondent attempted to deem IV push "unsafe" and "ineffective." * * *[4]

Phenergan's warning label has been subject to the FDA's strict regulatory oversight since the 1950s. For at least the last 34 years, the FDA has focused specifically on whether IV-push administration of Phenergan is "safe" and "effective" when performed in accordance with Phenergan's label. The agency's ultimate decision—to retain IV push as one means for administering Phenergan, albeit subject to stringent warnings—is reflected in the plain text of Phenergan's label (sometimes in boldfaced font and all-capital letters). And the record contains ample evidence that the FDA specifically considered and reconsidered the strength of Phenergan's IV-push-related warnings in light of new scientific and medical data. The majority's factual assertions to the contrary are mistaken.

The FDA's focus on IV push as a means of administering Phenergan dates back at least to 1975. In August of that year, several representatives from both the FDA and Wyeth met to discuss Phenergan's warning label. At that meeting, the FDA specifically proposed "that Phenergan Injection should not be used in Tubex®." Tubex is a syringe system used exclusively for IV push. An FDA official explained that the agency's concerns arose from medical-malpractice lawsuits involving IV push of the drug and that the FDA was aware of "5 cases involving amputation where the drug had been administered by Tubex together with several additional cases involving necrosis." Rather than contraindicating Phenergan for IV push, however, the agency and Wyeth agreed "that there was a need for better instruction regarding the problems of intraarterial injection."

The next year, the FDA convened an advisory committee to study, among other things, the risks associated with the Tubex system and IV push. At the conclusion of its study, the committee recommended an additional IV-push-specific warning for Phenergan's label but did not recommend eliminating IV push from the drug label altogether. In response to the committee's recommendations, the FDA instructed Wyeth to make several changes to strengthen Phenergan's label, including the addition of upper case warnings related to IV push. * * *

In its 1987 labeling order, the FDA cited voluminous materials to "suppor[t]" its new and stronger warnings related to IV push and the preferability of IV drip. One of those articles specifically discussed the relative advantages and disadvantages of IV drip compared to IV push, as well as the costs and benefits of administering Phenergan via IV push. The FDA also cited published case reports from the 1960s of gangrene caused by

---

4. To be sure, Congress recognized the principles of conflict preemption in the FDCA. See Drug Amendments of 1962, § 202, 76 Stat. 793 ("Nothing in the amendments made by this Act to the Federal Food, Drug, and Cosmetic Act shall be construed as invalidating any provision of State law ... unless there is a direct and positive conflict between such amendments and such provision of State law"). But a provision that simply recognizes the background principles of conflict preemption is not a traditional "saving clause," and even if it were, it would not displace our conflict-preemption analysis.

the intra-arterial injection of Phenergan, and the FDA instructed Wyeth to amend Phenergan's label in accordance with the latest medical research. The FDA also studied drugs similar to Phenergan and cited numerous cautionary articles—one of which urged the agency to consider contraindicating such drugs for IV use altogether.[9] * * * [T]he FDA also cited numerous articles that singled out the inner crook of the elbow—known as the "antecubital fossa" in the medical community—which is both a commonly used injection site and a universally recognized high-risk area for inadvertent intra-arterial injections. * * * Based on this and other research, the FDA ordered Wyeth to include a specific warning related to the use of the antecubital space for IV push.

When respondent was injured in 2000, Phenergan's label specifically addressed IV push in several passages * * * [and] devoted almost a full page to discussing the "Tubex system," which, as noted above, is used only to administer the drug via IV push. While Phenergan's label very clearly authorized the use of IV push, it also made clear that IV push is the delivery method of last resort. The label specified that "[t]he preferred parenteral route of administration is by deep intramuscular injection." If an intramuscular injection is ineffective, then "it is usually preferable to inject [Phenergan] through the tubing of an intravenous infusion set that is known to be functioning satisfactorily." Finally, if for whatever reason a medical professional chooses to use IV push, he or she is on notice that "INADVERTENT INTRA-ARTERIAL INJECTION CAN RESULT IN GANGRENE OF THE AFFECTED EXTREMITY." Phenergan's label also directs medical practitioners to choose veins wisely when using IV push * * * * Thus, it is demonstrably untrue that, as of 2000, Phenergan's "labeling did not contain a specific warning about the risks of IV-push administration." And whatever else might be said about the extensive medical authorities and case reports that the FDA cited in "support" of its approval of IV-push administration of Phenergan, it cannot be said that the FDA "paid no more than passing attention to" IV push; nor can it be said that the FDA failed to weigh its costs and benefits.

For her part, respondent does not dispute the FDA's conclusion that IV push has certain benefits. At trial, her medical practitioners testified that they used IV push in order to help her "in a swift and timely way" when she showed up at the hospital for the second time in one day complaining of "intractable" migraines * * * * Unfortunately, the physician's assistant

9. See Enloe et al., Hazards of Intra-Arterial Injection of Hydroxyzine, 16 Can. Anaesthetists' Soc'y J. 425, 427 (1969) (discussing hydroxyzine—an antihistamine with chemical properties similar to those of Phenergan—and suggesting its "temporary" benefits can never outweigh the risks of intra-arterial injection). With full knowledge of those risks, FDA retained IV push for Phenergan, although the agency required Wyeth to incorporate observations from the Enloe article into Phenergan's label. In contrast, at some time around 1970, the FDA prohibited all intravenous use of hydroxyzine. The FDA's decision to regulate the two drugs differently—notwithstanding (1) the agency's knowledge of the risks associated with both drugs and (2) the agency's recognition of the relevance of hydroxyzine-related articles and case reports in its regulation of Phenergan—further demonstrates that the FDA intentionally preserved IV-push administration for Phenergan.

who treated respondent in this case disregarded Phenergan's label and pushed the drug into the single spot on her arm that is *most* likely to cause an inadvertent intra-arterial injection. * * *

[I]t is irrelevant that the FDA's preamble does not "bear the force of law" because the FDA's labeling decisions surely do. It is well within the FDA's discretion to make its labeling decisions through administrative adjudications rather than through less-formal and less-flexible rulemaking proceedings, and we have never previously held that our preemption analysis turns on the agency's choice of the latter over the former. * * * [T]he FDA's explanation of the conflict between state tort suits and the federal labeling regime, set forth in the agency's amicus brief, is not even mentioned in the Court's opinion. Instead of relying on the FDA's explanation of its own regulatory purposes, the Court relies on a decade-old and now-repudiated statement, which the majority finds preferable. * * *

By their very nature, juries are ill-equipped to perform the FDA's cost-benefit-balancing function. * * * [P]atients like respondent are the only ones whom tort juries ever see, and for a patient like respondent—who has already suffered a tragic accident—Phenergan's risks are no longer a matter of probabilities and potentialities. In contrast, the FDA has the benefit of the long view. Its drug-approval determinations consider the interests of all potential users of a drug * * * * And the FDA conveys its warnings with one voice, rather than whipsawing the medical community with 50 (or more) potentially conflicting ones. After today's ruling, however, parochialism may prevail.

The problem is well illustrated by the labels borne by "vesicant" drugs, many of which are used for chemotherapy. As a class, vesicants are much more dangerous than drugs like Phenergan, but the vast majority of vesicant labels—like Phenergan's—either allow or do not disallow IV push. Because vesicant extravasation can have devastating consequences, and because the potentially lifesaving benefits of these drugs offer hollow solace to the victim of such a tragedy, a jury's cost-benefit analysis in a particular case may well differ from the FDA's. * * * The fact that the labels for such drugs allow IV push is striking—both because vesicants are much more dangerous than Phenergan, and also because they are so frequently extravasated. Regardless of the FDA's reasons for not contraindicating IV push for these drugs, it is odd (to say the least) that a jury in Vermont can now order for Phenergan what the FDA has chosen not to order for [vesicants]. * * *

NOTES AND QUESTIONS

1. *What's left after* Levine? Justice Stevens did not completely close the door to the possibility of impossibility preemption, but he seemed to reduce it primarily to a factual judgment for the trial judge to make and typically in state court (is that appropriate?). In any event, lower courts will have to decide how much stronger a showing would demonstrate an actual conflict between federal and state law. See, e.g., Mason v. SmithKline Beecham

Corp., 596 F.3d 387, 393–95 (7th Cir.2010) (finding even less evidence that the FDA would have barred the manufacturer of Paxil® (paroxetine) from warning about the risk of suicide in young adults); cf. Dowhal v. Smith-Kline Beecham Consumer Healthcare, 88 P.3d 1 (Cal.2004) [excerpted in Chap. 1(E)(2)] (finding implied preemption of California's reproductive toxicity warning requirement as applied to OTC smoking cessation products governed by NDAs notwithstanding ambiguous correspondence between various interested parties and the FDA). Assume that Wyeth had followed the CBE rule, unilaterally adding some additional risk information (though it is hard to imagine what more it might have said that this jury would have deemed adequate) and filing an NDA supplement, only to have the FDA reject the submission and instruct the company to revert to its originally approved labeling? As suggested in earlier chapters, of course, the agency likely would handle any concerns with greater subtlety, perhaps informally asking the sponsor to resubmit the NDA supplement with milder language more palatable to the agency (along similar lines, why do you think that the FDA evidently has never brought an enforcement action against a sponsor for unilaterally adding risk information?). Will *Levine* motivate manufacturers to resist such agency informality and insist instead on creating an administrative paper trail? Or assume that the FDA had approved Phenergan solely for IV use and that Ms. Levine had argued broadly that this route of administration (both push and drip) should have been contraindicated (in effect, that the NDA should be withdrawn)—might the majority regard her (more far-reaching) claim as preempted?

2. *FDA's preamble stunt*. As recounted in *Levine*, in the preamble to its rule revising the content and format of package inserts, the FDA included an extensive implied preemption analysis applicable to tort claims (and not limited to claims that would conflict with the details covered by that rule). See 71 Fed. Reg. 3922, 3934–36, 3969 (2006). The move triggered howls of protest. See David A. Kessler & David C. Vladeck, A Critical Examination of the FDA's Efforts to Preempt Failure-to-Warn Claims, 96 Geo. L.J. 461 (2008); Thomas O. McGarity, Corporate Accountability for Scientific Fraud: Ketek and the Perils of Aggressive Agency Preemption, 58 Emory L.J. 287 (2008); Catherine M. Sharkey, Preemption by Preamble: Federal Agencies and the Federalization of Tort Reform, 56 DePaul L. Rev. 227 (2007); Alicia Mundy, FDA Memos Undercut Stance on Preempting Drug Suits, Wall St. J., Oct. 30, 2008, at A3. As the Court explained in *Levine*, the FDA soon thereafter revised the CBE regulation (though in a way that would not necessarily have prevented Wyeth from adding risk information to the package insert). What if, instead, the agency had revoked the CBE rule altogether and, in the accompanying preamble, explained that this meant sponsors could no longer make any unilateral revisions in previously approved labeling? Not surprisingly, the new administration has gone in the other direction on the implied preemption question. See Philip Rucker, Obama Curtails Bush's Policy of "Preemption," Wash. Post, May 22, 2009, at A3.

3. *Childhood vaccines*. Chief Justice Roberts and Justice Scalia (who had authored the opinion in *Riegel* for all but two members of the Court) joined in Justice Alito's dissent in *Levine*. Obviously, the lack of an express preemption clause applicable to prescription drugs provides the central explanation for the otherwise seemingly inexplicable difference in treatment of FDA-approved pharmaceutical products and Class III medical devices. Just two years after *Levine*, in a case involving childhood vaccines, Justice Scalia penned the majority opinion in a 6–2 decision finding express (though hardly unambiguous) preemption of all design defect claims under the NCVIA (which, as previously discussed, created a federal no-fault compensation program and erected defenses to tort claims in order to discourage victims from opting out). See Bruesewitz v. Wyeth LLC, 131 S.Ct. 1068, 1080 (2011) (concluding that the statute "reflects a sensible choice to leave complex epidemiological judgments about vaccine design to the FDA and the National Vaccine Program rather than juries"). Although the dissenting opinion never made reference to the more plaintiff-friendly consumer expectations test of design defect still in widespread use at the time of the statute's enactment, it offered a more persuasive interpretation of the relevant provision as reflecting a congressional decision to codify *Rest. (2d)* § 402 comment k, which some courts at the time had read to require that plaintiffs demonstrate the availability of a feasible alternative design (and other courts had interpreted as providing blanket immunity from strict liability but not negligence-based design defect claims). See id. at 1086, 1089–91, 1094, 1096 (Sotomayor, J., dissenting). See generally Nitin Shah, Note, When Injury Is Unavoidable: The Vaccine Act's Limited Preemption of Design Defect Claims, 96 Va. L. Rev. 199 (2010); Eva B. Stensvad, Note, Immunity for Vaccine Manufacturers: The Vaccine Act and Preemption of Design Defect Claims, 95 Minn. L. Rev. 315 (2010); Deborah F. Buckman, Annotation, Construction and Application of Preemption Provisions of NCVIA, 39 A.L.R. Fed.2d 155 (2009 & 2011 Supp.).

4. *Generic drugs*. Curious questions have arisen when patients injured by generic drug products pursue failure-to-warn claims, see Chap. 7(A)(3), and, just two years after *Levine*, the Supreme Court confronted an implied preemption defense in such a case. For the most part, the FDA insists that generic drugs use the same labeling as the reference listed drug. See Chap. 3(A)(2). Deferring to the agency's interpretation of its CBE regulation (at least as it existed before 2007) as available only to manufacturers of brand-name drugs, the Court held that this categorically preempted inadequate warning claims against manufacturers of generic drugs even if those companies had failed to request (as arguably required by agency policy) that the FDA consider revising the labels for all versions of that drug. See PLIVA, Inc. v. Mensing, 131 S.Ct. 2567, 2574–79 (2011). In his opinion for the majority, Justice Thomas found a direct conflict between federal and state law; the mere possibility that the defendants could have persuaded the FDA to persuade the brand-name manufacturer to add a warning so that they then could include that same warning in their labeling did not overcome this facial conflict. See id. at 2578–79; id. at 2581 ("[W]hen a party cannot satisfy its state duties without the federal government's special permission and assistance, which is dependent on the exercise of judgment by a federal agency, that party cannot independently satisfy those state duties for preemption purposes."). The four dissenters pointed out that the same contingency had existed in *Levine* (insofar as the CBE regulation allowed innovator companies to make unilateral revisions to risk labeling only during an interim period before the FDA decided whether or not to allow it) without the Court in that case finding any conflict between federal and state law. See id. at 2588–90 & n.10 (Sotomayor, J., dissenting); id. at 2582 ("Until today, the mere possibility of impossibility had not been enough to establish preemption."). Notwithstanding the Court's effort to distinguish *Levine*, does the similarity between the two cases noted by the dissenters mean that a bare majority of the justices (three of whom had, after all, dissented in *Levine*) already doubts the continuing viability of *Levine*'s holding?

5. *OTC products*. In 1997, Congress amended the FDCA to preempt state regulation of nonprescription drugs, but it expressly saved products liability claims. See 21 U.S.C. § 379r; 64 Fed. Reg. 13,254, 13,272 (1999); see also J. Warren Rissier, Note, The FDA's Proposed Labeling Rules for Over-the-Counter Drugs and Preemption of State Tort Law, 71 S. Cal. L. Rev. 1387 (1998); cf. Green v. BDI Pharm., 803 So.2d 68, 74–75 (La.Ct.App.2001) (finding express preemption of a failure-to-warn claim involving an OTC ephedrine product, ignoring entirely the impact of the savings clause). Although the savings clause would not foreclose an implied preemption argument, it would seem to fare poorly in the wake of *Levine*. See Gaeta v. Perrigo Pharms. Co., 630 F.3d 1225 (9th Cir.2011). But how about OTC drugs subject to monographs rather than NDAs—after all, under these classwide regulations, the FDA (rather than any particular sponsor) dictates the precise content of labeling and allows essentially no (even fairly trivial) deviations?

6. *Further commentary*. See Ashutosh Bhagwat, Wyeth v. Levine and Agency Preemption: More Muddle, or Creeping to Clarity?, 45 Tulsa L. Rev. 197 (2009); Elizabeth J. Cabraser, When Worlds Collide: The Supreme Court Confronts Federal Agencies with Federalism in Wyeth v. Levine, 84 Tul. L. Rev. 1275 (2010); Mary J. Davis, The Battle over Implied Preemption: Products Liability and the FDA, 48 B.C. L. Rev. 1089 (2007); Richard A. Epstein, The Case for Field Preemption of State Laws in Drug Cases, 103 Nw. U. L. Rev. 463 (2009); Margaret Gilhooley, Drug Preemption and the Need to Reform the FDA Consultation Process, 34 Am. J.L. & Med. 539 (2008); Peter H. Schuck, FDA Preemption of State Tort Law in Drug Regulation: Finding the Sweet Spot, 13 Roger Williams U. L. Rev. 73 (2008); Douglas G. Smith, Preemption After Wyeth v. Levine, 70 Ohio St. L.J. 1435 (2009); David C. Vladeck, Deconstructing Wyeth v. Levine: The New Limits on Implied Conflict Preemption, 59 Case W. Res. L. Rev. 883 (2009); Anthony Gostanian, Note, How the FDA Can Overturn Wyeth v. Levine, 36 Am. J.L. & Med. 248 (2010).

3. TORT CLAIMS AGAINST THE FDA

In the event that a patient injured by a pharmaceutical product or medical device is unable to sue the manufacturer—whether because of preemption, a regulatory compliance defense, or bankruptcy—the FDA itself might become a target of tort litigation for authorizing the sale of an allegedly defective product.

Berkovitz v. United States

486 U.S. 531 (1988).

■ MARSHALL, JUSTICE:

The question in this case is whether the discretionary function exception of the Federal Tort Claims Act (FTCA or Act), 28 U.S.C. § 2680(a), bars a suit based on the government's licensing of an oral polio vaccine and on its subsequent approval of the release of a specific lot of that vaccine to the public.

On May 10, 1979, Kevan Berkovitz, then a 2–month-old infant, ingested a dose of Orimune, an oral polio vaccine manufactured by Lederle Laboratories. Within one month, he contracted a severe case of polio. The disease left Berkovitz almost completely paralyzed and unable to breathe without the assistance of a respirator. The Communicable Disease Center, an agency of the federal government, determined that Berkovitz had contracted polio from the vaccine.

Berkovitz, joined by his parents as guardians, subsequently filed suit against the United States in federal district court.[1] The complaint alleged that the United States was liable for his injuries under the FTCA because the Division of Biologic Standards (DBS), then a part of the National Institutes of Health, had acted wrongfully in licensing Lederle Laboratories to produce Orimune and because the Bureau of Biologics of the Food and Drug Administration (FDA) had acted wrongfully in approving release to the public of the particular lot of vaccine containing Berkovitz's dose. According to petitioners, these actions violated federal law and policy regarding the inspection and approval of polio vaccines.

The government moved to dismiss the suit for lack of subject-matter jurisdiction on the ground that the agency actions fell within the discretionary function exception of the FTCA. * * * [T]he discretionary function exception will not apply when a federal statute, regulation, or policy specifically prescribes a course of action for an employee to follow. In this event, the employee has no rightful option but to adhere to the directive. And if the employee's conduct cannot appropriately be the product of judgment or choice, then there is no discretion in the conduct for the discretionary function exception to protect.

Moreover, assuming the challenged conduct involves an element of judgment, a court must determine whether that judgment is of the kind that the discretionary function exception was designed to shield. The basis for the discretionary function exception was Congress' desire to "prevent

---

1. Petitioners also sued Lederle Laboratories in a separate civil action. That suit was settled before the instant case was filed.

judicial 'second-guessing' of legislative and administrative decisions grounded in social, economic, and political policy through the medium of an action in tort." United States v. Varig Airlines, 467 U.S. 797, 814 (1984). The exception, properly construed, therefore protects only governmental actions and decisions based on considerations of public policy. See Dalehite v. United States, 346 U.S. 15, 36 (1953) ("Where there is room for policy judgment and decision there is discretion"). In sum, the discretionary function exception insulates the government from liability if the action challenged in the case involves the permissible exercise of policy judgment. * * *

In restating and clarifying the scope of the discretionary function exception, we intend specifically to reject the government's argument, pressed both in this Court and the court of appeals, that the exception precludes liability for any and all acts arising out of the regulatory programs of federal agencies. That argument is rebutted first by the language of the exception, which protects "discretionary" functions, rather than "regulatory" functions. The significance of Congress' choice of language is supported by the legislative history. As this Court previously has indicated, the relevant legislative materials demonstrate that the exception was designed to cover not all acts of regulatory agencies and their employees, but only such acts as are "discretionary" in nature. * * *

Petitioners' suit raises two broad claims. First, petitioners assert that the DBS violated a federal statute and accompanying regulations in issuing a license to Lederle Laboratories to produce Orimune. Second, petitioners argue that the Bureau of Biologics of the FDA violated federal regulations and policy in approving the release of the particular lot of Orimune that contained Kevan Berkovitz's dose. We examine each of these broad claims by reviewing the applicable regulatory scheme and petitioners' specific allegations of agency wrongdoing. Because the decision we review adjudicated a motion to dismiss, we accept all of the factual allegations in petitioners' complaint as true and ask whether, in these circumstances, dismissal of the complaint was appropriate.

Under federal law, a manufacturer must receive a product license prior to marketing a brand of live oral polio vaccine. In order to become eligible for such a license, a manufacturer must first make a sample of the vaccine product. This process begins with the selection of an original virus strain. The manufacturer grows a seed virus from this strain; the seed virus is then used to produce monopools, portions of which are combined to form the consumer-level product. Federal regulations set forth safety criteria for the original strain, the seed virus, and the vaccine monopools. Under the regulations, the manufacturer must conduct a variety of tests to measure the safety of the product at each stage of the manufacturing process. Upon completion of the manufacturing process and the required testing, the manufacturer is required to submit an application for a product license to the DBS. In addition to this application, the manufacturer must submit data from the tests performed and a sample of the finished product. * * * These statutory and regulatory provisions require the DBS, prior to issuing a product license, to receive all data the manufacturer is required to submit, to examine the product, and to make a determination that the product complies with safety standards.

Petitioners' first allegation with regard to the licensing of Orimune is that the DBS issued a product license without first receiving data that the manufacturer must submit showing how the product, at the various stages of the manufacturing process, matched up against regulatory safety standards. The discretionary function exception does not bar a cause of action based on this allegation. The statute and regulations described above require, as a precondition to licensing, that the DBS receive certain test data from the manufacturer relating to the product's compliance with regulatory standards. The DBS has no discretion to issue a license without first receiving the required test data; to do so would violate a specific statutory and regulatory directive. Accordingly, to the extent that petitioners' licensing claim is based on a decision of the DBS to issue a license without having received the required test data, the discretionary function exception imposes no bar.

Petitioners' other allegation regarding the licensing of Orimune is difficult to describe with precision. Petitioners contend that the DBS licensed Orimune even though the vaccine did not comply with certain regulatory safety standards. This charge may be understood in any of three ways. First, petitioners may mean that the DBS licensed Orimune without first making a determination as to whether the vaccine complied with regulatory standards. Second, petitioners may intend to argue that the DBS specifically found that Orimune failed to comply with certain regulatory standards and nonetheless issued a license for the vaccine's manufacture. Third, petitioners may concede that the DBS made a determination of compliance, but allege that this determination was incorrect. Neither petitioners' complaint nor their briefs and argument before this Court make entirely clear their theory of the case.

If petitioners aver that the DBS licensed Orimune either without determining whether the vaccine complied with regulatory standards or after determining that the vaccine failed to comply, the discretionary function exception does not bar the claim. Under the scheme governing the DBS's regulation of polio vaccines, the DBS may not issue a license except upon an examination of the product and a determination that the product complies with all regulatory standards. The agency has no discretion to deviate from this mandated procedure. Petitioners' claim, if interpreted as alleging that the DBS licensed Orimune in the absence of a determination that the vaccine complied with regulatory standards, therefore does not challenge a discretionary function. Rather, the claim charges a failure on the part of the agency to perform its clear duty under federal law. When a suit charges an agency with failing to act in accord with a specific mandatory directive, the discretionary function exception does not apply.

If petitioners' claim is that the DBS made a determination that Orimune complied with regulatory standards, but that the determination was incorrect, the question of the applicability of the discretionary function exception requires a somewhat different analysis. In that event, the question turns on whether the manner and method of determining compliance with the safety standards at issue involve agency judgment of the kind protected by the discretionary function exception. Petitioners contend that the determination involves the application of objective scientific standards, whereas the government asserts that the determination incorporates considerable "policy judgment." In making these assertions, the parties have framed the issue appropriately; application of the discretionary function exception to the claim that the determination of compliance was incorrect hinges on whether the agency officials making that determination permissibly exercise policy choice. The parties, however, have not addressed this question in detail, and they have given us no indication of the way in which the DBS interprets and applies the regulations setting forth the criteria for compliance. Given that these regulations are particularly abstruse, we hesitate to decide the question on the scanty record before us. We therefore leave it to the district court to decide, if petitioners choose to press this claim, whether agency officials appropriately exercise policy judgment in determining that a vaccine product complies with the relevant safety standards.

The regulatory scheme governing release of vaccine lots is distinct from that governing the issuance of licenses. The former set of regulations places an obligation on manufacturers to examine all vaccine lots prior to distribution to ensure that they comply with regulatory standards. These regulations, however, do not impose a corresponding duty on the Bureau of Biologics. Although the regulations empower the Bureau to examine any vaccine lot and prevent the distribution of a noncomplying lot, they do not require the Bureau to take such action in all cases. The regulations generally allow the Bureau to determine the appropriate manner in which to regulate the release of vaccine lots, rather than mandating certain kinds of agency action. The regulatory scheme governing the release of vaccine lots is substantially similar in this respect to the scheme discussed in *Varig*.

Given this regulatory context, the discretionary function exception bars any claims that challenge the Bureau's formulation of policy as to the appropriate way in which to regulate the release of vaccine lots. In addition, if the policies and programs formulated by the Bureau allow room for implementing officials to make independent policy judgments, the discretionary function exception protects the acts taken by those officials in the exercise of this discretion. The discretionary function exception, however, does not apply if the acts complained of do not involve the permissible exercise of policy discretion. Thus, if the Bureau's policy leaves no room for an official to exercise policy judgment in performing a given act, or if the act simply does not involve the exercise of such judgment, the discretionary function exception does not bar a claim that the act was negligent or wrongful. Cf. Indian Towing Co. v. United States, 350 U.S. 61, 69 (1955) (holding that a negligent failure to maintain a lighthouse in good working order subjected the government to suit under the FTCA even though the initial decision to undertake and maintain lighthouse service was a discretionary policy judgment).

Viewed in light of these principles, petitioners' claim regarding the release of the vaccine lot from which Kevan Berkovitz received his dose survives the government's motion to dismiss. Petitioners allege that, under the authority granted by the regulations, the Bureau of Biologics has adopted a policy of testing all vaccine lots for compliance with safety standards and preventing the distribution to the public of any lots that fail to comply. Petitioners further allege that notwithstanding this policy, which allegedly leaves no room for implementing officials to exercise independent policy judgment, employees of the Bureau knowingly approved the release of a lot that did not comply with safety standards. Thus, petitioners' complaint is directed at a governmental action that allegedly involved no policy discretion. Petitioners, of course, have not proved their factual allegations, but they are not required to do so on a motion to dismiss. If those allegations are correct—that is, if the Bureau's policy did not allow the official who took the challenged action to release a noncomplying lot on the basis of policy considerations—the discretionary function exception does not bar the claim. Because petitioners may yet show, on the basis of materials obtained in discovery or otherwise, that the conduct challenged here did not involve the permissible exercise of policy discretion, the invocation of the discretionary function exception to dismiss petitioners' lot release claim was improper. * * *

PROBLEM #8. *PASSING THE BUCK*

Recall from Chapter 3(B) that the FDA has begun to allow third parties accredited by the agency to conduct reviews of premarket notifications for certain medical devices. See 21 U.S.C. § 360m. Imagine that one such organization, PMNs-r-Us, receives a § 510(k) submission from a manufacturer of resin casting tape (used to immobilize broken bones). After a brief debate between the engineering and medical experts over lunch, the organization concludes that a minor difference in the device's technological characteristics as compared to the predicate device does not render the product any less safe or effective, so it transmits a report to the FDA recommending premarket clearance. As the agency does with all such reports under its third party review program, an administrative assistant quickly checks the report for any obvious gaps before issuing a letter to the manufacturer. It turns out that review organization, in its hasty review, misjudged the potential risks associated with the design, and a patient is severely burned when his arm is put in a cast. In addition to bringing a products liability claim against the manufacturer, can he sue either the FDA or PMNs-r-Us for negligence?

NOTES AND QUESTIONS

1. *The record of tort litigation against the FDA.* After *Berkovitz*, lower courts concluded that the DBS had unjustifiably failed to implement the applicable requirements. See In re Sabin Oral Polio Vaccine Prods. Liab. Litig., 984 F.2d 124, 125–28 (4th Cir.1993). Courts routinely hold, however, that the FDA's product approval decisions fall within the FTCA's discretionary functions exception. See, e.g, Forsyth v. Eli Lilly & Co., 904 F.Supp. 1153 (D.Haw.1995); see also Deborah F. Buckman, Annotation, Liability of United States, Under Federal Tort Claims Act, for Damages Caused by Ingestion or Administration of Government–Approved Drugs, Vaccines, and Medications, 173 A.L.R. Fed. 431, § 8 (2001 & 2011 Supp.). For an analysis of the FTCA's application to private entities engaged in governmental functions, see Lars Noah, Deputizing Institutional Review Boards to Police (Audit?) Biomedical Research, 25 J. Legal Med. 267, 276 n.43 (2004).

2. *The old swine flu vaccine fiasco.* In 1976, responding to fears of an emerging influenza pandemic, the federal government initiated a mass immunization campaign, but pharmaceutical manufacturers refused to supply vaccines without protection from tort liability. Congress responded by amending the FTCA to allow the filing of tort claims against the government instead. See Pub. L. No. 94–380, 90 Stat. 1113 (1976) (codified at 42 U.S.C. § 247b); see also Thomas E. Baynes, Jr., Liability for Vaccine Related Injuries: Public Health Considerations and Some Reflections on the Swine Flu Experience, 21 St. Louis U. L.J. 44 (1977). After a number of vaccine recipients reported developing Guillain–Barré Syndrome, the immunization program ceased, and the tort litigation against the United States commenced. See, e.g., Novak v. United States, 865 F.2d 718 (6th Cir.1989); see also Mills v. United States, 764 F.2d 373, 378 (5th Cir.1985) (holding that a warning of the risk of anaphylactic shock was adequate); Ducharme v. Merrill–National Lab., 574 F.2d 1307, 1309–10 (5th Cir.1978) (rejecting constitutional objections to granting tort immunity to vaccine manufacturers); Arnold W. Reitze, Jr., Federal Compensation for Vaccination Induced Injuries, 13 B.C. Envtl. Aff. L. Rev. 169, 170–88 (1986). The government paid out more than $100 million in claims. See David Brown, A Shot in the Dark: Swine Flu's Vaccine Lessons, Wash. Post, May 27, 2002, at A9. In 2002, and notwithstanding this experience, the federal government assumed financial responsibility for injuries from smallpox vaccinations, though only under limited circumstances. See 42 U.S.C. § 233(p) (covering claims for injuries caused by the administration of smallpox countermeasures during a declared health emergency); Ceci Connolly, Homeland Bill Covers Smallpox Shot Liability, Wash. Post, Nov. 16, 2002, at A13; see also George W. Conk, Reactions and Overreactions: Smallpox Vaccination, Complications, and Compensation, 14 Fordham Envtl. L.J. 439 (2003).

3. *Vaccinating soldiers.* As discussed in Chapter 2(C), the Department of Defense inoculated military personnel during Operation Desert Storm with experimental vaccines against anthrax and other biowarfare agents. It has been suggested that these treatments contributed to the development of Gulf War Syndrome. See David Brown, Funding Continues for Illness Scientists Dismiss: Gulf Syndrome Has Believers in Congress, Wash. Post, Dec. 3, 2006, at A1. Even if soldiers could trace some injury to the use of these vaccines, the government would be immune (so to speak) to any tort litigation under another FTCA exception applicable to military operations and personnel. See 28 U.S.C. § 2680(j); Minns v. United States, 155 F.3d

445 (4th Cir.1998). Furthermore, any private companies supplying products to the military according to government specifications might enjoy protection from tort claims under the government contractor defense. See Ammend v. BioPort, Inc., 322 F.Supp.2d 848, 877–79 (W.D.Mich.2004) (anthrax vaccine); see also Carole A. Loftin, Note, Expansion of the Government Contractor Defense: Applying Boyle to Vaccine Manufacturers, 70 Tex. L. Rev. 1261 (1992); Scott Hensley & Ron Winslow, Drug Companies Contemplate New Role as "Biodefense Contractors," Wall St. J., Nov. 12, 2001, at B1.

C. CAUSATION DIFFICULTIES

Although products liability claims against sellers of prescription drugs and medical devices will raise issues of actual and proximate causation that often arise in other types of tort litigation, two stand out as peculiar to this class of cases. First, as products that may cause long latency diseases rather than acute injuries, pharmaceutical injury lawsuits have influenced the way that courts deal with cause-in-fact problems, in drug and device as well as toxic tort litigation. Second, in dealing with mass tort claims against the manufacturers of diethylstilbestrol (DES), courts have created special rules for the identification of responsible parties, which for the most part have remained unique to drug product litigation.

1. EPIDEMIOLOGICAL DATA

Daubert v. Merrell Dow Pharmaceuticals, Inc.

509 U.S. 579 (1993).

■ BLACKMUN, JUSTICE:

In this case we are called upon to determine the standard for admitting expert scientific testimony in a federal trial. Petitioners Jason Daubert and Eric Schuller are minor children born with serious birth defects. They and their parents sued respondent in California state court, alleging that the birth defects had been caused by the mothers' ingestion of Bendectin, a prescription antinausea drug marketed by respondent. Respondent removed the suits to federal court on diversity grounds.

After extensive discovery, respondent moved for summary judgment, contending that Bendectin does not cause birth defects in humans and that petitioners would be unable to come forward with any admissible evidence that it does. In support of its motion, respondent submitted an affidavit of Steven H. Lamm, physician and epidemiologist, who is a well-credentialed expert on the risks from exposure to various chemical substances. Doctor Lamm stated that he had reviewed all the literature on Bendectin and human birth defects—more than 30 published studies involving over 130,000 patients. No study had found Bendectin to be a human teratogen (i.e., a substance capable of causing malformations in fetuses). On the basis of this review, Doctor Lamm concluded that maternal use of Bendectin during the first trimester of pregnancy has not been shown to be a risk factor for human birth defects.

Petitioners did not (and do not) contest this characterization of the published record regarding Bendectin. Instead, they responded to respondent's motion with the testimony of eight experts of their own, each of whom also possessed impressive credentials. These experts had concluded that Bendectin can cause birth defects. Their conclusions were based upon "in vitro" (test tube) and "in vivo" (live) animal studies that found a link between Bendectin and malformations; pharmacological studies of the chemical structure of Bendectin that purported to show similarities between the structure of the drug and that of other substances known to cause birth defects; and the "reanalysis" of previously published epidemiological (human statistical) studies.

The district court granted respondent's motion for summary judgment. The court stated that scientific evidence is admissible only if the principle upon which it is based is " 'sufficiently established to have general acceptance in the field to which it belongs.' " The court concluded that petitioners' evidence did not meet this standard. Given the vast body of epidemiological data concerning Bendectin, the court held, expert opinion which is not based on epidemiological evidence is not admissible to establish causation. Thus, the animal-cell studies, live-animal studies, and chemical-structure analyses on which petitioners had relied could not raise by themselves a reasonably disputable jury issue regarding causation. Petitioners' epidemiological analyses, based as they were on recalculations of data in previously published studies that had found no causal link between the drug and birth defects, were ruled to be inadmissible because they had not been published or subjected to peer review.

The United States Court of Appeals for the Ninth Circuit affirmed. Citing *Frye v. United States*, 293 F. 1013, 1014 (D.C.App.1923), the court stated that expert opinion based on a scientific technique is inadmissible unless the technique is "generally accepted" as reliable in the relevant scientific community. * * * The court emphasized that other courts of appeals considering the risks of Bendectin had refused to admit reanalyses of epidemiological studies that had been neither published nor subjected to peer review. Those courts had found unpublished reanalyses "particularly problematic in light of the massive weight of the original published studies supporting [respondent's] position, all of which had undergone full scrutiny from the scientific community." Contending that reanalysis is generally accepted by the scientific community only when it is subjected to verification and scrutiny by others in the field, the court of appeals rejected petitioners' reanalyses as "unpublished, not subjected to the normal peer review process and generated solely for use in litigation." The court concluded that petitioners' evidence provided an insufficient foundation to allow admission of expert testimony that Bendectin caused their injuries and, accordingly, that petitioners could not satisfy their burden of proving causation at trial. * * *

In the 70 years since its formulation in the *Frye* case, the "general acceptance" test has been the dominant standard for determining the admissibility of novel scientific evidence at trial. * * * The merits of the *Frye* test have been much debated, and scholarship on its proper scope and application is legion. Petitioners' primary attack, however, is not on the content but on the continuing authority of the rule. They contend that the *Frye* test was superseded by the adoption of the Federal Rules of Evidence [in 1975]. We agree. * * *

Here there is a specific Rule that speaks to the contested issue. Rule 702, governing expert testimony, provides: "If scientific, technical, or other specialized knowledge will assist the trier of fact to understand the evidence or to determine a fact in issue, a witness qualified as an expert by knowledge, skill, experience, training, or education, may testify thereto in the form of an opinion or otherwise."* Nothing in the text of this Rule establishes "general acceptance" as an absolute prerequisite to admissibility. Nor does respondent present any clear indication that Rule 702 or the Rules as a whole were intended to incorporate a "general acceptance" standard. The drafting history makes no mention of *Frye*, and a rigid "general acceptance" requirement would be at odds with the "liberal thrust" of the Federal Rules and their "general approach of relaxing the traditional barriers to 'opinion' testimony." Given the Rules' permissive backdrop and their inclusion of a specific rule on expert testimony that does not mention " 'general acceptance,' " the assertion that the Rules somehow assimilated *Frye* is unconvincing. *Frye* made "general acceptance" the exclusive test for admitting expert scientific testimony. That austere standard, absent from, and incompatible with, the Federal Rules of Evidence, should not be applied in federal trials.

That the *Frye* test was displaced by the Rules of Evidence does not mean, however, that the Rules themselves place no limits on the admissibility of purportedly scientific evidence. Nor is the trial judge disabled from screening such evidence. To the contrary, under the Rules the trial judge must ensure that any and all scientific testimony or evidence admitted is not only relevant, but reliable.

The primary locus of this obligation is Rule 702, which clearly contemplates some degree of regulation of the subjects and theories about which an expert may testify. * * * The subject of an expert's testimony must be "scientific ... knowledge." The adjective "scientific" implies a grounding in the methods and procedures of science. Similarly, the word "knowledge" connotes more than subjective belief or unsupported speculation. The term "applies to any body of known facts or to any body of ideas inferred from such facts or accepted as truths on good grounds." Webster's Third New Int'l Dictionary 1252 (1986). Of course, it would be unreasonable to conclude that the subject of scientific testimony must be "known" to a

* Effective December 1, 2000, an amendment to Rule 702 inserted at the end the following new text: ", if (1) the testimony is based upon sufficient facts or data, (2) the testimony is the product of reliable principles and methods, and (3) the witness has applied the principles and methods reliably to the facts of the case." 192 F.R.D. 340, 418 (2000).

certainty; arguably, there are no certainties in science. But, in order to qualify as "scientific knowledge," an inference or assertion must be derived by the scientific method. Proposed testimony must be supported by appropriate validation—i.e., "good grounds," based on what is known. In short, the requirement that an expert's testimony pertain to "scientific knowledge" establishes a standard of evidentiary reliability.

Rule 702 further requires that the evidence or testimony "assist the trier of fact to understand the evidence or to determine a fact in issue." This condition goes primarily to relevance. "Expert testimony which does not relate to any issue in the case is not relevant and, ergo, non-helpful." The consideration has been aptly described by Judge Becker as one of "fit." "Fit" is not always obvious, and scientific validity for one purpose is not necessarily scientific validity for other, unrelated purposes. The study of the phases of the moon, for example, may provide valid scientific "knowledge" about whether a certain night was dark, and if darkness is a fact in issue, the knowledge will assist the trier of fact. However (absent creditable grounds supporting such a link), evidence that the moon was full on a certain night will not assist the trier of fact in determining whether an individual was unusually likely to have behaved irrationally on that night. Rule 702's "helpfulness" standard requires a valid scientific connection to the pertinent inquiry as a precondition to admissibility.

That these requirements are embodied in Rule 702 is not surprising. Unlike an ordinary witness, see Rule 701, an expert is permitted wide latitude to offer opinions, including those that are not based on firsthand knowledge or observation. Presumably, this relaxation of the usual requirement of firsthand knowledge * * * is premised on an assumption that the expert's opinion will have a reliable basis in the knowledge and experience of his discipline.

Faced with a proffer of expert scientific testimony, then, the trial judge must determine at the outset, pursuant to Rule 104(a), whether the expert is proposing to testify to (1) scientific knowledge that (2) will assist the trier of fact to understand or determine a fact in issue.[11] This entails a preliminary assessment of whether the reasoning or methodology underlying the testimony is scientifically valid and of whether that reasoning or methodology properly can be applied to the facts in issue. We are confident that federal judges possess the capacity to undertake this review. Many factors will bear on the inquiry, and we do not presume to set out a definitive checklist or test. But some general observations are appropriate.

Ordinarily, a key question to be answered in determining whether a theory or technique is scientific knowledge that will assist the trier of fact will be whether it can be (and has been) tested. "Scientific methodology

11. Although the *Frye* decision itself focused exclusively on "novel" scientific techniques, we do not read the requirements of Rule 702 to apply specially or exclusively to unconventional evidence. Of course, well-established propositions are less likely to be challenged than those that are novel, and they are more handily defended. Indeed, theories that are so firmly established as to have attained the status of scientific law, such as the laws of thermodynamics, properly are subject to judicial notice under Federal Rule of Evidence 201.

today is based on generating hypotheses and testing them to see if they can be falsified; indeed, this methodology is what distinguishes science from other fields of human inquiry." * * *

Another pertinent consideration is whether the theory or technique has been subjected to peer review and publication. Publication (which is but one element of peer review) is not a sine qua non of admissibility; it does not necessarily correlate with reliability, and in some instances well-grounded but innovative theories will not have been published. Some propositions, moreover, are too particular, too new, or of too limited interest to be published. But submission to the scrutiny of the scientific community is a component of "good science," in part because it increases the likelihood that substantive flaws in methodology will be detected. The fact of publication (or lack thereof) in a peer reviewed journal thus will be a relevant, though not dispositive, consideration in assessing the scientific validity of a particular technique or methodology on which an opinion is premised. Additionally, in the case of a particular scientific technique, the court ordinarily should consider the known or potential rate of error, and the existence and maintenance of standards controlling the technique's operation.

Finally, "general acceptance" can yet have a bearing on the inquiry. A "reliability assessment does not require, although it does permit, explicit identification of a relevant scientific community and an express determination of a particular degree of acceptance within that community." Widespread acceptance can be an important factor in ruling particular evidence admissible, and "a known technique which has been able to attract only minimal support within the community" may properly be viewed with skepticism.

The inquiry envisioned by Rule 702 is, we emphasize, a flexible one. Its overarching subject is the scientific validity—and thus the evidentiary relevance and reliability—of the principles that underlie a proposed submission. The focus, of course, must be solely on principles and methodology, not on the conclusions that they generate.

Throughout, a judge assessing a proffer of expert scientific testimony under Rule 702 should also be mindful of other applicable rules. Rule 703 provides that expert opinions based on otherwise inadmissible hearsay are to be admitted only if the facts or data are "of a type reasonably relied upon by experts in the particular field in forming opinions or inferences upon the subject." Rule 706 allows the court at its discretion to procure the assistance of an expert of its own choosing. Finally, Rule 403 permits the exclusion of relevant evidence "if its probative value is substantially outweighed by the danger of unfair prejudice, confusion of the issues, or misleading the jury." Judge Weinstein has explained: "Expert evidence can be both powerful and quite misleading because of the difficulty in evaluating it. Because of this risk, the judge in weighing possible prejudice against probative force under Rule 403 of the present rules exercises more control over experts than over lay witnesses."

We conclude by briefly addressing what appear to be two underlying concerns of the parties and *amici* in this case. Respondent expresses apprehension that abandonment of "general acceptance" as the exclusive requirement for admission will result in a "free-for-all" in which befuddled juries are confounded by absurd and irrational pseudoscientific assertions. In this regard respondent seems to us to be overly pessimistic about the capabilities of the jury and of the adversary system generally. Vigorous cross-examination, presentation of contrary evidence, and careful instruction on the burden of proof are the traditional and appropriate means of attacking shaky but admissible evidence. Additionally, in the event the trial court concludes that the scintilla of evidence presented supporting a position is insufficient to allow a reasonable juror to conclude that the position more likely than not is true, the court remains free to direct a judgment and likewise to grant summary judgment. These conventional devices, rather than wholesale exclusion under an uncompromising "general acceptance" test, are the appropriate safeguards where the basis of scientific testimony meets the standards of Rule 702.

Petitioners and, to a greater extent, their *amici* exhibit a different concern. They suggest that recognition of a screening role for the judge that allows for the exclusion of "invalid" evidence will sanction a stifling and repressive scientific orthodoxy and will be inimical to the search for truth. It is true that open debate is an essential part of both legal and scientific analyses. Yet there are important differences between the quest for truth in the courtroom and the quest for truth in the laboratory. Scientific conclusions are subject to perpetual revision. Law, on the other hand, must resolve disputes finally and quickly. The scientific project is advanced by broad and wide-ranging consideration of a multitude of hypotheses, for those that are incorrect will eventually be shown to be so, and that in itself is an advance. Conjectures that are probably wrong are of little use, however, in the project of reaching a quick, final, and binding legal judgment—often of great consequence—about a particular set of events in the past. We recognize that, in practice, a gatekeeping role for the judge, no matter how flexible, inevitably on occasion will prevent the jury from learning of authentic insights and innovations. That, nevertheless, is the balance that is struck by rules of evidence designed not for the exhaustive search for cosmic understanding but for the particularized resolution of legal disputes. * * *

"General acceptance" is not a necessary precondition to the admissibility of scientific evidence under the Federal Rules of Evidence, but the Rules of Evidence—especially Rule 702—do assign to the trial judge the task of ensuring that an expert's testimony both rests on a reliable foundation and is relevant to the task at hand. Pertinent evidence based on scientifically valid principles will satisfy those demands. The inquiries of the district court and the court of appeals focused almost exclusively on "general acceptance," as gauged by publication and the decisions of other courts. Accordingly, the judgment of the court of appeals is vacated, and the case is remanded for further proceedings consistent with this opinion. It is so ordered.

■ REHNQUIST, CHIEF JUSTICE (concurring in part and dissenting in part):

* * * The Court concludes, correctly in my view, that the *Frye* rule did not survive the enactment of the Federal Rules of Evidence, * * * but the Court nonetheless proceeds to construe Rules 702 and 703 very much in the abstract, and then offers some "general observations." * * *

The various briefs filed in this case are markedly different from typical briefs, in that large parts of them do not deal with decided cases or statutory language—the sort of material we customarily interpret. Instead, they deal with definitions of scientific knowledge, scientific method, scientific validity, and peer review—in short, matters far afield from the expertise of judges. This is not to say that such materials are not useful or even necessary in deciding how Rule 702 should be applied; but it is to say that the unusual subject matter should cause us to proceed with great caution in deciding more than we have to, because our reach can so easily exceed our grasp. * * *

I defer to no one in my confidence in federal judges; but I am at a loss to know what is meant when it is said that the scientific status of a theory depends on its "falsifiability," and I suspect some of them will be, too. I do not doubt that Rule 702 confides to the judge some gatekeeping responsibility in deciding questions of the admissibility of proffered expert testimony. But I do not think it imposes on them either the obligation or the authority to become amateur scientists in order to perform that role. I think the Court would be far better advised in this case to decide only the questions presented, and to leave the further development of this important area of the law to future cases.

Daubert v. Merrell Dow Pharmaceuticals, Inc.

43 F.3d 1311 (9th Cir.1995).

■ KOZINSKI, CIRCUIT JUDGE:

* * * For the most part, we don't know how birth defects come about. We do know they occur in 2–3% of births, whether or not the expectant mother has taken Bendectin. Limb defects are even rarer, occurring in fewer than one birth out of every 1000. But scientists simply do not know how teratogens (chemicals known to cause limb reduction defects) do their damage: They cannot reconstruct the biological chain of events that leads from an expectant mother's ingestion of a teratogenic substance to the stunted development of a baby's limbs. Nor do they know what it is about teratogens that causes them to have this effect. No doubt, someday we will have this knowledge, and then we will be able to tell precisely whether and how Bendectin (or any other suspected teratogen) interferes with limb development; in the current state of scientific knowledge, however, we are ignorant.

Not knowing the mechanism whereby a particular agent causes a particular effect is not always fatal to a plaintiff's claim. Causation can be proved even when we don't know precisely *how* the damage occurred, if there is sufficiently compelling proof that the agent must have caused the damage *somehow*. One method of proving causation in these circumstances is to use statistical evidence. If 50 people who eat at a restaurant one evening come down with food poisoning during the night, we can infer that the restaurant's food probably contained something unwholesome, even if none of the dishes is available for analysis. This inference is based on the fact that, in our health-conscious society, it is highly unlikely that 50 people who have nothing in common except that they ate at the same restaurant would get food poisoning from independent sources.

It is by such means that plaintiffs here seek to establish that Bendectin is responsible for their injuries. They rely on the testimony of three groups of scientific experts. One group proposes to testify that there is a statistical link between the ingestion of Bendectin during pregnancy and limb reduction defects. These experts have not themselves conducted epidemiological (human statistical) studies on the effects of Bendectin; rather, they have reanalyzed studies published by other scientists, none of whom reported a statistical association between Bendectin and birth defects. Other experts proffered by plaintiffs propose to testify that Bendectin causes limb reduction defects in humans because it causes such defects in laboratory animals. A third group of experts sees a link between Bendectin and birth defects because Bendectin has a chemical structure that is similar to other drugs suspected of causing birth defects.

The opinions proffered by plaintiffs' experts do not, to understate the point, reflect the consensus within the scientific community. The FDA—an agency not known for its promiscuity in approving drugs—continues to approve Bendectin for use by pregnant women because "available data do not demonstrate an association between birth defects and Bendectin." Every published study here and abroad—and there have been many—concludes that Bendectin is not a teratogen. In fact, apart from the small but determined group of scientists testifying on behalf of the Bendectin plaintiffs in this and many other cases, there doesn't appear to be a single scientist who has concluded that Bendectin causes limb reduction defects. * * *

Federal judges ruling on the admissibility of expert scientific testimony face a far more complex and daunting task in a post-*Daubert* world than before. * * * The first prong of *Daubert* puts federal judges in an uncomfortable position. The question of admissibility only arises if it is first established that the individuals whose testimony is being proffered are experts in a particular scientific field; here, for example, the Supreme Court waxed eloquent on the impressive qualifications of plaintiffs' experts. Yet something doesn't become "scientific knowledge" just because it's uttered by a scientist; nor can an expert's self-serving assertion that his conclusions were "derived by the scientific method" be deemed conclusive * * * * As we read the Supreme Court's teaching in *Daubert*, therefore, though we are largely untrained in science and certainly no match for any of the witnesses whose testimony we are reviewing, it is our responsibility to determine whether those experts' proposed testimony amounts to "scientific knowledge," constitutes "good science," and was "derived by the scientific method."

The task before us is more daunting still when the dispute concerns matters at the very cutting edge of scientific research, where fact meets theory and certainty dissolves into probability. As the record in this case illustrates, scientists often have vigorous and sincere disagreements as to what research methodology is proper, what should be accepted as sufficient proof for the existence of a "fact," and whether information derived by a particular method can tell us anything useful about the subject under study.

Our responsibility, then, unless we badly misread the Supreme Court's opinion, is to resolve disputes among respected, well-credentialed scientists about matters squarely within their expertise, in areas where there is no scientific consensus as to what is and what is not "good science," and occasionally to reject such expert testimony because it was not "derived by the scientific method." Mindful of our position in the hierarchy of the federal judiciary, we take a deep breath and proceed with this heady task. * * *

Our task, then, is to analyze not what the experts say, but what basis they have for saying it. Which raises the question: How do we figure out whether scientists have derived their findings through the scientific method or whether their testimony is based on scientifically valid principles? * * * [T]he Court did list several factors federal judges can consider in determining whether to admit expert scientific testimony under Fed. R. Evid. 702: whether the theory or technique employed by the expert is generally accepted in the scientific community; whether it's been subjected to peer review and publication; whether it can be and has been tested; and whether the known or potential rate of error is acceptable. We read these factors as illustrative rather than exhaustive; similarly, we do not deem each of them to be equally applicable (or applicable at all) in every case. Rather, we read the Supreme Court as instructing us to determine whether the analysis undergirding the experts' testimony falls within the range of accepted standards governing how scientists conduct their research and reach their conclusions.

One very significant fact to be considered is whether the experts are proposing to testify about matters growing naturally and directly out of research they have conducted independent of the litigation, or whether they have developed their opinions expressly for purposes of testifying. That an expert testifies for money does not necessarily cast doubt on the reliability of his testimony, as few experts appear in court merely as an eleemosynary gesture. But in determining whether proposed expert testimony amounts to good science, we may not ignore the fact that a scientist's normal workplace is the lab or the field, not the courtroom or the lawyer's office.

That an expert testifies based on research he has conducted independent of the litigation provides important, objective proof that the research comports with the dictates of good science. For one thing, experts whose findings flow from existing research are less likely to have been biased toward a particular conclusion by the promise of remuneration; when an expert prepares reports and findings before being hired as a witness, that record will limit the degree to which he can tailor his testimony to serve a party's interests. Then, too, independent research carries its own indicia of reliability, as it is conducted, so to speak, in the usual course of business and must normally satisfy a variety of standards to attract funding and institutional support. Finally, there is usually a limited number of scientists actively conducting research on the very subject that is germane to a particular case, which provides a natural constraint on parties' ability to shop for experts who will come to the desired conclusion. That the testimony proffered by an expert is based directly on legitimate, preexisting research unrelated to the litigation provides the most persuasive basis for concluding that the opinions he expresses were "derived by the scientific method."

We have examined carefully the affidavits proffered by plaintiffs' experts, as well as the testimony from prior trials that plaintiffs have introduced in support of that testimony, and find that none of the experts based his testimony on preexisting or independent research. While plaintiffs' scientists are all experts in their respective fields, none claims to have studied the effect of Bendectin on limb reduction defects before being hired to testify in this or related cases.

If the proffered expert testimony is not based on independent research, the party proffering it must come forward with other objective, verifiable evidence that the testimony is based on "scientifically valid principles." One means of showing this is by proof that the research and analysis supporting the proffered conclusions have been subjected to normal scientific scrutiny through peer review and publication.

Peer review and publication do not, of course, guarantee that the conclusions reached are correct; much published scientific research is greeted with intense skepticism and is not borne out by further research. But the test under *Daubert* is not the correctness of the expert's conclusions but the soundness of his methodology. That the research is accepted for publication in a reputable scientific journal after being subjected to the usual rigors of peer review is a significant indication that it is taken seriously by other scientists, i.e., that it meets at least the minimal criteria of good science. If nothing else, peer review and publication "increase the likelihood that substantive flaws in methodology will be detected."

Bendectin litigation has been pending in the courts for over a decade, yet the only review the plaintiffs' experts' work has received has been by judges and juries, and the only place their theories and studies have been published is in the pages of federal and state reporters. None of the plaintiffs' experts has published his work on Bendectin in a scientific journal or solicited formal review by his colleagues. Despite the many years the controversy has been brewing, no one in the scientific community—except defendant's experts—has deemed these studies worthy of verification, refutation or even comment. It's as if there were a tacit understanding within the scientific community that what's going on here is not science at all, but litigation.

Establishing that an expert's proffered testimony grows out of pre-litigation research or that the expert's research has been subjected to peer review are the two principal ways the proponent of expert testimony can show that the evidence satisfies the first prong of Rule 702. Where such evidence is unavailable, the proponent of expert scientific testimony may attempt to satisfy its burden through the testimony of its own experts. For such a showing to be sufficient, the experts must explain precisely how they went about reaching their conclusions and point to some objective source—a learned treatise, the policy statement of a professional association, a published article in a reputable scientific journal or the like—to show that they have followed the scientific method, as it is practiced by (at least) a recognized minority of scientists in their field.

Plaintiffs have made no such showing. As noted above, plaintiffs rely entirely on the experts' unadorned assertions that the methodology they employed comports with standard scientific procedures. In support of these assertions, plaintiffs offer only the trial and deposition testimony of these experts in other cases. While these materials indicate that plaintiffs' experts have relied on animal studies, chemical structure analyses and epidemiological data, they neither explain the methodology the experts followed to reach their conclusions nor point to any external source to validate that methodology. We've been presented with only the experts' qualifications, their conclusions and their assurances of reliability. Under *Daubert*, that's not enough. * * *

In elucidating the second requirement of Rule 702, *Daubert* stressed the importance of the "fit" between the testimony and an issue in the case * * * * Here, the pertinent inquiry is causation. In assessing whether the proffered expert testimony "will assist the trier of fact" in resolving this issue, we must look to the governing substantive standard, which in this case is supplied by California tort law.

Plaintiffs do not attempt to show causation directly; instead, they rely on experts who present circumstantial proof of causation. Plaintiffs' experts testify that Bendectin is a teratogen because it causes birth defects when it is tested on animals, because it is similar in chemical structure to other suspected teratogens, and because statistical studies show that Bendectin use increases the risk of birth defects. Modern tort law permits such proof, but plaintiffs must nevertheless carry their traditional burden; they must prove that their injuries were the result of the accused cause and not some independent factor. In the case of birth defects, carrying this burden is made more difficult because we know that some defects—including limb reduction defects—occur even when expectant mothers do not take Bendectin, and that most birth defects occur for no known reason.

California tort law requires plaintiffs to show not merely that Bendectin increased the likelihood of injury, but that it more likely than not caused their injuries. In terms of statistical proof, this means that plaintiffs must establish not just that their mothers' ingestion of Bendectin increased somewhat the likelihood of birth defects, but that it more than doubled it—only then can it be said that Bendectin is more likely than not the source of their injury. Because the background rate of limb reduction defects is one per thousand births, plaintiffs must show that among children of mothers who took Bendectin the incidence of such defects was more than two per thousand.[13]

None of plaintiffs' epidemiological experts claims that ingestion of Bendectin during pregnancy more than doubles the risk of birth defects. To evaluate the relationship between Bendectin and limb reduction defects, an epidemiologist would take a sample of the population and compare the frequency of birth defects in children whose mothers took Bendectin with the frequency of defects in children whose mothers did not. The ratio derived from this comparison would be an estimate of the "relative risk" associated with Bendectin. For an epidemiological study to show causation under a preponderance standard, * * * the study must show that children whose mothers took Bendectin are more than twice as likely to develop limb reduction birth defects as children whose mothers did not.[16] While plaintiffs' epidemiologists make vague assertions that there is a statistically significant relationship between Bendectin and birth defects, none states that the relative risk is greater than two. These studies thus would not be helpful, and indeed would only serve to confuse the jury, if offered to prove rather than refute causation. A relative risk of less than two may suggest teratogenicity, but it actually tends to *dis*prove legal causation, as it shows that Bendectin does not double the likelihood of birth defects. * * *

PROBLEM #9. *AN EXERCISE IN EPIDEMIOLOGY*

You are the trial judge in a products liability case against the manufacturer of a prescription drug ("Rx") used during pregnancy. The plaintiff's mother ingested the product, and the plaintiff was born with serious birth defects. The manufacturer's warning to physicians simply advised that

---

13. No doubt, there will be unjust results under this substantive standard. If a drug increases the likelihood of birth defects, but doesn't more than double it, some plaintiffs whose injuries are attributable to the drug will be unable to recover. There is a converse unfairness under a regime that allows recovery to everyone that may have been affected by the drug. Under this regime, all potential plaintiffs are entitled to recover, even though most will not have suffered an injury that can be attributed to the drug. One can conclude from this that unfairness is inevitable when our tools for detecting causation are imperfect and we must rely on probabilities rather than more direct proof. * * *

16. A statistical study showing a relative risk of less than two could be combined with other evidence to show it is more likely than not that the accused cause is responsible for a particular plaintiff's injury. For example, a statistical study may show that a particular type of birth defect is associated with some unknown causes, as well as two known potential causes—e.g., smoking and drinking. If a study shows that the relative risk of injury for those who smoke is 1.5 as compared to the general population, while it is 1.8 for those who drink, a plaintiff who does not drink might be able to reanalyze the data to show that the study of smoking did not account for the effect of drinking on the incidence of birth defects in the general population. By making the appropriate comparison—between non-drinkers who smoke and non-drinkers who do not smoke—the teetotaller plaintiff might be able to show that the relative risk of smoking for her is greater than two. * * *

epidemiological studies found an increase in birth defects but that it was not statistically significant (failing the conventional requirement of $p<0.05$). Plaintiff brings strict products liability claims, alleging design defect and failure to warn. The manufacturer moves for summary judgment, arguing (1) that the design of Rx could not be deemed defective because, in risk-utility terms, there was no risk at all; (2) that its warning accurately conveyed all that was known about the supposed risks; and (3) that, even if Rx was "defective" in terms of its design or warnings, the plaintiff has failed to prove that Rx actually caused his injuries. Experts for the manufacturer and the plaintiff, respectively, introduced the following studies to address the central question of causation:

- Epidemiological study (association between Rx and birth defects):

	No Rx	Rx
Pregnancies:	10,000	1,000
Birth defects:	100	12
Incidence:	1.0%	1.2%
		Relative risk: 1.2

- An unpublished "reanalysis" of the raw data by the plaintiff's expert (she has excluded 1,000 reports from the data set for the non-Rx population and 500 reports from the data set for the Rx population):

	No Rx	Rx
Pregnancies:	9,000	500
Birth defects:	45	6
Incidence:	0.5%	1.2%
		Relative risk: 2.4

How do you rule (we have not yet covered the questions raised by arguments (1) and (2), so skip them for now)?

NOTES AND QUESTIONS

1. *It's not over until the fat lady sings.* The body of scientific information relevant to causation issues represents a moving target for courts. In some instances, a litigant will argue on appeal that newly discovered information justifies granting a motion for a new trial, but courts usually decline:

> Although science is a constantly evolving process, the law depends upon a high level of certainty once an outcome has been determined. A trial can be no more than a resolution of an immediate dispute on the basis of present knowledge; its outcome must turn upon the teachings

> of science as understood at the time of trial as best can be discerned through the presentations of the parties. Where scientific facts are at issue, it is not unexpected, given the nature of the process, that the passage of time will bring forth further scientific data and inquiry relating to the ultimate scientific fact at issue. To reopen the trial's determination of scientific truth, however, runs squarely into the fundamental principle of certainty.

Merrell Dow Pharm., Inc. v. Oxendine, 649 A.2d 825, 831 (D.C.1994). Even so, the court remanded this Bendectin case, and, more than a decade after the original judgment for the plaintiff, the trial court granted extraordinary relief from the judgment based on newly acquired scientific evidence. See Oxendine v. Merrell Dow Pharm., Inc., 1996 WL 680992, at *31–35 (D.C.Super.Ct.1996).

2. *A postscript on the Bendectin saga.* As one commentator noted, "the wave of Bendectin litigation ultimately cost manufacturers so much that they stopped marketing the product. Although no jury verdict that Bendectin causes birth defects has ever been upheld on appeal, plaintiffs have received a favorable verdict in approximately 36% of the cases that have gone to trial. The risk of juror error coupled with high litigation costs led manufacturers to withdraw Bendectin from the market notwithstanding the continuing assessment by the FDA and the scientific community that Bendectin provides benefits exceeding its risks." W. Kip Viscusi, Corporate Risk Analysis: A Reckless Act?, 52 Stan. L. Rev. 547, 584 (2000); see also Michael Green, Bendectin and Birth Defects (1996); Joseph Sanders, The Bendectin Litigation: A Case Study in the Life Cycle of Mass Torts, 43 Hastings L.J. 301 (1992); Joseph Sanders, From Science to Evidence: The Testimony on Causation in the Bendectin Cases, 46 Stan. L. Rev. 1 (1993). In one verdict reversed on appeal, the jury had awarded the plaintiff almost $34 million. See Merrell Dow Pharm., Inc. v. Havner, 953 S.W.2d 706 (Tex.1997). Someday a generic version of Bendectin may be introduced in the United States market in part because the withdrawal of the drug left an unmet therapeutic need for pregnant women with severe nausea resulting in weight loss and dehydration that sometimes necessitated hospitalization. See Gina Kolata, Controversial Drug Makes a Comeback, N.Y. Times, Sept. 26, 2000, at F1; see also Liz Szabo, "Drug Drought" for Pregnancy: It's Considered Risky to Develop Medications for Expectant Moms, USA Today, June 4, 2008, at 1D (reporting that the litigation involving Bendectin spooked the industry more generally).

3. *Extension of* Daubert*'s admissibility formula.* The United States Supreme Court has continued expanding the "gatekeeping" role of trial judges in ruling on the admissibility of expert testimony. See, e.g., Kumho Tire Co. v. Carmichael, 526 U.S. 137, 147–57 (1999) (applying *Daubert* to testimony from an engineer that was based on his experience and observation rather than scientific research); General Elec. Co. v. Joiner, 522 U.S. 136, 142–43 (1997) (holding that an appellate court should review a trial judge's decision to exclude expert scientific testimony with a deferential abuse of discretion standard). As in *Kumho Tire*, the expert testimony may relate to the nature and source of an alleged defect rather than the question of whether any such defect caused the plaintiff's injury. See, e.g., Fuesting v. Zimmer, Inc., 594 F.Supp.2d 1043 (C.D.Ill.2009) (excluding expert testimony linking the failure of plaintiff's prosthetic knee to the manufacturer's sterilization technique using gamma irradiation, which allegedly triggered polyethylene delamination from oxidation), aff'd, 362 F.App'x 560 (7th Cir.2010). States remain divided about adopting *Daubert*. Compare, e.g., E.I. du Pont de Nemours & Co. v. Robinson, 923 S.W.2d 549 (Tex.1995) (following this approach), with Dow Chem. Co. v. Mahlum, 970 P.2d 98 (Nev.1998) (rejecting it in the course of affirming a plaintiff's verdict in a silicone-gel breast implant case); see also Blackwell v. Wyeth, 971 A.2d 235, 255–61 (Md.2009) (upholding the exclusion, under the state's version of the *Frye* general acceptance admissibility standard, of the plaintiffs' expert linking thimerosal with autism in genetically susceptible children). See generally Heather G. Hamilton, Note, The Movement from Frye to Daubert: Where Do the States Stand?, 38 Jurimetrics J. 201 (1998); Alice B. Lustre, Annotation, Post–Daubert Standards for Admissibility of Scientific and Other Expert Evidence in State Courts, 90 A.L.R.5th 453 (2001 & 2011 Supp.).

4. Daubert*'s application in medical products liability litigation*. Not surprisingly, *Daubert* has come to play quite a prominent role in the resolution of products liability lawsuits against pharmaceutical and medical device manufacturers. See, e.g., Norris v. Baxter Healthcare Corp., 397 F.3d 878, 881–87 (10th Cir.2005) (holding that case reports and differential diagnosis linking silicone-gel breast implants to systemic autoimmune disease were insufficient in the face of substantial contrary epidemiological evidence); Rider v. Sandoz Pharm. Corp., 295 F.3d 1194, 1202–03 (11th Cir.2002) (joining a number of courts that have found plaintiffs' evidence linking the lactation suppressant Parlodel® (bromocriptine mesylate) to hemorrhagic strokes inadmissible); In re Viagra Prods. Liab. Litig., 572 F.Supp.2d 1071 (D.Minn.2008) (excluding some of plaintiffs' expert testimony linking erectile dysfunction drug with vision disorder); In re Bextra & Celebrex Mktg. Sales Practice, 524 F.Supp.2d 1166 (N.D.Cal.2007) (excluding experts who opined that Pfizer's COX–2 inhibitors caused cardiovascular events at low doses, but admitting such testimony with regard to high doses); Doe v. Ortho–Clinical Diagnostics, Inc., 440 F.Supp.2d 465 (M.D.N.C.2006) (granting defendant's motion for summary judgment after excluding the plaintiff's expert testimony linking thimerosal in RhoGAM to autism); In re Phenylpropanolamine (PPA) Prods. Liab. Litig., 289 F.Supp.2d 1230 (W.D.Wash.2003) (finding sufficient evidence that the PPA in Dexatrim® could have caused the plaintiff's stroke); see also David A. Freedman & Philip B. Stark, The Swine Flu Vaccine and Guillain–Barré Syndrome: A Case Study in Relative Risk and Specific Causation, Law & Contemp. Probs., Fall 2001, at 49; Judith S. Novick, Use of Epidemiological Studies to Prove Legal Causation: Aspirin and Reye's Syndrome, a Case in Point, 22 Tort & Ins. L.J. 536 (1987); Bruce R. Parker, Understanding Epidemiology and Its Use in Drug and Medical Device Litigation, 65 Def. Counsel J. 35 (1998).

5. *Impaneling court-appointed scientific experts.* Two of the federal judges who were assigned to different class action lawsuits against the manufacturers of silicone-gel breast implants decided to impanel independent experts, as authorized by Federal Rule of Evidence 706, to evaluate the proffered testimony on whether silicone might trigger auto-immune disorders such as scleroderma and lupus. In both instances, the panels reviewed the available data and concluded that no causal association existed. See Hall v. Baxter Healthcare, 947 F.Supp. 1387, 1392–94 (D.Or.1996); Barbara S. Hulka et al., Experience of a Scientific Panel Formed to Advise the Federal Judiciary on Silicone Breast Implants, 342 New Eng. J. Med. 812 (2000) (providing insights by several members of one such panel); Laurens Walker & John Monahan, Scientific Authority: The Breast Implant Litigation and Beyond, 86 Va. L. Rev. 801 (2000); Thomas M. Burton, Implant Makers Get a Boost from Report, Wall St. J., Dec. 2, 1998, at B1 (describing the conclusions of a panel appointed by Judge Sam Pointer of the U.S. District Court for the Northern District of Alabama); see also Soldo v. Sandoz Pharm. Corp., 244 F.Supp.2d 434, 442, 503–04, 528–29, 576–77 (W.D.Pa.2003) (using such a panel, which split 2–1, in the course of deciding that the plaintiff had failed to produce admissible evidence linking Parlodel to her stroke); Howard M. Erichson, Mass Tort Litigation and Inquisitorial Justice, 87 Geo. L.J. 1983, 1986–95 (1999) (urging expanded use of court-appointed experts); Lawrence S. Pinsky, Comment, The Use of Scientific Peer Review and Colloquia to Assist Judges in the Admissibility Gatekeeping Mandated by Daubert, 34 Hous. L. Rev. 527, 554–78 (1997) (recommending similar approaches).

6. *Requiring a doubling of the risk.* Although hardly uncontroversial, a number of courts have followed the Ninth Circuit's approach in *Daubert* of requiring epidemiological evidence of a relative risk greater than 2.0. See Bartley v. Euclid, Inc., 158 F.3d 261, 273 (5th Cir.1998); In re Breast Implant Litig., 11 F.Supp.2d 1217, 1225–28 (D.Colo.1998); see also Merrell Dow Pharm., Inc. v. Havner, 953 S.W.2d 706, 717–20 (Tex.1997) (cautioning against using it as a "litmus test," and noting that some epidemiologists demand a relative risk above 3.0); Marder v. G.D. Searle & Co., 630 F.Supp. 1087, 1092 (D.Md.1986) (finding no causation where the relative risk in one study of the copper IUD was 1.9, and the 95% confidence interval ranged from 0.9 to 4.0); Theodore Eisenberg & Martin T. Wells, Statins and Adverse Cardiovascular Events in Moderate–Risk Females: A Statistical and Legal Analysis with Implications for FDA Preemption Claims, 5 J. Empirical Legal Stud. 507 (2008); David L. Faigman et al., How Good Is Good Enough? Expert Evidence Under Daubert and Kumho, 50 Case W. Res. L. Rev. 645, 659–67 (2000); Lucinda M. Finley, Guarding the Gate to the Courthouse: How Trial Judges Are Using Their Evidentiary Screening Role to Remake Tort Causation Rules, 49 DePaul L. Rev. 335, 347–76 (1999); Susanne L. Flanders, Note, A Tough Pill to Swallow: The Insurmountable Burden in Toxic Tort Claims Against Manufacturers of Children's Medications, 16 J.L. & Pol'y 305 (2007); cf. Lars Noah, An Inventory of Mathematical Blunders in Applying the Loss-of-a-Chance Doctrine, 24 Rev. Litig. 369 (2005) (explaining how a similar causation difficulty in medical malpractice cases has managed to befuddle most judges, lawyers, and commentators).

7. *Further commentary*. See Federal Judicial Center, Reference Manual on Scientific Evidence (3d ed. 2011); David E. Bernstein, Expert Witnesses, Adversarial Bias, and the (Partial) Failure of the Daubert Revolution, 93 Iowa L. Rev. 451 (2008); Edward K. Cheng & Albert H. Yoon, Does Frye or Daubert Matter? A Study of Scientific Admissibility Standards, 91 Va. L. Rev. 471 (2005); Sander Greenland & Charles Poole, Problems in Common Interpretations of Statistics in Scientific Articles, Expert Reports, and Testimony, 51 Jurimetrics J. 113 (2011); Thomas O. McGarity, Our Science Is Sound Science and Their Science Is Junk Science: Science-based Strategies for Avoiding Accountability and Responsibility for Risk-producing Products and Activities, 52 U. Kan. L. Rev. 897 (2004); A. Leah Vickers, Daubert, Critique and Interpretation: What Empirical Studies Tell Us About the Application of Daubert, 40 U.S.F. L. Rev. 109 (2005); Symposium, A Cross–Disciplinary Look at Scientific Truth: What's the Law to Do?, 73 Brook. L. Rev. 847 (2008).

Zuchowicz v. United States

140 F.3d 381 (2d Cir.1998).

■ CALABRESI, CIRCUIT JUDGE:

* * * On February 18, 1989, Mrs. Zuchowicz filled a prescription for the drug Danocrine at the Naval Hospital pharmacy in Groton, Connecticut. The prescription erroneously instructed her to take 1600 milligrams of Danocrine per day, or twice the maximum recommended dosage. The defendant has stipulated that its doctors and/or pharmacists were negligent and violated the prevailing standard of medical care by prescribing this wrong dosage. Mrs. Zuchowicz took the 1600 milligrams of Danocrine each day for the next month. Thereafter, from March 24 until May 30, she took 800 milligrams per day. While taking Danocrine she experienced abnormal weight gain, bloating, edema, hot flashes, night sweats, a racing heart, chest pains, dizziness, headaches, acne, and fatigue. On May 30, she was examined by an obstetrician/gynecologist in private practice who told her to stop taking the Danocrine.

During the summer, she continued to experience severe fatigue and chest tightness and pain, and began having shortness of breath. In October 1989, she was diagnosed with primary pulmonary hypertension (PPH), a rare and fatal disease in which increased pressure in an individual's pulmonary artery causes severe strain on the right side of the heart. At the time she was diagnosed with the disease, the median life expectancy for PPH sufferers was 2.5 years. Treatments included calcium channel blockers and heart and lung transplantation. Mrs. Zuchowicz was on the waiting list for a lung transplant when she became pregnant. Pregnant women are not eligible for transplants, and pregnancy exacerbates PPH. Mrs. Zuchowicz gave birth to a son on November 21, 1991. She died one month later * * * *

PPH is very rare. A National Institute[s] of Health registry recorded only 197 cases of PPH from the mid–1980s until 1992. It occurs predominantly in young women. Exogenous agents known to be capable of causing PPH include birth control pills, some appetite suppressants, chemotherapy drugs, rapeseed oil, and L–Tryptophan. According to the district court's findings of fact, the disease involves the interplay of the inner layers of the pulmonary blood vessels known as the endothelium and the vascular smooth muscle. The endothelium releases substances called vasodilators and vasoconstrictors, which dilate and constrict the blood vessels. These substances can also cause growth of the vascular smooth muscle. Experts currently believe that an imbalance in vasodilators and vasoconstrictors plays a part in the development of pulmonary hypertension. If too many vasoconstrictors are released, the blood vessels contract, the endothelial cells die, and the vascular smooth muscle cells proliferate. These actions create increased pulmonary vascular resistance.

Danocrine has been extensively studied and prescribed since the late 1960s for endometriosis. According to the testimony of plaintiff's expert Dr. W. Paul D'Mowski, who personally performed much of the initial research on the drug, Danocrine is safe and effective when administered properly. Based on studies by Dr. D'Mowski and others, Danocrine was approved by the Food and Drug Administration (FDA) for use in dosages not to exceed 800 mg/day. Mrs. Zuchowicz was accidentally given a prescription instructing her to take twice this amount—1600 mg/day. According to Dr. D'Mowski no formal studies of the effects of Danocrine at such high doses have been performed, and very, very few women have received doses this high in any setting.

The rarity of PPH, combined with the fact that so few human beings have ever received such a high dose of Danocrine, obviously impacted on the manner in which the plaintiff could prove causation. The number of persons who received this type of overdose was simply too small for the plaintiff to be able to provide epidemiological, or even anecdotal, evidence linking PPH to Danocrine overdoses. The plaintiff (Mrs. Zuchowicz's husband and executor), therefore, based his case primarily on the testimony of two expert witnesses, Dr. Richard Matthay, a physician and expert in pulmonary diseases, and Dr. Randall Tackett, a professor of pharmacology who has published widely in the field of the effects of drugs on vascular tissues. In rendering a judgment for the plaintiff, the district court relied heavily on the evidence submitted by these two experts. The defendant challenges both the admissibility and the sufficiency of their testimony.

Dr. Richard Matthay is a full professor of medicine at Yale and Associate Director and Training Director of Yale's Pulmonary and Critical Care Section. He is a nationally recognized expert in the field of pulmonary medicine, with extensive experience in the area of drug-induced pulmonary diseases. Dr. Matthay examined and treated Mrs. Zuchowicz. His examination included taking a detailed history of the progression of her disease, her medical history, and the timing of her Danocrine overdose and the onset of her symptoms.

Dr. Matthay testified that he was confident to a reasonable medical certainty that the Danocrine caused Mrs. Zuchowicz's PPH. When pressed, he added that he believed the overdose of Danocrine to have been responsible for the disease. His conclusion was based on the temporal relationship between the overdose and the start of the disease and the differential etiology method of excluding other possible causes. While Dr. Matthay did not rule out all other possible causes of pulmonary hypertension, he did exclude all the causes of secondary pulmonary hypertension. On the basis of Mrs. Zuchowicz's history, he also ruled out all previously known drug-related causes of primary pulmonary hypertension.

Dr. Matthay further testified that the progression and timing of Mrs. Zuchowicz's disease in relation to her overdose supported a finding of drug-induced PPH. Dr. Matthay emphasized that, prior to the overdose, Mrs. Zuchowicz was a healthy, active young woman with no history of cardiovascular problems, and that, shortly after the overdose, she began experiencing symptoms of PPH such as weight gain, swelling of hands and feet, fatigue, and shortness of breath. He described the similarities between the course of Mrs. Zuchowicz's illness and that of accepted cases of drug-induced PPH, and he went on to discuss cases involving classes of drugs that are known to cause other pulmonary diseases (mainly anti-cancer drugs). He noted that the onset of these diseases, which are recognized to be caused by the particular drugs, was very similar in timing and course to the development of Mrs. Zuchowicz's illness.

Dr. Randall Tackett is a tenured, full professor of pharmacology and former department chair from the University of Georgia. He has published widely in the field of the effects of drugs on vascular tissues. Dr. Tackett testified that, to a reasonable degree of scientific certainty, he believed that the overdose of Danocrine, more likely than not, caused PPH in the plaintiff by producing: 1) a decrease in estrogen; 2) hyperinsulinemia, in which abnormally high levels of insulin circulate in the body; and 3) increases in free testosterone and progesterone. Dr. Tackett testified that these hormonal factors, taken together, likely caused a dysfunction of the endothelium leading to PPH. Dr. Tackett relied on a variety of published and unpublished studies that indicated that these hormones could cause endothelial dysfunction and an imbalance of vasoconstrictor effects. * * *

[T]he district court carefully undertook and fulfilled its role in making the evaluation required by *Daubert*—a "preliminary assessment of whether the reasoning or methodology underlying the testimony is scientifically valid and of whether that reasoning or methodology properly can be applied to the facts in issue." Where, as in this case, the district court decides to admit the testimony of well-credentialed experts relying on scientific methodology, we should and will be reluctant to upset that decision as an abuse of discretion. In the district court, the defendant made substantially the same arguments, regarding the validity of the methods used by Dr. Matthay and Dr. Tackett in reaching their conclusions, that it now raises on appeal. The district court rejected these arguments, stating that the plaintiff's experts "based their opinions on methods reasonably relied on by experts in their particular fields." We do not believe that the district court's decision in this regard was erroneous, let alone manifestly so. * * *

The defendant argues that, even assuming that the testimony of the plaintiff's experts was admissible, the district court's finding that the Danocrine overdose more likely than not caused Mrs. Zuchowicz's illness was clearly erroneous. The defendant contends that, since Danocrine has never been previously linked to PPH, the district court's conclusion that the drug caused Mrs. Zuchowicz's illness was impermissible. For the reasons stated below, we reject the defendant's arguments. * * *

Mrs. Zuchowicz's PPH was, more likely than not, caused by Danocrine. While it was not possible to eliminate all other possible causes of pulmonary hypertension, the evidence presented showed that the experts had not only excluded all causes of secondary pulmonary hypertension, but had also ruled out all the previously known drug-related causes of PPH. In addition, Dr. Matthay testified, based on his expertise in pulmonary diseases, that the progression and timing of Mrs. Zuchowicz's illness in relationship to the timing of her overdose supported a finding of drug-induced PPH to a reasonable medical certainty. In this respect, we note that in the case before us, unlike many toxic torts situations, there was not a long latency period between the onset of symptoms and the patient's exposure to the drug that was alleged to have caused the illness. Rather, as Dr. Matthay testified, the plaintiff began exhibiting symptoms typical of drug-induced PPH shortly after she started taking the Danocrine. Under the circumstances, we cannot say that the fact finder was clearly erroneous in determining that, more probably than not, the Danocrine caused Mrs. Zuchowicz's illness.

To say that Danocrine caused Mrs. Zuchowicz's injuries is only half the story, however. In order for the causation requirement to be met, a trier of fact must be able to determine, by a preponderance of the evidence, that the defendant's negligence was responsible for the injury. In this case, defendant's negligence consisted in prescribing an overdose of Danocrine to Mrs. Zuchowicz. For liability to exist, therefore, it is necessary that the fact finder be able to conclude, more probably than not, that the overdose was the cause of Mrs. Zuchowicz's illness and ultimate death. The mere fact that the exposure to Danocrine was likely responsible for the disease does not suffice.

The problem of linking defendant's negligence to the harm that occurred is one that many courts have addressed in the past. A car is speeding and an accident occurs. That the car was involved and was a cause of the crash is readily shown. The accident, moreover, is of the sort that rules prohibiting speeding are designed to prevent. But is this enough to support a finding of fact, in the individual case, that speeding was, in fact, more probably than not, the cause of the accident? * * *

At one time, courts were reluctant to say in such circumstances that the wrong could be deemed to be the cause. They emphasized the logical fallacy of *post hoc, ergo propter hoc*, and demanded some direct evidence connecting the defendant's wrongdoing to the harm. All that has changed, however. And, as is so frequently the case in tort law, Chief Judge Cardozo in New York and Chief Justice Traynor in California led the way. In various opinions, they stated that: if (a) a negligent act was deemed wrongful because that act increased the chances that a particular type of accident would occur, and (b) a mishap of that very sort did happen, this was enough to support a finding by the trier of fact that the negligent behavior caused the harm. Where such a strong causal link exists, it is up to the negligent party to bring in evidence denying but for cause and suggesting that in the actual case the wrongful conduct had not been a substantial factor.

Thus, in a case involving a nighttime collision between vehicles, one of which did not have the required lights, Judge Cardozo stated that lights were mandated precisely to reduce the risk of such accidents occurring and that this fact sufficed to show causation unless the negligent party demonstrated, for example, that in the particular instance the presence of very bright street lights or of a full moon rendered the lack of lights on the vehicle an unlikely cause. See Martin v. Herzog, 126 N.E. 814, 816 (N.Y.1920). The general acceptance of this view is both signaled and explained by Prosser, which states categorically:

> And whether the defendant's negligence consists of the violation of some statutory safety regulation, or the breach of a plain common law duty of care, the court can scarcely overlook the fact that the injury which has in fact occurred is precisely the sort of thing that proper care on the part of the defendant would be intended to prevent, and accordingly allow a certain liberality to the jury in drawing its conclusion.

W. Page Keeton et al., Prosser and Keeton on the Law of Torts § 41, at 270 (5th ed.1984). * * *

The reason the FDA does not approve the prescription of new drugs at above the dosages as to which extensive tests have been performed is because all drugs involve risks of untoward side effects in those who take them. Moreover, it is often true that the higher the dosage the greater is the likelihood of such negative effects. At the approved dosages, the benefits of the particular drug have presumably been deemed worth the risks it entails. At greater than approved dosages, not only do the risks of tragic side effects (known and unknown) increase, but there is no basis on the testing that has been performed for supposing that the drug's benefits outweigh these increased risks. It follows that when a negative side effect is demonstrated to be the result of a drug, and the drug was wrongly prescribed in an unapproved and excessive dosage (i.e. a strong causal link has been shown), the plaintiff who is injured has generally shown enough to permit the finder of fact to conclude that the excessive dosage was a substantial factor in producing the harm.

In fact, plaintiff's showing in the case before us, while relying on the above stated principles, is stronger. For plaintiff introduced some direct evidence of causation as well. On the basis of his long experience with drug-induced pulmonary diseases, one of plaintiff's experts, Dr. Matthay, testified that the timing of Mrs. Zuchowicz's illness led him to conclude that the overdose (and not merely Danocrine) was responsible for her catastrophic reaction. Under the circumstances, we hold that defendant's attack on the district court's finding of causation is meritless. * * *

NOTES AND QUESTIONS

1. *The* Zuchowicz *follies?* The case involved a claim of medical malpractice in the use of a prescription drug, and it raised questions about both the admissibility and weight of the expert evidence on causation (note that, as a lawsuit against the government under the Federal Tort Claims Act, the trial judge rather than a jury served as the fact-finder). In what sense did each of the expert's testimony satisfy *Daubert*'s admissibility criteria? As for Dr. Matthay, is it enough that a treating physician interested in managing a patient's condition would, after "ruling out" other possible explanations, recommend discontinuing the use of a drug? Cf. Ruggiero v. Warner–Lambert Co., 424 F.3d 249, 254 (2d Cir.2005) (sustaining the trial judge's decision to exclude plaintiff's expert testimony linking Rezulin® to cirrhosis of the liver based on a differential diagnosis but without any independent evidence for ruling in the drug as a possible cause); In re Breast Implant Litig., 11 F.Supp.2d 1217, 1230 (D.Colo.1998) ("[T]he cause of many diseases remains unknown; therefore, a clinician who suspects that a substance causes a disease in some patients very well might conclude that the substance caused the disease in the plaintiff simply because the clinician has no other explanation."). Is time-of-onset enough to "rule in" Danocrine as the prime culprit (and does the lack of improvement after its discontinuation weaken the inference of causation, or would that only be true in the case of acute and reversible side effects)? Cf. Porter v. Whitehall Lab., Inc., 9 F.3d 607, 614–15 (7th Cir.1993) (excluding plaintiff's expert testimony, based on nothing more than temporal proximity, that a 30–day prescription of ibuprofen triggered renal failure); Wooley v. Smith & Nephew Richards, Inc., 67 F.Supp.2d 703 (S.D.Tex.1999) (holding a mere temporal association between implant and injury insufficient).

Would a medical journal publish an article (as opposed to merely a case report) written by Dr. Matthay that concluded, on the basis of his single patient-encounter, that Danocrine causes PPH (or, more to the point, that high doses of the drug did so)?! Would the plaintiff's case have been more compelling if she had previously consumed regular doses of Danocrine with no evidence of any ill effects? What if the plaintiff had offered only Prof. Tackett as an expert on causation—would his hypothesis about the mechanism of action suffice (and where had he gotten that information, animal studies)? Was there any evidence that Mrs. Zuchowicz had experienced these underlying hormonal changes while taking Danocrine? Note that, twenty years after Mrs. Zuchowicz's death, the FDA evidently has not ordered any revision of Danocrine's label to mention a risk of PPH. In contrast, the agency had done so when approving Redux® (dexfenfluramine), though it withdrew this diet drug in part because PPH appeared to occur at a higher than expected frequency among users. See E.D. Michelakis & E.K. Weir, Anorectic Drugs and Pulmonary Hypertension: From the Bedside to the Bench, 321 Am. J. Med. Sci. 292 (2001); Steven R. Salbu, The FDA and Public Access to New Drugs: Appropriate Levels of Scrutiny in the Wake of HIV, AIDS, and the Diet Drug Debacle, 79 B.U. L. Rev. 93, 126, 128–30 (1999).

The *Zuchowicz* court justified affirming the judgment by invoking a burden-shifting rule used in cases of negligence per se, but is that even applicable in this case (contrast *Stanton*, supra)? Did the FDA set the maximum dose in order to reduce the risk of PPH (or is it enough that the label indicated a maximum dose to reveal the absence of safety research at higher doses)? Was it unlawful for the physicians to exceed the maximum recommended dose?! What if they had exceeded that dose only slightly? Short of discovering that the patient took another drug known to cause PPH, how might the defendants try to rebut this shifted burden of proof on causation? Cf. Baker v. Dalkon Shield Claimants Trust, 156 F.3d 248, 251–53 (1st Cir.1998) (reversing the exclusion of defendant's expert who suggested alternative causes based on a differential diagnosis); Wheat v. Pfizer, Inc., 31 F.3d 340, 343 (5th Cir.1994) (agreeing that plaintiff's hepatitis probably resulted from something other than the drug).

2. *Epidemiology or bust?* In the absence of epidemiological studies, courts more readily accept other types of evidence. See Kennedy v. Collagen Corp., 161 F.3d 1226, 1229–30 (9th Cir.1998); Ambrosini v. Labarraque, 101 F.3d 129, 135–41 (D.C.Cir.1996) (reversing the exclusion of plaintiff's expert testimony that Depo–Provera® caused birth defects where the epidemiological evidence was unclear); Hyman & Armstrong, P.S.C. v. Gunderson, 279 S.W.3d 93, 102–09 (Ky.2008) (sustaining a sizeable jury verdict in favor of the plaintiffs where a patient suffered a fatal postpartum seizure, which their experts linked to her use of Parlodel); Vassallo v. Baxter Healthcare Corp., 696 N.E.2d 909, 917–18 (Mass.1998) [excerpted in Chap. 7(A)(1)] (allowing plaintiff's expert to link atypical autoimmune disease to silicone-gel breast implants notwithstanding the absence of supporting epidemiological data). For instance, one court explained that the plaintiff's "treating physicians based their conclusions on the microscopic appearance of his liver, the Tylenol found in his blood upon his admission to the hospital, the history of several days of Tylenol use after regular alcohol consumption, and the lack of evidence of a viral or any other cause of liver failure. [His experts on liver disease] relied upon a similar methodology; history, examination, lab and pathology data, and study of the peer-reviewed literature." Benedi v. McNeil–P.P.C., Inc., 66 F.3d 1378, 1384 (4th Cir.1995). Finally, how should a court handle an unimpeachably designed epidemiological study that finds a strong association which most experts view as entirely implausible (i.e., a spurious result)? See Rob Stein, Antibiotics May Raise Risk for Breast Cancer, Wash. Post, Feb. 17, 2004, at A1.

3. *Doctors and* Daubert. How should judges evaluate non-epidemiological evidence? Several courts have concluded that *Daubert* does not apply to diagnostic judgments by physicians. See Westberry v. Gislaved Gummi AB, 178 F.3d 257 (4th Cir.1999); Heller v. Shaw Indus., Inc., 167 F.3d 146, 155–

58 (3d Cir.1999); Globetti v. Sandoz Pharm. Corp., 111 F.Supp.2d 1174 (N.D.Ala.2000). Other courts have applied *Daubert* in such cases. See Guinn v. AstraZeneca Pharms. LP, 602 F.3d 1245, 1252–57 (11th Cir.2010) (affirming the exclusion of expert testimony linking the antipsychotic Seroquel® (quetiapine fumarate) to plaintiff's weight gain and diabetes based on a differential diagnosis that entirely failed to rule out numerous other likely explanations for her condition); Moore v. Ashland Chem., Inc., 151 F.3d 269, 275 n.7 (5th Cir.1998) (en banc); see also Lars Noah, Medicine's Epistemology: Mapping the Haphazard Diffusion of Knowledge in the Biomedical Community, 44 Ariz. L. Rev. 373, 378–82 (2002) (drawing parallels between *Daubert* and the "evidence-based medicine" (EBM) movement); id. at 382–406, 434, 465 (summarizing the tenets of EBM, noting some of its limitations, and explaining that many physicians fail to attain this ideal). See generally Jean M. Eggen, Clinical Medical Evidence of Causation in Toxic Tort Cases: Into the Crucible of Daubert, 38 Hous. L. Rev. 369 (2001); Wendy M. Ertmer, Note, Just What the Doctor Ordered: The Admissibility of Differential Diagnosis in Pharmaceutical Product Litigation, 56 Vand. L. Rev. 1227 (2003); Ian S. Spechler, Note, Physicians at the Gates of Daubert: A Look at the Admissibility of Differential Diagnosis Testimony to Show External Causation in Toxic Tort Litigation, 26 Rev. Litig. 739 (2007). In a controversial move, some medical associations have subjected their members' expert testimony to a form of "peer review." See Adam Liptak, Doctors' Testimony Under Scrutiny, N.Y. Times, July 6, 2003, § 1, at 10; see also Jennifer A. Turner, Going After the "Hired Guns": Is Improper Expert Witness Testimony Unprofessional Conduct or the Negligent Practice of Medicine?, 33 Pepp. L. Rev. 275 (2006).

4. *Differential diagnosis (etiology) for dummies.* Many courts and commentators do not seem to appreciate that "differential diagnosis" represents an iterative (one might even say "hit-or-miss") process that ultimately depends on the strength of the underlying research base in defining the probabilities of various explanations for a patient's condition. Of course, physicians do the best that they can in the face of uncertainty, and they may try any variety of things until hitting upon the seemingly correct answer. It's not, however, anything terribly scientific. See Lars Noah, Letter, Standards for Medical Expert Testimony, 288 JAMA 2971 (2002) ("I daresay that most physicians, especially those offering a differential diagnosis in support of a plaintiff's claim of causation as a 'reasonable medical certainty' (instead of as a working hypothesis intended for treatment and subject to revision), fall short of the ideal imagined by the proponents of EBM."); see also Edward J. Imwinkelried, The Admissibility and Legal Sufficiency of Testimony About Differential Diagnosis (Etiology): Of Under– and Over–Estimations, 56 Baylor L. Rev. 391 (2004). Diagnoses of persons other than the plaintiff, which may be published as "case reports" in the medical literature, would provide only anecdotal evidence of general causation. See Glastetter v. Novartis Pharm. Corp., 107 F.Supp.2d 1015, 1030–31 (E.D.Mo.2000), aff'd, 252 F.3d 986 (8th Cir.2001); Nelson v.

American Home Prods. Corp., 92 F.Supp.2d 954, 969 (W.D.Mo.2000); Willert v. Ortho Pharm. Corp., 995 F.Supp. 979, 981 (D.Minn.1998).

5. *Causation under the NCVIA*. The National Childhood Vaccine Injury Act, discussed briefly in Chapter 5(A), may impose less demanding standards for awarding compensation. See Althen v. HHS, 418 F.3d 1274, 1278–80 (Fed.Cir.2005); Whitney S. Waldenberg & Sarah E. Wallace, When Science Is Silent: Examining Compensation of Vaccine–Related Injuries When Scientific Evidence of Causation Is Inconclusive, 42 Wake Forest L. Rev. 303 (2007); Brandon L. Boxler, Note, What to Do with Daubert: How to Bring Standards of Reliable Scientific Evidence to the National Vaccine Injury Compensation Program, 52 Wm. & Mary L. Rev. 1319 (2011); Katherine E. Strong, Note, Proving Causation Under the Vaccine Injury Act: A New Approach for a New Day, 75 Geo. Wash. L. Rev. 426 (2007). But see Moberly v. HHS, 592 F.3d 1315, 1322–26 (Fed.Cir.2010) (refuting such claims). This more flexible approach has not, however, helped those parents who insist that vaccines can cause autism. See Hazlehurst v. HHS, 604 F.3d 1343, 1345 (Fed.Cir.2010); Joelle A. Moreno, It's Just a Shot Away: MMR Vaccines and Autism and the End of the Daubertista Revolution, 35 Wm. Mitchell L. Rev. 1511 (2009); cf. Michael J. Donovan, Comment, The Impact of "Hurricane" Hannah: The Government's Decision to Compensate in One Girl's Vaccine Injury Case Could Drastically Alter the Face of Public Health, 50 Jurimetrics J. 229 (2010); Gordon Shemin, Comment, Mercury Rising: The Omnibus Autism Proceeding and What Families Should Know Before Rushing out of Vaccine Court, 58 Am. U. L. Rev. 459 (2008).

6. *Causal chains*. Cause-in-fact does not seal the deal for a plaintiff. See, e.g., Skerl v. Arrow Int'l, Inc., 202 F.Supp.2d 748 (N.D.Ohio 2001) (holding that a malfunction in an implanted morphine pump was not the proximate cause of the patient's broken hip that occurred after her untreated pain required a physician visit for a morphine injection that later caused her to fall out of bed); see also Morguson v. 3M Co., 857 So.2d 796 (Ala.2003) (holding that the unforeseeable misuse of a perfusion pump by the surgical team amounted to a superseding cause of the patient's death). What about cases where a drug or device allows a user to engage in an activity that carries its own risks of injury? Cf. Brumley v. Pfizer, Inc., 149 F.Supp.2d 305, 313–14 (S.D.Tex.2001) ("Plaintiffs contend that Viagra allowed Mr. Brumley to engage in vigorous sexual intercourse, and that the exertion from this activity caused Mr. Brumley to suffer a fatal heart attack.... Plaintiffs also appear to be arguing that, independent of an inadequate warning, Viagra was unreasonably dangerous because it permitted Mr. Brumley to perform an act that he would not have otherwise."); id. (calling this theory "creative," but concluding that the drug's effectiveness was not the proximate cause of the patient's death even if it qualified as the "but for" cause). Chapter 7 will revisit proximate causation issues in connection with claims based on inadequate warnings.

7. *Injuries to third parties*. One type of recurring fact pattern involving pharmaceuticals poses proximate causation puzzles: a patient taking a drug product may inflict an injury on a third party who then wants to sue the manufacturer. For instance, a drug may cause sedation in the user who then drives an automobile and causes an accident. See Abby Goodnough & Katie Zezima, Drivers on Prescription Drugs: Dangerous, but Hard to Convict, N.Y. Times, July 25, 2010, at A1; see also Joy v. Eastern Maine Med. Ctr., 529 A.2d 1364 (Me.1987) (addressing the duty of health care providers to warn in such cases); cf. Gipson v. Kasey, 150 P.3d 228, 229, 233–34 (Ariz.2007) (holding that a patient who gave away oxycodone owed a duty to others injured by misuse). Or, as happened in *Grundberg*, a psychoactive drug (Halcion®) allegedly causes the patient to kill someone else. See Rimbert v. Eli Lilly & Co., 577 F.Supp.2d 1174, 1234 (D.N.M. 2008) (Prozac®); Angela M. Walker, Note, Rx: Take Two of These and Sue Me in the Morning: The Emergence of Litigation Regarding Psychotropic Medication in the United States and Europe, 19 Ariz. J. Int'l & Comp. L. 775 (2002); Emily Heller, Drug Maker Hit with $8M Verdict: Jury Finds Maker of Paxil Responsible for Multiple Shooting Deaths, Nat'l L.J., June 25, 2001, at A5. In such cases, it may be difficult to differentiate between side effects and efficacy failures (e.g., a subpotent antidepressant) as the trigger for the patient's criminal behavior. Cf. Michael A. Rosenhouse, Annotation, Liability of Prescription Drug Manufacturer for Drug User's Suicide or Attempted Suicide, 45 A.L.R.6th 385 (2009 & 2011 Supp.).

2. MARKET SHARE LIABILITY

Even when questions of defect and actual causation are straightforward, for instance where the manufacturer failed to warn of a known risk of illness that is strongly associated with a particular product (also known as a "signature" disease), the plaintiff still must identify who sold it.

Hymowitz v. Eli Lilly & Co.

539 N.E.2d 1069 (N.Y.1989).

■ WACHTLER, CHIEF JUDGE:

Plaintiffs in these appeals allege that they were injured by the drug diethylstilbestrol (DES) ingested by their mothers during pregnancy. They seek relief against defendant DES manufacturers. While not class actions, these cases are representative of nearly 500 similar actions pending in the courts in this State; the rules articulated by the court here, therefore, must do justice and be administratively feasible in the context of this mass litigation. With this in mind, we now resolve the issue twice expressly left open by this court, and adopt a market share theory, using a national market, for determining liability and apportioning damages in DES cases in which identification of the manufacturer of the drug that injured the plaintiff is impossible. * * *

The history of the development of DES and its marketing in this country has been repeatedly chronicled. Briefly, DES is a synthetic substance that mimics the effect of estrogen, the naturally formed female hormone. It was invented in 1937 by British researchers, but never patented. In 1941, the Food and Drug Administration (FDA) approved the new drug applications (NDAs) of 12 manufacturers to market DES for the treatment of various maladies, not directly involving pregnancy. In 1947, the FDA began approving the NDAs of manufacturers to market DES for the purpose of preventing human miscarriages; by 1951, the FDA had concluded that DES was generally safe for pregnancy use, and stopped requiring the filing of NDAs when new manufacturers sought to produce the drug for this purpose. In 1971, however, the FDA banned the use of DES as a miscarriage preventative, when studies established the harmful latent effects of DES upon the offspring of mothers who took the drug. Specifically, tests indicated that DES caused vaginal adenocarcinoma, a form of cancer, and adenosis, a precancerous vaginal or cervical growth. * * *

All DES was of identical chemical composition. Druggists usually filled prescriptions from whatever was on hand. Approximately 300 manufacturers produced the drug, with companies entering and leaving the market continuously during the 24 years that DES was sold for pregnancy use. The long latency period of a DES injury compounds the identification problem; memories fade, records are lost or destroyed, and witnesses die. Thus the pregnant women who took DES generally never knew who produced the drug they took, and there was no reason to attempt to discover this fact until many years after ingestion, at which time the information is not available. * * *

In a products liability action, identification of the exact defendant whose product injured the plaintiff is, of course, generally required. In DES cases in which such identification is possible, actions may proceed under established principles of products liability. The record now before us, however, presents the question of whether a DES plaintiff may recover against a DES manufacturer when identification of the producer of the specific drug that caused the injury is impossible. * * *

[T]he accepted tort doctrines of alternative liability and concerted action are available in some personal injury cases to permit recovery where the precise identification of a wrongdoer is impossible. * * * [U]se of the alternative liability doctrine generally requires that the defendants have better access to information than does the plaintiff, and that all possible tortfeasors be before the court. See Summers v. Tice, 199 P.2d 1 (Cal.1948). It is also recognized that alternative liability rests on the notion that where there is a small number of possible wrongdoers, all of whom breached a duty to the plaintiff, the likelihood that any one of them injured the plaintiff is relatively high, so that forcing them to exonerate themselves, or be held liable, is not unfair.

In DES cases, however, there is a great number of possible wrongdoers, who entered and left the market at different times, and some of whom no longer exist. Additionally, in DES cases many years elapse between the ingestion of the drug and injury. Consequently, DES defendants are not in any better position than are plaintiffs to identify the manufacturer of the

DES ingested in any given case, nor is there any real prospect of having all the possible producers before the court. Finally, while it may be fair to employ alternative liability in cases involving only a small number of potential wrongdoers, that fairness disappears with the decreasing probability that any one of the defendants actually caused the injury. This is particularly true when applied to DES where the chance that a particular producer caused the injury is often very remote. Alternative liability, therefore, provides DES plaintiffs no relief.

Nor does the theory of concerted action, in its pure form, supply a basis for recovery. This doctrine, seen in drag racing cases, provides for joint and several liability on the part of all defendants having an understanding, express or tacit, to participate in "a common plan or design to commit a tortious act." * * * [D]rug companies were engaged in extensive parallel conduct in developing and marketing DES. There is nothing in the record, however, beyond this similar conduct to show any agreement, tacit or otherwise, to market DES for pregnancy use without taking proper steps to ensure the drug's safety. Parallel activity, without more, is insufficient to establish the agreement element necessary to maintain a concerted action claim. Thus this theory also fails in supporting an action by DES plaintiffs.

In short, extant common-law doctrines, unmodified, provide no relief for the DES plaintiff unable to identify the manufacturer of the drug that injured her. This is not a novel conclusion; in the last decade a number of courts in other jurisdictions also have concluded that present theories do not support a cause of action in DES cases. Some courts, upon reaching this conclusion, have declined to find any judicial remedy for the DES plaintiffs who cannot identify the particular manufacturer of the DES ingested by their mothers. Other courts, however, have found that some modification of existing doctrine is appropriate to allow for relief for those injured by DES of unknown manufacture.

We conclude that the present circumstances call for recognition of a realistic avenue of relief for plaintiffs injured by DES. These appeals present many of the same considerations that have prompted this court in the past to modify the rules of personal injury liability, in order "to achieve the ends of justice in a more modern context," and we perceive that here judicial action is again required to overcome the " 'inordinately difficult problems of proof' " caused by contemporary products and marketing techniques.

Indeed, it would be inconsistent with the reasonable expectations of a modern society to say to these plaintiffs that because of the insidious nature of an injury that long remains dormant, and because so many manufacturers, each behind a curtain, contributed to the devastation, the cost of injury should be borne by the innocent and not the wrongdoers. This is particularly so where the Legislature consciously created these expectations by reviving hundreds of DES cases [after it modified the statute of limitations to start running only after a victim reasonably would discover an actionable injury]. Consequently, the ever-evolving dictates of justice and fairness, which are the heart of our common-law system, require formation of a remedy for injuries caused by DES.

We stress, however, that the DES situation is a singular case, with manufacturers acting in a parallel manner to produce an identical, generically marketed product, which causes injury many years later, and which has evoked a legislative response reviving previously barred actions. Given this unusual scenario, it is more appropriate that the loss be borne by those that produced the drug for use during pregnancy, rather than by those who were injured by the use, even where the precise manufacturer of the drug cannot be identified in a particular action. We turn then to the question of how to fairly and equitably apportion the loss occasioned by DES, in a case where the exact manufacturer of the drug that caused the injury is unknown.

The past decade of DES litigation has produced a number of alternative approaches to resolve this question. Thus, in a sense, we are now in an enviable position; the efforts of other courts provided examples for contending with this difficult issue, and enough time has passed so that the actual administration and real effects of these solutions now can be observed. With these useful guides in hand, a path may be struck for our own conclusion. * * *

In *Sindell v. Abbott Lab.*, 607 P.2d 924 (Cal.1980), the court synthesized the market share concept by modifying the *Summers v. Tice* alternative liability rationale in two ways. It first loosened the requirement that all possible wrongdoers be before the court, and instead made a "substantial share" sufficient. The court then held that each defendant who could not prove that it did not actually injure plaintiff would be liable according to that manufacturer's market share. The court's central justification for adopting this approach was its belief that limiting a defendant's liability to its market share will result, over the run of cases, in liability on the part of a defendant roughly equal to the injuries the defendant actually caused.

In the recent case of *Brown v. Superior Court*, 751 P.2d 470 (Cal.1988), the California Supreme Court resolved some apparent ambiguity in *Sindell* and held that a manufacturer's liability is several only, and, in cases in which all manufacturers in the market are not joined for any reason, liability will still be limited to market share, resulting in a less than 100% recovery for a plaintiff. Finally, it is noteworthy that determining market shares under *Sindell* proved difficult and engendered years of litigation. After attempts at using smaller geographical units, it was eventually determined that the national market provided the most feasible and fair solution, and this national market information was compiled.

Four years after *Sindell v. Abbott Lab.*, the Wisconsin Supreme Court followed with *Collins v. Lilly & Co.*, 342 N.W.2d 37 (Wis.1984). Deciding the identification issue without the benefit of the extensive California litigation over market shares, the Wisconsin court held that it was prevented from following *Sindell* due to "the practical difficulty of defining and proving market share." Instead of focusing on tying liability closely to the odds of actual causation, as the *Sindell* court attempted, the *Collins* court took a broader perspective, and held that each defendant is liable in proportion to the amount of risk it created that the plaintiff would be injured by DES. Under the *Collins* structure, the "risk" each defendant is liable for is a question of fact in each case, with market shares being relevant to this determination. Defendants are allowed, however, to exculpate themselves by showing that their product could not have caused the injury to the particular plaintiff.

The Washington Supreme Court, writing soon after *Collins v. Lilly & Co.*, took yet another approach. See Martin v. Abbott Lab., 689 P.2d 368 (Wash.1984). * * * Under the Washington scheme, defendants are first allowed to exculpate themselves by proving by the preponderance of the evidence that they were not the manufacturer of the DES that injured plaintiff. Unexculpated defendants are presumed to have equal market shares, totaling 100%. Each defendant then has the opportunity to rebut this presumption by showing that its actual market share was less than presumed. If any defendants succeed in rebutting this presumption, the liability shares of the remaining defendants who could not prove their actual market share are inflated, so that the plaintiff received a 100% recovery. The market shares of defendants is a question of fact in each case, and the relevant market can be a particular pharmacy, or county, or State, or even the country, depending upon the circumstances the case presents. See George v. Parke–Davis, 733 P.2d 507 (Wash.1987).

Turning to the structure to be adopted in New York, we heed both the lessons learned through experience in other jurisdictions and the realities of the mass litigation of DES claims in this State. Balancing these considerations, we are led to the conclusion that a market share theory, based upon a national market, provides the best solution. As California discovered, the reliable determination of any market smaller than the national one likely is not practicable. Moreover, even if it were possible, of the hundreds of cases in the New York courts, without a doubt there are many in which the DES that allegedly caused injury was ingested in another State. Among the thorny issues this could present, perhaps the most daunting is the spectre that the particular case could require the establishment of a separate market share matrix. We feel that this is an unfair, and perhaps impossible burden to routinely place upon the litigants in individual cases.

Nor do we believe that the Wisconsin approach of assessing the "risk" each defendant caused a particular plaintiff, to be litigated anew as a question of fact in each case, is the best solution for this State. Applied on a limited scale this theory may be feasible, and certainly is the most refined approach by allowing a more thorough consideration of how each defendant's actions threatened the plaintiff. We are wary, however, of setting loose, for application in the hundreds of cases pending in this State, a theory which requires the fact finder's individualized and open-ended assessment of the relative liabilities of scores of defendants in every case. Instead, it is our perception that the injustices arising from delayed recoveries and inconsistent results which this theory may produce in this State outweigh arguments calling for its adoption.

Consequently, for essentially practical reasons, we adopt a market share theory using a national market. We are aware that the adoption of a national market will likely result in a disproportion between the liability of individual manufacturers and the actual injuries each manufacturer caused in this State. Thus our market share theory cannot be founded upon the belief that, over the run of cases, liability will approximate causation in this State. Nor does the use of a national market provide a reasonable link between liability and the risk created by a defendant to a particular plaintiff. Instead, we choose to apportion liability so as to correspond to the over-all culpability of each defendant, measured by the amount of risk of injury each defendant created to the public-at-large. Use of a national market is a fair method, we believe, of apportioning defendants' liabilities according to their total culpability in marketing DES for use during pregnancy. Under the circumstances, this is an equitable way to provide plaintiffs with the relief they deserve, while also rationally distributing the responsibility for plaintiffs' injuries among defendants.

To be sure, a defendant cannot be held liable if it did not participate in the marketing of DES for pregnancy use; if a DES producer satisfies its burden of proof of showing that it was not a member of the market of DES sold for pregnancy use, disallowing exculpation would be unfair and unjust. Nevertheless, because liability here is based on the over-all risk produced, and not causation in a single case, there should be no exculpation of a defendant who, although a member of the market producing DES for pregnancy use, appears not to have caused a particular plaintiff's injury. It is merely a windfall for a producer to escape liability solely because it manufactured a more identifiable pill, or sold only to certain drugstores. These fortuities in no way diminish the culpability of a defendant for marketing the product, which is the basis of liability here.

Finally, we hold that the liability of DES producers is several only, and should not be inflated when all participants in the market are not before the court in a particular case. We understand that, as a practical matter, this will prevent some plaintiffs from recovering 100% of their damages. However, we eschewed exculpation to prevent the fortuitous avoidance of liability, and thus, equitably, we decline to unleash the same forces to increase a defendant's liability beyond its fair share of responsibility.[3]

---

3. The dissenter misapprehends the basis for liability here. We have not by the backdoor adopted a theory of concerted action. We avoided extending this theory, because its concomitant requirement of joint and several liability expands the burden on small manufacturers beyond a rational or fair limit. This result is reached by the dissent, not by the majority, so that criticism on this front is misplaced. We are confronted here with an unprecedented identification problem and have provided a solution that rationally apportions liability. We have heeded the practical lessons learned by other jurisdictions, resulting in our adoption of a national market theory with full knowledge that it concedes the lack of a logical link between liability and causation in a single case. The dissent ignores these lessons and, endeavoring to articulate a theory it perceives to be closer to traditional law, sets out a construct in which liability is based upon chance, not upon the fair assessment of the acts of defendants. Under the dissent's theory, a manufacturer with a large market share may avoid liability in many cases just because it manufactured a memorably shaped pill. Conversely, a small manufacturer can be held jointly liable for the full amount of every DES injury in this State simply because

■ MOLLEN, JUDGE (concurring in part and dissenting in part):

* * * I am also in complete agreement with the majority's view that the market share theory of liability, based upon a national market, is an appropriate means by which to accord DES plaintiffs an opportunity to seek recovery for their injuries. However, I respectfully disagree with the majority's conclusion that there should be no exculpation of those defendants who produced and marketed DES for pregnancy purposes, but who can prove, by a preponderance of the evidence, that they did not produce or market the particular pill ingested by the plaintiff's mother. Moreover, in order to ensure that these plaintiffs receive full recovery of their damages, as they are properly entitled to by any fair standard, I would retain the principle of imposing joint and several liability upon those defendants which cannot exculpate themselves.

The emergence of the market share concept of liability in the field of products liability reflects a recognition by several jurisdictions throughout the United States that due to the incidence of mass production and marketing of various drugs and fungible goods, consumers are many times harmed by a product which is not easily traceable to a specific manufacturer, particularly in those situations where the harm occurred many years prior to the discovery of the injuries and the cause thereof. Such is the situation in the DES cases now before us. * * *

Significantly, both the Supreme Courts of Wisconsin and Washington in the *Collins* and *Martin* cases, as did the Supreme Court of California in *Sindell*, provided that the joined or impleaded defendants may exculpate themselves from liability if they can establish, by a preponderance of the evidence, that they did not produce or market the particular DES pill taken by the plaintiff's mother. * * * In fact, *none* of the jurisdictions which have adopted varying theories of collective liability in DES cases has refused to permit exculpation of those defendants which have been able to prove that they could not have produced or marketed the pill which caused the particular plaintiff's injuries, thereby recognizing that to preclude exculpation would directly and unnecessarily contravene the established common-law tort principles of causation. * * *

I would adopt a market share theory of liability, based upon a national market, which would provide for the shifting of the burden of proof on the issue of causation to the defendants and would impose liability upon all of the defendants who produced and marketed DES for pregnancy purposes, except those who were able to prove that their product could not have caused the injury. Under this approach, DES plaintiffs, who are unable to

the shape of its product was not remarkable, even though the odds, realistically, are exceedingly long that the small manufacturer caused the injury in any one particular case. Therefore, although the dissent's theory based upon a "shifting the burden of proof" and joint and several liability is facially reminiscent of prior law, in the case of DES it is nothing more than advocating that bare fortuity be the test for liability. When faced with the novel identification problem posed by DES cases, it is preferable to adopt a new theory that apportions fault rationally, rather than to contort extant doctrines beyond the point at which they provide a sound premise for determining liability.

identify the actual manufacturer of the pill ingested by their mother, would only be required to establish (1) that the plaintiff's mother ingested DES during pregnancy; (2) that the plaintiff's injuries were caused by DES; and (3) that the defendant or defendants produced and marketed DES for pregnancy purposes. Thereafter, the burden of proof would shift to the defendants to exculpate themselves by establishing, by a preponderance of the evidence, that the plaintiff's mother could not have ingested their particular pill. Of those defendants who are unable to exculpate themselves from liability, their respective share of the plaintiff's damages would be measured by their share of the national market of DES produced and marketed for pregnancy purposes during the period in question.

I would further note that while, on the one hand, the majority would not permit defendants who produced DES for pregnancy purposes to exculpate themselves, the majority at the same time deprives the plaintiffs of the opportunity to recover fully for their injuries by limiting the defendants' liability for the plaintiff's damages to several liability. In my view, the liability for the plaintiff's damages of those defendants who are unable to exculpate themselves should be joint and several thereby ensuring that the plaintiffs will receive full recovery of their damages. In addition to being fair to the DES plaintiffs, the imposition of joint and several liability is consistent with that portion of the revival statute which specifically exempted DES claims from those provisions which provide, with certain exceptions, for several liability of joint tort-feasors. Moreover, in order to ease the financial burden on the specific defendants named in the lawsuit, the defendants would have the option of seeking contribution from their fellow defendants for damages in excess of each defendant's particular market share, and a defendant should be permitted leave to implead those DES manufacturers who the plaintiff has not joined, in order to ensure, where possible, full contribution. Admittedly, adherence to joint and several liability could result in a disproportion between a defendant's potential liability for the damages suffered by the plaintiff and defendant's actual national market share; however, the opportunity to present exculpatory evidence reduces the risk of imposing liability on innocent defendants.

The application of the aforesaid principles, although somewhat innovative and a modification of traditional tort law (i.e., the burden of proof is on the plaintiff to prove proximate causation), would, in view of the exigent circumstances, be in furtherance of a valid public policy of imposing the burden of bearing the cost of severe injuries upon those who are responsible for placing into the stream of commerce the causative instrumentality of such injuries. Adherence to this principle would not be too dissimilar from the accepted doctrine of res ipsa loquitur which provides, in essence, that where an instrumentality which caused the plaintiff's injuries was in the exclusive control of the defendant and the accident which occurred is one which would not ordinarily happen without negligence, these facts are sufficient to justify an inference of negligence and to shift the burden upon the defendant of coming forward with an explanation. Thus, this approach, unlike that taken by the majority, does not represent an unnecessary and radical departure from basic principles of tort law. By characterizing this approach as "nothing more than advocating that bare fortuity be the test for liability" the majority fails to perceive that this is no more and no less than a basic principle of tort law; i.e., a plaintiff may not recover for his or her injuries from a defendant who could not have caused those injuries. When the majority eliminates this fundamental causative factor as a basis for recovery, it effectively indulges in the act of judicial legislating. I would further note that if the Legislature had intended to adopt this radical approach which is at total variance with traditional tort law, it could readily have done so when it enacted the revival statute for, among others, DES plaintiffs. Its refusal to do so can certainly not be deemed to be an invitation to this court to assume the legislative role.

Judged by the aforesaid standard, I conclude that the trial courts' orders in *Tigue & Margolies v. Squibb & Sons* (decided herewith) and *Dolan v. Lilly & Co.* (decided herewith), to the extent that they denied the summary judgment motions of the defendant The Upjohn Company (Upjohn) in both actions and the defendant Rexall Drug Company (Rexall) in the *Tigue* action, were improper. In *Tigue*, Mrs. Tigue, the plaintiff's mother, testified that the DES pill she ingested while she was pregnant with the plaintiff was a white, round tablet. Similarly, Myrna Margolies' mother testified that the DES pill she ingested was a dark red, hard, round pill. Mr. Margolies, the plaintiff's father, also recalled that the pills were a reddish color and Mrs. Margolies' obstetrician stated that the DES pill he prescribed to his patients was not an Upjohn product. Moreover, in the *Dolan* action, Mrs. Dolan, the plaintiff's mother, stated that the DES pill she took was a white, round, hard tablet. This fact was corroborated by Mr. Dolan's testimony. Finally, it was established that Upjohn's DES pill which was produced and marketed for pregnancy purposes, was in the form of a "perle" which is a pharmaceutical term for a dose form consisting of a soft elastic capsule containing a liquid center. Based on the evidence submitted in support of Upjohn's summary judgment motions in these two cases, I would conclude that the plaintiffs have failed to adduce sufficient proof in admissible form to raise a triable issue of fact as to whether their mothers ingested an Upjohn DES pill. Accordingly, Upjohn's motion for summary judgment in those actions should have been granted. * * *

Rexall's motion for summary judgment should have been granted since the plaintiffs failed to raise a triable issue of fact as to whether their mothers could have ingested a Rexall DES product during the pregnancies in question. The evidence submitted in support of Rexall's motion established that until 1978, Rexall sold its products, including its DES pill, exclusively to Rexall Drug Stores. The testimony of the plaintiffs' parents, Mrs. Tigue and Mr. and Mrs. Margolies, established that they had purchased their DES prescriptions from non-Rexall pharmacies during the periods of their respective pregnancies, i.e., 1960 and 1953. Based on this uncontroverted evidence demonstrating Rexall's noninvolvement in these plaintiffs' injuries, Rexall's motion for summary judgment should have been granted. * * *

NOTES AND QUESTIONS

1. *Inculpation and exculpation.* After *Hymowitz*, a lower court refused to dismiss from a lawsuit a California company that had never sold DES in New York or any adjacent states. See In re New York County DES Litig., 615 N.Y.S.2d 882, 885 (App.Div.1994) (rejecting an objection to the exercise of personal jurisdiction); see also In re DES Market Share Litig., 591 N.E.2d 226 (N.Y.1992) (rejecting the argument that the market share theory represented an equitable claim for which the plaintiff would have no right to a jury trial). What if the plaintiff had found her mother's prescription records identifying the particular manufacturer of DES? Would *Hymowitz* require her to use a market share theory, which would mean recovering less than 100% of her damages? Why does the court only allow exculpation by manufacturers of DES marketed solely for non-pregnancy indications? Isn't it possible, given the prevalence of off-label prescribing, that such a manufacturer actually supplied the DES that injured a particular plaintiff? See Miles Lab., Inc. v. Superior Ct., 184 Cal.Rptr. 98 (Ct.App. 1982). For additional background on this litigation, see Romualdo P. Eclavea, Annotation, Products Liability: Diethylstilbestrol (DES), 2 A.L.R.4th 1091 (1980); Robert N. Hoover et al., Adverse Health Outcomes in Women Exposed In Utero to Diethylstilbestrol, 365 New Eng. J. Med. 1304 (2011); Leef Smith, The DES Legacy, Wash. Post, Sept. 23, 2003, at F1.

2. *Relationship to class actions and choice of law.* The progenitor market share decision, *Sindell v. Abbott Laboratories*, 607 P.2d 924 (Cal.1980), represented a statewide class action lawsuit against manufacturers of DES, and the court defined the relevant market share as limited to the state of California. In that context, perhaps, a theory of proportional liability has far greater appeal. In *Hymowitz*, the court justified using a national market share in part because some of the plaintiffs' mothers may have ingested DES in other states, but then New York tort law may not apply in any event. See Armata v. Abbott Lab., 747 N.Y.S.2d 863 (App.Div.2002) (applying the law of another state that had not definitively adopted market share rule for DES cases); see also Braune v. Abbott Lab., 895 F.Supp. 530 (E.D.N.Y.1995) (applying Georgia law).

3. *Other formulations.* See Conley v. Boyle Drug Co., 570 So.2d 275, 283 (Fla.1990) (adopting the narrowest possible definition of the relevant market); Abel v. Eli Lilly & Co., 343 N.W.2d 164 (Mich.1984) (modified alternative liability theory); see also Rest. (3d) § 15 cmt. c ("The Institute leaves to developing law the question of whether, given the appropriate factors, a rule of proportional liability should be adopted. However, if a court does adopt some form of proportional liability, the liability of each defendant is properly limited to the individual defendant's share of the market."); Richard E. Kaye, Annotation, "Concert of Activity," "Alternate Liability," "Enterprise Liability," or Similar Theory as Basis for Imposing Liability upon One or More Manufacturers of Defective Uniform Product, in Absence of Identification of Manufacturer of Precise Unit or Batch Causing Injury, 63 A.L.R.5th 195, §§ 4, 8 (1998 & 2011 Supp.).

4. *Jurisdictions rejecting market share theory even in DES cases.* See, e.g., Galvin v. Eli Lilly & Co., 488 F.3d 1026 (D.C.Cir.2007) (applying Kansas law); Wood v. Eli Lilly & Co., 38 F.3d 510 (10th Cir.1994) (applying Oklahoma law); Tidler v. Eli Lilly & Co., 851 F.2d 418 (D.C.Cir.1988) (applying Maryland and D.C. law); Smith v. Eli Lilly & Co., 560 N.E.2d 324 (Ill.1990); Sutowski v. Eli Lilly & Co., 696 N.E.2d 187 (Ohio 1998); see also Doe v. Baxter Healthcare Corp., 380 F.3d 399, 407–10 (8th Cir.2004) (explaining, in a case involving blood factor concentrates, that Iowa has rejected market share liability, adding that the alternative liability theory did not apply on the facts); Shackil v. Lederle Lab., 561 A.2d 511 (N.J.1989) (DPT vaccine); Senn v. Merrell–Dow Pharm., Inc., 751 P.2d 215 (Or.1988) (same). DES cases also have failed on other grounds peculiar to this drug. See, e.g., Grover v. Eli Lilly & Co., 591 N.E.2d 696, 700 (Ohio 1992) ("When a pharmaceutical company [supplies] drugs to a woman, the company, under ordinary circumstances, does not have a duty to her daughter's infant who will be conceived twenty-eight years later.").

5. *Manufacturing defect claims.* In DES cases, each and every unit sold contained the same defect. Does market share liability make less sense in cases where only some of the units sold by some manufacturers contain a defect? Contrast Sheffield v. Eli Lilly & Co., 192 Cal.Rptr. 870 (Ct.App. 1983) (rejecting market share theory in a case of a defective batch of polio vaccine), with Smith v. Cutter Biological, Inc., 823 P.2d 717 (Haw.1991) (allowing use of market share theory in a case of tainted blood factor concentrates). Along similar lines, courts will refuse to certify class action lawsuits involving medical technologies if there are significant differences among plaintiffs in their use and exposure (as well as differences in the applicable tort laws of the various states). See In re American Med. Sys., Inc., 75 F.3d 1069, 1081 (6th Cir.1996) (penile prostheses); In re Propulsid Prod. Liab. Litig., 208 F.R.D. 133 (E.D.La.2002); Baker v. Wyeth–Ayerst Lab., 992 S.W.2d 797, 801 (Ark.1999) (diet drugs); Janssen Pharm., Inc. v. Bailey, 878 So.2d 31, 45–49 (Miss.2004) (Propulsid®); see also Janssen Pharm., Inc. v. Armond, 866 So.2d 1092, 1099 (Miss.2004) ("Propulsid claims arise from an 'immature tort.' Because scientific, legal, and factual issues related to 'immature torts' are novel and unsettled, mass joinder is inappropriate and 'until enough trials have occurred so that the contours of various types of claims within the ... litigation are known, courts should proceed with extreme caution in consolidating claims.'" (quoting In re Bristol–Myers Squibb Co., 975 S.W.2d 601, 603 (Tex.1998))); Young K. Lee, Note, Beyond Gatekeeping: Class Certification, Judicial Oversight, and the Promotion of Scientific Research in "Immature" Pharmaceutical Torts, 105 Colum. L. Rev. 1905 (2005).

6. *Medical devices.* A lower court in New York declined to apply *Hymowitz* to litigation against breast implant manufacturers, offering the following explanation:

> This court finds that market share liability should not be applied to breast implants because such products are not fungible and the manufacturers of the implants can often be identified. There are differences

> in the design and composition of the implants; the warning inserts in each of the products vary; and the products are not generically marketed. Most importantly, the majority of women involved in the breast implant litigation have been able to identify all or some of the manufacturers of their implants. This ability to identify most of the manufacturers is important since both market share and concert of action liability theories came into play so plaintiffs could have recourse to the courts where product identification was impossible. The rationale of the Court of Appeals decision in *Hymowitz* was that market share liability was necessary because the DES was an identical generically marketed product, as a result of which the manufacturers of the product could not be identified. In the present case, silicone breast implant manufacturers make identifiable products, marketed under specific manufacturer names. The reality of a plaintiff's plight when product identification cannot be made is like any other plaintiff who claims injury from a product that has been lost or destroyed. So drastic a departure from traditional tort law is not warranted here.

In re New York State Silicone Breast Implant Litig., 631 N.Y.S.2d 491, 494 (Sup.Ct.1995), aff'd mem., 650 N.Y.S.2d 558 (App.Div.1996); see also Albright v. Upjohn Co., 788 F.2d 1217 (6th Cir.1986) (holding that the plaintiff's lawyer should have been sanctioned under FRCP Rule 11 for naming several manufacturers of tetracycline where the plaintiff's still available medical records had identified only a few of these drug companies as the source of antibiotics that she had received as a child); Thomas C. Willcox, Note, The Application of a Due Diligence Requirement to Market Share Theory in DES Litigation, 19 U. Mich. J.L. Reform 771 (1986).

7. *Further commentary.* See Frederick H. Fern & Leslie S. McHugh, Market Share Liability for Pharmaceuticals: The Distinction Between DES and DPT, 11 J. Legal Med. 391 (1990); Mark A. Geistfeld, The Doctrinal Unity of Alternative Liability and Market–Share Liability, 155 U. Pa. L. Rev. 447 (2006); Daniel J. Grimm, Note, Accounting for Risk Disparity: An Alternative to Market Share Liability, 2006 Colum. Bus. L. Rev. 549; Andrew R. Klein, Beyond DES: Rejecting the Application of Market Share Liability in Blood Products Litigation, 68 Tul. L. Rev. 883 (1994); Allen Rostron, Beyond Market Share Liability: A Theory of Proportional Share Liability for Nonfungible Products, 52 UCLA L. Rev. 151 (2004).

CHAPTER 6

PRODUCTION FAILURES

This chapter addresses products liability claims against sellers of prescription drugs and medical devices that are premised on manufacturing and design defects. A discussion of the more typical failure-to-warn claims is reserved for the next chapter on informational defects.

A. MANUFACTURING DEFECTS

Parkinson v. Guidant Corp.

315 F.Supp.2d 741 (W.D.Pa.2004).

■ DIAMOND, DISTRICT JUDGE:

* * * The Pennsylvania Supreme Court has adopted Section 402A of the *Restatement (Second) of Torts* * * * * Although no Pennsylvania court has addressed the "properly prepared" caveat to comment k, it must be assumed that, as with inadequate warnings, the only recognized basis of liability for an improperly prepared product is negligence, as the foregoing Pennsylvania cases make clear that § 402A strict liability is not applicable at all to cases governed by comment k.[1] * * *

[P]laintiffs assert that ACS [Advanced Cardiovascular Systems, Inc., a wholly owned subsidiary of Guidant Corp.] breached a duty owed to plaintiffs by improperly manufacturing a guidewire which fractured in the course of Rowan Parkinson's angioplasty procedure on May 11, 1999, resulting in emergency bypass surgery to remove the fractured tip and resulting in numerous ongoing health difficulties, particularly with Rowan Parkinson's legs. In support of that claim, plaintiffs have proffered the expert testimony of Norman Johanson, a mechanical engineer, and Ronald Crooks, a metallurgist, who are prepared to testify [based in part on destructive testing of the product, see Parkinson v. Guidant Corp., 315 F.Supp.2d 754, 757–59 (W.D.Pa.2004),] that the guidewire at issue contained certain manufacturing flaws that weakened the wire making it more

1. The court recognizes that Pennsylvania law on this issue is somewhat unique and other jurisdictions have held that comment k to § 402A precludes only design defect strict liability claims while permitting manufacturing defect and failure-to-warn defect strict liability claims under comment k's caveats. The *Restatement (Third) of Torts* § 6 also recognizes a manufacturing defect theory for prescription drugs and medical devices. However, this court, sitting in diversity jurisdiction, is bound by Pennsylvania law, and the Pennsylvania Supreme Court unambiguously has held that § 402A strict liability does *not* apply in any way to prescription drugs. * * *

susceptible to fracture and which, in fact, resulted in the premature fracture of the guidewire. Moreover, plaintiffs have proffered the expert testimony of Dr. George Moy, the interventional cardiologist who performed Rowan Parkinson's angioplasty procedure, who is prepared to testify as a medical causation expert that the fractured guidewire caused the bypass surgery and subsequent injuries to Mr. Parkinson.

The court finds that the foregoing evidence, if believed, is such that a reasonable jury could return a verdict for plaintiffs on a negligence claim. Of course, ACS challenges the conclusions of Moy, Crooks and Johanson, but at the summary judgment stage, the facts must be viewed in a light most favorable to plaintiffs. The ultimate issue of ACS's liability for negligence in improperly preparing the guidewire rests with a jury and is not for this court to make as a matter of law.

Moreover, even if the foregoing direct evidence is insufficient to establish negligence in this case, it may be possible for plaintiffs to establish negligence under the doctrine of res ipsa loquitur. Res ipsa loquitur is a rule of circumstantial evidence which allows a plaintiff, without direct evidence of the elements of negligence, to present a case to the jury based on an inference of negligence. Instead of directly proving the elements of ordinary negligence, the plaintiff provides evidence of facts and circumstances surrounding his injury that make the inference of the defendant's negligence reasonable. Under the doctrine of res ipsa loquitur, it may be inferred that harm suffered by a plaintiff is caused by a defendant's negligence when: (1) the event is of a kind which ordinarily does not occur in the absence of negligence; [and] (2) other responsible causes, including the conduct of the plaintiff and third persons, are sufficiently eliminated by the evidence * * * *

Plaintiffs have proffered the following facts to support an inference of res ipsa loquitur. First, plaintiffs contend that tip separation of a guidewire is not an incident that ordinarily occurs in the absence of negligence. In support, they will offer the testimony of Moy, who asserts that the tip separation in plaintiff's procedure is the only occurrence of tip fracture in the 650+ procedures in which he has used a guidewire. Plaintiffs also have proffered evidence indicating that Dr. Moy was not negligent in using the guidewire, including deposition testimony of Dr. Lima who conducted plaintiff's bypass operation and reviewed the cinescope of Dr. Moy's angioplasty procedure.

Defendants argue that plaintiffs are not entitled to a res ipsa loquitur inference arising from the foregoing facts because: (1) there is evidence in the record that tip separation conceivably can occur even in the absence of negligence; and (2) there is evidence that the negligence of Moy in torquing or twisting the wire against resistance was the cause of the guidewire fracture. However, Pennsylvania case law has made clear that, in order to show that an accident was of a type which ordinarily does not occur in the absence of negligence, a plaintiff need not prove that the accident *could not* occur in the absence of negligence, but must only show that it is more probable than not that the plaintiff's injuries were caused by defendant's negligence. Likewise, a plaintiff is not required to exclude all other possible causes of the accident beyond a reasonable doubt * * * *

Here, the court, viewing the evidence in a light most favorable to plaintiffs, finds that the res ipsa loquitur inference might reasonably be drawn by a jury in this case, as the evidence before the court is sufficient for a reasonable juror to conclude that the guidewire fracture more probably than not was the result of defendants' negligence in manufacturing it. Of course, whether plaintiffs will be entitled to a res ipsa loquitur charge will be dependent on the evidence actually offered and admitted at trial. However, the court believes that it would be premature at this stage of the litigation to preclude plaintiffs from seeking a res ipsa loquitur charge since the evidence presented at trial may well show that they are entitled to one. As plaintiffs have proffered sufficient evidence of either direct negligence or circumstantial evidence under res ipsa loquitur which, if believed, would allow a reasonable juror to return a verdict in plaintiffs' favor, ACS's motion for summary judgment on Count I of plaintiffs' complaint will be denied. * * * *

McCorvey v. Baxter Healthcare Corp.

298 F.3d 1253 (11th Cir.2002).

■ KRAVITCH, CIRCUIT JUDGE:

* * * [Charles] McCorvey underwent a transurethral resection of his prostate, a surgical procedure, after which a * * * catheter [manufactured by C.R. Bard, Inc. and distributed by Baxter Healthcare Corp.] was inserted in his bladder. Written instructions accompanied 30 cc Bard catheters advising that the device should be filled with no more than 36 cc's of sterile water, but McCorvey's doctor inserted 50 cc's of saline solution into the balloon portion of the catheter before insertion to test the device, then deflated the balloon. The catheter was placed inside McCorvey uninflated, and once inside him the balloon portion was again inflated with 50 cc's of saline solution. Deposition testimony by McCorvey's medical experts indicated that it was general medical practice to fill catheters to such volumes.

Six hours after insertion, the balloon portion of McCorvey's catheter spontaneously erupted and fragmented inside of him. Doctors extracted the catheter, which hospital employees discarded. McCorvey alleges that he experienced persistent symptoms of frequent urinary outflows, urgency with urination, and pain due to the catheter's eruption, even after its removal. Approximately a year and a half after McCorvey's initial operation, a doctor found an additional fragment of the balloon portion of the catheter lodged inside McCorvey's prostate. McCorvey underwent yet another procedure to remove the additional fragment, after which the hospital employees photographed and then discarded it. * * *

In Florida strict product liability actions, a legal inference is created that the subject product was defective at both the time of injury and the time of sale when that product "malfunctions during normal operation."

Cassisi v. Maytag Co., 396 So.2d 1140 (Fla.Ct.App.1981). * * * [T]he medical expert affidavits here establish that filling a 30 cc-capacity catheter to 50 cc's, despite Bard's recommendations to the contrary, is normal use, and constitutes standard urological practice.[2] * * * [T]he common "misuse" involved here is sufficient to establish that the occurrence in question, i.e., the fragmentation and spontaneous eruption of the catheter inside of McCorvey, "differs either from the manufacturer's intended result or from other units of the same product line," which according to expert testimony, were regularly inflated to similar levels.[3] We consider these facts sufficient to show that the catheter here erupted during the course of normal operation. * * *

[A]lthough any alternatives to a manufacturing defect as possible causes of the catheter's eruption, including McCorvey's doctor having over-inflated the catheter beyond manufacturer recommendations, are not enough to override the *Cassisi* inference, they may be highly relevant at trial. * * * [S]ummary judgment for the defendants would be inappropriate here. They remain free, however, to offer argument and evidence at trial that might negate McCorvey's inference of product defect and rebut his prima facie case. * * *

■ HILL, CIRCUIT JUDGE (dissenting):

* * * It is my experience from childhood that balloons will inherently burst if overinflated. * * * The majority interprets Florida products liabili-

2. Indeed, one of these affidavits was offered by a doctor who had personally handled and inserted hundreds of catheters, almost all manufactured by Bard, and who averred that "[w]hile C.R. Bard, Inc. apparently recommends that the inflation capacity of a 30 cc balloon used in Charles McCorvey to be 35 cc's of sterile water, the customary and standard practice for urologists is to inflate these 30 cc balloons to at least 50 cc's when traction of the catheter is required; venous bleeding is halted with traction and cannot be stopped in any other fashion." He continued, "[t]he catheter which fragmented inside Charles McCorvey was inflated to approximately 50 cc's which fits squarely within the standard of medical practice for urologists in and outside of Florida. I customarily fill these same catheters to 50 cc's with saline or water and this has been my practice over at least the past 21 years." This doctor offered that the inflation of the subject catheter to 50 cc's before insertion was "appropriate" and "usual." He also conducted his own experiment with a catheter of identical dimension as the one placed in McCorvey. He filled the device to 60 cc's of sterile water and placed twenty pounds on the inflated balloon for 72 hours, "which is far greater pressure than found in a bladder of a human being." The catheter which was the subject of this experiment did not deflate or fragment, as did McCorvey's.

3. The dissent finds it irrelevant to the determination of whether a *Cassisi* inference applies that McCorvey's catheter was subject to treatment and handling no different than hundreds, if not thousands, of the same catheters, which did not spontaneously fragment. We cannot agree. We find it extremely significant that, based upon McCorvey's expert medical affidavits, the inflation of Bard catheters beyond their recommended levels did not normally result in eruption. Clearly something was different between these non-erupting catheters and McCorvey's catheter; taking all inferences in favor of McCorvey, we must assume that this difference was not a variation in the inflation levels of the catheters. We therefore can infer, under *Cassisi,* that the difference was that McCorvey's catheter suffered from a manufacturing defect, while the other Bard catheters which were filled with the same amounts of water or solution did not. We stress, however, that the defendants remain free to rebut this inference at trial and point to the over-inflation of McCorvey's catheter as a possible reason for eruption and fragmentation here.

ty tort law to hold that this set of facts creates an inference that the catheter, with its 30 cc balloon, was defective because it fractured when overinflated by 66% of its stated capacity. The inference created by this interpretation is that, if the balloon burst when 166% of the amount of liquid it was capable of receiving was forced into it, then it also would have burst had the doctor inserted 100%, or the correct amount! I am not willing to conclude that this inference, which, to me, appears illogical, is correct * * * *

Davenport v. Medtronic, Inc.

302 F.Supp.2d 419 (E.D.Pa.2004).

■ KELLY, SENIOR DISTRICT JUDGE:

* * * The Activa [Tremor Control System] is a prescription medical device that was bilaterally implanted in [Richard] Davenport to help relieve him of symptoms associated with Parkinson's disease. * * * The Activa consists of three distinct implanted components: (1) the implantable pulse generator (IPG), (2) the extension lead, and (3) the intra-cranial lead. First, the IPG is the power source for the Activa and it is inserted in the recipients's thorax. The IPG is composed of a sealed, oval-shaped, metal container that houses a special battery and programmable electronics that dictate the electric charge generated by the battery. Second, the extension is a thin insulated wire that connects the IPG and the lead. The extension transports the electrical pulses from the IPG to the lead. Finally, the lead is a thin insulated wire that enters the brain. The lead has a series of tiny electrodes at one end that convey electrical pulses from the extension to the tissues in the brain. * * *

The Activa operates by electronically stimulating the targeted tissues in the brain that control movement and muscle function through a process called deep brain stimulation (DBS). DBS is intended to interrupt the messages to the brain that cause the symptoms of Parkinson's disease (i.e., tremors) and suppress these symptoms. As a result of DBS, patients are theoretically supposed to achieve greater control over their bodily movements. It should be noted that the surgical implantation of the Activa is done in two stages. In stage one, a hole is drilled into the cranium of the patient and the electrodes are introduced into the brain. The second stage of the procedure calls for the implantation of the IPG in the chest area. The IPG is then programmed using an external console and the system is completely activated. * * *

[O]n July 31, 1997, "the FDA approved the PMA application for the [Activa] as indicated for unilateral thalamic stimulation for suppression of essential and Parkinsonian tremor." [Almost five years later, the agency approved a PMA supplement for bilateral use of the device.] * * * Davenport met with Dr. Michael Munz of Temple University Hospital to discuss bilateral implantation of the Activa as therapy for his symptoms. Dr. Munz informed Davenport that the bilateral implantation would be an "off-label use of the [Activa] for his particular case." * * *

On November 9, 1998, Dr. Munz performed a surgical bilateral implant of Activa systems on Davenport. After surgery was completed, the Activa systems were activated and Davenport found that many of the symptoms of his Parkinson's disease became suppressed. * * * Within a month or two after surgery, Davenport began to experience problems. For example, the IPGs began to turn off and on for no apparent reason. Moreover, Davenport began feeling fluttering sensations in his chest. The problems with the IPGs and the fluttering sensations continued for months. * * * Davenport visited Dr. Munz in March of 1999 for an evaluation. In conjunction with this visit, Medtronic representative Denise Kelly interrogated Davenport's Activa devices. Kelly was able to identify two possible explanations for Davenport's complaints: (1) the IPGs had been placed too close to each other or (2) bodily fluid had leaked into one IPG.

On April 14, 1999, Dr. Munz removed the IPGs and implanted two new IPGs, keeping the previously implanted extensions. Dr. Munz attempted to place the new IPGs farther apart from one another in an attempt to prevent any future complications. In performing the operation, Dr. Munz noticed that a strand of fatty material had grown in one of the explanted IPG connectors, the mechanism that attached the IPG to the extension. At this time, Dr. Munz hypothesized that the fatty material had created a "fluid short" that was the cause of Davenport's complications.

On October 5, 1999 (approximately six months after his second surgery), Davenport had additional problems with the Activa systems. * * * Again, Kelly interrogated the Activa systems on behalf of Medtronic. Kelly found that the IPGs were functioning normally, but found that electricity was not flowing properly to the contacts in the brain. Subsequently, Davenport was transferred to Temple University Hospital, where he was put under the care of Dr. Jack Jallo since Dr. Munz had left the hospital. On October 6, 1999, Dr. Jallo performed another surgery on Davenport to evaluate the Activa systems. Initially, Dr. Jallo interrogated the IPGs and found that they were functioning properly. After analysis of the extension components of the systems revealed no problems, Dr. Jallo hypothesized by a process of elimination (since there are only three separate components to each Activa system) that the Activa systems were not functioning normally because there were fractures in the leads that extended into the brain. Revision and replacement of the leads was discussed at the time, but Davenport was unwilling to commit to the surgery that would be required. The Activa systems were turned off and Davenport was discharged from Temple Hospital on October 9, 1999 [with the devices still in his body but deactivated]. Subsequently, Davenport suffered further medical problems. * * *

In fulfilling its burden at this summary judgment stage, Medtronic has directed the court to concrete and substantial evidence that Davenport's Activa systems met all FDA/PMA standards. For example, Medtronic submitted to the court traceability records that indicate that all components of the specific Activa systems at issue were manufactured and tested in accordance with FDA/PMA requirements. Further, * * * Medtronic tested the IPGs that were explanted from Davenport on April 14, 1999. As stated by Medtronic and specifically conceded by Davenport in his response to the instant motion, "[b]oth IPGs passed Medtronic's final functional test, confirming that they satisfied the PMA-approved functional and performance requirements." Moreover, as stated by Medtronic and conceded by Davenport, "Medtronic also performed extensive interaction characterization testing of the two IPGs, including a series of tests specifically requested by [Davenport's] expert, and found no interaction between the IPGs that would explain plaintiff's complaints of sensations within his chest adjacent to the IPGs." Significantly, Davenport has not performed any tests on the IPGs * * * *

Davenport has pointed to the fact that tissue was found in the IPG connector in an attempt to show the IPGs were not manufactured in accordance with FDA/PMA requirements. Davenport states that "the presence of fatty material where the FDA requirement mandates that there be no such material constitutes failure of this product to meet FDA standards." * * * [Plaintiff's electrical engineering expert Ted] Milo stated in his expert reports that these devices should be sealed and water-tight * * * * [Although Mr. Milo claims that he read through relevant portions of the PMA's nearly 60,000 pages,] we find no reference in the reports to any FDA/PMA requirements that were allegedly breached if the IPG connector was not completely water-tight. While Milo's report mentions the impact of "failed insulation" within his reports, he does not point to any FDA/PMA requirements in relation to the sealed nature of the IPGs. Instead, Milo's report makes broad conclusory statements such as the "IPGs implanted in November of 1998 should not malfunction as it did in Mr. Davenport unless these devices were defective." * * * Even accepting every inference for Davenport at this stage in the litigation (i.e., that a "fluid short" in the IPG caused Davenport's complications), Davenport and his expert have simply not produced sufficient evidence to support the claim that Medtronic failed to comply with FDA/PMA requirements in the manufacturing of the IPGs at issue.

Davenport also directs the court to the fact that the leads malfunctioned after Davenport's second surgery in an attempt to show that the leads did not meet FDA/PMA standards. * * * Again, after a thorough examination of Milo's expert reports, the court finds no reference in the reports to any FDA/PMA requirement that was not met even if these leads became fractured or frayed while in Davenport's body. Even at this stage, Davenport and his expert cannot simply point to the malfunction itself to prove that the leads were not manufactured in accordance with FDA/PMA specifications. Accepting every inference for Davenport at this stage in the litigation (i.e., that frayed or fractured leads caused Davenport's complications), Davenport and his expert have not produced sufficient evidence to support the claim that Medtronic failed to comply with FDA/PMA requirements in the manufacturing of the leads. * * *

Davenport's counsel could only make the conclusory assertion that some FDA/PMA requirement must not have been met since tissue was found in the IPGs, the leads malfunctioned and Davenport experienced problems. This argument ignores the fact that there may have been other causes for Davenport's issues with the Activa systems, notwithstanding that the devices were manufactured within FDA/PMA standards.[24] * * * Davenport's strict product liability and negligent manufacturing claims only survive preemption because they are based on the premise that the Activa systems at issue were not in compliance with FDA/PMA standards. Medtronic has presented substantial evidence that Davenport's Activa devices were manufactured within FDA/PMA standards. In response, Davenport has made only conclusory allegations and has not presented this court with sufficient evidence to create a triable issue of fact on this issue. Therefore, summary judgment in Medtronic's favor is appropriate * * * *

NOTES AND QUESTIONS

1. *Restatement formulations*. As the court in *Parkinson* conceded, its interpretation of the "properly prepared" language in comment k to *Rest. (2d)* § 402A may have departed from the norm. See Transue v. Aesthetech Corp., 341 F.3d 911, 917–19 (9th Cir.2003) (rejecting the trial judge's conclusion in a breast implant case that this language connoted a negligence standard applicable to manufacturing defect claims). The *Products Liability Restatement* uses the same standard to define prescription drug and medical device manufacturing defects as it does for other consumer goods. See Rest. (3d) § 6(b)(1) (cross-referencing § 2(a), which provides that a product "contains a manufacturing defect when the product departs from its intended design even though all possible care was exercised in the preparation and marketing of the product"). Thus, if a product is "out of specifications" for any reason, it is defective, which reflects a true strict liability standard. See Lars Noah, This Is Your Products Liability Restatement on Drugs, 74 Brook. L. Rev. 839, 841 (2009). What if every unit sold contains the same alleged flaw—is that better understood as a defectively designed product? Cf. id. at 916 ("I assume, for instance, that, after the recent discovery that foreign suppliers of the active ingredient used in heparin surreptitiously had substituted a dangerous material, the finished good manufacturers would face manufacturing defect claims.").

2. *Manufacturing defect cases*. See Martin v. American Med. Sys., Inc., 116 F.3d 102, 103, 105 (4th Cir.1997) (allowing a patient to pursue a breach of express warranty claim for an implant that was not sterile); Ferren v. Richards Mfg. Co., 733 F.2d 526, 528–30 (8th Cir.1984) (affirming judgment for plaintiff where metal defect in hip implant caused injury, but reversing

---

24. Notably, some of Medtronic's Activa literature warned both doctors and patients of some of the complications that Davenport experienced. For example, the Lead Implant Manual warned that "leads may fail to function for a variety of causes, including but not limited to, medical complications, body rejection phenomena, or failure by breakage or by breach of their insulation covering." Further, the Medtronic Physician and Hospital Manual warned that "IPGs are used with extensions, which are implanted in the extremely hostile environment of the human body. IPGs may fail to function for a variety of causes, including but not limited to, medical complications, body rejection phenomena, or component failure."

award of punitive damages); Moore v. Sulzer Orthopedics, Inc., 337 F.Supp.2d 1002 (N.D.Ohio 2004) (dismissing as preempted one claim where the plaintiff failed to allege any departure from GMPs); Pozefsky v. Baxter Healthcare Corp., 194 F.R.D. 438 (N.D.N.Y.2000); In re Copley Pharm., Inc., "Albuterol" Prods. Liab. Litig., 158 F.R.D. 485, 487–88 (D.Wyo.1994) (certifying a class action on behalf of patients who were injured by bacterial contamination of four batches of a bronchodilator drug later recalled by the manufacturer); see also Thomas M. Burton, Baxter Says Its Dialysis Filters Appear to Have Played Role in Patients' Deaths, Wall St. J., Nov. 6, 2001, at A3.

3. *Circumstantial evidence of product defect.* Prescription drugs usually are dispensed in small quantities and rapidly metabolized, and explanted medical devices may not be preserved for testing. In such cases, courts may allow plaintiffs to rely on circumstantial evidence of product defectiveness. See Oja v. Howmedica, Inc., 111 F.3d 782, 792–93 (10th Cir.1997) (reversing a directed verdict against a plaintiff's strict liability manufacturing defect claim involving a hip implant); Readel v. Vital Signs, Inc., 174 F.Supp.2d 754 (N.D.Ill.2001) (denying summary judgment to the seller of a respiratory system valve on a manufacturing defect claim); Mozes v. Medtronic, Inc., 14 F.Supp.2d 1124, 1128–29 (D.Minn.1998) (rejecting res ipsa loquitur where manufacturer of pacemaker leads offered numerous post-sale explanations for failure); Reiter v. Zimmer Inc., 897 F.Supp. 154 (S.D.N.Y.1995) (denying a motion for summary judgment because experts for the plaintiff—injured when bone cement used during hip replacement surgery hardened prematurely—raised genuine issues about the defendant's compliance with GMP and PMA requirements where records showed that the batch of cement twice failed a "cure test" and the manufacturer should have discarded the batch rather than try to salvage it by altering the proportion of ingredients); see also Rest. (3d) § 3(b) (rule for inference of defectiveness). In order for a plaintiff to make use of a malfunction theory, however, post-sale explanations for the defect generally must be rebutted. See Fane v. Zimmer, Inc., 927 F.2d 124, 129–32 (2d Cir.1991) (affirming a directed verdict for manufacturer where a metal brace may have broken because of patient misuse); Rogers v. Johnson & Johnson Prods., Inc., 565 A.2d 751 (Pa.1989) (holding that the manufacturer of components for a plaster splint, which caused serious burns when applied to a patient's leg in a hospital, was not entitled to a directed verdict against an inferential manufacturing defect claim where the plaintiff successfully had rebutted its evidence of medical malpractice as the likely cause); Fulton v. Pfizer Hosp. Prods. Group, 872 S.W.2d 908, 910–12 (Tenn.Ct.App.1993) (reversing judgment for a plaintiff because no evidence supported the inference that some manufacturing defect caused the pegs in a knee replacement to shear off); Rohde v. Smiths Med., 165 P.3d 433, 438–40 (Wyo.2007) (affirming summary judgment for the manufacturer of a venous access device (whose catheter tubing fractured several months after it was inserted into the patient's chest) because the plaintiff's failure to exclude other likely causes (particularly compression of the patient's clavicle and first rib exacerbated by his weight gain) defeated an inference of defectiveness). These decisions all involved medical devices. Why might a circumstantial manufacturing defect case rarely succeed against sellers of pharmaceutical products?

4. *Trying to get the inside scoop.* To the extent that plaintiffs must identify violations of FDA requirements to avoid preemption in cases involving PMA'd devices, they may encounter additional evidentiary obstacles (can they no longer ask a jury to infer a defect from the apparent occurrence of a malfunction?). Cf. Funk v. Stryker Corp., 631 F.3d 777 (5th Cir.2011) (hip implant); Clark v. Medtronic, Inc., 572 F.Supp.2d 1090, 1094 (D.Minn.2008) ("If negligence were the only cause of a Class III device's failure, there would be no need for the MDA's ongoing reporting requirements.... Plaintiff is ultimately wrong when he assumes that premarket approval guarantees the device is completely safe."). Parties to tort litigation generally cannot subpoena agency employees to testify. See 21 C.F.R. § 20.1; David P. Graham & Jacqueline M. Moen, Discovery of Regulatory Information for Use in Private Products Liability Litigation: Getting Past the Road Blocks, 27 Wm. Mitchell L. Rev. 653 (2000). But see In re Vioxx Prods. Liab. Litig., 235 F.R.D. 334 (E.D.La.2006). Even so, when it approves a product or initiates enforcement action, the FDA leaves a paper trail that parties may wish to use in a products liability case. See, e.g., Sabel v. Mead Johnson & Co., 737 F.Supp. 135, 140–44 (D.Mass.1990) (rejecting hearsay objection to the introduction of a letter from an FDA reviewer to the sponsor recommending revisions in risk labeling). In addition, plaintiffs may try to use the Freedom of Information Act. See Chap. 4(A)(1) (notes following *Tummino*). Finally, of course, manufacturers leave their own paper trails. See, e.g., Melody Petersen & Alex Berensen, Papers Indicate That Bayer Knew of Dangers of Its Cholesterol Drug, N.Y. Times, Feb. 22, 2003, at A1; Mary W. Walsh, Judge to Unseal Documents on the Eli Lilly Drug Zyprexa, N.Y. Times, Sept. 6, 2008, at C4; see also Patricia L. Andel, Inapplicability of the Self–Critical Analysis Privilege to the Drug and Medical Device Industry, 34 San Diego L. Rev. 93 (1997); Daniel R. Cahoy, Medical Product Information Incentives and the Transparency Paradox, 82 Ind. L.J. 623 (2007).

B. DESIGN DEFECTS

1. SETTLING ON A SENSIBLE STANDARD

Hansen v. Baxter Healthcare Corp.

764 N.E.2d 35 (Ill.2002).

■ KILBRIDE, JUSTICE:

* * * Baxter designs, manufactures and distributes IV tubing sets to hospitals nationwide. These IV sets are prescription medical devices used to deliver fluids, such as blood products, medicines, or nutrients. An IV set consists of tubing and a connector, allowing it to be attached to other sections of tubing or to a catheter inserted into a patient's venous system.

There are two types of connectors: "friction-fit" and "Luer-lock." The friction-fit type consists of two mating tapered fittings. A medical professional must push the ends of the two fittings together with sufficient force to maintain a leak-proof connection. The Luer-lock type is similar to a friction-fit connector but also has a threaded collar that screws onto the hub of the catheter. In its patent application, Baxter stated that the Luer-lock was designed to overcome the problem of inadvertent disconnection that occurs with friction-fit connectors. Baxter continued to distribute both friction-fit and Luer-lock connectors to hospitals.

In March 1991, Andrina [Hansen] was admitted to Mt. Sinai Hospital for treatment of stomach ulcers. Following successful surgery, fluids were administered intravenously to Andrina through her jugular vein. This procedure is known as a "central line" application. Unfortunately, the Baxter friction-fit connector used to connect the IV tube to a catheter came apart, causing Andrina to suffer a seizure. She also suffered an air embolism resulting in brain damage, paralysis and, ultimately, death. * * *

At trial, plaintiff called Baxter employees as adverse witnesses to establish the propensity of the friction-fit connectors to disconnect unintentionally and to prove that Luer-locking devices provided a more secure connection. According to Margaret Foss, a registered nurse and Baxter vice-president, Baxter was aware at the time Andrina was injured that friction-fit connectors sometimes failed due to patient movement. Foss admitted that this could cause air embolisms in central line applications. She conceded that friction-fit connectors were inadequate for central line use and that, in such instances, medical professionals should use Luer-locks. She testified, however, that Baxter did not encourage sales representatives to recommend Luer-locks for central line applications. Instead, Baxter simply made both products available to its customers. * * *

Neil Sheehan testified as plaintiff's expert witness without objection. Sheehan is a mechanical engineer and had worked for several companies that developed and sold IV components. Sheehan had personally designed and, in some cases, patented medical devices, including IV equipment. He explained that the main problem with using a friction-fit connector was that the amount of force needed to disconnect it depended on several factors, including (1) the force used to connect it; (2) its composition; (3) the method used to sterilize it; and (4) variations in molding. Thus, the strength of the connection varied as different persons used different friction-fit connectors at different times. Generally, however, if the connection was made with less force, it was more likely to fail.

Sheehan also described the technical aspects of the Luer-lock. He stated that a Luer-lock prevents the accidental disconnection of IV lines and that it is four to five times stronger than a friction-fit. * * * In his opinion, the friction-fit connector became obsolete once the Luer-lock became available. In addition, Sheehan stated that it was foreseeable that friction-fit connectors might be used in a central line application. He opined, however, that a friction-fit connection was not a safe design in *any* application and that it was especially hazardous when used in a central vein. He also believed that if medical personnel had used a Luer-lock connector, Andrina's injury would have been prevented.

Dr. William Schumer, chief of surgery at Mt. Sinai Hospital, testified that decisions regarding the purchase of medical supplies were made by a nursing products committee. He said that Luer-locks were not used at Mt. Sinai prior to the incident, and he believed that most hospitals did not use them at that time. He stated that he assumed friction-fit connectors were safe because they were readily available in the market. * * *

In its case in chief, Baxter presented testimony from two expert witnesses. First, William McVay, a "medical device consultant" with a degree in mechanical engineering, testified as an expert witness. He agreed that only Luer-locks should be used in central line applications. McVay acknowledged that Baxter was aware of the dangers of using friction-fit connectors in central lines but believed that Baxter was not obliged to reveal this information. Next, Kathleen Medica, a registered nurse with a master's degree, testified as an expert witness for Baxter. In her opinion, a friction-fit connector was much more likely to fail than a Luer-lock, although she did not know whether this was a well-known complication in the field. She acknowledged that some nurses may never have had the experience of a friction-fit coming apart.

After hearing the evidence, the jury returned a general verdict for the decedent's estate [in excess of $18 million, which the trial judge reduced by almost $3 million to reflect the amount of a settlement with other defendants sued for medical malpractice]. * * * We agree that the record contains sufficient conflicting evidence to raise factual questions concerning the comparative knowledge of Baxter and that of the medical community concerning both the danger of using friction-fits in central lines and the need to use only Luer-locks in these applications.

The record indicates that Baxter's employees knew of the inherent dangers of friction-fits * * * * In contrast, the testimony from persons on the medical staff at Mt. Sinai shows that they had significantly less knowledge. The chairperson of the nursing products committee testified that hospital staff relied on product manufacturers to advise them regarding the appropriate uses of a product. The nurse responsible for the actual purchase and distribution of medical supplies at Mt. Sinai testified that, in March 1991, she did not know the difference between a friction-fit connector and a Luer-lock and that she did not know that friction-fit connectors should not be used in central lines.

Moreover, Dr. Norbert Strohmayer, the fifth-year resident who assisted at Andrina's surgery, was unaware of any literature describing the frequency of unintentional separation with friction-fit connectors, despite reading and subscribing to several well-known medical journals. He was also unaware of the force necessary to disconnect a friction-fit connector. In addition, Dr. Ricky Maddox, who actually placed the catheter in Andrina's jugular vein, stated that he was unfamiliar with Luer-lock connectors and did not learn about them until after the incident. * * *

Baxter gave the medical community no warning at all about the need to use Luer-locks in central line applications. Thus, this issue was properly submitted to the jury. The jury's general verdict for plaintiff could have been reasonably based on a finding that Baxter's knowledge with respect to the use of friction-fit connectors was superior to that of the medical community and thus Baxter breached its duty to warn. * * *

[In pursuing a design defect claim, a plaintiff can select one of two approaches.] The first way is commonly referred to as the consumer expectation test. The second is called the risk-utility or risk-benefit test. The appellate court held that under either test, the evidence justified a finding of defective design. We agree.

1. *The Consumer Expectation Test.* In affirming the jury's verdict, the appellate court held that it was not against the manifest weight of the evidence for the jury to find that the friction-fit device failed to meet Andrina's reasonable expectation that it would function properly. Baxter contends that the health-care professional (rather than the patient) should be deemed "the consumer" for purposes of the consumer expectation test. * * *

Baxter refers us to *Shanks v. Upjohn Co.,* 835 P.2d 1189 (Alaska 1992). In that case, the court concluded that a prescription drug is defectively designed and imposes strict liability on its manufacturer if it fails to perform as safely as an ordinary doctor would expect, when used by the patient in an intended and reasonably foreseeable manner. In a footnote, the court observed:

> With certain types of prescription drugs, the role of the doctor in the decision to use a specific product is significantly reduced. Examples of such atypical prescription products include contraceptives, where the patient initiates and directs the usage, drugs administered in a clinical setting with little or no physician involvement, or drugs marketed under a strategy designed to appeal directly to the consuming public. These are areas where courts have held that manufacturers have a duty to warn patients directly. In strict liability design cases involving such products, it may be appropriate to apply the "ordinary consumer expectation" test rather than the "ordinary doctor expectation test."

Shanks, 835 P.2d at 1195 n.7.

In the case before us, the evidence showed that the decision to purchase friction-fit connectors was made exclusively by the nursing products committee at Mt. Sinai. The chairperson of that committee testified that the hospital staff relied on the product manufacturer to advise them of the proper uses for the product. The person who actually purchased the friction-fit connectors from Baxter's sales representative was not a physician and did not know that those devices should not be used in central line applications. Since the purchase of the product had little physician involvement, it would appear that the facts in this case are similar to those described in the *Shanks* footnote. In such cases, the application of the "ordinary consumer" expectation test, rather than the "ordinary physician" expectation test, is appropriate.

Moreover, in *Haudrich v. Howmedica, Inc.,* 662 N.E.2d 1248 (Ill.1996), plaintiff sought recovery on a strict liability theory against the manufacturer of a knee prosthesis that failed prematurely, causing personal injuries. The evidence was conflicting as to whether the device failed because of a design defect, a manufacturing defect, or both. In any event, this court held that the evidence was sufficient to support a finding that the plaintiff was injured by an unreasonably dangerous condition of the knee device. The court stated: "sufficient evidence was presented to support a finding that the device failed to perform in a manner reasonably expected in light of its nature and intended function and subjected the plaintiff to an unreasonable risk of harm beyond that contemplated by an ordinary person." Although the *Haudrich* court was not presented with the argument that the contemplation of the doctors, rather than the patient, should be controlling, that case clearly used the "ordinary person" standard in applying the consumer expectation test.

Andrina, who was conscious after surgery, could have reasonably expected that her IV catheter connection, if properly designed and manufactured, would be safe to use for its intended purpose. She was the person who would be harmed if the device failed. The expert testimony adduced at trial was sufficient to establish that the design of the device was defective and that this defective design caused her injury. Thus, we agree with the appellate court's conclusion that the jury's decision did not contradict the manifest weight of the evidence.

2. *The Risk–Utility Test.* Baxter also argues that the appellate court erred in finding that the jury's verdict could be supported under the risk-utility test. The appellate court held that the record supported a finding that a connector existed that would prevent foreseeable harm without hindering its function or significantly increasing its price. * * * The record in this case contains sufficient evidence to establish that the Luer-lock collar was designed to, and would have, prevented an unintentional disconnection at a cost of between three and five cents per unit. This record is sufficient to sustain a finding of unreasonable dangerousness under a risk-utility analysis. Baxter argues, however, that a risk-utility analysis is inappropriate in this case because the device in question is simple and because the risks are well-known to the medical community that uses the device. * * * Even though the doctors assumed the friction-fit device was safe to use in central line applications, the reasonable conclusion is that the danger in the friction-fit was not obvious, nor was the mechanism simple. * * *

Baxter also argues that if the risk-utility test is to be applied in the defective design analysis, then we should apply the standard defined by the new *Restatement (Third) of Torts.* That standard would allow a finding of unreasonably dangerous design only if reasonable health-care providers, knowing the foreseeable risks and therapeutic benefits, would not prescribe the device for any class of patients. Baxter did not argue this point in the trial court and it was asserted for the first time in Baxter's reply brief in the appellate court. The appellate court, however, made no reference to this argument in its opinion. * * * We decline, therefore, to address this issue. We do not foreclose the consideration of the *Restatement (Third) of Torts* standard in another case where it is raised at trial and is appropriately briefed and argued. * * *

NOTES AND QUESTIONS

1. *Technological leapfrogging.* What if the difference in cost between the two types of IV connectors was far more than a few cents? See Peter Waldman, Intravenous Bags, Tubes Redesigned for Safety, Wall St. J., Apr. 19, 2006, at D3; cf. Lars Noah, Assisted Reproductive Technologies and the Pitfalls of Unregulated Biomedical Innovation, 55 Fla. L. Rev. 603, 648 (2003) (suggesting that a "plaintiff might argue that—in light of the current state of the art—the older fertility drugs are defectively designed insofar as the risk of multifetal pregnancy now outweighs their limited benefits when compared to alternative, safer [though more expensive] ARTs"). Would the design defect claim have proceeded differently if Baxter adequately had warned hospital personnel, but they continued to purchase and use the friction-fit connector? Does Baxter have a duty only to warn of the risk of inadvertent disconnection or must it also draw attention to a superior device (and what if only a competitor sold this new and improved design)? How far might a seller's duty to educate sophisticated users of medical technologies extend (e.g., reminders about correct surgical technique)? See Marks v. OHMEDA, Inc., 871 So.2d 1148, 1156 (La.Ct.App. 2004) (sustaining the apportionment of full responsibility to the manufacturer of an anesthesia machine for carbon monoxide poisoning suffered by a patient where it had failed to warn hospital employees of this risk); cf. Wright v. Abbott Lab., Inc., 259 F.3d 1226, 1233–35 (10th Cir.2001) (concluding that the manufacturer of concentrated saline solution adequately had warned of the product's risks and did not also have to encourage hospitals to store the product separately from unconcentrated saline in order to minimize the risk of medication mix-ups); Demmler v. SmithKline Beecham Corp., 671 A.2d 1151, 1154–55 (Pa.Super.Ct.1996) (rejecting an inadequate warning claim for the failure to specify the appropriate therapy in the event that a listed side effect occurred). Chapter 7 focuses on the duty to warn.

2. *Consumer expectations vs. risk-utility balancing.* One of the most significant and controversial aspects of the new *Restatement* concerned its rejection of the warranty-inspired consumer expectations test still used by some jurisdictions in design defect cases in favor of a risk-utility test that asks whether a reasonable alternative design exists that would have avoided the plaintiff's injury. See Rest. (3d) § 2 & cmts. d–g; id. at 44–94 (providing an exhaustive survey of the case law and scholarly literature addressing this question). As mentioned in *Hansen* and elaborated below, the *Products Liability Restatement* announced a still different test for prescription drugs and devices, id. § 6(c), though a number of courts continue to use basic risk-utility balancing in such cases. See, e.g., In re Mentor Corp. ObTape Transobturator Sling Prods. Liab. Litig., 711 F.Supp.2d 1348, 1356–57, 1364–65, 1369–78 (M.D.Ga.2010) (denying the defendant's motions for summary judgment on risk-utility based design defect (and other) claims brought against the manufacturer of a suburethral sling used to treat women with stress urinary incontinence where the plaintiffs' admissible expert testimony indicated that this implanted device (a non-woven, thermally bonded polypropylene mesh tape with non-uniform pores, most smaller than 40 microns) was more prone to degradation—and to causing vaginal erosion and infection—than woven, macroporous (> 75 microns) mesh products marketed for the same use); Webster v. Pacesetter, Inc., 259 F.Supp.2d 27, 31–33 (D.D.C.2003) (holding that the plaintiff failed to establish that a reasonable alternative design existed for a pacemaker lead); Dyer v. Danek Med., Inc., 115 F.Supp.2d 732, 738–39 (N.D.Tex.2000) ("Plaintiffs have failed to clearly identify a safer design alternative [for a pedicle screw], which is a prerequisite for a finding of design defect."); Merck & Co. v. Garza, 277 S.W.3d 430, 440 (Tex.Civ.App. 2008) (rejecting design defect claim where "[t]he only proof of a safer alternative design offered by plaintiffs was a patent application for a pain-relief drug designed by Merck that combines the gastro-protective qualities of Vioxx with the cardio-protective qualities of aspirin").

In jurisdictions that retain the consumer expectations test, how would courts resolve design defect claims against sellers of prescription drugs where plaintiffs testify that, even though warned of a statistically remote risk of a serious injury, they never imagined that such a fate would befall them? Or how should fact-finders assess the reasonableness of patients' expectations about the functionality and durability of implanted devices? See Rosburg v. Minnesota Mining & Mfg. Co., 226 Cal.Rptr. 299, 303–05 (Ct.App.1986) (allowing expert testimony about the limited life expectancy of a breast implant to rebut the plaintiff's belief that the device should last a lifetime); Schindler v. Sofamor, Inc., 774 A.2d 765 (Pa.Super.Ct.2001) (spinal fixation device could not be expected to last forever in case of nonfusion); see also Stephen Smith, As Americans Age, So Do Their Implants, Boston Globe, July 18, 2005, at C1. For one unusual design defect claim premised on a seemingly trivial problem with a life-saving implant, see Bravman v. Baxter Healthcare Corp., 794 F.Supp. 96, 102 (S.D.N.Y.1992) (rejecting claim that an artificial heart valve was defective because it emitted an annoying clicking noise), aff'd, 984 F.2d 71, 76 (2d Cir.1993) ("Despite the alleged noise problems experienced by some patients, the ... heart valve has an impressive record of prolonging the lives of its recipients."), though the appellate court remanded the failure-to-warn claim for trial. See id. at 74–75; see also id. at 74 & n.2 (quoting from Edgar Allan Poe's story "The Tell–Tale Heart"); cf. Barnaby J. Feder, That Must Be Bob at the Door. I Hear His New Hip Squeaking, N.Y. Times, May 11, 2008, at A1 ("Beyond annoyance and embarrassment, many patients and their surgeons fear that the squeaky ceramic hips may signal that the joints are wearing out prematurely.... Already, dozens of patients have elected to endure subsequent surgeries to replace the noisy hips. Some have sued Stryker, the pioneer and market leader ....").

California uses both tests, depending on the complexity of the product. See Brown v. Superior Ct., 751 P.2d 470, 477–78 (Cal.1988) (explaining that the consumer expectations test has no place in cases involving prescription drugs); West v. Johnson & Johnson Prods., Inc., 220 Cal.Rptr. 437, 452 (Ct.App.1985) (allowing a plaintiff to use the consumer expectations test in a design defect claim against the manufacturer of a tampon that caused toxic shock syndrome); see also Green v. Smith & Nephew AHP, Inc., 629 N.W.2d 727 (Wis.2001) (rejecting the risk-utility standard on a design defect claim against the seller of latex gloves used by health care workers, and holding that the defendant could be held strictly liable even if it could not have known of the risk of allergic reactions at the time of sale). Other courts have recognized that the consumer expectations test is more apt for nonprescription drugs than for items requiring professional intervention. Even in cases involving OTC products, in jurisdictions that continue to use both tests for design defect, some courts allow plaintiffs to opt for a risk-utility standard because otherwise an adequate warning might defeat a design claim based on consumer expectations. See Reece v. Good Samaritan Hosp., 953 P.2d 117, 122–23 (Wash.Ct.App.1998). But see Haddix v. Playtex Family Prods. Corp., 138 F.3d 681, 684–86 (7th Cir.1998) (affirming summary judgment for a tampon manufacturer because the plaintiff could not choose to use the risk-utility test for such a simple product and her design defect claim failed under the consumer expectations test where the labeling included a clear warning of the risk of toxic shock syndrome).

3. *Contraceptive devices.* Intrauterine devices (IUDs) have triggered significant products liability litigation, including claims that certain devices suffered from design defects. See Jay M. Zitter, Annotation, Liability of Manufacturer or Seller for Injury or Death Allegedly Caused by Use of Contraceptive, 54 A.L.R.5th 1, § 20 (1997 & 2011 Supp.). The most notorious involved the Dalkon Shield, which used a multifilamented tail string that transferred bacteria into the uterus at a far higher rate than other IUDs, causing pelvic inflammatory disease and occasional septic abortions. See In re A.H. Robins Co., 880 F.2d 709 (4th Cir.1989) (summarizing the history of this litigation, and affirming a class certification order and settlement agreement); Palmer v. A.H. Robins Co., 684 P.2d 187 (Colo.1984) (affirming a judgment for one plaintiff). In the end, the Dalkon Shield caused more than 200,000 injuries and almost 20 deaths in the United States. For extended accounts of this mass tort, see Ronald J. Bacigal, The Limits of Litigation: The Dalkon Shield Controversy (1990); Georgene M. Vairo, The Dalkon Shield Claimants Trust, 61 Fordham L. Rev. 617 (1992). Subsequent lawsuits alleged design defects against the maker of the CU–7, an IUD that the FDA had regulated as a drug by virtue of the chemical action of the copper used in the device (in the years before it had the power to require premarket approval for medical devices), based on claims that the use of a polypropylene withdrawal string was more likely than a polyethylene string to retract into the uterus where it might cause a perforation or pelvic inflammatory disease. See Adams v. G.D. Searle & Co., 576 So.2d 728, 731–34 (Fla.Ct.App.1991) (reversing summary judgment for the defendant on a design defect claim).

Ezagui v. Dow Chemical Corp.

598 F.2d 727 (2d Cir.1979).

■ LUMBARD, CIRCUIT JUDGE:

* * * Parke–Davis developed Quadrigen during the 1950s as a quadruple antigen product, combining diphtheria toxoids, tetanus toxoids, Salk polio vaccine, and pertussis (whooping cough) vaccine. Vaccines confer protection against diseases by introducing antigens into the body which stimulate the production of immunizing antibodies. This process occurs when lymphocytes, cells contained in the lymph glands, absorb the antigens and produce an antitoxin against the particular disease. With some infectious diseases, such as diphtheria and tetanus, it has been possible to isolate the soluble toxin or poison excreted by these bacteria and to inactivate this toxin with formaldehyde, thereby converting the toxin into what is called a toxoid. This toxoid helps immunize the body against disease by stimulating the production of antibodies, but the toxoid will not cause disease because it has lost its poisonous qualities.

By contrast, the bacterial organism which causes pertussis is so complex as to make impossible the isolation and deactivation of the toxin or poison. Since the ingredient in the pertussis bacteria which stimulates the production of protective antibodies has not been isolated, Parke–Davis and other drug companies have manufactured pertussis vaccine consisting of whole pertussis bacteria, treated to reduce their propensity to cause the disease. Because this treatment cannot completely deactivate the relevant toxin, reactions to pertussis vaccine are more frequent than are reactions to other vaccines.

In the early 1940s, drug manufacturers developed a method for combining pertussis vaccine with diphtheria and tetanus toxoids in a three-way antigen product known as "DTP" and marketed by Parke–Davis under the trade name "Triogen." This combination allowed one shot to do the work of three and was regarded as an important advance. This three-in-one combination produced no apparent increase in toxicity or reactivity.

In 1953 Dr. Jonas Salk developed a polio vaccine. Following commercial development of the Salk Vaccine, Parke–Davis decided to add the new polio vaccine to its "Triogen" product in order to develop a four-way antigen product, whereby one shot would protect against polio as well as diphtheria, tetanus, and pertussis. This new product Parke–Davis marketed under the trade name Quadrigen, beginning in July 1959.

Combining the older Triogen product with the new Salk polio vaccine, however, required a change in preservative which many investigators later believed caused the marked increase in adverse medical reactions experienced with the use of Quadrigen. All vaccines packed in multidose vials require a preservative to maintain their sterility. Prior to the development of the Salk polio vaccine, the universal preservative was merthiolate. Although originally intended to maintain sterility, merthiolate was later shown to act as a stabilizer of the vaccine, decreasing toxicity but maintaining potency. Merthiolate, however, adversely affected the polio vaccine.

Accordingly, Parke–Davis selected a different preservative for use in Quadrigen. This preservative was benzethonium chloride, or Phemerol, which was Parke–Davis' trade name for this product. Later research, however, indicated that use of Phemerol caused certain endotoxins in the pertussis vaccine to leak out from the bacterial cell into the fluid which was injected. One of these endotoxins, the lipopolysaccharide, was known to cause a fever which could lead to convulsions and brain damage, as occurred in this case. From the time when they first began to investigate the marked increase in adverse reactions reported by doctors using Quadrigen [prior to the occurrence of this injury], until very recently, Parke–Davis research personnel have been on record as believing that the leakage of these endotoxins was responsible for the measured increase in adverse medical reactions associated with Quadrigen, an increase which finally led to the withdrawal of Quadrigen from the market in November 1962. (The return in 1962 to the older three-in-one product, administered with a separate polio vaccine, reduced the incidence of adverse medical reactions to their pre-Quadrigen levels.) * * *

A jury could reasonably conclude from this evidence that the pertussis vaccine is capable of causing encephalopathy such as that experienced by Mark Ezagui, and that the combination in Quadrigen of the pertussis vaccine with other chemicals materially increased this risk. * * *

PROBLEM #10. *COMBINATION VACCINES*

A researcher in England has suggested that the measles, mumps, and rubella (MMR) vaccine causes autism (a serious neurological disorder), hypothesizing that this represents a synergistic effect when the components are used in combination. See Andrew J. Wakefield et al., Ileal–Lymphoid–Nodular Hyperplasia, Non–Specific Colitis, and Pervasive Developmental Disorder in Children, 351 Lancet 637 (1998). Two years later, the CBS news program "60 Minutes" aired the story. Subsequent research found no connection. See David Brown, Experts Find No Vaccine–Autism Link, Wash. Post, May 19, 2004, at A2 (reporting that the Institute of Medicine also discounted another theory, which had implicated the preservative thimerosal widely used until recently in childhood vaccines); see also John F. Burns, British Council Bars Doctor Who Linked Vaccine with Autism, N.Y. Times, May 25, 2010, at A4; Kate Kelland, Lancet Retracts Paper Linking Vaccine to Autism, Wash. Post, Feb. 3, 2010, at A2. Assume just for the sake of argument that MMR causes autism at a rate of one–in–10,000 children receiving the vaccine (and that using each of the components separately at six month intervals would not reduce their effectiveness). The manufacturers respond that the single combined dose is more convenient (and therefore makes it more likely that kids will get vaccinated). How would a court engage in risk-utility balancing in a case such as this?

NOTES AND QUESTIONS

1. *Childhood vaccines.* The claim in *Ezagui* involved an unusual interaction between the pertussis component and a preservative. More frequently, plaintiffs have assailed the design of the whole-cell pertussis vaccine in isolation. The plaintiffs in these cases have suggested that "fractionated" and "acellular" forms of the pertussis vaccine represented reasonable alternative designs that would not have caused their injuries even though neither form was approved by the FDA during the relevant times. Most courts granted the manufacturer summary judgment on these design defect claims. See Ackley v. Wyeth Lab., Inc., 919 F.2d 397, 398–404 (6th Cir. 1990); id. at 401 ("Without an FDA license to produce another design, Wyeth was legally prohibited from distributing either a fractionated cell or an acellular vaccine ...."); Pease v. American Cyanamid Co., 795 F.Supp. 755, 757, 760 (D.Md.1992) (explaining that the FDA did not approve an acellular version until 1991, and then only as a booster because of doubts about its effectiveness in infants); White v. Wyeth Lab., Inc., 533 N.E.2d 748, 753 (Ohio 1988); see also Arthur Allen, Whooping Cough Makes a Comeback, Wash. Post, Sept. 28, 2010, at E1 ("In the view of some pertussis experts, the [acellular] vaccines in use since the mid–1990s aren't as effective as some of the vaccines they replaced."); Gardiner Harris, Vaccine Cleared Again as Autism Culprit, N.Y. Times, Aug. 26, 2011, at A19 ("In retrospect, the whole-cell pertussis vaccine may have played little role in the underlying illness in many of these children [with Dravet syndrome, a severe form of epilepsy,] other than to serve as its first trigger."). See generally Francis M. Dougherty, Annotation, Products Liability: Pertussis Vaccine Manufacturers, 57 A.L.R.4th 911 (1987 & 2011 Supp.). Nonetheless, a few courts handling such cases have allowed the design defect issue to go to the jury. See Graham v. Wyeth Lab., 666 F.Supp. 1483, 1496–98 (D.Kan.1987); Toner v. Lederle Lab., 732 P.2d 297, 308 (Idaho 1987). Recall from Chapter 5(A) that Congress displaced much of this tort litigation when it enacted the National Childhood Vaccine Injury Act.

2. *Valuing convenience.* Assume that the elevated risk of injury in *Ezagui* had been less serious—can one justify any increase in risk that does not enhance the therapeutic effect of the product but simply reduces the number of injections required? Cf. Rob Stein, Vaccine Promises More Protection, Fewer Shots: FDA Approves Round of Three Inoculations That Protects Infants Against Five Diseases, Wash. Post, Dec. 17, 2002, at A2 (reporting that the development of low fevers represented the sole additional side effect). What if an oral dosage reformulation eliminated the need to provide the vaccine by injection? Cf. Tricia Bishop, Finding Ways to Make Drugs Go Down Easier: From Lollipops to Nasal Sprays, Companies Develop New Delivery Systems for Old Medicines, Balt. Sun, Aug. 27, 2006, at

1C; Justin Gillis, FDA Approves Inhalable Insulin, Wash. Post, Jan. 28, 2006, at A1 (explaining that the agency's "decision confronts millions of Americans—diabetics make up 7 percent of the population—with a complicated new strategic problem, requiring them to figure out how much long-range risk they're willing to incur for the convenience, and possibly greater disease control, of using inhaled insulin"). Conversely, alternatives to oral formulations avoid the digestive track, which may allow for lower dosages and fewer side effects. See Mary Duffy, Patch Raises New Hope for Beating Depression, N.Y. Times, Dec. 3, 2002, at F7. Pharmaceutical manufacturers often try to design time-released or other dosage forms as easier for patients than having to remember to take several pills during the course of a day. See Shankar Vedantam, Implants May Reshape Schizophrenia Treatment, Wash. Post, Nov. 16, 2002, at A1 (reporting that long-acting antipsychotics delivered by injection could reduce problems with patient non-compliance); see also Alicia Ault, Two for Whom? Combo Pills May Help Patients—and Are Sure to Help Drug Firms, Wash. Post, Feb. 17, 2004, at F1; Ranit Mishori, Coming Soon: New Ways to Take Drugs, Without Needles or Pills, Wash. Post, Feb. 8, 2005, at F1. More convenient dosage forms may, however, present additional risks—for instance, increases in skin temperature may cause transdermal patches to release dangerously elevated doses of the active ingredient. See Dawn Fallik, Experts: Patches + Heat = Danger, Phila. Inquirer, Mar. 5, 2006, at A18 (describing some of the resulting litigation).

3. *High-dose estrogen contraceptives.* Oral contraceptives contain varying levels of estrogen. In the early 1970s, scientists found that high-dose versions posed a greater risk of cerebral thrombosis. Although the higher-dose versions were thought to be no more effective at preventing pregnancy than the available lower-dose versions, doctors sometimes prescribed the higher-dose versions to patients who suffered "break-through bleeding" when using the lower-dose products, a bothersome side effect that may reduce patient compliance with daily dosing directions and, thereby, reduce effectiveness. Courts typically left an analysis of this trade-off to juries. See Brochu v. Ortho Pharm. Corp., 642 F.2d 652, 654–55 & n.4 (1st Cir.1981); Ortho Pharm. Corp. v. Heath, 722 P.2d 410, 414–16 (Colo.1986); Glassman v. Wyeth Lab., 606 N.E.2d 338, 340–41, 343 (Ill.App.Ct.1992). As it turns out, lower dosage formulations are less effective even when taken as prescribed. See Anna W. Mathews, FDA Mulls Birth–Control Standards, Wall St. J., Jan. 19, 2007, at B5; see also Michael Mason, Pressing to Look Closer at Blood Clots and the Pill, N.Y. Times, Feb. 13, 2007, at F5 (reporting that "third-generation" low-dose contraceptives may pose heightened risks); U.S. Orders Review of Risks of Some Birth Control Pills, N.Y. Times, June 1, 2011, at B5 (reporting that a pair of recent studies found up to a threefold greater risk of blood clots in women taking drospirenone (e.g., Yaz®) than other oral contraceptives). In the event of a contraceptive efficacy failure, could a woman assert a "wrongful birth" claim against the manufacturer (as courts have allowed, though typically with limited damages, in the event of negligently performed sterilization procedures)? What about the design choices involving products that halt the menstrual cycle altogether? See Rob Stein, Birth Control Pill That Stops Periods Wins FDA Approval, Wash. Post, May 23, 2007, at A1 (Lybrel®); see also Shari Roan, Now, a Birth Control Bonanza, L.A. Times, July 10, 2006, at F1 (describing continuous dosing schedules and implants with the same effect); cf. Anne M. Chaker, Doctors Back off Birth–Control Patch, Wall St. J., Nov. 22, 2005, at D1 (reporting that the FDA has added a warning about elevated estrogen levels associated with a once-a-week transdermal product); Gardiner Harris & Alex Berenson, Drug Makers Near Old Goal: A Legal Shield, N.Y. Times, Apr. 6, 2008, at A1 ("More than 3,000 women and their families have sued Johnson & Johnson, asserting that users of the Ortho Evra patch suffered heart attacks, strokes and, in 40 cases, death.").

4. *Complexities with risk-utility balancing*. First, how would a jury manage to determine whether any existing (much less theoretical) alternative designs would provide at least the same therapeutic benefit in every case that a physician may encounter? Second, how would a jury assess the risk profile of an alternative treatment? Although they may be able to compare the relative risks of existing products, it is impossible for scientists, let alone courts, to predict with any accuracy the likely safety profile of purely theoretical alternative molecular structures. (In contrast to durable goods where engineers might opine that a particular design modification could improve product safety, it is impossible to anticipate the likely safety and effectiveness of a new molecular entity, which is why the FDA requires extensive clinical trials.) Third, how would a jury decide, for example, which of the following effects of an alternative design would justify a finding that an existing design was defective: (1) reducing by 50% a one–in–100,000 chance of a serious acute side effect such as anaphylactic shock, (2) eliminating an unquantified risk of chronic disease such as cancer (extrapolated from animal studies) that the FDA concluded justified only a precautionary statement in labeling, (3) eliminating a one–in–1,000 risk of blindness, or (4) eliminating a common (one–in–five chance) but nonserious side effect such as nausea or drowsiness? These are difficult judgments routinely faced by the FDA and medical professionals, and they will depend on the countervailing benefits of the drug or device and the needs of a particular patient. See Grundberg v. Upjohn Co., 813 P.2d 89, 99 (Utah 1991) ("To determine whether a drug's benefit outweighs its risk is inherently complex because of the manufacturer's conscious design choices regarding the numerous chemical properties of the product and their relationship to the vast physiologic idiosyncracies of each consumer for whom the drug is designed.").

Williams v. Ciba–Geigy Corp.

686 F.Supp. 573 (W.D.La.), aff'd mem., 864 F.2d 789 (5th Cir.1988).

■ VERON, DISTRICT JUDGE:

In this diversity matter under Louisiana law, the plaintiff Carolyn Sue Williams has sued the defendant Ciba–Geigy Corporation in negligence and products liability seeking damages arising out of Stephens–Johnson syndrome, a serious skin condition known to be an adverse reaction to the defendant's product Tegretol (carbamazepine), a prescription drug the plaintiff had taken under a physician's supervision. The defendant moved for summary judgment * * * *

[I]t is presumptively inappropriate for a jury to apply the pure risk-utility test of "unreasonably dangerous per se" [i.e., defective even in the absence of a reasonable alternative design] to a known and warned-of risk of a prescription drug. Such risks have already been considered in the arduous risk-utility scrutiny of the expert Food and Drug Administration's approval procedures. The plaintiff desirous of having such a risk submitted to a jury must affirmatively show the propriety of the court's so doing. Rather than simply permitting juries to apply, haphazardly and case-by-case, the risk-utility test whenever harm results, the court must require, as a part of the plaintiff's burden of producing evidence, an articulable basis for disregarding the FDA's determination that the drug should be available. For instance, a fact question may arise where the plaintiff produces evidence tending to show that FDA approval was based on erroneous data or on an assumption that the incidence of harmful effects would be significantly lower than the actual incidence the plaintiff can objectively demonstrate. Or, the plaintiff may make out a fact question by producing evidence tending to show that notwithstanding the utility of the drug, the qualitative and quantitative harmful effects, although known and warned of, are such that reasonable minds could conclude that the FDA manifestly erred in its finding that the societal benefits of access to the drug are not outweighed by the risks. * * *

The defendant has submitted a copy of the package insert provided with Tegretol, a copy of the Tegretol entry in the *Physician's Desk Reference* (*PDR*), and the affidavits of five of the plaintiff's treating physicians, all of whom consider the warnings of Stevens–Johnson syndrome adequate and four of whom further consider Tegretol not to be "defective." The plaintiff has submitted as her opposition exhibits bibliographical listings accompanied by abstracts of the contents of each listing * * * * There is no evidence that the FDA's initial or continuing permission to market Tegretol is based on erroneous data or assumptions. Nor does the record reflect what the condition was, in the plaintiff's case, that caused Tegretol to be prescribed.

Tegretol is effective for two basic medical purposes: for the control of epileptic symptoms including psychomotor and grand mal seizures, and for relief of trigeminal neuralgia. * * * [A] layperson might define "trigeminal neuralgia" as suddenly recurring or intensifying severe pain focused roughly in the center of the head below the brain.

No evidence in the record tends to impugn the utility of Tegretol. There is no showing that any drug other than carbamazepine is effective in treating trigeminal neuralgia. Tegretol is indicated only for those sufferers of psychomotor and grand mal seizures who do not respond to, or are endangered by, more conventional anticonvulsants which have serious side effects of their own (one of the most common is phenobarbitol). One of the abstracts submitted by plaintiff outlines dangers of treating liver-damaged patients with carbamazepine, especially in conjunction with other hepatotoxic drugs, however the "[a]uthors stress that physicians should not be discouraged from using carbamazepine as a valuable anticonvulsant." The consequences of the nonavailability of Tegretol for those patients who suffer serious seizures, which can be fatal if not controlled, but who cannot take other anticonvulsants, would be grave indeed.

Proper "risk" evidence for purposes of the risk-utility test is not a mere roster of isolated incidents. Rather, "risk" in a vaccine or pharmaceutical case, as with other cases, concerns not only the qualitative harmful effect, but also the quantitative harm or "incidence" of serious adverse effects, that is, the ratio of instances of harm compared to the total use or consumption of the product. Although the danger may be devastating to those individuals who experience the worst effects, the incidence may be statistically small and the composite risk may not outweigh the value of a high utility drug. There is no question that the qualitative harmful effect of carbamazepine for some individuals can be devastating, indeed fatal, especially where interaction with other prescription drugs is a factor. Many of the possible non-fatal side effects are serious and loathsome conditions, some reversible, some not.

The quantitative risk evidence, however, is very scant. The vast majority of the abstracts submitted by plaintiff simply attribute side effects in particular cases to carbamazepine. Many of the side effects attributed to the drug result from other anticonvulsants as well. * * * [Reported toxic effects] include non-serious effects attributed to Tegretol such as drowsiness, dizziness, unsteadiness, and nausea. A high incidence of *overall* toxic effects in a strong drug such as an anticonvulsant for epilepsy is of little probative value in regard to risk-utility. Cancer chemotherapy may well entail a 100% incidence of relatively serious toxic effects, yet its utility undoubtedly outweighs the *certainty* of the poisoning, nausea, hair loss, and weight loss involved. * * * [A]ssuming the approximately 10–12% risk of severe side effects [in patients given carbamapezine], where doctors have prescribed this drug for patients with the indicated severe and life-threatening conditions and no alternative hope for treatment, reasonable minds could not find this incidence too high.

Finally, * * * [i]n the case of prescription drugs which are unavailable to the consumer except by prescription from the treating physician, warning information listed in the *PDR* should be considered as part and parcel to the product. In this case, the package insert contains substantially or identically the same warnings and information listed in the *PDR*. These warnings are very clear, frank, and comprehensive about the dangers of the drug and ways of reducing the risk. These warnings so greatly diminish the product's danger-in-fact that for this reason alone no reasonable trier of fact could conclude that this highly utile medicine is unreasonably dangerous per se. * * *

Restatement (Third) of the Law of Torts: Products Liability § 6 (American Law Inst. 1998):

(c) A prescription drug or medical device is not reasonably safe due to defective design if the foreseeable risks of harm posed by the drug or medical device are sufficiently great in relation to its foreseeable therapeutic benefits that reasonable health-care providers, knowing of such foreseeable risks and therapeutic benefits, would not prescribe the drug or medical device for any class of patients.

Comment f. *Manufacturers' liability for defectively designed prescription drugs and medical devices*. Subsection (c) reflects the judgment that, as long as a given drug or device provides net benefits for a class of patients, it should be available to them, accompanied by appropriate warnings and instructions. Learned intermediaries must generally be relied upon to see that the right drugs and devices reach the right patients. However, when a drug or device provides net benefits to no class of patients—when reasonable, informed health-care providers would not prescribe it to any class of patients—then the design of the product is defective and the manufacturer should be subject to liability for the harm caused.

A prescription drug or device manufacturer defeats a plaintiff's design claim by establishing one or more contexts in which its product would be prescribed by reasonable, informed health-care providers. That some individual providers do, in fact, prescribe defendant's product does not in itself suffice to defeat the plaintiff's claim. Evidence regarding the actual conduct of health-care providers, while relevant and admissible, is not necessarily controlling. The issue is whether, objectively viewed, reasonable providers, knowing of the foreseeable risks and benefits of the drug or medical device, would prescribe it for any class of patients. Given this very demanding objective standard, liability is likely to be imposed only under unusual circumstances. The court has the responsibility to determine when the plaintiff has introduced sufficient evidence so that reasonable persons could conclude that plaintiff has met this demanding standard.

An illustration accompanying comment f was inspired by the following unusual decision.

Tobin v. Astra Pharmaceutical Products, Inc.

993 F.2d 528 (6th Cir.1993).

■ GUY, CIRCUIT JUDGE:

* * * In 1986, Kathy Tobin was 19 years old and pregnant with twins. Her expected date of delivery was in early April 1987. Other than a mitral valve prolapse, or heart murmur, a rather common finding in reproductive-age women, Tobin was a healthy young woman. In mid-October 1986, Tobin was hospitalized for dehydration. She was having difficulty keeping down food and fluids and required hydration. Her condition was diagnosed

as viral in origin. She was released after a few days and her pregnancy progressed. In January 1987, Tobin was admitted to the hospital for management of preterm labor. She was given an injection of magnesium sulphate and then was placed on an oral maintenance dose of ritodrine. Dosage levels varied, being increased when contractions returned.

Tobin testified that after each dose of ritodrine her pulse would race and her heart felt as if "it was going to jump out of my skin;" her face would also flush and her hands and legs would swell. She was advised that these symptoms were normal side effects of ritodrine. On March 9, 1987, Tobin's obstetricians reduced the dosage because of her rapid heart rate. On March 16, 1987, Tobin informed her doctors that she could not breathe when lying down, and she was told to further reduce the ritodrine dosage. At 1:30 a.m. on March 17, she was admitted to the hospital with symptoms of tachypnea (rapid breathing), dyspnea (shortness of breath), and a gallop rhythm of the heart. At this time, it also was noted that Tobin had a grade I/IV systolic murmur of the heart. X-rays revealed that she had pulmonary edema (fluid in the lungs) and cardiomegaly (enlargement of the heart) caused by congestive heart failure. An electrocardiogram revealed advanced dilated cardiomyopathy. Ritodrine was discontinued, and that afternoon plaintiff delivered healthy twins having a gestational age of 37 weeks.

On March 20, Tobin was discharged from the hospital with instructions to follow up with a cardiologist. The next day she was readmitted for treatment of congestive heart failure, cardiomyopathy, and pulmonary edema. After five days in the hospital, she was again released. She was readmitted on April 10, and on April 15 a mechanical heart, or ventricular assist device, was inserted until a donated heart for a heart transplant could be found. On April 16, Tobin underwent a heart transplant.

Plaintiff filed suit against Duphar B.V., the corporation in the Netherlands that manufactures ritodrine, and against Astra Pharmaceutical, Duphar's United States distributor. After removal to federal court on diversity grounds, the district court granted Duphar's motion to dismiss for lack of personal jurisdiction. Plaintiff proceeded against Astra. After a two-week trial, the jury returned a verdict in favor of the plaintiff. The jury awarded Tobin approximately $4.5 million, finding Astra liable on the basis of defective design and failure to warn for the conditions that led to her heart transplant. The district court denied Astra's motion for j.n.o.v. or in the alternative for a new trial, and Astra timely appealed. * * *

Ritodrine belongs to a class of compounds known as betamimetics. These compounds mimic adrenaline, a natural hormone. A betamimetic, or beta-receptor agonist, exerts its effect by stimulating beta-adrenergic receptors. There are at least two sub-groups of beta receptors, beta–1 and beta–2. The heart contains beta–1 receptors, which, when stimulated, result in an increased heart rate and a rise in systolic pressure concomitant with a decrease in diastolic pressure. The force with which the heart contracts also increases. Stimulation of beta–2 receptors inhibits contractility of smooth muscle, such as that contained in the uterus.

Ritodrine, which at low doses preferentially affects beta–2 receptors, is administered to pregnant women to arrest premature labor. The drug, however, may also exert pronounced beta–1 effects. Ritodrine may unmask occult heart conditions and is specifically contraindicated when a patient suffers from cardiac disease.

Both plaintiff's causation expert, Dr. Waller, and defendant's causation expert, Dr. O'Connell, testified that Tobin's viral infection in October 1986 resulted in myocarditis, an inflammation of the heart muscle. Dr. O'Connell testified that approximately 70 percent of us have been infected by a virus that causes myocarditis and that at least 50 percent of us actually have had the virus infect our heart, and therefore, by definition, have had myocarditis. But Dr. O'Connell testified that most people recover without ever having known it. Dr. Waller's main causation theory was that Tobin would have recovered from the myocarditis, just like the vast majority of people, if it had not been for the added strain of the ritodrine. Dr. O'Connell, on the other hand, testified that plaintiff's cardiomyopathy could be explained by the myocarditis and her twin pregnancy which placed additional strain on her heart. Dr. Waller also felt that there was evidence that ritodrine had a direct effect on plaintiff's heart. * * *

Under Kentucky law, the test for whether a product is in a defective condition and unreasonably dangerous to the user is whether an ordinarily prudent manufacturer, being fully aware of the risks, would have placed the product on the market. Plaintiff argues that the only way to decide whether an ordinarily prudent manufacturer would place a product on the market is to balance the product's risks, its harmful side effects, against its benefits. Defendant argues that Kentucky has never adopted the risk/benefit analysis proffered by plaintiff. * * *

In a nutshell, plaintiff claims that oral ritodrine is bereft of benefits as far as improving neonatal outcome.[8] Weighing no benefits against the serious risks posed by the drug and suffered by the plaintiff, it is clear, plaintiff asserts, that the risks outweigh the benefits and thus no "ordinarily prudent manufacturer" would put the drug on the market. Astra maintains that oral ritodrine is effective in prolonging pregnancy, and therefore in improving neonatal outcome, and that the risks to maternal and fetal health associated with oral ritodrine are outweighed by the benefits of reducing neonatal morbidity and mortality. Astra also maintains that, because of FDA approval, ritodrine's effectiveness is not open to question.

Plaintiff's expert in this area was Dr. Mortensen. Dr. Mortensen, a pediatrician with a master's degree in pharmacology and trained in toxicology, reviewed the test results that were submitted to the FDA with the New Drug Application in 1974. Dr. Mortensen also reviewed several articles discussing betamimetic drugs in general and ritodrine in specific. * * * Dr.

8. Plaintiff does acknowledge that there may be some benefit in improving the overall quality of life for the mother during the remainder of the pregnancy by avoiding repetitive hospitalization.

Mortensen has experience in clinical studies on the efficacy of drugs. Her testimony centered on the testing procedures used in various studies of the efficacy of ritodrine and the interpretation of the test results. Her testimony on the clinical studies investigating ritodrine was properly allowed.

Before addressing the arguments concerning efficacy, we must first address whether plaintiff should have been allowed to litigate the efficacy issue at all. Defendant argues that "[p]laintiff should not have been permitted to litigate this issue, because it is a mockery of the scientific analysis employed by the FDA and the Advisory Committee which conclusively found that ritodrine was efficacious." We reject the argument that FDA approval preempts state product liability claims based on design defect. * * *

FDA approval is evidence which the jury may consider in reaching its verdict. The jury may weigh FDA approval as it sees fit, especially in a case where the plaintiff has presented evidence to support an articulable basis for disregarding an FDA finding—in this case the finding that ritodrine was effective. Tobin presented an articulable basis for disregarding the FDA's finding that ritodrine was effective in improving neonatal outcome: the individual studies relied on by the FDA were insufficient to support a finding of efficacy as found by the FDA Advisory Committee, and the pooled data requested by the Advisory Committee w[ere] statistically invalid.

To understand the arguments of the parties concerning ritodrine's effectiveness, it is necessary to review the New Drug Application that was submitted to the FDA and the results of the required clinical trials, along with subsequent articles that have been published discussing ritodrine. Approval of a new drug by the FDA requires a showing of substantial evidence of efficacy based upon adequate and well-controlled studies. The required clinical studies on ritodrine consisted of Phase I (16 studies in healthy patients to determine safety), Phase II (5 studies in preterm labor patients to determine efficacy), and Phase III (11 studies in preterm labor patients comparing ritodrine patients to non-ritodrine controls to determine safety and efficacy).

The clinical trials were designed to measure a gain in days in the length of pregnancy as a measure of efficacy under the assumption that any increase in the gestational period would reduce neonatal morbidity and mortality. The Phase III studies consisted of tests of oral ritodrine's effectiveness based on three separate testing procedures: a placebo series, in which oral ritodrine was compared to the use of a placebo; an ethanol series comparing ritodrine to the use of ethanol; and a series referred to as the "Creasy studies," in which all patients were treated with injections of intramuscular ritodrine and then half received oral maintenance doses of ritodrine while the other half received placebos. In the Creasy studies, any recurrences of premature labor were treated with injections of intramuscular ritodrine.

After the data from these studies w[ere] submitted to the FDA, the FDA Advisory Committee on Fertility and Maternal Health Drugs found that the required clinical trials failed to demonstrate efficacy. Specifically, "the tenor of the committee was that there was not substantial data to support the efficacy of ritodrine for the treatment of premature labor." The Advisory Committee found that three of the Phase III placebo-controlled studies were flawed because they included women who were not actually in preterm labor. Because the remaining individual studies did not have a sufficient number of patients to establish statistical significance regarding improvement in neonatal outcome, the Advisory Committee requested the data be pooled and resubmitted. The initial data w[ere] presented in terms of gain in days; it did not include statistics on neonatal outcome or mortality. The Advisory Committee requested that, when the data w[ere] resubmitted, it should include such information. The manufacturer was asked to pool the data from all the studies for an all-patient analysis; stratify all of the patients by gestational age; and analyze neonatal mortality, birth weight, and the incidence of respiratory distress syndrome.

Dr. Peter, who participated in the proceedings before the FDA, testified at trial that this pooled data do[] not represent statistically valid results. * * * Dr. Little of the committee commented that "obviously, it is not reasonable to pool data." Yet, on the basis of the originally submitted data, which the Advisory Committee had found did not contain substantial evidence to support a finding of efficacy, and the newly reworked data, the committee recommended approval.

The FDA made its own determination regarding efficacy. FDA regulations require that efficacy be established by "at least two 'adequate and well-controlled' studies." Warner–Lambert Co. v. Heckler, 787 F.2d 147, 151 (3d Cir.1986). The FDA determined that four of the Phase III studies met this test, and approved ritodrine in 1980. The four studies are referred to by the names of the project leaders: Fuchs, Barden, Creasy, and Sivasambo. Plaintiff introduced evidence regarding the methodology and conclusions of each study.

In the Fuchs study, the control group of mothers were treated with intravenous ethanol and no follow-up, while ritodrine patients were given initial intravenous doses of ritodrine and follow-up oral doses. The control group was further along in gestation based on each mother's last menstrual period, and the group was found to be in more advanced labor, in that they were more dilated, than the ritodrine group. The Sivasambo study compared ritodrine to librium, which according to recent studies actually increases uterine activity. The Creasy study, described above, did not have an adequate control group, in that all patients were given intramuscular injections of ritodrine at the onset of premature labor and again if contractions returned. In a later publication, Dr. Creasy stated that "further studies have not proved that oral maintenance will decrease the incidence of preterm birth.... [T]hey do show that such an approach will decrease the need for repetitive hospitalization, thus improving the overall quality of life for the remainder of the pregnancy." The final study relied on by the FDA, the Barden study, involved a total of only 25 patients—some given oral ritodrine and others given a placebo.

Astra's evidence focused on the effect of oral ritodrine in prolonging the term of pregnancy, and then separately showed that extending the term of pregnancy improves neonatal outcome. Plaintiff refuted this claim with evidence that, while ritodrine may produce a short-term gain in prolonging pregnancy, there is no evidence of improved neonatal outcome. Plaintiff introduced articles written after the FDA approval. * * *

We do not sit to review the findings of the FDA; our only role in this appeal is to decide if there was sufficient evidence on which the jury could base its verdict. Plaintiff introduced evidence, through the cross-examination of Astra officials, that a reasonably prudent manufacturer would not market ritodrine if the evidence of its efficacy was inconclusive. Plaintiff also introduced sufficient evidence regarding the various clinical studies concerning the efficacy of ritodrine. The jury found that ritodrine, as manufactured and marketed by Astra, was in a defective condition and unreasonably dangerous to plaintiff. We find that there was sufficient evidence before the jury to conclude that a prudent manufacturer knowing all the risks would not market ritodrine. * * *

NOTES AND QUESTIONS

1. *Not ready for prime time?* The court's opinion in *Tobin* is remarkable. First, although it refers to later studies, the court does not base its decision on post-approval data; instead, it allows a jury to conclude (with the assistance, of course, of the parties' experts) that the FDA blew it by using a surrogate marker (i.e., gestational age) for a clinical end-point (i.e., neonatal health) and by accepting a sub-group analysis using clinical trials that the agency's advisory committee viewed as methodologically flawed. (Does it matter that the FDA had not approved any other tocolytic agents as of 1993, or that neonatal intensive care was more primitive when it approved ritodrine in 1980?) In effect, despite its protestations to the contrary, the court holds that Astra should not have begun marketing even after it received FDA approval. See Lars Noah, This Is Your Products Liability Restatement on Drugs, 74 Brook. L. Rev. 839, 870 n.132 (2009) ("I fail to see how this involves any less an exercise in 'rank speculation' than trying to decide whether the FDA might approve a hypothesized alternative design . . . ; indeed, absent some confession of error by the agency, . . . it seems even less appropriate to invite a jury to engage in this sort of reassessment . . . ."). Second, the court marginalizes ritodrine's evident effectiveness in reducing the need for repeated hospitalizations during the pregnancy. Why doesn't this count? In effect, the court turns a complex risk-utility judgment (using data from less than ideal clinical trials) into a no-brainer by allowing the jury to conclude that the drug is totally ineffective (meaning that any risk makes the product's design defective). Although this patient suffered a severe injury that may have resulted from use of the drug, the labeling did warn of some cardiac risks, and the court focuses only on utility. Third, the court gives exaggerated significance to the comments of the advisory committee, disregarding the fact that the FDA had undertaken a lengthy internal review and had no obligation to abide by the committee's recommendations. In 1992, based on newly published research, another FDA advisory committee concluded that oral ritodrine lacked effectiveness at current dosages. See id. at 871 n.135; cf. Deborah Kotz, Drug Aims to Reduce Risk of Premature Labor, Boston Globe, Feb. 5, 2011, at A5 (reporting the much anticipated FDA approval of an injectable synthetic progesterone product); Alison Young, FDA Flags Risks on Pregnancy Drug: Strongest Safety Warning Issued for Popular Terbutaline, USA Today, Feb. 18, 2011, at 3A (reporting that the agency mandated a black box warning of potentially fatal cardiac risks associated with the off-label use of terbutaline to prevent pre-term labor, adding that the government doubts its efficacy).

2. *Time dimension and the state-of-the-art.* As explained at greater length in Chapter 7(A), product manufacturers need only warn of risks "knowable" at the time of sale. Similarly, their obligation to adopt reasonable alternative designs only applies to those redesigns knowable at the time of sale (a.k.a., "the state-of-the-art"). Although a complex issue even in run-of-the-mill products liability cases, it becomes especially tricky with technologically sophisticated products subject to lengthy premarket review by administrative agencies. If risk information comes to light late in the process, sellers generally still can make labeling modifications before sale, but designs become fixed earlier in the R & D process. If the test asks about the availability of a reasonable alternative design, should the question focus on risks and redesigns knowable at the time when the seller (1) discovers the compound, (2) begins clinical trials, (3) files an application with the FDA, (4) receives agency approval, (5) introduces the product into commercial distribution, or (6) sells the unit that injures the plaintiff? Recall that the investigational process unavoidably continues after product approval. Should the test ask instead about the state-of-the-art at the time of the plaintiff's injury, or perhaps even at the time of trial? Do manufacturers ask for trouble when they introduce purportedly "new and improved" line extensions, especially if they continue to sell an old stand-by?

3. *Rest. (2d) § 402A comment k vs. Rest. (3d) § 6(c).* As discussed in the previous chapter, some courts interpreted comment k as extending blanket immunity from strict products liability claims against sellers of prescription drugs and medical devices, but this did not foreclose design defect claims sounding in negligence (or perhaps even strict liability design defect claims if the product was not properly prepared or labeled). The new *Restatement* offers a unitary standard for judging design defect claims in such cases. If you represented a defendant in a jurisdiction that has not yet sided with either formulation, which would you advocate? Does the apparent mischief in *Tobin* color your assessment? Compare Wimbush v. Wyeth, 619 F.3d 632, 641–46 (6th Cir.2010) (reversing summary judgment granted to the defendant on the basis of implied preemption of a negligence claim brought on behalf of a patient who died from primary pulmonary hypertension asserting that the manufacturer should never have brought the diet drug Redux® (dexfenfluramine) to market notwithstanding receipt of FDA approval with labeling that warned of precisely this risk); id. at 645 (favorably citing *Tobin* as involving a case of "pre-approval design defect"), with Madsen v.

American Home Prods. Corp., 477 F.Supp.2d 1025, 1034, 1037 (E.D.Mo. 2007) (assuming that the Iowa Supreme Court would use section 6 to resolve informational and design defect claims against the manufacturer of fenfluramine and dexfenfluramine, and granting the defendant summary judgment on a design defect claim in light of uncontested testimony that some physicians would have continued prescribing these withdrawn diet drugs to some of their obese patients even after learning of the risk of valvular heart disease). Courts have not exactly rushed to embrace the *Restatement*'s new test for design defects involving prescription drugs and devices. See, e.g., Doe v. Solvay Pharm., Inc., 350 F.Supp.2d 257, 266–68 (D.Me.2004) (quoting § 6, but retaining a risk-utility standard); Bryant v. Hoffman–La Roche, Inc., 585 S.E.2d 723, 727 (Ga.Ct.App.2003); Freeman v. Hoffman–La Roche, Inc., 618 N.W.2d 827, 839–40 (Neb.2000). Although the court in *Hansen* left the question open, a few years later a lower state court declined to adopt § 6(c), instead applying a modified consumer expectations test that allowed the defendant to introduce evidence of countervailing utilities of the challenged design. See Mele v. Howmedica, Inc., 808 N.E.2d 1026, 1038–42, 1045–46 (Ill.App.Ct.2004); see also id. at 1037–38 ("Even if implantees have no expectation specific to this particular part of the artificial hip, they may have relevant expectations about the safety of the artificial hip as a whole.... The trial court correctly rejected the proposal to assess risks from the standpoint of the ordinary doctor.").

Lars Noah, *This Is Your Products Liability Restatement on Drugs*

74 BROOK. L. REV. 839 (2009).

* * * Instead of asking whether a reasonable alternative design (RAD) exists, the new test asks whether a fully-informed health care provider would ever select the product for any class of patients. Although a good deal clearer than its predecessor [i.e., comment k], section 6(c) of the *Products Liability Restatement* has proven to be no less controversial or subject to misunderstanding.

Insofar as the availability of safer substitutes undoubtedly would impact a reasonable physician's decision, section 6(c) does not differ so terribly from the risk-utility test of section 2(b). In a subsequent article, the Reporters clarified that RADs would remain relevant in this limited fashion. They clearly meant, however, to avoid a test that focused on the availability of hypothetical RADs in part because full substitutability seemed far harder to predict in this context: the Reporters insisted that a purported RAD serve all potential classes of patients, and they rejected any reference to Rx drugs that had not yet received approval from the [FDA].

Taking a cue from the medical profession promised a firmer basis for making such tricky judgments, especially when coupled with an assumption of full information. The Reporters had in mind an aspirational rather than simply a custom-based standard, even though, in practice, a fully-informed health care provider represents a largely unattainable ideal. In cases involving genuinely—and, if properly labeled, unabashedly—worthless and dangerous drugs,[27] plaintiffs should have no particular difficulty finding qualified experts willing to testify that no reasonable physician would have used such a drug in any class of patients, which, apart from a malpractice claim against the prescribing physician, would provide the basis for a design defect claim unless the manufacturer nonetheless managed to identify such a class.

By asking what a reasonable physician would select, the test presumably did not mean fully-informed only about the risks and benefits of the particular drug; instead, it imagined an expert with knowledge about the peculiar needs of the patient as well as perspective about the entire range of (drug and non-drug) options available for treatment. Thus, section 6(c) has less to do with reasonable alternative designs than with the broader (though related) question of substitutability. Indeed, manufacturers might fare better under section 2(b) in cases where fully-informed physicians would prefer a surgical procedure over a prescription product with a challenged but unalterable design. * * *

1. *MUDs and Child's Play*

Section 6(c) shares important similarities with another contentious pocket of design defect scrutiny. Although elsewhere the *Products Liability Restatement* rejected the proposition that some types of products (e.g., cigarettes and handguns) may create such a high risk of injury and have so little social utility that they should be regarded as defective even without proof of a RAD, the Reporters conceded that some products, such as toy guns that shoot hard rubber pellets, may suffer from a "manifestly unreasonable" design (MUD) if courts defined the relevant product category (and substitutes) too narrowly. In short, if no parent in their right mind would purchase such a product, then a jury could conclude that the manufacturer should not have made it available in the first place (in effect, to protect children against the foolishness of their parents and their own lack of judgment).

Because prescription drugs often represent a class onto themselves without clear substitutes, and because their purchase requires assent from a person more sophisticated than the end user, section 6(c) created a similar standard for judging design defects. Although paternalism in medicine has acquired a bad reputation, patients seek out professional assistance precisely because they lack the expertise to make such choices unaided. * * * Similarly, section 2(b) imagines that the utility of some products may outweigh their risk only when used by a subset of potential consumers (e.g., adults or experts), which then requires that labeling define the appropriate subset.* In short, rather than the "unprecedented" (even

---

27. Of course, it seems entirely implausible that the labeling for an FDA-approved drug would ever contraindicate use in all potential classes of patients.

* [As explained later in the article (p.884),] [c]ritics have objected that section 6(c) conflicts with the well-accepted proposition that product manufacturers should not get to warn their way out of a duty to adopt reasonable alternative designs. * * * [T]his complaint fails to appreciate the centrality of labeling in helping to define a pharmaceutical product's niche.

"radical") new test assailed by critics, section 6(c) announces a blended standard drawn from entirely familiar tests for judging design defects in other contexts.

Some commentators have criticized section 6(c) for insulating both lifesaving and lifestyle (read "trivial") prescription products, but they make the same mistake as those who would call lawfully marketed products that appeal to some (wrong-headed?) consumers defectively designed even in the absence of a RAD (and in the face of an adequate warning). One central objection to the recognition of a broader form of "product category" liability is that it would allow courts to decide that lawfully marketed products should not be available to consumers. Of course, a jury verdict does not amount to an injunction against further sales of a product, and defenders of a more expansive standard of liability for design defects would say that it simply amounts to an obligation to pay for harm caused (and to spread those costs among all users who may derive utility from the product). If nothing else has emerged from the otherwise confused preemption jurisprudence of the last fifteen years, however, the Supreme Court has left little doubt about the potential regulatory effect of tort judgments.

A conclusion that a prescription drug has a design defect may well amount to a command that would deprive other patients of access to the product. If a manufacturer has provided an adequate warning to the health care providers responsible for selecting an intervention for a particular patient, a jury generally would have no basis for deciding that a drug had no legitimate use in any class of patients, even if a physician may have erred in selecting it for the plaintiff. As it did in recognizing MUDs in only the narrowest of circumstances, the *Products Liability Restatement* crafted a design defect standard for prescription products to guard against the risk of such judicial tunnel-vision. * * *

Although a reasonable manufacturer test [preferred by some courts and commentators] sounds like the other side of the same coin as the reasonable physician test, it may not provide a suitable safeguard for patient welfare. On the one hand, some manufacturers may persist in marketing drugs past the point of genuine obsolescence; on the other hand, overly conscientious pharmaceutical manufacturers may remove drugs from the marketplace even though reasonable physicians would have continued prescribing them for a subset of patients. Once serious risks with an approved drug become known, risk-averse firms may not see much countervailing revenue in continuing to serve a narrow patient population, and patients deprived of a drug from which they derived therapeutic benefits would have no claim for continued access. Thus, framing the question from the perspective (or through the lens) of a reasonable health care provider better guards against the twin dangers of tunnel-vision (risk-utility judged solely from a plaintiff's perspective) and preference aggregation (risk-utility evaluated from a societal perspective), both of which might unduly sacrifice the needs of a minority of patients for whom the risk-utility balance differs from either the particular victim or the norm.†

2. *Snowflakes (and Cost–Consciousness) in Medical Practice*

Section 6(c) appropriately recognizes the variability in patient response and the inadvisability of considering a particular product design as the best choice for treating a condition in every case. When it comes to pharmaceutical interventions, one size does not fit all. The requirements of patients vary widely, depending on factors such as the nature of their symptoms, progression of the underlying disease, presence of any concurrent conditions or use of other medications, and sensitivity to (or tolerance of) specific side effects. For example, differences in metabolic patterns depending on age, gender, and ethnic background may indicate selection of a drug for some patients even if its risk-utility balance is less favorable for most other persons in the population.

Physicians frequently must try different medications at different dosages until they find the one that seems to work best in a particular patient, and they may have to try various combinations. In some cases, a patient proves to be refractory to the "drug of choice" but responds well to a second- or third-line (often more dangerous) therapeutic agent. This may happen, for instance, when a patient encounters a resistant strain of a common infectious agent. These characteristics make pharmaceutical products fundamentally unlike most consumer goods, which anyone equipped with basic information could select and use successfully to achieve the product's intended purpose.

In theory, of course, there always might be at least one hypothetical patient who does not tolerate or mysteriously fails to respond to every other alternative treatment in whom a reasonable physician—at a loss for any other ideas—would try a particular drug. The Reporters had made it clear, however, that this possibility would not suffice to demonstrate the existence of a class of patients for whom physicians appropriately might select a drug. Labeling helps in this connection: indications (and contraindications) may specify those subpopulations of patients with a condition in whom use of the drug would (or would not) be appropriate. Occasionally after drug withdrawal, the FDA permits continued use by an even more

† [As explained later in the article (pp.872–73),] one cannot say that the infamous teratogen thalidomide suffers from a design defect. Currently approved by the FDA for the treatment of skin lesions associated with Hansen's disease (leprosy), though contraindicated for use in pregnancy (and accompanied by various other mechanisms designed to help ensure that physicians and patients take this limitation on use seriously), this drug appropriately passes the section 6(c) test. One wonders whether thalidomide would fare as well under a less structured risk-utility balancing approach in a case where a pregnant leprosy patient had used the drug: (1) from the perspective of her terribly deformed child, the risk clearly outweighs the utility; (2) from the perspective of the mother, the risk to her offspring also undoubtedly outweighs the drug's utility to her (after all, less effective and more dangerous, but non-teratogenic, options such as glucocorticoids might have worked for her); and (3) from a societal perspective, the specter of a wave of birth defects arising from the very real possibility of the irresponsible use of this drug by physicians and patients might well outweigh the utility to the relatively small (and still stigmatized) community of leprosy sufferers. Section 6(c) does a better job of managing such cases than either a particularized or aggregate form of risk-utility balancing.

narrowly defined class of patients. Finally, courts could take a cue from the FDA's orphan drug regulations, which require that manufacturers identify a "medically plausible" subset of patients with a relatively common condition if they seek the incentives available for products designed to treat "rare" diseases.*

In contrast to the multi-factor test of section 2(b) of the *Products Liability Restatement*, section 6(c), with its inquiry limited to "therapeutic benefits" and using a physician-based frame of reference, may fail to protect legitimate design choices and prescribing decisions. In particular, it may undervalue matters of patient convenience, even though in practice this may have genuine public health consequences. For instance, simplified dosing or delivery may improve patient compliance with prescribed treatment. Changes in dosage forms may, however, present trade-offs between safety, efficacy, and convenience. * * *

Moreover, in judging the design of older prescription drugs, the reasonable physician standard (and section 6(c)'s emphasis on "*therapeutic* benefits") might make manufacturers more vulnerable to defect claims than the risk-utility test that governs other consumer products and takes cost into account.[80] * * * Imagine a new biotechnology drug that is safer and more effective in every type of patient with a certain condition, but it costs $50,000 annually as compared to $500 for the old standby; from a purely medical standpoint, no reasonable physician would prescribe the older product, at least not unless affordability got factored into the equation. With time, older medical technologies will fade from the scene, but manufacturers may persist in marketing them, especially if cost-conscious purchasers continue to demand "safe enough" prescription drugs. Section 6(c) appropriately discourages the continued marketing of genuinely obsolete prescription products that pose undue risks to patients when the FDA has not acted to withdraw these products, but it also should incorporate section 2(b)'s willingness to factor affordability and convenience into the equation.

3. *Myths About Designer (and "Lifestyle") Drugs*

Section 6(c) recognizes that pharmaceuticals are not designed in the same sense as other consumer goods; instead, new drugs are discovered. The advent of new techniques of "rational drug design," which some commentators point to when disputing the supposed distinctiveness of pharmaceutical products, will not fundamentally change things anytime soon. A pharmaceutical manufacturer cannot market a theoretical redesign until it discovers this allegedly superior drug, subjects it to the full battery of preclinical and clinical testing over a period of several years, and then patiently waits for the FDA's blessing. Hypothesized redesigns have unpre-

---

* [In addition, as explained later in the article (p.922), pharmacogenomic] research may help to identify subgroups of patients for whom reasonable physicians would prescribe a certain drug in the face of a plaintiff's allegations of defective design.

80. If the reasonable physician standard governed design defect claims against automobile manufacturers, would vehicles that sacrificed some amount of passenger safety for greater affordability (or merely aesthetics) get driven from the marketplace?

dictable safety and efficacy profiles, which makes it impossible for an expert to predict whether it would pass muster with the FDA.

In some cases, a design defect may relate to the proportions of (or interactions between) ingredients used in a combination drug product rather than the design of the separately approved chemicals themselves. Design issues also may relate to fixed dosage levels. Even minor changes in formulation (e.g., different inactive ingredients) would, however, require the submission of a new drug approval (NDA) supplement to the FDA with supporting data to demonstrate bioavailability of the active ingredient. For instance, OxyContin® caused deaths among abusers who had managed to defeat the delayed-release mechanism by crushing or dissolving the pills. After the filing of several lawsuits, the manufacturer announced plans to add an ingredient that could deactivate the oxycodone when crushed, but the changed formulation would have to await FDA approval. In fact, these reformulation efforts have encountered roadblocks.[†] [They also may pose a potentially difficult question about making a trade-off between therapeutic utility to legitimate users and health risks to abusers.]

Apart from laboring under misimpressions about the ease of redesigning prescription drugs, critics of efforts to constrain design defect scrutiny point out that pharmaceutical products do not all have equally high utility. * * * Some commentators would hold manufacturers of "lifestyle" drugs to a higher standard. One laundry list of such products included treatments for erectile dysfunction (ED), arthritis, obesity, and urinary incontinence, but it failed to explain the reasons for lumping these disparate drugs together: was it that they offered primarily symptomatic relief (or targeted a mere risk factor) and required chronic use? Aside from problems of recreational abuse, are powerful analgesics properly dismissed as merely "lifestyle" drugs? Contraceptives sometimes get trivialized in this fashion.

Even if not elevated to the vaunted status of a genuine "disease," bothersome conditions (e.g., irritable bowel syndrome) and disfiguring ailments (e.g., cystic acne) undoubtedly have adverse effects on the sufferers' quality of life, which can take an emotional and financial toll on them. If not unduly dangerous, the FDA does permit marketing of prescription products that presumably everyone would label as "lifestyle" drugs (e.g., wrinkle reducers), though even unmistakably cosmetic products such as Botox® may have secondary therapeutic uses. In the final analysis, all drugs are, to one degree or another, lifestyle drugs.[117]

---

† In 2010, more than two years after filing its application, Purdue Pharma finally received approval for such a reformulation. See Abby Goodnough & Katie Zezima, Drug Is Harder to Abuse, but Users Persevere, N.Y. Times, June 16, 2011, at A21 (reporting that OxyContin OP "is the first painkiller reformulated to deter abuse, according to the F.D.A., which is now studying several proposed reformulations of other opiate drugs").

117. A similarly vague dividing line exists with regard to medical procedures, treating "elective" surgeries as nonessential (or, at least, non-emergency). Even so, unmistakably lifesaving procedures technically also should qualify as elective insofar as respect for autonomy means that patients have a right to decline treatment.

In theory, section 6(c)'s reference to "therapeutic benefits" and use of a physician-based standard might expose "lifestyle" drugs to unforgiving design defect scrutiny. Although it appears that the Reporters meant to include even "cosmetic" products that required the intervention of a health care provider, courts may refuse to credit these separately published glosses on the blackletter formulation. If taken at face value, section 6(c) could have the effect of delegating judgments about the utilities of prescription products to reasonable physicians whose professional training presumably would give us a far narrower range of legitimate clinical endpoints, which would make some pharmaceutical manufacturers more vulnerable to design defect claims than they would have been under the more flexible and consumer-oriented standard of section 2(b).

Aside from questions about the special utility of prescription drugs, some commentators have argued that, unlike other consumer goods, these products rarely cause third-party effects, but this claim of distinctiveness strikes me as clearly incorrect. It disregards, for instance, recurring litigation over birth defects (including cases where the drug has no intended use related to pregnancy), sedation (as it relates to automobile accidents and the like), and psychosis. It also seemingly disregards claims related to abuse and diversion. Finally, though not so far as I know litigated, efficacy failures may permit contagious diseases to spread to others, pharmaceuticals may cause harm to health care workers, and medical technologies may have deleterious environmental consequences. Prescription products have many distinctive characteristics, but an absence of third-party effects is not one of them. * * *

NOTES AND QUESTIONS

1. *Let's get real.* The excerpted article then provided a detailed discussion of several illustrations previously offered by both proponents and critics of *Rest. (3d)* § 6(c): Yutopar® (ritodrine), Thalomid® (thalidomide), Proscar® (finasteride), polio vaccines, and Accutane® (isotretinoin). See id. at 869–84; see also id. at 868–69 ("The operation of section 6(c) becomes more concrete when applied to particular fact patterns, real or imagined (as I note repeatedly below, these turn out to be far more imagined than real, but that alone does not defeat the effort to draw relevant insights from these case studies)."). Can you think of any other medical technologies (from earlier in the casebook, current headlines, or personal experience) that would help to test (and perhaps refute) some or all of these arguments about the operation and desirability of the new *Restatement*'s special test for design defects involving Rx products?

2. *Judging experimental technologies?* In recalling some of the tort litigation excerpted in Chapter 2(A) & (C) (related to clinical trials and brought against parties other than product manufacturers), consider this unexplained discrepancy:

> The *Products Liability Restatement* does not separately address investigational products, even though these appeared to be a central concern

> in the *Second Restatement*'s comment k to section 402A. * * * The last decade has witnessed growing tort litigation on behalf of subjects injured during clinical trials, though claims against the suppliers of investigational products remain fairly uncommon. Insofar as section 6 turns on differential access rather than deference to FDA approval decisions, it should encompass investigational products accessible only to subjects enrolled in trials and under the strict supervision of clinical investigators, even though the research aims to answer the very questions that lay at the heart of design and informational defect claims * * *

Id. at 905–06. Given the typical absence of any meaningful knowledge about either the risks or benefits of an investigational product (coupled with the fact that clinical trials do not involve a genuine physician-patient encounter), would the design defect standard instead have to ask whether a reasonable investigator would enroll a particular individual as a subject in such a study (using the sort of factors that an IRB must consider before approving a protocol)? If, rather than done as part of a clinical trial, a physician uses a still investigational product in a patient, would it suffice under § 6(c) to demonstrate that the product has shown some promise in treating persons who have no other viable therapeutic options?

3. *Fitting the pieces together*. In reading Chapter 7(B)(2), keep in mind that unresolved

> questions [exist] about the interrelationship between the design and warning provisions of the *Products Liability Restatement*. If an exception to the learned intermediary rule covers a particular case, such as mass immunizations, should that also render inapplicable section 6(c)'s physician-based design defect standard in favor of the more open-ended test of section 2(b)? How about the far less common contraceptive exception—if section 6(d)(2) would allow a failure-to-warn claim because the learned intermediary has fallen out of the picture, would that also render inapplicable the protective design defect standard of section 6(c)? * * *

Id. at 895–96. Putting aside any ambiguities in these blackletter rules, do the previously noted decisions involving childhood vaccines and contraceptives help in deciding whether § 6(c) should apply to such products?

4. *Drugs vs. medical devices*. Section 6(c) of the new *Restatement* applies equally to prescription drugs and devices. This corresponds with the case law applying *Rest. (2d)* § 402A comment k to sellers of certain medical devices, especially implants, but are there any arguments for differentiating between these two broad categories of medical technologies for purposes of engaging in design defect scrutiny?

> For a variety of reasons, design defect claims involving medical devices do not pose nearly the same difficulties that arise with prescription pharmaceuticals. Although the Reporters explained emphatically (and persuasively) that "drug designs *are* different," they have not offered a similarly detailed defense of their decision to apply the

> special design defect standard to medical devices. Moreover, while other commentators have offered a range of both criticism and praise of section 6(c) with reference to the treatment of pharmaceutical products, it seems that not one of them has endorsed its extension to prescription devices. Instead, the contours of express federal preemption as a defense to tort claims against medical device manufacturers, which has evolved fitfully and attracted its share of criticism, may better define those contexts where courts should decline to engage in duplicative design defect review—namely, those devices that have undergone full premarket review and approval, at least where the FDA has made a particular judgment about a feature challenged by the plaintiff.
>
> In sharp contrast to prescription drugs, medical devices are built rather than discovered. Innovation in this field tends to be incremental, and the FDA's premarket screening mechanism accommodates the introduction of new and slightly improved models of medical devices. In addition, devices generally should not present the same unpredictable (and variable) responses encountered with metabolized drugs, though anatomical variation exists (as does variation in the skill of surgeons). In short, the risk-utility standard does not seem nearly as inapt in this context, and perhaps juries can more easily judge the trade-offs made in the course of designing devices. Nonetheless, focusing on the presence of a learned intermediary (and the public policy rationales for limiting the liability of sellers that supply products of value to some patients), the *Products Liability Restatement* does not differentiate between prescription drugs and medical devices.

Id. at 913–14. Some courts already have applied § 6(c) to implanted devices. See, e.g., Wheat v. Sofamor, S.N.C., 46 F.Supp.2d 1351 (N.D.Ga. 1999); Sita v. Danek Med., Inc., 43 F.Supp.2d 245, 255 (E.D.N.Y.1999); cf. Anderson v. Siemens Corp., 335 F.3d 466, 470–71 (5th Cir.2003) (declining to apply § 6 to an ICU ventilator with a malfunctioning alarm because it did not qualify as a prescription product). For additional case law involving design defect (and other) claims against medical device firms, see Romualdo P. Eclavea, Annotation, Products Liability in Connection with Prosthesis or Other Product Designed to Be Surgically Implanted in Patient's Body, 1 A.L.R.4th 921 (1980 & 2011 Supp.); Debra T. Landis, Annotation, Products Liability: Medical Machinery Used in Plaintiff's Treatment, 34 A.L.R.4th 532 (1984 & 2011 Supp.); Robin Miller, Annotation, Products Liability: Cardiac Pacemakers, 23 A.L.R.6th 223 (2007 & 2011 Supp.).

5. *Further commentary*. See Michael D. Green, Prescription Drugs, Alternative Designs, and the Restatement (Third): Preliminary Reflections, 30 Seton Hall L. Rev. 207 (1999) (symposium); James A. Henderson, Jr., Prescription Drug Design Liability Under the Proposed Restatement (Third) of Torts: A Reporter's Perspective, 48 Rutgers L. Rev. 471 (1996); David G. Owen, Dangers in Prescription Drugs: Filling a Private Law Gap in the Healthcare Debate, 42 Conn. L. Rev. 733 (2010); Dustin R. Marlowe,

Note, A Dose of Reality for Section 6(c) of the Restatement (Third) of Torts: Products Liability, 39 Ga. L. Rev. 1445 (2005).

2. EXEMPTING BIOMATERIALS SUPPLIERS

In re TMJ Implants Products Liability Litigation

97 F.3d 1050 (8th Cir.1996).

■ BOWMAN, CIRCUIT JUDGE:

This appeal arises from a multidistrict litigation proceeding, consolidating approximately 280 products liability actions * * * Plaintiffs-appellants are the recipients of the Proplast TMJ Interpositional Implant, a prosthetic device used to correct temporomandibular joint (TMJ) disorders. The TMJ connects the upper and lower jaw; it facilitates normal movement of the jawbone. When the articulating surface of the jawbone that fits into the TMJ becomes diseased, normal mobility can be restored by implanting a prosthetic device like the Proplast TMJ Interpositional Implant. The gravamen of the complaint is that the implants failed, abrading the surrounding bone and causing pain to the recipients.

The implants were invented, designed, tested, manufactured, packaged, and sold by Vitek, Inc., a now bankrupt company founded by Dr. Charles Homsy. Du Pont and Durafilm are the named defendants in this action, however, because they manufactured and supplied some of the raw materials that were used to construct the implants—including polytetrafluoroethylene powder and fiber (PTFE resin) and fluorinated ethylene propylene film (FEP film). Du Pont manufactured both of these materials and sold them under the familiar Teflon trademark. Durafilm distributed FEP film, but did not manufacture it. PTFE resin and FEP film are chemically inert with a wide variety of safe industrial uses. PTFE is used to manufacture everything from bearings in jet aircraft to non-stick surfaces on frying pans. FEP film is used in applications ranging from pipe insulation to solar collectors.

In the late 1960s, Dr. Homsy invented the implant biomaterial Proplast while conducting prosthesis research at Methodist Hospital in Houston, Texas. Proplast is a spongy and highly porous coalesceable gel designed to promote tissue attachment. Dr. Homsy founded Vitek in 1969 to manufacture and distribute his Proplast prosthetic devices while he continued his research at Methodist Hospital. To make Proplast, Vitek combined PTFE resin with carbons and solvents and then subjected this mixture to an eight-step patented process of heating, compressing, and drying. The implant itself is formed by molding the Proplast into the required shape and laminating one side of it with translucent FEP film. The FEP film layer replaced the meniscus or articulating surface of the TMJ and was designed to protect the underlying Proplast from wear in load-bearing joints like the TMJ. Surgeons positioned the implant so that the Proplast side would be anchored eventually by tissue growth while the FEP film side abutted the lower jaw to shield against wear. The chain of distribution for

PTFE resin and FEP film thus began with Du Pont or Durafilm as the initial suppliers, then continued on to Vitek as the finished product manufacturer, and finally ended with the recipients as the ultimate users of the finished product. Each implant, while selling for at least fifty dollars, contained only a few cents' worth of PTFE resin and FEP film.

When Du Pont learned that Dr. Homsy intended to use its Teflon products for medical purposes, Du Pont advised the purchasing agent at Methodist Hospital by a March 13, 1967, letter that its Teflon products were not made for medical applications and that Du Pont had not conducted the necessary long-term studies to determine the suitability of fluorocarbons for medical use. Du Pont's letter also noted several published scientific reports indicating that pure Teflon implants wore badly and had a tendency to disintegrate in load-bearing joints. Consequently, Du Pont required the hospital to sign a disclaimer, acknowledging Du Pont's warnings and agreeing to use its own independent medical and legal judgment as to the safety of Teflon in the implants. * * *

Based on years of clinical studies with Proplast implants in animals and humans and his extensive experience in the manufacturing and marketing of prosthetic devices, Dr. Homsy believed that Proplast was an excellent implant material. Indeed, two FDA advisory committees stated that "the safety and effectiveness of [Proplast] has been established through long-term clinical trials." The FDA authorized the sale of Proplast TMJ implants in 1983. By the late 1980s, however, it had become apparent that the FEP film abraded into particles despite the additional precautions Vitek had taken to ensure that this would not happen. In November 1989, Du Pont informed Vitek and Dr. Homsy that it would no longer fill Vitek's orders for Teflon because of concerns about lawsuits spawned by the disintegrating implants. In January 1991, the FDA ordered Proplast implants removed from the market because of their fragmentation and irritation to human tissue.

The recipients filed this action against the defendants, asserting strict liability and negligence claims. * * * The recipients argue that the district court erred in granting summary judgment against them because they have raised factual issues as to whether FEP film was defectively designed. The recipients insist that, even though FEP film has many safe industrial uses and is not inherently dangerous or defective for all uses, the film was defectively designed for its "reasonably foreseeable" use in the implants. In other words, they claim that FEP film was designed defectively, not because it malfunctioned, but because when incorporated into the implants it caused the implants to function in an unreasonably dangerous manner. We reject this argument because * * * the defect was in the overall design of the implants and not in the FEP film. FEP film is a mere building-block material suitable for many safe uses. The recipients' argument boils down to nothing more than the fact that Vitek decided to use what proved to be an unsuitable material to manufacture its implants. The erroneous and unfortunate decision to use FEP film in the design of the implant was made by Vitek, however, not by Du Pont or Durafilm. * * * Therefore, as courts in other TMJ implant cases already have held, we hold that the defendants were entitled to summary judgment on the design defect claim.

While the law of design defect clearly extends liability to finished product manufacturers like Vitek, it rarely imposes strict liability on component part suppliers who merely sell their multi-use parts to manufacturers of finished products. The critical inquiry focuses on determining the reason why the component part turned out to be unsuitable for use in the finished product. "If the failure was due to a flaw in the component part, then the component part is itself defective and the cause for the assembled product being defective." In such cases, the component part maker may be held strictly liable. Apperson v. E.I. du Pont de Nemours & Co., 41 F.3d 1103, 1106 (7th Cir.1994) ("Strict liability may extend to manufacturers of component parts for injuries caused by design or manufacturing defects in the component part itself."). If, on the other hand, the finished product was unreasonably dangerous because the component part was unsuited for the particular use that the finished product manufacturer chose to make of it, then the defect is in the design of the finished product rather than in the design of the component part. In these cases, it is the finished product manufacturer and not the component part supplier that may be held strictly liable. * * *

Making suppliers of inherently safe raw materials and component parts pay for the mistakes of the finished product manufacturer would not only be unfair, but it also would impose an intolerable burden on the business world, especially where, as here, the raw material or component part (the FEP film) accounts for only a few cents' worth of the cost of the entire finished product (the Proplast TMJ implant). See Kealoha v. E.I. du Pont de Nemours & Co., 844 F.Supp. 590, 595 (D.Haw.1994) ("[T]he cost to a manufacturer of an inherently safe raw material to insure against all conceivable misuse of his product would be prohibitively expensive."), aff'd, 82 F.3d 894, 901 (9th Cir.1996). As another panel of this court has determined in a previous TMJ case, "[i]t would be unreasonable and impractical to place the burden of testing and developing all devices that incorporate Teflon as a component on Du Pont." Rynders v. E.I. Du Pont de Nemours & Co., 21 F.3d 835, 842 (8th Cir.1994). Suppliers of versatile materials like chains, valves, sand, gravel, etc., cannot be expected to become experts in the infinite number of finished products that might conceivably incorporate their multi-use raw materials or components. *Kealoha*, 844 F.Supp. at 594 ("[T]here would be no end to potential liability if every manufacturer of nuts, bolts and screws could be held liable when their hardware was used in a defective product."). * * *

There is no allegation that FEP film, in and of itself, is inherently dangerous. Indeed, the recipients concede that FEP film has many safe industrial uses. As the Seventh Circuit noted, "Clearly, Teflon is a raw material with many safe uses; it only became dangerous when Vitek incorporated it into a highly specialized medical device, the Proplast TMJ Implant." *Apperson*, 41 F.3d at 1106; see also Jacobs v. E.I. du Pont de Nemours & Co., 67 F.3d 1219, 1241 (6th Cir.1995). In these circumstances, the responsibility to design a safe medical device is Vitek's alone because, as the finished product manufacturer, it knew the specific end-use it intended to make of the FEP film and was in a far better position to evaluate the film's safety for that particular end-use. Summary judgment thus was properly granted for the defendants on the design defect claim. * * *

■ HEANEY, CIRCUIT JUDGE (dissenting):

The majority expands the component part supplier doctrine to shield from liability even those suppliers who knew how their product was going to be used and knew that the intended use posed grave danger to the ultimate consumers. I cannot accept such blanket protection for component part manufacturers. In this case, I would permit the recipients' claims to go to a jury for a determination of what DuPont knew and whether it had a duty to prohibit the sale of Teflon for use in human implants, or at least to provide adequate warnings to Vitek of those known risks.

Underlying the component part supplier doctrine is the premise that the manufacturer of a finished product is generally in a better position to detect its potential dangers than the manufacturer of only a part of the product. Certainly, a finished product manufacturer is responsible for dangers that result from the product design or from the manner in which a component part is integrated into the finished product. As a corollary, manufacturers of a component part generally will not know about such dangers and should not be required to research every possible application of its nondefective, multi-use product.

But the facts of this case place it outside the parameters of the general component part supplier doctrine. The recipients have presented evidence sufficient for a jury to find that DuPont knew Vitek was going to use the Teflon in the TMJ implants. There is also evidence that DuPont knew that Teflon, used in load-bearing human implants, no matter how the implants were designed, can disintegrate and cause injury to implant recipients. DuPont was aware of several studies demonstrating this precise risk. Moreover, a chemist who worked for DuPont for over thirty years testified that a known characteristic of all Teflon, including FEP film, is that it severely fragments after constant contact with and pressure from sharp edges.

This is not a case, as the majority contends, of an "erroneous decision to incorporate what turned out to be an unsuitable material." Rather, the evidence suggests that DuPont was fully aware of the serious risk of harm Teflon posed when used in human implants. To hold DuPont responsible for these known risks would not require component part suppliers to research every possible application of its product; it recognizes DuPont's actual knowledge, without any further research or speculation. Nor are the recipients claiming that DuPont should have designed FEP film differently, as the majority suggests, but that if DuPont knew the film was inappropriate for use in human implants, it should not have continued to supply the film.

There is significant "social utility" in making DuPont accountable for what it knew and for its failure to prevent harm to the ultimate consumers. While Vitek may have been in the better position to evaluate the film's safety for the particular use, DuPont's position may well have been sufficient for it to have known of the harm Teflon posed in the human implants. It is my position that where the component part manufacturer knows that its product is going to be used in a particular fashion and knows that, no matter what the design, the product poses a danger to the ultimate consumer, it cannot escape from liability.

NOTES AND QUESTIONS

1. *Searching high and low for a culprit in the Proplast fiasco.* With the manufacturer bankrupt (and Dr. Homsy having fled the country), plaintiffs naturally sought to pin the blame on others. In addition to targeting DuPont, they unsuccessfully pursued claims against hospitals and surgeons who had implanted the TMJ devices. See Chap. 8. In one curious case, some plaintiffs even tried going after a dental school faculty member who had served as a scientific advisor to Vitek. See Adelmann–Chester v. Kent, 33 So.3d 187, 195, 198–201 (La.Ct.App.2009) (affirming summary judgment for the professor and his university on the products liability claims because they did not qualify as manufacturers or professional vendors). But see id. at 203 (Belsome, J., dissenting) ("It is not disputed that Dr. Kent designed the shape of the glenoid fossa . . . , and, as the majority notes, obtained several design patents regarding the shape of the implants and drafted package inserts for some Vitek devices."). For more on the history behind Vitek, see Bruce Ingersoll & Rose Gutfeld, Medical Mess: Implants in Jaw Joint Fail, Leaving Patients in Pain and Disfigured, Wall St. J., Aug. 31, 1993, at A1.

2. *The high price of success.* DuPont ultimately prevailed in all of the TMJ lawsuits filed against it for supplying raw materials. In addition to the decisions cited above, see, e.g., Anguiano v. E.I. Du Pont De Nemours & Co., 44 F.3d 806 (9th Cir.1995); LaMontagne v. E.I. Du Pont De Nemours & Co., 41 F.3d 846 (2d Cir.1994); Klem v. E.I. DuPont De Nemours & Co., 19 F.3d 997, 1003 (5th Cir.1994). DuPont expended significant resources, however, for its string of victories during the decade that this litigation lasted, paying far more in legal fees than it ever earned on this minor application. See Gary Taylor, A Discovery by DuPont: Hidden Costs of Winning, Nat'l L.J., Mar. 27, 1995, at B1 (reporting one estimate that the company spent more than $40 million defending itself).

3. *Breast implant litigation.* After the largest manufacturer of silicone-gel breast implants filed for bankruptcy protection from the numerous products liability claims, see In re Dow Corning Corp., 211 B.R. 545, 551–54 (Bankr.E.D.Mich.1997), plaintiffs' lawyers began pursuing Dow Chemical as the supplier of the raw silicone. See, e.g., Dow Chem. Co. v. Mahlum, 970 P.2d 98 (Nev.1998) (upholding a compensatory damage award of $4.2 million, but reversing a punitive damage award of $10 million). Dow

Chemical usually prevailed, and the lawsuits filed against other companies that had supplied silicone to other manufacturers of breast implants have not succeeded. See In re Silicone Gel Breast Implants Prods. Liab. Litig., 996 F.Supp. 1110 (N.D.Ala.1997); Artiglio v. Corning Inc., 957 P.2d 1313 (Cal.1998); see also Cabrera v. Cordis Corp., 134 F.3d 1418, 1422–23 (9th Cir.1998) (affirming the exclusion of plaintiff's expert testimony in her claims against the manufacturer of a hydrocephalus shunt composed of silicone). Even so, spooked by lawsuits of these sorts, Dow discontinued supplying silicone for other important medical device applications such as hydrocephalus shunts. See RAND Sci. & Tech. Policy Inst., Biomaterials Availability: Potential Effects on Medical Innovation and Health Care, Issue Paper No. 194, Jan. 2000, at 17, 32; see also Barnaby J. Feder, Implant Industry Is Facing Cutback by Top Suppliers, N.Y. Times, Apr. 25, 1994, at A1.

4. *Legislative reaction.* In response to fears of an emerging shortage of raw materials needed to make life-saving medical devices, Congress enacted the Biomaterials Access Assurance Act of 1998, 21 U.S.C. §§ 1601–1606. Under this statute, which displaces applicable state law, a biomaterials supplier that neither manufactured nor sold the allegedly defective implant would face tort liability only if it "failed to meet contractual requirements or specifications" when it furnished raw materials or component parts. See id. § 1604. When named in a lawsuit as a co-defendant, the biomaterials supplier receives certain procedural benefits, including protection from sweeping discovery requests and an opportunity to seek an expedited dismissal with prejudice or summary judgment if the plaintiff cannot establish that the supplier also made or sold the implant or furnished nonconforming biomaterials. See id. § 1605. The biomaterials supplier remains subject to impleader, but only if the claimant or device manufacturer can persuade the trial judge that the negligence or intentionally tortious conduct of the previously dismissed biomaterials supplier caused the harm, and that the manufacturer cannot or should not shoulder the full amount of any tort judgment. See id. § 1606; see also 66 Fed. Reg. 17,562 (2001) (announcing the availability of a draft guidance for implementing a procedure to petition the FDA for a declaration concerning a biomaterials supplier's compliance with establishment registration requirements). See generally Ann M. Murphy, Note, The Biomaterials Access Assurance Act of 1998 and Corporate Supplier Liability: Who You Gonna Sue?, 25 Del. J. Corp. L. 715 (2000).

5. *Bulk supplier doctrine.* Even outside of the biomaterials context, companies that sell raw materials or components that are incorporated into finished products will rarely face tort liability. See White v. Weiner, 562 A.2d 378 (Pa.Super.Ct.1989) (upholding summary judgment for a company that had supplied bulk active ingredient to another company that manufactured a prescription drug that caused a patient's death); see also Rest. (3d) § 5 (setting forth the bulk supplier doctrine); Lars Noah, This Is Your Products Liability Restatement on Drugs, 74 Brook. L. Rev. 839, 917 n.337 (2009) ("This standard roughly parallels section 6(c) insofar as it declines to impose liability for a design defect for injuries caused by a product supplied to a sophisticated purchaser so long as it has some reasonably safe uses."). But cf. Fisher v. Professional Compounding Ctrs. of Am., 311 F.Supp.2d 1008, 1019–21 (D.Nev.2004) (holding that suppliers of bulk fenfluramine used to compound diet drugs had failed to ensure that pharmacists knew of the risks associated with this drug substance). See generally Jeffrey W. Kemp & Lindsy N. Alleman, The Bulk Supplier, Sophisticated User, and Learned Intermediary Doctrines Since the Adoption of the Restatement (Third) of Torts, 26 Rev. Litig. 927 (2007). Will the pending tort claims against manufacturers of the vaccine preservative thimerosal (noted in Chap. 5(A)) founder on the bulk supplier doctrine?

C. Fear of Malfunction

Willett v. Baxter International, Inc.

929 F.2d 1094 (5th Cir.1991).

■ Wisdom, Circuit Judge:

The plaintiff, Gene Earl Willett, sued the defendants, Baxter Healthcare Corporation and Carbomedics, Inc., seeking to recover for his fear that his allegedly defective heart valve, manufactured by the defendants, would fail. Mrs. Albert Spriggins, and her husband, intervened in the action, seeking the same recovery. * * * In January of 1988, Dr. White E. Gibson III, a New Orleans cardiovascular surgeon, replaced deteriorating heart valves in both Willett and Mrs. Spriggins with artificial heart valves manufactured by the defendants. In June of 1988, Willett read an article in his local paper that discussed Baxter's voluntary suspension of the marketing of the valves. * * *

Each artificial heart valve has two leaves, made of pyrolitic carbon, that control the flow of blood through the valve. The voluntary recall was prompted by several reports of a phenomenon known as "leaflet escape." Leaflet escape refers to the in vivo escape of one of the two leaflets that controls the flow of blood through the valve.

The plaintiff and the intervenor alleged that their valves were defective in that pyrolitic carbon was not well-suited for use in heart valves because of the possibility of stress fractures in the material. The plaintiff and the intervenor do not deny that their valves are currently functioning properly. Instead, they seek damages for their fear that their valves will fail in the future. * * *

[A]pproximately 19,614 patients received these valves between 1982 and the first quarter of 1990. Since the valves were first implanted, only seventeen cases of leaflet escape have been reported. Of the seventeen reported cases, fifteen involved mitral valves, and two involved aortic valves. All seventeen cases occurred in valves manufactured before April of 1986. The valves of both the plaintiff and the intervenor were manufactured after April of 1986. Of the valves manufactured since April of 1986, no failures have been reported.[4]

From the evidence, a reasonable jury could conclude that leaflet escape is caused by stress fractures in the pyrolitic carbon. From the evidence, it appears that pyrolitic carbon is very resistant to the start of a stress fracture. But once a stress fracture has begun, the fracture will grow at a fairly steady rate, and may eventually lead to leaflet escape.

Baxter published at least three clinical reports documenting the leaflet escape problem in January of 1987, November of 1987, and January of 1988. The articles described the failures that had occurred to date. While the reports stated that the cause (or causes) of the failures was uncertain, the articles suggested that the problem may have been caused by improper surgical technique. Specifically, the reports suggested that, during the surgical procedure, a valve may have been scratched or improperly exposed to certain chemicals. This scratch or improper exposure created a weak spot in the leaflet, where a stress fracture could begin.

In contrast, the plaintiff and the intervenor argue that the manufacturing process inevitably leads to weak spots in the leaflets. They rely on the deposition testimony of one Dr. Harvey Miller Flower, taken from the sealed court records. According to Dr. Flower, soot pockets can form in pyrolitic carbon during manufacture. If not discovered, the soot pocket might weaken the leaflet sufficiently that a stress fracture can begin. Notably, the expert did not testify that another material was more suitable than pyrolitic carbon for use in the valves, or that a different manufacturing or quality control process could have reduced a theoretical soot pocket problem. Dr. Flower also did not testify as to how often undiscovered soot pockets would develop given the manufacturing and quality control process used by the defendants.

The plaintiff and the intervenor provided no evidence that their particular valves actually suffered from a soot pocket problem, and no evidence that their valves were not performing as designed. On the contrary, their surgeon, Dr. Gibson stated, in his affidavit, that the valves implanted in both Willett and Mrs. Spriggins were functioning normally. He also stated that, to a reasonable degree of medical certainty, the valve replacement had saved their lives and greatly improved their quality of life. The district court granted summary judgment in favor of the defendants. The district court held that the valves were functioning normally and were therefore not defective * * * *

First, to establish that a product is unreasonably dangerous per se, a plaintiff must show that the likely harm of the product outweighs its benefit. Based on the summary judgment evidence, a reasonable jury could

4. It is unclear whether the defendants changed their manufacturing or quality control process in April of 1986. As a result, it is unclear why the more recently manufactured valves have not failed. The defendants may have solved the problem, or it may simply be that the valves fail over time, and sufficient time has not passed for the more recently manufactured valves to fail.

not find that the pyrolitic carbon heart valves are unreasonably dangerous per se. The undisputed evidence establishes that the valves have extended over nineteen thousand lives. While the valve replacement was not successful in every case, the undisputed evidence established that, even with the risk of leaflet escape, a patient has a much greater chance for life with the valve replacement than without the replacement. From the record, the only reasonable conclusion is that the clear life-saving benefits of the heart valve outweigh its risks.

Second, the plaintiff and the intervenor argue that the existence of soot pockets in some valves is sufficient to create a factual issue as to whether their valves have soot pockets. While we agree that a soot pocket may be a manufacturing defect, the mere possibility of a manufacturing defect is not sufficient to establish the fact of a manufacturing defect in the valves implanted in the plaintiff and the intervenor.

Third, the plaintiff and the intervenor argue that pyrolitic carbon is not suited for use in a heart valve, and that its use establishes a defect in the design of the product. * * * [A] plaintiff would have to present evidence that the defendants knew or should have known of an alternative, either for the heart valve itself or for the pyrolitic carbon in the heart valve, with a failure rate lower than the failure rate established by the summary judgment evidence for the pyrolitic carbon heart valves. The plaintiff and the intervenor presented no evidence of a less risky alternative. * * *

While we recognize that the fear of an unknowable, but potentially fatal, defect in a heart valve is perfectly rational, and almost certainly sincere, we have serious concerns about permitting recovery for such fear absent actual failure of the valve.[20] We do not decide these issues, though, because of our resolution of the defect issue. * * *

PROBLEM #11. *HANDLING Y2K PARANOIA*

In 1989, Walter Stiles, age 49, underwent surgery to implant a pacemaker to assist his failing heart. He received a Cardiotronic Model #75, a

---

20. The plaintiff and the intervenor argue that there is no difference between allowing recovery for fear and mental anguish as an element of damages if the product in fact fails, and for the fear and mental anguish that the product will fail. We see one critical difference that we illustrate using the facts in this case. Under the current law, if the seventeen persons whose valves actually failed establish a defect, then they can recover mental anguish as a component of their damages. The damages of the seventeen are presumably incorporated into the price of the product and spread among the nineteen thousand who have purchased the valve. In contrast, under the plaintiff's theory, all nineteen thousand would be able to seek recovery for their fear. Again, the probable recovery would be included in the price, but instead of spreading a concentrated loss over a large group, each patient would cover his own probable fear recovery (plus the costs of litigation) by paying a higher price for the heart valve in the first instance. Because no loss-spreading occurs, the money flows in a circle, from each patient (in the form of a higher price) to the company back to the same patient (in the form of a fear recovery), with a substantial portion of the higher price skimmed off for attorneys' fees. In addition, the higher price will place the product beyond the economic reach of at least some of the patients, forcing them to turn to the next best (affordable) alternative. We see little reason to adopt such a system.

medical device first approved by the FDA in 1985. Like many other electronic appliances sold nowadays, the pacemaker was designed with an imbedded computer chip. The chip, which monitored the pacemaker's power source and circuitry, allowed a physician to scan the device periodically without requiring any invasive procedures. During semiannual visits to Mr. Stiles' regular physician, Dr. Laura Manning, the readouts for the pacemaker consistently showed nothing abnormal in its operation.

In 1996, reports began to surface in the media about the so-called "Year 2000 problem" or "millennium bug" in older computer chips. Because dates used only the last two digits of the year, concerns developed that computers would, on Jan. 1, 2000, instead interpret the year as 1900. A great deal of effort and money went into making computers Year 2000 (Y2K) compliant. Upon hearing these reports, Mr. Stiles became alarmed that his pacemaker would malfunction on Jan. 1, 2000. He asked Dr. Manning about this at his Dec. 1998 checkup, but she dismissed his concerns as unfounded. Dr. Manning explained that, at worst, the scanned readouts would provide an incorrect date but there was no reason to fear a malfunction. Mr. Stiles was initially relieved, but he again became worried during the summer of 1999 after having done some additional research on the Internet. Several web sites warned of impending disasters for recipients of pacemakers and other electronic implants. One Internet site directed him to a surgeon in a nearby city, Dr. Ronald Akers, who offered explants of old pacemakers and replacements with Y2K compliant models.

Mr. Stiles was quite agitated when he arrived at Dr. Akers' office and demanded the explant procedure, which Dr. Akers scheduled for Dec. 20, 1999. Realizing that even a short delay could spell disaster, Mr. Stiles became increasingly fearful that he would die at the stroke of midnight on New Year's Eve. In the meantime, the FDA sent an urgent "Dear Doctor" letter warning surgeons against unjustified explant procedures because most pacemakers used computer chips that were not "date aware." On Dec. 15th, the office assistant for Dr. Akers called Mr. Stiles and left a message on his answering machine, saying only that his surgery had been cancelled. Upon arriving at home that evening, Stiles heard the message and became despondent. During a restless night, he suffered a stroke that left him in a permanently vegetative state. Mr. Stiles' pacemaker worked perfectly for another two years until he finally died while in the hospital. His estate plans to sue the manufacturer, Cardiotronic Corp. What claims might Mr. Stiles' estate might bring and what are their probable chances of success?

NOTES AND QUESTIONS

1. *Latent defects and emotional distress*. Other courts have rejected fear of malfunction claims. See Angus v. Shiley Inc., 989 F.2d 142, 147–48 (3d Cir. 1993); Walus v. Pfizer, Inc., 812 F.Supp. 41, 44–45 (D.N.J.1993) (collecting cases); Pfizer, Inc. v. Farsian, 682 So.2d 405, 407–08 (Ala.1996), conformed to certified question, 97 F.3d 508 (11th Cir.1996). These cases vaguely resemble toxic tort litigation brought by persons exposed to hazardous substances who seek to recover for their enhanced future risk of developing cancer. Lawsuits involving the recalled diet drugs fenfluramine and dexfenfluramine (Redux®) posed these issues as well insofar as plaintiffs alleged that they feared developing heart valve abnormalities. See Richard B. Schmitt, Woman Wins $56.6 Million in AHP Case, Wall St. J., Apr. 9, 2001, at B7. In some cases, plaintiffs do not even allege emotional distress. For instance, after the withdrawal of Duract® prompted by safety concerns, a nationwide class action lawsuit was brought on behalf of healthy users and insurers seeking only to recover their economic losses. See Rivera v. Wyeth–Ayerst Lab., 283 F.3d 315, 319–21 (5th Cir.2002) (dismissing lawsuit for lack of standing); id. at 319 ("Rivera would like her money back. The plaintiffs do not claim Duract caused them physical or emotional injury, was ineffective as a pain killer, or has any future health consequences to users."); id. at 320 ("The plaintiffs claim that Wyeth violated the implied warranty of merchantability by selling a defective drug, but then aver that the drug was not defective as to them.").

2. *Recalls, prophylactic explant surgery, and medical monitoring.* If a medical device manufacturer recalls an implant, courts generally have allowed recipients to recover the costs associated with explant surgery and accompanying emotional distress. See Larsen v. Pacesetter Sys., Inc., 837 P.2d 1273, 1286–87 (Haw.1992). If, however, explant surgery is not medically-indicated but undertaken at the patient's insistence, courts have rejected such claims. See O'Brien v. Medtronic, Inc., 439 N.W.2d 151 (Wis.Ct.App.1989). Where defects may require explantation in limited circumstances, plaintiffs may request medical monitoring costs. See In re Telectronics Pacing Sys., Inc., 172 F.R.D. 271, 276–78, 284–87 (S.D.Ohio 1997), rev'd on other grds., 221 F.3d 870 (6th Cir.2000); see also Sutton v. St. Jude Med. S.C., Inc., 419 F.3d 568 (6th Cir.2005) (holding that plaintiff had standing to pursue a class action lawsuit for medical monitoring expenses on behalf of cardiac bypass patients who received an allegedly defective aortic connector and faced an increased risk of injury); In re St. Jude Med., Inc., 425 F.3d 1116, 1121–23 (8th Cir.2005) (reversing certification of class action for medical monitoring of recipients of the recalled Silzone® heart valve). This peculiar remedy has become increasingly popular in pharmaceutical litigation. See David M. Studdert et al., Medical Monitoring for Pharmaceutical Injuries: Tort Law for the Public's Health?, 289 JAMA 889 (2003); see also Wood v. Wyeth–Ayerst Lab., 82 S.W.3d 849, 856–59 (Ky.2002) (recognizing this trend, but declining to join it in a fenfluramine case); Sinclair v. Merck & Co., 948 A.2d 587, 594–96 (N.J. 2008) (same, in a Vioxx case); Tamara J. Dodge, Comment, Raging Hormones?: The Legal Obstacles and Policy Ramifications to Allowing Medical Monitoring Remedies in Hormone Replacement Therapy Suits, 21 Wis. Women's L.J. 263 (2006). To what extent does this form of relief allow plaintiffs to dodge some of the tricky causation difficulties discussed in the previous chapter?

3. *Fear mongering.* What about fears that later prove to be entirely unfounded? For instance, even if the scientific community now accepts the proposition that Bendectin did not cause birth defects, could patients still have sought emotional distress damages for the uncertainty that existed at the time that they used the drug? See Margaret A. Berger & Aaron D. Twerski, Uncertainty and Informed Choice: Unmasking Daubert, 104 Mich. L. Rev. 257 (2005) (arguing that plaintiffs should be allowed to pursue such claims when drug manufacturers fail to warn them of uncertain risks). But see Lars Noah, Platitudes About "Product Stewardship" in Torts: Continuing Drug Research and Education, 15 Mich. Telecomm. & Tech. L. Rev. 359, 373–81 (2009) (roundly criticizing this idea). What if plaintiffs' lawyers and consumer activists had whipped up public hysteria about supposed risks with a product (as happened in the case of silicone-gel breast implants and the widespread fears of autoimmune disease)—would that amount to a superseding cause and absolve the manufacturers of liability? What if such hysteria caused people to forego the use of valuable therapeutic agents (e.g., parents who refused vaccines for their children because of unfounded fears about autism, resulting in an outbreak of a preventable viral illness). See Gardiner Harris, Measles Cases Grow in Number, and Officials Blame Parents' Fear of Autism, N.Y. Times, Aug. 22, 2008, at A16; see also Neil Genzlinger, Vaccinations: A Hot Debate Still Burning, N.Y. Times, Apr. 27, 2010, at C3 (noting "celebrity advocacy by Jenny McCarthy and Jim Carrey," adding that the Internet "is the reason that vaccines will never be fully exonerated, no matter how many studies clear them"). Could the victims sue the manufacturers for failing to have sufficiently reassuring data on hand?!

4. *Class action settlements.* Each high profile drug withdrawal or device recall precipitates its own flood of litigation (including claims of failures to warn that are discussed in the next chapter) and often results in a global settlement agreement. See, e.g., In re Diet Drugs Prods. Liab. Litig., 385 F.3d 386 (3d Cir.2004) (approving Wyeth's $3.75 billion class action settlement); In re Vioxx Prod. Liab. Litig., 650 F.Supp.2d 549, 551–53 (E.D.La. 2009) (summarizing the multidistrict litigation and $4.85 billion settlement); In re Zyprexa Prods. Liab. Litig., 649 F.Supp.2d 18, 21–28 (E.D.N.Y. 2009) (recounting the regulatory history related to Eli Lilly's atypical antipsychotic olanzapine as it related to the "massive and highly complex multidistrict litigation" alleging, among other things, that the manufacturer provided inadequate warnings of the risk of weight gain and diabetes); Stephanie Saul, Pfizer in $894 Million Drug Settlement, N.Y. Times, Oct. 18, 2008, at B2 (Bextra and Celebrex); see also In re Baycol Prods. Liab. Litig., 218 F.R.D. 197, 204 (D.Minn.2003) ("To date, no court of appeals decision has approved class certification of an action involving prescription drugs."); Barbara J. Rothstein et al., A Model Mass Tort: The PPA Experience, 54 Drake L. Rev. 621 (2006); Danielle Oakley, Note, Is Multidistrict Litigation a Just and Efficient Consolidation Technique? Using Diet Drug Litigation as a Model to Answer This Question, 6 Nev. L.J. 494 (2006). Disputes still may arise about claims filed by plaintiffs who participated in the class settlement. See, e.g., Plaintiffs' Attorneys Dispute Allegations That They Induced Doctors to Inflate Claims, 30 Prod. Safety & Liab. Rep. (BNA) 876 (2002) (discussing problems in the administration of $3.75 billion nationwide class action settlement of the fen-phen litigation).

Bowling v. Pfizer, Inc.

922 F.Supp. 1261 (S.D.Ohio), aff'd mem., 103 F.3d 128 (6th Cir.1996).

■ NANGLE, DISTRICT JUDGE:

* * * Between 1979 and 1986, Shiley, Inc., a wholly-owned subsidiary of Pfizer, Inc., manufactured a human-implant heart valve known as the Bjork–Shiley convexo/concave heart valve ("c/c heart valve" or "valve"). Somewhere between 50,000 and 100,000 of the valves were implanted in patients world-wide. By 1992, approximately 450 of these valves had fractured resulting in approximately 300 deaths. The valves continue to fracture today and it is anticipated that they will continue to do so in the future.

As early as 1984, consumer groups such as the Washington, D.C.-based Public Citizen, Inc., claimed that the c/c heart valve posed a serious public health threat because it had design and manufacture defects which caused it to have an abnormally high risk of fracture. Defendants have steadfastly denied that the c/c heart valve is any more likely to fracture than any other valve available on the market at that time; however, when Public Citizen petitioned the Food and Drug Administration in 1990 to require defendants to notify implantees of the risks associated with the valves, defendants voluntarily agreed to undertake to find and notify implant patients and their physicians of the alleged risks posed by the valves.

The c/c heart valve has engendered a substantial amount of litigation. Individuals implanted with valves that have fractured, as well as individuals with properly functioning valves, have brought suit against defendants in jurisdictions across the United States. In every suit involving a valve that had actually fractured, defendants were able to settle the case with a confidential agreement. In cases where there had been no fracture, however, defendants were able to get at least 27 courts to dismiss the suits on the ground that there is no right of recovery for emotional distress arising from a valve implantee's fear that a properly functioning valve might fracture in the future.

Although defendants had generally been successful at settling all fracture cases and getting non-fracture cases dismissed, the litigation and attendant poor publicity was nevertheless taking its toll. Defendants were having to devote substantial resources to defending the nation-wide litigation, and a California court denied their motion for summary judgment in a case where a plaintiff had a properly functioning c/c heart valve. Furthermore, criticism of the valve and of the defendants in newspaper articles, television programs and even congressional hearings began to mount. Thus, as Judge Spiegel observed in his order finding the proposed settlement to be fair, defendants had ample reason to settle all claims involving their c/c heart valves.

All of the named plaintiffs in this action had properly functioning c/c heart valves when their complaint was filed on April 19, 1991. The causes of action asserted in their complaint included negligence, strict liability, negligent misrepresentation, fraudulent misrepresentation, intentional infliction of emotional distress, and negligent infliction of emotional distress; and the relief sought included compensatory damages, medical monitoring, and punitive damages. * * *

The settlement applies to all living persons currently implanted with c/c heart valves (approximately 50,000 people) and their current spouses, except those who file valid and timely requests for exclusion. The settlement has three primary components: The Patient Benefit Fund, The Medical and Psychological Consultation Fund, and The Fracture Compensation Mechanism.

A. The Patient Benefit Fund

The Patient Benefit Fund is a guaranteed fund of $37.5 million, which may increase to as much as $75 million, that is to be used to fund research and development and valve replacement surgery ("explanation") for qualifying class members. The settlement requires defendants to deposit $12.5 million following "Final Approval of the Settlement," and then $6.25 million annually starting on the second anniversary of the Final Approval of the Settlement. Once the defendants have contributed $37.5 million to the Fund, they are entitled to go before the court and argue that further research would be fruitless and that they should not, therefore, be required to make further contributions to the Fund. If they are unsuccessful in their argument, then they are required to continue the annual contribution of $6.25 million until they have deposited a total of $75 million.

In order to administer the benefits available under the Patient Benefit Fund, the settlement creates a seven-member Supervisory Panel to manage the research and to determine whether a class member qualifies for a particular benefit. The Panel is to be comprised of six experts and one layman and all of the fees and expenses of the Panel are to be paid from this Fund. The specific benefits available under the Fund are:

Research and Development. The fund will pay for research and development of diagnostic techniques to identify implantees who have a significant risk of valve fracture, and research to reduce and properly characterize the risks associated with valve replacement surgery.

Payment of Expenses Associated with Explant Surgery. Payment of the usual and customary expenses for valve replacement surgery that are not covered by a third-party payor (i.e. insurance company, government, etc.), where surgery is necessitated by risk of valve fracture.

$38,000.00 for Miscellaneous Expenses. Payment of $38,000.00 to each member who undergoes an explant surgery approved by the Panel and who does not suffer death or permanent bodily injury. This payment is to cover miscellaneous costs of post-hospitalization care, meals, travel, etc.

Temporary Loss of Income. Member's actual lost income, up to $1,500.00 per week for a maximum of 16 total weeks, resulting from a member's inability to work because of hospitalization and recuperation from a qualifying valve replacement surgery. The amount payable is reduced by any payments available from a third-party payor, such as worker's compensation, sick pay, disability insurance, etc. The lost income is only payable from the sixteenth through fifty-second week after surgery.

Permanent Loss of Income. If, after one year, a member is partially disabled from explant surgery and, as a result, suffers a diminished earning capacity and/or extraordinary medical expenses, then he will receive compensation for future income loss that is not covered by workmen's compensation, a disability policy or other third-party source.

Alternative Payment for Death or Permanent Total Disability. If valve replacement surgery results in death or permanent total disability, then a member is entitled to: (1) The same payment available to a member whose valve actually fractures under the Valve Compensation Mechanism; or (2) compensation as set by an arbitration procedure.

Payment for FDA Approved Diagnostic Procedure. If the Food and Drug Administration approves a technique for diagnosing valves with a high risk of fracture, then the Supervisory Panel may use the money from the Fund to pay for the use of the technique on class members where it is reasonably medically necessary.

Additionally, this portion of the settlement permits a class member, who qualifies for valve replacement surgery but chooses not to undergo surgery, to bring an action for damages for alleged emotional distress from fear of fracture of a working valve if the class member has not received any fracture compensation under the settlement. Finally, in the event that class members continue to qualify for explant surgery after the Fund is fully expanded to $75 million, the settlement obligates defendants to continue to pay all of the members' qualifying expenses and benefits listed above even though defendants' total contribution to the Fund would exceed $75 million.

B. The Medical and Psychological Consultation Fund

The Medical and Psychological Consultation Fund is a fund of at least $80 million, which could increase to as much as $130 million, that is intended to provide class members with funds to obtain medical and psychological consultation. The Fund will provide an equal cash payment of between $2,500.00 and $4,000.00 to each member, depending upon how many class members make a claim. Defendants are also required, under this part of the settlement, to pay an additional $10 million into the Fund, which is to be paid to spouses of valve implantees ("Spousal Compensation Fund"). * * *

C. The Valve Fracture Mechanism

The third component of the settlement, the Valve Fracture Mechanism, provides an implantee whose valve has fractured with one of three options for seeking compensation. The first option is a sort of insurance program whereby compensation is determined by a set of formulas that take into account a claimant's family status, age, income and country of residence. The compensation available to a United States resident, for example, ranges from a minimum of $500,000.00 to a maximum of $2,000,000.00, while the payment to members from other countries may be something less but is in no event less than $50,000.00. The settlement creates a Foreign Fracture Panel, which will determine fair compensation for fracture claimants who are residents of countries other than the United States.

The second alternative available to a fracture claimant under the mechanism is binding arbitration. The claimant can bring his or her claim before a three-member panel, whose decision is final and binding. The third option is to bring suit against defendants in an appropriate forum, with all claims and defenses preserved. * * *

An important issue of settlement interpretation that has arisen is whether a class member implanted with a valve that suffers a so-called "single-leg fracture" or "single-strut separation" qualifies for explanation benefits and/or compensation under the Fracture Mechanism. Class and Special Counsel took the position that a member suffering a single-leg separation should receive the same treatment under the settlement that a member suffering a full, dual-leg fracture receives.[12] Defendants disagreed, taking the position that a single-leg separation is qualitatively different from a full, dual-leg fracture and, as a result, a class member suffering such a separation should not be entitled to the same benefits as a member suffering a complete fracture. The parties resolved the issue through an agreement that Class Counsel would negotiate with the defendants each single-leg fracture case on an individual basis. * * *

---

12. It is the court's understanding that, when only one of the two legs on the c/c valve fractures, the valve continues to function; whereas, when both legs fracture, the valve stops functioning.

CHAPTER 7

Informational Defects

In products liability litigation, failure-to-warn claims have become quite common, supplanting the more traditional and difficult to prove claims such as those alleging defects in manufacture or design. Although prescription drugs by their very nature are most often the subject of lawsuits alleging failures to warn, medical devices and OTC drugs also have been faulted for informational defects. Two difficult questions arise: is there any obligation to warn of a particular risk and, if such a duty exists, was any warning already provided with the product adequate.

A. Triggering the Duty to Warn

1. Unknowable Risks

Feldman v. Lederle Laboratories

479 A.2d 374 (N.J.1984).

■ Schreiber, Justice:

* * * Tetracyclines are a group of antibiotics that was first introduced in 1948. They were produced by different drug manufacturers that marketed the drugs under various trade names.

Defendant first marketed Declomycin in 1959. The *Physicians' Desk Reference* (*PDR*), a book used by doctors to determine effects of drugs, contains data furnished by drug manufacturers about drugs, their compositions, usages, and reactions. The 1959 *PDR* entry for Declomycin stated that it had a greater antibiotic potency that made it possible to achieve therapeutic activity with less weight of antibiotic; it had a reduced renal clearance rate that produced a prolongation of the antibacterial levels in the body; and it was therapeutically equally effective as other tetracyclines in infections caused by organisms sensitive to the tetracyclines. The *PDR* is produced annually. Until the 1965 or 1966 edition, the *PDR* did not mention that tooth discoloration was a possible side effect of Declomycin. Since 1965 or 1966 the *PDR* has stated that the drug, when administered to infants and children, could cause tooth discoloration that would be permanent if the drug were given during the developmental stage of the permanent teeth.

Plaintiff, Carol Ann Feldman, was born on February 8, 1960. Her father, Dr. Harold Feldman, asserted that he prescribed Declomycin for her approximately seven or more times from September or October, 1960, when she was eight or nine months old, until the end of 1963. She was given this drug to prevent secondary infections when she had different childhood diseases. In his words, "[i]t was a very effective drug for what I was using it for." He had been introduced to the drug by a medical representative employed by the defendant. The representative gave him a number of samples to be distributed to patients. Plaintiff's baby teeth were discolored gray-brown. Her permanent teeth were more deeply discolored, being primarily gray. The parties agreed that this discoloration had resulted from use of a tetracycline, although they disputed whether Declomycin was the particular tetracycline involved. * * *

The respective experts, Dr. Bonda for the plaintiff and Dr. Guggenheimer for the defendant, agreed that scientific literature existed by 1960 that referred to tooth staining being caused by tetracycline. Dr. Bonda specifically mentioned a 1956 article by Dr. Andre reciting that tetracycline accumulated in mineralized portions of growing bones and teeth of mice; an article by Dr. Milch in the July 1957 *Journal of the National Cancer Institute* reporting that laboratory animals had yellow fluorescents in bones, including teeth, following dosages of tetracycline; a second article by Dr. Milch in the July 1958 issue of the *Journal of Bone and Joint Surgery* again describing fluorescents in the bones and incisor teeth of rodents that had been fed tetracycline; a 1959 article by Dr. Swackman noting that, of 50 children with cystic fibrosis who had received massive doses of tetracycline, 40 had dark tooth staining; a 1960 letter from Dr. Sigrelli, a Columbia University professor, to the *Pediatric Journal* observing that patients with cystic fibrosis of the pancreas who had received tetracyclines as an antibiotic suffered severe discoloration of their teeth, possibly as a result of their tetracycline use; a May 1961 article by Dr. Sigrelli in the *New Jersey/New York State Dental Journal* containing the same information; and an essay by Dr. Bevlander on "The Effect of the Administration of Tetracycline on the Development of Teeth" in the October 1961 issue of the *Journal of Dental Research* reflecting the adverse effect of tetracycline on developing teeth in young laboratory animals. Dr. Bonda concluded the defendant should have begun to investigate the possible effects of all forms of tetracycline on teeth no later than 1956, when the Andre article appeared.

Defendant's expert, Dr. Guggenheimer, on the other hand, noted that before 1962 the literature on tooth discoloration concerned only patients with cystic fibrosis who had been receiving massive doses of tetracyclines. He pointed out that Dr. Milch's papers described only fluorescents, not tooth staining. He testified that Declomycin did not become available until 1959 and that it would take 2½ years for permanent teeth developing in 1959 to erupt. The completion of accurate controlled studies of multiple well-documented cases would have been the only way one could really know whether Declomycin caused tooth discoloration in permanent teeth. Dr. Guggenheimer's testimony is unclear as to whether a correlation between tetracycline and tooth discoloration had been established in 1962. One reading of his testimony indicates that such a correlation was not known to exist and that only by hindsight could that conclusion be drawn. It is also possible to interpret his opinion to be that such correlation had been established in 1962. In any event it is significant that Dr. Guggenheimer gave no opinion as to 1963.

On November 16, 1962, Dr. Swanzey, defendant's Director of Regulatory Agencies Relations, wrote to the Federal Food and Drug Administration (FDA) that the defendant proposed to add to the labels on all its tetracycline products the following warning: "During therapy tetracyclines may form a stable calcium complex in bone-forming tissue with no known harmful effects. Use of any tetracycline during teeth development in the neonatal period or early childhood may cause discoloration of the teeth." Dr. Swanzey explained that it was not necessary to obtain FDA approval before placing a warning on a label, but it was the practice to do so. On cross-examination, however, he indicated that, although no FDA approval was needed to write letters to doctors informing them of this correlation, labeling the product without FDA approval could be considered a misbranding.

The FDA acknowledged receipt of Dr. Swanzey's letter on December 3, 1962, and advised him that the FDA "has been acutely interested by the increasing number of new and/or undesirable effects accompanying or following the use of these products," and would notify the defendant "as soon as any conclusion is reached." Dr. Swanzey telephoned Dr. Barzilai of the FDA, who advised against putting any statement in a circular proposed to be distributed by the defendant and that the FDA had the matter under study. On January 15, 1963, Dr. Swanzey sent to the FDA two articles on bone effects, including a copy of the Bevlander article. Dr. Swanzey also spoke with Dr. Sigrelli, who advised that staining would occur with some tetracyclines, but he had not observed that it occurred with Declomycin.

The FDA, in a letter dated February 4, 1963, proposed that the defendant insert the following warning statement in "all" its tetracycline products:

> Tetracyclines may form a stable calcium complex in any bone forming tissue with no serious harmful effects reported thus far in humans. However, use of any tetracycline drug during tooth development (= last trimester of pregnancy, neonatal period and early childhood) may cause discoloration of the teeth (= yellow-grey-brownish). This effect occurs mostly during long-term use of the drug but it has also been observed in usual short treatment courses.

Dr. Swanzey responded that the suggested statement was satisfactory and would be incorporated in its literature. He added that he assumed that the directive was applicable to Declomycin as well as other tetracycline drugs. The FDA replied that "[t]here is practically no specific clinical evidence to substantiate such a labeling requirement" for Declomycin and the warning would have to appear only on labeling of other tetracycline drugs. On April 12, 1963, the FDA made it clear that the warning statement was to refer not to tetracyclines generally but only to the specific brand names of the implicated products.

In 1963, the defendant received complaints from eight doctors that Declomycin was causing tooth staining. In May, 1963 the defendant referred the FDA again to the side effect of Declomycin. Commencing in mid-December 1963, after receipt of FDA approval, it included the same warning in the Declomycin literature as in other tetracyclines. * * *

This is a strict liability warning case. The product has been made as the manufacturer intended. The plaintiff does not contend that it contained a manufacturing defect. Declomycin's purpose was to act as did other tetracyclines—as an antibiotic. However, it had several advantages over other antimicrobial therapeutics. The plaintiff does not dispute this. Indeed, there is no evidence that plaintiff's usage of Declomycin was not adequate in this respect. Nor was there any proof that it was improperly designed. The crux of the plaintiff's complaint is that her doctor should have been warned of a possible side effect of the drug in infants, discoloration of teeth. * * *

The emphasis of the strict liability doctrine is upon the safety of the product, rather than the reasonableness of the manufacturer's conduct. It is a product-oriented approach to responsibility. Generally speaking, the doctrine of strict liability assumes that enterprises should be responsible for damages to consumers resulting from defective products regardless of fault. The doctrine differs from a negligence theory, which centers on the defendant's conduct and seeks to determine whether the defendant acted as a reasonably prudent person. This difference between strict liability and negligence is commonly expressed by stating that in a strict liability analysis, the defendant is assumed to know of the dangerous propensity of the product, whereas in a negligence case, the plaintiff must prove that the defendant knew or should have known of the danger. This distinction is particularly pertinent in a manufacturing defect context.

When the strict liability defect consists of an improper design or warning, reasonableness of the defendant's conduct is a factor in determining liability. The question in strict liability design defect and warning cases is whether, assuming that the manufacturer knew of the defect in the product, he acted in a reasonably prudent manner in marketing the product or in providing the warnings given. Thus, once the defendant's knowledge of the defect is imputed, strict liability analysis becomes almost identical to negligence analysis in its focus on the reasonableness of the defendant's conduct. * * *

[A]s to warnings, generally conduct should be measured by knowledge at the time the manufacturer distributed the product. Did the defendant know, or should he have known, of the danger, given the scientific, technological, and other information available when the product was distributed; or, in other words, did he have actual or constructive knowledge of the danger? The *Restatement (Second) of Torts* has adopted this test in comment j to section 402A * * * * Under this standard negligence and strict liability in warning cases may be deemed to be functional equivalents. Constructive knowledge embraces knowledge that should have been known based on information that was reasonably available or obtainable and should have alerted a reasonably prudent person to act. Put another way, would a person of reasonable intelligence or of the superior expertise of the defendant charged with such knowledge conclude that defendant should have alerted the consuming public?

Further, a manufacturer is held to the standard of an expert in the field. A manufacturer should keep abreast of scientific advances. * * * Implicit in the requirement that such a manufacturer is held to the standard applicable to experts in the field is the notion that at least in some fields, such as those impacting on public health, a manufacturer may be expected to be informed and affirmatively to seek out information concerning the public's use of its own product.

Furthermore, a reasonably prudent manufacturer will be deemed to know of reliable information generally available or reasonably obtainable in the industry or in the particular field involved. Such information need not be limited to that furnished by experts in the field, but may also include material provided by others. Thus, for example, if a substantial number of doctors or consumers had complained to a drug manufacturer of an untoward effect of a drug, that would have constituted sufficient information requiring an appropriate warning. See Hoffman v. Sterling Drug, Inc., 485 F.2d 132, 146 (3d Cir.1973) (in judgment for plaintiff alleging negligence and strict products liability in failure-to-warn case against prescription drug manufacturer of Aralen, court found jury question whether defendants used foresight appropriate to their enterprise in view of the number of letters from physicians reporting visual injury in patients using Aralen and subsequent medical literature). * * *

In strict liability warning cases, unlike negligence cases, however, the defendant should properly bear the burden of proving that the information was not reasonably available or obtainable and that it therefore lacked actual or constructive knowledge of the defect. The defendant is in a superior position to know the technological material or data in the particular field or specialty. The defendant is the expert, often performing self-testing. It is the defendant that injected the product in the stream of commerce for its economic gain. As a matter of policy the burden of proving the status of knowledge in the field at the time of distribution is properly placed on the defendant.

One other aspect with respect to warnings based on subsequently obtained knowledge should be considered. Communication of the new warning should unquestionably be given to prescribing physicians as soon as reasonably feasible. Although a manufacturer may not have actual or constructive knowledge of a danger so as to impose upon it a duty to warn, subsequently acquired knowledge, both actual and constructive, also may obligate the manufacturer to take reasonable steps to notify purchasers and consumers of the newly-discovered danger.

The timeliness of the warning issue is obliquely present in this case. It is possible that Dr. Feldman already had Declomycin on hand when defendant became aware of Declomycin's side effect. If that state of affairs existed, defendant would have had an obligation to warn doctors and others promptly. This most assuredly would include those to whom defendant had already furnished the product. The extent and nature of post-distribution warnings may vary depending on the circumstances, but in the context of this case, the defendant at a minimum would have had a duty of advising physicians, including plaintiff's father, whom it had directly solicited to use Declomycin. * * *

[The defendant also argued] that it could not lawfully have modified the warnings without FDA approval, an approval that was not obtained until the end of 1963. It raised this defense even though its witness, Dr. Swanzey, testified there was "no prohibition" against inserting the additional warning without FDA approval. * * * We note that the regulation did not prevent a drug manufacturer from adding an additional warning as soon as it was aware of its necessity. Nor has counsel submitted to us any FDA administrative decision to the contrary effect. It would seem anomalous for the FDA to have prevented a drug manufacturer from advising the public immediately of a newly discovered danger while waiting for FDA approval. * * * Furthermore, in 1965 the regulation was amended to require that drug manufacturers inform the public immediately of newly discovered dangers before waiting for the FDA to act. * * *

The trial court erred in fixing the date at which defendant's actual or constructive knowledge was to be measured. It was undisputed that plaintiff had received Declomycin or another tetracycline from approximately September, 1960 until the end of 1963. When the trial court considered the motion, it referred to the conflict in the evidence on whether defendant knew or should have known of the correlation between an infant's ingestion of Declomycin and tooth discoloration in 1960, when the plaintiff first began receiving the drug.

However, the evidence is overwhelming that, at least by mid-November 1962, defendant had sufficient information to warrant that it warn doctors of the possible tooth discoloration effects of Declomycin when administered to infants. According to Dr. Swanzey, then defendant's Director of Regulatory Agency Relations, defendant had "strong suspicions" of the connection between tetracyclines and the discoloration of the teeth by the end of 1962. However, the defendant's actions indicate that its awareness at that time went beyond the stage of suspicion. There was no equivocation in its letter to the FDA on November 16, 1962. The letter proposed that defendant add to the labels on all its tetracycline products, including Declomycin, the following warning: "Use of *any* tetracycline during teeth development in the neonatal period or early childhood may cause discoloration of the teeth." * * *

Apart from plaintiff's evidence to the effect that defendant should have known of the side effect as early as 1960, the record overwhelmingly demonstrates that defendant actually knew of the danger by the end of 1962. Defendant nonetheless continued to market the drug in 1963 and plaintiff continued to ingest the drug that year. * * * In that event defendant would be responsible at least for the enhancement of the condition. We reverse and remand for a new trial.

Carlin v. Superior Court (Upjohn Co.)

920 P.2d 1347 (Cal.1996).

■ MOSK, JUSTICE:

* * * Plaintiff Wilma Peggy Carlin brought an action for damages against Upjohn for injuries she assertedly sustained from ingesting the drug Halcion, which was prescribed for her by a physician between 1987 and 1992. * * * Upjohn demurred, alleging, inter alia, that Carlin failed to state facts sufficient to constitute a cause of action for strict liability * * * * It argues that California courts have "long refused to expand the scope of potential liability of prescription pharmaceutical manufacturers beyond traditional negligence principles." Not so. In prior cases, we have expressly and repeatedly applied a strict liability standard to manufacturers of prescription drugs for failure to warn of known or reasonably scientifically knowable risks. We merely reaffirm those precedents here.

In *Anderson v. Owens–Corning Fiberglas Corp.*, 810 P.2d 549 (Cal. 1991), we summarized prior case law and outlined the general principles of strict liability as they have been applied by California courts for over three decades. * * * Although *Anderson* involved an action against a manufacturer of asbestos, we relied extensively on cases involving a variety of products, *including prescription drugs*. In particular, we were guided by our prior decision in *Brown v. Superior Court*, 751 P.2d 470 (Cal.1988), in which we refused to extend strict liability to the failure to warn of risks that were unknown or *unknowable* at the time of distribution. * * *

We recognized that the knowledge or knowability requirement for failure to warn infuses some negligence concepts into strict liability cases. Indeed, in the failure-to-warn context, strict liability is to some extent a hybrid of traditional strict liability and negligence doctrine. As we explained, however, "the claim that a particular component 'rings of' or 'sounds in' negligence has not precluded its acceptance in the context of strict liability." Indeed, "the strict liability doctrine has incorporated some well-settled rules from the law of negligence and has survived judicial challenges asserting that such incorporation violates the fundamental principles of the doctrine." Thus, although *Anderson*, following *Brown*, incorporated certain negligence concepts into the standard of strict liability for failure to warn, it did not thereby adopt a simple negligence test.

"[F]ailure to warn in strict liability differs markedly from failure to warn in the negligence context. * * * [I]n strict liability, as opposed to negligence, the reasonableness of the defendant's failure to warn is immaterial. Stated another way, a reasonably prudent manufacturer might reasonably decide that the risk of harm was such as not to require a warning as, for example, if the manufacturer's own testing showed a result contrary to that of others in the scientific community. Such a manufacturer might escape liability under negligence principles. In contrast, under strict liability principles the manufacturer has no such leeway; the manufacturer is liable if it failed to give warning of dangers that were known to the scientific community at the time it manufactured or distributed the product." Similarly, a manufacturer could not escape liability under strict liability principles merely because its failure to warn of a known or reasonably scientifically knowable risk conformed to an industry-wide practice of failing to provide warnings that constituted the standard of reasonable care.

We explained the policy behind our strict liability standard for failure to warn as follows: " 'When, in a particular case, the risk qualitatively (e.g., of death or major disability) as well as quantitatively, on balance with the end sought to be achieved, is such as to call for a true choice judgment, medical or personal, the warning must be given. . . .' Thus, the fact that a manufacturer acted as a reasonably prudent manufacturer in deciding not to warn, while perhaps absolving the manufacturer of liability under the negligence theory, will not preclude liability under strict liability principles if the trier of fact concludes that, based on the information scientifically available to the manufacturer, the manufacturer's failure to warn rendered the product unsafe to its users."

Upjohn and amici curiae argue that applying *Anderson* will place manufacturers of prescription drugs in an untenable position because they must comply with regulations set by the Food and Drug Administration, which may preclude them from labeling drugs with warnings of certain side effects. They also contend that *Anderson* would result in overlabeling of pharmaceuticals. Neither claim withstands scrutiny.

We are unpersuaded by Upjohn's argument that a strict liability standard for failure to warn about known or reasonably scientifically knowable risks from prescription drugs is inconsistent with federal regulatory policy. Upjohn concedes that FDA regulations do not expressly preempt common law tort remedies for failure to warn or occupy the entire field of regulation. As numerous courts have concluded, Congress evinced no intention of preempting state tort liability for injuries from prescription drugs.

We disagree with Carlin's argument, however, that FDA regulations are essentially irrelevant in a common law action for failure to warn. We reiterate that strict liability for failure to warn *is not absolute liability*. Under *Anderson*, drug manufacturers are not strictly liable for a risk that was not known or reasonably scientifically knowable. In this context, it is significant that the FDA *precludes* drug manufacturers from warning about every conceivable adverse reaction; they may warn only if there exists significant medical evidence of a possible health hazard. * * *

In appropriate cases, FDA action or inaction, though not dispositive, may be admissible under *Anderson* to show whether a risk was known or reasonably scientifically knowable. Similarly, a drug manufacturer could present evidence to show that there was no "reasonably scientifically knowable risk" because, at the time of distribution, the cause of the alleged adverse effect was too speculative to have been reasonably attributable to the drug by a scientist conducting state-of-the-art research. Thus, when a plaintiff's claim is based on an allegation that a particular risk was "reasonably scientifically knowable," an inquiry may arise as to what a reasonable scientist operating in good faith should have known under the circumstances of the evidence. As we emphasized in *Anderson*, we do not altogether reject strict liability in the failure-to-warn context—for drugs or any other products—simply because some considerations of reasonableness sounding in negligence may be required.

Moreover, in the case of an alleged "known" risk, if state-of-the-art scientific data concerning the alleged risk was fully disclosed to the FDA and it determined, after review, that the pharmaceutical manufacturer *was not permitted to warn*—e.g., because the data w[ere] inconclusive or the risk was too speculative to justify a warning—the manufacturer could present such evidence to show that strict liability cannot apply; the FDA's conclusion that there was, in effect, no "known risk" is controlling.

We are also unpersuaded by Upjohn's assertion that applying strict liability to claims of injury for failure to warn will inevitably result in manufacturers inundating consumers with warnings of even speculative risks from prescription drugs. In *Finn v. G.D. Searle & Co.*, 677 P.2d 1147 (Cal.1984), we addressed the potential problems of overlabeling: "[E]xperience suggest[s] that if every report of a possible risk, no matter how speculative, conjectural, or tentative, imposed an affirmative duty to give some warning, a manufacturer would be required to inundate physicians indiscriminately with notice of any and every hint of danger, thereby inevitably diluting the force of any specific warning given."

The application of the failure-to-warn theory to pharmaceuticals requires determinations whether available evidence established a causal link between an alleged side effect and a prescription drug, whether any warning should have been given, and, if so, whether the warning was adequate. These are issues of fact involving, inter alia, questions concerning the state of the art, i.e., what was known or reasonably knowable by the application of scientific and medical knowledge available at the time of manufacture and distribution of the prescription drug. They also necessarily involve questions concerning whether the risk, in light of accepted scientific norms, was more than merely speculative or conjectural, or so remote and insignificant as to be negligible. Moreover, in the case of prescription drugs, the duty to warn runs *to the physician*, not to the patient. Thus, a pharmaceutical manufacturer may not be required to provide warning of a risk known to the medical community.

Nor does Upjohn offer any sound public policy rationale for departing from *Anderson* concerning the liability of manufacturers of prescription drugs for failure to warn of known or reasonably scientifically knowable risks. Thus, we are unpersuaded by the argument, purportedly derived from our reasoning in *Brown*, that manufacturers of prescription drugs should be exempt from the strict liability duty to warn because they might otherwise refrain from developing and marketing drugs, including "cutting-edge vaccines to combat human immunodeficiency virus (HIV)" and other diseases. Our rationale in *Brown*, which involved strict liability for *design defects*, is inapplicable: unlike strict liability for design defects, strict liability for failure to warn does not potentially subject drug manufacturers to liability for flaws in their products that they have not, and could not have, discovered. Drug manufacturers need only warn of risks that are *actually known or reasonably scientifically knowable.*

Upjohn offers no clear or sufficient basis for concluding that research and development will inevitably decrease as a result of imposing strict liability for failure to warn of *known or reasonably scientifically knowable* risks; indeed, requiring manufacturers to internalize the costs of failing to determine such risks may instead *increase* the level of research into safe and effective drugs. In any event, we see no reason to depart from our conclusion in *Anderson* that the manufacturer should bear the costs, in terms of preventable injury or death, of its own failure to provide adequate warnings of known or reasonably scientifically knowable risks. As we observed: "Whatever may be reasonable from the point of view of the manufacturer, the user of the product must be given the option either to refrain from using the product at all or to use it in such a way as to minimize the degree of danger." * * *

■ KENNARD, JUSTICE (concurring in part and dissenting in part):

The manufacture of prescription drugs, a multi billion-dollar industry, has provided many of the 20th century's greatest success stories and some of its worst tragedies. Because they cure disease, alleviate pain, and prolong life, prescription drugs have been a great benefit to society. But prescription drugs sometimes cause severe complications and side effects, inflicting great anguish as well as temporary and even permanent disability on some individuals.

This court's task in the present case is to set rules defining prescription drug manufacturers' tort liability for personal injuries caused by their products' side effects. More particularly, the task is to determine under what circumstances a drug manufacturer should be held liable in tort for personal injury damages proximately caused by a failure to warn about the possibility of a particular drug complication. * * *

At first glance, the majority's holding—that a prescription drug manufacturer need warn only of those risks that are "known or reasonably scientifically knowable"—appears quite reasonable. A close look, however, reveals that the majority imposes on a manufacturer a duty to warn of any risk that arguably may exist. The sheer breadth of that duty threatens two fundamental public interests. First, the majority's holding will result in the problems of overwarning this court has previously recognized, thereby undermining the public interest in consumer protection. Second, by subjecting prescription drug manufacturers to excessive liability, the majority's standard jeopardizes the important public interest of encouraging the development, availability, and affordability of beneficial prescription drugs.

To discern what the majority means by the phrase "known or reasonably scientifically knowable" is no easy task. Throughout its opinion, the majority itself gives different descriptions of the meaning of that phrase. The majority's various characterizations of "knowability" lead me to conclude that the majority considers a risk to be "knowable," even though not actually known to the manufacturer, if the risk at the time of distribution had been or reasonably could have been scientifically identified. The word "risk" simply means the possibility of a loss. Because the majority does not suggest that the degree of probability of loss is of any significance, the majority seemingly equates the identification of a bare possibility of harm with "knowability" and hence a duty to warn. Thus, under the majority's holding, once a prescription drug plaintiff proves that a risk has been or reasonably could have been identified by the scientific community, the manufacturer has a duty to warn regardless of whether warning is otherwise appropriate or reasonable. * * *

In my view, the majority's holding goes too far in imposing liability, because it fails to recognize the complexity involved in scientifically identifying a risk as meaningful and in determining whether a warning is appropriate. As this court has noted, the quality of scientific evidence "may range from extremely vague to highly certain." Scientific studies suggesting associations between products and injuries may themselves be subjected to legitimate question as to the validity of their methods and the soundness of their conclusions. The majority's apparent standard that a prescription drug manufacturer is strictly liable for failure to warn of any "knowable" risk fails to recognize, much less deal with, the complexity of scientific evaluations.

A possible result of such a standard is the destruction of the viability of any warnings. * * * The problems of overwarning are exacerbated if warnings must be given even as to very remote risks, which drug manufacturers may find necessary under the vague standard that the majority adopts today. "Not only would such remote risk warnings crowd out potentially useful warnings but they would also focus consumer attention on the fairy tale bogeyman. One cannot cry wolf without paying the price over the long term."

According to the majority, its standard of liability would not result in inundating consumers with too many warnings, because the manufacturer's duty to warn runs to the physician rather than the patient, and because there is no duty to warn of obvious dangers. It is true, as the majority states, that a prescription drug manufacturer has no duty to ensure that a warning given a physician reaches the patient. But even physicians, the "learned intermediaries," may be overwhelmed by excessive warnings. As this court has recognized, both common sense and experience suggest that to require a manufacturer "to inundate physicians indiscriminately with notice of any and every hint of danger" inevitably dilutes "the force of any specific warning given." And, contrary to the majority's assertion, the absence of a duty to warn of known or obvious dangers has little import in the context of prescription drugs, because few of the sophisticated potential risks of prescription drugs could be considered obvious.

The majority's holding exposes prescription drug manufacturers to such broad liability that they may restrict or cease the development and distribution of life-sustaining and lifesaving drugs, thereby defeating a strong public interest. * * * The concern repeatedly voiced by the courts and legal commentators that the imposition of excessive liability on prescription drug manufacturers may discourage the development and availability of life-sustaining and lifesaving drugs is well founded * * * * To require prescription drug manufacturers to warn of all scientifically knowable risks, as the majority holds, exposes them to excessive liability. Such exposure creates a powerful disincentive on the part of prescription drug manufacturers to develop essential medications, especially when it is joined with the extensive liability exposure for alleged inadequacy of warnings given. * * *

Justice Baxter's dissent [which is not included with this excerpt] expresses the view that a prescription drug manufacturer's liability for failure to warn should be based solely upon negligence principles. Under that approach, a manufacturer is liable for failure to warn only if the plaintiff establishes that a reasonable manufacturer in similar circumstances would have issued warnings. The dissent agrees with the majority that the legal theories of negligent failure to warn and strict liability failure to warn are two different theories of liability: negligence looks to the reasonableness of a manufacturer's conduct while strict liability considers it irrelevant. According to the dissent, the same policy considerations that led this court in *Brown* to adopt a negligence standard for prescription drug design defects apply with equal force when, as here, the alleged defect is a failure to warn of risks associated with the drug.

The dissent cites four reasons for its conclusion. First, it mentions that several commentators have concluded that a product's warning may be characterized as a subset of the product's design. Second, the dissent points out that products liability law has always recognized that prescription drugs may require different legal treatment than other products, and that the tentative draft of the *Restatement Third of Torts* incorporates negligence principles into its new standard for prescription drug manufacturer products liability. Third, it notes that the prescription drug industry is heavily regulated by the federal Food and Drug Administration (FDA), and that one of the FDA's primary functions is to evaluate drug warnings. Fourth, the dissent points out that the imposition of strict liability for failure to warn on prescription drug manufacturers would inhibit and delay the development and marketing of essential drugs.

The negligence standard advocated by the dissent preserves the public interest in the development and availability of life-sustaining and lifesaving drugs because prescription drug manufacturers would be liable only if their decision not to warn was unreasonable. But the dissent's approach would unnecessarily weaken the legal protection afforded injured consumers under products liability law. As mentioned at the outset, a principal objective of products liability law is to relieve injured consumers of the problems of proof inherent in negligence and contractual warranty, common law concepts that were initially applied to consumers injured by defective products. The dissent's approach runs counter to this important goal. * * *

In short, the majority's strict liability standard is too harsh towards the manufacturer of prescription drugs, while the dissent is too harsh towards the injured consumer. I propose an intermediate approach, one that fairly accommodates the competing public policies. Unlike the majority, I would not impose liability on prescription drug manufacturers for their failure to warn of every arguable risk, but only of those risks supported by credible scientific evidence or that upon reasonable inquiry would be supported by credible scientific evidence. * * * In determining the admissibility of new scientific techniques, this court has held that evidence of a technique is admissible only if it has gained acceptance in the particular scientific field to which it belongs. * * * Evidence of a risk would be scientifically credible if the data upon which it is based, the methodology employed, and its conclusions identifying the existence of a risk comply with generally accepted scientific methodology and analysis. Scientific evidence that postulates the possibility of a risk or that is otherwise speculative or conjectural would be inadequate. Also, the relevant inquiry relates to the credibility of the scientific evidence in light of accepted scientific norms, not to the personal professional beliefs or preferences of an otherwise qualified expert.

The plaintiff's identification of such a risk would not by itself subject the manufacturer to liability for failure to warn of the risk associated with the drug prescribed. Against the benefits that may be gained by a warning must be balanced the dangers of overwarning and of less meaningful warnings crowding out necessary warnings, the problems of remote risks, and the seriousness of the possible harm to the consumer. But requiring a plaintiff to prove that these factors supported the giving of a warning would force the plaintiff to independently obtain and evaluate all relevant scientific information bearing on these factors. Because such information is not readily accessible to plaintiffs, who may also lack the resources necessary to analyze and evaluate the information, it would impose too heavy a burden on plaintiffs to require them to prove that a warning should have been given because of factors such as the magnitude of the risk in relation to other risks, the seriousness of the harm, and the probability of the harm. Therefore, I would shift to the manufacturer the burden of proving justification for the failure to warn of the risk established by the consumer's prima facie case.

To satisfy its burden, the manufacturer would have to show that its failure to warn was reasonable in relation to the identified risk. The manufacturer, for instance, could introduce evidence that the risk did not pose a serious threat to health, that it was remote, that the number or relative severity of other risks justified a failure to warn, or that the scientific association between the drug and the risk was weak. The manufacturer's compliance with product safety statutes or regulations such as those of the FDA would also be relevant, but not necessarily controlling.[1]

1. I agree with the majority that a prescription drug manufacturer cannot be held liable for failure to warn if it was precluded from issuing a warning by the FDA. A contrary conclusion would be unreasonable because it would make manufacturer compliance with both

The same is true of industry standards and practices to the extent they relate to the reasonableness of the manufacturer's decision not to warn.

In my view, this allocation of the burden of proof is appropriate given the manufacturer's superior access to and capability of evaluating the relevant scientific information; it also furthers a goal of products liability law of relieving injured consumers from evidentiary burdens that may be too onerous. Is this solution perfect? Perhaps not. But it does attempt to strike a fair balance between two distinct public interests: compensating consumers injured by defective products, and encouraging the development of prescription drugs, many of which are life sustaining and lifesaving. * * *

The continuing debate over the proper standard of liability for prescription drug warning defects has largely been framed as though the only available alternatives were strict liability and negligence. Both the majority and the dissent in this case address the issue from within that limited framework. For the reasons stated above, however, I am convinced that the framework must be discarded in order to craft a standard of liability that achieves a just resolution of competing public policies. * * *

Restatement (Third) of the Law of Torts: Products Liability § 6 (American Law Inst. 1998):

Comment g. *Foreseeability of risks of harm in prescription drug and medical device cases*. Duties concerning the design and marketing of prescription drugs and medical devices arise only with respect to risks of harm that are reasonably foreseeable at the time of sale. Imposing liability for unforeseeable risks can create inappropriate disincentives for the development of new drugs and therapeutic devices. Moreover, because actuaries cannot accurately assess unknown and unknowable risks, insuring against losses due to unknowable risks would be problematic. Drug and medical device manufacturers have the responsibility to perform reasonable testing prior to marketing a product and to discover risks and risk-avoidance measures that such testing would reveal.

NOTES AND QUESTIONS

1. *When does a risk become knowable?* Courts do not impose a duty to warn of unknowable risks associated with drugs or medical devices. See Moore v. Vanderloo, 386 N.W.2d 108, 116 (Iowa 1986); Castrignano v. E.R. Squibb & Sons, Inc., 546 A.2d 775, 782 (R.I.1988) (refusing to hold the manufacturer of DES liable "for failure to warn of risks inherent in a drug

federal and state laws impossible. I also agree with the majority that FDA regulations and action or inaction would be admissible as probative of whether a manufacturer should have warned of a risk.

[because] it neither knew nor could have known by the application of scientific knowledge available at the time of distribution that the drug could produce the undesirable effects suffered by plaintiff"). In *Feldman*, Lederle did not dispute at trial that Declomycin caused tooth discoloration, whereas, in *Carlin*, Upjohn denied that Halcion had caused any injury. Note that courts generally do not follow *Feldman*'s burden shifting (by imputing knowledge to the manufacturer) approach. See Rest. (3d) § 2 cmt. m & 102–07; see also Grenier v. Medical Eng'g Corp., 243 F.3d 200, 205 (5th Cir.2001) (dismissing the plaintiff's failure-to-warn claim because she "presented no evidence about the cause, frequency, severity, or consequences of 'gel bleed' with regard to the [silicone breast] implants at issue in this case"). It is, of course, difficult to identify at what point knowledge about a putative hazard gives rise to a duty to warn. Think back to Problem #9 (Chap. 5(C)(1)) involving published epidemiological studies finding no statistically significant association between Rx and birth defects. Was there any obligation to warn (or, to revisit the question about materiality in securities fraud litigation from Chapter 3(C), was there any duty to disclose to investors)? Some courts have found such a duty on the basis of extremely weak evidence that a substance may have caused an injury. See, e.g., Hermes v. Pfizer, Inc., 848 F.2d 66, 68 (5th Cir.1988) (adverse event reports); Wells v. Ortho Pharm. Corp., 788 F.2d 741, 745–46 (11th Cir.1986) (manufacturer of spermicide had duty to warn of possible teratogenicity notwithstanding the FDA's conclusion that these drugs did not cause birth defects). For instance, some courts have held that a reasonable jury could have found a failure to warn of a risk not revealed during clinical trials because of knowledge that a chemically similar product created such a risk. See Thom v. Bristol–Myers Squibb Co., 353 F.3d 848, 854–55 (10th Cir.2003) (Serzone®); Wagner v. Roche Lab., 671 N.E.2d 252, 256–58 (Ohio 1996) (Accutane®); Barson v. E.R. Squibb & Sons, 682 P.2d 832, 836 (Utah 1984) (reports that progesterone caused birth defects should have alerted manufacturer of progesterone-derivative to its teratogenic potential); see also Mulligan v. Lederle Lab., 786 F.2d 859, 864–65 (8th Cir.1986) (sustaining verdict for plaintiff where the manufacturer previously had received reports of similar but not identical adverse reactions). Other courts demand greater substantiation of a risk allegedly posed by a product before imposing a duty to warn of that risk. See, e.g., Stupak v. Hoffman–La Roche, Inc., 326 F.App'x 553, 558–60 (11th Cir.2009) (affirming summary judgment for drug manufacturer on strict liability failure-to-warn claim, concluding that 17 "inconclusive case reports (out of millions of Accutane prescriptions) is simply insufficient to support an allegation that Roche knew or should have known that Accutane could cause suicide without premonitory symptoms"); Smith v. Ortho Pharm. Corp., 770 F.Supp. 1561, 1582 (N.D.Ga.1991) (rejecting failure-to-warn claim because there was no "reasonably reliable" evidence that spermicide caused birth defects).

2. *Duty to test?* Some courts recognize a duty to engage in premarket testing, which in practice may come close to imputing time-of-sale knowledge of risks. See Kociemba v. G.D. Searle & Co., 707 F.Supp. 1517, 1528–

29 (D.Minn.1989) ("[T]he duty to test is a subpart ... of the duty to warn."); Rest. (3d) § 2 cmt. m ("The harms that result from unforeseeable risks—for example, in the human body's reaction to a new drug, medical device, or chemical—are not a basis of liability. Of course, a seller bears responsibility to perform reasonable testing prior to marketing a product and to discover risks and risk-avoidance measures that such testing would reveal. A seller is charged with knowledge of what reasonable testing would reveal."); cf. Valentine v. Baxter Healthcare Corp., 81 Cal.Rptr.2d 252, 265 (Ct.App.1999) (explaining that, while the manufacturer of silicone-gel breast implants had "an ongoing duty to warn of side effects 'known or knowable' in the scientific community," the "imposition of liability for breach of an independent duty to conduct long-term testing, where the causal link to the known harm to plaintiff is the unknown outcome of testing that was not done, would be beyond the pale of any California tort doctrine we can identify"). What would a plaintiff have to prove in a case premised on a failure to conduct reasonable premarket testing? See Lars Noah, Platitudes About "Product Stewardship" in Torts: Continuing Drug Research and Education, 15 Mich. Telecomm. & Tech. L. Rev. 359, 364 (2009) ("Drug-drug interactions provide an illustration of the potential difficulties in defining a broader duty to test. Obviously, if a manufacturer discovers a dangerous interaction during clinical trials or post-market surveillance, then it would have a duty to communicate information about the risk. What if, however, a patient experiences a previously unknown acute drug interaction and argues that the manufacturer should have tested for it? A strict liability standard that focused on the knowability of this risk seemingly would ask only whether a manufacturer could have checked for the interaction, while a negligence standard would recognize the impracticality of testing for every conceivable drug-drug interaction."); see also Duff Wilson, Heart Warning Added to Label on Popular Antipsychotic Drug, N.Y. Times, July 19, 2011, at B7 (discussing multiple drug interactions with Seroquel® discovered more than a decade after initial FDA approval).

3. *Defensive labeling*. The FDA generally frowns upon "defensive" labeling. See Thomas Scarlett, The Relationship Among Adverse Drug Reaction Reporting, Drug Labeling, Product Liability, and Federal Preemption, 46 Food Drug Cosm. L.J. 31, 40 (1991) ("Although the FDA is not rigidly opposed to adding more precautionary information to labeling, it is conscious of the problem of information overload ... [and it] would not acquiesce in defensive labeling that lacked medical support."). For instance, the agency rejected manufacturers' proposals to contraindicate or otherwise warn against use of their drugs by pregnant women, proposals evidently prompted by the valid fear that birth defects might wrongly be associated with the use of those drugs during pregnancy and therefore expose the manufacturer to potentially meritless but costly products liability litigation. See F–D–C Rep. ("The Pink Sheet"), Dec. 21, 1992, at 3; see also Dowhal v. SmithKline Beecham Consumer Healthcare, 88 P.3d 1 (Cal.2004) [excerpted in Chap. 1(E)(2)] (discussing labels for nicotine replacement products). The agency also has directed manufacturers to remove risk information from existing labeling after concluding that there was insufficient data to justify a particular contraindication. See F–D–C Rep. ("The Pink Sheet"), May 24, 1993, at T & G–1.

4. *Regulatory compliance redux.* Recall from Chapter 5 that most courts treat compliance with FDA requirements as relevant but not dispositive. See, e.g., Wells v. Ortho Pharm. Corp., 788 F.2d 741, 746 (11th Cir.1986) ("An FDA determination that a warning is not necessary may be sufficient for federal regulatory purposes but still not be sufficient for state tort law purposes."). In support of the general refrain that federal regulations represent only minimum safety requirements open to supplementation by juries, *Feldman* and other courts have noted that additional or more forceful warnings may be added to labeling without prior FDA approval, which the Supreme Court emphasized when it rejected an implied preemption defense in *Wyeth v. Levine*, 555 U.S. 555 (2009) [excerpted in Chap. 5(B)(2)]. Even if a manufacturer may add a warning in advance of receiving agency approval, the additional warning may not be used if, after reviewing the NDA supplement, the FDA rejects the modified language. The possibility of agency disapproval means that manufacturers typically await at least informal clearance before changing product labeling. See 71 Fed. Reg. 3922, 3934 (2006). Although *Carlin* suggests otherwise, even a refusal by the FDA to allow the addition of a warning may not protect a manufacturer from tort liability for failing to include precisely that warning. See, e.g., Wooderson v. Ortho Pharm. Corp., 681 P.2d 1038, 1057 (Kan.1984) (ignoring FDA letter to a manufacturer rejecting addition of requested warning).

5. *Are warnings costless?* When resolving failure-to-warn claims against sellers of drugs and devices, many courts appear to regard additional labeling information as essentially costless. See, e.g., Ross Lab. v. Thies, 725 P.2d 1076, 1079 (Alaska 1986); Cooley v. Carter–Wallace Inc., 478 N.Y.S.2d 375, 376–77 (App.Div.1984) ("Since the cost of providing warnings is often minimal, the balance usually weighs in favor of an obligation to warn."). Other courts pay more attention to the "information costs" in such cases, at least for patient labeling. See, e.g., Doe v. Miles Lab., Inc., 927 F.2d 187, 194 (4th Cir.1991) ("If pharmaceutical companies were required to warn of every suspected risk that could possibly attend the use of a drug, the consuming public would be so barraged with warnings that it would undermine the effectiveness of these warnings ...."); Boruski v. United States, 803 F.2d 1421, 1427 (7th Cir.1986) (rejecting the plaintiff's argument that the warning "ought to be so strong, regardless of medical experience, as to frighten people from receiving the beneficial aspects of the [vaccination] program"); cf. Richard A. Epstein, Legal Liability for Medical Innovation, 81 Cardozo L. Rev. 1139, 1150 (1987) ("The full costs of overwarning would only be known if legal actions were available to people deterred from taking needed therapy by excessive warnings.").

6. *Information overload for doctors.* As mentioned in *Carlin*, physicians may not be immune to the consequences of overwarning of prescription drug risks. See Thomas v. Hoffman–LaRoche, 949 F.2d 806, 816 n.40 (5th Cir.1992) (noting that the imposition of liability for failure to warn about reported but unconfirmed adverse experiences with prescription medications could "force drug manufacturers to list, and perhaps contraindicate, every possible risk"). In the event that labeling included warnings of all possible side effects, the cacophony of risk information could undermine a doctor's ability to appreciate warnings about meaningful hazards. See id. ("If manufacturers so respond to the possibility of liability, physicians will begin to ignore or discount the warnings provided by the drug manufacturers. Permitting a jury to find liability on such a basis would undermine the important role of warnings as a device to communicate vital information to physicians."); Janssen Pharm., Inc. v. Bailey, 878 So.2d 31, 55–59 (Miss. 2004) (noting that plaintiffs had argued "that Propulsid became a victim of label fatigue" by virtue of the five revisions to the package insert (sometimes accompanied by "Dear Doctor" letters) issued over the course of five years to convey increasingly alarming risk information, and concluding that this presented a question for the fact-finder); see also Lars Noah, The Imperative to Warn: Disentangling the "Right to Know" from the "Need to Know" About Consumer Product Hazards, 11 Yale J. on Reg. 293, 381–91 (1994); Scott Hensley, Liability Worries Cloud Drug Labels, Wall St. J., July 5, 2005, at D3. There is a danger that physicians may alter their prescribing decisions in response to warnings about trivial drug risks, either by taking all warnings less seriously or taking trivial warnings too seriously. Even if physicians are not misled by warnings about trivial risks, they may nonetheless avoid using perfectly safe and effective therapeutic agents for fear of malpractice liability if they disregard a warning. See Chap. 8(A).

Vassallo v. Baxter Healthcare Corp.

696 N.E.2d 909 (Mass.1998).

■ Greaney, Justice:

* * * In February 1977, at the age of forty-eight, Mrs. Vassallo underwent breast implantation surgery. The silicone gel breast implants that Mrs. Vassallo received were manufactured by Heyer–Schulte Corporation in October 1976. Through a series of corporate transactions, the defendants assumed responsibility for breast implant products manufactured by Heyer–Schulte.

In 1992, Mrs. Vassallo underwent a mammogram after complaining of chest pains that extended up under her left armpit. The mammogram revealed that her breast implants possibly had ruptured. The silicone gel implants were subsequently removed in April 1993, and were replaced with saline implants. During the course of the explant surgery, the surgeon noted severe, permanent scarring of Mrs. Vassallo's pectoral muscles which she attributed to the silicone gel. The implants themselves were encapsulated in scar tissue with multiple nodules of silicone granulomas. Dissection of the scar tissue capsules revealed that the left implant had ruptured, releasing free silicone gel, while the right implant was intact, but had several pinholes through which silicone gel could escape.

The plaintiff's pathology expert, Dr. Douglas Shanklin, indicated that, based on the cellular responses shown in the pathology slides of Mrs. Vassallo's breast tissue taken at the time of explant, the rupture had been longstanding, perhaps for several years. According to Dr. Shanklin, Mrs. Vassallo's pathology slides showed silicone granulomas, giant cells, lymphocytes, and macrophages, all of which indicated a chronic immunological and inflammatory reaction to the silicone implants. Dr. Shanklin also identified deposits of silica and lymphocytic vasculitis, which, he testified, were evidence that Mrs. Vassallo suffered from an autoimmune disease caused by the silicone gel. * * *

There was also extensive testimony as to knowledge, attributable to the defendants, of the risks of silicone gel breast implants up to the time of Mrs. Vassallo's implant surgery in 1977. According to Heyer–Schulte's own internal correspondence, the company was aware of a "Talk Paper," issued by the United States Food and Drug Administration in 1976, that documented migration to the brain, lungs, and heart, and death following injections of liquid silicone into the human body. In 1976, Heyer–Schulte received a report of an animal study, partially funded by Heyer–Schulte and conducted using miniature silicone gel implants supplied by Heyer–Schulte, that documented migration of gel from ruptured implants to the surrounding connective tissues and local inflammatory responses with fibroblastic activity and giant cell formation. The authors of the study stated: "The present tendency by manufacturers of breast implants towards ever thinner envelopes and a filler that is getting further away from gel and closer to silicone liquid must be looked at in the light of these experimental findings, and the question must be asked whether the possible advantages of these changes outweigh the disadvantages."

Heyer–Schulte was also aware that some of their implants were rupturing, having received 129 complaints of ruptured gel implants in 1976. In fact, the president of Heyer–Schulte had written in 1975 that "[p]resently, mammary implants have been designed to be increasingly fragile in response to plastic surgeons' demand for softness, realistic feel and mobility." As a result, Heyer–Schulte knew that its implants were "not consistent as far as durability or destructibility is concerned." The encapsulation of the implant, and the viscous nature of the silicone gel, made it difficult to detect that a rupture had occurred, allowing the silicone to leak into the body for long periods before explantation. By 1975, Heyer–Schulte also knew that, even without a rupture of the implant shell, the silicone gel could leak (known as "gel bleed") through to the exterior surface of the implant and possibly produce "detrimental effect[s]" in the body.

Despite this knowledge of the possible adverse long-term consequences of leaking silicone in the body, Heyer–Schulte conducted few animal, and no clinical, studies to document the safety and efficacy of its silicone gel implants. When Heyer–Schulte began using silicone gel manufactured by Dow Corning in 1976, they relied primarily on the animal testing conducted by Dow Corning, despite the observations of a Heyer–Schulte scientist that "the data ... [did] not answer questions concerning migration," and "was lacking in quality and left many questions unanswered." Heyer–Schulte did conduct toxicity testing on the Dow Corning gel; the gel passed the seven-day and thirty-day toxicity tests, but failed the ninety-day toxicity test based on the microscopic tissue evaluation that showed considerably greater fibrous tissue reaction and inflammation to the silicone gel than to the control material. There is no indication in the record that Heyer–Schulte ever repeated this ninety-day toxicity test, and the company continued to use the Dow Corning gel in the manufacture of their silicone gel breast implants.

Heyer–Schulte did furnish warnings to physicians concerning their silicone gel implants in a product insert data sheet (PIDS). The 1976 version of the PIDS that accompanied Mrs. Vassallo's implants included warnings that the implant shell could be easily cut or ruptured by excessive stresses, and that Heyer–Schulte could not guarantee gel containment in the case of a rupture. The warnings did not address the issue of gel bleed, the fact that a rupture could result from normal stresses and could persist undetected for a significant time period, or the consequences of gel migration in the body. The PIDS also contained a list of potential complications associated with breast implants, but this list did not address the risks of chronic inflammation, permanent tissue scarring, or possible effects on the immune system. Proposed revisions to the PIDS, which would have included "a warning to the effect that uncontained silicone gel may have untoward consequences," and complications of "migration of the silicone, with mild to severe consequences, including reduction of breast size and absorption of the silicone by the blood and lymph systems, resulting in damage to the liver and kidneys," were rejected by Heyer–Schulte's president in March 1976. The president did issue a letter to doctors dated August 23, 1976, which stated that "[i]f a shell is torn[] with time and normal stresses the gel will migrate," and that "mild inflammation and polynuclear giant cell response characterized as mild foreign body reaction" had been associated with the silicone gel implants. Once again, this letter did not completely address the potential effects of silicone migration on the body's immune system. Mrs. Vassallo stated that, if she had known that the implants could cause permanent scarring, chronic inflammation, and problems with her immune system, she would not have gone ahead with the implantation procedure. * * *

The judge properly allowed the plaintiffs to introduce evidence of complaints made to Heyer–Schulte on a year-by-year basis with an appropriate cautionary instruction to the jury that the complaints were "not admitted for the truth of what the complaints say," but for the jury's "consideration of what Heyer–Schulte was being told and was learning about its product." The complaints of substantially similar defects and consequences were admissible as evidence of notice to Heyer–Schulte of defects in the integrity of its product about which it had failed to warn. * * *

Because the plaintiffs' recoveries can be upheld on the jury's findings of negligence, we need not address the defendants' claims of error concerning the breach of warranty count. We take this opportunity, however, to consider the defendants' argument that we should change our products liability law concerning the implied warranty of merchantability * * * to adopt a "state of the art" standard that conditions a manufacturer's liability on actual or constructive knowledge of the risks.

Our current law, regarding the duty to warn under the implied warranty of merchantability, presumes that a manufacturer was fully informed of all risks associated with the product at issue, regardless of the state of the art at the time of the sale, and amounts to strict liability for failure to warn of these risks. This rule has been justified by the public policy that a defective product, "unreasonably dangerous due to lack of adequate warning[s], [is] not fit for the ordinary purposes for which [it is] used regardless of the absence of fault on [a defendant's] part." * * * [W]e recognize that we are among a distinct minority of States that applies a hindsight analysis to the duty to warn.

The majority of States, either by case law or by statute, follow the principle expressed in *Restatement (Second) of Torts* § 402A comment j (1965), which states that "the seller is required to give warning against [a danger], if he has knowledge, or by the application of reasonable, developed human skill and foresight should have knowledge, of the ... danger." See Restatement (Third) of Torts: Products Liability, Reporters' Note to comment m, at 104 (1998) ("An overwhelming majority of jurisdictions supports the proposition that a manufacturer has a duty to warn only of risks that were known or should have been known to a reasonable person"). * * * The thin judicial support for a hindsight approach to the duty to warn is easily explained. The goal of the law is to induce conduct that is capable of being performed. This goal is not advanced by imposing liability for failure to warn of risks that were not capable of being known. * * *

We have stated that liability under the implied warranty of merchantability in Massachusetts is "congruent in nearly all respects with the principles expressed in *Restatement (Second) of Torts* § 402A." The main difference has been our application of a hindsight approach to the duty to warn of (and to provide adequate instructions regarding) risks associated with a product. * * * In recognition of the clear judicial trend regarding the duty to warn in products liability cases, and the principles stated in *Restatement (Third) of Torts: Products Liability*, § 2(c) and comment m, we hereby revise our law to state that a defendant will not be held liable under an implied warranty of merchantability for failure to warn or provide instructions about risks that were not reasonably foreseeable at the time of sale or could not have been discovered by way of reasonable testing prior to marketing the product. A manufacturer will be held to the standard of knowledge of an expert in the appropriate field, and will remain subject to a continuing duty to warn (at least purchasers) of risks discovered following the sale of the product at issue. * * *

NOTES AND QUESTIONS

1. *Adverse events and the duty to investigate.* Even if initial reports of adverse reactions do not trigger a duty to warn, companies may be held liable if they have not at least undertaken further inquiries or requested FDA approval of an additional warning as soon as a new hazard is discovered. See, e.g., Lindsay v. Ortho Pharm. Corp., 637 F.2d 87, 91 (2d Cir.1980) ("The duty is a continuous one, requiring the manufacturer to keep abreast of the current state of knowledge of its products as gained through research, adverse reaction reports, scientific literature, and other available methods."); see also Rest. (3d) § 10 cmt. b (With regard to "prescription drugs and devices, courts traditionally impose a continuing duty of reasonable care to test and monitor after sale to discover product-related risks."); Sean M. Basquill, Comment, Prescription Drug Liability and Postmarketing Surveillance: A Modest Proposal, 25 Temp. J. Sci. Tech. & Envtl. L. 69 (2006).

2. *Post-sale duty to warn.* A product seller may have a duty to warn when after-acquired information reveals a risk of injury unknowable at the time of sale. See Rest. (3d) § 10. Thus, courts have insisted that companies send out letters or use their sales representatives in order to reach health care providers with newly discovered risk information. See Sterling Drug, Inc. v. Yarrow, 408 F.2d 978 (8th Cir.1969). Sellers would find it more difficult, of course, to track down patients who have received a drug or device in order to provide warnings, which explains why courts apply a more forgiving negligence-based standard. See Stanger v. Smith & Nephew, Inc., 401 F.Supp.2d 974, 982–83 (E.D.Mo.2005) (recognizing a post-sale duty to warn (but not to recall) after the manufacturer discovered that an artificial knee component had a limited shelf life). Courts generally do not impose a tort duty to recall defective products, but a failure to act reasonably in undertaking a recall may justify imposing liability for any resulting injuries. See Rest. (3d) § 11; cf. Cupek v. Medtronic, Inc., 405 F.3d 421 (6th Cir.2005) (holding that such claims against an approved device were preempted).

3. *When does a knowable risk become significant?* Another factor relevant to whether a duty to warn exists is the magnitude of the risk posed by the product. In one case, the court held that the manufacturer had a duty to warn of the less than one-in-a-million risk of contracting polio from a vaccine because the risk of contracting polio as a result of not using the vaccine was equally small. See Davis v. Wyeth Lab., Inc., 399 F.2d 121, 130 n.16 (9th Cir.1968); see also Tomer v. American Home Prods. Corp., 368 A.2d 35, 40 (Conn.1976). But see Odom v. G.D. Searle & Co., 979 F.2d 1001, 1003–04 (4th Cir.1992) (rejecting plaintiff's proposed contraindication for an IUD, noting that any additional suggested warning "must bear some reasonable relation to the 1.84% risk" of pelvic inflammatory disease and resulting ectopic pregnancy); Kearl v. Lederle Lab., 218 Cal.Rptr. 453, 468 (Ct.App.1985) ("[W]hatever duty a manufacturer may have to inform of risks associated with nonuse of a product, such a duty most certainly cannot be imposed when the relationship between use and nonuse is statistically close (and quite possibly immeasurable) and the probability of injury from either course is extremely remote.").

4. *Allergic reactions.* Manufacturers have an obligation to warn when they knew or should have known that hypersensitive individuals may suffer serious injury. See Basko v. Sterling Drug, Inc., 416 F.2d 417, 430 (2d Cir.1969); see also Michael K. Barrett, Comment, Latex Gloves: Medical–Legal Issues for Health Care Professionals, 22 J. Legal Med. 263 (2001); cf. Friedman v. Merck & Co., 131 Cal.Rptr.2d 885 (Ct.App.2003) (rejecting a negligent infliction of emotional distress claim against distributors of tuberculosis test for responding to an inquiry by stating that it was "vegan-safe" even though it contained bovine serum). Claims against manufacturers of OTC drugs often involve unexpected allergic reactions. See Burlison v. Warner–Lambert Co., 842 F.2d 991 (8th Cir.1988) (cough drop manufacturer had no duty to warn in the absence of evidence that it knew or should have known of possible allergic reactions); Daley v. McNeil Consumer Prods. Co., 164 F.Supp.2d 367, 373–74 (S.D.N.Y.2000) (same, Lactaid®); see also Rest. (3d) § 2(c) cmt. k ("[A] warning is required when the harm-causing ingredient is one to which a substantial number of people are allergic."); id. illus. 13 (if product contains aspirin, manufacturer would only need to disclose this ingredient). Advances in genetics could impact the resolution of such litigation in the future:

> [Pharmacogenetic research] may expand the limited duty to warn of allergic reactions. Historically, such claims rarely succeeded, either because the manufacturer could not have known of the risk of allergic reactions, or because a warning would not have altered the consumer's decision to use a product if they did not know of their susceptibility. Pharmacogenomics may eliminate both of these obstacles to recovery in drug products liability cases. For instance, in a class action lawsuit premised on a failure-to-warn theory, the plaintiffs alleged that the manufacturer of a vaccine against Lyme disease should have recommended that patients first get a genetic test for the HLADR4+ allele, which occurs in thirty percent of the population and produces an autoimmune reaction in response to an outer surface protein found on the vaccine. As pharmacogenomic research reveals more such genetic variations, drug companies can expect to encounter an expansion in this sort of litigation.

Lars Noah, This Is Your Products Liability Restatement on Drugs, 74 Brook. L. Rev. 839, 923 (2009); see also Chap. 11(C)(2) (elaborating on pharmacogenomics).

2. UNINTENDED USES

Proctor v. Davis

682 N.E.2d 1203 (Ill.App.Ct.1997).

■ HARTMAN, JUSTICE:

Plaintiffs Meyer Proctor and Marjorie Proctor filed this medical malpractice and products liability action against Dr. Michael J. Davis and the Upjohn Company, alleging serious injury resulting from Dr. Davis' injection of the corticosteroid Depo–Medrol, manufactured by Upjohn, directly into Meyer Proctor's left eye on November 7, 1983. A jury exonerated Dr. Davis, but found against Upjohn, awarding Proctor compensatory damages of $3,047,819.76, and punitive damages of $124,573,750, the latter of which the circuit court remitted to $35 million. Proctor and Upjohn appealed from that judgment. * * *

In 1959, the Food and Drug Administration (FDA) approved Upjohn's "New Drug Application" (NDA) for Depo–Medrol, a sterile, aqueous suspension containing methyl prednisone acetate, a corticosteroid, for treatment of various inflammatory bodily disorders. The FDA's approval was limited to intramuscular (in the muscle), intra-articular (in the joint), and intralesional (in a lesion) injections. According to the evidence, Depo–Medrol is an insoluble, toxic material, which is intended to be released in the body over a period of six to eight weeks in human tissue with adequate blood supply; however, the human eye does not possess such a blood supply. Depositing Depo–Medrol into the eye meant that the drug would remain in the eye for a relatively long time. Because of its insolubility, its crystals had an effect on the body's response to it when inserted, including increased intraocular pressure and other trauma. It became a foreign body in the eye, which was very difficult, if not impossible, to remove once injected into the eye.

Shortly after Depo–Medrol's FDA limited approval, two ophthalmologists contacted Upjohn independently, each wishing to use the drug clinically for the treatment of ophthalmic conditions through an unapproved method of administration—periocular (near the eye) injections.[1] This use of Depo–Medrol was neither approved by the FDA nor listed on Depo–Medrol's label (off-label use). Nevertheless, Upjohn immediately provided both with vials of Depo–Medrol without cautioning them that no animal studies had been initiated to test the reaction of the drug upon living tissue before embarking upon human use. Instead, Dr. Porter Crawford, an Upjohn employee responsible for monitoring Depo–Medrol at the time, encouraged this unapproved off-label use * * * * Dr. Crawford sent vials of Depo–Medrol to the inquiring doctor and asked him to let him know when he needed additional supplies. Dr. Crawford also noted that Upjohn would "be anxious to learn how it performs when used this way."

Upjohn dispensed not only vials of Depo–Medrol but, also, financial assistance to doctors who would use Depo–Medrol for the unapproved off-label use of periocular injections, granting one in 1959 $3,000. This doctor later wrote Upjohn that he had given two talks in Chicago in the fall of 1960, extolling the use of Depo–Medrol for subconjunctival injections * * * * Upjohn asked the doctor to prepare a write-up of his cases or publish an article in order to document this off-label use for possible FDA

---

1. At trial, defendant Dr. Davis testified that he believed that by 1983, the technique of periocular injections was widely used in the medical community; he believed physicians were using this technique an estimated one million times each year. Physicians had previously used periocular injections with other steroids to avoid the side effects from other methods of administration, and to provide more direct action on the point of inflammation in the eye. As a new, longer-acting steroid, Depo–Medrol appeared to offer advantages for this type of use. Dr. Davis did not then know of the drug's dangerous propensities, or he would not have used it.

approval. Upjohn noted that "not too many people are actually using this type of therapy and your good results suggest that the work should be scattered about."

Upjohn itself undertook the task of "scattering about" the unapproved off-label use of Depo–Medrol to the medical community. In 1961, an article on the use of Depo–Medrol was written by the experimenting doctor to whom Upjohn had given $3,000. This doctor informed Dr. Crawford, on August 31, 1961, of the completion of the article, noting separately, however, that he was unable to use any of his animal experiments because the results were "very unsatisfactory." Proctor's expert, Dr. Philip Walson, who reviewed this correspondence, believed the omission of the animal studies created a serious problem because collected data was ignored, and the animal studies, although "unsatisfactory," should have been included in the article touting this use of Depo–Medrol.

Upjohn nevertheless ordered and distributed 2,500 reprints of the article, 500 for "hospital sales" and 2,000 for "sales education," thus becoming part of the "literature" to which the ophthalmic community was exposed. On November 16, 1961, Upjohn requested reprints of another experimenting doctor's article for distribution, which also mentioned the use of subconjunctival injections of Depo–Medrol. More "fodder" priming the sales pump. * * *

The practice of publicizing unapproved uses of drugs, when sponsored by the pharmaceutical company, is not approved by the FDA as proper advertising; it results in continuing, unapproved, potentially dangerous use. Dr. [Samuel] Stubbs was aware that those experimenting physicians would subsequently write publications which appeared in medical journals, for which Upjohn paid secretarial and editorial expenses. These writings, of course, would be addressed to the medical community and become available to ophthalmologists, thereby becoming, incredibly, part of the current medical literature attempting to establish the standard of medical expertise.

In 1965, Dr. Stubbs collected articles in the medical literature and prepared a report for internal use by Upjohn. Based on that report, he and his immediate supervisor recommended that Upjohn consider filing a supplemental NDA to obtain FDA approval for periocular administration of the drug. Without FDA approval, Upjohn could not include that use of Depo–Medrol as an approved method of administration on the drug's labeling. In order to supplement the NDA to provide for periocular administration of Depo–Medrol, Upjohn knew that it was "likely that animal tissue tolerance studies" would have to be performed. Upjohn elected not to pursue a supplemental NDA for periocular administration. * * *

Upjohn knew of potential adverse reactions to the drug, of which it learned over a period of preceding years from drug experience reports (DERs),[9] yet its labeling never referred to unapproved periocular injection

9. * * * Between the first marketing of Depo–Medrol and the injection of Meyer Proctor that led to this suit, Upjohn received 23 reports indicating adverse experiences associated with

of the drug, neither listing it as an appropriate method of administration, including any recommended dosages, nor stating any warnings regarding periocular use. Ophthalmologists, not having been advised of adverse reactions, began making extensive use of periocular injections of Depo–Medrol because the benefits seemingly outweighed the risks. Defendant Dr. Davis, himself, and four others testified to routine periocular administration of the drug.

In October 1980, in response to the FDA's global restructuring of labeling for all corticosteroids, Upjohn proposed a revised Depo–Medrol package insert. The proposed insert included the following statement:

> "ADVERSE REACTIONS REPORTED WITH NONRECOMMENDED ROUTES OF ADMINISTRATION * * * Ophthalmic: (Subconjunctival)—Redness and itching, obtuse, slough at injection site, increased intraocular pressure, decreased vision. (Retrobulbar)—Blindness."

In September 1983, the FDA informed Upjohn that it should not make its proposed changes, but rather should "continue using currently approved labeling" until it received "notification" from the agency. The FDA also told Upjohn that "[i]f important new labeling information becomes available, you should revise your approved product labeling under 21 C.F.R. 314.8." The circuit court excluded this evidence.

In April 1983, Meyer Proctor, a retired public relations worker, consulted Dr. Davis with complaints of blurred vision. Dr. Davis diagnosed Proctor's condition as uveitis, an inflammation of the eye, which can be chronic and can lead to permanent blindness. Dr. Davis began treating this condition with steroid medications applied to both of Proctor's eyes by means of eye drops, which proved to be of only limited value. In May 1983, Proctor developed cystoid macular edema (CME) as a complication of the uveitis, and the vision in his left eye deteriorated to the level of legal blindness. Dr. Davis referred him to a retinal-vitreal specialist for further evaluation and treatment, who concurred in the diagnosis of CME and prescribed Nalfon, a nonsteroidal anti-inflammatory medication. Some improvement in Proctor's vision occurred, but his sight was not restored to normal. After treating Proctor for several months, the specialist referred him back to Dr. Davis, recommending the use of a nonsteroidal anti-inflammatory drug (such as Nalfon), or the systemic or periocular administration of a steroid (such as Depo–Medrol) if continued impairment of vision made further treatment necessary.

On August 1, 1983, Dr. Davis examined Proctor and reinstituted treatment with Nalfon; however, his vision again began to deteriorate. On August 9, 1983, Dr. Davis decided to use periocular injections of Depo–Medrol to treat Proctor's condition, one shot around each eye. Within

---

its use. The DERs based on these communications were forwarded to the FDA, usually accompanied by a cover letter stating that the use involved was not recommended. Three of these reports (one in 1977 and two in 1983) concerned vision loss following periocular injections with unintentional intraocular injection. Additionally, the medical literature had reported other instances of accidental intraocular injections of corticosteroids like Depo–Medrol, some of which were followed by vision loss.

several weeks, Proctor's vision improved almost to normal, but in November 1983, Proctor experienced renewed problems with the vision in his left eye. In response, on November 7, 1983, Dr. Davis administered another periocular injection of Depo–Medrol near that eye.

All the ophthalmologists who testified at trial regarding the standard of care concluded that Dr. Davis' decision to administer Depo–Medrol via periocular injection both in August and again in November of 1983 was appropriate and within the applicable standard of care. None suggested that anything known at the time, or subsequently discovered, would have made this treatment inappropriate. There were risks associated with this treatment, however. Dr. Davis himself testified that in November 1983 he knew that an inadvertent intraocular injection was a risk of any periocular injection; Depo–Medrol could be "toxic" if inadvertently injected into the eye and cause damage to the eye, including blindness; he had never penetrated the globe of the eye (made an intraocular injection) in more than 1,600 prior periocular injections of Depo–Medrol in his entire career; and, he believed he would be able to deliver the drug to its intended location without incident in this instance.

During the November 7, 1983 injection, however, Dr. Davis mistakenly inserted the needle and Depo–Medrol into Proctor's left eye. Dr. Davis then referred Proctor to a specialist for evaluation and treatment, who determined that the appropriate treatment was observation, waiting for the drug to clear from the eye, and watching for possible retinal detachment, which eventually occurred. Proctor underwent surgery on November 23, 1983, the Depo–Medrol was removed from Proctor's left eye, and the retina was reattached. The retina again detached, however, and two subsequent operations, on December 13 and 29, 1983, failed to reattach it. In April 1984, Proctor's left eye, having become blind and painful, was surgically removed. * * *

Upjohn first argues that, after considering all the evidence in the case in the light most favorable to Proctor, it was entitled to either judgment notwithstanding the verdict or a new trial because Proctor failed to prove that a warning was required, because the risk was too remote to require a warning, and because the specialized medical community was already aware of the risks. * * *

From the evidence it is clear that Upjohn knew or should have known that Depo–Medrol is an insoluble, toxic material which, because of its insolubility, when inserted in the eye, became a foreign body, and was very difficult, if not impossible, to remove. * * * The evidence revealed that Upjohn knew of Depo–Medrol's dangerous propensities before the instant occurrence took place in 1983; yet, there was no reference in the 1983 label or insert that subconjunctival use of Depo–Medrol as practiced upon Proctor in this case was not recommended by Upjohn, nor that FDA approval was never secured for such application. * * *

The record demonstrates that by 1961, Upjohn had learned that some ophthalmologists were administering Depo–Medrol through periocular injection as an "off-label" use. Upjohn fostered and encouraged this unapproved use as experimentation on human beings with no prior basic scientific studies having been made. This unauthorized use, encouraged by Upjohn, became more widespread in the next two decades, although Upjohn never secured FDA approval for it and never set forth the use, warnings or directions for such periocular injections on its labels or in its literature. None of the dangers attendant to such use, or any reported deleterious side effects which may have developed of which Upjohn was apprised through DERs, were made known to the prescribing or treating physicians who made this unauthorized off-label use of it. Dr. Davis testified that he did not know of the drug's dangerous propensities, or he would not have used it. Dr. Thomas Deutsch, Upjohn's own expert, asserted that, until he testified in this case, he did not know Depo–Medrol would be difficult or impossible to remove once injected into the eye. * * *

A manufacturer of ethical drugs cannot evade its responsibilities of warning physicians of dangers and risks attendant to the use of its products, by hoping, as in the present case, that the doctors will learn of the dangers themselves. Upjohn's duty to warn was nondelegable; the failure of prescribing and treating physicians to learn of the risks of a drug from other sources does not relieve the manufacturer of liability for harm resulting from its own failure to adequately warn. Here, Upjohn knew of the risks, yet did not share this knowledge with members of the profession acting in decision-making capacities in administering drugs to their patients, and encouraged unapproved use and misleading publicity. * * *

Significantly, Upjohn knew how to warn, and did warn doctors against certain uses of Depo–Medrol by advising them, for example, against intrathecal administration of this drug, which it printed on the insert distributed with the drug in 1983, before the instant insertion of Depo–Medrol into Proctor's eye. Upjohn, in another line or two of print on the insert, easily could have mentioned potential adverse reactions to the drug when injected intraocularly, of which it had learned over a period of preceding years from the DERs. Information regarding questionable reactions or side effects to this Upjohn product contained in DERs in Upjohn's possession was not shared by it with the medical community by any other means. According to Dr. Walson, being on notice of that kind of information from the 1960s up to 1983, there were methodologies and scientific means available to Upjohn to confirm or disaffirm the toxicity of the drug. In his opinion, Upjohn should have included a warning on its label or package insert which said, in effect, do not use the drug in that way, and if so used, this is what may be seen. This was never done. In light of this imbalance of access to information about adverse propensities of Depo–Medrol, it cannot be concluded that physicians had knowledge of the risks equal to Upjohn's. * * *

A drug company cannot absolve itself from the duty to warn by pointing to the unauthorized use of its drug by physicians with whom it has not shared its knowledge of dangerous side effects and injury. Violation of its duty to warn is even more egregious in this case since, as the evidence heard by the jury demonstrated, Upjohn encouraged and participated in disseminating misleading information concerning the use of its drug to the "learned intermediaries," through financial support, technical assistance, and abundant supplies of the drug during the period when Upjohn was receiving adverse information concerning this use of the drug. * * *

The evidence convincingly supports the conclusion that Upjohn promoted, encouraged and advertised the off-label use of Depo–Medrol by providing financial and technical assistance to a limited number of members of the medical community without attempting to communicate to these physicians and the medical community at large the dangers and risks attendant to this use. Although it is assumed that physicians will keep abreast of current medical literature, here, part of the flawed literature was generated by Upjohn. Upjohn even sought to "plant the seed" in doctors' minds about contributing to the literature, and thereby help to mislead the specialized ophthalmic community as to the potential harmful effects attendant to the intraocular injection of a drug which could be impossible to remove. To conclude that the existence of literature in such a case constitutes knowledge on the part of doctors and the medical community equal to that of a drug's manufacturer, would encourage more writings of the type found in this case, fostered by the very defendant upon whom responsibility should be fixed. Such an insidious situation as here existed should be neither countenanced, encouraged nor condoned. The evidence demonstrates that Upjohn knew or should have known of the risks and dangers attendant to the use of Depo–Medrol, thereby requiring warning. Upjohn simply failed to do so. * * *

Upjohn's most persuasive argument is that the punitive damages awarded are excessive and should be reduced. In reviewing punitive damage awards, the question of excessiveness turns on whether the amount is so large that it outruns the justification for exacting punitive damages, namely retribution and deterrence of future outrageous conduct. A reviewing court considers the degree of reprehensibility of defendant's conduct, the relationship between the punitive damage award and the harm caused by the conduct, defendant's gain from the misconduct, and the financial condition of defendant. This court's inquiry is thus one of degree: when arrayed along the spectrum of wrongful acts, was the conduct at issue here so extraordinarily outrageous as to justify extraordinary punitive damages? The circuit court, in its review of the punitive damages awarded, answered that question in the affirmative, although it remitted the jury's award by almost 75%. The original award of more than $124 million amounted to precisely 7% of Upjohn's net worth; the remitted amount is still more than 2% of the company's net worth and more than eleven times the amount of compensatory damages awarded.

When we consider the factors set out by the United States Supreme Court and Illinois courts, we find that the amount of punitive damages awarded in this case far outruns the justification for imposing punitive damages. We agree with the circuit court that Upjohn's conduct was sufficiently reprehensible to support an award of punitive damages, however, there is no reasonable relationship between the amount of the punitive damages and the harm caused by the conduct. Further, although Upjohn is a large corporation with a net worth of approximately $1.7 billion, punishment in the amount of 2% of its net worth is excessive in the extreme. * * * We believe that a punitive damage award twice that of the compensatory damage award will send a strong message to pharmaceutical manufacturers of the necessity to warn of the known potential adverse effects of their drugs. The twin goals of retribution and deterrence would both be met by such an award. Pursuant to Supreme Court Rule 366, we enter a remittitur of the punitive damages to $6,095,639.52. * * *

■ DiVito, Justice (dissenting):

Meyer Proctor suffered a painful and tragic injury. For that, however, Upjohn bears no responsibility. Succinctly stated, Proctor's injury was the result of an accident involving Dr. Davis' use of a needle, and Upjohn could not have prevented, nor was it responsible for, the doctor's mistake. Judgment notwithstanding the verdict should have been granted because Upjohn had no duty to warn and, even if it did, there was no showing that any alleged failure to warn was a proximate cause of Proctor's injury. Alternatively, reversal and a new trial are warranted because the circuit court improperly excluded critical evidence favorable to Upjohn. * * *

The majority holds that Upjohn is liable for Proctor's injury because it knew that Depo–Medrol was toxic and difficult to remove if injected into the eye, and it failed to warn ophthalmologists of these risks. The record, however, does not justify that conclusion because it contains ample evidence that the medical community, including Dr. Davis, was aware of the risks associated with periocular injection of Depo–Medrol. Drs. Walson, Deutsch, Giles, and Fagman testified that the possibility of intraocular injection was a well-known risk of periocular use of Depo–Medrol. Dr. Walson, plaintiffs' own expert, also testified that he thought that, in 1983, ophthalmologists were aware that inadvertent intraocular injection of Depo–Medrol had caused the loss of an eye for some patients. In addition, there were several reports in the medical literature describing incidents in which vision loss resulted from an inadvertent intraocular injection of Depo–Medrol. Physicians are held to a standard of medical expertise and may be expected to have knowledge of current medical literature. * * *

Not only were the risks associated with periocular use of Depo–Medrol well-known to the medical community, they were also evident to Dr. Davis. Although he testified that he did not know that Depo–Medrol could not be easily removed once injected into the eye, Dr. Davis knew that injecting it into the eye could lead to blindness. From reading medical literature, he knew that accidental intraocular injection was possible and that piercing of the eyeball could cause damage, including blindness. He also testified that he knew Depo–Medrol was toxic to the eye. Even as a medical resident, he and his fellow medical residents were well aware of the drug's toxicity and knew that it should not be used intraocularly. * * *

With respect to the removability of the drug, the relevant question is whether Upjohn had greater knowledge than the medical community about any difficulty in removing Depo–Medrol from the eye. Dr. Stubbs, Upjohn's medical monitor for Depo–Medrol, testified that, based on information in the medical literature available in 1983 and information in drug experience reports sent to Upjohn, he did not believe that Depo–Medrol would be particularly difficult to remove from the eye. Likewise, in the course of testifying about instances reported in the literature concerning the injection of Depo–Medrol into the eye, Dr. Walson made a similar statement concerning the removability of the drug. In addition, two of the three drug experience reports received by Upjohn that described an intraocular injection of Depo–Medrol reported that the Depo–Medrol had been removed by performing a vitrectomy. Thus, the record before us does not support the conclusion that Upjohn had greater knowledge than the medical community of any difficulty in removing the drug in the event of an inadvertent intraocular injection.

Even with the evidence viewed in the light most favorable to plaintiffs, therefore, Upjohn had no duty to warn in this case. The record demonstrates that the medical community and Dr. Davis were well-aware of the potential danger associated with periocular injection of Depo–Medrol and that Upjohn did not have superior knowledge of these risks. * * *

Dr. Davis did testify that he would not have given Proctor a periocular injection of Depo–Medrol had he known it was difficult to remove and might cause blindness. Certainly, it was the role of the jury to evaluate his credibility and to resolve conflicts in the evidence. Nevertheless, judgment notwithstanding the verdict was appropriate because, even viewing the evidence in the light most favorable to plaintiffs, it is clear that, despite his testimony to the contrary, Dr. Davis' treatment decision would have been the same had he received the warnings plaintiffs contend were required.

Dr. Davis' testimony that he would not have treated Proctor with periocular injection of Depo–Medrol if he had received these warnings was completely contradicted by the remainder of his testimony. For example, he testified that he had found this treatment to be safe and effective and had used it without problem on 1,600 occasions prior to the accidental injection of Proctor's eye. In fact, he had used it to restore Proctor's vision when no other treatment had worked. Also contrary to his testimony that he would not have used Depo–Medrol periocularly if he had known the risks, Dr. Davis testified that, at the time he treated Proctor, he was aware that accidental intraocular injection and blindness were possible consequences of periocular injection of Depo–Medrol. Perhaps the best indicator of how knowledge of these risks would have affected his treatment decision was his testimony that, even after he accidentally penetrated Proctor's eye, he continued to treat patients with periocular injections of Depo–Medrol.

Dr. Davis' testimony that periocular injection of Depo–Medrol was the only treatment alternative for Proctor also contradicted his testimony that warnings would have changed his treatment decision. The majority states that there were alternative treatments available, but the record does not support this conclusion. Dr. Davis explained that further use of Nalfon was not a feasible alternative because it had been used without success to treat Proctor's condition. Dr. Davis also explained that intramuscular, that is, systemic, administration of steroids, was contraindicated by certain health conditions Proctor had. As for the majority's suggestion that Dr. Davis could have used a different formulation of Depo–Medrol, the record does not indicate that a different formulation would have been effective. By contrast, Dr. Davis knew that periocular injection was an effective treatment for Proctor because it had restored his vision in the past, and it was not contraindicated by Proctor's other medical conditions.

The testimony of other ophthalmologists also indicated that the warning plaintiffs claim was required would not have changed Dr. Davis' treatment decision. Expert witnesses, Drs. Giles, Fagman, and Deutsch, all testified that Davis' decision to inject Depo–Medrol periocularly was in accordance with the applicable standard of care. Dr. Giles also testified that, even after he accidentally injected Depo–Medrol intraocularly, he continued to treat patients using periocular injection of the drug and found it to be safe and efficacious. It is clear from this evidence that the ophthalmologic community, including Dr. Davis, considered Depo–Medrol to be an appropriate treatment for Proctor's condition and found periocular injection of this drug to be safe and effective despite the possibility of intraocular injection and vision loss.

This uncontradicted evidence compelled the jury to conclude that Upjohn's alleged failure to warn was not a proximate cause of Proctor's injury. The only proximate cause of Proctor's loss of his eye was Dr. Davis' accidental injection of Depo–Medrol into the eye rather than periocularly. Consequently, the circuit court should have granted the motion for judgment notwithstanding the verdict. * * *

The circuit court excluded evidence of post–1983 usage of Depo–Medrol, but Upjohn made offers of proof that, after 1983, Drs. Giles, Deutsch, and Fagman continued to use periocular injection of Depo–Medrol to treat their patients. The evidence that, even after 1983, ophthalmologists continued to view periocular injection of Depo–Medrol as a safe and efficacious treatment severely undermines the argument that Dr. Davis would have treated Proctor differently had he known more about the drug. Moreover, such evidence was highly relevant to the issue of punitive damages. The circuit court erred in excluding this evidence.

The majority holds that this evidentiary ruling was proper because it was consistent with the court's exclusion of post–1983 labeling changes. The majority's "consistency" rationale, however, is not persuasive because, although there are public policy considerations that support the exclusion of the evidence of post–1983 labeling changes, there is no legitimate basis for the exclusion of the evidence of post–1983 usage. Generally, evidence of subsequent remedial measures is inadmissible in negligence and product liability actions for public policy reasons: courts do not want to discourage defendants from making safety improvements, evidence of subsequent remedial measures is not probative, and the jury may view this evidence as proof of negligence. These policy concerns supported the circuit court's exclusion of the post–1983 labeling changes, but they do not justify the exclusion of the post–1983 usage of Depo–Medrol. * * *

Also troubling is the circuit court's exclusion of evidence of Upjohn's attempt to add a warning to its labeling and its exclusion of evidence of FDA labeling controls. * * * Illinois courts have held that evidence of compliance with federal requirements, including FDA requirements, is admissible. The majority distinguishes these cases, however, on the basis that the parties in those cases demonstrated compliance, and Upjohn did not prove that it complied with FDA requirements in this case. The majority, therefore, concludes that Upjohn was not entitled to present evidence of its attempted labeling change or of FDA labeling requirements because these were not relevant either to its duty to warn or to punitive damages. * * *

Even absent proof of compliance, the evidence of Upjohn's attempted labeling change and FDA labeling requirements was highly relevant to the issue of punitive damages because it tended to show that Upjohn's conduct was not willful and wanton. * * * Furthermore, there was no basis for concluding from the record that Upjohn was not complying with an FDA directive when it continued to use labeling that did not contain a warning with respect to ophthalmic use. In response to the FDA's request for format changes to all corticosteroid labels, Upjohn submitted a supplemental application, in which it proposed to revise the Depo–Medrol label to, among other things, include a new warning for ophthalmic uses. In September 1983, the FDA informed Upjohn that it was conducting further review of the labeling format and instructed it to continue to use existing labeling until the FDA notified it of the status of its supplemental application. * * * It was, therefore, logical for Upjohn to wait for the FDA to act on its pending application and to follow the FDA's instruction to use its existing labeling until the FDA notified it of the status of its application. Had the jury been allowed to consider this letter, it may have reached the same conclusion as to Upjohn's actions. * * *

The Depo–Medrol labeling included a warning against intrathecal use because the FDA required this warning. It is not clear what sort of warnings, if any, the FDA would have permitted for periocular use. The FDA must approve all post-marketing labeling changes and, therefore, would not necessarily have permitted Upjohn to "easily" include a warning involving periocular use of the drug. In fact, the record demonstrates that when Upjohn submitted such a warning, it took the FDA several years to respond, and the response instructed Upjohn to continue to use its existing labeling. * * *

Finally, the majority's description of Upjohn's activities with respect to the off-label use of Depo–Medrol must be addressed. * * * Off-label use of drugs is not unusual or illegal, and even the FDA has acknowledged that off-label use of a drug may be appropriate and rational. In addition, contrary to the majority's implication that Upjohn acted improperly by funding research into off-label uses and distributing reprints of articles discussing off-label uses, these practices have been common among drug manufacturers. Dr. Stubbs testified that it was not unusual to supply drugs to physicians who requested them, that fulfilling reprint requests was part of normal sales education, and that, in 1963 and 1964, it was normal for drug manufacturers to compensate doctors for secretarial help in preparing case reports and to supply writing support services. The FDA has recently restricted the manner in which manufacturers may communicate with physicians about off-label uses, but its policy with respect to such communications was not as strict during the period of time relevant to this suit. The majority offers no authority for its suggestion that Upjohn's activities would not have been approved by the FDA and the record does not permit such a conclusion. * * *

NOTES AND QUESTIONS

1. *What's wrong with this picture?* How might Upjohn have described the risk (as revealed by the footnotes excerpted with the majority's opinion, three cases of blindness following accidental intraocular injection had been reported over a 23 year period and associated with an off-label use that occurred approximately one million times in 1983)? How might an ophthalmologist react to such information? Consider this assessment:

> [T]he majority agreed that a jury could have found Upjohn's warnings [to physicians] inadequate (and its conduct outrageous!), in part for failing to disclose that periocular use was not FDA approved (even though that would have been obvious from the silence in the indications statement) and that it was not recommended (even though that would have represented an entirely false statement about the existing standard of care in the ophthalmological community).

Lars Noah, Platitudes About "Product Stewardship" in Torts: Continuing Drug Research and Education, 15 Mich. Telecomm. & Tech. L. Rev. 359, 372 (2009); see also id. ("The jury verdict included more than $3 million in compensatory damages for the loss of an eye that, until the physician tried Depo–Medrol, seemed destined for blindness ...."); id. at 371 n.53 ("[T]he appellate court rejected Upjohn's decision-causation argument, agreeing that the trial judge acted properly in excluding evidence that Dr. Davis and the plaintiffs' experts had continued engaging in this off-label use even after the accident.... When the jury credited Dr. Davis's testimony that he would not have used the drug if Upjohn had warned him of the risks associated with periocular use, however, it would seem to undercut injury causation insofar as Depo–Medrol had offered the last best hope of saving Mr. Proctor's deteriorating eye."). Even when a manufacturer specifically warns of a risk, efforts to downplay the seriousness of the risk and encourage off-label use may provide the basis for punitive damages. See Wyeth v. Rowatt, 244 P.3d 765, 779–85 (Nev.2010) (affirming a punitive damage award of almost $58 million (plus $23 million in compensatory damages)—remitted from the jury's verdict of $99 million (plus $35 million in compensatory damages)—for three patients who claimed that hormone replacement therapy caused their breast cancers, notwithstanding purported compliance with FDA labeling requirements, given evidence of deceptive marketing and other company efforts to dilute the warnings that it had provided).

2. *The relevance of FDA labeling decisions.* In a case similar to *Proctor*, the court credited the testimony from a former FDA Commissioner who had explained that the agency "would not have allowed Upjohn to contact physicians or send a 'Dear Doctor' letter regarding the intrathecal use of Depo–Medrol because it was not an approved use for the drug." Hahn v. Richter, 628 A.2d 860, 863 (Pa.Super.Ct.1993); cf. Denise Gellene, Avastin Use in Eyes Irks Genentech, L.A. Times, Oct. 17, 2005, at C1 (reporting that ophthalmologists have used a colon cancer drug off-label on more than 1,000 patients with macular degeneration, and that the manufacturer "is in discussions with the [FDA] to modify the Avastin label to state that the drug is not for ophthalmic use"). Why might the FDA resist such labeling? Indeed, would Upjohn face heightened exposure to tort liability if it had decided to add such a warning without FDA approval? Recall that the *Feldman* court at least allowed the manufacturer to introduce evidence concerning the FDA's initial resistance to the proposed addition of a warning. Even absent a general duty to warn against off-label uses, if a manufacturer submits a supplemental application seeking approval of a new indication that the agency denies, should the manufacturer have an obligation to disclose that fact in its labeling? Cf. Richards v. Upjohn Co., 625 P.2d 1192, 1196 (N.M.Ct.App.1980) (because an intramuscular antibiotic solution "had been on the market for over ten years before the recommendation to use it topically was withdrawn," the manufacturer may have had a specific duty to warn against what was now an off-label use).

3. *Foreseeable misuse.* Manufacturers must warn of the hazards associated with both the intended use and any foreseeable misuse of a product. It is generally no defense that a plaintiff's injury resulted from misuse if the manufacturer was aware that such misuse might take place and could have warned against it. See Knowlton v. Deseret Med., Inc., 930 F.2d 116, 122–23 (1st Cir.1991) (device manufacturer knew that its catheter was being used in open-heart surgery); Felice v. Valleylab, Inc., 520 So.2d 920, 926 (La.Ct.App.1987) (manufacturer of electrosurgical device could foresee that it might be used in performing circumcisions and therefore had a duty to warn of the accompanying risk of severe burns); see also Erony v. Alza Corp., 913 F.Supp. 195 (S.D.N.Y.1995) (allowing an inadequate warning claim to proceed on behalf of a teenager who died after sucking on his father's discarded Duragesic® (fentanyl) patches). But cf. Foister v. Purdue Pharma, L.P., 295 F.Supp.2d 693, 703–06 (E.D.Ky.2003) (granting defendants' motion for summary judgment because the plaintiffs had intentionally altered and abused OxyContin, in disregard of the directions that accompanied their prescriptions or after purchasing the drug illegally); id. at 695 (rejecting "the plaintiffs' 'victimization' mentality"). The basis for liability becomes still stronger where a manufacturer actively encouraged an unapproved use. See Knipe v. SmithKline Beecham, 583 F.Supp.2d 602, 627–29 (E.D.Pa.2008) (holding that the manufacturer of the antidepressant Paxil® (paroxetine) had a duty to warn of the risk of suicide associated with its off-label use in pediatric patients); id. at 623–24, 639–41 (pointing to evidence that the manufacturer had encouraged this use, which might support a punitive damage award); Richard C. Ausness, "There's Danger Here, Cherie!": Liability for the Promotion and Marketing of Drugs and Medical Devices for Off–Label Uses, 73 Brook. L. Rev. 1253 (2008); Mark A. Ford, Note, Another Use of OxyContin: The Case for Enhancing Liability for Off–Label Drug Marketing, 83 B.U. L. Rev. 429 (2003).

4. *Unforeseeable misuse.* Manufacturers would not have to anticipate "gross misuse" of a drug by a physician. See Rhoto v. Ribando, 504 So.2d 1119, 1124–25 (La.Ct.App.1987); see also Phelps v. Sherwood Med. Indus., 836 F.2d 296, 304 (7th Cir.1987) (holding that a jury could find the off-label use of a catheter in open-heart surgery an unforeseeable misuse of the device by the physician); Robak v. Abbott Lab., 797 F.Supp. 475, 476 (D.Md.1992) ("[T]he manufacturer had no duty to warn of any deleterious effects that might be associated with misuse of the product, i.e., its use for treatment of a non-indicated condition."); cf. Alston v. Caraco Pharm., Inc., 670 F.Supp.2d 279, 286–87 (S.D.N.Y.2009) (dismissing inadequate warning claims of prisoner who became addicted to the opioid analgesic Ultram® (tramadol) and allegedly suffered an injury from his criminal misuse of this prescription drug). See generally Lars Noah, Constraints on the Off–Label Uses of Prescription Drug Products, 16 J. Prods. & Toxics Liab. 139 (1994); Kaspar J. Stoffelmayr, Comment, Products Liability and "Off–Label" Uses of Prescription Drugs, 63 U. Chi. L. Rev. 275 (1996).

3. Generic Drugs

Even though generic drugs now account for more than two-thirds of dispensed prescriptions, until recently they have played almost no discernible role in products liability litigation. In the last few years, courts have begun to confront challenging questions presented when plaintiffs assert tort claims for injuries caused by the use of generic drugs. First, special difficulties may arise when resolving lawsuits filed against the manufacturers of such products; second, as revealed in the following case, plaintiffs sometimes seek to press claims against the manufacturers of the brand-name products as well.

Conte v. Wyeth, Inc.

85 Cal.Rptr.3d 299 (Ct.App.2008).

■ Siggins, Judge:

* * * The defendants in these consolidated appeals manufacture and market metoclopramide, which [Elizabeth] Conte's physician [Dr. Robert Elsen] prescribed in its generic and name-brand form, Reglan, to treat her gastroesophageal reflux disease. Wyeth manufactures and markets Reglan. Defendants Purepac Pharmaceutical Company, Teva Pharmaceutical USA, Inc., and Pliva, Inc. manufacture generic versions of metoclopramide.

Conte developed tardive dyskinesia, a debilitating and incurable neurological disorder. She alleges she developed her condition as a result of taking metoclopramide for almost four years between August 2000 and April 2004. It is undisputed that Conte took only the generic version of the medication, not Reglan. She claims that defendants knew or should have known of a widespread tendency among physicians to misprescribe Reglan and generic metoclopramide for periods of 12 months or longer, even though the medication is only approved for 12 weeks of use, because the drugs labeling substantially understates the risks of serious side-effects from extended use. * * *

She argues that Wyeth can be liable for her injuries because a name-brand manufacturer that disseminates information about its product owes a duty of care to ensure the information's accuracy to any doctor who prescribes the drug in reasonable reliance on that information, even if the patient ends up taking the name-brand product's generic equivalent. Wyeth argues, and the trial court agreed, that it cannot be held liable to Conte for her injuries caused by generic metoclopramide because Wyeth has no duty to users of the generic version of its products, which are produced by other manufacturers. * * *

The complaint alleges that Wyeth made intentional and/or negligent misrepresentations about the safety of metoclopramide, the risks of its long-term use, and the likelihood of its serious side effects. [Conte] does not allege that Wyeth is strictly liable because inadequate warnings rendered its product unreasonably dangerous. Rather, she charges that Wyeth failed to use due care when disseminating its product information.[8] * * * For this reason, Wyeth's reliance on numerous strict products liability cases for the rule that a plaintiff in a products liability case must prove the defendant made or sold the allegedly defective product that causes injury sheds no light on the issue presented for our consideration.

Our decision today is rooted in common sense and California common law. We are not marking out new territory by recognizing that a defendant that authors and disseminates information about a product manufactured and sold by another may be liable for negligent misrepresentation where the defendant should reasonably expect others to rely on that information and the product causes injury, even though the defendant would not be liable in strict products liability because it did not manufacture or sell the product. See Hanberry v. Hearst Corp., 81 Cal.Rptr. 519 (Ct.App.1969) (misrepresentation claim permitted against magazine publisher that endorsed manufacturer's product). * * *

In California, the general rule is that "all persons have a duty to use ordinary care to prevent others from being injured as the result of their conduct." Randi W. v. Muroc Joint Unified Sch. Dist., 929 P.2d 582 (Cal.1997). More specifically, when our Supreme Court has considered misrepresentations that implicate a risk of physical harm to others, it has looked to the rules set forth in the Restatement Second of Torts * * *

8. Nor, contrary to Wyeth's suggestion, is there any indication in the record that Conte is proceeding under a market-share liability theory, see Sindell v. Abbott Labs., 607 P.2d 924 (Cal.1980), on the basis of the similarities between Reglan and generic metoclopramide.

Section 311 provides that "[o]ne who negligently gives false information to another is subject to liability for physical harm caused by action taken by the other in reasonable reliance upon such information, where such harm results (a) to the other, or (b) to such third persons as the actor should expect to be put in peril by the action taken." * * *

In California, as in most states, pharmacists have long been authorized by statute to fill prescriptions for name-brand drugs with their generic equivalents unless the prescribing physician expressly forbids such a substitution. It is therefore highly likely that a prescription for Reglan written in reliance on Wyeth's product information will be filled with generic metoclopramide. And, because by law the generic and name-brand versions of drugs are biologically equivalent, it is also eminently foreseeable that a physician might prescribe generic metoclopramide in reliance on Wyeth's representations about Reglan. In this context, we have no difficulty concluding that Wyeth should reasonably perceive that there could be injurious reliance on its product information by a patient taking generic metoclopramide.

In addition to foreseeability, California law also identifies various policy factors courts are to consider when they determine whether a duty of care exists in a novel situation. * * * If it is established that Dr. Elsen relied on Wyeth's product warnings when he prescribed metoclopramide and Conte's long-term use of the medication led to her condition, a close link between Wyeth's non-disclosure of its long-term effects and Conte's condition is readily apparent. * * * [I]f Wyeth misrepresented the risks of taking its medication, any moral culpability it might bear for that misrepresentation is not lessened if the person who is harmed by his or her reliance on it happened to ingest the generic version as a result, rather than Wyeth's Reglan brand.

We are unpersuaded by Wyeth's assertion that imposing liability would undermine the goal of preventing future harm because it would chill innovation in the pharmaceutical industry. No evidence was introduced on summary judgment to support this supposition, much less to permit an informed balancing of such a risk against the harm to patients that might be prevented by recognizing a duty of care. * * * While there is much that could and will be said in various fora about the burdens, societal consequences, cost, and insurance implications of Wyeth's potential liability, the limited record on summary judgment does not provide the information necessary to inform such a debate. These broader consequences of the duty we identify today cannot be considered on the limited facts in the record. * * *

In the absence of California authority directly on point, Wyeth urges us to follow law from other jurisdictions that have rejected the proposition that name-brand drug manufacturers may be liable under theories of misrepresentation for injuries resulting from the use of a generic equivalent. The seminal case principally relied upon by the trial court is *Foster v. American Home Products Corp.*, 29 F.3d 165 (4th Cir.1994). In *Foster*, the parents of an infant who died after ingesting generic promethazine sued

Wyeth, the name-brand manufacturer of Phenergan. The complaint alleged negligence, strict liability, breach of warranty and negligent misrepresentation. As here, Wyeth moved for summary judgment on all counts on the ground that it did not manufacture the drug given to the plaintiffs' child.

The federal district court granted summary judgment in Wyeth's favor on the negligence, strict liability and breach of warranty counts. As to the plaintiffs' negligent misrepresentation theory, however, the court found it was immaterial that Wyeth did not manufacture the drug the child ingested. The trial court reasoned that Wyeth could be liable for the injury, without reference to any products liability-based theory, if (1) it made false representations about the drug's safety for treating infants; and (2) the prescribing doctor relied on those representations in prescribing generic promethazine. The court of appeals reversed. Applying Maryland law, it held the manufacturer of a name-brand prescription drug cannot be held liable under a theory of negligent misrepresentation for an injury arising from the use of a generic version of the drug. * * *

As foreseeability is the principal determinant of duty, the foreseeability of harm to consumers of the generic drug in reliance on information disseminated about the name-brand version should have some significance in considering whether a duty of care arises in these circumstances. But *Foster* does not address that point. Instead, it concludes—without further discussion—that no duty lies because "Brandy Foster was injured by a product that Wyeth did not manufacture." Id. at 171. But that is the very question posed—not the answer. *Foster* also supports its holding with various policy reasons that we consider unpersuasive. It reasons it would be unfair to allow misrepresentation actions against name-brand manufacturers for injuries caused by generic drugs because name-brand makers bear the expense of developing, testing, and formulating labeling information for new medications, while generic manufacturers merely "rid[e their] coattails" by duplicating the innovator's successful drugs and labels. Id. at 170. * * * [W]hat is unfair about requiring a defendant to shoulder its share of responsibility for injuries caused, at least in part, by its negligent or intentional dissemination of inaccurate information? * * *[16]

We are also reluctant to create an exception to the general rule of duty based on the very limited "fairness" analysis permitted on the summary judgment record before us. While we have no reason to doubt that generic manufacturers do not invest the same time and expense in research and development of their products as innovators, there are countervailing factors that may warrant an outcome on policy analysis that is different than *Foster*'s. For example, the innovator who brings a new drug to market enjoys unique advantages, such as the initial period of patent-protection

---

16. We are not persuaded by the trial court's warning that allowing misrepresentation claims in these circumstances would, in effect, "hold the pioneer manufacturer liable as insurer" for its generic competitors. The liability in question here is based on reasonable and foreseeable reliance on the manufacturer's misleading written information about the risks of a drug, not on information disseminated by a generic competitor or on defects in the formulation or manufacture of the competitor's drug. * * *

from competition, the fiscal rewards of name-brand recognition and the commensurate ability to charge a higher price for its product, even after its exclusive marketing position expires. While Wyeth predicts that holding it subject to the duty to avoid injurious misrepresentations would impose "permanent and uncontrolled liability" "in perpetuity, for all injuries allegedly caused by generic equivalents," these dire consequences are neither self-evident nor substantiated by the record. * * * We are aware that in declining to follow *Foster* we depart from the majority of courts to have wrestled with this particular issue. See Colacicco v. Apotex, Inc., 432 F.Supp.2d 514, 540–41 (E.D.Pa.2006) (compilation of federal district court rulings following *Foster*). * * *

[Conte's] appellate brief states explicitly: "No evidence indicates that the generic defendants disseminated any information concerning their metoclopramide products aside from price lists (distributed to pharmacies) and package inserts, distributed with wholesale shipments, as required by 21 C.F.R. § 201.100. No evidence suggests that Dr. Elsen relied on either the price lists or the package inserts for generic metoclopramide, if and when he ordered or wrote Ms. Conte's Reglan prescription." This concession leads implacably to the conclusion that Conte cannot prove that any of the three generic makers is responsible for her injury. Given the state of the evidence, we think it would be inappropriate to consider the federal preemption issues presented in this appeal. * * * We affirm [though on other grounds] the grant of summary judgment in favor of each of the three generic defendants. * * *

NOTES AND QUESTIONS

1. *More on metoclopramide*. More than four years after Ms. Conte stopped taking the drug, the FDA ordered all manufacturers of metoclopramide to include a prominent warning of the risk of tardive dyskinesia. See Jill U. Adams, Metoclopramide: Another "Black Box" Warning, L.A. Times, Mar. 9, 2009, at E3; see also Christopher Kenney et al., Metoclopramide, an Increasingly Recognized Cause of Tardive Dyskinesia, 48 J. Clinical Pharmacology 379, 381–82 (2008). The California Supreme Court declined to review the case. See Bob Egelko, Way Clear for Suit Against Wyeth, S.F. Chron., Jan. 22, 2009, at B8 (noting that the appellate court did not address separate claims of malpractice asserted against Conte's physician). In what sense had Wyeth promoted the use of metoclopramide (as opposed to Reglan®)? Elsewhere in its opinion, the court conceded that "there is no evidence in this case that Dr. Elsen relied on information provided by sales representatives for either Wyeth or the generic manufacturers." *Conte*, 85 Cal.Rptr. at 319 n.19. Brand-name companies often cease advertising once generic competitors enter the marketplace. See Jayanta Bhattacharya & William B. Vogt, A Simple Model of Pharmaceutical Price Dynamics, 46 J.L. & Econ. 599, 609, 619 (2003). Although federal law requires it, see Chap. 4(A), wouldn't brand-name companies prefer not to use the "established name" of the drug in their labeling?

2. *Trying to make sense of such crossover litigation.* The court in *Conte* encountered an odd set of facts insofar as company A's product caused the plaintiff's injury, but company A's allegedly tortious behavior in connection with the marketing of that product could not have caused her injury, while company B's product could not have caused the plaintiff's injury, but company B's allegedly tortious behavior in connection with the marketing of that product arguably caused her injury. Although superficially akin to market share liability, see Chap. 5(C)(2), why was the court correct to decline invoking *Sindell*? Notwithstanding the court's reassurance (in n.16) that manufacturing and design defects would pose entirely different questions, could one not still argue that misleading information disseminated by the brand-name company caused the plaintiff's exposure to the defective generic version? Finally, although *Conte* arose in the context of generic substitution, might it also justify imposing liability on the manufacturer of the leading brand-name product for risks common to an entire drug class if a patient receives a slightly different ("me too") drug (a.k.a. therapeutic substitution)? For a scathing critique of the court's reasoning, see Lars Noah, Adding Insult to Injury: Paying for Harms Caused by a Competitor's Copycat Product, 45 Tort Trial & Ins. Prac. L.J. 673, 684–95 (2010). For more sympathetic accounts, see Allen Rostron, Prescription for Fairness: A New Approach to Tort Liability of Brand–Name and Generic Drug Manufacturers, 60 Duke L.J. 1123 (2011); Beatrice S. Resendes, Note, The Extinct Distinction of Privity: When a Generic Drug Label Fails to Warn, the Drug's Pioneer Should Be Liable as Component Part Supplier of the Warning Label, 32 T. Jefferson L. Rev. 95 (2009).

Most courts remain dubious about *Conte*'s approach. See, e.g., Mensing v. Wyeth, Inc., 588 F.3d 603, 612–14 (8th Cir.2009), rev'd in part on other grounds, 131 S.Ct. 2567 (2011); Schrock v. Wyeth, Inc., 601 F.Supp.2d 1262, 1266–67 (W.D.Okla.2009); Moretti v. Wyeth, Inc., 2009 WL 749532, No. 2:08–cv–00396–JCM–(GWF), at *4 (D.Nev. Mar. 20, 2009) (characterizing *Conte* as an outlier in the course of granting defendants summary judgment on essentially identical facts); Swicegood v. Pliva, Inc., 543 F.Supp.2d 1351, 1355–58 (N.D.Ga.2008); Flynn v. American Home Prods. Corp., 627 N.W.2d 342, 350 (Minn.Ct.App.2001); see also Doe 2 v. Ortho–Clinical Diagnostics, Inc., 335 F.Supp.2d 614, 626–28 (M.D.N.C.2004) (holding that the company that originally discovered and patented the mercury-based preservative thimerosal, which later was copied by other manufacturers and used in their vaccines and other drug products, owed no duty to warn users). But see Weeks v. Wyeth, Inc., 2011 WL 1216501 (M.D.Ala. 2011); Kellogg v. Wyeth, 762 F.Supp.2d 694 (D.Vt.2010); Clark v. Pfizer Inc., No. 1819, 2008 Phila. Ct. Com. Pl. LEXIS 74, at *20–29 (Mar. 14, 2008) (allowing misrepresentation claim where the manufacturer of Neurontin® (gabapentin) had promoted it for off-label uses and the plaintiff was injured by generic versions). See generally Kenneth Sills, Annotation, Liability of Name Brand Drug Manufacturer for Injury or Death Resulting from Use of Prescription Drug's Generic Equivalent, 56 A.L.R.6th 161 (2010).

3. *Suing generic product manufacturers.* As noted at the end of Chapter 5(B)(2), the Supreme Court found implied preemption of failure-to-warn claims against manufacturers of generic drugs. See PLIVA, Inc. v. Mensing, 131 S.Ct. 2567 (2011) (involving metoclopramide's tardive dyskinesia risk). (Does that render the earlier decision in *Conte* any more palatable?) Assuming that a plaintiff managed to surmount any causation and preemption obstacles, might generic drug manufacturers find themselves in a weaker litigating position than their brand-name brethren? For instance, in trying to mount a risk-utility defense against design defect claims, will their lack of access to the clinical trials underlying the NDA for the innovator product place them at an evidentiary disadvantage? Also, if an innovator company introduces a new and slightly improved (and more expensive) version of the original drug, then (at least given the narrow focus on "therapeutic benefits" for judging utility in § 6(c) of the *Products Liability Restatement*) manufacturers of generic versions of the original drug seemingly could not point to cost savings in response to allegations of product obsolescence. In addition, do you think that courts would apply a more forgiving standard of knowability?

Although generic manufacturers would have to abide by any risk labeling changes that the FDA mandates for the brand-name version (and any failure to do so would support a negligence per se claim), generic drugs may encounter peculiar problems when it comes to off-label uses: if an innovator company receives FDA approval for a new indication, then it may receive three years of additional market exclusivity for that use—this would not prevent the prescribing of the generic version for that new use, but the labeling for the generic drug will not include any information (including, in all likelihood, risk information) associated with that new use. In the event that a patient suffers an injury while using the generic version (which completely failed to mention risks associated with the new indication approved only for the brand-name version), would a court find some way of finessing this problem? If a physician prescribed the generic version for the new indication after consulting the labeling of the innovator drug, would that insulate the generic manufacturer from a failure-to-warn claim? Cf. Miles Labs., Inc. v. Superior Court, 184 Cal.Rptr. 98, 103 (Ct.App.1982) (allowing a claim for failure to warn of risks of use during pregnancy against the manufacturer of a DES product labeled solely for use in male (prostate cancer) patients because it might have been dispensed in place of other DES products labeled for the prevention of miscarriages).

B. Scope of the Duty to Warn

1. The Learned Intermediary Rule

Larkin v. Pfizer, Inc.

153 S.W.3d 758 (Ky.2004).

■ Cooper, Justice:

[The plaintiff developed Stevens–Johnson syndrome and toxic epidermal necrolysis while taking a pair of prescription drugs. The package inserts included references to these side effects as uncommon adverse reactions, but the plaintiff's physician had failed to mention the risk to his patient.] This matter reaches us by a request for certification of a question of law from the United States Court of Appeals for the Sixth Circuit * * *: "Whether the learned intermediary doctrine should apply in Kentucky to a case involving an allegation that a manufacturer of a prescription drug failed to warn the ultimate consumer of risks associated with that drug, even though the manufacturer informed the prescribing physician of those risks?" * * *

The American Law Institute has stated the rule as follows:

> A prescription drug or medical device is not reasonably safe due to inadequate instructions or warnings if reasonable instructions or warnings regarding foreseeable risks of harm are not provided to:
>
> (1) prescribing and other health-care providers who are in a position to reduce the risks of harm in accordance with the instructions or warnings; or
>
> (2) the patient when the manufacturer knows or has reason to know that health-care providers will not be in a position to reduce the risks of harm in accordance with the instructions or warnings.

Restatement (Third) of Torts: Products Liability § 6(d) (1998). * * * "The obligation of a manufacturer to warn about risks attendant to the use of drugs and medical devices that may be sold only pursuant to a health-care provider's prescription traditionally has required warnings directed to health-care providers and not to patients.... Subsection (d)(1) retains the 'learned intermediary' rule." Id. cmt. b. * * * Although the rule largely applies to prescription drugs, some courts have extended it to cases involving prescription medical implants and devices. Thus, the ALI included such devices within the purview of section 6(d). Obviously, the rule applies only to prescription drugs and devices and not to over-the-counter products. * * *

Three basic rationales have been articulated to support the rule. The first and best rationale is that the prescribing physician is in a superior position to impart the warning and can provide an independent medical decision as to whether use of the drug is appropriate for treatment of a particular patient. * * * The second rationale for the rule is that manufacturers lack effective means to communicate directly with each patient. The third rationale for the rule is that imposing a duty to warn upon the manufacturer would unduly interfere with the physician-patient relationship. Furthermore, since the typical manufacturer's warning provides a list with scores of potential side effects, no matter how minute the possibility of occurrence, the lay consumer might overreact to such warnings and forego beneficial, or even vital, medical treatment. * * * Thus, providing an adequate warning to the prescribing physician relieves the manufacturer of its duty to warn the patient regardless of how or if the physician warns the patient. * * *

To date, the courts of thirty-four states have specifically adopted the learned intermediary rule by common law decision. * * * Furthermore, federal courts applying state laws have either interpreted the laws of nine other states and Puerto Rico as having adopted the rule or a facsimile thereof, or predicted that those jurisdictions would ultimately adopt it. No court that has directly addressed the issue as an exception to the common law duty to warn has rejected the learned intermediary rule * * *

[T]he Larkins claim that adoption of the learned intermediary rule is a matter of public policy that should be left to the legislature. * * * [W]e do not view the adoption of an almost universally accepted exception to a common law rule as a matter of public policy. Only three jurisdictions have adopted the learned intermediary rule by statute, and all three enacted their statutes after their courts had adopted the rule by common law. Furthermore, the learned intermediary rule is consistent with our informed consent statute, which anticipates that doctors will inform their patients of any risks or dangers inherent in proposed treatment * * *

Finally, we reject the argument that adopting the learned intermediary rule would immunize manufacturers of prescription drugs from products liability claims. Manufacturers still have a duty to warn; the rule only identifies the party to be warned, i.e., the health care provider who prescribes the drugs. If the manufacturer fails to adequately warn the prescribing health care provider, the manufacturer is directly liable to the patient for damages resulting from that failure. Accordingly, * * * we now adopt *Restatement (Third) of Torts: Products Liability* § 6(d). The posture of this case does not require us to decide which, if any, of the recognized exceptions to this rule should be adopted in Kentucky.

■ WINTERSHEIMER, JUSTICE (dissenting):

* * * The so-called learned intermediary doctrine provides a type of summary immunization for pharmaceutical manufacturers and makes the adequacy of warnings to the ultimate consumer a question of law for the court and not a question of fact for the jury. In Kentucky, the Product Liability Act applies to all damage claims arising from use of products, regardless of legal theory advanced. KRS 411.300(1). * * * Nowhere in the Product Liability Act is there an incorporation of the common law defense of the learned intermediary doctrine. Instead, the majority has made such legislation by judicial fiat, but it is an unfortunate addition for the reasons below.

This court should take notice of the abundantly obvious fact that the development of direct to consumer pharmaceutical advertising has indelibly changed the realities of physician/patient relationships. Anyone who watches television is regularly bombarded with a variety of pharmaceutical products which suggest that the ultimate consumer ask his physician to prescribe a particular advertised product. * * * There is no question that pharmaceutical manufacturers believe they have very effective methods to communicate directly with consumers. * * * Given that the manufacturers are now directly marketing and benefiting by increased sales, they must also assume increased share in the risks and duties pertinent to selling a product.

Pharmaceutical companies are in the best position to ensure that adequate warnings are provided to customers. * * * This case can have a profound effect on the health and well being of individuals in this Commonwealth. It is an important matter of public policy that should be properly decided by the legislature. The matter needs public and legislative debate which is supported by evidence of its value or otherwise. Such a process can best be obtained through legislative investigative hearings as a matter of public policy. Kentucky product liability law is statutory and amendments to the law are within the discretion of the General Assembly.

NOTES AND QUESTIONS

1. *No doubt about it?* Notwithstanding the court's 4–3 decision, the majority correctly observed that, at the time, no other jurisdiction had declined to adopt the learned intermediary rule. See Ehlis v. Shire Richwood, Inc., 367 F.3d 1013, 1017 (8th Cir.2004) (noting the nearly universal adoption of this doctrine); see also Diane S. Kane, Annotation, Construction and Application of Learned–Intermediary Doctrine, 57 A.L.R.5th 1 (1998 & 2011 Supp.). Even so, commentators routinely question its desirability. See, e.g., Timothy S. Hall, Reimagining the Learned Intermediary Rule for the New Pharmaceutical Marketplace, 35 Seton Hall L. Rev. 193 (2004); Nancy K. Plant, The Learned Intermediary Doctrine: Some New Medicine for an Old Ailment, 81 Iowa L. Rev. 1007 (1996). How compelling do you find the rationales mentioned by the majority? Is there some other way of addressing the dissent's concern about the impact of direct-to-consumer advertising? Three years after *Larkin*, and taking a cue from the dissenting opinion, West Virginia became the first jurisdiction to reject the learned intermediary doctrine altogether. See State ex rel. Johnson & Johnson Corp. v. Karl, 647 S.E.2d 899, 908–10 (W.Va.2007); see also Vitatoe v. Mylan Pharms., Inc., 696 F.Supp.2d 599, 608–10 (N.D.W.Va. 2010) (refusing to apply Louisiana's learned intermediary doctrine to a failure-to-warn claim arising out of a drug injury that occurred there because it would offend the public policy of the forum state!); Rimbert v. Eli Lilly & Co., 577 F.Supp.2d 1174, 1214–24 (D.N.M.2008) (predicting that the New Mexico courts would reject the doctrine); Kyle T. Fogt, Note, The Road Less Traveled: West Virginia's Rejection of the Learned Intermediary Doctrine in the Age of Direct-to-Consumer Advertising, 34 J. Corp. L. 587 (2009).

2. *Medical devices.* As pointed out in *Larkin*, the learned intermediary rule also applies to implantable medical devices. See, e.g., Toole v. Baxter Healthcare Corp., 235 F.3d 1307, 1313–14 (11th Cir.2000); Sita v. Danek Med., Inc., 43 F.Supp.2d 245 (E.D.N.Y.1999); see also Ellis v. C.R. Bard, Inc., 311 F.3d 1272, 1279–88 (11th Cir.2002) (applying Georgia's learned intermediary doctrine to a prescription device, and rejecting the plaintiff's argument that FDA regulations preempted application of this rule, in a case where a nurse allowed family members to activate morphine pump while visiting a patient in the hospital).

3. *Excluding nonprescription products*. The *Larkin* court also accurately explains that the learned intermediary rule applies only to prescription drugs and devices, but what exactly accounts for that limitation? Consider the following:

> The increasing movement of prescription pharmaceuticals to the OTC marketplace, whether at the manufacturer's behest or otherwise, may justify rethinking the stark doctrinal distinctions that have emerged. With inadequate warning claims, the differential treatment seems inevitable—after all, FDA approval of OTC sale usually removes the learned intermediary from the selection process and turns on the agency's judgment that average consumers will manage to comprehend instructions and warnings. Even so, the relatively recent phenomenon of advertising prescription drugs directly to consumers, as well as the advent of Internet prescribing and dispensing, may have made these products more similar to OTC drugs. It is not clear whether these changes throw into doubt the traditional protections afforded to prescription drugs, as some have argued, or instead suggest that these protections also might extend to increasingly potent and useful nonprescription drugs.

Lars Noah, Treat Yourself: Is Self–Medication the Prescription for What Ails American Health Care?, 19 Harv. J.L. & Tech. 359, 379–80 (2006); see also id. at 379 ("In switching a product, the FDA invariably abridges the package insert, which means that some of the risk information previously communicated to physicians will not appear on the label of the OTC drug. When a consumer then experiences such a known but undisclosed side effect, the manufacturer may find itself hard-pressed to defend against a failure-to-warn claim."). Might it make sense to apply the rule in those situations where physicians administer or recommend the use of a nonprescription drug?

4. *Functions of warnings*. Warnings can serve either to promote safe use of a product or to disclose unavoidable risks so that the user can make a more informed risk-benefit decision. As explained in the comments accompanying § 6 of the *Restatement (Third)*:

> Failure to instruct or warn is the major basis of liability for manufacturers of prescription drugs and medical devices. When prescribing health-care providers are adequately informed of the relevant benefits and risks associated with various prescription drugs and medical devices, they can reach appropriate decisions regarding which drug or device is best for specific patients. Sometimes a warning serves to inform health-care providers of unavoidable risks that inhere in the drug or medical device. By definition, such a warning would not aid the health-care provider in reducing the risk of injury to the patient by taking precautions in how the drug is administered or the medical

> device is used. However, warnings of unavoidable risks allow the health-care provider, and thereby the patient, to make an informed choice whether to utilize the drug or medical device. Beyond informing health-care providers, a drug or device manufacturer may have a duty under the law of negligence to use reasonable measures to supply instructions or warnings to nonprescribing health-care providers who are in positions to act on such information so as to reduce or prevent injury to patients.

Rest. (3d) § 6 cmt. d (1998); see also id. § 2 cmt. i.

5. *Impacts on litigation.* The learned intermediary rule has important practical consequences. When reduced to the question of whether the warning conveyed to a physician or other health care provider was adequate, plaintiffs will find it more difficult to get a case to a jury. See, e.g., Odom v. G.D. Searle & Co., 979 F.2d 1001, 1003 (4th Cir.1992); Willett v. Baxter Int'l, Inc., 929 F.2d 1094, 1099 (5th Cir.1991). Although physicians may have an incentive to shift blame to the manufacturer, often they will testify that they understood the warnings provided in the package insert. See Hall v. Merck, Sharp & Dohme, 774 F.Supp. 604, 606–07 (D.Kan.1991); Wooten v. Johnson & Johnson Prods. Inc., 635 F.Supp. 799, 802–04 (N.D.Ill.1986); cf. John A. Cohan, Psychiatric Ethics and Emerging Issues of Psychopharmacology in the Treatment of Depression, 20 J. Contemp. Health L. & Pol'y 115, 158 (2003) (noting Eli Lilly's promise to indemnify physicians sued for prescribing Prozac®); Michael D. Tomatz, Note, Prozac: Is It the Next Rising Giant in Products Liability?, 12 Rev. Litig. 704, 711 & n.41, 713–14 (1993) (same). This stands in contrast to a typical plaintiff's testimony that the warning communicated to them seemed insufficient. Moreover, plaintiffs may have to produce expert testimony to support an inadequacy claim. See Montagnon v. Pfizer, Inc., 584 F.Supp.2d 459, 462–63 (D.Conn.2008) (osteoporosis warning for Depo–Provera® injectable contraceptive); Colville v. Pharmacia & Upjohn Co., 565 F.Supp.2d 1314, 1321 (N.D.Fla.2008) (same). This stands in contrast to a consumer-directed warning to which jurors can often apply their own experience.

2. EXCEPTIONS

Only in situations where an individualized prescribing decision is unlikely to be made (for example, when vaccines are being administered to patients in a mass immunization program) would a manufacturer have to provide a warning directly to the patient. See Plummer v. Lederle Lab., 819 F.2d 349, 356 (2d Cir.1987) ("If the drug is given under clinic-type conditions the manufacturer is obligated to warn consumers directly."); Allison v. Merck & Co., 878 P.2d 948, 958 n.16 (Nev.1994); see also Mazur v. Merck & Co., 964 F.2d 1348, 1365–69 (3d Cir.1992) (holding that a vaccine manufacturer satisfied this duty by delegating to the CDC the responsibility for disseminating patient labeling); Walker v. Merck & Co., 648 F.Supp. 931, 934–35 (M.D.Ga.1986) (treating nurses as learned intermediaries when they administered vaccine), aff'd mem., 831 F.2d 1069 (11th Cir.1987); Wyeth–Ayerst Lab. Co. v. Medrano, 28 S.W.3d 87, 92–93

(Tex.Civ.App.2000) (same, in case of an implanted contraceptive). With regard to childhood vaccines, however, federal legislation has overridden the mass immunization exception. See 42 U.S.C. § 300aa–22(c). A few courts have extended the mass immunization exception to other products, such as contraceptives, for which a physician may not make an individualized judgment in prescribing a particular medication. See, e.g., Hill v. Searle Lab., 884 F.2d 1064, 1071 (8th Cir.1989) (IUDs); Odgers v. Ortho Pharm. Corp., 609 F.Supp. 867, 878–79 (E.D.Mich.1985) (oral contraceptives). The overwhelming majority of courts do not, however, recognize any exception for contraceptive drugs or devices. See, e.g., West v. G.D. Searle & Co., 879 S.W.2d 412 (Ark.1994); Martin v. Ortho Pharm. Corp., 661 N.E.2d 352, 356 (Ill.1996); see also Doe v. Solvay Pharm., Inc., 350 F.Supp.2d 257, 272 (D.Me.2004) (declining to extend the rationales underlying the contraceptive exception to an antidepressant prescribed for the treatment of obsessive-compulsive disorder).

Restatement (Third) of the Law of Torts: Products Liability § 6 (American Law Inst. 1998):

Comment e. *Direct warnings to patients.* Warnings and instructions with regard to drugs or medical devices that can be sold legally only pursuant to a prescription are, under the "learned intermediary" rule, directed to health-care providers. Subsection (d)(2) recognizes that direct warnings and instructions to patients are warranted for drugs that are dispensed or administered to patients without the personal intervention or evaluation of a health-care provider. An example is the administration of a vaccine in clinics where mass inoculations are performed. In many such programs, health-care providers are not in a position to evaluate the risks attendant upon use of the drug or device or to relate them to patients. When a manufacturer supplies prescription drugs for distribution to patients in this type of unsupervised environment, if a direct warning to patients is feasible and can be effective, the law requires measures to that effect.

Although the learned intermediary rule is generally accepted and a drug manufacturer fulfills its legal obligation to warn by providing adequate warnings to the health-care provider, arguments have been advanced that in two other areas courts should consider imposing tort liability on drug manufacturers that fail to provide direct warnings to consumers. In the first, governmental regulatory agencies have mandated that patients be informed of risks attendant to the use of a drug. A noted example is the FDA requirement that birth control pills be sold to patients accompanied by a patient package insert. In the second, manufacturers have advertised a prescription drug and its indicated use in the mass media. Governmental regulations require that, when drugs are so advertised, they must be accompanied by appropriate information concerning risk so as to provide balanced

> advertising. The question in both instances is whether adequate warnings to the appropriate health-care provider should insulate the manufacturer from tort liability.
>
> Those who assert the need for adequate warnings directly to consumers contend that manufacturers that communicate directly with consumers should not escape liability simply because the decision to prescribe the drug was made by the health-care provider. Proponents of the learned intermediary doctrine argue that, notwithstanding direct communications to the consumer, drugs cannot be dispensed unless a health-care provider makes an individualized decision that a drug is appropriate for a particular patient, and that it is for the health-care provider to decide which risks are relevant to the particular patient. The Institute leaves to developing case law whether exceptions to the learned intermediary rule in these or other situations should be recognized.

Even so, the accompanying reporters' note asserted that several courts and commentators seem favorably predisposed to recognizing such exceptions. See id. at 155. (In earlier drafts, the reporters had proposed including these exceptions in the blackletter formulation as well as in the comments.) For details on this drafting history, and a highly critical response to the reporters' description of the available case law, see Lars Noah, Advertising Prescription Drugs to Consumers: Assessing the Regulatory and Liability Issues, 32 Ga. L. Rev. 141, 161–80 (1997).

Edwards v. Basel Pharmaceuticals

933 P.2d 298 (Okla.1997).

■ Summers, Vice Chief Justice:

* * * Alpha Edwards brought a wrongful death action for the death of her husband. He died of a nicotine-induced heart attack as a result of smoking cigarettes while wearing two Habitrol nicotine patches. Habitrol is manufactured by Basel Pharmaceuticals. Plaintiff's theory of liability was that the warnings given in conjunction with the Habitrol patches were inadequate to warn her husband of the fatal risk associated with smoking and overuse of the product. A relatively thorough warning was given to physicians providing the Habitrol patch, but the insert provided for the user did not mention the possibility of a fatal or cardiac related reaction to a nicotine overdose, cautioning that an "overdose might cause you to faint." * * *

When direct warnings to the user of a prescription drug have been mandated by a safety regulation promulgated for the protection of the user, an exception to the learned intermediary doctrine exists, and failure on the part of the manufacturer to warn the consumer can render the drug unreasonably dangerous. According to the material certified by the federal court, the FDA has found a need to require that prescriptions for nicotine patches be accompanied by warnings to the ultimate consumer as well as to the physician, as is required in the distribution of oral contraceptives and intrauterine devices. * * *

The question then becomes whether the manufacturer has fulfilled its legal obligation once the warnings are approved by the FDA and transmitted to the user. Basel contends that because it complied with FDA requirements it had no further duty to warn Mr. Edwards. Jurisdictions split on their answer to this question. * * * It may be that in certain instances compliance with FDA warning procedures will satisfy all state law requirements. But although compliance with FDA standards may prove an effective starting ground, it is not necessarily conclusive. The adequacy of warnings is determined by state law. Our result could improve the safety of prescription drugs by requiring that both standards are met. * * *

In the present case it appears the manufacturer clearly had knowledge of the dangers associated with the Habitrol patch; it furnished detailed warnings to the prescribing physicians. However, as to the warnings the late Mr. Edwards received in his Habitrol insert, state products liability law must be applied to determine their adequacy. * * *

Perez v. Wyeth Laboratories Inc.

734 A.2d 1245 (N.J.1999).

■ O'HERN, JUSTICE:

Our medical-legal jurisprudence is based on images of health care that no longer exist. At an earlier time, medical advice was received in the doctor's office from a physician who most likely made house calls if needed. The patient usually paid a small sum of money to the doctor. Neighborhood pharmacists compounded prescribed medicines. Without being pejorative, it is safe to say that the prevailing attitude of law and medicine was that the "doctor knows best." Pharmaceutical manufacturers never advertised their products to patients, but rather directed all sales efforts at physicians. In this comforting setting, the law created an exception to the traditional duty of manufacturers to warn consumers directly of risks associated with the product as long as they warned health-care providers of those risks.

For good or ill, that has all changed. Medical services are in large measure provided by managed care organizations. Medicines are purchased in the pharmacy department of supermarkets and often paid for by third-party providers. Drug manufacturers now directly advertise products to consumers on the radio, television, the Internet, billboards on public transportation, and in magazines. * * * The question in this case, broadly stated, is whether our law should follow these changes in the marketplace or reflect the images of the past. We believe that when mass marketing of prescription drugs seeks to influence a patient's choice of a drug, a pharmaceutical manufacturer that makes direct claims to consumers for the efficacy of its product should not be unqualifiedly relieved of a duty to provide proper warnings of the dangers or side effects of the product. * * *

This appeal concerns Norplant, a Food and Drug Administration (FDA)-approved, reversible contraceptive that prevents pregnancy for up to five years. The Norplant contraceptive employs six thin, flexible, closed capsules that contain a synthetic hormone, levonorgestrel. The capsules are implanted under the skin of a woman's upper arm during an in-office surgical procedure characterized by the manufacturer as minor. A low, continuous dosage of the hormone diffuses through the capsule walls and into the bloodstream. Although the capsules are not usually visible under the skin, the outline of the fan-like pattern can be felt under the skin. Removal occurs during an in-office procedure, similar to the insertion process.

We have no doubt of the profound public interest in developing new products for reproductive services. We intend no disparagement of the product when we recite plaintiffs' claims concerning the efficacy of Norplant. The procedural posture that brings this case before us requires that we accept as true plaintiffs' version of the facts. The motion to dismiss was in the nature of a motion for judgment on the pleadings.

According to plaintiffs, Wyeth began a massive advertising campaign for Norplant in 1991, which it directed at women rather than at their doctors. Wyeth advertised on television and in women's magazines such as *Glamour*, *Mademoiselle* and *Cosmopolitan*. According to plaintiffs, none of the advertisements warned of any inherent danger posed by Norplant; rather, all praised its simplicity and convenience. None warned of side effects including pain and permanent scarring attendant to removal of the implants. * * *

In 1995, plaintiffs began to file lawsuits in several New Jersey counties claiming injuries that resulted from their use of Norplant. Plaintiffs' principal claim alleged that Wyeth, distributors of Norplant in the United States, failed to warn adequately about side effects associated with the contraceptive. Side effects complained of by plaintiffs included weight gain, headaches, dizziness, nausea, diarrhea, acne, vomiting, fatigue, facial hair growth, numbness in the arms and legs, irregular menstruation, hair loss, leg cramps, anxiety and nervousness, vision problems, anemia, mood swings and depression, high blood pressure, and removal complications that resulted in scarring. * * *

The trial court dismissed plaintiffs' complaints, concluding that even when a manufacturer advertises directly to the public, and a woman is influenced by the advertising campaign, "a physician is not simply relegated to the role of prescribing the drug according to the woman's wishes." Consequently, the court held that the learned intermediary doctrine applied. According to the court, the physician retains the duty to weigh the benefits and risks associated with a drug before deciding whether the drug is appropriate for the patient. * * * The Appellate Division affirmed the trial court's grant of summary judgment in favor of defendants and its determination that the learned intermediary doctrine applied. * * *

[T]he New Jersey Products Liability Act provides:

> An adequate product warning or instruction is one that a reasonably prudent person in the same or similar circumstances would have provided with respect to the danger and that communicates adequate information on the dangers and safe use of the product, taking into account the characteristics of, and the ordinary knowledge common to, the persons by whom the product is intended to be used, or in the case of prescription drugs, taking into account the characteristics of, and the ordinary knowledge common to, the prescribing physician. If the warning or instruction given in connection with a drug or device or food or food additive has been approved or prescribed by the federal Food and Drug Administration under the "Federal Food, Drug, and Cosmetic Act," 52 Stat. 1040, 21 U.S.C. § 301 et seq., . . . a rebuttable presumption shall arise that the warning or instruction is adequate. . . .

N.J.S.A. 2A:58C–4.

The Senate Judiciary Committee Statement that accompanied L.1987, c.197 recites: "The subsection contains a general definition of an adequate warning and a special definition for warnings that accompany prescription drugs, since, *in the case of prescription drugs, the warning is owed to the physician*." See N.J.S.A. 2A:58C–1 (providing the Committee Statement) (emphasis added). At oral argument, counsel for Wyeth was candid to acknowledge that he could not "point to a sentence in the statute" that would make the learned intermediary doctrine applicable to the manufacturers' direct marketing of drugs, but rather relied on the Committee Statement. Although the statute provides a physician-based standard for determining the adequacy of the warning due to a physician, the statute does not legislate the boundaries of the doctrine. * * * [I]n 1987, direct-to-consumer marketing of prescription drugs was in its beginning stages. * * *

Our dissenting member suggests that we should await legislative action before deciding that issue. * * * If we decline to resolve the question, we are making the substantive determination that the learned intermediary doctrine applies to the direct marketing of drugs, an issue recently debated but left unanswered by the drafters of the *Restatement*. Either course, then, requires us to adopt a principle of law. The question is which is the better principle. * * *

Judge John Minor Wisdom explained the rationale behind the learned intermediary doctrine. His perspective reflects the then-prevalent attitude about doctor-patient relationships:

> This special standard for prescription drugs is an understandable exception to the *Restatement*'s general rule that one who markets goods must warn foreseeable ultimate users of dangers inherent in [the] products. . . . Prescription drugs are likely to be complex medicines, esoteric in formula and varied in effect. As a medical expert, the prescribing physician can take into account the propensities of the drug, as well as the susceptibilities of [the] patient. [The physician's] task [is to weigh] the benefits of any medication against its potential

> dangers. The choice [the physician] makes is an informed one, an individualized medical judgment bottomed on a knowledge of both patient and palliative. Pharmaceutical companies then, who must warn ultimate purchasers of dangers inherent in patent drugs sold over the counter, in selling prescription drugs are required to warn only the prescribing physician, who acts as a "learned intermediary" between manufacturer and consumer.

Reyes v. Wyeth Lab., Inc., 498 F.2d 1264, 1276 (5th Cir.1974) (footnote and citation omitted).

A more recent review summarized the theoretical bases for the doctrine as based on four considerations.

> First, courts do not wish to intrude upon the doctor-patient relationship. From this perspective, warnings that contradict information supplied by the physician will undermine the patient's trust in the physician's judgment. Second, physicians may be in a superior position to convey meaningful information to their patients, as they must do to satisfy their duty to secure informed consent. Third, drug manufacturers lack effective means to communicate directly with patients, making it necessary to rely on physicians to convey the relevant information. Unlike [over-the-counter products], pharmacists usually dispense prescription drugs from bulk containers rather than as unit-of-use packages in which the manufacturer may have enclosed labeling. Finally, because of the complexity of risk information about prescription drugs, comprehension problems would complicate any effort by manufacturers to translate physician labeling for lay patients. For this reason, even critics of the rule do not suggest that pharmaceutical companies should provide warnings only to patients and have no tort duty to warn physicians.

Lars Noah, Advertising Prescription Drugs to Consumers: Assessing the Regulatory and Liability Issues, 32 Ga. L. Rev. 141, 157–59 (1997) (footnotes omitted).

These premises: (1) reluctance to undermine the doctor-patient relationship; (2) absence in the era of "doctor knows best" of need for the patient's informed consent; (3) inability of drug manufacturer to communicate with patients; and (4) complexity of the subject; are all (with the possible exception of the last) absent in the direct-to-consumer advertising of prescription drugs.

First, with rare and wonderful exceptions, the " 'Norman Rockwell' image of the family doctor no longer exists." Id. at 180 n.78. Informed consent requires a patient-based decision rather than the paternalistic approach of the 1970s. The decision to take a drug is "not exclusively a matter for medical judgment." Second, because managed care has reduced the time allotted per patient, physicians have considerably less time to inform patients of the risks and benefits of a drug. "In a 1997 survey of 1,000 patients, the FDA found that only one-third had received information from their doctors about the dangerous side effects of drugs they were taking.'' Third, having spent $1.3 billion on advertising in 1998, drug manufacturers can hardly be said to ''lack effective means to communicate directly with patients'' when their advertising campaigns can pay off in close to billions in dividends. Consumer-directed advertising of pharmaceuticals thus belies each of the premises on which the learned intermediary doctrine rests. * * *

Concerns regarding patients' communication with and access to physicians are magnified in the context of medicines and medical devices furnished to women for reproductive decisions. In *MacDonald v. Ortho Pharmaceutical Corp.*, 475 N.E.2d 65 (Mass.1985), the plaintiff's use of oral contraceptives allegedly resulted in a stroke. The Massachusetts Supreme [Judicial] Court explained several reasons why contraceptives differ from other prescription drugs and thus ''warrant the imposition of a common law duty on the manufacturer to warn users directly of associated risks.'' For example, after the patient receives the prescription, she consults with the physician to receive a prescription annually, leaving her an infrequent opportunity to ''explore her questions and concerns about the medication with the prescribing physician.'' Consequently, the limited participation of the physician leads to a real possibility that their communication during the annual checkup is insufficient. The court also explained that because oral contraceptives are drugs personally selected by the patient, a prescription is often not the result of a physician's skilled balancing of individual benefits and risks but originates, instead, as a product of patient choice. Thus, ''the physician is relegated to a . . . passive role.'' Patient choice is an increasingly important part of our medical-legal jurisprudence. New Jersey has long since abandoned the ''professional standard'' in favor of the objectively-prudent-patient rule, recognizing the informed role of the patient in health-care decisions. * * *

When a patient is the target of direct marketing, one would think, at a minimum, that the law would require that the patient not be misinformed about the product. It is one thing not to inform a patient about the potential side effects of a product; it is another thing to misinform the patient by deliberately withholding potential side effects while marketing the product as an efficacious solution to a serious health problem. Further, when one considers that many of these ''life-style'' drugs or elective treatments cause significant side effects without any curative effect, increased consumer protection becomes imperative, because these drugs are, by definition, not medically necessary. * * *

FDA regulations are pertinent in determining the nature and extent of any duty of care that should be imposed on pharmaceutical manufacturers with respect to direct-to-consumer advertising. Presently, any duty to warn physicians about prescription drug dangers is presumptively met by compliance with federal labeling. * * * We believe that in the area of direct-to-consumer advertising of pharmaceuticals, the same rebuttable presumption should apply when a manufacturer complies with FDA advertising, labeling and warning requirements. That approach harmonizes the manufacturer's duty to doctors and to the public when it chooses to directly advertise its products, and simultaneously recognizes the public interest in informing patients about new pharmaceutical developments. * * * For all practical purposes, absent deliberate concealment or nondisclosure of after-acquired knowledge of harmful effects, compliance with FDA standards should be virtually dispositive of such claims. By definition, the advertising will have been "fairly balanced." * * *

The more difficult question is whether the role of the physician breaks the chain of causation. Although the physician writes the prescription, the physician's role in deciding which prescription drug is selected has been altered. * * * We have described proximate cause as an expression as much of policy as it is an expression of the effect of sequential events. A proximate cause need not be the sole cause of harm. It suffices if it is a substantial contributing factor to the harm suffered. * * * As a matter of policy then, we could hold that even if deceptive advertising were a substantial contributing factor influencing a patient's choice of a medicine, the intervening role of the physician should insulate the manufacturer who has engaged in deceptive trade practices. * * *

Obviously, the physician is almost always the essential link between the patient and the pharmaceutical. Most ads for drugs caution the patient to consult with a physician. * * * However, we must consider as well a case in which a diabetic patient might have been influenced by advertising to request a drug from a physician without being warned by the manufacturer or the physician of the special dangers posed to a diabetic taking the drug. If an overburdened physician does not inquire whether the patient is a diabetic, the question remains whether the manufacturer should be relieved entirely of responsibility. In the case of direct marketing of drugs, we believe that neither the physician nor the manufacturer should be entirely relieved of their respective duties to warn. Pharmaceutical manufacturers may seek contribution, indemnity or exoneration because of the physician's deficient role in prescribing that drug. * * *

[T]he dramatic shift in pharmaceutical marketing to consumers is based in large part on significant changes in the health-care system from fee-for-service to managed care. Managed care companies negotiate directly with pharmaceutical companies and then inform prescribers which medications are covered by the respective plans. Because managed care has made it more difficult for pharmaceutical companies to communicate with prescribers, the manufacturers have developed a different strategy, marketing to consumers. * * * * The direct marketing of drugs to consumers generates a corresponding duty requiring manufacturers to warn of defects in the product. The FDA has established a comprehensive regulatory scheme for direct-to-consumer marketing of pharmaceutical products. Given the presumptive defense that is afforded to pharmaceutical manufacturers that comply with FDA requirements, we believe that it is fair to reinforce the regulatory scheme by allowing, in the case of direct-to-consumer marketing of drugs, patients deprived of reliable medical information to establish that the misinformation was a substantial factor contributing to their use of a defective pharmaceutical product.

Before concluding, we acknowledge that the procedural posture of this case casts defendant's product in an unfair light. Because the case arises on a motion for summary judgment, we are obliged to view the issues in the light most favorable to the claimants. We have no doubt that substantial proofs will be marshaled to show that Norplant is a safe and efficacious product and that Wyeth's advertising, if any, was fairly balanced. An agreed statement of facts submitted to the trial court suggested as much. And Norplant probably does not afford the best context in which to address the general question whether direct-to-consumer marketers of pharmaceutical products are unqualifiedly relieved of a duty to warn consumers of the dangerous propensities of a product. After all, in the case of Norplant, the role of the physician can never be insubstantial because only a physician may implant the device. Just as it is difficult to legislate a rule for every foreseeable circumstance, so too it is difficult to create a special rule of law for a hybrid [drug-device] product such as Norplant.

We are called upon, however, to resolve a question of law that will apply equally as well to an unprincipled marketer of pharmaceutical products as to a principled marketer. To place the issue in context, consider if prescription diet drugs were heavily advertised without warning of a known potential for heart damage. * * * That is the normative situation for which we must decide if a pharmaceutical manufacturer is free to engage in deceptive advertising to consumers. We believe that the answer in such a case should be no. Any question of fairness in imposing on the direct marketer of a product such as Norplant a duty to warn the targeted consumers will be resolved in the proximate cause analysis. * * *

■ POLLOCK, JUSTICE (dissenting):

With disarming understatement, the majority opinion raises profound questions about the purpose of judicial opinions, the role of courts, and the separation of powers. In raising those questions, the majority rejects the Legislature's endorsement of the learned intermediary doctrine as set forth in N.J.S.A. 2A:58C–4. The majority opinion sustains itself only by ignoring the plain language of an unambiguous statute, the New Jersey Products Liability Act (NJPLA), and by substituting its own policy preference for that of the Legislature. Contrary to the majority opinion, the point of this dissent is not that the court should await legislative action. Rather, the point is that the Legislature has already acted. * * *

New Jersey courts consistently have recognized the vitality of the learned intermediary doctrine. In 1987, the Legislature codified the learned intermediary doctrine in the NJPLA. Thus, although the learned intermediary doctrine remains a common-law rule in most states, it is now a statutory rule in New Jersey. * * * Analysis of the status of the learned intermediary doctrine thus depends on the intent of the Legislature. * * *

The majority has mischaracterized both the statute and the rationale for the learned intermediary doctrine. Contrary to the majority opinion, the statute directs that the warning is owed to the physician not "because drugs were then marketed to the physician," but because the physician is in the best position to make an individualized evaluation of the risks of drugs and warn the patient of those risks. The patient, moreover, cannot obtain the drugs without a prescription written by a physician. Underlying the majority opinion is the assumption that the Legislature in 1987 could not have anticipated the mass-marketing of prescription drugs. That assumption, however, has no basis in the record. * * *

Given the statutory basis for the learned intermediary doctrine in New Jersey, recourse to the *Restatement (Third) of Torts: Products Liability* § 6 (1998) is gratuitous. Furthermore, the *Restatement* generally endorses the traditional rule that a drug manufacturer's duty to warn is owed to the health-care provider, not the consumer. The *Restatement* suggests, however, that it may be appropriate to impose a duty to warn the patient directly "when the manufacturer knows or has reason to know that health-care providers will not be in a position to reduce the risks of harm in accordance with the instructions or warnings." Here, the *Restatement* does not apply for two reasons. First, as prestigious as any *Restatement* may be, it cannot supersede a governing statute. Second, the surgical implantation of Norplant requires the significant involvement of a health-care provider who must make an individualized evaluation of the risk to the patient. Such involvement stands in contrast to the "diminished role as an evaluator or decision maker" that is a predicate for liability under the *Restatement*. That involvement also distinguishes the implantation of Norplant from the administration of mass inoculations, which proceed without an individualized evaluation of the risks to the patient. * * *

Norplant is a poor vehicle to import so momentous a change. Unlike other drugs that concern the majority, the record reveals that Norplant cannot be purchased in a supermarket, is not promoted by health maintenance organizations, approved by compliant physicians to placate overbearing patients, or implanted over the Internet. Through the incorporation of presumed facts, the majority has created a phantom record to support the creation of its exception to the learned intermediary doctrine. That exercise has led the majority to wander from the confines of the present case.

Norplant is not an over-the-counter drug; it can be obtained only with a doctor's prescription. To insert Norplant, a physician or other health-care professional anesthetizes an area in a patient's upper arm, makes a one-eighth-inch incision, and implants six capsules just below the patient's skin. Similar surgery is required to remove the capsules. The use of Norplant thus requires the significant involvement of the prescribing physician. Even Norman Rockwell would recognize the procedure as one performed in accordance with the traditional physician-patient relationship. Presumably, Wyeth's mass-marketing campaign has increased the demand for Norplant and led many women to request it by name. In some contexts, the extent to which pharmaceutical companies seek to influence consumers, like the extent to which they seek to influence physicians, may be disturbing. Here, however, the mass-marketing campaign apparently was ineffectual; none of the bellwether plaintiffs saw any advertising about Norplant. The invasiveness of the Norplant procedure, moreover, would give any patient pause and a physician cause to evaluate the risks. * * *

The majority identifies four premises underlying the learned intermediary doctrine that it asserts are inapplicable when a manufacturer advertises the drug directly to consumers * * * * Contrary to the majority, those four considerations remain relevant to the implantation of Norplant. First, the Norplant System must be implanted surgically. Implicit in the performance of a surgical procedure is respect for the physician-patient relationship. "[T]he physician is in the best position to take into account the propensities of the drug and the susceptibilities of the patient, and to give a highly individualized warning to the ultimate user based on the physician's specialized knowledge." Second, the physician is the only person who can communicate with the patient to obtain the patient's informed consent to the procedure. Third, a pharmaceutical company, such as Wyeth, cannot provide an adequate warning to each individual consumer about the potential side-effects and risks associated with the device. Each patient has individualized risks associated with surgical procedures. Lastly, the Norplant implant, far more than other birth control devices, is a complex contraceptive system that requires detailed instructions and warnings.

To soften the impact of its opinion, the majority creates a rebuttable presumption that a warning is adequate if it complies with FDA regulations. Regrettably, the court has not granted the parties the opportunity to address the creation, nature, or sufficiency of such a presumption. To the extent that such a presumption is essential to the majority's rationale, the parties should have been given that opportunity. * * *

NOTES AND QUESTIONS

1. *An exceptional exception?* It took more than a decade before another court adopted the exception to the learned intermediary doctrine announced in *Perez*. See Centocor, Inc. v. Hamilton, 310 S.W.3d 476, 505–08 (Tex.Ct.App.2010); id. at 486–90, 508 & n.18, 512–14, 516–18 (applying this exception in a case where the manufacturer of Remicade® had supplied an infusion center with instructional videotapes for patients that failed to mention the rare risk (revealed in the package insert) of developing lupus-like syndrome, and affirming sizeable compensatory and punitive damage awards); cf. Banner v. Hoffmann–La Roche Inc., 891 A.2d 1229, 1236–37 (N.J.App.Div.2006) (declining to apply *Perez* where Accutane® manufacturer simply had provided brochures for doctors to use with their patients). Most courts squarely presented with the question have declined to recognize the DTCA exception. See, e.g., In re Norplant Contraceptive Prods. Liab. Litig., 165 F.3d 374 (5th Cir.1999); Beale v. Biomet, Inc., 492 F.Supp.2d 1360, 1376 (S.D.Fla.2007); Cowley v. Abbott Labs., Inc., 476 F.Supp.2d 1053, 1060 n.4 (W.D.Wis.2007); In re Meridia Prods. Liab. Litig., 328 F.Supp.2d 791, 812 n.19 (N.D.Ohio 2004), aff'd, 447 F.3d 861, 865 (6th Cir.2006); Vitanza v. Upjohn Co., 778 A.2d 829 (Conn.2001). If plaintiffs in a case like *Perez* had seen and relied on the advertisements, might they assert a misrepresentation claim (see Rest. (3d) § 9), or would the learned intermediary rule present the same duty limitation absent an exception? See Miller v. Pfizer Inc., 196 F.Supp.2d 1095, 1119–22 (D.Kan.2002) (applying the learned intermediary rule to a misrepresentation claim brought against the manufacturer of Zoloft®). How about subjects enrolled in clinical trials that sponsors had advertised in print or on television?

2. *The PPI exception.* Contrary to *Edwards*, several courts have rejected the suggestion that the mandatory or voluntary distribution of PPIs would eliminate the learned intermediary rule. See, e.g., MacPherson v. Searle & Co., 775 F.Supp. 417, 425 (D.D.C.1991); Presto v. Sandoz Pharm. Corp., 487 S.E.2d 70, 73–74 (Ga.Ct.App.1997); Martin v. Ortho Pharm. Corp., 661 N.E.2d 352, 356 (Ill.1996). One court suggested that the learned intermediary rule would not protect a manufacturer against a claim for failure to warn the public of a drug recall. See Nichols v. McNeilab, Inc., 850 F.Supp. 562, 564–65 (E.D.Mich.1993) (distinguishing the notification of a drug withdrawal prompted by safety concerns from the risk information conveyed to patients at the time that a drug is initially prescribed); see also Francesca L. Kritz, Recalls: Who Knew?, Wash. Post, Oct. 22, 2002, at F1 (reporting that patients often do not receive notifications of drug recalls).

3. *Regulatory compliance.* In *Perez*, the court held that compliance with FDA requirements would create a presumption that the risk information communicated to consumers was adequate. This presumption is, however, rebuttable. See McDarby v. Merck & Co., 949 A.2d 223, 256–61 (N.J.App. Div.2008); id. at 229–48 (recounting in detail the regulatory history of Vioxx in relation to postapproval research and marketing of the drug); see also Rowe v. Hoffman–La Roche, Inc., 917 A.2d 767, 773–76 (N.J.2007) (applying Michigan's conclusive presumption rather than New Jersey's rebuttable presumption that FDA-approved labeling provides adequate warnings). Furthermore, recall from Chapter 5(B)(2) that few states other than New Jersey have codified an FDA compliance defense, and, as suggested in *Edwards*, most courts do not credit compliance with FDA labeling rules. See MacDonald v. Ortho Pharm. Corp., 475 N.E.2d 65, 70–71 (Mass.1985) (explaining that "compliance with FDA requirements, though admissible to demonstrate lack of negligence, is not conclusive"); cf. Catherine M. Sharkey, Drug Advertising Claims: Preemption's New Frontier, 41 Loy. L.A. L. Rev. 1625 (2008) (explaining that FDA regulation of DTCA would not likely preempt consumer fraud claims).

4. *Keeping doctors in the loop.* In thinking about the desirability of these various exceptions, one should not lose sight of the fact that a medical professional will continue to intervene in the decision to prescribe a drug or device and make the final judgment about its relative risks and benefits for a particular patient. See Seley v. G.D. Searle & Co., 423 N.E.2d 831, 840 (Ohio 1981) ("The decision to use oral contraception, although involving a higher degree of patient choice than is generally associated with a prescribing decision, remains a joint one made by both doctor and patient."); William E. Boden & George A. Diamond, DTCA for PTCA—Crossing the Line in Consumer Health Education?, 358 New Eng. J. Med. 2197, 2200 (2008) ("[A drug-eluting] stent can be selected and implanted only by someone with a very sophisticated medical understanding .... It seems almost unimaginable ... that a cardiologist would accede to a patient's request for a particular stent on the basis of the information gleaned from a television ad."). As explained in the next chapter, it would constitute professional malpractice to do otherwise.

5. *Further commentary*. See Richard B. Goetz & Karen R. Growdon, A Defense of the Learned Intermediary Doctrine, 63 Food & Drug L.J. 421 (2008); Michelle M. Mello et al., Direct-to-Consumer Advertising and Shared Liability for Pharmaceutical Manufacturers, 289 JAMA 477 (2003); Victor E. Schwartz et al., Marketing Pharmaceutical Products in the Twenty–First Century: An Analysis of the Continued Viability of Traditional Principles of Law in the Age of Direct-to-Consumer Advertising, 32 Harv. J.L. & Pub. Pol'y 333 (2009); Jennifer Girod, Note, The Learned Intermediary Doctrine: An Efficient Protection for Patients, Past and Present, 40 Ind. L. Rev. 397 (2007); Andrea M. Greene, Note, Pharmaceutical Manufacturers' Liability for Direct Marketing and Over–Promotion of Prescription Drugs to Product Users, 26 Am. J. Trial Advoc. 661 (2003); Kate Miller, Note, Hormone Replacement Therapy in the Wake of the Women's Health Initiative Study: An Opportunity to Reexamine the Learned Intermediary Doctrine, 12 Wm. & Mary J. Women & L. 239 (2005).

Lars Noah, *This Is Your Products Liability Restatement on Drugs*

74 Brook. L. Rev. 839 (2009).

* * * Until the central feature that defines the marketing of prescription drugs—namely, the requirement that a medical professional authorize the purchase by a particular patient—is modified, the learned intermediary rule does not lose its force simply because a company chooses to promote its product directly to consumers. * * * Although essentially no one doubts that direct advertising has altered the dynamic between patients and their physicians when considering the use of a drug promoted in this fashion, * * * doctors would continue playing a central role. The majority [in *Perez*] also never explained how such advertising rendered inapplicable concerns that supplying comprehensive risk information directly to patients might cause them to discontinue needed treatments,[260] much less that a manufacturer could do this in a way reasonably comprehensible to laypersons. * * * Evidently the majority thought that Norplant, like some of the other examples it had cited, did not qualify as a therapeutically important product, echoing suggestions made by some commentators that another exception to the learned intermediary doctrine should apply to "lifestyle" drugs and devices, whether or not directly advertised to consumers. * * *

260. Extensive warnings conveyed directly by pharmaceutical manufacturers might make patients lose trust in their physicians or discontinue necessary drug therapies because of undue anxiety about the reported side effects that the physician felt did not deserve mention or emphasis in a particular case—after all, advertisements emphasize benefits and come before the patient visits a physician, while PPIs emphasize risks and reach patients only upon drug dispensing.

What the plaintiffs wanted * * * was not clearer risk information in advertisements that they may not have seen (or remembered); instead, they sought printed warnings to accompany the drugs when later dispensed to them. * * * The *Perez* majority hastened to add that, as provided by state statute, the defendant would enjoy a rebuttable (or stronger) presumption of adequacy so long as the warnings complied with FDA requirements. This reflects a potentially serious misunderstanding of the intended purpose of the agency's advertising rules (and it also fails to appreciate the entirely flimsy nature of the FDA's recent non-rule pronouncements on the subject): these do not attempt to fulfill a risk disclosure function so much as to ensure fair balance.

If the plaintiffs had not, in fact, seen any Norplant ads, then compliance with agency requirements designed to prevent misleading advertising could hardly have satisfied the new-found duty to warn patients directly. If extended to broadcast ads, where the FDA's "requirements" appear in technically non-binding (and hardly unambiguous) guidance documents, then the compliance defense would offer essentially no protection unless courts understood the manner in which agency expectations operate as de facto requirements. * * * If courts recognized an advertising exception to the learned intermediary rule (or abrogated it entirely), then pharmaceutical manufacturers would have to find a way of disseminating PPIs, ensure that these inserts contained references to all possible side effects in nontechnical language, and, in the unlikely event that they managed to design such an unassailable warning, hope that a jury would not decide that continued advertising to consumers diluted the effectiveness of this warning. * * *

Extending a parallel suggested previously in connection with the design defect standard, manufacturers of toys and other goods accessible to young children have a duty to warn their parents. If manufacturers choose to advertise directly to youngsters, and the kids then whine until their parents purchase inappropriate products, the manufacturers still would owe no duty to warn the kids directly (though, if overpromotion dilutes the force of information already supplied to adult purchasers, then it might well provide the basis for an inadequate warning claim). Although such promotional efforts may deserve criticism (and efforts at prohibition), presumably no one would argue that recognizing a largely incoherent duty to warn children directly offered a second-best solution to the problem.

By definition, adequate consumer labeling cannot be designed for prescription drugs. * * * [P]roducts that continue to require prescription labeling reflect the agency's judgment that professional intervention remains necessary to ensure their safe use. The FDA has in the past mandated PPIs for some drugs to supplement the labeling provided to physicians, and it continues to encourage their broad use, but no one suggests that PPIs should fully replace professional labeling. Direct advertising further encourages active participation by consumers in prescribing decisions, a favorable development that courts should not reward by expanding the tort duties of drug manufacturers and, because consumer-directed warnings inevitably would fall short, discouraging such advertising in the future. * * *

3. Other Sources of Information

In re Factor VIII or IX Concentrate Blood Products Litigation

25 F.Supp.2d 837 (N.D.Ill.1998).

■ Grady, District Judge:

* * * Plaintiffs in this multidistrict litigation are hemophiliacs and the personal representatives of deceased hemophiliacs who used certain blood products known as "factor concentrates" to treat their hemophilia and, as a result, became infected with the HIV virus. The defendant National Hemophilia Foundation (NHF) is a nonprofit organization that provided information to hemophiliacs about blood products in the 1980s. * * * NHF membership includes chapters (usually on a statewide basis), medical providers and the leading members of the plasma industry. Part of its stated mission is to promote "programs of research; patient, public and professional education; and patient, family and community services." The NHF also develops medical treatment standards or recommendations which are disseminated and relied upon by physicians in their treatment of persons with hemophilia.

The plaintiffs allege that the NHF established itself as the "preeminent authority" and "principal educator" on medical treatment issues impacting persons with hemophilia. The plaintiffs also assert that, early in the AIDS epidemic, the NHF assumed a leadership role in informing, guiding and educating hemophiliacs, their treaters and the media regarding the proper treatment of hemophilia in light of the AIDS risk.

The primary theory of liability is that the NHF was negligent in providing information and advice to its members and for the benefit of the hemophilia community at large. The allegations are that the NHF made false, incorrect and misleading statements regarding the safety of factor concentrates manufactured and distributed by the other defendants in this litigation. Plaintiffs charge that the NHF negligently recommended use of the concentrates when it should have known of the danger of viral contamination, failed to warn its members about that danger, failed to recommend timely recall of the concentrates and failed to disclose certain relationships between NHF board members and the defendant manufacturers. In addition to the negligence allegations, it is claimed that the NHF violated certain fiduciary duties owing to the plaintiffs. Plaintiffs claim that, as a result of the NHF's actions, they and their decedents relied on the NHF, used the concentrates and became infected with the HIV virus. In many cases the infections have resulted in death.

In moving for summary judgment, the NHF argues that its First Amendment rights to free speech and free press would be abridged if courts were to impose liability on it because of its communications. * * * A threshold issue is whether sufficient governmental action exists to implicate the First Amendment. The NHF claims that the imposition of tort liability would be sufficient. This is correct. * * *

The NHF begins by arguing that its publications are noncommercial speech and because of that status can lose protection in only four circumstances—libel, obscenity, incitement and fighting words. * * * It reasons that it is entitled to full First Amendment protection from liability in this litigation unless we find that its speech falls into one of the four unprotected categories. We disagree with the NHF's view of the law. No Supreme Court case has held that the[se] four categories of speech * * * are an exhaustive enumeration of unprotected speech. * * *

The NHF argument is belied by a considerable body of law denying First Amendment protection in situations not involving obscenity, libel, incitement or fighting words. For example: speech that invades privacy, speech that breaches a promise of confidentiality, speech that infringes a copyright, speech that is harassing, speech that infringes a performer's right of publicity, and speech that constitutes fraudulent misrepresentation. Some of these cases are significant for another reason: they illustrate the well-established principle that the protections of the First Amendment do not shield the press from laws of general applicability. * * * It is, of course, true that when the press is confronted with potential liability for the content of its publications, there is a danger of chilling vigorous public discourse. The Supreme Court has recognized this tension in the context of tort liability for defamation. * * *

In regard to plaintiffs' allegations of negligent mistakes in the NHF's publications, the NHF argues that liability cannot be imposed for misstatement alone. * * * The problem with the NHF's argument is that it does not explain why a specific standard articulated in the context of a public figure's ability to recover under libel and invasion of privacy theories applies to this case. The libel and privacy cases did not articulate a broad standard for cases where a defendant is sued for misstatements of fact. Instead, those cases were context-specific, applying only to libel suits brought by public figures. * * *

In this case, the interest of society in providing redress for the grave injuries alleged should be weighed against the danger of chilling the NHF's communications. Here, the chilling effect may be greater because of the large number of claimants. * * * We are not persuaded that this potential chilling effect outweighs the public interest in redressing the kinds of injuries alleged here. For one reason, liability here would not extend to "all the world." The facts of this case involve an organization supplying information to its known membership and, by extension, to the limited community of persons suffering from hemophilia. Moreover, this case involves injuries that are different in nature and gravity from the injuries complained of in [other cases]. * * *

It is essential to recognize the exact nature of the interests being asserted in this litigation. On the one hand, there is the interest of the plaintiffs in redressing serious personal injury and death caused by reliance on erroneous information concerning the safety of medical products. On the other hand, there is the interest of the defendant in being immune from liability for negligent communication of misinformation that has resulted in serious injury or death. The litigation presents no question as to whether there should be liability for erroneous communications which are not negligent or which do not cause serious injury.

Medical and scientific opinions can differ, of course, and there is often a wide range of opinions on a particular medical question. It is traditional in negligence law to distinguish between negligence and errors in judgment, with no liability arising from the latter. But it is also traditional for liability to be imposed upon medical practitioners who fail to use ordinary care in arriving at recommendations that proximately cause injury to patients. The recommendation is a form of expression, since it can be conveyed only orally or in writing, but the First Amendment has never been thought to bar an action for medical malpractice based on such written or spoken expression in a medical context. We see no material difference between such an action and the claims presented here.

The situation would be entirely different if plaintiffs were seeking to impose strict liability upon the NHF for its communications. In that event, the First Amendment would surely be implicated and we would be persuaded by the NHF's argument that there must be open and candid public debate on all medical issues and that the courts should not inhibit nonprofit organizations from contributing to that debate. But the argument is not apposite to negligence liability. In seeking to avoid liability altogether, even for negligent conduct, the NHF simply fails to recognize the interests protected by negligence law (in general or in this particular case) or the need to balance those interests against the values of free speech.

We conclude that negligence law, a law of general applicability, provides a constitutionally acceptable accommodation between the competing interests asserted here, and that the First Amendment does not protect the NHF from liability for the negligent acts and omissions alleged by the plaintiffs in this consolidated litigation.[11] * * *

[I]n response to the plaintiffs' argument that the NHF had a duty to speak concerning several matters,[13] the NHF cites two Supreme Court cases and argues that the First Amendment provides a right not to speak. We reject this argument for several reasons. First, the two cited cases are from areas of law not analogous to this one. Second, there is no case authority for the proposition that the First Amendment provides immunity

---

11. * * * [T]he determination of whether First Amendment protection exists is different from the determination of whether a duty exists in tort law. The issue before the court is not whether a duty existed in this situation, it is whether and to what extent the NHF is protected by the First Amendment. * * *

13. Plaintiffs argue that the NHF had: (1) a duty to disclose the financial and other relationships of its board with the blood products manufacturers; (2) a duty to disclose all potential risks involved in using the factor concentrates; (3) a duty to warn hemophiliacs about the risk of the sexual transmission of AIDS; and (4) a duty to disclose statements by a certain Dr. Bruce Evatt.

for defendants in failure to warn cases. Third, adopting the NHF's view of the First Amendment would ignore decades of tort law, dating back to at least 1892, holding that manufacturers can be liable for failing to warn consumers about dangers of their products. We see no principled basis on which the duty to warn could be imposed on manufacturers while organizations such as the NHF would be exempted on First Amendment grounds. * * *

NOTES AND QUESTIONS

1. *First amendment redux.* Does a court's imposition of a duty to warn raise any of the free speech concerns discussed in Chapter 4(C)? See James M. Beck, Constitutional Protection of Scientific and Educational Activities from Tort Liability: The First Amendment as a Defense to Personal Injury Litigation, 37 Tort & Ins. L.J. 981 (2002). Courts generally refuse to impose strict liability against publishers of informational books, including texts that provide therapeutic advice. See Jones v. J.B. Lippincott Co., 694 F.Supp. 1216 (D.Md.1988) (rejecting tort claims brought by a student who suffered an injury from trying a remedy for constipation listed in a nursing textbook). The courts view the content of such books as an intangible not covered by products liability doctrines, and they also express concerns about chilling the dissemination of information. See Libertelli v. Hoffman–La Roche, 565 F.Supp. 234 (S.D.N.Y.1983) (dismissing tort claim against the publisher of the PDR for failing to warn of Valium's addictive potential); Rest. (3d) § 19 cmt. d. These objections seem misplaced, however, especially when one compares the courts' willingness to entertain failure-to-warn claims. See Lars Noah, Authors, Publishers, and Products Liability: Remedies for Defective Information in Books, 77 Or. L. Rev. 1195, 1212 (1998) ("The conceptual separation between the product itself and information contained within the product, so evident in cases declining to hold authors and publishers strictly liable, is absent in the prescription drug liability context."). But cf. Smith v. Linn, 563 A.2d 123, 126 (Pa.Super.Ct.1989) (rejecting, in the course of immunizing the author of a diet book from a wrongful death claim brought on behalf of a reader who followed the recommendations, the suggested parallel to failure-to-warn claims against drug manufacturers), aff'd, 587 A.2d 309 (Pa.1991).

2. *Liability for negligence in supplying therapeutic information.* The court did not decide whether the NHF owed any tort duties to the plaintiffs, though recall from Chapter 7(A)(3) the *Conte* court's willingness to allow users of generic drugs to pursue negligent misrepresentation claims against the brand-name manufacturer even though it had not supplied the product that caused the patient's injury. A few courts have allowed tort claims to proceed against the American Association of Blood Banks for failing to recommend to its members certain screening procedures designed to prevent the use of HIV-infected blood. See Snyder v. American Ass'n of Blood Banks, 676 A.2d 1036 (N.J.1996); Weigand v. University Hosp. of NYU Med. Ctr., 659 N.Y.S.2d 395 (Super.Ct.1997). But see N.N.V. v. American Ass'n of Blood Banks, 89 Cal.Rptr.2d 885 (Ct.App.1999) (rejecting such a claim). Some commentators have argued that injured patients should get to assert similar claims against medical societies responsible for the drafting of practice guidelines. See Matthew R. Giannetti, Note, Circumcision and the American Academy of Pediatrics: Should Scientific Misconduct Result in Trade Association Liability?, 85 Iowa L. Rev. 1507, 1546–66 (2000); Megan L. Sheetz, Note, Toward Controlled Clinical Care Through Clinical Practice Guidelines: The Legal Liability for Developers and Issuers of Clinical Pathways, 63 Brook. L. Rev. 1341 (1997); see also Brian H. Lamkin, Comment, Medical Expert Systems and Publisher Liability: A Cross–Contextual Analysis, 43 Emory L.J. 731 (1994). Courts remain divided on the question. Compare Cali v. Danek Med., Inc., 24 F.Supp.2d 941, 949–50 (W.D.Wis.1998) (rejecting fraud claims against medical societies for sponsoring seminars at which allegedly unsafe uses of pedicle screws in spinal fusion were discussed), with Coleman v. Danek Med., Inc., 43 F.Supp.2d 629 (S.D.Miss.1998) (holding that FDAMA's protections of the practice of medicine would not preclude such a claim).

C. Measuring the Adequacy of Warnings

If a duty to warn does exist in a particular case, the complete failure to provide any warning of the risk would represent an actionable breach. The question becomes more difficult when a manufacturer has conveyed a warning of the risk in question to the appropriate persons but the plaintiff alleges that the warning was inadequate.

1. Warning Health Professionals

Felix v. Hoffmann–LaRoche, Inc.

540 So.2d 102 (Fla.1989).

■ Grimes, Justice:

* * * This was a suit for the wrongful death of a child attributed to the ingestion of Accutane by his mother during pregnancy. Accutane is a drug prescribed for serious and disfiguring cases of acne which was approved for marketing in the United States by the Food and Drug Administration in 1982. The mother took the drug late in 1982 while she was pregnant upon the prescription of her physician. The child was born with severe birth defects which led to his early demise.

A critical issue in the case was whether the manufacturer of the drug furnished adequate warnings of the dangers of using the drug during pregnancy. The relevant text of the package insert at that time stated:

> CONTRAINDICATIONS: Teratogenicity was observed in rats at a dose of isotretinoin of 150 mg/kg/day. In rabbits a dose of 10 mg/kg/day was teratogenic and embryotoxic, and induced abortion. There are no adequate and well-controlled studies in pregnant women. Because teratogenicity has been observed in animals given isotretinoin, patients

who are pregnant or intend to become pregnant while undergoing treatment should not receive Accutane. Women of childbearing potential should not be given Accutane unless an effective form of contraception is used, and they should be fully counseled on the potential risks to the fetus should they become pregnant while undergoing treatment. Should pregnancy occur during treatment, the physician and patient should discuss the desirability of continuing the pregnancy....

WARNINGS: Although no abnormalities of the human fetus have been reported thus far, animal studies with retinoids suggest that teratogenic effects may occur. It is recommended that contraception be continued for one month or until a normal menstrual period has occurred following discontinuation of Accutane therapy....

PRECAUTIONS: *INFORMATION FOR PATIENTS*:.... Women of childbearing potential should be instructed to use an effective form of contraception when Accutane therapy is required. (See CONTRAINDICATIONS AND WARNINGS)....

PREGNANCY: Category X. See "CONTRAINDICATIONS" section.

Dr. Greenwald prescribed Accutane to the mother for a cystic acne condition of her face and shoulders which had persisted for many years. He characterized Accutane as a miracle drug for people with acne. Dr. Greenwald testified that he understood the warnings which accompanied the drug and said that "category X" meant that the drug should not be used during pregnancy. He also stated that he had prior knowledge of the teratogenic propensities of Accutane from independent research and reading and from seminars he had attended. He defined "teratogenicity" as "the ability of something to turn out a teratogen" and the term "teratogen" as "a mutant, deformed something—a deformed part, a deformed being, a deformed person, a monster, if you will, something very abnormal." Dr. Greenwald testified that he warned the mother against the use of Accutane if she were to become pregnant. The mother denied having received such a warning. * * *

At the outset, it is clear that the manufacturer's duty to warn of Accutane's dangerous side effects was directed to the physician rather than the patient. This is so because the prescribing physician, acting as a "learned intermediary" between the manufacturer and the consumer, weighs the potential benefits against the dangers in deciding whether to recommend the drug to meet the patient's needs. Furthermore, there is no contention that the warning given in this case contained any misstatements. While there have been subsequent incidents of children born with birth defects after their mothers ingested Accutane, there had been no Accutane related teratogenicity in human infants prior to the ingestion of the drug in this case. * * *

[P]etitioner argues that the adequacy of a drug warning can never be decided as a matter of law. Respondents suggest that a pharmaceutical manufacturer would be much less likely to make the capital investment in research, development, obtaining FDA approval, and marketing of a potentially beneficial drug which is accompanied by serious side effects if faced with the knowledge that, no matter how accurate and well-phrased the warning, a jury could decide its adequacy every time the side effect occurred.

While in many instances the adequacy of warnings concerning drugs is a question of fact, we hold that it can become a question of law where the warning is accurate, clear, and unambiguous. The courts of many other jurisdictions have reached the same conclusion. In the instant case, the district court of appeal acknowledged that whether a warning is adequate is usually a jury question. However, in this case the court held that "[i]t is inconceivable that reasonable persons could disagree as to the adequacy of the warnings in conveying to physicians that the prescription drug, Accutane, is dangerous to pregnant women and should not have been prescribed." We agree. While the word "teratogenicity" is not one with which all consumers might be familiar, we are convinced that, as to physicians, the warning concerning the dangerous side effects of Accutane was quite clear.

The district court of appeal also held that even if it could be said that there was a factual dispute concerning the adequacy of the warning, any breach of the duty to warn in this case could not have been the proximate cause of the damage. The court reached this conclusion because the prescribing physician testified that he fully understood the warnings and also had prior knowledge of the teratogenic propensity of Accutane. Therefore, we agree that any inadequacy in the Accutane warning could not have been the proximate cause of the birth defects in this case. Insofar as the liability of the manufacturer is concerned, it makes no difference that the mother testified that Dr. Greenwald did not warn her of the danger of taking Accutane while she was pregnant. While this would present a factual issue in a claim against the doctor, the drug manufacturer could not be penalized for the failure of the doctor to impart knowledge concerning the dangers of the drug of which the doctor had been warned and was aware. * * *

NOTES AND QUESTIONS

1. *Measuring adequacy.* During the next two decades, and in spite of increasingly alarming warnings, more than 2,000 women became pregnant while taking Accutane. See Sandra G. Boodman, Too Hard to Take, Wash. Post, Sept. 5, 2006, at F1. What does that poor track record suggest? Cf. Lars Noah, Too High a Price for Some Drugs?: The FDA Burdens Reproductive Choice, 44 San Diego L. Rev. 231, 236 (2007) ("Over the last two decades, and in parallel with the FDA's incremental approach to addressing Accutane's teratogenicity, victims have pursued tort litigation against Hoffmann–La Roche. For the most part, courts have rejected inadequate warning claims."); id. at 256 (discussing the limited range of claims available against physicians in such cases); Steven Bushong, Controversial Acne Drug: Accutane off Shelves, but Lawsuits Live, Columbus Dispatch, July 3,

2009, at 1A. Courts generally require that a warning be communicated with the degree of urgency necessary to cause the user to exercise the level of caution commensurate with the potential danger. See Weilbrenner v. Teva Pharms. USA, Inc., 696 F.Supp.2d 1329, 1339–40 (M.D.Ga.2010); Bennett v. Madakasira, 821 So.2d 794, 805–07 (Miss.2002). See generally Janet Fairchild, Annotation, Liability of Manufacturer or Seller for Injury or Death Allegedly Caused by Failure to Warn Regarding Danger in Use of Vaccine or Prescription Drug, 94 A.L.R.3d 748 (1979 & 2011 Supp.). For instance, plaintiffs in drug cases will sometimes complain that a side effect listed in the Adverse Reactions section should instead have appeared in the Warnings or even Contraindications section of the package insert. A warning also may be judged inadequate if its tone, placement, or typeface makes it unlikely to attract the physician's attention. When a product's labeling warns of the very injury suffered by the plaintiff in clear and precise terms, the manufacturer may succeed on summary judgment. See, e.g., Ziliak v. AstraZeneca LP, 324 F.3d 518, 521 (7th Cir.2003) (inhaled corticosteroid); Adams v. Synthes Spine Co., 298 F.3d 1114, 1118–19 (9th Cir.2002) (surgical plate); Stahl v. Novartis Pharm. Corp., 283 F.3d 254, 264–68 (5th Cir.2002) (Lamisil®); id. at 268 ("[W]hen a particular adverse effect is clearly and unambiguously mentioned in a warning label and the prescribing physician unequivocally states that he or she was adequately informed of that risk by the warning, the manufacturer has satisfied its duty to warn ...."); id. (reference to risk of cholestatic hepatitis made it obvious to physicians that liver failure and death could result); id. at 269–72 (finding no inadequacy in the instructions for monitoring liver function); Ralston v. Smith & Nephew Richards, Inc., 275 F.3d 965, 975–76 (10th Cir.2001) (orthopedic nail, where labeling included statement that another product was more durable); Parkinson v. Guidant Corp., 315 F.Supp.2d 741, 748–49 (W.D.Pa.2004) (guidewire used in angioplasty).

2. *Causation.* If prescribing physicians testify that a stronger warning would not have altered their choice of drug, then plaintiffs cannot satisfy causation requirements. See Dietz v. Smithkline Beecham Corp., 598 F.3d 812, 816 (11th Cir.2010); Gove v. Eli Lilly & Co., 394 F.App'x 817 (2d Cir.2010); Ackermann v. Wyeth Pharms., 526 F.3d 203, 209–14 (5th Cir. 2008); Hoffmann–La Roche Inc. v. Mason, 27 So.3d 75, 77 (Fla.Ct.App. 2009); cf. Mauldin v. Upjohn Co., 697 F.2d 644, 646–47 (5th Cir.1983) (holding that a jury could find that a stronger warning would have altered the physician's behavior notwithstanding his contrary testimony); Tongate v. Wyeth Lab., 580 N.E.2d 1220, 1228–31 (Ill.App.Ct.1991) (same). Also, if a physician had not consulted the package insert, the failure to warn did not cause the patient's injury. See Motus v. Pfizer Inc., 358 F.3d 659, 661 (9th Cir.2004) ("Because the doctor testified that he did not read the warning label that accompanied Zoloft or rely on information provided by Pfizer's detail men before prescribing the drug to Mr. Motus, the adequacy of Pfizer's warnings is irrelevant ...."). Similarly, if a physician fails to diagnose a condition in a patient that would make a warning relevant in the selection of the drug, then any inadequacy in the warning would not have caused the injury. See Dyson v. Winfield, 113 F.Supp.2d 35, 43

(D.D.C.2000); see also Haggerty v. Wyeth Ayerst Pharm., 782 N.Y.S.2d 842, 844 (App.Div.2004) (alleged failure to warn was not the proximate cause of injury where the physician had intended to administer an entirely different vaccine but made a mistake). If a physician consciously decides not to relay a warning provided by a manufacturer, any inadequacy in that warning would not qualify as the cause of the patient's injury. See Krasnopolsky v. Warner–Lambert Co., 799 F.Supp. 1342, 1347 (E.D.N.Y.1992).

3. *Dilution.* The use of qualifying language may dilute the impact of an otherwise satisfactory warning. See, e.g., Tinnerholm v. Parke, Davis & Co., 285 F.Supp. 432, 451 (S.D.N.Y.1968) (finding that a warning had been "water[ed] down" by the "shrewd use of descriptive adjectives"), modified, 411 F.2d 48 (2d Cir.1969); McFadden v. Haritatos, 448 N.Y.S.2d 79, 81 (App.Div.1982) (statement that side effects of drug are usually reversible "tends to qualify and dilute the whole of the [adverse reactions] section's admonition"); see also McNeil v. Wyeth, 462 F.3d 364, 368 (5th Cir.2006); Thom v. Bristol–Myers Squibb Co., 353 F.3d 848, 853–54 (10th Cir.2003) (holding that the adequacy of a warning presented a question for the jury where the package insert was "equivocal" in referring to reports of adverse effect as "rare" and only "temporally associated" but for which "causal relationship . . . had not been established"); Michael Imbroscio & Gabriel Bell, Adequate Drug Warnings in the Face of Uncertain Causality: The Learned Intermediary Doctrine and the Need for Clarity, 107 W. Va. L. Rev. 847 (2005) (criticizing this decision).

4. *Overpromotion.* A manufacturer's promotion of a product also may render an otherwise complete warning inadequate. See, e.g., Brown v. Glaxo, Inc., 790 So.2d 35, 40–41 (La.Ct.App.2000); Holley v. Burroughs Wellcome Co., 348 S.E.2d 772, 777 (N.C.1986); see also Hyman & Armstrong, P.S.C. v. Gunderson, 279 S.W.3d 93, 111–12, 121–22 (Ky.2008) (sustaining a sizeable jury verdict, including $11.25 million in punitive damages, in favor of the plaintiffs on an inadequate warning claim where a patient suffered a fatal postpartum seizure linked to her use of the lactation suppressant Parlodel® (bromocriptine mesylate)); Phillip J. Winger, Note, Pharmaceutical Overpromotion Liability: The Legal Battle over Rural Prescription Drug Abuse, 93 Ky. L.J. 269 (2004–2005). See generally Janet Fairchild, Annotation, Promotional Efforts Directed Toward Prescribing Physician as Affecting Prescription Drug Manufacturer's Liability for Product–Caused Injury, 94 A.L.R.3d 1080 (1979 & 2011 Supp.). In one peculiar case, a court held that a warning might be inadequate even if the risk of the very injury suffered by the plaintiff was clearly disclosed, on the grounds that the plaintiff might have been deterred from taking the drug had the risk of some other more serious injury been fully disclosed. See Sanderson v. Upjohn Co., 578 F.Supp. 338, 339–40 (D.Mass.1984); see also McMahon v. Eli Lilly & Co., 774 F.2d 830, 834–35 (7th Cir.1985). But cf. Canesi v. Wilson, 685 A.2d 49, 54 (N.J.App.Div.1996), aff'd in part, 730 A.2d 805 (N.J.1999).

5. *Method of communication.* Even a specific and prominent warning may be found inadequate if it has not been communicated through the most effective channels. For instance, a number of courts have demanded the use of methods other than labeling to convey information to physicians about prescription drug risks, in part because physicians rarely see the actual product they have prescribed for any particular patient. See Sterling Drug, Inc. v. Yarrow, 408 F.2d 978, 992 (8th Cir.1969) ("[I]t was not unreasonable to find that the appellant should have employed all its usual means of communication ... to warn the prescribing physicians of these dangers."); Finn v. G.D. Searle & Co., 677 P.2d 1147, 1169 n.20 (Cal.1984) (Bird, C.J., dissenting) ("These include advertising and promotional literature, letters to the medical profession and oral communications by sales representatives."). In particular, several courts have focused on the use of pharmaceutical company sales representatives to convey precautionary information about prescription drugs to physicians. See Yarrow v. Sterling Drug, Inc., 263 F.Supp. 159, 163 (D.S.D.1967) [excerpted in Chap. 4(B)(1)], aff'd, 408 F.2d 978, 990–94 (8th Cir.1969) (pharmaceutical company held liable for failure to warn of newly discovered side effects, notwithstanding letters it had sent to physicians, because it had not used its sales representatives to convey the information); see also Wallace v. Upjohn Co., 535 So.2d 1110, 1117 (La.Ct.App.1988) (sales persons would not be personally liable for failing to warn physicians). When companies use their sales representatives to disseminate information about possible new side effects, some courts have criticized them for not sending a "Dear Doctor" letter instead. See Sterling Drug, Inc. v. Cornish, 370 F.2d 82, 84 (8th Cir.1966); Hoffman v. Sterling Drug, Inc., 485 F.2d 132, 146–47 (3d Cir.1973) (noting that "some doctors did not take the time to speak to detail men, some did not always accept the product cards or brochures offered, and some did not always listen to what the detail men said about a drug"); see also id. at 146 ("Nor was mailing drug literature to physicians necessarily an effective way to reach them.... [T]he jury could reasonably have found that a considerable amount of such literature winds up in the wastebasket and is not adequate to advise doctors concerning matters of utmost importance."). Thus, product labeling alone may sometimes fail to satisfy the duty to warn. Just as in hindsight the content of warning statements may always seem inadequate, a manufacturer's choice of mechanisms for presenting these warnings may always appear to be less than perfect.

Bernhardt v. Pfizer, Inc.

2000 WL 1738645 (S.D.N.Y.2000).

■ McKENNA, DISTRICT JUDGE:

Lawrence D. Bernhardt and Arnold Liebman have filed product liability actions against Pfizer, Inc. for claims arising out of their use of Cardura, a prescription drug manufactured by defendant. Presently before this court is defendant's motion for judgment on the pleadings pursuant to Fed. R. Civ. P. 12(c) with respect to plaintiffs' claim for mandatory injunctive relief in the form of an emergency notice sent to Cardura users and their physicians. * * *

Pfizer manufactures and markets the antihypertensive drug doxazosin under the brand name "Cardura" for the treatment of hypertension. In 1994, the National Heart, Lung and Blood Institute (NHLBI), a division of the National Institutes of Health (NIH), began an eight-year study called Antihypertensive and Lipid Lowering Treatment to Prevent Heart Attack Trial ("ALLHAT") which included in its scope the comparison of doxazosin to chlorthalidone in the treatment of hypertension. On March 8, 2000, the NHLBI issued a press release announcing that it was discontinuing this part of the ALLHAT study because doxazosin "was found less effective than [chlorthalidone] in reducing some forms of cardiovascular disease." Plaintiffs claim that the ALLHAT findings demonstrate that "Cardura users are twice as likely to be hospitalized for congestive heart failure and have a significantly higher chance of suffering from certain serious cardiac events, including strokes, as compared with patients" who took chlorthalidone to treat hypertension. Plaintiffs seek an order requiring Pfizer to send a notice to Cardura users and their physicians regarding the ALLHAT findings with respect to Cardura. The proposed notice to physicians would state, among other things, that a study by NHLBI "has demonstrated that Cardura (doxazosin) is less effective in preventing heart failure compared to a widely used diuretic drug, chlorthalidone," and the proposed notice to patients, among other things, the same. * * *

Under the doctrine of primary jurisdiction, a district court may refer a matter within its original jurisdiction to the appropriate administrative agency if doing so will "promot[e] proper relationships between the courts and administrative agencies charged with particular regulatory duties." * * * Plaintiffs are not arguing that the ALLHAT findings trigger a statutory or regulatory notification requirement or that Pfizer's inaction violates the FDCA. Rather, plaintiffs ask this court to determine, on the basis of presumably scientific and medical principles to be developed at an adversary preliminary injunction hearing, that the ALLHAT findings warrant a notice to all Cardura users and their physicians. The FDA, not this court, has the relevant expertise.

Congress has granted the FDA the authority to ensure that drugs are safe and effective. The FDA approves the labeling of a drug as part of the new drug approval process. Such labeling is "broadly defined" and has been found to include the "Dear Doctor" and "Dear Patient" notices requested by plaintiffs. See Walls v. Armour Pharm. Co., 832 F.Supp. 1467, 1482–83 (M.D.Fla.1993). The FDA also has the authority to either alert Cardura users and their physicians if it determines that Cardura creates "an imminent danger to health or gross deception of the consumer," or to request Pfizer to revise the labeling for Cardura. Finally, plaintiffs have the ability to request the FDA to take either action pursuant to a "citizen petition" provision. The above review of the relevant regulatory scheme convinces this court that whether the notice requested by plaintiffs is warranted is a decision that has been squarely placed within the FDA's informed expert discretion. * * *

NOTES AND QUESTIONS

1. *Exhausting administrative remedies.* After their setback in the courts, the *Bernhardt* plaintiffs filed a citizen petition with the agency. See Rita Rubin, Taking on a Drug Giant: Two Patients File Suit Against Pfizer, USA Today, May 23, 2001, at 1D. An FDA advisory committee recommended, however, against issuing the requested notice. See Melody Petersen, Panel Suggests Wait in Telling Doctors About Hypertension Drug, N.Y. Times, May 25, 2001, at C11. Once a plaintiff has established the knowability of an unexpected adverse event, should the FDA's decision about the appropriate response (presumably though not invariably calibrated to the certainty and severity of the identified risk) foreclose an inquiry into alternative risk management strategies that might have been available to the seller (including, of course, the option of withdrawing the product from the marketplace)? In other words, to what extent should courts go beyond the basic duty to warn and entertain claims that parallel other regulatory options at the agency's disposal when new risk information comes to light?

2. *Differentiating between types of court-ordered relief.* Would the court's analysis have differed on a post-sale failure-to-warn claim brought by a patient injured by Cardura® one year after the release of the NIH study? Was the problem in *Bernhardt* that the plaintiffs had sought relief prematurely, or was it the nature of the relief that they had requested? If we assume that awarding damages for failing to disseminate warnings that the FDA declined to mandate has a regulatory (deterrent) effect, is the injunction requested here really any different? In a class action lawsuit brought on behalf of users of the antidepressant Paxil®, the plaintiffs requested an injunction barring the manufacturer from claiming in television ads that the drug was not habit-forming. See In re Paxil Litig., 2002 WL 31375497 (C.D.Cal.2002) (rejecting the defendant's preemption and primary jurisdiction arguments, but declining to issue a preliminary injunction because the plaintiffs were unlikely to succeed on the merits in the face of the FDA's conclusions). Putting aside the matter of timing and relief sought, might deferring to the agency's primary jurisdiction implicate the plaintiffs' Seventh Amendment rights to a jury trial?

2. WARNING PATIENTS

Questions about the adequacy of warnings directed to patients arise in two contexts. First, a court might decide that the learned intermediary rule does not apply in a particular case. Second, a failure-to-warn claim may relate to a nonprescription drug or medical device.

Hahn v. Sterling Drug, Inc.

805 F.2d 1480 (11th Cir.1986).

■ PER CURIAM:

* * * On December 19, 1982, four year old Valerie Anne Hahn swallowed one and one-half ounces of Campho–Phenique, an over-the-counter

topical analgesic. One half hour later, she was convulsing, vomiting, and for a time she stopped breathing. After treatment at the Rockdale County Hospital, she was transferred to the intensive care unit at the Henrietta Eggleston Children's Hospital. After an approximate 24–hour stay in the intensive care unit, Valerie was released and has suffered no permanent disability from the incident.

Earlier in the evening of the 19th, the Hahns allowed their seven year old child to use Campho–Phenique to treat a cold sore. This child evidently misplaced the lid to the container. There was some speculation that the seven year old administered the medicine to Valerie.

Valerie's parents sued Sterling Drug, alleging that Campho–Phenique was a defective product because the warning on the container was inadequate and for the further reason that the product did not have a child-proof cap. The complaint sounds in tort and strict liability. The district court directed a verdict for the defendant, holding that the warning on the package was adequate and that reasonable men could not arrive at a contrary verdict. The warning label on the defendant's product contains the following:

> WARNING: Keep this and all medicines out of children's reach. In case of accidental ingestion, seek professional assistance or contact a poison control center immediately.
>
> DIRECTIONS: For external use: apply with cotton three or four times daily.

Appellants contend that they produced evidence from which a jury could conclude that the danger posed by the product when ingested by small children was great enough to require a more stringent warning. The Hahns rely principally on the testimony of their toxicology expert, Dr. Albert P. Rauber, Professor of Pediatrics at Emory University and also Medical Director of the Georgia Poison Center. Dr. Rauber testified that the warning was very general and that its effect is "watered down" by the fact that the same warning appears on numerous products that are not harmful (i.e., Flintstone Vitamins and Hydrocortisone Cream). Rauber said he was not "satisfied" with the Campho–Phenique label.

The Hahns point to several other facts which could have led a jury to believe that the warning was inadequate. First, the Hahns themselves testified that they had read the label in its entirety and were still unaware that the product could harm their child if ingested. Second, Sterling was aware that many children had been injured after ingesting the product, yet the product continued to use the same warning. Third, the product was known to be quite toxic, and as such it required a more dramatic warning. Fourth, the warning was in a smaller print than other messages on the label. The Hahns say that this was confusing even though the warning was in bold-face type. Fifth, the direction "for external use" was not followed by the word "only." Sixth, the label stated that the product may be used on the gums, possibly indicating to a reasonable person that internal use might be acceptable. Seventh, the label was silent as to the possibility of seizures and respiratory failure if taken internally. Eighth, the warning to contact the poison control center was insufficient since it would have been just as easy to put the word "poison" on the label. Also, the warning is said to be more like a "helpful hint meant merely to please and placate a concerned parent and not a clue that the contents of the bottle are poisonous."

Appellee, of course, argues that no reasonable person could find that the warning on the Campho–Phenique label was inadequate. Sterling relies on Dr. Rauber's admission during cross examination that the warning advised a reasonable person that the product was potentially toxic and that ingestion might create "grave danger." The district court agreed. The court below held that both the references to external use and to the poison control center in combination with the reference to keep this and all medicines out of the reach of children were sufficient to convey the message to an average adult that there is a risk of serious harm if the child swallows the medicine.

At oral argument, Sterling's attorneys conceded that they could not refer to the court any case decided in the Eleventh Circuit or in the Georgia courts which held that the adequacy of a product manufacturer's warning is a proper subject for a directed verdict. * * * As we understand the decided cases in this area of law, the simple question is whether the warning is adequate, given the unsafe nature of the product. It is appropriate for a jury to determine that adequacy. While the jury may or may not consider the intelligence and experience of the consumer-plaintiff, that does not play a part in our rationale in determining whether or not the question should or should not be presented to a jury. * * *

Another issue brought up on appeal that is not a basis for our reversal of the district court but may be important on retrial is whether certain documents should have been admitted at trial. Appellant complained that the district court abused its discretion in refusing to admit into evidence a Food and Drug Administration report that compiled statistics of other ingestions of Campho–Phenique, as well as other documents, on the ground that the reports were irrelevant. Evidence is relevant if it tends to make the existence of any fact that is of consequence to the determination of the action more probable or less probable than it would be without the evidence. It is not clear from the record below whether the plaintiff established that the prior incidents occurred under conditions substantially similar to those of this case, but if upon retrial it develops that the conditions were similar and the evidence of prior accidents might be relevant to either the defendant's notice, the magnitude of danger involved, the defendant's ability to correct known defects, the lack of safety for intended uses, the strength of the product, the standard of care, or the causation, such evidence should not be excluded. * * *

Ramirez v. Plough, Inc.

863 P.2d 167 (Cal.1993).

■ KENNARD, JUSTICE:

* * * Plaintiff Jorge Ramirez, a minor, sued defendant Plough, Inc., alleging that he contracted Reye's syndrome as a result of ingesting a nonprescription drug, St. Joseph Aspirin for Children (SJAC), that was manufactured and distributed by defendant. * * *

In March 1986, when he was less than four months old, plaintiff exhibited symptoms of a cold or similar upper respiratory infection. To relieve these symptoms, plaintiff's mother gave him SJAC. Although the product label stated that the dosage for a child under two years old was "as directed by doctor," plaintiff's mother did not consult a doctor before using SJAC to treat plaintiff's condition. Over a two-day period, plaintiff's mother gave him three SJAC tablets. Then, on March 15, plaintiff's mother took him to a hospital. There, the doctor advised her to administer Dimetapp or Pedialyte (nonprescription medications that do not contain aspirin), but she disregarded the advice and continued to treat plaintiff with SJAC.

Plaintiff thereafter developed Reye's syndrome, resulting in severe neurological damage, including cortical blindness, spastic quadriplegia, and mental retardation. First described by the Australian pathologist Douglas Reye in 1963, Reye's syndrome occurs in children and teenagers during or while recovering from a mild respiratory tract infection, flu, chicken pox, or other viral illness. The disease is characterized by severe vomiting and irritability or lethargy, which may progress to delirium and coma. In 1982, the Centers for Disease Control estimated that Reye's syndrome affected 600 to 1200 children and teenagers in this country each year. The disease is fatal in 20 to 30 percent of cases, with many of the survivors sustaining permanent brain damage. The cause of Reye's syndrome was unknown in 1986 (and apparently remains unknown), but by the early 1980s several studies had shown an association between ingestion of aspirin during a viral illness, such as chicken pox or influenza, and the subsequent development of Reye's syndrome. These studies prompted the United States Food and Drug Administration (FDA) to propose a labeling requirement for aspirin products warning of the dangers of Reye's syndrome. The FDA published a regulation to this effect on March 7, 1986. * * * In 1988, the FDA revised the required warning to state explicitly that Reye's syndrome is reported to be associated with aspirin use, and it made the regulation permanent.

Even before the federal regulation became mandatory, packages of SJAC displayed this warning: "Warning: Reye Syndrome is a rare but serious disease which can follow flu or chicken pox in children and teenagers. While the cause of Reye Syndrome is unknown, some reports claim aspirin may increase the risk of developing this disease. Consult doctor before use in children or teenagers with flu or chicken pox." The package insert contained the same warning, together with this statement:

"The symptoms of Reye syndrome can include persistent vomiting, sleepiness and lethargy, violent headaches, unusual behavior, including disorientation, combativeness, and delirium. If any of these symptoms occur, especially following chicken pox or flu, call your doctor immediately, even if your child has not taken any medication. REYE SYNDROME IS SERIOUS, SO EARLY DETECTION AND TREATMENT ARE VITAL."

These warnings were printed in English on the label of the SJAC that plaintiff's mother purchased in March 1986. At that time, plaintiff's mother, who was born in Mexico, was literate only in Spanish. Because she could not read English, she was unable to read the warnings on the SJAC label and package insert. Yet she did not ask anyone to translate the label or package insert into Spanish, even though other members of her household could have done so. Plaintiff's mother had never heard, seen, or relied upon any advertising for SJAC in either English or Spanish. In Mexico, she had taken aspirin for headaches, both as a child and as an adult, and a friend had recommended SJAC.

Plaintiff, by and through his mother as guardian ad litem, filed suit against defendant in August 1989, alleging causes of action for fraud, negligence, and product liability, all premised on the theory of failure to warn about the dangers of Reye's syndrome. * * *

Defendant moved for summary judgment, submitting uncontradicted evidence of the facts as stated above. Defendant argued that it was under no duty to label SJAC with Spanish language warnings, that the English language label warnings were adequate, and that the adequacy of the English warnings was ultimately inconsequential in this case because plaintiff's mother did not read the warnings or have them translated for her. On the motion for summary judgment, the parties agreed that over 148 languages are spoken in the United States. Plaintiff adduced evidence that defendant realized that Hispanics, many of whom have not learned English, constituted an important segment of the market for SJAC, and that defendant had acted on this knowledge by using Spanish language advertisements for SJAC in Los Angeles and New York. The court granted summary judgment. In its order granting the motion, the court stated that there was "no duty to warn in a foreign language" and no causal relationship between plaintiff's injury and defendant's activities. Plaintiff appealed from the judgment for defendant.

The court of appeal reversed. It reasoned that although the question of duty is an issue for the court, the existence of a duty to warn here was undisputed, the actual dispute being as to the adequacy of the warning given. The court noted that the adequacy of a product warning is normally a question of fact, and that a defendant moving for summary judgment has the burden of proving an affirmative defense or the nonexistence of an element of the plaintiff's cause of action. Given the evidence of defendant's knowledge that SJAC was being used by non-English-literate Hispanics, and the lack of evidence as to the costs of Spanish language labeling, the reasonableness of defendant's conduct in not labeling SJAC with a Spanish language warning was, the court concluded, a triable issue of fact.[3] * * *

The FDA has stated that it "encourages the preparation of labeling to meet the needs of non-English speaking or special user populations so long as such labeling fully complies with agency regulations." But the controlling regulation requires only that manufacturers provide full English labeling for all nonprescription drugs except those "distributed solely in the Commonwealth of Puerto Rico or in a Territory where the predominant language is one other than English." The regulation further states that if the label or packaging of any drug distributed in the 50 states contains "any representation in a foreign language," then all required "words, statements, and other information" must appear in the foreign language as well as in English. Finally, the regulation states that "use of label space for any representation in a foreign language" is not a basis to exempt a manufacturer from the general obligation to make required language prominent and conspicuous.

California law parallels and reinforces federal law on the points discussed here. The Health and Safety Code mandates conspicuous English language warnings in section 25900, which provides: "Cautionary statements which are required by law, or regulations adopted pursuant to law, to be printed upon the labels of containers in which dangerous drugs, poisons, and other harmful substances are packaged shall be printed in the English language in a conspicuous place in type of conspicuous size in contrast to the typography, layout, or color of the other printed matter on the label." Although warnings in English are expressly required, no California statute requires label or package warnings in any other language. * * *

[Other] statutes demonstrate that the [California] Legislature is able and willing to define the circumstances in which foreign-language communications should be mandated. Given the existence of a statute expressly requiring that package warnings on nonprescription drugs be in English, we think it reasonable to infer that the Legislature has deliberately chosen not to require that manufacturers also include warnings in foreign languages. The same inference is warranted on the federal level. The FDA's regulations abundantly demonstrate its sensitivity to the issue of foreign-language labeling, and yet the FDA regulations do not require it. Presumably, the FDA has concluded that despite the obvious advantages of multilingual package warnings, the associated problems and costs are such that at present warnings should be mandated only in English.

On this point, the FDA's experience with foreign-language patient package inserts for prescription drugs is instructive. Recognizing that "the United States is too heterogeneous to enable manufacturers, at reasonable cost and with reasonable simplicity, to determine exactly where to provide

3. * * * [A]lthough symbols and pictograms can be used effectively to warn that a substance is flammable or toxic, or to explain its preparation and use, it is doubtful that they are at present able to convey the more complex warning information typically required for nonprescription drugs. In any event, the issue presented for decision in this case is whether manufacturers must warn in foreign languages, not by means of symbols or pictograms.

alternative language inserts," the FDA for a time required manufacturers, as an alternative to multilingual or bilingual inserts, to provide Spanish language translations of their patient package inserts on request to doctors and pharmacists. But the FDA later noted that manufacturers were having difficulty obtaining accurate translations, and eventually it abandoned altogether the patient package insert requirement for prescription drugs.

Were we to reject the applicable statutes and regulations as the proper standard of care, there would be two courses of action open to us. The first would be to leave the issue for resolution on a case-by-case basis by different triers of fact under the usual "reasonable person" standard of care. This was the approach that the court of appeal adopted in this case. As a practical matter, such an open-ended rule would likely compel manufacturers to package all their nonprescription drugs with inserts containing warnings in multiple foreign languages because, simply as a matter of foreseeability, it is foreseeable that eventually each nonprescription drug will be purchased by a non-English-speaking resident or foreign tourist proficient only in one of these languages. The burden of including warnings in so many different languages would be onerous, would add to the costs and environmental burdens of the packaging, and at some point might prove ineffective or even counterproductive if the warning inserts became so large and cumbersome that a user could not easily find the warning in his or her own language.

The other alternative would be to use our seldom-exercised power to judicially declare a particularized standard of care, giving precise guidance on this issue. But this determination would involve matters that are peculiarly susceptible to legislative and administrative investigation and determination, based upon empirical data and consideration of the viewpoints of all interested parties. A legislative body considering the utility of foreign-language label warnings for nonprescription medications would no doubt gather pertinent data on a variety of subjects, including the space limitations on nonprescription drug labels and packages, the volume of information that must be conveyed, the relative risks posed by the misuse of particular medications, the cost to the manufacturer of translating and printing warnings in languages other than English, the cost to the consumer of multilingual package warnings in terms of higher prices for, or reduced availability of, products, the feasibility of targeted distribution of products with bilingual or multilingual packaging, the number of persons likely to benefit from warnings in a particular language, and the extent to which nonprescription drug manufacturers as a group have used foreign-language advertisements to promote sales of their products. Legislation and regulations would no doubt reflect findings on these and other pertinent questions.

Lacking the procedure and the resources to conduct the relevant inquiries, we conclude that the prudent course is to adopt for tort purposes the existing legislative and administrative standard of care on this issue. The feasibility and advisability of foreign-language labeling for nonprescription drugs will, no doubt, be reviewed periodically by the FDA and other concerned agencies. Indeed, we are conscious that our decision here may prompt review of this issue by the California Legislature. That is as it should be, for further study might persuade the Legislature, the FDA, or any other concerned agency to revise the controlling statutes or regulations for nonprescription drugs. * * *

We do not, of course, foreclose the possibility of tort liability premised upon the *content* of foreign-language advertising. For example, we do not decide whether a manufacturer would be liable to a consumer who detrimentally relied upon foreign-language advertising that was materially misleading as to product risks and who was unable to read English language package warnings that accurately described the risks. No such issue is presented here. Although plaintiff presented evidence that defendant advertised its product in Spanish, the record contains no evidence of the content of that advertising. And, in any event, plaintiff's mother could not have relied upon defendant's advertising because she admittedly did not see or hear it.

For these reasons, we reject plaintiff's attempt to place on nonprescription drug manufacturers a duty to warn that is broader in scope and more onerous than that currently imposed by applicable statutes and regulations. The FDA has stressed that "it is in the best interest of the consumer, industry, and the marketplace to have uniformity in presentation and clarity of message" in the warnings provided with nonprescription drugs. To preserve that uniformity and clarity, to avoid adverse impacts upon the warning requirements mandated by the federal regulatory scheme, and in deference to the superior technical and procedural lawmaking resources of legislative and administrative bodies, we adopt the legislative/regulatory standard of care that mandates nonprescription drug package warnings in English only.

Plaintiff contends that defendant should be held liable for his injuries even if, as we have concluded, defendant was not required to include Spanish language warnings with SJAC. Plaintiff insists there are other bases of liability that are within the scope of the complaint and that were raised in both the trial court and the court of appeal.

The first alternative ground of liability is an alleged defect in the English language labeling. Plaintiff maintains that the product label represented that SJAC was safe to administer to a child suffering from a common cold. Plaintiff argues that because a cold is a viral illness, and because Reye's syndrome is associated with aspirin use during or while recovering from viral illnesses, defendant should have warned against the use of SJAC for children experiencing or recovering from the symptoms of the common cold. The evidence submitted on the motion for summary judgment precludes liability on this ground. Plaintiff's mother, who administered the SJAC to plaintiff, neither read nor obtained translation of the product labeling. Thus, there is no conceivable causal connection between the representations or omissions that accompanied the product and plaintiff's injury.

The other alternative ground of liability is that defendant should not have marketed SJAC at all because the risks of Reye's syndrome clearly outweighed any benefit to be derived from the product, particularly in light of the availability of non-aspirin pain relievers. We conclude, however, as a matter of law, that defendant may not be held liable for failing to withdraw its product from the market in early 1986, when plaintiff's mother purchased and used it. (Defendant did cease distribution of SJAC effective December 31, 1986.) Although devastating, Reye's syndrome was then and remains now a rare and poorly understood illness. A few scientific studies had shown an association between aspirin and Reye's syndrome, but the methodology of those studies had been questioned and the FDA had determined that further studies were needed to confirm or disprove the association. Pending completion of those studies, the FDA concluded that product warnings were an adequate public safety measure. Although the FDA's conclusion is not binding on us, we think it deserves serious consideration. Plaintiff has submitted nothing that causes us to doubt the FDA's judgment in this matter that in early 1986 aspirin could be considered a reasonably safe product for administration to children, when distributed with appropriate warnings. * * *

■ MOSK, JUSTICE (concurring):

* * * Evidence of the content, timing, duration, and scope of distribution of foreign-language advertising bears substantially on the question whether a non-English-literate consumer has been materially misled about product risks, and a trial court must consider that evidence if properly presented. The majority do not define "materially misleading as to product risks," leaving that issue for another day—a day likely to arrive soon, given the high probability that foreign-language media will continue to expand in California.

Popular advertisements for over-the-counter drugs generally emphasize their therapeutic effects, not the harmful or fatal consequences of inadvertent misuse. Yet the proper use and inadvertent misuse of drugs occur in very similar ways: swallowing one pill may prove therapeutic, but more may be fatal. Hence, a foreign-language pharmaceutical advertisement will be "materially misleading as to product risks" if a company extols a drug's health benefits in the advertisement yet does not warn a non-English-literate consumer of the risks of misuse in a manner reasonably calculated to reach that consumer before the product is consumed or applied.

If there is such a misrepresentation, then a jury ordinarily should decide the defendant's tort liability. To conclude that notice must be reasonably calculated to reach the non-English-literate consumer is not necessarily to decide that the foreign-language warning must appear in or on the promotional material itself, or on the product's warning label. Notice on a drug's product label, in the foreign languages in which the drug is advertised, not to take or apply the drug before reading a package insert's detailed warning in those languages may, depending on the facts, be sufficient to warn of hazards and yet satisfy federal law. In general, I believe that as long as an over-the-counter drug manufacturer gives reasonable notice, by any legal means, of possible side effects in a foreign language to a non-English-literate consumer whose purchase has been induced in that language, it has met the standard of conduct California tort law demands.

PROBLEM #12. *PULLING IT ALL TOGETHER*

Your client, Jorge Diaz, suffered serious injuries after ingesting Noflux, a recently approved prescription drug indicated for the treatment of gastroesophageal reflux disease. The package insert included a warning of the adverse event that he had suffered. The manufacturer had aggressively promoted the drug in television advertisements on Univision, a Spanish-language cable television station. These spots complied with the FDA's guidance on broadcast advertising [excerpted in Chap. 4(B)(2)], except that the company had not made a copy of the brief summary available in Spanish as the agency had "strongly encouraged." Mr. Diaz (who is not fluent in English) saw these ads, as had his physician (Gloria Gonzalez), and he specifically requested that Dr. Gonzalez prescribe it for his use. After taking a cursory medical history, Dr. Gonzalez (who is fluent in English) gave her patient several samples of Noflux that one of the manufacturer's detail reps had left with her. Assume that the highest court in your jurisdiction has cited both *Perez* and *Ramirez* with approval. What are your prospects?

NOTES AND QUESTIONS

1. *Multilingual labeling*. The FDA regulation addressing foreign language warnings for drug products provides only limited guidance. See 21 C.F.R. § 201.15(c). It does require Spanish labeling for drugs sold in Puerto Rico. Even so, if a prescription drug manufacturer failed to comply with that requirement, but the physician was able to read the English labeling, a plaintiff bringing an inadequate warning claim would fail to establish causation. See Pierluisi v. E.R. Squibb & Sons, Inc., 440 F.Supp. 691 (D.P.R.1977). In issuing its final regulation mandating a Reye syndrome warning, the FDA explained that manufacturers could voluntarily provide the information in a foreign language. See 53 Fed. Reg. 21,633, 21,636 (1988). Notwithstanding the FDA's earlier problems in mandating multilingual PPIs, the Centers for Disease Control (CDC) required that health-care providers supply patients with vaccine information pamphlets in certain foreign languages. See 56 Fed. Reg. 51,798, 51,800 (1991) (promising to provide manufacturers with acceptable translations in Spanish, French, Vietnamese, and Chinese). Under the Clinton administration, HHS issued a requirement that health care providers make interpreters available for Medicaid patients who cannot speak English, a condition of participation that the American Medical Association assailed as excessively burdensome. See Language Gap, Wash. Post, May 1, 2001, at T6.

Couldn't Plough at least have included the following disclaimer in the labeling of St. Joseph's Aspirin for Children: "Si usted no sabe leer en inglés, por favor no use este producto, hasta que se le haya brindado entrenamiento adecuado." The EPA may require that the labeling of pesticides include just such a disclaimer ("If you cannot read English do not use this product until properly instructed.") in the language(s) spoken by foreseeable users. See 40 Fed. Reg. 28,242, 28,251 (1975); see also Hubbard–Hall Chem. Co. v. Silverman, 340 F.2d 402, 405 (1st Cir.1965) (holding that a jury could find the warning on a pesticide inadequate for users who could not read English "because of its lack of a skull and bones or other comparable symbols"); Stanley Indus., Inc. v. W.M. Barr & Co., 784 F.Supp. 1570, 1576 (S.D.Fla.1992) (same). See generally Glenda Labadie–Jackson, Warning: Silence Can Cause Severe Harm: Spanish Language and Civil Liability for Inadequate Warnings and Instructions, 11 Harv. Latino L. Rev. 85 (2008); Marjorie A. Caner, Annotation, Products Liability: Failure to Provide Product Warning or Instruction in Foreign Language or to Use Universally Accepted Pictographs or Symbols, 27 A.L.R.5th 697 (1995 & 2011 Supp.); Labels in English Pose Risk in Multilingual Nation, N.Y. Times, May 20, 2001, § 1, at 30.

2. *Warnings for nonprescription drugs and devices*. Labeling directed to consumers must include clear instructions for avoiding or minimizing the risk. See Cooley v. Carter–Wallace Inc., 478 N.Y.S.2d 375, 379–80 (App.Div. 1984) ("Mere directions for the proper use of a product which fail to warn of specific dangers and risks of harm if the directions are not followed may be inadequate."); see also O'Gilvie v. International Playtex, Inc., 821 F.2d 1438, 1441–43 (10th Cir.1987) (tampons); Torsiello v. Whitehall Lab., 398 A.2d 132, 137–40 (N.J.App.Div.1979) (aspirin products); Michael v. Warner/Chilcott, 579 P.2d 183, 187 (N.M.Ct.App.1978) (sinus medication).

3. *Adequacy of PPIs and regulatory compliance*. Again, contrary to *Ramirez*, compliance generally provides no defense to claims of inadequacies in warnings provided to patients. In several cases, for instance, courts have allowed juries to find that the specific warnings provided to patients by manufacturers of oral contraceptives were inadequate even though the labeling fully complied with FDA's PPI regulation. See, e.g., McEwen v. Ortho Pharm. Corp., 528 P.2d 522, 534 (Or.1974). In one case involving labeling for oral contraceptives, warnings emphasizing the risk of "fatal" adverse reactions but failing to use the word "stroke" were found potentially inadequate because a jury might conclude that the resulting permanent disability is a fate worse than death. See MacDonald v. Ortho Pharm. Corp., 475 N.E.2d 65, 72 (Mass.1985); see also Petty v. United States, 740 F.2d 1428, 1437 (8th Cir.1984) ("[T]he risk of death may be conceptually remote, whereas a more specific warning detailing the known risk of serum sickness and its symptoms would alert recipients more concretely to the risks that they actually were assuming."). But see Mampe v. Ayerst Lab., 548 A.2d 798, 801 (D.C.Ct.App.1988) ("We seriously doubt that promotional materials which warn of death as a possible reaction to a drug could be inadequate to warn of a consequence any less severe."); Kurer v. Parke, Davis & Co., 679 N.W.2d 867, 876–80 (Wis.Ct.App.2004). If the plaintiff discarded the allegedly inadequate PPI without reading it, an inadequate warning claim will fail on causation grounds. See E.R. Squibb & Sons, Inc. v. Cox, 477 So.2d 963, 971 (Ala.1985) (insulin).

4. *Translating complex information for laypersons.* Recall from Chapter 2 that informed consent for participation in clinical trials is geared toward an 8th grade reading level. (The FDA's consumer information brochures are pitched even lower, designed to be understood by those functioning at a 5th grade reading level.) It will be awfully difficult to "dumb down" prescription drug information written for educated medical professionals in a way that will reach most of the population. Many adults in the United States qualify as functionally illiterate, and an even higher percentage experience difficulties in comprehending health information. See Council on Scientific Affairs, Health Literacy, 281 JAMA 552 (1999); Lauran Neergaard, Doctors' Orders, Drug Labels Often Misunderstood, Phila. Inquirer, Apr. 9, 2004, at A3 (reporting an estimate from the Institute of Medicine that 90 million Americans have limited health literacy); Deborah Franklin, And Now, a Warning About Labels, N.Y. Times, Oct. 25, 2005, at F1 (documenting widespread confusion about pictograms in warning stickers affixed by pharmacists on prescription drug bottles).

D. A Duty to Design Better Access Restrictions?

Lars Noah, *Platitudes About "Product Stewardship" in Torts: Continuing Drug Research and Education*

15 Mich. Telecomm. & Tech. L. Rev. 359 (2009).

* * * Genuine product stewardship * * * go[es] beyond labeling to include choices about how and to whom a seller markets a drug. Such a theory might morph into a design defect claim, viewing the drug product as a package or bundle that includes choices about how patients may secure access to it. Just as regulatory officials have become more creative in adopting risk management plans, tort litigation might encourage manufacturers to craft such programs. For instance, with teratogens such as thalidomide and isotretinoin, plaintiffs might pursue negligent marketing claims on the theory that a prescription drug manufacturer should have further restricted distribution. * * *

Although the *Products Liability Restatement* finds a bright line distinguishing prescription and nonprescription products, which it then uses to justify different rules for the former category (because of the power of differential marketing), pharmaceuticals actually lie along a continuum. For instance, stricter prescription requirements apply to controlled substances and certain teratogens (and the most restrictive access restrictions apply to investigational drugs supplied to subjects enrolled in a clinical trial). Although most people use prescription drugs on an outpatient basis, physicians order the administration of some medications in hospitals and other controlled settings. * * *

Conversely, the relatively recent phenomenon of advertising prescription drugs directly to consumers, as well as the advent of Internet prescribing and dispensing, may have made these products more similar to OTC drugs. Some commentators have suggested that drug manufacturers have a duty to cut off supplies to Internet companies that engage in irresponsible online prescribing and dispensing. Serious practical difficulties would, however, complicate any such effort. More controversially, if general practitioners engaged in patterns of dangerous overprescribing, then a plaintiff might claim that the drug manufacturer had a duty to limit access to only some subset of responsible physicians (perhaps only specialists or physicians who have registered with the manufacturer after attesting to their knowledge of the risks involved in the use of a product).

More than twenty years ago, in *Swayze v. McNeil Laboratories, Inc.*, [807 F.2d 464 (5th Cir.1987),] a federal court rejected such a claim. In that case, a child had suffered respiratory depression (and eventually died) after a certified registered nurse anesthetist (CRNA) administered an excessive dose of Sublimaze® (fentanyl) during surgery. The nurse had, without any supervision by an anesthesiologist, selected this powerful narcotic agent from among various alternatives, administered an inappropriately high dose, monitored the patient's response, and decided how to counteract the drug's effects at the conclusion of the surgery. Although a clear violation of state law governing prescribing privileges, CRNAs routinely made these sorts of choices because of a shortage of licensed anesthesiologists. The plaintiff had argued, among other things, that the manufacturer—knowing of this widespread practice of irresponsible use—should have restricted sales of the drug "to hospitals which establish and enforce appropriate procedures to assure that Sublimaze is prescribed and administered in compliance with state law." The federal district court granted a directed verdict to the defendant, and a divided court of appeals affirmed. The dissenting judge, however, thought that "McNeil could have prevented liability by removing, selectively, the drug from hospitals that could not ensure that qualified doctors would prescribe."

Perhaps recognition of such claims would represent a form of product stewardship that courts resolving tort litigation should embrace. More so than proposed new obligations to engage in potentially endless testing or to communicate essentially meaningless disclaimers, a duty to consider the adoption of distribution restrictions would better promote risk minimization. Obviously, some negligent marketing claims might create tension with emerging FDA policies in this area (though conflicts seem far less likely to arise than in the area of labeling), and they also could adversely impact patient access, but this potential extension of drug products liability strikes me as more worthy of exploration than the other approaches that have attracted attention in recent years.

NOTES AND QUESTIONS

1. *Negligent marketing theories*. Recall that comment k to *Rest. (2d)* § 402A had referred separately to "proper marketing" and proper warnings as prerequisites (along with proper preparation) for exempting sellers of unavoidably unsafe products from strict liability (design defect) claims. Under what circumstances might a drug fail to meet this requirement? See Lars Noah, This Is Your Products Liability Restatement on Drugs, 74 Brook. L. Rev. 839, 887 n.203 (2009) ("Imagine ... that the manufacturer had sold OxyContin without the required legend for Schedule II controlled substances (or, worse yet, without even the Rx legend, which would make it available on OTC shelves alongside analgesics such as acetaminophen and ibuprofen); I assume that—whether called a design defect, informational defect, or negligent marketing claim—such a case would fall under the defectiveness per se rubric."); see also In re TMJ Implants Prods. Liab. Litig., 97 F.3d 1050, 1060 (8th Cir.1996) (Heaney, J., dissenting) (suggesting that the manufacturer of Teflon should have ceased supplying this raw material to a medical device company because it knew of dangers associated with this application) [excerpted in Chap. 6(B)(2)]; Richard C. Ausness, Will More Aggressive Marketing Practices Lead to Greater Tort Liability for Prescription Drug Manufacturers?, 37 Wake Forest L. Rev. 97, 136 (2002) (forecasting that negligent marketing claims will be brought against manufacturers of prescription drugs when patients suffer injuries as a result of dispensing by unscrupulous Internet pharmacies); Margaret Gilhooley, When Drugs Are Safe for Some but Not Others: The FDA Experience and Alternatives for Products Liability, 36 Hous. L. Rev. 927, 946 (1999) ("The best case for applying a distribution limit, if products liability law were to be extended to recognize a new type of defect, relates to misuse of a drug that poses grave risks not only to the immediate users, but also to the wider public."); cf. id. at 945 ("Limiting the distribution of drugs, however, is too novel to be an appropriate basis for a finding of products liability."). Might plaintiffs use such a theory to assail the common practice of supplying samples of Rx drugs to physicians because this promotes more casual dispensing or increases the risk of diversion by allowing easy access to office staff who lack prescribing privileges? Could excessive involvement by agents of therapeutic product sellers in the delivery of care to a particular patient itself become actionable? See Michael J. Summerhill & Aaron M. Chandler, Company Representatives in the Operating and Treatment Room: How to Navigate the Ever–Expanding Theories of Liability for Medical Device and Pharmaceutical Companies, 12 DePaul J. Health Care L. 253 (2009).

2. *OTC drugs*. In *Ramirez*, the plaintiffs argued that, given the risk of Reye's syndrome and the availability of substitutes, OTC children's aspirin should not have been sold at all. Is this a form of risk-utility balancing borrowed from the standard for design defects? Although rejected by the court, how far might such a theory of liability go?

In addition to making drugs more vulnerable to both inadequate warning and design defect claims, switching a prescription pharmaceu-

> tical product to OTC status may prompt injured parties to pursue a peculiar theory of recovery akin to negligent marketing. If an OTC drug with otherwise unassailable labeling and design causes an injury, then the victim might argue that the product should have been made available only under professional medical supervision and never sold directly to consumers. Such a claim would represent something of a hybrid between more traditional defects in labeling and design, challenging a manufacturer's choice about appropriate channels for distributing potentially hazardous products in a way that resembles novel (and so far largely unsuccessful) theories asserted against gun sellers. In particular, such claims find their closest parallel in lawsuits alleging that manufacturers of certain types of weapons or ammunition should not have sold these products to civilians, instead limiting their distribution to law-enforcement professionals and the military.

Lars Noah, Treat Yourself: Is Self–Medication the Prescription for What Ails American Health Care?, 19 Harv. J.L. & Tech. 359, 381 (2006). If the FDA had authorized OTC sale, which would make continued Rx marketing unlawful, would implied federal preemption bar such a claim? Would pharmacies and other retailers find themselves vulnerable to negligent marketing claims insofar as they have exercised the power to hold some OTC products "behind the counter"?

CHAPTER 8

UTILIZATION ERRORS AND MEDICAL MALPRACTICE

Courts face unique difficulties in dealing with malpractice claims involving the use of medical technologies. In evaluating the tort liability of health care providers, courts must consider how those providers use or dispense drugs and devices in order to define the appropriate standard of liability.

In most cases, each entity in the chain of distribution—from the manufacturer down to the retailer—may face strict liability for selling a defective product, even if it played no role in introducing the defect. Injuries caused by counterfeit drugs do not, however, fit into this paradigm. See Ashworth v. Albers Med., Inc., 410 F.Supp.2d 471, 476–82 (S.D.W.Va. 2005) (dismissing various claims against Pfizer for alleged injuries caused by counterfeit versions of its drug Lipitor® (atorvastatin calcium)); id. at 482 ("[T]here exists no duty on the manufacturer at common law to ensure that its products are counterfeit-proof."); Fagan v. AmerisourceBergen Corp., 356 F.Supp.2d 198, 204–07, 215 (E.D.N.Y.2004) (dismissing claims against the manufacturer of Epogen® where counterfeiters had diverted, substantially diluted, and then sold the drug in the gray market); id. at 207–11 (allowing negligence claims against the distributor to proceed); cf. Stephanie F. Aleong, Green Medicine: Using Lessons from Tort Law and Environmental Law to Hold Pharmaceutical Manufacturers and Authorized Distributors Liable for Injuries Caused by Counterfeit Drugs, 69 U. Pitt. L. Rev. 245 (2007).

As explained in Chapter 6(B)(2), bulk suppliers generally need not fear liability. Moreover, at the other end of the chain of distribution, the *Restatement (Third) of the Law of Torts: Products Liability* effectively exempts retailers and users of prescription drugs and devices from most forms of strict liability:

> (e) A retail seller or other distributor of a prescription drug or medical device is subject to liability for harm caused by the drug or device if:
>
> (1) at the time of sale or other distribution the drug or medical device contains a manufacturing defect as defined in § 2(a) [i.e., when the product departs from its intended design even though all possible care was exercised in the preparation and marketing of the product]; or
>
> (2) at or before the time of sale or other distribution of the drug or medical device the retail seller or other distributor fails to exercise reasonable care and such failure causes harm to persons.

Rest. (3d) § 6. In other words, hospitals and pharmacies are not treated as retailers within the chain of distribution except in cases of manufacturing defects. (Are physicians considered "other distributor[s]," or do they fall entirely outside of the chain of distribution?) In cases of design or informational defects, hospitals and pharmacies are liable only if they acted negligently—why is that?

The comment accompanying § 6(e) justified this approach as follows:

> The rule governing most products imposes liability on wholesalers and retailers for selling a defectively designed product, or one without adequate instructions or warnings, even though they have exercised reasonable care in marketing the product. Courts have refused to apply this general rule to nonmanufacturing retail sellers of prescription drugs and medical devices and, instead, have adopted the rule stated in Subsection (e). That rule subjects retailers to liability only if the product contains a manufacturing defect or if the retailer fails to exercise reasonable care in connection with distribution of the drug or medical device. In so limiting the liability of intermediary parties, courts have held that they should be permitted to rely on the special expertise of manufacturers, prescribing and treating health-care providers, and governmental regulatory agencies. They have also emphasized the needs of medical patients to have ready access to prescription drugs at reasonable prices.

Id. cmt. h; see also Anderson v. Siemens Corp., 335 F.3d 466, 471 n.10 (5th Cir.2003) (holding that the distributor of a ventilator used in a hospital ICU was not a "retailer" within the meaning of *Rest. (3d)* § 6(e)). Thus, as a general rule, physicians, pharmacists, and hospitals whose patients suffer harm from the use of a prescription drug or device are judged by ordinary negligence standards. Is this really any different from the rules applied to manufacturers of such products? Also, given the policy arguments elaborated in the materials that follow, does it make sense to impose strict liability for manufacturing defects on retailers (aren't these precisely the cases where the need to subject those at the bottom of the chain of distribution to strict liability seems the weakest)?

A. LIABILITY OF USERS AND PRESCRIBERS

Physicians "distribute" medical products in the sense that they utilize these items (or authorize their dispensing) in connection with providing medical services, but courts generally have concluded that physicians are not in the chain of distribution for products liability purposes. Nevertheless, physicians have legal obligations in connection with the use of medical technologies—they must exercise due care in selecting appropriate products for treating individual patients; they must inform patients of the associated risks; and they must, of course, utilize the technology in a non-negligent fashion.

Magrine v. Krasnica

227 A.2d 539 (N.J.Super.Ct.1967), aff'd, 250 A.2d 129 (N.J.1969).

■ LYNCH, JUDGE:

The novelty of this case lies in the attempt by plaintiff, a patient of defendant dentist, to extend the rule of "strict liability" against defendant for personal injuries caused by the breaking of a hypodermic needle in plaintiff's jaw while being used by defendant in an injection procedure. The break was due to a latent defect in the needle. Novelty, of itself, does not foreclose consideration of plaintiff's contentions in this field of developing tort law. Neither does it justify a headlong leap to impose strict liability unless, based on proper policy considerations and reason, such liability should be found. Plaintiff concedes that there is no precedent—anywhere—holding a dentist, or any other "user" of an article, strictly liable for injuries caused by a latent defect therein. * * *

[Defendant] was administering a local anesthetic with a hypodermic needle inserted into the left temporomandibular space, a point at the extreme end of the lower gum beyond the last tooth. The needle extended 1–5/8″ beyond the syringe. It had been assembled by the doctor just before the injection and had been used approximately eight times for about three weeks prior to the accident. It is the custom of the doctor to use about four needles a month and to discard them at the end of the month. As the injection was being made the needle "separated" at the hub, the place where the needle entered the syringe, leaving the entire 1–5/8″ length of the needle in plaintiff's jaw. Defendant does not know what caused the needle to break, but he believes there must have been some sort of defect in it. He does not know from whom he purchased the needle. * * *

We have seen the rapid development of the "strict liability" concept in the products liability field. * * * Plaintiff's argument moves from the major premise that "strict liability" is not confined to "sales," through the minor premise that the basic policy considerations of the doctrine apply to the use of a needle by a dentist, and concludes that he should be held liable though free from negligence. Since the major premise is established, it therefore remains for us to analyze the policy considerations projected by our decisions and other authorities and determine to what extent, if any, they postulate a judgment for plaintiff. * * *

[I]n all of our recent cases strict liability was imposed (except with respect to a retail dealer) upon those who were in "a better position" in the sense that they created the danger (in making the article) * * * or possessed a better capacity or expertise to control, inspect and discover the defect than the party injured. In these respects the dentist here was in no better position than plaintiff. He neither created the defect nor possessed any better capacity or expertise to discover or correct it than she. It is further very clear that strict liability was imposed in our New Jersey cases for the basic reason that those so held liable put the product "in the stream of trade and promote its purchase by the public." * * * Defendant dentist did not put the needle in the stream of commerce or promote its purchase.

It may be logically argued that the foregoing analysis does not effectively distinguish defendant from the retail dealer who, for example, sells food in a sealed container, or otherwise has no opportunity to discover a defect in the article he sells, and who nevertheless is liable for breach of warranty. In this respect such retail dealer is in no better position to discover the defect than the dentist here. Nevertheless, the situations are distinct. In the first place, the Uniform Sales Act and the Uniform Commercial Code, legislative enactments, apply to sales and there can be no judicial construction which could deny a warranty against a retail seller. At common law the implied warranty was originally confined to food. Even so, several courts have refused to impose warranty liability on the "innocent" retailer who has no means of discovering the defect in the goods. Such reasoning is not without a concept of fairness. * * * Of more meaningful significance is a recognition that the essence of the transaction between the retail seller and the consumer relates to the article sold. The seller is in the business of supplying the product to the consumer. It is that, and that alone, for which he is paid. A dentist or a physician offers, and is paid for, his professional services and skill. That is the essence of the relationship between him and his patient. * * *

Plaintiff also invokes the policy consideration of "spreading of the risks"—the concept which suggests that defendant could cover his liability by insurance, or he could be held harmless by impleading his supplier or manufacturer. The "risk distributing theory" is a relevant consideration. But again, we must appreciate the context in which it has been applied in our cases. * * * [A party] who put the goods in the stream of commerce * * * may fairly be assumed to have substantial assets and volume of business, and a large area of contacts over which the risk can be widely spread. It is the "large-scale" enterprise which should bear the loss. The impact of liability upon such a defendant is minuscule in comparison with that of an individual dentist or physician. His means of "spreading the risk" could be by insurance or impleading his supplier or manufacturer. "Malpractice" insurance, however, does not cover implied warranty unless the policy "expressly covers contract claims." In this very case defendant dentist is represented not only by counsel for his insurance carrier but also by his personal counsel because the carrier denies coverage. In any event, there are definite limits as to how far the argument of "risk-spreading" by insurance can go. * * *

So, here, if the dentist or physician were to obtain insurance covering strict liability for equipment failure, the risk would be spread upon his patients by way of increased fees. Can anyone gainsay the fact that medical and dental costs, and insurance therefor, are already bearing hard there? * * * As a matter of principle, the spreading of losses to their patients subverts, rather than supports, the policy consideration that the loss should be imposed on those best able to withstand it, i.e., the manufacturer or other entity which puts the article into the stream of commerce. The "risk distribution" theory has some weight, but not nearly enough when laid beside other more basic considerations. * * *

Something can be said, by way of logical argument, in plaintiff's favor, for the policy consideration that if the dentist be held liable he, as the retail seller of food in a sealed container, can implead the manufacturer and thus be used as a conduit to place the loss where it belongs. This, too, should be regarded as only a "makeweight" argument. While we fully appreciate the appeal of the suggestion that the retail dealer—or the dentist here—is the most convenient conduit to "fight out" liability with the ultimate manufacturer, we are not satisfied that in this case such circuity of action is appropriate. * * * [D]efendant "does not know from whom the needle was purchased; he testified on oral depositions that the needle was manufactured by a certain Precision Bur Co. of New York, New York, but in answers to interrogatories Dr. Krasnica had suggested other possible manufacturers." Thus, plaintiff is not without remedy to reach the supplier by proper use of discovery procedures. If it be shown that identification of the supplier does not eventuate in this particular case, and both plaintiff and defendant are denied recourse to him, then our answer is that this is a "hard case" from which bad law should not flow. It is not the usual situation, for ordinarily the manufacturer can be reached.

In our view it would be bad law to sustain plaintiff's contentions because the relevant policy considerations do not justify imposition of strict liability upon a dentist in the first, or last, instance. Further, the vast body of malpractice law, presumably an expression of the public policy involved in this area of health care, imposes upon a dentist or physician liability only for negligent performance of his services—negligent deviation from the standards of his profession. In the performance of his professional skill he has control of what he does. As to the instrument he uses, he has no control with respect to a latent defect therein. Why, then, should he be held strictly liable for the instruments he uses, as to which he has no control over latent defects, and liable only for negligence in the performance of his professional services, which he does control? * * *

We must consider, also, the consequences if we were to adopt the rule of strict liability here. The same liability, in principle, should then apply to any user of a tool, other equipment or any article which, through no fault of the user, breaks due to a latent defect and injures another. It would apply to any physician, artisan or mechanic and to any user of a defective article—even to a driver of a defective automobile. In our view, no policy consideration positing strict liability justifies application of the doctrine in such cases. No more should it here. * * * Judgment for defendant.

NOTES AND QUESTIONS

1. *Exemption from strict products liability.* Notwithstanding changes in the profession since the decision in *Magrine*, courts continue to reject strict products liability claims against physicians:

> In analyzing this question, we must consider whether the essence of the transaction is the provision of a service or a product. We hold that health care providers who perform breast implant procedures are, in

> essence, providing a service. Although the breast implant procedure requires the use of a product, the implant, the health care provider is fundamentally and predominantly offering a service. The provider must have medical knowledge and skill to conduct the procedure. He must advise the patient of the medical consequences and must recommend to the patient the preferable type of procedure. The product may not be purchased independently of the service. One does not "buy" a breast implant procedure in the same way as one would buy a product, such as a lawn-mower. At its heart, the breast implant procedure is a service and not a product.

In re Breast Implant Prod. Liab. Litig., 503 S.E.2d 445, 449 (S.C.1998); see also infra Chap. 8(B)(2) (explaining that hospitals are exempt from strict liability as well). But see Richard L. Cupp, Jr., Sharing Accountability for Breast Implants: Strict Products Liability and Medical Professionals Engaged in Hybrid Sales/Service Cosmetic Product Transactions, 21 Fla. St. U. L. Rev. 873 (1994) (discussing the benefits of applying strict products liability to plastic surgeons who "sell" cosmetic implant devices to patients); see also Detwiler v. Bristol–Myers Squibb Co., 884 F.Supp. 117, 121–22 (S.D.N.Y.1995) (allowing a patient to assert a strict products liability claim against a physician who had modified liquid silicone for use in cosmetic injection because he was acting in the capacity of a manufacturer); Natasha Singer, The Little Botox Shop Around the Corner, N.Y. Times, Apr. 19, 2007, at G3. The distinction between sales and services extends beyond the medical context. See Rest. (3d) § 19(b) & cmt. f. Thus, just as strict liability does not apply to surgeons who implant devices, persons who install new appliances generally face tort liability only if they acted unreasonably under the circumstances. For a different approach to holding physicians strictly liable, see Wright v. Jeckle, 16 P.3d 1268 (Wash.Ct.App. 2001) (reinstating plaintiff's claim that the physician's advertising and sale of diet drugs constituted inappropriate entrepreneurial activities in violation of the state's consumer protection act).

2. *Categories of physician negligence.* Physicians have been found negligent in their utilization of medical technologies under a variety of circumstances. See Linda A. Sharp, Annotation, Malpractice: Physician's Liability for Injury or Death Resulting from Side Effects of Drugs Intentionally Administered to or Prescribed for Patients, 47 A.L.R.5th 433 (1997 & 2011 Supp.).

a. *Negligent prescribing.* Courts have found physicians negligent for prescribing drugs that are medically inappropriate for their patients. See, e.g., Edwards v. Tardif, 692 A.2d 1266 (Conn.1997) (wrongful death action based on negligent prescribing without examination of patient); Atlanta Obstet. & Gyn. Group v. Coleman, 398 S.E.2d 16 (Ga.1990) (negligent selection of drug); Bazel v. Mabee, 576 N.W.2d 385 (Iowa Ct.App.1998) (physician negligent for using betadine despite patient's known allergy); Hogle v. Hall, 916 P.2d 814 (Nev.1996) (sustaining a jury verdict for a child who suffered severe birth defects against a physician who negligently had prescribed Accutane during the mother's pregnancy); Lynch v. Bay Ridge

Obstet. & Gyn. Assoc., 532 N.E.2d 1239 (N.Y.1988) (allowing claim against physician for negligently failing to diagnose a pregnancy and then prescribing a drug that was contraindicated for use in pregnant women); Berkowitz v. Kingsboro, 651 N.Y.S.2d 116 (App.Div.1996) (summary judgment reversed based on claim that physician was negligent in selecting drug to treat infection); Eiss v. Lillis, 357 S.E.2d 539 (Va.1987) (negligent failure to monitor patient's drug therapy); see also Thomas L. Hafemeister & Richard M. Gulbrabdsen, Jr., The Fiduciary Obligation of Physicians to "Just Say No" If an "Informed" Patient Demands Services That Are Not Medically Indicated, 39 Seton Hall L. Rev. 335 (2009). Physicians who prescribe drugs over the Internet based only on a cursory (virtual) examination of a patient may face malpractice claims.

b. *Failures to warn.* Another category of negligence concerns physician failures to warn the patient of risks associated with the use of the prescribed drug. See, e.g., Hutchinson v. United States, 915 F.2d 560, 562–63 (9th Cir.1990) (doctor held liable for not warning patient of the risks involved with use of asthma medication); Bowman v. Songer, 820 P.2d 1110, 1113–15 (Colo.1991) (dermatologist negligent for failing to warn patient of risk of sun exposure during use of topical prescription drug); Tenuto v. Lederle Lab., 687 N.E.2d 1300 (N.Y.1997) (physician had a duty to warn plaintiff of risk of contracting polio from child who had received a polio vaccine); Shadrick v. Coker, 963 S.W.2d 726 (Tenn.1998) (informed consent requires physician to inform patient that medical device was not FDA approved); see also Margaret Z. Johns, Informed Consent: Requiring Doctors to Disclose Off–Label Prescriptions and Conflicts of Interest, 58 Hastings L.J. 967 (2007); Lars Noah, Informed Consent and the Elusive Dichotomy Between Standard and Experimental Therapy, 28 Am. J.L. & Med. 361, 364–70 (2002). Physicians also may have duties to warn former patients when new risk information comes to light about a previously prescribed drug or implanted device. See, e.g., Harris v. Raymond, 715 N.E.2d 388, 394–95 (Ind.1999). In some jurisdictions, third parties involved in traffic accidents with a person driving under the influence of a sedating medication may have a claim against the patient's physician in case of a failure to warn of this side effect. See, e.g., Coombes v. Florio, 877 N.E.2d 567, 572–75 (Mass.2007) (plurality); Burroughs v. Magee, 118 S.W.3d 323 (Tenn.2003) (holding, however, that the third party could not assert a claim for negligent prescribing); Osborne v. United States, 567 S.E.2d 677 (W.Va. 2002); cf. Janet Brewer, Violent Behavior Associated with Acetylcholinesterase Inhibitors and Liability of Prescribers of Donepezil, 16 Widener L.J. 111 (2006).

c. *Undermedicating.* Courts have begun to entertain tort claims against physicians for undertreating pain that would have responded to powerful analgesic products. See James R. Blaufuss, Note, A Painful Catch–22: Why Tort Liability for Inadequate Pain Management Will Make for Bad Medicine, 31 Wm. Mitchell L. Rev. 1093 (2005); Rima J. Oken, Note, Curing Healthcare Providers' Failure to Administer Opioids in the Treatment of Severe Pain, 23 Cardozo L. Rev. 1917, 1968–81 (2002). Occasionally, a patient will allege that a physician committed malpractice for failing to switch the patient to a newly approved product that might have worked more effectively. See Reese v. Stroh, 907 P.2d 282, 283–84 (Wash.1995) (noting that the physician had justified his decision based in part on the fact that the FDA had approved the product using surrogate rather than clinical end-points); cf. Bell v. Maricopa Med. Ctr., 755 P.2d 1180, 1182 (Ariz.Ct.App.1988) (alleging malpractice for the failure to use an approved drug for an off-label use); Bridges v. Shelby Women's Clinic, 323 S.E.2d 372, 374–76 (N.C.Ct.App.1984) (same).

d. *Errors in drug administration*. Finally, when health care professionals administer a different drug than the one prescribed or an improper dosage of the correct drug, courts may find these professionals liable. See, e.g., Baylis v. Wilmington Med. Ctr., Inc., 477 A.2d 1051 (Del.1984) (negligence claim based on improper dose of a drug); Leiker v. Gafford, 778 P.2d 823 (Kan.1989) (negligence for administering excessive dose of a drug); Harrison v. Axelrod, 599 N.Y.S.2d 96 (App.Div.1993) (nurse negligent for administering incorrect dose of prescription drug solution).

Kelley v. Associated Anesthesiologists, Inc.

589 N.E.2d 1050 (Ill.App.Ct.1992).

■ MCCUSKEY, JUSTICE:

* * * Plaintiff, Bryan Kelley, brought an action in medical malpractice against defendants, Associated Anesthesiologists, Inc. and John C. Burdon, M.D. (collectively "Dr. Burdon"), and in products liability against defendant, Burroughs Wellcome Co. Plaintiff's action involved a surgical operation performed during his recovery from an automobile accident. * * *

Dr. Burdon first administered sodium pentothal to put plaintiff to sleep. Dr. Burdon then administered a drip solution of succinylcholine (a muscle relaxant marketed by Burroughs as Anectine) to allow the insertion of a breathing tube into plaintiff's throat. After one unsuccessful attempt at intubation, Dr. Burdon increased the flow of succinylcholine to further relax plaintiff. Plaintiff was then successfully intubated. Plaintiff was removed from the gurney and turned to a prone position on the operating table. Immediately after plaintiff was turned, Dr. Burdon was unable to get a pulse. * * * Plaintiff was revived, but was without a heartbeat for approximately 29 minutes. The drip solution of succinylcholine was inadvertently left on during a portion of this time. Plaintiff is now severely impaired. * * *

The jury returned a verdict in favor of plaintiff and against Dr. Burdon and Burroughs. Based upon counterclaims for contribution filed by defendants, the jury apportioned the verdict 90% against Dr. Burdon and 10% against Burroughs. The trial court entered judgment on the verdicts rendered on plaintiff's claims and on defendants' counterclaims. Burroughs' main contention on appeal is that the trial court erred in denying Burroughs' motion for judgment notwithstanding the verdict. Burroughs argues that plaintiff failed to show causation between his injury and

Burroughs' alleged failure to contraindicate administration of Anectine to patients exhibiting symptoms like plaintiff's. * * *

Dr. Burdon testified he was aware of the contents of the package insert. The package insert specifically warned that Anectine may induce hyperkalemia and cardiac arrest in patients recovering from "severe trauma," or in patients with "extensive denervation of skeletal muscle." Evidence presented at trial supported these statements. Dr. Burdon testified the package insert correctly summarized medical literature on the subject, and appropriately listed those persons at risk to experience a hyperkalemic reaction to succinylcholine. Dr. Burdon also testified he was aware of the risk of administering succinylcholine to denervated patients. He stated he had used succinylcholine before on extensively denervated patients without adverse results.

Expert testimony established it was basic knowledge to anesthesiologists that the administration of succinylcholine to an extensively denervated patient entailed the risk of hyperkalemia leading to cardiac arrest. Plaintiff's experts opined the administration of succinylcholine to plaintiff caused hyperkalemia and cardiac arrest, and that Dr. Burdon's failure to stop the flow of succinylcholine delayed efforts to revive plaintiff.

No direct proof was presented which showed Burroughs' product was the proximate cause of plaintiff's injury. No testimony was presented that the package insert was unreasonably dangerous, or that Burroughs' failure to "positively contraindicate" use of Anectine in extensively denervated patients proximately caused plaintiff's injury. Experts for the parties testified it is not necessary to absolutely contraindicate the use of succinylcholine in patients with denervated muscle. The experts further acknowledged the package insert's use of the language with "great caution" was not inappropriate.

Crucial to Dr. Burdon's decision to administer succinylcholine was his determination that plaintiff was not extensively denervated, and therefore not at risk with respect to succinylcholine. Dr. Burdon based his belief on professional literature on the subject and his personal experience in nearly 40 years of practice. Dr. Burdon testified that plaintiff had suffered neither the type nor quantity of "severe" trauma necessary to place plaintiff at risk for cardiac arrest from a hyperkalemic reaction to succinylcholine. Evidence at trial, however, showed that plaintiff was indeed extensively denervated. Since Dr. Burdon failed to identify plaintiff as someone at risk with respect to the administration of succinylcholine, the package insert could not have played a causative role in his injuries. Dr. Burdon never felt plaintiff was in the class of persons in which succinylcholine should be prohibited or used with great caution. * * *

The manner in which Dr. Burdon administered Anectine to plaintiff was not recommended by the package insert. The drip method used by Dr. Burdon was recommended only for long (rather than short) surgical procedures. The insert also stated the 0.2% solution used by Dr. Burdon was the highest recommended dosage rather than the lowest recommended diluted solution (0.1%). Dr. Burdon testified he felt he was administering Anectine cautiously by using it for a brief period of time. He also testified that a 0.2% solution is the amount he would customarily administer.

The record demonstrates that Dr. Burdon understood the risks involved in administering succinylcholine. Dr. Burdon had used succinylcholine daily for over 30 years. One year prior to the incident, he had read the package insert for Anectine. He had also read the history and content of medical literature regarding succinylcholine. He had used succinylcholine in the past with denervated patients. Even if the insert had absolutely contraindicated the use of succinylcholine in extensively denervated patients, Dr. Burdon would not have heeded the prohibition because he had failed to diagnose plaintiff as being extensively denervated. Under these circumstances, the package insert could not have proximately caused the injury to plaintiff.

We conclude that the trial court should have granted Burroughs' motion for judgment n.o.v. because plaintiff failed to prove the product was unreasonably dangerous or that Burroughs' failure to absolutely contraindicate use of the product in extensively denervated patients was the proximate cause of plaintiff's injury. Accordingly, the judgment of the trial court is vacated as to Burroughs. Based upon our findings, we enter judgment against defendants, Associated Anesthesiologists, Inc. and John C. Burdon, M.D., for the entire amount of the jury verdict.

Tanuz v. Carlberg

921 P.2d 309 (N.M.Ct.App.1996).

■ APODACA, JUDGE:

* * * Plaintiff complained of TMJ pain and was diagnosed as suffering from bilateral derangement of the TMJ. In September 1983, defendant surgically implanted TMJ implants manufactured by Vitek, Inc. The implants were manufactured using Proplast, a teflon-based substance patented by Vitek. At the time, the Vitek implants were being touted as having a greater success rate than other treatments. Defendant advised plaintiff to return for routine follow-up care and to return if she experienced pain or discomfort.

On April 27, 1984, plaintiff returned to defendant's office, complaining of pain in her TMJs. Defendant's notes from that visit indicate that plaintiff had failed to make her appointments after the previous visit. He referred her to Dr. Jameson to have her splint replaced. Plaintiff did not see Dr. Jameson after the referral and failed to continue follow-up treatment with defendant, contrary to his advice. In 1987, plaintiff began experiencing TMJ pain and self-treated this pain with over-the-counter medication. * * * In October 1993, plaintiff contacted defendant's office after watching a television show that discussed problems with Vitek implants. Defendant surgically removed plaintiff's implants in February 1994.

Plaintiff filed her complaint against defendant in June 1994. In addition to her strict liability claim, plaintiff alleged that defendant was negligent in failing to warn her of the dangers posed by the Vitek implants. Specifically, plaintiff alleged that defendant should have contacted her before any official warnings from the manufacturer about the product had arisen, based solely on problems he himself had experienced with his own patients and a growing awareness in the medical community that Vitek implants posed dangers to patients. Plaintiff also alleged that, when Vitek and the Food and Drug Administration alerts appeared in 1990 and 1991, defendant made inadequate attempts to locate her. * * *

Plaintiff does not contend that defendant was negligent when he inserted the implants in 1983 or when he assumed care for their removal in 1993 and 1994. * * * [T]he central issue in this case is not whether defendant owed a duty to exercise reasonable care as information became known later, but whether defendant breached the duty or applicable standard of care. Breach is an issue for the fact finder unless no reasonable minds could differ. In a medical malpractice action, a plaintiff is required to establish breach through expert medical testimony unless the fact finder can resort to common knowledge. * * *

Defendant testified that Proplast was showing a 93–97% success rate at the time of plaintiff's initial surgery. Before surgery, defendant discussed with plaintiff the nature of the procedure and informed her that her pain may never go away. He told her that the implant could break up, that it was incapable of regeneration, and that anything that is incapable of regeneration can deteriorate. After plaintiff's surgery, none of the major problems defendant discussed with plaintiff at the informed consent meeting occurred. At the time of the last visit, however, he recommended continued follow-up care. Defendant stated that he saw 1400 patients a year, and, as a result, he could not be a "babysitter" for their appointments.

Defendant removed Vitek implants from two of his patients in March (before plaintiff's last visit) and June 1984. He clinically observed that these patients were getting good results initially but that their erosion problems and pain would return. By the end of 1985, he had removed fifteen implants, constituting a 60% failure rate. At this time, he determined he would no longer use these implants in his patients. The problems he experienced with the implants occurred within the first or second year after surgery, after which time the situation had stabilized. * * *

When asked why he had not attempted to contact plaintiff after her April 1984 visit, defendant responded that he advised her during this visit to see Dr. Jameson for a splint, and he assumed that she was treated by Dr. Jameson. When Vitek issued the first safety alert in 1990, defendant informed his front desk to send it to all of his patients who had implants. Plaintiff was on the mailing list in 1990 and his office assumed that she was reached because the letter was never returned. In October 1991, his office sent an FDA recall notice to plaintiff and it was returned as undeliverable. Defendant's office assumed that there had been a change of address between 1990 and 1991 because the earlier mailing had not been returned. As a result, his office attempted to contact her at her last known address, listed as the Red River Fish Hatchery on her 1983 intake form and was told she had moved and no one at the fish hatchery knew her new address. He was told by his staff that they went through the records and had used all the abilities that they could have used to contact her. * * *

We believe the testimony noted above shows that the trial court reasonably determined plaintiff failed to meet her burden that defendant breached the applicable standard of care. Specifically, defendant's testimony established that, although there was mounting evidence against the safety of the Vitek implants throughout the 1980s, it was not known until the safety alerts were issued that the Proplast material itself was to blame. This fact is important because, up until that time, it was reasonable for defendant to conclude that the implants themselves were not inherently defective and that the success or failure with a given patient could be attributed to other causes, such as surgical technique or movement of the implant over time. As such, it was reasonable for defendant to assume that plaintiff was not experiencing problems because she did not return to his office, as she was advised to do should she have problems. * * * Although defendant's 60% failure rate was alarming on its face, the trial court could reasonably rely on defendant's additional testimony that the problems he experienced with these patients surfaced shortly after their surgery and, as a result, it was reasonable to assume that plaintiff was asymptomatic.

It was also reasonable for the trial court to disbelieve plaintiff's assertion that defendant's efforts in 1990 and 1991 to locate plaintiff were inadequate. It was reasonable to assume that plaintiff received the 1990 alert because the letter was not returned. * * * [W]e agree that more steps might have been taken to locate plaintiff [e.g., certified letters, phone calls, efforts to contact family members], but this factor was most likely considered by the trier-of-fact in the context of defendant's advice to plaintiff to return if she began to experience problems. In other words, the trial court could have determined that it would be reasonable to assume that the efforts to locate plaintiff did not have to exceed those taken because plaintiff would return to see defendant or another physician if her implants began to fail. Although the evidence presented by plaintiff was sufficient to sustain a finding to the contrary, we are compelled under our standard of review to affirm the trial court's determination that defendant did not breach his duty or the applicable standard of care.

We hold that a physician may not be held strictly liable as a matter of policy for the use of a manufactured implant later shown to be defective. We also hold that a physician has a duty to warn a patient of information obtained following a medical procedure. Under the facts of this case, however, it was reasonable for the trial court, sitting as fact finder, to conclude that plaintiff had failed to meet her burden of proof that defendant breached his duty. * * *

NOTES AND QUESTIONS

1. *Report on errors in medicine.* The Institute of Medicine (IOM) has issued an influential series of reports documenting the frequency and causes of errors in the provision of health care. See, e.g., Linda T. Kohn et al., To Err Is Human: Building a Safer Health System (2000); Gardiner Harris, Report Finds a Heavy Toll from Medication Errors, N.Y. Times, July 21, 2006, at A12; see also David Classen, Editorial, Medication Safety: Moving from Illusion to Reality, 289 JAMA 1154 (2003); Jeff Donn, Are We Taking Too Many Drugs?, Newsday, Apr. 19, 2005, at B13 (reporting estimates of "3.6 million adverse drug reactions a year," including medication errors, that lead to more than 125,000 fatalities). What is the most significant barrier to reducing such events? See Stephen G. Pauker et al., Editorial, Creating a Safer Health Care System: Finding the Constraint, 294 JAMA 2906 (2005); Sandra G. Boodman, No End to Errors, Wash. Post, Dec. 3, 2002, at F1; Denise Grady, Study Finds No Progress in Safety at Hospitals, N.Y. Times, Nov. 25, 2010, at A1. In order to track and ultimately prevent patient injuries resulting from improper choice of medication (or inappropriate doses), hospitals and other institutions must be able to identify when such an injury occurs and what error caused the injury. The most obvious source of this information is the treating physician. Consider the competing pressures physicians experience in such circumstances. How might the system alleviate these pressures in order to encourage error reporting and ultimately facilitate error prevention? See Lucian L. Leape, Reporting of Adverse Events, 347 New Eng. J. Med. 1633 (2002); Melissa Chang, Note, Promoting Patient Safety: Creating a Workable Reporting System, 18 Yale J. on Reg. 383 (2001).

2. *Mix-ups and handwriting disasters.* More than one thousand pairs of prescription drugs have similar names that may lead to confusion. For example, compare Celebrex® (for arthritis), Cerebyx® (for seizures), and Celexa® (for depression). See FDA, Minimizing Medical Products Errors: A Systems Approach, Jan. 8, 1998 (noting estimates that look-alike and sound-alike drug names cause 20 to 25% of medical errors). The FDA ordered several manufacturers to change their labels in order to highlight differences between similar-sounding drug names. See Lauren Neergaard, FDA Pushes to Curb Drug Mix-ups, Boston Globe, Jan. 2, 2002, at E4 (describing label changes using a mixture of upper- and lower-case letters and colors to draw attention to differences in product names). The use of abbreviations coupled with notoriously poor penmanship contributes to the confusion between drug names and also may result in patients receiving inappropriate dosages of the intended drug. See Bernadette Tansey, Nonprofit, FDA Seek to Change Doctors' Prescription Habits, S.F. Chron., June 15, 2006, at A4. In one case, a jury ordered a physician, hospital, and pharmacist to pay $450,000 to the family of a man who died of a heart attack after taking an overdose of Plendil® (a blood pressure drug) when he should have received Isordil® (an angina drug) because the prescription was illegible. See Bruce Japsen, Drug Name Confusion a Hazard, Chi. Trib., July 30, 2000, at A1. Some hospitals have resorted to forcing their staff physicians to attend handwriting classes. See Rene Sanchez, For Doctors' Scrawl, Handwriting's on the Wall, Wash. Post, May 16, 2000, at A1. Although computerized prescribing systems should reduce such errors, they do not represent a fail-safe alternative. See Ross Koppel et al., Role of

Computerized Physician Order Entry Systems in Facilitating Medication Errors, 293 JAMA 1197 (2005); Judith Graham & Cynthia Dizikes, Technology May Be Risky for Patients: Baby's Death Shows How Computerized Data Can Cause Medical Mishaps, Chi. Trib., June 27, 2011, at A1; Rob Stein, Automated Systems for Drugs Examined: Computers Can Add to Errors, Wash. Post, Dec. 21, 2004, at A3; see also Ceci Connolly, Few Doctors Sign Off on Online Prescribing, Wash. Post, Nov. 25, 2008, at F1.

3. *New technology and malpractice.* The opportunities for physician negligence increase with advances in medical knowledge and technology. See Mark F. Grady, Why Are People Negligent? Technology, Nondurable Precautions, and the Medical Malpractice Explosion, 82 Nw. U. L. Rev. 293, 298–99, 312 (1988) ("[W]ith the advent of dialysis, there are many compliance opportunities and when someone forgets to test a solution or check a shunt and harm results, there is a negligence claim that could not have existed before dialysis technology was introduced."); Michael D. Greenberg, Medical Malpractice and New Devices: Defining an Elusive Standard of Care, 19 Health Matrix 423 (2009); Sharona Hoffman & Andy Podgurski, e-Health Hazards: Provider Liability and Electronic Health Record Systems, 24 Berkeley Tech. L.J. 1523 (2009); Margaret Lent, Note, The Medical and Legal Risks of the Electronic Fetal Monitor, 51 Stan. L. Rev. 807, 828 (1999) (explaining that "several courts have indicated that a physician has a specific duty to 'keep abreast of progress,' " which "obligate[s] physicians to read, interpret, and apply the latest research regarding the drugs, techniques, and procedures employed in their specialities"). For a discussion of the peculiar malpractice issues that may arise in connection with fertility treatments, see Lars Noah, Assisted Reproductive Technologies and the Pitfalls of Unregulated Biomedical Innovation, 55 Fla. L. Rev. 603, 633–48 (2003). Advances in medical technologies also may complicate the resolution of other types of malpractice claims. See Lars Noah, An Inventory of Mathematical Blunders in Applying the Loss-of-a-Chance Doctrine, 24 Rev. Litig. 369, 387–88 (2005) (predicting that, with the arrival of improved pharmaceutical treatments for cancer, the "opportunities for computational errors in resolving [delayed diagnosis] cases will increase").

4. *Package inserts and the standard of care.* Courts have struggled in determining the appropriate status of prescription drug labeling in medical malpractice cases. See David C. Minneman, Annotation, Medical Malpractice: Drug Manufacturer's Package Insert Recommendations as Evidence of Standard of Care, 82 A.L.R.4th 166 (1990 & 2011 Supp.). In some jurisdictions, the package insert may serve as prima facie evidence of the applicable standard of care. See, e.g., Fournet v. Roule–Graham, 783 So.2d 439, 442–44 (La.Ct.App.2001); Thompson v. Carter, 518 So.2d 609, 612–13 (Miss.1987). In other jurisdictions, it may provide only some relevant evidence on that score. See, e.g., Mozer v. Kerth, 586 N.E.2d 759, 763–64 (Ill.App.Ct.1992); Bissett v. Renna, 710 A.2d 404, 407 (N.H.1998) (holding that "the PDR, by itself, is insufficient to establish the standard of care required of the defendant"); Ramon v. Farr, 770 P.2d 131, 134–35 (Utah 1989); cf. Young v. Cerniak, 467 N.E.2d 1045, 1057–58 (Ill.App.Ct.1984) ("[W]e are aware of no case which holds that a drug manufacturer's recommendation regarding dosage, unaccompanied by any warning of adverse consequences if the recommendation is not followed, is proof of the standard of care.''). In still other jurisdictions, the package insert may amount to inadmissible hearsay. See, e.g., Rosario v. N.Y. City Health & Hosp. Corp., 450 N.Y.S.2d 805, 807 (App.Div.1982). If phrased as a "contraindication," of course, precautionary information would effectively amount to a direction to the physician never to use the drug in those circumstances. See Richardson v. Miller, 44 S.W.3d 1, 8 n.2, 16–17 (Tenn. Ct.App.2000) (holding that the trial judge had erred in excluding label that had specifically warned against the off-label use selected by the physician); see also Lars Noah, Medicine's Epistemology: Mapping the Haphazard Diffusion of Knowledge in the Biomedical Community, 44 Ariz. L. Rev. 373, 435 (2002) ("Oddly enough, notwithstanding the clear rigor of this [FDA] process, proponents of EBM [evidence-based medicine] never mention package inserts as a valuable source of evidence-based recommendations for practitioners.'').

Morlino v. Medical Center of Ocean County

706 A.2d 721 (N.J.1998).

■ POLLACK, JUSTICE:

* * * On March 5, 1990, four weeks before she was due to deliver her baby, [Angela] Morlino visited the emergency room of the Medical Center. She was diagnosed with "acute pharyngitis," commonly known as a sore throat, and was given a prescription for 500 milligrams of amoxicillin, an antibiotic in the penicillin family. Morlino returned to the emergency room of the Medical Center on March 20. She again sought treatment for a sore throat. Dr. Dugenio took her history, examined her, and diagnosed her condition as acute pharyngitis. He also ordered a variety of tests. * * * Two days later, the results of Morlino's throat culture confirmed the presence of *Hemophilus influenza* bacteria. The culture also revealed that Morlino's infection was resistant to numerous antibiotics such as ampicillin, cephalosporin, erythromycin, clindamycin, nafcillin, and penicillin.

Even before receiving the throat culture results, Dr. Dugenio considered prescribing Cipro. He consulted the PDR, a compilation of information about prescription drugs that is published annually and distributed to the medical professional free of charge. A typical entry includes the trade and chemical names of the drug, a description of the drug, indications and contraindications for its use, warnings, adverse reactions, administrations and dosage, and information on managing and adjusting the dosage of the drug. Generally, the information in a package insert, which accompanies prescription drugs, is the same as that in the PDR.

The PDR contains the following warning for Cipro:

> CIPROFLOXACIN SHOULD NOT BE USED IN CHILDREN OR PREGNANT WOMEN. The oral administration of ciprofloxacin caused lameness in immature dogs. Histopathological examination of the weight-bearing joints of these dogs revealed permanent lesions of the cartilage.

Additionally, the PDR characterizes drugs for pregnant women based on the degree to which the drug manufacturer has ruled out a risk to the fetus. Cipro was in "Use–In–Pregnancy Category C," which means:

> Risk cannot be ruled out. Human studies are lacking, and animal studies are either positive for fetal risk, or lacking as well. However, potential benefits may justify the potential risk.

From the PDR warnings, Dr. Dugenio understood that he should prescribe Cipro for a pregnant patient only if the potential benefit to the patient outweighed the risk to her and the fetus. In weighing the risks and benefits, Dr. Dugenio was concerned that the *Hemophilus influenzae* bacteria, if untreated, could lead to more serious illnesses, such as infectious mononucleosis, pneumonia, and meningitis. These illnesses could pose serious risks to Morlino and her fetus. The PDR, he noted, did not state that the use of Cipro in pregnant women is contraindicated. * * *

In affirming, the Appellate Division held that the trial court did not err by refusing to read verbatim that part of the two PDR warnings stating that Cipro should not be used by pregnant women and that the "risk cannot be ruled out." The Appellate Division identified three approaches concerning the use of the manufacturer's insert and the parallel PDR warning to establish a medical standard of care. The first approach, adopted by this court in *Sanzari v. Rosenfeld*, 167 A.2d 625 (1961), "is that product packaging inserts do not establish a standard of care but are admissible to show what the physician knew or should have known about the drug." According to the Appellate Division, out-of-state cases support two other approaches. "The second approach is to allow product inserts (and the PDR) into evidence to show the standard of care, provided expert testimony is also presented to explain the standard of care to the jury." The third approach "is that the product insert, standing alone without expert testimony, is evidence of negligence by the physician who fails to adhere to its rules." Rejecting the first and third approaches, the Appellate Division adopted the rule that package inserts and their parallel PDR references may be considered by the jury along with expert testimony to determine the appropriate standard of care. * * *

[T]he jury viewed "blow-ups" of the PDR's relevant sections and heard extensive expert testimony concerning the PDR. Morlino's experts testified about the PDR warnings and their opinion concerning the prescription of Cipro. The experts relied, in part, on the PDR to establish the standard of care and to describe the risk/benefit analysis required for Category C drugs. Also, Dr. Dugenio admitted that he had learned from the PDR not only of the risks of giving Cipro to a pregnant woman, but also of the necessity for a risk/benefit analysis. * * *

[W]e agree with the Appellate Division that the jury was free to consider the PDR warnings on questions of both Dr. Dugenio's knowledge and the standard of care applicable to his conduct. We further hold that the jury may consider package inserts and parallel PDR references, when they are supported by expert testimony, to determine the appropriate standard of care in a medical malpractice case. * * * Physicians frequently rely on the PDR when making decisions concerning the administration and dosage of drugs. Often, the drug manufacturer, which has developed and tested the drug, may be in a better position than the physician to determine the appropriate usage and dosage of drugs.

Nevertheless, drug manufacturers do not design package inserts and PDR entries to establish a standard of medical care. Manufacturers write drug package inserts and PDR warnings for many reasons including compliance with FDA requirements, advertisement, the provision of useful information to physicians, and an attempt to limit the manufacturer's liability. After a drug has been on the market for a sufficient period of time, moreover, physicians may rely more on their own experience and the professional publications of others than on a drug manufacturer's advertisements, inserts, or PDR entries.

Those considerations highlight the reasons expert testimony must accompany the introduction of PDR warnings to establish the applicable standard of care in prescribing a drug. Additionally, expert testimony often is needed to explain the information contained in package inserts or the PDR. Drug manufacturers write explanations and warnings for doctors, not the general public. Comprehension of the terms and their significance may depend on medical expertise. Accordingly, we hold that package inserts and PDR references alone do not establish the standard of care. It follows that a physician's failure to adhere to PDR warnings does not by itself constitute negligence. Reliance on the PDR alone to establish negligence would both obviate expert testimony on an issue where it is needed and could mislead the jury about the appropriate standard of care. * * * Allowing the admission of PDR warnings without accompanying expert testimony could transform drug manufacturers into judges of acceptable medical care. The effect would be to force doctors to follow the PDR's recommendations or run the risk of liability for malpractice.

Whether to prescribe a drug and, if so, what drug to prescribe are issues that demand careful consideration. The decision to prescribe a particular drug ultimately is a matter of judgment for the physician. In addition to considering the individual patient, the physician may consider all available information concerning a drug. The information may include the manufacturer's inserts and PDR warnings, as well as medical journals, advice from colleagues, and the physician's own experience. To confine the treatment choices to those expressly permitted in the PDR would be too restrictive. Such an approach also would be inconsistent with the FDA's position that physicians are not bound by PDR recommendations. * * *

B. LIABILITY OF SUPPLIERS AND DISPENSERS

1. PHARMACISTS

Murphy v. E.R. Squibb & Sons, Inc.

710 P.2d 247 (Cal.1985).

■ MOSK, JUSTICE:

* * * Plaintiff filed an action for personal injuries allegedly resulting from DES taken by her mother in 1951 and 1952 during pregnancy for the

purpose of reducing the risk of miscarriage. The complaint sought damages on the theory of strict liability, alleging that the drug was defectively designed, with the result that plaintiff developed clear cell adenocarcinoma at the age of 23. As defendants, plaintiff joined Exclusive Prescription Pharmacy Corporation where plaintiff's mother purchased the DES, and E.R. Squibb & Sons, Inc. * * *

[P]harmacists perform a broad range of tasks, from selling razor blades and dental floss to treating patients in a health care facility by ordering laboratory tests and administering drugs by injection and acting as consultants regarding medication prescribed for patients at such facilities. The discussion which follows relates only to the duties in a community pharmacy of a pharmacist who fills prescriptions for drugs on the order of a physician or other medical care provider, and who has used due care in compounding and labeling the drug.

There are no cases in California deciding whether a retail pharmacy is strictly liable for injuries caused by an inherent defect in a drug. In Florida, North Carolina, and New York a pharmacy is held not to be strictly liable for defects in a prescription drug. These cases rely on section 402A of the *Restatement Second of Torts*, which declares that unavoidably unsafe products such as drugs are not defective if they are accompanied by an appropriate warning, and that a seller is only required to warn of defects of which he knew or should have known. * * *

As might be anticipated, the parties differ sharply as to whether the main function of a pharmacist is to provide a service or to sell a product. Plaintiff asserts that the duties of a pharmacist in filling a prescription do not differ from those of any other retailer: he reads the prescription, fills the container with the proper type and dosage of the medication required, types up a label, attaches it to the container, and exchanges the medication for payment by the customer. In essence, argues plaintiff, a pharmacist is the functional equivalent of "an experienced clerk at a hardware store."

Exclusive paints a dramatically different picture of the role of the pharmacist, characterizing him as a professional who provides an important health service. They point out that with a few exceptions specified by statute, only a physician or a licensed pharmacist may compound or dispense prescription drugs. * * * A pharmacist is required not only to assure that the drug prescribed is properly selected, measured and labeled but * * * he must be alert to errors in prescriptions written by doctors, and contact the doctor in case of doubts or questions regarding the drug prescribed. In addition, the pharmacist may discuss with the patient the proper use of the drug and the potential side effects, and must be aware of the possibility of harmful interaction between various medications which the pharmacist knows the patient is using. * * *

It seems clear to us that the pharmacist is engaged in a hybrid enterprise, combining the performance of services and the sale of prescription drugs. It is pure hyperbole to suggest, as does plaintiff, that the role of the pharmacist is similar to that of a clerk in an ordinary retail store. * * * A pharmacist must not only use skill and care in accurately filling and labeling a prescribed drug, but he must be aware of problems regarding the medication, and on occasion he provides doctors as well as patients with advice regarding such problems. In counseling patients, he imparts the same kind of information as would a medical doctor about the effects of the drugs prescribed. A key factor is that the pharmacist who fills a prescription is in a different position from the ordinary retailer because he cannot offer a prescription for sale except by order of the doctor. In this respect, he is providing a service to the doctor and acting as an extension of the doctor in the same sense as a technician who takes an X-ray or analyzes a blood sample on a doctor's order.

Nevertheless, it cannot be disputed that a sale in fact occurs. There is an obvious distinction between the doctor who provides a patient with a prescription for a defective drug, a dentist who uses a faulty drill, or a hospital that uses a defective needle during surgery, and a pharmacist who fills a prescription. The pharmacist is in the business of selling prescription drugs, and his role begins and ends with the sale. His services are rendered only in connection with the sale, and a patient who goes to a pharmacy to have a prescription filled generally is seeking to purchase the drug rather than to obtain the advice of the pharmacist. By contrast, the doctor, dentist and hospital in the cases cited above are not in the business of selling the drug or device; they use the product in the course of treatment as one element in their efforts to effect a cure, and furnishing the services does not depend on sale of a product.

Ordinarily, in deciding whether the sale or service aspect of an enterprise predominates, we would confine our consideration to the type of factors discussed above. In the case of a pharmacy, however, we must broaden our inquiry. The Legislature has provided that the practice of pharmacy is not only a profession, but also a "dynamic patient-oriented health service that applies a scientific body of knowledge to improve and promote patient health by means of appropriate drug use and drug related therapy." * * *

If pharmacies were held strictly liable for the drugs they dispense, some of them, to avoid liability, might restrict availability by refusing to dispense drugs which pose even a potentially remote risk of harm, although such medications may be essential to the health or even the survival of patients. Furthermore, in order to assure that a pharmacy receives the maximum protection in the event of suit for defects in a drug, the pharmacist may select the more expensive product made by an established manufacturer when he has a choice of several brands of the same drug. As [one] amicus brief warns, "Why choose a new company's inexpensive product, which has received excellent reviews in the literature for its quality, over the more expensive product of an established multinational corporation which will certainly have assets available for purpose of indemnification 10, 20, or 30 years down the line?" * * *

Finally, plaintiff contends that even if the pharmacist is personally exempt from strict liability because he provides a service, the "merchandising organization which employs him ... should not be so exempted." Plaintiff cites no authority in support of this claim, and we perceive no basis in law or rationale for accepting it. The fact that a pharmacy may be owned by an enterprise which also deals in ordinary merchandise does not justify the conclusion that it should be held strictly liable when it performs a service. Moreover, the policy justifying the grant of immunity from strict liability to the practice of pharmacy would only be effectuated if the pharmacy operation itself is exempted. For the reasons stated above, we conclude that the trial court was correct in granting judgment on the pleadings to Exclusive.

■ BIRD, CHIEF JUSTICE (dissenting):

* * * The issue is whether retail druggists and pharmacies, which sell prescription drugs to consumers, are engaged primarily in selling a product or in performing a service. The simple answer is that in the marketing of prescription drugs by retail druggists, as in the marketing of automobiles and other consumer products, the sale aspect predominates over any incidental service provided to the consumer. * * * [S]trict liability applies if the purchase of a product is the "primary objective" or "essence" of the transaction. Strict liability is inapplicable only where the transaction is limited to the provision of a service and does not involve the sale of a product or where the service aspect predominates and any sale included in the transaction is incidental to the provision of the service. * * *

Only 22 percent of patients who purchase prescription drugs are counseled by the retail druggist, who spends an average of only one and one-half hours a day performing this service. Thus, in the vast majority of prescription drug sales transactions, the customer receives only a product and no services from the retail druggist. The predominance of the sale is also reflected by the fixed prices the retail druggist charges for prescription drugs, based on a markup from wholesale cost rather than an hourly fee calculation. The majority dismiss as "pure hyperbole" plaintiff's suggestion that the retail druggist's role is similar to that of a clerk in an "ordinary" retail store. Yet, the average hardware store clerk probably devotes as much or more time to counseling customers on the applications and proper use of the items offered for sale by the store. I doubt that the majority would have any difficulty concluding that the essence of the transaction between the hardware clerk and the customer is a sale rather than a service.

The majority, diverging from the inquiry into the nature of the transaction, contend that the educational and professional standards which must be met to obtain a pharmacist's license somehow dictate the conclusion that the retail druggist and the pharmacy are primarily engaged in the provision of a service. An almost mystical significance is attributed to the retail druggist's admitted expertise and professional status. * * * Nowhere do they explain how the retail druggist's professional status converts the business of selling prescription drugs, in which the provision of services plays a subordinate role, into a business in which the service aspect predominates.

The majority also draw contradictory conclusions from the high standards of knowledge and professional responsibility to which retail druggists are held. On the one hand, they stress the retail druggist's extensive knowledge of the properties, proper dosages, contraindications and side-effects of prescription drugs as support for the view that the retail druggist is primarily a seller of services rather than products. Yet, if anything, the retail druggist's expertise supports the imposition of strict liability. Armed with extensive knowledge of the products he or she sells, the retail druggist may be better equipped than other retailers to identify defective products. This capacity was a prime consideration supporting the application of strict liability to retailers. "[The] retailer himself may play a substantial part in insuring that the product is safe or may be in a position to exert pressure on the manufacturer to that end; the retailer's strict liability thus serves as an added incentive to safety."

On the other hand, the majority stress the statutory and professional restrictions that limit the retail druggist's discretion. Since a retail druggist may not sell a prescription drug except on a doctor's order and is prohibited from substituting a different drug (other than a generic equivalent), they suggest that it would be unfair to treat retail druggists like other retailers who are not subject to such restraints. This reasoning misses the point. The retailer's capacity to select the product sold has never been held to be a prerequisite to the imposition of strict liability. On the contrary, the doctrine has been held to apply to a wholesale-retail tire distributor who supplied whatever tires the manufacturer specified. This rule is consistent with the well-established principle that a retailer is strictly liable even though not equipped to test the product sold. It is also consistent with the focus of the strict liability doctrine on the product rather than on the conduct of the defendant. * * *

NOTES AND QUESTIONS

1. *Exemption from strict liability.* Most jurisdictions decline to apply strict liability to pharmacists. See, e.g., Madison v. American Home Prods. Corp., 595 S.E.2d 493 (S.C.2004); see also In re Yasmin and Yaz (Drospirenone) Marketing, Sales Practices & Prods. Liab. Litig., 692 F.Supp.2d 1012, 1021–24 (S.D.Ill.2010) (dismissing implied warranty claims against pharmacy that dispensed oral contraceptive); In re Rezulin Prod. Liab. Litig., 133 F.Supp.2d 272, 292 (S.D.N.Y.2001) ("[A]lmost every state that has considered the issue has declined to find pharmacists liable for breach of either implied or express warranty with respect to properties of prescription drugs."). But see Heredia v. Johnson, 827 F.Supp. 1522, 1524 (D.Nev.1993) (declining to grant the pharmacy's motion for summary judgment on a strict liability claim for an alleged failure to transmit the manufacturer's warning to a consumer about a drug's risks). See generally David J. Marchitelli, Annotation, Liability of Pharmacist Who Accurately Fills Prescription for Harm Resulting to User, 44 A.L.R.5th 393 (1996 & 2011 Supp.). Does the fact that many pharmacies today employ "techs" to help fill prescriptions alter your view of the proper characterization of their role? How about pharmacy chains that offer 24 hour drive through service? Cf. Rhonda L. Rundle, Getting Your Drugs from a Vending Machine, Wall St. J., June 21, 2005, at D1 (discussing efforts to use ATM-like kiosks to dispense prescription drug refills). The majority in *Murphy* refers to the exception for "unavoidably unsafe" products under *Rest. (2d)* § 402A comment k, which we discussed in Chapter 5(A). Does this in fact ever suggest freeing pharmacists of all strict products liability claims? Recall that the new *Restatement* exempts retailers and end users of prescription drugs and medical devices from strict products liability except in cases of manufacturing defects. See Rest. (3d) § 6(e). Furthermore, pharmacies that sell OTC drugs and devices would face the same strict liability claims as any other retailer of consumer products. See Morales v. American Home Prods. Corp., 214 F.Supp.2d 723, 726 (S.D.Tex.2002); see also Lars Noah, Treat Yourself: Is Self–Medication the Prescription for What Ails American Health Care?, 19 Harv. J.L. & Tech. 359, 382–83 (2006) ("[R]etailers may have greater flexibility than manufacturers after an Rx-to-OTC switch when it comes to regulating consumer access to such products, as demonstrated by chains that opted for behind-the-counter sales of drugs containing pseudoephedrine, which may make them more vulnerable to negligent marketing claims if they fail to adopt such safeguards."); cf. Lars Noah, This Is Your Products Liability Restatement on Drugs, 74 Brook. L. Rev. 839, 922 (2009) ("Similarly, if an exception to the learned intermediary rule applies (e.g., mass immunization, contraceptives, DTCA), then it seemingly would undermine the professional-status rationale underlying the exclusion of doctors and pharmacists from the chain of distribution for such drugs.").

2. *Liability for processing errors*. When a pharmacist dispenses the wrong drug, the wrong dosage, or with the wrong label, he or she may be liable in negligence if the error harms the patient. In these circumstances, no matter how well-trained and careful a pharmacist may be, the processing error itself usually suffices to prove negligence. See, e.g., Lou v. Smith, 685 S.W.2d 809 (Ark.1985) (pharmacist who altered prescription to correct an assumed prescribing error held liable after a child suffered a severe reaction to the drug); Forbes v. Walgreen Co., 566 N.E.2d 90, 91 (Ind.Ct. App.1991) (pharmacist liable for dispensing incorrect medication); Walter v. Wal–Mart Stores, Inc., 748 A.2d 961, 967–68 (Me.2000); see also Eric M. Grasha, Note, Discovering Pharmacy Error: Must Reporting, Identifying, and Analyzing Pharmacy Dispensing Errors Create Liability for Pharmacists?, 63 Ohio St. L.J. 1419 (2002); Christopher Rowland, CVS Faces Pharmacy Reviews: Settlement with State Comes After Scores of Prescription Errors, Boston Globe, Feb. 10, 2006, at C1 (reporting that "pharmacies typically experience a 3 percent error rate"). See generally Timothy E. Travers, Annotation, Druggist's Civil Liability for Injuries Sustained as a Result of Negligence in Incorrectly Filling Drug Prescriptions, 3 A.L.R.4th 270 (1981 & 2011 Supp.). Although it resembles strict liability for a manufacturing defect, a presumption of negligence in the case of processing errors differs from *Rest. (3d)* § 6(e)(1), where retailers face strict liability for dispensing a product with a manufacturing defect that they could not have detected. Cf. Fagan v. AmerisourceBergen Corp., 356 F.Supp.2d 198, 213 (E.D.N.Y.2004) ("[S]ince there is an allegation that the label on the Epogen was facially defective [and indicative of counterfeiting], the instant case does not involve a latent defect; but rather a patent defect, for which [the mail-order pharmacy] may be held liable for failing to discover upon reasonable inspection."); Harco Drugs, Inc. v. Holloway, 669 So.2d 878 (Ala.1995) (pharmacist should have double-checked prescription because it was illegible and an oncologist normally would not have prescribed a cardiology drug).

3. *Negligent compounding*. Negligence in compounding a drug that results in an injury might provide the basis for holding the pharmacist liable. See, e.g., Brown v. Southern Baptist Hosp., 715 So.2d 423, 426 n.2, 431 (La.Ct.App.1998); Schroeder v. Lester E. Cox Med. Ctr., 833 S.W.2d 411, 416–19, 422 (Mo.Ct.App.1992). Should compounding have broader doctrinal significance in making pharmacists subject to strict products liability? Cf. Fontanez v. Parenteral Therapy Assoc., 974 So.2d 1101, 1105–06 (Fla.Ct. App.2007) (rejecting strict liability but allowing a breach of implied warranty claim); id. at 1105 ("[T]he risk of harm associated with the use of a drug which somehow became contaminated during the compounding process should be borne by the one best able to implement procedures to prevent the contamination, not by a consumer who is powerless to protect himself or herself."). But cf. Dove v. Ruff, 558 N.E.2d 836, 837–40 (Ind.Ct.App. 1990) (rejecting strict liability where physician had engaged in compounding). See generally Lars Noah, This Is Your Products Liability Restatement on Drugs, 74 Brook. L. Rev. 839, 922 (2009) ("To the extent that pharmacogenomics blurs the line between manufacturing and compounding, courts may have to revisit the sales-service distinction as it applies to pharmaceutical products.").

Schaerrer v. Stewart's Plaza Pharmacy, Inc.

79 P.3d 922 (Utah 2003).

■ WILKINS, JUSTICE:

* * * In June 1995, Schaerrer met with her physician, Dr. Jeffrey W. Johnson, who prescribed fenfluramine and phentermine as a weight loss measure. Schaerrer took fenfluramine and phentermine as prescribed from June 1995 through June 1997. She was originally prescribed twenty-milligram fenfluramine tablets to be taken three times daily and a generic phentermine capsule to be taken once daily. Schaerrer purchased her prescriptions from Woolsey's Pharmacy until October 1996.

Between November 1996 and June 1997, Schaerrer filled five prescriptions for fenfluramine and phentermine from Stewart's Plaza Pharmacy. Schaerrer switched pharmacies when a friend who worked at a doctor's office told her about a "one-a-day fen-phen" capsule available from Stewart's. Although he had never heard of a one-a-day fen-phen capsule, over the course of eight months Dr. Johnson wrote Schaerrer five prescriptions for sixty milligrams of fenfluramine and twenty milligrams of phentermine to be taken once daily. Dr. Johnson testified that he never independently investigated the one-a-day fen-phen capsule and that he assumed the pharmacy had determined the product's safety.

Stewart's began offering the one-a-day fen-phen capsule after Stewart Koeven, a pharmacist and the proprietor of the pharmacy, compounded raw fenfluramine manufactured by Professional Compounding Centers of America, Inc. (PCCA), phentermine powder manufactured by several pharmaceutical companies, methylcellulose as a time-release agent, and lactose as a filler. After creating his one-a-day fen-phen capsule, Koeven distributed samples of it to local physicians for experimental use with their patients. Eventually, Stewart's began receiving and filling prescriptions for the one-a-day fen-phen capsule. Koeven testified that neither he nor Stewart's Plaza Pharmacy ever tested the safety or efficacy of the compounded drug.

Schaerrer began experiencing nausea, chest pains, and dizziness in early 1997. She stopped taking fenfluramine and phentermine in mid-July 1997, and shortly after required open heart surgery to repair two damaged heart valves. * * * Based on the stipulation that Stewart's actions in compounding the one-a-day fen-phen capsule did not make the fenfluramine more dangerous, and their argument that it was simply following typical pharmaceutical practice, Stewart's claims it is a protected pharmacist, not a manufacturer. Because a pharmacist cannot dispense certain drugs without a valid physician's prescription, Stewart's maintains that a pharmacist should be immune from strict products liability suits. * * *

Schaerrer alleges that Stewart's has stepped outside the bounds of appropriate compounding pharmacist behavior through the following conduct: (1) creating a new drug product (2) prior to receipt of a valid prescription order for the product, (3) marketing the new product to local physicians, and (4) providing samples of the new product to local physicians for distribution to their patients. Since Stewart's cannot be strictly liable as a pharmacist, there must be sufficient evidence that Stewart's was no longer acting as a pharmacy, and instead had become a drug manufacturer when it created the one-a-day fen-phen capsule.

According to Stewart Koeven's testimony, he noticed that a number of the patients who filled their prescriptions for fenfluramine and phentermine at his pharmacy were not complying with their prescriptions. Specifically, according to Koeven, they were not taking all of the Pondimin (fenfluramine) that their physicians prescribed. In approximately May of 1996, Koeven decided, based on his experience as a pharmacist with other time-release products, that a time-release version of the standard regime prescribed by physicians in the area might improve patient compliance. He contacted the physicians whose patients had been having compliance problems to determine whether they would be interested in the compounded drug product. The physicians expressed interest, and Koeven created sample capsules for some of the physicians to distribute to ten to twelve patients. Eventually, Koeven began receiving and filling prescription orders for his compounded one-a-day fen-phen capsules. * * *

[M]uch of Stewart's conduct falls within the guidelines of acceptable pharmaceutical practice in Utah. Consulting with physicians regarding the compliance problems of their patients, designing a new drug product that is not otherwise available based on numerous prescriptions previously written by physicians, and dispensing the new drug product directly to patients only after receipt of a valid prescription order all appear to be legitimate activities for a licensed pharmacist. We find no statutory prohibition against such behavior, nor do the parties cite any authority on such a prohibition. * * *

For over ten years, the FDA has expressed concern that increasing numbers of pharmacies are engaged in manufacturing behavior "that is clearly outside the bounds of traditional pharmacy practice." FDA Office of Regulatory Affairs, Compliance Policy Guide § 460.200 (May 2002). * * * While the policy statements of the FDA are by no means binding on this court, they do provide meaningful guidance on a question that few, if any, courts in this country have yet considered. According to the facts alleged in this case, Stewart's only act that might have run afoul of these prohibitions is the first—that no compounding occur in advance of a prescription except in limited quantities in relation to future prescriptions. * * * However, it is clear that the FDA does not see all pre-prescription compounding as clearly indicative of manufacturing behavior, nor do we. Some pre-prescription compounding activity is appropriate, particularly if the purpose and scale of the activity is in line with the traditional role that pharmacies play in the health care process. * * *

There is no indication from the record that Stewart's was conducting a large-scale, speculative, compounding business similar to that of a commercial pharmaceutical drug manufacturer. Nor was Stewart's using commercial scale equipment, compounding drugs for resale or wholesale distribution, or, as Schaerrer emphasizes, compounding a drug already available in the marketplace. Finally, there are no allegations that Stewart's violated any state or federal regulations governing the use of FDA-regulated drugs or the practice of pharmacy.

We do find the distribution of sample one-a-day fen-phen capsules to local physicians problematic, and perhaps indicative of the type of marketing used by large-scale drug manufacturers. However, the parties have provided no authority, nor do we find any, for the proposition that pharmacies must limit their advertising efforts to written materials and other strategies that do not include limited distribution of product samples. The fact remains that the pharmacy did not distribute the samples directly to patients, and cannot profit from any sale of one-a-day fen-phen without a valid prescription. The physician remains a gatekeeper between the compounded drug and the patient, and continues to control the patient's access to all prescription drugs.

Furthermore, strict liability for manufacturers exists in large part as a deterrent and a method of allocating the risk of loss among those best equipped to deal with it. Compounding pharmacies provide a unique and valuable service in our health care system, one which we have no reason to deter at this point. Nor do we believe that pharmacies are in a good position to insure against, or take steps to reduce the risk of, harm done by the drugs used in their compounded products through additional warnings. So long as the pharmacy is acting within the rules and regulations set forth by the state and federal governments for the practice of pharmacy, providing compounded drug products to patients after receipt of a physician's prescription, and confining themselves to the traditional scope of pharmaceutical care, we need not shift the pharmacy into the category of drug manufacturer for the purpose of strict products liability.

The conduct alleged in this case is not that of a drug manufacturer. Everything that Stewart's did was in the context of a compounding pharmacist. Stewart's may have overstepped the bounds of appropriate pre-prescription compounding or marketing activity, but that question is best reserved for state and federal regulators. For a pharmacy to cross the line and become a manufacturer, there must be evidence of large-scale compounding activity, third party resale or wholesale distribution efforts, or other significant indicators of questionable and non-traditional pharmaceutical behavior. A pharmacy taking steps to improve compliance within a small group of patients in the local community it serves through legitimate marketing efforts and without violating state or federal regulations is not strictly liable as a manufacturer for the compounded drug product that it provides. The learned intermediary rule shields pharmacists from strict products liability so long as they are engaged in the practice of pharmacy. Whether their pharmaceutical practice is improper or excessive is a question of negligence, not strict liability, so long as the conduct occurs within the standard framework of pharmacists. * * *

Morgan v. Wal–Mart Stores, Inc.

30 S.W.3d 455 (Tex.Ct.App.2000).

■ PATTERSON, JUSTICE:

The issue presented is whether pharmacists have a duty under Texas law to warn of potentially adverse reactions to prescription drugs. Jacquelyn Morgan and Charles Pettus sued Wal–Mart Stores, Inc. individually and as heirs to the estate of their minor child, Cameron Pettus. Plaintiffs alleged that Cameron's death in August 1993 was caused by an adverse reaction to Desipramine, a prescription drug sold to Morgan for Cameron's use by a Wal–Mart pharmacist. A jury found that Wal–Mart's negligent failure to warn of the known dangers of Desipramine was a proximate cause of Cameron's death, and the trial court assessed actual damages of $1,012,000, together with pre- and post-judgment interest. We reverse the judgment of the trial court and render a take-nothing judgment in favor of Wal–Mart. * * *

Cameron began taking Desipramine [for attention deficit hyperactivity disorder] in April 1991 at age twelve * * * * The parties agree that no

Wal–Mart pharmacist orally counseled Morgan about Desipramine's possible side effects; they also agree that Wal–Mart did not give Morgan the drug manufacturer's package insert, which contains substantial technical information about Desipramine, including warnings of potential adverse reactions. Pursuant to valid prescriptions from Dr. Schroeder, Morgan purchased Desipramine three more times at Wal–Mart, the last time in February 1993. Morgan testified that at no time did a Wal–Mart pharmacist advise her of anything with respect to the drug.

Irene Franklin, a pharmacist at the Wal–Mart where Morgan purchased Desipramine, testified that during a typical ten-hour shift in 1992 and 1993, she filled about 150 prescriptions. Although Franklin could not recall meeting Morgan, Franklin identified a Wal–Mart business record indicating that on October 24, 1992, she filled a prescription for 25 milligrams of Desipramine for Cameron Pettus. Franklin testified that Wal–Mart computers generate two documents each time a prescription is filled. The first document is a prescription label; the second document contains the patient's receipt and information from a national database about the drug, such as its generic name, common uses, and possible side effects. Franklin testified that it is common practice at Wal–Mart to staple the sheet containing the receipt and drug information to the outside of the bag in which the drug is placed. Morgan specifically denied receiving from Wal–Mart any printed warnings about Desipramine, although she acknowledged that she disposed of all paperwork related to the drug after Cameron's death. * * *

[P]laintiffs alleged Wal–Mart was negligent in the sale of Desipramine "by failing to properly warn intended users of the hazards and harms associated with the use of the product." Plaintiffs contended that Wal–Mart's negligence was the proximate cause of Cameron's health problems and death, as well as their own mental anguish, loss of consortium, and loss of family relationship. * * * On appeal, Wal–Mart argues that as a matter of law its pharmacists had no duty to warn of the potential dangers of Desipramine because that duty rested with the prescribing physician. * * *

While it is apparent then that Wal–Mart owed the plaintiffs a duty to dispense Desipramine in accordance with Dr. Schroeder's prescription, no Texas court has yet considered whether a pharmacist is also obligated to warn customers of potential hazards or side effects of prescribed drugs. A majority of courts considering this question have held that a pharmacist has no such duty when the prescription is proper on its face and neither the physician nor the manufacturer has required that the pharmacist give the customer any warning. The reluctance of courts to hold pharmacists liable for injuries caused by drugs accurately dispensed according to the terms of a valid prescription can be attributed to the application of the "learned intermediary" doctrine, which typically acts as an exception to a manufacturer's duty to warn customers in products liability cases. According to this doctrine, the manufacturer of a prescription drug has a duty to adequately warn the prescribing physician of the drug's dangers. The physician, relying on his medical training, experience, and knowledge of the individual patient, then chooses the type and quantity of drug to be prescribed. The physician assumes the duty to warn the patient of dangers associated with a particular prescribed drug.

A leading case in which the learned intermediary doctrine was applied to a negligence action against a pharmacy is *McKee v. American Home Products Corp.*, 782 P.2d 1045 (Wash.1989). In *McKee*, the plaintiff received prescriptions from her doctor for an appetite suppressant known as Plegine. The Physician's Desk Reference entry for Plegine cautions that it is a potentially addictive amphetamine; therefore, its use should be discontinued within a few weeks to avoid addiction. Notwithstanding, McKee's doctor authorized refills of the drug for ten years, and two pharmacists filled the prescriptions without warning McKee of the possible side effects of extended use. McKee sued the drug manufacturer, the prescribing physician, and the pharmacists for damages sustained as a result of her addiction to Plegine. McKee argued that her pharmacists were negligent in selling her Plegine without warning of its adverse effects and for failing to provide her the drug manufacturer's package insert.

In a 5–4 decision, the Washington Supreme Court concluded that the learned intermediary doctrine, normally applied to the relationship among physician, patient, and manufacturer, applied with equal force to the relationship among physician, patient, and pharmacist. The court reasoned that in both circumstances, the physician was in the best position to "relate the propensities of the drug to the physical idiosyncrasies of the patient." The court therefore held that McKee's pharmacists did not have a duty to warn her of the dangerous propensities of Plegine, nor were they legally obligated to give her the drug manufacturer's package insert containing such warnings. This holding is consistent with the decisions of many other states that have addressed the issue of whether to impose on pharmacists a duty to warn of adverse side effects. * * *

[I]n *Pysz v. Henry's Drug Store*, 457 So.2d 561 (Fla.Ct.App.1984), a pharmacist had filled the plaintiff's prescription for Quaaludes for more than nine years. Pysz alleged that the pharmacist's failure to warn him of the addictive propensities of Quaaludes constituted negligence. The Florida appeals court stated that although a pharmacist might in some instances possess greater knowledge than a physician of the adverse effects of drugs, "it is the physician who has the duty to know the drug that he is prescribing and to properly monitor the patient." The court concluded that the pharmacist, who had properly filled a lawful prescription, had no duty to warn the plaintiff of adverse reactions and affirmed the trial court's dismissal of Pysz's complaint. * * *

In *Stebbins v. Concord Wrigley Drugs, Inc.*, 416 N.W.2d 381 (Mich.Ct. App.1987), Bonnie Stebbins was seriously injured when a car driven by a man taking the antidepressant Tofranil struck her car. Stebbins settled with the other driver and sued his prescribing physician and pharmacist for negligence, alleging that they had failed to warn the patient of Tofranil's side effects, which include drowsiness. The Michigan appeals court began its consideration of the pharmacist's liability by citing the general rule that pharmacists owe patients a high standard of care in filling prescriptions and may be held liable for negligently dispensing a drug other than that prescribed. Relying on *Pysz*, the court concluded that "a pharmacist has no duty to warn the patient of possible side effects of a prescribed medication where the medication is proper on its face and neither the physician nor the manufacturer has required that any warning be given to the patient by the pharmacist." The court emphasized that its decision did not apply to a situation in which a pharmacist knows of a particular patient's unique medical problems or where a pharmacist fills incompatible prescriptions. * * *

In *Jones v. Irvin*, 602 F.Supp. 399 (S.D.Ill.1985), the plaintiff alleged she had suffered injuries as a result of her consumption of an excessive amount of Placidyl and other prescribed drugs. The Illinois district court concluded that K–Mart had no duty to notify the customer that she was being overmedicated because the duty to warn of a prescription drug's adverse effects falls squarely on the prescribing physician. Furthermore, the court placed upon the patient the duty to notify the physician of other drugs the patient is taking and upon the drug manufacturer the duty to notify the physician of any adverse effects in administering the drug. The court concluded that "placing these duties to warn on the pharmacist would only serve to compel the pharmacist to second guess every prescription a doctor orders in an attempt to escape liability." As in *Pysz* and *Stebbins*, the district court stressed the narrow application of its holding, stating that it applied only to prescription drugs and that pharmacists still owed customers the highest degree of prudence in filling a prescription. * * *

While a majority of courts that have considered whether a pharmacist has a duty to warn a patient of the adverse side effects of prescription medication has rejected the imposition of such a duty, unusual factual situations have arisen in which courts have felt compelled to impose a duty beyond mechanically dispensing drugs pursuant to a physician's directions. For example, in *Hand v. Krakowski*, 453 N.Y.S.2d 121 (App.Div.1982), a doctor prescribed certain psychotropic drugs to an alcoholic patient. The drugs were contraindicated with the use of alcohol. Although its records identified the patient as an alcoholic, the pharmacy dispensed the drugs to her over a period of six years without warning her of the danger. The patient died at age fifty-five of pancreatitis associated with a severe degree of cirrhosis. The New York appellate court reversed the summary judgment granted in favor of the defendant pharmacy. The court held that because the dispensing pharmacists knew that the decedent was an alcoholic and knew, or should have known, that the prescribed drugs were contraindicated with alcohol, a fact question existed regarding whether they had a duty to warn the patient of the danger involved. * * *

In sum, courts holding that pharmacists owe their customers a duty beyond accurately filing prescriptions do so based on the presence of additional factors, such as known contraindications, that would alert a reasonably prudent pharmacist to a potential problem. We do not dispute that a pharmacist may be held liable for negligently filling a prescription in such situations, but we cannot discern from the relevant case law a trend towards imposing a more general duty to warn. Nor do we conclude that existing Texas statutory law imposes such a duty. The plaintiffs contend that under the Texas Pharmacy Act and the administrative rules adopted pursuant to the Act, pharmacists have a general duty to warn customers of potential adverse side effects. Plaintiffs argue that the duty arises by implication from the mention of "patient counseling" in the Act's definition of "practice of pharmacy," as well as from several references to pharmacists counseling or communicating with patients in the Administrative Code. Plaintiffs emphasize the Code's repeated references to pharmacists communicating to patients information regarding "common severe side effects or adverse effects or interactions."

While these administrative rules demonstrate that pharmacists in Texas are trusted professionals with varied and important responsibilities, they cannot be reasonably read to impose a legal duty to warn patients of the adverse effects of prescription drugs. The imposition of a generalized duty to warn would unnecessarily interfere with the relationship between physician and patient by compelling pharmacists seeking to escape liability to question the propriety of every prescription they fill. Furthermore, a patient faced with an overwhelming number of warnings from his or her pharmacist may decide not to take a medication prescribed by a physician, who has greater access to and knowledge of the patient's complete medical history and current condition than the pharmacist. Instead of imposing such an onerous and counterproductive duty, the administrative rules reinforce the notion that, although pharmacists act as final auditors of the technical accuracy of a prescription and its appropriateness with respect to a patient's known condition and medication record, they do not possess the extensive knowledge of a physician with respect to a patient's complete medical history and are thus not legally obligated to warn a patient of adverse drug reactions.

Therefore, we hold that any liability of Wal–Mart's for negligently filling Cameron's prescription for Desipramine must be based on neglect in the face of information on which a reasonably prudent pharmacist would have acted. Having reviewed the entire record, we find no basis to conclude that the Wal–Mart pharmacists breached their duty of care when they filled Cameron's prescription for Desipramine. Dr. Schroeder prescribed Desipramine to treat Cameron's ADHD. * * * [A]lthough Cameron experienced severe discomfort while taking Desipramine, at no time did even one of the many doctors that examined him warn Cameron, Morgan, or Pettus of the potential adverse side effects of Desipramine or contact the pharmacists to instruct them to give such a warning. Indeed, the record reveals that the doctors did not attribute Cameron's ailments to Desipramine at all.

Furthermore, it is undisputed that Wal–Mart sold Desipramine to Morgan according to the terms of Dr. Schroeder's prescription. Plaintiffs do not allege that Wal–Mart possessed any special knowledge of Cameron's medical history that would impose upon it an additional duty to warn him,

Morgan, or Pettus of the particular dangers of Desipramine. Nor do the plaintiffs contend that Wal–Mart was or should have been aware of any contraindications. * * *

We acknowledge that the pharmacist's role has changed in the last few decades from a mere dispenser of medication to a trusted professional who plays a vital role in patient treatment. We understand that modern pharmacies employ advanced computer systems that can analyze drug interactions in seconds, thus preventing the sale of potentially fatal drugs to consumers, and we encourage the use of such systems. Nonetheless, in light of the learned intermediary doctrine, which we find applicable to the relationship among physician, patient, and pharmacist, we hold that pharmacists have no generalized duty to warn patients of potential adverse reactions to prescription drugs absent some special circumstances not present here. We do not imply that pharmacists may not warn patients of potential adverse reactions or dangerous side effects; we merely hold that pharmacists are not legally obligated to do so. * * *

NOTES AND QUESTIONS

1. *Negligent failures to warn.* Should the learned intermediary rule operate to relieve pharmacists from a duty to warn patients in the same way (and for the same reasons) that it insulates manufacturers? See In re Yasmin and Yaz (Drospirenone) Marketing, Sales Practices & Prods. Liab. Litig., 692 F.Supp.2d 1012, 1018–20 (S.D.Ill.2010) (dismissing inadequate warning claims against a pharmacy that dispensed oral contraceptives); DiGiovanni v. Albertson's, Inc., 940 N.E.2d 73, 75–77 (Ill.App.Ct.2010) (holding that a pharmacy owed no duty to warn a patient of a known drug-drug interaction that proved to be fatal); Nichols v. Central Merch., Inc., 817 P.2d 1131 (Kan.Ct.App.1991) (pharmacy has no duty to warn of possible birth defects associated with a prescription drug); see also Springhill Hosps., Inc. v. Larrimore, 5 So.3d 513, 519–21 (Ala.2008) (holding that a hospital pharmacist, who initially had alerted an ER physician of an inappropriately high starting oral dose of colchicine for gout, owed no duty to provide the physician with additional information about the maximum safe daily dosage). Should physicians always be the ultimate arbiters of the appropriateness of prescription drug therapy for a particular patient? Some courts have recognized a broader duty to warn. See Dooley v. Everett, 805 S.W.2d 380 (Tenn.Ct.App.1990) (pharmacy liable for failure to warn customer of drug interaction); see also Cottam v. CVS Pharmacy, 764 N.E.2d 814, 819–23 (Mass.2002) (concluding that, although it owes no general duty to warn of a prescription drug's potential side effects, at least absent any specific knowledge of risks faced by a particular patient, a pharmacy does have a duty to provide comprehensive warnings once it voluntarily chooses to supply instructional labeling that lists some side effects); cf. Rite Aid Corp. v. Levy–Gray, 894 A.2d 563 (Md.2006) (affirming verdict for plaintiff on breach of express warranty claim based on inaccuracy in pharmacy-prepared instructional pamphlet for doxycycline). See generally Brian L. Porto, Annotation, Civil Liability of Pharmacists or Druggists for Failure to

Warn of Potential Drug Interactions in Use of Prescription Drug, 79 A.L.R.5th 409 (2001 & 2011 Supp.).

What if the pharmacist knows of a particular patient's vulnerability? See, e.g., Lasley v. Shrake's Country Club Pharmacy, Inc., 880 P.2d 1129 (Ariz.Ct.App.1994) (mail order pharmacy may have a duty to warn long-time customer of danger of addiction from a prescription drug); Happel v. Wal–Mart Stores, Inc., 766 N.E.2d 1118 (Ill.2002) (pharmacy had duty to warn physician or patient of risks with prescription drug known to be contraindicated for that patient's use); Ferguson v. Williams, 374 S.E.2d 438 (N.C.Ct.App.1988) (although pharmacist has no duty to advise a customer about a drug, if pharmacist has specific knowledge about the customer's special sensitivities and undertakes to advise the customer, pharmacist has duty to provide the customer with accurate advice). Under what circumstances, if any, should the pharmacist have an obligation to question the physician's prescribing decision? Contrast Fakhouri v. Taylor, 618 N.E.2d 518 (Ill.App.Ct.1993) (pharmacist had no duty to warn customer where prescribed drug dose exceeded the dose recommended in the package insert), with Dee v. Wal–Mart Stores, Inc., 878 So.2d 426 (Fla.Ct. App.2004) (holding that pharmacist may have acted negligently in filling a four month old prescription for an opioid analgesic that allegedly was "unreasonable on its face" for failing to include an expiration date); Riff v. Morgan Pharmacy, 508 A.2d 1247 (Pa.Super.Ct.1986) (pharmacist has a duty to warn patient or physician when incomplete prescription information creates a risk of substantial harm to the patient).

2. *Failures to monitor drug therapy.* In 1990, Congress required that states participating in the federal Medicaid program create prospective drug utilization review standards for pharmacists. See 42 U.S.C. § 1396r–8. Pharmacists must evaluate whether the drug prescribed by the physician is appropriate for that patient and also offer to provide counseling. See Michael J. Holleran, The Pharmaceutical Access and Prudent Purchasing Act of 1990: Federal Law Shifts the Duty to Warn from Physician to Pharmacist, 26 Akron L. Rev. 77 (1992); Steven W. Huang, The Omnibus Reconciliation Act of 1990: Redefining Pharmacists' Legal Responsibilities, 24 Am. J.L. & Med. 417 (1998). This codification of the pharmacist's duty to monitor prescription drug therapy coincided with the development of a line of cases exploring the contours and limits of a duty in tort. See, e.g., Powers v. Thobhani, 903 So.2d 275 (Fla.Ct.App.2005); Hooks SuperX, Inc. v. McLaughlin, 642 N.E.2d 514 (Ind.1994) (holding that, where a pharmacy customer is having a prescription for a drug refilled at an unreasonably faster rate than the rate prescribed, the pharmacist has a duty to suspend refills pending directions from the prescribing physician); Baker v. Arbor Drugs, 544 N.W.2d 727 (Mich.Ct.App.1996) (where pharmacy advertised that its computer monitoring system would warn of therapeutic duplication and drug interactions, pharmacy had duty to monitor prescriptions as advertised); cf. Pappas v. Clark, 494 N.W.2d 245 (Iowa Ct.App.1992) (customer's fraudulent acquisition of prescription drugs from pharmacy barred claim that pharmacist negligently failed to monitor the customer's prescription drug use).

3. *Further commentary*. See David B. Brushwood, Pharmacy Malpractice Law and Regulations (2d ed. 1998); Kimberly A. Burns & Alan R. Spies, A Pharmacist's Duty to Warn: Promoting the Acceptance of a Consistent Legal and Professional Standard, 47 Duq. L. Rev. 1 (2009); Jaclyn Casey, Note, Prescription for Compromise: Maintaining Adequate Pharmacist Care Contraindicates Imposition of a General Duty to Warn, 17 Wash. U. J.L. & Pol'y 287 (2005); Lauren Fleisher, Note, From Pill–Counting to Patient Care: Pharmacists' Standard of Care in Negligence Law, 68 Fordham L. Rev. 165 (1999); Alison G. Myhra, The Pharmacist's Duty to Warn in Texas Reconsidered Within a National Framework, 27 Rev. Litig. 607 (2008); Heather A. Weisser, Note, Abolishing the Pharmacist's Veto: An Argument in Support of a Wrongful Conception Cause of Action Against Pharmacists Who Refuse to Provide Emergency Contraception, 80 S. Cal. L. Rev. 865 (2007).

2. Hospitals

Cafazzo v. Central Medical Health Services, Inc.

668 A.2d 521 (Pa.1995).

■ Montemuro, Justice:

In this case of first impression, we are presented with the question of whether a hospital and a physician can be held subject to strict liability under the *Restatement (Second) of Torts* § 402A for defects in a product incidental to the provision of medical services.

In 1986, appellant Albert Cafazzo underwent surgery for implantation of a mandibular prosthesis. In 1992, some time after it was discovered that this device was defective, a complaint was filed against appellees, the physician who performed the surgery and the hospital where the operation took place, claiming that "all defendants sell, provide or use certain prosthetic devices," and that they should be held strictly liable as having "provided, sold or otherwise placed in the stream of commerce products manufactured by Vitek, Inc., known as Proplast TMJ Implants." The complaint alleged that the prosthesis was defectively designed, unsafe for its intended use, and lacked any warning necessary in order to ensure safety. * * *

In this instance, the manufacturer is in bankruptcy, and unable to sustain liability. Thus, an alternative, and solvent, payor was sought. All other considerations were subordinated to this objective, hence the unequivocal necessity, in appellants' view, for appellees to be designated as sellers irrespective of the actual facts of this matter. However, to ignore the ancillary nature of the association of product with activity is to posit surgery, or indeed any medical service requiring the use of a physical object, as a marketing device for the incorporated object. This is tantamount to deciding that the surgical skills necessary for the implantation of, e.g., mandibular prostheses, are an adjunct to the sale of the implants. Moreover, under such a theory, no product of which a patient in any medical setting is the ultimate consumer, from CT scanners to cotton balls, could escape the assignment of strict liability. Clearly, the relationship of hospital and/or doctor to patients is not dictated by the distribution of such products, even if there is some surcharge on the price of the product. As the New York Court of Appeals has aptly stated:

> Concepts of purchase and sale cannot be separately attached to the healing materials . . . supplied by the hospital for a price as part of the medical services. That the property or title to certain items of medical material may be transferred, so to speak, from the hospital to the patient during the course of medical treatment does not serve to make such a transaction a sale. "Sale" and "transfer" are not synonymous, and not every transfer of personal property constitutes a sale.

Perlmutter v. Beth David Hosp., 123 N.E.2d 792, 794 (N.Y.1954). The thrust of the inquiry is thus not on whether a separate consideration is charged for the physical material used in the exercise of medical skill, but what service is performed to restore or maintain the patient's health. The determinative question becomes not what is being charged, but what is being done. * * *

[W]hile the implant was incidental to the surgical procedure here, it was a necessary adjunct to the treatment administered, as were the scalpel used to make the incision, and any other material objects involved in performing the operation, all of which fulfill a particular role in provision of medical service, the primary activity. Once the illness became evident, treatment of some kind became a matter of necessity to regain health. When one enters the hospital as a patient he goes there, not to buy medicines or pills, not to purchase bandages or iodine or serum or blood, but to obtain a course of treatment in the hope of being cured of what ails him. * * *

[E]ven assuming that providers of medical services could reasonably be termed sellers, in examining the test relied upon by appellants to "prove" their major premise, the policy reasons for strict liability are not present. * * * First, as to the availability of some entity for redress, medical personnel and hospitals are already subject to liability, albeit only where the quality or quantity of the services they provide may be called into question. It is perfectly reasonable to assume, for example, that a physician or hospital possesses the necessary skill and expertise to select a product for use in medical treatment which is fit for its intended purpose. An error of choice might indeed be attributed to negligence or ignorance. However, no allegation has been made that the selection of the Vitek TMJ was made either carelessly or intentionally despite knowledge of its defects. To assign liability for no reason other than the ability to pay damages is inconsistent with our jurisprudence. Where the liability is sought to be imposed on a party which is not a seller under 402A, such liability would indeed be assigned for no reason at all.

Next comes the matter of whether applying strict liability would provide an incentive to safety. As the Superior Court correctly pointed out, the safety of the product depends on the judgment of those connected to the research, development, manufacture, marketing and sale of the product. Moreover, the safety testing and licensing for use of medical devices is a responsibility specifically undertaken by the federal government. Therefore, imposing liability for a poorly designed or manufactured product on the hospitals and doctors who use them on the assurances of the FDA is highly unlikely to effect changes of this sort. Again, selection of the wrong product becomes a matter of professional negligence for which recovery is available. * * *

The net effect of this cost spreading [under a rule of strict liability] would further endanger the already beleaguered health care system. As a practical matter costs would merely be absorbed by the insurers of physicians and hospitals, whose charges would reflect the increase in policy rates without corresponding improvement to any aspect of the health care system. Rather, research and innovation in medical equipment and treatment would be inhibited. The Supreme Court of Wisconsin in *Hoven v. Kelble*, 256 N.W.2d 379 (Wis.1977), has observed, albeit in a slightly different context, that, on balance, the peculiar characteristics of medical services outweigh any of the reasons which might exist to assign strict liability in the medical setting. These include the tendency to be experimental, which would certainly be adversely affected if 402A were applicable; a dependence on factors beyond the control of the professional; and a lack of certainty or assurance of the desired result. In short, medical services are distinguished by factors which make them significantly different in kind from the retail marketing enterprise at which 402A is directed. * * *

■ CAPPY, JUSTICE (dissenting):

* * * [T]his defendant is in a better position than the consumer to prevent the circulation of defective products. The majority commences its analysis of this point by recognizing that the focus of this inquiry is on whether there is "some ongoing relationship with the manufacturer from which some financial advantage inures to the benefit of the latter and which confers some degree of influence on the [putative seller]." The majority, however, rapidly loses sight of its objective. It deduces that since the defendants here have an extensive list of products at their disposal, * * * then the defendants here should also be held immune from strict liability. * * * Such reasoning would lead to the absurd result that a department store, with an inventory of tens of thousands of items, would be less likely to be held strictly liable than the local, family-run convenience store with its modest inventory. Such a "test" does not advance the goals of strict liability, but rather perverts them. * * *

Parker v. St. Vincent Hospital

919 P.2d 1104 (N.M.Ct.App.1996).

■ HARTZ, JUDGE:

[In this case, another TMJ implant recipient sued the hospital under a theory of strict liability. She also sued the hospital on a negligence claim, arguing that the hospital breached a duty to investigate the safety of the implants before supplying and allowing their use in the hospital. The district court granted summary judgment to the defendants.]

According to the weight of authority, a hospital is not a distributor of medical supplies, even though it may bill separately for the item and charge the patient a markup over the hospital's cost. The courts have generally held that the essence of the hospital's role is the provision of services, regardless of whether a product is involved. We are not convinced by this analysis. To be sure, the chief function of hospitals is to provide a service. But when a product is provided as part of the service, and the service provider bills separately for the product, the rule that has emerged outside of the hospital context is that the provision of the product is a distribution for purposes of strict products liability. To depart from this characterization of such a transaction for the special case of hospitals would, in our view, generate unnecessary confusion. If there are sound policy reasons for not imposing strict products liability on hospitals, those policy reasons should be addressed directly, not obscured by artificial semantic distinctions. * * *

[O]ne could expect that the cost of liability arising from defects in a particular product would be shared by those purchasing any product sold by the distributor. For example, the Hospital's liability expenses arising from defective design of an implant would probably be borne by patients using any medical product for which the Hospital is a distributor. The price of pacemakers may go up because of defective jaw implants. To the extent that the cost of injury caused by a defective product is borne by persons who have no occasion to use the product, the first policy [i.e., cost spreading] is not advanced. * * *

[T]he fact that it is easier to prove that a product is defectively designed than to prove that there was negligence in designing the product has a perverse effect in [the hospital] context because ordinarily there is no possibility that a distributor other than the manufacturer created a design defect. That would surely be the case when the hospital does not alter the product and the product is used for its intended purpose. In that event there could be no negligent design by the hospital. * * *

[Although the rationale that strict liability encourages suppliers to select reputable manufacturers when purchasing products] makes sense for other products, it encounters a powerful contrary public policy with regard to medical products. Improving medical care is a national priority. Improvement encompasses both advances in treatment and greater access to care, which is impeded by high costs. In this light, should hospitals be encouraged to deal only with the preeminent suppliers of medical products who have a track record of "well-designed" products and have the financial resources to pay for any injuries caused by defective products? Such encouragement could, for example, impact heavily on the use of generic drugs. * * * Our perception is that public policy strongly favors medical innovation and the use of less expensive alternative products. Protection to the public comes from the expertise of physicians who select the products and, at least to some extent, from regulation by the Food and Drug Administration (FDA). * * *

[T]o the extent that imposition on hospitals of strict products liability for defective design would cause hospitals to devote more resources to reviewing the designs of products it distributes, that additional effort might be contrary to public policy. If, for example, hospitals were to acquire the expert staff and devote the other resources necessary to evaluate the designs of the medical products used in the hospital, hospitals would incur substantial additional costs that would be passed on to its patients. Yet such measures might well provide little benefit in medical care, and could even cause harm. To make each hospital a mini-FDA could duplicate effort while producing a less reliable result because of the much smaller data base. For example, if a hospital must rely on a small sample of uses of a particular product, random fluctuations may cause the hospital to conclude that a product is unsafe (and should not be used at the hospital) when more extensive, better data establish otherwise. * * *

NOTES AND QUESTIONS

1. *Sales vs. service.* See Rest. (3d) § 20 cmt. d ("[I]n a strong majority of jurisdictions, hospitals are held not to be sellers of products they supply in connection with the provision of medical care, regardless of the circumstances."). Consider the following assessment:

> [S]ome commentators have suggested that hospitals should qualify as links in the chain of distribution.... For the most part, however, courts refuse to treat hospitals as members of the chain of distribution on the notion that they provide a service (indeed, even more so than retail pharmacies, they look like sophisticated purchasers rather than mere retailers). Courts do not care that hospitals nowadays generate itemized bills that charge for everything used by a patient (often with a substantial mark-up), may enter into exclusive (and lucrative) purchasing agreements with particular wholesalers and manufacturers (almost the way an automobile dealership does), and may have the clout to influence manufacturers' design choices. Moreover, hospitals have the expertise to select and inspect drugs and devices—and patients presumably depend on hospitals to exercise that expertise—to say nothing of their active role in storage and handling.

Lars Noah, This Is Your Products Liability Restatement on Drugs, 74 Brook. L. Rev. 839, 923–25 (2009); see also Blankenship v. Ethicon, Inc., 656 S.E.2d 451, 458–59 (W.Va.2007) (rejecting plaintiffs' effort to characterize tort actions against hospitals that allegedly used improperly sterilized absorbable (Vicryl®) sutures as products liability rather than medical malpractice claims); cf. id. at 462–63 (Starcher, J., dissenting in part) (quoting *Rest. (3d)* § 6(e) as support for the proposition that hospitals should be deemed in the chain of distribution for manufacturing defects).

See generally Robert R. Willis, Comment, Strict Products Liability and Hospitals: Liability of the Modern Hospital and the Use of Surgically Implanted Medical Products, Tools, and Prosthetic Devices, 34 W. St. U. L. Rev. 191 (2007); Linda A. Sharp, Annotation, Liability of Hospital or Medical Practitioner Under Doctrine of Strict Liability in Tort, or Breach of Warranty, for Harm Caused by Drug, Medical Instrument, or Similar Device Used in Treating Patient, 65 A.L.R.5th 357 (2001 & 2011 Supp.). Under what circumstances, if any, should a hospital be vicariously liable (itself a form of strict tort liability) for an employee's negligent failure to select the most appropriate therapeutic product (i.e., how much control does the hospital exert over an individual physician's selection of a drug or medical device to treat a patient within its walls)?

2. *A duty to investigate the safety of technology used in the hospital?* In *Parker,* the court separately considered the plaintiff's negligence claim alleging that the hospital owed a duty to investigate the safety of the TMJ implants before allowing the devices to be used at the hospital. Although it remanded the case for consideration of this issue, the court observed that, "[i]f a duty to investigate would require considerable effort and expense by hospitals, resulting in higher costs for medical care, but would add little to patient safety, it would be unwise to impose the duty. Safety would not be enhanced, for example, if the hospital were merely duplicating efforts by the FDA, particularly given that the hospital would have a far smaller data base to work from, which could lead it to draw inaccurate inferences. On the other hand, if, as alleged by an expert witness provided by plaintiffs, hospitals already have a duty under federal law to conduct the sort of investigation plaintiffs would require, then there may be little reason not to impose liability on a hospital that injures a patient because of failure to perform that duty with due care." 919 P.2d at 1112. What kinds of medical products might be cheaply and efficiently inspected by a hospital prior to use (and therefore might justify a negligence claim if the inspection failed to detect a problem)?

3. *Negligence claims against hospitals.* See, e.g., Newmann v. United States, 938 F.2d 1258 (11th Cir.1991) (holding a government hospital liable for failure to monitor drug therapy); Kelley v. Wiggins, 724 S.W.2d 443 (Ark.1987) (clinic held negligent in administering drug); Fleming v. Baptist Gen. Convention, 742 P.2d 1087 (Okla.1987) (allowing a negligence claim against a hospital and physician for improper administration of an injectable drug subcutaneously rather than intravenously); Edinburg Hosp. Auth. v. Trevino, 941 S.W.2d 76 (Tex.1997); Harris County Hosp. Dist. v. Estrada, 872 S.W.2d 759 (Tex.Ct.App.1993) (allowing claim against hospital for patient death due to prescribing error that could have been prevented with proper function of hospital charting system).

PROBLEM #13. *THE MALFUNCTIONING PACEMAKER*

Walter Stewart has experienced periodic arrhythmias and tachycardia (racing heartbeat), so his cardiologist arranges for him to receive a pacemaker to prevent his heart from beating erratically. Dr. James Grant, a surgeon with staff privileges at Providence Hospital, successfully attaches the leads of a pacemaker manufactured by Cardiotronica to the correct portions of the heart muscle and then runs a test to check that the pacemaker is functioning properly. Finally, he uses a device to program the pacemaker to respond in specific ways whenever Mr. Stewart's heart begins an abnormal rhythm. (The programming device has been supplied by Cardiotronica free of charge to the hospital in exchange for the hospital's agreement to encourage its staff physicians to select Cardiotronica pacemakers for their patients.) Unfortunately, the programming device malfunctions, causing the pacemaker to send rapid electrical pulses to Mr. Stewart's heart. Before Dr. Grant and his team can disconnect the pacemaker, Mr. Stewart experiences cardiac arrest and suffers permanent disability. His adult daughter wants to sue Providence Hospital, Cardiotronica, and Dr. Grant. What claims can she make on her father's behalf, and what are her chances of success?

Chin v. St. Barnabas Medical Center

734 A.2d 778 (N.J.1999).

■ HANDLER, JUSTICE:

* * * Angelina Chin died at the age of forty-five from a massive air embolism during a diagnostic hysteroscopy at St. Barnabas Medical Center. An hysteroscopy is a procedure used to determine abnormalities in a woman's uterus. The doctor uses an hysteroscope, a wand-like instrument with a lens at one end, to view the walls of a woman's uterus on a television monitor. The physician's view of the uterus is enhanced by stretching the uterine walls with a continuous flow of fluid into the uterus. Typically, this type of medical procedure involves minimal risk. In the case of Ms. Chin, however, gas was pumped into her uterus rather than fluid, causing the gas to be introduced into her coronary arteries and resulting in the air embolism that killed her. The record clearly demonstrates that the embolism was the direct result of an incorrect hook-up of the hysteroscope.

Ms. Chin's treating physician, defendant Dr. Herbert Goldfarb, performed the procedure using an hysteroscope manufactured by defendant C.R. Bard, Inc. This type of hysteroscope, called the Hystero–Flo Pump, uses a pump driven by compressed nitrogen to create a vacuum that forces fluid to be drawn into a tube. The fluid passes through the tube, into the hysteroscope unit and finally into the patient's uterus. In order to perform this function, the Bard Hystero–Flo Pump has several tubes. An "irrigation tube" draws fluid into the woman's uterus and a "suction tube" draws waste fluid out of the uterus. Both are connected to the pump. A third tube connects the nitrogen source to the pump. Lastly, an "exhaust hose" carries the by-product of the nitrogen that drives the pump; it is attached to the gas line coming off the pump. When the exhaust hose arrives from the manufacturer, it is attached by three wire clips to indicate that it should remain away from the operating field and remain non-sterile.

In addition to Dr. Goldfarb, three nurses were in the operating room during this procedure. Defendants Nurse Teresa Leib and Nurse Immacula Louis–Charles were assigned to the procedure. Because Leib and Louis–Charles had no experience, familiarity, or training on the Hystero–Flo Pump, they asked defendant Nancy Hofgesang, a nurse who had some experience with the equipment, to assist. She acted as circulating nurse, although she was not officially scheduled by the hospital to be there.

During Ms. Chin's operation, one of the tubes was incorrectly connected to the hysteroscope, causing a closed circuit pathway that permitted the nitrogen gas to enter Ms. Chin's uterus and resulted in the embolism. Defendants presented several theories regarding which tube was wrongly attached. Because Dr. Goldfarb removed the tubes from the pump shortly after Ms. Chin went into cardiac arrest, their exact configuration was ascertainable only by inference. * * *

At trial, defendants presented conflicting testimony regarding which party or parties incorrectly hooked up the apparatus. At the close of evidence, defendant C.R. Bard moved for a directed verdict. The trial court granted the motion and none of the remaining parties argue that C.R. Bard is liable for the death of Ms. Chin. * * * The jury awarded plaintiff two million dollars in damages. It apportioned liability against the several defendants: Dr. Goldfarb, 20% liable; Nurse Leib, 20% liable; Nurse Hofgesang, 25% liable; St. Barnabas Medical Center, 35% liable. Nurse Louis–Charles was found not liable for the death of Ms. Chin. * * *

The primary issue in this case is the application of the principles set forth in our plurality opinion in *Anderson v. Somberg*, 338 A.2d 1 (N.J. 1975). In that case, the court rejected the traditional allocation of the burden of proof; rather than resting with the plaintiff, the burden of proof was shifted to the defendants. Thus, in a case governed by *Anderson*, the jury is instructed that at least one defendant must be found liable and that the defendants bear the burden of exonerating themselves from liability.

The facts in *Anderson v. Somberg* help in understanding the reasoning behind this exception to the usual allocation of burdens of proof. In *Anderson*, a surgical instrument broke during surgery and was lodged in the plaintiff's spinal canal, requiring multiple surgeries and resulting in severe and permanent physical injuries. The plaintiff, who was unconscious at the time, could not be blamed for the mishap. The plaintiff sued his physician, the hospital, the medical supply distributor and the manufacturer of the instrument. No explanation other than the negligence or fault of one of the defendants was available as the cause of the accident. Nevertheless, because the plaintiff could not prove which defendant caused the accident, the jury returned a verdict of no cause of action for each of the defendants. The evidence led to the inference that the break in the medical instrument may have been caused by weak metal, a crack during manufacture, cumulative misuse by other surgeons, or misuse by the operating surgeon. Hence, one, some or all of the defendants indisputably caused the instrument to break; a determination that no defendant was responsible would be an unjust result. * * *

Under the principles of *Anderson v. Somberg*, the plaintiff must show three things in order to shift the burden of proof to the defendants. First, the plaintiff must herself be entirely blameless. The fact pattern to which the principles of *Anderson* most readily apply is where a plaintiff was "clearly helpless or anesthetized" when her injury occurred. Second, the injury must be one that bespeaks negligence on the part of one or more of the defendants. Third, all the potential defendants must be before the court. That is, all those defendants who participated in the chain of events causing plaintiff's injury must be represented. * * *

All three requirements for the application of *Anderson* have been met. Angelina Chin, who was unconscious, helpless, and utterly blameless, suffered a fatal injury that bespeaks negligence on the part of one or more of the defendants. It is not contested that the air embolism could have been caused only by negligent use of the hysteroscope. All the potential defendants, that is, all those who participated in the chain of events leading up to Ms. Chin's injury, were sued in this case. * * * The verdict in this case reflects that the jury reached its determination conscientiously on sufficient evidence. The jurors thoroughly considered the evidence and exonerated Nurse Louis–Charles. Consistent with the jury's verdict, all the testimony indicated that this nurse was not at fault. * * * The jury, weighing the conflicting testimony and contradictory evidence, found various levels of liability among defendants. There is nothing irrational about these findings of fact and they are supported by the evidence. * * *

NOTES AND QUESTIONS

1. *Strict liability in disguise.* Does *Anderson v. Somberg* amount to a rule of strict liability extended to all links in the chain of distribution? See Maciag v. Strato Med. Corp., 644 A.2d 647 (N.J.App.Div.1994) (reversing summary judgment in favor of device manufacturer, physicians, and hospital, and remanding for trial so that each defendant could explain why it should not be held accountable for the plaintiff's injuries). No other jurisdiction has followed New Jersey's approach. Should manufacturers shoulder more responsibility for such foreseeable mistakes? See Gardiner Harris, U.S. Inaction Lets Look–Alike Tubes Kill Patients, N.Y. Times, Aug. 21, 2010, at A1.

2. *Durable medical equipment.* Courts have held that hospitals must have adequate equipment to furnish the medical services that they offer in a non-negligent manner. In *Washington v. Washington Hospital Center*, 579 A.2d 177 (D.C.1990), the plaintiff suffered a permanent catastrophic brain injury from oxygen deprivation while under general anesthesia. She alleged that the Washington Hospital Center (WHC), a tertiary care hospital, was negligent in failing to provide the anesthesiologists with an end-tidal carbon dioxide monitoring device that allows for the early detection of insufficient oxygen in time to prevent brain injury. After reviewing the expert testimony, statements from professional associations, and articles about anesthesiology practice published in peer-reviewed journals, the court concluded that a reasonable juror could find that the standard of care required WHC to supply such monitors at the time of the plaintiff's injury. With the emergence of sophisticated information technologies in medical practice, claims of institutional liability increasingly may become the focal point of efforts to reduce medical errors. See Nicolas P. Terry, When the "Machine That Goes Ping" Causes Harm: Default Torts Rules and Technologically–Mediated Health Care Injuries, 46 St. Louis U. L.J. 37 (2002); see also Robert L. Wears & Marc Berg, Editorial, Computer Technology and Clinical Work: Still Waiting for Godot, 293 JAMA 1261 (2005).

3. *Radiation overdoses and other mishaps.* In some instances, health care facilities enthusiastically embrace the latest machinery but fail to do an adequate job of training and supervising the employees responsible for its safe use. For instance, serious patient injuries have resulted from errors by technicians who operate various types of complex radiation-emitting equipment used in diagnosis and treatment. See Walt Bogdanich, While Technology Surges, Radiation Safeguards Lag, N.Y. Times, Jan. 27, 2010, at A1; see also Donald G. McNeil, Jr., M.R.I. Scanners' Strong Magnets Are Cited in a Rash of Accidents, N.Y. Times, Aug. 19, 2005, at A1 ("As the number of magnetic resonance imaging scanners in the country has soared from a handful in 1980 to about 10,000 today, and as magnets have quadrupled in power, careless accidents [involving certain types of metal objects] have become more frequent."). Undue human reliance on increasingly sophisticated computer controls for these devices may be partly to blame. In light of such problems, should manufacturers have to adopt still more fool-proof designs (or might that only make things worse)? See Walt Bogdanich, Seeking to Cut Radiation Errors, F.D.A. Toughens Process for Approving Equipment, N.Y. Times, Apr. 9, 2010, at A12; CT Scan Makers to Install Radiation Controls, Boston Globe, Feb. 26, 2010, at A2. Aside from errors, the overuse of CT scanners has raised some eyebrows. See Michael S. Lauer, Elements of Danger—The Case of Medical Imaging, 361 New Eng. J. Med. 841 (2009); Rebecca Smith–Bindman, Is Computed Tomography Safe?, 363 New Eng. J. Med. 1 (2010); Gardiner Harris, Scientists Say F.D.A. Ignored Warnings on Radiation Exposure, N.Y. Times, Mar. 29, 2010, at A14 ("The average lifetime dose of diagnostic radiation has increased sevenfold since 1980, driven in part by the increasing popularity of CT scans. Such scans can deliver the radiation equivalent of 400 chest X-rays. An estimated 70 million CT ... scans are performed in the United States every year, up from three million in the early 1980s, and as many as 14,000 people may die every year of radiation-induced cancers as a result, researchers estimate.").

4. *Reprocessing single-use only devices.* In the early 1980s, device manufacturers began developing and marketing increasingly sophisticated medical devices and surgical instruments. Because of concerns about the difficulty of sterilizing such devices after use (and perhaps to promote sales), manufacturers began to label these devices as "disposable" and "single-use devices" (SUDs). Hospitals, however, re-used certain SUDs in order to cut costs. This practice has become widespread and can have frightening results. For example, some hospitals have reused surgical instruments that had originally been used to operate on patients with Creutzfeldt–Jakob Disease, but, because ordinary sterilization procedures do not destroy the prions that cause this disease, subsequent patients may have been exposed. See Alec Klein, Reused Devices, Surgery's Deadly Suspects: Patients May Be Exposed to Rare Brain Disease from Prior Operations, Wash. Post, Dec. 30, 2005, at A3 ("Over the past five years, dozens of patients in at least four U.S. hospitals have been potentially exposed to the disease because their surgeons reused medical instruments first used on patients who had the rare brain disorder ...."). Such reprocessing and re-use of SUDs makes hospitals vulnerable to negligence claims. As one commentator has explained, the duty of care "includes efforts to establish and maintain appropriate reprocessing protocols and to insure that reuse of the device is safe and presents no increased risk of harm or injury to the patient." Emil P. Wang, Regulatory and Legal Implications of Reprocessing and Reuse of Single–Use Medical Devices, 56 Food & Drug L.J. 77, 93–95 (2001); see also Janice M. Hogan & Thomas Colonna, Products Liability Implications of Reprocessing and Reuse of Single–Use Medical Devices, 53 Food & Drug L.J. 385 (1998). Why not impose strict products liability in such cases (recall from Chapter 1(C) that the FDA now regulates hospitals engaged in reprocessing in the same manner as original equipment manufacturers)?

PART III

ECONOMICS AND INNOVATION

CHAPTER 9

PRICING AND PAYMENT SYSTEMS

In 2009, national health care expenditures totaled approximately $2.5 trillion, which accounted for 17.6 percent of the gross domestic product. See Robert Pear, Health Spending Rose in '09, but at Low Rate, N.Y. Times, Jan. 6, 2011, at A19 (reporting that 10 percent of that amount went to prescription drug costs); see also Janet Moore, Device Group Says Its Prices Are Stable, Minn. Star Trib., July 15, 2011, at 2D ("Spending on medical devices and diagnostic equipment ... totaled $147 billion [in 2009], or 5.9 percent of total national health expenditures"); Tony Pugh, Health Costs Running a Fever, Seattle Times, Feb. 22, 2006, at A3 (reporting estimates from CMS that "health-care spending will double to $4 trillion a year over the next decade" and that "prescription-drug spending will reach $446 billion in 2015, up from $203 billion in 2005"). Several factors account for this country's growing tab for therapeutic products: increased utilization, escalating prices charged for existing products, and the substitution of newer (and more expensive) products. See Jeff Donn, Are We Taking Too Many Drugs?, Newsday, Apr. 19, 2005, at B13 (reporting that 130 million Americans use prescription drugs every month, filling 3.5 billion prescriptions and resulting in more than $250 billion in sales by the pharmaceutical industry); see also Ceci Connolly, 2003 Drug Spending up Despite Pressure to Cut Costs, Wash. Post, Mar. 16, 2004, at A4 ("Cholesterol-lowering drugs Lipitor and Zocor, antidepressants Zyprexa and Zoloft, and heartburn medications Nexium and Prevacid each had sales in excess of $3 billion.").

This chapter examines how drugs and devices are paid for in this country. Reimbursement mechanisms directly affect the adoption and use of therapeutic products by health care providers. Securing FDA approval will represent a hollow victory unless insurers agree to pay for advanced (and increasingly expensive) medical technologies. See Barnaby J. Feder, When FDA Says Yes, but Insurers Say No, N.Y. Times, July 6, 2005, at C1 (reporting that agency licensure of Johnson & Johnson's implantable spinal disk failed to impress public and private health insurers, and noting that other approved medical devices have encountered similar resistance); Jeanne Whalen, Hurdles Multiply for Latest Drugs, Wall St. J., Aug. 1, 2011, at B1 ("Today, [FDA] regulatory approval means the push to create a new hit drug is just beginning. Getting increasingly frugal insurers and government health systems to cough up money for an expensive new drug ... is often an even tougher fight, and one drug companies are throwing vast resources into fighting."); see also Sally Squires, The Selling of the Stent, Wash. Post, Sept. 16, 2003, at F1 (reporting that manufacturers of drug-eluting stents simultaneously submitted their clinical trial results to

FDA and CMS, resulting in "the first medical device to receive approval for Medicare reimbursement prior to FDA approval"). For a snapshot of the approaches used in ten other major markets, see Richard Kingham & Joanna Wheeler, Government Regulation of Pricing and Reimbursement of Prescription Medicines: Results of a Recent Multi–Country Review, 64 Food & Drug L.J. 101 (2009).

A. INSURANCE COVERAGE OF MEDICAL TECHNOLOGIES

1. PUBLIC INSURANCE PROGRAMS

The Medicare and Medicaid insurance programs, which together cover almost 80 million individuals, fall under the authority of the Centers for Medicare & Medicaid Services (CMS), formerly known as the Health Care Financing Administration (HCFA) and housed within HHS. Medicare covers primarily elderly individuals, while Medicaid programs, which are administered at the state level, cover primarily poor or disabled individuals. For useful overviews, see John K. Iglehart, The American Health Care System: Medicaid, 340 New Eng. J. Med. 403 (1999); Timothy S. Jost, Governing Medicare, 51 Admin. L. Rev. 39 (1999); Marilyn Moon, Medicare, 344 New Eng. J. Med. 928 (2001).

Apart from drugs administered to patients in hospitals and skilled nursing facilities, Medicare originally paid for only a limited group of prescription drugs: immunosuppressants for organ transplant recipients, certain drugs for kidney disease patients, some anti-cancer agents, and hemophilia drugs. In 2003, Congress enacted the Medicare Prescription Drug, Improvement, and Modernization Act (MMA), creating Part D to cover outpatient prescription drugs starting in 2006 for beneficiaries in fee-for-service plans. See Pub. L. No. 108–173, 117 Stat. 2066 (2003); see also 70 Fed. Reg. 4194 (2005) (codified as amended at 42 C.F.R. pt. 423). The probable cost to the federal government, initially estimated as $400 billion over the first ten years, continues to balloon and attract criticism. See Ceci Connolly, Officials Defend Cost of Medicare Drug Benefit, Wash. Post, Feb. 17, 2005, at A7 (reporting a price tag for the first decade running two to three times higher than originally forecast); David Wessel, GAO Says Medicare Drug Benefit Will Cost More Than $6 Trillion, Wall St. J., Dec. 20, 2004, at A4 (reporting the long-term estimated liability just to cover all current workers and retirees); cf. Robert Pear, Federal Costs Dropping Under New Medicare Drug Plan, Administration Reports, N.Y. Times, Feb. 3, 2006, at A20 ("One reason for the lower cost is the intense competition among private insurers offering drug coverage."). Whatever the ultimate tab, the MMA ensures that coverage choices made by the federal government will become even more influential. See Robert Pear, Medicare Law Prompts a Rush for Lobbyists, N.Y. Times, Aug. 23, 2005, at A1 (reporting estimates that "Medicare and Medicaid will account for 37 percent of all spending on prescription drugs next year, up from 20 percent this year" and that "Medicare will spend more than $1 trillion on prescription drugs in the next 10 years," adding that "private insurers often look to Medicare as a guide in deciding what services to cover and how much to pay"); see also Stephen Heuser, Medicare Eases Fee Cuts, and Boston Scientific Fears, Boston Globe, Aug. 2, 2006, at F1 (explaining that CMS decisions dramatically affect the fortunes of medical device firms).

In its basic contours, the Part D benefit operates as follows: for an average premium of approximately $30 per month now, Medicare beneficiaries can purchase drug coverage subject to a deductible of $250 per year, 25% co-pays on the next $2,000 spent, no coverage for the next $2,850 spent (a gap referred to as the "doughnut hole"), and 5% co-pays on any additional amounts spent during the year (so-called "catastrophic" coverage), but only drugs included on a plan's formulary would count. See Robert Pear, Medicare Beneficiaries Confused and Angry over Gap in Drug Coverage, N.Y. Times, July 30, 2006, § 1, at 14; see also Bruce Stuart et al., Riding the Rollercoaster: The Ups and Downs in Out-of-Pocket Spending Under the Standard Medicare Drug Benefit, Health Aff., July–Aug. 2005, at 1022 (evaluating the likely effects of these rules). The program relies on private insurers to offer seniors a variety—or, as some have complained, a bewildering array—of options (differing primarily in the lists of drugs covered, which can change monthly while beneficiaries could only change plans once a year). See Susan Levine, Seniors Find Medicare Drug Plan Options Bewildering, Wash. Post, Nov. 19, 2005, at A1 (describing confusion over the wide array of premiums, deductibles, co-payments, and exceptions found among the dozens of plans available); Richard Wolf, Medicare Drug Premiums Steady, USA Today, Sept. 29, 2006, at 1A. Physicians and pharmacists also have found it difficult to navigate the various new formulary and prior authorization systems for Medicare beneficiaries. See Julie Appleby, Medicare Red Tape Snares Drugs, USA Today, Feb. 28, 2006, at 1B; Robert Pear, Rules of Medicare Drug Plans Slow Access to Benefits, N.Y. Times, Feb. 14, 2006, at A17 ("Most states have at least 40 Medicare drug plans."). Fearing that employers who provide health insurance for retirees might decide to drop their drug benefits, the government offered generous subsidies for maintaining coverage. See Robert Pear, Retirees Are Paying More for Health Benefits, Study Says, N.Y. Times, Dec. 15, 2004, at A27.

Poorer beneficiaries (defined as those with incomes at or below 150% of the poverty line) would face lower (or no) premiums, deductibles, and co-pays. See Edward Walsh & Bill Brubaker, Drug Benefit's Impact Detailed: Many Will Face Big Out-of-Pocket Costs, Wash. Post, Nov. 26, 2003, at A10; see also Ceci Connolly, Millions Not Joining Medicare Drug Plan: Despite Outreach, Poor Seniors Miss out on Low–Cost Coverage, Wash. Post, Feb. 21, 2006, at A1. Senior citizens and the disabled who had received drug coverage through Medicaid programs (so-called "dual eligibles") but had not already switched were automatically (and randomly) enrolled in one of the new Medicare plans, which created confusion among beneficiaries unaware of the switch or confused by the less generous coverage under Medicare. See Ceci Connolly, The States Step in as Medicare Falters: Seniors Being Turned Away, Overcharged Under New Prescription Drug Program, Wash. Post, Jan. 14, 2006, at A1; see also Julie Kristen Lappas, Note, Changing Horses in the Middle of the Stream: The Medicare Part D Bidding Process and Its Effect on the Stability of Dual Eligible Beneficiaries, 38 Pub. Cont. L.J. 487 (2009). The switch of dual eligibles to Medicare drug plans promised to reduce state Medicaid expenditures substantially, but the federal government got to recoup these amounts. See Robert Pear, States Protest Contributions to Drug Plan, N.Y. Times, Oct. 18, 2005, at A24 (reporting that the CBO "estimate[d] that the required state contributions, also known as clawback payments, will total" $130 billion over the first decade); see also Evan Halper, State to Sue U.S. over Medicare, L.A. Times, Feb. 2, 2006, at B3 (explaining that some states have challenged the formulas used to calculate these payments). Some of the Medicare drug benefit's more prominent features get mentioned where relevant in the materials that follow. See generally Timothy S. Jost, The Most Important Health Care Legislation of the Millennium (So Far): The Medicare Modernization Act, 5 Yale J. Health Pol'y L. & Ethics 437 (2005); Elliot Golding, Medicare Part D: Rights Without Remedies, Bars to Relief, and Miles of Red Tape, 77 Geo. Wash. L. Rev. 1044 (2009); David Pratt, The New Medicare Part D Prescription Drug Benefit, 17 Alb. L.J. Sci. & Tech. 337 (2007).

Apart from the fact that full implementation got deferred until 2014 (and subject to the possibility that the courts or Congress will unravel all or part of it), the health reform legislation enacted in 2010 will have fewer direct impacts on payment for medical technologies. See Patient Protection and Affordable Care Act (PPACA), Pub. L. No. 111–148, 124 Stat. 804 (2010). Medicare Part D's doughnut hole will gradually close over the course of a decade. See David S. Hilzenrath, Higher Drug Prices Feared After "Doughnut Hole" Plan, Wash. Post, Sept. 21, 2010, at A6 (reporting that initially seniors will receive a 50% discount on affected purchases); see also Richard L. Kaplan, Analyzing the Impact of the New Health Care Reform Legislation on Older Americans, 18 Elder L.J. 213 (2011). The drug and device industries agreed to help underwrite implementation of the law: under a newly imposed annual fee, the IRS will allocate an amount fixed by statute ($2.5 billion for 2011) among branded prescription drug manufacturers that supply pharmaceuticals to government-covered entities, and device makers face a 2.3% excise tax starting in 2013. One of the centerpieces of the new law requires that private health insurers offer policies to individuals and small companies that provide an "essential benefits" package, including payment for prescription drugs and devices, but left the details to HHS (using benefits provided under typical employer plans as a guide). See PPACA § 1302; N.C. Aizenman, "Basic" Gets Tricky in the Health–Care Law, Wash. Post, Jan. 15, 2011, at A2 ("Should health insurers have to cover treatment of Lyme disease ... [o]r infertility treatments? Can they limit the number of chemotherapy rounds allowed cancer patients? ... [A]n independent advisory group convened by the Obama administration launched what is likely to be a long and emotional process to answer such questions."). Separately, the industry has expressed some alarm about the prospect of price controls imposed by the Independent Payment Advisory Board (IPAB), a new high-level group responsible for making recommendations to reduce Medicare costs that would become binding unless Congress acts to reject them. See N.C. Aizenman, Panel Charged with Medicare Cost-cutting Under Fire for Powers, Wash. Post, Aug. 14, 2011, at A5; Tracy Jan, Biotech Fights Medicare Cost Panel, Boston Globe, June 27, 2011, at A1; see also Mark V. Pauly, What If Technology Never Stops Improving? Medicare's Future Under Continuous Cost Increases, 60 Wash. & Lee L. Rev. 1233 (2003).

Friedrich v. HHS

894 F.2d 829 (6th Cir.1990).

■ LIVELY, SENIOR CIRCUIT JUDGE:

* * * The Medicare Act consists of two parts or programs. Part A provides insurance against the cost of institutional health services. Part B, the portion at issue here, is a voluntary, supplemental medical insurance program that covers 80 percent of the "reasonable charge" for a number of services, including certain physician services, x-rays, lab tests and medical supplies. The purpose of this section is to complement existing insurance coverage for the aged and disabled. Part B is financed through monthly fee charges to the beneficiaries and funding from the government. * * *

Because of the substantial dimensions of the program, Part B is managed for the Secretary by "carriers," insurance companies who administer the payment of qualifying claims. The Secretary pays the carriers' costs resulting from claims administration and the carriers, acting as the Secretary's agents, in turn determine whether a claimed item or service is covered by the program. The carriers make this determination in strict accordance with the Medicare statute and the regulations, instructions and guidelines promulgated by the Secretary. * * *

[U]nder Part B, the Secretary and the insurance carriers are required to deny reimbursement for services that are not "reasonable and necessary for the diagnosis or treatment" of a claimant's illness or injury. 42 U.S.C. § 1395y(a)(1). A finding of what services are "reasonable and necessary" is often made on a case-by-case basis by the carrier. In more difficult cases, however, the Health Care Financing Administration (HCFA), a component of the Department of Health & Human Services (HHS), will make an assessment and then issue a "national coverage determination" clearly indicating to the carriers whether the particular item should be considered covered or not. National coverage determinations issued by HCFA are published in the Part B Carriers Manual (the Manual) and are therefore binding on the carriers and their hearing officers.

In making its assessment of reasonableness and necessity HCFA often relies on the Public Health Service (PHS) for an evaluation of the safety and effectiveness of a particular service and the extent to which it has been accepted by the medical community. Within PHS, every review of this kind is undertaken by the Office of Health Technology Assessment (OHTA) of the National Center for Health Services Research and Health Care Technology Assessment (NCHSRHCTA). OHTA usually places a notice in the *Federal Register* announcing that an assessment is underway and soliciting comments from interested parties. During the assessment process OHTA also seeks information and recommendations from governmental agencies such as the National Institutes of Health (NIH) and the Food and Drug Administration (FDA). OHTA also consults with professional organizations and medical specialty groups to determine whether the procedure is generally accepted by the medical community as being safe and effective, and conducts a review of the medical literature. HCFA then issues a national coverage determination based on its consideration of PHS's recommendations.

The service at issue here, chelation therapy, is a treatment for atherosclerosis (obstructed arteries). The treatment consists of intravenous injections of disodium edetate solution. Proponents of the treatment believe that the disodium edetate, which binds ("chelates") with calcium, removes the calcium-containing plaque that clogs arteries. According to the government, however, this treatment has been widely discredited by the general medical community as being ineffective and unsafe.

An examination of the record indicates that as early as 1970, HCFA had issued instructions restricting Medicare coverage of disodium edetate to treatment for hypercalcemia, ventricular arrhythmias, heart block associated with digitalis toxicity and scleroderma. This position was apparently embraced at the urging of PHS, which had consulted with various medical organizations and the FDA. As early as 1970 the FDA-approved labeling for the drug stated that disodium edetate was indicated for the severe conditions mentioned above, but not "for the treatment of generalized arteriosclerosis associated with advancing age."

The HCFA instructions on disodium edetate remained in effect until 1980, when HCFA replaced most specific drug coverage determinations with general criteria for intermediary and carrier use in determining coverage. The new 1980 criteria permitted payment for any use of an FDA-approved drug determined by the carrier to be reasonable and necessary, except for those uses specifically disapproved by the FDA or for which coverage might be precluded by a national instruction.

Subsequent to the issuance of the 1980 Carriers Manual, HCFA requested that NCHSRHCTA review chelation therapy and make a recommendation as to Medicare coverage. NCHSRHCTA published a notice in the *Federal Register* announcing its planned assessment and requesting interested parties to submit relevant information. NCHSRHCTA additionally sought evaluations of chelation therapy from a number of professional organizations and medical specialty groups. As a result of this notice a large number of opinions by physicians and various medical organizations were obtained. Based on this information, NCHSRHCTA issued a comprehensive report and assessment recommending that the Medicare program not cover chelation therapy. HCFA responded to the assessment by issuing a national coverage determination in February 1982 instructing intermediaries and carriers not to pay for chelation therapy under Medicare. * * *

The plaintiff Michael J. Friedrich, a Medicare Part B beneficiary, requested reimbursement for expenses related to chelation therapy. Friedrich received these treatments in February, March and April of 1983. The total cost of these services was $410.70. The plaintiff's insurance carrier, Nationwide Mutual Insurance, refused to reimburse the claimant for these expenses.

On May 19, 1983, plaintiff filed a claim with Nationwide seeking review of the earlier denial of his claim. The plaintiff's claim was again denied by letter on June 24, 1983. On July 25, 1983, Friedrich requested a carrier hearing review. This hearing was held on March 19, 1984. At the hearing both the plaintiff and his physician, Dr. Frackleton, testified as to the benefits of chelation therapy for the treatment of atherosclerosis. The witnesses also submitted written material. The Secretary offered no contrary evidence. On April 25, 1984, the hearing officer found that "although the evidence and testimony presented at this hearing was impressive and implies the efficacy of chelation therapy as a viable alternative to conventional treatment for coronary artery disease, this does not alter the instructions contained in the carrier's manual that EDTA chelation therapy for the treatment or prevention of atherosclerosis is not covered." Reimbursement was denied on this basis. * * *

The plaintiff argues that the chelation therapy determination represented a departure from Medicare's general policy with respect to coverage. It argues that the general policy is to treat drugs approved for marketing by the FDA as satisfying the statutory "reasonable and necessary" requirement for Medicare reimbursement. He emphasizes the fact that a passage in the Manual states that the disqualification of chelation therapy is an exception to Medicare's general policy on coverage of drugs. The same statement continues, however, by stating that the general rule is to treat FDA-approved drugs prescribed by a physician as covered "if the Medicare contractor determines the use is reasonable and necessary." The Secretary asserts that the purpose of the determination was to restate the Department's consistent policy that, though considered reasonable and necessary for treatment of some illnesses, chelation therapy does not satisfy this statutory requirement when used for the treatment of atherosclerosis.

The record reveals that as early as 1970 the Department of Health, Education and Welfare had advised by notices in the *Federal Register* that disodium edetate was not considered effective for the treatment of generalized arteriosclerosis. (Atherosclerosis is a stage of the chronic disease arteriosclerosis.) The Secretary states that this has been the consistent position of the Department and that the 1982 national coverage determination did not represent a change of position.

In 1980 the Secretary began the practice of examining some drugs individually rather than qualifying all FDA-approved drugs if they were found by the Part B carriers to be reasonable and necessary. The 1982 determination implemented this new policy. In effect, it made the determination of reasonableness and necessity with respect to a particular use of chelation therapy rather than leaving that determination to the carriers. The Secretary states that in doing so, he created no new rights or duties; he merely applied the statutory requirements to a particular use of a given drug and method of treatment. The "new policy" referred to in the Manual is the *method* of dealing with FDA-approved drugs, not a new policy with respect to the reasonableness or necessity for use of chelation therapy in the treatment of atherosclerosis. * * * The record as a whole convinces us that the Secretary has been consistent in his determination that chelation therapy is not reasonable and necessary for the diagnosis or treatment of atherosclerosis. Thus the 1982 determination did not represent a departure from a previous evaluation of this medical procedure. * * *

The Medicare program covers the full range of modern medicine and pharmacology. It is comprehensive and operates through a complex structure. National standards are essential if there is to be uniformity and equality in the administration of Medicare. The Secretary has chosen to seek uniformity by requiring Part B carriers to abide by all regulations in the Manual. It is inconceivable to us that the Secretary might be required to comply with the full panoply of APA notice and comment requirements in promulgating national standards for individual drugs and medical procedures. This is a classic case of a rule that fits perfectly the "common theme" of the § 553(b)(A) exception for rules that "accommodate situations where the policies promoted by public participation in rulemaking are outweighed by the countervailing considerations of effectiveness, efficiency, expedition and reduction in expense."

The Medicare Act mandates that only reasonable and necessary medical services are reimbursable. The national coverage determination does not "fill the gaps" in the statute. Thus, it creates no new law. Rather, it interprets the statutory language "reasonable and necessary" as applied to a particular medical service or method of treatment. The district court erred in concluding that the determination is a legislative rule and therefore is invalid for failure of the Secretary to comply with the requirements of 5 U.S.C. § 553(b). * * *

The first step in deciding a procedural due process claim is to identify the interest to which the due process attaches. Here, Friedrich claimed a property interest in Medicare benefits * * * * The only legitimate claim of entitlement under Medicare is to those services that are reasonable and necessary. There is no legitimate claim of entitlement to a given medical procedure just because a doctor prescribes it or a patient requests it. The record in this case reveals that the plaintiff had no more than a unilateral expectation that he would receive reimbursement under the Medicare program for chelation therapy. * * *

The record discloses that NCHSRHCTA received and considered large volumes of material, mostly anecdotal, in favor of chelation therapy before HCFA made its final evaluation and issued the national coverage determination in February 1982. We have found the evaluation procedure valid as meeting the requirements for promulgation of an interpretative rule.

Friedrich does not have a due process right to have his individual claim considered de novo in the face of the Secretary's determination. Having made a national coverage determination, the Secretary is not required to defend it in response to individual claims by every person who disagrees with the decision to deny coverage. The fact that the hearing officer was bound by the determination did not deny Friedrich process to which he was due. * * *

Goodman v. Sullivan

712 F.Supp. 334 (S.D.N.Y.1989).

■ WALKER, DISTRICT JUDGE:

* * * Plaintiff was suffering from a progressive speech impediment. In February 1985, plaintiff's physician suggested that plaintiff undergo a diagnostic test known as a magnetic resonance imaging procedure (MRI) to determine the underlying cause of his condition. Plaintiff underwent a MRI and subsequently presented a claim for $675.00 for the cost of the test to the Medicare Part B carrier in his area. The carrier denied plaintiff reimbursement for the MRI on the ground that MRIs were not covered under Medicare Part B as of February 1985. * * *

Plaintiff claims, however, that the regulation denying coverage for any medical procedures unapproved by the Secretary violates 42 U.S.C. § 1395 in that it is contrary to the Act's mandate that the Secretary: (a) pay for all medically necessary treatment and, (b) not interfere with the practice of medicine. Plaintiff maintains that no regulation can establish an irrebuttable presumption of the lack of medical necessity without countermanding the Act. * * * That the Secretary eventually approved MRIs for reimbursement is immaterial. As noted previously, plaintiff does not merely challenge the Secretary's policy regarding MRIs. Rather, plaintiff broadly challenges the validity of the Secretary's regulation denying coverage for any techniques unapproved by the Secretary. * * *

While Congress created specific exclusions from coverage and provided that in no case may payment be made for any expenses incurred for items and services which "are not reasonable and necessary for the diagnosis or treatment of illness or injury," 42 U.S.C. § 1395y(a)(1)(A), it never provided that payment must be made at all times when services are deemed "medically necessary." Neither plaintiff nor the court can locate such language either in the Act or in the legislative history. Rather, Congress delegated to the Secretary the authority to promulgate regulations for administering the Medicare program, and provided the Secretary with great discretion in determining what items or services will be covered under Medicare Part B. The Secretary is specifically provided with discretion in considering whether diagnostic tests shall be covered in 42 U.S.C. § 1395x(s).

Plaintiff mistakenly contends that once a physician has concluded that a service or item is medically necessary, the Secretary cannot deny reimbursement. Congress has not provided that all medically necessary items or services must be covered under Medicare Part B. * * * [T]he rules promulgated by the Secretary do not conflict with the Act but, rather, stay well within the general intent of Congress in enacting Part B of Medicare. Moreover, the court finds no evidence that either the Secretary's decision to deny plaintiff MRI benefits or the Secretary's regulations themselves interfere with the practice of medicine. * * *

CMS, Notice, *Revised Process for Making Medicare National Coverage Determinations*

68 Fed. Reg. 55,634 (2003).

* * * [W]e published a notice of intent to engage in rulemaking for coverage criteria (May 16, 2000, 65 Fed. Reg. 31,124) and had a subsequent town hall meeting. Given that there are substantial competing interests about the coverage criteria, we believe it best not to pursue rulemaking. In the meantime, as we have done in the past 35 years, we would continue to need to make coverage decisions and interpret what is "reasonable and necessary." We believe that in the interest of expediting NCDs [national coverage determinations] and making the process as predictable as possible that, in the interim, nonbinding sector-specific guidance documents would be helpful. Sector-specific guidance documents refer to how our expectations and evaluation of evidence may differ in some respects depending on the nature of the topic under review. Evidence can vary greatly, for example, between a diagnostic and an item of DME [durable medical equipment] or between a near-term fatal condition and a life-long chronic condition. * * *

In general, an NCD is a national policy statement granting, limiting, or excluding Medicare coverage for a specific medical item or service. Often, an NCD is written in terms of a particular patient population that may receive (or not receive) Medicare reimbursement for a particular item or service. An NCD is binding on all Medicare carriers, fiscal intermediaries (FIs), quality improvement organizations (QIOs), health maintenance organizations (HMOs), competitive medical plans (CMPs), and health care prepayment plans (HCPPs). * * *

We contract with private insurance companies, referred to as carriers and FIs, to process Medicare claims; that is, claims-payment contractors. Local QIOs are also involved in the claims adjudication process. We refer to all of these entities as "Medicare contractors." Medicare contractors review and adjudicate claims to ensure that Medicare payments are made only for those items or services covered under Medicare Part A or Part B. In the absence of a specific NCD, coverage determinations are made locally by the Medicare contractors within the boundaries established by the law. Sometimes these determinations are made on a claim-by-claim basis. Medicare contractors will also publish local coverage determinations (LCDs) that will provide guidance to the public and medical community within a specified geographic area. * * *

Both CMS and the FDA review scientific evidence, and may review the same evidence, to make purchasing and regulatory decisions, respectively. However, CMS and its contractors make coverage determinations and the FDA conducts premarket review of products under different statutory standards and different delegated authority. Whereas the FDA must determine that a product is safe and effective as a condition of approval, CMS must determine that the product is reasonable and necessary as a condition of coverage under section 1862(a)(1)(A) of the Act. CMS adopts FDA determinations of safety and effectiveness, and CMS evaluates whether or not the product is reasonable and necessary for the Medicare population. Although an FDA-regulated product must receive FDA approval or clearance (unless exempt from the FDA premarket review process) for at least one indication to be eligible for Medicare coverage, except for Category B devices under an IDE clinical trial, FDA approval/clearance alone does not generally entitle that device to coverage. * * *

During our review of an NCD request, we may require an HTA [Health Technology Assessment] to complete our review. Generally, an HTA provides an independent analysis of all scientific and clinical evidence available on a particular health care technology. We may request an HTA when there is conflicting or complex medical and scientific literature available, or when we believe an independent analysis of all relevant literature will assist us in determining whether an item or service is reasonable and necessary. We may also request an HTA in preparation for an upcoming MCAC [Medicare Coverage Advisory Committee] meeting. We will obtain services from the Agency for Healthcare Research and Quality or a third party with the requisite experience in HTA and evidence-based medicine to ensure the technical competence and fairness of the HTA. * * *

The primary role of the MCAC is to provide independent, expert advice and assistance to us in making sound coverage decisions based upon the reasoned application of scientific evidence. Voting members must possess the scientific and technical competence commensurate with this purpose. In addition, a consumer and industry representative serve as nonvoting members on each panel. * * * The MCAC meetings are open to the public, and time is allotted for public comment on the particular coverage issue under consideration. * * *

The NCD (issued as a program memorandum, manual instruction, *Federal Register* notice, or CMS ruling) will include the effective date when our Medicare contractors will implement any change in payment that may result from the NCD. * * * [A]n NCD is binding on all Medicare contractors; that is, carriers, FIs, QIOs, HMOs, CMPs, and HCPPs. NCDs that expand coverage are binding on Medicare+Choice plans. We will also publish a reference to each national coverage decision in the *Federal Register* as part of our quarterly listing of program issuances. * * *

NOTES AND QUESTIONS

1. *NCDs*. The agency repeatedly has failed to adopt clear criteria used for making coverage decisions. See Jacqueline Fox, The Hidden Role of Cost:

Medicare Decisions, Transparency and Public Trust, 79 U. Cin. L. Rev. 1 (2010); Muriel R. Gillick, Medicare Coverage for Technological Innovations—Time for New Criteria?, 350 New Eng. J. Med. 2199 (2004); Eleanor D. Kinney, Medicare Coverage Decisionmaking and Appeal Procedures: Can Process Meet the Challenge of New Medical Technology?, 60 Wash. & Lee L. Rev. 1461 (2003); Sean R. Tunis, Why Medicare Has Not Established Criteria for Coverage Decisions, 350 New Eng. J. Med. 2196 (2004); Jane Zhang, Medicare Official Key to Spending, Wall St. J., Oct. 27, 2009, at A6; see also Peter J. Neumann et al., Medicare's National Coverage Decisions for Technologies, 1999–2007, 27 Health Aff. 1620 (2008). Courts generally have rejected challenges to restrictive NCDs. See, e.g., Aitken v. Shalala, 986 F.Supp. 57 (D.Mass.1997); Bosko v. Shalala, 995 F.Supp. 580 (W.D.Pa. 1996); see also Timothy S. Jost, Health Care Rationing in the Courts: A Comparative Study, 21 Hastings Int'l & Comp. L. Rev. 639 (1998) (finding significant judicial deference). In one of its most significant recent coverage determinations, CMS expanded eligibility for implantable cardioverter-defibrillators (ICDs). See David Brown, Medicare to Cover Heart Devices, Wash. Post, June 7, 2003, at A4; Robert Pear, Medicare to Expand Coverage of Heart Devices, N.Y. Times, Jan. 20, 2005, at A16; see also Barnaby J. Feder, U.S. Expands Some Stent Reimbursement Coverage, N.Y. Times, Mar. 18, 2005, at C4 (reporting that Medicare broadened payment for carotid stenting six months after the FDA approved the first device for use in this procedure); Rick Weiss & David Brown, Medicare Will Pay for Alzheimer's Scan: Doubts About the Technology Lead Agency to Cover Only Some Patients, Wash. Post, Sept. 17, 2004, at A2 (reporting that CMS authorized coverage for PET scans in only a narrow subset of suspected Alzheimer's patients). Private insurers often follow the lead of CMS in making coverage decisions.

2. *To cover or not to cover?* Just a couple of months after the FDA approved Provenge® (sipuleucel-T), an active cellular immunotherapy for advanced prostate cancer, CMS announced that it would initiate a review to decide whether it would cover the $93,000 tab per patient for an average life extension of four months (less than two months more than standard chemotherapy but with a better quality of life). See Andrew Pollack, New Drugs Fight Prostate Cancer, but at High Cost, N.Y. Times, June 28, 2011, at A1 ("Medicare officials denied that price was the reason for the review. But some patient advocates and politicians portrayed the review as a step toward rationing. Private insurers are also paying only if drugs are used according to the label ...."); Rob Stein, Medicare Renews Debate on Health Costs, Wash. Post, Nov. 8, 2010, at A1 (quoting an NCI official's conclusion that $270,000/life year was excessive); id. ("Although Medicare is not supposed to take cost into consideration when making such rulings, the decision to launch a formal examination has raised concerns among cancer experts, drug companies, lawmakers, prostate cancer patients and advocacy groups."); see also Andrew Pollack, Medicare Will Cover Prostate Cancer Drug, N.Y. Times, Mar. 31, 2011, at B2 (reporting that CMS decided to issue a proposed NCD that would cover Provenge only for patients with the particular stage of cancer specified in approved labeling);

cf. Andrew Pollack, Approval for Drug That Treats Melanoma, N.Y. Times, Mar. 26, 2011, at B1 (reporting that the sponsor of Yervoy® (ipilimumab), another novel immunotherapy providing a similarly modest average extension of survival in advanced cancer patients, announced that it would charge $120,000 for a full course of treatment). Most CMS coverage decisions have a decidedly ad hoc quality to them. See, e.g., Reed Abelson, Heart Scans Still Covered by Medicare, N.Y. Times, Mar. 13, 2008, at C1 (CT angiography); Denise Grady, Studies Question Using Cement for Spine Fractures, N.Y. Times, Aug. 6, 2009, at A18 ("Medicare had no national policy on vertebroplasty and had been letting states decide."); Stephanie Saul, (Not So) Standard Procedure, N.Y. Times, Dec. 17, 2008, at B1 (reporting uneven coverage decisions for CyberKnife, a device for treating prostate cancer, adding that "[t]he disparities result from a policy principle as old as Medicare itself, in which officials in Washington leave many reimbursement decisions to the discretion of 15 regional contractors around the country"); id. ("[O]ver the years, Medicare has resolved only about 300 such [new technology] questions with blanket national coverage rulings. Meanwhile, thousands of other coverage policies have been—and continue to be—decided region by region."); see also Patricia S. Keenan et al., Biotechnology and Medicare's New Technology Policy: Lessons from Three Case Studies, 25 Health Aff. 1260 (2006).

3. *Opportunities for synergy between FDA and CMS?* Although relevant, FDA approval does not ensure Medicare coverage. See Christopher D. Zalesky, Considering Change to CMS's National Coverage Decision Process: Applying Lessons Learned from FDA as a Regulator of Access to Healthcare Technology, 57 Food & Drug L.J. 73 (2002). In fact, CMS has made some of its recent coverage determinations conditional on patient tracking to confirm safety and effectiveness (in essence, a CMS-imposed Phase IV study requirement). See Gina Kolata, Medicare Covering New Treatments, but with a Catch, N.Y. Times, Nov. 5, 2004, at A1; Andrew Pollack, Gene Test for Dosage of Warfarin Is Rebuffed, N.Y. Times, May 5, 2009, at B3; Rick Weiss, Medicare to Cover Cardiac Device: Plan Raises Issue of Line Between Care and Research, Wash. Post, Jan. 20, 2005, at A1 (explaining that the NCD for ICDs "represents the most aggressive effort yet to use the federal insurance plan for the elderly as a backdoor way to learn more about what works and what does not in medicine"); see also Sandra J. Carnahan, Medicare's Coverage with Study Participation Policy: Clinical Trials or Tribulations?, 7 Yale J. Health Pol'y L. & Ethics 229 (2007); Lars Noah, Coerced Participation in Clinical Trials: Conscripting Human Research Subjects, 62 Admin. L. Rev. 329, 342–66 (2010) (responding to the NIH's published defenses of the ethical propriety of this policy); id. at 362 ("[S]emantic quibbles should not distract from efforts to judge the acceptability of conditions on public health insurance coverage that would obligate patients to 'volunteer' for research, and the various indignities that come with it, in order to secure access to a needed item or service."); id. at 366 ("CMS has discovered a creative way to use its leverage over beneficiaries in order to generate useful information.... The CSP policy appears to run afoul of federal research regulations, which only represent ethical minima in any event. Indeed, the agency's effort to skirt those regulations and justify its ethically dubious initiative rather than to steer well clear of existing restrictions itself sets a poor example for the broader research community.").

4. *Differentiating among devices.* In an earlier proposal, HCFA explained that "FDA approval for the marketing of a medical device will not necessarily lead to a favorable coverage recommendation, particularly if FDA requirements have been met by means of a [PMN rather than a PMA]." 54 Fed. Reg. 4302, 4307 (1989) ("This is because a section 510(k) notice generally does not involve clinical data showing safety and effectiveness."), superseded, 64 Fed. Reg. 22,619, 22,622 (1999). Conversely, the lack of FDA approval will not necessarily foreclose coverage. See 42 C.F.R. § 405.201–.211 (distinguishing between experimental and non-experimental IDEs); Cedars–Sinai Med. Ctr. v. Shalala, 939 F.Supp. 1457 (C.D.Cal.1996) (invalidating an earlier policy refusing to cover any IDEs), rev'd on other grds. after remand, 177 F.3d 1126 (9th Cir.1999). Even for devices subject to PMA requirements, recall that the FDA applies a more flexible standard than used for drugs, which may undermine efforts to secure insurance coverage after device approval. See, e.g., Sandra G. Boodman, Now There's a Device to Treat Depression: If Only There Were Solid Evidence That It Works, Wash. Post, Mar. 21, 2006, at F1 (reporting that, after the FDA approved a narrow antidepressant indication for the vagus nerve stimulator (VNS, a.k.a. "a pacemaker for the brain" previously approved to treat severe epilepsy) on the basis of a single and uncontrolled clinical trial, thousands of patients sought authorization from their insurers to undergo the $25,000 implantation procedure: "So far neither the federal government nor private insurers have agreed to cover VNS for depression on a routine basis, although many have approved individual cases.... Two recent technology assessments by major insurance companies have concluded there is insufficient evidence to find that VNS works for depression."); Purva Patel, The Word for Cyberonics Is No: Medicare Says It Won't Pay for Use of Device to Treat Depression, Hous. Chron., May 5, 2007, at D1 (same); Jessica Sidman, Artificial Spinal Disc Generates Controversy: Effectiveness Is Questioned, USA Today, July 26, 2006, at 8D.

5. *Medicare drug benefit.* CMS will not issue NCDs for out-patient prescription drugs, leaving the development of formularies to the private insurers offering plans to Medicare beneficiaries, subject to certain guidelines. Insurers must cover at least two drugs within each of 146 identified therapeutic categories (or distinct classes within such broader categories). See Robert Pear, Advisory Panel Lists Drugs It Wants New Law to Cover, N.Y. Times, Jan. 4, 2005, at A12 (reporting concerns that, under guidelines prepared by the U.S. Pharmacopeia, insurers theoretically could decline to cover entire subclasses of newer drugs such as statins for lowering cholesterol or SSRIs for treating depression). In reviewing proposals from insurers seeking to participate, however, CMS has demanded fairly comprehensive coverage of widely prescribed drugs. See Robert Pear, Medicare Insists on Wider Choice in Drug Benefits, N.Y. Times, June 15, 2005, at A1 ("[T]he government has been insisting that they cover not just one or two drugs to treat each disease, but most or substantially all the drugs available for certain conditions.''); see also R. Jeffrey Smith & Jeffrey H. Birnbaum, Drug Bill Demonstrates Lobby's Pull, Wash. Post, Jan. 12, 2007, at A1 (''Drug companies spent more on lobbying than any other industry between 1998 and 2005—$900 million, according to the nonpartisan Center for Responsive Politics.''). The inclusion of erectile dysfunction (ED) drugs, which could cost $2 billion during the first decade of the Medicare drug benefit, triggered criticism. See Robert Pear, Companies Fight to Ensure Coverage for Erectile Drugs, N.Y. Times, Feb. 22, 2005, at A12; Sheryl G. Stolberg, House Rejects Coverage of Impotence Pills, N.Y. Times, June 25, 2005, at A10. The MMA already had craved out from coverage anxiety drugs such as Xanax®. In addition, even though CMS now regards obesity as a disease (and may pay for bariatric surgery), it will not cover weight-loss medications. See Daniel Akst, Shedding Pounds with Medicare, N.Y. Times, July 25, 2004, § 3, at 1; cf. Rob Stein, N.C. Health Insurer to Offer Coverage for Weight Problems, Wash. Post, Oct. 13, 2004, at A2.

6. *Coverage under Medicaid.* Section 1927(d)(2) of the Social Security Act provides that when a state chooses to include outpatient drugs within its Medicaid program it must cover (with a very few exceptions) all FDA-approved prescription drugs for their medically accepted indications. See Visser v. Taylor, 756 F.Supp. 501, 505–07 (D.Kan.1990) (preliminarily enjoining Medicaid program from refusing to cover Clozaril® (clozapine) for a patient with treatment-resistant schizophrenia, and ordering that the state include this antipsychotic drug on its formulary); cf. Armen H. Merjian, A Choice Between Food and Medicine: Denning v. Barbour and the Struggle for Prescription Drug Coverage Under the Medicaid Act, 13 Scholar 201 (2010) (describing pending litigation that challenges Mississippi's decision to impose strict monthly caps on the number of prescription drugs that it will reimburse). Most states currently provide such coverage (with CMS picking up two-thirds of the tab), and spending on prescription drugs amounted to $20 billion in 2009. See Anna Edney & Drew Armstrong, Report Faults Medicaid Drug Spending, Wash. Post, Mar. 29, 2011, at A19 (adding that, according to an AEI study, the program overspent by more than $300 million by ''purchasing 20 brand-name drugs instead of available generic copies'').

Weaver v. Reagen

886 F.2d 194 (8th Cir.1989).

■ ROSS, CIRCUIT JUDGE:

* * * On March 20, 1987, the Food and Drug Administration (FDA) announced its approval of AZT under the brand name Retrovir, for the treatment of AIDS. The labeling approved by the FDA for AZT stated:

> Retrovir capsules are indicated for the management of certain adult patients with symptomatic HIV infection (AIDS and advanced [AIDS-related complex (ARC)]) who have a history of cytologically confirmed Pneumocystis carinii pneumonia (PCP) or an absolute CD4 (T4 help-

er/inducer) lymphocyte count of less than 200/mm in the peripheral blood before therapy is begun.

At the time this action was filed on July 6, 1987, the State of Missouri did not provide any Medicaid coverage for AZT. Three days after the suit was filed, the Missouri Department of Social Services promulgated an emergency rule, providing Medicaid coverage of AZT under certain diagnoses or conditions. Adopted as a permanent rule with minor modifications effective November 12, 1987, Missouri regulations now provide coverage for AZT [using] * * * language [that] is virtually identical to FDA's approval statement for the drug.

At the present time, the drug AZT is the only approved treatment of AIDS or ARC. While there are treatments for particular opportunistic infections which the AIDS patient may develop, AZT is the only approved drug which acts on the HIV virus itself. Although plaintiff Glenn Weaver, who had suffered from pneumocystis carinii pneumonia (PCP), became eligible for Medicaid coverage of AZT as a result of the change in the Missouri Medicaid rules, the present action was continued when other plaintiffs were granted leave to intervene.

The new plaintiffs suffered with AIDS and certain AIDS indicator diseases, but did not meet the restricted medical conditions necessary for coverage of AZT under Missouri's Medicaid rule (history of PCP or an absolute CD4 lymphocyte count below 200). For example, plaintiff Mark Momot was diagnosed as infected with the AIDS virus and suffering from oropharyngeal/esophageal candidiasis, an AIDS indicator disease, as well as significant diarrhea, fever, sweats and lymphadenopathy. In order to prevent or retard the progression of the disease to a more serious illness, his personal physician prescribed AZT. However, because Momot had no history of PCP and his CD4 count had not dropped below 200, Missouri Medicaid denied coverage of his AZT prescription because "he did not meet the diagnosis criteria set forth in the state regulation." * * *

The trial court held that defendants' rule limiting Medicaid coverage of AZT to only those recipients who meet certain diagnostic criteria or conditions violated federal Medicaid law. The district court found that AZT is medically necessary treatment for individuals in the plaintiff class who do not fit within the restrictive criteria of Missouri's Medicaid rule. The court, therefore, enjoined Missouri officials from denying coverage of AZT to "persons eligible for Medicaid and infected with the AIDS virus." * * *

Title XIX of the Social Security Act, commonly known as the Medicaid Act, is a federal-state cooperative program designed to provide medical assistance to persons whose income and resources are insufficient to meet the costs of medical care. Although a state's participation is voluntary, once a state chooses to participate in the program it must comply with federal statutory and regulatory requirements, including the requirement that participating states provide financial assistance for in-patient hospital services, out-patient hospital services, laboratory and x-ray services, skilled nursing facilities and physicians' services. The participating state may also elect to provide other optional medical services such as prescription drugs.

Once a state chooses to offer such optional services it is bound to act in compliance with the Act and the applicable regulations in the implementation of those services, including the requirement that "each service must be sufficient in amount, duration, and scope to reasonably achieve its purpose."

Although a state has considerable discretion in fashioning its Medicaid program, the discretion of the state is not unbridled: "[A state] may not arbitrarily deny or reduce the amount, duration, or scope of a required service . . . to an otherwise eligible recipient solely because of the diagnosis, type of illness or condition." 42 C.F.R. § 440.230(c). "Appropriate limits [may be placed] on a service based on such criteria as medical necessity or utilization control procedures." Id. § 440.230(d). Moreover, the state's plan for determining eligibility for medical assistance must be " 'reasonable' and 'consistent with the objectives' of the Act." This provision has been interpreted to require that a state Medicaid plan provide treatment that is deemed "medically necessary" in order to comport with the objectives of the Act.

In the present case, defendants argue that their reliance on the FDA's approval statement in limiting coverage of AZT to only those patients who meet certain medical criteria is a reasonable exercise of their discretion to place limitations on covered services based on medical necessity and utilization controls. We do not find this argument persuasive.

Contrary to defendants' assertions, FDA approved indications were not intended to limit or interfere with the practice of medicine nor to preclude physicians from using their best judgment in the interest of the patient. Instead, the FDA new drug approval process is intended to ensure that drugs meet certain statutory standards for safety and effectiveness, manufacturing and controls, and labeling, and to ensure that manufacturers market their drugs only for those indications for which the drug sponsor has demonstrated "substantial evidence" of effectiveness. * * * Thus, the fact that FDA has not approved labeling of a drug for a particular use does not necessarily bear on those uses of the drug that are established within the medical and scientific community as medically appropriate. It would be improper for the State of Missouri to interfere with a physician's judgment of medical necessity by limiting coverage of AZT based on criteria that admittedly do not reflect current medical knowledge or practice.

It is also defendants' position on appeal that prescribing AZT outside the FDA approved indications is per se "experimental" in the sense that there is no scientific data derived from clinical trials documenting the efficacy and safety of AZT use outside the FDA guidelines. According to defendants, because such AZT use is experimental, it can never be deemed medically necessary treatment. In our view, defendants' definition of "experimental" in this context is overly broad. * * * [T]he prescription of AZT beyond its labeled indications is not experimental. The record here establishes that physicians commonly prescribe AZT for patients who have neither a history of PCP nor a CD4 count below 200. Plaintiffs' experts stated that based on their own practice, professional literature, conferences, and contacts with other physicians, AZT is generally accepted by the medical community as an effective and proven treatment for AIDS patients who do not meet the criteria in the FDA indications. * * *

Defendants' expert, Dr. John Mills, a professor of medicine at the University of California at San Francisco, does not controvert the affidavits of plaintiffs' experts in which they conclude that AZT may be medically necessary for AIDS patients who do not meet the restrictive diagnostic criteria in Missouri's regulation. Although Dr. Mills stated that the use of AZT beyond labeled indications was experimental in the sense that scientific studies had not conclusively determined its effectiveness, Dr. Mills agreed that "doctors commonly exercise professional medical judgment and prescribe drugs for uses not within the indications articulated by the FDA." Specifically with regard to AZT, Dr. Mills stated that "doctors commonly prescribe AZT for patients not meeting those two criteria" (history of PCP or CD4 count below 200) and in fact, Dr. Mills himself testified that he has prescribed AZT outside the FDA indications. * * *

Missouri's Medicaid rule constitutes an irrebuttable presumption that AZT can never be medically necessary treatment for AIDS patients who have neither a history of PCP nor a CD4 count below 200. The record here establishes that such a presumption is unreasonable in light of the widespread recognition by the medical community and scientific literature that AZT is the only known antiviral treatment for individuals with AIDS.

The Medicaid statute and regulatory scheme create a presumption in favor of the medical judgment of the attending physician in determining the medical necessity of treatment. In denying coverage of AZT to the plaintiff class, the defendants have done nothing to overcome that presumption except to rely on the FDA approval process in a manner expressly rejected by the FDA. In the face of widespread recognition by the medical community and the scientific and medical literature that AZT is the only available treatment for most persons with AIDS, we find that Missouri Medicaid's approach to its coverage of the drug AZT is unreasonable and inconsistent with the objectives of the Medicaid Act. * * *

NOTES AND QUESTIONS

1. *Affording antivirals*. The latest research confirms the value of starting antiretroviral treatment immediately rather than waiting for CD4 counts to fall below a certain threshold. See Donald G. McNeil, Jr., Early Therapy for H.I.V. Said to Cut Spread, N.Y. Times, May 13, 2011, at A1. Many individuals with HIV or AIDS cannot, however, afford the drug cocktails using protease-inhibitors that typically cost more than $10,000 annually. Even if patients have private health insurance, they may exceed the maximum coverage limits of their policies. See Sharona Hoffman, AIDS Caps, Contraceptive Coverage, and the Law: An Analysis of the Federal Anti–Discrimination Statutes' Applicability to Health Insurance, 23 Cardozo L. Rev. 1315 (2002); see also Jonathan Bor, Living Longer with HIV: Report Finds Patient Can Live Average 24 Years, Pay $385,000, Balt. Sun,

Nov. 11, 2006, at 1A. Now that antiviral treatments have become the standard of care, should government-funded programs pay for these drugs when patients cannot? AIDS Drug Assistance Programs exist but have only limited resources. See Vanessa Fuhrmans, Medical Dilemma: Costly New Drugs for AIDS Means Some Go Without, Wall St. J., Jan. 13, 2004, at A1 ("[E]xpensive drugs such as Fuzeon [approximately $20,000 annually] are helping create a kind of rationing of HIV care common in poor nations but, until now, rarely seen in the U.S."); Shefali S. Kulkarni, States Cutting Back Support for HIV Patients, Wash. Post, May 24, 2011, at A3; see also Steven R. Keener, Note, A Comparative Analysis of the Origins and Structure of Public Health Financing for HIV Care in the United States and England, 83 Notre Dame L. Rev. 1357 (2008).

2. *Medicare and Medicaid coverage of off-label uses.* CMS provides Medicare reimbursement for approved drugs prescribed for a use approved by the FDA or, in the case of certain anti-cancer agents, for a use supported by a study appearing in the peer-reviewed medical literature or a citation in one of several identified medical compendia. See 42 U.S.C. § 1395x–(t)(2)(B)(ii); see also Gardiner Harris, Medicare Takes Steps Broadening Coverage of Cancer Care, N.Y. Times, Nov. 2, 2004, at A18 (reporting that CMS is "increasingly agreeing to pay for unproven treatments only for those who agree to participate in clinical trials"). As the next case reveals, confusion has arisen about the extent to which off-label uses must be covered under Part D. In contrast, in a provision added to the statute after the decision in *Weaver*, Congress authorized Medicaid reimbursement of prescription drug expenses only for off-label uses appearing in certain medical compendia.

Layzer v. Leavitt

770 F.Supp.2d 579 (S.D.N.Y.2011).

■ BAER, DISTRICT JUDGE:

* * * In 2003 Congress passed the Medicare Prescription Drug, Improvement, and Modernization Act (MMA), under which a plan sponsor is required to provide coverage of qualified prescription drugs. Section 1395w–102(e) of the MMA defines what may be considered a "covered Part D drug." The definition refers to the term "medically accepted indication" as defined at 42 U.S.C. § 1396r–8(k)(6): "any use for a covered outpatient drug which is approved under the [FDCA] or the use of which is supported by one or more citations included or approved for inclusion in any of [three compendia]." The Secretary [of HHS] promulgated a regulation implementing the definition, and it requires that to be a "covered Part D drug" a drug must be prescribed for a "medically accepted indication." 42 C.F.R. § 423.100. In this case, coverage of the plaintiffs' drugs was denied because the uses for which the drugs were prescribed were not approved or listed in any of these compendia. Because FDCA approval is not an issue in this case, the "medically accepted indication" requirement set forth in 42 C.F.R § 423.100 will simply be referred to as the "compendia requirement."

[Judith M.] Layzer is a Medicare beneficiary with granulose cell tumor, a rare form of ovarian cancer. Several oncologists urged her to take the drug Cetrotide to control her cancer, including Robert Bast, M.D., her oncologist at the University of Texas M.D. Anderson Cancer Center, who prescribed the drug for Mrs. Layzer for several years. According to Dr. Bast, Cetrotide retards the growth of Mrs. Layzer's cancer and prevents her tumors from hemorrhaging. He has warned that the medicine "is essential for my patient. There is no substitute at this time." * * * Other physicians have echoed the conclusion that Cetrotide is critical to Mrs. Layzer's treatment. Peer-reviewed medical literature has also recognized the unique and effective capacity of Cetrotide to treat ovarian cancer. Mrs. Layzer's plan sponsor denied full coverage, stating that Cetrotide "is a fertility agent" and "not covered under Medicare Part D."

[Ray J.] Fisher is a Medicare beneficiary diagnosed with myotonic muscular dystrophy type 2, a rare and degenerative form of muscular dystrophy that results in muscle weakness and cardiac abnormalities, among other things. The drug Increlex proved significantly helpful in slowing or stopping the deterioration of Mr. Fisher's muscle; it also helped him regain strength and range of motion and allowed him to function without a hand-arm tremor. Mr. Fisher's physician, Richard Moxley, M.D., director of research at the Rochester Medical Center's Neuromuscular Disease Center, noted that Increlex has "helped to optimize [Mr. Fisher's] quality of life and maintain his present level of independence." Mr. Fisher's plan sponsor denied coverage, explaining that Increlex "is not FDA approved for the diagnosis provided."

On appeal, the respective denials of coverage were affirmed by a Medicare Part D Independent Review Entity, which concluded that the plan sponsors were not required to provide coverage because the drugs were not being used for a medically accepted indication. It explained that "a medically accepted indication means a use that is approved by the FDA or a use that is supported by one or more citations in . . . drug compendia." The plaintiffs' respective denials were again affirmed by administrate law judges [ALJs]. * * * Plaintiffs appealed to the Medicare Appeals Council, which affirmed the denials of coverage, noting that it too was bound to follow 42 C.F.R. § 423.100 and lacked authority to consider whether that regulation was inconsistent with the statute.

Plaintiffs seek review in this court and argue that the compendia requirement should be set aside as inconsistent with the Act. * * * I start with the definitional language:

(1) Except as provided in this subsection . . . , the term "covered part D drug" means—

(A) a drug that may be dispensed only upon a prescription and that is described in subparagraph (A)(i), (A)(ii), or (A)(iii) of section 1396r–8(k)(2) of this title; or

(B) a biological product described in clauses (i) through (iii) of subparagraph (B) of such section . . . ,

> *and such term includes* a vaccine licensed under section 262 of this title ... and any use of a covered part D drug for a medically accepted indication [as defined in § 1396r–8(k)(6)].
>
> (2) Exclusions....
>
> (3) Application of general exclusion provisions....

42 U.S.C. § 1395w–102(e) (emphasis added). Looking only at § 102(e)(1)(A)–(B), plaintiffs' drug use would be covered because (A) and (B) are written in the disjunctive, and (A) merely requires FDA approval for reimbursement. However, the dispute centers on the final paragraph before subparagraph (2). Specifically, the parties disagree on whether to construe the phrase "and such term includes" as illustrative (introducing several examples) or as definitional (introducing additional factors required to meet the definition). * * *

One district court has concluded that the plain language of the statutory scheme indicates that "the medically accepted indication clause must be read as a limitation." Kilmer v. Leavitt, 609 F.Supp.2d 750, 754 (S.D.Ohio 2009). That court reasoned that

> Congress specifically and expressly included "such term," which means that this court must credit that usage as having some point—i.e., to make clear that the definition was continuing and that "includes" means in context essentially "also means" or "as well as" so that the "such term includes ..." clause means "a drug that is used for a medically accepted indication."

For the following reasons, I respectfully disagree.

The [Social Security] Act provides that the word " 'includes' ... when used in a definition contained in this chapter shall not be deemed to exclude other things otherwise within the meaning of the term defined." 42 U.S.C. § 1301(b). In other words, the term "includes" as used in the definition does not introduce an exhaustive category of covered Part D drugs because it does not exclude "other things" that would fall within the preceding definition. * * * Moreover, if "includes" introduces further limiting terms, both limitations cited in the paragraph must be addressed. As drafted, they are connected by the word "and" which requires the conclusion that they are conjunctive requirements, i.e., a covered Part D drug would have to be (1) a vaccine licensed under § 262 *and* (2) used for a medically accepted indication. The Secretary does not argue for such an interpretation but only that a drug which meets the requirements of subsection (A) or (B) must also be used for a medically accepted indication. In that formulation, the two requirements should be joined by the word "or." The fact that they are not indicates further discord between the Secretary's interpretation and the statutory language.

The Secretary argues that the word "includes" must be read as definitional because the clause that follows "is highly specific, undermining any suggestion that the clause was intended as merely one example of what might be considered a covered drug." The Secretary fails to explain why a specific clause must be definitional rather than illustrative. The Secretary argues its interpretation is required to avoid surplusage. He contends that plaintiffs' interpretation would cover *all* FDA-approved drugs, and "drugs used for a medically accepted indication" would be a superfluous category because such drugs fall wholly under the larger category of "all FDA-approved drugs." Defendant further argues that Congress would not have taken such care to define "medically accepted indication" if it had meant it to be "mere surplusage." The force of this argument is eroded by the fact that the term "medically accepted indication" is found in a different subchapter of Title 42, 42 U.S.C. § 1396r–8(k)(6). It is merely cross-referenced in the subchapter at issue here. Plaintiffs' interpretation does not render the term superfluous because the term exists elsewhere.

The Secretary's next argument is based on statutory context. He argues that there were two definitions of "medically accepted indication" in the Act, and the fact that the definition cited to the narrower rather than the broader [one] is further proof that Congress intended for there to be a compendia requirement. Had Congress intended to allow off-label uses, the Secretary opines, it could have done so by citing the broader definition of "medically accepted indication." In fact, Congress subsequently expanded the definition of "medically accepted indication" at issue here to allow for certain off-label uses. See 42 U.S.C. § 1395w–102(e)(4)(A)(i).[5] However, * * * the fact that Congress made a choice as to which definition to reference sheds no light on whether it meant that reference to be illustrative or definitional. * * *

More compelling statutory construction arguments confirm that Congress did not intend to impose a compendium requirement. In general, remedial legislation should be broadly construed. In particular, the Second Circuit has said that the Social Security Act should be "liberally construed in favor of beneficiaries." The "intent" of the Act "is inclusion rather than exclusion," and a more inclusive definition is consistent with these exhortations. Additionally, the definition "should be interpreted to avoid untenable distinctions and unreasonable results whenever possible."

The Secretary's interpretation would create arbitrarily fine and unreasonable distinctions between uses that are covered in the compendia and those that are not. Significantly, as Judge Smith [one of the ALJs] suggested, the compendia requirement precludes coverage of effective yet newly discovered prescription drug treatments—particularly for rare diseases—because FDA-approved uses often lag behind knowledge about actual effective treatment. As Judge Smith explained, the "lack of the 'required' compendium listing is likely due to the rarity of [Mrs. Layzer's] cancer."

---

5. On July 15, 2008, Congress passed the Medicare Improvements for Patients and Providers Act of 2008 (MIPPA), Pub. L. No. 110–275. Under MIPPA, effective January 1, 2009, the relevant definition of "medically accepted indication" was expanded to include drugs utilized in an anticancer chemotherapeutic regimen even if supported solely by peer-reviewed medical literature, i.e., the compendia requirement no longer applies to this category of drug use. See 42 U.S.C. § 1395w–102(e)(4)(A)(i). Mrs. Layzer brought a separate administrate action pursuant to MIPPA, and was awarded Part D coverage of her Cetrotide prescription, effective January 1, 2009. She continues to seek coverage for Part D benefits that were denied prior to 2009.

The more rare the disease, the more difficult it is for researchers to (1) determine which drugs provide effective treatment and (2) secure FDA approval to use the drugs for that particular treatment.

Finally, the compendia requirement is defeated by the principle of *expressio unius est exclusio alterius,* "the mention of one thing implies the exclusion of the other." Because subparagraph (2), which is titled "Exclusions," contains a number of express exclusions, it is implied that the language in subparagraph (1) should not be construed to express additional exclusions. It does not make sense that Congress would create both (1) a general definition with exceptions imbedded; and (2) a list of explicit exceptions immediately following. This is confirmed by the fact that the definition begins with the proviso "Except as provided in this subsection." This indicates that Congress did not intend to import the definition of "medically accepted indication" in § 1396r–8(k)(6) as a limiting element of the definition.

Because I conclude on the basis of the statutory text and canons of construction that Congress did not intend to impose the compendia requirement, I need not turn to the legislative history. The parties' various arguments relating to the legislative history of the MMA and MIPPA provide little or no help in resolving the question at bar. * * * Nonetheless, the Secretary's argument that Congress has acquiesced in his interpretation merits some discussion. He points out that the regulation at issue, 42 C.F.R. § 423.100, was brought to the attention of Congress, yet Congress failed to controvert that regulation when it revised the statute by passing MIPPA on July 15, 2008. * * * The congressional acquiescence theory is unpersuasive * * * * *Bellevue* relied on congressional acquiescence to determine that a regulation was reasonable. See Bellevue Hosp. Ctr. v. Leavitt, 443 F.3d 163, 176 (2d Cir.2006). In other words, it was a *Chevron* step two case and did not rely on the acquiescence theory to determine whether the statute was ambiguous but rather whether the regulation filling in the ambiguous statute was reasonable. * * *

Because the reasons stated for denying coverage of plaintiffs' medications rested on an unsound interpretation of the law, the denial is reversed and the Secretary is directed to provide the appropriate coverage * * * *

Edmonds v. Levine

417 F.Supp.2d 1323 (S.D.Fla.2006).

■ KLEIN, MAGISTRATE JUDGE:

* * * Plaintiffs Jack Edmonds, Susan Weschke, and Gaylord Payne are Medicaid recipients who are challenging a policy of the Florida Agency for Health Care Administration (AHCA) to deny reimbursement under the federal Medicaid program for prescriptions for the drug Neurontin and/or its generic equivalent, gabapentin, except when prescribed for four indications or uses: adjunctive therapy for partial seizures (including partial

seizure refractory); postherpetic neuralgia; diabetic neuropathy; and amyotrophic lateral sclerosis (ALS). * * * Plaintiffs suffer from neuropathic pain resulting from conditions other than the four identified above. Plaintiffs and their treating physicians or psychiatrists claim that Neurontin is one of the first-line medications for neuropathic pain, is a relatively safe and inexpensive drug widely used to treat nerve-related pain and some psychiatric disorders, and is medically necessary for the treatment of their conditions. * * *

The Medicaid Act's provisions for coverage of outpatient prescription drugs are set forth in 42 U.S.C. § 1396r–8. The Act provides coverage for the "medically accepted indication" of "any covered outpatient drug." The term "medically accepted indication" is defined as "any use for a covered outpatient drug which is approved under the Federal Food, Drug, and Cosmetic Act or the use of which is supported by one or more citations included or approved for inclusion in any of the compendia described in subsection (g)(1)(B)(i) of this section." Id. § 1396r–8(k)(6). There are three compendia listed in subsection (g)(1)(B)(i): United States Pharmacopeia–Drug Information (USP), American Hospital Formulary Service Drug Information (AHFS), and DrugDex Information System. Thus, the Medicaid Act directs states to reimburse any use for a covered outpatient drug which is either (1) approved by the [FDA] or (2) supported by one or more citations in any congressionally-recognized compendia.

The FDA has approved Neurontin, a covered outpatient prescription drug, for two uses: adjunctive therapy for partial seizures and postherpetic neuralgia. There are many off-label uses for Neurontin, all of which thus call into play the question of whether such uses are "supported by one or more citations included ... in any of the compendia." Florida covers the two FDA-approved uses, and two other off-label uses of Neurontin, adopting its own criteria for deciding that those are the only two such uses which are properly supported by citation in the compendia. It is the meaning of the phrase "supported by one or more citations included ... in any of the compendia" upon which this case turns.

While the Medicaid Act requires a state paying for outpatient prescription drugs to reimburse for "medically accepted indications," the Act does permit states to limit coverage under certain circumstances. Under § 1396r–8(d)(1)(B), a state may *exclude* a drug from coverage, that is, *deny* reimbursement, under four circumstances: if the prescribed use is not for a medically accepted indication (i.e., either FDA approved or supported by citation in a compendium); if the drug is listed in § 1396r–8(d)(2) or is subsequently determined by the Secretary of HHS by regulation to be subject to clinical abuse or inappropriate use; if the drug is subject to restriction pursuant to an agreement between the state and drug manufacturer; or if the drug has been excluded by a state-established formulary. The only one of the four circumstances listed above which is at issue here is whether the disputed uses are for medically accepted indications. The parties agree that the other three of these circumstances do not exist here. Neurontin is not on the list of restricted drugs delineated in § 1396r–

8(d)(2) nor has it been restricted by HHS regulation; there is no agreement between Neurontin's manufacturer and the State of Florida to restrict coverage; and Florida has not established a drug formulary. * * *

A drug formulary, which is developed by a committee of physicians, pharmacists, and other appropriate individuals or the state's drug use review board, is a list of Medicaid-eligible drugs for which the state will provide reimbursement when prescribed for medically accepted indications. §§ 1396r–8(d)(4)(A)–(B). The Medicaid Act permits a state (through its formulary committee) to remove a Medicaid-eligible drug from the formulary, with the result that the drug will no longer be covered for reimbursement, if the drug that "does not have a significant, clinically meaningful therapeutic advantage in terms of safety, effectiveness, or clinical outcome" over other drugs included in the formulary. § 1396r–8(d)(4)(C). The committee's decision to exclude a drug from the formulary is generally limited to issues of clinical safety and effectiveness. The committee must provide a written explanation, available to the public, of the basis for excluding a drug from the formulary. * * *

Because through the formulary process a state can exclude from coverage drugs that otherwise would be eligible for reimbursement under the Medicaid Act, Congress has devised a process whereby a doctor who wishes to prescribe an excluded drug may seek an exception to the exclusion (and thus obtain reimbursement for that drug). The Medicaid Act requires a state, when it establishes a formulary, to also establish a prior authorization program that is consistent with § 1396r–8(d)(5). Subsection (d)(5) provides that a state may require, "as a condition of coverage or payment for a covered outpatient drug," prior authorization, or approval, of the drug before it is dispensed. The only two statutory requirements for a prior authorization program are that the state must respond to the prescribing doctor within 24 hours of his request for prior authorization, and a 72–hour supply of the drug must be made available in an emergency situation. * * *

Congress has authorized two very distinct prior authorization programs; the one discussed above which is created in conjunction with a drug formulary which permits the state to have final authority to exclude a drug, and the one like Florida's which covers all Medicaid-eligible drugs and conditions payment for any such drug upon a doctor contacting the state before the drug is dispensed. * * * Under Florida's program, when a doctor who wishes to prescribe a drug that is subject to the prior authorization program contacts the state pharmacist, that individual advises the doctor of the availability of other drugs that allegedly have comparable therapeutic value but are less expensive * * * * Ultimately, though, the *doctor* retains the authority to override any suggestions made by the AHCA state pharmacist and obtain approval of, and eventual reimbursement for, the doctor's first-choice drug. However, under the formulary prior authorization program, a prescribing doctor may ask the state to cover a Medicaid-eligible drug that has been excluded from the formulary, but ultimately, the state can deny the request for coverage, meaning it is the *state* which retains the final authority over coverage for non-formulary drugs. * * *

The Medicaid Act permits a state to exclude or otherwise restrict coverage for drugs that are listed in § 1396r–8(d)(2). Subparagraph (d)(2) is a list of drugs or classes of drugs that Congress has determined may be excluded from coverage or otherwise restricted. The Secretary of HHS must by regulation periodically update this list of drugs or their medical uses "which the Secretary has determined, based on data collected by surveillance and utilization review programs of State medical assistance programs, to be subject to clinical abuse or inappropriate use." Through a drug utilization review program, a state may advise the Secretary of drugs that are subject to gross overuse or inappropriate or medically unnecessary care.[5] Until the Secretary amends the list of excluded drugs to include a particular drug, however, the state may not exclude that drug from coverage except through its formulary committee based solely on clinical factors. * * *

In the spring of 2004, following news reports that Neurontin was being widely prescribed for off-label uses and that reimbursement for the drug by state Medicaid programs was significant, the Florida Legislature passed legislation authorizing AHCA, at its discretion, to require prior authorization for the off-label uses of Medicaid-covered prescribed drugs, including Neurontin. * * * AHCA responded to this legislation by changing its policy on Neurontin reimbursements for Medicaid recipients, effective July 1, 2004. Prior to July 1, 2004, AHCA reimbursed *all* Neurontin prescriptions. Under the new policy, AHCA decided to cover Neurontin for the two FDA-approved uses, and for off-label uses only when the uses for which the drug was prescribed were substantiated as being safe and effective by double-blind, placebo-controlled, randomized clinical trials. * * * [I]f a provider submits a prior authorization form and indicates that Neurontin is being prescribed for something other than one of the four approved conditions, AHCA denies reimbursement. * * *

The following sections in the DrugDex chapter on Neurontin are relevant in this lawsuit. Section 4.5, entitled "Therapeutic Uses," lists 54 uses for Neurontin including both the two FDA-approved and 52 off-label

5. States are required to implement drug use review programs in order to assure that prescriptions are appropriate, medically necessary, and not likely to result in adverse medical results. § 1396r–8(g)(1). These drug use review programs "assess data on drug use against predetermined standards, consistent with" the drug compendia listed in § 1396r–8(g)(1)(B)(i) and peer-reviewed medical literature. These programs must (a) prospectively review drug therapy before prescriptions are filled or delivered to Medicaid recipients, and (b) retrospectively "identify patterns of fraud, abuse, gross overuse, or inappropriate or medically unnecessary care, among physicians, pharmacists and [Medicaid recipients], or associated with specific drugs." Then, on an annual basis, each state must submit a report to the HHS Secretary which includes, among other things, a description of the nature and scope of the prospective and retrospective drug use review programs. Thus, this provision establishes a scheme whereby states can identify drugs that are subject to gross overuse or inappropriate or medically unnecessary care, then formally present that information to the Secretary, who must periodically update the list of restricted drugs after determining, based on this information, which drugs are subject to clinical abuse or inappropriate use.

uses. For each of the 54 uses, DrugDex includes an overview which reflects whether the FDA has approved Neurontin for that particular use, and a rating of the efficacy ("effective," "possibly effective," and "ineffective") and documentation of Neurontin ("excellent," "good," "fair," and "poor") for that use. DrugDex also includes a summary of the support for each use. Support ranges from a single case study for some of the uses to randomized placebo-controlled double-blind clinical studies for other uses. Section 6.0 is entitled "References" and contains citations to 178 articles reviewed by the editors of DrugDex. Some of the articles address uses for Neurontin that are not listed in the "Therapeutic Uses" section. Section 4.3 is entitled "Place in Therapy" and references one of the two FDA-approved uses for Neurontin. Finally, Section 4.6 is entitled "Comparative Efficacy and Evaluation with Other Similar Therapeutic Agents" and compares the efficacy of Neurontin with other drugs in treating a few conditions, including diabetic peripheral neuropathy. * * *

Although AHCA has every right, and indeed an obligation, to ensure that it is not covering drugs that are subject to clinical abuse or misuse, it must act within the confines of the Medicaid law. The state must follow the procedures for excluding Medicaid-eligible drugs like Neurontin that are set out § 1396r–8(d). Through a properly-constituted formulary committee, the state may establish a drug formulary and then, for clinical reasons, exclude Neurontin for certain off-label uses from the formulary. Alternatively, through its annual drug utilization review report, the state may advise the Secretary of HHS that Neurontin is subject to clinical abuse or inappropriate use. However, until the HHS Secretary amends the HHS regulation to add Neurontin or specified uses thereof to the list of excluded drugs, the state may not stop covering the drug for most uses based simply on its own determination that the drug is being abused or misused. Finally, the only other way the state can deny reimbursement for off-label uses of Neurontin is by concluding that the drug is being prescribed for non-"medically accepted indications," which is what AHCA has done. * * *

AHCA's construction of § 1396r–8(k)(6) renders superfluous the second phrase of the term "medically accepted indication." The statute provides for coverage of drugs that are prescribed for (1) FDA-approved uses or (2) off-label uses supported by citation in the compendia. AHCA reads the second phrase to mean only those uses that are supported by double-blind, placebo-controlled, randomized clinical trials. But this is the same standard employed for FDA-approved uses. Requiring off-label uses to be supported by the same standard as FDA-approved uses is the equivalent of saying the same thing twice. If Congress had intended that "medically accepted indications" must be supported by double-blind, placebo-controlled, randomized clinical trials, it would have said so. * * *

In 1993, Congress amended the definition of "medically accepted indication" to add the phrase which is at the heart of this case: "or the use of which is supported by one or more citations included or approved for inclusion in any of the compendia described in subsection (g)(1)(B)(i)." Pub. L. No. 103–66, § 13602(a)(2)(B)(iii), 107 Stat. 312, 619. A few years later, in 1997, Congress updated subsection (g)(1)(B)(i) to add DrugDex to the approved list of compendia. See Pub. L. No. 105–33, § 4756, 111 Stat. 251, 527. Several years later, in 2003, Congress *again* updated the list of approved compendia by eliminating American Medical Association Drug Evaluations from subsection (g)(1)(B)(i). See Pub. L. No. 108–173, § 101(e)(9)(B), 117 Stat. 2066, 2152. The court must presume that Congress knew what it was doing when it added "supported by citation in the compendia" to the term "medically accepted indication," and further, that it understood the differences in the compendia's organization, format, and editorial practices when it added DrugDex as an approved compendium. These statutory changes over the years substantiate the notion that Congress intended coverage for off-label uses, many of which would obviously not be supported by the same strict criteria required for FDA approval. Had Congress intended otherwise, it would have been easy to amend the term "medically accepted indication" to add the phrase "that meet the same testing criteria for approval required by the FDA," for any such off-label uses.

Commentary by the federal agency charged with implementing the Medicaid law lends support for plaintiffs' argument that the Medicaid Act covers many off-label uses which are not supported by the same strict criteria required for FDA approval. After Congress added DrugDex to the list of approved compendia, the head of HHS' Center for Medicaid and State Operations notified state Medicaid directors of the change by saying:

> The addition of DrugDex also means that some additional indications would be considered "medically accepted indications" for purposes of [§ 1396r–8(k)(6)]. This will * * * require coverage of additional off-label uses of FDA approved drugs for the indications that are listed in the DrugDex monographs. As before, prior approval policies can be put in place (e.g., to require another drug to be used first for that indication), but prior authorization cannot be used to simply deny the off-label DrugDex-identified indication for a drug.

AHCA has done just that in contravention of the Center's stated policy: employed the prior authorization program to deny coverage of certain drugs.

Significantly, AHCA has arbitrarily determined that a double-blind, placebo-controlled, randomized clinical trial is the standard it will apply, disregarding the fact that the Act directs coverage when a use is supported by citation in a compendia, a different standard. Under AHCA's interpretation, nothing would prevent a state Medicaid agency from deciding to apply an entirely different standard altogether. Counsel for AHCA acknowledged at the preliminary injunction hearing that a state could go behind what is listed in the compendia and make its own determination as to whether a particular use is sufficiently supported by clinical evidence. Thus, a state Medicaid agency could choose any standard it wants, either more rigid, or less stringent, employing whatever reasoning it chooses as a justification to eliminate covered uses. Moreover, the state could change its criteria at any time. It could even disregard the compendia entirely in making its choices.

* * * That means that fifty states could establish their own criteria for denying coverage of a Medicaid-eligible drug without going through the formulary process or employing the other methods delineated in the statute for excluding a drug. The court finds that this approach contravenes provisions of the Medicaid Act and Congress' intent to establish uniformity in Medicaid drug coverage. It would contravene the statutory scheme which sets forth very specific criteria and means by which a state may exclude coverage for specific drugs or uses of such drugs.

To the extent that AHCA uses the compendia, and DrugDex in particular, AHCA is deciding on its own what is "supported by citation," as is evidenced by its decision to pay for two of the three uses which are listed as "ineffective" (i.e., partial seizures-refractory and ALS) and to not pay for others which are deemed "effective" (e.g., multiple sclerosis complications including, e.g., trigeminal neuralgia, which happens to be listed in AHFS). This renders the "supported by citation" provision in the statute irrelevant to AHCA's determination, and means that AHCA is disregarding the federal statute when it makes its own determination based on its own criteria, irrespective of the drug's citation in DrugDex.

Furthermore, AHCA has ignored the fact that AHFS, another congressionally-approved compendium, cites several off-label uses for Neurontin in addition to the two FDA-approved uses. The editors of AHFS do not indicate what level of clinical support exists for any of the uses cited in the compendium, so AHCA would provide reimbursement only for the two FDA-approved uses listed in this compendium. But again, this reads the "supported by citation in any of the compendia" phrase out of the statute, and effectively negates AHFS as a source for any off-label uses, in clear violation of the statute. In essence, AHCA is attacking the motives and methodology of the editors of all of the compendia. However, Congress has already stamped its imprimatur on these compendia by including them in § 1396r–8(g)(1)(B)(i). AHCA may not substitute its own judgment for that of Congress.

AHCA argues that as the state agency charged with administering Florida's Medicaid program, this court should accord substantial deference to its interpretation of the federal and state Medicaid statutes it administers. Consistently, however, federal courts have held that interpretations of federal law by *state* agencies are not entitled to such deference. * * * It also bears note that AHCA, by excluding coverage pursuant to the prior authorization program, has gone beyond what the Florida Legislature authorized it to do. The Florida Legislature obviously recognized the limitations of the Medicaid Act in excluding drugs, and recognized the limitations of Florida's prior authorization program. The law passed in 2004 permitted AHCA, at its discretion, to require prior authorization for the off-label use of Medicaid-covered prescribed drugs such as Neurontin. See Fla. Stat. § 409.912(39)(a)(13) (2005). Nothing in the law authorized AHCA to *exclude* certain uses from coverage, which it has improperly done through implementation of its new Neurontin policy. * * *

Plaintiffs acknowledge it would be inappropriate to cover any drug listed for any use in any section of DrugDex, and argue instead that all the uses listed in the "Therapeutic Uses" section of DrugDex should be considered "medically accepted indications." They argue that since the "Place in Therapy" section mentions only one of the two FDA-approved uses for Neurontin (for seizures), reference to this section alone would render both clauses of § 1396r–8(k)(6) (FDA-approved uses and uses which are supported by citation) meaningless. Plaintiffs suggest that relying on the "References" section alone would be nonsensical since it includes citations to uses for Neurontin that are not even listed in the "Therapeutic Uses" section. And they discount reliance on the "Comparative Efficacy" section because it simply compares Neurontin to other drugs for several therapeutic uses.

Plaintiffs say, then, that the only possible construction of the statute vis-a-vis DrugDex is that the 54 off-label uses listed in the "Therapeutic Uses" section are "supported by citation" as defined in 42 U.S.C. § 1396r–8(k)(6). Plaintiffs acknowledge that the "Therapeutic Uses" section encompasses three uses that are rated as "ineffective," but they point out that defendant already covers two of those uses (partial seizures refractory and ALS). No other construction of the statute leads to a consistent reasonable result. Plaintiffs also point out that the Medicaid Act does not require a use listed in a compendium to be rated "effective." The statute reads that a use must be "supported by one or more citations included . . . in any of the compendia." It says nothing about a use having been evaluated in terms of efficacy by the compendia's editors. Plaintiffs argue that defendant has "superimposed" an "effectiveness" criteria on the term "medically accepted indication;" doing so renders Congress's reference to the *other* compendia, which do *not* include classifications of effectiveness, meaningless. * * *

The compendia citations do not create an irrebuttable presumption, because the state can always adopt a formulary or avail itself of the other methods for exclusion of a drug which have been adopted in the federal statutory scheme. Here, though, AHCA adopted its own *ad hoc* procedure for excluding Neurontin from coverage. By applying a more stringent test for drug coverage than the one set out by Congress, AHCA is effectively denying coverage for those drugs it is legally required to cover. * * *

Plaintiffs in this case are not seeking monetary damages but rather, prospective injunctive relief. They are asking this court to enjoin defendant, as head of the state Medicaid agency, from continuing to implement a policy which they say (and which this court has found) violates the federal Medicaid Act. They seek to force defendant to adopt a written policy which complies with the Medicaid Act and ensures coverage of Neurontin for those uses recognized in the Medicaid law, and to take appropriate action to ensure that affected individuals are notified of the change in policy and advised that previously-denied prescriptions for Neurontin can be resubmitted for reimbursement to AHCA. * * *

Plaintiffs are low-income residents of Florida who cannot pay for their own health care. Their poverty qualifies them for participation in the

Florida Medicaid program, which guarantees them prompt access to essential medical services. Plaintiffs' treating physicians have concluded, after assessing their patient's conditions and medical histories, including other drugs prescribed and reactions thereto, that Neurontin is medically necessary and indicated for the treatment of plaintiffs' conditions. Plaintiffs claim that as a result of defendant's refusal to cover Neurontin for their conditions (because they are not among the four that AHCA has approved for coverage), they and other Medicaid recipients like them are being denied essential medical treatment, and that the resultant harm is imminent and irreparable.

AHCA counters that plaintiffs have failed to show they would suffer irreparable harm if they are no longer able to take Neurontin. It is AHCA's position that any harm is speculative and remote, because Neurontin has not been shown to have any curative effect on any of the indications for which AHCA is denying reimbursement, and in any event, there are alternative drugs covered by AHCA that have been proven to be safe and effective in treating the conditions from which plaintiffs suffer. * * * AHCA is denying Medicaid benefits to which plaintiffs are legally entitled. The denial of medical benefits, and resultant loss of essential medical services, constitutes an irreparable harm to these individuals. * * * Issuance of an injunction to enforce the federal Medicaid Act is without question in the public interest, and the court finds that plaintiffs have satisfied all prongs of the injunction standard. * * *

NOTES AND QUESTIONS

1. *Is listing an off-label use in one of the compendia sufficient?* See United States ex rel. Rost v. Pfizer, Inc., 253 F.R.D. 11, 16 (D.Mass.2008) ("[A] more recent statement of the Center for Medicaid and State Operations undermines this holding [in *Edmonds*], by explaining that '[t]he statute requires coverage of off-label uses of FDA-approved drugs for indications that are supported (as opposed to listed) in the compendia.' "); see also Joshua Cohen et al., Off–Label Use Reimbursement, 64 Food & Drug L.J. 391, 396 (2009) ("Compendia have become a de facto reference for public sector reimbursement of off-label uses, particularly with respect to antineoplastics."). Is there any problem with delegating to the publishers of compendia the power to dictate coverage under public insurance programs? Cf. Chap. 1(B)(1) (notes following *Ova II*).

2. *Medicaid coverage exceptions.* States may choose to exclude or restrict access to certain types of drugs, including barbiturates, benzodiazepines, weight loss drugs, fertility agents, and drugs used for cosmetic purposes, cough/cold relief, and smoking cessation. States may decline to cover the abortifacient mifepristone, which the federal government has refused to reimburse in any event. See Amy Goldstein, Medicaid Coverage of RU–486 Limited, Wash. Post, Mar. 31, 2001, at A9. Conversely, a policy requiring coverage of ED drugs has attracted vocal criticism. See David F. Chavkin, Medicaid and Viagra: Restoring Potency to an Old Program?, 11 Health

Matrix 189 (2001); Erin L. Connolly, Note, Constitutional Issues Raised by States' Exclusion of Fertility Drugs from Medicaid Coverage in Light of Mandated Coverage of Viagra, 54 Vand. L. Rev. 451 (2001); Carole L. Stewart, Comment, Mandated Medicaid Coverage of Viagra: Raising the Issues of Questionable Priorities, the Need for a Definition of Medical Necessity, and the Politics of Poverty, 44 Loy. L. Rev. 611 (1998). See generally Emile L. Loza, Access to Pharmaceuticals Under Medicaid Managed Care: Federal Law Compiled and State Contracts Compared, 55 Food & Drug L.J. 449 (2000).

3. *Covering medical devices.* States must cover home health services, including medical supplies and equipment. See 42 U.S.C. § 1396a(a)(13)(B)–(C); 42 C.F.R. § 440.70(b)(3). As one commentator has noted, "[i]n many states, to have an item of durable medical equipment (DME) covered by a state's Medicaid program, the item must be listed as a covered item in a state's preapproved list, and a Medicaid recipient's physician must certify that the item is medically necessary for the health of the recipient." Jennifer K. Squillario, Comment, Medicaid and Durable Medical Equipment: An Ongoing Battle Between Expense and Health, 59 Md. L. Rev. 669, 669–70 (2000) (adding that "[t]he lists are rarely updated"); see also Esteban v. Cook, 77 F.Supp.2d 1256, 1262 (S.D.Fla.1999) (invalidating $582 cap on wheelchairs for adults with severe mobility impairment, explaining that, "once the state voluntarily elects to provide wheelchairs to eligible Medicaid recipients, it must provide wheelchairs [including more expensive customized and motorized models] that are sufficient in amount, duration and scope to achieve their purpose").

4. *Medicaid waivers.* Individual states may petition CMS for permission to implement experimental programs or demonstration projects that deviate from federal requirements. See 42 U.S.C. § 1315; see also Diane Rowland, Medicaid—Implications for the Health Safety Net, 353 New Eng. J. Med. 1439 (2005); Amy Goldstein, States' Changes Reshape Medicaid: New Restrictions Aim to Save Money, Wash. Post, June 12, 2006, at A1. A number of states operate their Medicaid programs under waivers. Oregon sparked controversy when it proposed a waiver that would allow it to expand its Medicaid coverage to all persons living below the poverty line by specifically ranking covered medical products and services according to their effectiveness and cost, and funding only items that ranked above a particular cut-off point. See Howard M. Leichter, Oregon's Bold Experiment: Whatever Happened to Rationing?, 24 J. Health Pol. Pol'y & L. 147 (1999); Nancy K. Stade, The Use of Quality-of-Life Measures to Ration Health Care: Reviving a Rejected Proposal, 93 Colum. L. Rev. 1985 (1993); Caitlin J. Halligan, Note, "Just What the Doctor Ordered": Oregon's Medicaid Rationing Process and Public Participation in Risk Regulation, 83 Geo. L.J. 2697 (1995); see also Andrew Pollack, A Panel Decides Washington State's Health Care Costs, N.Y. Times, Mar. 22, 2011, at B1 (describing the work of a neighboring state's Health Technology Assessment committee, which "explicitly considers the cost of treatments in making its decisions, akin to Britain's National Institute for Health and Clinical Excellence"). In 2008, Oregon took an entirely different approach when it decided to use a lottery to select among 90,000 new Medicaid applicants because the state could only afford to cover an additional 10,000 individuals. See Gina Kolata, First Study of Its Kind Shows Benefits of Providing Medical Insurance to Poor, N.Y. Times, July 7, 2011, at A14.

2. PRIVATE PAYERS

Sibley–Schreiber v. Oxford Health Plans, Inc.

62 F.Supp.2d 979 (E.D.N.Y.1999).

■ DEARIE, DISTRICT JUDGE:

* * * Plaintiffs bring this class action seeking declaratory judgment, injunctive relief, and to recover damages resulting from defendants' wrongful denial of insurance coverage for the prescription medicine Viagra. * * * Viagra was approved by the FDA as an effective treatment for erectile dysfunction on March 27, 1998. Prior to Viagra, the prescribed course of treatment for erectile dysfunction included painful, complicated, and expensive injections, suppositories, and pumps. These methods were covered, and continue to be covered, under defendants' insurance policies.

On May 1, 1998, defendants stopped paying for Viagra and announced that it would issue a final policy regarding coverage within 45 days (the "no pay" period). On June 15, 1998, Oxford publicly announced that it would pay for only six Viagra pills per month regardless of the number of pills prescribed by the physician (the "six pill" policy). Each plaintiff claims to suffer from "organic impotence." Each plaintiff further alleges that his physician prescribed Viagra soon after the FDA had approved its use for impotence. Plaintiffs challenge defendants' denial of coverage during the 45 day period and the six pill policy.

Defendants argue that plaintiffs failed to exhaust the administrative claims process provided by the insurance plans before filing the instant action. Each plaintiff, however, communicated with defendants on numerous occasions in an effort to get an exception from defendants' publicly announced policies. Each of the named plaintiffs submitted affidavits detailing their efforts at securing coverage for the prescribed medication. * * *

Section 503(2) of the Employee Retirement Income Security Act (ERISA) requires that "every employee benefit plan shall ... afford a reasonable opportunity to any participant whose claim for benefits has been denied for a full and fair review by the appropriate named fiduciary of the decision denying the claim." 29 U.S.C. § 1133 (1998). There is no statutory requirement that plaintiffs exhaust administrative processes before filing an action in federal court. However, relying on § 1133, "courts have 'developed the requirement that a claimant should ordinarily follow internal plan procedures and exhaust internal plan remedies before seeking judicial relief under ERISA.' " * * *

Exhaustion of the statutorily required administrative process is not always required. Most notably, exhaustion is excused "where claimants make a 'clear and positive showing' that pursuing available administrative remedies would be futile." To fall within the futility doctrine, claimants must "show that it is certain that their claim will be denied on appeal, not merely that they doubt an appeal will result in a different decision." The exhaustion doctrine, however, does not require plaintiffs to "engage in meaningless acts or to needlessly squander resources as a prerequisite to commencing litigation." Courts have been unwilling to conclude that pursuit of the administrative process is futile absent evidence that a plaintiff sincerely attempted to resolve its dispute extrajudicially. Certainly, an allegation of futility is not satisfied by the mere showing that a claim was denied when initially presented to the insurance company. Nor is futility demonstrated by the fact that the members of a review committee consist of the insurance company's management rather than a neutral arbitrator. * * *

According to plaintiffs' affidavits, numerous telephone calls were made to defendants in an effort to get an exception to the "no pay" and six pill policies. Plaintiffs' physicians were required to, and did, submit letters of medical necessity, in some cases on more than one occasion. In one instance, a treating physician interceded on behalf of his needy patient. Regardless of the efforts and opinions of plaintiffs' physicians, defendants consistently denied coverage during the 45 day no-pay period and coverage beyond six pills after that policy was announced. * * *

Assuming arguendo that plaintiffs were aware of their need to pursue all administrative appeals and the procedure for pursuing such appeals, there is overwhelming evidence that such efforts would have been futile. While an insured's belief, even in good faith, cannot by itself justify bypassing a contractually binding review process, there are circumstances here, not genuinely in dispute, that make it perfectly clear, as the course of events now confirms, that Oxford would not make any exceptions to the announced policy. Each of the four named plaintiffs called defendants on numerous occasions and received the same "no exceptions" answer to their repeated pleas for consideration. * * *

The named plaintiffs in this case acted entirely reasonably. When faced with Oxford's sudden denial of coverage, they contacted the insurer directly or with the help of the employer's representative for reconsideration and an explanation. They persisted in their request for coverage; they provided medical documentation; they pursued their claims up the hierarchy of Oxford's bureaucracy, and, quite understandably, came eventually to recognize that relief would not come from Oxford at any level. Ultimately, Oxford proved them right. Nevertheless, Oxford now argues that they stopped too soon and despite their entirely reasonable efforts, that misjudgment has cost them the opportunity to press their claims before this court.

Oxford's position seems particularly untenable when seen in the light of the policy language itself. In neither policy handbook is the insured instructed that administrative remedies must be utilized. These materials are strangely silent on the exhaustion requirement that Oxford now embraces with such enthusiasm. Like the named plaintiffs, insureds are left to their own devices, instructed that they should use the grievance procedure and may file a claim or may appeal, as the exhaustion requirement lurks in the background waiting to be deployed should a frustrated policyholder seek to initiate judicial proceedings. The scenario offends notions of fairness and common sense.

In re Union Pacific R.R. Employment Practices Litig.

479 F.3d 936 (8th Cir.2007).

■ GRUENDER, CIRCUIT JUDGE:

Brandi Standridge and Kenya Phillips, as class representatives [for approximately 1,500 female employees], sued Union Pacific Railroad Company for sexual discrimination under Title VII of the Civil Rights Act of 1964, as amended by the Pregnancy Discrimination Act of 1978 (PDA). * * * Union Pacific, a freight company headquartered in Omaha, Nebraska, provides health care benefits to those of its employees who are covered by collective bargaining agreements * * * through one of five plans. While the plans provide benefits for services such as routine physical exams, tetanus shots and drug and alcohol treatments, they exclude coverage of allergy serum, immunization agents, biological sera and drugs that treat infertility. They also exclude both male and female contraceptive methods, prescription and nonprescription, when used for the sole purpose of contraception. Union Pacific only covers contraception when medically necessary for a non-contraceptive purpose such as regulating menstrual cycles, treating skin problems or avoiding serious health risks associated with pregnancy. * * *

The district court held that Union Pacific violated Title VII, as amended by the PDA, because "it treats medical care women need to prevent pregnancy less favorably than it treats medical care needed to prevent other medical conditions that are no greater threat to employees' health than is pregnancy." In re Union Pac. R.R. Employment Practices Litig., 378 F.Supp.2d 1139, 1149 (D.Neb.2005). * * *

Title VII provides that "[i]t shall be an unlawful employment practice for an employer ... to discriminate against any individual with respect to his compensation, terms, conditions, or privileges of employment, because of such individual's ... sex." 42 U.S.C. § 2000e–2(a)(1). Congress created the PDA to amend this provision in response to the Supreme Court's holding that the exclusion of pregnancy benefits did not violate Title VII. See Gen. Elec. Co. v. Gilbert, 429 U.S. 125, 145–46 (1976). The PDA provides:

> The terms "because of sex" or "on the basis of sex" include, but are not limited to, because of or on the basis of pregnancy, childbirth, or related medical conditions; and women affected by pregnancy, childbirth, or related medical conditions shall be treated the same for all employment-related purposes, including receipt of benefits under fringe benefit programs, as other persons not so affected but similar in

their ability or inability to work.... This subsection shall not require an employer to pay for health insurance benefits for abortion, except where the life of the mother would be endangered if the fetus were carried to term, or except where medical complications have arisen from an abortion.

42 U.S.C. § 2000e(k).

Neither the circuit courts nor the Supreme Court has considered whether the PDA applies to contraception. The Supreme Court, though, has discussed the scope of the PDA in *Newport News Shipbuilding & Dry Dock Co. v. EEOC*, 462 U.S. 669 (1983), and *International Union, United Automobile, Aerospace & Agricultural Implement Workers of America, UAW v. Johnson Controls, Inc.*, 499 U.S. 187 (1991). * * * In *Krauel v. Iowa Methodist Medical Center*, 95 F.3d 674, 679 (8th Cir.1996), we applied these Supreme Court precedents and held that the PDA does not extend to infertility treatments. We concluded that the phrase "related medical conditions" in the PDA refers only to medical conditions associated with "pregnancy" and "childbirth," the specific terms that precede the general phrase. Infertility is "strikingly different" from pregnancy and childbirth because infertility prevents conception, while pregnancy, childbirth and medical conditions related to them can occur only after conception. Therefore, *Krauel* holds that infertility is "outside of the PDA's protection because it is not pregnancy, childbirth, or a related medical condition." Id. at 679–80. * * *

While contraception may certainly affect the causal chain that leads to pregnancy, we have specifically rejected the argument that a causal connection, by itself, results in a medical condition being "related to" pregnancy for PDA purposes. * * * [C]ontraception is not "related to" pregnancy for PDA purposes because, like infertility treatments, contraception is a treatment that is only indicated prior to pregnancy. Contraception is not a medical treatment that occurs when or if a woman becomes pregnant; instead, contraception prevents pregnancy from even occurring. See Merriam–Webster's Collegiate Dictionary 271 (11th ed.2005) (defining contraception as the "deliberate prevention of conception or impregnation"). As in *Krauel,* the result in *Johnson Controls* does not require coverage of contraception because contraception is not a gender-specific term like "potential pregnancy," but rather applies to both men and women like "infertility." In conclusion, the PDA does not require coverage of contraception because contraception is not "related to" pregnancy for PDA purposes and is gender-neutral.

We are not persuaded by the contention of Standridge and Phillips and the amici members of Congress [five Senators and twenty-five members of the House] that Congress intended to address the coverage of prescription contraception in the PDA. In their views, the PDA was a "broad response" to the *Gilbert* decision, and Congress wanted to protect women in all areas concerning pregnancy, including the prevention of it. However, the plain language of the PDA makes no reference to contraception. Additionally, the House and Senate legislative histories do not mention contraception. This silence by Congress on the issue of contraception cannot be interpreted to expand the PDA to cover contraception.

We also do not agree with Standridge and Phillips's argument that the PDA's express exclusion of coverage of abortion, without an accompanying express exclusion of coverage for contraception, implies an intent to include coverage of contraception. Abortion is "the termination of a pregnancy," Merriam–Webster's Collegiate Dictionary 3, while contraception prevents pregnancy from even occurring. While we do not need to decide whether the PDA would cover abortion without this exclusion, abortion arguably would be "related to" pregnancy in a manner that contraception is not because abortion can only occur when a woman is pregnant. In contrast, there would be no reason for Congress to expressly exclude a treatment that is not "related to" pregnancy for PDA purposes, such as contraception.

Finally, we are not persuaded by the EEOC [Equal Employment Opportunity Commission] decision that interpreted the PDA as requiring employers to cover prescription contraception for women if they cover "other prescription drugs and devices, or other types of services, that are used to prevent the occurrences of other medical conditions." EEOC Commission Decision on Coverage of Contraception (Dec. 14, 2000). * * * The decision addressed a policy that denied coverage of prescription contraception but included coverage of the surgical contraceptive methods of vasectomies and tubal ligations. Union Pacific's coverage is different because it excludes coverage of all contraception for women and men, both prescription and surgical. Additionally, the decision compares prescription contraception to the broadest possible spectrum of other preventive treatments and services without citing a persuasive basis for doing so. Furthermore, the EEOC did not issue any guidance on the issue of coverage of prescription contraception until 22 years after the enactment of the PDA. The delay brings into question the consistency and persuasiveness of the EEOC's position. Therefore, we find this decision unpersuasive on the question before us. * * *

Along with its argument that the PDA does not require coverage of contraception, Union Pacific argues that its exclusion of contraception coverage does not discriminate against its female employees under a general Title VII analysis. * * * In determining whether Union Pacific treated the similarly situated male employees more favorably than the protected female employees, we must compare the health benefits that Union Pacific's plans provided for men and women. The district court * * * found that the health plans treated men more favorably because the plans covered preventive medicines and services such as medication for male-pattern baldness, routine physical exams, tetanus shots, and drug and alcohol treatments. Union Pacific argues that the district court's comparator was too broad because it treated pregnancy as a disease that needed to be prevented instead of focusing on the narrow issue of contraception.

We decline to address whether pregnancy is a "disease." Instead, we simply hold that the district court erred in using the comparator "medicines or medical services [that] prevent employees from developing diseases or conditions that pose an equal or lesser threat to employees' health than does pregnancy." As previously discussed, this case concerns Union Pacific's coverage of contraception for men and women. The proper comparator is the provision of the medical benefit in question, contraception. Union Pacific's health plans do not cover any contraception used by women such as birth control, sponges, diaphragms, intrauterine devices or tubal ligations or any contraception used by men such as condoms and vasectomies. Therefore, the coverage provided to women is not less favorable than that provided to men. Thus, there is no violation of Title VII. * * *

■ BYE, CIRCUIT JUDGE (dissenting):

* * * When one looks at the medical effect of Union Pacific's failure to provide insurance coverage for prescription contraception, the inequality of coverage is clear. This failure only medically affects females, as they bear all of the health consequences of unplanned pregnancies. An insurance policy providing comprehensive coverage for preventative medical care, including coverage for preventative prescription drugs used exclusively by males, but fails to cover prescription contraception used exclusively by females, can hardly be called equal. * * * That its policy does not provide coverage for condoms is unsurprising—Union Pacific has not identified any health insurance policy which would provide coverage for nonprescription, contraceptive devices available in drug stores and gas stations nationwide. As for vasectomies, even if we were to look at its exclusion of coverage for vasectomies, the policy nonetheless discriminates against females. When a policy excludes coverage for vasectomies, the medical effect of this exclusion is born entirely by women, as the record demonstrates women are the only gender which can become pregnant.

The court holds Union Pacific's failure to cover prescription contraception is not covered by the PDA because prescription contraception use occurs prior to pregnancy. * * * While the plain language of the PDA does not specifically include pre-pregnancy conditions, there is some indication Congress intended the act to cover pre-pregnancy discrimination. Congress used the phrase "related medical conditions." The word "related" indicates the PDA covers more than mere pregnancy. In this case, the district court relied on the second clause of the PDA which is drafted even more broadly than the first, covering "women *affected by* pregnancy, childbirth, or related medical conditions." 378 F.Supp.2d at 1143 (emphasis added) ("Because the PDA plainly * * * applies to 'women affected by pregnancy' and not merely to pregnant women, the clear language of the statute requires that [Union Pacific's] Plans treat the risk of pregnancy no less favorably than the Plans treat other similar health risks."). Finally, * * * use of the phrase "include, but are not limited to" mandates a broad reading of the PDA because it suggests Congress was being illustrative rather than exclusive with the list following the phrase. The PDA's legislative history also promotes a broad construction of the act to include pre-pregnancy. Representative Ronald Sarasin explained the PDA gives a woman "the right . . . to be financially and legally protected *before,* during, and after her pregnancy." 124 Cong. Rec. 38574 (daily ed. Oct. 14, 1978) (statement of Rep. Sarasin, a manager of the House version of the PDA) (emphasis added).

Even if Congress did not intend the PDA to cover pre-pregnancy discrimination, the Supreme Court ostensibly broadened the scope of the PDA to include pre-pregnancy discrimination in *Johnson Controls*. The Court found classifying employees on the basis of childbearing capacity, whether or not they were already pregnant, "must be regarded, for Title VII purposes, in the same light as explicit sex discrimination." 499 U.S. at 199. In *Johnson Controls*, a battery manufacturer enforced a gender-based, fetal-protection policy excluding fertile women (women who were pregnant or capable of becoming pregnant) from working in jobs where they would be exposed to lead. The bias was clear, as the policy at issue excluded only women. Id. at 197. The Court used the PDA to bolster its holding [that] the policy discriminated on its face as it "explicitly classifies on the basis of potential for pregnancy." The choice to treat all "female employees as potentially pregnant" was discriminatory. * * * The court suggests *Krauel* drew the line at pregnancy, and held the PDA does not apply to infertility treatments because infertility, by its definition, occurs prior to pregnancy. In my assessment, *Krauel* cannot draw such a bright line because of *Johnson Controls*. * * *

Potential pregnancy, like infertility, by its definition occurs prior to conception. The same can be said for the use of prescription contraception. The reason *Krauel* determined the PDA did not apply to an employer's failure to cover infertility treatments, even in light of *Johnson Controls*, was because infertility, unlike potential pregnancy, is a gender-neutral affliction. After *Krauel*, denial of coverage for infertility treatments does not implicate the PDA because infertility affects both men and women. The court suggests infertility treatments and contraception are both pre-pregnancy and this fact makes the difference. Although both are used prior to conception, when one looks at the medical effect of the denial of insurance coverage, prescription contraception is easily distinguishable from infertility treatments. * * * Without contraception, a sexually active, fertile woman is almost certain to become pregnant. Once pregnant, only the woman's health is affected. Infertility, by contrast, is a word used to describe a number of medical conditions affecting both men and women. When a man or a woman is infertile, he or she is unable to contribute to reproduction as his or her reproductive organs do not function properly. Infertility treatments may correct the medical condition of infertility in both men and women, allowing them to effectively make the necessary contribution to reproduction. Thus, prescription contraception and infertility treatments are like apples and oranges. Although both relate to pregnancy in a general sense, prescription contraception is, unlike fertility treatments, at its very core gender-specific. As such, a PDA claim based on a failure to provide prescription contraception coverage is not foreclosed by *Krauel*. * * *

[T]he court also holds Union Pacific's policy does not discriminate against women under Title VII, because the policy excludes contraception coverage for both men and women. Because I agree with the district court's comparison—between the insurance coverage provided to men and woman for all types of preventative medicine—I also dissent with regard to this holding. Whether something constitutes discrimination under Title VII, as amended by the PDA, is a matter of comparison. * * *

The history of the PDA supports the district court's choice of comparators. The PDA was enacted specifically to overrule the reasoning employed by the majority in *Gilbert* and to adopt the reasoning of the *Gilbert* dissenters. See Newport News, 462 U.S. at 678–79 & n.17 (noting the legislative history of the PDA demonstrates Congress viewed the *Gilbert* dissenters as expressing the true principle and meaning of Title VII when they explained it was facially discriminatory for an employer to offer protection against all risks but for pregnancy and "the appropriate classification was 'between persons who face a risk of pregnancy and those who do not' "). In *Gilbert*, the Court refused to require employers to cover pregnancy in their short-term disability plans, noting that without the pregnancy coverage, plans for men and women were equal and covered the same risks. 429 U.S. at 138–40. In his dissent, Justice Stevens argued this was discriminatory because the employer treated absenteeism based on pregnancy differently than all other types of absenteeism. Id. at 161 (Stevens, J., dissenting). Likewise, Justice Brennan explained it was discriminatory for a company to devise "a policy that, but for pregnancy, offers protection for all risks, even those that are 'unique to' men or heavily male dominated." Id. at 160 (Brennan, J., dissenting). Put another way, the *Gilbert* dissenters recognized, to be equal, a plan would have to cover for the uniquely female risk of pregnancy, although this required giving women additional benefits men would not receive.

Under this reasoning, as prescription contraception is a treatment for (or a method to control the occurrence and timing of) the uniquely female condition of potential pregnancy, the exclusion of this coverage in a plan providing other preventative coverage is discriminatory. Union Pacific provides coverage for a wide range of preventative medicines and procedures, including coverage for prescription drugs used exclusively by males to prevent benign prostatic hypertrophy. Union Pacific specifically excludes coverage for prescription contraception when used for a preventative purpose. Under the reasoning of the *Gilbert* dissenters, as adopted by Congress with the PDA, this is discriminatory. Women are uniquely and specifically disadvantaged by Union Pacific's failure to cover prescription contraception. Because I believe such a policy is violative of Title VII, as amended by the PDA, I respectfully dissent. Although the district court's decision might appear to grant women benefits above and beyond those of men, the PDA requires such benefits be included in an otherwise comprehensive health care plan.

NOTES AND QUESTIONS

1. *Insurance coverage and "lifestyle" drugs.* Private insurance coverage for outpatient drugs did not become common until after 1980. See Patricia

M. Danzon & Mark V. Pauly, Health Insurance and the Growth in Pharmaceutical Expenditures, 45 J.L. & Econ. 587 (2002) (evaluating this development). Health plans generally do not cover items—such as baldness preparations and wrinkle treatments—that improve quality of life rather than treat a disease. See William M. Sage, Managed Care's Crimea: Medical Necessity, Therapeutic Benefit, and the Goals of Administrative Process in Health Insurance, 53 Duke L.J. 597 (2003); Annotation, What Services, Equipment, or Supplies Are "Medically Necessary" for Purposes of Coverage Under Medical Insurance, 75 A.L.R.4th 763 (1990 & 2011 Supp.). Some insurers decline to cover ED drugs, while other policies cover such products subject to various restrictions. See, e.g., Harrow v. Prudential Ins. Co., 279 F.3d 244 (3d Cir.2002); Scholl v. QualMed, Inc., 103 F.Supp.2d 850 (E.D.Pa. 2000) (dismissing for failure to exhaust administrative remedies a class action suit demanding "full coverage" of Viagra® under a health plan's drug benefit clause); cf. David Kirby, Party Favors: Pill Popping as Insurance, N.Y. Times, June 21, 2004, at F1 (describing the growing recreational use of ED drugs); Jane Spencer, His and Hers Sex Drugs, Wall St. J., Nov. 4, 2003, at D1 (reporting increased medical attention to female sexual dysfunction). Don't ED drugs help to overcome one underlying cause of male infertility? Which categories of drugs would you consider to be "medically necessary" if you were a benefits manager for an insurance company? How about vaccines that guard against STDs or drugs (e.g., cholesterol-lowering statins) that obviate the need to make difficult lifestyle changes (e.g., diet and exercise)? Cf. Jonathan Klick & Thomas Stratmann, Diabetes Treatments and Moral Hazard, 50 J.L. & Econ. 519 (2007) (finding that state insurance coverage mandates discourage lifestyle modification efforts); Lars Noah, Platitudes About "Product Stewardship" in Torts: Continuing Drug Research and Education, 15 Mich. Telecomm. & Tech. L. Rev. 359, 381–84 (2009) ("In the final analysis, all drugs are, to one degree or another, lifestyle drugs."). Even though they have recognized therapeutic uses, legislators evidently regard Botox and tanning beds as entirely frivolous products. See Julie H. Davis, Plastic Surgeons Fight Proposed Excise Tax: Strategy to Pay for Health Care Headed for Vote, Boston Globe, Nov. 20, 2009, at A2 (reporting that a proposed additional 5% fee on procedures such as Botox injections and breast implant surgery, dubbed the "Botax," encountered stiff industry resistance); N.C. Aizenman, Some Customers Heated over Indoor "Tan Tax," Which Was Part of Health-care Law, Wash. Post, July 8, 2010, at A5 (noting passage instead of a 10% surcharge on the use of tanning beds).

2. *Excluding infertility treatments.* Is the distinction suggested by the dissent in *Union Pacific* persuasive? Whatever the underlying cause of a couple's infertility, and whoever undergoes treatment to overcome that difficulty, won't the "medical effects" of successful treatment get experienced solely by the female? Other courts have sided with the holding in *Krauel* that the exclusion of infertility treatments was not discriminatory. See Saks v. Franklin Covey Co., 316 F.3d 337 (2d Cir.2003); see also Lars Noah, Assisted Reproductive Technologies and the Pitfalls of Unregulated Biomedical Innovation, 55 Fla. L. Rev. 603, 616–17 (2003) (explaining that noncoverage remains the norm and reduces the influence of insurers over the utilization of ARTs); Katherine E. Abel, Note, The Pregnancy Discrimination Act and Insurance Coverage for Infertility Treatment: An Inconceivable Union, 37 Conn. L. Rev. 819 (2005); cf. Katherine Pratt, Deducting the Costs of Fertility Treatment: Implications of Magdalin v. Commissioner for Opposite–Sex Couples, Gay and Lesbian Same–Sex Couples and Single Women and Men, 2009 Wis. L. Rev. 1283; Anna L. Benjamin, Note, The Implications of Using the Medical Expense Deduction of I.R.C. Section 213 to Subsidize Assisted Reproductive Technology, 79 Notre Dame L. Rev. 1117 (2004).

3. *Excluding contraceptives.* Would the introduction of a prescription contraceptive product for men simplify or complicate the analysis? See Pam Belluck, Interest and Scientific Advances Lead to Progress on Contraceptive for Men, N.Y. Times, July 24, 2011, at A13. The fact that many insurers decided to cover ED drugs brought renewed attention to the tradition of excluding contraceptives. See Carey Goldberg, Insurance for Viagra Spurs Coverage for Birth Control, N.Y. Times, June 30, 1999, at A1; see also Kathryn Kindell, Comment, Prescription for Fairness: Health Insurance Reimbursement for Viagra and Contraceptives, 35 Tulsa L.J. 399 (2000). Coverage of prescription contraceptives remains spotty. See Tamar Lewin, Agency Finds Many Health Plans Should Cover Contraceptive Costs, N.Y. Times, Dec. 15, 2000, at A1. A few earlier district court decisions found PDA violations in such circumstances. See Stocking v. AT & T Corp., 436 F.Supp.2d 1014, 1016–17 (W.D.Mo.2006); Erickson v. Bartell Drug Co., 141 F.Supp.2d 1266, 1270–71 (W.D.Wash.2001); see also Stephen F. Befort & Elizabeth C. Borer, Equitable Prescription Drug Coverage: Preventing Sex Discrimination in Employer–Provided Health Plans, 70 La. L. Rev. 206 (2009); Phyra M. McCandless, Comment, The Fallacy of Mandating Contraceptive Equity: Why Laws That Protect Women with Health Insurance Deepens Institutional Discrimination, 42 U.S.F. L. Rev. 1115 (2008). Several states have passed "contraceptive equity" bills requiring insurers that cover prescription drugs to include birth control. See Katie E. Carlson, Note, A Study of the Effectiveness of Mandated State Contraceptive Coverage in Iowa and Missouri and the Case for a Federal Law, 54 Drake L. Rev. 509 (2006); Breena M. Roos, Note, The Quest for Equality: Comprehensive Insurance Coverage of Prescription Contraceptives, 82 B.U. L. Rev. 1289 (2002); see also N.C. Aizenman, No Insurance Co–Payments for Birth Control, U.S. Says, Wash. Post, Aug. 2, 2011, at A1 (reporting that new federal regulations implementing the health reform legislation require insurers to start providing full coverage of all FDA-approved prescription contraceptives); Robert Pear, Panel Calling for Free Contraceptive Coverage, N.Y. Times, July 20, 2011, at A1 (noting that "[m]ost private insurance provides contraceptive coverage, but co-payments have increased in recent years"). Such laws have, however, encountered objections based on religious principles. See Catholic Charities of Diocese of Albany v. Serio, 7 N.Y.3d 510, 825 N.Y.S.2d 653, 859 N.E.2d 459 (2006) (rejecting free exercise challenges to such a requirement); Janice Lee, Note,

A Quick Fix Solution for the Morning After: An Alternative Approach to Mandatory Contraceptive Coverage, 9 Geo. J.L. & Pub. Pol'y 189 (2011).

4. *OTC products*. Health insurers generally exclude nonprescription drugs from coverage, even when "prescribed" by a physician, and they also may restrict coverage of any Rx products remaining in a class of drugs when one of them gets switched OTC. See Joshua P. Cohen et al., Switching Prescription Drugs to Over the Counter, 330 Brit. Med. J. 39, 40 (2005); Bruce Japsen, New Pain Rising in Heartburn Drug Costs: Insured Prilosec Users to Pay More Over the Counter, Chi. Trib., July 31, 2003, at 1. In addition, the federal tax deduction allowed for medical expenses exceeding 7.5% of adjusted gross income includes uncovered expenses for prescription drugs but not OTC products (except for insulin). See Tax Equity and Fiscal Responsibility Act of 1982, Pub. L. No. 97–248, § 202(b), 96 Stat. 324 (codified as amended at 26 U.S.C. § 213(a)–(b)); see also Lance W. Rook, Listening to Zantac: The Role of Non–Prescription Drugs in Health Care Reform and the Federal Tax System, 62 Tenn. L. Rev. 107, 133–39 (1994) (advocating that the federal tax deduction be extended to expenditures on OTC drugs); id. at 138–39 ("[T]he prescription/non-prescription distinction was probably a shorthand way to exclude inexpensive medication from health care insurance and tax benefits.... [This] might have been acceptable when there was a correlation between expense and the prescription requirement ... [but] no longer makes sense."); cf. Sandra Block, IRS Rulings Make Medical Flexible Spending Accounts More Attractive, USA Today, Sept. 30, 2003, at 3B (reporting that employers now can offer flex accounts that would include purchases of OTC drugs among eligible expenses).

5. *Off-label uses*. Private payers often resist covering off-label uses of approved drugs or devices. See, e.g., Coram Healthcare Corp. v. Wal–Mart Stores, Inc., 238 F.Supp.2d 586, 590–91 (S.D.N.Y.2002) (upholding insurer's refusal to cover off-label use of intravenous immunoglobulin (IVIG) in MS patient); Bernard Wysocki, Jr., "Wonder Drug" Stops Bleeding, but Cost Is High, Wall St. J., Mar. 17, 2004, at B1 (reporting that public and private insurers are unlikely to pay $5,000 a shot for NovoSeven®, a biotech drug approved to treat a rare form of hemophilia but widely used to stop bleeding in severe trauma cases). Thus, an insurer might cover an expensive new drug to treat a particular type of cancer upon FDA approval but decline to reimburse it when used to treat a different type of cancer. See Robert E. Wittes, Cancer Weapons, out of Reach, Wash. Post, June 15, 2004, at A23 (explaining that, as the prices become astronomical, insurers will become even less willing to pay for off-label uses); see also Amy D. Marcus, Price Becomes Factor in Cancer Treatment, Wall St. J., Sept. 7, 2004, at D1 (explaining that co-payments and caps may put expensive new drugs out of reach even when covered by insurance); Susan Okie, Cancer Drug Approved Quickly: Gleevec Dramatically Effective Against a Type of Leukemia, Wash. Post, May 11, 2001, at A2 (describing a new treatment costing up to $2,400 per month, and noting that the drug's manufacturer plans to subsidize the drug's cost for uninsured patients). In such a case, the patient may have to pay out of pocket, unless the manufacturer is providing the drug gratis as part of a formal clinical trial.

3. COVERAGE FOR EXPERIMENTAL TREATMENTS

Shumake v. Travelers Insurance Co.

383 N.W.2d 259 (Mich.Ct.App.1985).

■ ALLEN, JUDGE:

In this declaratory judgment action, plaintiffs sought reimbursement for Laetrile (amygdalin) and related nutritional therapy prescribed for James Shumake by his physician, Philip E. Binzel, M.D. Dr. Binzel determined that Shumake suffered from a metabolic disorder, a diagnosis he reached based primarily on the fact that Shumake had developed lung cancer. The Laetrile and nutritional supplements were prescribed as a treatment for the metabolic disorder. The trial court held that under the terms of the policy, plaintiffs were entitled to reimbursement in the amount of $17,478.20. Defendant appeals as of right.

Plaintiffs were insured under a group health insurance policy issued by defendant Travelers Insurance Company to James Shumake's former employer, Service Reproduction Company. On May 26, 1978, Shumake underwent surgery for removal of the right upper lobe of his right lung after a cancerous tumor was discovered. His prognosis was guarded, with doctors estimating his chances of survival over the ensuing five years as between 15 and 25 percent. Shumake consulted a general practitioner, Dr. Binzel, who prescribed a course of treatment involving a regimen of Laetrile, enzymes and vitamins, and certain nutritional guidelines. Defendant paid all expenses associated with this treatment from June, 1978, to January 31, 1981. Defendant then notified plaintiffs that expenses for Laetrile and Laetrile-related nutritional supplements were not covered under the subject insurance policy.

The policy at issue provides coverage for 80 percent of "covered medical expenses" which are "necessarily [incurred]." "Covered medical expense" is defined as:

> [The] actual expense to the Employee of the reasonable charges (as defined) not hereinafter excepted incurred by the Employee on account of himself or his Dependent upon the recommendation and approval of the attending physician for the services and supplies listed below and required in connection with the treatment of the Employee or his Dependent for any [accidental bodily injury or sickness].

Included in the list of covered medical expenses are "medical supplies," which are defined to include "[drugs] and medicines covered by written prescription of a physician." The insurance policy does not contain any exclusion which would specifically preclude coverage for Laetrile and Laetrile-related nutritional supplements. Nonetheless, defendant maintains that coverage was properly denied * * * *

Dr. Binzel testified that he did not order laboratory tests because numerous tests would be required to isolate specific nutritional deficiencies and the tests would have been costly. Moreover, he believed that the presence of cancer was indicative of a metabolic disorder and that monitoring the patient's response during the course of therapy was a preferred method for determining whether deficiencies were being adequately treated. It appears from the record before us that Laetrile practitioners generally operated on the central premise that cancer resulted from metabolic imbalances. Proponents believed that if the disorder could be cured, the body's defense mechanisms would then operate to avert a recurrence of cancer.

This issue appears to pose two distinct concerns. First, defendant places substantial weight on the treatment agreement indicating that Shumake was being treated for a metabolic disorder and not for cancer. Yet, the metabolic disorder and the cancer were intricately related. The purpose of the treatment was to enhance the body's defense mechanisms so that they would take over to ward off cancer. The treatment would never have been prescribed if Shumake had not contracted cancer. By way of affidavit, Binzel stated that he was treating Shumake "for lung cancer and its attendant side effects." Moreover, the crux of defendant's argument on the question of whether Laetrile therapy was "necessarily incurred" is the assertion that the treatment was ineffective in the treatment of cancer—not that it was ineffective in the treatment of a metabolic disorder. Regardless of the efficacy of treatment and the disclaimers in the agreement, we believe that the inescapable result is that Shumake received this treatment because of the cancer. Since we have already determined that he was suffering from a "sickness" as a result of the cancer, coverage cannot be denied on this basis.

In addition, defendant's argument relative to whether Shumake was sick goes to a basic tenet upon which Laetrile practitioners operated, i.e., that cancer was indicative of a metabolic disorder. Although defendant presented substantial evidence which challenges the logic of this reasoning, defendant failed to negate the fact that at the time Shumake's treatment commenced there was a strong and viable minority in the medical community which adhered to these basic tenets and believed that Laetrile was an effective means of controlling cancer. We recognize that the weight of authority held a contrary view. However, we are not prepared to determine as a matter of law that a diagnosis subject to conflicting medical opinions is fallacious merely because a majority of the medical community would arrive at a [different] conclusion. Accordingly, we believe that the evidence presented was sufficient to establish a "sickness."

The next issue presented for our consideration is whether Laetrile and related nutritional treatments were necessarily incurred covered medical expenses and required in connection with Shumake's treatment. Defendant maintains that the treatments have been demonstrated to be ineffective and that, as a result, they cannot be regarded as necessary or required for the treatment of cancer.

The trial court found that "necessarily incurred" was an ambiguous term. It then relied on [a previous decision] to hold that the necessity of a medical treatment or expense should be determined by the attending physician. Defendant points out that such a construction of medical necessity could lead to absurd results. For example, such a construction of the policy would require coverage where a physician prescribed bizarre or archaic treatments, such as bloodletting, simply because the physician deemed it necessary. Defendant therefore urges us to follow the reasoning of *Free v. Travelers Ins. Co.*, 551 F.Supp. 554 (D.Md.1982), which, in construing an identical provision of an insurance policy, found that the language was unambiguous. The *Free* court went on to hold that Laetrile could not be regarded as necessary for the treatment of cancer since the evidence presented at trial overwhelmingly indicated that Laetrile had no value in the treatment of cancer.

We cannot agree with the initial premise of the *Free* opinion, that the terms "necessarily incurred" and "required" for treatment are unambiguous. [The court then reviewed prior decisions equating "necessary" with "appropriate," concluding that necessary means "wise in the light of facts known at the time rendered" and "reasonably calculated to shorten and relieve an ordeal of agonizing pain and thereby effectuate the most rapid recovery possible."] * * *

Since the terms "necessary" and "required" are capable of diverse connotations, we find that the provisions in the subject insurance policy are indeed ambiguous. It is a well-established principle that ambiguities in an insurance contract are to be construed against the insurer which drafts the policy and resolved in favor of the insured. A policy should not be construed to defeat coverage unless the language so requires since the purpose of insurance is to insure.

The language "necessarily incurred" or "required" implies that some entity must exercise judgment in determining when a medical expense will be covered. When the insurer does not reserve the right to exercise that judgment itself by way of an exclusion, we believe that the approach of the trial judge * * * is reasonable. A physician is generally better equipped than lawyers and judges to discern what is medically necessary. Cognizant that a rubber stamp approach to a physician's unfettered exercise of discretion could result in coverage for inane treatments, we decline to hold that any treatment or expense is necessary or required merely because it is deemed so by a physician. However, we do hold that a physician's judgment should be accorded deference. Moreover, since medicine is an evolving science in which treatments are at one time regarded as valid and later discredited, we hold that a decision as to necessity shall be reviewed in light of knowledge which existed at the time the decision was rendered.

Employing such a standard does not dispense with this issue since the gist of defendant's argument is that Laetrile falls within the category of inane cancer treatments and was recognized as ineffective at all times during which Mr. Shumake received treatment. In support of these contentions, defendant relies on the decision of the Commissioner of Food and

Drugs on Laetrile, dated July 29, 1977. See 42 Fed. Reg. 39,768. Further, defendant points to a study on Laetrile which was commissioned by the National Cancer Institute. The results of this study were originally published on January 28, 1982. See Moertel, A Clinical Trial of Amygdalin (Laetrile) in the Treatment of Human Cancer, 306 New Eng. J. Med. 201 (1982). * * *

[T]he FDA concluded that there was "no basis in law or in fact for the use of Laetrile or related substances in the treatment of cancer." A review of the Commissioner's report discloses that, although the FDA acknowledged that Laetrile was generally regarded as ineffective by qualified experts, the FDA did not categorically conclude that Laetrile was ineffective. Rather, the FDA's determination was based on a lack of scientific evidence which might have demonstrated that Laetrile was safe and effective. In other words, Laetrile proponents failed to meet the requisite burden of proof. * * * [The court then reviewed the *Rutherford* litigation cited in Chapter 2(D).]

Our review of the Commissioner's report and the *Rutherford* decisions reveals that there was no definitive determination in the scientific community or the courts with respect to Laetrile's effectiveness throughout 1980. Effectiveness had not been proven or disproven. Indeed, these decisions indicate that the debate on Laetrile was still raging in 1980 and that notable institutions were still investigating its use. Moreover, a number of states enacted statutes which permitted intrastate distribution of Laetrile despite the FDA's ban on interstate distribution. Due to the diversity of opinion and Laetrile's questionable status at that time, we believe that a physician could properly exercise discretion so as to determine that Laetrile was necessary and required for the treatment of cancer during this period.

Publication of the Moertel study, however, appears to have terminated the controversy over Laetrile's effectiveness. After administering Laetrile to various control groups while following the regimens recommended by leading Laetrile practitioners, the researchers concluded that:

> [no] substantive benefit was observed in terms of cure, improvement, or stabilization of cancer, improvement of symptoms related to cancer, or extension of life span. The hazards of amygdalin therapy were evidenced in several patients by symptoms of cyanide toxicity or by blood cyanide levels approaching the lethal range. * * * Amygdalin (laetrile) is a toxic drug that is not effective as a cancer treatment.

We have not been provided with any indication that the findings of the Moertel study have been challenged by subsequent studies. At oral argument, plaintiffs' counsel conceded that Laetrile is now recognized as ineffective. In the absence of documentation to refute the Moertel study findings, we would not hold in the future that Laetrile is a necessarily incurred medical expense or required for treatment. However, based on the time frame when these treatments were administered to Shumake and the controversy which was transpiring, we hold that Dr. Binzel's decision as to necessity should be accorded deference.

Finally, defendant argues that the nutritional supplements were not covered under the policy since they could be acquired without a prescription. The policy provides coverage for "drugs and medicines covered by the written prescription of a physician." It is uncontroverted that the nutritional supplements at issue were covered by Binzel's written prescriptions. The policy did not limit its definition of "medical supplies" to drugs which could only be secured with a physician's prescription. Moreover, defendant acknowledged that it provided coverage for nutritional supplements for patients receiving radiation treatments and chemotherapy since malnutrition is often associated with these treatments. Further, Binzel stated that one reason why he prescribed these nutritional supplements was so that he could closely control the dosages that Shumake would receive, a factor which presumably cannot be monitored with medicines that are sold over-the-counter. Since the policy language did not limit coverage to what are generally recognized as "prescription drugs," and the language used must be construed against the insurer, we find that coverage for the nutritional supplements was provided under the terms of the policy. * * *

Richard S. Saver, Note, *Reimbursing New Technologies: Why Are the Courts Judging Experimental Medicine?*

44 STAN. L. REV. 1095 (1992).

* * * As most health care payers, both public and private, generally exclude coverage for experimental medical technologies, answering the question of whether a treatment is experimental answers a much more pressing question—who pays? * * * Natural tensions arise between health care payers who want to limit reimbursement to treatments proven as safe and effective, and individual patients who care more about access to promising treatments. This characterizes the nature of the underlying dispute in experimental exclusion cases. Such cases also often involve multilateral conflicts between patients, medical specialists who use "innovative" technologies, health payers, private sector research advocates, and others. As a result, the experimental exclusion cases severely test the judiciary's ability to resolve competing interests, technical questions, and moral claims about medical technology. * * *

The case law of experimental exclusion is remarkably inconsistent. Decisions involving similarly situated plaintiffs are often resolved inequitably, in part because courts supply their own varied standards for determining when a treatment is "experimental." Because the facts of these cases are distinguishable, no generally accepted legal definition of "experimental" exists. Definitions also vary because of the different contexts in which experimental exclusion cases occur. The public payers (the federal and state governments) run entitlement programs, whereas the private payers (such as insurers) enter into consensual arrangements. In theory, patients and payers have different expectations and obligations, depending on whether the insurance coverage is offered by a self-insured, public, or private payer. Thus, "experimental" may have different meanings depending upon who is spending money on health care. As a result, great uncertainty remains as to what technologies may be excluded as nonreimbursable experimentation.

When public payers are involved, courts interpret "experimentation" in light of the excessively broad definitions offered by the Medicare and Medicaid legislation. The key statutory language for Medicare, the federal health insurance program covering services for the elderly and disabled, states that payment shall not be made for items or expenses which are "not reasonable and necessary." The Health Care Financing Administration (HCFA), which runs Medicare and Medicaid, equates this with a test of whether the technologies are "safe" and "effective" and not "experimental." However, no regulations have clarified these terms. Indeed, HCFA recognizes that the Medicare law is vague, leaving most coverage questions to the fiscal intermediaries and other Medicare contractors who review payment claims. These Medicare contractors vary widely in their determinations.

In more difficult cases, HCFA issues a "national coverage decision" to indicate to carriers whether a particular technology is covered. Courts may be called upon to review these decisions, yet judicial scrutiny usually focuses on whether proper administrative procedures were followed, and not on the criteria used by HCFA to label a technology experimental. When courts do address these criteria directly, they often mechanically quote from the Medicare pamphlets, which are not much more specific or informative than the statutory language. At best, courts scrutinize whether the determination of a technology's status is reasonable "based on current medical opinion."

The case law surrounding Medicaid, the combined federal-state health insurance program for the poor, is equally vague. The Medicaid statute does not set out specific coverage limitations, but courts have granted states considerable power to determine what services are covered, including the power to exclude experimental services. States are given so much discretion that the Medicaid statute could be read to allow states to exclude even "medically necessary" services, [so] judicial inquiry into whether a technology is experimental is made irrelevant. In any event, Medicaid disputes that end up in court rarely address directly the criteria for labeling a technology as experimental. Courts often defer to the opinion of the prescribing physician, which suggests one approach for determining experimental status. Other courts, however, have recognized that this can result in unfair and inconsistent determinations of benefits. Most of this litigation focuses on the question of who decides what constitutes a "medical necessity." The case law remains relatively silent as to how the term should be construed.

As is true with the public payers, private insurers typically depend upon exclusionary language denying liability for "experimental" technology. Usually insurers include explicit limitations in health plans. Most courts take the approach that such experimental exclusion clauses, without more descriptive language or criteria, are ambiguous. And, because insurance law favors construing ambiguous language against the insurer (in part to discourage unfair contracts of adhesion) courts generally read ambiguous language in health insurance contracts to cover disputed technologies. In some cases, an insurer can overcome the harshness of the ambiguities rule by showing its interpretation of the exclusion clause is reasonable. In most instances, however, courts are reluctant to rely on insurer-supplied definitions of "experimental" if the contract itself did not make them explicit.

Insurers may be unwilling to develop more explicit criteria for experimental status, in part fearing that plans that make noncoverage more visible will drive away customers. Some have relied upon one partially successful strategy for avoiding the ambiguities rule: reserving the right to prescreen for experimental technologies. If patients obtain treatment without first seeking authorization, they may be denied benefits for breach of contract. Insurers can also prevail if their contracts set out clear review and arbitration procedures to resolve whether a particular treatment will be covered.

While courts differ to some extent about when they will apply the ambiguities rule, how they will apply the rule is even less certain. After declaring experimental exclusion clauses ambiguous, courts have supplied their own varying and convoluted definitions for what is "medically necessary" and what is "experimental." A frequently employed variant of the ambiguities rule is the doctrine of "reasonable expectations." Under this doctrine, courts construe insurance policies in light of the reasonable expectations of the insured. This is really the same principle in practical operation as the ambiguities rule. If the insurer intends not to cover something for which the insured could reasonably expect to be reimbursed, then "notice of noncoverage must be conspicuous, plain and clear."

Courts have used the reasonable expectations concept to expand coverage for disputed technologies. Some commentators criticize the reflexive use of the doctrine, arguing that insureds do not reasonably expect coverage for unproven technologies and that from the ex ante position, insureds would rather avoid contracting for costly technology that raises premiums but provides uncertain medical benefit. However, the problem of changing perspectives, which can be quite dramatic where health care is concerned, makes any characterization of the ex ante position somewhat suspect. Moreover, this critique may be incorrect in its assumption that insureds would typically opt for lower premiums as opposed to greater potential protection. This is especially true when the individual costs and benefits of access to promising medical treatments are not counter-balanced by equivalent adjustments to premiums. In any event, courts have difficulty employing the ex ante view when hearing the tragic cases of patients facing life threatening disease. In such "hard cases," there are undeniable sympathies to mandate expanded coverage, regardless of doctrinal justifications.

The imprecise manner in which courts employ either the reasonable expectations doctrine or the ambiguities rule presents efficiency problems. The different approaches to expanding or contracting coverage impair the ability of insurers to rely on legal rules to narrow their insurance risk pools. Insurers compete for the relatively low risk customers in a given pool, luring them away by offering lower premiums that are closer to the customers' expected losses. According to conventional, free market interpretations, the narrowing of pools increases competition, which in turn increases total insurance availability by lowering fees.

In theory, courts could promote efficiency by using the reasonable expectations principle to force insurers to describe more accurately what technologies their policies will cover. But the variation in court decisions makes it difficult for insurers to assess their exposure under this doctrine. Such uncertainty may chill insurers because they are not sure what expenses they will be required to reimburse. Moreover, courts may be indulging in hyperbole when they identify certain expectations as reasonable, given the complexity of typical health insurance policies. Where master health contracts run to 65 pages, perhaps it is time to question how well courts can gauge what insureds "reasonably expect." * * *

Although the judiciary has been criticized for ordering payment for experimental treatment too often, it is difficult to assess patient-plaintiffs' rate of success. For a number of reasons, many patients denied payment for novel technologies never even make it to court. At a time of illness, some patients simply cannot marshal the resources for litigation. Others, facing a limited time horizon in which to begin treatment, will conclude that a lawsuit will take too long. A favorable court decision may provide an empty victory because the plaintiff's condition has changed and the technology can no longer be applied. Furthermore, limitations on damages may make litigation impractical or unappealing. If a plaintiff recovers on a contract theory, the judgment will likely cover only the dollar amount of the disputed claim. The additional expense and burden of litigation itself may be worthwhile only in the rarer situation where a patient can pursue a tort action and possibly recover punitive damages. Further, many cases that could be successfully litigated are settled out of court. By agreeing to settle, the insurer deprives other beneficiaries in the same position of a legal interpretation of the relevant provisions of the policy. Only the most determined or most litigious patients are likely to prevail. * * *

Health care payers may also employ strategies, including delaying the evaluation of technologies, to discourage beneficiaries' appeals. For example, one California HMO, after waiting eight months to evaluate a patient's claim that the cancer drug Interferon should be covered, canceled its coverage for all the members in the patient's workplace. According to a Gallup poll of oncologists, one patient in eight never receives the physician's preferred treatment because of such reimbursement struggles. * * *

Courts have developed several benchmarks to define experimental status. Different approaches have, of course, been combined by courts. But it is useful to examine each in isolation and consider the problems such standards pose. In the first instance, courts rely on evidence that a physician has prescribed a particular technology. Such a standard is, however, circular. * * * [C]ourts also rely on evaluations in the medical literature. This approach has the benefit of relying on more rigorously developed and evaluated data than the prescriptive habits of individual physicians. But many new technologies do not generate primary evaluative data. In addition, few medical technologies enjoy an uncritical reception before they are accepted into general practice. Consensus about new treatments may have more to do with whether the treatments follow current fashions in medical theory and less to do with how well they work. * * * A more troubling aspect of this approach is the inevitable time lag between a technology's acceptance in the medical community and its mainstream publication. * * * In a variation on the literature survey standard, courts may rely upon physician experts who testify about accepted practices in the relevant community of specialists or academic centers. * * *

Several payers have proposed one additional and increasingly controversial standard, suggesting that a technology should be considered experimental unless a government agency such as the FDA approves its use. This standard would normally apply only to cases involving drugs and devices, having little relevance for technologies left untested by government agencies. Where health contracts have ambiguous terms, courts have hesitated to use this standard. But where contracts contain specific language requiring the approval of government agencies, courts have denied reimbursement for treatments based on unapproved technologies. Payers have undoubtedly advanced the "agency approval" standard as a way of curtailing costs, but it is most unfair, as it cuts against medical custom. Government agencies have limited objectives when evaluating new technologies. * * * Insisting on agency approval for all uses of a drug would result not only in lost treatment opportunities, but would also dramatically increase costs, as repeated FDA evaluations would be required. In fact, payers that now routinely deny reimbursement for off-label therapy may unintentionally contribute to the inflation of overall health care costs. To avoid anticipated coverage battles, many clinicians hospitalize patients, where reimbursement for off-label therapy is easier to obtain, rather than administering treatments in the cheaper outpatient setting. * * *

An FDA approval standard would also, as a practical matter, exclude much of the information generated by physicians practicing in highly specialized fields such as oncology. Modern chemotherapy involves the use of "cocktails," the combination of many different drugs in constantly changing dosage levels and time intervals. There is no convenient way for the FDA to review such combined modality therapy. And for other uses of oncology drugs, it is not feasible to perform the kind of clinical trials necessary to obtain FDA approval. * * * Therefore, if courts relied exclusively on agency approval as the standard for nonexperimentation, payers would unfairly benefit from government inaction. * * *

NOTES AND QUESTIONS

1. *What's "experimental"?* For instance, a few physicians reported dramatic success after injecting a cement approved by the FDA for a different use into broken vertebrae, and "vertebroplasty" quickly became a standard procedure—even in the absence of any supporting research, proponents successfully lobbied insurers for coverage and, in 2004, Medicare spent more than $20 million on the procedure. See Gina Kolata, Spinal Cement Draws Patients and Questions, N.Y. Times, Aug. 28, 2005, § 1, at 1 (reporting "concern[s] about the procedures' widespread and largely uncritical acceptance"); see also Andrew Pollack, Hot Chemotherapy Bath: Patients See Hope, Critics Hold Doubts, N.Y. Times, Aug. 12, 2011, at A1. Why isn't that considered "experimental"? Recall from Chapter 2 that this question has regulatory consequences—do the different contexts justify using different definitions of the term? The court in *Weaver* had rejected the argument made by Missouri officials that the off-label use of AZT made it "experimental" and therefore excluded from coverage under Medicaid.

2. *Coverage disputes.* Patients with advanced breast cancer brought numerous challenges to refusals by their insurers to cover high-dose chemotherapy with autologous bone marrow transplantation (HDC–ABMT), an expensive and dangerous experimental treatment that ultimately proved to be entirely ineffective. See, e.g., Pitman v. Blue Cross & Blue Shield of Okla., 217 F.3d 1291 (10th Cir.2000); Bechtold v. Physicians Health Plan, 19 F.3d 322 (7th Cir.1994); Bushman v. State Mut. Life Assur. Co. of Am., 915 F.Supp. 945 (N.D.Ill.1996); see also Peter D. Jacobson & Stefanie A. Doebler, "We Were All Sold a Bill of Goods:" Litigating the Science of Breast Cancer Treatment, 52 Wayne L. Rev. 43 (2006); cf. Westover v. Metropolitan Life Ins. Co., 771 F.Supp. 1172 (M.D.Fla.1991) (upholding plan's denial of plaintiff's claim for chelation therapy benefits to treat atherosclerosis on the grounds that the treatment was experimental).

3. *Further commentary.* See Joseph B. Clamon, Does My Health Insurance Cover It? Using Evidence–Based Medicine and Binding Arbitration Techniques to Determine What Therapies Fall Under Experimental Exclusion Clauses in Health Insurance Contracts, 54 Drake L. Rev. 473 (2006); Sharona Hoffman, A Proposal for Federal Legislation to Address Health Insurance Coverage for Experimental and Investigational Treatments, 78 Or. L. Rev. 203 (1999); E. Haavi Morreim, From the Clinics to the Courts: The Role Evidence Should Play in Litigating Medical Care, 26 J. Health Pol. Pol'y & L. 409 (2001); Natalie Regoli, Insurance Roulette: The Experimental Treatment Exclusion and Desperate Patients, 22 QLR 697 (2004); Janet L. Richards, Geography Is Destiny: Disparate Insurance Coverage for Cancer Clinical Trials Demands a Federal Mandate, 76 UMKC L. Rev. 141 (2007); Dorothy Puzio, Note, Health Insurance Coverage for Emerging Medical Technologies: A New Approach, 38 Tort Trial & Ins. Prac. L.J. 1019 (2003).

B. TECHNOLOGY ASSESSMENT AND PHARMACOECONOMICS

Technology assessment involves a broader inquiry than the FDA's product approval processes. Regulatory reviews focus entirely on the safety and effectiveness of a product for a particular use. The FDA generally does not consider data pertaining to the costs and benefits of a new drug or device, or how that new technology compares with currently marketed products or alternative treatments such as surgical interventions. See Maxwell J. Mehlman, Health Care Cost Containment and Medical Technology: A Critique of Waste Theory, 36 Case W. Res. L. Rev. 778, 788 (1986) (explaining that the FDA "has occasionally, albeit rarely, denied approval to market a drug on the basis that it was less safe or less effective than an alternative already on the market"). When it approves extremely costly new cancer treatments or cardiac assist devices, for which no cheaper substitutes exist, the agency does not ask about the value of extending the lives of critically ill patients by a few months. See Alex Berenson, Cancer Drugs Offer Hope, but at Huge Expense, N.Y. Times, July 12, 2005, at A1 (reporting that Avastin® can cost a colon cancer patient $54,000 per year and that Erbitux® can run to $100,000 annually); Rob Stein, FDA Approves Artificial Heart for Those Awaiting Transplant: Doctors Hail the $100,000 Device, but Critics Question Whether Cost Is Justified, Wash. Post, Oct. 19, 2004, at A3. When the FDA decided to narrow Avastin's indications based on postapproval research, critics assailed the move for inappropriately taking costs into account. See Alicia Mundy, Roche Drug Faces FDA Curb—Agency Plans to Revoke Approval of Avastin for Breast Cancer, Drawing Protests, Wall St. J., Dec. 17, 2010, at B4; cf. Andrew Pollack, Blue Shield of California Won't Cover Breast Cancer Drug, N.Y. Times, Oct. 3, 2011, at B3 (reporting that, even if the FDA decided to remove Avastin's breast cancer indication, CMS had no immediate plans to stop reimbursing for what would become an off-label use).

Although CMS (and HCFA before it) attracted criticism for proposing to use cost as an explicit factor in making Medicare coverage determinations, public and private insurers (and health care providers) inevitably make such judgments, even if the trade-offs lack visibility and rigorous analysis. In the public sector, the Agency for Healthcare Research and Quality (AHRQ) conducts technology assessments at the request of other federal agencies. The now-defunct Office of Technology Assessment (OTA) also prepared important reports about the relative costs and benefits of a wide variety of medical technologies. See OTA, Identifying Health Technologies That Work: Searching for Evidence (1994).

Office of Technology Assessment, *Health Care Technology and Its Assessment in Eight Countries*

OTA–BP–H–140 (1995).

* * * Apart from inflation and its effects on wages and the costs of goods, the increase in resource use is the primary reason for rising health care costs. Nations seeking to control these costs must control the growth and/or use of resources—an effort that inevitably has involved trying to control the processes by which health care technologies are developed, evaluated, adopted, and used.

Yet even without rising costs, controlling technology seems necessary. Choices among technologies have to be made—this occurs at different levels of health care systems. Some choices are made at the national or regional policy level, as when laws and regulations prevent the purchase of equipment or the provision of certain services. Most choices, however, are at the operational level of clinical practice: made by hospital administrators, heads of clinical departments, and health care providers working day to day. The ability to influence these choices, and the means through which that influence is exerted are prominent health policy issues. * * *

As a new technology appears to be of value, clinicians begin to use it and patients begin to ask for it. Diffusion may culminate with the technology's attainment of an appropriate level of use or with the technology's abandonment, either because it was of no value or because a more effective technology has been developed. The technology also may be used too much or too little, as often seems to be the case. In recent years a great deal of attention has been paid to the possibility of assessing the benefits, risks, and costs of technologies before they come into general use and employing the results of these assessments to guide technology adoption and use. * * *

Medical imaging remained relatively unchanged until the computed tomography (CT) scanner was introduced to the market by the EMI Co. in 1972. The CT scanner is a diagnostic device that combines x-ray equipment with a computer and a cathode-ray tube (a television-like device) to produce images of cross-sections of the human body. The principle of CT scanning was developed by the English physicist Hounsfield; he succeeded in producing the first scan of an object in 1967, and in 1971 he was able to scan the head of a live patient. Commercialization of the CT scanner in 1972 initiated a revolution in the field of diagnostic imaging. * * *

CT scanning was rapidly and enthusiastically accepted by the medial community. Despite concerns about its high cost—up to and more than $1 million—it diffused extraordinarily rapidly and came into widespread use throughout the world. * * * Although no randomized studies of the value of CT scanning were done in its early years, clinical experience gradually accumulated that indicated its usefulness in many conditions. It is now a fully accepted diagnostic technology. Magnetic resonance imaging (MRI) is a more recent innovation in the field of medical imaging, based on nuclear magnetic resonance (NMR). * * *

MRI produces images of cross-sections of the human body similar to those produced by CT scanning, with some important differences. A CT scanner depicts the x-ray opacity of body structure. MRI images depict the density or even the chemical environment of hydrogen atoms. These various properties are not necessarily correlated. MRI has several advantages. It gives a high contrast sensitivity in its images, and it can distinguish between various normal and abnormal tissues. Blood flow, circulation of the cerebrospinal fluid, and contraction and relaxation of organs can be assessed. Tissues surrounded by bone can be represented. Also, MRI does not employ potentially dangerous ionizing radiation, as do CT scanning and other imaging methods. It is not necessary to inject toxic contrast agents, as is often done with CT scanning (although contrast agents are being used more and more frequently with MRI scanning). MRI allows for a choice of different imaging planes without moving the patient; CT scanning can produce an image of only one plane at a time, and some planes are not scannable. Finally, images can be obtained from areas of the body where CT scanning fails to produce clear images.

Despite its potential, the initial diffusion of MRI in most countries was less rapid than had been the case with CT scanners. Introduction and diffusion were slowed because of the economic recession in the early 1980s. At the same time health authorities were unwilling to invest heavily in MRI before any thorough evaluation had taken place. Questions such as these were asked: Is present MRI an advance in imaging technology as compared with CT scanning? Does it produce useful information at a reasonable cost? Does it produce diagnostic information not otherwise available?

MRI has been repeatedly and formally assessed since its introduction. * * * These assessments agree that MRI is a reliable diagnostic device that produces information that can be quite useful. However, evaluation of MRI scanning has been far from optimal. For example, a literature review published in 1988 found that 54 evaluations did poorly when rated by commonly accepted scientific standards, such as use of a "gold standard" comparison of blinded readers of the images (i.e., the expert doing the reading does not know the status of the patient). Only one evaluation had a prospective design. Also, over the period examined there was no improvement in quality of research over time, and this problem continued in later years.

Literature shows that MRI is probably superior to CT, its main competitor, for detection and characterization of posterior fossa (brain) lesions and spinal cord myelopathies, imaging in multiple sclerosis, detecting lesions in patients with refractory partial seizures, and detailed display for guiding complex therapy, as for brain tumors. In other diseases the efficacy of MRI is similar to that of CT. In fact, the best designed study, carried out in a heterogeneous group of patients * * * in a matched pair design, found that sensitivity and specificity of CT scanning were somewhat better than those of MRI. As for the diagnostic or therapeutic impact, little information is available. Investigators in Norway found that 33 percent of patients had their main diagnosis changed by MRI scanning. Plans for surgery changed in 20 percent of the patients, and plans for radiotherapy changed in 8 percent.

Although most MRI scans are of the brain, a specific advantage of MRI lies in diagnosis of spinal cord problems, where MRI may replace myelography, an x-ray procedure involving injection of a potentially dangerous dye. In the spinal cord two studies have examined the relative accuracy of MRI in relation to myelography and CT. The studies found that MRI and CT were roughly equivalent in terms of true positive results but that both were superior to myelography. MRI is gradually replacing both CT scanning and myelography. * * *

The capital cost of an MRI scanner varies greatly, depending particularly on the strength of the magnets. A basic unit costs at least $1,115,000 per year in the mid–1980s. Only about one-third of this operating cost is accounted for by the capital investment in the scanner itself. Other expenses include space, personnel, equipment, and maintenance. The cost per scan in one mid–1980s study was between $370 and $550, and the fee paid for the scan was $500. (The costs apparently do not include payment to the physician.) Other studies have demonstrated that the costs of an MRI scan are considerably more than those of a CT scan. * * *

MRI costs may be offset by replacement of other diagnostic procedures, particularly myelography. Although myelography requires hospitalization of at least one day, MRI can be done on an outpatient basis. It does not appear to have replaced other modalities, such as CT scanning in the brain, except that it is used preferentially in suspected posterior fossa tumors. In general, however, replacement of other procedures by MRI has not been demonstrated. The result is a considerable increase in costs. The basic issues with CT scanning and MRI scanning is that they provide similar information. It has been difficult to demonstrate much advantage with MRI. * * *

Amy L. Wax, *Technology Assessment and the Doctor–Patient Relationship*

82 VA. L. REV. 1641 (1996).

* * * There are many examples of new medical technologies for which cost is extremely high, and benefit is slight, marginal or unproven. For example, in treating metastatic breast cancer, the use of bone marrow transplantation is extremely expensive, potentially traumatic and risky. Virtually every well-controlled study has failed to show that the treatment has any statistically significant effect on duration of survival. Similarly, a number of drugs recently approved by the FDA show modest, short-lived or ambiguous effects. Demonstrating that these drugs have any benefit whatsoever requires trials of many thousands of patients. Scientists must conduct sophisticated and sometimes problematic statistical analyses in an often unsuccessful attempt to identify subgroups of patients who might be helped by the drug. With respect to diagnostic techniques the situation is not much different. New scanners, screening techniques, and blood tests significantly add to medical expenditures overall, but frequently present only a marginal improvement over existing methods, provide a net health benefit that is very difficult to measure, or have a high error rate that confounds their usefulness.

Careful, accurate, and sophisticated outcomes assessment is the best, and indeed, the only reliable way to identify and measure the magnitude of the costs and benefits of many new therapies. Even under the most rigorous and well-controlled circumstances, it is technically very difficult to quantify with any confidence the effects of innovations that represent only marginal improvements over existing techniques or interventions. Necessarily, measurements are subject to various kinds of error and require assumptions that render them little more than best estimates. These observations apply not just to innovative therapies, but also to established treatments, some of which will also be of questionable or marginal value in some or all patients who have received treatment.

But, even with all of its imperfections and difficulties, technology assessment's irreplaceable role in documenting the cost-benefit ratio makes the technique vitally important to the optimal operation of bedside rationing. Technology assessment allows conscientious physicians to think through the possible approaches to diagnosis and treatment in a systematic and informed manner, rather than relying on intuition, anecdote and limited personal experience. Armed with information about medical benefit, efficacy, side effects and overall expense, physicians who have a scientifically sound understanding of the likely costs and effects of treatment choices can formulate more reasoned treatment plans for individual patients in the least harmful and most cost-effective way. * * * [I]t also allows physicians to pinpoint areas of uncertainty and to advise patients about what is known and unknown concerning the effects of new and existing options. If patients can be made to appreciate the (sometimes flimsy) scientific basis for some interventions, they may go along more readily with recommendations that certain particularly expensive therapies or procedures be forgone or put off.

Some examples show how information technology can foster patient-physician joint decision-making that resolves towards less rather than more interventionist care. Mark Hall illustrates the kind of bottom-up rationing that frequently occurs in practice by offering a hypothetical based loosely on a physician's handling of a knee injury his wife received while playing tennis. He states that his wife's physician estimated that there was a ninety percent chance that the injury was a ligament strain (ordinarily treated by resting the affected limb), and a ten percent chance that the injury was a more severe ligament tear, which in turn had a ten percent chance of leading to permanent impairment if left untreated. The most definitive resolution of the diagnostic uncertainty would have been to perform a magnetic resonance imaging scan (costing twelve hundred dollars) immediately. The physician, after consulting with the patient, decided against ordering the scan. A quick recovery proved the gamble harmless.

As Hall points out, this situation does not present the kind of dramatic life-or-death dilemma that dominates the rationing literature. The reality is far less riveting. Through his hypothetical, Hall attempts to provide a more realistic picture of the small, incremental and routine decisions that physicians make every day—decisions like "declining to order a confirming diagnostic test or an extra day in the hospital, prescribing a less expensive drug, or avoiding a referral to a specialist." For each of these decisions, the stakes are comparatively small for individual patients, but the costs of indulging extreme risk aversion at every point add up in the aggregate to significantly greater expense for the system.

Hall's example also illustrates that it is a mistake to think of every medical judgment that can be characterized as not doing everything possible as a sharp departure from norms of acceptable medical practice. First, in most routine cases of medical diagnosis and treatment, it is not readily apparent precisely what doing everything possible would mean. There are often a number of ways to approach a particular medical problem, especially since details of presentation always differ from patient to patient. Flexible conventions, selectively applied through the exercise of individual judgment, are the essence of ordinary medical practice, and can give rise to many alternative strategies for dealing with day-to-day medical scenarios. A measured and gradually escalating sequence of tests and interventions often represents the most acceptable course of action. * * *

Although Hall's story is not primarily about the use of cutting edge technologies, it presents a good example of the kind of decision-making at the margin—decision-making that invites "the prudent trimming of incrementally beneficial services"—that physicians must engage in when determining whether and how to use innovative drugs or treatments. But in order to make decisions at the margins it is necessary to know where the margins are. Hall does not comment on the source or reliability of the probability estimates used in his anecdote. It is easy to devise numbers for use in a hypothetical, but only technology assessment can generate accurate data in a form that can be applied to real-life decision-making. * * *

Paul C. Sorum, *Limiting Cardiopulmonary Resuscitation*

57 ALB. L. REV. 617 (1994).

Researchers at Duke University, studying the outcomes and costs of care of 146 patients who suffered cardiac arrests on the general medical and surgical wards between 1988 and 1991, found that only eighty-four (58%) were revived and only seven (5%) were subsequently able to leave the hospital and lead "meaningful lives" for a period of time. The high cost of caring for the eighty-four initial survivors totaled $1.1 million, or $13,000 per person, due in large part to the expensive care each received in intensive care units after their resuscitations. The researchers pointed out that the cost was about $150,000 for each "meaningful" survivor and, therefore, concluded that "doctors should be reluctant to recommend CPR to people who are gravely ill."

This argument is invalid for four reasons. First, the argument applies equally well to many other treatments routinely given to quite sick or fragile people—e.g., antibiotics that prevent death from pneumonia, chemotherapy that delays the spread of cancer, surgery that relieves a bowel obstruction. In each of these cases, as in the case of a cardiac arrest, if the patients are left to die rather than given treatment, money will be saved (assuming they do die). If monetary savings provide a valid basis to withhold CPR, why not withhold other treatments that have equally high (or higher) monetary consequences?

Second, this amount of money, which initially seems staggering, may not seem so unacceptable upon further examination. It may not be fair to eliminate consideration of the seventy-nine initial survivors who died prior to discharge from the hospital. Their added period of life * * * may very well have been meaningful and valuable to them and their families. Furthermore, $150,000 might not be a high price for preserving a "meaningful" life. To begin with, it would help to know the length and quality of the survivors' lives. This may alter the cost-effectiveness when expressed as cost per year of life gained (rather than as number of survivors) and when adjusted for any decrease in the patients' quality of life (i.e., when expressed as cost per "quality-adjusted life year"). The limited data in other studies on outcomes after discharge suggest that the patients' longevity is limited largely by their age and pre-existing diseases, not by their cardiac arrest, and is quite good; 50% of the survivors live between one and three years or even longer. Furthermore, the patients' mental and physical capacities remain mostly intact. Therefore, the cost per quality-adjusted life year might well be far less than $150,000.

To understand such a cost, it would help to look at the cost-effectiveness of other interventions. [One study has] compared a variety of accepted treatments in terms of the additional dollars spent (as compared with the alternative treatment) for each quality-adjusted life year gained: neonatal intensive care for 1000–1499 gram babies, $5,100; the use of low osmolar contrast media for radiographic studies in patients at high risk for subsequent kidney failure, $22,600; neonatal intensive care for 500–999 gram babies, $30,900; bone marrow transplant for acute nonlymphocytic leukemia, $59,300. The Center for Risk Analysis at the Harvard School of Public Health has compiled the published cost-effectiveness analyses of over 500 interventions intended to prevent premature deaths. The median cost, in 1991 dollars, of interventions in medicine (including measures to prevent, screen for, diagnose, and treat illness) was $17,000 per year of life saved (not adjusted for quality). In consumer product safety the median was $19,000, in transportation safety it was $60,000, in environmental control it was $350,000, and in occupational safety the median cost was $370,000 per year of life saved. The consensus of experts in cost-effectiveness analysis is that in general a medical intervention is cost-effective if the procedure's additional cost, as compared with the costs of the alternatives, is less than $40,000–50,000 for each quality-adjusted life year gained.

Using this guideline to evaluate the allocation of intensive care resources, it is noteworthy, for example, that the charges for intensive care for critically ill patients aged sixty-five and older have been calculated as only $21,768 for each year of life saved (not adjusted for quality of life). On the other hand, the cost per year of life gained by treating critically ill cancer patients in the intensive care unit was found to be $82,845 for patients with solid tumors and $189,399 for those with hematologic malignancies. In the case of CPR, the adjustment of the costs of CPR in the Duke study, in light of the duration and quality of the experiences of the transient and long-term survivors, might well bring the cost per quality-adjusted life year into the range of the guideline of $40,000–50,000 per quality-adjusted life year.

The third criticism of the cost argument is that it unfairly attributes to successful CPR all the costs of subsequent care, implying that once the decision to undertake CPR is made, the option of letting the patient die is lost and the physicians' hands become tied, i.e., they have no choice but to give and continue expensive treatment. In fact, depending on the results of CPR, the patient or patient's surrogate and the physician can decide (either after the CPR or, by advance directives, before) to limit treatment. If they do not, the cost of treatment—which will be far more expensive than CPR itself—must be attributed to that decision, not solely to the decision to undertake CPR. * * *

NOTES AND QUESTIONS

1. *Evidence-based medicine through technology assessment.* Information about the comparative outcomes of two technologies to diagnose or treat the same condition allows health care providers to select the most useful technology from among the available options. See Donald M. Berwick, Disseminating Innovations in Health Care, 289 JAMA 1969 (2003); see also Barry Meier, Doctors, Too, Ask: Is This Drug Right?, N.Y. Times, Dec. 30, 2004, at C1 (reporting efforts to conduct and disseminate "evidence-based reviews" of drugs); Walecia Konrad, For Those with Diabetes, Older Drugs Are Often Best, N.Y. Times, May 28, 2011, at B6; Christopher Rowland, Consumer Reports Turns Focus to Prescription Drugs, Boston Globe, Dec. 10, 2004, at A1. Sometimes older technologies remain entrenched when newer, better technologies are available; at other times, newer, more expensive technologies replace older therapies without demonstrable added benefit. See Lars Noah, Medicine's Epistemology: Mapping the Haphazard Diffusion of Knowledge in the Biomedical Community, 44 Ariz. L. Rev. 373, 387–88, 393–94 (2002); Denise Grady, Many Defibrillators Implanted Unnecessarily, Study Says, N.Y. Times, Jan. 5, 2011, at A12; Gina Kolata, Though Results Are Unproved, Robotic Surgery Wins Converts, N.Y. Times, Feb. 14, 2010, at A1 ("[R]obot-assisted prostate surgery costs more—about $1,500 to $2,000 more per patient. And it is not clear whether its outcomes are better ...."); Rob Stein, Experts Debate CyberKnife for Prostate Cancer: Safety, Effectiveness of Device at Issue, Wash. Post, Nov. 28, 2008, at A3 ("[P]atients and many doctors tend to assume that just because something is new, it is better."); Shankar Vedantam, In Antipsychotic, Newer Isn't Better: Drug Find Shocks Researchers, Wash. Post, Oct. 3, 2006, at A1; Keith J. Winstein, A Simple Health–Care Fix Fizzles out, Wall St. J., Feb. 11, 2010, at A1 (discussing the continued (over)use of cardiac stents notwithstanding the publication of a cost-effectiveness study demonstrating that far less expensive drug treatments would work equally well for many patients with chest pain). Payers may well ask whether any added increment of safety or effectiveness is worth the added expense. See

Lee Goldman, Editorial, Cost–Effectiveness in a Flat World—Can ICDs Help the United States Get Rhythm?, 353 New Eng. J. Med. 1513 (2005) (pegging "the usually accepted threshold" at $35,000–50,000 per QALY); Maria Cheng, British Agency Makes Tough Choices on Costly Drugs: Cap for an Additional Year of Life Is Usually $47,000, Wash. Post, May 26, 2009, at F6 (discussing the U.K.'s National Institute for Health and Clinical Excellence (NICE)); Ross Kerber, We're Extending Our Lives, but at What Price?, Boston Globe, Sept. 26, 2005, at E1 (reporting that "healthcare economists often use $100,000 per added year of life as the maximum benefit worth paying by" Medicare); cf. Binyamin Appelbaum, A Life's Value? It May Depend on the Agency, N.Y. Times, Feb. 17, 2011, at A1 (reporting that the FDA "declared that life was worth $7.9 million last year, up from $5 million in 2008").

2. *Cost-effectiveness of newer technologies*. Are the latest pharmaceuticals and medical devices worth the additional cost? See, e.g., Arthur Allen, Mixed Reactions to Lupus Drug: It Can Work Well, but Some Experts Fret over Its High Price and Limited Usefulness, Wash. Post, June 14, 2011, at E1 (reporting that the monoclonal antibody Benlysta® (belimumab) costs $35,000 annually); Ian Austen, A Leg with a Mind of Its Own, N.Y. Times, Jan. 3, 2002, at G1 ("The C–Leg [prosthesis], which was introduced to the United States market in 1999, costs $40,000 to $50,000, compared with $15,000 for a non-electronic hydraulic model."); Lyndsey Layton, New Study Questions Effectiveness of Popular Cholesterol Drugs, Wash. Post, Nov. 16, 2009, at A6 (discussing doubts about ezetimibe (Zetia® and Vytorin®), which reduces bad cholesterol by a different mechanism than statins). When a new product effectively treats a serious disease for which no alternative therapy exists, how does one make such a judgment? More typically, a new product offers at best some marginal advantage over existing treatments for a condition, but does that simplify or complicate the inquiry? See Deborah Schrag, The Price Tag on Progress: Chemotherapy for Colorectal Cancer, 351 New Eng. J. Med. 317 (2004); Marilyn Chase, Cancer Tab: Pricey Drugs Put Squeeze on Doctors, Wall St. J., July 8, 2008, at A1; Denise Gellene, New Cancer Drugs Are Driving up Cost of Care, L.A. Times, May 14, 2005, at C1 (reporting that the switch from standard chemotherapy agents to "targeted" drugs has, for instance, doubled the average life expectancy of patients with inoperable colon cancer (to 22 months), while treatment costs increased 500–fold (to $250,000)); Rachel Zimmerman, Drug Slows a Deadly Cancer, Study Finds, but Price Is Steep, Wall St. J., June 16, 2005, at D2 (reporting that Velcade®, a newly approved proteasome inhibitor that costs more than $45,000 for a nine month course of treatment, allowed multiple myeloma patients to live an average of three months longer than those given the standard treatment of dexamethasone, a generic corticosteroid that costs $170 and causes fewer serious side effects). See generally Douglas Mossman, Unbuckling the "Chemical Strait-jacket": The Legal Significance of Recent Advances in the Pharmacological Treatment of Psychosis, 39 San Diego L. Rev. 1033 (2002); Alastair J.J. Wood, Editorial, When Increased Therapeutic Benefit Comes at Increased Cost, 346 New Eng. J. Med. 1819 (2002).

One investigator concluded that replacing older drugs with newer (and more expensive) drugs reduces morbidity, mortality, and total medical expenditures. See Frank R. Lichtenberg, Are the Benefits of Newer Drugs Worth Their Cost? Evidence from the 1996 MEPS, Health Aff., Sept.–Oct. 2001, at 241, 250; Frank R. Lichtenberg, Op–Ed.,Yes, New Drugs Save Lives, Wash. Post, July 11, 2007, at A15 ("[L]ongevity increased the most in those states where access to newer drugs—measured by their mean 'vintage,' or FDA approval year—in Medicaid and Medicare programs has increased the most."); see also David M. Cutler et al., The Value of Antihypertensive Drugs: A Perspective on Medical Innovation, 26 Health Aff. 97 (2007); Ani B. Satz, Toward Solving the Health Care Crisis: The Paradoxical Case for Universal Access to High Technology, 8 Yale J. Health Pol'y L. & Ethics 93 (2008). How would a health insurer that restricts access to control costs respond to this study's findings? Might a policy that covered only generic drugs still be defensible in the sense that it ensured payment for the state-of-the-art as it had existed approximately one decade earlier (and as it still exists in many industrialized countries where price controls have slowed the introduction of expensive innovations) or allowed patients to rely on still older (and generally cheaper) nonprescription drugs? Cf. Kevin Outterson, The Vanishing Public Domain: Antibiotic Resistance, Pharmaceutical Innovation and Intellectual Property Law, 67 U. Pitt. L. Rev. 67, 73 (2005) ("Rich consumers pay for and receive the latest innovations (2005 medicine), while the poor might well be satisfied with the less effective, but much less expensive, 1991 all-generic pharmacopoeia."); Linda A. Johnson, A Wave of Expiring Patents Will Bring Plunging Prices on Prescription Drugs, Wash. Post, July 26, 2011, at A18. Patients with the resources and willingness to pay out-of-pocket would continue to have access to the more expensive and cutting-edge medical technologies, while everyone else could get access (through public or private insurance) to a set of less advanced though more affordable (good enough?) therapeutic products. Cf. Aaron L. Nelson et al., Much Cheaper, Almost as Good: Decrementally Cost–Effective Medical Innovation, 151 Annals Internal Med. 662 (2009); S. Karene Witcher, In the Land Down Under, A Model for National Drug Insurance, Wall St. J., Aug. 31, 2000, at B1. After all, in other product markets (e.g., automobiles), consumers must pay a premium for special features (e.g., crash avoidance technologies)—are medical technologies fundamentally different?

3. *Clot busters*. Two drugs for treating blood clots in heart attack patients appear to be equally effective. The older, off-patent drug, streptokinase, costs between $76 and $300 per dose. The newer agent, a biotechnology product called tissue plasminogen activator (tPA), costs $2,200 per dose. In 1990, two-thirds of the patients treated after heart attack received tPA for a total cost of $210 million, while the streptokinase therapy for the remaining third of the patients cost only $5 million. Many physicians have questioned this prescribing trend in light of studies that found no differences in comparative efficacy. The manufacturer of tPA promoted the drug aggressively by identifying arguable flaws in the data and by warning physicians that they may subject themselves to malpractice liability if they prescribe streptokinase. See Andrew Pollack, The Battle of the Heart Drugs, N.Y. Times, June 30, 1991, at A1; see also Robert McNutt & Arthur Evans, Editorial, Accelerated tPA Versus Streptokinase for Suspected Myocardial Infarction: Waiting for Our Mountain Dew, 15 Med. Decision Making 395 (1995). In contrast, tPA has shown clear benefits when rapidly administered to stroke victims, but health care providers fail to use it. See Laurie Tarkan, Absence of Urgency: A Deadly Problem When Strokes Occur, N.Y. Times, Feb. 13, 2001, at F7 ("Only 2 percent to 3 percent of stroke patients actually receive the new drug, whereas 30 percent to 40 percent of them could benefit from it."); see also Thomas M. Burton, Medicare to Directly Cover Use of a Genentech Stroke Drug, Wall St. J., Aug. 4, 2005, at D6 (reporting that this change in policy by CMS may overcome hospitals' reluctance to use tPA).

4. *Drug-eluting stents*. As an alternative to more invasive coronary artery bypass surgery, cardiologists developed angioplasty, a procedure that uses a catheter to thread a tiny inflatable balloon into a clogged artery in order to clear the blockage, though the resulting inflammation and scarring often caused another blockage ("restenosis") and required repeating the procedure. Starting in the late 1980s, physicians began inserting stents (wire-mesh devices) as scaffolding to keep the vessels open after angioplasty, which partially reduced the occurrence of re-blockages. In 2003, the FDA approved a stent imbedded with a slowly released drug that further reduced restenosis (Johnson & Johnson's Cypher® stent), but the device initially cost more than $3,000, almost four times as much as traditional stents. See Sally Squires, The Selling of the Stent, Wash. Post, Sept. 16, 2003, at F1. A back-of-the-envelope cost-effectiveness analysis looked unfavorable: switching from bare-metal to drug-eluting stents prevented restenosis in approximately 7% of patients (avoiding almost $15,000 in additional treatment costs per patient), which meant that, if 100 angioplasty patients received the new stents (and an average of two stents per procedure), a hospital could anticipate savings of approximately $100,000 after spending an extra $450,000 for the newer devices. See id.; cf. Ron Winslow, J & J Study Says New Heart Stent Is Cost–Effective, Wall St. J., Mar. 31, 2003, at B5 (reporting that a more sophisticated analysis, which assumed avoidance of restenosis in 19% of patients, supported routine use of the devices). Is anything important missing from this picture? Notwithstanding questions about cost-effectiveness, drug-eluting stents have become enormously popular (accounting for most stents used in angioplasty), the introduction of a competing device (Boston Scientific's Taxus® stent) helped to reduce prices (to about $2,300), further research has allayed some of the safety and efficacy concerns, and other manufacturers have still newer types in development, including one that eventually dissolves. See Avery Johnson, New Generation of Cardiac Stents Awaits FDA Approval, Wall St. J., Mar. 8, 2007, at D1; see also Barnaby Feder, A Heart Stent Gets a Reprieve from Doctors, N.Y. Times, Nov. 12, 2007, at A1.

5. *Screening for cancer*. A firestorm erupted after public health officials recommended revisions in guidelines for mammography that would delay the start of routine screening for breast cancer and reduce its frequency for most women. See Gina Kolata, Mammogram Debate Took Group by Surprise, N.Y. Times, Nov. 20, 2009, at A1; see also Denise Grady, Guidelines Push Back Age for Cervical Cancer Tests, N.Y. Times, Nov. 20, 2009, at A1. Further advances in imaging technologies raise interesting questions about cost-effectiveness. See Charles Stein, A Picture out of Focus, Boston Globe, June 25, 2002, at D1; Rob Stein, High–Tech Mammograms Faulted: Computer Systems Don't Detect More Tumors, Study Finds, Wash. Post, Apr. 5, 2007, at A7. For example, spiral computed tomography, a faster and potentially more accurate type of CT scan, may allow physicians to find smaller lung tumors than traditional x-ray technology. Because spiral CT scans cost at least $300 per scan, some commentators have questioned whether screening at-risk persons for lung cancer will detect lung tumors earlier enough to increase the cure rate for an otherwise frequently fatal disease. Critics suggest that, although patients with lung tumors detected through spiral CT may live longer than patients whose tumors are discovered through conventional scans, the extended life expectancy associated with scanning may be illusory—patients simply live longer after diagnosis because they get diagnosed earlier. See Lars Noah, An Inventory of Mathematical Blunders in Applying the Loss-of-a-Chance Doctrine, 24 Rev. Litig. 369, 385 (2005) (discussing lead-time bias and other statistical artifacts in cancer screening). A clinical trial of spiral CTs finally seems to have settled at least this question. See Gardiner Harris, Scans Cut Deaths by Lung Cancer Among Smokers, N.Y. Times, Nov. 5, 2010, at A1; cf. Rob Stein, CT Scans for Lung Cancer Ignite Debate over Need: Experts Split on Whether Benefits Outweigh Risks of Widespread Testing, Wash. Post, Aug. 16, 2011, at A1.

Another new type of scanning technology, positron emission tomography (PET), raises similar issues of costs and benefits. See Rhonda L. Rundle, PET Scanners Become New Rx for Diagnostics, Wall St. J., May 6, 2003, at B1; see also Rick Weiss, A Tale of Politics: PET Scans' Change in Medicare Coverage, Wash. Post, Oct. 14, 2004, at A1 (describing intense lobbying that secured reimbursement for limited use in Alzheimer's patients). PET scans measure abnormal metabolic activity in cells and therefore can identify cancer cells, which typically operate at a higher metabolic rate than normal cells. Ordinary CT scans may show abnormal tissue as darkened masses within the body, but, without a biopsy, there is no way to determine whether the abnormality is cancerous. PET scans thus can potentially prevent unnecessary biopsy procedures. Medicare now covers the $2,000 scans for a variety of suspected cancerous conditions, but experts suggest that more study is needed to determine whether the costly technology will deliver benefits in the form of reduced treatment costs or extended lifespans. One of the most difficult questions is how to determine the "testing threshold"—that is, the pretest probability that the patient has the disease for which the diagnostic test, if performed, will affect therapeutic choices: "at what probabilities of malignancy is it beneficial or cost-effective to avoid further diagnostic testing or to treat patients empirically? . . . Given the need to balance the risks of diagnostic tissue sampling of lung masses with the risks of failure to diagnose cancer, along with the unknown benefit of early diagnosis of lung cancer, the question of which patients to evaluate is clinically very important." Ethan Balk & Joseph Lau, PET Scans and Technology Assessment: Deja Vu?, 285 JAMA 936 (2001). These same commentators also emphasized the need to evaluate the usefulness of PET in comparison with other relevant technologies, such as CT and MRI, in a controlled clinical trial. See id.; see also Liz Kowalczyk, New CT Scanners Offer Faster Diagnoses: Hospitals Betting on Costly Devices, Boston Globe, Apr. 30, 2006, at A1 (discussing similar questions about the diagnosis of heart disease).

6. *Pulling out all of the stops.* After years of inadequate treatment for sepsis, a frequently fatal blood infection, hospitals had (until withdrawn in 2011) access to drotrecogin (recombinant human activated protein C), a marginally more effective but much costlier new treatment (sold under the brand-name Xigris®). See Braden J. Manns et al., An Economic Evaluation of Activated Protein C Treatment for Severe Sepsis, 347 New Eng. J. Med. 993 (2002). In response to disappointing sales, the manufacturer launched an unusual multi-pronged campaign designed to spur demand: funding and then publicizing a survey about rationing in ICUs, securing a new diagnostic code for severe sepsis, urging states to require tracking of sepsis cases, and lobbying for special Medicare reimbursement. See Peter Q. Eichacker et al., Surviving Sepsis: Practice Guidelines, Marketing Campaigns, and Eli Lilly, 355 New Eng. J. Med. 1640 (2006); Antonio Regalado, Who Gets Health Care? Rationing in an Age of Rising Costs, Wall St. J., Sept. 18, 2003, at A1 ("Lilly successfully petitioned [CMS] for 'new technology' status for Xigris, winning a special dispensation for 50% reimbursement from the federal government, up to $3,400. It was the first time such approval was given."). Even more remarkably, the manufacturer initially had launched a marketing campaign that warned hospitals of potential tort liability if they failed to stock the drug. See Thomas M. Burton, Can Hospitals Afford Not to Prescribe Eli Lilly's Pricey New Sepsis Drug Xigris?, Wall St. J., Sept. 11, 2001, at B1. Based on what you learned in Chapter 8, is this a realistic concern? Cf. Peter D. Jacobson & C. John Rosenquist, The Use of Low–Osmolar Contrast Agents: Technological Change and Defensive Medicine, 21 J. Health Pol. Pol'y & L. 243, 250–53 (1996) (finding that liability concerns played only a secondary role in adoption of a costly new technology). The CDC also may engage in a bit of scare mongering. See Steven Woloshin et al., A Shot of Fear, Wash. Post, Oct. 25, 2005, at F1 ("To promote vaccine use, many in the public health community have overstated the risk of flu-related death and the effectiveness of the vaccine in preventing it."); see also Rob Stein, European Reports Call WHO's H1N1 Policy Tainted by Drug Makers, Wash. Post, June 5, 2010, at A14 (describing a pair of reports that accused the World Health Organization "of exaggerating the threat posed by the [swine flu] virus and failing to disclose possible influence by the pharmaceutical industry").

7. *Cost consciousness, medical ethics, and patient care.* Does maximum utilization of the newest technologies necessarily promote the highest standards of patient care? Once hospitals invest in expensive new equipment, the threshold for recommending surgical interventions over less costly (and, from the hospital's perspective, less remunerative) alternatives may decline. Apart from the possibility that patients will receive riskier and more expensive treatments, physicians have warned their colleagues that overreliance on technology can depersonalize the physician-patient relationship and, ultimately, hinder patient care. See Chiedozie I. Udeh, New Technologies in Medicine, 283 JAMA 2592 (2000) ("Technology also brings with it the potential for misuse and overuse.... We often forget that for patients and their families, the best physician is rarely the one with all the latest technology. It is usually the one who takes time to carefully examine the patient, discuss the treatment plan, or simply holds a patient's hand to allay his or her fears."); Jennifer Obel, Losing the Touch, Wash. Post, June 17, 2003, at F1; see also Chap. 11(D)(2) (exploring the connection between the ethical concept of medical futility and the pervasiveness of "bedside rationing" of medical technologies). Is cost-consciousness an ethical imperative for physicians (i.e., do they have obligations to the public at large not to squander scarce health care resources)? See Michael J. Malinowski, Capitation, Advances in Medical Technology, and the Advent of a New Era in Medical Ethics, 22 Am. J.L. & Med. 331 (1996); Reed Abelson, Insurers Test New Cancer Pay Systems, N.Y. Times, Oct. 20, 2010, at B1; see also Eric Cassell, The Sorcerer's Book: Medicine's Rampant Technology, 23 Hastings Ctr. Rep. 32 (1993); David Seedhouse, Why Bioethicists Have Nothing Useful to Say About Health Care Rationing, 21 J. Med. Ethics 288 (1995).

8. *Further commentary*. See Matthew D. Adler, QALYs and Policy Evaluation: A New Perspective, 6 Yale J. Health Pol'y L. & Ethics 1 (2006); Einer Elhauge, The Limited Regulatory Potential of Medical Technology Assessment, 82 Va. L. Rev. 1525 (1996); Mita K. Giacomini, The Which–Hunt: Assembling Health Technologies for Assessment and Rationing, 24 J. Health Pol. Pol'y & L. 715 (1999); Nikolas H. Goldberg et al., Availability of Comparative Efficacy Data at the Time of Drug Approval in the United States, 305 JAMA 1786 (2011); Thomas J. Parisi, Comment, How Much Did You Pay for Your Heart: Is a Centralized Entity Performing Health Technology Assessment with Cost–Effectiveness Analysis the Answer to the Rising Costs of Health Care?, 49 Jurimetrics J. 285 (2009).

PROBLEM #14. *PREYING ON PARENTAL PARANOIA*

Each year, nearly 100,000 infants are hospitalized with respiratory syncytial virus (R.S.V.) infections, leading to bronchitis or pneumonia and a fatality rate of approximately 1%. Synagis® (palivizumab) is a monoclonal antibody that interferes with infection by R.S.V.; it does not prevent such infections but reduces their severity. A clinical trial conducted by MedImmune, the manufacturer of Synagis, found that the drug cuts in half the risk that an infant with R.S.V. infection will be hospitalized. (An independent study estimated that, for every seventeen patients who received Synagis, the treatment would keep one of those patients out of the hospital.) MedImmune poured substantial resources into the marketing of its product, including direct-to-consumer advertising. One television spot showed a doctor giving oxygen to an infant in the hospital with the following voice-over: "If you knew what R.S.V. could do to your precious baby, it would take your breath away. If your baby was born prematurely, call your pediatrician now and ask about Synagis, before it's too late." (Such campaigns apparently paid dividends for the company—in 2005, worldwide sales of the drug surpassed $1 billion.)

Stephanie Webster (now six months old) was born six-weeks prematurely but, after a 10–day stay in the hospital, was discharged and has been healthy ever since. After seeing MedImmune's TV ad, however, her mother Rhonda immediately called Stephanie's pediatrician and made an appointment for the next day. (Rhonda wasn't sure what R.S.V. was, but she feared that Stephanie might catch it—with winter just around the corner, Stephanie was already fighting a cold and coughing a bit.) After examining Stephanie, the pediatrician told Rhonda that the cough was nothing to worry about and that the child did not need the expensive series of Synagis injections (a total of five shots at a cost of $6,000). Rhonda had done a little research on the Internet, and she insisted that Stephanie was at risk for a serious R.S.V. infection and that she be given Synagis. The Websters' insurance plan covers the drug only for premature babies with other risk factors (e.g., staying in day care, living with a parent who smokes, or having siblings in school who could spread the virus at home), none of which apply to Stephanie (Rhonda said that they will pay out of pocket if their insurance plan refuses coverage). Should the pediatrician give Stephanie the drug? See Melody Petersen, Doctors Caught in the Middle: Ad Campaign Has Parents Asking for a Costly Drug, N.Y. Times, Jan. 31, 2001, at C1. Is the insurance reimbursement policy too restrictive? See Laura Landro, Weighing Which Babies Get a Costly Drug—Small Numbers Who Benefit May Not Justify $6,000 Price of Preventive RSV Therapy, Wall St. J., Apr. 16, 2008, at D1.

Note, *Will Health Care Economic Information Lead to Therapeutic–Class Warfare or Welfare?*

111 HARV. L. REV. 2384 (1998).

* * * [P]harmaceutical companies are engaged in an increasingly fierce struggle to develop potent drugs, ensure efficient distribution chains, and seize larger market shares. The stakes are enormous: given the size of the market, "even a small share can mean large revenues." In recent years, the terrain has shifted as managed care organizations (MCOs) have emerged as serious market players. MCOs wield enormous influence because they determine which drugs are included on their formularies, which are "lists of drug products approved by the [FDA], arranged by therapeutic category, along with the reimbursement rate for the drug." Formulary inclusion gives a drug manufacturer a tactical advantage over competitors within its therapeutic class.

As prescription drug costs have continued to rise, MCOs have become increasingly concerned with structuring drug utilization schemes that optimize consumer health while minimizing economic expenditures. MCOs hope to reduce overall costs, even at the expense of greater short-term costs, by factoring in the costs and benefits of current health care interventions that prevent later, more expensive illnesses. To do so, MCOs need health care economic information to assess the cost-effectiveness of a given drug to determine whether it should be included on the formulary.

Until recently, however, FDA stifled this information. Rather than adopting an economic standard for evaluating health care economic claims, FDA applied the same clinical-based standard that it used to determine drug effectiveness. * * * Although a few companies submitted the requisite two adequate and well-controlled studies and ultimately gained approval to make specific pharmacoeconomic claims, many opted to forego this route—because of time and cost concerns—in favor of alternative marketing strategies. Thus, due to FDA's restrictive approach to cost-effectiveness claims, the development and dissemination of health care economic information languished.

Congress recognized the importance of health care economic information to MCOs when it considered the FDA Modernization Act of 1997. Having identified this need, Congress responded by including a health care economic provision in the FDA Modernization Act. This provision defines "health care economic information" to mean "any analysis that identifies, measures, or compares the economic consequences, including the costs of the represented health outcomes, of the use of a drug to the use of another drug, to another health care intervention, or to no intervention." Congress lowered the standard of proof that a manufacturer must meet to substantiate health care economic claims. Under the new framework, Congress now only requires pharmaceutical companies to base health care economic claims on "competent and reliable scientific evidence." Not surprisingly, this new standard is largely context-driven: "the nature of the evidence required to support various components of health care economic analyses depends on which component of the analysis is involved." * * *

[H]ealth care economic information provided by pharmaceutical companies will not be considered a false, misleading, or illegal new drug claim as long as it "directly relates to an [approved] indication," as reflected in the approved physician package insert. This section explicitly prohibits drug manufacturers from making any pharmacoeconomic claims relating to unapproved uses of an approved drug. For example, "economic claims based on preventing disease progression would ordinarily not be considered to be directly related to an approved indication for the treatment of symptoms of a disease, for a drug for which the use in prevention of disease progression has not been approved."

Lastly, Congress used this provision to change the default rule for health care economic claims from a requirement of prior approval to one of permissive publication. As noted above, FDA required drug manufacturers to gain premarket approval of any health care economic claim—if it was used in labeling—before publicizing it. Although FDA's current postmarketing reporting regulations still require drug manufacturers to submit health care economic information to FDA at the time such information is initially provided to a formulary committee or other managed care provider, drug manufacturers are now allowed to market their claims immediately. * * *

Although the FDA Modernization Act explicitly defines the output of CEA [cost effectiveness analysis], it fails to address methods that will be used to generate that output. The wide disparity in methods currently used to conduct CEA renders the resulting pharmacoeconomic information suspect. A recent survey of MCO decisionmakers found that they considered current health care economic information only "moderately useful" in making drug purchasing decisions, although they ascribed a much higher value to the future usefulness of such information. * * *

One problem that arises from the use of divergent methodologies is the way that researchers identify and calculate the relevant costs that should be included in the numerator of the cost-effectiveness ratio. Although economic theory dictates that a "change in the use of a resource caused by its health intervention should be valued at its opportunity cost," researchers have had a hard time applying this theory in practice. A similar host of problems confronts researchers trying to identify and calculate the relevant benefits that should be included in the denominator of the cost-effectiveness ratio. A comprehensive cost-benefit analysis would weigh all of the benefits accruing to society, even if those benefits do not accrue directly to the MCO. Yet, researchers know that MCOs have an incentive to discount purely societal benefits. Furthermore, researchers have struggled to express these benefits in a meaningful way. One scientific panel suggested incorporating these health benefits variables into a standard unit of measurement called "quality-adjusted life-years" (QALYs). However, "there are a number of methodologic challenges involved in estimating QALYs, including: how to classify health states; whose preferences to use in judging the desirability of the health states; how to measure preferences; and how to adjust for time preferences."

Even if researchers accurately identify and measure the health care costs and benefits associated with a given treatment, three other sources of uncertainty remain. First, researchers must estimate the effectiveness of given treatment interventions. "The quality and validity of a CEA depend crucially on the quality of the underlying data that describe the effectiveness of interventions and the course of illness without intervention." Typically, researchers develop a model based on primary and secondary data sources to estimate effectiveness. On a primary level, researchers might rely on studies conducted specifically to inform the CEA. On a secondary level, researchers might rely on reports of randomized controlled trials, observational studies, uncontrolled experiments, or descriptive series. However, FDA's previous position that "effects need to be demonstrated by adequate and well-controlled studies" rather than simply estimated through "meta-analyses, assumptions[,] or expert opinion" posed a serious obstacle to the development of workable models. It is unclear whether, or how, FDA will alter its treatment of modeling assumptions under the new law. In addition, the new statute only allows consideration of approved drug uses, not off-label uses, even if the latter represent the medical standard of care.

Second, researchers must incorporate consistent discount rates and time preferences. In calculating the cost-effectiveness ratio of a treatment, researchers must calculate the net present value of the costs and benefits. One problem that arises in this calculation is that CEAs frequently incorporate different discount rates that hamper cross-study comparisons. * * * Third, some CEAs fail to address the uncertainty that results from their dependence on a multitude of frequently debatable assumptions. "Cost-effectiveness analyses are subject to uncertainty with regard to estimates of effectiveness, the course of illness, [health-related quality-of-life] consequences and preferences, and health care utilization and costs." Depending on the nature of the assumption and the relative importance of the variable, health care economic outcomes can be significantly affected. However, some studies fail to incorporate appropriate sensitivity analyses that would place the relevant assumptions in an understandable context.

The free market, by itself, is not likely to address completely these methodological shortcomings. * * * The new framework for health care economic information leaves in place the existing incentives for bias and also exacerbates the incentive for researchers to make biased assumptions. First, researchers are still required to make numerous, often subtle assumptions in order to develop workable models. Because most CEAs are done for marketing purposes, "the assumptions made in constructing the models and the data used in the analysis ... could be biased." * * *

Second, the new framework provides added incentives for bias. The lower standard of proof—competent and reliable scientific evidence—suggests that researchers can afford to make some of the questionable assumptions that they may have been reluctant to make under the stricter standard. Thus, this new standard may actually increase the number of low-quality studies that purport to offer conclusive health care economic information. One expert's observation of CEAs under the former standard is revealing: "There are very few well-done pharmacoeconomic studies in the literature; many are quick and dirty studies done for marketing and promotion. They are beginning to denigrate and give a bad name to the research area." Even if the lower standard will not exacerbate existing incentives for bias, it does nothing to ameliorate these incentives.

Market forces will ameliorate some, but not all, of the incentives to produce low-quality pharmacoeconomic information. Specifically, drug manufacturers, pharmaceutical organizations, and MCOs have incentives to provide or demand high-quality economic information. For instance, a manufacturer of a cost-effective drug can distinguish its product by submitting the CEA for publication in a peer review journal. Journals would effectively screen CEAs for the highest quality studies, and then give those studies their endorsement by publishing them. Although not every CEA would be sufficiently thorough and unbiased, MCOs would have a pool of high-quality, published studies from which to select drugs for their formulary lists. * * *

NOTES AND QUESTIONS

1. *Pharmacoeconomic research.* Drug manufacturers occasionally sponsor studies pitting their product against a competitor's drug (or another form of treatment) in the hope of demonstrating superiority in relative safety, effectiveness, and/or cost. These sometimes have surprising results. See Thomas M. Burton, Older Treatment for Manic Illness May Be Superior, Wall St. J., Dec. 12, 2000, at B1 (reporting on research sponsored by the manufacturer of Zyprexa® which found that another drug works just as well in treating bipolar disorder with fewer side effects and at half the cost); Ron Winslow, Blood Feud: For Bristol–Myers, Challenging Pfizer Was a Big Mistake, Wall St. J., Mar. 9, 2004, at A1 ("It's rare for pharmaceutical companies to mount head-to-head studies of their drug against a competitor's product because of the risk of unfavorable results."); id. (reporting that a comparative trial of cholesterol-lowering drugs sponsored by the manufacturer of Pravachol® demonstrated the superiority of Lipitor®); AstraZeneca Study on Crestor Appears to Backfire, L.A. Times, Sept. 3, 2011, at B4 (reporting that comparative trial of statins failed to show any significant advantage over Lipitor); see also Michael Hochman & Danny McCormick, Characteristics of Published Comparative Effectiveness Studies of Medications, 303 JAMA 951 (2010). Pharmacoeconomics, which seeks to document the cost effectiveness of drugs, has attracted sharp methodological criticisms. See Suzanne R. Hill et al., Problems with the Interpretation of Pharmacoeconomic Analyses, 283 JAMA 2116 (2000); Drummond Rennie & Harold S. Luft, Editorial, Pharmacoeconomic Analyses: Making Them Transparent, Making Them Credible, 283 JAMA 2158, 2158–59 (2000).

2. *Conflicts of interest.* Some critics have argued that pharmaceutical manufacturers may stack the deck when they design comparative studies in an effort to ensure a favorable result. See Shankar Vedantam, Comparison of Schizophrenia Drugs Often Favors Firm Funding Study, Wash. Post, Apr. 12, 2006, at A1; see also Benjamin P. Falit, Curbing Industry Sponsors' Incentive to Design Post–Approval Trials That Are Suboptimal for Informing Prescribers but More Likely Than Optimal Designs to Yield Favorable Results, 37 Seton Hall L. Rev. 969 (2007). Greater government funding offers one solution, but groups with vested interests may resist such initiatives. See Ceci Connolly, Comparison Shopping for Medicine: Obama's Stimulus Package Funds Research on Cutting Costs, Wash. Post, Mar. 17, 2009, at A2; see also Eleanor D. Kinney, Comparative Effectiveness Research Under PPACA: Can New Bottles Accommodate Old Wine?, 37 Am. J.L. & Med. (forthcoming 2011); David Brown, Finding What Works Best: "Comparative Effectiveness Research" Evaluates Treatment Options, Wash. Post, Aug. 16, 2011, at E1 (discussing recent federal initiatives).

3. *Regulating the distribution of pharmacoeconomic information.* Historically, the FDA strictly limited the use of comparative claims. See 21 C.F.R. § 202.1(e)(6)(ii); David A. Kessler et al., Therapeutic–Class Wars: Drug Promotion in a Competitive Marketplace, 331 New Eng. J. Med. 1350, 1352 (1994); Peter J. Neumann et al., The FDA and Regulation of Cost–Effectiveness Claims, Health Aff., Fall 1996, at 54, 59–61 (criticizing the agency's traditional demand for randomized controlled trials to substantiate pharmacoeconomic claims). In 1997, Congress liberalized these restrictions by allowing drug companies to disseminate "health care economic information" so long as it is based on "competent and reliable scientific evidence." Pub. L. No. 105–115, § 114(a), 111 Stat. 2296, 2312 (1997) (codified at 21 U.S.C. § 352(a)). Manufacturers could not, however, provide pharmacoeconomic information to individual health care professionals because of congressional concerns that physicians would not have the time or skill needed to interpret research on the cost effectiveness of drugs. See H.R. Rep. No. 105–310, at 65 (1997); see also Anna W. Mathews, Detective Work: Reading the Fine Print, Insurers Question Studies of Drugs, Wall St. J., Aug. 24, 2005, at A1. This more paternalistic stance stands in sharp contrast to the provision in the same statute that had liberalized the rules on the distribution of enduring materials that discuss off-label uses. Does it also raise the sort of First Amendment problems discussed in Chapter 4(C)?

C. DRUG PRICING AND PRICE CONTROLS

1. FEDERAL EFFORTS AT PRICE CONTROLS

TAP Pharmaceuticals v. HHS

163 F.3d 199 (4th Cir.1998).

■ MOTZ, CIRCUIT JUDGE:

TAP Pharmaceuticals, Inc. * * * seeks to challenge a Medicare reimbursement policy. That policy reduces the amount of reimbursement paid for Lupron, a prostate cancer drug manufactured by TAP, to the amount paid for Zoladex, a competing prostate cancer drug made by another drug company. The district court concluded that the interests asserted by TAP in this action do not fall within the "zone of interests" protected by the Medicare Part B program, and that therefore TAP lacked standing to sue. Although we rely on reasons somewhat different than those set forth by the district court, we reach the same conclusion. Accordingly, we affirm.

Lupron and Zoladex treat prostate cancer by means of the same basic chemical mechanism, and they achieve the same level of effectiveness. The two drugs have different rates of action, however, and their particular chemical formulations implicate different adverse reactions. Lupron is administered in liquid form by an intramuscular injection with a 22–gauge needle, while Zoladex is administered as a pellet injected under the skin with a larger, 14– or 16–gauge needle. The larger needle used in administering Zoladex may occasionally cause complications, such as keloid scarring or bleeding hematoma, which are less likely to occur with a Lupron injection. The manufacturer of Zoladex suggests that, at the option of the physician or the patient, a local anesthetic and bandage be used in administering the drug. Such procedures are unnecessary with Lupron. Some doctors prefer Lupron to Zoladex because of its less invasive means of administration.

Many patients who receive Lupron or Zoladex have a portion of their health care costs covered by Medicare Part B, a federal program that provides supplementary medical insurance to the elderly. Generally, Medicare Part B covers "reasonable and necessary" medical services for the "diagnosis or treatment of illness or injury or to improve the functioning of a malformed body member." Though Medicare Part B does not cover most prescription medication, it does cover drugs, like Lupron and Zoladex, which are typically administered by doctors during office or hospital visits. 42 U.S.C. § 1395x(s)(2)(A). Medicare reimburses doctors for a percentage of the cost of such drugs.

In October 1996, Palmetto Government Benefits Administrators, which administers Medicare Part B benefits in South Carolina under the authority of the Health Care Financing Administration and the United States Department of Health and Human Services, adopted the policy that TAP seeks to challenge here. The policy provides that doctors will be reimbursed for the cost of Lupron only at the reimbursement level of the less-expensive Zoladex. Prior to its adoption, Palmetto reimbursed expenditures for each drug on the basis of that drug's own cost.

Palmetto based this change in policy on its conclusion that "there is no therapeutic difference between" the two drugs, although it later acknowledged that TAP's Lupron has a greater duration of action. In the most recent version of the Lupron policy, Palmetto states that "there is no demonstrable difference in clinical efficacy" between Lupron and Zoladex. This latest version of the policy also loosens the restriction on Lupron reimbursement. It allows patients who wish to receive Lupron to make up the difference in cost between Lupron and Zoladex on their own, and it provides that "if there are true medical indications requiring the use of [Lupron] instead of [Zoladex], Medicare will consider reimbursement for the difference in cost if an invoice and documentation of the medical necessity accompanies the claim." * * *

TAP alleges that the new Lupron reimbursement policy violates a Medicare regulation providing that reimbursement for drugs such as Lupron must be "based on the lower of the estimated acquisition cost or the national wholesale average price of the drug." 42 C.F.R. § 405.517(b). TAP asserts that basing reimbursement for Lupron on the cost of Zoladex, rather than on the cost of Lupron itself, violates this regulation. Although the regulation has now been superseded by a 1997 amendment to the Act, which provides that payment for covered drugs is to be made at 95% of the average wholesale price, 42 U.S.C. § 1395u(*o*)(1), TAP's contention regarding the regulation applies equally well to the statute as amended. Both base reimbursement on the cost of the drug used, while the new Lupron policy bases reimbursement on the cost of another drug. TAP also alleges that * * * Palmetto's conclusion that "there is no therapeutic difference between" Lupron and Zoladex lacked a scientific basis and so its adoption of the new Lupron policy in reliance upon this conclusion was arbitrary and capricious; * * * and finally that Palmetto's reimbursement policy violated 42 U.S.C.A. § 1395y(a)(1)(A), which prohibits payment for any item that is not "reasonable and necessary." * * *

The government maintains that the only interest arguably protected by the Medicare Part B program is the interest "of the elderly in receiving affordable medical insurance," and that TAP's commercial interests are at odds with this statutory goal. In support of this position, the government cites the statute's provision of insurance for the cost of "reasonable and necessary" medical care. The government argues that this statutory language shows Congress's sole intention in enacting this legislation to have been that of protecting the financial integrity of the Medicare program.

TAP contends that the most important interest protected by the Medicare Part B program is the provision of excellent medical care to the elderly. It accordingly denies that the "reasonable and necessary" language in the statute involves a cost limitation, as the government has argued; instead, TAP maintains that the phrase has long been interpreted by the government itself to mean merely "safe and effective." TAP also argues that the government's failed attempts to promulgate a regulation introducing a cost-based limitation show that the existing regulatory scheme has no such limitation. TAP heavily relies on a phrase in the legislative history stating that Medicare Part B seeks "to make the best of modern medicine more readily available to the aged." TAP contends that its commercial interests in selling as much Lupron as possible coincide with this statutory goal.

Both parties provide a distorted picture of the interests "arguably protected" by Medicare Part B. Their conflicting positions suggest what our examination of the statute, the regulations, and the legislative history leads us to conclude: Medicare Part B, like many statutes, embodies a compromise between ideals of achievement and economic feasibility that puts its basic purposes in tension. The Act seeks to "make the best of modern medicine more readily available to the aged," but it tries to do so by covering only "reasonable and necessary" care in a manner that will ensure the financial integrity of the system. Perhaps the clearest indication of the statute's competing goals appears in its provision establishing that health care services will generally be covered at a statutorily-defined percentage of their cost. Through this provision, the Act makes all levels of reasonable and necessary medical care more readily available to the aged, while at the same time discouraging excessive expenditure by requiring beneficiaries to pay for a proportionate share of the cost of the services they use.

To have standing, however, TAP need not assert an interest that coincides precisely with the balance struck by Congress between the Act's conflicting purposes; rather, it need only show that its "interests affected by the agency action" are "among" those that Congress arguably sought to protect. Considering only the statute's interest in providing high-quality medical care does not lead to a resolution favorable to TAP, however. Contrary to TAP's assertions, the interest that it asserts here is not the same as the statute's interest in making the best of medicine more readily available to the aged. TAP seeks to increase distribution of Lupron, but it does not specifically allege that Lupron is the best of medicine, and it has not otherwise definitively contended that Lupron is "better" than Zoladex.

Even if we regard TAP's more general allegations as asserting the superiority of Lupron, the statute's interest in "making the best of modern medicine more readily available to the aged" would not coincide with TAP's interest. Quotation of the entire sentence in which this much-cited fragment of legislative history occurs makes the difference plain: "The provision of insurance against the covered costs would encourage the participating institutions, agencies, and individuals to make the best of modern medicine more readily available to the aged." This statement expresses an expectation that, as a result of the coverage of health care costs under Medicare Part B, hospitals, health care agencies, and doctors will become less reluctant to provide high-quality medical care to elderly patients. Medicare Part B is here envisioned as a means of rectifying a situation in which health care providers denied first-rate services to the aged because they lacked insurance. The main import of the statement, then, is that the statute seeks to make the best of medicine "more readily available" than it would be in the absence of Medicare Part B. The Lupron policy achieves this statutory purpose: Lupron is still covered, reimbursement for a portion of its cost is still provided, and Lupron is thus made more readily available to the aged than it would be in the absence of Medicare Part B. TAP's interest in attacking the Lupron policy must therefore be in something other than making the best of medicine more available in the sense articulated in the legislative history.

TAP actually seeks not to make Lupron "more readily available" than it would be without Medicare Part B, but rather to make it more available than it is now, under the Lupron policy. In this sense, TAP's asserted claim strives for something very different than that which the legislative history identifies as a statutory goal. Moreover, TAP objects to the present reimbursement policy not because it fails to make Lupron more available, but because it fails to make Lupron available on the same basis as Zoladex. The legislative history stating that the statute seeks "to make the best of modern medicine more readily available to the aged," however, cannot be read to express an interest in making different treatments for the same condition available on the same basis. The interest of TAP that is "affected by the agency action in question," therefore, does not coincide with the statute's interest in making the best of medicine more available to Medicare recipients. * * *

NOTES AND QUESTIONS

1. *(Under)standing.* Would beneficiaries have standing to challenge this local coverage determination (LCD)? What about a physician who had decided that a patient should receive Lupron® but then does not get full reimbursement and switches to Zoladex® for subsequent injections? If the medical necessity exception in the revised policy makes this seem unlikely, assume it away—in fact, to pose the question more starkly, assume that CMS adopted an NCD against ever reimbursing any amount for Lupron. If some Medicare coverage is always better than none at all, then can no one challenge restrictive payment policies no matter how seemingly irrational? Similar issues may arise with devices. For example, Medicare covers 70% of the cost of artificial knee replacement, leaving beneficiaries with thousands of dollars to pay out of pocket (unless they also have Medigap coverage) and resulting in the underutilization of this safe and effective procedure. See Alicia Ault, Federal Panel Gives High Marks to Joint Replacement Surgery, N.Y. Times, Dec. 16, 2003, at F5; see also Alex Berenson, Medicare Cuts Payout on 2 Cancer Drugs, N.Y. Times, Dec. 7, 2007, at C3.

2. *EPO sticker shock.* As part of covered care for patients of any age with renal disease, Medicare pays for erythropoietin (EPO), a biotechnology product approved by the FDA in 1989 to treat anemia problems caused by chronic renal failure. Under HCFA's interim policy for EPO reimbursement, the total costs reached $265 million—an average of $5,300 per patient for EPO alone. HCFA quickly opted to revise the way it calculated payments for EPO (by changing reimbursement rates and dosage units to reflect actual practice), but the newer approach failed to lower the cost to the agency for EPO. See OTA, Health Care Technology and Its Assessment in Eight Countries, OTA–BP–H–140, at 317–18 (1995); see also Paul Elias, Drugs Save Lives, but Who Will Pay?, Miami Herald, May 27, 2003, at B8 (reporting that CMS has encountered similar difficulties with other "orphan" drugs); Andrew Pollack, Stronger Warnings on 3 Drugs for Anemia, N.Y. Times, Nov. 9, 2007, at C3; Rob Stein, Medicare Law Hurts Cancer Patients: Some Find It Harder to Get Chemotherapy, Wash. Post, Feb. 14, 2004, at A1 (describing criticism of efforts to rationalize reimbursement for the administration of anti-cancer agents). With annual payments climbing over $1 billion, CMS requested a comparative trial between two EPO products, Procrit® and Aranesp® (which costs almost three times as much), but this effort got bogged down in methodological (and political) disputes. See Gardiner Harris, Two Cancer Drugs, No Comparative Data, N.Y. Times, Feb. 26, 2004, at C1; see also Gardiner Harris, F.D.A. Urges Less Use of Anemia Drugs, N.Y. Times, June 25, 2011, at B1 ("The medicines have cost the federal government more than $60 billion since they were introduced in 1989, and for years they were the biggest single drug expense in the federal Medicare program."). Although Congress had directed AHRQ to conduct cost-effectiveness research, it prohibited CMS from using the results to withhold coverage of a prescription drug. See MMA, Pub. L. No. 108–173, § 1013, 117 Stat. 2066 (2003); see also PPACA, Pub. L. No. 111–148, § 6301(c), 124 Stat. 119, 740 (2010) (to be codified at 42 U.S.C. § 1320e–1) (same); Richard S. Saver, Health Care Reform's Wild Card: The Uncertain Effectiveness of Comparative Effectiveness Research, 159 U. Pa. L. Rev. 2147, 2166–70 (2011).

3. *Unlawful industry practices in seeking reimbursement from government programs.* TAP was charged with bribing physicians to prescribe Lupron and conspiring with a physician to receive inflated Medicare reimbursement for the drug. Although that case settled in 2001, the government has pursued similar cases against other pharmaceutical companies for excessive billing to both the Medicare and Medicaid programs. See Ricardo Alonso–Zaldivar, Medicaid Overpaying for Drugs, U.S. Auditors Say, L.A. Times, June 29, 2005, at A25 (reporting "estimate[s] that there could be as many as 200 to 250 pending federal and state lawsuits against drug manufacturers alleged to have cheated Medicaid"); Anna Edney, Drug-firm Executives Under New Scrutiny in Medicare Fraud, Wash. Post, Nov. 9, 2010, at A15 (discussing plans to make increased use of debarment sanction); Jonathan D. Rockoff, Improper Sales of Medicines Targeted: Drug Firms Have Paid Fines of $3.5 Billion Since 2001 for Wrongful Promotions, Balt. Sun, May 7, 2006, at 1A. The manufacturer of Zoladex got into hot water as well. See In re Pharm. Indus. Average Wholesale Price Litig., 582 F.3d 156 (1st Cir. 2009) (affirming a $13 million damage award in a class action lawsuit brought by patients and insurers under a state consumer protection statute against AstraZeneca for publishing inflated average wholesale prices for this drug). Although the marketing techniques and reimbursement issues differ substantially, device manufacturers have begun to attract their own share of attention from prosecutors. See Barry Meier, Sales Tactics on Implants Raise Doubts, N.Y. Times, June 1, 2011, at B1; see also Gardiner Harris, Doctor Faces Suits over Cardiac Stents, N.Y. Times, Dec. 6, 2010, at A15; Mary W. Walsh, Senate Panel Weighs Tighter Rules for Hospital Suppliers, N.Y. Times, Sept. 15, 2004, at C4. See generally Thomas N. Bulleit, Jr. & Joan H. Krause, Kickbacks, Courtesies or Cost–Effectiveness?: Application of the Medicare Antikickback Law to the Marketing and Promotional Practices of Drug and Medical Device Manufacturers, 54 Food & Drug L.J. 279 (1999); Fred Eaton & Jaimee Reid, Mirror, Mirror on the Wall—Evaluating Fair Market Value for Manufacturer–Physician Consulting Arrangements, 65 Food & Drug L.J. 141 (2010).

4. *Qui tam litigation.* The False Claims Act allows private parties to bring lawsuits on behalf of (and share in any proceeds with) the United States in cases of fraud involving government programs. A few such *qui tam* cases have accused manufacturers of causing health care providers to bill Medicare for products ineligible for payment. See Rost v. Pfizer, Inc., 507 F.3d 720 (1st Cir.2007) (off-label marketing of hGH); United States ex rel. Gilligan v. Medtronic, Inc., 403 F.3d 386 (6th Cir.2005) (concluding that courts lacked jurisdiction over claim that the manufacturer of pacemaker leads had failed to secure FDA approval for device modifications because a prior public disclosure of the alleged fraud had put the government on notice); Dingle v. Bioport Corp., 388 F.3d 209 (6th Cir.2004) (same, involving a defense contractor manufacturing anthrax vaccine); United States ex rel. Schmidt v. Zimmer, Inc., 386 F.3d 235 (3d Cir.2004) (reversing summary judgment for defendant where surgeon alleged that the manufacturer of orthopedic implants had offered kickbacks to hospital chain for purchasing products that would get billed to Medicare); id. at

244–45 (holding that a manufacturer could face liability under the False Claims Act where it caused, even if only indirectly, another party to file a fraudulent claim for payment from the government); cf. In re Cardiac Devices Qui Tam Litig., 221 F.R.D. 318 (D.Conn.2004) (allowing an action initiated by a manufacturer's sales representative against more than 100 hospitals that had received payments for services to patients enrolled in clinical trials of numerous different investigational devices not eligible for Medicare reimbursement). See generally Vicki W. Girard, Punishing Pharmaceutical Companies for Unlawful Promotion of Approved Drugs: Why the False Claims Act Is the Wrong Rx, 12 J. Health Care L. & Pol'y 119 (2009); Sandra H. Johnson, Polluting Medical Judgment? False Assumptions in the Pursuit of False Claims Regarding Off–Label Prescribing, 9 Minn. J.L. Sci. & Tech. 61 (2008); Dayna B. Matthew, The Moral Hazard Problem with Privatization of Public Enforcement: The Case of Pharmaceutical Fraud, 40 U. Mich. J.L. Reform 281 (2007); Alex T. Paradiso, Note, Prosecutorial Regulation of Off–Label Promotion: Side Stepping the Courts and Congress to Levy a Tax on Suspect "Big Pharma" Marketing, 60 Syracuse L. Rev. 161 (2009). Recent amendments may facilitate the prosecution of such actions in the future. See Fraud Enforcement and Recovery Act of 2009, Pub. L. No. 111–21, § 4, 123 Stat. 1617, 1621.

5. *Direct purchases and the Medicare drug benefit.* The federal government buys substantial quantities of prescription drugs and devices for use in a variety of programs. By virtue of its sheer size, the government can negotiate for favorable prices, at least if it can coordinate its purchases. See Scott Hensley, Big Buyers Push for Steep Price Cuts from Drug Makers, Wall St. J., June 22, 2006, at B1; Robert Pear, Companies Fight to Ensure Coverage for Erectile Drugs, N.Y. Times, Feb. 22, 2005, at A12 (reporting that the VA pays half the regular price for Viagra); Shankar Vedantam, HHS's Varying Costs for Cipro Criticized, Wash. Post, Oct. 26, 2001, at A16. Responding to fears over the prospect of federal price controls, Congress expressly forbade CMS from negotiating for discounts from drug manufacturers. Although the private insurers offering plans to Medicare beneficiaries would remain free to seek discounts, critics continue to assail this concession to the pharmaceutical industry and have proposed to repeal the provision. See Amy Goldstein, AARP to Seek a Better Drug Benefit, Wash. Post, Jan. 28, 2006, at A7; Tomas J. Philipson, Op–Ed., A Dangerous Medicare Proposal, Wall St. J., July 26, 2011, at A17; see also Christopher Lee, New Drug Benefit Questioned: Democrats' Report Cites Lower Prices from VA and in Canada, Wash. Post, Nov. 23, 2005, at A4 ("[T]he average prices of 10 popular drugs [e.g., Celebrex, Lipitor, Plavix, Prevacid and Zocor] being offered to Medicare recipients through 10 well-known insurance plans were 80 percent higher than prices negotiated for the government by Veterans Affairs. The Medicare prices were 60 percent higher than average prices paid by Canadian consumers, the report found.").

6. *Rebate agreements.* In 1990, Congress enacted a law designed to reduce prices on drugs that the federal government purchases or reimburses by demanding that manufacturers give it the benefit, through a rebate or otherwise, of the "best price" that the manufacturer has given any other purchaser. See 42 U.S.C. § 1396r–8(a)(1) (requiring a rebate of at least 15% of the average manufacturer price). Manufacturers must enter into a rebate agreement with the federal government or individual states in order for their drugs to be covered under the Medicaid program. See id. § 1396(b). Under such an agreement, a manufacturer provides a rebate to the states each quarter based on information submitted by the states for the amount of drugs paid for under Medicaid. See Bruce N. Kuhlik, The Medicaid Prescription Drug Rebate and Improved Access to Medicines Requirements of the Omnibus Budget Reconciliation Act of 1990, 46 Food Drug Cosm. L.J. 363 (1991); see also In re Pharm. Indus. Average Wholesale Price Litig., 321 F.Supp.2d 187 (D.Mass.2004) (denying motions to dismiss claims brought by states alleging that manufacturers fraudulently overstated the AWPs of their prescription drugs in an effort to circumvent the definition of "best price" under federal Medicaid rebate requirements, and rejecting an implied preemption defense); Robert Pear, Medicaid Pays Less Than Medicare for Many Prescription Drugs, U.S. Report Finds, N.Y. Times, Aug. 16, 2011, at A10 ("The minimum rebate for a brand-name drug was increased last year to 23 percent of the average price that manufacturers receive for sales of the product to retail pharmacies. Drug companies must pay additional rebates to Medicaid if a drug's price rises faster than general inflation ...."). In 1992, Congress added a requirement that manufacturers extend these same discounted prices to certain local entities that provide medical care to the poor, though HHS has done a poor job of ensuring compliance. See Astra USA, Inc. v. Santa Clara County, 131 S.Ct. 1342 (2011) (rejecting breach of contract claims for overcharges asserted by local entities as third-party beneficiaries to the boilerplate Pharmaceutical Pricing Agreement executed by each drug manufacturer); see also id. at 1350 ("Instead, in the PPACA, Congress directed HRSA to create a formal dispute resolution procedure, institute refund and civil penalty systems, and perform audits of manufacturers."). After 2003, the shift of drug coverage for low-income elderly and certain other beneficiaries from Medicaid to Medicare promised to reduce the rebate obligations of manufacturers. See Milt Freudenheim, A Windfall from Shifts to Medicare, N.Y. Times, July 18, 2006, at C1; Diedtra Henderson, Prescription Sales Gain Under Medicare Plan, Boston Globe, July 25, 2006, at C1.

2. State Efforts at Price Controls

Pharmaceutical Research & Mfrs. of Am. v. Thompson

362 F.3d 817 (D.C.Cir.2004).

■ Henderson, Circuit Judge:

The appellants, the Pharmaceutical Research and Manufacturers of America (PhRMA) and two non-profit organizations * * * , appeal the district court's summary judgment rejecting their challenge to the "Michigan Best Practices Initiative" (Initiative), a low-cost state prescription drug coverage program—for beneficiaries of Medicaid and of two non-Medicaid state health programs—which was designed by the State of Michigan and approved by the Secretary of the United States Department of Health and Human Services. Under the Initiative, if a drug manufacturer does not sign each of two specified rebate agreements with Michigan—one to provide rebates for drugs the state purchases for Medicaid recipients and the other to provide identical rebates for drugs the state purchases for the two non-Medicaid state health programs—the drug will be covered under the programs subject to "prior authorization."

The appellants argue, as they did below, that the Initiative violates (1) the "formulary" provision of the Medicaid outpatient drug payment statute, 42 U.S.C. § 1396r–8(d)(4), because it excludes from its drug formulary those drugs for which prior authorization is required; (2) the general statutory mandate that Medicaid services be provided in a manner consistent with the best interests of the recipients, id. § 1396a(a)(19); and (3) the Commerce Clause of the United States Constitution because it requires manufacturers to charge the same prices both within and without Michigan. Because the district court correctly rejected each of these arguments, we affirm the summary judgment.

The Medicaid program, jointly funded by the federal government and the states, pays for medical services to low-income persons pursuant to state plans approved by the Secretary. See 42 U.S.C. § 1396a(a)–(b). The statutory rebate provisions require that, in order for a state to receive Medicaid payments for a covered outpatient drug, the drug's manufacturer must have entered into an agreement to rebate a specified portion of the drug's price pursuant to a state plan approved by the Secretary. Id. § 1396r–8(a)(1). In recent years, some states have gone beyond the required Medicaid rebate agreement and "have enacted supplemental rebate programs to achieve additional cost savings on Medicaid purchases as well as for purchases made by other needy citizens." The Initiative is one such supplemental program.

The Initiative began in October 2001 when Michigan's governor convened the Pharmacy & Therapeutics Committee, made up of physicians and pharmacists, with instructions to review the "Michigan Pharmaceutical Product List" (MPPL), a listing of all drugs covered by any program operated by Michigan's Department of Community Health (DCH), including those requiring prior authorization. The Committee studied 40 therapeutic drug classes and in each class designated two or more as "Therapeutically Advantageous," that is, as having a clinical advantage over other drugs in the class without regard to cost. These "best in class" drugs were designated as "Preferred Drugs" and were included on the MPPL for automatic reimbursement under the Initiative. The best-in-class drug available at the lowest cost anywhere in the United States (taking into account the mandatory Medicaid rebate) was designated as the "reference drug" and all drugs in the class priced comparably with it were also listed on the MPPL as Preferred Drugs for automatic reimbursement. All remaining drugs were labeled "non-preferred drugs" and were listed on the MPPL with an asterisk signifying required prior authorization for reimbursement—unless the manufacturer signed both a "Supplemental Drug–Rebate

Agreement'' (Medicaid Agreement) requiring the manufacturer to rebate to the state the difference between the price of the drug and the price of the reference drug for Medicaid purchases and a ''Non–Medicaid State Funded Rebate Agreement'' (Non–Medicaid Agreement), extending the additional rebate to Michigan's non-Medicaid state prescription drug programs.

In fall 2001 DCH submitted to the [HHS] Secretary a proposed State Plan Amendment to Michigan's State Medicaid Plan incorporating the Initiative's provisions for approval pursuant to 42 U.S.C. § 1396. The Secretary approved use of the Medicaid Agreement in a letter dated January 24, 2002 and of the additional Non–Medicaid Agreement in a letter dated December 5, 2002. The Secretary limited approval of the non-Medicaid rebate program, however, to only two of the four Michigan health programs for which it was proposed: the Elder Prescription Insurance Company Program (EPIC), which provides prescription drug coverage to low-income seniors, and the Maternity Outpatient Medical Service (MOMS), which provides prenatal care, including drug coverage, to low-income, adolescent and incarcerated females and to Medicaid beneficiaries eligible for emergency services only.

On June 28, 2002, PhRMA filed this action challenging the Secretary's approval of the prior authorization provisions in both the Medicaid Agreement and the Non–Medicaid Agreement. DCH intervened on the side of the Secretary and the non-profits intervened in support of PhRMA. In a decision dated March 28, 2003, the district court granted summary judgment in favor of the Secretary and DCH. PhRMA and the non-profits filed timely appeals.

After the district court entered judgment, the United States Supreme Court issued its decision in *PhRMA v. Walsh*, 538 U.S. 644 (2003), which affirmed the First Circuit's vacatur of a preliminary injunction preventing implementation of Maine's Medicaid-covered outpatient drug program which, like Michigan's, requires prior authorization for a Medicaid drug if its manufacturer has not agreed to provide rebates both for Medicaid and for non-Medicaid state prescription drug programs. In *Walsh* the Supreme Court expressly rejected PhRMA's challenges to Maine's program based on Medicaid's ''best interests'' requirement, albeit without a majority opinion, and, by a majority, on the Commerce Clause. The analyses in *Walsh* enlighten ours here.

We review the district court's grant of summary judgment de novo pursuant to the Administrative Procedure Act and therefore will uphold the Secretary's decision unless it is ''arbitrary, capricious, an abuse of discretion, or otherwise not in accordance with law,'' 5 U.S.C. § 706(2)(A). There is some question, however, what level of deference the court should accord the Secretary's interpretation of the Medicaid drug payment statute. Ordinarily we review an agency's interpretation of a statute it is charged with implementing under the familiar and deferential two-part framework of *Chevron U.S.A. Inc. v. NRDC*, 467 U.S. 837 (1984). The appellants assert, however, that the Secretary's decisions approving the Initiative are due only minimal deference, if any * * * *

This argument overlooks the nature of the Secretary's authority. This is not a case of implicit delegation of authority through the grant of general implementation authority. In the case of the Medicaid payment statute, the Congress expressly conferred on the Secretary authority to review and approve state Medicaid plans as a condition to disbursing federal Medicaid payments. See 42 U.S.C. § 1396 ("The sums made available under this section shall be used for making payments to States which have submitted, and had approved by the Secretary, State plans for medical assistance."). In carrying out this duty, the Secretary is charged with ensuring that each state plan complies with a vast network of specific statutory requirements, including the prescription rebate agreement provision in section 1396r–8. Through this "express delegation of specific interpretive authority," the Congress manifested its intent that the Secretary's determinations, based on interpretation of the relevant statutory provisions, should have the force of law. The Secretary's interpretations of the Medicaid Act are therefore entitled to *Chevron* deference. * * *

[T]he appellants argue, as in *Walsh*, that the Medicaid Agreement violates the general statutory requirement that a state Medicaid plan "provide such safeguards as may be necessary to assure that eligibility for care and services under the plan will be determined, and such care and services will be provided, in a manner consistent with simplicity of administration and the best interests of the recipients." 42 U.S.C. § 1396a(a)(19). Specifically, they argue that, by making a drug available to Medicaid beneficiaries without prior authorization only if the drug's manufacturer has signed the Non–Medicaid Agreement, the Initiative benefits EPIC and MOMS participants at the expense of Medicaid beneficiaries and therefore is not in the best interests of Medicaid recipients. We reject this argument as well.

We first consider whether the Secretary's interpretation of section 1396a(a)(19) is permissible under *Chevron* and find that it is. The Secretary construes the best interests requirement to allow a state to establish a Medicaid prior authorization program in order to secure rebates on drugs for non-Medicaid populations if "a state demonstrates 'through appropriate evidence that the prior authorization program will further the goals and objectives of the Medicaid program.' " Specifically, the Secretary concluded that "by making prescription drugs accessible to the EPIC and MOMS populations, which are closely related to Medicaid populations in terms of financial and medical need, it is reasonable to conclude that these populations (and in the case of the MOMS program, their children) will maintain or improve their health status and be less likely to become Medicaid eligible." Conversely, in the Secretary's view, the failure to implement the Non–Medicaid Agreement could require cuts in the two non-Medicaid programs that "will necessarily result in some individuals enrolling in Medicaid, and for others, lead to a decline in their health status and resources that will result in Medicaid eligibility or increased Medicaid expenses" and the "[i]ncreased Medicaid enrollments and expenditures for newly qualified Medicaid recipients will strain already scarce Medicaid resources in a time of State budgetary shortfalls."

The Secretary's conclusion that a prior authorization program that serves Medicaid goals in this way can be consistent with Medicaid recipients' best interests, as required by section 1396a(a)(19), is reasonable on its face. If the prior authorization program prevents borderline populations in non-Medicaid programs from being displaced into a state's Medicaid program, more resources will be available for existing Medicaid beneficiaries. Six Justices in *Walsh* acknowledged that such an effect can be in the best interests of Medicaid beneficiaries. The plurality decision there, authored by Justice Stevens and joined by Justices Souter and Ginsburg, relied on precisely this reasoning in determining that Maine's program served the best interests of Medicaid recipients. In her separate opinion, Justice O'Connor, joined by Chief Justice Rehnquist and Justice Kennedy, also suggested that this rationale, although "not self-evident," would suffice if supported by facts in the record.

Having concluded the Secretary's statutory interpretation is permissible, we must next consider whether his specific determination that the Initiative serves valid Medicaid goals is "arbitrary, capricious, an abuse of discretion, or otherwise not in accordance with law." We conclude that it is not. The two Michigan non-Medicaid programs, unlike Maine's program (or the two other Michigan programs for which the Secretary declined to approve a Medicaid prior authorization requirement), are open only to "borderline" populations many of whom may become Medicaid beneficiaries without the support of EPIC and MOMS. The EPIC program provides prescription drug benefits to seniors age 65 and older with household income levels below 200% of the federal poverty level. Michigan estimated that 3% of its beneficiaries (the figure used in similar calculations by the neighboring states of Indiana and Wisconsin), or 3,000 persons, would convert to Medicaid without the EPIC program. Based on an average monthly cost per member of $1,220, Michigan calculated that EPIC saves the state Medicaid program $44,147,760 per year. * * * [In addition], Michigan estimated MOMS saved Medicaid $4,646,002 per year. While the record support for Michigan's estimates is less than overwhelming, it is sufficient to persuade us the Secretary's determination of Medicaid-related benefit is not arbitrary, particularly given the absence of any demonstrable significant impediment to Medicaid services from Michigan's prior authorization requirement.

The undisputed evidence establishes that the Initiative's prior authorization procedure affords Medicaid beneficiaries reasonable and prompt access to those drugs subject to prior authorization. Under the Initiative, DCH's pharmacy benefits manager immediately authorizes a prior authorization drug if (1) the drug is needed "due to a specific medical condition or necessity, such as a drug allergy"; (2) the beneficiary has used the drug for several months and changing drugs is "medically inadvisable"; (3) the beneficiary has tried available drugs in the class and experienced "treatment failure or side effects"; or (4) the drug works better in combination with other medications the beneficiary uses. If the drug fits none of these categories, the request is "immediately forwarded" to a pharmacist who "after further conversation with the physician" either authorizes the drug or "informs the physician of his right to appeal to a DCH physician." If the request is not "immediately resolved with a DCH physician," the treating physician may prescribe an emergency 72–hour supply. Perhaps most important, at the end of the prior authorization process, "the prescribing physician has the final say as to whether or not the requested drug will be approved" provided he can "attest to medical necessity." And the available data confirm that in practice the prior authorization requirement has proved neither burdensome nor overly time-consuming.

Finally, PhRMA contends the Initiative violates the Commerce Clause because it "has the 'practical effect' of controlling out-of-state prices." PhRMA reasons that a manufacturer that wishes to raise the price of a drug in a particular state must consider the effect of the change on drug sales in Michigan. As an example, the appellants note that "if the manufacturer is considering lowering the price of a [reference] drug, doing so would require the manufacturer to lower the price of other drugs in the same therapeutic class in Michigan if it wishes to avoid prior authorization." PhRMA's theory rests on an attenuated and speculative causal relationship between the Initiative's prior authorization requirement and the price a manufacturer charges for a reference drug out-of-state and, as the district court recognized, the claimed effect, if any, "will occur only sporadically and incidentally." Most important, any interstate effect on prices is the result not of provisions peculiar to the Initiative, but of the federal Medicaid rebate statute which requires that the rebate reflect the difference between the "average manufacturer price" and the "best price," that is, "the lowest price available from the manufacturer during the rebate period to any wholesaler, retailer, provider, health maintenance organization, nonprofit entity, or governmental entity within the United States." 42 U.S.C. § 1396r–8(c)(A), (C). It is this federal provision that requires interstate price conformity. Thus, here, as in *Walsh*, the state prior authorization program "does not 'regulate the price of an[] out-of-state transaction by its express terms or its inevitable effect.' "

Biotechnology Industry Organization v. District of Columbia

496 F.3d 1362 (Fed.Cir.2007).

■ GAJARSA, CIRCUIT JUDGE:

* * * The D.C. City Council has adopted specific legislation which prohibits any patented drug from being sold in the District for an excessive price. The operative section of the [Prescription Drug] Excessive Pricing Act reads:

> It shall be unlawful for any drug manufacturer or licensee thereof, excluding a point of sale retail seller, to sell or supply for sale or impose minimum resale requirements for a patented prescription drug that results in the prescription drug being sold in the District for an excessive price.

D.C. Code § 28–4553. The legislation was adopted after the Council determined that:

> The excessive prices of prescription drugs in the District of Columbia [are] threatening the health and welfare of the residents of the District as well as the District government's ability to ensure that all residents receive the health care they need, and these excessive prices directly and indirectly cause economic harm to the District and damage the health and safety of its residents.... [I]t is incumbent on the government of the District of Columbia to take action to restrain the excessive prices of prescription drugs.

Id. § 28–4551. * * * [T]he Act took effect on December 10, 2005.

The statutory term "excessive price" is not specifically defined. The statute states that "[a] prima facie case of excessive pricing shall be established where the wholesale price of a patented prescription drug in the District is over 30% higher than the comparable price in any high income country in which the product is protected by patents or other exclusive marketing rights." Id. § 28–4554(a). If such prima facie excessive pricing is shown, the burden shifts to the defendant to prove:

> that a given prescription drug is not excessively priced given demonstrated costs of invention, development and production of the prescription drug, global sales and profits to date, consideration of any government funded research that supported the development of the drug, and the impact of price on access to the prescription drug by residents and the government of the District of Columbia.

Id. § 28–4554(b). A "high income country" is defined as one of "the United Kingdom, Germany, Canada, or Australia." Id. § 28–4552(2).* The Act provides for both public and private enforcement: "Any affected party, including the District of Columbia, shall have standing to file a civil suit in a court of competent jurisdiction for a violation of this chapter and to seek a remedy, including declaratory and injunctive relief." Id. § 28–4555(a). The term "affected party" is itself broadly defined as "any person directly or indirectly affected by excessive prices of patented prescription drugs, including any organization representing such persons or any person or organization representing the public interest." Id. § 28–4552(1). The Act provides for a wide array of remedies [including fines, treble damages, attorneys fees and costs]. Id. § 28–4555(b).

---

* [Later in its opinion the court noted that the Act's sponsor had used the following illustrations when the proposal was debated before the City Council:]

> Once a lawsuit is filed the prescription drug manufacturer will be afforded an opportunity to explain why its prices are not excessive.... For instance, under the new law Merck may have the opportunity to explain why District residents pay 166 percent more for the cholesterol drug Zocor than the citizens of Germany. Or Pfizer could defend its reasoning for charging District residents 323 percent more for its arthritis drug Celebrex than the residents of Australia.

Remarks of D.C. Councilmember Catania, Sept. 20, 2005.

On October 12, 2005, plaintiff Pharmaceutical Research and Manufacturers of America (PhRMA) filed suit in the United States District Court for the District of Columbia, alleging that the Act was invalid in light of the Commerce Clause of the Constitution and that it was preempted by the federal patent laws. Fifteen days later, plaintiff Biotechnology Industry Organization (BIO) filed a similar suit. Both plaintiffs are industry organizations whose membership includes manufacturers of patented pharmaceuticals. The district court consolidated the two actions, heard oral argument, and on December 22, 2005 issued an opinion and order finding the Act to be preempted by the patent laws and enjoining its enforcement. PhRMA v. District of Columbia, 406 F.Supp.2d 56 (D.D.C.2005). * * *

There is no express provision in the patent statute that prohibits states from regulating the price of patented goods * * * * The plaintiffs urge that the Act conflicts with Congress's intention to provide their members and other pharmaceutical patent holders with the pecuniary reward that follows from the right to exclude granted by a patent. * * * The fundamental goal of the patent law is spelled out in the Constitution: "To promote the Progress of Science and useful Arts, by securing for limited Times to Authors and Inventors the exclusive Right to their respective Writings and Discoveries." U.S. Const. art. I, § 8, cl. 8. Inventors are impelled to invest in creative effort by the expectation that, through procurement of a patent, they will obtain a federally protected "exclusive right" to exclude others from making, using, or selling embodiments of their invention. Patentees value the right to exclude in part because the ability to foreclose competitors from making, using, and selling the invention may allow them an opportunity to obtain above-market profits during the patent's term. * * *

Congress, too, has acknowledged the central role of enhanced profits in the statutory incentive scheme it has developed. In the legislative history of the Drug Price Competition and Patent Term Restoration Act of 1984 (popularly known as the "Hatch–Waxman Act"), the House Committee on Energy and Commerce observed:

> Patents are designed to promote innovation by providing the right to exclude others from making, using, or selling an invention. They enable innovators to obtain greater profits than could have been obtained if direct competition existed. These profits act as incentives for innovative activities.

H.R. Rep. No. 98–857, at 17 (1984), reprinted in 1984 U.S.C.C.A.N. 2647, 2650.

Of course, the patent laws are not intended merely to shift wealth from the public to inventors. Their purpose is to "promote the Progress of ... useful Arts," ultimately providing the public with the benefit of lower price through unfettered competition. * * * These two objectives—to reward innovators with higher profits and to keep prices reasonable for consumers—are in dialectic tension. * * * Congress, as the promulgator of patent policy, is charged with balancing these disparate goals. The present patent system reflects the result of Congress's deliberations. Congress has decided that patentees' present amount of exclusionary power, the present length of patent terms, and the present conditions for patentability represent the best balance between exclusion and free use. * * *

The Act's operation stands largely—indeed, exclusively—within the scope of the patent laws, and its effect is to shift the benefits of a patented invention from inventors to consumers. By penalizing high prices—and thus limiting the full exercise of the exclusionary power that derives from a patent—the District has chosen to re-balance the statutory framework of rewards and incentives insofar as it relates to inventive new drugs. In the District's judgment, patents enable pharmaceutical companies to wield too much exclusionary power, charging prices that are "excessive" for patented drugs. The Act is a clear attempt to restrain those excessive prices, in effect diminishing the reward to patentees in order to provide greater benefit to District drug consumers. This may be a worthy undertaking on the part of the District government, but it is contrary to the goals established by Congress in the patent laws. The fact that the Act is targeted at the patent right is apparent on its face. It applies only to patented drugs. D.C.Code § 28–4553. The District has thus seen fit to change federal patent policy within its borders. The underlying determination about the proper balance between innovators' profit and consumer access to medication, though, is exclusively one for Congress to make. * * *

■ DYK, CIRCUIT JUDGE (dissenting from denial of rehearing en banc*):

* * * In my view the panel's decision in this case presents an important issue of broad significance beyond the District of Columbia, warranting our en banc attention. * * * [A]ny state law regulating the prices of patented pharmaceutical products would likely be preempted as a result of the panel's holding. While the D.C. statute in this case appears to be invalid because of its poor drafting, the panel's opinion suggests that even legitimate price regulation is invalid. * * *

The problem with the D.C. Act, in my view, is that in a misguided effort to accommodate the patent statutes, it seeks to establish patent policy and thus is subject to field preemption. This is so because the statute requires the D.C. courts (in addressing the defense to excessive pricing) to determine what price is necessary to spur innovation, see D.C.Code § 28–4554(b), a policy determination that Congress surely did not intend to leave to the states. This is not, however, the ground for the panel decision here, which rests on conflict preemption. In my view, a price discrimination provision presents no conflict with the purpose of the federal patent law.

Despite its poor drafting, which inadvertently invades the field of patent policy, the main thrust of the D.C. Act is designed to prevent price discrimination between sales of patented pharmaceutical products in the District and in certain other countries that confer exclusivity. In this respect, the D.C. Act reflects the significant public concern about the disparity between drug prices in the United States and other industrialized nations with pharmaceutical patent protection. See generally U.S. Dep't of Commerce, Pharmaceutical Price Controls in OECD Countries: Implica-

* Biotechnology Indus. Org. v. District of Columbia, 505 F.3d 1343, 1348 (Fed.Cir.2007).

tions for U.S. Consumers, Pricing, Research and Development, and Innovation (2004). The District determined that it was important to regulate this price discrimination to protect public health, due to concern that such price discrimination would deny access to important pharmaceutical products to some District residents who are unable to afford needed medicines. It is limited to patented drugs because that is the area in which the price discrimination and access issues exist. * * *

[T]he panel finds a conflict between the D.C. Act and a supposed policy of the patent law to allow patent holders to reap maximum profits during the term of the limited monopoly on use of the invention. This seems to me incorrect. First, the patent laws are not designed to confer immunity from antitrust-type regulation. Congress has not conferred any right on a patentee "to enlarge the scope of the patent monopoly by using the [exclusionary] power it confers to restrain competition" except to the extent that the patent law confers exclusivity. Thus, for example, sellers of patented products have no special right to fix the price at which the patented products are sold. Second, the panel errs in suggesting that the purpose of the patent statutes is to allow a patentee to reap maximum profits during the exclusivity period * * * * A patent grant is designed not to allow the patent holder to exploit the grant for the maximum profit that the market will bear, but merely to confer a right of exclusivity. The panel's assertion to the contrary is inconsistent with longstanding Supreme Court precedent. * * *

[P]atent law does not preempt or conflict with state and federal statutes regulating or prohibiting the sale of patented products. * * * The legislative history of the Hatch–Waxman Act shows no more than a desire to allow exclusivity because it would result in higher profits. A law that does nothing to interfere with exclusivity also does nothing to interfere with this purpose. There is not a word in the cited legislative history of the Hatch–Waxman Act suggesting any concern about state price regulation of patented pharmaceutical products. The D.C. Act does not conflict with the purposes of federal patent law because the D.C. Act's limitations on price discrimination do not in any way interfere with any patent holder's right to exclusivity. The D.C. Act does not authorize any other person to make, use, or sell any patented products. * * *

It is clear that, to the extent that the D.C. Act prohibits price discrimination to ensure public access to important medications, it falls within the core of the states' traditional powers, triggering a strong presumption against preemption. The patent laws were not designed to immunize patent holders from legitimate state regulation in the states' traditional legislative spheres. A prohibition on price discrimination may or may not be desirable legislation. But the decision of whether to preempt such legislation is for the Congress to make, and not this court. * * *

NOTES AND QUESTIONS

1. *Patent policy preemption puzzles.* If the D.C. Act allowed for compulsory licensing of patented drugs, then it clearly would conflict with the patent law's grant of exclusivity (as Judge Dyk conceded); what if, instead, D.C. officials imposed a special excise tax on sellers of excessively priced drugs (putting aside for the moment the fact that this probably would exacerbate the problem as such taxes simply get passed along to purchasers)? Would the D.C. Act have passed muster if only it had applied equally to all (rather than just patented) prescription drugs, even though "excessive pricing" presumably would arise only rarely after patent expiration occurs given the prospect of generic competition? What if officials in one state found that identical brand-name drugs sold for substantially less in neighboring states—could they pursue charges of price discrimination in violation of state antitrust laws without impermissibly conflicting with federal patent policy? What if D.C. officials regarded the sale of an FDA-approved product as posing a serious danger to the public health—could they ban its local sale, notwithstanding the resulting interference with the patent-holder's ability to generate a profit? See generally Serena Lipski, Comment, Excessive Pricing and Pharmaceuticals: Why the Federal Patent Act Does Not Preempt State Regulation of Pharmaceutical Prices, 39 U. Tol. L. Rev. 913 (2008).

2. *Jumping on the bandwagon.* The District of Columbia also considered "taking" an even more radical step. See Susan Levine, Eminent Domain Urged as Tool to Cut Drug Costs, Wash. Post, Mar. 17, 2005, at T3. Other states have opted for more modest approaches in trying to assist their citizens with prescription drug purchasing, including subsidies and tax credits. The industry successfully challenged Vermont's plan, which allowed participants to receive drug discounts of up to 30% and required pharmaceutical companies to assume the burden of the price differential. See PhRMA v. Thompson, 251 F.3d 219 (D.C.Cir.2001) (invalidating HHS's waiver of certain Medicaid requirements). See generally Timothy S. Jost, Pharmaceutical Research and Manufacturers of America v. Walsh: The Supreme Court Allows the States to Proceed with Expanding Access to Drugs, 4 Yale J. Health Pol'y L. & Ethics 69 (2004); Paula Tironi, Pharmaceutical Pricing: A Review of Proposals to Improve Access and Affordability of Prescription Drugs, 19 Annals Health L. 311 (2010); Timothy J. Cahill, Comment, Curing the Legal Deficiencies of Proposed State and Federal Prescription Drug Discount Programs, 70 U. Cin. L. Rev. 1341 (2002); Kimberley Fox et al., State Pharmacy Discount Programs: A Viable Mechanism for Addressing Prescription Drug Affordability?, 60 N.Y.U. Ann. Surv. Am. L. 187 (2004).

3. *Medicaid formularies and prior authorization.* Putting aside efforts to extend the reach of favorable pricing beyond Medicaid beneficiaries, states have had to grapple with rising drug budgets in their programs. See Robert Pear & James Dao, States Trying New Tactics to Reduce Spending on Drugs, N.Y. Times, Nov. 21, 2004, § 1, at 35 (describing several different initiatives including the use of buyers' cooperatives); Stephanie Saul, Battle Lines Are Forming over Rapidly Rising Drug Prices, N.Y. Times, Jan. 31, 2006, at C1; see also Shaila Dewan, In Mississippi, Soaring Costs Force Deep Medicaid Cuts, N.Y. Times, July 2, 2005, at A8 (reporting that, with a few exceptions, beneficiaries in one state can fill no more than five prescriptions per month and no more than two for brand-name drugs); Michael Luo, Drug Costs Run Free Under New York Medicaid, N.Y. Times, Nov. 23, 2005, at A1 (contrasting the success of various initiatives adopted in other states). Several states have developed lists of preferred drugs and require that physicians treating Medicaid patients seek prior authorization for any products that do not appear in the formulary. See Richard Perez–Pena, 22 States Limiting Doctors' Latitude in Medicaid Drugs, N.Y. Times, June 16, 2003, at A1. The industry failed in its challenge to Florida's policy of exempting drugs from prior authorization requirements only if the manufacturer agreed to offer the state an additional 10% rebate. See PhRMA v. Meadows, 304 F.3d 1197 (11th Cir.2002). In lieu of providing these extra rebates, some drug manufacturers offered to establish "disease management programs," providing case workers to help Medicaid beneficiaries with chronic conditions such as diabetes and asthma to comply with recommended treatments (including prescribed pharmaceuticals) and promising to reduce total expenditures for such patients. See Melody Petersen, Drug Makers Expand Their Medicaid Role, N.Y. Times, Apr. 23, 2003, at C1 (reporting that officials in Florida and other states have allowed companies to proceed with these initiatives); cf. Marc Kaufman, States Get a Big Dose of Drugmakers' Cash, Wash. Post, Apr. 6, 2006, at A2 (reporting that, in response to the growth of efforts at reducing drug costs, the "industry spent more than $44 million on lobbying state governments in 2003 and 2004"); Melody Petersen, Making Drugs, Shaping the Rules, N.Y. Times, Feb. 1, 2004, § 3, at 1 (describing an aggressive industry campaign to ensure that state guidelines for antipsychotics recommend use of their newer products). See generally Brook Ames, Note, Paying Less for Celebrex: A Comparative Study of Medicaid Prescription Drug Cost–Containment Programs and a Recommendation for Medicare's Increasing Drug Costs, 85 B.U. L. Rev. 517 (2005); Nora Flaherty, Note, Medicaid "Preferred Drug Lists": Florida as a Model for Analysis, 11 Elder L.J. 77 (2003); Jagan N. Ranjan, Note, Medicaid and the Unconstitutional Dimensions of Prior Authorization, 101 Mich. L. Rev. 602 (2002).

4. *Generic substitution laws.* An older approach to concerns about escalating prices authorized generic substitution by pharmacists. See Inwood Lab. v. Ives Lab., 456 U.S. 844, 847 n.4 (1982) ("Since the early 1970s, most States have enacted laws allowing pharmacists to substitute generic drugs for brand name drugs under certain conditions."); Pharmaceutical Soc'y of N.Y. v. Lefkowitz, 586 F.2d 953 (2d Cir.1978) (holding that the potential savings to consumers justified the minimal burden on interstate commerce and that the physician override provision protected the integrity of the doctor-patient relationship and the prescribing process); see also Ranit Mishori, Giving You Just What the Doctor Ordered: Generics Save Money, but Sometimes Physicians Don't Prescribe Them, Wash. Post, July 12, 2011, at E1 (discussing a survey that found approximately five percent of prescription orders indicated "Dispense as Written," adding that Massachusetts recently made it more difficult for physicians to prevent generic substitution in this manner). As noted in Chapter 3(A)(2), concerns have arisen about slight differences between brand-name and generic equivalents that might adversely impact patients. As a result, some states have exempted certain classes of drugs from these substitution laws. See, e.g., Abbott Labs. v. Mylan Pharms., Inc., 15 So.3d 642, 645–46, 656–57 (Fla.Ct. App.2009); see also Jonathan D. Rockoff, Cost of Medicine Could Increase: Brand–Name Drugmakers Target Generic Prescriptions, Balt. Sun, June 17, 2008, at 1A (noting recent laws passed in Tennessee and Utah that prohibit the substitution of antiepileptic agents); Sarah Rubenstein, Pill Push: Industry Fights Switch to Generics for Epilepsy—Big Drug Makers Help Patient Groups Lobby, Wall St. J., July 13, 2007, at A1.

5. *Therapeutic substitution.* A more extreme approach to cost-cutting involves therapeutic substitution—a practice mandating the substitution of cheaper drugs within the same therapeutic class despite lack of evidence of equivalent safety or effectiveness. See John C. Ballin, Therapeutic Substitution: Usurpation of the Physician's Prerogative, 257 JAMA 528 (1987); Am. College of Physicians, Therapeutic Substitution and Formulary Systems, 113 Annals Internal Med. 160 (1990); Glenn Ruffenach, When Druggists Second–Guess Doctors, Wall St. J., May 9, 1988, at A25 (describing a law in the state of Washington permitting therapeutic substitution). Thus, as happened in the case of cholesterol-lowering statins, when generic versions of one drug in a class become available, other similar drugs may lose significant market share even though still under patent. See Scott Hensley, As Generics Pummel Its Drugs, Pfizer Faces Uncertain Future, Wall St. J., Jan. 5, 2006, at A1.

6. *Bargain hunting across the border.* The D.C. Act had adopted as a benchmark drug prices in the U.K., Germany, Australia, and Canada. Individuals living in other parts of the country have found their own ways to take advantage of the often dramatic pricing disparities. See Lars Noah, NAFTA's Impact on the Trade in Pharmaceuticals, 33 Hous. L. Rev. 1293, 1311–14 (1997); Elizabeth Mehren, Bargain Drug Prices Spark Border Crossings, L.A. Times, Dec. 4, 2000, at A1; see also Sarah Lunday, When Purchasing Medicine in Mexico, Buyer Beware, N.Y. Times, Apr. 17, 2001, at F5 (describing concerns about improper manufacturing, labeling, and storage of prescription drugs available in Mexico). In 2000, Congress enacted legislation that would have authorized pharmacists and wholesalers to reimport prescription drugs from certain countries, including Canada. See Medicine Equity and Drug Safety Act, Pub. L. No. 106–387, § 745, 114 Stat. 1549A–35. The law never went into effect, however, because the Secretary of HHS declined to make the findings necessary to trigger this provision. See William Davis, Comment, The Medicine Equity and Drug Safety Act of 2000: Releasing Gray Market Pharmaceuticals, 9 Tul. J. Int'l & Comp. L. 483 (2001); cf. Eric Lipton, Lawmakers Agree to Spend $1.2 Billion on Tightening Border, N.Y. Times, Sept. 26, 2006, at A21 ("Congressional negotiators also added a measure to the bill [FY2007 appropriations for the Department of Homeland Security, Pub. L. No. 109–295, § 535] that would allow Americans to buy as much as a 90–day supply of prescription drugs in Canada ... and then return home with them."). As explained in the following excerpt, Congress tried once again, but HHS did not change its views.

Vermont v. Leavitt

405 F.Supp.2d 466 (D.Vt.2005).

■ SESSIONS, CHIEF JUDGE:

In Beebe Plains, Vermont, there is a street, appropriately named Canusa Avenue, that runs right along the United States–Canada border. Houses on the northern side of the street are in Canada while houses on the southern side are in Vermont. If a resident of the northern side of Canusa Avenue needs medication to control high cholesterol, he or she can purchase a 90–day supply of 20 milligram Lipitor for $170. On the southern side of the street, Vermont residents will have to dig much deeper if they need to purchase the same drug. The same 90–day supply of Lipitor costs about $330 in the United States.

This price differential is far from unique. On average, brand-name drug prices are approximately 70% higher in the United States. Congressional Research Serv., Importing Prescription Drugs: Objectives, Options, and Outlook 7–8 (2004). It has been estimated that United States consumers would have saved $59.7 billion if, during 2004, they had purchased all brand-name drugs at Canadian prices. Id. at 29. To put that figure in context, it is more than the gross national products of Kuwait, Iceland and Jamaica combined.

Given the dramatic difference between United States and Canadian drug prices, it is unsurprising that many Americans are interested in buying prescription drugs in Canada. "Nearly five million shipments, comprising about 12 million prescription drug products with a value of approximately $700 million entered the U.S. from Canada alone in 2003." HHS Task Force on Drug Importation, Report on Prescription Drug Importation, ix (Dec. 2004). As residents of a border state, most Vermonters can drive to Canada within two or three hours. Thus, Vermont residents are more likely to buy prescription drugs in Canada than most other Americans.

Vermont regulators have been concerned about high domestic drug prices and the increase in ad hoc, personal importation of Canadian drugs by Vermont residents. In response to these concerns, plaintiff Vermont Agency of Administration (VAA) submitted a citizen petition to the Food and Drug Administration (FDA) requesting that the FDA allow the Vermont State Employee Medical Benefit Plan (VTSEMBP) to "establish a program for the orderly individual importation of prescription medications." * * *

Vermont explained that it wanted "authority to contract with providers to create a system under which its members have the option of forwarding a prescription to a Canadian firm where the prescription would be reviewed by a physician familiar with the member's medical history and re-written as a Canadian prescription, which would be forwarded to a licensed Canadian pharmacy to be filled and sent by mail to the member in the United States." Accordingly, Vermont requested the FDA to "issue regulations or otherwise commit to exercise its enforcement discretion to allow the VTSEMBP to establish a program for the orderly individual importation of prescription medications in a manner that promotes the safety and health of its members." In the alternative, the petition requested that the FDA "issue guidance that such a program would be lawful under the statutes and regulations enforced by the Commissioner of Food and Drugs." Finally, Vermont requested that "the FDA promptly establish regulations to provide for importation of prescription drugs from Canada into the [United States]" as provided by section 1121 of the Medicare Prescription Drug, Improvement, and Modernization Act, Pub. L. No. 108–173, 117 Stat. 2066 (2003) (MMA).

In its petition, Vermont noted that the FDA is not currently committing resources to controlling importation by individuals of prescription medications from outside the United States for their own use. Vermont claimed that, because of the close proximity to Canada, "[t]he reality is that many plan members regularly travel to Canada and have the ability to bring back prescription medications under the published FDA enforcement policy." Given that prescription medications are cheaper in Canada, "members are likely to import prescription medications on an ad hoc, personal level." Vermont argued that, when this occurs, VTSEMBP does not "have an opportunity to intervene to minimize the risks associated with prescription medications obtained outside the U.S., as identified by the FDA."

Vermont suggested that, by granting the petition, the FDA would enable VTSEMBP to minimize any health risks associated with importing drugs. As part of its program, Vermont would contract with service providers with knowledge regarding which prescription drugs sold in Canada are manufactured in FDA-approved facilities. The petition suggests that "[i]f the plan was able to bring such Canadian prescription purchases back into our plan mechanism, as opposed to after-the-fact reimbursement as occurs with any other out-of-network purchase, we may be able to make those purchases subject to other safety and health promotion features of our pharmacy benefit management program, such as drug-interaction warnings and disease management."

The FDA denied Vermont's citizen petition eight months after it was filed. In its response, the FDA discussed the import provisions of the Federal Food, Drug and Cosmetic Act (FDCA). In the FDA's view, the FDCA creates a "closed" system which strictly limits the importation of prescription medications. * * * The FDA also rejected Vermont's request that the FDA promptly issue regulations as called for by section 1121 of the MMA to facilitate the wholesale importation of prescription medications from Canada. The FDA noted that, under the MMA, it can only issue such regulations "if the Secretary of Health and Human Services ... certifies that implementing the program would (1) pose no additional risk to the public health and safety and (2) result in a significant reduction in the cost of drugs to the American consumer." * * *

The FDA also contested some of the policy arguments raised in Vermont's petition. The FDA claimed that:

> In our experience, many drugs obtained from foreign sources that purport and appear to be the same as U.S.-approved prescription drugs have been of unknown quality. In examining imported drugs sent through the mail, FDA has identified so-called "foreign versions" of FDA-approved drugs sent through the mail, improperly labeled drugs, drugs that failed to meet special storage conditions, drugs requiring close physician monitoring, and drugs containing addictive controlled substances. Such findings show the serious risks posed by the illegal importation of prescription drugs. The agency cannot provide adequate assurance that the drug products delivered to consumers in the United States from foreign countries are the same products approved by FDA or that they are safe and effective for their intended uses. * * *

The policy debates surrounding drug importation are contentious and complex. However, this case presents the court with a pure question of law. The FDA claims that, under the law, it was unable to provide any of the relief Vermont requested in its citizen petition. This means that the court must determine if Vermont's proposal was permitted under the relevant federal statutes. * * *

Under 21 U.S.C. § 381(d)(1), no prescription drug "which is manufactured in a State and exported may be imported into the United States unless the drug is imported by the manufacturer of the drug." There are only two exceptions to this rule. First, the Secretary may authorize importation for emergency use. Second, importation may be permitted under the MMA's importation provisions.

The MMA contains a provision that authorizes the Secretary of HHS to "promulgate regulations permitting pharmacists and wholesalers to import prescription drugs from Canada into the United States." 21 U.S.C. § 384(b). The MMA also provides that the Secretary "may grant to individuals, by regulation or on a case-by-case basis, a waiver of the prohibition of importation of a prescription drug or device or class of prescription drugs or devices, under such conditions as the Secretary determines to be appropriate." Id. § 384(j)(2)(A). Thus, the MMA contemplates both commercial and individual importation. * * * "This section shall become effective only if the Secretary certifies to the Congress that the implementation of this section will—(A) pose no additional risk to the public's health and safety; and (B) result in a significant reduction in the cost of covered products to the American consumer." Id. § 384(*l*). Secretary Leavitt and his predecessor, former Secretary Thompson, have declined to issue a certification under this subsection.

The MMA superseded the Medicine Equity and Drug Safety Act of 2000 (MEDS Act). Like the MMA, the MEDS Act authorized the Secretary of HHS to pass regulations allowing commercial importation of prescription drugs. The MEDS Act also contained a certification provision conditioning importation on a certification to Congress. Former Secretaries Thompson and Shalala declined to issue a certification to Congress under the MEDS Act. Thus, when Congress enacted the MMA's certification provision, it was aware that, during the previous three years, the Secretary of HHS had declined to issue a certification under a very similar provision.

There is no question that Vermont's proposed program would violate the FDCA. For example, whenever Vermont assisted in the re-importation of a drug manufactured in the United States, it would violate 21 U.S.C. § 331(t). This will be true regardless of whether VTSEMBP or the members themselves import the drugs. VTSEMBP will violate section 331(t) if it "causes" its members to import drugs in violation of 21 U.S.C. § 381(d)(1). Thus, as Vermont's proposed plan would be highly likely to include drugs manufactured in the United States, it would lead to violations of section 331(t). Similarly, Vermont's plan is likely to violate 21 U.S.C. § 331(a). Many Canadian drugs will have packaging and labeling that is not approved by the FDA. Also, many Canadian drugs may not have been manufactured according to GMP (even if these drugs are pharmacologically identical to drugs approved by the FDA). Thus, VTSEMBP would violate 21 U.S.C. § 331(a) by causing these drugs to be introduced into interstate commerce.

As Vermont's proposed plan violates the FDCA, the crucial issue is whether the MMA provides authorization for the plan. Vermont argues that its proposed program is permitted under the MMA. Vermont is incorrect. Under section 384(*l*), the relevant provisions of the MMA only become effective if the Secretary certifies to Congress that importation is safe and cost-effective. As the Secretary has not made this certification, the MMA offers no support for Vermont's program. Vermont argues that, as a matter of statutory construction, the certification provision only applies to the commercial importation provisions of section 384 and not to the personal importation provisions. * * *

Under Vermont's interpretation, when Congress wrote "this section" it actually meant "subsections (b)–(h) but not subsections (a) and (j)." This is a convoluted and implausible interpretation. Moreover, Vermont's position is undermined by the fact that Congress used the term "subsection" in other provisions of section 384. Clearly, when Congress intended to refer only to a particular subsection, it used the appropriate language. * * * Overall, the only sensible way to read the statute is to assume that Congress intended the certification provision to apply to the whole of section 384. As the Secretary has not made the required certification, section 384 provides no authorization for Vermont's proposed plan.

Vermont claims that section 384(*l*) improperly delegates legislative power to the Executive Branch. * * * [I]f the certification provision were severed from the statute then the MMA would authorize commercial and personal importation from Canada. * * * Vermont suggests that the MMA "confers unbridled discretion on the Secretary to decide whether or not" the MMA's importation provisions will become effective. If this were true, the MMA would violate the intelligible principle test. However, Vermont mischaracterizes the MMA. * * * [T]he MMA's certification provision provides clear guidance to the Secretary of HHS by directing the Secretary to consider safety and cost-effectiveness. This is not unbridled discretion.

The Supreme Court has consistently upheld delegations that provide less guidance. * * *

Vermont also claims that the MMA is unconstitutional because of its conditional nature. Section 384 is unusual in that it only becomes effective if the Secretary issues a certification. According to Vermont, the certification provision gives the Secretary the authority to decide what the law is. The MMA is not unconstitutional because of its conditional nature. The Constitution "does not require that Congress find for itself every fact upon which it desires to base legislative action." Yakus v. United States, 321 U.S. 414, 424 (1944). The Constitution only requires that "Congress has specified the basic conditions of fact upon whose existence or occurrence, ascertained from relevant data by a designated administrative agency, it directs that its statutory command shall be effective." Id. at 424–25. * * *

Moreover, even if section 384(*l*)(1) were an unconstitutional delegation of authority, this would not help Vermont. This is because the provision may not be severed from the rest of section 384. It is evident that Congress would not have enacted the other provisions of section 384 standing alone. To hold otherwise would be to assume that Congress was indifferent as to whether the Secretary considered an importation program to be safe and cost-effective. The plain language of section 384(*l*)(1) says otherwise. * * *

[T]he FDA concluded that "it would be extremely unlikely that the State of Vermont could ensure that all the Canadian drugs that VTSEMBP helped its members obtain were in full compliance with all laws and regulations applicable to FDA-approved drug products." * * * Admittedly, the FDA's conclusion appears in isolation on the fourth page of the decision letter. Nevertheless, the FDA provides a full explanation for this conclusion earlier in the letter. The second page of the decision letter contains a thorough outline of the FDCA's structure. For example, the letter explains that only the original United States manufacturer may import a prescription drug back into the United States. The letter also explains that Canadian drugs often do not satisfy the FDA's requirements concerning manufacturing or labeling. The FDA also cited a recent federal court decision enjoining commercial importation of Canadian drugs. Overall, the FDA adequately explained why Vermont's proposal is likely to conflict with the requirements of the FDCA. * * *

Vermont's complaint must be dismissed as it requests relief the court has no authority to grant. Vermont's citizen petition asked the FDA to approve a program that was, and remains, illegal. Thus, the FDA did not act arbitrarily or capriciously by denying the petition. Also, as of August 4, 2004, the Secretary had not unreasonably delayed action regarding the certification provision of section 384(*l*)(1).

NOTES AND QUESTIONS

1. *Made in Canada.* Similar challenges to the Secretary's failure to issue the necessary certification fared no better. See Montgomery County v. Leavitt, 445 F.Supp.2d 505 (D.Md.2006); see also In re Canadian Import

Antitrust Litig., 470 F.3d 785 (8th Cir.2006) (affirming the dismissal of a class action lawsuit, which alleged that manufacturers had acted to discourage pharmacies in Canada from dispensing prescription drugs to American patients, because the plaintiffs' desire to import cheaper drugs violated federal law). Notwithstanding judicial set-backs and continuing opposition from the FDA, several states persist in facilitating the importation of drugs as a way of helping their citizens save money. See Marc Kaufman, FDA, States at Odds over Drugs, Wash. Post, Feb. 22, 2004, at A11; Gretchen Ruethling, Five Drug–Importing States Add Two Countries as Sources, N.Y. Times, July 19, 2005, at A17 ("Australia and New Zealand join Canada, Britain and Ireland as medication sources for the program, I–SaveRx, which was created by Illinois and Wisconsin in October and has been joined by Kansas, Missouri and Vermont."). The subject has attracted substantial debate—in the short term, visible cost savings must be balanced against concerns about assuring safety; in the longer-term, importing foreign price controls eventually might discourage R & D (but, then again, those foreign countries have enjoyed something of a free-ride, leaving American consumers to shoulder more than their fair share of the costs of innovation). See generally Aaron S. Kesselheim & Niteesh K. Choudhry, The International Pharmaceutical Market as a Source of Low–Cost Prescription Drugs for U.S. Patients, 148 Annals Internal Med. 614 (2008); Robert S. Nakagawa, Prescription Drug Systems and Price Control in Canada, 15 J.L. & Pol'y 1103 (2007); Kevin Outterson, Pharmaceutical Arbitrage: Balancing Access and Innovation in International Prescription Drug Markets, 5 Yale J. Health Pol'y L. & Ethics 193 (2005); Paige E. Goodwin, Note, Right Idea, Wrong Result—Canada's Access to Medicines Regime, 34 Am. J.L. & Med. 567 (2008); Jennifer L. Halser, Comment, Canadian Pharmacies: A Prescription for a Public Health Disaster, 54 DePaul L. Rev. 543 (2005); Devin Taylor, Note, Importing a Headache for Which There's No Medicine: Why Drug Reimportation Should and Will Fail, 15 J.L. & Pol'y 1421 (2007). Importation also threatens to create shortages in Canada as manufacturers restrict supplies. See Tamsin Carlisle, What's Left for Canadians If Americans Buy Their Drugs?, Wall St. J., Nov. 4, 2003, at D3; Ceci Connolly, Pfizer Cuts Supplies to Canadian Drugstores, Wash. Post, Feb. 19, 2004, at A10. The Medicare drug benefit has reduced demand. See Fewer Americans Are Buying Drugs from Canada, Wall St. J., Feb. 22, 2006, at D2 (reporting a 30% decline).

2. *Pharmacy dispensing fees*. In covering prescription drugs purchased by beneficiaries, Medicaid reimburses for both the product and the costs associated with dispensing it. New York pharmacists challenged a statute that created a co-payment system to cover pharmacy dispensing costs but that also required pharmacists to dispense drugs to Medicaid recipients who were unable to afford the co-payment. One court held that the statutory scheme was preempted by federal law insofar as it resulted in the reduction of payments to pharmacists: "To the extent that pharmacies do not receive full compensation, some are likely to drop out of the Medicaid program and reduce the number of providers of health care to poor individuals. And, if they continue as providers, they will simply pass on the costs of the uncollected co-payments to the public at large." Pharmaceutical Soc'y of N.Y. v. Department of Social Serv., 50 F.3d 1168, 1175 (2d Cir.1995); see also Pennsylvania Pharmacists Ass'n v. Houstoun, 283 F.3d 531 (3d Cir.2002) (reviewing a challenge to pharmacy reimbursement rates under state Medicaid program); Florida Pharmacy Ass'n v. Cook, 17 F.Supp.2d 1293 (N.D.Fla.1998) (same); cf. Elizabeth Agnvall, A New Type of Pharmacist Seeks to Help People Manage Complex Drug Regimens, Wash. Post, Dec. 14, 2004, at F1 ("[M]anaged care companies that will provide Medicare drugs must create a drug therapy management program, designed to pay pharmacists to counsel patients with multiple chronic diseases such as diabetes, asthma and hypertension.").

Pharmaceutical Care Mgmt. Ass'n v. Rowe

429 F.3d 294 (1st Cir.2005).

■ TORRUELLA, CIRCUIT JUDGE:

This appeal arises from an attempt by plaintiff-appellant Pharmaceutical Care Management Association (PCMA) to challenge the provisions of Maine's Unfair Prescription Drug Practices Act (UPDPA), Me. Rev. Stat. Ann. tit. 22, § 2699 (2005). PCMA brought suit against defendant-appellee G. Steven Rowe, Attorney General of the State of Maine, seeking to obtain an order enjoining enforcement of the UPDPA [on a variety of grounds, including ERISA preemption, taking property without just compensation or due process, infringing on free speech, and offending dormant Commerce Clause principles]. * * * [W]e affirm the decision of the district court [to grant the defendant's motion for summary judgment].

PCMA is a national trade association of pharmacy benefit managers (PBMs). PBMs are major players in the delivery of health care in the United States. They act as middlemen in the lucrative business of providing prescription drugs. They serve as intermediaries between pharmaceutical manufacturers and pharmacies on the one hand (as the district court noted, the "supply" side of the trade) and health benefit providers (e.g., insurers, self-insured entities, health maintenance organizations, and public and private health plans) on the other (the "demand" side). The services that PBMs extend are designed to facilitate the provision of prescription drug benefits to the people who utilize the services of the health benefit providers.

For example, PBMs often provide health benefit providers with access to an established network of pharmacies, where customers of the health benefit providers can obtain drugs at certain set prices. PBMs negotiate volume discounts and rebates with drug manufacturers by pooling substantial numbers of health benefit providers. This pooling gives the PBMs tremendous market power to demand concessions from the manufacturers. PBMs also provide drug utilization review services and "therapeutic interchange programs" (in other words, substituting a drug for the one actually prescribed by a doctor).

In this role as intermediary, however, PBMs have the opportunity to engage in activities that may benefit the drug manufacturers and PBMs financially to the detriment of the health benefit providers. For example, in cases of "therapeutic interchange," a PBM may substitute a more expensive brand name drug for an equally effective and cheaper generic drug. This is done so that the PBM can collect a fee from the manufacturer for helping to increase the manufacturer's market share within a certain drug category. Similarly, a PBM might receive a discount from a manufacturer on a particular drug but not pass any of it on to the health benefit provider, keeping the difference for itself. The health benefit provider, however, often has no idea that a PBM may not be working in its interest. This lack of awareness is the result of the fact that there is little transparency in a PBM's dealings with manufacturers and pharmacies. * * *

With the aim of placing Maine health benefit providers in a better position to determine whether PBMs are acting against their interests, and, correspondingly, to help control prescription drug costs and increase access to prescription drugs, the Maine Legislature enacted the UPDPA in the spring of 2003. The UPDPA imposes a number of requirements on those PBMs that choose to enter into contracts in Maine with "covered entities"—meaning health benefit providers and including, in part, insurance companies, the state Medicaid program, and employer health plans. Such PBMs are required to act as fiduciaries for their clients and adhere to certain specific duties. For example, they must disclose conflicts of interest, disgorge profits from self-dealing, and disclose to the covered entities certain of their financial arrangements with third parties. The disclosures made by the PBMs to the covered entities are protected by confidentiality. None of the disclosures are available to the public. * * *

PCMA argues that the UPDPA violates the Commerce Clause under the more lenient test set out by the Supreme Court in *Pike v. Bruce Church, Inc.*, 397 U.S. 137, 142 (1970). Under that test—to be used when the state statute at issue regulates evenhandedly and has only incidental effects on interstate commerce—courts employ a balancing approach whereby they examine whether the state's interest is legitimate and whether the burden on interstate commerce clearly exceeds the local benefits. * * *

The aim of the UPDPA is to reduce the costs of, and increase the public's access to, prescription drugs. The law was designed to deal with "one of the serious problems of our time." PCMA, for its part, thinks these benefits are not likely to materialize as a result of the UPDPA. It is not the place of this court, however, to pass judgment on the wisdom of the policies adopted by the Maine legislature. Furthermore, as the district court points out, under *Pike,* it is the *putative* local benefits that matter. It matters not whether these benefits actually come into being at the end of the day. On the "burden" side of the *Pike* balancing equation, PCMA only asserts that as a result of the UPDPA, certain PBMs will no longer do business in Maine. * * * Given the set of competing concerns we are presented with here, we think the district court was correct in asserting that PCMA "failed to provide the court with any great weight to place on the excessive burden side of the scale." When measuring PCMA's concern about its members' profits against the increased access to prescription drugs for Maine citizens, the local benefits clearly outweigh any incidental burden on interstate commerce. * * *

■ BOUDIN, CHIEF JUDGE (concurring):

* * * PCMA's First Amendment claim is completely without merit. So-called "compelled speech" may under modern Supreme Court jurisprudence raise a serious First Amendment concern where it effects a forced association between the speaker and a particular viewpoint. What is at stake here, by contrast, is simply routine disclosure of economically significant information designed to forward ordinary regulatory purposes—in this case, protecting covered entities from questionable PBM business practices. There are literally thousands of similar regulations on the books—such as product labeling laws, environmental spill reporting, accident reports by common carriers, SEC reporting as to corporate losses and (most obviously) the requirement to file tax returns to government units who use the information to the obvious disadvantage of the taxpayer. The idea that these thousands of routine regulations require an extensive First Amendment analysis is mistaken. * * * The [applicable rational basis] test is so obviously met in this case as to make elaboration pointless.

3. PRIVATE EFFORTS AT PRICE CONTROLS

Patricia M. Danzon & Li–Wei Chao, *Does Regulation Drive out Competition in Pharmaceutical Markets?*

43 J.L. & ECON. 311 (2000).

Most countries regulate manufacturer prices for pharmaceuticals, either directly (France and Italy) or indirectly through controls on insurance reimbursement (Japan) or profits (the United Kingdom). Regulation is often justified by the assumption that price competition is weak for several reasons: patents intentionally limit competition and lead to product differentiation that may be intensified by promotion, insurance makes patients insensitive to prices, and physicians who are primary decision makers may not know product prices and/or may be imperfect agents for patients. * * *

Optimal competition policy and the extent of competition in practice differ over the life cycle of a new molecule. Originator products are granted patent protection to provide an opportunity to recoup research and development (R & D) expense. Patents bar competition from generic imitators for the life of the patent, which corresponds to roughly the first 10–12 years of life on the market. However, patent-protected drugs may face competition from "therapeutic substitutes"—drugs with different active ingredients but similar therapeutic effects. After patent expiration, generic imitators can enter the market with minimal R & D expense. * * * [T]here is a strong presumption that price competition between generic substitutes of patent-expired drugs is socially beneficial, assuming that the patent term and structure are designed to yield the socially desired return on R & D.

[I]n the United States, many people who were insured for physician and hospital services had no coverage for outpatient drugs and, hence, faced the full price. In addition, many of those with coverage had plans with generic substitution programs, which set a maximum allowable charge (MAC) for generically equivalent drugs and require the patient to pay any excess of the actual price over the MAC * * * * [B]y the 1990s all states had repealed antisubstitution laws and authorized pharmacists to substitute generic equivalents unless the physician explicitly writes "dispense as written." Managed care plans and Medicaid encourage generic substitution for off-patent drugs by paying a maximum allowable charge (MAC, or reference price) for generically equivalent products. * * *

In the United States, manufacturer prices are unregulated. Since the mid–1980s, managed care has changed the nature of competition. Health maintenance organizations (HMOs) and other pharmacy benefit managers (PBMs) create formularies of "preferred" drugs that physicians and patients are encouraged to use. The ability to shift demand toward one or two preferred products within a group of therapeutic substitutes has increased demand elasticity in the managed care sector, which has enabled PBMs to negotiate discounts from list prices for branded products. * * *

NOTES AND QUESTIONS

1. *Determinants of drug prices.* See Jayanta Bhattacharya & William B. Vogt, A Simple Model of Pharmaceutical Price Dynamics, 46 J.L. & Econ. 599 (2003); Carmelo Giaccotto et al., Drug Prices and Research and Development Investment Behavior in the Pharmaceutical Industry, 48 J.L. & Econ. 195 (2005); F.M. Scherer, The Pharmaceutical Industry—Prices and Progress, 351 New Eng. J. Med. 927 (2004); see also Alex Berenson, A Cancer Drug's Big Price Rise Disturbs Doctors and Patients, N.Y. Times, Mar. 12, 2006, § 1, at 1 (reporting a dramatic price increase for an old chemotherapy agent with a small but captive market: "In some drug categories, such as cholesterol-lowering treatments, many drugs compete, keeping prices relatively low. But when a medicine does not have a good substitute, its maker can charge almost any price."); id. ("After years of defending high prices as necessary to cover the cost of research or production, industry executives increasingly point to the intrinsic value of their medicines as justification for prices."); Stephen Heuser, Shire Drug Gets FDA Approval, Boston Globe, July 25, 2006, at C1 (reporting that Elaprase®, which treats an extremely rare genetic condition, would set a record for most expensive pharmaceutical treatment at about $300,000 annually). After it received FDA approval for the preterm labor drug Makena® (hydroxyprogesterone caproate), which came with seven years of market exclusivity as an "orphan" drug, KV Pharmaceutical attracted sharp criticism for deciding to charge $1,500 per dose (approximately $30,000 total during the course of a pregnancy) because previously available compounded versions had sold for no more than $20 per dose. See Rob Stein, Price Tag Soars on Preterm Birth Drug, Wash. Post, Mar. 29, 2011, at A1 (adding that an FDA official suggested that it might approve a generic version of the same drug for a different indication, which would then allow physicians to use it off-label); see also Rob Stein, FDA Won't Obstruct Cheap Alternative to Makena, Wash. Post, Mar. 31, 2011, at A5 (reporting that the FDA "took the unusual step of announcing that it would" not act to prevent continued pharmacy compounding); Andrew Zajac, Pregnancy Drug's Price Reduced, L.A. Times, Apr. 2, 2011, at AA2 (reporting a revised but still controversial price of $690 per dose); cf. Jonathan D. Rockoff, An Old Gout Drug Gets New Life and a New Price, Riling Patients, Wall St. J., Apr. 12, 2010, at B1 (reporting that the FDA's grant of three years of market exclusivity for Colcrys® (colchicine) resulted in a dramatic price increase).

2. *Formularies*. Health plans may use a variety of mechanisms to control the prescribing of drugs for their beneficiaries. In an open formulary plan, the insurer agrees to pay for any drug prescribed to the beneficiary, although the insurer may circulate to physicians a list of preferred drugs. At the other extreme, health plans using a closed formulary approach categorically refuse to pay for any nonformulary drug product. Closed formularies typically include the most cost-effective drug in each group of therapeutically-interchangeable drugs. Partially-closed formularies attempt to balance the cost-effectiveness of closed formularies with the prescribing freedom of open formularies. Thus, the partially-closed formulary limits choice with respect to drugs in the most commonly-prescribed therapeutic categories, but otherwise uses an open-formulary approach. Finally, some plans now employ clinical formularies (either closed or partially-closed) for the treatment of specific conditions, such as asthma or stomach ulcers. See Mark A. Buckles, Electronic Formulary Management and Medicaid: Maximizing Economic Efficiency and Quality of Care in the Age of Electronic Prescribing, 11 U. Fla. J.L. & Pub. Pol'y 179, 183–85 (2000); see also Connecticut v. Physicians Health Serv. of Conn., Inc., 103 F.Supp.2d 495 (D.Conn.2000) (suit on behalf of state health plan enrollees challenging formulary system); Arnold J. Rosoff, The Changing Face of Pharmacy Benefits Management: Information Technology Pursues a Grand Mission, 42 St. Louis U. L.J. 1 (1998); Daniel L. Freidlin, Note, Just Say No: The Cipro Craze and Managed Care—Applying the Hand Formula to Managed Care Decisions, 30 Hofstra L. Rev. 1329 (2002). Patients whose physicians prescribe drugs outside of the formulary may face higher co-payments or may be billed for the full cost of the drug. An increasing number of MCOs allow physicians to override formularies in certain situations, but penalties for deviation from formularies and pre-approval requirements probably limit the number of successful overrides. See AMA Council on Ethical & Judicial Aff., Managed Care Cost Containment Involving Prescription Drugs, 53 Food & Drug L.J. 25, 28 (1998). Do the economic efficiencies of drug formularies justify their potentially negative impact on patient care? What sorts of ethical issues arise with the imposition of strict formulary requirements? And are there any benefits associated with prior authorization requirements for non-formulary drugs apart from cost savings? Cf.

Stephanie Saul, V.A. Limits Glaxo Drug Widely Used for Diabetes, N.Y. Times, Oct. 18, 2007, at C3 (reporting that the Department removed Avandia® (rosiglitazone) from its formulary based on safety concerns notwithstanding the FDA's more modest response). Might an insurer face tort liability if its cost-containment mechanisms failed to discover and prevent inappropriate prescribing (e.g., Accutane for pregnant patients, Celebrex in patients who would do equally well with an NSAID, or apparently excessive quantities of opioid analgesics)?

3. *Professional concerns about drug formularies.* The American Medical Association strongly encourages physicians to keep abreast of managed care formularies so that they can prescribe drugs effectively for patients:

> Managed care organizations establish drug formulary systems so that physicians will supplement medical judgment with cost considerations in drug selection. To ensure optimal patient care, various ethical requirements must be established for formulary application.
>
> (1) Physicians who participate in managed care plans should maintain awareness of plan decisions about drug selection by staying informed about pharmacy and therapeutics (P & T) committee actions and by ongoing personal review of formulary composition....
>
> (2) Physicians should be particularly vigilant to ensure that formulary decisions adequately reflect the needs of individual patients and that individual needs are not unfairly sacrificed by decisions based on the needs of the average patient. Physicians are ethically required to advocate for additions to the formulary when they think patients would benefit materially and for exceptions to the formulary on a case-by-case basis when justified by the health care needs of particular patients....
>
> (3) Limits should be placed on the extent to which managed care plans use incentives or pressures to lower prescription drug costs. Financial incentives are permissible when they promote cost-effectiveness, not when they require withholding medically necessary care. Physicians should not be made to feel that they jeopardize their compensation or participation in a managed care plan if they prescribe drugs that are necessary for their patients but that may also be costly....
>
> (4) Managed care plans should develop and implement educational programs on cost-effective prescribing practices. Such initiatives are preferable to financial incentives or pressures by health maintenance organizations or hospitals, which can be ethically problematic.
>
> (5) Patients must be informed of the methods used by their managed care plans to limit prescription drug costs. During enrollment, the plan should disclose the existence of formularies, the provisions for cases in which the physician prescribes a drug that is not included in the formulary and the incentives or other mechanisms used to encourage physicians to consider costs when prescribing drugs. In addition, plans should disclose any relationships with pharmaceutical

> benefit management companies or pharmaceutical companies that could influence the composition of the formulary. If physicians exhaust all avenues to secure a formulary exception for a significantly advantageous drug, they are still obligated to disclose the option of the more beneficial, more costly drug to the patient, so that the patient can decide whether to pay out-of-pocket.

AMA Council on Ethical & Judicial Aff., Managed Care Cost Containment Involving Prescription Drugs, Rep. E–8.135 (1996); see also Donald P. Hay & Linda K. Hay, Diagnosing and Treating Depression in a Managed Care World, 42 St. Louis U. L.J. 55, 57–58 (1998) (criticizing formularies for excluding new generations of costly antidepressant drugs that pose fewer risks for some patients); Peter J. Neumann, Evidence–Based and Value–Based Formulary Guidelines, Health Aff., Jan.–Feb. 2004, at 124.

4. *Incentive-based formularies.* Instead of restricting reimbursement to only those drugs included in a formulary, insurers increasingly have established a more flexible system of "tiers" with varying co-payments. See Haiden A. Huskamp et al., The Effect of Incentive–Based Formularies on Prescription–Drug Utilization and Spending, 349 New Eng. J. Med. 2224, 2225 (2003) ("57 percent of workers in the United States who had drug benefits were enrolled in plans with a three-tier formulary."); Geoffrey F. Joyce et al., Employer Drug Benefit Plans and Spending on Prescription Drugs, 288 JAMA 1733, 1733 (2002) ("These plans typically set the lowest co-payment for generic drugs, the middle co-payment for formulary or preferred brands, and the highest co-payment for nonformulary brands."); Cindy P. Thomas, Incentive–Based Formularies, 349 New Eng. J. Med. 2186, 2188 (2003) ("Some insurers have created a fourth, 'lifestyle,' tier for more discretionary or 'cosmetic' drugs ...."); cf. Julie Appleby, Medicare Expands Tier Pricing System, USA Today, Jan. 4, 2006, at 3B (reporting that 40% of plans being offered to Medicare beneficiaries have four tiers and that, "[i]n that fourth tier—where Medicare patients will most commonly pay 25% to 33% of the cost of the drug rather than a flat dollar amount—are such expensive treatments as Remicade and Enbrel for rheumatoid arthritis, Procrit and Aranesp for anemia and Copaxone and Betaseron for multiple sclerosis"). Other approaches include co-insurance (i.e., co-pays as a percentage of the drug price rather than a flat amount) and "reference-pricing" (i.e., capping reimbursement at the average price charged for all drugs in a therapeutic class). What are the pros and cons of these different cost-sharing mechanisms, and can you suggest any others? As co-payment levels have increased, especially in the non-preferred tier, these arrangements may begin to have the same effects as a restrictive formulary. See Thomas H. Lee & Ezekiel J. Emanuel, Tier 4 Drugs and the Fraying of the Social Compact, 359 New Eng. J. Med. 333 (2008); Vanessa Fuhrmans, Higher Co–Pays May Take Toll on Health, Wall St. J., May 19, 2004, at D1; Barbara Martinez, Drug Co–Pays Hit $100, Wall St. J., June 28, 2005, at D1; see also John Hsu et al., Unintended Consequences of Caps on Medicare Drug Benefits, 354 New Eng. J. Med. 2349 (2006). Some brand-name manufacturers have tried to counterbalance such disincentives by offering discounts directly to patients. See Jeffrey Krasner, Drug Coupons May Be No Bargain, Boston Globe, Apr. 6, 2006, at D1. Were patients better off before public and private health insurers began to cover outpatient prescription drugs insofar as manufacturers would find it harder to charge what they do today knowing that few individuals could afford to pay sticker prices out of their own pockets, or has such coverage facilitated expensive innovation that otherwise might not have taken place?

5. *Pill splitting.* When tablets come in different dosages (though often for similar prices per tablet), some insurers encourage or require the substitution of half as many tablets as prescribed but at twice the dosage and with directions that the patient split the drug in half (some tablets are "scored" in the middle to facilitate cutting). See Victoria Colliver, Prescription for Costly Health Care, S.F. Chron., May 30, 2006, at C1; Tara Parker–Pope, Health Insurers Push Pill Splitting as a Way to Save Money on Drugs, Wall St. J., Nov. 22, 2005, at D1; see also Timmis v. Permanente, 2004 WL 2943993 (Cal.Ct.App.2004) (rejecting an unfair business practice claim against one HMO's pill-splitting program). Do you foresee any potential problems with such policies?

In re Brand Name Prescription Drugs Antitrust Litig.

288 F.3d 1028 (7th Cir.2002).

■ Posner, Chief Judge:

The plaintiffs in this Sherman Act price-fixing case appeal from the grant of summary judgment to the defendants. The plaintiffs had opted out from a large antitrust litigation, other phases of which are discussed at 123 F.3d 599 (7th Cir.1997), and 186 F.3d 781 (7th Cir.1999) * * * * The plaintiffs are retail sellers of prescription drugs, and the defendants that are the appellees are wholesale sellers of such drugs, that is, the plaintiffs' suppliers. The plaintiffs argue that the wholesalers conspired with the manufacturers of the drugs to deny the plaintiffs discounts they would have received had it not been for the conspiracy. The manufacturers are also defendants but they are not before us. They remain, their liability as yet unresolved, in the district court. * * *

The plaintiffs' theory is that the manufacturers agreed not to give discounts to pharmacies and other retail sellers and enlisted the wholesalers to police the agreement by means of a "chargeback" system that the wholesalers had adopted early in the 1980s. Then as later, manufacturers of brand-name prescription drugs engaged in price discrimination. That is, a manufacturer would sell the same product, costing the same to make and sell, at different prices to different customers. The lowest price, presumably, covered the manufacturer's cost (for there is no allegation that the manufacturers were engaged in predatory pricing or forced by adverse business conditions to sell at distress prices), implying that the higher prices in the discriminatory price schedule generated revenues in excess of cost.

That sounds like monopoly pricing, but we must be careful here to distinguish between fixed and variable costs. Many of the costs of a new drug are incurred before manufacturing for sale begins—costs of research, of development, of obtaining patents, of obtaining FDA approval, and so forth. A price equal to just the cost of manufacturing and selling the drug, the cost that varies with the amount of the drug sold (the marginal cost, in other words, as distinct from the average total cost of the drug), would therefore not cover the product's total costs. The firm could try to cover those costs by charging a uniform markup over marginal cost, but if customers vary in their willingness to pay for a particular drug, the firm may do better to charge different prices to different customers or groups of customers.

A customer's willingness to pay will be a function of the customer's options. In the drug industry, as it happens, hospitals and HMOs, because they "control" to a considerable extent the physicians whom they employ or contract with, are in a good position to effect the substitution of generic equivalents for brand-name prescription drugs. They therefore are unwilling to pay as much for the brand-name drugs as the typical drugstore, which simply fills the physician's prescription—and physicians are often indifferent to the price of the drug they are prescribing.

If brand-name drugs were interchangeable not only with generics but with each other, then unless the manufacturers colluded they would be unable to discriminate in price between hospitals and HMOs on the one hand and drugstores on the other hand. The high markup in the price to the disfavored customers would be competed away. Suppose marginal cost is $5 and price $10; at any price above $5, the seller obtains some contribution to his fixed costs, and so a seller who starts out with a price of $10 will be tempted to shade it to attract sales from his rivals and this competitive process will continue until price is bid down to $5. If, however, the drugs are not interchangeable, whether because of chemical differences protected by patents against being duplicated or because of perceived differences having to do with a manufacturer's reputation or his advertising or other promotional activity on behalf of particular brands, then each manufacturer might be able to engage in price discrimination.

Price discrimination is in fact quite common in competitive industries; think only of the difference in price between hardback and paperback books, a difference that almost always exceeds the difference in the marginal cost of the two types; or the difference in ticket prices between the same first-run and subsequent-run movie; or discounts for senior citizens. As long as competitive products are not perfect substitutes to all consumers, the fact of their being competitive does not preclude discriminatory pricing. The publishing industry is extremely competitive but, as just noted, price discrimination is the norm in it. Just as copyrights give the publisher a temporary monopoly of each book he publishes, so patents give manufacturers of drugs a temporary monopoly of each drug he manufactures. These monopolies create preconditions for discriminatory pricing.

Yet even in the case of the differentiated product protected from immediate competitive duplication by a patent, copyright, or trade secret, price discrimination would be feasible only if the manufacturer could prevent (or at least limit) arbitrage—the erasure of a price difference not attributable to a cost difference (that is, a discriminatory price difference) by a middleman's buying from the favored customers and reselling to the disfavored. (Or the favored customer might overbuy and resell the surplus directly to the disfavored one.) And that brings us to the chargeback system.

Suppose that a manufacturer wanted hospitals to be able to buy its drugs for 10 percent less than pharmacies, and so it granted its wholesalers a 10 percent discount on all sales intended for resale to hospitals. The wholesaler would have an incentive to overstate the number of those sales and divert the excess above those necessary to meet the hospitals' demand to the pharmacies. Suppose the retail price suggested by the manufacturer for some drug was $10 to pharmacies and $9 to hospitals, and the price charged by the manufacturer to wholesalers for sales destined for pharmacies was $5 and the price for sales destined for hospitals was $4.50. Any quantities of the drug that the wholesaler obtained for $4.50 and resold to a pharmacy would yield the wholesaler $5.50 per sale ($10–$4.50) rather than $5, and so the wholesalers might end up buying their entire supply for $4.50 per unit on the representation that they were selling only to hospitals. The result would be a reduction in the manufacturer's revenue from sales destined for pharmacies from $5 to $4.50, its anticipated revenue from sales destined for hospitals.

Enter the chargeback system, whereby the manufacturer contracts directly with the retail level of distribution, the hospitals and the pharmacies in our example. Continuing with the example, the manufacturer promises a hospital a 10 percent discount, the hospital so informs its wholesaler, the wholesaler reduces its price to the hospital accordingly, and then the wholesaler, which had bought the drug for $5, bills the manufacturer 50 thus preserving its own margin. To get the 50it must present proof that it sold the drug to a customer authorized to buy at a discount. There is no way the wholesaler can pay only $4.50 for a drug that he resells to a pharmacy for $10. Arbitrage by wholesalers is thus prevented.

Price discrimination by a firm that is not a monopolist and is not colluding with its competitors is generally not an antitrust violation at all; as we said, it is common in competitive industries. It is particularly difficult to object to it when, as in the case of drugs or books, a producer has heavy fixed costs, so that a price equal to marginal cost would not be compensatory. The alternative in such a case to price discrimination is as we said a high uniform markup over marginal cost, and there is no reason to think it a superior alternative to a differential pricing scheme. Indeed often, as quite probably in the book case and possibly in the drug case as well, the differential scheme enables the industry to achieve a larger output than with a uniform price. If the average hardback book is priced at $25 and the average paperback at $9, and if publishers were constrained to price them on the basis of the cost difference and as a result set a price of (say) $18 for hardbacks and $16 for paperbacks, they would probably lose more sales at the low end than they gained at the high end, and if so their total output would be less.

Since price discrimination is not (in general) unlawful, neither are efforts to prevent arbitrage. An agreement by distributors to adopt a system for preventing arbitrage, the better to serve their suppliers, would surely not be a per se violation of the antitrust laws, as the principal effect of invalidating it might simply be to induce the manufacturers to take over the wholesale function themselves. In any event, the charge here is not that a "horizontal" agreement to ban arbitrage is unlawful (there is a hint of such a charge in the plaintiffs' brief, but it is insufficiently developed to preserve the issue for our review), but that the defendant wholesalers joined a conspiracy by manufacturers of brand-name prescription drugs to fix prices, the wholesalers' role in the conspiracy being to prevent arbitrage that would undermine the manufacturers' price-fixing scheme.

To make the charge stick, the plaintiffs would have had to prove two things. The first was that the manufacturers conspired to fix prices. The second was that the wholesalers joined the conspiracy by adopting the chargeback system. We said that manufacturers of differentiated products can engage in price discrimination unilaterally, because each manufacturer has a little monopoly power. But in addition manufacturers who have no individual monopoly power may find it feasible and attractive to engage in price discrimination collusively, that is, to agree on a discriminatory schedule of prices.

Suppose the defendant drug manufacturers cannot charge a very high price to hospitals because if they do the hospitals will simply substitute generics, but that drugstores have no such option. Then it would make sense for the manufacturers, even if their brand-name drugs were fungible, to agree (if they thought they could get away with it and that the agreement would be effective) to charge a higher price for drugs destined for drugstores and a lower price for drugs destined for hospitals. But if they reach their customers through wholesalers, they need a way of preventing the wholesalers from engaging in arbitrage; and the chargeback system is that way. That is, the chargeback system is equally efficacious whether used to prevent arbitrage against individual price discrimination or arbitrage against collusive price discrimination. In the second case the chargeback system would have the additional benefit to the conspiring manufacturers of preventing any of them from cheating on their coconspirators (the bane of conspiracy) by trying to lure the high-margin customers (the drugstores in our example) with prices slightly below the agreed-upon price to disfavored customers.

It is not easy to distinguish factually between the two forms of discrimination—one legal, the other illegal—in the setting of this case, since, as we said, the defendant manufacturers do sell differentiated products. The plaintiffs (who remember are the disfavored purchasers, the drugstores and other retail sellers) did present considerable evidence that some of them, at least, have competitive options just as good as those of some of the favored purchasers. For example, in a number of states pharmacists have the legal right, unless the prescribing physician expressly forbids, to substitute a chemically identical drug for the one prescribed. The refusal of the defendant manufacturers to grant discounts to pharmacies in such states must mean, the plaintiffs argue, that the manufacturers have agreed to hold the line on discounts. This is not an impressive argument, because if pharmacies have the same competitive options as hospitals, why would the manufacturers' cartel charge different prices to pharmacies and to hospitals? Stated differently, if the manufacturers can by agreement avoid giving discounts to pharmacies, why do they give discounts to hospitals that are identically situated so far as competitive options, such as generics, are concerned?

We need not pursue this issue, because the district court has not yet determined whether the manufacturers conspired among themselves. Assuming they did, the plaintiffs would still have to prove that the wholesalers joined the conspiracy. They would have to show not only that the wholesalers knew that the manufacturers' price discrimination which the chargeback system assists was collusive rather than individual, but also that the wholesalers agreed with the manufacturers to support that price discrimination by means of the chargeback system.

There is authority for prohibiting as a violation of the Sherman Act or of section 5 of the Federal Trade Commission Act an agreement that facilitates collusive activity—for example, a basing-point pricing system, or a system of exchanging price information, or industry-wide adoption in contracts with customers of most-favored-nation clauses (which make discounting more costly by requiring that a discount to one buyer be granted to all buyers protected by such clauses). But that is not the theory of this case. The theory is that the wholesalers joined the manufacturers' conspiracy. And of that there is too little evidence to permit a reasonable jury to infer the wholesalers' guilt.

There is first of all no evidence that the wholesalers *knew* that the manufacturers' price discrimination was collusive rather than individual. To argue that because the uniform refusal to grant discounts even to pharmacies that seemed to have competitive options as good as hospitals and HMOs smacks of collusion the wholesalers knew that the manufacturers were colluding is too much of a stretch; it would amount to basing an inference of conspiracy on negligence, a careless failure to tumble to the nature of one's suppliers' business methods. It would mean that any time a seller asked a distributor not to engage in arbitrage the distributor would be in peril of being found to have conspired with the seller to fix prices should it turn out that the price discrimination engaged in by the seller was collusive rather than individual.

An inference of knowledge would be particularly shaky here because, so far as appears, the chargeback system was adopted before the alleged collusion of the manufacturers began and because the system is supported by commercial reasons independent of any desire to prevent arbitrage, let alone to facilitate collusive pricing. Without the chargeback system or some simulacrum, a hospital or other purchaser of brand-name prescription drugs that was entitled to a discount would have to pay the full price to the wholesaler and then ask the manufacturer for a rebate. The delay entailed in that system would give these purchasers something the wholesalers dreaded, namely an incentive to buy directly from the manufacturers. The chargeback system enabled the purchasers to obtain their discount at the moment of purchase, just as they would have done had they bought directly from the manufacturers. It was a wholesaler survival tactic. * * *

[W]e cannot find anything [in the record] to create more than the barest suspicion that the wholesalers knew the manufacturers were colluding (at present only a hypothesis, we remind) and knowing this decided to help them by means of the chargeback system. Most of it is evidence that the manufacturers were engaged in collusive pricing. This evidence was deemed sufficient by the district court to defeat the *manufacturers'* motion for summary judgment, but it was hardly strong enough to compel or even permit an inference that the wholesalers knew the manufacturers were colluding. (In a trial of the same claim by the plaintiffs who did not opt out of the class action, the manufacturers were exonerated of the only price-fixing charge in which the wholesalers may have been implicated. 186 F.3d at 784–88.) There is evidence that the chargeback system was intended to discourage arbitrage; undoubtedly it was, but that is consistent with the wholesalers' believing, whether correctly or not, that the manufacturers' price discrimination was individual rather than collusive.

The plaintiffs' best evidence is testimony concerning meetings of the wholesalers' trade association at which manufacturers were present (not that there is anything suspicious in general about suppliers talking to distributors). All the testimony concerns retail buying groups. At one meeting the wholesalers asked the manufacturers whether the latter would be selling directly to groups of buyers, bypassing the wholesalers, and were relieved to be assured that they would not be. This could be a form of compensation for the wholesalers' preventing arbitrage that would thwart collusive price discrimination by the manufacturers, but that is sheer conjecture. * * *

The plaintiffs' evidence is consistent with the existence of an overarching conspiracy of which the wholesalers were members. But it is equally consistent with there being either no conspiracy at all or one of which the wholesalers were unaware, let alone of which they were members. * * * On this record, no reasonable jury could find for the plaintiffs, and so the judgment of the district court must be affirmed.

NOTES AND QUESTIONS

1. *Price discrimination litigation.* Shortly before trial on the claims against the manufacturers, the parties settled. See Drug Mart Pharmacy Corp. v. American Home Prods. Corp., 378 F.Supp.2d 134, 136 n.2 (E.D.N.Y.2005); see also id. at 138–40 (granting summary judgment to the manufacturers on separate Robinson–Patman Act claims for conspiring to price discriminate). See generally Dennis S. Corgill, Distributing Products Under the Nonprofit Institutions Act: Price Discrimination, Arbitrage, and Fraud in the Pharmaceutical Industry, 2001 B.Y.U. L. Rev. 1383; Asha S. Geire, Comment, Price Wars and Patent Law: Reducing the Cost of Health Care Through Medical Device Price Transparency, 12 Tul. J. Tech. & Intell. Prop. 239 (2009); Aimee M.W. Pollak, Note, Should the Exemption from the Robinson–Patman Act Apply to Pharmaceutical Purchases by Nonprofit HMOs?, 73 N.Y.U. L. Rev. 965 (1998); Symposium, Soaring Prices for Prescription Drugs: Just Rewards for Innovations or Antitrust Violations?, 39 U.S.F. L. Rev. 1 (2004).

2. *Antitrust issues in drug marketing.* Federal prosecutors have investigated whether several drug companies, including Bristol–Myers Squibb, engaged in inappropriate marketing practices in order to persuade physicians to prescribe their products. The company apparently gave oncologists certain drugs free of charge in exchange for agreements to purchase other Bristol–Myers products. The company also "bundled" its oncology drugs in order to increase the marketability of its lesser-selling products. See David S. Cloud, U.S. Scrutinizes Sales Practices of Bristol–Myers, Wall St. J., Feb. 27, 2001, at A3; see also Courtney E. Curtis, Comment, Under the Section 2 Microscope: Do Pfizer's Bundled Rebates and Exclusive Dealing Contracts Violate the Sherman Antitrust Act?, 35 Sw. U. L. Rev. 207 (2006). Some drug manufacturers purchased PBMs, creating the potential for preferential treatment of their products in transactions with a PBM's customers. See Allison D. Garrett & Robert Garis, Leveling the Playing Field in the Pharmacy Benefit Management Industry, 42 Val. U. L. Rev. 33 (2007); Mark Meador, Comment, Squeezing the Middleman: Ending Underhanded Dealing in the Pharmacy Benefit Management Industry Through Regulation, 20 Annals Health L. 77 (2011); see also Reed Abelson & Michael J. de la Merced, Drug Benefit Managers Plan Merger, N.Y. Times, July 22, 2011, at B1 (reporting serious antitrust doubts about a proposed combination between two of the three largest PBMs). Chapter 10(C) considers these and other antitrust issues.

D. SUPPLY SHORTAGES

Lars Noah, *Triage in the Nation's Medicine Cabinet: The Puzzling Scarcity of Vaccines and Other Drugs*

54 S.C. L. REV. 741 (2003).

The tragic events of September 11, 2001, and the still mysterious mailing of weaponized anthrax spores one month later, awakened this country to the risks of bioterrorism and brought attention to what has become a growing problem: shortages of antibiotics, vaccines, and other medical technologies. Although this situation poses concerns about our readiness in the event of a bioterrorist attack, it has more mundane and potentially serious public health implications. In addition, while it should come as no great surprise that we have inadequate supplies of treatments for smallpox and anthrax, persistent shortages of common childhood vaccines and other critical pharmaceuticals seem inexplicable. * * *

The affected products include a couple of long-used combination vaccines—one to protect against diphtheria, tetanus, and pertussis (DTP), and another one to protect against measles, mumps, and rubella (MMR)—along with two newer vaccines—one to protect against pneumonia, and another one to protect against varicella (chickenpox). * * * Dozens of other essential pharmaceutical products also have run low in the last couple of years, including the anticoagulant heparin, the antiviral drug ganciclovir, several antiemetics, diuretics, antiepileptic agents, injectable corticosteroids, and neuromuscular blocking agents. * * *

Usually, short supplies of drugs do not increase the risks to patient health because effective therapeutic substitutes remain available, but occasionally these shortfalls do endanger patients. Vaccine shortages can interfere with mass immunization efforts, and, with time, they would threaten to unravel some of the remarkable gains made against infectious diseases during the last half century. Even when substitute vaccines exist, they may represent older formulations that offer somewhat reduced safety, efficacy, and/or convenience. Similarly, patients who have come to depend on a particular medication to treat a chronic health condition may suffer if unable to secure supplies. In addition, alternative suppliers may introduce separate safety concerns. For instance, when the manufacturer of betamethasone experienced quality control problems and had to halt production temporarily, physicians and hospitals in one region of the country turned to a local pharmacy with requests to compound this injectable corticosteroid from available bulk materials, but the product became contaminated and resulted in two deaths and dozens of injuries among patients. * * *

Apart from manufacturing problems, drug shortages may arise from deliberate decisions by pharmaceutical companies to cease or drastically reduce production of a product because profits have declined. Compounds that have lost their patent protection typically command far lower prices, and manufacturers often will prefer to focus on a newer product designed to replace its predecessor and generate more substantial revenues. In 1997, in an effort to minimize the short-term supply disruptions caused by corporate decisions to cease marketing critical pharmaceuticals, Congress mandated that sole suppliers of such products notify the FDA at least six months ahead of time so that the agency can alert physician and patient organizations. * * *

Although tort liability received most of the blame in the past, two other factors may help to account for the latest round of shortages: stringent federal control of manufacturing facilities and cost-containment efforts that erode profit margins. * * * Public and private insurers are more likely to reimburse or supply pharmaceuticals regarded as essential to health, but the desire to guarantee patient access unwittingly may weaken the industry's economic incentives for producing adequate supplies of these therapeutic agents. Bulk purchases by government agencies or pressures exerted by large insurers can depress prices to the point that it makes little business sense for a company to continue manufacturing a particular product.

Vaccines do not represent a terribly lucrative business compared to other pharmaceutical lines. Indeed, their success in eradicating dreaded infectious diseases of the past creates a risk of eventual obsolescence, as had happened with the smallpox vaccine until very recently. Government-mandated immunizations for children ensure a steady demand for many vaccines, but, in contrast to prevalent chronic diseases that may require daily and indefinite use, individuals may receive a particular vaccine on only a few occasions over the course of their lifetimes. To make matters worse, many individuals do not purchase vaccines, relying instead on supplies made available by public health departments. In 1993, Congress created the Childhood Immunization Initiative, which ensured free vaccines to all eligible children. This statute directed the CDC to increase their purchasing of pediatric vaccines but limited price increases on government contracts to the rate of inflation. * * *

In response to the latest round of vaccine shortages, interested parties have begun serious efforts to find solutions to the problem. The previous discussion suggests a pair of responses. First, the FDA needs to facilitate rather than impede the production of critical pharmaceuticals. The agency now does a better job of getting essential drugs to the market, but it needs to help keep them on the market as well. When it initially licenses products, the FDA gives priority to reviewing drugs and biologics intended for the treatment of life-threatening conditions for which effective therapies do not yet exist; it needs to do the same when it inspects facilities and resolves disputes involving GMP requirements. At the very least, the FDA must demonstrate additional flexibility in case of a serious supply shortage. Second, cost-containment strategies need to give way to some mechanism for paying a premium for critical pharmaceutical products or at least providing their manufacturers with generous tax incentives. * * *

The creation of emergency stockpiles represents another response to the threat of shortages, much like the strategic petroleum reserve established after the OPEC oil embargo. In 1982, the federal government began stockpiling childhood vaccines. On a couple of occasions, the CDC has tapped into this reserve in order to cover temporary shortfalls caused by production difficulties. Although the agency continues to maintain the stockpile at its original levels, the program has stagnated somewhat in the face of resource constraints.

More recently, the federal government created a National Pharmaceutical Stockpile (NPS) of a range of drugs designed for rapid deployment in the event of public health emergencies. When bioterrorism emerged as a threat to civilians, some feared shortages of antibiotics effective in the treatment of anthrax. In addition, the relatively few remaining doses of the vaccine for smallpox, a disease eradicated decades earlier, triggered research into the possibility of diluting the available supplies in order to stretch the doses while waiting for manufacturers to ramp up production under government contracts to purchase 300 million doses. The CDC has added both products to the NPS, and it also has purchased a large supply of potassium iodide, a drug that provides some protection against thyroid damage from radioactive fallout.

Stockpiles offer a stopgap measure for covering limited shortfalls in supply, but they do not address the underlying causes of scarcity. They also present serious logistical difficulties that limit their usefulness, and resource constraints make it unlikely that the federal government would ever manage to establish—much less maintain—a truly comprehensive selection of critical pharmaceuticals for a sizeable patient population. Instead, drug stockpiles will play an increasingly important but still limited role as part of an emergency response strategy.

An even more radical strategy calls for active public sector involvement in the production of critical pharmaceuticals. Compulsory licensing, which forces a patent holder to allow the use of an invention by others in exchange for a fixed royalty, offers one mechanism for doing so, and some commentators have suggested patent buyouts by the federal government as a mechanism for controlling price and availability problems with critical drug products. * * * [A]lthough the United States does not have separate legislation authorizing compulsory licensing of patents for pharmaceutical products, the Tucker Act provides a right of action for the unlicensed use of a patent by the federal government. To the dismay of the pharmaceutical industry, the government threatened to use this authority in order to acquire inexpensive supplies of the antibiotic Cipro® (ciprofloxacin) for treating persons exposed to anthrax. * * *

Some commentators have suggested even more aggressive government involvement in producing critical drugs, but past experience with public control of vaccine manufacturing suggests caution. * * * The public health departments in a couple of states produce their own supplies of certain childhood vaccines, but doing this for numerous critical pharmaceuticals on a national scale seems both impractical and inadvisable. In 1992, the Institute of Medicine recommended the creation of a "surge" production capacity for critical vaccines under public ownership, and it reiterated this proposal shortly after the latest terrorist attacks. Some commentators have, however, questioned the wisdom of undertaking such an effort * * * * Instead of trying to displace private manufacturers, the federal government should try to help ensure that market conditions are conducive to the production of ample supplies by multiple sources.

For a variety of reasons, shortages of vaccines and other critical pharmaceutical products have increased in the last few years. Pressures emanating from regulatory agencies, courts, and insurers have conspired to make this line of the pharmaceutical business less than attractive. The FDA's implementation of GMP requirements, especially those governing the production of vaccines and other biologics, have created compliance difficulties for manufacturers; the threat of tort liability continues to drive some drug companies from particular markets; and cost-containment pressures resulting from bulk government purchases or declining levels of insurance reimbursement have eroded profit margins. Under these conditions, the pharmaceutical industry's focus on blockbuster drugs for lifestyle uses or chronic health conditions should come as no great surprise.

This is a multi-faceted problem that does not admit of any single or simple solution, but the government should not respond in ways that further weaken market incentives. Instead, it should try to encourage private manufacturers to continue supplying critical pharmaceutical products. A number of steps would help improve the business climate: more flexible regulation of manufacturing facilities, greater protection from the vagaries of tort liability, and the avoidance of excessive cost controls. In addition, the government should bolster its emergency stockpiles, but it must take care to avoid suggestions that the public sector should take over the entire operation, because then we really would have only a single supplier that would risk many of the same shortcomings that government-run monopolies have encountered in other fields.

NOTES AND QUESTIONS

1. *No shortage of shortages.* See Jennifer C. Dooren, Drug Shortages Distress Hospitals, Wall St. J., Feb. 1, 2011, at A4; Scott Hensley & Bernard Wysocki, Jr., As Industry Profits Elsewhere, U.S. Lacks Vaccines, Antibiotics, Wall St. J., Nov. 8, 2005, at A1; Christopher K. Hepp, Critical U.S. Drug Shortage Worsening, Phila. Inquirer, Dec. 12, 2010, at C1 ("Much of the problem seems to reside among generic medications, particularly sterile injectable drugs ...."); Rita Rubin, Drug Shortages Forcing Risky Alternatives, USA Today, Feb. 3, 2011, at 3A ("Anesthesiology and oncology have been hit particularly hard."); Paula Span, Drive to Stem Shingles Meets Few Expectations, N.Y. Times, July 12, 2011, at D1 (reporting that only 10% of eligible older adults have received the shingles vaccine (Zostavax®), partly because of recurring supply shortages); Rob Stein, U.S. Drug Shortages Threatening Those Whose Lives Depend on Crucial Remedies, Wash. Post, May 2, 2011, at A10 ("A record 211 medications became scarce in 2010—triple the number in 2006—and at least 89 new shortages have been recorded through the end of March ...."); id. ("Consolidation in the pharmaceutical industry has left only a few manufacturers for many older, less profitable products, meaning that when raw material runs short, equipment breaks down or government regulators crack down, the snags can quickly spiral into shortages."); see also Valerie Jensen & Bob A. Rappaport, The Reality of Drug Shortages—The Case of the Injectable Agent Propofol, 363 New Eng. J. Med. 806 (2010); Gardiner Harris, Obama Tries to Speed Response to Shortages in Vital Medicines, N.Y. Times, Oct. 31, 2011, at A1; Andrew Pollack, Shift to Ozone–Friendly Inhaler Is Leading to Shortages and Rising Prices, N.Y. Times, May 12, 2006, at C1; cf. Rob Stein, Lethal Injection Drug Being Phased Out, Wash. Post, Jan. 22, 2011, at A1 ("The U.S. company that makes a drug most states use in lethal injection announced Friday that it would no longer produce the powerful anesthetic, a decision that throws capital punishment in the United States into disarray."). The marketplace does, however, appear to offer adequate incentives for new vaccine development. See Matt Richtel, Warding off Diseases, Many Vaccines at a Time, N.Y. Times, May 16, 2007, at H5 (describing "a broad renaissance in vaccine research and development"); Daniel Costello, Vaccine Industry Is Being Revived, L.A. Times, Jan. 28, 2007, at A1.

2. *Pandemic fears.* Shortages often arise because of perennial difficulties in producing vaccines against influenza, and the recent emergence of potentially virulent new strains such as H5N1 (avian flu) and novel H1N1 (swine flu) only exacerbate these problems. See Rob Stein, Vaccine System Remains Antiquated: New Production Techniques Are Mostly Years Away from Being Implemented, Wash. Post, Nov. 24, 2009, at F1 ("While several companies are trying to ready their new techniques in case the H1N1 pandemic worsens, most of these remain years away from contributing significantly to the world's capacity to respond to a deadly new pathogen."); Shankar Vedantam & Michael Rosenwald, Ever–Changing Virus Challenges Drugmakers, Wash. Post, May 2, 2009, at A8; see also Mary P. Flaherty, Some Suppliers Jack up Flu Vaccine Price, Wash. Post, Oct. 14, 2004, at A2 (describing price gouging); Michael D. Shear & Rob Stein, Why Such a Shortage of Swine Flu Vaccine? Administration Points to Drugmakers, and Both Point to Science, Wash. Post, Oct. 27, 2009, at A1 ("Public anxiety has surged as the swine flu sweeps across the country and doctors and clinics are forced to turn away many people."); cf. Rob Stein, Millions of H1N1 Vaccine Doses May Be Discarded: Expiration Date Looms for Supplies Left Unused as Demand Declined, Wash. Post, Apr. 1, 2010, at A1 ("[L]ess than half of the 229 million doses of H1N1 vaccine the government bought to fight the pandemic have been administered—leaving an estimated 71.5 million doses that must be discarded if they are not used before they expire . . . , the latest twist in the $1.6 billion program—the most ambitious immunization campaign in U.S. history."). The government has backed efforts to improve manufacturing processes to allow for the rapid production of adequate vaccine supplies in the event of a pandemic. See Andrew Pollack, Scientists See Success in Flu Vaccine Made by Faster Method, N.Y. Times, Feb. 16, 2011, at A17 (discussing HHS-sponsored trial of cell culture production); Andrew Zajac, Government to Overhaul Plans for Bioterror, Flu, L.A. Times, Aug. 20, 2010, at A13 ("Acknowledging that the development of medical countermeasures against bioterrorism threats and pandemic flu is lagging, federal authorities . . . announced a $1.9–billion makeover of the system for identifying and manufacturing drugs and vaccines for public health emergencies."); see also Bernard Wysocki, Jr., Missing Medicine—Emergency Response: Fearing Avian Flu, Bioterror, U.S. Scrambles to Fill Drug Gap, Wall St. J., Nov. 9, 2005, at A1 ("A popular idea among some foundations and economists in recent years is to create a guaranteed bounty for new drugs that market forces wouldn't normally supply.").

Even if adequate supplies exist to meet normal demand, the widespread outbreak of a serious disease would overwhelm existing inventories of antibiotics, antivirals, and hospital equipment. See Christopher Lee, U.S. Flu Outbreak Plan Criticized: It Does Not Anticipate Strain on Hospitals, Local Health Officials Say, Wash. Post, Feb. 2, 2008, at A3 ("A serious outbreak and its fallout would probably ... trigger shortages of beds, ventilators, drugs, masks, gloves and other supplies ...."); Donald G. McNeil, Jr., Experts Say Medical Ventilators Are in Short Supply in Event of Bird Flu Pandemic, N.Y. Times, Mar. 12, 2006, § 1, at 24 ("A typical hospital ventilator costs $30,000, and hospitals, operating on thin profit margins, say they cannot afford to buy and store hundreds of units that may never be used. Cheaper alternatives can be deployed in a crisis, but doctors say they are grossly inadequate to deal with a flu pandemic."). For instance, shortages of antiviral treatments have arisen during recent flu scares. See David Brown, CDC Says Most Won't Need Drugs for Flu, Wash. Post, Sept. 9, 2009, at A7 ("The guidance is aimed at getting optimal benefit from Tamiflu and Relenza while preventing overuse, hoarding and shortages of the drugs, as was seen briefly during the spring outbreak of swine flu."); Rob Stein, Tamiflu Shortages Have Parents on Wild Dose Chase: Liquid Form of Drug Used to Treat Youngest Victims of Swine Flu Is in Short Supply, Wash. Post, Oct. 29, 2009, at A1. Indeed, pandemic fears have led to personal stockpiling (hoarding) of antivirals. See David Brown, Run on Drug for Avian Flu Has Physicians Worried, Wash. Post, Oct. 22, 2005, at A1; see also Mary B. Marcus, Companies Given Chance to Stockpile Anti–Flu Drug, USA Today, June 27, 2008, at 4A (reporting that Roche has created a program allowing large businesses to pre-order supplies of Tamiflu for their work forces). For further commentary on these issues, see Bradley J. Condon & Tapen Sinha, The Effectiveness of Pandemic Preparations: Legal Lessons from the 2009 Influenza Epidemic, 22 Fla. J. Int'l L. 1 (2010); Lawrence O. Gostin & Benjamin E. Berkman, Pandemic Influenza: Ethics, Law, and the Public's Health, 59 Admin. L. Rev. 121 (2007); Symposium, Preparing for Pandemic Influenza, 39 Seton Hall L. Rev. 1103 (2009).

3. *Bioterrorism preparedness*. Although bioterrorism has received substantial attention and an influx of resources designed to detect and respond to such a threat, most experts conclude that this country remains woefully unprepared. See Renae Merle, Bioterror Antidote—Unfulfilled Prescription: After Four Years, Scant Progress on Bush's BioShield Plan, Wash. Post, Jan. 16, 2007, at D1; Bernard Wysocki, Jr., US Struggles for Drugs to Counter Biological Threats, Wall St. J., July 11, 2005, at A1. The government's effort to inoculate half a million first-responders against smallpox, which some critics regarded as entirely unjustified, reached less than 10% of its goal and caused serious side effects in a few individuals. See Ceci Connolly, Mixed Report on Smallpox Inoculations, Wash. Post, Dec. 7, 2005, at A5. The emergency drug stockpile has, however, improved dramatically. See Spencer S. Hsu, Modest Gains Against Ever–Present Bioterrorism Threat, Wash. Post, Aug. 3, 2008, at A10 ("The Strategic National Stockpile, an emergency cache of critical pharmaceuticals that can be sent within 12 hours to counter outbreaks, has been greatly expanded .... [It] has 60 million treatment courses of antibiotics for anthrax and pneumonic plague .... About 300 million doses of smallpox vaccine can also be shipped."); see also id. ("Officials say that the government is retooling efforts to encourage drug companies to invest in BioShield projects, and that the effort is paying off in new antitoxins for anthrax and botulism."); Renae Merle, Deal for Smallpox Vaccine Could Jump–Start BioShield, Wash. Post, June 7, 2007, at D1 ("The government has agreed to spend as much as $1.6 billion to buy millions of doses of a smallpox vaccine tailored for people with impaired immunity."); cf. id. ("[Project BioShield] has been plagued by delays, scientific hurdles and management problems and has completed few of its goals .... [HHS recently] withdrew plans to buy 100,000 doses of a radiation sickness treatment, saying none of the available drugs met requirements."); David Brown, If Bioterrorists Strike, Letter Carriers Might Deliver Antibiotics, Wash. Post, Oct. 2, 2008, at A2 ("Before that pilot project can begin, however, the [FDA] must approve distribution of the drug for this purpose, which is not currently part of its label ...."); Renae Merle, GAO Report Cites Waste in Anthrax Vaccine Cache, Wash. Post, Oct. 23, 2007, at D3; Andrew Pollack, Anxiety over Radiation Drives a Sales Surge for a Drug Against Thyroid Cancer, N.Y. Times, Mar. 16, 2011, at A13 ("[T]he situation in Japan could rekindle calls for the United States government to provide potassium iodide tablets to more people who live near American nuclear power plants. The suppliers of the three versions of potassium iodide approved by the [FDA], none of which require a prescription, said they were struggling to keep up with demand."); Matthew L. Wald, Plan to Store Anti–Radiation Pills Is Overdue, N.Y. Times, Oct. 23, 2004, at A15 ("Potassium iodide is cheap, about 20 cents for a 24–hour dose, and if kept away from light and moisture, it will last for years in storage. But the number of people who might someday need the drug is in the tens of millions or higher.").

4. *Rationing*. When shortages of critical medical technologies arise, public health officials and health care providers may have to grapple with difficult questions about how to allocate their limited supplies. Chapter 11(D)(2) considers some of these issues in greater detail.

CHAPTER 10

Managing Incentives for Innovation

A. Intellectual Property Protections

More than sixty years ago, when asked whether he planned to patent his new polio vaccine, Dr. Jonas Salk replied by asking "Can you patent the sun?" How times have changed.

1. Patentable Subject Matter

Diamond v. Chakrabarty

447 U.S. 303 (1980).

■ Burger, Chief Justice:

* * * In 1972, respondent Chakrabarty, a microbiologist, filed a patent application, assigned to the General Electric Co. The application asserted 36 claims related to Chakrabarty's invention of "a bacterium from the genus Pseudomonas containing therein at least two stable energy-generating plasmids, each of said plasmids providing a separate hydrocarbon degradative pathway." This human-made, genetically engineered bacterium is capable of breaking down multiple components of crude oil. Because of this property, which is possessed by no naturally occurring bacteria, Chakrabarty's invention is believed to have significant value for the treatment of oil spills.

Chakrabarty's patent claims were of three types: first, process claims for the method of producing the bacteria; second, claims for an inoculum comprised of a carrier material floating on water, such as straw, and the new bacteria; and third, claims to the bacteria themselves. The patent examiner allowed the claims falling into the first two categories, but rejected claims for the bacteria. His decision rested on two grounds: (1) that micro-organisms are "products of nature," and (2) that as living things they are not patentable subject matter under 35 U.S.C. § 101. * * *

The Court of Customs and Patent Appeals, by a divided vote, reversed on the authority of its prior decision in *In re Bergy*, 563 F.2d 1031, 1038 (C.C.P.A.1977), which held that "the fact that microorganisms ... are alive ... [is] without legal significance" for purposes of the patent law.[1] * * *

---

1. *Bergy* involved a patent application for a pure culture of the micro-organism Streptomyces vellosus found to be useful in the production of lincomycin, an antibiotic.

The Commissioner of Patents and Trademarks again sought certiorari, and we granted the writ as to both *Bergy* and *Chakrabarty*. Since then, *Bergy* has been dismissed as moot, leaving only *Chakrabarty* for decision.

The Constitution grants Congress broad power to legislate to "promote the Progress of Science and useful Arts, by securing for limited Times to Authors and Inventors the exclusive Right to their respective Writings and Discoveries." Art. I, § 8, cl. 8. The patent laws promote this progress by offering inventors exclusive rights for a limited period as an incentive for their inventiveness and research efforts. The authority of Congress is exercised in the hope that "[t]he productive effort thereby fostered will have a positive effect on society through the introduction of new products and processes of manufacture into the economy, and the emanations by way of increased employment and better lives for our citizens."

The question before us in this case is a narrow one of statutory interpretation requiring us to construe 35 U.S.C. § 101, which provides: "Whoever invents or discovers any new and useful process, machine, manufacture, or composition of matter, or any new and useful improvement thereof, may obtain a patent therefor, subject to the conditions and requirements of this title." Specifically, we must determine whether respondent's micro-organism constitutes a "manufacture" or "composition of matter" within the meaning of the statute. * * *

In choosing such expansive terms as "manufacture" and "composition of matter," modified by the comprehensive "any," Congress plainly contemplated that the patent laws would be given wide scope. The relevant legislative history also supports a broad construction. The Patent Act of 1793, authored by Thomas Jefferson, defined statutory subject matter as "any new and useful art, machine, manufacture, or composition of matter, or any new or useful improvement [thereof]." The Act embodied Jefferson's philosophy that "ingenuity should receive a liberal encouragement." Subsequent patent statutes in 1836, 1870, and 1874 employed this same broad language. In 1952, when the patent laws were recodified, Congress replaced the word "art" with "process," but otherwise left Jefferson's language intact. The Committee Reports accompanying the 1952 Act inform us that Congress intended statutory subject matter to "include anything under the sun that is made by man."

This is not to suggest that § 101 has no limits or that it embraces every discovery. The laws of nature, physical phenomena, and abstract ideas have been held not patentable. Thus, a new mineral discovered in the earth or a new plant found in the wild is not patentable subject matter. Likewise, Einstein could not patent his celebrated law that $E = mc^2$; nor could Newton have patented the law of gravity. Such discoveries are "manifestations of ... nature, free to all men and reserved exclusively to none."

Judged in this light, respondent's micro-organism plainly qualifies as patentable subject matter. His claim is not to a hitherto unknown natural phenomenon, but to a nonnaturally occurring manufacture or composition of matter * * * * [T]he patentee has produced a new bacterium with markedly different characteristics from any found in nature and one having the potential for significant utility. His discovery is not nature's handiwork, but his own; accordingly it is patentable subject matter under § 101. * * *

The petitioner's second argument is that micro-organisms cannot qualify as patentable subject matter until Congress expressly authorizes such protection. His position rests on the fact that genetic technology was unforeseen when Congress enacted § 101. From this it is argued that resolution of the patentability of inventions such as respondent's should be left to Congress. The legislative process, the petitioner argues, is best equipped to weigh the competing economic, social, and scientific considerations involved, and to determine whether living organisms produced by genetic engineering should receive patent protection. * * *

Congress has performed its constitutional role in defining patentable subject matter in § 101; we perform ours in construing the language Congress has employed. In so doing, our obligation is to take statutes as we find them, guided, if ambiguity appears, by the legislative history and statutory purpose. Here, we perceive no ambiguity. The subject-matter provisions of the patent law have been cast in broad terms to fulfill the constitutional and statutory goal of promoting "the Progress of Science and the useful Arts" with all that means for the social and economic benefits envisioned by Jefferson. Broad general language is not necessarily ambiguous when congressional objectives require broad terms. * * *

A rule that unanticipated inventions are without protection would conflict with the core concept of the patent law that anticipation undermines patentability. Mr. Justice Douglas reminded that the inventions most benefiting mankind are those that "push back the frontiers of chemistry, physics, and the like." Congress employed broad general language in drafting § 101 precisely because such inventions are often unforeseeable.

To buttress his argument, the petitioner, with the support of amicus, points to grave risks that may be generated by research endeavors such as respondent's. The briefs present a gruesome parade of horribles. Scientists, among them Nobel laureates, are quoted suggesting that genetic research may pose a serious threat to the human race, or, at the very least, that the dangers are far too substantial to permit such research to proceed apace at this time. We are told that genetic research and related technological developments may spread pollution and disease, that it may result in a loss of genetic diversity, and that its practice may tend to depreciate the value of human life. These arguments are forcefully, even passionately, presented; they remind us that, at times, human ingenuity seems unable to control fully the forces it creates—that with Hamlet, it is sometimes better "to bear those ills we have than fly to others that we know not of."

It is argued that this Court should weigh these potential hazards in considering whether respondent's invention is patentable subject matter under § 101. We disagree. The grant or denial of patents on micro-organisms is not likely to put an end to genetic research or to its attendant risks. The large amount of research that has already occurred when no researcher had sure knowledge that patent protection would be available suggests that legislative or judicial fiat as to patentability will not deter the scientific mind from probing into the unknown any more than Canute could command the tides. Whether respondent's claims are patentable may determine whether research efforts are accelerated by the hope of reward or slowed by want of incentives, but that is all.

What is more important is that we are without competence to entertain these arguments—either to brush them aside as fantasies generated by fear of the unknown, or to act on them. The choice we are urged to make is a matter of high policy for resolution within the legislative process after the kind of investigation, examination, and study that legislative bodies can provide and courts cannot. That process involves the balancing of competing values and interests, which in our democratic system is the business of elected representatives. Whatever their validity, the contentions now pressed on us should be addressed to the political branches of the government, the Congress and the Executive, and not to the courts. * * *

Congress is free to amend § 101 so as to exclude from patent protection organisms produced by genetic engineering. Cf. 42 U.S.C. § 2181(a), exempting from patent protection inventions "useful solely in the utilization of special nuclear material or atomic energy in an atomic weapon." Or it may chose to craft a statute specifically designed for such living things. But, until Congress takes such action, this Court must construe the language of § 101 as it is. The language of that section fairly embraces respondent's invention. * * *

Association for Molecular Pathology v. PTO

653 F.3d 1329 (Fed.Cir.2011).

■ LOURIE, CIRCUIT JUDGE:

* * * "DNA sequencing" or "gene sequencing" refers to the process by which the precise linear order of nucleotides in a DNA segment or gene is determined. A gene's nucleotide sequence in turn encodes for a linear sequence of amino acids that comprise the protein encoded by the gene, e.g., the BRCA1 gene encodes for the BRCA1 protein. Most genes have both "exon" and "intron" sequences. Exons are DNA segments that are necessary for the creation of a protein, i.e., that code for a protein. Introns are segments of DNA interspersed between the exons that, unlike exons, do not code for a protein.

The creation of a protein from a gene comprises two steps: transcription and translation. * * * For transcription, the DNA double helix is unwound and each nucleotide on the non-coding, or template, DNA strand is used to make a complementary RNA molecule of the coding DNA strand, i.e., adenine on the template DNA strand results in uracil in the RNA molecule, thymine results in adenine, guanine in cytosine, and cytosine in guanine. The resulting "pre-RNA," like the DNA from which it was generated, contains both exon and intron sequences. Next, the introns are physically excised from the pre-RNA molecule, in a process called "splicing," to produce a messenger RNA (mRNA). * * * Following transcription, the resulting mRNA is "translated" into the encoded protein. Genes, and their corresponding mRNAs, encode proteins via three nucleotide combinations called codons. Each codon corresponds to one of the twenty amino acids that make up all proteins or a "stop" signal that terminates protein translation. For example, the codon adenine-thymine-guanine (ATG, or [AU]G in the corresponding mRNA), encodes the amino acid methionine. * * *

DNA sequencing is used in clinical diagnostic testing to determine whether a gene contains mutations associated with a particular disease or risk of a particular disease. * * * Genomic DNA can be extracted from its cellular environment using a number of well-established laboratory techniques. A particular segment of DNA, such as a gene, can then be excised or amplified from the DNA to obtain the isolated DNA segment of interest. DNA molecules can also be synthesized in the laboratory. One type of synthetic DNA molecule is complementary DNA (cDNA). cDNA is synthesized from mRNA using complementary base pairing in a manner analogous to RNA transcription. The process results in a double-stranded DNA molecule with a sequence corresponding to the sequence of an mRNA produced by the body. Because it is synthesized from mRNA, cDNA contains only the exon sequences, and thus none of the intron sequences, from a native gene sequence.

Mutations in the BRCA genes correlate with an increased risk of breast and ovarian cancer. The average woman in the United States has around a twelve to thirteen percent risk of developing breast cancer in her lifetime. Women with BRCA mutations, in contrast, face a cumulative risk of between fifty to eighty percent of developing breast cancer and a cumulative risk of ovarian cancer of between twenty to fifty percent. Diagnostic genetic testing for the existence of BRCA mutations is therefore an important consideration in the provision of clinical care for breast or ovarian cancer. This testing provides a patient with information on her risk for hereditary breast and ovarian cancers, and thus aids in the difficult decision regarding whether to undertake preventive options, including prophylactic surgery. Diagnostic results can also be an important factor in structuring an appropriate course of cancer treatment, since certain forms of chemotherapy are more effective in treating cancers related to BRCA mutations.

The inventors of the patents in suit identified the genetic basis of BRCA1 and BRCA2–related cancers using an analysis called positional cloning. Relying on a large set of DNA samples from families with inherited breast and ovarian cancers, the inventors correlated the occurrence of cancer in individual family members with the inheritance of certain marker DNA sequences. This allowed the inventors to identify, or "map," the physical location of the BRCA genes within the human genome and to isolate the BRCA genes and determine their exact nucleotide sequences. This in turn allowed Myriad to provide BRCA diagnostic testing services to women.

Myriad filed the first patent application leading to the patents in suit covering isolated BRCA1 DNA and associated diagnostic methods in August 1994. * * * [Less than four years later,] Myriad demanded a royalty under its patents from Dr. [Harry] Ostrer based on his clinical BRCA-related activities [at NYU Medical Center]. * * * At the same time, as Ostrer was aware, Myriad was asserting its patent rights against other similarly situated parties * * * [including] a patent infringement suit by Myriad against the University of Pennsylvania, which was later dismissed without prejudice after the University agreed to cease all accused BRCA testing services. Myriad also sued Oncormed for patent infringement based on its BRCA genetic testing services. As a result of Myriad's patent enforcement actions, Dr. Ostrer was forced to send all patient samples to Myriad, now the sole provider of BRCA diagnostic testing services. * * *

[S]ince Myriad published its discoveries of the BRCA1 and BRCA2 genes in October 1994 and March 1996, respectively, over 18,000 scientists have conducted research on the BRCA genes and over 8,600 research papers have been published. * * * [A]lthough [scientists may] conduct gene sequencing, they are forbidden from informing their research subjects of the results of their BRCA tests without first sending the samples to Myriad. * * *

[N]ow to the merits of Myriad's appeal of the district court's summary judgment decision, which held all fifteen challenged composition and method claims invalid under § 101. * * * [T]he Supreme Court has drawn a line between compositions that, even if combined or altered in a manner not found in nature, have similar characteristics as in nature, and compositions that human intervention has given "markedly different," or "distinctive," characteristics. Applying this test to the isolated DNAs in this case, we conclude that the challenged claims are drawn to patentable subject matter because the claims cover molecules that are markedly different—have a distinctive chemical identity and nature—from molecules that exist in nature. * * *

Native DNA exists in the body as one of forty-six large, contiguous DNA molecules. Each DNA molecule is itself an integral part of a larger structural complex, a chromosome. In each chromosome, the DNA molecule is packaged around histone proteins into a structure called chromatin, which in turn is packaged into the chromosomal structure. Isolated DNA, in contrast, is a free-standing portion of a native DNA molecule, frequently a single gene. Isolated DNA has been cleaved (i.e., had covalent bonds in its backbone chemically severed) or synthesized to consist of just a fraction of a naturally occurring DNA molecule.

For example, the BRCA1 gene in its native state resides on chromosome 17, a DNA molecule of around eighty million nucleotides. Similarly, BRCA2 in its native state is located on chromosome 13, a DNA of approximately 114 million nucleotides. In contrast, isolated BRCA1 and BRCA2, with introns, each consists of just 80,000 or so nucleotides. And without introns, BRCA2 shrinks to just 10,200 or so nucleotides and BRCA1 to just around 5,500 nucleotides. Furthermore, claims 5 and 6 of the '282 patent

[U.S. Patent 5,747,282] cover isolated DNAs having as few as fifteen nucleotides of a BRCA sequence. Accordingly, BRCA1 and BRCA2 in their isolated state are not the same molecules as DNA as it exists in the body; human intervention in cleaving or synthesizing a portion of a native chromosomal DNA imparts on that isolated DNA a distinctive chemical identity from that possessed by native DNA. * * *

[I]solated DNA is not purified DNA. Purification makes pure what was the same material, but was previously impure. Although isolated DNA must be removed from its native cellular and chromosomal environment, it has also been manipulated chemically so as to produce a molecule that is markedly different from that which exists in the body. * * * [I]n nature, isolated DNAs are covalently bonded to such other materials. Thus, when cleaved, an isolated DNA molecule is not a purified form of a natural material, but a distinct chemical entity. In fact, some forms of isolated DNA require no purification at all, because DNAs can be chemically synthesized directly as isolated molecules. * * * The covalent bonds in this case separate one chemical species from another.

Plaintiffs argue that because the claimed isolated DNAs retain the same nucleotide sequence as native DNAs, they do not have any "markedly different" characteristics. This approach, however, looks not at whether isolated DNAs are markedly different—have a distinctive characteristic—from naturally occurring DNAs, as the Supreme Court has directed, but at one similarity: the information content contained in isolated and native DNAs' nucleotide sequence. Adopting this approach, the district court disparaged the patent eligibility of isolated DNA molecules because their genetic function is to transmit information. We disagree, as it is the distinctive nature of DNA molecules as isolated compositions of matter that determines their patent eligibility rather than their physiological use or benefit. Uses of chemical substances may be relevant to the non-obviousness of these substances or to method claims embodying those uses, but the patent eligibility of an isolated DNA is not negated because it has similar informational properties to a different, more complex natural material that embodies it. The claimed isolated DNA molecules are distinct from their natural existence as portions of larger entities, and their informational content is irrelevant to that fact. We recognize that biologists may think of molecules in terms of their uses, but genes are in fact materials having a chemical nature and, as such, are best described in patents by their structures rather than their functions. * * *

It is suggested that holding isolated DNAs patent eligible opens the door to claims covering isolated chemical elements, like lithium; minerals found in the earth, like diamonds; atomic particles, like electrons; and even organs, like a kidney, and a leaf from a tree. None of these examples, however, as far as we can discern, presents the case of a claim to a composition having a distinctive chemical identity from that of the native element, molecule, or structure. Elemental lithium is the same element whether it is in the earth or isolated; the diamond is the same lattice of carbon molecules, just with the earth removed; the kidney is the same kidney, the leaf the same leaf. Some may have a changed form, quality, or use when prepared in isolated or purified form, but we cannot tell on this record whether the changes are sufficiently distinctive to make the composition markedly different from the one that exists in nature. * * *

It is estimated that the PTO has issued 2,645 patents claiming "isolated DNA" over the past twenty-nine years and that, by 2005, had granted 40,000 DNA-related patents covering, in non-native form, twenty percent of the genes in the human genome. In 2001, the PTO issued *Utility Examination Guidelines*, which reaffirmed the agency's position that isolated DNA molecules are patent eligible, and Congress has not indicated that the PTO's position is inconsistent with § 101. If the law is to be changed, and DNA inventions excluded from the broad scope of § 101 contrary to the settled expectation of the inventing community, the decision must come not from the courts, but from Congress.

We turn next to Myriad's challenged method claims. * * * We conclude that Myriad's claims to "comparing" or "analyzing" two gene sequences fall outside the scope of § 101 because they claim only abstract mental processes. The claims recite, for example, a "method for screening a tumor sample," by "comparing" a first BRCA1 sequence from a tumor sample and a second BRCA1 sequence from a non-tumor sample, wherein a difference in sequence indicates an alteration in the tumor sample. * * * Although the *application* of a formula or abstract idea in a process may describe patentable subject matter, Myriad's claims do not apply the step of comparing two nucleotide sequences in a process. Rather, the step of comparing two DNA sequences is the entire process claimed. To escape this result, Myriad attempts to read into its method claims additional, transformative steps. As described above, Myriad reads into its claims the steps of (1) extracting DNA from a human sample, and (2) sequencing the BRCA DNA molecule, arguing that both steps necessarily precede the step of comparing nucleotide sequences. The claims themselves, however, do not include either of these steps. * * *

In *Prometheus* [*Laboratories, Inc. v. Mayo Collaborative Services*, 628 F.3d 1347, 1350 (Fed.Cir.2010)], the patents claimed methods for optimizing the dosage of thiopurine drugs administered to patients with gastrointestinal disorders. As written, the claimed methods included the steps of (a) "administering" a thiopurine drug to a subject, and/or (b) "determining" the drug's metabolites levels in the subject, wherein the measured metabolite levels are compared with predetermined levels to optimize drug dosage. In holding that the claims satisfied § 101, this court concluded that, in addition to the "administering" step being transformative, the "determining" step was both transformative and central to the purpose of the claims. Specifically, the court held that because the metabolite levels could not be determined by mere inspection, the determining step necessarily required a transformation: "Some form of manipulation . . . is necessary to extract the metabolites from a bodily sample and determine their concentration." Id. at 1357. Moreover, we concluded that this transformation was not just insignificant extra-solution activity or necessary data-gathering steps, but was central to the claims, because determining the metabolite levels was what enabled the optimization of drug dosage.

Myriad's claims, in contrast, do not include the step of "determining" the sequence of BRCA genes by, e.g., isolating the genes from a blood sample and sequencing them, or any other necessarily transformative step. Rather, the comparison between the two sequences can be accomplished by mere inspection alone. Accordingly, Myriad's claimed methods of comparing or analyzing nucleotide sequences fail to satisfy the machine-or-transformation test, and are instead directed to the abstract mental process of comparing two nucleotide sequences. The claims thus fail to claim a patent-eligible process under § 101.

Lastly, we turn to Myriad's method claim directed to a method for screening potential cancer therapeutics via changes in cell growth rates. * * * Specifically, the claim recites a method that comprises the steps of (1) "growing" host cells transformed with an altered BRCA1 gene in the presence or absence of a potential cancer therapeutic, (2) "determining" the growth rate of the host cells with or without the potential therapeutic, and (3) "comparing" the growth rate of the host cells. The claim thus includes more than the abstract mental step of looking at two numbers and "comparing" two host cells' growth rates. The claim includes the steps of "growing" transformed cells in the presence or absence of a potential cancer therapeutic, an inherently transformative step involving the manipulation of the cells and their growth medium. * * * Accordingly, we hold that claim 20 of the '282 patent claims patentable subject matter * * *

■ MOORE, CIRCUIT JUDGE (concurring in part and concurring in judgment):

* * * [J]ust because the same series of letters appears in both the chromosome and an isolated DNA sequence does not mean they are the same molecule. While the isolated DNA molecules claimed in this case are undoubtedly inspired by the corresponding naturally occurring sequence present on the chromosome, man must create these isolated DNA molecules. This can be accomplished by building them de novo using chemical or biological means, or by chemically altering the larger polymer to cleave off adjacent portions. Isolation of a DNA sequence is more than separating out impurities: the isolated DNA is a distinct molecule with different physical characteristics than the naturally occurring polymer containing the corresponding sequence in nature. These differences, of course, are directly related to the change in chemical bonds in the isolated DNA. Instead of being connected to many thousands of additional nucleotides at the 3' and 5' ends of the sequence in question, as is the case in the chromosome, the isolated DNA molecules terminate in, for example, a hydroxyl and a phosphate group, respectively. * * *

The cDNA claims present the easiest analysis. * * * [S]ince cDNA has all of the introns removed, and only contains the coding nucleotides, it can be used to express a protein in a cell which does not normally produce it. Of course, the claimed isolated cDNA is inspired by nature—after all, naturally occurring RNA is the template upon which cDNA is constructed. Because it is used as a template, however, cDNA has a complementary sequence of nucleotides, and therefore has a completely different nucleotide sequence than the RNA. Moreover, DNA has a different chemical structure than RNA, including a different base (T instead of U, respectively) and sugar units (deoxyribose instead of ribose, respectively). This results in, among other things, greater stability for the DNA sequence as compared to the RNA sequence. cDNA sequences thus have a distinctive name, character, and use, with markedly different chemical characteristics from either the naturally occurring RNA or any continuous DNA sequence found on the chromosome. The claimed isolated cDNA sequences are the creation of man, made using biological tools and the naturally occurring mRNA as a template. * * *

DNA sequences that have the same pattern of DNA bases as a natural gene, in whole or in part, present a more difficult issue. Unlike the isolated cDNA molecules, whose sequence is not present in nature, these kinds of isolated DNA claims include nucleotide sequences which are found in the human body, albeit as part of a much larger molecule, the chromosome. * * * [T]he claimed isolated DNA molecules, which are truncations (with different ends) of the naturally occurring DNA found as part of the chromosome in nature, are not naturally produced without the intervention of man. * * *

The shorter isolated DNA sequences have a variety of applications and uses in isolation that are new and distinct as compared to the sequence as it occurs in nature. For example, these sequences can be used as primers in a diagnostic screening process to detect gene mutations. These smaller isolated DNA sequences—including isolated radiolabeled sequences mirroring those on the chromosome—can also be used as the basis for probes. Naturally occurring DNA cannot be used to accomplish these same goals. Unlike the isolated DNA, naturally occurring DNA simply does not have the requisite chemical and physical properties needed to perform these functions. * * * Man has whittled the chromosomal DNA molecule down to a 15 nucleotide sequence—defining the parts to be retained and discarded. And the result is a product with a function (primer or probe) that is entirely different from the full gene from which it was obtained. * * *

Longer strands of isolated DNA, in particular isolated strands which include most or all of the entire gene, are a much closer case. * * * All of the same structural arguments apply to any length of isolated DNA so, like the shorter strands, an isolated DNA coding for a gene does have a literal chemical difference from the gene as it appears on the chromosome. Different ends in a 15 nucleotide sequence have greater significance than different ends in a 6,000 nucleotide sequence. Unlike the shorter strands of isolated DNA, * * * the full length gene is too large to be used as a probe. Likewise, an entire isolated gene appears unsuitable for use as a primer in genetic screening for mutations in that same gene. As such, the chemical and structural differences in an isolated DNA sequence which includes most or all of a gene do not clearly lead to significant new utility as compared to nature. Whether an isolated gene is patentable subject matter depends on how much weight is allocated to the different structure as compared to the similarity of the function to nature.

If I were deciding this case on a blank canvas, I might conclude that an isolated DNA sequence that includes most or all of a gene is not patentable subject matter. Despite the literal chemical difference, the isolated full length gene does not clearly have a new utility and appears to simply serve the same ends devised by nature, namely to act as a gene encoding a protein sequence. This case, however, comes to us with a substantial historical background. * * * [T]hese settled expectations tip the scale in favor of patentability.[5] * * *

The settled expectations of the biotechnology industry—not to mention the thousands of issued patents—cannot be taken lightly and deserve deference. This outpouring of scientific creativity, spurred by the patent system, reflects a substantial investment of time and money by the biotechnology industry to obtain property rights related to DNA sequences. * * * If the Executive decided to change course in the Patent Office, and decline to issue new patents to isolated genes, it would not impact these existing property rights. This, however, is not what the Executive argues in this case. Instead the Solicitor General argues for an entirely different interpretation of the law that would destroy existing property rights. Although the dissent points out that *Chakrabarty* overturned the Patent Office's practice of denying patents to microorganisms, there is a clear difference between allowing additional patent protection where none previously existed, and denying patent protection decades (or centuries) after the fact, thereby eliminating a large number of property rights. * * *

It is tempting to use our judicial power in this fashion, especially when the patents in question raise substantial moral and ethical issues related to awarding a property right to isolated portions of human DNA—the very thing that makes us humans, and not chimpanzees. The Solicitor General's invitation is tempting, but I must decline the opportunity to act where Congress remains silent. * * * Judicial restraint is particularly important here because an entire industry developed in the decades since the Patent Office first granted patents to isolated DNA. * * * Changing course years after the fact will only serve to punish those companies who made the reasonable decision to invest large amounts of time and money into the identification, isolation, and characterization of genes. Unsettling the expectations of the biotechnology industry now, based on nothing more than unsupported supposition, strikes me as far more likely to impede the progress of science and useful arts than advance it. * * *

In fact, Congress has at least implicitly approved of the Patent Office's policy of awarding patents on genes and DNA sequences. * * * Far from

---

5. My analysis of the claims at issue assumes that they do not include an isolated, full length chromosome. I do not believe that a claim to an entire chromosome, for example chromosome 17, is patentable subject matter. First, there is no indication that the chromosome in isolation has markedly different characteristics compared to the chromosome in nature. Second, unlike claims to isolated genes, there is no indication of either settled expectations or extensive property rights for claims to isolated chromosomes. * * *

oblivious to the patenting of genes, members of Congress previously introduced bills which would put a moratorium on gene patents, authorize funding for the study of whether genes ought to be patentable, and exempt from patent infringement anyone who uses patented genes for non-commercial research purposes or medical practitioners who use genetic diagnostic tests. None of these became law. * * *

■ BRYSON, CIRCUIT JUDGE (concurring in part and dissenting in part):

* * * At the outset, it is important to identify the inventive contribution underlying Myriad's patents. Myriad was not the first to map a BRCA gene to its chromosomal location. That discovery was made by a team of researchers led by Dr. Mary–Claire King. And Myriad did not invent a new method of nucleotide sequencing. Instead, it applied known sequencing techniques to identify the nucleotide order of the BRCA genes. Myriad's discovery of those sequences entailed difficult work, and the identified sequences have had important applications in the fight against breast cancer. But the discovery of the sequences is an unprotectable fact, just like Dr. King's discovery of the chromosomal location of the BRCA1 gene.

Of course, Myriad is free to patent applications of its discovery. As the first party with knowledge of the sequences, Myriad was in an excellent position to claim applications of that knowledge. Many of its unchallenged claims are limited to such applications. Yet some of Myriad's challenged composition claims effectively preempt any attempt to sequence the BRCA genes, including whole-genome sequencing. In my view, those claims encompass unpatentable subject matter, and a contrary ruling is likely to have substantial adverse effects on research and treatment in this important field. * * *

Myriad is claiming the genes themselves, which appear in nature on the chromosomes of living human beings. The only material change made to those genes from their natural state is the change that is necessarily incidental to the extraction of the genes from the environment in which they are found in nature. While the process of extraction is no doubt difficult, and may itself be patentable, the isolated genes are not materially different from the native genes. In this respect, the genes are analogous to the "new mineral discovered in the earth," or the "new plant found in the wild" that the Supreme Court referred to in *Chakrabarty*. It may be very difficult to extract the newly found mineral or to find, extract, and propagate the newly discovered plant. But that does not make those naturally occurring items the products of invention.

The same is true for human genes. Like some minerals, they are hard to extract from their natural setting. Also like minerals, they can be used for purposes that would be infeasible if they remained in their natural setting. And the process of extracting minerals, or taking cuttings from wild plants, like the process of isolating genetic material, can result in some physical or chemical changes to the natural substance. But such changes do not make extracted minerals or plant cuttings patentable, and they should not have that effect for isolated genes. In each case, merely isolating the products of nature by extracting them from their natural location and making those alterations attendant to their extraction does not give the extractor the right to patent the products themselves. * * *

[T]here is no magic to a chemical bond that requires us to recognize a new product when a chemical bond is created or broken, but not when other atomic or molecular forces are altered. * * * Weaker interatomic forces will be broken when, for example, a dirty diamond is cleaned with water or another solvent, but that does not make the clean diamond a human-made invention. Nor should it make a difference for purposes of patentability if the portion of a wild plant that is collected for purposes of later regeneration is separated from the original plant by chemical means or by scissors. * * *

The government as amicus curiae argues that patenting the BRCA genes would be like patenting the element lithium. Isolated lithium does not occur naturally because it reacts with air and water and thus is found in nature only as part of a chemical compound, ionically bound to other elements. Once isolated, lithium has many industrial applications, and in order to isolate lithium, it is necessary to break ionic bonds in the lithium compounds that are found in nature. But the majority acknowledges that elemental lithium (like other elements) would not be patentable subject matter because it "is the same element whether it is in the earth or isolated."

The principles underlying that analysis apply to genetic material as well. In order to isolate the BRCA gene, it is necessary to break chemical bonds that hold the gene in its place in the body, but the genetic coding sequence that is the subject of each of the BRCA gene claims remains the same whether the gene is in the body or isolated. The majority, however, does not agree that the cases are analogous, and indeed appears to have adopted the following rule: Isolated atoms are not patent eligible, but isolated molecules are.

Apart from the arbitrariness of such a rule, if we are to apply the conventional nomenclature of any field to determine whether Myriad's isolated DNA claims are "new," it would seem to make more sense to look to genetics, which provides the language of the claims, than to chemistry. * * * The isolated BRCA genes are identical to the BRCA genes found on chromosomes 13 and 17. They have the same sequence, they code for the same proteins, and they represent the same units of heredity. During the transcription phase of protein synthesis, the BRCA genes are separated from chromosomal proteins. The transcription process then proceeds from a starting point called the promoter to a stopping point often called the terminator. The only difference between the naturally occurring BRCA genes during transcription and the claimed isolated DNA is that the claimed genes have been isolated according to nature's predefined boundaries, i.e., at points that preserve the ability of the gene to express the protein for which it is coded.

In that respect, extracting a gene is akin to snapping a leaf from a tree. Like a gene, a leaf has a natural starting and stopping point. It buds during spring from the same place that it breaks off and falls during autumn. Yet prematurely plucking the leaf would not turn it into a human-made invention. That would remain true if there were minor differences between the plucked leaf and the fallen autumn leaf, unless those differences imparted "markedly different characteristics" to the plucked leaf. * * * [T]o argue that the isolated BRCA gene is patentable because in its native environment it is part of a much larger structure is no more persuasive than arguing that although an atom may not be patentable, a subatomic particle is patentable because it was previously part of a larger structure, or that while a tree is not patentable, a limb of the tree becomes a patentable invention when it is removed from the tree.

Of course, it is an over-simplification to say that something that can be characterized as "isolated" or "extracted" from its natural setting always remains a natural product and is not patentable. One could say, for example, that a baseball bat is "extracted" or "isolated" from an ash tree, but in that case the process of "extracting" the baseball bat necessarily changes the nature, form, and use of the ash tree and thus results in a manmade manufacture, not a naturally occurring product. In that setting, man has defined the parts that are to be retained and the parts that are to be discarded. The result of the process of selection is a product with a function that is entirely different from that of the raw material from which it was obtained.

In the case of the BRCA genes, by contrast, nature has defined the genes as independent entities by virtue of their capacity for protein synthesis and, ultimately, trait inheritance. Biochemists extract the target genes along lines defined by nature so as to preserve the structure and function that the gene possessed in its natural environment. In such a case, the extraction of a product in a manner that retains the character and function of the product as found in nature does not result in the creation of a human invention. * * *

Cases involving the "purification" of a natural substance employ similar analysis. Our predecessor court recognized that merely purifying a naturally occurring substance does not render the substance patentable unless it results in a marked change in functionality. On the other hand, the purified natural substance is patentable if the "purification" results in a product with such distinct characteristics that it becomes "for every practical purpose a new thing commercially and therapeutically." Parke–Davis & Co. v. H.K. Mulford Co., 189 F. 95, 103 (C.C.S.D.N.Y.1911) [adrenaline]; see also Merck & Co. v. Olin Mathieson Chem. Corp., 253 F.2d 156, 161–64 (4th Cir.1958) (holding that a purified composition of vitamin B–12 was patentable because the purification process resulted in a product that was therapeutically effective, whereas the natural form was not). * * *

What is claimed in the BRCA genes is the genetic coding material, and that material is the same, structurally and functionally, in both the native gene and the isolated form of the gene. The structural differences between the claimed "isolated" genes and the corresponding portion of the native genes are irrelevant to the claim limitations, to the functioning of the genes, and to their utility in their isolated form. The use to which the genetic material can be put, i.e., determining its sequence in a clinical setting, is not a new use; it is only a consequence of possession. In order to sequence an isolated gene, each gene must function in the same manner in the laboratory as it does in the human body. * * *

I agree with the court that the claims to BRCA cDNA are eligible for patenting. The cDNA cannot be isolated from nature, but instead must be created in the laboratory. Although that process occurs with natural machinery, the end product is a human-made invention with distinct structure because the introns that are found in the native gene are removed from the cDNA segment. Additionally, the cDNA has a utility not present in the naturally occurring BRCA DNA and mRNA because cDNA can be attached to a promoter and inserted into a non-human cell to drive protein expression.

However, I disagree with the court as to the two claims to short segments of DNA having at least 15 nucleotides. Claim 6 of the '282 patent covers any sequence of the BRCA1 cDNA that is at least 15 nucleotides long. That claim encompasses each BRCA1 exon, even though each exon is naturally defined by transcription. Moreover, because small sequences of DNA are repeated throughout the three billion nucleotides of the human genome, the claim covers portions of the cDNA of more than 4% of human genes. It also covers portions of the DNA of nearly all human genes. Accordingly, efforts to sequence almost any gene could infringe claim 6 even though Myriad's specification has contributed nothing to human understanding of other genes.

Myriad could easily have claimed more narrowly to achieve the utility it attaches to segments of cDNA. It contends that those segments can be used as probes and primers. DNA probes must be chemically altered or "tagged" before they can be so used, and Myriad could have claimed the tagged segments to achieve probe functionality. A claim to tagged segments would not encompass the BRCA1 exons. As to primer functionality, many of the cDNA segments will not work. Some will be too long. Some will be too short. Some will be palindromic and fold in on themselves. Myriad could have identified a subset of the segments that work as primers * * * *

While Myriad has emphasized the biotechnology industry's need of patent protection to encourage and reward research in this difficult and important field, there is another side to the coin. Broad claims to genetic material present a significant obstacle to the next generation of innovation in genetic medicine—multiplex tests and whole-genome sequencing. New technologies are being developed to sequence many genes or even an entire human genome rapidly, but firms developing those technologies are encountering a thicket of patents. In order to sequence an entire genome, a firm would have to license thousands of patents from many different licensors. * * *

The comments that the PTO issued at the time of its 2001 guidelines in response to suggestions that isolated human genes were not patentable are, frankly, perfunctory. Because those comments, at least on their face, do not reflect thorough consideration and study of the issue, I do not regard them as worthy of much weight in the analysis of this complex question. * * * The Department of Justice filed a brief on behalf of the United States in this court taking the position that Myriad's gene claims (other than the cDNA claims) are not patent-eligible. Although the PTO did not "sign" the brief and we are left to guess about the status of any possible continuing interagency disagreements about the issue, the Department of Justice speaks for the Executive Branch, and the PTO is part of the Executive Branch, so it is fair to assume that the Executive Branch has modified its position from the one taken by the PTO in its 2001 guidelines and, informally, before that. * * *

Although my colleagues believe our analysis of the legal question in this case should be influenced by purported expectations of the inventing community based on the PTO's past practice of issuing patents on human genes, that is in effect to give the PTO lawmaking authority that Congress has not accorded it. There is no collective right of adverse possession to intellectual property, and we should not create such a right. * * *

NOTES AND QUESTIONS

1. *What now for Myriad and gene patents?* Does the court's unanimous decision to invalidate Myriad's primary method patents (was it just a matter of poor drafting?) in any way limit the company's ability to enforce its composition patents (i.e., are competing laboratories any freer now to offer their own BRCA diagnostic testing)? Does the court's unanimous decision to sustain the whole cDNA patents suffice to protect Myriad's testing monopoly, or did the company also have to prevail on the isolated DNA claims? See Andrew Pollack, Patents Safe, a Company Tries to Keep Its Secrets, N.Y. Times, Aug. 25, 2011, at B1 (reporting that Myriad plans to rely more heavily on trade secret protections in the future and has already stopped sharing the results of its research into relevant mutations). Insofar as the court's decision to sustain the isolated DNA patents only reflects a plurality, how far apart are the opinions of Judges Lourie and Moore (to the extent that they lack any shared rationale, does this leave the broader question unresolved, and might it prompt an en banc rehearing)? Insofar as DOJ failed to persuade the court, does its change of heart during the course of this litigation have any impact on the continuing vitality of the PTO's policy? See Andrew Pollack, In a Policy Reversal, U.S. Says Genes Should Not Be Eligible for Patenting, N.Y. Times, Oct. 30, 2010, at B1. Lastly, in an extended discussion not included in the above excerpt, the court unanimously concluded that, among all of the various named plaintiffs, only Dr. Ostrer (who alone continued to express a firm desire to provide BRCA testing services to patients) had satisfied standing requirements—does it then seem at all odd that the court also would reach the validity of the last method claim, which related to drug discovery? For more on the standing issues in the case, see Jenny L. Maxey, Comment, A Myriad of Misunderstanding Standing: Decoding Judicial Review for Gene Patents, 113 W. Va. L. Rev. 1033 (2011).

Ultimately, of course, the Supreme Court very well could choose to have the last word, putting aside the possibility that Congress might amend the statute to delineate the patentability of isolated genes. These questions have drawn—and no doubt will continue to attract—plenty of scholarly attention. See, e.g., John M. Conley, Gene Patents and the Product of Nature Doctrine, 84 Chi.-Kent. L. Rev. 109 (2009); Eileen M. Kane, Patent-Mediated Standards in Genetic Testing, 2008 Utah L. Rev. 835; Oskar Liivak, Maintaining Competition in Copying: Narrowing the Scope of Gene Patents, 41 U.C. Davis L. Rev. 177 (2007); Lawrence M. Sung, Medical Alert: Alarming Challenges Facing Medical Technology Innovation, 6 J. Bus. & Tech. L. 35 (2011); Kourtney Baltzer, Note, A Clearinghouse: The Solution to Clearing up Confusion in Gene Patent Licensing, 24 Harv. J.L. & Tech. 519 (2011); Jonah D. Jackson, Note, Something Like the Sun: Why Even "Isolated and Purified" Genes Are Still Products of Nature, 89 Tex. L. Rev. 1453 (2011); Krysta Kauble, Comment, Patenting Everything Under the Sun: Invoking the First Amendment to Limit the Use of Gene Patents, 58 UCLA L. Rev. 1123 (2011).

2. *Prometheus unbound.* As recounted by Judge Lourie in *AMP v. PTO*, the Federal Circuit previously had sustained method patents for metabolite testing to optimize doses of a class of drugs used to treat certain autoimmune diseases, a decision which twice has attracted the attention of the Supreme Court. See Prometheus Labs., Inc. v. Mayo Collaborative Servs., 581 F.3d 1336 (Fed.Cir.2009), vacated and remanded, 130 S.Ct. 3543 (2010) (for reconsideration in light of Bilski v. Kappos, 130 S.Ct. 3218 (2010), which held that claims to methods of hedging risk are not patentable processes because they attempt to patent abstract ideas), after remand, 628 F.3d 1347 (Fed.Cir.2010), cert. granted, 131 S.Ct. 3027 (2011); see also Stephen Pessagno, Note, Prometheus and Bilski: Pushing the Bounds of Patentable Subject Matter in Medical Diagnostic Techniques with the Machine-or-Transformation Test, 36 Am. J.L. & Med. 619 (2010). In addition, the court previously had sustained the validity of a claim for the process of correlating various homocysteine levels with vitamin B deficiencies. See Metabolite Lab. Inc. v. Laboratory Corp. of Am., 370 F.3d 1354 (Fed.Cir.2004), cert. dismissed, 548 U.S. 124 (2006); see also Joseph P. Anderson, III, Comment, Distinguishing Patentable Process Claims from Unpatentable Laws of Nature in the Medical Technology Field, 59 Ala. L. Rev. 1203 (2008). How about genetic tests designed to identify patients with particular mutations that may affect drug selection or dosing? Does it depend on linking the test to a particular drug as opposed to tests identifying differences in liver metabolizing enzymes that might affect dosing for a broad range of drugs? For further discussion of the emerging field of pharmacogenomics, see Chap. 11(C)(2).

3. *Patentable subject matter.* Although most traditional medical technologies are clearly patentable, biotechnology continues to pose some difficult questions for the patent system. See David E. Adelman & Kathryn L. DeAngelis, Patent Metrics: The Mismeasure of Innovation in the Biotech Patent Debate, 85 Tex. L. Rev. 1677 (2007); Linda J. Demaine & Aaron X. Fellmeth, Reinventing the Double Helix: A Novel and Nonobvious Reconceptualization of the Biotechnology Patent, 55 Stan. L. Rev. 303 (2002); Robin Feldman, Rethinking Rights in Biospace, 79 S. Cal. L. Rev. 1 (2005); Allen K. Yu, Within Subject Matter Eligibility—A Disease and a Cure, 84 S. Cal. L. Rev. 387 (2011); Peter Lee, Note, Patents, Paradigm Shifts, and Progress in Biomedical Science, 114 Yale L.J. 659 (2004); Jennifer L. Schuster, Note, Combining the Components of Life: The Application of Patent Extraterritoriality Doctrine to Biotechnology, 83 Ind. L.J. 363 (2008).

4. *Novelty run amok?* The Court in *Chakrabarty* declined to consider the government's arguments concerning the potential hazards associated with genetic engineering, explaining that such questions of policy were best left to Congress. Do you agree that the PTO should pay no attention to broader societal questions? See Margo A. Bagley, Patent First, Ask Questions Later: Morality and Biotechnology in Patent Law, 45 Wm. & Mary L. Rev. 469 (2003); Sapna Kumar & Arti Rai, Synthetic Biology: The Intellectual Property Puzzle, 85 Tex. L. Rev. 1745 (2007). How should it handle anticipated future developments in regenerative medicine using stem cells? See Amy R. Davis, Note, Patented Embryonic Stem Cells: The Quintessential "Essential Facility"?, 94 Geo. L.J. 205 (2005); Joshua Whitehill, Note, Patenting Human Embryonic Stem Cells: What Is So Immoral?, 34 Brook. J. Int'l L. 1045 (2009); see also Jonathan Grossman, Comment, Human Embryos, Patents, and the Thirteenth Amendment, 55 U. Kan. L. Rev. 731 (2007); Dean Calbreath, Decision Could Boost Stem Cell Research: Wisconsin Group's Patent Rejected, San Diego Union–Trib., May 4, 2010, at A5 (reporting that the PTO reversed an examiner on the latest of three patents granted to WARF). The PTO rejected an application for a technique that purportedly blended embryonic cells from a human and a primate. See Rick Weiss, U.S. Denies Patent for a Too–Human Hybrid, Wash. Post, Feb. 13, 2005, at A3 (explaining that the agency had issued patents for bacteria, yeast, and more than 400 modified animals, but had a longstanding policy against patenting human organisms, and adding that this issue "put[s] the patent office in an awkward position of being the federal arbiter of what is human"); see also Pub. L. No. 109–108, § 623, 119 Stat. 2290, 2342 (2005) ("None of the funds appropriated or otherwise made available under this Act may be used to issue patents on claims directed to or encompassing a human organism."); Ryan Hagglund, Patentability of Human–Animal Chimeras, 25 Santa Clara Computer & High Tech. L.J. 51 (2008).

5. *Medical procedure patents.* Consider the following:

> In many contexts, information represents a "public good," which means that it will be undersupplied unless the government mandates its production or rewards those who produce it. The FDA's premarket review mechanisms and other controls generate substantial information about drugs and medical devices. No similar regulatory regime exists with regard to surgical techniques and other types of therapeutic interventions, which has led a few commentators to suggest extending federal regulatory authority into this area.

Intellectual property protections offer a different mechanism for generating information about medical advances. The patent laws attempt to encourage innovation and the dissemination of new technology by rewarding those who first publicize their inventions. Again, the availability of patent protection for pharmaceutical products and medical devices has facilitated substantial private investments in the production of information related to those therapeutic interventions. In some cases, Congress has supplemented these incentives by granting product manufacturers additional market exclusivity periods in order to generate valuable but otherwise undersupplied biomedical information ....

In the last decade, controversy has erupted over efforts to patent advances in surgical techniques. In 1996, Congress responded by amending the statute to exempt health care providers from any liability for infringing patented medical procedures, which effectively rendered novel medical techniques unpatentable subject matter. Several commentators have objected that this legislation may reduce the incentive to undertake research and disseminate information about the safety and effectiveness of innovative procedures.

Absent comparable incentives for generating information about the whole range of available therapies, health care professionals may receive a distorted picture of the relative safety and effectiveness of their different options. This asymmetrical knowledge base—where a great deal is known about both the risks and the benefits of drugs but fairly little about nonpharmaceutical treatments—may result in suboptimal therapeutic choices. For instance, a recent clinical trial demonstrated that brain surgery effectively treated patients who suffered from temporal-lobe epilepsy and did not respond to anticonvulsants. Although the technique has long existed, few eligible patients underwent this surgical procedure, in part because previously no one had undertaken an RCT [randomized controlled trial] to establish its efficacy. Of course, the new study may not rapidly alter existing treatment patterns, but knowledge production must precede diffusion into practice.

Lars Noah, Medicine's Epistemology: Mapping the Haphazard Diffusion of Knowledge in the Biomedical Community, 44 Ariz. L. Rev. 373, 447–49 (2002); see also Michelle M. Mello & Aaron S. Kesselheim, Medical Process Patents—Monopolizing the Delivery of Health Care, 355 New Eng. J. Med. 2036 (2006); Emily C. Melvin, Note, An Unacceptable Exception: The Ramifications of Physician Immunity from Medical Procedure Patent Infringement Liability, 91 Minn. L. Rev. 1088 (2007); cf. Bruce N. Kuhlik, The Assault on Pharmaceutical Intellectual Property, 71 U. Chi. L. Rev. 93, 95 (2004) ("[T]he end product of the investment in most cases consists overwhelmingly in the *information* that is generated about the drug's safety and effectiveness, rather than in the physical properties of the compound. At least for small-molecule products, it may be a relatively straightforward exercise to reverse engineer a drug product that conforms to the physical chemical specifications of the original ...."). Apart from these policy concerns, the statutory provision, 35 U.S.C. § 287(c), also presents some curious technical questions: How should the compounding of drugs (by pharmacists or physicians) be treated (e.g., could a pharmacist secure a process patent to cover novel procedures for compounding a drug using substances no longer protected by composition patents)?

2. PATENT PREREQUISITES

University of Rochester v. G.D. Searle & Co.

358 F.3d 916 (Fed.Cir.2004).

■ LOURIE, CIRCUIT JUDGE:

* * * Traditional non-steroidal anti-inflammatory drugs (NSAIDs) such as aspirin, ibuprofen, ketoprofen, and naproxen are believed to function by inhibiting the activity of enzymes called cyclooxygenases. Cyclooxygenases catalyze the production of a molecule called prostaglandin H2, which is a precursor for other prostaglandins that perform various functions in the human body.

In the early 1990s, scientists discovered the existence and separate functions of two distinct cyclooxygenases, referred to as "COX–1" and "COX–2." COX–1 is expressed (i.e., produced biologically) in the gastrointestinal tract, where it is involved in the production of prostaglandins that serve a beneficial role by, for example, providing protection for the stomach lining. COX–2 is expressed in response to inflammatory stimuli, and is thought to be responsible for the inflammation associated with diseases such as arthritis. It is now known that the traditional NSAIDs inhibit both COX–1 and COX–2, and as a result they not only reduce inflammation, but also can cause undesirable side effects such as stomach upset, irritation, ulcers, and bleeding.

After the separate functions of COX–1 and COX–2 were discovered, it was hypothesized that it would be possible to reduce inflammation without gastrointestinal side effects if a method could be found for selectively inhibiting the activity of COX–2 (i.e., inhibiting the activity of COX–2 without inhibiting COX–1 activity). To that end, [University of] Rochester scientists developed a screening assay for use in determining whether a particular drug displayed such selectivity, and filed a U.S. patent application directed to their developments in 1992. After filing a series of continuation, continuation-in-part, and divisional applications derived from that 1992 application, the scientists eventually received United States Patent 5,837,479 in 1998, covering methods "for identifying a compound that inhibits prostaglandin synthesis catalyzed by mammalian prostaglandin H synthase–2 (PGHS–2)."

From a division of the application that led to the '479 patent, the scientists also obtained, on April 11, 2000, the '850 patent [United States Patent 6,048,850]. The '850 patent contains three independent claims and five dependent claims. * * * [A]ll eight claims are directed to methods "for selectively inhibiting PGHS–2 activity in a human host" by "administering a non-steroidal compound that selectively inhibits activity of the PGHS–2 gene product to [or in] a human host in need of such treatment." On the day the '850 patent issued, Rochester sued G.D. Searle & Co., Inc., Monsanto Co., Pharmacia Corp., and Pfizer Inc. (collectively, "Pfizer"), alleging that Pfizer's sale of its COX–2 inhibitors Celebrex® and Bextra® for treatment of inflammation infringed the '850 patent, and seeking injunctive and monetary relief. * * *

An issued patent enjoys a presumption of validity, 35 U.S.C. § 282, that can be overcome only through clear and convincing evidence, U.S. Surgical Corp. v. Ethicon, Inc., 103 F.3d 1554, 1563 (Fed.Cir.1997). Accordingly, a party "seeking to invalidate a patent at summary judgment must submit such clear and convincing evidence of invalidity." Eli Lilly & Co. v. Barr Lab., Inc., 251 F.3d 955, 962 (Fed.Cir.2001). * * *

Section 112 provides, in relevant part, that:

> The specification shall contain a written description of the invention, and of the manner and process of making and using it, in such full, clear, concise, and exact terms as to enable any person skilled in the art to which it pertains, or with which it is most nearly connected, to make and use the same, and shall set forth the best mode contemplated by the inventor of carrying out his invention.

35 U.S.C. § 112, ¶ 1 (2000). Three separate requirements are contained in that provision: * * * the "written description requirement," the "enablement requirement," and the "best mode requirement," respectively. The United States Supreme Court also recently acknowledged written description as a statutory requirement distinct not only from the best mode requirement, but also from enablement. See Festo Corp. v. Shoketsu Kinzoku Kogyo Kabushiki Co., 535 U.S. 722, 736 (2002) ("[A] number of statutory requirements must be satisfied before a patent can issue. The claimed subject matter must be useful, novel, and not obvious. In addition, the patent application must *describe, enable, and set forth the best mode* of carrying out the invention. These latter requirements must be satisfied before issuance of the patent, for exclusive patent rights are given in exchange for disclosing the invention to the public." (emphasis added)).

Although there is often significant overlap between the three requirements, they are nonetheless independent of each other. Thus, an invention may be described without an enabling disclosure of how to make and use it. A description of a chemical compound without a description of how to make and use it, unless within the skill of one of ordinary skill in the art, is an example. Moreover, an invention may be enabled even though it has not been described. Such can occur when enablement of a closely related invention A that is both described and enabled would similarly enable an invention B *if* B were described. A specification can likewise describe an invention without enabling the practice of the full breadth of its claims. Finally, still further disclosure might be necessary to satisfy the best mode requirement if otherwise only an inferior mode would be disclosed.

The "written description" requirement serves a teaching function, as a "quid pro quo" in which the public is given "meaningful disclosure in exchange for being excluded from practicing the invention for a limited period of time." Enzo Biochem, Inc. v. Gen–Probe Inc., 323 F.3d 956, 970 (Fed.Cir.2002). Rochester argues, however, that this teaching, or "public notice," function,[5] although "virtually unchanged since the 1793 Patent Act," in fact "became redundant with the advent of claims in 1870." We disagree. * * *

> [T]he appearance of mere indistinct words in a specification or a claim, even an original claim, does not necessarily satisfy that requirement.... A description of an anti-inflammatory steroid, i.e., a steroid (a generic structural term) described even in terms of its function of lessening inflammation of tissues fails to distinguish any steroid from others having the same activity or function. A description of what a material does, rather than of what it is, usually does not suffice.... The disclosure must allow one skilled in the art to visualize or recognize the identity of the subject matter purportedly described.

Enzo, 323 F.3d at 968. Similarly, for example, in the nineteenth century, use of the word "automobile" would not have sufficed to describe a newly invented automobile; an inventor would need to describe what an automobile is, viz., a chassis, an engine, seats, wheels on axles, etc. Thus, generalized language may not suffice if it does not convey the detailed identity of an invention. In this case, there is no language here, generalized or otherwise, that describes compounds that achieve the claimed effect. * * *

We see no reason for the rule to be any different when non-genetic materials are at issue; in fact, where there might be some basis for finding a written description requirement to be satisfied in a genetics case based on the complementariness of a nucleic acid and, for example, a protein, that correspondence might be less clear in a non-genetic situation. In *Enzo,* we explained that functional descriptions of genetic material can, in some cases, meet the written description requirement if those functional characteristics are "coupled with a known or disclosed correlation between function and structure, or some combination of such characteristics." 323 F.3d at 964. DNA and RNA are each made up of just four building blocks that interact with each other in a highly predictable manner. Each of those building blocks, or "nucleotides," is characterized by a unique "base": In the case of DNA, the four nucleotides include the bases adenine, thymine, cytosine, and guanine; RNA also includes adenine, cytosine, and guanine, but contains the base uracil in place of thymine. Adenine on one strand of

---

5. We and the Supreme Court have frequently used the term "public notice" in connection with claims and discussion of the doctrine of equivalents, the point being that the public is entitled to notice of what the inventor has claimed and the Patent and Trademark Office has agreed should be the subject of a patent's limited right to exclude. However, while the role of the claims is to give public notice of the subject matter that is protected, the role of the specification is to teach, both what the invention is (written description) and how to make and use it (enablement).

DNA binds, or "hybridizes," to thymine on the other; in RNA, adenine binds to uracil; and in either DNA or RNA, cytosine binds to guanine. Given the sequence of a single strand of DNA or RNA, it may therefore have become a routine matter to envision the precise sequence of a "complementary" strand that will bind to it. Therefore, disclosure of a DNA sequence might support a claim to the complementary molecules that can hybridize to it.

The same is not necessarily true in the chemical arts more generally. Even with the three-dimensional structures of enzymes such as COX–1 and COX–2 in hand, it may even now not be within the ordinary skill in the art to predict what compounds might bind to and inhibit them, let alone have been within the purview of one of ordinary skill in the art in the 1993–1995 period in which the applications that led to the '850 patent were filed. Rochester and its experts do not offer any persuasive evidence to the contrary. As the district court pointed out:

> Tellingly, . . . what plaintiff's experts do *not* say is that one of skill in the art would, from reading the patent, understand what compound or compounds—which, as the patent makes clear, are necessary to practice the claimed method—would be suitable, nor would one know how to find such a compound except through trial and error. . . . Plaintiff's experts opine that a person of ordinary skill in the art would understand from reading the '850 patent what method is claimed, but it is clear from reading the patent that one critical aspect of the method—a compound that selectively inhibits PGHS–2 activity—was hypothetical, for it is clear that the inventors had neither possession nor knowledge of such a compound.

Univ. of Rochester v. G.D. Searle & Co., 249 F.Supp.2d 216, 229 (W.D.N.Y. 2003). * * *

Regardless whether a compound is claimed per se or a method is claimed that entails the use of the compound, the inventor cannot lay claim to that subject matter unless he can provide a description of the compound sufficient to distinguish infringing compounds from non-infringing compounds, or infringing methods from non-infringing methods. * * * Pfizer points out that the district court found that the '850 patent does not disclose the structure or physical properties of any of the compounds required to practice the claimed methods, and that the structure of such compounds cannot be deduced from any known structure-function correlation. Pfizer agrees with the district court that the '850 patent discloses nothing more than a hoped-for function for an as-yet-to-be-discovered compound, and a research plan for trying to find it. * * *

The '850 patent does contain substantial description of the cyclooxygenases, including the nucleotide sequences of coding and promoter regions of the genes that encode human COX–1 and COX–2 and a comparison of those sequences. The patent also describes in detail how to make cells that express either COX–1 or COX–2, but not both, as well as "assays for screening compounds, including peptides, polynucleotides, and small organic molecules to identify those that inhibit the expression or activity of the

PGHS–2 gene product; and methods of treating diseases characterized by aberrant PGHS–2 activity using such compounds.'' Such assay methods are in fact claimed in the '479 patent, i.e., Rochester's *other* patent based on the same disclosure.

The '850 patent specification also describes what can be done with any compounds that may potentially be identified through those assays, including formulation into pharmaceuticals, routes of administration, estimation of effective dosage, and suitable dosage forms. As pointed out by the district court, however, the '850 patent does not disclose just ''*which* 'peptides, polynucleotides, and small organic molecules' have the desired characteristic of selectively inhibiting PGHS–2.'' Without such disclosure, the claimed methods cannot be said to have been described. * * * Rochester did not present any evidence that the ordinarily skilled artisan would be able to identify any compound based on its vague functional description as ''a non-steroidal compound that selectively inhibits activity of the PGHS–2 gene product.''[7] * * *

The patent's claims all require a COX–2 selective compound, but no COX–2 selective compound is disclosed in the patent, and it is undisputed that there was no pre-existing awareness in the art of any compound having COX–2 selective activity. * * *[10] Because the court did not err in holding the '850 patent to be invalid for failing to comply with the written description requirement of 35 U.S.C. § 112, ¶ 1, and in granting summary judgment in favor of Pfizer on that ground, the decision of the district court is affirmed.

In re Brana

51 F.3d 1560 (Fed.Cir.1995).

■ PLAGER, CIRCUIT JUDGE:

Miguel F. Brana, et al. (applicants), appeal the March 19, 1993 decision of the United States Patent and Trademark Office (PTO) Board of Patent Appeals and Interferences * * * * On June 30, 1988, applicants filed patent application Serial No. 213,690 (the '690 application) directed to 5–nitrobenzo[de]isoquinoline–1,3–dione compounds, for use as antitumor sub-

---

7. Indeed, if compounds that selectively inhibit activity of the PGHS–2 gene product *had* been known in the art, it is difficult to see how the claims of the '850 patent would have satisfied the novelty requirement of 35 U.S.C. § 102. After all, the novelty of those claims, if any, would appear to reside in the fact that COX–2 selective inhibitors were previously unknown. * * *

10. Although we have treated the issue in this case as one of written description, as it was argued and decided below, underlying that question is the fundamental issue whether Rochester actually invented the subject matter it claimed in the '850 patent as required by 35 U.S.C. § 102(f). As the Supreme Court has cautioned, ''a patent is not a hunting license. It is not a reward for the search, but compensation for its successful conclusion.'' Here the patentee has done no more than invent a search method, i.e., a method of identifying a selective COX–2 inhibitor, much less did it invent, as claimed in the '850 patent, a method of using any such compound to selectively inhibit COX–2 in humans. Under these circumstances, it might appear that the patentee also failed to satisfy the requirements of section 102(f).

stances * * * * These claimed compounds differ from several prior art benzo[de]isoquinoline–1,3–dione compounds due to the presence of a nitro group (O_2N) at the 5–position and an amino or other amino group (NR^3R^4) at the 8–position of the isoquinoline ring.

The specification states that these non-symmetrical substitutions at the 5– and 8–positions produce compounds with "a better action and a better action spectrum as antitumor substances" than known benzo[de]isoquinolines, namely those in K.D. Paull et al., Computer Assisted Structure–Activity Correlations, Drug Research, 34(II), 1243–46 (1984). Paull describes a computer-assisted evaluation of benzo[de]iso-quinoline–1,3–diones and related compounds which have been screened for antitumor activity by testing their efficacy *in vivo* against two specific implanted murine (i.e., utilizing mice as test subjects) lymphocytic leukemias, P388 and L1210. These two *in vivo* tests are widely used by the National Cancer Institute (NCI) to measure the antitumor properties of a compound. Paull noted that one compound in particular * * * (hereinafter "NSC 308847"), was found to show excellent activity against these two specific tumor models. Based on their analysis, compound NSC 308847 was selected for further studies by NCI. In addition to comparing the effectiveness of the claimed compounds with structurally similar compounds in Paull, applicants' patent specification illustrates the cytotoxicity of the claimed compounds against human tumor cells, *in vitro*, and concludes that these tests "had a good action." * * *

At issue in this case is an important question of the legal constraints on patent office examination practice and policy. The question is, with regard to pharmaceutical inventions, what must the applicant prove regarding the practical utility or usefulness of the invention for which patent protection is sought. This is not a new issue; it is one which we would have thought had been settled by case law years ago. * * *

The first basis for the Board's decision was that the applicants' specification failed to disclose a specific disease against which the claimed compounds are useful, and therefore, absent undue experimentation, one of ordinary skill in the art was precluded from using the invention. In support, the Commissioner argues that the disclosed uses in the '944 application, namely the "treatment of diseases" and "antitumor substances," are similar to the nebulous disclosure found insufficient in [a previous case]. * * * Applicants' specification, however, also states that the claimed compounds have "a better action and a better action spectrum as antitumor substances" than known compounds, specifically those analyzed in Paull. As previously noted, Paull grouped various benzo[de]isoquinoline–1,3–diones, which had previously been tested *in vivo* for antitumor activity against two lymphocytic leukemia tumor models (P388 and L1210), into various structural classifications and analyzed the test results of the groups (i.e., what percent of the compounds in the particular group showed success against the tumor models). Since one of the tested compounds, NSC 308847, was found to be highly effective against these two lymphocytic leukemia tumor models, applicants' favorable comparison implicitly asserts that their claimed compounds are highly effective (i.e., useful) against lymphocytic leukemia. An alleged use against this particular type of cancer is much more specific than the vaguely intimated uses rejected by the courts in [prior cases].

The Commissioner contends, however, that P388 and L1210 are not diseases since the only way an animal can get sick from P388 is by a direct injection of the cell line. The Commissioner therefore concludes that applicants' reference to Paull in their specification does not provide a specific disease against which the claimed compounds can be used. We disagree. As applicants point out, the P388 and L1210 cell lines, though technically labeled tumor models, were originally derived from lymphocytic leukemias in mice. Therefore, the P388 and L1210 cell lines do represent actual specific lymphocytic tumors; these models will produce this particular disease once implanted in mice. If applicants were required to wait until an animal naturally developed this specific tumor before testing the effectiveness of a compound against the tumor *in vivo*, as would be implied from the Commissioner's argument, there would be no effective way to test compounds *in vivo* on a large scale. * * *

The second basis for the Board's rejection was that, even if the specification did allege a specific use, applicants failed to prove that the claimed compounds are useful. Citing various references, the Board found, and the Commissioner now argues, that the tests offered by the applicants to prove utility were inadequate to convince one of ordinary skill in the art that the claimed compounds are useful as antitumor agents. * * *

The references cited by the Board, Pazdur and Martin, do not question the usefulness of any compound as an antitumor agent or provide any other evidence to cause one of skill in the art to question the asserted utility of applicants' compounds. Rather, these references merely discuss the therapeutic predictive value of *in vivo* murine tests—relevant only if applicants must prove the ultimate value in humans of their asserted utility. Likewise, we do not find that the nature of applicants' invention alone would cause one of skill in the art to reasonably doubt the asserted usefulness. The purpose of treating cancer with chemical compounds does not suggest an inherently unbelievable undertaking or involve implausible scientific principles. Modern science has previously identified numerous successful chemotherapeutic agents. * * * Taking these facts—the nature of the invention and the PTO's proffered evidence—into consideration we conclude that one skilled in the art would be without basis to reasonably doubt applicants' asserted utility on its face. The PTO thus has not satisfied its initial burden. Accordingly, applicants should not have been required to substantiate their presumptively correct disclosure to avoid a rejection under the first paragraph of § 112.

We do not rest our decision there, however. Even if one skilled in the art would have reasonably questioned the asserted utility, i.e., even if the PTO met its initial burden thereby shifting the burden to the applicants to offer rebuttal evidence, applicants proffered sufficient evidence to convince one of skill in the art of the asserted utility. In particular, applicants provided through Dr. Kluge's declaration test results showing that several compounds within the scope of the claims exhibited significant antitumor activity against the L1210 standard tumor model *in vivo*. Such evidence alone should have been sufficient to satisfy applicants' burden. The prior art further supports the conclusion that one skilled in the art would be convinced of the applicants' asserted utility. As previously mentioned, prior art * * * disclosed structurally similar compounds which were proven *in vivo* against various tumor models to be effective as chemotherapeutic agents. Although it is true that minor changes in chemical compounds can radically alter their effects on the human body, evidence of success in structurally similar compounds is relevant in determining whether one skilled in the art would believe an asserted utility.

The Commissioner counters that such *in vivo* tests in animals are only preclinical tests to determine whether a compound is suitable for processing in the second stage of testing, by which he apparently means *in vivo* testing in humans, and therefore are not reasonably predictive of the success of the claimed compounds for treating cancer in humans. The Commissioner, as did the Board, confuses the requirements under the law for obtaining a patent with the requirements for obtaining government approval to market a particular drug for human consumption. See Scott v. Finney, 34 F.3d 1058, 1063 (Fed.Cir.1994) ("Testing for the full safety and effectiveness of a prosthetic device is more properly left to the Food and Drug Administration (FDA). Title 35 does not demand that such human testing occur within the confines of Patent and Trademark Office (PTO) proceedings.").

Our court's predecessor has determined that proof of an alleged pharmaceutical property for a compound by statistically significant tests with standard experimental animals is sufficient to establish utility. In re Krimmel, 292 F.2d 948, 953 (C.C.P.A.1961). In concluding that similar *in vivo* tests were adequate proof of utility the court in *In re Krimmel* stated:

> We hold as we do because it is our firm conviction that one who has taught the public that a compound exhibits some desirable pharmaceutical property in a standard experimental animal has made a significant and useful contribution to the art, even though it may eventually appear that the compound is without value in the treatment in humans.

Id. at 953. Moreover, NCI apparently believes these tests are statistically significant because it has explicitly recognized both the P388 and L1210 murine tumor models as standard screening tests for determining whether new compounds may be useful as antitumor agents. * * *

On the basis of animal studies, and controlled testing in a limited number of humans (referred to as Phase I testing), the Food and Drug Administration may authorize Phase II clinical studies. Authorization for a Phase II study means that the drug may be administered to a larger number of humans, but still under strictly supervised conditions. The purpose of the Phase II study is to determine primarily the safety of the drug when administered to a larger human population, as well as its potential efficacy under different dosage regimes. FDA approval, however, is not a prerequisite for finding a compound useful within the meaning of the patent laws. Usefulness in patent law, and in particular in the context of pharmaceutical inventions, necessarily includes the expectation of further research and development. The stage at which an invention in this field becomes useful is well before it is ready to be administered to humans. Were we to require Phase II testing in order to prove utility, the associated costs would prevent many companies from obtaining patent protection on promising new inventions, thereby eliminating an incentive to pursue, through research and development, potential cures in many crucial areas such as the treatment of cancer. In view of all the foregoing, we conclude that applicants' disclosure complies with the requirements of 35 U.S.C. § 112 ¶ 1. * * *

Fujikawa v. Wattanasin

93 F.3d 1559 (Fed.Cir.1996).

■ CLEVENGER, CIRCUIT JUDGE:

Yoshihiro Fujikawa et al. appeal from two decisions of the Board of Patent Appeals and Interferences of the United States Patent & Trademark Office granting priority of invention in two related interferences to Sompong Wattanasin * * * * These interferences pertain to a compound and method for inhibiting cholesterol biosynthesis in humans and other animals. The compound count recites a genus of novel mevalonolactones. The method count recites a method of inhibiting the biosynthesis of cholesterol by administering to a "patient in need of said treatment" an appropriate dosage of a compound falling within the scope of the compound count.

The real parties in interest are Sandoz Pharmaceuticals Corporation, assignee of Wattanasin, and Nissan Chemical Industries, Ltd., assignee of Fujikawa. The inventive activity of Fujikawa, the senior party, occurred overseas. Fujikawa can thus rely only on his effective filing date, August 20, 1987, to establish priority. 35 U.S.C. § 102(g) (1994).* Whether Wattanasin is entitled to priority as against Fujikawa therefore turns on two discrete questions. First, whether Wattanasin has shown conception coupled with diligence from just prior to Fujikawa's effective filing date until reduction to practice. Second, whether Wattanasin suppressed or concealed the invention between reduction to practice and filing. * * *

The Board divided Wattanasin's inventive activity into two phases. The first phase commenced in 1979 when Sandoz began searching for drugs which would inhibit the biosynthesis of cholesterol. Inventor Wattanasin was assigned to this project in 1982, and during 1984–1985 he synthesized

* As required by an international agreement, Congress subsequently amended this provision to eliminate the differential treatment of foreign entities in claiming priority to an invention. See Pub. L. No. 106–113, § 4806, 113 Stat. 1501 (1999). In 2011, Congress amended the statute to give priority to the first filer.

three compounds falling within the scope of the compound count. When tested *in vitro,* each of these compounds exhibited some cholesterol-inhibiting activity, although not all the chemicals were equally effective. Still, according to one Sandoz researcher, Dr. Damon, these test results indicated that, to a high probability, the three compounds "would be active when administered *in vivo* to a patient to inhibit cholesterol biosynthesis, i.e. for the treatment of hypercholesteremia or atherosclerosis." Notwithstanding these seemingly positive results, Sandoz shelved Wattanasin's project for almost two years, apparently because the level of *in vitro* activity in two of the three compounds was disappointingly low.

By January 1987, however, interest in Wattanasin's invention had revived, and the second phase of activity began. Over the next several months, four more compounds falling within the scope of the compound count were synthesized. In October, these compounds were tested for *in vitro* activity, and each of the four compounds yielded positive results. Again, however, there were significant differences in the level of *in vitro* activity of the four compounds. Two of the compounds in particular, numbered 64–935 and 64–936, exhibited *in vitro* activity significantly higher than that of the other two compounds, numbered 64–933 and 64–934.

Soon after, in December 1987, the three most active compounds *in vitro* were subjected to additional *in vivo* testing. For Sandoz, one primary purpose of these tests was to determine the *in vivo* potency of the three compounds relative to that of Compactin, a prior art compound of known cholesterol-inhibiting potency. From the results of the *in vivo* tests, Sandoz calculated an ED_{50} [effective dose for achieving 50% inhibition] for each of the compounds and compared it to the ED_{50} of Compactin. * * *

During this period, Sandoz also began to consider whether, and when, a patent application should be filed for Wattanasin's invention. Several times during the second phase of activity, the Sandoz patent committee considered the question of Wattanasin's invention but decided that it was too early in the invention's development to file a patent application. Each time, however, the patent committee merely deferred decision on the matter and specified that it would be taken up again at subsequent meetings. Finally, in January 1988, with the *in vivo* testing completed, the Committee assigned Wattanasin's invention an "A" rating which meant that the invention was ripe for filing and that a patent application should be prepared. The case was assigned to a Ms. Geisser, a young patent attorney in the Sandoz patent department with little experience in the pharmaceutical field.

Over the next several months the Sandoz patent department collected additional data from the inventor which was needed to prepare the patent application. This data gathering took until approximately the end of May 1988. At that point, work on the case seems to have ceased for several months until Ms. Geisser began preparing a draft sometime in the latter half of 1988. * * * [T]he draft was completed in November and, after several turn-arounds with the inventor, ultimately filed in March of 1989. * * *

We first address Fujikawa's argument that Wattanasin's *in vitro* and *in vivo* tests failed to establish a practical utility for either the compound or method count. The Board held that the *in vitro* tests established a practical utility for the compound and that the *in vivo* tests established a practical utility for both the compound and method counts. For the reasons set out below, we affirm these findings of the Board.

For over 200 years, the concept of utility has occupied a central role in our patent system. Indeed, "[t]he basic *quid pro quo* contemplated by the Constitution and the Congress for granting a patent monopoly is the benefit derived by the public from an invention with substantial utility." Consequently, it is well established that a patent may not be granted to an invention unless substantial or practical utility for the invention has been discovered and disclosed. Similarly, actual reduction to practice, which constitutes in law the final phase of invention, cannot be established absent a showing of practical utility.

In the pharmaceutical arts, our court has long held that practical utility may be shown by adequate evidence of any pharmacological activity. * * * Such activity constitutes a practical utility because "[i]t is inherently faster and easier to combat illnesses and alleviate symptoms when the medical profession is armed with an arsenal of chemicals having known pharmacological activities. Since it is crucial to provide researchers with an incentive to disclose pharmacological activities in as many compounds as possible, we conclude that adequate proof of any such activity constitutes a showing of practical utility."

It may be difficult to predict, however, whether a novel compound will exhibit pharmacological activity, even when the behavior of analogous compounds is known to those skilled in the art. Consequently, testing is often required to establish practical utility. But the test results need not absolutely prove that the compound is pharmacologically active. All that is required is that the tests be "reasonably indicative of the desired [pharmacological] response." In other words, there must be a sufficient correlation between the tests and an asserted pharmacological activity so as to convince those skilled in the art, to a reasonable probability, that the novel compound will exhibit the asserted pharmacological behavior. * * *

Fujikawa contends that Wattanasin has failed to establish an adequate correlation between *in vitro* and *in vivo* results in the field of cholesterol-inhibiting compounds to permit Wattanasin to rely on affirmative *in vitro* results to establish a practical utility for the compound. The Board determined that Wattanasin had reduced the compound count to practice in October 1987 when several compounds falling within the scope of the genus count exhibited activity *in vitro*. In reaching that conclusion, the Board relied on testimony from those skilled in the art that the *in vitro* results convinced them that the claimed compounds would exhibit the desired pharmacological activity when administered *in vivo*. * * *

Having determined that Wattanasin was the de facto first inventor, the remaining question before the Board was whether Wattanasin had suppressed or concealed the invention between the time he reduced to practice and the time he filed his patent application. Suppression or concealment of the invention by Wattanasin would entitle Fujikawa to priority. * * * Admittedly, Sandoz was not overly efficient in preparing a patent application, given the time which elapsed between its reduction to practice in late 1987 and its ultimate filing in March 1989. Intentional suppression, however, requires more than the passage of time. It requires evidence that the inventor intentionally delayed filing in order to prolong the period during which the invention is maintained in secret. Fujikawa presented no evidence that Wattanasin delayed filing for this purpose. On the contrary, all indications are that throughout the period between reduction to practice and filing, Sandoz moved slowly (one might even say fitfully), but inexorably, toward disclosure. We therefore hold that Wattanasin did not intentionally suppress or conceal the invention in this case.

Absent intentional suppression, the only question is whether the 17 month period between the reduction to practice of the compound, or the 15 month period between reduction to practice of the method, and Wattanasin's filing justify an inference of suppression or concealment. The Board held that these facts do not support such an inference. * * *

In our view, the circumstances in this case place it squarely within the class of cases in which an inference of suppression or concealment is not warranted. We acknowledge, of course, that each case of suppression or concealment must be decided on its own facts. Still, the rich and varied case law which this court has developed over many years provides some guidance as to the type of behavior which warrants an inference of suppression or concealment. In this case Wattanasin delayed approximately 17 months between reduction to practice and filing. During much of that period, however, Wattanasin and Sandoz engaged in significant steps towards perfecting the invention and preparing an application. For example, we do not believe any lack of diligence can be ascribed to Wattanasin for the period between October and December 1987 when *in vivo* testing of the invention was taking place. Similarly, at its first opportunity following the *in vivo* testing, the Sandoz patent committee approved Wattanasin's invention for filing. This takes us up to the end of January 1988.

Over the next several months, until May 1988, the Sandoz patent department engaged in the necessary collection of data from the inventor and others in order to prepare Wattanasin's patent application. We are satisfied from the record that this disclosure-related activity was sufficient to avoid any inference of suppression or concealment during this period. Also, as noted above, the record indicates that by August 1988, Ms. Geisser was already at work preparing the application, and that work continued on various drafts until Wattanasin's filing date in March 1989. Thus, the only real period of unexplained delay in this case is the approximately three month period between May and August of 1988.

Given a total delay of 17 months, an unexplained delay of three months, the complexity of the subject matter at issue, and our sense from the record as a whole that throughout the delay Sandoz was moving, albeit slowly, towards filing an application, we conclude that this case does not warrant an inference of suppression or concealment. Consequently, we affirm the Board on this point. * * *

NOTES AND QUESTIONS

1. *Novel and useful?* In order to receive patent protection, an invention must satisfy requirements of novelty and usefulness. Novelty requires, among other things, that the invention not have been in public use (as opposed to experimental use) in the United States for more than one year prior to the filing of a patent application. See 35 U.S.C. § 102(b); see also Baxter Int'l, Inc. v. COBE Lab., Inc., 88 F.3d 1054, 1058–61 (Fed.Cir.1996) (finding an absence of novelty because a researcher at NIH who lacked any relationship with the inventor had not restricted access to a modified centrifuge that he used for separating blood components); Eli Lilly & Co. v. Zenith Goldline Pharm., Inc., 364 F.Supp.2d 820 (S.D.Ind.2005) (rejecting arguments pressed by potential generic competitors that the patent covering the atypical antipsychotic olanzapine (Zyprexa®) was invalid on grounds of anticipation, obviousness, double patenting, or prior public use, or unenforceable due to inequitable conduct); Pfizer Inc. v. Ranbaxy Lab. Ltd., 405 F.Supp.2d 495, 512–26 (D.Del.2005) (same, with regard to patents covering atorvastatin calcium (Lipitor®)). Pharmaceutical companies generally apply for patents before starting clinical (and sometimes even pre-clinical) trials with a new molecular entity. See Robert Schaffer et al., Clinical Trials May Bar Drug's Patent Protection, Nat'l L.J., May 22, 2000, at B14; see also Tricia Bishop, For Biotechs, Guarding Concepts Is Critical, Balt. Sun, Apr. 30, 2006, at 4C; John Careyrou, Eli Lilly Faces Patent Challenge from a Long–Ago Collaboration, Wall St. J., May 10, 2006, at A1 (describing dispute with researchers who claim to have cloned the Protein C gene that provided the basis for the development of the sepsis drug Xigris®); cf. In re Omeprazole Patent Litig., 536 F.3d 1361, 1372–75 (Fed.Cir.2008) (upholding the lower court's finding that a patent claiming use of an enteric coating with an inert water-soluble subcoating to surround the drug core in the proton pump inhibitor Prilosec® had not been reduced to practice and ready for patenting until completion of clinical trials demonstrating the utility of this particular formulation).

2. *Section 112 requirements and biotech.* As the court explained in *University of Rochester*, 35 U.S.C. § 112 requires (1) written description, (2) enablement, and (3) disclosure of the best mode. See Chiron Corp. v. Genentech, Inc., 363 F.3d 1247, 1254–58 (Fed.Cir.2004) (holding that a patent claim construed to encompass newer methods for producing certain monoclonal antibodies could not claim priority where these genetic modification techniques became known only after filing of the original application, which therefore failed to satisfy the written description requirement, and remained nascent before the filing of continuation applications, which therefore failed to satisfy the enablement requirement); Amgen Inc. v. Hoechst Marion Roussel, Inc., 314 F.3d 1313, 1330–39, 1352–57 (Fed.Cir. 2003) (rejecting written description and enablement objections to patents covering recombinant erythropoietin (Epogen®), but remanding objections based on obviousness and anticipation); Bayer AG v. Schein Pharm., Inc., 301 F.3d 1306, 1313–23 (Fed.Cir.2002) (holding that patent covering ciprofloxacin (Cipro®) satisfied the best mode requirement). The courts have struggled in deciding how to apply the written description requirement to biotech patents. See Ariad Pharms., Inc. v. Eli Lilly & Co., 598 F.3d 1336 (Fed.Cir.2010) (en banc) (reaffirming that § 112 imposes a written description requirement separate from enablement, and reversing a judgment of infringement against the manufacturer of Evista® and Xigris® after concluding that the patent claims covering substances designed to modulate the action of nuclear factor kappa B (NF-kB) were invalid for lacking such a description); see also Christopher M. Holman, Is Lilly Written Description a Paper Tiger?: A Comprehensive Assessment of the Impact of Eli Lilly and Its Progeny in the Courts and PTO, 17 Alb. L.J. Sci. & Tech. 1 (2007); Dmitry Karshtedt, Limits on Hard-to-Reproduce Inventions: Process Elements and Biotechnology's Compliance with the Enablement Requirement, 3 Hastings Sci. & Tech. L.J. 109 (2011); William C. Mull, Note, Using the Written Description Requirement to Limit Broad Patent Scope, Allow Competition, and Encourage Innovation in Biotechnology, 14 Health Matrix 393 (2004); Symposium, Biotechnology Patents Get Special Treatment, 46 Ariz. L. Rev. 441 (2004).

3. *Inequitable conduct defense.* Even valid patents may lose protection from infringement if acquired on the basis of material and intentional misrepresentations to the PTO. See AstraZeneca Pharms. LP v. Teva Pharms. USA, Inc., 583 F.3d 766 (Fed.Cir.2009) (affirming the lower court's finding that the holder of the composition patent on the atypical antipsychotic Seroquel® (quetiapine) had not engaged in inequitable conduct); Purdue Pharma L.P. v. Endo Pharm., Inc., 438 F.3d 1123, 1128–35 (Fed.Cir.2006) (affirming the trial judge's finding that the prosecution of patents for controlled release oxycodone (OxyContin®) incorrectly had implied that claims of utility made to distinguish invention from prior art reflected clinical research, but reversing conclusion of inequitable conduct because of inadequate evidence of intent to deceive); see also id. at 1134 ("[T]he quantum of proof necessary for FDA approval [of a comparative labeling claim of superior titrability] is significantly higher than that required by the PTO."). See generally Shashank Upadhye, Liar Liar Pants on Fire: Towards a Narrow Construction for Inequitable Conduct as Applied to the Prosecution of Medical Device and Drug Patent Applications, 72 UMKC L. Rev. 669 (2004).

4. *Further commentary.* See Murray L. Eiland, The Role of the Individual Inventor in Pharmaceutical Patents, 18 U. Balt. Intell. Prop. L.J. 1 (2009); Kristen Nugent, Patenting Medical Devices: The Economic Implications of Ethically Motivated Reform, 17 Annals Health L. 135 (2008); Benjamin N. Roin, Unpatentable Drugs and the Standards of Patentability, 87 Tex. L. Rev. 503 (2009); A. Meaghin Burke, Comment, New Approaches to Pharmaceutical Patent Law: Why Current Patent Jurisprudence Is Inappropriate as Applied to the Unique Characteristics of Chemical Compounds, 75 Miss. L.J. 1143 (2006).

3. TYPES OF PATENTS

a. COMPOSITION PATENTS

Sanofi–Synthelabo v. Apotex, Inc.

550 F.3d 1075 (Fed.Cir.2008).

■ NEWMAN, CIRCUIT JUDGE:

* * * The patent at issue is United States Patent No. 4,847,265 (the '265 patent), owned by Sanofi–Synthelabo and related companies, and covers the pharmaceutical * * * Plavix [clopidogrel bisulfate]. The product has the property of inhibiting the aggregation of blood platelets and is used to treat or prevent blood-thrombotic events such as heart attacks and strokes. * * * Clopidogrel is the common name of the dextrorotatory isomer of the chemical compound named methyl alpha–5(4,5,6,7–tetrahydro(3,2–c)thienopyridyl)(2–chlorophenyl)-acetate [MATTPCA]. * * *

Apotex, Inc. filed an abbreviated new drug application (ANDA) in November 2001 for FDA approval to sell clopidogrel bisulfate, stating, pursuant to 21 U.S.C. § 355(j)(2)(A)(vii)(IV), that it believed the '265 patent to be invalid. Such "paragraph IV certification" is defined as an act of infringement for litigation purposes * * * * Sanofi duly filed suit for infringement, and Apotex counterclaimed that the '265 patent is invalid on several grounds and unenforceable. The suit initiated a thirty-month stay of FDA approval of Apotex's ANDA, as provided by 21 U.S.C. § 355(j)(5)(B)(iii). A proposed settlement was not achieved, the statutory stay expired, the FDA approved the Apotex ANDA, and Apotex commenced sale of its generic clopidogrel bisulfate product on August 8, 2006. * * * [More than three weeks later, the district court issued a preliminary injunction, and, almost ten months thereafter, it] ruled that the '265 patent is valid and enforceable. This appeal is focused on the question of patentability of this dextrorotatory isomer in view of its known racemate described in earlier Sanofi patents, specifically, Sanofi's United States Patent No. 4,529,596 (the '596 patent) and Canadian Patent No. 1,194,875 (the '875 patent). Both reference patents are derived from the same French priority filing and are prior art against the '265 patent. * * *

In 1972 Sanofi scientists were seeking products that might have improved anti-inflammatory properties, and in the course of this work discovered that certain compounds of the class known as thienopyridines (compounds having a thiene ring fused to a pyridine ring) have the property of inhibiting blood platelet aggregation. Sanofi scientists, led by Dr. Jean–Pierre Maffrand, pursued this direction of research. The record states that they initially synthesized and evaluated several hundred chemical modifications and derivatives of thienopyridines, seeking optimum antiplatelet aggregation properties with minimal undesirable effects. They eventually selected for development the compound * * * [given] the common name "ticlopidine." After lengthy development, including animal and human trials, in 1991 ticlopidine was approved in the United States for use as an anti-thrombotic agent. This approval, however, was accompanied by required warnings concerning possible adverse effects, for reports had been received of rarely occurring but serious blood disorders, neutropenia and thrombotic thrombocytopenic purpura, associated with prolonged usage of ticlopidine. Thus Sanofi continued its search for a product that would have the therapeutic benefits of ticlopidine but without the adverse properties.

Sanofi synthesized and evaluated several hundred additional thienopyridine derivatives, including a class of compounds * * * wherein one of the hydrogen atoms on the bridge carbon atom is replaced with an ester, carboxylic acid, or amide group. This class is the subject of the '596 patent (and the counterpart Canadian '875 patent) * * * [Designations] X and Y [in a drawing of the molecule's structure not included in this excerpt] can be any of a number of substituents, as identified in the patents; the district court found that there are thirty-seven possibilities for X and 1710 choices for Y. The patents state that compounds of this class exhibit good anti-platelet aggregation properties and are well tolerated.

Focusing on the '596 patent, the specification includes twenty-one examples of specific compounds, including a compound designated as PCR 4099, which Sanofi synthesized in July 1980. In PCR 4099 the substituent attached to the bridge carbon is the methyl ester group ($-COOCH_3$), and X is chlorine in the 2-position * * * PCR 4099 as the hydrochloride salt was selected for commercial development as a potential replacement for ticlopidine in light of its improved platelet inhibition and toxicity profile. However, PCR 4099 still raised toxicity concerns, for at very high doses it caused convulsions in laboratory animals. Thus the research efforts continued, concurrently with the clinical and commercial development of PCR 4099.

Sanofi states that about 1500 compounds in this general class were synthesized, of which about 600, including PCR 4099, were chiral thienopyridines. "Chiral" is defined as "describ[ing] asymmetric molecules that are mirror images of each other, i.e., they are related like right and left hands. Such molecules are also called enantiomers and are characterized by optical activity." Enantiomers are spatial isomers, also called stereoisomers, wherein the isomeric compounds have the same chemical formula and the same chemical structure, but differ in their orientation in three-dimensional space. Such stereoisomers can exist for all molecules that contain an asymmetric carbon atom. An "asymmetric carbon" is a carbon atom to which four different substituents are attached, whereby, due to the tetrahedral structure of carbon bonds in three dimensions, the spatial orientation of substituents attached to a carbon atom varies. When there is only one asymmetric carbon atom in the molecule and thus only two stereoisomers, these isomers are called enantiomers. Enantiomers are identified and distinguished by their optical characteristics when a purified solution of the separated isomers is exposed to plane-polarized light. One enantiomer will rotate plane-polarized light to the right (and thus is called the dextrorotatory or *d*- or (+) isomer), and the other rotates plane-polarized light to the left (called the levorotatory or *l*- or (–) isomer). * * * Enantiomers generally are formed in equal amounts, to produce what is called a racemate; the racemate is optically neutral.

In the district court, experts for both sides explained the difficulty of separating enantiomers, for they are identical except for the spatial arrangement at one of the carbon atoms. Sanofi scientists had previously separated the enantiomers of two thienopyridines and had found that the separated enantiomers showed no advantage over the racemates. The first such separation was conducted in 1978 for a compound designated PCR 1033 * * * * About three years later, Sanofi separated the enantiomers of a compound designated PCR 3233 * * * * [N]o other racemates were separated until, in November 1985, Dr. Maffrand decided to study the enantiomers of PCR 4099. The separation for PCR 4099 was assigned to Mr. Alain Badorc, the chemist who had separated the enantiomers of PCR 1033 and 3233. * * *

The record shows five months of experimentation by Mr. Badorc and eventually the successful separation using a technique called diastereomeric salt formation. This procedure, which originated with Louis Pasteur, is based on the trial of diverse salt-forming compositions and conditions, in the hope of coming upon a lucky combination of reagents that will preferentially select one of the enantiomers and crystallize from the solution in optically pure form. In Mr. Badorc's successful experiment, he prepared thirty compositions of PCR 4099 and various resolving acids at various concentrations and in various solvents, and after about one month crystals formed in the composition containing (+)camphorsulfonic acid and PCR 4099 in a 4:10 ratio, dissolved in acetone. This combination eventually yielded the pure levorotatory enantiomer, and isolation of the pure dextrorotatory enantiomer followed * * * *

Sanofi then determined the biological properties of the enantiomers of PCR 4099 and found that they had the rare characteristic of "absolute stereoselectivity": the dextrorotatory enantiomer provided all of the favorable antiplatelet activity but with no significant neurotoxicity, while the levorotatory enantiomer produced no antiplatelet activity but virtually all of the neurotoxicity. The experts for both sides agreed that, while it was generally known that enantiomers can exhibit different biological activity, this degree and kind of stereoselectivity is rare and could not have been predicted. The experts explained that in the usual case, if one enantiomer is more biologically active than the other, that activity includes the adverse as well as the beneficial properties.

In view of these results, in April 1987 Sanofi terminated commercial development of the racemate PCR 4099, which had been proceeding since 1980 and had reached Phase I human trials at a cost stated to be tens of millions of dollars. More years of development ensued for the dextrorotatory enantiomer, to which Sanofi gave the common name "clopidogrel." Sanofi also found that the hydrochloride salt, which had been suitable for processing and tableting the racemate PRC 4099, was not suitable for clopidogrel. After further research, Sanofi found that the hydrogen sulfate salt (also called the bisulfate) was suitable for tableting. FDA approval of clopidogrel bisulfate was achieved in the United States in 1998, allowing introduction of the product Plavix.

Sanofi filed a patent application directed to clopidogrel and certain salts and pharmaceutical compositions, in France on February 17, 1987 and then in the United States and other countries. The United States patent is the '265 patent in suit. The '265 specification explains that the racemate of the same chemical formula was described in the earlier French '247 patent, which corresponds to the earlier U.S. '596 patent. The '265 patent discusses the unusual stereoselectivity of the biological properties as between the dextrorotatory and the levorotatory enantiomers. The United States patent examiner, who had also examined the '596 patent, allowed the claims after requiring that the '265 claims make clear that the dextro and levoenantiomers are "substantially separated." Apotex stipulated that claim 3 of the '265 patent is literally infringed by its product. The district court, after full trial including extensive expert testimony provided by both sides, ruled that claim 3 is valid and enforceable. Apotex appeals the court's rulings on the issues of anticipation and obviousness * * * *

Claimed subject matter is "anticipated" when it is not new; that is, when it was previously known. Invalidation on this ground requires that every element and limitation of the claim was previously described in a single prior art reference, either expressly or inherently, so as to place a person of ordinary skill in possession of the invention. See Schering Corp. v. Geneva Pharms., Inc., 339 F.3d 1373, 1379 (Fed.Cir.2003). An anticipating reference must be enabling; that is, the description must be such that a person of ordinary skill in the field of the invention can practice the subject matter based on the reference, without undue experimentation. See Amgen Inc. v. Hoechst Marion Roussel, Inc., 457 F.3d 1293, 1306–07 (Fed.Cir. 2006); Elan Pharms., Inc. v. Mayo Found. for Med. Educ. & Research, 346 F.3d 1051, 1054 (Fed.Cir.2003). Anticipation is a question of fact, and the district court's finding of this issue is reviewed for clear error. See Merck & Co. v. Teva Pharms. USA, Inc., 347 F.3d 1367, 1369 (Fed.Cir.2003).

The district court identified the limitations stated in claim 3 of the '265 patent as (1) the bisulfate salt of (2) the dextrorotatory enantiomer of (3) the compound MATTPCA (4) substantially separated from the levorotatory enantiomer. The references on which Apotex relied were the '596 patent or its Canadian '875 counterpart. Apotex argued that either reference not only shows the racemate PCR 4099, but also its addition salts and enantiomeric forms. * * * The '596 specification states: "These compounds having an asymmetrical carbon may exist in the form of two enantiomers. The invention relates both to each enantiomer and their mixture." However, as the witnesses agreed, all of the compounds in the '596 patent are racemates, and neither the twenty-one specific examples nor any other part of the specification shows their separation into enantiomers. The district court reasoned that a person of ordinary skill in the field of the invention would not have been guided to either the dextrorotatory enantiomer of PCR 4099 or its bisulfate salt.

Apotex argues that the district court erred in law, and that it suffices that the reference shows the specific racemate PCR 4099 and states that the compounds in the reference have enantiomers and that the enantiomers are included in the invention. Apotex states that the separation of enantiomers is routine, even if time-consuming or requiring some experimentation, and thus that the separation need not have been performed or described in the reference. Apotex states that the properties of the enantiomers of PCR 4099 are inherently and necessarily present in its known racemate, such that when the enantiomers are separated the previously observed properties are "immediately recognized" in one or the other enantiomer.

Apotex stresses that the '596 patent's Example 1 is specific to PCR 4099, and the '596 claims refer to "addition salts with pharmaceutically acceptable mineral or organic acids" and "both enantiomeric forms or their mixture." The counterpart Canadian '875 patent states that when the desired structure is obtained it "is isolated and, if desired, its enantiomers are separated and/or it is salified by mineral or organic acid action." Apotex concedes that the references do not show any separated enantiomers or describe how to separate them, but argues that such detail is not required because persons of ordinary skill would know the existing techniques for separating enantiomers. Apotex thus argues that the dextrorotatory enantiomer of MATTPCA cannot be deemed novel, as a matter of law.

However, as the district court recognized, that is not the correct view of the law of anticipation, which requires the specific description as well as enablement of the subject matter at issue. To anticipate, the reference "must not only disclose all elements of the claim within the four corners of the document, but must also disclose those elements 'arranged as in the claim.'" The district court analyzed the question as whether a generic disclosure necessarily anticipates everything within the genus, and recognized that the answer depends on the factual aspects of the specific disclosure and the particular products at issue. * * * In this case the district court correctly declined to find that the references' general statements that these compounds consist of enantiomers constituted an anticipating disclosure of the separated dextrorotatory enantiomer of PCR 4099. * * * The knowledge that enantiomers may be separated is not "anticipation" of a specific enantiomer that has not been separated, identified, and characterized. * * *

The parties also debated the question of enablement with respect to anticipation. The district court found that the asserted references are not enabling, for they contain no guidance as to how to separate the enantiomers of PCR 4099. Based on the evidence adduced at trial, the court concluded that absent such guidance, undue experimentation would be required. * * * Apotex states that it is irrelevant whether the separation of this specific enantiomer is shown in the references, because a person of ordinary skill in this field would know all of the existing techniques for separating stereoisomers, and would presumptively succeed in this particular separation. Apotex points out that the method that was eventually used by Sanofi was a well-known method, even if it involved some experimentation. * * *

The '596 patent reference states only that "if desired, its enantiomers are separated," and similarly for the Canadian counterpart. The district court found that these references contain no description of how to separate the enantiomers of PCR 4099, and that "[d]iscovering which method and what combination of variables is required is sufficiently arduous and uncertain as to require undue experimentation, even by one skilled in the relevant art." This finding has not been shown to be clearly erroneous. In *Forest Laboratories, Inc. v. Ivax Pharmaceuticals, Inc.*, 501 F.3d 1263, 1268–69 (Fed.Cir.2007), this court recognized the known difficulty of separating enantiomers and the unpredictability of their properties, and held that a reference that stated that a compound has enantiomers did not enable the separation of those enantiomers, where the reference did not teach how to obtain the enantiomer. * * *

The determination of obviousness is made with respect to the subject matter as a whole, not separate pieces of the claim. For chemical compounds, the structure of the compound and its properties are inseparable considerations in the obviousness determination. Precedent establishes the analytical procedure whereby a close structural similarity between a new chemical compound and prior art compounds is generally deemed to create a prima facie case of obviousness, shifting to the patentee the burden of coming forward with evidence of nonobviousness. The evidence may take various forms, as relevant in the particular case. See, e.g., Takeda Chem. Indus., Ltd. v. Alphapharm Pty., Ltd., 492 F.3d 1350, 1358, 1362–63 (Fed.Cir.2007) (prima facie case depends on whether the prior art provided a suggestion or reason to choose a specific lead compound for modification, or to make the specific modification of the compound at issue); Eisai Co. v. Dr. Reddy's Labs., Ltd., 533 F.3d 1353, 1359 (Fed.Cir.2008) (same). * * *

The district court assumed that Apotex had made a prima facie case of obviousness based on the reference patents' disclosure of the PCR 4099 racemate, the statements in the patents concerning enantiomers, and the general knowledge that enantiomers may be separated and may differ from each other in biological properties. * * * [T]he court held that the unpredictable and unusual properties of the dextrorotatory enantiomer and the therapeutic advantages thereby provided, weighed in favor of nonobviousness, and that Apotex had not met its burden of establishing otherwise.

Apotex argues that the recognition in the prior art that PCR 4099 is composed of enantiomers outweighs the effect of any unexpected or unpredictable properties of the separated dextrorotatory enantiomer. Apotex asserts that Sanofi's previous selection of PCR 4099 as a promising replacement for ticlopidine would have led a skilled artisan to start with PCR 4099 as a lead compound for further research. Apotex states that it was well known that enantiomers can have different levels of biological activity even if the exact allocation of properties is unpredictable, thereby rendering it obvious to separate the enantiomers and determine their properties. Apotex contends that the only features of clopidogrel bisulfate arguably not explicit in the prior art—the separation of the dextro- from the levorotatory enantiomer and its preparation as a bisulfate salt—required no more than well-known chemical techniques. Apotex cites known examples of other chiral compounds that exhibit stereoselectivity and argues that the general knowledge that a favorable allocation of properties is possible suffices to render the separation obvious to a person of ordinary skill.

Apotex thus argues that there was motivation to separate the enantiomers of PCR 4099 and that a person of ordinary skill in the field would have been able to do so using known procedures, even if some experimentation was required, and then, upon separation of the enantiomers, routine testing would have revealed the favorable allocation of properties in the dextrorotatory isomer. Apotex asserts that it is not material that this allocation was unknown in advance and unpredictable and that what matters is whether a person of ordinary skill would have had a reasonable probability of success in the separation and evaluation of the enantiomer, citing *Pfizer, Inc. v. Apotex, Inc.*, 480 F.3d 1348, 1364 (Fed.Cir.2007), wherein this court observed that "case law is clear that obviousness cannot be avoided simply by a showing of some degree of unpredictability in the art so long as there was a reasonable probability of success."

Sanofi responds by challenging Apotex's view of the law and citing the evidence on the factual premises of these arguments. At trial the expert witnesses for both sides agreed that a person of ordinary skill in this field in the mid–1980s would have known that enantiomers can exhibit different biological activities. However, the experts also agreed that it was not predictable whether such differences, if any, would be weak, moderate, or strong, or how they would be manifested. The experts agreed that no known scientific principle allows prediction of the degree to which stereoisomers will exhibit different levels of therapeutic activity and toxicity. The experts agreed that weak stereoselectivity of biological properties is more common than strong stereoselectivity and that absolute stereoselectivity is rare. Sanofi witnesses testified as to the research team's belief, based on the earlier separations of two other thienopyridines, that separation of enantiomers was unlikely to be productive. Apotex's expert, when asked whether one could predict in advance the therapeutic and toxic properties of the enantiomers, stated: "No. I certainly don't believe you could predict that without separating them and trying it. I can't imagine anybody presuming anything else." The experts also agreed that activity and toxicity were more likely to be positively correlated, such that a reduction in toxicity would be expected also to reduce the beneficial activity. Witnesses also explained that it was known that for compounds whose biological activity is delivered through metabolism within the body, the acid environment in the stomach or other metabolic processes often restores the racemic state, thereby removing any potential benefit of a separated enantiomer. On the basis of this trial evidence, the district court found that a person of ordinary skill in this field would not reasonably have predicted that the dextrorotatory enantiomer would provide all of the antiplatelet activity and none of the adverse neurotoxicity. Clear error has not been shown in this finding, and in the conclusion of nonobviousness based thereon.

The district court also discussed the evidence concerning the process of separating the enantiomers of PCR 4099. Apotex argued that Sanofi's separation procedure was well known and therefore that the separated components of the known racemate were obvious as a matter of law, whether or not they were deemed to have unexpected properties. The district court observed that in 1987 there were at least ten techniques that had been used to separate enantiomers and that they all required experimentation to determine whether they could be successful for a particular compound, including choices of reagents, solvents, concentrations, temperature, and a variety of other conditions. The court observed that Pasteur's diastereomeric salt formation technique had long been described in chemistry textbooks, but that the textbooks also explain that the method is difficult and that there is no "infallible recipe" for obtaining separation. * * * Mr. Badorc's eventual success came only after several failures using other known strategies for enantiomer separation. The court observed that although Sanofi had previously separated the enantiomers of two other thienopyridines, the diastereomeric salt formation method had succeeded in one case but failed in the other. The court also found that a person of ordinary skill would have recognized that it could be more difficult to separate the enantiomers of PCR 4099 than the two other compounds that Mr. Badorc had previously separated, because it would be understood by chemists that the methyl ester substituent in PCR 4099 could make it more susceptible to re-racemization and thus resistant to successfully obtaining a separated product.

The district court found that this separation was not a simple or routine procedure and that success in separation, as well as the allocation of properties, was unpredictable. The court observed that Apotex did not cite any reference showing or suggesting any reliable method of separation for any analogous compounds. The court described the separation as a "paradigm of trial and error" and found that "neither the chemists at Sanofi nor a person of ordinary skill in the art could have reasonably expected that the separate enantiomers of PCR 4099 could be obtained at the time that Sanofi was contemplating whether to investigate them and, if obtained, they could not have predicted by what method and configuration." The court found that Sanofi's expenditure of tens of millions of dollars for several years of development of the racemate PCR 4099, before separating the enantiomers, also weighed against finding that separation would have been obvious. Again, Apotex has demonstrated no clear error in the extensive finding of the district court concerning the difficulty and unpredictability of the separation of these enantiomers. These unchallenged findings undermine Apotex's argument in this appeal that the separation of the enantiomers would have been obvious. Only with hindsight knowledge that the dextrorotatory enantiomer has highly desirable properties can Apotex argue that it would have been obvious to select this particular racemate and undertake its arduous separation. The application of hindsight is inappropriate where the prior art does not suggest that this enantiomer could reasonably be expected to manifest the properties and advantages that were found for this particular dextrorotatory isomer.

Concerning the bisulfate salt, the district court found no evidentiary support for Apotex's argument that the '596 patent taught the dextrorotatory enantiomer of PCR 4099 as the bisulfate salt. The PCR 4099 racemate is shown in the '596 patent as the hydrochloride, not the bisulfate. The district court observed that the scientific literature listed eighty acids as candidates for forming salts with basic drug compounds, fifty-three of which acids had been used in FDA-approved drugs. The experts of both parties agreed that whether a pharmaceutically suitable crystalline salt will form from a particular acid-base combination is unpredictable. The district court distinguished the facts of this case from those of *Pfizer*, 480 F.3d 1348, where there was evidence that based on the prior art a person of ordinary skill would have narrowed the possible salts to only a few including the claimed besylate, whereas here Sanofi presented evidence that the prior art taught away from the use of sulfuric acid with an enantiomer, for strong acids could encourage re-racemization. Apotex has shown no clear error in the district court's finding, based on the trial evidence, that the facts distinguish this case from those in *Pfizer*.

Based on all of these findings, the district court concluded: "Whether or not it may have been 'obvious to try' separating the enantiomers of PCR 4099 and, secondarily, preparing its dextrorotatory enantiomer as a bisulfate salt, the wide range of possible outcomes and the relative unlikelihood that the resulting compound would exhibit the maximal increase in antiplatelet aggregation activity and the absence of neurotoxicity makes clopidogrel bisulfate non-obvious." Apotex argues that the district court applied an incorrect inquiry and that the correct inquiry is not whether the results obtained with the separated enantiomer were unexpected but whether it would have been obvious to separate and test the enantiomers, based on the general knowledge that enantiomers can exhibit different properties. * * *

The determination of obviousness is dependent on the facts of each case. In *Forest Laboratories*, 501 F.3d at 1269, this court affirmed that the (+) enantiomer of citalopram would not have been obvious in light of the known racemate, when it was shown that the therapeutic properties of the (+) enantiomer were unexpected. In contrast, in *Aventis Pharma Deutschland GmbH v. Lupin, Ltd.*, 499 F.3d 1293, 1302 (Fed.Cir.2007), this court held that the ramipril isomer's potency was "precisely what one would expect, as compared to a mixture containing other, inert or near-inert stereoisomers." Apotex argues that *Aventis* is the closer analogy, but the evidence was directly contrary to that position. The district court entered extensive findings in this case on the unexpected and unpredictable properties of clopidogrel * * * *

Apotex also argues that the district court did not take adequate account of the Supreme Court's holding in *KSR Int'l Co. v. Teleflex Inc.*, 550 U.S. 398, 416 (2007), that the "combination of familiar elements according to known methods is likely to be obvious when it does no more than yield predictable results." Apotex states that Sanofi did no more than separate the enantiomers and determine their properties and that the properties were predictably those of the racemate, allocated between the enantiomers. Sanofi points out that this case does not concern a "combination of familiar elements" as in the *KSR* mechanical device made by combining known components to produce a combination having the properties of the known components. The evidence at trial well supported the finding that the result of this separation of enantiomers was unpredictable. We discern no error in the district court's implicit recognition that the principles of *KSR* do not affect the conclusion herein.

The district court thoroughly discussed the many issues and arguments raised by Apotex. We discern no error in the district court's findings that, on the state of the prior art, a person of ordinary skill would not have had the expectation that separating the enantiomers would be likely to produce an isomer having absolute stereoselectivity as to both the favorable antiplatelet activity and the unfavorable neurotoxicity. The totality of these findings, and the correct application of law, well support the district court's conclusion that invalidity had not been established by clear and convincing evidence.

NOTES AND QUESTIONS

1. *Mirror, mirror on the wall.* What if another company had separated the enantiomers of PCR 4099 and developed the bisulfate form of the dextrorotatory enantiomer—could Sanofi have sued for infringement of its earlier '596 patent assuming that it had not expired by then (and that, with regard to the question of enablement, it would instead offer the sort of expert testimony that Apotex had introduced in this case)? What if the degree of stereoselectivity had been less dramatic and, therefore, less unexpected? Conversely, if PCR 4099 had not appeared as the lead example of the thousands of compounds in the general class covered by the '596 patent, would Apotex not even have gotten the (limited) benefit of a prima facie case of obviousness? What exactly differentiates the court's approach to the questions of anticipation and obviousness (might one subsume the other, and are both simply aspects of the broader question of novelty)? See Miles J. Sweet, Note, The Patentability of Chiral Drugs Post–KSR: The More Things Change, the More They Stay the Same, 24 Berkeley Tech. L.J. 129 (2009); see also Quincy Chen, Destroying a Pharmaceutical Patent for Saving Lives?: A Case Study of Sanofi–Synthelabo v. Apotex, Inc., 21 Alb. L.J. Sci. & Tech. 125 (2011) (explaining that antitrust objections had prevented an effort to settle the litigation); cf. Michael Strong, FDA Policy and Regulation of Stereoisomers: Paradigm Shift and the Future of Safer, More Effective Drugs, 54 Food & Drug L.J. 463 (1999) (discussing the regulatory issues posed by enantiomers).

2. *(Non)obviousness.* Although it did not involve a medical technology, the Supreme Court's decision in *KSR International Co. v. Teleflex Inc.*, 550

U.S. 398 (2007), which enunciated a more expansive and flexible standard for determining obviousness, seemed to render pharmaceutical patents increasingly vulnerable to invalidation on that ground. As suggested by the court's opinion in *Sanofi–Synthelabo*, the latest case law on this question has been mixed. Compare In re Kubin, 561 F.3d 1351 (Fed.Cir.2009) (upholding the PTO's decision to reject on grounds of obviousness a patent application for a gene sequence encoding "the natural killer cell activation inducing ligand"); Bayer Schering Pharma AG v. Barr Labs., Inc., 575 F.3d 1341, 1346–50 (Fed.Cir.2009) (invalidating patent for the oral contraceptive Yasmin® (drospirenone) because micronization without enteric coating was obvious to try even though a person having ordinary skill in the art might have predicted (incorrectly as it turns out) that this would prove to be counterproductive by increasing the rate of isomerization in stomach acid), with id. at 1351 (Newman, J., dissenting) ("The law does not hold it 'obvious to try' experiments that contravene conventional knowledge, and that are not deemed reasonably likely to succeed."); Daiichi Sankyo Co. v. Matrix Labs., Ltd., 619 F.3d 1346, 1353–57 (Fed.Cir.2010) (affirming lower court's nonobviousness determination on the compound claim for the third-generation angiotensin receptor blocker Benicar® (olmesartan medoxomil)); Proctor & Gamble Co. v. Teva Pharms. USA, Inc., 566 F.3d 989, 996–98 (Fed.Cir.2009) (upholding an infringement judgment in favor of the owner of the composition patent for the osteoporosis drug Actonel® (risedronate), noting that the extremely unpredictable nature of bisphosphonates demonstrated nonobviousness); Ortho–McNeil Pharm., Inc. v. Mylan Labs., Inc., 520 F.3d 1358, 1364–65 (Fed.Cir.2008) (affirming summary judgment for holder of patent for anticonvulsant Topomax® (topiramate), emphasizing that obviousness not be determined with the benefit of hindsight). See generally Rebecca S. Eisenberg, Pharma's Nonobvious Problem, 12 Lewis & Clark L. Rev. 375 (2008); Tom Irving et al., Nonobviousness in the U.S. Post–KSR for Innovative Drug Companies, 34 U. Dayton L. Rev. 157 (2009); Scott D. Locke & William D. Schmidt, Protecting Pharmaceutical Inventions in a KSR World, 50 IDEA 1 (2009); Janice M. Mueller, Chemicals, Combinations, and "Common Sense": How the Supreme Court's KSR Decision Is Changing Federal Circuit Obviousness Determinations in Pharmaceutical and Biotechnology Cases, 35 N. Ky. L. Rev. 281 (2008); Diane C. Renbarger, Note, Putting the Brakes on Drugs: The Impact of KSR v. Teleflex on Pharmaceutical Patenting Strategies, 42 Ga. L. Rev. 905 (2008); Andrew V. Trask, Note, "Obvious to Try": A Proper Patentability Standard in the Pharmaceutical Arts?, 76 Fordham L. Rev. 2625 (2008).

Zenith Laboratories, Inc. v. Bristol–Myers Squibb Co.

19 F.3d 1418 (Fed.Cir.1994).

■ PLAGER, CIRCUIT JUDGE:

The question in this declaratory judgment action is whether a drug compound, which in its manufactured state does not infringe the patent in suit, becomes infringing as a result of transitory chemical changes that occur *in vivo*, that is, as a result of ingestion by the patient. * * *

The chemical compound cefadroxil, an antibiotic of the cephalosporin family effective against bacteria that are resistant to penicillin, was described and claimed in United States Patent No. 3,489,752 (the '752 patent), which issued in 1970; the owner was Bristol. The claims of the '752 patent covered any and all forms of cefadroxil—they described the chemical compound per se. The '752 patent expired in 1987.

In the meantime, Bristol set to work to find a commercially useful crystalline form of the compound that would overcome problems related to manufacture of the product so that it would be usable by humans. The task of developing a commercial production process was assigned to certain of Bristol's chemists. They developed what became known as the Bouzard monohydrate, named after one of the discoverers—a new crystalline form of cefadroxil. Unlike prior forms of cefadroxil, Bouzard monohydrate possesses certain characteristics in its pre-ingested, powdered form, related to bulk density, solubility, and stability (manufacturing-related characteristics), which make it particularly suitable for packaging into capsules.

The Bouzard monohydrate was the subject of the single claim in the '657 patent:

> 1. Crystalline 7–[D-α-amino-α-(p-hydroxyphenyl-)acetamido]–3–methyl–3–cephem–4–carboxylic acid monohydrate exhibiting essentially the following x-ray diffraction properties: [a 37–line table of relative intensities exhibited by Bouzard monohydrate at various scan angles].

In July 1988, Zenith, the plaintiff in this declaratory judgment action, contracted with a Spanish company, Gema, S.A. of Barcelona, to become the exclusive United States distributor of the form of cefadroxil manufactured by Gema and known as cefadroxil DC. Cefadroxil DC is a hemihydrate form of cefadroxil and thus differs structurally from Bouzard monohydrate. * * * Zenith and Gema sought abbreviated approval on the grounds that cefadroxil DC was bioequivalent to a form of cefadroxil monohydrate (other than Bouzard monohydrate) which had already been approved by the FDA for commercial sale. In October 1990, the FDA granted approval.[3] * * *

Bristol conceded that cefadroxil DC, being a hemihydrate, did not literally infringe the '657 patent in its pre-ingested form. Bristol nevertheless argued that Zenith was liable under the patent on two grounds: Zenith's product infringed under the doctrine of equivalents; and Zenith's product converted into the patented compound in the patient's stomach, and thus the sale of cefadroxil DC would induce infringement of the '657 patent * * * *

---

3. The record suggests that the FDA subsequently reconsidered and rescinded this approval after Bristol filed with the FDA a citizens petition seeking to block approval on the grounds cefadroxil DC was a hemihydrate and thus not bioequivalent to cefadroxil monohydrate. * * *

We begin with claim construction: whether the claim of the '657 patent, properly construed, covers Bouzard crystals which might form momentarily in a patient's stomach. Zenith argues that, due to statements made by Bristol during the '657 prosecution, the '657 claim is limited to the pre-ingested, powdered form of Bouzard monohydrate. In those statements Bristol particularly emphasized the superior manufacturing-related benefits of the pre-ingested form of Bouzard monohydrate in relation to prior forms of cefadroxil. Bristol, it is argued, thus relinquished coverage of any forms of cefadroxil DC that do not exhibit these manufacturing-related characteristics—that would obviously include any Bouzard monohydrate formed in a patient's stomach.

Zenith has a point. Prosecution history serves as a limit on the scope of claims by excluding any interpretation of the claim language that would permit the patentee to assert a meaning for the claim that was disclaimed or disavowed during prosecution in order to obtain claim allowance. The prosecution history in this case is replete with arguments by Bristol that the importance of this invention was the discovery of a way to manufacture the known compound so as to make it commercially available for medical treatment.

The difficulty with Zenith's argument, however, is in the nature of the sole claim in the patent. The claim as written and allowed simply describes a compound having specified chemical properties. The question before us is not one of validity: whether the claim would be patentable over the prior art if the suggested restriction were not applicable. The question here is one of infringement: whether there is anything in the claim as issued that limits it to the pre-ingested form * * * *

Zenith's argument suffers from additional infirmities. The '657 claim is a claim for a compound. Its patentability thus derives from the structure of the claimed compound in relation to prior compounds. The relevance to patentability of the properties or characteristics exhibited by the compound is limited to assessing the significance of the structural distinctions of the claimed compound over the prior art. Second, as we later note in more detail, it is not at all clear that the statements concerning these characteristics played a determinative or even significant role in the Patent and Trademark Office's decision to grant the patent. We conclude, therefore, that while the claim as issued is limited to the crystalline form of cefadroxil exhibiting the specified x-ray diffraction pattern, it is not limited to the compound in its pre-ingested form with the manufacturing characteristics which Bristol emphasized during prosecution.

We turn next to the question of whether Bouzard monohydrate is actually found in the stomach of patients who ingest cefadroxil DC. One answer is that no one knows—the scientific fact appears to be that there is no known way to actually sample the contents of patients' stomachs at the precise moment and conduct the x-ray diffraction analyses required to ascertain if all 37 lines described in the patent are present. For its proof Bristol offered instead the testimony of its principal scientific witness, Dr. Harry Brittain, who described various studies and experiments simulating the environment of the human stomach which were conducted under his auspices; Zenith countered with the testimony of its principal scientific witness, Dr. Martha Greenblatt. The trial judge, after hearing all the evidence, concluded that the Bouzard monohydrate in fact does inevitably form in the patient's stomach after ingestion of cefadroxil DC. * * *

In order to establish its case, Bristol had to show that the accused compound infringed the claim contained in the patent. This required Bristol to show that the diffraction pattern of cefadroxil DC following its conversion *in vivo* displayed the same diffraction pattern as that of the claimed compound. The district court, instead of requiring the comparison of the accused compound following conversion to be made with the lines specified in the claim, allowed Bristol to make the comparison with the diffraction pattern exhibited by a sample (the reference pattern) of a material considered by Bristol to be the patented compound.

As we have repeatedly said, it is error for a court to compare in its infringement analysis the accused product or process with the patentee's commercial embodiment or other version of the product or process; the only proper comparison is with the claims of the patent. The difficulty was compounded. The x-ray diffraction pattern exhibited by Bristol's sample (the reference pattern) consisted of a table of only 30 lines of relative intensities. Of this total, the court only compared 22 lines to corresponding lines recited in the claim. Based on its comparison, the court concluded the two were sufficiently similar to permit Bristol to use the reference pattern in its infringement analysis. In fact, the number of lines recited in the claim is 37. Thus, 15 of the lines recited in the claim (representing about 40% of the total) were not considered by the court in its comparison. Although the term "essentially" recited in the claim permits some leeway in the exactness of the comparison with the specified 37 lines of the claim, it does not permit ignoring a substantial number of lines altogether. It is the claim that sets the metes and bounds of the invention entitled to the protection of the patent system.

On the basis of this evidence the trial court concluded that when cefadroxil DC is ingested Bouzard monohydrate is created in a patient's stomach, that that constitutes an infringing use, and that therefore the sale of cefadroxil DC by Zenith would constitute inducement of infringement under 35 U.S.C. § 271(b). Since the finding of infringement was based on testimony which incorporated an improper comparison, and since that comparison was an essential element in the conclusion that infringement occurred, the conclusion that Zenith by selling cefadroxil DC would engage in inducement of infringement is insupportable. Zenith is correct that there was a failure of proof as to whether any crystals, assumed to form in the stomach from ingested cefadroxil DC, literally infringe the '657 claim. In the absence of evidence comparing the '657 claim with the cefadroxil DC after ingestion Bristol has failed to establish any infringing use and therefore we must reverse the district court's conclusion that Zenith's sale of cefadroxil DC induces infringement of the '657 patent. * * *

To prove infringement under the doctrine of equivalents, Bristol bore the burden of showing that cefadroxil DC was the equivalent of Bouzard monohydrate. A necessary part of the function/way/result equivalency analysis is the *function* of the substituted element as seen in the context of the patent, the prosecution history, and the prior art.

In view of Bristol's numerous statements in the prosecution history regarding the superior manufacturing-related benefits of the Bouzard crystal in relation to the prior forms of cefadroxil, it is clear that the primary, if not the only, function of the Bouzard crystal form of the drug as compared to other forms is to facilitate pre-ingestion manufacturing. No other intended function is described or suggested. Since any unanticipated production of the Bouzard crystal in the patient's stomach as a result of ingesting cefadroxil DC does not even remotely perform that function, the "function" part of the function/way/result test of equivalency is not met. As a matter of law, there can be no infringement under the doctrine of equivalents.

Bristol cites a number of cases to demonstrate that the doctrine of equivalents has been applied to find infringement in situations involving *in situ* or *in vivo* conversions. However, these cases do not support Bristol's argument. In [several cases], * * * the substituted compound or ingredient converted *in vivo* or *in situ* to the compound or ingredient called for by the claim, and performed the same function as that of the claim. The infringer was thus using the equivalent element to perform the same function as the claimed compound, a typical case for doctrine of equivalents application.

Even assuming that cefadroxil DC converts *in vivo* to Bouzard monohydrate in measurable amounts, that particular crystalline form does not perform the function of facilitating encapsulation. On the record before us, the trial court was correct in his judgment that Bristol had failed to establish infringement under the doctrine of equivalents. * * *

NOTES AND QUESTIONS

1. *Digestion and the doctrine of equivalents.* For a similar decision rejecting an infringement claim based on *in vivo* conversion, see Marion Merrell Dow Inc. v. Baker Norton Pharm., Inc., 948 F.Supp. 1050, 1053–57 (S.D.Fla.1996) (terfenadine acid metabolite), dismissed mem., 152 F.3d 941 (Fed.Cir.1998); see also SmithKline Beecham Corp. v. Apotex Corp., 403 F.3d 1331, 1341–46 (Fed.Cir.2005) (invalidating composition patent for paroxetine hydrochloride hemihydrate (Paxil®) because the earlier patent for the anhydrate version (an unstable crystalline form of this polymorph, some of which converts to a hemihydrate) inherently anticipated the later discovery, obviating the need to address the infringement argument based on *in vivo* conversion); cf. Abbott Labs. v. Sandoz, Inc., 566 F.3d 1282, 1291–95 (Fed.Cir.2009) (en banc) (holding that process terms in "product-by-process" claims limit the scope of composition patents in the sense that identical products made by different processes would not infringe); id. at 1298 (panel opinion) ("Abbott also asserts that Lupin effectively admitted infringement by equivalents when it claimed before the [FDA] that its cefdinir generic was a bioequivalent to Abbott's Omnicef product.... Bioequivalency is a regulatory and medical concern aimed at establishing that two compounds are effectively the same for pharmaceutical purposes. In contrast, equivalency for purposes of patent infringement requires an element-by-element comparison of the patent claim and the accused product, requiring not only equivalent function but also equivalent way and result."). See generally D. Alan White, Comment, The Doctrine of Equivalents: Fairness and Uncertainty in an Era of Biologic Pharmaceuticals, 60 Emory L.J. 751 (2011).

2. *Remedies for infringement.* The holder of a patent may seek an injunction and/or damages for lost profits. For instance, Johnson & Johnson's medical device subsidiary Cordis was awarded almost $600 million in damages from two competitors who allegedly infringed its patent on a stent used to open coronary arteries. See Margaret C. Fisk, Patent Victories Reflect 2000 Trend, Nat'l L.J., Feb. 19, 2001, at A1; see also Thomas M. Burton, Jury Says St. Jude Medical Violated Guidant Heart–Defibrillator Patent, Wall St. J., July 5, 2001, at B2 (reporting on a verdict of $140 million). In cases of willful infringement, the plaintiff may recover additional damages. See Stryker Corp. v. Intermedics Orthopedics, Inc., 96 F.3d 1409 (Fed.Cir.1996) (affirming the trial judge's finding of willful infringement of a patent for a modular hip implant and an award of double lost profits, plus attorneys fees, totaling more than $72 million); Minnesota Mining & Mfg. Co. v. Johnson & Johnson Orthopaedics, Inc., 976 F.2d 1559 (Fed.Cir.1992) (affirming the trial judge's finding of willful infringement of patents for resin-based casting tapes and an award of double lost profits totaling more than $110 million).

b. METHOD-OF-USE PATENTS

Eli Lilly & Co. v. Barr Laboratories, Inc.

251 F.3d 955 (Fed.Cir.2001).

■ Gajarsa, Circuit Judge:

* * * On January 10, 1974, Lilly filed application Serial No. 432,379 ("the '379 application") containing claims for a class of compounds, therapeutic methods of using those compounds, and pharmaceutical compositions comprising those compounds. The '379 application named Bryan B. Molloy and Klaus K. Schmiegel as inventors. After its filing, the '379 application engendered a progeny of divisional applications, continuation applications, and patents that rivals the Hapsburg legacy. When the last patent stemming from the '379 application issued in December 1986, the application had spawned four divisional applications, three continuation applications, and six patents. During that twelve-year period, Lilly obtained six patents relating to fluoxetine hydrochloride [the active ingredient in Prozac®]—the '081 and '549 patents, as well as U.S. Patent Nos. 4,018,895 ("the '895 patent"), 4,194,009 ("the '009 patent"), 4,590,213 ("the '213 patent"), and 4,329,356 ("the '356 patent"). The '213 and '356 patents did not stem from the '379 application, and during the course of this litigation, Lilly disclaimed those patents.

The '009 patent, which expired in April 1994, claimed a class of pharmaceutical compounds, including fluoxetine hydrochloride, for administration in psychotropically effective amounts. The '895, '213, and '356 patents related to methods for treating particular ailments by administering a pharmaceutical compound within a class of compounds that includes fluoxetine hydrochloride. Specifically, the '895 patent, which expired in April 1994, concerned the treatment of humans suffering from depression; the '213 patent concerned the treatment of humans suffering from anxiety; and the '356 patent concerned the treatment of animals suffering from hypertension. * * * On March 31, 1986, Lilly filed continuation application Serial No. 846,448, claiming the benefit of the 1974 filing date of the '379 application under 35 U.S.C. § 120. On December 2, 1986, the application matured into the '549 patent. Claim 7 of the '549 patent, which depends on claim 4, relates to blocking the uptake of the monoamine serotonin in an animal's brain neurons through administration of the compound N-methyl–3–(p-trifluoromethylphenoxy)–3–phenylpropylamine hydrochloride—commonly referred to as fluoxetine hydrochloride. * * *

Through a statutorily prescribed term, Congress limits the duration of a patentee's right to exclude others from practicing a claimed invention. The judicially-created doctrine of obviousness-type double patenting cements that legislative limitation by prohibiting a party from obtaining an extension of the right to exclude through claims in a later patent that are not patentably distinct from claims in an earlier patent. * * * [A]n obviousness-type double patenting analysis entails two-steps. First, as a matter of law, a court construes the claim in the earlier patent and the claim in the later patent and determines the differences. Second, the court determines whether the differences in subject matter between the two claims render the claims patentably distinct. * * *

The relevant portion of claim 1 of the '213 patent is directed to a method for treating anxiety in a human by administering an effective amount of fluoxetine or a pharmaceutically-acceptable salt thereof. Claim 7 of the '549 patent covers a method of blocking the uptake of serotonin by brain neurons in animals by administering the compound fluoxetine hydrochloride. A person of ordinary skill in the art would have recognized that fluoxetine hydrochloride is a pharmaceutically-acceptable salt of fluoxetine. In fact, hydrochloride salts are the most common pharmaceutically acceptable salts of basic drugs, and hence are obvious compounds.

Therefore, the only difference between claim 1 of the '213 patent and claim 7 of the '549 patent is that the former addresses a method of treating anxiety in humans with fluoxetine hydrochloride while the latter claims a method of using fluoxetine hydrochloride to block serotonin uptake in animals. Having recognized the difference between the claims at issue, we must decide whether this difference renders the claims patentably distinct. * * * In this case, it is clear from all of the evidence proffered by Barr that the natural result flowing from administration of fluoxetine hydrochloride is inhibition of serotonin uptake.

Therefore, the limitation of claim 7 of the '549 patent directed to blocking serotonin uptake by use of fluoxetine hydrochloride is an inherent characteristic of the administration of fluoxetine hydrochloride for any purpose, including the treatment of anxiety. A patentable distinction does not lie where a later claim is anticipated by an earlier one. That is, a later patent claim that fails to provide novel invention over an earlier claim is not patentably distinct from the earlier claim. * * * [C]laim 7 of the '549 patent simply describes the process by which fluoxetine hydrochloride physically acts on individuals who receive the drug. That is, fluoxetine hydrochloride inherently blocks serotonin uptake upon administration. Therefore, no patentable distinction rests between administering fluoxetine hydrochloride for treatment of anxiety and inhibition of serotonin uptake by administration of fluoxetine hydrochloride.

The only other difference between claim 1 of the '213 patent and claim 7 of the '549 patent is that the former is directed to humans while the latter is directed to animals. Humans are a species of the animal genus. Our case law firmly establishes that a later genus claim limitation is anticipated by, and therefore not patentably distinct from, an earlier species claim. * * * [T]he double patenting issue in this case is solely a matter of law. We have compared the differences between the claims at issue as a whole and conclude that they are not patentably distinct. Therefore, we reverse the district court's denial of the portion of Barr's motion for summary judgment contending that claim 7 of the '549 patent is invalid for obviousness-type double patenting over claim 1 of the '213 patent. * * *

NOTES AND QUESTIONS

1. *Maximizing patent protection.* The "double patenting" doctrine prevents an applicant from extending its patent protection by claiming a slight variant of an earlier invention. See Sun Pharm. Indus., Ltd. v. Eli Lilly & Co., 611 F.3d 1381 (Fed.Cir.2010) (method-of-use patent for Gemzar® (gemcitabine) as a cancer treatment held invalid); id. at 1386 ("[O]bviousness-type double patenting encompasses any use for a compound that is disclosed in the specification [as a utility] of an earlier patent claiming the compound and is later claimed as a method of using that compound."). Lilly's strategy of seeking "second generation" patents (a.k.a. patent stacking or evergreening) is not uncommon or inevitably unsuccessful. See Melody Petersen, Lilly Set Back in Prozac Patent Case, N.Y. Times, Aug. 10, 2000, at C1 ("Efforts to extend the monopoly on a popular brand-name drug are common in the pharmaceutical industry .... [O]ften companies file numerous patent applications on different aspects of the same drug—different uses of the drug, for example, or slightly different formulations—to try to get even more years of exclusive sales."); see also Julie Appleby & Jayne O'Donnell, Consumers Pay as Drug Firms Fight over Generics, USA Today, June 6, 2002, at 1A ("The average number of patents on a drug has gone from two to 10 in the past two decades, according to the generic-drug industry."). Method-of-use patents, which identify a previously undisclosed utility, offer one mechanism for doing so. See Fonar Corp. v. General Elec. Co., 107 F.3d 1543, 1550–51 (Fed.Cir.1997) (affirming judgment for holder of patent for the use of MRI scanners in multi-angle oblique imaging); Glaxo Wins Lawsuit over Drug Patent, Wall St. J., Aug. 24, 2004, at D3. They only work, however, if the ANDA filer seeks approval for the patented additional use, which would not occur if, for instance, the pioneer never had secured FDA approval for that use. See Warner–Lambert Co. v. Apotex Corp., 316 F.3d 1348 (Fed.Cir.2003) (rejecting a claim by the manufacturer of Neurontin® (gabapentin), which was labeled only for treating epilepsy but widely used in patients with neurodegenerative diseases, that approval of a generic version would infringe (or induce infringement of) its method patent covering such off-label uses); Allergan, Inc. v. Alcon Lab., Inc., 324 F.3d 1322, 1332–34 (Fed.Cir.2003) (same, with regard to the patented off-label uses of the glaucoma drug Alphagan® (brimonidine)); cf. Merck & Co. v. Teva Pharm. USA, Inc., 395 F.3d 1364, 1372–77 (Fed.Cir.2005) (invalidating a method-of-use patent covering the once-weekly formulation of Fosamax® on grounds of obviousness).

As elaborated in the next part of this chapter, whether or not second generation patents succeed in blocking generic competitors, they may lead to line extensions that enjoy some patent protection as well as non-patent market exclusivity periods granted by the FDA. See Daniel I. Gorlin, Staving off Death: A Case Study of the Pharmaceutical Industry's Strategies to Protect Blockbuster Franchises, 63 Food & Drug L.J. 823, 832–64 (2008) (contrasting the different tactics employed by the manufacturers of Prilosec® (omeprazole) and Claritin® (loratadine) as their original patents expired); see also Schering Corp. v. Geneva Pharm., Inc., 339 F.3d 1373, 1378–82 (Fed.Cir.2003) (affirming a decision that the compound claims in the patent for desloratadine (Clarinex®), a metabolite formed upon ingestion of loratadine, were invalid because inherently anticipated by prior art even though not disclosed in the earlier (and now expired) compound patent for loratadine); Duff Wilson, As Generics Near, Makers Tweak Erectile Drugs, N.Y. Times, Apr. 14, 2011, at B1.

2. *Composition vs. use patents.* What if someone other than the holder of the composition patent discovered an unanticipated use? If the owner of the composition patent agreed to license the product (or if that earlier patent had expired), what kind of protection would a method-of-use patent offer in a regulatory environment that tolerates off-label use (are the shortcomings primarily practical ones)? Method-of-use patents have less value than composition patents, but does that make them entirely valueless? For instance, would not the holder of the method patent have recourse against other sellers for inducing infringement if they promoted the off-label use of their products? Would it make any difference if the holder of the composition patent never secured FDA approval for the originally anticipated uses? (Reconsider these questions after learning about the various market exclusivity incentives discussed in Chapter 10(B).) Is there any inconsistency between the patentability of new uses for medical technologies and the previously discussed non-patentability of medical procedures? Cf. Shankar Vedantam, Botox Appears to Ease Depression Symptoms, Wash. Post, May

21, 2006, at A9 (reporting that a dermatologist had applied for a method-of-use patent after discovering this potential off-label use for the injectable cosmetic product). For an illustration of the possible consequences of the differences between composition patents and far less attractive (and, therefore, often not sought) method-of-use patents, see Charles A. Black, The Cure for Deadly Patent Practices: Preventing Technology Suppression and Patent Shelving in the Life Sciences, 14 Alb. L.J. Sci. & Tech. 397, 419–22 (2004) (explaining that the composition patents secured for H2–receptor antagonists gave sellers the incentive to promote these products for symptomatic relief (i.e., suppression of stomach acid) even though researchers had discovered that off-patent (and far cheaper) antibiotics often could cure the underlying condition (i.e., an ulcer)); cf. Peter Landers, Nosed Out? With New Patent, Mayo Clinic Owns a Cure for the Sniffles, Wall St. J., Apr. 30, 2003, at A1 (reporting that a researcher had secured method-of-use patents for antifungal agents to treat sinusitis and chronic asthma, and contrasting this situation with the failure of researchers to do so for the use of antibiotics in treating ulcers). See generally Rebecca S. Eisenberg, The Problem of New Uses, 5 Yale J. Health Pol'y L. & Ethics 717 (2005); Richard A. Castellano, Note, Patent Law for New Medical Uses of Known Compounds and Pfizer's Viagra Patent, 46 IDEA 283 (2006).

3. *Conditional sales.* Although the sale and purchase of replacement parts for a patented medical device generally would not amount to acts of infringement, see Kendall Co. v. Progressive Med. Tech., Inc., 85 F.3d 1570, 1573–76 (Fed.Cir.1996), the reuse of a patented medical device sold for "single use only" may do so. See Mallinckrodt, Inc. v. Medipart, Inc., 976 F.2d 700, 708–09 (Fed.Cir.1992) (allowing the patent holder to bring an infringement claim to enforce such a restriction even if it had an anticompetitive effect); see also B. Braun Med., Inc. v. Abbott Lab., 124 F.3d 1419, 1426–27 (Fed.Cir.1997) (applying the same analysis to a usage restriction imposed by the holder of a patent for an IV tip that reduced the risk of accidental needle sticks when selling it as a component for a kit distributed by another company). One commentator has suggested that the practice of encouraging patients to purchase and then split higher-dose pills than prescribed may infringe a seller's method-of-use patent. See Nicolas G. Barzoukas, Pill Splitting Raises Issues of Safety and Patent Coverage, Nat'l L.J., May 22, 2000, at B9.

C. PROCESS PATENTS

Eli Lilly & Co. v. American Cyanamid Co.

82 F.3d 1568 (Fed.Cir.1996).

■ BRYSON, CIRCUIT JUDGE:

The ongoing struggle between "pioneer" drug manufacturers and generic drug distributors has once more come before our court. Eli Lilly and Company, the "pioneer" drug manufacturer in this case, has filed suit for patent infringement against the appellees, who are involved in various ways in the distribution of a particular generic drug. Lilly sought a preliminary injunction, arguing that the importation and sale of the generic drug in this country infringed Lilly's patent on a process for making a related compound. * * *

The pharmaceutical product at issue in this case is a broad-spectrum antibiotic known as "cefaclor." Cefaclor is a member of the class of cephalosporin antibiotics, all of which are based on the cephem nucleus. Although there are many different cephem compounds, only a few have utility as antibiotic drugs. Each of the known commercial methods for producing cefaclor requires the production of an intermediate cephem compound known as an enol. Once the desired enol cephem intermediate is obtained, it is then subjected to several processing steps in order to produce cefaclor.

Lilly developed cefaclor and patented it in 1975. Until recently, Lilly has been the exclusive manufacturer and distributor of cefaclor in this country. In addition to its product patent on cefaclor, Lilly obtained several patents covering different aspects of the manufacture of cefaclor, including processes for producing enol cephem intermediates. Many of those patents have now expired.

In 1995, Lilly purchased the patent at issue in this case, U.S. Patent No. 4,160,085 (the '085 patent). Claim 5 of that patent defines a method of producing enol cephem compounds, including what is called "compound 6," an enol cephem similar to the one Lilly uses in its process for manufacturing cefaclor. The '085 patent will expire on July 3, 1996.

Compound 6 differs from cefaclor in three respects. Although both compound 6 and cefaclor are based on the cephem nucleus, compound 6 has a hydroxy group at the 3–position on the cephem nucleus, a para-nitrobenzyl carboxylate ester at the 4–position, and a phenylacetyl group at the 7–position. Cefaclor has different groups at each of those positions: it has a chlorine atom at the 3–position, a free carboxyl group at the 4–position, and a phenylglycyl group at the 7–position. Each of those differences between compound 6 and cefaclor contributes to the effectiveness of cefaclor as an orally administered antibiotic drug. The free carboxyl group at the 4–position is believed important for antibacterial activity; the chlorine increases cefaclor's antibiotic potency; and the phenylglycyl group enables cefaclor to be effective when taken orally.

To produce cefaclor from compound 6 requires four distinct steps. First, the hydroxy group is removed from the 3–position and is replaced by a chlorine atom, which results in the creation of "compound 7." Second, compound 7 is subjected to a reaction that removes the phenylacetyl group at the 7–position, which results in the creation of "compound 8." Third, a phenylglycyl group is added at the 7–position, which results in the creation of "compound 9." Fourth, the para-nitrobenzyl carboxylate ester is removed from the 4–position, which results in the creation of cefaclor.

On April 27, 1995, defendants Zenith Laboratories, Inc., and American Cyanamid Company obtained permission from the Food and Drug Administration to distribute cefaclor in this country. Defendant Biocraft Laboratories, Inc., had applied for FDA approval to manufacture and sell cefaclor in the United States but had not yet obtained that approval. All three have obtained large quantities of cefaclor that were manufactured in Italy by defendant Biochimica Opos, S.p.A.

On the same day that Zenith and Cyanamid obtained FDA approval to sell cefaclor in this country, Lilly obtained the rights to the '085 patent and filed suit against Zenith, Cyanamid, Biocraft, and Opos. In its complaint, Lilly sought a declaration that the domestic defendants' importation of cefaclor manufactured by Opos infringed Lilly's rights under several patents, including the '085 patent. Lilly also requested a preliminary injunction, based on the alleged infringement of claim 5 of the '085 patent, to bar the defendants from importing or inducing the importation of cefaclor manufactured by Opos. * * *

The Process Patent Amendments Act of 1988 was enacted to close a perceived loophole in the statutory scheme for protecting owners of United States patents. Prior to the enactment of the 1988 statute, a patentee holding a process patent could sue for infringement if others used the process in this country, but had no cause of action if such persons used the patented process abroad to manufacture products, and then imported, used, or sold the products in this country. * * * Congress changed the law by making it an act of infringement to import into the United States, or to sell or use within the United States "a product which is made by a process patented in the United States ... if the importation, sale, or use of the product occurs during the term of such process patent."

A concern raised during Congress's consideration of the process patent legislation was whether and to what extent the new legislation would affect products other than the direct and unaltered products of patented processes—that is, whether the new statute would apply when a product was produced abroad by a patented process but then modified or incorporated into other products before being imported into this country. Congress addressed that issue by providing that a product that is "made by" a patented process within the meaning of the statute "will ... not be considered to be so made after—(1) it is materially changed by subsequent processes; or (2) it becomes a trivial and nonessential component of another product." 35 U.S.C. § 271(g).

That language, unfortunately, is not very precise. Whether the product of a patented process is a "trivial and nonessential component" of another product is necessarily a question of degree. Even less well defined is the question whether the product of a patented process has been "materially changed" before its importation into this country. While applying that statutory language may be relatively easy in extreme cases, it is not at all easy in a closer case such as this one. * * * [T]he language of the statute refers to changes in the product; the statute permits the importation of an item that is derived from a product made by a patented process as long as that product is "materially changed" in the course of its conversion into the imported item. The reference to a "changed" product is very hard to square with Lilly's proposed test, which turns on the quite different question of whether the use or sale of the imported item impairs the economic value of the process patent. * * *

In the chemical context, a "material" change in a compound is most naturally viewed as a significant change in the compound's structure and properties. Without attempting to define with precision what classes of changes would be material and what would not, we share the district court's view that a change in chemical structure and properties as significant as the change between compound 6 and cefaclor cannot lightly be dismissed as immaterial. Although compound 6 and cefaclor share the basic cephem nucleus, which is the ultimate source of the antibiotic potential of all cephalosporins, the cephem nucleus is common to thousands of compounds, many of which have antibiotic activity, and many of which are dramatically different from others within the cephem family. Beyond the cephem nucleus that they have in common, compound 6 and cefaclor are different in four important structural respects, corresponding to the four discrete chemical steps between the two compounds. While the addition or removal of a protective group, standing alone, might not be sufficient to constitute a "material change" between two compounds (even though it could dramatically affect certain of their properties), the conversion process between compound 6 and cefaclor involves considerably more than the removal of a protective group. * * *

Acknowledging that the task of determining whether a product was "materially changed" prior to its importation would ultimately be left to the courts, the Committee then set out a "two-phased test" to "give the courts congressional guidance in what may be a difficult determination." The first part of the test restated the test set forth in the House report, i.e., that a product "will be considered made by the patented process ... if it would not be possible or commercially viable to make that product but for the use of the patented process." The Senate report provided an analysis of how the first part of the test should be applied in the case of chemical intermediates. The report explained:

> If the only way to have arrived at Y is to have used the patented process at some step, e.g., producing X as an intermediate, Y is infringing. If there is more than one way to have arrived [at] Y, but the patented process is the only commercially viable way to have done so, Y is infringing. If there are commercially viable non-infringing processes to have arrived at X, the connection between the patented process for producing chemical X and the ultimate product, chemical Y, is broken, and Y would be a non-infringing product having satisfied both phases of the test.

As we noted above, the record makes clear that there is at least one commercially viable process for making cefaclor that does not involve the patented method of synthesizing enol cephems (including compound 6). Opos does not use that non-infringing process, but under the test set forth in the Senate report, it is enough to defeat the claim of infringement that there is another way of producing the intermediate, even if the alleged infringer does not use that alternative process.

The Senate Committee described the second portion of the two-part test for identifying a "material change" as follows:

> A product will be considered to have been made by a patented process if the additional processing steps which are not covered by the patent do not change the physical or chemical properties of the product in a manner which changes the basic utility of the product [produced] by the patented process. However, a change in the physical or chemical properties of a product, even though minor, may be "material" if the change relates to a physical or chemical property which is an important feature of the product produced by the patented process. Usually a change in the physical form of a product (e.g., granules to powder, solid to liquid) or minor chemical conversion (e.g., conversion to a salt, base, acid, hydrate, ester, or addition or removal of a protecti[ve] group) would not be a "material" change.

It seems fairly clear that under this second part of the test, the change from compound 6 to cefaclor would be regarded as a material change. The chemical properties of the two compounds are completely different, the "basic utility" of the products is different, and the chemical structure of the two products is significantly different. The changes between compound 6 and cefaclor go far beyond the minor changes that the report described as not material, such as the conversion to a salt, base, acid, hydrate or ester, or the removal of a protective group. * * *

Lilly also challenges the district court's conclusion that it failed to show that it would suffer irreparable harm if the district court did not grant a preliminary injunction in this case. We conclude that the court did not commit clear error in finding that Lilly failed to prove irreparable harm; the court therefore acted within its discretion in denying Lilly's request for preliminary relief. Because Lilly has not made a strong showing on the issue of infringement, it is not entitled to a presumption of irreparable harm. Nor did the district court commit clear error in rejecting Lilly's arguments that, apart from the presumption, it would suffer irreparable harm in the absence of a preliminary injunction. In particular, the district court found that, under the specific circumstances of this case, "an award of money damages would be an adequate remedy in the event that Lilly ultimately establishes" infringement. In light of the structure of the cefaclor market, the court found that calculating lost profits would be a relatively simple task. The court also found that the two distributors who have been authorized by the FDA to sell cefaclor in this country have adequate assets to satisfy any judgment likely to be awarded if Lilly were to prevail on the merits of its infringement claim.

Lilly contends that the loss of profits on sales of cefaclor because of competition from the appellees will result in irreparable injury to Lilly's overall pharmaceutical research efforts. As the district court pointed out, however, that claim of injury is not materially different from any claim of injury by a business that is deprived of funds that it could usefully reinvest. If a claim of lost opportunity to conduct research were sufficient to compel a finding of irreparable harm, it is hard to imagine any manufacturer with a research and development program that could not make the same claim and thus be equally entitled to preliminary injunctive relief. Such a rule would convert the "extraordinary" relief of a preliminary injunction into a standard remedy, available whenever the plaintiff has shown a likelihood of success on the merits. * * *

■ RADER, CIRCUIT JUDGE (concurring):

* * * The court's majority places great emphasis on the legislative history to resolve the meaning of "material change"—a curious approach given its recognition that the legislative history contains "something . . . for each side." The enactment history is far from dispositive in this case. The record of the enactment of this provision evinces a bitter battle between the pharmaceutical industry and its generic industry competitors. In the first place, neither combatant could convince either house of Congress to enact a statutory standard clearly favorable to their segment of the industry. * * * Without a clear resolution in the statutory language, the battleground shifted to the committee reports. On this front, each combatant could find lobbyists to lace the reports with tutorials to the courts about applying the ambiguous provisions of section 271(g) in future litigation.

With a focus on future litigation, these committee reports became particularly unenlightening as an aid to interpret statutory language. These reports surrendered any pretext of informing members of Congress about the meaning of pending bills before a vote on the floor. Instead, these tutorials, by their own admission, addressed judicial officers, not legislative officers. * * * [T]he directly conflicting and confusing tests set forth in the section analysis leave little doubt that they were inserted by lobbyists for use in future litigation by their clients. In sum, the enactment history maps all the graves on this inconclusive legislative battleground, but shows no route away from the combat zone. * * *

Sadly this decision will create another massive loophole in the protection of patented processes. This decision will, in effect, deny protection to holders of process patents on intermediates as opposed to "final" products. This decision denies protection to a patented process anytime it is not the only way to make an intermediate, even if it is the most economically efficient way to produce the intermediate. In view of the purpose of the statute, compound 6 and cefaclor are essentially the same product. Compound 6 has no commercial use in the U.S. market except to make cefaclor. The patented process is thus in use to make compound 6—a product only four simple, well-known steps from cefaclor. The record shows no other current commercial use of compound 6.

Rather than attempting to distill an elixir from this intoxicating witches brew of enactment history, this court should interpret "material change" consistent with the overriding purpose of the Act—to provide protection to process patent holders. With its eye firmly fixed on the purpose of the Act, this court would avoid eliminating processes for intermediates from the protections of the 1988 Act.

Bio–Technology General Corp. v. Genentech, Inc.

80 F.3d 1553 (Fed.Cir.1996).

■ LOURIE, CIRCUIT JUDGE:

* * * Human growth hormone (hGH) is a 191–amino acid polypeptide hormone secreted by the anterior pituitary gland. It has important metabolic effects, including stimulation of protein synthesis and cellular uptake of amino acids. Genentech is the assignee of two patents relating to hGH that are at issue in this lawsuit. The first patent, U.S. Patent 4,601,980, is directed to a recombinant DNA method for producing a 191– or 192–amino acid human growth hormone product that is identical, or essentially identical, and functionally equivalent to the natural hormone. The product is useful in treating hypopituitary dwarfism in children.

Prior to the '980 invention, hGH could be obtained for therapeutic use only by extracting it from the pituitary glands of human cadavers. Known recombinant DNA methods for producing hGH were deficient; they yielded not only the amino acid sequence of the protein, but also a "leader sequence" of additional amino acids at the beginning of the protein. In the natural synthesis of hGH, the leader sequence enables the protein to emerge from a pituitary cell after expression; the leader is then enzymatically removed. When the product is recombinantly expressed in a bacterial host, however, the leader is not removed and it renders the resulting product biologically inactive.

The invention claimed in the '980 patent solved this problem by providing a method for directly expressing a human growth hormone expression product without a leader sequence. The inventors started with complementary DNA (cDNA) encoding hGH and its leader sequence, and cleaved the cDNA encoding the leader sequence along with a portion of the codons encoding hGH to obtain a cDNA fragment containing hGH codons 24–191. Next, they synthesized a DNA fragment corresponding to the 23 missing codons plus a "start" codon, and fused that DNA fragment to the cDNA fragment. They inserted the resulting semi-synthetic gene into bacterial cells, which directly expressed a 192–amino acid product, met-hGH, consisting of the hGH molecule and one additional amino acid, methionine ("met"), coded for by the start codon. Met-hGH has essentially the same biological activity as the natural hormone, hGH. The '980 patent teaches that the amino acid, methionine, may be cleaved intracellularly in the bacterial host to produce a product that is identical to the natural hormone. Genentech sells met-hGH and hGH under the trademarks Protropin® and Humatrope®, respectively.

The second patent in suit, U.S. Patent 4,342,832, also assigned to Genentech, contains essentially the same disclosure as the '980 patent. The '832 patent claims, however, are directed to a method for constructing a replicable cloning vehicle (e.g., a plasmid) capable, in a microbial organism, of expressing a particular polypeptide (e.g., human growth hormone).

Like Genentech, BTG [Bio–Technology General] manufactures hGH by recombinant DNA techniques using a plasmid that contains a semi-synthetic gene engineered to express hGH without a leader sequence. BTG incorporates the plasmid into bacteria, which then express insoluble met-hGH in the form of biologically-inactive inclusion bodies. In a final step, BTG carries out a purification process that involves recovering soluble met-hGH free of inclusion bodies and cleaving the extra methionine residue to produce the final product, biologically-active hGH. BTG manufactures hGH in Israel, and it plans to import the product for sale in the United States under the trademark Bio–Tropin®. BTG filed an Investigational New Drug Application (IND) for hGH with the Food and Drug Administration (FDA) in 1985. * * * The FDA approved the NDA in May 1995.

In January 1995, BTG sued Genentech in district court, seeking a declaratory judgment that the '980 and '832 patents are invalid, unenforceable, and not infringed by BTG. Genentech counterclaimed for infringement and moved for a preliminary injunction, arguing that BTG's importation of hGH into the United States would infringe the '980 and '832 patents. After a hearing, the district court found that Genentech had established a reasonable likelihood of success on the merits of its counterclaim * * * *

Claim 2 of the '980 patent reads as follows:

> 2. A method for producing human growth hormone which method comprises [1] culturing bacterial transformants containing recombinant plasmids which will, in a transformant bacterium, express a gene for human growth hormone unaccompanied by the leader sequence of human growth hormone or other extraneous protein bound thereto, and [2] isolating and purifying said expressed human growth hormone. * * *

Claim 2 uses broad, generic language to define the steps of isolating and purifying the recombinantly produced hGH product. Nothing in the claim language, specification, or prosecution history suggests that the claim is limited to any particular technique for isolating and purifying the product. Further, BTG's process meets these claim limitations. In its NDA, for example, BTG characterized its recovery of soluble, biologically-active hGH from insoluble, biologically-inactive met-hGH in the form of inclusion bodies as a "purification" step. Similarly, at the preliminary injunction hearing there was expert testimony that these processes constitute a "purification" step within the meaning of claim 2. Thus, BTG's process clearly involves "isolating and purifying [the] expressed human growth hormone," as generically defined in claim 2. * * *

The more difficult question is whether hGH is "a product which is made by a process patented in the United States," even though claim 1 of the '832 patent is directed to a method for producing a replicable cloning vehicle (e.g., a plasmid), not hGH. * * * The legislative history precisely anticipated this fact situation and indicated Congress's intent that infringement of a process for making a plasmid is not to be avoided by using it to express its intended protein. Moreover, the '832 patent itself explicitly contemplates that the patented process will be used as part of an overall process for producing hGH; indeed, the patent discloses in detail how to make hGH by carrying out the claimed process and other necessary steps. Thus, it cannot be said as a matter of law that the production of hGH is too remote from the claimed process of making a replicable cloning vehicle. We therefore find no error in the court's conclusion that hGH is a product that is "made by" the '832 patented process. * * *

BTG next argues that the district court's finding of irreparable harm is clearly erroneous. We disagree. The court correctly held that Genentech was entitled to a presumption of irreparable harm because Genentech made a strong showing of infringement and validity, and BTG's asserted defenses lacked substantial merit. BTG did not come forward with persuasive evidence to rebut the presumption of irreparable harm. In addition, the district court determined that Genentech would be harmed if BTG were allowed to enter the market because Genentech would lose revenues and goodwill, and would be required to reduce its research and development activities. BTG has not demonstrated that these findings are clearly erroneous. * * *

NOTES AND QUESTIONS

1. *Tangibility*. The court was not done with trying to resolve ambiguities in the statute introduced by the Process Patent Amendments. See Bayer AG v. Housey Pharm., Inc., 340 F.3d 1367, 1372–78 (Fed.Cir.2003) (holding that patents covering a method for readily identifying whether a test substance either inhibits or activates a target protein were not infringed within the meaning of section 271(g), which only addressed processes for manufacturing tangible products and not methods for generating information that later facilitated the development of pharmaceutical products); see also Amgen Inc. v. F. Hoffmann–La Roche Ltd., 580 F.3d 1340, 1377–80 (Fed.Cir.2009) (affirming jury conclusion that pegylation did not materially change bioengineered EPO). See generally Katherine A. Helm, Note, Outsourcing the Fire of Genius: The Effects of Patent Infringement Jurisprudence on Pharmaceutical Drug Development, 17 Fordham Intell. Prop. Media & Ent. L.J. 153 (2006); Lauren Shuttleworth, Note, Is 35 U.S.C. Section 271(f) Keeping Pace with the Times?: The Law After the Federal Circuit's Cardiac Pacemakers Decision, 29 J.L. & Com. 117 (2010).

2. *Patent buyouts*. Some commentators have suggested "patent buyouts" as a mechanism for controlling price and availability problems with critical pharmaceutical products. See James A. Kodak, Drug Patent Purchasing: A Potent Means of Lowering Drug Prices While Encouraging Innovation, 13 Quinnipiac Health L.J. 39 (2009); see also James Love & Tim Hubbard, Prizes for Innovation of New Medicines and Vaccines, 18 Annals Health L. 155 (2009); David W. Opderbeck, Patents, Essential Medicines, and the Innovation Game, 58 Vand. L. Rev. 501 (2005); Amanda Mitchell, Comment, Tamiflu, the Takings Clause, and Compulsory Licenses: An Exploration of the Government's Options for Accessing Medical Patents, 95 Cal. L. Rev. 535 (2007); Eduardo Porter, Do New Drugs Always Have to Cost So Much?, N.Y. Times, Nov. 14, 2004, § 3, at 5. Such proposals also might help to resolve a quandary involving antibiotics: with the spread of resistance, patents provide a necessary incentive for the development of new classes of these drugs but also create pressures to maximize their sales during the limited term of the patent even though public health authorities would prefer to delay widespread use of newer antimicrobial agents as long as possible. See Kevin Outterson, The Legal Ecology of Resistance: The Role of Antibiotic Resistance in Pharmaceutical Innovation, 31 Cardozo L. Rev. 613 (2010); Jessica P. Schulman, Comment, Patents and Public Health: The Problems with Using Patent Law Proposals to Combat Antibiotic Resistance, 59 DePaul L. Rev. 221 (2009).

3. *Compulsory licensing schemes*. Several industrialized countries have limited compulsory licensing rules applicable to medical technologies either where necessary to combat a threat to public health or after a period of non-use by the patent holder. See Reed Boland, RU 486 in France and England: Corporate Ethics and Compulsory Licensing, 20 Law Med. & Health Care 226, 230 (1992); see also Richard A. Epstein & F. Scott Kieff, Questioning the Frequency and Wisdom of Compulsory Licensing of Pharmaceutical Patents, 78 U. Chi. L. Rev. 71 (2011); Samuel M. Borowski, Comment, Saving Tomorrow from Today: Preserving Innovation in the Face of Compulsory Licensing, 36 Fla. St. U. L. Rev. 275 (2009). Until 1993, Canada used a compulsory licensing system as a mechanism to control the pricing of pharmaceuticals: companies were permitted to market generic copies of drugs still under patent upon payment of minimal royalties to the patent holder. See Novopharm Ltd. v. Janssen Pharm. N.V., 41 C.P.R.3d 194 (Can.1992) (refusing to require more than a 4% royalty); see also An Act to Amend the Patent Act, 1993 S.C., ch. 2, § 3 (Can.); Edward Hore, A Comparison of United States and Canadian Laws as They Affect Generic Pharmaceutical Market Entry, 55 Food & Drug L.J. 373 (2000); George Tsai, Note, Canada's Access to Medicines Regime: Lessons for Compulsory Licensing Schemes Under the WTO Doha Declaration, 49 Va. J. Int'l L. 1063 (2009). Compulsory licensing remains an option for public health emergencies. See Taiwo A. Oriola, Against the Plague: Exemption of Pharmaceutical Patent Rights as a Biosecurity Strategy, 2007 U. Ill. J.L. Tech. & Pol'y 287; Shankar Vedantam & Terence Chea, Drug Firm Plays Defense in Anthrax Scare: For Now, U.S. Declines to Suspend Bayer's Patent and Authorize Generic Cipro, Wash. Post, Oct. 20, 2001, at A4 (reporting that Canada had invoked its compulsory licensing authority for this antibiotic).

4. *Technology transfer between industrialized and developing countries*. Historically, other countries, especially Third World nations, provided little or no intellectual property protection for pharmaceuticals. See F.M. Scherer, The Pharmaceutical Industry and World Intellectual Property Standards, 53 Vand. L. Rev. 2245 (2000); Theresa B. Lewis, Comment, Patent Protection for the Pharmaceutical Industry: A Survey of the Patent Laws of Various Countries, 30 Int'l Law. 835 (1996). Developing countries have sought to justify patent piracy, particularly in connection with medical technologies, as a human rights imperative. See Uche Ewelukwa, Patent Wars in the Valley of the Shadow of Death: The Pharmaceutical Industry,

Ethics, and Global Trade, 59 U. Miami L. Rev. 203 (2005); Lissett Ferreira, Note, Access to Affordable HIV/AIDS Drugs: The Human Rights Obligations of Multinational Pharmaceutical Corporations, 71 Fordham L. Rev. 1133 (2002); Symposium, Access to Medicines in the Developing World: International Facilitation or Hindrance?, 20 Wis. Int'l L.J. 451 (2002); see also William W. Fisher & Talha Syed, Global Justice in Healthcare: Developing Drugs for the Developing World, 40 UC Davis L. Rev. 581 (2007); David Brown, Pfizer Donating 135 Million Doses of Anti–Blindness Drug, Wash. Post, Nov. 12, 2003, at A7; Justin Gillis, Cure for Neglected Diseases: Funding, Wash. Post, Apr. 25, 2006, at D1 (reporting that substantial donations from charitable foundations have spurred research into tropical diseases by pharmaceutical companies). Conversely, these countries argue that industrialized nations have exploited the rich biological resources of the Third World in the search for new pharmaceuticals. See Cynthia M. Ho, Biopiracy and Beyond: A Consideration of Socio-cultural Conflicts with Global Patent Policies, 39 U. Mich. J.L. Reform 433 (2006); see also Katie Bates, Note, A Penny for Your Thoughts: Private and Collective Contracting for Traditional Medicinal Knowledge Modeled on Bioprospecting Contracts in Costa Rica, 41 Ga. L. Rev. 961 (2007).

Responding to demands for access to affordable AIDS drugs in Africa and elsewhere, governments have undertaken special initiatives to supply treatments. See David Brown, We Can Treat AIDS, but Who Will Pay for It? A Rich–Poor Divide Remains, 30 Years into the Global Epidemic, Wash. Post, May 31, 2011, at E1 (reporting that, with $16 billion spent last year, more than "6 million people in the developing world are now receiving life-extending ART [antiretroviral therapy], . . . less than half the 14.6 million HIV-infected people who should be getting treatment under the World Health Organization's latest guidelines"). These have tended, however, to supply only older treatment options. See Jay Purcell, Note, Adverse Clinical and Public Health Consequences of Limited Anti–Retroviral Licensing, 25 Berkeley Tech. L.J. 103 (2010); see also Horace E. Anderson, Jr., We Can Work It out: Co-op Compulsory Licensing as the Way Forward in Improving Access to Anti-retroviral Drugs, 16 B.U. J. Sci. & Tech. L. 167 (2010); Alexandra G. Watson, Note, International Intellectual Property Rights: Do TRIPS' Flexibilities Permit Sufficient Access to Affordable HIV/AIDS Medicines in Developing Countries?, 32 B.C. Int'l & Comp. L. Rev. 143 (2009); Donald G. McNeil, Jr., Pharmaceutical Company Agrees to Share AIDS and Hepatitis Drugs with Patent Pool, N.Y. Times, July 12, 2011, at D6. What other types of drugs might qualify as sufficiently critical to justify such distribution programs? See Cynthia M. Ho, Access to Essential Medicines, 82 Chi.–Kent. L. Rev. 1469 (2007); Symposium, Access to HPV Vaccines: Human Rights and Global Health, 35 Am. J.L. & Med. 247 (2009); David Brown, In High–Stakes Fight over Non-infectious Diseases, an Old Issue, Wash. Post, Sept. 20, 2011, at A2 (reporting that a new global fight against noncommunicable diseases has posed questions about whether Doha's compulsory licensing mechanism might extend to drugs used to treat conditions such as heart disease and cancer).

5. *Free trade agreements*. Under the auspices of the World Trade Organization (WTO), which includes 140 nations as members and accounts for 90% of global trade, the Trade–Related Aspects of Intellectual Property Rights (TRIPS) Agreement sought to harmonize patent laws around the world, and it required that signatories grant at least 20 years of protection to novel and useful pharmaceutical products and processes. See TRIPS arts. 27.1 & 33; see also Aaron X. Fellmeth, Secrecy, Monopoly, and Access to Pharmaceuticals in International Trade Law: Protection of Marketing Approval Data Under the TRIPS Agreement, 45 Harv. Int'l L.J. 443 (2004); Jean O. Lanjouw, A New Global Patent Regime for Diseases: U.S. and International Legal Issues, 16 Harv. J.L. & Tech. 85 (2002). TRIPS and other free trade agreements have spurred revisions in domestic patent laws. See, e.g., Amy Kapczynski, Harmonization and Its Discontents: A Case Study of TRIPS Implementation in India's Pharmaceutical Sector, 97 Cal. L. Rev. 1571 (2009); Janice M. Mueller, The Tiger Awakens: The Tumultuous Transformation of India's Patent System and the Rise of Indian Pharmaceutical Innovation, 68 U. Pitt. L. Rev. 491 (2007); Naomi A. Bass, Note, Implications of the TRIPS Agreement for Developing Countries: Pharmaceutical Patent Laws in Brazil and South Africa in the 21st Century, 34 Geo. Wash. Int'l L. Rev. 191 (2002). For drugs patented after May 15, 1997, the WTO prohibits routine compulsory licensing, but, in case of a national emergency, a signatory may authorize compulsory licensing of patented pharmaceuticals if necessary to protect the public health. See Aditi Bagchi, Note, Compulsory Licensing and the Duty of Good Faith in TRIPS, 55 Stan. L. Rev. 1529 (2003). Subsequent developments may have watered down these restrictions somewhat. See Frederick M. Abbott & Jerome H. Reichman, The Doha Round's Public Health Legacy: Strategies for the Production and Diffusion of Patented Medicines Under the Amended TRIPS Provisions, 10 J. Int'l Econ. L. 921 (2007); Daniel R. Cahoy, Confronting Myths and Myopia on the Road from Doha, 42 Ga. L. Rev. 131 (2007); Sara Germano, Note, Compulsory Licensing of Pharmaceuticals in Southeast Asia: Paving the Way for Greater Use of the TRIPS Flexibility in Low– and Middle–Income Countries, 76 UMKC L. Rev. 273 (2007); Riadh Quadir, Note, Patent Stalemate? The WTO's Essential Medicines Impasse Between Pharmas and Least Developed Countries, 61 Rutgers L. Rev. 437 (2009); see also Brook K. Baker, Ending Drug Registration Apartheid: Taming Data Exclusivity and Patent/Registration Linkage, 34 Am. J.L. & Med. 303 (2008); Anand Giridharadas, U.S. Pushes to Limit Generic Drug Rights: Agreements Seek to Extend Monopolies in Exchange for Improvements in Trade, Int'l Herald Trib., Apr. 19, 2006, at 1 (reporting that the United States has extracted concessions related to pharmaceutical patents in bilateral trade negotiations, including limitations on the compulsory licensing power narrower than permitted in TRIPS).

4. GENERIC DRUGS AND PATENT EXTENSION

Bayer AG v. Elan Pharmaceutical Research Corp.

212 F.3d 1241 (Fed.Cir.2000).

■ SCHALL, CIRCUIT JUDGE:

Bayer AG and Bayer Corporation own United States Patent No. 5,264,446. The '446 patentclaims a pharmaceutical composition that contains nifedipine crystals of a defined specific surface area (SSA). The patent also claims the composition's method of preparation and a method of treatment using the composition. Bayer sued Elan Pharmaceutical Research Corporation and Elan Corporation, PLC in the United States District Court for the Northern District of Georgia alleging infringement by Elan of the '446 patent * * * based on Elan's filing of an abbreviated new drug application (ANDA) seeking approval by the Food and Drug Administration (FDA) of a generic version of Bayer's Adalat CC, Bayer's commercial embodiment of the pharmaceutical composition claimed in the '446 patent. * * *

[T]he Hatch–Waxman Act amended the Federal Food, Drug, and Cosmetic Act as well as the patent laws. See Bristol–Myers Squibb Co. v. Royce Lab., Inc., 69 F.3d 1130, 1131–32 (Fed.Cir.1995); Dupont Merck Pharm. Co. v. Bristol–Myers Squibb Co., 62 F.3d 1397, 1399–401 (Fed.Cir. 1995). Under the FDCA, as amended by the Act, a pharmaceutical manufacturer submits an ANDA when seeking expedited FDA approval of a generic version of a drug previously approved by the FDA (a "listed drug"). An ANDA can be filed if the generic drug manufacturer's active ingredient is the "bioequivalent" of the listed drug. When submitting an ANDA, a manufacturer must certify one of four statements concerning the applicable listed drug: (i) the listed drug is not patented (a "Paragraph I certification"); (ii) the listed drug's patent has expired (a "Paragraph II certification"); (iii) the expiration date of the listed drug's patent (a "Paragraph III certification"); or (iv) the listed drug's patent "is invalid or . . . it will not be infringed by the manufacture, use, or sale of the new drug" covered by the ANDA (a "Paragraph IV certification"). 21 U.S.C. § 355(j)(2)(A)(vii)(I)–(IV). If an ANDA is certified under Paragraph IV, the applicant must notify the patent's owner of the certification.

An ANDA certified under Paragraphs I or II is approved immediately after meeting all applicable scientific and regulatory requirements. An ANDA certified under Paragraph III must, even after meeting all applicable scientific and regulatory requirements, wait for approval until the listed drug's patent expires. An ANDA certified under Paragraph IV is approved immediately after meeting all applicable scientific and regulatory requirements unless the listed drug's patent owner brings suit for infringement under 35 U.S.C. § 271(e)(2)(A) within forty-five days of receiving the notice required under 21 U.S.C. § 355(j)(2)(B). If suit is brought, the FDA is required to suspend approval of the ANDA, and the FDA cannot approve the ANDA until the earliest of three dates: (i) the date of the court's decision that the listed drug's patent is either invalid or not infringed; (ii) the date the listed drug's patent expires if the court finds the listed drug's patent infringed; or (iii) subject to modification by the court, the date that is thirty months from the date the owner of the listed drug's patent received notice of the filing of a Paragraph IV certification.

The Act modified the patent laws to provide that "[i]t shall not be an act of infringement to make, use, or sell . . . a patented invention . . . solely for uses reasonably related to the development and submission of information under a Federal law which regulates the manufacture, use, or sale of drugs." 35 U.S.C. § 271(e)(1). A Paragraph IV certification, however, is deemed to be an act of infringement "if the purpose of such a submission is to obtain approval under the [FDCA] to engage in the commercial manufacture, use, or sale of a drug . . . claimed in a patent or the use of which is claimed in a patent before the expiration of such a patent." 35 U.S.C. § 271(e)(2)(A); see also Glaxo, Inc. v. Novopharm, Ltd., 110 F.3d 1562, 1567 (Fed.Cir.1997). "If the court determines that the patent is not invalid and that infringement would occur, and that therefore the ANDA applicant's paragraph IV certification is incorrect, the patent owner is entitled to an order that FDA approval of the ANDA containing the paragraph IV certification not be effective until the patent expires." *Royce Lab.*, 69 F.3d at 1135.

The application that matured into the '446 patent was filed on August 20, 1981; the '446 patent issued on November 23, 1993. The '446 patent relates to solid pharmaceutical compositions, such as tablets, that contain nifedipine crystals of a given SSA, combined with a solid diluent that is adapted for formation into tablets. Nifedipine is a compound that acts on the body's circulation—a coronary vasodilator—and is used to control such medical conditions as high blood pressure. The '446 patent attempts, through its claimed SSA for nifedipine crystals, to address the problem of poor solubility—absorption of nifedipine into the blood—while still maintaining a sustained presence of nifedipine in the blood, i.e., high bioavailability. The patent seeks to achieve its objective without using such disadvantageous means as large-sized tablets, which are hard to swallow, or liquid formulations, which are very expensive and require protection from light.

The '446 patent contains twelve independent claims; the claims cover actual compositions of the nifedipine drug, methods of making the drug, and methods of treatment using the drug. Each claim specifies a SSA range for the nifedipine crystal used. Claim 1, which Bayer asserts against Elan, is representative of the composition claims and recites the broadest SSA range:

> 1. A solid pharmaceutical composition comprising as the active ingredient an effective amount of nifedipine crystals with a specific surface area of 1.0 to 4 m^2/g, in admixture with a solid diluent, to result in a sustained release of nifedipine.

Elan submitted an ANDA to the FDA on April 30, 1997, seeking approval for a product that is bioequivalent to Bayer's Adalat CC product. Elan's ANDA covers a once-daily formulation of nifedipine—an extended release tablet dosage form containing 30 mg of nifedipine. With its ANDA, Elan filed a Certificate of Quality and Analysis (COA). The COA related to an analysis performed by * * * an independent laboratory, on April 17, 1996 with respect to the micronized—finely ground—nifedipine provided to

Elan by its nifedipine supplier, Arzneimittelwerk Dresden GmbH (AWD). According to the COA, the measured SSA of the micronized AWD nifedipine crystals was 6.15 m^2/g. The tablets made from these micronized nifedipine crystals and tested for the ANDA process are referred to by the parties as the "biobatch." Elan also filed with its ANDA a Paragraph IV certification, in which it stated that its nifedipine composition did not infringe the '446 patent * * * *

Determination of a claim of infringement involves a two step inquiry. First, the claims are construed, a question of law in which the scope of the asserted claims is defined. Second, the claims, as construed, are compared to the accused device. This is a question of fact. To prevail, the plaintiff must establish by a preponderance of the evidence that the accused device infringes one or more claims of the patent either literally or under the doctrine of equivalents.

Literal infringement requires the patentee to prove that the accused device contains each limitation of the asserted claim(s). If any claim limitation is absent from the accused device, there is no literal infringement as a matter of law. The district court, in deciding the issue of literal infringement, first looked to Elan's ANDA, noting that it "sets a specification for its proposed product of a specific surface area greater than 5 m^2/g." The district court also observed that AWD, Elan's nifedipine supplier, cannot sell nifedipine with a SSA under 4.7 m^2/g to anyone who will use or sell a product containing AWD's nifedipine in the United States. In addition, the court stated that results in the COA indicated that Elan's biobatch tablets had a SSA of 6.15 m^2/g. Faced with this evidence, the court found that Bayer had offered only "unsubstantiated assertions" that there was uncertainty as to whether Elan and AWD would meet Elan's ANDA specification. Thus, Bayer had failed to meet its burden of defeating summary judgment by showing a genuine issue of material fact with respect to the issue of literal infringement of the '446 patent. The district court concluded by noting that Bayer could sue Elan for infringement if Elan begins manufacturing for commercial sale a product with a SSA within 1.0 to 4 m^2/g, as claimed by the '446 patent.

Bayer's first argument on appeal is that a genuine issue of material fact exists as to whether Elan's biobatch infringes the '446 patent. Bayer contends that an infringing biobatch is material evidence of infringement under 35 U.S.C. § 271(e)(2). In that regard, Bayer asserts that there is no evidence as to the SSA of Elan's micronized nifedipine crystals just before the crystals were mixed to make biobatch tablets, and it points to certain evidence that nifedipine crystals grow over time before being mixed into tablets, thereby causing the SSA of the crystals to decrease. Bayer also argues that there are genuine issues of material fact as to whether Elan will be able to comply with its SSA specification and thus produce a noninfringing product. Bayer asserts that Elan has not specified a validated test protocol or test equipment to measure the SSA of its nifedipine. It also asserts that Elan has not produced any samples, or test data from samples, under the requirements set forth in Elan's amended ANDA specification. * * *

The focus, under § 271(e)(2)(A), is on "what the ANDA applicant will likely market if its application is approved, an act that has not yet occurred." *Glaxo*, 110 F.3d at 1569. "[T]his hypothetical inquiry is properly grounded in the ANDA application and the extensive materials typically submitted in its support." Id. Therefore, it is proper for the court to consider the ANDA itself, materials submitted by the ANDA applicant in support of the ANDA, and any other relevant evidence submitted by the applicant or patent holder. However, if the ANDA "is to sell [a] well-defined compound," then the "ultimate question of infringement is usually straightforward."

We believe that the specification in Elan's ANDA mandates a finding of no literal infringement. Elan's specification indicates that "the specific surface area of the micronized nifedipine is to be 5 m^2/g or greater," and that this SSA "will be reflected in certification of analysis provided by Elan's supplier (AWD)." Elan further defines its specification by noting that it is "Elan's intention to measure specific surface area on the micronized nifedipine material prior to use (within 5 working days prior to blend manufacture) to ensure that the 5 m^2/g specification for specific surface area is met. Material not meeting this specification will not be used for manufacture." Thus, according to Elan's ANDA specification, nifedipine used in its drug cannot have a SSA of less than 5 m^2/g within five working days prior to manufacturing. Significantly, Bayer does not allege that within five working days, the nifedipine's SSA will decrease from 5 m^2/g to a literally infringing size of 4 m^2/g or less. Therefore, under the ANDA specification, Elan cannot literally infringe the '446 patent.

Bayer's focus on the biobatch, whose test data was submitted with Elan's ANDA, is misplaced for two reasons. First, the Act specifically provides an ANDA applicant immunity from allegations of infringement for acts that are necessary in preparing an ANDA. The production of a biobatch, and the submission of a COA regarding this biobatch, are required in the ANDA application process. Thus, even if the biobatch falls within the scope of the claims, the Act specifically indicates that such actions by Elan cannot constitute infringement. In addition, the focus of the infringement inquiry under 35 U.S.C. § 271(e)(2)(A) is on the product that will be sold after the FDA's approval of the ANDA, not on the biobatch that is produced to facilitate FDA approval. The filing of an ANDA is considered an act of infringement under § 271(e)(2)(A), but this "act" is merely a vehicle "to create case or controversy jurisdiction to enable a court to promptly resolve" a dispute concerning an infringement that will happen in the future.

Second, the specification in Elan's ANDA defines its product in a way that directly addresses the question of infringement—the SSA of the nifedipine crystals. Elan is bound by this specification. The dispute between the parties concerns the SSA of the nifedipine that Elan will use in its drug. Elan stated to the FDA that the SSA of its nifedipine composition will not be less than 5 m^2/g, clarifying in an amendment that the SSA will be 5 m^2/g or more five working days before manufacturing. Elan is required, under 21 C.F.R. § 314.94(a)(9), to comply with 21 C.F.R. § 314.50(d)(1)(i) and state the ANDA drug's specification, including its particle size and the process controls used in manufacturing to assure the specification is met. Elan, in its initial ANDA and answers to FDA questions, provided this information and sought approval under 21 U.S.C. § 355(j) based on its specification.

If any of the statements in Elan's specification are false, Elan is subject to civil penalties and the withdrawal of the approval of its drug. Additionally, if Elan introduces a drug into interstate commerce without complying with the approval requirements of 21 U.S.C. § 355, it is subject to various additional penalties, including an injunction, criminal sanctions, seizure of the unapproved drug, and debarment of its corporation and individual officials from submitting or assisting in the submission of an ANDA in the future. Elan also would be subject to criminal prosecution for making false statements to the FDA under 18 U.S.C. § 1001, conspiring to defraud the United States under 18 U.S.C. § 371, and obstructing proceedings before a federal agency under 18 U.S.C. § 1501. If Elan changes its ANDA, it must file the changes with the FDA, and if the changes are to the drug's specification, Elan must obtain approval for the changes before they can be made. In short, the only drug Elan can produce upon approval of the ANDA at issue is a drug that does not literally infringe the '446 patent.

Bayer is correct that in *Glaxo*, we approved of the district court looking to a biobatch for help in deciding the issue of infringement. However, the biobatch in *Glaxo* was properly considered because the ANDA specification in that case did not define the compound in a manner that directly addressed the issue of infringement. The compound in *Glaxo* existed in multiple crystalline forms and mixtures, possibly containing either Form 1 or Form 2 ranitidine hydrochloride (RHCl), and the asserted patent covered mixtures that contained Form 2 RHCl. Thus, the ANDA at issue, which permitted the marketed product to have a Form 1 RHCl purity as low as 90%, did not address the question of infringement—whether a drug produced under the ANDA would contain Form 2 RHCl. Here, however, the ANDA directly addresses the question of infringement; it recites that the SSA of Elan's drug will be 5 m^2/g or above. Thus, we have before us an ANDA specification that, in the words of *Glaxo*, describes a "well-defined compound," and thus "the ultimate question of infringement is . . . straightforward." 110 F.3d at 1569. Elan's biobatch does not control the issue of infringement. * * *

If an asserted claim does not literally read on an accused product, infringement may still occur under the doctrine of equivalents if there is not a substantial difference between the limitations of the claim and the accused product. Infringement under the doctrine of equivalents is a question of fact. Prosecution history estoppel is one limitation on the scope of equivalents that a patentee can claim under the doctrine of equivalents and is a question of law. Prosecution history estoppel can occur as a result of (i) amendments made to overcome patentability rejections or (ii) arguments made during prosecution that show "a clear and unmistakable surrender of subject matter."

In addressing whether there was a genuine issue of material fact as to infringement by Elan under the doctrine of equivalents, the district court looked to see whether prosecution history estoppel prevented Bayer from claiming a SSA beyond the upper limit of 4 m^2/g set forth in claim 1 of the '446 patent. In that connection, the court examined the entire prosecution history of the '446 patent to determine what subject matter, if any, a competitor would reasonably conclude was surrendered by Bayer. The court noted that, during prosecution, Bayer argued that the SSA range of 0.5 to 6 m^2/g originally claimed in claim 1 provided unexpected results, but the examiner did not agree. The court further noted that, in response to the examiner's rejection * * *, Bayer amended claims 1 through 3 by changing the SSA range to 1.0 to 4 m^2/g and canceled claim 4. The district court also considered declarations submitted by Bayer, as well as arguments made by Bayer's attorney, to support Bayer's claim of an unexpected, plateau-like effect for a SSA range of 1.0 to 4 m^2/g, with high bioavailability dropping off outside this range. Based on this evidence, the district court determined, as a matter of law, that Bayer had surrendered subject matter outside the claimed range of 1.0 to 4 m^2/g * * * *

We need not resolve the question of why Bayer amended its claims and whether its reasons related to patentability because it is clear that, regardless of why it amended its claims, when it did so it unmistakably surrendered coverage to SSAs above 4 m^2/g. As a result, it is precluded from asserting that the nifedipine composition that is the subject of Elan's ANDA infringes the '446 patent under the doctrine of equivalents. * * *

In determining whether there has been a clear and unmistakable surrender of subject matter, the prosecution history must be examined as a whole. See Pharmacia & Upjohn Co. v. Mylan Pharm., Inc., 170 F.3d 1373, 1376 (Fed.Cir.1999). * * * Bayer repeatedly argued that its claimed range of 1.0 to 4 m^2/g produced unique results and was a superior and inventive range. At the same time, the declarations it submitted praised the benefits of the 1.0 to 4 m^2/g SSA range, claiming that this range exhibited a plateau-like effect by producing the maximum dissolution of nifedipine into the blood. * * * This case is very similar to *Pharmacia*. There, we concluded that a patentee had relinquished claim coverage to any type of lactose that was not spray-dried. During prosecution, the patentee argued that the use of spray-dried lactose was "a critical feature" of the claimed invention and that using lactose that was not spray-dried resulted in a pharmaceutical powder that was not readily processed. We held that these statements were "reasonably interpreted as a broad disclaimer of what the invention was not." 170 F.3d at 1378. * * * In this case, during prosecution, Bayer emphasized the inventive nature of its claimed SSA range and the disadvantages of SSAs outside its claimed range. Thus, Bayer's statements, in total, amount to a "clear and unmistakable surrender," so that a competitor would reasonably believe that Bayer had surrendered SSAs outside the claimed range. * * *

NOTES AND QUESTIONS

1. *The Hatch–Waxman compromise.* As explained in *Bayer*, Congress enacted legislation in 1984 to facilitate the introduction of generic drugs without undermining incentives for innovation. See Glaxo, Inc. v. Novopharm, Ltd., 110 F.3d 1562, 1568 (Fed.Cir.1997) ("[The] legislation [was] designed to benefit makers of generic drugs, research-based pharmaceutical companies, and not incidentally the public. The Hatch–Waxman Act, inter alia, allows makers of generic drugs to market generic versions of patented drugs as soon as possible after expiration of the relevant patents, while providing patent holders with limited extensions of patent term in order to recover a portion of the market exclusivity lost during the lengthy process of development and FDA review."). Another court summarized the different ways that the Hatch–Waxman Act simplified clearance of generic drugs:

> Before 1984, a company that wished to make a generic version of an FDA-approved brand-name drug had to file another NDA. Preparation of the second NDA was as time-consuming and costly as the original, because the application had to include new studies showing the drug's safety and effectiveness. In 1984, Congress ... simplified the procedure for obtaining approval of generic drugs.... Subsequent applicants who wished to manufacture generic versions of the original drug were ... allowed to rely on the FDA's previous determination that the drug is safe and effective. As a result of the ANDA innovation under Hatch–Waxman, generic makers can obtain expedited approval to market generic versions of drugs that have undergone the rigors of "pioneer" approval under the NDA process. Moreover, generic makers are permitted to manufacture and use drugs protected by a patent(s) if the otherwise infringing activity is related to the development and submission of an ANDA. Finally, Hatch–Waxman establishes an ANDA certification process, whereby generic makers can obtain expedited approval for their ANDAs before expiration of the pioneer maker's patent.

Mylan Pharm., Inc. v. Henney, 94 F.Supp.2d 36, 39 (D.D.C.2000), vacated as moot, 276 F.3d 627 (D.C.Cir.2002). Because of implementation problems discussed later in this chapter, Congress revised certain aspects of this legislation. See Medicare Prescription Drug, Improvement, and Modernization Act of 2003, Pub. L. No. 108–173, tit. XI(A), 117 Stat. 2448; Colleen Kelly, The Balance Between Innovation and Competition: The Hatch–Waxman Act, the 2003 Amendments, and Beyond, 66 Food & Drug L.J. 417 (2011). When it created a regulatory pathway for the approval of generic biologic products, however, Congress deviated in several important respects from the patent provisions of the Hatch–Waxman Act. See Pub. L. No. 111–148, tit. VII(A), 124 Stat. 804 (2010); Michael P. Dougherty, The New Follow-on-Biologics Law: A Section by Section Analysis of the Patent

Litigation Provisions in the Biologics Price Competition and Innovation Act of 2009, 65 Food & Drug L.J. 231 (2010); see also Chap. 11(A).

2. *Timing is everything.* Patent holders can wait more than 45 days to file an infringement claim against an ANDA filer, though then they lose the benefit of an automatic 30–month stay on FDA approval of generics. Cf. Mutual Pharm. Co. v. Pfizer Inc., 307 F.Supp.2d 88, 93–95 (D.D.C.2004) (dismissing a declaratory judgment action brought by the second filer of an ANDA against the pioneer manufacturer after the latter failed to bring a patent infringement claim within 45 days of receiving plaintiff's paragraph IV certification). Conversely, upon receiving FDA approval, generic competitors do not have to delay marketing until the conclusion of any infringement lawsuits (though the failure to wait would expose them to liability for damages if they ultimately lose). See Julie Schmit, Drugmakers Gamble Big on Generics, USA Today, Aug. 24, 2004, at 1B (calling this strategy "launch at risk"); see also Sanofi–Synthelabo v. Apotex Inc., 488 F.Supp.2d 317 (S.D.N.Y.) (preliminarily enjoining sales of an FDA-approved generic version of Plavix® because the brand-name manufacturer was likely to prevail on the merits of its patent infringement claims), aff'd, 470 F.3d 1368 (Fed.Cir.2006). In 2003, Congress amended the statutes by allowing ANDA filers to seek a declaratory judgment to establish "patent certainty" before launch in the event that the NDA holder declined to bring an infringement action within 45 days. See Teva Pharms. USA, Inc. v. Novartis Pharms. Corp., 482 F.3d 1330, 1340–46 & n.5 (Fed.Cir.2007) (allowing ANDA filer to pursue such an action where the NDA holder had strategically brought an infringement claim on its composition patent but not (yet) on its four method patents). In other settings, the Declaratory Judgment Act provides only limited opportunities for potential competitors to test the validity of patents. See Medimmune, Inc. v. Genentech, Inc., 427 F.3d 958, 962–65 (Fed.Cir.2005) (holding that, where the manufacturer of Synagis® continued to pay royalties under its license to use a patented process covering monoclonal antibodies, the court lacked jurisdiction to entertain a challenge to the patent), rev'd, 549 U.S. 118 (2007).

3. *Patent term restoration.* Under Hatch–Waxman, pharmaceutical companies may receive patent extensions for time lost awaiting FDA approval as well as half of the time expended in preapproval clinical trials, but the extension is capped at five years. See 35 U.S.C. § 156; see also Fisons plc v. Quigg, 876 F.2d 99 (Fed.Cir.1989) (sustaining the PTO's decision that line extensions (i.e., new uses and dosage forms) of a previously approved active ingredient were not eligible for patent term extension because these did not represent the first permitted commercial marketing or use of the product, rejecting the manufacturer's argument that the statutory reference to "product" meant the whole approved drug product rather than just the active ingredient); Pfizer Inc. v. Ranbaxy Lab. Ltd., 405 F.Supp.2d 495, 511–12 (D.Del.2005) (rejecting objections to patent term extension granted to the manufacturer of Lipitor® (atorvastatin calcium)), aff'd in part, 457 F.3d 1284 (Fed.Cir.2006); cf. Merck & Co. v. Hi–Tech Pharmacal Co., 482 F.3d 1317, 1321–24 (Fed.Cir.2007) (holding that a patent term extension under § 156 may be applied to a patent subject to a terminal disclaimer (i.e., accepting the expiration date of an earlier patent) filed to overcome an obviousness-type double-patenting rejection); Kate S. Gaudry, Uncharted Territories of the Patent–Restoration Due–Diligence Challenge, 66 Food & Drug L.J. 121 (2011). Occasionally, companies succeed in persuading Congress to enact private bills granting them patent extensions on particular products. See Richard M. Cooper, Legislative Patent Extensions, 48 Food & Drug L.J. 59 (1993). Even so, the effective (i.e., post-approval) patent life of pharmaceuticals is seven years shorter on average than that enjoyed by patented products in other industries. See Bruce N. Kuhlik, The Assault on Pharmaceutical Intellectual Property, 71 U. Chi. L. Rev. 93, 96–97 (2004).

Photocure ASA v. Kappos

603 F.3d 1372 (Fed.Cir.2010).

■ Newman, Circuit Judge:

* * * The patent term extension statute was enacted in recognition of the lengthy procedures associated with regulatory review of a new drug product, for the patent term continues to run although the product cannot be sold or used until authorized by the [FDA]. The statute was designed to restore a portion of the patent life lost during the period of regulatory review, in order to preserve the economic incentive for development of new therapeutic products. The following provisions are relevant to this case:

> (a) The term of a patent which claims a product, a method of using a product, or a method of manufacturing a product shall be extended in accordance with this section . . . , if . . .
>
> (4) the product has been subject to a regulatory review period before its commercial marketing or use;
>
> (5)(A) except as provided in subparagraph (B) or (C) [not here relevant], the permission for the commercial marketing or use of the product after such regulatory review period is the first permitted commercial marketing or use of the product under the provision of law under which such regulatory review period occurred . . . .
>
> (f) For purposes of this section:
>
> (1) The term "product" means: (A) A drug product. . . .
>
> (2) The term "drug product" means the active ingredient of—(A) a new drug, antibiotic drug, or human biological product (as those terms are used in the [FDCA] and the [PHSA]), . . . including any salt or ester of the active ingredient, as a single entity or in combination with another active ingredient.

35 U.S.C. § 156.

The drug product Metvixia, whose active ingredient is MAL [methyl aminolevulinate] hydrochloride, is used in photochemotherapy or photodynamic therapy to treat actinic keratoses, which are precancerous cell growths on the skin. When the Metvixia cream is applied to the skin, the MAL hydrochloride concentrates in the cells to be treated. The cells use

MAL hydrochloride to form an excess amount of a naturally-occurring, light sensitive compound called protoporphyrin IX ("Pp"). On exposure to light, the Pp is activated and a chemical reaction ensues that kills the precancerous cells.

MAL hydrochloride was a new chemical compound, and [it] was patented in U.S. Patent No. 6,034,267 ("the '267 patent") on the basis of its improved therapeutic properties as compared with the known compound aminolevulinic acid [ALA] hydrochloride. MAL is the methyl ester of ALA. ALA hydrochloride had previously received FDA approval for the same therapeutic use. The specification of the '267 patent discusses and exemplifies the biological and physiological advantages of the MAL product over the ALA product; MAL is characterized as "better able to penetrate skin and other tissues," as a "better enhancer[] of Pp production than ALA," and as providing "improved selectivity for the target tissue to be treated." Separate patentability of the MAL product and its use is not disputed.

The product containing MAL hydrochloride was a "new drug" * * * and required full FDA approval. The clinical and other tests for demonstration of safety and efficacy of the MAL hydrochloride product consumed four and a half years. After FDA approval was received, Photocure applied for the statutory extension of the term of the '267 patent. The PTO consulted with the FDA, in accordance with the[ir] memorandum of understanding, 52 Fed. Reg. 17,830 (1987). The FDA advised that MAL hydrochloride had received regulatory approval for the designated use. The FDA also pointed out that MAL hydrochloride is an ester of the previously FDA-approved ALA hydrochloride, and proposed that the requirements of [35 U.S.C.] § 156(a)(5)(A) were not met.

The PTO then denied the requested term extension, stating that "active ingredient" in § 156(f)(2) does not mean the product that was approved by the FDA, but rather means the "active moiety" of that product. The PTO held that MAL hydrochloride is the "same 'product' " as ALA hydrochloride because the "underlying molecule" of MAL is ALA, and the PTO stated that "ALA is simply formulated differently in the two different drugs." The PTO held that since a drug product containing ALA hydrochloride was previously approved by the FDA, the FDA's marketing approval of the MAL hydrochloride product was not the first commercial marketing or use of that "product." * * *

MAL hydrochloride is a different chemical compound from ALA hydrochloride, and it is not disputed that they differ in their biological properties, warranting separate patenting and separate regulatory approval, although their chemical structure is similar. Thus the district court held that MAL hydrochloride and ALA hydrochloride are different "products" with different "active ingredients," as the terms are used in § 156, explaining that "a compound can only qualify as the 'active ingredient' of a drug if that compound itself is present in the drug" * * * * See Glaxo Operations UK Ltd. v. Quigg, 894 F.2d 392, 393–95 (Fed.Cir.1990) (extending term of patent on a new separately patentable ester, although salts of the same acid had previously been approved); Hoechst–Roussel Pharms., Inc. v. Lehman,

109 F.3d 756, 759 n.3 (Fed.Cir.1997) ("For purposes of patent term extension, this active ingredient must be present in the drug product when administered."). * * *

As this court held in *Glaxo*, "section 156(f)(2)'s operative terms, individually and as combined in the full definition, have a common and unambiguous meaning, which leaves no gap to be filled in by the administering agency." 894 F.2d at 398. * * * The PTO's statutory interpretation, which would exclude MAL hydrochloride from term extension, is contrary to the statutory purpose, for MAL is the active ingredient of a new and improved drug product. The district court correctly applied 35 U.S.C. § 156 to extend the term of the patented product that is subject to regulatory review. We affirm the ruling that the patent on MAL hydrochloride is subject to term extension.

Eli Lilly & Co. v. Medtronic, Inc.

496 U.S. 661 (1990).

■ Scalia, Justice:

In 1984, Congress enacted the Drug Price Competition and Patent Term Restoration Act of 1984, which amended the FDCA and the patent laws in several important respects. The issue in this case concerns the proper interpretation of a portion of § 202 of the 1984 Act, codified at 35 U.S.C. § 271(e)(1). That paragraph, as originally enacted, provided:

> It shall not be an act of infringement to make, use, or sell a patented invention (other than a new animal drug or veterinary biological product (as those terms are used in the Federal Food, Drug, and Cosmetic Act and the Act of March 4, 1913)) solely for uses reasonably related to the development and submission of information under a Federal law which regulates the manufacture, use, or sale of drugs.

The parties dispute whether this provision exempts from infringement the use of patented inventions to develop and submit information for marketing approval of medical devices under the FDCA. * * * [P]etitioner interprets the statutory phrase, "a Federal law which regulates the manufacture, use, or sale of drugs," to refer only to those individual provisions of federal law that regulate drugs, whereas respondent interprets it to refer to the entirety of any Act (including, of course, the FDCA) at least some of whose provisions regulate drugs. * * *

If § 271(e)(1) referred to "a Federal law which *pertains* to the manufacture, use, or sale of drugs" it might be more reasonable to think that an individual provision was referred to. But the phrase "a Federal law which *regulates* the manufacture, use, or sale of drugs" more naturally summons up the image of an entire statutory scheme of regulation. The portion of § 271(e)(1) that immediately precedes the words "a Federal law" likewise seems more compatible with reference to an entire Act. It refers to "the development and submission of information *under* a Federal law" (emphasis added). It would be more common, if a single section rather than an entire scheme were referred to, to speak of "the development and submission of information *pursuant* to a Federal law," or perhaps "*in compliance with* a Federal law." Taking the action "under a Federal law" suggests taking it in furtherance of or compliance with a comprehensive scheme of regulation. * * *

On the other side of the ledger, however, one must admit that while the provision more naturally means what respondent suggests, it is somewhat difficult to understand why anyone would *want* it to mean that. Why should the touchstone of noninfringement be whether the use is related to the development and submission of information under a provision that happens to be included within an Act that, *in any of its provisions*, not necessarily the one at issue, regulates drugs? * * * As far as the text is concerned, therefore, we conclude that we have before us a provision that somewhat more naturally reads as the court of appeals determined [to cover medical devices], but that is not plainly comprehensible on anyone's view. Both parties seek to enlist legislative history in support of their interpretation, but that sheds no clear light. We think the court of appeals' interpretation is confirmed, however, by the structure of the 1984 Act taken as a whole. * * *

The parties agree that the 1984 Act was designed to respond to two unintended distortions of the 17–year patent term produced by the requirement that certain products must receive premarket regulatory approval. First, the holder of a patent relating to such products would as a practical matter not be able to reap any financial rewards during the early years of the term. When an inventor makes a potentially useful discovery, he ordinarily protects it by applying for a patent at once. Thus, if the discovery relates to a product that cannot be marketed without substantial testing and regulatory approval, the "clock" on his patent term will be running even though he is not yet able to derive any profit from the invention.

The second distortion occurred at the other end of the patent term. In 1984, the Court of Appeals for the Federal Circuit decided that the manufacture, use, or sale of a patented invention during the term of the patent constituted an act of infringement even if it was for the sole purpose of conducting tests and developing information necessary to apply for regulatory approval. Since that activity could not be commenced by those who planned to compete with the patentee until expiration of the entire patent term, the patentee's de facto monopoly would continue for an often substantial period until regulatory approval was obtained. In other words, the combined effect of the patent law and the premarket regulatory approval requirement was to create an effective extension of the patent term.

The 1984 Act sought to eliminate this distortion from both ends of the patent period. Section 201 of the Act established a patent-term extension for patents relating to certain products that were subject to lengthy regulatory delays and could not be marketed prior to regulatory approval. The eligible products were described as [including medical devices.] * * * Section 201 provides that patents relating to these products can be extended up to five years if, inter alia, the product was "subject to a regulatory review period before its commercial marketing or use," and "the permission for the commercial marketing or use of the product after such regulatory review period [was] the first permitted commercial marketing or use of the product under the provision of law under which such regulatory review period occurred." 35 U.S.C. § 156(a).

The distortion at the other end of the patent period was addressed by § 202 of the Act. That added to the provision prohibiting patent infringement, 35 U.S.C. § 271, the paragraph at issue here * * * * This allows competitors, prior to the expiration of a patent, to engage in otherwise infringing activities necessary to obtain regulatory approval. * * *

It seems most implausible to us that Congress, being demonstrably aware of the *dual* distorting effects of regulatory approval requirements in this entire area—dual distorting effects that were roughly offsetting, the disadvantage at the beginning of the term producing a more or less corresponding advantage at the end of the term—should choose to address both those distortions only for drug products; and for other products named in § 201 should enact provisions which not only leave in place an anticompetitive restriction at the end of the monopoly term but simultaneously expand the monopoly term itself, thereby not only failing to eliminate but positively aggravating distortion of the 17–year patent protection. It would take strong evidence to persuade us that this is what Congress wrought, and there is no such evidence here.

Apart from the reason of the matter, there are textual indications that §§ 201 and 202 are meant generally to be complementary. That explains, for example, § 202's exception for "a new animal drug or veterinary biological product (as those terms are used in the Federal Food, Drug, and Cosmetic Act and the Act of March 4, 1913)." Although new animal drugs and veterinary biological products are subject to premarket regulatory licensing and approval under the FDCA, neither product was included in the patent-term extension provision of § 201. They therefore were excepted from § 202 as well. Interpreting § 271(e)(1) as the court of appeals did here appears to create a perfect "product" fit between the two sections. All of the products eligible for a patent term extension under § 201 are subject to § 202 * * * * No interpretation we have been able to imagine can transform § 271(e)(1) into an elegant piece of statutory draftsmanship. To construe it as the court of appeals decided, one must posit a good deal of legislative imprecision; but to construe it as petitioner would, one must posit that and an implausible substantive intent as well. * * *

■ KENNEDY, JUSTICE (dissenting):

* * * Section 271(e)(1), in my view, does not privilege the testing of medical devices such as the cardiac defibrillator. When § 271(e)(1) speaks of a law which regulates drugs, I think that it does not refer to particular enactments or implicate the regulation of anything other than drugs. It addresses the legal regulation of drugs as opposed to other products. Thus, while the section would permit a manufacturer to use a drug for the purpose of obtaining marketing approval under the FDCA, it does not

authorize a manufacturer to use or sell other products that, by coincidence, the FDCA also happens to regulate. * * *

The Court asserts that Congress could have specified this result in a clearer manner. That is all too true. But we do not tell Congress how to express its intent. Instead, we discern its intent by assuming that Congress employs words and phrases in accordance with their ordinary usage. In this case, even if Congress could have clarified § 271(e)(1), the Court ascribes a most unusual meaning to the existing language. * * *

Congress did not act in an irrational manner when it drew a distinction between drugs and medical devices. True, like medical devices, some drugs have a very high cost. Testing a patented medical device, however, often will have greater effects on the patent holder's rights than comparable testing of a patented drug. As petitioner has asserted, manufacturers may test generic versions of patented drugs, but not devices, under abbreviated procedures. These procedures, in general, do not affect the market in a substantial manner because manufacturers may test the drugs on a small number of subjects, who may include healthy persons who otherwise would not buy the drug. By contrast, as in this case, manufacturers test and market medical devices in clinical trials on patients who would have purchased the device from the patent holder. * * *

NOTES AND QUESTIONS

1. *Research exception.* In *Merck KGaA v. Integra Lifesciences I, Ltd.*, 545 U.S. 193 (2005), the Court again gave this provision a broad interpretation:

> Basic scientific research on a particular compound, performed without the intent to develop a particular drug or a reasonable belief that the compound will cause the sort of physiological effect the researcher intends to induce, is surely not "reasonably related to the development and submission of information" to the FDA. It does not follow from this, however, that § 271(e)(1)'s exemption from infringement categorically excludes either (1) experimentation on drugs that are not ultimately the subject of an FDA submission or (2) use of patented compounds in experiments that are not ultimately submitted to the FDA. Under certain conditions, we think the exemption is sufficiently broad to protect the use of patented compounds in both situations.
>
> As to the first proposition, it disregards the reality that, even at late stages in the development of a new drug, scientific testing is a process of trial and error. In the vast majority of cases, neither the drugmaker nor its scientists have any way of knowing whether an initially promising candidate will prove successful over a battery of experiments. That is the reason they conduct the experiments.... For similar reasons, the use of a patented compound in experiments that are not themselves included in a "submission of information" to the FDA does not, standing alone, render the use infringing. The relationship of the use of a patented compound in a particular experiment to the "development and submission of information" to the FDA does not

> become more attenuated (or less reasonable) simply because the data from that experiment are left out of the submission that is ultimately passed along to the FDA. Moreover, many of the uncertainties that exist with respect to the selection of a specific drug exist as well with respect to the decision of what research to include in an IND or NDA.

Id. at 205–07; see also Ian Jaquette, Note, Implications of the Supreme Court's Decision for the People Who Matter Most . . . the Consumer, 33 Am. J.L. & Med. 97 (2007); cf. NeoRx Corp. v. Immunomedics, Inc., 877 F.Supp. 202, 206–12 (D.N.J.1994) (holding that scale-up production and shipment overseas to conduct clinical trials in support of FDA approval would be exempt, but shipment to foreign regulatory authorities to secure their approval would not be). But cf. Biogen, Inc. v. Schering AG, 954 F.Supp. 391, 397 (D.Mass.1996) (holding that this safe harbor did not apply where a company "had spent $24 million to stockpile and prepare to market Avonex immediately upon the anticipated, imminent FDA approval in order to access promptly the lucrative market for beta interferon drugs to combat multiple sclerosis"). See generally Sarah J. Chickos, Navigating the Safe Harbor: Guidance from the Courts on Qualifying for the 35 U.S.C. 271(e)(1) Exemption from Patent Infringement of Health Care Related Inventions, 24 J. Contemp. Health L. & Pol'y 43 (2007); Andrew S. Baluch, Note, Relating the Two Experimental Uses in Patent Law: Inventor's Negation and Infringer's Defense, 87 B.U. L. Rev. 213 (2007); R. Andrew Schwentker, Note, Experimenting with the Experimental–Use Exception: Proposals for a Tax Alternative, 76 Geo. Wash. L. Rev. 426 (2008).

2. *Research tools.* In *Merck v. Integra*, the Supreme Court declined to "express a view about whether, or to what extent, § 271(e)(1) exempts from infringement the use of 'research tools' in the development of information for the regulatory process." 545 U.S. at 205 n.7. This open question has attracted a good deal of scholarly attention. See Peter Y. Lee, Inverting the Logic of Scientific Discovery: Applying Common Law Patentable Subject Matter Doctrine to Constrain Patents on Biotechnology Research Tools, 19 Harv. J.L. & Tech. 79 (2005); Michael S. Mireles, An Examination of Patents, Licensing, Research Tools, and the Tragedy of the Anticommons in Biotechnology Innovation, 38 U. Mich. J.L. Reform 141 (2004); Caroline A. Crenshaw, Note, Patents and Patients: Who Is the Tragedy of the Anticommons Impacting and Who Is Bearing the Cost of High–Priced Biotechnological Research?, 9 Minn. J.L. Sci. & Tech. 913 (2008); Dev A. Ghose, Comment, A Proposal to Modify the Utility Standard for Patenting Biotechnology Research Tools, 56 Emory L.J. 1661 (2007). Aside from doctrinal solutions, commentators have proposed a range of approaches to this and related problems. See Donna M. Gitter, Resolving the Open Source Paradox in Biotechnology: A Proposal for a Revised Open Source Policy for Publicly Funded Genomic Databases, 43 Hous. L. Rev. 1475 (2007); Hillary Greene, Patent Pooling Behind the Veil of Uncertainty: Antitrust, Competition Policy, and the Vaccine Industry, 90 B.U. L. Rev. 1397 (2010); Emily Marden, Open Source Drug Development: A Path to More Accessible Drugs and Diagnostics?, 11 Minn. J.L. Sci. & Tech. 217 (2010); Stephen M. Maurer, Open Source Drug Discovery: Finding a Niche (Maybe Several), 76

UMKC L. Rev. 405 (2007); Alfred C. Server et al., Reach–Through Rights and the Patentability, Enforcement, and Licensing of Patents on Drug Discovery Tools, 1 Hastings Sci. & Tech. L.J. 21 (2009); Courtney C. Scala, Note, Making the Jump from Gene Pools to Patent Pools: How Patent Pools Can Facilitate the Development of Pharmacogenomics, 41 Conn. L. Rev. 1631 (2009).

3. *Medical devices.* Lower courts have extended the Supreme Court's application of the exception to medical devices. See Abtox, Inc. v. Exitron Corp., 122 F.3d 1019, 1027–29 (Fed.Cir.1997) (applying the exception to research performed on a Class II device prior to marketing); Telectronics Pacing Sys., Inc. v. Ventritex, Inc., 982 F.2d 1520, 1523 (Fed.Cir.1992) (holding that company demonstrations of an implantable defibrillator subject to an IDE at medical conferences "constitute an exempt use reasonably related to FDA approval, because device sponsors are responsible for selecting qualified investigators and providing them with the necessary information to conduct clinical testing"); Intermedics, Inc. v. Ventritex, Inc., 775 F.Supp. 1269 (N.D.Cal.1991), aff'd mem., 991 F.2d 808 (Fed.Cir. 1993); Shashank Upadhye, Understanding Patent Infringement Under 35 U.S.C. Section 271(e): The Collisions Between Patent, Medical Device and Drug Laws, 17 Santa Clara Computer & High Tech. L.J. 1 (2000); see also J. Matthew Buchanan, Medical Device Patent Rights in the Age of FDA Modernization: The Potential Effect of Regulatory Streamlining on the Right to Exclude, 30 U. Tol. L. Rev. 305 (1999).

5. Copyright Protection

SmithKline Beecham v. Watson Pharmaceuticals, Inc.

211 F.3d 21 (2d Cir.2000).

■ WINTER, CHIEF JUDGE:

* * * On January 13, 1984, SmithKline obtained FDA approval to sell 2 mg strength Nicorette for prescription-only use. Later, on June 8, 1992, the FDA approved prescription-only use of 4 mg Nicorette. Finally, on February 9, 1996, the FDA approved both 2 mg and 4 mg Nicorette for OTC sale. Pursuant to 21 U.S.C. § 355(c)(3)(D)(iv), SmithKline obtained a three-year period of exclusivity—essentially an extension of the effective term of SmithKline's Nicorette patent based on additional clinical testing—for OTC sale of Nicorette.

SmithKline's user's guide and audiotape were developed in the course of its research into producing a method of, and product for, quitting smoking. To obtain approval for the OTC sale of Nicorette, SmithKline submitted various versions of the guide and tape to the FDA for review. Between July 1993 and February 1996, SmithKline made approximately 70 changes to the guide and the tape at the FDA's request. Most of the changes related to factual matters, safety, and efficacy. The tape and guide were ultimately included as part of Nicorette's FDA-approved OTC labeling. On April 21, 1998, SmithKline registered a federal copyright for the guide and audiotape script. On February 9, 1999, the day when its exclusivity period for Nicorette expired, SmithKline registered a copyright for the words and music on the tape.

Shortly thereafter, appellees Watson Pharmaceuticals, Inc., Watson Laboratories, Inc., and Circa Pharmaceuticals, Inc. (collectively "Watson") obtained FDA approval for the OTC marketing of a generic version of nicotine gum intended to compete directly with Nicorette. To obtain that approval from the FDA, Watson had to comply with the requirement imposed by the Hatch–Waxman Amendments that "the labeling proposed for [its] new drug [be] the same as the labeling approved for" Nicorette. Thus, Watson's generic nicotine gum was "accompanied by a user guide and audio tape that [we]re virtually identical to SmithKline's."

Before Watson could sell its product to the public, SmithKline initiated the present copyright action, alleging willful infringement of its guide and tape. The district court granted a preliminary injunction that effectively stopped Watson from shipping or selling its product. The district court relied on a March 1999 FDA letter recounting that the agency had explained to Watson that "the 'same labeling' requirement d[oes] not require that the generic's behavioral support materials be identical to the innovator's materials" and indeed that "generic sponsors, like all other sponsors of nicotine-based smoking cessation aids, have discretion to design their own audio support materials." Based on this representation, the district court "concluded that the FDA would have permitted Watson to use a user's guide and audio tape that deviated to some extent from SmithKline's materials . . . [and] that were sufficiently different in wording and otherwise to avoid copyright concerns."

Subsequently, the FDA altered its position. In the face of the preliminary injunction, Watson revised its guide and tape to render them "comparable, but not identical, to SmithKline's." However, on November 23, 1999, the FDA rejected the revised user guide. The FDA "advised Watson that it would approve a revised version of Watson's 'previously approved labeling,' i.e., the virtually identical user's guide previously approved by the FDA." To assist Watson, the FDA "marked up a copy of the previously approved user guide" and bracketed certain portions of text which could be in appropriate cases deleted or "substituted with new text . . . similar to the original in tone, content and length." Nevertheless, the bracketed guide gave Watson "very little leeway to deviate from the previously approved user guide." In essence, therefore, the FDA "determined that Watson had to copy verbatim substantially all of the text used in the SmithKline" user's guide.

In December, representatives of the FDA attended a conference with the district court, at which time the court asked the FDA to " 'revisit' the question of whether portions of Watson's proposed user's guide could be rewritten to change the text 'a little bit' to address the copyright concerns." On December 15, the FDA wrote the court and advised that it had "decline[d] to change its approach to Watson's labeling" and that it could not address copyright concerns because it "ha[d] never been directed by

Congress to consider potential copyright rights in approving generic drug labeling." In a supplemental decision issued the same day, the FDA "adhered to its decision to require Watson to copy verbatim most of the SmithKline" user guide. In light of the FDA's position, the district court dissolved the preliminary injunction, citing also Watson's efforts to revise its materials, the prejudice caused Watson by delay, and the public interest in a generic nicotine gum product. * * *

We do not doubt that SmithKline has demonstrated the existence of substantial issues under the copyright laws, at least when they are considered in isolation. SmithKline's guide and tape are creative works in which it has a substantial investment, and they are integral to both the marketing and use of Nicorette. Watson's guide and tape are concededly in large part copies of SmithKline's copyrighted materials. Moreover, Watson intends to use the guide and tape in marketing a product in direct competition with SmithKline's gum. Absent more, the propriety of a preliminary injunction would seem clear.

Watson asserts that this copying, having been dictated by the FDA, is a "fair use" protected under 17 U.S.C. § 107. The United States, in its amicus curiae brief, argues instead that in submitting its copyrighted materials for FDA approval, SmithKline gave the FDA an implied, nonexclusive license to permit or require generic drug applicants to copy the user's guide and audiotape in their own nicotine gum packaging. Neither fair use nor implied license is clearly a defense in the present circumstances. Watson's use of SmithKline's copyrighted works in its labeling is rather different from the sorts of copying traditionally deemed to constitute a fair use, e.g., copying for "purposes such as criticism, comment, news reporting, teaching . . . , scholarship, or research." Moreover, courts have found implied licenses only in "narrow" circumstances where one party "created a work at [the other's] request and handed it over, intending that [the other] copy and distribute it."

However, we see little need for further examination of these possible defenses. If either were to prevail, some new law, essentially judge-made, would have to be fashioned. In our view, the case can more easily be disposed of on the straightforward ground that the Hatch–Waxman Amendments to the FDCA not only permit but require producers of generic drugs to use the same labeling as was approved for, and is used in, the sale of the pioneer drug, even if that label has been copyrighted. Because those Amendments were designed to facilitate rather than impede the approval and OTC sale of generic drugs, the FDA's requirement that Watson use much of SmithKline's label precludes a copyright infringement action by SmithKline. SmithKline's copyright claim is therefore meritless, and we need not address either the fair use or implied license defenses. * * *

The Hatch–Waxman Amendments reflect the FDA's view that clinical retesting of generic drugs was "unnecessary and wasteful because the drug ha[d] already been determined to be safe and effective," as well as "unethical because it [would] require[] that some sick patients take placebos and be denied treatment known to be effective." H. Rep. No. 98–857, Part I, at

16 (1984), reprinted in 1984 U.S.C.C.A.N. 2647, 2649. Bypassing redundant human testing would also speed up FDA approval for generic entrants and thus introduce price competition more rapidly once the pioneer producer's patent and exclusivity periods expired. See Mead Johnson Pharm. Group v. Bowen, 838 F.2d 1332, 1333 (D.C.Cir.1988) (interpreting congressional purpose of Hatch–Waxman Amendments to be "increas[ing] competition in the drug industry by facilitating the approval of generic copies of drugs").

Except for human clinical tests, the ANDA requires a manufacturer to submit to the FDA the same items as required in the NDA, as well as information to show that the generic drug has the same active ingredients, means of administration, dosage form, strength, pharmacological or therapeutic class, and labeling as the already-approved pioneer drug, and that the generic drug does not infringe any outstanding patents. With specific regard to labeling, the Hatch–Waxman Amendments require that an ANDA "show that the labeling proposed for the [generic] drug is the same as the labeling proposed for the [pioneer] drug ... except for changes required because of [approved] differences [between the pioneer and generic drug] or because the [generic] drug and [pioneer] drug are produced or distributed by different manufacturers." 21 U.S.C. § 355(j)(2)(A)(v). The FDCA defines "label" and "labeling" for these purposes as "a display of written, printed, or graphic matter upon the immediate container of any article" or "accompanying such article," 21 U.S.C. § 321(k) & (m), which the FDA has broadly interpreted to include "[b]rochures, booklets, ... sound recordings, ... and similar pieces of printed, audio, or visual matter descriptive of a drug." 21 C.F.R. § 202.1(*l*)(2).

Applying the Hatch–Waxman Amendments to the present appeal, SmithKline's copyright claim fails. First, its copyrighted user's guide and audiotape constitute "labeling" for purposes of the Hatch–Waxman Amendments. SmithKline has not contended otherwise and understandably so. The guide and tape clearly fall within the statutory and regulatory definitions quoted immediately above. Moreover, they were submitted to the FDA as part of SmithKline's quest for administrative approval of OTC sales of Nicorette. The guide and tape were approved only after more than two years of administrative consideration and after that consideration had led to some 70 changes in the guide and tape at the FDA's request.

Second, the FDA's requirement that Watson use copious amounts of SmithKline's copyrighted material is not a misapplication of the Hatch–Waxman Amendments. As noted, the Amendments require that the labeling for the generic drug be the "same" as the labeling for the pioneer drug. To be sure, as SmithKline noted at oral argument, "same" may be something less than "identical." However, where the language of a document is the "same" as that of a copyrighted work, the former usually infringes the latter. Certainly, a legislative drafter would believe that a sameness requirement would lead to the creation of works that would easily fall within the copyright law's infringement test of "substantial similarity."[2] Indeed, the legislative history of the Hatch–Waxman Amendments suggests that whatever difference may exist between "same" and "identical" is narrow and intended to prevent misstatements rather than infringement:

> [A]n ANDA must contain adequate information to show that the proposed labeling for the generic drug is the same as that of the listed drug. The Committee recognizes that the proposed labeling for the generic drug may not be exactly the same. For example, the name and address of the manufacturers would vary as might the expiration dates for the two products. Another example is that one color is used in the coating of the listed drug and another color is used in that of the generic drug. The FDA might require the listed drug maker to specify the color in its label. The generic manufacturer, which has used a different color, would have to specify a different color in its label.

H. Rep. No. 98–857, Part I, at 22 (1984), reprinted in 1984 U.S.C.C.A.N. 2647, 2655.

Third, if SmithKline's copyright claim has merit, then Watson cannot realistically use the ANDA process to sell its generic nicotine gum because it will either have to change the label and lose FDA approval or be enjoined from using a label that infringes SmithKline's copyright. We are thus faced with a conflict between two statutes. The Hatch–Waxman Amendments require generic drug producers to use labeling that will infringe upon copyrights in labels of pioneer drugs. The Copyright Act seems to prohibit such copying. However, applying the familiar canon that, where two laws are in conflict, courts should adopt the interpretation that preserves the principal purposes of each,[3] the conflict is less stark and more easily resolved than it might seem.

The purposes of the Hatch–Waxman Amendments would be severely undermined if copyright concerns were to shape the FDA's application of the "same" labeling requirement. The Amendments were intended to facilitate the introduction of generic competitors once a pioneer drug's patent term and exclusivity periods had ended by allowing the generic

2. Some courts have held that infringement of a copyright in commercial labeling must involve verbatim or near-verbatim copying. However, this heightened standard typically involves a copyrighted label of a "fact-based work," and SmithKline's guide and tape are substantially more creative than the typical commercial labels afforded copyright protection. We need not decide whether the traditional "substantial similarity" infringement test or a heightened "verbatim or near-verbatim" test applies to the instant case. As discussed infra, the plain language of the Hatch–Waxman Amendments, their legislative history, and their interpretation by the FDA all require manufacturers of generic drugs to copy the labeling of pioneer drugs "near-verbatim" to obtain ANDA approval, and this statutory mandate necessarily trumps any copyright interest in the label at issue.

3. In addition to looking to conflicting statutes' principal purposes, courts have traditionally given weight to statutes' priority of enactment and specificity in reconciling conflicts. Here, of course, both time of enactment and specificity favor our interpretation: the Hatch–Waxman Amendments were enacted subsequent to the Copyright Act of 1976, and the Copyright Act's broad generality contrasts with the Hatch–Waxman Amendments' specific generic drug approval scheme.

producer to piggy-back upon the pioneer producer's successful FDA application. For example, human testing by the generic producer is not required because it would be time- and resource-consuming even though redundant. For the very same reason, the creation and approval of new labels is avoided by the "same" labeling requirement. If labels that were "substantially similar" to copyrighted labels on pioneer drugs had to be avoided, the administrative process of approving a new label would, in cases like the present one, drain the resources of the FDA and generic producer—not to mention the problem of successive generic producers avoiding infringement of multiple copyrighted labels. Avoiding such infringement would also delay the introduction of the generic product without advancing public health and safety to any perceptible degree. For that reason, Congress left no room for such redundant proceedings and adopted the "same" labeling requirement. The FDA cannot be faithful to that requirement, however, without requiring labels that will often violate copyrights. If copyright law were to prevail, producers of generic drugs will always be delayed in—and quite often prohibited from—marketing the generic product, results at great odds with the purposes of the Hatch–Waxman Amendments.

No such severe undermining of the purpose of the copyright laws would follow from the rejection of SmithKline's claim, however. The creation of labels to be approved by the FDA, such as SmithKline's user's guide and audio tape, is ancillary to the FDA's administrative process. The creativity of the author is focused not only on pleasing and medicating ultimate consumers but also on obtaining the administrative approval of labeling necessary to FDA approval of a drug that will be protected from competition both for the period of the patent term and FDCA exclusivity periods.

Our point here is not only that Congress would have provided explicitly that the Hatch–Waxman Amendments trump the copyright laws had it foreseen the statutory conflict exposed by the present action, although we firmly believe that to be obvious. Our point is also that the profit sought by the creator of the pioneer drug label flows primarily from the administrative approval of the drug and the patent and exclusivity periods free from competition that follow. The pertinent purpose of the copyright laws—to encourage the production of creative works by according authors a property right in their works so that authors will not have to share profits from their labors with free riders—is not seriously implicated by allowing the "same" labeling requirement to trump a copyright under the Hatch–Waxman Amendments.[5] It is simply not conceivable that, if we reject

5. Although commercial labeling is clearly copyrightable, see 1 Nimmer on Copyright § 2.08[G], at 2–135 ("It is clear that [17 U.S.C. §] 102(a)(5) includes prints and labels used for articles of merchandise under the general protection accorded to pictorial, graphic and sculptural works."), it has been recognized that the "danger lurking in copyright protection for labels is that the tail threatens to wag the dog—proprietors at times seize on copyright protection for the label in order to leverage their thin copyright protection over the text . . . on the label into a monopoly on the typically uncopyrightable product to which it is attached." Id. § 2.08[G][2], at 2–138. "Used in that fashion, the copyright serves 'primarily as a means of harassing competitors,' and thus fails 'nine times out of ten.' " Id. at 2–139. Here, although

SmithKline's claim, pioneer drug producers will so fear the copying of labels by future generic drug producers that some pioneer producers—or even one of them—will lack the incentive to create labeling needed for FDA approval.

We emphasize that we do not read the Hatch–Waxman Amendments to repeal other rights under the Copyright Act of copyright owners in SmithKline's circumstances. Even though such an owner cannot enforce its copyright against generic drug manufacturers who are required by the Hatch–Waxman Amendments to copy labeling and who do no more than that, it still retains a copyright, if otherwise valid, in the label and might well pursue copyright claims against potential infringers in other circumstances, e.g., use of the copyrighted material in non-labeling advertisements. * * *

NOTES AND QUESTIONS

1. *Constitutional perspective*. Might the FDA's interpretation have violated the Takings Clause? See John C. O'Quinn, Protecting Private Intellectual Property from Governmental Intrusion: Revisiting SmithKline and the Case for Just Compensation, 29 Pepp. L. Rev. 435, 460, 517–23 (2002) (arguing that the question was close enough to justify a narrower construction of the Hatch–Waxman Act pursuant to the avoidance canon); see also id. at 444–60 (criticizing the court's decision on other grounds). Separately, the agency has insisted that ANDAs adopt the same labeling even if the brand-name drug manufacturer retains a separate method patent covering a particular direction for use, which effectively stalls generic entry even after the composition patent has expired. See Julie Dohm, Comment, Expanding the Scope of the Hatch–Waxman Act's Patent Carve-out Exception to the Identical Drug Labeling Requirement: Closing the Patent Litigation Loophole, 156 U. Pa. L. Rev. 151 (2007).

2. *Copyright in another context*. Some scholars have suggested using copyright to protect discoveries of naturally occurring DNA sequences. See Christopher M. Holman, Copyright for Engineered DNA: An Idea Whose Time Has Come?, 113 W. Va. L. Rev. 699 (2011); Stephen R. Wilson, Copyright Protection for DNA Sequences: Can the Biotech Industry Harmonize Science with Song?, 44 Jurimetrics J. 409 (2004).

6. TRADEMARKS AND LANHAM ACT LITIGATION

Eli Lilly & Co. v. Natural Answers, Inc.

86 F.Supp.2d 834 (S.D.Ind.), aff'd, 233 F.3d 456 (7th Cir.2000).

■ HAMILTON, DISTRICT JUDGE:

Plaintiff Eli Lilly & Company manufactures and sells fluoxetine hydrochloride under the federally registered trademark Prozac®. Prozac is a

---

the labeling at issue is more creative than that in the "familiar" commercial labeling cases, SmithKline's copyright claim is arguably weaker than even the typical commercial labeling case, because the copyrighted text was submitted to obtain FDA approval and consequent market exclusivity.

prescription drug used to treat clinical depression and some other psychological conditions. Defendant Natural Answers, Inc. manufactures and sells a blend of St. John's Wort and several other herbs under the name Herbrozac. Natural Answers has been advertising Herbrozac over the Internet as "a very potent and synergistic formula, designed to promote Mood Elevation," and as "a powerful, and effective all-natural and herbal formula alternative to [the] prescription drug Prozac." Lilly has sued Natural Answers and its founder, Brian Alexander Feinstein, under the Lanham Act for federal trademark infringement and for dilution of Prozac as a famous trademark. On December 16, 1999, Lilly moved for a preliminary injunction to prevent Natural Answers from continuing to market its product using both the Herbrozac name and references to Prozac in its Internet advertising. * * *

Since 1988, using the trademark Prozac, plaintiff Lilly has sold fluoxetine hydrochloride throughout the United States and in many countries around the world. Lilly has marketed the medicine primarily to treat depression. The medicine has also proven useful in treating bulimia nervosa and obsessive-compulsive disorder. Lilly owns United States Trademark Registration No. 1357582 for Prozac as used for pharmaceutical products. The registration was issued September 3, 1985, and has become incontestable as a matter of law.

As a prescription drug, Prozac is not freely available to patients who seek to use it to relieve depression or other conditions. A licensed physician must prescribe the medicine, and a licensed pharmacist must fill the prescription for the patient. Lilly's advertising of Prozac has been aimed at physicians and pharmacists, and not directly to potential consumers. Prozac is the best-selling prescription antidepressant in the United States. Since 1988, doctors have prescribed Prozac more than 240 million times for more than 17 million Americans. Prozac sales in the United States alone have totaled more than $12 billion since 1988.

Over the last eleven years, fluoxetine hydrochloride and the Prozac mark have received an extraordinary amount of attention from the news media. The product has achieved extraordinary fame in American culture. Prozac is the best known brand of a new generation of medications that have been developed and are being developed to treat not only depression but a host of other psychological conditions more effectively than has been possible before.

Lilly has submitted a sampling of newspaper and magazine articles and books about Prozac that evidence this fame. In 1993, for example, Penguin Books USA published Peter D. Kramer's book *Listening to Prozac*, and in 1994, the Berkley Publishing Group published Elizabeth Wurtzel's *Prozac Nation: Young and Depressed in America*. Both books were national best-sellers. * * * Lilly has submitted an article from the *Baltimore Sun* of September 21, 1993, that sums up the fame Prozac achieved within just a few years of its initial launch as a brand. After referring to the use of

Prozac in punch lines in a Woody Allen film and a *New Yorker* poem, the author wrote:

> Prozac entered the popular lexicon almost immediately after its introduction six years ago. It's been on the cover of *Newsweek* and shared the stage with Phil and Geraldo; it continues to turn up in the monologues of comedians and the cultural references of the ironic. It's a designer label, a buzzword, a brand name familiar to not only the 4.5 million Americans who have taken it, but also those who wonder if they, too, might find a cure for whatever ails them in the little green-and-off-white capsule.

As further evidence of Prozac's fame, searches of computerized databases turned up extraordinary numbers of responses. A search of the Internet for "Prozac" using the Altavista search engine on November 29, 1999, found 63,150 web pages. A November 29, 1999, search of the Westlaw database ALLNEWS for the word Prozac and a date after 1997 produced more than 10,000 stories. The Westlaw database Dow Jones Major Newspapers covers only 48 major newspapers. A November 29, 1999, search of that database for "Prozac" over the last ten years turned up more than 12,000 references, or an average of more than 250 stories for each newspaper included in the database.

Defendant Natural Answers' Herbrozac is part of a line of products that Natural Answers calls Herbscriptions. These products are manufactured from a variety of herbs and other natural substances. Natural Answers markets these products over the Internet from a site marked <www.naturalanswers.com/>. Natural Answers has not yet arranged for distribution through "brick-and-mortar" retail stores, but it is actively seeking to do so. * * * As compared to Lilly, which is a worldwide pharmaceutical company established in 1876, with annual sales in the billions of dollars, Natural Answers launched its business in 1999 and has one full-time employee, founder Brian Feinstein. * * *

Natural Answers tries to walk a fine line in its business. On one hand, Natural Answers attempts to draw a sharp distinction between its herbal formula dietary supplements and the drugs manufactured by pharmaceutical companies like Lilly. * * * The FDA treats Natural Answers' dietary supplements as "foods" that are not subject to the FDA's drug approval process. This regulatory treatment of the products as "foods," however, requires Natural Answers to make clear in its labeling that its products are not FDA-approved and are "not intended to diagnose, treat, cure, or prevent any disease." 21 U.S.C. §§ 321(ff), 343(r)(6)(C). Nevertheless, Natural Answers wants to market its products as natural alternatives to manufactured pharmaceuticals. * * *

One way in which Natural Answers tries to suggest the benefits of its products is by giving them names that suggest an association with well-known drug brands or families of drugs. As explained below in the discussion of the similarity of the marks in question, the association between Prozac and Herbrozac is strong and intentional. Natural Answers chose a name similar to Prozac rather than a name similar to other antidepressant drugs because Prozac is the most famous and best-selling antidepressant drug. * * * [T]he other product names in the Herbscriptions line attempt to suggest similar associations. Natural Answers promotes Herbalium as a formula to promote "deep relaxation," and the name is intended to suggest an association with the brand-name drug Valium. Natural Answers promotes Vita–Agra as enhancing men's sexual performance, and the name is intended to suggest an association with the Pfizer brand-name drug Viagra®. Natural Answers promotes Herbocet as a pain reliever, and its name is intended to suggest an association with a family of pain relief drugs using the suffix "cet," such as Lorcet, Darvocet, and Percocet. Natural Answers promotes HerbenolPM as suitable for headaches and a good night's sleep, and the name is intended to suggest an association with TylenolPM®. Natural Answers promotes Herbasprin for pain relief, and the name is intended to suggest an association with aspirin. Similarly, the name of the Natural Answers product Herbadryl is intended to suggest an association with Benadryl®. * * *

The legal line between pharmaceutical drugs and herbal remedies has begun to blur in the market place. Several major pharmaceutical companies have recently begun marketing herbal products based, as Herbrozac is, on St. John's Wort. These companies include Warner–Lambert and SmithKline Beecham. This phenomenon lends weight to a possibility that is legally important. It would not be unreasonable for a number of consumers who see or hear the name Herbrozac not only to associate the name with Prozac but also to assume or expect that there is some affiliation between the two. Even though the two products are distributed differently and are subject to very different regulatory regimes, they obviously are marketed to address similar if not identical conditions. The fact that some other major pharmaceutical companies are now marketing herbal products in general, and especially herbal products for mood elevation tends to lend some support to the possibility of confusion with respect to association or affiliation. * * *

To succeed on a trademark infringement claim, a plaintiff must establish that it has a protectable trademark and that the alleged infringer's use of that trademark is likely to cause confusion among consumers. * * * In assessing the likelihood of confusion, the court must consider several factors: (1) the degree of similarity between the parties' marks in appearance and suggestion (or actual copying); (2) the similarity of the products; (3) the area and manner of concurrent use; (4) the degree of care likely to be exercised by consumers; (5) the strength of complainant's mark; (6) actual confusion; and (7) intent to palm off by the infringer. This list of factors is not intended to be a mechanical checklist. No one factor is decisive, and the court must weigh all the facts and circumstances of the particular marks, products, and parties. There are a myriad of variables to be considered, but the most important are the similarity of the marks, the intent of the claimed infringer, and evidence of actual confusion. * * *

There is a strong similarity between the marks Prozac and Herbrozac, in terms of sight, sound, and meaning. Herbrozac includes five of the six letters of Prozac. As for the sixth, the "B" sound in Herbrozac is very similar to the "P" sound at the beginning of Prozac. The net effect is a message that effectively states "herbal Prozac." * * *

There are important differences and similarities between these two products. Herbrozac is not a drug. It is a dietary supplement available directly to consumers who choose to take it. The maker of Herbrozac may not lawfully claim that the product is intended to diagnose, treat, or cure a disease. By contrast, Prozac is a prescription drug that has been proven safe and effective in treating clinical depression and other conditions. There are also physical differences between the products that should not be overlooked. Herbrozac comes in large capsules with a distinctly herbal odor. Prozac comes in small green and off-white pills.

Despite these differences, the difference between a drug and a dietary supplement is primarily an artificial construct of the law, not necessarily a real difference between products. The artificial distinction between drug and dietary supplement is one that Natural Answers seeks to preserve for legal purposes but to obscure for marketing purposes. Natural Answers markets Herbrozac as an alternative to Prozac and other antidepressant drugs. * * * [A] dietary supplement based on herbs lies, for purposes of trademark law, in the natural line of expansion for a manufacturer of pharmaceutical drugs, especially where a drug and dietary supplement are intended and used to affect the same body functions and/or structures. That is, Natural Answers is trying to position its Herbrozac in the closest "competitive proximity" to Prozac that the food and drug laws will possibly allow. * * *

Lilly does not contend that consumers are likely to believe that Herbrozac capsules are really Prozac. Such confusion is not likely because one cannot even purchase Prozac without a prescription from a licensed physician, who is not at all likely to confuse one product for another. Lilly contends, however, that the similarity of the trademarks is likely to confuse some consumers as to whether there is some affiliation or association between the sources of the two products. The Lanham Act applies to use of a product name that "is likely to cause confusion, or to cause mistake, or to deceive as to the affiliation, connection, or association of such person with another person, or as to the origin, sponsorship, or approval of his or her goods, services, or commercial activities by another person." 15 U.S.C. § 1125(a)(1). * * *

The Prozac mark is unusually strong. First, it is a fanciful word that carries no meaning apart from its use to identify a product. It does not describe or suggest the function of the product it names. When the seller of a product coins a word just for the product, as Lilly did with Prozac, trademark protection is at its highest.

Natural Answers asserts that Prozac is now so famous that it has become a "generic" term no longer entitled to trademark protection. A trademark becomes generic when it comes to describe, in common usage in the United States, a class of goods rather than an individual product. * * * Where the plaintiff's trademark has been registered with the United States

Patent and Trademark Office, the plaintiff is entitled to a presumption that the mark is not generic, and the burden of proof is on the defendant to come forward with evidence showing that the mark is generic. * * * A trademark can become exceptionally strong and famous without becoming generic, as suggested by the examples of Coca–Cola® and Kodak®.

Natural Answers has not shown that Prozac is likely to be deemed generic. There is no evidence that any other competitors have used the term in a generic way, let alone that Lilly has tolerated such use.[4] There is no evidence that Lilly itself has used the term in a generic way. The parties have not submitted dictionary definitions tending to show the term has seeped into common usage in a generic sense. The media references actually before the court do not use the term "Prozac" in a generic way. They use the term instead to identify plaintiff Lilly's product. They tend to focus on Prozac more than other brands, but they do not use the term "Prozac" to refer to a whole class of different antidepressant drugs. In fact, the references to the new class of antidepressant drugs, of which Prozac is the most widely sold, are much more descriptive: "selective serotonin re-uptake inhibitors." Nor is there any evidence of persons in the trade that the term "Prozac" has taken on a generic meaning, nor has Natural Answers presented any public surveys about the meaning of the term. * * *

Lilly has not presented any evidence of actual confusion here. That is not surprising. Lilly filed suit and sought a preliminary injunction before Herbrozac had reached a level of even $2000 in total sales. In fact, a respectable consumer survey would probably require sampling reactions of more consumers than have actually purchased Herbrozac to date. * * *

Considering all the factors as set forth above, the court concludes that Lilly has shown an unusually strong case on the issue of likelihood of confusion. Most important here are the unusual strength of Lilly's Prozac mark, the strong similarity between Prozac and Herbrozac, and defendant's intentional selection of the Herbrozac name precisely because of its similarity to Prozac for the purpose of suggesting an association or affiliation between the products. Add to this mixture the fairly close "competitive proximity" of the two products, especially as pharmaceutical companies expand into the herbal and dietary supplement business, and Lilly has made a powerful showing of likelihood of success on its claim for trademark infringement.

---

4. Like many defendants in trademark cases, Natural Answers has tried to portray itself as a tiny David being bullied by a gigantic Goliath. For the holder of a famous trademark on a successful product, however, there is little alternative because the risk of inaction is so great. Delay or failure in enforcing trademark rights will usually give rise to a laches defense. Thus, even when the infringing use is on a new product produced in small volume by a tiny start-up company, the holder of the trademark and the court must assume that the defendant's new product will achieve great commercial success. If the holder of the famous trademark waits, a growing competitor may argue laches. If the holder ignores the first infringer, a later infringer with a more successful product may try to use the holder's failure to contest the small infringing use as evidence of abandonment or of generic meaning.

[In addition, on its separate claim for dilution of a famous trademark,] Lilly has shown that it is likely to prevail in showing that the Herbrozac mark blurs the Prozac mark. Herbrozac is a new product with little national recognition. However, if other manufacturers were to follow Natural Answers' footsteps in naming products, the Prozac mark would become less and less distinctive. * * * [The court issued a preliminary injunction ordering Natural Answers to discontinue using the name Herbrozac.]

NOTES AND QUESTIONS

1. *Trademark infringement.* Recall from Chapter 4(A) that the FDA has begun to pay attention to drug nomenclature in an effort to reduce prescribing errors caused by confusingly similar brand-names. See Dana M. Herberholz, Curing Confusion: An Overview of the Regulatory Complexities of Obtaining Pharmaceutical Trademarks and a Prescription for Reform, 8 Minn. J.L. Sci. & Tech. 97 (2007). Apart from these types of regulatory concerns, the use of similar brand-names may trigger private litigation. See Erva Pharm., Inc. v. American Cyanamid Co., 755 F.Supp. 36 (D.P.R.1991) (holding that a company selling the erectile dysfunction drug Supra® in violation of various FDA requirements could not sue for trademark infringement by a competitor); see also Karl Storz Endoscopy Am., Inc. v. Surgical Tech., Inc., 285 F.3d 848, 854–57 (9th Cir.2002) (allowing Lanham Act claim to proceed against a company that rebuilt broken endoscopes for hospitals without altering the original trademark etched on to the devices because this practice might confuse surgeons about the source of the unit). Similar sorts of issues arise in connection with so-called "trade dress" protection. See CIBA–GEIGY Corp. v. Bolar Pharm. Co., 719 F.2d 56 (3d Cir.1983); David M. Fritch, Should "the Purple Pill" by Any Other Drug Company Still Be as Purple? The Changing Face of Trade Dress Protection for Pharmaceutical Manufacturers, 47 IDEA 171 (2006); Signe H. Naeve, Heart Pills Are Red, Viagra Is Blue ... When Does Pill Color Become Functional? An Analysis of Utilitarian and Aesthetic Functionality and Their Unintended Side Effects in the Pharmaceutical Industry, 27 Santa Clara Computer & High Tech. L.J. 299 (2011); Gina Kolata, Pills Morph as Patients Try to Cope, N.Y. Times, July 12, 2011, at D5 (reporting concerns about patient confusion because generic versions typically use different shapes and colors than the brand-name drug (as well as other generics) for which they may be substituted).

2. *Battling "gray market" imports.* When U.S. companies license the sale of their products overseas, they sometimes find that the foreign licensees attempt to export them back for sale to American consumers. These so-called "gray market" imports are not counterfeits, but they have a similar impact because their lower prices undercut sales by the domestic license holder. Companies have turned to the Lanham Act in an effort to block such imports. See Summit Tech., Inc. v. High–Line Med. Instruments Co., 922 F.Supp. 299, 307–11 (C.D.Cal.1996) (rejecting a Lanham Act claim brought by the manufacturer of an excimer laser system used by ophthalmologists against a company that purchased units in foreign markets for reimportation into the United States); see also Shira R. Yashor, Note, Competing in the Shadowy Gray: Protecting Domestic Trademark Holders from Gray Marketeers Under the Lanham Act, 59 U. Chi. L. Rev. 1363 (1992); cf. Polymer Tech. Corp. v. Mimran, 37 F.3d 74, 77–81 (2d Cir.1994) (rejecting trademark infringement claims asserted by the manufacturer of a contact lens solution intended only for sale to health professionals against retailers who sold the product directly to consumers). Recall from the previous chapter that Congress enacted legislation authorizing the FDA to allow the re-importation of drugs, but, until the agency chooses to implement that law, most types of gray market imports would run afoul of existing restrictions. See United States v. Milstein, 481 F.3d 132, 135–37 (2d Cir.2007) (upholding conviction and sentence, which included restitution order of $3.5 million to trademark owners); United States v. Genendo Pharm., N.V., 485 F.3d 958 (7th Cir.2007); Lars Noah, NAFTA's Impact on the Trade in Pharmaceuticals, 33 Hous. L. Rev. 1293, 1303–09 (1997); see also Jeffery Atik & Hans H. Lidgard, Embracing Price Discrimination: TRIPS and the Suppression of Parallel Trade in Pharmaceuticals, 27 U. Pa. J. Int'l Econ. L. 1043 (2006); Robert C. Bird & Peggy E. Chaudhry, Pharmaceuticals and the European Union: Managing Gray Markets in an Uncertain Legal Environment, 50 Va. J. Int'l L. 719 (2010); Julia A. Moore, Note, Parallel Trade, Unparallel Laws: An Examination of the Pharmaceutical Parallel Trade Laws of the United States, the European Union and the World Trade Organization, 6 Rich. J. Global L. & Bus. 77 (2006).

Rhone–Poulenc Rorer Pharmaceuticals, Inc. v. Marion Merrell Dow, Inc.

93 F.3d 511 (8th Cir.1996).

■ LOKEN, CIRCUIT JUDGE:

* * * Defendant Marion Merrell Dow (MMD) introduced the first diltiazem drug, Cardizem, in 1982. The FDA approved Cardizem for the treatment of angina; it was also widely prescribed to treat hypertension. In 1989, MMD introduced a sustained release Cardizem product that is taken twice per day. MMD then developed Cardizem CD, a sustained release drug that is taken only once per day. The FDA approved Cardizem CD for hypertension and for angina. Diltiazem was a pioneer new drug, which means that the Cardizem products enjoyed a ten-year period of market exclusivity under the [transitional provisions of the] Hatch–Waxman amendments to the Food, Drug, and Cosmetics Act. Cardizem products were immensely successful, generating sales of $1.1 billion in 1992 alone. By the early 1990s, competing drug manufacturers were anxious to penetrate the diltiazem market with less costly alternatives.

[Plaintiff Rhone–Poulenc Rorer (RPR)] launched its diltiazem drug in June 1992. RPR's Dilacor XR, a once-per-day sustained release tablet, initially received FDA new drug approval for the treatment of hypertension but not angina. FDA approval as a new drug, which is more rigorous than approval as a generic substitute, allowed Dilacor XR to compete with

Cardizem CD during the latter's period of market exclusivity. FDA classified Dilacor XR as a "BC" drug—one that is not necessarily "bioequivalent"—rather than a bioequivalent "AB" drug. Pharmacists may freely substitute among AB drugs, but only a prescribing physician may substitute one BC drug for another.

Given this FDA classification, to significantly penetrate the diltiazem market RPR had to persuade physicians to prescribe its low-cost product, Dilacor XR, as a substitute for Cardizem CD. MMD of course wanted to persuade the same audience that this is an inappropriate substitution. With this issue as the battleground, the two companies launched advertising campaigns for the allegiance of doctors, pharmacists, and hospitals. Because these are sophisticated consumers, the battle was waged with technical advertisements in professional journals and with marketing presentations by each company's sales representatives. RPR sought to convince prescribing physicians that Dilacor XR is the "same as, only cheaper" than Cardizem CD. MMD's message was, in essence, "not same as," and maybe not cheaper.

The nature of the competing false advertising claims can be briefly summarized. MMD's defensive advertising began with literature telling its sales representatives that Dilacor XR might be only seventy-five percent as bioavailable as Cardizem CD. After agreeing to discontinue that unsubstantiated claim, MMD's next wave of promotional materials advised sales representatives, doctors, and pharmacists that studies showed Dilacor XR only fifty percent as bioavailable as Cardizem CD. In its third wave of advertising, MMD released a four-page brochure in April 1993 reporting the results of a comparative study conducted by an outside laboratory, the "6730 Study." The results, as reported by MMD: "Dilacor XR delivers 81% of a 180–mg dose relative to Cardizem CD" and "74% of a 540–mg dose." RPR sued, contending that these false comparative bioavailability claims violate the Lanham Act.

Throughout this period, RPR's advertising urged doctors and pharmacists to switch their patients from Cardizem products to the low-cost Dilacor XR. In its counterclaims, MMD attacked this advertising as falsely telling medical professionals that Dilacor XR is freely substitutable for Cardizem products when in fact Dilacor XR is not FDA-approved for angina, physicians should monitor patients who switch from Cardizem CD because Dilacor XR does not have "similar bioavailability," and the two drugs are absorbed differently when taken with a meal (the "food effect").

After a bench trial, the district court found that MMD's early literature claiming that Dilacor XR has only seventy-five percent or fifty percent bioavailability violated the Lanham Act. It enjoined MMD from making those claims. However, it found that MMD's advertising based upon the 6730 Study was not false, and it declined to award RPR money damages because RPR failed to prove damage resulting from MMD's earlier false advertising. * * *

The Lanham Act prohibits "commercial advertising or promotion [that] misrepresents the nature, characteristics, qualities, or geographic origin of [the advertiser's] or another person's goods, services, or commercial activities." 15 U.S.C. § 1125(a)(1)(B). * * * Thus, the issue before us is whether that advertising was false because the 6730 Study is not a sufficiently reliable basis for comparing the bioavailability of Dilacor XR and Cardizem CD. At trial, RPR presented expert testimony that the 6730 Study was flawed in design and execution, plus evidence that two RPR studies, the "113 Study" and the "115 Study," did not have these flaws and refuted the bioavailability conclusions of the 6730 Study. MMD countered with expert testimony supporting the 6730 Study's methodology and attacking the RPR studies. After weighing this conflicting evidence, the district court concluded that the 6730 Study is a valid study "conducted by standards accepted within the scientific community and consistent with FDA principles." * * *

After carefully reviewing this evidence, we conclude the district court's finding that MMD did not falsely advertise the 6730 Study must be upheld. * * * We note that Lanham Act liability for "tests prove" advertising requires proof that the tests are not "sufficiently reliable" to support the advertised conclusion with "reasonable certainty." To ensure vigorous competition and to protect legitimate commercial speech, courts applying this standard should give advertisers a fair amount of leeway, at least in the absence of a clear intent to deceive or substantial consumer confusion.

RPR also argues that it was entitled to money damages for MMD's earlier false advertising. The Lanham Act provides that a successful plaintiff "shall be entitled" to recover "any damages sustained." 15 U.S.C. § 1117(a). Plaintiff must prove both actual damages and a causal link between defendant's violation and those damages. * * * RPR attempted to prove that MMD's false advertising resulted in $40 to $56 million of lost Dilacor XR sales. However, the district court found that Dilacor XR sales "exceeded [RPR's] initial predictions" and that "Dilacor XR is as well-positioned as should be reasonably expected at this stage in its product history with or without [MMD's] anti-Dilacor campaigns." These findings are not clearly erroneous and are directly responsive to RPR's damage theory. Thus, the district court did not abuse its remedial discretion in declining to award RPR damages. Likewise, because MMD discontinued its earlier false advertising and did not violate the Lanham Act in advertising the 6730 Study results, the court did not abuse its discretion in declining to order MMD to conduct corrective advertising.

The district court found that RPR's advertisements conveyed a false hidden message encouraging indiscriminate substitution of Dilacor XR for Cardizem CD. It ordered RPR to engage in corrective advertising regarding the fact that Dilacor XR is not FDA-approved to treat angina, the need to monitor and titrate patients who switch from Cardizem CD to Dilacor XR, and Dilacor XR's food effect. RPR concedes that its advertisements encouraged physicians to consider the two drugs freely substitutable, and it does not appeal the order that it must effectively disclose the need to monitor and titrate patients who switch drugs. But RPR does contend that the district court erred in ordering corrective advertising disclosing that Dilacor XR is not approved to treat angina and has a "food effect."

Regarding the limited FDA approval issue, RPR notes that it has truthfully advertised Dilacor XR as approved for the treatment of hypertension. The district court erred, RPR argues, because a Lanham Act plaintiff alleging that advertising is false because it conveys a false implicit message must prove actual consumer confusion, and MMD presented no such proof. See Johnson & Johnson–Merck Consumer Pharm. Co. v. SmithKline Beecham Corp., 960 F.2d 294, 297–98 (2d Cir.1992). We note that other Second Circuit cases have said that implicit falsity "should be tested by public reaction," not that a plaintiff such as MMD must prove confusion by consumer research. But we need not resolve that issue because consumer confusion need not be proved if advertising is literally false.[4]

In assessing whether advertising is literally false, "a court must analyze the message conveyed in full context." Here, the record clearly supports the district court's finding that RPR's advertisements were literally false. The court focused on RPR advertisements featuring images such as two similar gasoline pumps or airline tickets with dramatically different prices, accompanied by the slogan, "Which one would you choose." The court found that these ads falsely represented that the two drugs may be indiscriminately substituted, in effect, a representation that Dilacor XR "has certain qualities that it in fact does not actually have." Because the implicit message was literally false, the issue became one of remedy—what corrective advertising would be appropriate. The district court determined that the false message would be remedied if RPR adequately explained the differences in the two products, including the fact that Dilacor XR is not approved to treat angina. There was no abuse of discretion in adopting that remedy. * * *

Sandoz Pharmaceuticals Corp. v. Richardson–Vicks

902 F.2d 222 (3d Cir.1990).

■ BECKER, CIRCUIT JUDGE:

* * * Sandoz manufactures and sells various pharmaceutical products. Its offerings include Triaminic–DM and Triaminicol, leading cough medicines which may be used by children as well as adults. Like Sandoz, Vicks produces and markets a wide array of pharmaceuticals, but, unlike Sandoz, it has not had a market leader in the over-the-counter (OTC) children's cough medicine market. In the fall of 1989, Vicks sought to develop such a leader by introducing a new product, Pediatric 44.

---

4. Furthermore, MMD presented evidence of consumer confusion. One physician testified that an RPR representative told him that RPR's formulation of diltiazem "is the same as Cardizem CD." MMD produced affidavits from other physicians stating that they had been told by RPR representatives that the drugs are the same. MMD also produced RPR physician surveys suggesting that consumers viewed the two products as interchangeable.

Before its nationwide release of Pediatric 44, Vicks developed a consumer advertising campaign which claimed that Pediatric 44 "starts to work the instant they [the children] swallow" by "shielding irritated cough receptors on contact." Vicks planned to carry this message to consumers via television commercials and print advertisements in consumer magazines, and to pediatricians via "information sheets" mailed to doctors. In addition to claiming that Pediatric 44 "starts working from the very first swallow," the information sheets also state that "Pediatric Formula 44 provides more cough relief in the first thirty minutes [than] those thin, watery cough medicines." To support this statement, the Vicks circular used a bar graph which compared Pediatric 44 with "the leading OTC cough syrup," and showed Pediatric 44 apparently outperforming the competitor.

Vicks's advertising claims with regard to Pediatric 44 are based on the effect of certain locally-acting, inert sugary liquids known as "demulcents," which operate directly on cough receptors in the recipient's throat and respiratory passages. Demulcents are topically acting antitussives, in contrast to centrally acting antitussives, which are the traditional cough antidotes. Because these demulcents work on contact, Vicks claims that Pediatric 44 begins to reduce coughs as soon as it is swallowed.

Vicks performed various tests to support this conclusion. The record contains test results which support, if only marginally, Vicks's arguments that Pediatric 44 starts to work right away, that there is a scientific basis for this claim, and that Pediatric 44 is superior to its competitors. However, the FDA has never approved any "demulcents" as effective for the relief of coughs, and whether Vicks's level of testing could meet the high standards for drug approval set by the FDA is far from certain.[5] * * *

The first question of law we must address is whether a plaintiff can prevail under the Lanham Act by showing simply that the defendant's advertising claims about its OTC drug's effectiveness are inadequately substantiated under federal guidelines, without also showing that the claims are literally false or are misleading to the consuming public. Sandoz's prime contention on appeal is that it can.

The FTC has the authority under Sections 5 and 12 of the FTC Act, 15 U.S.C. §§ 45 & 52, to find that an inadequately substantiated advertising claim regarding a non-prescription drug is deceptive or misleading, and

---

5. * * * To this point, Vicks has only completed induced cough studies on Pediatric 44. These tests employed healthy subjects whose coughs were artificially induced by the inhalation of citric acid aerosol. Of the five tests performed, each test showed a statistically significant reduction in coughs by the subjects after they received Pediatric 44 as compared to before they received any cough medicine. All but one of the tests, however, were statistically inconclusive regarding whether Pediatric 44 reduced coughs more effectively than Robitussin, a leading OTC children's cough medicine. * * * Vicks undertook, but eventually abandoned, two attempts to measure the effectiveness of Pediatric 44 utilizing "disease state" studies, i.e., studies using individuals actually suffering from upper respiratory infections or other cough-inducing illnesses. Disease state studies are considered more accurate measures of a drug's effectiveness because the drug is tested on subjects actually suffering from the symptoms the drug allegedly combats.

thus illegal. Sandoz argues that the language in the FTC Act prohibiting "any false advertising" is functionally indistinguishable from the language in the Lanham Act prohibiting "any false description or representation." Therefore, according to Sandoz, "it would be absurd" to conclude that an inadequately substantiated claim can violate Sections 5 and 12 of the FTC Act but not Section 43(a) of the Lanham Act.

Vicks, on the other hand, states that Sandoz cannot succeed merely by showing that Vicks's advertising claims are not supported by enough evidence to warrant FDA approval. Rather, Vicks maintains that Sandoz must prove that insufficient substantiation misleads consumers or pediatricians. * * * The key distinctions between the FTC and a Lanham Act plaintiff turns on the burdens of proof and the deference accorded these respective litigants. The FTC, as a plaintiff, can rely on its own determination of deceptiveness. In contrast, a Lanham Act plaintiff must prove deceptiveness in court. * * * [C]onsumer testimony proving actual deception is not necessary when the FTC claims that an advertisement has the capacity to deceive or mislead the public. A Lanham Act plaintiff, on the other hand, is not entitled to the luxury of deference to its judgment. Consequently, where the advertisements are not literally false, plaintiff bears the burden of proving actual deception by a preponderance of the evidence. Hence, it cannot obtain relief by arguing how consumers *could* react; it must show how consumers *actually do* react. * * * We hold that it is not sufficient for a Lanham Act plaintiff to show only that the defendant's advertising claims of its own drug's effectiveness are inadequately substantiated under FDA guidelines; the plaintiff must also show that the claims are literally false or misleading to the public. * * *

Sandoz failed to advance actual evidence of consumer misinterpretation. Furthermore, Sandoz's counsel in oral argument before this court admitted that Sandoz had not proven either that the ingredient in Pediatric 44 designed to shield cough receptors was ineffective or that Vicks's advertising claim was literally false. The district court carefully analyzed the evidence of Vicks's theoretical and empirical justifications for its advertising claims, and we cannot say that its finding that Sandoz did not establish that consumers were misled was clearly erroneous. * * *

[A] target audience's special knowledge of a class of products is highly relevant to any claim that it was misled by an advertisement for such a product. Sandoz never advanced any hard evidence that pediatricians would be misled by Vicks's information sheets or that they would believe that the assertions contained therein were supported by a greater degree of testing data than Vicks actually had compiled. We therefore conclude that the district court's finding that Sandoz had not proven that the pediatrician advertisements were misleading is also not clearly erroneous. * * *

We turn now to the question whether a Lanham Act false labeling claim exists against a manufacturer who lists an ingredient as "inactive" when FDA standards seem to require that such an ingredient be labeled as "active." Sandoz has presented no evidence showing that Pediatric 44's "inactive" label is misleading to the consuming public, and Sandoz did not actively pursue the argument, either here or in the district court, that the "inactive" label in question was deceptive. Instead, it alleges that the label contains a literally false description of the product. * * *

The Lanham Act is primarily intended to protect commercial interests. A competitor in a Lanham Act suit does not act as a " 'vicarious avenger' of the public's right to be protected against false advertising." Am. Home Prods. Corp. v. Johnson & Johnson, 672 F.Supp. 135, 145 (S.D.N.Y.1987). Instead, the statute provides a private remedy to a commercial plaintiff who meets the burden of proving that its commercial interests have been harmed by a competitor's false advertising. The FD & C Act, in contrast, is not focused on the truth or falsity of advertising claims. It requires the FDA to protect the public interest by "pass[ing] on the safety and efficacy of all new drugs and ... promulgat[ing] regulations concerning the conditions under which various categories of OTC drugs ... are safe, effective and not misbranded." Am. Home Prod. Corp. v. Johnson & Johnson, 436 F.Supp. 785, 797–98 (S.D.N.Y.1977), aff'd, 577 F.2d 160 (2d Cir.1978).

Sandoz argues that false labeling is actionable under the Lanham Act, and rather conclusively assumes that Vicks's listing of the demulcents in its Pediatric 44 as "inactive" is false. Assuming arguendo that false labeling is actionable under the Lanham Act, Sandoz cannot prevail on its labeling claim because it has not proved that Vicks's labeling is false. Sandoz's counsel argued to the district court that "[i]f [the demulcents] relieve coughs they're active. That's true as a matter of common sense and normal English." Such an interpretation of FDA regulations, absent direct guidance from the promulgating agency, is not as simple as Sandoz proposes.

The FDA has not found conclusively that demulcents must be labelled as active or inactive ingredients within the meaning of 21 C.F.R. § 210.3(b)(7).[10] We decline to find and do not believe that the district court had to find, either "as a matter of common sense" or "normal English," that which the FDA, with all of its scientific expertise, has yet to determine. Because "agency decisions are frequently of a discretionary nature or frequently require expertise, the agency should be given the first chance to exercise that discretion or to apply that expertise." Thus, we are unable to conclude that Vicks's labeling of Pediatric 44's demulcents as inactive is literally false, even if Vicks concurrently claims that these ingredients enable its medicine to work the instant it is swallowed.

Sandoz's position would require us to usurp administrative agencies' responsibility for interpreting and enforcing potentially ambiguous regulations. Jurisdiction for the regulation of OTC drug marketing is vested jointly and exhaustively in the FDA and the FTC, and is divided between them by agreement. Neither of these agencies' constituent statutes creates an express or implied private right of action, and what the FD & C Act and the FTC Act do not create directly, the Lanham Act does not create

10. Sandoz is free to petition the FDA to investigate these alleged labeling violations. Sandoz represents that it has embarked upon this path already. The fact that it has been unable to get a quick response from the FDA, however, does not create a claim for Sandoz under the Lanham Act.

indirectly, at least not in cases requiring original interpretation of these Acts or their accompanying regulations. * * *

NOTES AND QUESTIONS

1. *Private remedies for false advertising by competitors.* In addition to providing a private right of action for cases of trademark infringement, the Lanham Act has become an important weapon in the promotional battles between pharmaceutical companies. See Schering–Plough Healthcare Prods., Inc. v. Schwarz Pharma, Inc., 586 F.3d 500, 505, 508–13 (7th Cir.2009) (affirming the dismissal of false labeling claims asserted by the manufacturer of the OTC laxative drug Miralax® (polyethylene glycol 3350) against sellers of generic versions that continued to indicate Rx-only use because the FDA had not yet decided whether this caused the latter products to be misbranded); Schering Corp. v. Pfizer Inc., 189 F.3d 218 (2d Cir.1999) (reviewing allegations that sales representatives had made misleading claims for prescription antihistamines when detailing physicians); Axcan Scandipharm v. Ethex Corp., 585 F.Supp.2d 1067, 1073–77 (D.Minn. 2007) (rejecting the argument that the FDA enjoyed primary jurisdiction over allegations (and therefore barred Lanham Act claims) that the defendants had falsely implied that their prescription pancreatic-enzyme supplements were bioequivalent to the plaintiff's Ultrase® products); see also PhotoMedex, Inc. v. Irwin, 601 F.3d 919, 924–31 (9th Cir.2010) (affirming summary judgment for defendant that had represented its dermatological laser as "approved" even though the device arguably differed significantly from a prior model cleared under § 510(k)); id. at 924 ("Because the FDCA forbids private rights of action under that statute, a private action brought under the Lanham Act may not be pursued when, as here, the claim would require litigation of the alleged underlying FDCA violation in a circumstance where the FDA has not itself concluded that there was such a violation."); Suzanne Vranica, Pharmaceuticals Try Bolder Tactics: Pfizer Campaign Includes Rare Swing at Rival Drug in a Competitive Market, Wall St. J., Apr. 5, 2004, at B3 (reporting a controversy about a superiority claim for a migraine treatment made in advertisements directed to consumers).

2. *False advertising claims by consumers.* Purchasers do not have standing to sue under the Lanham Act. See Serbin v. Ziebart Int'l Corp., 11 F.3d 1163 (3d Cir.1993). Thus, federal law would offer no relief to consumers if, for instance, it turns out that antitussives do not work as advertised. See Rita Rubin, Cough Syrup Left out in the Cold: Over-the-Counter Drugs Don't Help, Report Says, USA Today, Jan. 10, 2006, at 1A. If a consumer did not suffer a personal injury that might allow a tortious misrepresentation or similar claim under common law, he or she might have recourse under state statutes that prohibit deceptive acts or practices and provide a private right of action. See Bober v. Glaxo Wellcome PLC, 246 F.3d 934 (7th Cir.2001) [excerpted in Chap. 4(B)(2)] (rejecting consumers' objections to nonsubstitutability claims for OTC Zantac 75 and Rx Zantac 150); Boos v. Abbott Lab., 925 F.Supp. 49, 54–56 (D.Mass.1996).

B. MARKET EXCLUSIVITY PERIODS

Because inventors usually apply for patents before clinical testing commences, manufacturers of new drugs and medical devices have only a portion of their patent term (which now runs 20 years from filing, plus any extension) left when they receive FDA approval. Recognizing that this may weaken the incentives for innovative activity, Congress established various periods of market exclusivity as a partial substitute. Although weaker than a patent because it only stalls FDA clearance of generic competitors, a period of market exclusivity can provide tremendous financial returns if it runs beyond the date of patent expiration. See William E. Ridgway, Note, Realizing Two–Tiered Innovation Policy Through Drug Regulation, 58 Stan. L. Rev. 1221, 1235–36 (2006) (explaining that this form of quasi-IP protection has become increasingly important); see also Ron A. Bouchard et al., The Pas de Deux of Pharmaceutical Regulation and Innovation: Who's Leading Whom?, 24 Berkeley Tech. L.J. 1461 (2009); Rebecca S. Eisenberg, The Role of FDA in Innovation Policy, 13 Mich. Telecomm. & Tech. L. Rev. 345 (2007).

1. NEW DRUGS AND MEDICAL DEVICES

Upjohn Co. v. Kessler

938 F.Supp. 439 (W.D.Mich.1996).

■ BELL, DISTRICT JUDGE:

* * * Upjohn originally developed minoxidil as an antihypertensive agent for the treatment of high blood pressure. When patients using the drug experienced unwanted hair growth, Upjohn began investigations into the use of the drug for treatment of hair loss. In 1988 the FDA approved Upjohn's new drug application (NDA) for Rogaine, a 2% minoxidil topical solution for the treatment of certain forms of male hair loss. In 1991 Upjohn received FDA approval for the use of Rogaine in the treatment of female hair loss. The FDA approvals limited Rogaine to sale as a prescription drug.

In September 1991, Upjohn initiated communications with the FDA regarding its desire to have Rogaine approved for over-the-counter sales. Such a switch from Rx to OTC status requires approval of a supplemental NDA by the FDA. Upjohn advised that Rogaine had proven to be a safe treatment and that a sufficiently large body of data had been collected that supported the Rx-to-OTC switch. On April 9, 1992, Upjohn representatives met with FDA representatives to discuss what information the FDA would require in order to evaluate the proposed Rx-to-OTC switch. Among the concerns raised by FDA representatives at this meeting were the low tolerance for any risk of serious adverse effects due to the cosmetic nature of the drug, the need to address cardiovascular risks and the need to address risks associated with gross over use of the product. Upjohn referenced the ongoing IV [intravenous] study in hypertensive patients that it was conducting in connection with its investigation into 5% minoxidil. On April 29, 1993, Upjohn submitted its supplemental NDA to the FDA for OTC Rogaine. Included in the supplemental NDA were the results of the IV study and an application for a 3 year period of exclusivity.

The FDA approved Upjohn's supplemental NDA for the Rx-to-OTC switch on February 9, 1996. Upjohn's patent for minoxidil expired on February 13, 1996. On April 5, 1996, the FDA informed Upjohn by telephone that its claim of exclusivity was denied. On the same date the FDA approved ANDAs for OTC Minoxidil Topical Solution 2% for intervenors Barre National and Lemmon. On April 9, 1996, the FDA approved a similar ANDA for Bausch & Lomb.

On April 12, 1996, Upjohn filed this action for declaratory and injunctive relief. Upjohn contends that the FDA's denial of its request for three years of market exclusivity and approval of the ANDAs prior to February 9, 1999, violates the market exclusivity provisions of the Act, was done arbitrarily and capriciously and not in accordance with law, was in excess of statutory authority, and constituted a taking of property without just compensation in violation of the Fifth Amendment. * * *

Upjohn was informed of the decision by telephone on April 5, 1996. In a subsequent telephone conversation Dr. Lipicky of the FDA explained that the agency's view was that the IV minoxidil study was not essential. Upjohn was also informed that the agency would not be preparing an explanatory letter * * * * [The administrative record that the agency certified to the court consisted primarily of a memorandum from Dr. Robert Temple, Director of the FDA's Office of Drug Evaluation, to Dr. Janet Woodcock, Director of the FDA's Center for Drug Evaluation and Research (CDER), dated March 20, 1996.]

[T]here are three conditions for approval of a three-year exclusivity period. [See 21 U.S.C. § 355(j)(4)(D)(iv).] In this case there is no dispute that the IV test was a new clinical test or that the test was sponsored by Upjohn. The only issue for the court's consideration is whether there was a rational basis for the FDA's determination that the IV test was not essential to approval. Upjohn contends that the question of whether the test was essential is straight forward and calls for no scientific expertise: the IV test was essential because it was required by the FDA.

Upjohn's argument fails because it is not supported by the evidence presented. There is no question that the FDA expressed its safety concerns at the April 9, 1992, meeting. There is no evidence, however, that the FDA required Upjohn to conduct the IV study as a condition for approval of the Rx-to-OTC switch. The FDA minutes reveal that the FDA representatives expressed several areas of concern: (1) risk of misuse—"What if someone uses more than the labeled dose? What are the blood levels of Rogaine when there is an increase in absorption or gross over use?;" (2) Dr. Botstein noted the need for a focused presentation on cardiovascular risks; and (3) Dr. Temple stated that given the nature of the benefits, a case must be made that there is no discernable risk in terms of serious adverse events. * * * Dr. Temple stated that by now Upjohn should have enough information to determine whether the warnings about cardiovascular events should be removed from the physician's insert. Dr. Lipicky and Dr. Temple commented that they were familiar with the post-marketing surveillance study that had been done in conjunction with the Rx Rogaine, and that the data from the post-marketing study would support the safety of Rogaine.

The 1992 discussion clearly centered on what should be included in the submission, and was not designed to critique the studies or available data. That data was not then before the FDA—the supplemental NDA would not be filed for another year. Nowhere is there any indication that the FDA ever suggested that the available data was insufficient or that the IV test was a necessary prerequisite for approval. In fact there was testimony from Upjohn's Dr. Data that subsequent to the meeting Upjohn seriously considered submitting the supplemental NDA without the IV study.

After submitting the supplemental NDA in 1993 with the completed IV study, Upjohn received numerous questions about the IV study from the FDA. The FDA's interest in the results of the study is not evidence that the FDA requested that the study be done. The FDA is not required to ignore evidence offered by a company in support of its request for approval merely because the evidence is not necessary to approval.

If the FDA did not require Upjohn to conduct the IV study as a condition to approval, was the IV study nevertheless essential to the FDA's ability to make its determination that Rogaine was safe for OTC use? The FDA has defined the term "essential to approval" in its regulations: "Essential to approval means, with regard to an investigation, that there are no other data available that could support approval of the application." 21 C.F.R. § 314.108(a). There is no question that the FDA had some safety concerns with respect to the OTC sale of Rogaine. Could that safety determination be made without reference to the IV test? Was there other available data which addressed FDA's concern about whether the margin of safety for topical minoxidil was sufficient to support OTC use? These questions involve evaluation of the clinical trial and the scientific and medical significance of that trial to FDA's final determination. They bring the court into the heart of a chemical and pharmacological debate that is within the peculiar expertise of the FDA. * * *

The court has reviewed Dr. Temple's 19–page memorandum devoted to the issue of whether Upjohn's IV study of minoxidil was essential to approval of OTC Rogaine. In this comprehensive memorandum Dr. Temple considered the fact that Dr. Lipicky, Director, Division of Cardio–Renal Drug Products, said that the IV study was essential to his approval recommendation because it helped answer questions about the safety of OTC minoxidil raised by the medical reviewer, Dr. Karkowsky. Dr. Temple also considered Dr. Karkowsky's safety review and the extent to which it analyzed and relied on the results of the IV study.

Dr. Temple agreed that in order to approve the Rx-to-OTC switch the FDA should have a high level of confidence that topical minoxidil will rarely, if ever, have significant hemodynamic effects. Nevertheless, he concluded that the IV study did not add significantly to the FDA's ability to reach this conclusion because (1) the IV study did not add much information about concentration-response relationships, at least as analyzed, and (2) neither the IV nor oral studies, as analyzed, shed light on individual responses—they do not help answer the question of whether the rare topical patients with concentrations in the 5–10 ng/ml range will have a response:

> My conclusion is that the original clinical data, including study 84, enhanced by 6 benign (so far as we can tell) years of marketing, and the cohort study, indicate a very satisfactory record of safety, one suitable for an OTC drug. This is not surprising given the documented large (order of magnitude) difference between blood levels after topical dosing and the blood levels associated with barely detectable effects (slight HR increase, no BP effect) after oral dosing with a 2.5 mg b.i.d. tablet. The IV study was not essential to this conclusion, although it supported it, because concentrations achieved overlapped with those in the study of oral minoxidil and gave little new information.

Upjohn contends that the Temple rationale is arbitrary and capricious because it relied on data available in or before 1988, prior to approval for Rx Rogaine and because the IV test was the only effective study to address the margin of safety issue. Upjohn also contends that the 6 benign years of Rx use are not very helpful to the safety issue because people with hypertension had been warned away from the drug through the package insert discussion on risk factors.

Upjohn's dispute with the Temple memorandum is fundamentally a scientific dispute in an area where this court lacks expertise and is required to give the FDA great deference. It appears to this court that although an opposite conclusion, i.e., that the IV test was essential, could have been supported on this record, Dr. Temple's decision did not come out of the blue. Prior to the final decision Upjohn learned that even Dr. Lipicky was leaning against exclusivity. The issue of exclusivity presented the agency with a close question that required more levels of agency attention than was routine. * * *

Dr. Temple's memorandum states in detail the grounds for the decision and the essential facts upon which the decision was based. It appears that he considered the statutory factors governing exclusivity, considered the relevant data, and arrived at a rational decision based upon the evidence. Nothing more is required. See Upjohn Mfg. Co. v. Schweiker, 681 F.2d 480, 483 (6th Cir.1982). The court cannot say that the agency's determination that the IV test was not essential was arbitrary and capricious. * * * In light of the fact that Upjohn has not shown a likelihood of success on the merits, the court does not believe injunctive relief is appropriate. Upjohn's motion for preliminary injunctive will accordingly be denied.

NOTES AND QUESTIONS

1. *Supplemental indications.* The statute provided five years of market exclusivity for the original NDA, coupled with three additional years for supplemental indications based on new research. One company argued that, once it approves such a supplement, the FDA could not approve an ANDA for the original indication(s) because the labeling for the generic would then not be the same as the innovator's product. In the course of rejecting this interpretation of the statute, the court explained the economic motivation for taking this position:

> BMS considers it cold comfort that the FDA would withhold approval of a generic version of captopril for some indications but not others; once the FDA approves the sale of generic captopril for hypertension, the agency can offer BMS no assurance that physicians and pharmacists will not substitute it for Capoten in the treatment of diabetic nephropathy [the supplemental indication for which the additional exclusivity period had not yet expired].

Bristol–Myers Squibb Co. v. Shalala, 91 F.3d 1493, 1496 (D.C.Cir.1996). Although the court held that the innovator company had alleged a sufficient injury to have standing to sue, see id. at 1498–99, it rejected the company's challenge to the FDA's regulation on the merits, see id. at 1499–500:

> [U]nder the Secretary's interpretation of the Act, a pioneer drug manufacturer that obtains approval for a supplemental indication based upon proprietary research will enjoy three years during which the FDA will not approve any ANDA that includes the supplemental indication. BMS claims that economic reality renders the protection offered by the Secretary largely an illusion. Perhaps so, but why? By BMS's own account, it is because the value of the protection the Congress most clearly conferred upon pioneers would be greater but for some state laws and health insurers that mandate substitution of generic drugs. That is not a sufficient basis upon which to conclude that the Congress intended to confer upon the manufacturers of pioneer drugs the much broader protection that BMS now seeks.

Even so, does that not risk creating "orphan" indications? See, e.g., Andrew Pollack, Drug Offers a Safer Option in Preventing Breast Cancer, Researchers Say, N.Y. Times, June 5, 2011, at A25 (reporting that the aromatase inhibitor exemestane, approved to prevent the recurrence of breast cancer, appears also to help prevent such cancers initially, but noting that the patent just expired so the prospect of generic competition "means that Pfizer, which sells Aromasin, has little incentive to seek regulatory approval" for this new indication, adding that "insurers might be reluctant to pay" for such an off-label use).

2. *Exclusivity after OTC switches.* Unlike Upjohn's experience with Rogaine, recall from Chap. 10(A)(5) that SKB received three years of additional market exclusivity after successfully switching Nicorette to nonprescription status. Similarly, after securing the long-delayed (and ultimately only partial) OTC switch of its emergency contraceptive product, see Chap. 4(A)(1), Barr Labs received this added exclusivity period for Plan B. See Diedtra Henderson, No–Competition Drugs Stir Controversy, Boston Globe, Nov. 13, 2006, at E1. Even if generic competitors previously had entered the prescription market, an OTC switch would force the FDA to withdraw ANDAs for the Rx versions (and, if the sponsor had secured supplemental exclusivity, ANDAs for OTC versions would have to wait three years). See, e.g., 73 Fed. Reg. 63,491, 63,491–92 (2008) (announcing proposed withdrawal of ANDAs for polyethylene glycol 3350); id. at 63,493 n.1 (explaining exceptions where a version of the original product remained subject to Rx-only use).

3. *Medical devices*. Because of the significant differences in approval systems, the market exclusivity periods provided by the Hatch–Waxman Act have no application to medical devices (though patent term extension and other provisions did apply equally to them). Nonetheless, the Safe Medical Devices Act of 1990 created a somewhat analogous approach for Class III devices subject to PMA requirements. Aside from possible patent constraints, a company wishing to market a device similar to one already approved by the FDA would have to assemble the same data as the innovator, but, six years after approval of a PMA for the same type of Class III device, subsequent manufacturers could file what amounts to an abbreviated PMA by cross-referencing the innovator's safety and effectiveness data. See 21 U.S.C. § 360j(h)(4).

4. *Turnabout is fair play*. When the patent and market exclusivity periods for an innovator drug wind down, manufacturers may respond by seeking approval of a "new and improved" version to combat the threat of generic competition against the original version of the drug. See Michael A. Carrier, A Real–World Analysis of Pharmaceutical Settlements: The Missing Dimension of Product Hopping, 62 Fla. L. Rev. 1009 (2010); Rebecca S. Yoshitani & Ellen S. Cooper, Pharmaceutical Reformulation: The Growth of Life Cycle Management, 7 Hous. J. Health L. & Pol'y 379 (2007); Jessie Cheng, Note, An Antitrust Analysis of Product Hopping in the Pharmaceutical Industry, 108 Colum. L. Rev. 1471 (2008). For instance, manufacturers may introduce sustained release formulations that require less frequent dosing or a different form of the active ingredient with greater safety and/or effectiveness. See Gardiner Harris, As a Patent Expires, Drug Firm Lines up Pricey Alternative, Wall St. J., June 6, 2002, at A1 (reporting that AstraZeneca introduced Nexium® (esomeprazole magnesium) for gastroesophageal reflux disease just as its blockbuster drug Prilosec® (omeprazole) faced generic competition); Andrew Pollack, A Drug's Second Act: Battling Jet Lag, N.Y. Times, Jan. 7, 2010, at B1 (discussing Cephalon's efforts to extend its Provigil® (modafinil) franchise by, prior to patent expiration, substantially increasing its price and introducing the relatively less expensive extended-release drug Nuvigil® (armodafinil) with additional indications); see also Walgreen Co. v. AstraZeneca Pharms. L.P., 534 F.Supp.2d 146, 149, 152–53 (D.D.C.2008) (dismissing antitrust claims against the manufacturer of Prilosec for introducing a slightly modified formulation (Nexium) and ceasing to advertise its original prescription formulation);

Abbott Labs. v. Teva Pharms. USA, Inc., 432 F.Supp.2d 408, 416–18 (D.Del.2006) (summarizing similar allegations in TriCor® (fenofibrate) antitrust litigation); Guy V. Amoresano, Branded Drug Reformulation: The Next Brand vs. Generic Antitrust Battleground, 62 Food & Drug L.J. 249 (2007). If the FDA approves such a product, the sponsor of the NDA will receive market exclusivity for either three years (same as a supplemental NDA for an additional indication based on new studies) or five years (same as an entirely new chemical entity). Although the agency may approve ANDAs for generic versions of the original product, the manufacturers of these less expensive copies may find it difficult to take market share from therapeutically superior or more convenient versions of the product.

5. *Active moieties*. The statute provides that, before approving an ANDA, the FDA must wait five years after the approval of an NDA "for a drug, no active ingredient (including any ester or salt of the active ingredient) of which has been approved in any other application." 21 U.S.C. § 355(j)(5)(D)(ii). In trying to interpret identical language used to grant ten years of exclusivity for new chemical entities approved between 1982 and 1984, one court found serious ambiguities in the provision. See Abbott Lab. v. Young, 920 F.2d 984 (D.C.Cir.1990). In 1982, the FDA had approved the anticonvulsant Depakote® (divalproex sodium), but the agency granted the sponsor only two years of market exclusivity under the Hatch–Waxman Act's transitional provisions because, four years earlier, the same company had received an NDA for the anticonvulsant Depakene® (valproic acid). Although their active ingredients differed, the two drugs had the same "active moiety" (and pharmacological action) because divalproex sodium converted into valproic acid once ingested, but Depakote produced fewer gastrointestinal side effects. The question for the court was whether Depakote's "active ingredient (including any ester or salt of the active ingredient)" had previously been approved, in which case the sponsor would receive the shorter period of market exclusivity. Although it was a salt of valproic acid, the FDA had never before approved a drug containing divalproex sodium or any ester or salt of that active ingredient. Over a sharp dissent, the court held that the language was ambiguous with regard to whether it referred to the active ingredient of the first or the second NDA, but it rejected as unreasonable the government's argument that the word "including" in the parenthetical introduced a nonexhaustive list of examples of similar forms of an active ingredient, which the FDA could interpret as also encompassing an active moiety. Conversely, the court rejected the sponsor's literal reading as implausible because it doubted that Congress had any reason for such an asymmetry (if the FDA had approved the NDA for valproic acid in 1982—after previously approving divalproex sodium—and the question focused on market exclusivity for Depakene, then everyone agrees that the sponsor would receive only two years of protection from generics). The court remanded this interpretive mess to the FDA for further consideration. See Pfizer Inc. v. Dr. Reddy's Lab., Ltd., 359 F.3d 1361, 1366 (Fed.Cir.2004) (explaining that the FDA subsequently promulgated a rule defining the phrase to encompass an active moiety, and applying this interpretation to identical language in a different Hatch–

Waxman provision so as to prevent approval of a paper NDA for a different salt of amlodipine (Norvasc®) before the end of its extended patent term); cf. Photocure ASA v. Kappos, 603 F.3d 1372 (Fed.Cir.2010) [excerpted in Chap. 10(A)(4)] (interpreting similar language related to eligibility for patent term extension).

Actavis Elizabeth LLC v. FDA

625 F.3d 760 (D.C.Cir.2010).

■ RANDOLPH, SENIOR CIRCUIT JUDGE:

* * * In 2005, New River Pharmaceuticals, the predecessor in interest to intervenor-defendant Shire Pharmaceuticals, sought approval to market lisdexamfetamine dimesylate for the treatment of attention deficit hyperactivity disorder under the brand name Vyvanse. Vyvanse received FDA approval on February 23, 2007. The agency determined that the drug was entitled to a five-year period of exclusivity under its regulations. In January 2009, Actavis submitted its abbreviated application for the generic drug lisdexamfetamine dimesylate. Its application referenced Vyvanse. The FDA returned Actavis' application unfiled because Vyvanse's period of market exclusivity had not expired. Actavis brought this suit in the district court under the Administrative Procedure Act, seeking to force the agency to rescind its grant of exclusivity to Vyvanse and to accept Actavis' abbreviated application. * * *

To understand Actavis' arguments, it is necessary briefly to describe the chemical structure of lisdexamfetamine dimesylate, the drug molecule in question. Lisdexamfetamine dimesylate is a salt of lisdexamfetamine. Since, under the agency's regulations, salts are not considered active moieties, the agency's analysis centered on the lisdexamfetamine molecule alone. Lisdexamfetamine consists of a portion of lysine, a common amino acid, connected to dextroamphetamine. These two parts are linked by an amide bond, a type of covalent bond that utilizes a nitrogen atom to perform the linking function. What is important is that once it enters the body, lisdexamfetamine undergoes a chemical conversion to produce dextroamphetamine. In industry parlance, this makes lisdexamfetamine a "prodrug" of dextroamphetamine. Drugs containing dextroamphetamine, but not lisdexamfetamine, had received FDA approval before New River filed its application for Vyvanse. * * *

The agency interprets its regulations to allow five-year exclusivity for drugs containing derivative molecules of previously approved "active moieties" when those derivative molecules contain non-ester covalent bonds [i.e., use linking atoms other than oxygen]. * * * When the drug molecule is not in the form of an ester, salt, or other noncovalent derivative, the FDA treats the entire molecule as that "responsible for the physiological or pharmacological action of the drug substance," and therefore a separate "active moiety." 21 C.F.R. § 314.108(a). Any drug that does not contain a previously approved active moiety is entitled to five-year exclusivity. This leaves certain types of prodrugs eligible for five-year exclusivity—namely, those that are not esters, salts, or other types of noncovalent derivatives. The FDA's interpretation is squarely within the language of its regulations. And since lisdexamfetamine contains an amide bond, the FDA properly treated it as an "active moiety" of its own.

Actavis spends the bulk of its briefs arguing that the FDA's interpretation is inconsistent with the clear meaning of the statute. Where Actavis sees clarity we see ambiguity. Under the Hatch–Waxman Amendments, five-year exclusivity is granted to drugs "no active ingredient (including any ester or salt of the active ingredient) of which" has been approved in a prior new drug application. 21 U.S.C. § 355(j)(5)(F)(ii). Actavis thinks this language prevents the FDA from granting five-year exclusivity to any drug containing a drug molecule (such as lisdexamfetamine) that eventually produces a previously approved drug molecule in the body. In addition, the company believes that the FDA's interpretation allowing such exclusivity upends the incentive scheme created by Congress and "eviscerates" the distinction between three- and five-year exclusivity.

Actavis relies mainly on the term "active ingredient," which it says obligates the FDA to identify the particular drug molecule that reaches the "site" of the drug's action. This molecule, Actavis argues, is necessarily the "active ingredient" of the drug in question, regardless of the form of the molecule before it enters the body. But there is nothing to indicate that Congress used the term in the sense Actavis urges. The Hatch–Waxman Amendments do not define active ingredient. The legislative history establishes only that Congress was concerned with providing incentives for innovation by granting five-year exclusivity to "new chemical entities" and is silent on what determines novelty.

The word "active," standing alone, does not get Actavis any further. Actavis argues that by using the term "active," Congress was requiring the FDA to determine the particular molecule that provides the drug's "activity," which it claims is limited to the drug's specific therapeutic effect. If this molecule has been previously approved, then five-year exclusivity is not warranted. But the FDA is right—or at least we have been given no reason to doubt—that the activity of a drug cannot be reduced to such a simple formulation. The agency has concluded that, for certain types of prodrugs, the entire pre-ingestion drug molecule should be deemed responsible for the drug's activity, which can include its "distribution within the body, its metabolism, its excretion, or its toxicity." There is no reason to believe Congress thought differently—or thought about it at all. * * *

Actavis argues that the FDA's current approach violates the statutory scheme, which it claims "reserves five-year exclusivity only for major innovations." In this view, a drug containing a derivative molecule such as lisdexamfetamine should be entitled, at most, to three years of exclusivity. To buttress its claim, Actavis offers a scenario in which drug companies such as Shire are able to maintain never-ending periods of five-year exclusivity for "minor" variations on already approved drug molecules simply by adding different covalent appendages to them.

In the FDA's view, drug derivatives such as lisdexamfetamine *are* "major innovations" deserving five-year exclusivity. The FDA's regulations leave many types of drug derivatives eligible only for three-year exclusivity. For example, an ester derivative of a previously approved drug molecule remains entitled to three-year exclusivity if the application required for its approval "contains reports of new clinical investigations ... essential to the approval of the application and conducted or sponsored by the applicant." 21 U.S.C. § 355(j)(5)(F)(iii). The FDA is *defining* the line between three- and five-year exclusivity, not eviscerating it. Actavis' prediction of multiple repeated periods of five-year exclusivity for minor variations on existing drug products assumes a view (contrary to the agency's) of what constitutes a minor variation. It also finds little support in reality. In the nearly two decades since the current FDA regulations came into effect, there is no such example, or at least none Actavis has identified. This is hardly surprising, given the time and effort required to gain approval under § 355(b).

Since nothing in the text, structure, purpose, or legislative history of the statute "speaks directly to the precise question at issue," the agency's interpretation must stand if it is reasonable. The FDA's policy is based on its view that drug derivatives containing non-ester covalent bonds are, on the whole, distinct from other types of derivative drugs such that the former are uniquely deserving of "new chemical entity" status and the resulting five-year exclusivity. The FDA explained its distinction in a 1989 response to a citizens' petition:

> It has been FDA's longstanding experience that even minor covalent structural changes are capable of producing not only major changes in the activity of a drug but changes that are not readily predicted.... In contrast to most changes in the covalent structure of a molecule, the formation of a salt or a complex, or of an ester, is not intended to, and generally cannot, alter the basic pharmacologic or toxicologic properties of the molecule.

We are hard pressed to second-guess the FDA's view, especially since it "rests on the agency's evaluations of scientific data within its area of expertise." At best, Actavis has offered evidence that some covalent structural changes do not alter the basic properties of the drug in question and that some noncovalent structural changes do. But agencies may "employ bright-line rules for reasons of administrative convenience, so long as those rules fall within a zone of reasonableness and are reasonably explained." The FDA has explained that its policy is based in part on the "difficulty in determining precisely which molecule, or portion of a molecule, is responsible for a drug's effects." Nothing in the record establishes that the FDA's approach is unreasonable. Given the complexity of the statutory regime, we defer to the agency's interpretation. * * * The district court's grant of summary judgment to the FDA and to Shire is affirmed.

2. "ORPHAN" PRODUCTS AND INDICATIONS

Baker Norton Pharmaceuticals, Inc. v. FDA

132 F.Supp.2d 30 (D.D.C.2001).

■ HARRIS, DISTRICT JUDGE:

This case involves three groups: plaintiff Baker Norton, defendants Food and Drug Administration and two government officials (collectively "the FDA defendants"), and defendant-intervenor Bristol–Myers Squibb (BMS). Before the court are three motions for summary judgment, submitted by each of the three groups. * * *

When the potential market for a drug is small because the target market is relatively small, it is difficult for a pharmaceutical manufacturer to recover the large research and development costs, and even more difficult to realize a worthwhile return on that investment. The Orphan Drug Act therefore was enacted in 1983 to provide an incentive to develop and test drugs for the treatment of "rare diseases or conditions," which is defined to include diseases or conditions affecting fewer than 200,000 Americans. According to the FDA, in the ten years prior to the passage of the Orphan Drug Act, only ten products for rare diseases were developed and approved for marketing without federal funding. Since the passage of the Orphan Drug Act, the FDA has approved at least 172 orphan drugs and biological products; furthermore, more than 700 orphan-designated products currently are being developed.

Designation and approval of a drug as an orphan drug provides certain benefits to the sponsor of the drug. For example, such a designation permits the FDA to assist the sponsor in studying the drug, and allows the sponsor to claim the benefit of certain tax incentives. 26 U.S.C. § 28. More importantly, orphan drug designation and approval confers seven years of non-patent marketing exclusivity.

In 1992, the FDA promulgated its final orphan drug regulations on how to implement the orphan drug exclusivity right. One of the regulations, 21 C.F.R. § 316.3(b)(13)(i), provided a definition for determining when two drugs are the "same drug" and thus the second drug may not be approved for market exclusivity. In essence, that regulation provides that two drugs will be considered the same drug if they contain the same active moiety, unless the second drug is deemed to be "clinically superior."

To be eligible for orphan drug exclusivity, a drug's sponsor must submit a request to the FDA for designation as an orphan drug. If the FDA determines that the drug targets a rare disease or condition, or that there is no reasonable expectation that the cost of developing and making a drug available will be recovered in the United States, the drug is designated as an orphan drug. Because the drug is designated as an orphan drug before it is approved, more than one applicant may receive orphan designation for what later may be deemed the same "drug" for treatment of the same disease or condition. * * *

Baker Norton developed a drug called Paxene, and BMS developed a drug called Taxol. Although the two drugs are manufactured differently, contain some different inactive ingredients (or "excipients"), and have different profiles of impurities, they both contain paclitaxel as their active component. Paclitaxel is the generic name of a naturally-occurring anticancer agent extracted in trace amounts from the Pacific yew tree. Both Taxol and Paxene dissolve paclitaxel in ethanol and polyethoxylated castor oil for delivery by injection into a patient's body. While the castor oil provides adequate solubility of the paclitaxel, it also promotes chemical degradation of the paclitaxel. A principal difference between Taxol and Paxene is how each controls the rate of degradation. One of the ways that BMS controls the degradation rate is by removing certain compounds by passing the castor oil over a solid absorbent. Baker Norton uses citric acid, an inactive ingredient, which changes the physical formation of components so as to reduce the rate of long-term degradation of the paclitaxel.

On March 31, 1997, Baker Norton submitted a new drug application requesting approval for Paxene. Among the potential uses of Paxene is for treating Kaposi's sarcoma, an AIDS-related cancer. Because Kaposi's sarcoma qualifies under the Orphan Drug Act as a "rare disease," Baker Norton also sought designation as an orphan drug. On April 15, 1997, the FDA granted orphan designation. [Previously], BMS requested orphan designation for Taxol for treatment of Kaposi's sarcoma on January 31, 1997, and it filed a supplemental new drug application for Taxol on February 4, 1997.[11] On March 25, 1997, the FDA granted Taxol orphan designation for Kaposi's sarcoma.

What ensued essentially was a race for orphan drug approval since both Taxol and Paxene had been granted orphan drug designation; whichever drug was approved first would receive the seven-year period of market exclusivity. On August 4, 1997, the FDA granted approval to BMS to market Taxol as a second-line treatment for Kaposi's sarcoma. On December 24, 1997, the FDA issued a letter decision to Baker Norton indicating that it had determined Paxene to be safe and effective and, in all other respects, approvable, but that it could not confer final approval until August 4, 2004, due to Taxol's period of exclusivity. Baker Norton could, however, obtain final approval for marketing prior to August 4, 2004, if it could show that Paxene and Taxol should not be considered the "same drug" as defined in 21 C.F.R. part 316. * * *

"There is a presumption in favor of the validity of administrative action, and courts are particularly deferential when an agency is interpreting its own statute and regulations." Pfizer v. Shalala, 1 F.Supp.2d 38, 44 (D.D.C.1998). Moreover, the "FDA's policies and its interpretation of its own regulations will be paid special deference because of the breadth of Congress' delegation of authority to FDA and because of FDA's scientific expertise." Berlex Lab., Inc. v. FDA, 942 F.Supp. 19, 25 (D.D.C.1996). * * * The court starts with the relevant statutory language of the Orphan Drug Act, which states in pertinent part: "[I]f the Secretary ... approves an application filed pursuant to section 355 ... for a drug designated under section 360bb of this title for a rare disease or condition, the Secretary may not approve another application under section 355 of this title ... for such drug for such disease or condition for a person who is not the holder of such approved application ... until the expiration of seven years from the

11. BMS filed a supplemental new drug application because the FDA previously had approved Taxol for ovarian cancer usages.

date of the approval of the approved application." 21 U.S.C. § 360cc(a). * * *

Baker Norton asserts that the FDA's regulation improperly equates the term "drug" in § 360cc(a) with an "active moiety," contrary to legislative intent. * * * Baker Norton asserts that Congress clearly intended for the term "drug" in the context of § 360cc(a) to mean a "finished drug product." Baker Norton reasons that the term "drug" in § 360cc(a) is used in the context of an "application for a drug" under section 355. 21 U.S.C. § 355, which governs applications for approval of new drugs, interprets an "application for a drug" to be an "application for a drug product," not just for an active ingredient or active moiety. When considering an application for a drug product, the inactive ingredients, as well as the manufacturing processes, are important and can distinguish one drug product from another. Because Congress chose to use the phrase "application for a drug" in § 360cc(a) and not another phrase, Baker Norton concludes that Congress clearly intended for the term "drug" to mean a drug product. * * *

Sections 355 and 360cc(a) are different statutory provisions with different purposes. Section 355 aims to protect public health and safety, which it accomplishes by considering the safety of all parts of any new drug proposed for entry in interstate commerce, whereas the Orphan Drug Act seeks to provide a meaningful financial incentive for the development of orphan drugs. What one statutory provision defines as a "drug" may not necessarily control another statutory provision's definition of a "drug," even when used in the same phrase. Courts have held that "it is not unusual for the same word to be used with different meanings in the same act, and there is no rule of statutory construction which precludes the courts from giving to the word the meaning which the legislature intended it should have in each instance." * * *

Given the multiple definitions of the term "drug," and the differing purposes that various statutory provisions can serve, the court cannot find that the definition of "drug" in § 360cc(a) is clear and unambiguous. The court finds it more likely that Congress left it to the FDA to determine which definition fits a particular statutory section. Other courts have agreed that the word "drug" in other statutory provisions can be inherently ambiguous, and may cover more than just a finished drug product. * * *

Because the court has determined that the meaning of § 360cc(a) is ambiguous, the court turns to whether the agency's interpretation is based on a permissible construction of the statute. First, Baker Norton asserts that instead of considering whether two drugs have the same "active moiety," the FDA should adopt a "functionality" test: that is, the FDA should consider whether other ingredients in the product may create a functionally different product. Such a test, Baker Norton contends, would prevent companies from claiming that two drugs with the same active moiety are "different" simply by adding ingredients of de minimis import and thereby compromise a prior company's market exclusivity. In Baker Norton's case, Paxene's use of citric acid creates a functionally different drug because the citric acid helps reduce the rate of degradation of paclitaxel. The FDA defendants and BMS assert that a functionality test would vitiate the market exclusivity provision because many drug products could contain the same active moiety yet be functionally different. Whether such a "functionality test" would improve the current regime, however, does not necessarily undermine the permissibility of the FDA's interpretation. Under the *Chevron* test, the court considers only whether the agency's interpretation is permissible, not whether a better interpretation exists.

Baker Norton also maintains that the FDA's regulation is not permissible because it violates the well-established doctrine that grants of monopolies should be narrowly construed. The court finds, however, that the FDA's interpretation does not produce so sweeping a monopoly as plaintiff would suggest: the market exclusivity rights are limited in time to seven years, and granted only for a particular drug for a particular use. Nothing prevents subsequent applicants from obtaining FDA approval for the same drug for a different use, or a different drug for the same use, or a clinically superior drug with the same active moiety for the same use.

The court finds that the FDA's interpretation is permissible. The interpretation of "same drug" appears to bear out the purpose behind the Orphan Drug Act. The preamble to the 1991 proposed regulations implementing the Orphan Drug Act states:

> With respect to small molecules, it appears sound, for the purposes of consideration of exclusive marketing under the Orphan Drug Act, to adopt a policy that regards two drugs as different if they differ with respect to the chemical structure of their active moieties. First, such differences are highly likely to lead to pharmacologic differences. Second, the development of an agent with a novel active moiety is not a financially or intellectually trivial matter; it represents a considerable effort and a substantial risk, as the results of changes in small molecules are difficult to predict.

56 Fed. Reg. 3338, 3341 (1991). Only one of the 40 comments received during the rulemaking stage suggested an alternate approach for distinguishing among different small-molecule drugs, and that alternate approach was rejected as unworkable.

The regulation's manner of determining "sameness" appears to promote the obvious legislative intent behind the Orphan Drug Act—to promote the development of orphan drugs. The financial incentive for companies to develop such drugs is provided by the period of market exclusivity, which would be undermined if other companies could develop drugs with the same active moiety but minor differences in inactive ingredients. The interests of patients who need such drugs are served by the approval of drugs which have the same active moiety but are clinically superior. See Arent v. Shalala, 70 F.3d 610, 615 (D.C.Cir.1995) ("[A] reviewing court's inquiry . . . is focused on discerning the boundaries of Congress' delegation of authority to the agency; and as long as the agency stays within that delegation, it is free to make policy choices in interpreting the statute, and such interpretations are entitled to deference."). The court therefore finds that the FDA's actions with regard to Baker Norton's application for approval of Paxene are not arbitrary and capricious, or in excess of statutory authority. Accordingly, the court denies plaintiff's motion for summary judgment, and grants the FDA and BMS's motions for summary judgment.

NOTES AND QUESTIONS

1. *Biotech's crutch.* Biotechnology pioneers took full advantage of the special statutory incentives offered to orphan drugs. See Geeta Anand, How Drugs for Rare Diseases Became Lifeline for Companies, Wall St. J., Nov. 15, 2005, at A1; see also Andrew Pollack, A Drug's Delayed Triumph, N.Y. Times, Mar. 16, 2010, at B1 (reporting that FDA approval of Xiaflex® (collagenase) for Dupuytren's contracture secured for its developers orphan drug exclusivity to go with their method-of-use patents); cf. Bernadette Tansey, Biotech Looks at Hair Loss: Research into Stem Cells, Gene Therapy, Cloning and Drugs Could Yield Multibillion-dollar Industry, S.F. Chron., Mar. 7, 2008, at C1. In the mid–1980s, two manufacturers sought orphan drug approval for recombinant hGH for the treatment of growth hormone deficiency in children. Previously, companies had derived hGH from the pituitary glands of human cadavers, but they withdrew these products after contamination incidents triggered a fatal neurological disease. See Paul Brown et al., Potential Epidemic of Creutzfeldt–Jakob Disease from Human Growth Hormone Therapy, 313 New Eng. J. Med. 728 (1985). Almost one year after approving Genentech's r-hGH product (Protropin®), which is derived from genetically engineered *E. coli* bacteria and differed from the natural protein only in the addition of a terminal methionine amino acid group, the FDA approved Eli Lilly's r-hGH product (Humatrope®), which had a protein structure identical to natural hGH. Genentech challenged the agency's decision as unlawfully interfering with its right to seven years of marketing exclusivity. The court sided with Eli Lilly, concluding that Humatrope qualified for orphan drug designation because it differed from the previously approved *natural* hGH products by virtue of the synthetic process used to produce it, which avoided the risk of contamination and filled an unmet need occasioned by their withdrawal from the market. See Genentech, Inc. v. Bowen, 676 F.Supp. 301, 312–13 (D.D.C.1987). The court declined, however, to address the separate and seemingly trickier question of whether Humatrope differed sufficiently from Protropin, by virtue of its lack of an added methionyl group, to permit approval before the expiration of Genentech's market exclusivity period.

2. *Perverse incentives.* A more recent orphan drug controversy involved a treatment for Fabry disease. Two companies developed recombinant versions of alpha-galactosidase, an enzyme missing in patients with this rare and fatal condition (Genzyme's Fabrazyme® and Transkaryotic Therapies' Replagal®). Both sponsors had received orphan product designations, and, in an apparently unprecedented situation, both filed their applications for approval within weeks of one another, attempting to take advantage of the less demanding evidence of effectiveness required under the agency's accelerated new drug approval process. An FDA advisory committee found weaknesses in the clinical trial results submitted with both applications, which some observers attributed to the "winner-take-all" aspect of the orphan drug rules that created pressures for each sponsor to rush its studies in an effort to beat the other to market, but the committee concluded that Genzyme had offered a somewhat stronger showing of effectiveness. See Naomi Aoki, FDA Review Deals Blow to TKT: Drug Panel Says Replagal Clinical Data Do Not Justify Approval, Boston Globe, Jan. 15, 2003, at D1; see also Aaron S. Kesselheim et al., Characteristics of Clinical Trials to Support Approval of Orphan vs Nonorphan Drugs for Cancer, 305 JAMA 2320 (2011). The agency approved Fabrazyme a few months later. See Marc Kaufman, FDA Approves "Orphan" Drug for Life–Threatening Disorder, Wash. Post, Apr. 25, 2003, at A9; see also Ron Winslow et al., Cancer Research Gets a Boost from New Methods of Treatment, Wall St. J., June 2, 2003, at A1 (reporting that similar problems have plagued the accelerated approval process for drugs designed to meet serious unmet needs).

3. *Clinical superiority.* The regulations provide that a new drug is "clinically superior" if it offers "[g]reater safety in a substantial portion of the target populations." 21 C.F.R. § 316.3(b)(3)(ii) (listing as an example of "greater safety" the elimination of "an ingredient or contaminant that is associated with relatively frequent adverse effects"); see also 57 Fed. Reg. 62,076, 62,078 (1992) (explaining that even "a small demonstrated ... diminution in adverse reactions may be sufficient to allow a finding of clinical superiority"). In *Berlex Laboratories, Inc. v. FDA*, 942 F.Supp. 19 (D.D.C.1996), the court deferred to these regulations in the course of upholding the FDA's decision to approve Biogen's biological drug Avonex®, a beta interferon product used to treat multiple sclerosis. Berlex, which sold the similar orphan drug product Betaseron®, objected because its seven year exclusivity period had not yet expired. The court sustained the FDA's finding that Avonex was not the same drug because it completely avoided one of the side effects (injection site necrosis) associated with Betaseron, disregarding Berlex's response that the overall safety profiles for the two products were comparable. See id. at 23–24. Five years later, Biogen faced the prospect that a competitor would trump its victory over Berlex. See Ronald Rosenberg, Serono Says Drug Better for Skirting Relapses, Boston Globe, May 9, 2001, at F4 (reporting that a comparative efficacy trial demonstrated that a new beta interferon product was clinically superior to Avonex in treating MS patients); see also Naomi Aoki, The Price of Success: Orphan Drug Act Has Spurred Advances and Disputes, Boston Globe, July 25, 2001, at F1.

4. *Contrasting the different forms of market exclusivity.* A patent generally gives the inventor a 20 year period (measured from the date of filing) of protection against all imitators, and not just in the United States. When the FDA approves a new chemical or molecular entity as a drug, the NDA sponsor receives a five year period of exclusivity, but only against generic applicants. If a sponsor later conducts additional studies in order to secure FDA approval of a supplemental NDA for a new use, it receives a three year period of exclusivity, but only against ANDAs for that particular use (though a full OTC switch works more powerfully). Orphan drug exclusivity provides a seven-year period of protection against both ANDAs and NDAs, but only for that use. See Sigma–Tau Pharm., Inc. v. Schwetz, 288 F.3d 141, 145–48 (4th Cir.2002) (holding that the approval of a second orphan indication (protected by a separate seven-year exclusivity period) did not prevent the FDA from approving generic versions for only the original (and no longer protected) orphan indication notwithstanding the likelihood of off-label prescribing of the generic drugs for the new indication). What, if anything, accounts for these differences? Might other types of incentives help? Cf. U.S. Presses Drugmakers on Neglected Disorders, Wash. Post, June 21, 2010, at A14 ("Regulators need new tactics, because an experiment two years ago to give priority review vouchers in exchange for new drugs for tropical diseases drew only one participant.").

5. *Orphan medical devices*. In 1988, Congress amended the Orphan Drug Act to provide a few of the same incentives to manufacturers of medical devices used to treat rare diseases or conditions. See Pub. L. No. 100–290, § 3, 102 Stat. 90 (1988).

6. *Further commentary*. See Peter S. Arno et al., Rare Diseases, Drug Development, and AIDS: The Impact of the Orphan Drug Act, 73 Milbank Q. 231 (1995); Robert A. Bohrer & John T. Prince, A Tale of Two Proteins: The FDA's Uncertain Interpretation of the Orphan Drug Act, 12 Harv. J.L. & Tech. 365 (1999); Anupam B. Jena et al., Altruism and Innovation in Health Care, 53 J.L. & Econ. 497 (2010); Frank R. Lichtenberg & Joel Waldfogel, Does Misery Love Company? Evidence from Pharmaceutical Markets Before and After the Orphan Drug Act, 15 Mich. Telecomm. & Tech. L. Rev. 335 (2009); David D. Rohde, The Orphan Drug Act: An Engine of Innovation? At What Cost?, 55 Food & Drug L.J. 125 (2000); Janice M. Hogan, Note, Revamping the Orphan Drug Act: Potential Impact on the World Pharmaceutical Market, 26 Law & Pol'y Int'l Bus. 523 (1995); see also Geneviève Michaux, EU Orphan Regulation—Ten Years of Application, 65 Food & Drug L.J. 639 (2010).

National Pharmaceutical Alliance v. Henney

47 F.Supp.2d 37 (D.D.C.1999).

■ ROBERTSON, DISTRICT JUDGE:

* * * The pediatric exclusivity provision of FDAMA took effect on November 21, 1997. On March 16, 1998, in compliance with section 355a(b), FDA published a "Draft Pediatric List" of approved drugs for which it suggested that additional pediatric information might produce health benefits in the pediatric population. * * * On May 20, 1998, within the 180–day period prescribed by section 355a(b), FDA published a final "List of Approved Drugs for Which Additional Pediatric Information May Produce Health Benefits in the Pediatric Population." On July 7, 1998, the FDA issued a document entitled "Guidance for Industry: Qualifying for Pediatric Exclusivity Under Section 505A of the Federal Food, Drug, and

Cosmetic Act.'' FDA has neither issued nor proposed regulations for implementing section 355a. It began issuing written requests for pediatric studies on specific drugs soon after publication of the Guidance document. * * *

The complaint alleges that FDA developed the Pediatric List improperly and that FDA's interpretation of the pediatric exclusivity provisions of section 355a is at variance with the statute. * * * The principal issue * * * is whether FDA has authority to grant additional exclusivity periods for drug product *lines* containing a single active moiety in exchange for a pediatric study covering a single drug *product*. * * * The main arguments of both sides focus, correctly, on the FDA's interpretation of the statute. Neither the language of section 355a nor anything in the nature of legislative history speaks directly to the question at issue. * * *

[The] question is whether FDA's interpretation of section 355a is ''based on a permissible construction of the statute.'' Plaintiff asserts that it is not, arguing that FDA has departed from other, consistent interpretations of the term ''drug'' throughout the [FDCA] to mean ''drug product,'' that Congress wanted extended pediatric exclusivity to be limited to the ''drug product'' studied in response to a request from FDA, and that FDA's construction conflicts with the statutory purpose of maximizing information about the use of drugs in children by removing the [dis]incentive to conduct research. There is little in the way of substantive information in this record, however, that supports these arguments. Congress did not prescribe the exact terms of the bargain it wanted struck with the research-based drug companies, leaving it to FDA to strike the appropriate balance. * * * [Plaintiffs also argue] that FDA acted arbitrarily and capriciously by including in the Pediatric List every drug approved for use in adults for indications that also appear in children. That argument is easily resolved by appropriate deference to the expertise of FDA. * * *

[B]ecause the likelihood of success is slim, plaintiffs would have to make a very substantial showing of severe irreparable injury in order to prevail on their motion [for a preliminary injunction]. * * * [G]eneric drug manufacturers will not realize profits from the sale of their products over the six-month periods of market exclusivity, but that effect was obviously contemplated by Congress when it enacted FDAMA. Plaintiffs have not shown that the loss of six months would allow the creation of impenetrable barriers to market entry or cause business failures among generic manufacturers.

FDAMA has a sunset provision for the year 2002. A report is due to Congress in 2001. The legislative incentive for the conduct of important pharmaceutical testing—which is not otherwise required of drug manufacturers—is thus of limited duration. * * * The public interest would be disserved by an injunction whose operation would be to remove the incentive for testing or actually to stop new testing. As for harm to the parties, it is true that generic drug manufacturers have something to lose and innovator drug manufacturers something to gain from the denial of a preliminary injunction, but that equation was set in place by the enactment of FDAMA. * * *

NOTES AND QUESTIONS

1. *Pediatric indications.* Recall that Eli Lilly & Co. failed in its effort to protect Prozac® with second generation patents. See Chap. 10(A)(3)(b). A few months after losing its appeal, the FDA granted the company a six month extension of its market exclusivity period for agreeing to undertake pediatric studies. See Eli Lilly Granted Extension on Prozac, L.A. Times, Nov. 16, 2000, at C2. Other manufacturers of blockbuster drugs nearing the end of their patent lives also have benefitted from this provision. See Mylan Lab., Inc. v. Thompson, 389 F.3d 1272 (D.C.Cir.2004) (rejecting a generic applicant's challenge to pediatric exclusivity awarded to the manufacturer of the Duragesic® (fentanyl) patch); Barr Lab., Inc. v. Thompson, 238 F.Supp.2d 236 (D.D.C.2002) (same, Novaldex® (tamoxifen)); Anna W. Mathews, So Young and So Many Pills—More than 25% of Kids and Teens in the U.S. Take Prescriptions on a Regular Basis, Wall St. J., Dec. 28, 2010, at D1 (reporting that youngsters are "taking a wide variety of other medications once considered only to be for adults, from statins to diabetes pills" and antihypertensives, adding that, in more than a third of the studies conducted under the FDA's program, "there have been surprising side effects, or results that suggested a smaller or larger dose was needed than had been expected"). Congress has twice extended the law, with fairly minor modifications, for another five year period, and it also created a mechanism for funding third-party research that could result in formulation or labeling changes in an approved drug. See Best Pharmaceuticals for Children Act of 2007, Pub. L. No. 110–85, tit. v, 121 Stat. 876; Karena J. Cooper, Pediatric Marketing Exclusivity, 57 Food & Drug L.J. 519 (2002); see also Rob Stein, A Gap in Knowledge About Kids, Medication, Wash. Post, Nov. 23, 2007, at A1 (reporting that funds for the third-party research failed to materialize).

2. *No such thing as a free lunch.* Although they require no direct expenditure of public money, such exclusivity incentives come at a price. See Aaron S. Kesselheim et al., Extensions of Intellectual Property Rights and Delayed Adoption of Generic Drugs: Effects on Medicaid Expenditures, 25 Health Aff. 1637 (2006); see also Rachel Zimmerman, Pharmaceutical Firms Win Big on Plan to Test Adult Drugs on Kids, Wall St. J., Feb. 5, 2001, at A1 (estimating that the additional six months of market exclusivity on the first 26 drugs to receive this extension will generate an extra $4 billion for the brand-name manufacturers, including nearly $1 billion each on Claritin and Prozac). Research suggests that this particular program has been worth it. See Jennifer S. Li et al., Economic Return of Clinical Trials Performed Under the Pediatric Exclusivity Program, 297 JAMA 480 (2007).

3. *Overlapping exclusivity.* What happens if the pediatric studies lead to a significant alteration in the labeling for the pioneer drug (e.g., adding a specific indication for use in adolescents, as happened with Prozac)? The sponsor of the NDA supplement could get six additional months of protection against any generic competition and/or three years of protection against generic competition on that labeling statement (but not on the drug itself). Cf. Liz Kowalczyk, Doctors Seek a Viagra Variant for Lung Ailment, Boston Globe, Aug. 3, 2001, at A1 (reporting that doctors have used sildenafil to treat pulmonary hypertension in infants, and adding that Pfizer could receive the six-month exclusivity period for pediatric testing as well as incentives for pursuing approval of an orphan indication but that neither would provide much of an incentive because the drug still enjoyed 12 years of patent life). Should the sponsor receive both exclusivity periods, and would they run sequentially or concurrently? See Juliet Eilperin, Bristol–Myers Presses for Patent, Wash. Post, Nov. 28, 2001, at A33 (reporting that the manufacturer of Glucophage® argued that it deserved an additional 3½ years of exclusivity, and against any generic competition, after discovering that children could benefit from this diabetes drug). When it extended the sunset date, Congress also closed this apparent loophole. See Alice Dembner, Pediatric Testing Program Extended: Drug Makers Keep Patent Incentive, Boston Globe, Dec. 20, 2001, at A8.

4. *Further commentary*. See Randall B. Clark, Speed, Safety, and Dignity: Pediatric Pharmaceutical Development in an Age of Optimism, 9 U. Chi. L. Sch. Roundtable 1 (2002); Lauren H. Breslow, Note, The Best Pharmaceuticals for Children Act of 2002: The Rise of the Voluntary Incentive Structure and Congressional Refusal to Require Pediatric Testing, 40 Harv. J. Legis. 133 (2003); Lisa Jerles, Note, The Best Pharmaceuticals for Children Act and the Pediatric Research Equity Act—Helping or Hurting America's Children?, 6 Cardozo Pub. L. Pol'y & Ethics J. 515 (2008); Kurt R. Karst, Comment, Pediatric Testing of Prescription Drugs: The FDA's Carrot and Stick for the Pharmaceutical Industry, 49 Am. U. L. Rev. 739 (2000); see also Aaron S. Kesselheim, Using Market–Exclusivity Incentives to Promote Pharmaceutical Innovation, 363 New Eng. J. Med. 19 (2010); Leslie Kushner, Note, Incentivizing Postmarketing Pharmaceutical Product Safety Testing with Extension of Exclusivity Periods, 19 Fordham Intell. Prop. Media & Ent. L.J. 519 (2009).

3. GENERIC EXCLUSIVITY

Purepac Pharmaceutical Co. v. Friedman

162 F.3d 1201 (D.C.Cir.1998).

■ RANDOLPH, CIRCUIT JUDGE:

"The active ingredients in most prescription drugs constitute less than 10% of the product; inactive 'excipients' (such as coatings, binders, and capsules) constitute the rest. The term 'generic drug' is used to describe a product that contains the same active ingredients but not necessarily the same excipients as a so-called 'pioneer drug' that is marketed under a brand name." United States v. Generix Drug Corp., 460 U.S. 453, 454–55 (1983). New drugs, including new generic drugs, may not be marketed without the Food and Drug Administration's approval. The Drug Price

Competition and Patent Term Restoration Act of 1984, Pub. L. No. 98–417, 98 Stat. 1585, revised the procedures for obtaining the FDA's approval. One of the provisions in the "Hatch–Waxman Amendments," as this Act is known, conferred on the first generic drug applicant a 180–day period during which it would be free of competition from generic applicants who file later. The FDA implemented this provision through a regulation. In *Mova Pharmaceutical Corp. v. Shalala*, 140 F.3d 1060 (D.C.Cir.1998), we sustained a district court injunction against the FDA's enforcement of one of the regulation's requirements, finding it inconsistent with the statute. In response to *Mova*, the FDA revised its system for granting the 180–day exclusivity period. The questions in this case concern the validity of the revision.

In July 1998, the FDA tentatively approved Purepac Pharmaceutical Company's application to market the generic drug ticlopidine hydrochloride, marketed by other companies under the brand-name "Ticlid." Although Purepac's application has become ready for final approval, the FDA is withholding action. Purepac must, the FDA insists, wait until the first ticlopidine applicant—Torpharm, a division of Apotex, Inc.—markets its product for 180 days. At the time of this writing, it is not certain when these 180 days will start running. The FDA has not yet finally approved Torpharm's application.

With matters thus at a standstill, Purepac decided to take legal action. It sued for an injunction and a declaratory judgment, challenging the validity of the FDA's post-*Mova* revision and claiming that Torpharm was not entitled to the 180–day exclusivity period because it had not been sued for patent infringement * * * *

In a paragraph IV certification, the generic applicant must give notice to the owner of the patent and to the holder of the approved application for the drug covered by the patent. FDA approval of the abbreviated application may be made "effective immediately," unless a patent infringement suit is brought against the applicant within forty-five days from the date the patent owner or application holder receives notice of the paragraph IV certification.

No one brought a patent infringement suit against Torpharm (or Purepac) and it is therefore unnecessary to describe the provisions dealing with the various contingencies of such a lawsuit. The section directly in dispute—the section conferring the 180–day period of exclusivity—reads as follows:

> If the application contains a certification described in subclause (IV) of paragraph (2)(A)(vii) and is for a drug for which a previous application has been submitted under this subsection cont[ain]ing such a certification, the application shall be made effective not earlier than one hundred and eighty days after (i) the date the Secretary receives notice from the applicant under the previous application of the first commercial marketing of the drug under the previous application, or (ii) the date of a decision of a court in an action described in clause (iii)

holding the patent which is the subject of the certification to be invalid or not infringed, whichever is earlier.

21 U.S.C. § 355(j)(5)(B)(iv), as amended by Pub. L. No. 105–115, 111 Stat. 2296 (1997).

The FDA's original regulation implementing this section, promulgated in 1994, * * * embodied what the parties and our *Mova* opinion call the "successful defense" requirement: the first generic applicant was entitled to the 180–day exclusivity period only after it had successfully defended a patent infringement suit. *Mova* held that this portion of the regulation was "inconsistent with the statutory text and structure." 140 F.3d at 1076. As the court read the statute, it provided that a later generic applicant could not start marketing its product for 180 days after either commercial marketing by the first applicant, or a court decision declaring the patent invalid or not infringed. Id. at 1069. The FDA's successful defense requirement read the commercial marketing "trigger" out of the statute. As a result, first applicants who were not sued could never receive the benefit of the exclusivity period.

After *Mova*, the FDA issued a "Guidance to Industry" announcing its intention to "formally" remove the successful defense requirement from the regulation and to conduct a rulemaking proceeding to issue new regulations under § 355(j)(5)(B)(iv). In the meantime, the FDA said it would follow the statute as *Mova* interpreted it. That is, the agency would inform "the first applicant to submit a substantially complete" abbreviated application, "with a paragraph IV certification," that the applicant was eligible for 180 days of market exclusivity even though it had not been sued for patent infringement. The FDA added that it expected first applicants to begin marketing their product "promptly upon approval."

In November 1998, while this case was pending, the FDA published an interim rule in the *Federal Register* amending its regulation to eliminate the successful defense requirement. See 21 C.F.R. § 314.107(c)(1). * * * Purepac maintains that the regulation containing the successful defense requirement did not entitle Torpharm to the 180–day exclusivity period because Torpharm had not been sued for patent infringement. As Purepac sees it, even after *Mova* the FDA still had to require, as a condition for exclusivity, that the first generic applicant be sued for patent infringement, although the FDA could no longer insist that the applicant defend the suit successfully. * * *

We see the FDA's revised system for granting exclusivity as consistent with the statute and with our *Mova* decision. Section 355(j)(5)(B)(iv) does not, on its face, require the first applicant to be sued in order to benefit from market exclusivity. It provides, as we said in *Mova*, that the 180–day exclusivity period for the first applicant begins running upon the occurrence of one of two events, whichever is earlier—commercial marketing by the first applicant, or a court decision in favor of the applicant. The second condition obviously presupposes a lawsuit. The first does not. The words of the statute provide no reason to think, as Purepac must, that the only "commercial marketing" contemplated in § 355(j)(5)(B)(iv) is marketing that takes place while the first applicant is defending a lawsuit or after the lawsuit has concluded. The regulation, as it now stands, is fully consistent with the statute. * * *

There is nothing irrational in the FDA's giving first applicants the 180-day exclusivity period even if they have not been sued. On its face, the statute does the same. Seen in this light, Purepac's real objection is to the words Congress used, not the FDA's revision of its regulation. * * * Purepac also offers a policy reason for reading a lawsuit requirement into § 355(j)(5)(B)(iv). If a first applicant is never sued for patent infringement, it is possible that neither of two "triggers" for the running of the 180 days of market exclusivity—commercial marketing or a judicial decision—would ever occur. Without a lawsuit there would be no judicial decision. If the applicant never begins marketing its product, the 180 days would never run and all later generic applicants would be barred from bringing their products to market. * * * For this reason, *Mova* described a narrower answer to the problem: for first applicants who are not sued, they must bring their products to market within a prescribed period in order to benefit from exclusivity. See 140 F.3d at 1071 n.11. There is some indication that the FDA will consider this alternative in the rulemaking promised in its Guidance, or in response to comments on its interim rule. That is the proper time and setting for Purepac to repeat its point and to offer its solution. * * *

Mylan Pharmaceuticals, Inc. v. Henney

94 F.Supp.2d 36 (D.D.C.2000), vacated as moot, 276 F.3d 627 (D.C.Cir.2002).

■ URBINA, DISTRICT JUDGE:

Pharmachemie, B.V. and Mylan Pharmaceuticals, Inc., generic manufacturers of the drug tamoxifen, bring separate actions against defendant Jane E. Henney, M.D., in her official capacity as Commissioner of the United States Food and Drug Administration, and against defendant Donna E. Shalala, in her official capacity as Secretary of the United States Department of Health and Human Services (collectively referred to as the "FDA"). The parties, whose tamoxifen drugs are used in the treatment of breast cancer, bring their actions under the Federal Food, Drug and Cosmetic Act (FDCA) and the Administrative Procedure Act (APA). Barr Laboratories is a manufacturer of the generic drug tamoxifen, currently exclusively licensed by the owner of the patent to market the drug.

Mylan and Pharmachemie both assert that the FDA acted arbitrarily and capriciously in rendering by letter dated March 2, 1999, its decision to grant Barr's request that the FDA stay approval of any version of the drug tamoxifen other than Barr's version. The effect of the March letter is that neither Mylan nor Pharmachemie has the opportunity to market their generic version of tamoxifen until the patent for tamoxifen expires on August 20, 2002. In essence, both maintain that the March letter violates the FDCA and runs contrary to the agency's own regulations. * * *

[A] generic maker seeking certification of his ANDA under paragraph III must wait for the pioneer maker's patent to expire and, consequently, will not infringe the patent. But a generic maker seeking certification of his ANDA under paragraph IV, on the grounds that the pioneer maker's patent is invalid, triggers a multi-tiered process that potentially enables him to obtain approval of his ANDA and market his generic drug before the pioneer maker's patent expires. * * *

As an incentive to the first generic maker to expose himself to the risk of costly patent litigation, the Hatch–Waxman regime provides that the first to file a paragraph IV certified ANDA is eligible for a 180–day period of marketing protection, commonly known as the 180–day exclusivity period. By its terms, the exclusivity incentive affords the first filer protection from competition from subsequent generic makers for 180 days beginning from the earlier of a commercial marketing or court decision. * * *

The facts material to disposition of this consolidated action date back to August 1985, when a pioneer maker secured the original patent for brand-name tamoxifen, which is a drug used in the treatment of breast cancer. On August 20, 1985, Imperial Chemicals Industries, PLC obtained U.S. Patent 4,536,516, covering tamoxifen. Imperial's subsidiary, Zeneca Inc., is the sole producer of tamoxifen under Imperial's patent. In December 1985, Barr Laboratories, a generic maker of tamoxifen, submitted an ANDA requesting FDA approval to market its own generic version of tamoxifen.

In September 1987, Barr amended its ANDA to include a paragraph IV certification and to challenge the validity of Imperial's tamoxifen patent. After amending its ANDA, Barr sent Imperial notice that it contended Imperial's patent was invalid. The FDA gave effect to Barr's amended paragraph IV certification. In other words, Barr became potentially eligible for the exclusivity incentive. After receiving notice of the challenge, Imperial sued Barr for patent infringement in the United States District Court for the Southern District of New York. On July 21, 1992, the Southern District held that Imperial's tamoxifen patent was invalid because Imperial deliberately, knowingly and fraudulently withheld material information from the Patent and Trademark Office. See Imperial Chem. Ind., PLC v. Barr Lab., Inc., 795 F.Supp. 619, 629 (S.D.N.Y.1992).

Imperial filed a notice of appeal with the United States Court of Appeals for the Federal Circuit, but, before any substantive review by the Federal Circuit, Imperial settled the case with Barr. The settlement was expressly conditioned on Barr's agreement to abandon its challenge to the validity of Imperial's patent. Barr would abandon its challenge by amending its paragraph IV certified ANDA back to a paragraph III certified ANDA. Pursuant to the settlement and as a result of the amendment back, Barr's ANDA was no longer eligible for approval until after August 20, 2002, the date that Imperial's tamoxifen patent was scheduled to expire. In exchange, Imperial paid Barr $21 million and granted Barr a license to market tamoxifen.

After settling the case but during the pendency of the appeal before the Federal Circuit, Imperial and Barr jointly moved to (1) vacate the July 21, 1992, judgment of the Southern District and (2) remand the case with instructions to dismiss without prejudice. The Federal Circuit issued a short order that granted the parties' request, finding that the "parties to the district court proceeding have entered into a settlement agreement resolving the entire dispute." * * *

Within a year of the Federal Circuit's vacatur of the Southern District's decision, in August 1994, Pharmachemie submitted a paragraph III ANDA for its generic version of tamoxifen. In January 1996, Mylan submitted a paragraph IV ANDA for its generic version of tamoxifen. In February 1996, Pharmachemie amended its ANDA to include a paragraph IV certification. After Mylan submitted its paragraph IV ANDA in January 1996, Zeneca sued Mylan for infringement. Because Zeneca brought a patent infringement action against Mylan within 45 days, the 30 month statutory stay of approval was triggered against Mylan and scheduled to expire on July 10, 1998. After Pharmachemie amended its ANDA to reflect a paragraph IV ANDA, Zeneca sued Pharmachemie for patent infringement within 45 days. The 30–month statutory stay was triggered and scheduled to expire in August 1998.

But in June 1998, approximately one month before Mylan's and two months before Pharmachemie's 30 month statutory stays were to expire, Barr filed a petition for stay with the FDA. The petition asked the FDA to continue to credit Barr with the exclusivity incentive to the exclusion of all other generic makers of tamoxifen. Specifically, Barr's petition asked the FDA not to approve any ANDA for a generic version of tamoxifen until 180 days after: (1) Barr's first commercial marketing of generic tamoxifen under its ANDA; or (2) the date of a final decision of a court holding the tamoxifen patent to be invalid or not infringed. Barr's petition came in the midst of the FDA's determination, in light of adverse court decisions, to overhaul its interpretation and application of the exclusivity incentive * * * *

In response to the petition, Janet Woodcock, M.D., Director of the FDA's Center for Drug Evaluation and Research, announced to Barr by letter dated March 2, 1999: "After careful review of your petition and supplement, as well as comments to the petition received by FDA, the Agency grants the petition for the following reasons ...." Thus, the FDA granted Barr's petition to preserve its exclusivity incentive and to exclude all other generic makers of tamoxifen. * * *

In its March letter, the FDA gives no effect to the Southern District's decision, rendered in Barr's favor, which held that Imperial's patent for tamoxifen was invalid. Although the district court's decision was vacated during the pendency of appeal and pursuant to a settlement agreement, the FDA, without explanation, sweepingly ignores the existence of the decision altogether. Page four of the March letter states: "Barr has settled its patent litigation without a decision of a court finding the patent invalid, not infringed or unenforceable." While subsequent ANDA applicants have challenged the tamoxifen patent, no court decisions have been rendered in those cases either. Thus, according to the FDA's interpretation, Barr's 180 days of marketing exclusivity has not yet been triggered since there is neither a court decision nor a commercial marketing of tamoxifen under Barr's ANDA. * * * From the plain, comprehensive and inclusive terms of 21 U.S.C. § 355(j)(5)(B)(iii) and (iv), the court discerns clear congressional intent that the draftsmen intended "a decision of a court" to mean all court decisions, whether subsequently vacated, settled, appealed or otherwise mooted. * * *

Moreover, viewed against the sparse legislative history and compromise, the FDA's March letter not only violates the plain language of the statute, but also conflicts with the purposes of Hatch–Waxman. * * * [T]his interpretation is demonstrably at odds with the statute's interest in affording market access and incentives for both generic and non-generic makers. This circuit once cautioned that in cases where the first applicant is never sued, the court-decision trigger will never be satisfied. Later ANDA applicants are thereby at the mercy of the first applicant's decision over when, and if, to market its product. The first applicant could wait indefinitely to begin selling its product, preventing other applicants from entering the market. The court pointed out that this "unfortunate scenario" could happen if the first applicant "colludes with the pioneer drug company to eliminate generic competition." While Imperial and Barr may not have intended to "collude," the chain of events culminating with the FDA's March letter has eliminated generic competition in the tamoxifen market. * * *

Second, the FDA's March letter precludes the possibility of competition in the tamoxifen market until 2002. Courts are advised that statutes should not be interpreted so as to create anticompetitive effects. While this canon may not apply with full force when the FDA is playing in the field of compromise, the FDA's interpretation of the statute as embodied by its March letter excessively favors Barr and Imperial's anticompetitive hold over tamoxifen. The effect of the FDA's interpretation is that from August 20, 1985, the date that Imperial was granted the tamoxifen patent, until August 20, 2002, the date the patent expires, the public will have access only to Imperial's version of tamoxifen, to the exclusion of any generic version of the drug. Barr and Imperial will have benefitted from exclusivity for nearly twenty years. Hatch–Waxman intended to provide an incentive for drug companies to explore new drugs, not a market "windfall" for crafty, albeit industrious, market players. * * *

On or about March 19, 1993, and pursuant to the settlement between Barr and Imperial's subsidiary Zeneca, Barr amended its ANDA from a paragraph IV certification back to a paragraph III certification. To date, Barr has not submitted any further amendments to its ANDA. Mylan and Pharmachemie thus contend that Barr's application can no longer be considered to continue a paragraph IV certification. * * * Regulation 314.94 provides: "An applicant shall submit an amended certification by letter or as an amendment to a pending application [or] an approved application. Once an amendment or letter is submitted, the application will no longer be considered to contain the prior certification." Regulation 314.94, promulgated pursuant to notice-and-comment rulemaking, has the force and effect of law, and must be applied by the agency as written. As written, Regulation 314.94 prohibits the FDA from imposing a 180–day delay period because of Barr's amendment back.

Although Barr changed its certification from a paragraph IV to a paragraph III certification, the agency has not interpreted its regulation to render Barr ineligible for exclusivity after the change. The FDA explains that this regulation regarding changes in patent certification "fulfills a purely administrative function." * * * When first presented, this argument inspired "laughter" and jest from the appeals court. * * * [T]his court continues to be baffled by the internal "housekeeping" argument. * * * In the absence of cogent explanation, the agency's failure to follow its own regulation is fatal. * * *

Because Mylan and Pharmachemie have demonstrated that the FDA's March letter is contrary to its plain meaning and purpose of 21 U.S.C. § 355(j)(5)(B)(iv) and Regulation 314.94, the parties are entitled to declaratory relief. This action will be remanded to the FDA for a permissible construction of the statute. * * *

NOTES AND QUESTIONS

1. *Other consequences.* In licensing Barr to sell the patented tamoxifen product, the settlement also had an impact on insurance reimbursement. See Del Greco v. CVS, 337 F.Supp.2d 475 (S.D.N.Y.2004) (dismissing patients' claims that a pharmacy benefit manager improperly applied its higher co-payment for brand-name products to prescriptions filled with Barr's tamoxifen). Purchasers filed lawsuits alleging that the settlement violated the antitrust laws, but a court dismissed these claims on various grounds. See In re Tamoxifen Citrate Antitrust Litig., 466 F.3d 187 (2d Cir.2006). Such issues receive more detailed consideration in the next part of this chapter.

2. *Encouraging generic companies to test the validity of innovator patents.* The prospect of receiving even a relatively short period of market exclusivity against other generics has encouraged companies to challenge patents on brand-name drugs. See Joseph A. Slobodzian, Patent Challenges Are Key to Generics, Nat'l L.J., Feb. 12, 2001, at B1; Saritha Rai, Indian Drug Maker Says It Will Keep Attacking Patents Despite Pfizer Loss, N.Y. Times, Dec. 20, 2005, at C7 (describing "the aggressive patent-breaking strategy" of generic drug manufacturers headquartered in India, and noting that Ranbaxy Labs "has 19 first-to-file applications pending on drugs with a total estimated brand value of $22.6 billion dollars"). But cf. Christopher S. Ponder, Comment, The Dubious Value of Hatch–Waxman Exclusivity, 45 Hous. L. Rev. 555 (2008) (concluding that this incentive has done more harm than good). In some instances, the generic companies have gone too far, and one court awarded attorneys fees and costs to the patent holder when the ANDA applicant filed a baseless paragraph IV certification. See Yamanouchi Pharm. Co. v. Danbury Pharmacal, Inc., 231 F.3d 1339 (Fed. Cir.2000); see also Glaxo Group Ltd. v. Apotex, Inc., 268 F.Supp.2d 1013, 1033 (N.D.Ill.2003); Eli Lilly & Co. v. Zenith Goldline Pharm., Inc., 264 F.Supp.2d 753, 759 (S.D.Ind.2003); cf. Eli Lilly & Co. v. Teva Pharms. United States, Inc., 557 F.3d 1346, 1350–51 (Fed.Cir.2009) (affirming a six-month extension of the 30–month stay where, shortly before trial of infringement claims asserted by the holder of a dozen patents on the osteoporosis drug Evista® (raloxifene), the defendant amended its ANDA to use a different particle-size specification and measuring methodology in an effort to avoid infringing one of the patents). Conversely, frivolous patent litigation by the pioneer may provide the basis for a private antitrust claim. See Nobelpharma AB v. Implant Innovations, Inc., 141 F.3d 1059, 1068–73 (Fed.Cir.1998).

3. *Permutations.* In one case, a court had to untangle the interaction between market exclusivity periods granted for NDA supplements and for the first-filed ANDA. Initially, Glaxo Wellcome filed an NDA for ranitidine hydrochloride (Zantac®) in 150 mg and 300 mg tablets, labeled as a prescription drug for the treatment of ulcers. GenPharm was the first company to file a substantially complete ANDA, and, upon the conclusion of patent infringement claims brought by Glaxo, it received a market exclusivity period of 180 days. Subsequently, Glaxo filed an NDA supplement for a lower dose (75 mg) ranitidine hydrochloride tablet with OTC labeling for the treatment of heartburn. Because this required the submission of new studies to secure FDA approval (contrast the *Upjohn* decision excerpted earlier in this chapter), Glaxo received three years of market exclusivity for OTC Zantac. Novopharm was the first company to file a substantially complete ANDA for the OTC product, so the FDA granted it 180 days of generic exclusivity to commence at the conclusion of Glaxo's period. TorPharm, another company that had filed an ANDA for OTC ranitidine, unsuccessfully challenged the agency's decision to provide this second generic exclusivity period as inconsistent with the statute because the different brand-name products grew out of the same patents previously challenged by GenPharm. See Apotex, Inc. v. Shalala, 53 F.Supp.2d 454, 459–62 (D.D.C.1999); see also Purepac Pharm. Co. v. Thompson, 354 F.3d 877, 888–90 (D.C.Cir.2004) (sustaining the FDA's decision as to which of two generic applicants qualified as the first filer entitled to generic exclusivity); Apotex Inc. v. FDA, 414 F.Supp.2d 61, 71 (D.D.C.2006) ("Assume that Company A submitted the first ANDA for Drug X, making a paragraph IV certification as to Patent 1. Company B subsequently submits its own ANDA for Drug X, making a paragraph IV certification as to Patent 2. If there is then a court decision holding Patent 2 invalid or not infringed as described in § 355(j)(5)(B)(iv), is the exclusivity period that Company A holds based upon its certification as to Patent 1 triggered by the court decision concerning Patent 2? Or would the exclusivity period only be triggered by a court decision finding Patent 1 invalid or not infringed?"); id. at 68 ("[U]nder FDA's view, distinct 180–day exclusivity entitlements may be awarded to multiple ANDA-applicants, or even to a single ANDA-applicant.''); id. at 74 (deferring to the FDA's resolution of this ambiguity); id. at 73 n.6 (noting that Congress rejected the FDA's interpretation when it amended these provisions in 2003); Dr. Reddy's Lab., Inc. v. Thompson, 302 F.Supp.2d 340, 359 (D.N.J.2003) (noting that the FDA may grant shared generic exclusivity to avoid ''an 'exclusivity stand-off' in which two or more ANDA applicants are eligible for exclusivity under a patent-by-patent analysis based upon their being first-to-file a paragraph IV certification on at least one patent listed for a drug, but no ANDA applicant can be granted final approval because the exclusivity periods of other ANDA applicants block approval'').

4. *Struggling to untangle generic exclusivity.* Courts have found it difficult to define exactly when the six month clock starts to run. See, e.g., Teva Pharm. USA, Inc. v. FDA, 441 F.3d 1 (D.C.Cir.2006) (rejecting as arbitrary and capricious the FDA's conclusion that the dismissal of a competitor's action was a ''court decision'' triggering a first-filer's exclusive marketing period); Mylan Pharm., Inc. v. Shalala, 81 F.Supp.2d 30, 36–42, 47 (D.D.C. 2000) (invalidating an FDA regulation providing that a court decision in favor of the ANDA sponsor accused of infringing a patent would trigger the 180–day exclusivity period only after opportunities for appeal had been exhausted); see also Teva Pharms. USA, Inc. v. EISAI Co., 620 F.3d 1341 (Fed.Cir.2010); Caraco Pharm. Labs., Ltd. v. Forest Labs., Ltd., 527 F.3d 1278 (Fed.Cir.2008) (allowing second ANDA filer with a paragraph IV certification to seek a declaratory judgment of noninfringement so as to trigger the first filer's exclusivity period); Ann K. Wooster, Annotation, Construction and Application of Hatch–Waxman Act, 180 A.L.R. Fed. 487 (2002 & 2011 Supp.). In 2003, Congress clarified this issue and a number of other matters. See David E. Korn et al., A New History and Discussion of 180–Day Exclusivity, 64 Food & Drug L.J. 335 (2009); Douglas A. Robinson, Note, Recent Administrative Reforms of the Hatch–Waxman Act: Lower Prices Now in Exchange for Less Pharmaceutical Innovation Later?, 81 Wash. U. L.Q. 829 (2003). As hinted at by the court in *Mylan* and elaborated in the next section, this question has implications for resolving antitrust claims against brand-name companies.

5. *Other exclusivity periods for generics.* Some generic drugs come to market through a ''paper NDA'' rather than an ANDA. These generics (sometimes called ''branded generics'') may receive a three-year market exclusivity period if the applicant had to conduct additional studies in order to secure FDA approval, and they also may receive six months of market exclusivity if the sponsor of the generic rather than the brand-name drug conducted pediatric studies. Apart from the possibility of receiving their own period of market exclusivity, paper NDAs allow the sponsor to circumvent the exclusivity rights of ANDA first-filers. See Leila Abboud & Anna W. Mathews, FDA to Allow Back Door for Some Generics, Wall St. J., Oct. 14, 2003, at B1; FDA Defends Its Use of Drug–Version Law: At Issue Is Whether the Agency Has Infringed the Patents by Approving Similar Versions of Medicines, Phila. Inquirer, Oct. 16, 2003, at C3 (reporting that the agency's approval of a modified form of Paxil® sold by Synthon undercut the exclusive rights held by Apotex to sell the first generic copy of this antidepressant).

6. *Sore losers?* The exclusivity period enjoyed by first filers only prevents the FDA from granting final approval to other ANDAs for 180 days; it does not bar the introduction of so-called "authorized generics" (i.e., drug product manufactured under the terms of the NDA but sold—by either the pioneer manufacturer or one of its licensees—using a different tradename and at a reduced price). See Teva Pharm. Indus. Ltd. v. Crawford, 410 F.3d 51 (D.C.Cir.2005) (rejecting a first filer's challenge to the agency's failure to prevent this practice); Saami Zain, Sword or Shield? An Overview and Competitive Analysis of the Marketing of Authorized Generics, 62 Food & Drug L.J. 739 (2007); Thomas Chen, Note, Authorized Generics: A Prescription for Hatch–Waxman Reform, 93 Va. L. Rev. 459 (2007); Diedtra Henderson, Ruling Likely to Limit How Low the Price of Generics Will Go as Zocor Patent Ends, Boston Globe, May 2, 2006, at E1 ("[These] have raised the ire of some generic-drug manufacturers and have triggered a federal investigation. Authorized generics released during the six-month period extend the revenue stream for brand manufacturers at the expense of such generic companies ...."). Why would a pioneer drug manufacturer introduce authorized generics? More curiously, why would a company ask the FDA to remove patents it had listed in the *Orange Book* instead of filing infringement claims against generic applicants? See Teva Pharms. USA, Inc. v. Sebelius, 595 F.3d 1303, 1316–18 (D.C.Cir.2010) (rejecting an FDA interpretation of the 2003 amendments that would allow brand-name manufacturers to deprive first filers of their generic exclusivity bonus by delisting a patent after the agency receives an ANDA with a paragraph IV certification); Teva Pharms., USA, Inc. v. Leavitt, 548 F.3d 103, 105–08 (D.C.Cir.2008) (upholding the FDA's denial of first-filer exclusivity requested by the manufacturer of a generic version of Risperdal® where its paragraph IV certification came a few months after the pioneer had delisted the patents even though the agency did not immediately revise print versions of the *Orange Book* to reflect this change).

C. COMPETITION AND ANTITRUST LAW

Arkansas Carpenters Health & Welf. Fund v. Bayer AG

604 F.3d 98 (2d Cir.2010).

PER CURIAM:

* * * Defendants Bayer AG and its subsidiary Bayer Corporation own the patent for the active ingredient in the antibiotic ciprofloxacin hydrochloride (Cipro). Defendants Barr Laboratories, Inc., Hoechst Marion Roussel, Inc. (HMR), and Watson Pharmaceuticals, Inc. were potential generic manufacturers of Cipro. Plaintiffs are direct purchasers of Cipro who allege that defendants violated federal antitrust law when they settled a patent infringement lawsuit by entering into collusive agreements that blocked the

entry of low-cost generic versions of Cipro into the prescription drug market.

Bayer is the owner of the patent relating to the active ingredient in Cipro, which has been described as the most prescribed antibiotic in the world. The Cipro patent, U.S. Patent No. 4,670,444, was issued on June 2, 1987, and was scheduled to expire on December 9, 2003. In 1991, Barr sought to market a generic version of Cipro pursuant to the expedited FDA approval process established by the Drug Price Competition and Patent Term Restoration Act of 1984 (the "Hatch–Waxman Act"), Pub. L. No. 98–417, 98 Stat. 1585. Under the Hatch–Waxman Act, a pharmaceutical company can seek approval to market generic versions of an approved branded drug without having to re-establish the drug's safety and effectiveness by filing an Abbreviated New Drug Application (ANDA).

Where, as here, a generic manufacturer seeks to enter the market before the expiration of the branded firm's patent, it must file a pre-expiration challenge ("paragraph IV" or "ANDA–IV" certification). 21 U.S.C. § 355(j)(2)(A)(vii)(IV). The ANDA–IV certification requires the generic firm * * * to state the basis for its claim of invalidity or noninfringement of the branded firm's patent, see id. § 355(j)(2)(B)(iv)(II). * * * The first generic firm to file an ANDA–IV is rewarded with a 180–day exclusive right to market its generic version of the drug. Id. § 355(j)(5)(B)(iv). However, only the first-filed ANDA–IV is eligible for the 180–day exclusivity period: even if the first filer loses, withdraws, or settles its challenge, subsequent filers do not become eligible for the exclusivity period.

Barr filed an ANDA–IV challenging Bayer's Cipro patent in October 1991. Bayer sued Barr for patent infringement in the Southern District of New York within 45 days of its receipt of notice of Barr's filing, triggering the Hatch–Waxman statutory stay. Barr subsequently entered into an agreement with other defendants herein, also potential generic manufacturers of Cipro, to share the costs and benefits of the patent litigation. In June 1996, the district court denied the parties' cross-motions for summary judgment. In January 1997—approximately two weeks prior to the scheduled trial—Bayer and Barr entered into a "reverse exclusionary payment" (or "pay-for-delay") settlement: that is, the patent holder (Bayer) agreed to pay the alleged infringer to settle the lawsuit, and in exchange, the alleged infringer agreed not to enter the market. Under the terms of the settlement agreement, Bayer agreed to (1) pay $49.1 million immediately; (2) make quarterly payments of between $12.5 and $17.125 million for the duration of the patent except for the last six months prior to the patent's expiration;[8] and (3) provide the generic manufacturers a guaranteed license to sell brand-name Cipro at a reduced rate for six months prior to the patent's expiration. In exchange, Barr conceded the patent's validity and agreed not to market a generic version of Cipro prior to the patent's expiration.[9]

---

8. * * * Settlement payments ultimately totaled $398.1 million.

9. Barr reserved its right to reinstate its ANDA–IV if Bayer's patent were later held to be invalid. Four generic manufacturers—Ranbaxy, Schein, Mylan, and Carlsbad—subsequent-

In 2000, direct and indirect purchasers of Cipro filed over thirty antitrust lawsuits against Bayer under federal and state law. These cases were consolidated by the Multi–District Litigation Panel in the Eastern District of New York. Plaintiffs allege that defendants' settlement exceeded the scope of Bayer's patent rights because Bayer effectively paid its potential competitors hundreds of millions of dollars not to challenge its patent. Plaintiffs also allege that the agreements were unlawful because Barr was permitted to reclaim the 180–day market exclusivity period if a subsequent challenger was successful in having the patent invalidated, and because the generic manufacturers agreed not to file any ANDA–IV certifications for products that relate to Cipro. But for the challenged agreements, plaintiffs assert that (1) Barr would have entered the market pending resolution of the patent litigation; (2) Barr would have prevailed in the litigation and entered the market; or (3) Bayer would have granted Barr a license to market a generic version of Cipro to avoid a trial on the patent's validity.

On cross-motions for summary judgment, the district court granted summary judgment for the defendants. In re Ciprofloxacin Hydrochloride Antitrust Litig., 363 F.Supp.2d 514, 548 (E.D.N.Y.2005). The court stated: * * *

> [I]n the absence of any evidence that the agreements created a bottleneck on challenges to the '444 Patent, or that they otherwise restrained competition beyond the scope of the claims of the '444 Patent, the agreements have not had any anti-competitive effects on the market for ciprofloxacin beyond that which are permitted under the '444 Patent. The fact that Bayer paid what in absolute numbers is a handsome sum to Barr to settle its lawsuit does not necessarily reflect a lack of confidence in the '444 Patent, but rather the economic realities of what was at risk. There is simply no precedent for plaintiffs' argument that the parties to a settlement are required to preserve the public's interest in lower prices. Such a rule would only result in parties being less likely to reach settlements, aside from undermining well-settled principles of patent law. Finally, to even attempt to quantify the public's interest in a patent settlement between private parties would require devaluing patents across the board, a result that would contravene the presumption of validity afforded by Congress and impact the very way patent licenses are handled in countless daily transactions.

Id. at 540–41. * * *

The Sherman Act provides that "[e]very contract, combination in the form of trust or otherwise, or conspiracy, in restraint of trade or commerce among the several States, or with foreign nations, is declared to be illegal."

---

ly challenged the Cipro patent. Ranbaxy's challenge was dismissed as moot in October 1999. Mylan's and Schein's consolidated challenges were dismissed at summary judgment and this dismissal was affirmed on appeal. Bayer AG v. Schein Pharm., Inc., 129 F.Supp.2d 705 (D.N.J.2001), aff'd, 301 F.3d 1306 (Fed.Cir.2002). Carlsbad's challenge was rejected after a nine-day bench trial. Bayer AG v. Carlsbad Tech., Inc., No. Civ. 01–867–B (S.D.Cal. Aug. 26, 2002).

15 U.S.C. § 1. Although by its terms, the Act prohibits "every" restraint of trade, the Supreme Court "has long recognized that Congress intended to outlaw only unreasonable restraints." Agreements that have a "predictable and pernicious anticompetitive effect, and . . . limited potential for procompetitive benefit" are deemed per se unlawful. Most conduct, however, is subject to so-called "rule of reason" analysis. Rule of reason analysis proceeds in three steps. First, the plaintiff bears the initial burden of showing that the defendant's conduct "had an *actual* adverse effect on competition as a whole in the relevant market." If plaintiff satisfies this burden, the burden then shifts to defendant to offer evidence that its conduct had pro-competitive effects. If defendant is able to offer such proof, the burden shifts back to plaintiff, who must prove that any legitimate competitive effects could have been achieved through less restrictive alternatives. * * *

The question, therefore, is whether patent settlements in which the generic firm agrees to delay entry into the market in exchange for payment fall within the scope of the patent holder's property rights, or whether such settlements are properly characterized as illegal market-sharing agreements. Authorities are divided on this question. The Federal Trade Commission (FTC), the U.S. antitrust enforcement agency charged with supervising the pharmaceutical industry, has long insisted that reverse exclusionary payment settlements violate antitrust law and has challenged numerous agreements as unreasonable restraints of trade. Although it initially took a different view, the United States [Department of Justice] has since maintained that reverse exclusionary payment settlements may violate antitrust laws. Many academic commentators share the United States's view.[12]

Most courts, by contrast, including this court, Joblove v. Barr Labs. Inc. (In re Tamoxifen Citrate Antitrust Litig.), 466 F.3d 187, 216 (2d Cir.2006), have held that the right to enter into reverse exclusionary payment agreements falls within the terms of the exclusionary grant conferred by the branded manufacturer's patent. See Ark. Carpenters Health & Welfare Fund v. Bayer AG (In re Ciprofloxacin Hydrochloride Antitrust Litig.), 544 F.3d 1323, 1333 (Fed.Cir.2008) [rejecting claims brought by indirect purchasers]; Schering–Plough Corp. v. FTC, 402 F.3d 1056, 1076 (11th Cir.2005). But see La. Wholesale Drug Co. v. Hoechst

12. See, e.g., C. Scott Hemphill, Paying for Delay: Pharmaceutical Patent Settlement As a Regulatory Design Problem, 81 N.Y.U. L. Rev. 1553, 1561–62 (2006) (arguing that a settlement should be accorded a presumption of illegality if the settlement both restricts the generic firm's ability to market a competing drug and includes compensation from the innovator to the generic firm); Herbert Hovenkamp et al., Anticompetitive Settlement of Intellectual Property Disputes, 87 Minn. L. Rev. 1719, 1759–60 (2003) (proposing that a defendant would overcome the presumptive unlawfulness of a reverse payment settlement by "showing both (1) that the ex ante likelihood of prevailing in its infringement lawsuit is significant, and (2) the size of the payment is no more than the expected value of litigation and collateral costs attending the lawsuit"). But see Alan Devlin, The Stochastic Relationship Between Patents and Antitrust, 5 J. Competition L. & Econ. 75, 108 (2009) ("[U]ncritical application of standard principles of competition law to information markets may be myopic.").

Marion Roussel, Inc. (In re Cardizem CD Antitrust Litig.), 332 F.3d 896, 908 (6th Cir.2003) (holding such agreements to be per se illegal); In re Terazosin Hydrochloride Antitrust Litig., 352 F.Supp.2d 1279 (S.D.Fla. 2005) (same).

Particularly relevant here is this court's decision in *Tamoxifen*. The plaintiffs in *Tamoxifen* challenged a reverse exclusionary payment settlement between Zeneca and Barr that the parties entered into after a district court had declared Zeneca's patent invalid. 466 F.3d at 193. At the 12(b)(6) stage, *Tamoxifen* rejected as speculative plaintiffs' allegation that Barr would have prevailed on appeal but for the settlement agreement. Id. at 203–04. Assuming the truth of plaintiffs' allegation that the exclusion payments exceeded the profits Barr would have obtained upon entering the market as a generic competitor, the *Tamoxifen* court determined that the plaintiffs had no antitrust claim because a patent holder is entitled to protect its "lawful monopoly over the manufacture and distribution of the patented product." Id. at 205, 208–09.

Notably, *Tamoxifen* expressly adopted aspects of the lower court's summary judgment decision in this case, holding: "Unless and until the patent is shown to have been procured by fraud, or a suit for its enforcement is shown to be objectively baseless, there is no injury to the market cognizable under existing antitrust law, as long as competition is restrained only within the scope of the patent." Id. at 213. The *Tamoxifen* court ruled that the settlement agreement did not exceed the scope of the patent where (1) there was no restriction on marketing non-infringing products; (2) a generic version of the branded drug would necessarily infringe the branded firm's patent; and (3) the agreement did not bar other generic manufacturers from challenging the patent. Id. at 213–15. * * *

Plaintiffs do not argue that the patent infringement lawsuit was a sham or that the Cipro patent was procured by fraud. Thus, the only reasonable basis for distinguishing *Tamoxifen* would be if plaintiffs demonstrated that the settlement agreement here, unlike in *Tamoxifen,* exceeded the scope of the Cipro patent. Plaintiffs cannot establish this because a generic version of Cipro would necessarily infringe Bayer's patent. *Tamoxifen* explained that unlike "formulation patents," which cover only specific formulations or delivery methods for a compound, a "compound patent" "by its nature, excludes all generic versions of the drug." 466 F.3d at 214. Bayer's Cipro patent is a compound patent. Thus, Barr's agreement to refrain from manufacturing generic Cipro encompasses only conduct that would infringe Bayer's patent rights. * * *

The *Tamoxifen* majority urged against addressing the probability that a patent was invalid and deferred to a patent holder's desire to settle patent challenges, concluding that a patent holder could reasonably decide to pay money, even more than a generic manufacturer would make on the market, to guarantee protection of its patent. See 466 F.3d at 210 ("[A] rule [limiting the amount of exclusion payments] would . . . fail to give sufficient consideration to the patent holder's incentive to settle . . . .").

Plaintiffs and amici also argue that *Tamoxifen* runs afoul of the purpose of the Hatch–Waxman Act. The purpose of the Hatch–Waxman Act was "to make available more low cost generic drugs." H.R. Rep. No. 98–857, pt. 1, at 14 (1984), reprinted in 1984 U.S.C.C.A.N. 2647, 2647. The Act sought to accomplish this objective by providing an incentive through the ANDA–IV certification procedure for generic manufacturers to challenge presumptively valid patents, which, if successful, would result in exclusivity for the first successful challenger and the entry of generic drugs into the market. The market entry of generic drugs arising from successful Hatch–Waxman challenges can result in significant savings to consumers. See Brief for AARP as Amicus at 8–9 (discussing generic manufacturers' challenges to the Prozac patent and Paxil patent where generic entry resulted in $2.5 and $2 billion in consumer savings, respectively).[17]

These policy arguments cannot be addressed here. As defendants note, this panel is bound by *Tamoxifen* "absent a change in law by higher authority or by way of an in banc proceeding." However, there are several reasons why this case might be appropriate for reexamination by our full court. First, the United States has itself urged us to repudiate *Tamoxifen,* arguing that *Tamoxifen* adopted an improper standard that fails to subject reverse exclusionary payment settlements to appropriate antitrust scrutiny. Brief for the United States as Amicus [filed at the court's request] at 6, 14–15. * * * While acknowledging that patent-holders are entitled to settle disputes over the validity of their patent, the United States proposes that excessive reverse payment settlements be deemed presumptively unlawful unless a patent-holder can show that settlement payments do not greatly exceed anticipated litigation costs. Id. at 27–32.

Second, there is evidence that the practice of entering into reverse exclusionary payment settlements has increased since we decided *Tamoxifen.* * * * Third, after *Tamoxifen* was decided, a principal drafter of the Hatch–Waxman Act criticized the settlement practice at issue here. See 148 Cong. Rec. S7565 (July 30, 2002) (remarks of Sen. Hatch) ("As coauthor of the [Hatch–Waxman Act], I can tell you that I find these type[s] of reverse payment collusive arrangements appalling."); see also 146 Cong. Rec. E1538–02 (Sept. 20, 2000) (remarks of Rep. Waxman) ("[R]equir[ing] companies seeking to reach secret, anticompetitive agreements to disclose them to the FTC ... [would] ensure that existing antitrust and drug approval laws are enforced to the letter.").

Fourth and finally, the *Tamoxifen* panel appears to have relied on an erroneous characterization of the Hatch–Waxman Act. *Tamoxifen* was based in no small part on the panel majority's statement that reverse exclusionary settlements "open[] the [relevant] patent to immediate challenge by other potential generic manufacturers, which did indeed follow—spurred by the additional incentive (at the time) of potentially securing the

---

17. One study found that generic manufacturers prevailed in 73% of the Hatch–Waxman lawsuits that were tried to verdict. See Brief for American Antitrust Institute as Amicus at 3 (citing Generic Drug Entry Prior to Patent Expiration, at vii (2002), available at http://www.ftc.gov/os/2002/07/genericdrugstudy.pdf).

180–day exclusivity period available upon a victory in a subsequent infringement lawsuit.'' 466 F.3d at 214. If understood as a legal conclusion this remark, that the statutory exclusivity period cedes to the first ANDA filer to successfully defend, was erroneous.

In addition, unlike *Tamoxifen,* which was decided at the 12(b)(6) [motion to dismiss] stage, this case involves a summary judgment decision based on a full record. This case could provide our full court with an opportunity to revisit the issues in play in *Tamoxifen* and to analyze the competing interests that underlie antitrust challenges to reverse payment settlements in light of the full record and the arguments of the parties and amici, including the United States, that have been raised in this appeal. We therefore invite plaintiffs-appellants to petition for in banc rehearing. * * *

NOTES AND QUESTIONS

1. *Not taking the bait.* The full court failed to take up the panel's invitation to revisit the issue, denying the petition for en banc rehearing. 625 F.3d 779 (2d Cir.2010). This prompted a dissent from one of the members of the panel (who also had dissented in *Tamoxifen*):

> [Since 2006, the FTC] has identified fifty-three pharmaceutical patent settlements involving exclusion payments. The Commission estimates that such settlements cost consumers approximately $3.5 billion per year. Further, such settlements serve no obvious redeeming social purpose. Put simply, what the patent holder purchases by means of an exclusion payment settlement is the continuation of a patent the patent holder must have thought had some significant probability of being declared invalid.... It should not be surprising, therefore, that our *Tamoxifen* decision has inspired vigorous criticism from a variety of sources. The United States ... has supported the plaintiffs' petition for en banc rehearing in this case. Also supporting the petition for rehearing are the majority of state attorneys general, the [FTC], the American Medical Association, and an impressive array of consumer groups and academic commentators.... The *Tamoxifen* majority recognized the "troubling dynamic" of permitting exclusion payments that "inevitably protect patent monopolies that are, perhaps, undeserved." 466 F.3d at 211. Subsequent experience has shown that the majority was right to be "troubled." ... It will be up to the Supreme Court or Congress to resolve the conflict among the courts of appeals.

Id. at 780–82 (Pooler, J., dissenting) (footnotes omitted). The Supreme Court denied a petition for certiorari. Louisiana Wholesale Drug Co. v. Bayer AG, 131 S.Ct. 1606 (2011).

2. *Judicial activity elsewhere.* For the most part, lower courts in other circuits continue to reject these sorts of antitrust claims. See, e.g., Kroger Co. v. Sanofi–Aventis, 701 F.Supp.2d 938 (S.D.Ohio 2010) (dismissing various purchasers' antitrust claims against the manufacturer of Plavix® (clopidogrel bisulfate) for lack of standing even though reverse payment settlements are treated as illegal per se in the Sixth Circuit); In re

AndroGel Antitrust Litig., 687 F.Supp.2d 1371, 1375–79 (N.D.Ga.2010) (dismissing FTC and several private antitrust complaints against the manufacturer of a testosterone-replacement drug for allegedly conspiring with generic competitors to delay launch of their competing versions). But see King Drug Co. v. Cephalon, Inc., 702 F.Supp.2d 514 (E.D.Pa.2010) (rejecting motions to dismiss FTC and several private antitrust complaints in a case involving Provigil® (modafinil)); Meijer, Inc. v. Barr Pharm., Inc., 572 F.Supp.2d 38 (D.D.C.2008) (applying rule of reason standard to a reverse payment settlement by the brand-name manufacturer of the oral contraceptive Ovcon®, and denying generic drug manufacturer's motion for summary judgment on antitrust claims brought by direct purchasers because there remained genuine issues of disputed fact).

3. *Regulatory activity*. The Federal Trade Commission has not relented. See Duff Wilson, F.T.C. Criticizes Agreements That Delay Generic Drugs, N.Y. Times, Sept. 1, 2011, at B2; see also Editorial, The "Pay for Delay" Rap, Wall St. J., Oct. 5, 2010, at A22 (complaining that FTC Chairman Jon "Leibowitz has been conducting his campaign with evangelical zeal," and noting that, after a string of judicial setbacks, he "has taken the unusual step of directly lobbying Congress to ban reverse settlements"). As revealed in the *Cipro* opinion, the Antitrust Division of the Department of Justice has partially come to agree with the FTC's views on this question. See Lyndsey Layton, FTC Sues in "Pay-for-Delay" Pact: Drugmaker Paid Rivals to Withhold Generic, Agency Says, Wash. Post, Feb. 3, 2009, at A4 ("The FTC has tried unsuccessfully to persuade the Supreme Court to hear two cases challenging such agreements in recent years, but each time, the Department of Justice argued that the high court should not take the case. Leibowitz said he believes the Justice Department under President Obama will be more supportive of the FTC's position."); see also Henry N. Butler & Jeffrey P. Jarosch, Policy Reversal on Reverse Payments: Why Courts Should Not Follow the New DOJ Position on Reverse–Payment Settlements of Pharmaceutical Patent Litigation, 96 Iowa L. Rev. 57 (2010).

4. *Congressional proposals*. Legislative proposals to restrict the practice have "recently gained momentum in Congress." Jillian Berman & Jayne O'Donnell, Bills Target Delays on Cheap Drugs, USA Today, Aug. 18, 2010, at 1B; see also Natasha Singer, Deals to Restrain Generic Drugs Face a Ban in Health Care Bill, N.Y. Times, Jan. 13, 2010, at B1. Even so, efforts in 2010 to tack these proposals into broader legislation failed. See Reed Abelson, In Health Care Reform, Boons for Hospitals and Drug Makers, N.Y. Times, Mar. 22, 2010, at B1; see also Editorial, Faint Progress on Drug Payoffs, N.Y. Times, Aug. 10, 2010, at A24 ("Meanwhile, the problem has been getting worse. The F.T.C. found that there have been more such pay-for-delay settlements in the first nine months of the current fiscal year than in any entire previous year.").

5. *Views of the European Union*. Although it did not file an amicus brief in the *Cipro* litigation, the EU has actively investigated the reverse payment problem. See Stephen Castle & James Kanter, European Antitrust Regulators Raid Large Drug Makers, N.Y. Times, Jan. 17, 2008, at C2;

James Kanter, Europe Is Studying Delays in Access to Generic Drugs, N.Y. Times, July 9, 2009, at B4; Jeanne Whalen & Peppi Kiviniemi, EU Blasts Drug Titans' Tactics—Report Says Roadblocks to Generic Rivals Cost $3.87 Billion, Wall St. J., Nov. 29, 2008, at B5; see also Melanie J. Brown, Note, Reverse Payment Settlements in the European Commission's Pharmaceutical Sector Inquiry Report: A Missed Opportunity to Benefit from U.S. Experience, 33 Colum. J.L. & Arts 377 (2010); Jonathan A. Hareid, Note, In Search of an Elixir: What Ails the Pharmaceutical Industry in Europe and How to Use the Competition Laws to Cure It, 10 Minn. J.L. Sci. & Tech. 727 (2009).

6. *Further commentary*. See Michael A. Carrier, Unsettling Drug Patent Settlements: A Framework for Presumptive Illegality, 108 Mich. L. Rev. 37 (2009); Bret Dickey et al., An Economic Assessment of Patent Settlements in the Pharmaceutical Industry, 19 Annals Health L. 367 (2010); C. Scott Hemphill, An Aggregate Approach to Antitrust: Using New Data and Rulemaking to Preserve Drug Competition, 109 Colum. L. Rev. 629 (2009); David W. Opderbeck, Rational Antitrust Policy and Reverse Payment Settlements in Hatch–Waxman Patent Litigation, 98 Geo. L.J. 1303 (2010); Lisa Allen, Note, Reviewing the Legality of Pharmaceutical Reverse Payment Settlements: The FTC Doesn't Get It Right, 8 Geo. J.L. & Pub. Pol'y 245 (2010); Sheila Kadura, Note, Is an Absolute Ban on Reverse Payments the Appropriate Way to Prevent Anticompetitive Agreements Between Branded– and Generic–Pharmaceutical Companies?, 86 Tex. L. Rev. 647 (2008).

Bristol–Myers Squibb Co. v. IVAX Corp.

77 F.Supp.2d 606 (D.N.J.2000), aff'd in part, 246 F.3d 1368 (Fed.Cir.2001).

■ WALLS, DISTRICT JUDGE:

Bristol–Myers Squibb, a drug manufacturer, has sued Zenith Goldline and IVAX Corporation for infringement of two patents owned by Bristol that claim methods of using the anti-cancer drug Taxol®, a drug based on a natural agent known as paclitaxel. The plaintiff alleges that Zenith Goldline, with the assistance of IVAX, has filed Abbreviated New Drug Application (ANDA) 75–297 with the Food and Drug Administration, to request approval to market paclitaxel. Bristol claims that the filing of the ANDA constitutes infringement of Bristol's rights under U.S. Patent No. 5,641,-803 ("the '803 patent") and No. 5,670,537 ("the '537 patent"), pursuant to the Hatch–Waxman Act, 35 U.S.C. § 271(e)(2)(A). Zenith Goldline and Baker Norton (a subsidiary of IVAX Corporation) assert numerous counterclaims based on federal antitrust provisions and state law. * * *

Paclitaxel is the FDA-designated generic term for an anti-cancer agent derived from the bark of the Pacific Yew tree. Its anti-cancer properties were discovered and developed by researchers at the National Cancer Institute (NCI), an institute of the National Institutes of Health (NIH), beginning in the 1960s. During this period, the federal government developed techniques to extract paclitaxel from yew tree bark and to create a clinically acceptable formulation for treating humans. In the early 1980s, the NCI conducted research and clinical trials concerning the use of paclitaxel to treat ovarian cancer. Eventually, the agency sought a commercial partner to bring a paclitaxel-based drug to market, and in 1991 the NCI and Bristol entered into a cooperative research and development agreement (CRADA) pursuant to the Federal Technology Transfer Act, 15 U.S.C. § 3710a(b).

In 1991 and 1993, Congress held investigatory hearings to determine the extent of Bristol's power to exclude competition pursuant to the CRADA, and to examine Bristol's pricing arrangements. Bristol made various oral and written statements during these hearings. Beginning in 1991, purportedly relying on public assurances by Bristol not to block competition in the development of paclitaxel-related drugs, Baker Norton began to conduct clinical trials involving the use of paclitaxel to treat breast cancer. In 1995, Baker Norton learned that the NCI had obtained U.S. Patent No. 5,496,846 ("the '846 patent"), known as the Wilson patent, which described the use of paclitaxel to treat breast cancer. Accordingly, Baker Norton sought a nonexclusive license to this patent in the spring of 1996 and formally applied to the NIH in September 1996. Soon after, NIH informed Baker Norton that no license was available because the agency had determined that the Wilson patent was a subject invention of the CRADA. Because Bristol had exercised its option under the CRADA for an exclusive license to this patent, Baker Norton's application was rejected.

Baker Norton, seeking to market a paclitaxel-based drug to treat Kaposi's sarcoma, a life-threatening form of cancer that often strikes persons with AIDS, developed and tested Paxene®, a paclitaxel-based drug. The counterclaimants allege that through Baker Norton's application to the NIH for a license to the Wilson patent, Bristol improperly learned that Baker Norton was preparing a New Drug Application to obtain "orphan drug" exclusive marketing privileges regarding the treatment of Kaposi's sarcoma. Orphan drug designation is a form of non-patent marketing exclusivity granted by the FDA pursuant to 21 U.S.C. § 360bb to encourage the development of drugs to treat rare diseases or conditions. The counterclaimants allege that in February 1997, with the assistance of data from NCI researchers, Bristol submitted to the FDA its own application for orphan drug status and a supplemental New Drug Application. These applications were approved, and Bristol was granted a seven-year period of marketing exclusivity. As a result, Baker Norton's New Drug Application, submitted in March 1997, was approved, but Baker Norton was barred from marketing Paxene to treat patients with Kaposi's sarcoma until 2004. * * *

Bristol maintains that because any injury to Baker Norton was the result of Bristol's valid efforts to obtain government action, such efforts are immunized from federal antitrust and state law liability by the *Noerr–Pennington* doctrine. * * * The counterclaimants protest that this doctrine does not immunize an entire course of wrongful acts simply because Bristol requested government approval and licenses as part of its allegedly tortious scheme. * * * Here, there is no question that the counterclaiming plaintiffs' injuries were the "direct result" of decisions made by government agencies. NCI chose to enter a licensing agreement with Bristol; likewise, the FDA made the decision to grant orphan drug exclusivity to the defendant drug company.* These decisions cannot fairly be characterized as the result of Bristol's private actions. * * *

The counterclaimants next argue that any antitrust immunity is shed by Bristol's engagement in a course of tortious conduct. They charge that: (1) Bristol improperly received Baker Norton's confidential business information and obtained an exclusive license to the Wilson patent only after it became aware that Baker Norton had expressed interest in obtaining a nonexclusive license to use paclitaxel to treat breast cancer; (2) Bristol obtained its license to the Wilson patent solely to block competition and has never attempted to bring a breast cancer therapy to market; (3) Bristol misappropriated Baker Norton's confidential business information, learned that Baker Norton was preparing to apply for orphan drug status to market paclitaxel to treat Kaposi's sarcoma and submitted its own request for orphan drug status. Additionally, (4) while the FDA was considering Baker Norton's application for orphan drug status, Bristol met privately with high-level FDA officials in an effort to block the application. * * * Baker Norton and Zenith Goldline assert that the *Noerr–Pennington* doctrine does not protect misconduct in ex parte proceedings before a government agency. * * *

If misconduct were evident, counterclaimants' argument would remain inadequate. In reviewing a publicity campaign that involved the circulation of propaganda which had been disguised as independent commentary, the *Noerr* Court rejected the argument that unethical business conduct could form a basis for antitrust liability. The Court held that even deliberate deception of the public and public officials was of no consequence to liability under the Sherman Act. * * *

In a final effort to save their antitrust claims, Baker Norton and Zenith Goldline proffer that when the government acts in a commercial role, rather than in its political or regulatory capacity, courts should apply a "commercial exception" to the *Noerr–Pennington* doctrine and reject assertions of immunity. They assert that the NCI and its parent NIH began an ongoing commercial relationship with Bristol in 1991, when NCI and Bristol entered the CRADA. They also allege that when NIH granted Bristol an exclusive license to the Wilson patent, the agency had been a commercial partner with Bristol for five years and was in the process of negotiating a royalty agreement under the licensing agreement. * * *

Antitrust immunity is not destroyed by a commercial relationship between the government and a private actor. If that were so, courts would be called upon to frustrate First Amendment rights [to petition] whenever

---

* A direct challenge to the agency's action was rejected one year after the decision in this case. See Baker Norton Pharm. v. FDA, 132 F.Supp.2d 30 (D.D.C.2001) [excerpted in Chap. 10(B)(2)].

the government stood to profit from its decisions. There is clear statutory authority to the federal agencies to enter into the CRADA, to grant the patent license, and to designate orphan drug exclusivity to Bristol. Without express declaration of Congress, the counterclaimants' proposed exception cannot swallow the [far]reaching rule of immunity or these statutory grants. The court finds that Bristol was engaged in protected petitioning conduct. The court grants Bristol's motion to dismiss the Sherman Act counterclaims of Baker Norton and Zenith Goldline to the extent that they allege conduct protected by the *Noerr–Pennington* doctrine. * * *

Both counterclaimants assert an estoppel claim, maintaining that Bristol promised during congressional hearings in 1991 and 1993 "that it would not bar all competition in the market for paclitaxel-based drugs and that its monopoly in the paclitaxel-based drug market was limited to . . . non-patent exclusivity." The purported promises include statements that: (1) Bristol did not have a monopoly on paclitaxel because the compound [as opposed to methods of administration] is not patentable; (2) Bristol did not have exclusive intellectual property rights to make paclitaxel; (3) any company could file a full [NDA] and market paclitaxel; (4) the NCI did not require a "reasonable pricing clause" in its CRADA with Bristol because paclitaxel is not patentable; (5) " '[c]ompetition' from 'generics' was 'a near certainty in the next several years. . . . [N]ear-term generic competition for Taxol is a certainty because Taxol is not a patented product;' " and (6) "While Taxol qualified for orphan drug status as a treatment for refractory ovarian cancer, BMS [Bristol] believed that the potential utility of Taxol could place it outside the spirit and intent of the Orphan Drug Act. Therefore, the company voluntarily relinquished Taxol orphan drug status . . . ."

Bristol moves to dismiss on two grounds: that "[s]tatements made to Congress fall—dead center—within the protected zone of petitioning the government," and second, that the counterclaimants have not alleged the elements of promissory estoppel. * * * Here, the statements made by Bristol were offered during congressional hearings headlined, "Exclusive Agreements Between Federal Agencies and Bristol–Myers Squibb Co. for Drug Development: Is The Public Interest Protected?" and, "Pricing of Drugs Codeveloped by Federal Laboratories and Private Companies." It is apparent that these claims were made in an effort to induce favorable government action, to encourage cooperation between government agencies and drug manufacturers and to defend Bristol's paclitaxel pricing system. It is also likely, as the counterclaimants allege, that these statements were made with anticompetitive intent. Yet, *Noerr* has long protected such a situation from antitrust scrutiny—and, in our circuit, it is likewise protected from state law liability. * * *

[I]t is clear that even misrepresentations made to induce government action are protected by the *Noerr–Pennington* doctrine. The counterclaim for promissory estoppel is barred. Baker Norton and Zenith Goldline have not adequately alleged that Bristol's alleged statements injured them directly. From the well-pled allegations, the court can infer only that their competitor made certain representations in its efforts to obtain government approval. The motion to dismiss the promissory estoppel counterclaim is granted. * * *

NOTES AND QUESTIONS

1. *Paying (twice?) for Taxol.* The General Accounting Office subsequently issued a report detailing the history behind the development of paclitaxel. See Peter Landers, U.S. Recoups Modest Sum on Taxol: NIH Says It Lacked Power to Pressure Bristol–Myers for Better Licensing Terms, Wall St. J., June 9, 2003, at B7 ("The government spent $183 million to research Taxol, the best-selling cancer drug in history with revenue of $9 billion. But it recouped only $35 million of that cost in licensing deals .... The report said that the government did achieve its primary goal of bringing the treatment quickly to patients."). The FTC looked into the dispute over Taxol. See Melody Petersen, Two Companies Under Inquiry on Generic Drug Actions, N.Y. Times, Sept. 7, 2000, at C6; see also Xechem, Inc. v. Bristol–Myers Squibb Co., 372 F.3d 899 (7th Cir.2004) (reversing dismissal of antitrust claims brought by a potential generic competitor); Gardiner Harris, Bristol–Myers Is Sued by 29 States over Its Efforts to Protect Taxol, Wall St. J., June 5, 2002, at A3.

2. *Licensing and pricing.* Taxol does not represent an exceptional case. See Alice Dembner, Public Handouts Enrich Drug Makers, Boston Globe, Apr. 5, 1998, at A1 ("NIH spent at least $1 billion on drug and vaccine development in fiscal 1996, but took in only $27 million in royalties from all products."); see also Public Citizen Health Research Group v. NIH, 209 F.Supp.2d 37 (D.D.C.2002) (upholding the agency's invocation of FOIA's exemption for confidential commercial information in declining to disclose royalties received on inventions licensed to pharmaceutical companies); Ron A. Bouchard, Balancing Public and Private Interests in the Commercialization of Publicly Funded Medical Research: Is There a Role for Compulsory Government Royalty Fees?, 13 B.U. J. Sci. & Tech. L. 120 (2007). Apart from complaints about forgone licensing revenues, questions have arisen about the high prices that some drug companies have charged for products developed with federal assistance. Until 1995, NIH had imposed a "reasonable pricing" requirement on products that emerged from a CRADA, which it dropped in the wake of criticism that this amounted to the imposition of price controls. See Peter S. Arno & Michael H. Davis, Why Don't We Enforce Existing Drug Price Controls? The Unrecognized and Unenforced Reasonable Pricing Requirements Imposed upon Patents Deriving in Whole or in Part from Federally–Funded Research, 75 Tul. L. Rev. 631 (2001); see also Ceci Connolly, NIH Declines to Enter AIDS Drug Price Battle, Wash. Post, Aug. 5, 2004, at A4. The government retains "march in" rights that would allow it to call for compulsory licensing of covered inventions. See John H. Raubitschek & Norman J. Latker, Reasonable Pricing—A New Twist for March-in Rights Under the Bayh–Dole Act, 22 Santa Clara Computer & High Tech. L.J. 149 (2005).

3. *Promoting technology transfer*. Under the Bayh–Dole Act, private entities may commercialize breakthroughs supported by government funding. See Pub. L. No. 96–517, § 6(a), 94 Stat. 3019 (1980) (codified as amended at 35 U.S.C. §§ 200–211); see also Board of Trustees of Stanford Univ. v. Roche Molecular Sys., Inc., 131 S.Ct. 2188 (2011) (resolving a dispute over ownership of patents on an HIV test); Platzer v. Sloan–Kettering Inst., 787 F.Supp. 360, 362 (S.D.N.Y.) ("The Bayh–Dole Act grants non-profit organizations exclusive title to inventions developed through federal funding and allows them to freely license such inventions for profit so long as such profit is used to fund additional scientific research."), aff'd mem., 983 F.2d 1086 (Fed.Cir.1992); James D. Clements, Improving Bayh–Dole: A Case for Inventor Ownership of Federally Sponsored Research Patents, 49 IDEA 469 (2009); Carl E. Gulbrandsen, Bayh–Dole: Wisconsin Roots and Inspired Public Policy, 2007 Wis. L. Rev. 1149; Ashley J. Stevens et al., The Role of Public–Sector Research in the Discovery of Drugs and Vaccines, 364 New Eng. J. Med. 535, 540 (2011) (finding that public-sector research institutions "have contributed to the discovery of 9.3 to 21.2% of all drugs involved in new-drug applications approved during the period from 1990 through 2007"); Gardiner Harris, Federal Research Center Will Help Develop Medicines, N.Y. Times, Jan. 23, 2011, at A1. Under the Federal Technology Transfer Act, Pub. L. No. 99–502, § 2, 100 Stat. 1785 (1986) (codified at 15 U.S.C. § 3710), agencies could enter into CRADAs, assigning to private entities the patents for any inventions developed in collaboration with government researchers. Some collaborations with industry occur under the table. See David Willman, NIH Audit Criticizes Scientist's Dealings: A Researcher Received More Than $100,000 from Drug Firms, L.A. Times, Sept. 10, 2006, at A1. See generally Arti K. Rai et al., Pathways Across the Valley of Death: Novel Intellectual Property Strategies for Accelerated Drug Discovery, 8 Yale J. Health Pol'y L. & Ethics 1 (2008); Sheila R. Shulman & Andrea Kuettel, Drug Development and the Public Health Mission: Collaborative Challenges at the FDA, NIH, and Academic Medical Centers, 53 Buff. L. Rev. 663 (2005); Andrew A. Toole, Does Public Scientific Research Complement Private Investment in Research and Development in the Pharmaceutical Industry?, 50 J.L. & Econ. 81 (2007).

4. *University involvement*. In tandem with the significant role played by the federal government, industry has forged increasingly close ties with academia. See David Blumenthal et al., Participation of Life–Science Faculty in Research Relationships with Industry, 335 New Eng. J. Med. 1734 (1996); see also Sharon Begley, Researchers Try to Cut New Path to the Pharmacy: As Companies Get Gun Shy, Nonprofits Make Drugs and Conduct Own Trials, Wall St. J., Jan. 12, 2004, at A1; David Wahlberg & Andrea Jones, Drug Deal Burnishes Emory's Reputation, Atlanta J.–Const., July 20, 2005, at 1A (reporting that Gilead Sciences paid $525 million for the rights to commercialize the AIDS drug Emtriva®, "the largest lump sum payment for intellectual property to any American university . . . [and] part of a trend of colleges cashing in on future rights to scientific discoveries instead of risking uncertain profits"). Universities have become active participants in patent litigation. See, e.g., Genentech, Inc. v. Regents of the

Univ. of Cal., 143 F.3d 1446 (Fed.Cir.1998); Regents of the Univ. of Minn. v. Glaxo Wellcome Inc., 44 F.Supp.2d 998 (D.Minn.1999); University of Colo. Fdn., Inc. v. American Cyanamid Co., 974 F.Supp. 1339 (D.Colo. 1997); see also University of Rochester v. G.D Searle & Co., 358 F.3d 916, 929 (Fed.Cir.2004) [excerpted in Chap. 10(A)(2)] (rejecting the argument that strict application of the written description requirement to invalidate a method patent for hypothetical COX–2 inhibitors would conflict with the policies underlying the Bayh–Dole Act or inhibit universities' technology transfer programs); John M. Golden, WARF's Stem Cell Patents and Tensions Between Public and Private Sector Approaches to Research, 38 J.L. Med. & Ethics 314 (2010); Rebecca Goulding et al., Alternative Intellectual Property for Genomics and the Activity of Technology Transfer Offices: Emerging Directions in Research, 16 B.U. J. Sci. & Tech. L. 194 (2010); Aaron S. Kesselheim & Jerry Avorn, University–Based Science and Biotechnology Products: Defining the Boundaries of Intellectual Property, 293 JAMA 850 (2005); Peter Landers, Method Actors: In Drug Market, Scientists Assert Power of Patents, Wall St. J., May 10, 2004, at A1. As academic researchers and their institutions receive financial stakes in their inventions, conflicts of interest may arise. See Annetine C. Gelijns & Samuel O. Thier, Medical Innovation and Institutional Interdependence: Rethinking University–Industry Connections, 287 JAMA 72 (2002); Hamilton Moses, III & Joseph P. Martin, Academic Relationships with Industry, 285 JAMA 933 (2001).

Lars Noah, *Sham Petitioning as a Threat to the Integrity of the Regulatory Process*

74 N.C. L. Rev. 1 (1995).

The Federal Trade Commission (FTC) recently announced plans to investigate the petitioning activities of companies in the pharmaceutical and medical device industries. Agency officials expressed concerns that firms were using frivolous patent litigation and petitions to the Food and Drug Administration (FDA) to limit competition and market entry. The financial stakes in these industries are often enormous, and even relatively short delays in FDA approval of competing products could prove extremely valuable to a company with an approved product already on the market. Mark Whitener, Acting Director of the FTC's Bureau of Competition, noted in 1994 that "there is a trend in this market for increasing intervention by pharmaceutical firms in judicial or regulatory proceedings," and he added that some of these efforts may violate the federal antitrust laws.

The FTC's current investigation prompts a number of important questions. Initially, one might ask whether there is any foundation to fears that firms in these or other industries are manipulating regulatory processes. In theory, at least, it seems that pharmaceutical manufacturers could make use of a variety of administrative procedures to delay or perhaps completely prevent market entry by potential competitors. * * *

[T]he next question is how best to minimize the risk of anticompetitive manipulation. By default rather than by design, application of the federal antitrust laws has become the preferred method of response by public and private litigants. Nevertheless, one might wonder whether the confidence expressed by the FTC in using the antitrust laws for these purposes is justified. Because the First Amendment protects persons' right to petition the government for redress of grievances, the Supreme Court has conferred broad immunity from antitrust scrutiny to businesses engaged in legislative lobbying, regulatory proceedings, and litigation. Although "sham petitioning" is excluded from this immunity, serious limitations exist with a remedial approach dependent on the proscriptions of the Sherman Act. * * * The antitrust laws, while perhaps a useful adjunct for combatting the most blatant abuses of regulatory procedure, can never substitute for active policing by agencies to maintain the integrity of their own processes. * * *

The FTC's investigation of petitioning activities in the pharmaceutical industry suggests that the drug approval process may be subject to manipulation by "incumbent firms," namely those companies with approved products already on the market. Although the following hypothetical is only a caricature, it represents a composite derived from a number of actual examples. For the sake of clarity, the illustration proceeds chronologically, first describing the drug approval process, and then identifying how one incumbent firm could try to repel potential competition at different time intervals after it has received all necessary approvals for its own product. * * *

Imagine that Alpha Pharmaceutical Company, the incumbent firm, requests orphan drug designation for a combination product ("Rx") for possible use in the treatment of a rare form of cancer. After evaluating the company's evidence that the expected patient population would not exceed 200,000, the FDA grants Alpha's request for orphan designation. Assume also that Rx includes two active ingredients, one of which happens to be regulated as a Schedule II controlled substance. Authority over controlled substances resides with a separate agency, the Drug Enforcement Administration (DEA) of the United States Department of Justice. Before clinical testing of Rx may proceed, Alpha must register as a manufacturer of controlled substances and receive an annual production quota from the DEA for the Schedule II component of the product. * * *

One year after Rx is approved, Alpha's competitor "Medica" seeks approval of an apparently similar orphan drug for the same intended use. Both companies had received orphan drug designations for their respective investigational products in the same year. Medica secured a limited DEA registration and procurement quota in order to conduct its own clinical trials in preparation of an NDA application, but Alpha was the first to receive final product approval from the FDA. Although Medica submits evidence that its product would be clinically superior to Rx, Alpha lodges its objection that approval of Medica's product would violate Alpha's statutory right to market exclusivity because the drugs are the same as defined under the FDA's implementing regulations. The agency thereupon rejects Medica's application.

Alpha's own orphan designation is, however, subsequently revoked because of a misrepresentation about the expected size of the patient population, a misrepresentation brought to the Agency's attention by Medica. Alpha therefore loses its seven-year period of market exclusivity for Rx because the product is no longer regarded as an orphan drug. Even so, the NDA for the product is unaffected, leaving Alpha with the more limited form of exclusivity afforded approved new drugs that do not qualify as orphan products—namely, five years of market exclusivity against makers of generic versions of the drug seeking abbreviated approval. Another company could submit a complete NDA application for the same drug during the exclusivity period if it had performed the necessary preclinical and clinical testing. Thus, Medica resubmits its application, and, after another lengthy review, the FDA approves the product. Medica is not initially able to market its product, however, because Alpha temporarily blocks Medica's full manufacturer registration and quota applications by filing objections with DEA.

Finally, when the limited exclusivity period for Rx lapses, Alpha faces the prospect of abbreviated NDA (ANDA) submissions by competitors seeking to market generic versions of this product. * * * Alpha, however, attempts to forestall agency approval of generics by filing a citizen petition asserting general bioequivalence problems that must be resolved before the FDA can evaluate any ANDA applications for this class of products. Even when the agency is prepared to approve generic versions of Rx, perhaps after a significant delay while it has grappled with these bioequivalence issues, Alpha may raise specific objections to the ANDA filings of individual companies.

If these efforts to prevent FDA approval of generic products ultimately prove unsuccessful, even though the company did manage to delay such approvals, Alpha might again attempt to use DEA processes to preserve its market position. Alpha also might file patent infringement lawsuits against the companies marketing generic versions of Rx. Finally, even after these competitors have received the necessary FDA approvals and DEA licenses, Alpha might try to convince state formulary committees not to include the generic products on the list of drugs reimbursable under Medicaid and other health insurance programs, again in hopes of retaining its existing market share.

Thus, an incumbent drug manufacturer may be able to utilize the regulatory processes of the FDA and DEA, as well as the states, in a variety of ways to delay and perhaps completely prevent market entry by competitors. It is precisely this sort of conduct in the pharmaceutical industry that the Federal Trade Commission recently identified as potentially abusive and worthy of closer investigation. This illustration prompts two important questions, namely, whether such conduct should be regarded as objectionable and, if so, whether the antitrust laws provide a meaningful response. To the extent that courts have restricted antitrust scrutiny in such cases, partly in recognition of the First Amendment right to petition, this Article suggests that greater attention should be paid to the procedural mechanisms available to administrative agencies for protecting the integrity of the regulatory process. * * *

Sham petitioning in the regulatory arena is not an unexpected phenomenon. Many commentators have recognized the strategic opportunities available to incumbent firms. As one scholar recently observed: "Entering a market nowadays can require approvals from a myriad of licensing boards, zoning commissions, and environmental regulators. A firm that is repeatedly opposed in such proceedings without regard to the legal merits can have its entry to the market delayed for a long time." In its 1988 enforcement guidelines, the Antitrust Division of the U.S. Department of Justice noted that the "use of governmental processes to disadvantage a competitor and thus to increase market power is in general a more plausible anticompetitive strategy than is pricing below cost because a firm may be able to trigger significant litigation costs and other administrative burdens at little cost to itself." Indeed, such opportunities for deterring market entry may have been part of the political bargain struck between lawmakers and regulated entities * * *

The fact that a petitioner intentionally causes delay in agency proceedings generally is not, by itself, sufficient to trigger the sham exception. Only in cases where delay appears to be the sole purpose underlying petitions that have no reasonable chance of success on the merits would *Noerr–Pennington* immunity be lost.

Objective baselessness may be difficult to prove in the administrative context, however, because agencies enjoy greater policymaking discretion than do the courts. Indeed, where the standards for approval of licenses and applications make reference to undefined considerations of public interest, it may be impossible to show that a competitor's objections were objectively baseless. Even when agencies must apply more particularized criteria in evaluating applications * * * , incumbent firms generally are free to press objections of this sort even though their only real interest in the matter is the threat of competition. For example, referring back to our drug approval hypothetical, it would be difficult to say that Alpha's objections to Medica's applications to the FDA and DEA, or its array of maneuvers to block generic competition—filing a citizen petition to raise general bioequivalence concerns, objecting to particular ANDAs and DEA registrations, and lobbying state drug formulary committees—are objectively baseless even if the company's ulterior purposes were entirely transparent.

There may be situations when an incumbent firm's claims before an agency clearly are indefensible as a matter of law, and courts have applied the sham exception in the few cases in which this was true. Similarly, a petition may be treated as a sham if its allegations lack any factual support (amounting to fraud), but simple inaccuracies or exaggerations generally would not suffice. Thus, in lobbying state formulary committees, Alpha could reiterate the bioequivalence concerns that it raised unsuccessfully with the FDA, but it could not claim that the generic approvals were procured by bribery of FDA officials if there was no basis for making such an allegation. * * *

One final set of noteworthy questions has arisen from litigation about the sham exception. From the outset, the Supreme Court suggested a sharp distinction between the political arena of the legislature and the adjudicatory setting of judicial and administrative proceedings, with the latter category benefitting from a more expansive sham exception and a correspondingly lesser degree of petitioning immunity. It is not, of course, simple to categorize agency decisionmaking as primarily legislative or adjudicatory. For instance, the various procedural devices available to Alpha Pharmaceuticals arise in settings that may be characterized as primarily legislative (e.g., the citizen petition regarding bioequivalence problems with generics, and the lobbying of state formulary committees) or adjudicative (e.g., objections raised during FDA product approval and DEA licensing proceedings). * * *

Because of the First Amendment interests at stake, courts have given the sham exception a narrow construction. Petitions to the government, therefore, are cloaked in a presumption that they have been brought in good faith. Thus, successful invocation of the sham exception is difficult because "[p]etitioners almost always genuinely desire government action, and [they] seldom have no possibility of getting it." * * *

As previously suggested, the largely unrestricted opportunity to participate brings with it the possibility for strategic manipulation of the regulatory process in pursuit of anticompetitive ends. Although openness and accessibility have long been considered hallmarks of good government, at some point rules favoring public participation may become counterproductive. The central question is whether the potential harms associated with sham petitioning will ever outweigh the values that are served by an open regulatory process. * * *

Although licenses issued by government are regarded as property under the due process clause, only the person whose license or application is at issue would have a sufficiently direct interest in the proceeding to trigger due process rights. For instance, in the hypothetical discussed above, Alpha Pharmaceuticals might have a constitutional right to raise objections if FDA approval of Medica's application would violate Alpha's statutory right to seven years of market exclusivity, but it would not have a similar right to object on some other basis once this period has expired. * * *

Courts have recognized that agencies possess considerable latitude in restricting the scope of an intervenor's participation in order to prevent dilatory tactics. As the Supreme Court once noted, "administrative proceedings should not be a game or a forum to engage in unjustified obstructionism." Moreover, in what appears to be a little-noticed provision, the APA itself directs agencies to take action on license applications with dispatch.

At present, however, many agencies halt proceedings or otherwise delay final decisionmaking when a third party raises objections. These procedures provide obvious invitations for anticompetitive abuse, especially if objections may be filed in a tardy or seriatim fashion. Indeed, intervention procedures may represent political concessions to existing members of a regulated industry as a tool for retarding market entry by potential competitors. They may also reinforce an agency's reluctance to act before all information has been considered; bureaucrats may be more concerned with unimpeachable decisionmaking than with the speedy resolution of matters.

On occasion, agencies do limit the opportunities for intervention in adjudicatory proceedings. When the FDA issued its orphan drug approval regulations, for example, it rejected suggestions that it create a preapproval challenge procedure because it feared that incumbents might try thereby "to delay the marketing of competitors' approvable" orphan drugs. Earlier this year, DEA eliminated the right of incumbents to demand a hearing on a competitor's application to manufacture controlled substances. As the agency explained when it first proposed this modification of its existing procedures:

> [C]urrently registered manufacturers use the regulatory hearing requirement to deter others from applying or to delay entry of competitors into their marketplace. As often as not, a company whose new application is opposed by a current manufacturer retaliates by opposing the annual renewal of the other's registration. This abuse of the regulatory hearing requirement adversely affects competition by delaying new registrations and results in the unnecessary expenditure of DEA resources * * * *

Although agencies permit and even encourage participation by persons with financial interests in licensing and other decisions, neither the constitutional right to petition nor guarantees of due process require that incumbent firms be given opportunities that may be used to block market entry by competitors.

MD Pharmaceutical, Inc. v. DEA

133 F.3d 8 (D.C.Cir.1998).

■ Sentelle, Circuit Judge:

This case arises out of the Drug Enforcement Administration's approval of an application submitted by Mallinckrodt Chemical, Inc. for registration as a bulk manufacturer of methylphenidate, a generic form of the drug commonly known by the brand name of Ritalin. MD Pharmaceutical, Inc., a current producer of methylphenidate, petitions for review * * * *

Methylphenidate is a Schedule II drug, which means that it has a high potential for abuse, that it has a currently accepted medical use, and that abuse of the drug may lead to severe psychological or physical dependence.

A company seeking to become a manufacturer of a Schedule II drug must apply for and obtain a certificate of registration from DEA. * * *

On June 20, 1995, DEA issued a final rule altering the certification process in two pertinent respects. Under the amended regulations, which went into effect on July 20 of that year, registered manufacturers retained the right to comment on another firm's application, but no longer had the right to a hearing on an application other than their own. 60 Fed. Reg. 32,099 (1995) (codified at 21 C.F.R. § 1301.43(a) (1996)). The second alteration concerned an applicant's ability to withdraw a pending application. * * *

On July 20, 1995, the date that the new regulations went into effect, Mallinckrodt submitted a letter to DEA requesting withdrawal of its 1994 and 1995 applications. On the same day, Mallinckrodt submitted a new application for registration as a bulk manufacturer of methylphenidate under the newly amended regulations. MD strenuously opposed the withdrawal of the applications, arguing that Mallinckrodt was simply trying to circumvent the hearing requirement under the old rules. * * *

Before reaching the merits, we must address the issue of whether MD has standing to challenge the actions taken by DEA. * * * DEA does not allege that MD has not suffered an injury in fact, nor that the action taken by the government has not caused the alleged injury. * * * MD's competitive injury is fairly traceable to DEA's decision to issue a certificate of registration to Mallinckrodt. * * *

[A] competitor need not be an intended beneficiary to fall within the zone of interests of an entry-restricting statute. * * * MD, as a manufacturer facing potential competition from Mallinckrodt, is a suitable challenger and thus falls within the zone of interests of the statute. When a regulatory system "by its very nature restricts entry into a particular field or transaction," firms that are already operating in the regulated industry have an interest in enforcing the restrictions on potential market entrants. Even though competitors may be motivated by something other than a desire to advance the public interest, they nonetheless fall within the zone of interests of an entry-restricting statute because their interests "are generally congruent with a statutory purpose to restrict entry." The Controlled Substance Act is a quintessential entry-restricting statute. * * * Even more so than traditional licensees, registered manufacturers of controlled substances have an interest in limiting the number of producing firms, because each new market entrant will produce a percentage of the aggregate production quota that would otherwise be produced by existing firms. * * *

MD emphasizes that it submitted detailed comments to DEA regarding Mallinckrodt's proposed registration, which received, in MD's estimation, only short-shrift attention from the agency. 61 Fed. Reg. 37,079 (1996). Petitioner reiterates several of the objections that it unsuccessfully raised before DEA, including Mallinckrodt's alleged history of noncompliance with DEA and FDA regulations, and evidence suggesting that there is adequate competition in the methylphenidate market. MD faults DEA for not dealing with these and other objections in greater detail and with greater specificity. Petitioner also criticizes the agency for failing to identify specific facts to support its conclusion that registration of Mallinckrodt would be consistent with the public interest. * * *

We hold that DEA gave an adequate explanation for its decision to register Mallinckrodt. DEA published an explanation that spans almost eight columns in the *Federal Register* and is largely devoted to answering the many objections raised by MD during the application process. * * * Taken as a whole, DEA's explanation demonstrates that it examined the data, considered the relevant factors, and made a reasonable judgment based on the record. We conclude that the explanation offered by DEA passes muster under the APA. * * *

We decline to reach the merits of MD's objections, however, because there is no longer any live issue with respect to Mallinckrodt's first two applications. * * * Insofar as MD claims that DEA's disposition of the first and second applications somehow tainted the grant of the third, such a claim must rest on the theory that third parties acquire, at the time an application is filed, a vested right in the procedural rules then applicable, which somehow is forever attached to later applications on the same subject. This is altogether untenable. * * *

NOTES AND QUESTIONS

1. *Waging "competition" on multiple fronts.* Innovator companies have continued to use various strategies in an effort to stave off generic competition. See Thomas M. Burton, Bested Interests: Why Generic Drugs Often Can't Compete Against Brand Names, Wall St. J., Nov. 18, 1998, at A1 ("Even when [citizen] petitions fail, they can keep generic drugs off the market for months or years."); Gardiner Harris, OxyContin Manufacturer Seeks Delay of Rivals, N.Y. Times, Jan. 13, 2004, at C4; Diedtra Henderson, Dose of Relief: Are Generic Drugs Just What the Cost–Cutters Ordered?, Boston Globe, Apr. 30, 2006, at D1 (noting an "increase in petitions innovator drug companies filed with the FDA, posing complex questions that slow FDA approvals" of generics); Marc Kaufman, Petitions to FDA Sometimes Delay Generic Drugs: Critics Say Companies Misusing Process, Wash. Post, July 3, 2006, at A1 (reporting an official estimate that, of the 170 citizen petitions pending before the agency, approximately 30% are "blocking petitions"); see also Stacey B. Lee, Is a Cure on the Way?—The Bad Medicine of Generics, Citizen Petitions, and Noerr–Pennington Immunity, 20 Kan. J.L. & Pub. Pol'y 98 (2010); Alicia Mundy, Senate Panel Hits Sanofi Payments, Wall St. J., May 25, 2011, at B3 (reporting that the manufacturer of Lovenox® contributed more than $5 million to medical groups who then agreed to file a purportedly independent citizen petition with the FDA questioning the bioequivalence of a proposed generic version of this blockbuster anticoagulant). Congress recently tried to address such blocking petitions. See FDAAA, Pub. L. No. 110–85, § 914, 121 Stat. 823, 953 (2007) (codified at 21 U.S.C. § 355(q)).

2. *Gaming "Orange Book" listings.* Some pioneer companies listed marginally-related patents in the FDA's *Orange Book*, which then requires a paragraph IV certification and obligates the agency to delay ANDA approval for 30 months if the patent holder initiates patent infringement litigation. See Apotex, Inc. v. Thompson, 347 F.3d 1335, 1340–41, 1346–47 (Fed.Cir.2003) (explaining that the manufacturer of Paxil® had secured five overlapping 30–month stays); American Bioscience, Inc. v. Thompson, 269 F.3d 1077 (D.C.Cir.2001); Jayne O'Donnell & Julie Appleby, FTC Scrutinizes Validity of Drugmakers' Patent Listings, USA Today, Jan. 8, 2002, at 1A. Courts have concluded that the FDA has no obligation to screen *Orange Book* listings for accuracy. See aaiPharma Inc. v. Thompson, 296 F.3d 227, 235–43 (4th Cir.2002) (where the holder of a patent on a polymorphic variant of the active ingredient in Prozac had failed to persuade the NDA holder to request listing, it could not demand that the FDA do so); id. at 237 ("The FDA defends this purely ministerial conception of its role in the Orange Book listing process by explaining that it lacks both the resources and the expertise to police the correctness of Orange Book listings."); see also Andrx Pharm., Inc. v. Biovail Corp., 276 F.3d 1368, 1376 (Fed.Cir.2002) (reversing a district court's order to shorten a second 30–month stay); In re Buspirone Patent Litig., 185 F.Supp.2d 363, 369–76 (S.D.N.Y.2002) (filing new patent information with the FDA for listing in the *Orange Book* does not qualify as petitioning entitled to *Noerr–Pennington* antitrust immunity or else falls within the sham exception). See generally Jacob S. Wharton, "Orange Book" Listing of Patents Under the Hatch–Waxman Act, 47 St. Louis U. L.J. 1027 (2003); Christine S. Paine, Comment, Brand–Name Drug Manufacturers Risk Antitrust Violations by Slowing Generic Production Through Patent Layering, 33 Seton Hall L. Rev. 479 (2003). The FDA revised its rules in the hopes of preventing this behavior. See 68 Fed. Reg. 36,676 (2003) (codified at 21 C.F.R. § 314.53); Leila Abboud, Bush Announces Plan to Hasten Generic Drugs, Wall St. J., June 13, 2003, at B8 (explaining that the rule sought to prevent the practice of "stacking" 30–month stays); see also Stephanie E. Piatt, Note, Regaining the Balance of Hatch–Waxman in the FDA Generic Approval Process: An Equitable Remedy to the Thirty–Month Stay, 59 N.Y.U. Ann. Surv. Am. L. 163 (2003).

3. *Legislative reforms.* In 2003, Congress amended the Hatch–Waxman Act. In addition to codifying some of the regulatory reforms announced earlier that same year by the FDA (especially in providing for only a single 30–month stay), the statute now requires antitrust review of settlement agreements by the FTC and DOJ, creates a 75–day window in which a first-filer must begin selling (or else lose the 180–day generic exclusivity period), and allows the filing of a declaratory judgment action under certain circumstances. See Medicare Prescription Drug, Improvement, and Modernization Act of 2003, Pub. L. No. 108–173, tit. XI(A), 117 Stat. 2448; cf. Novo Nordisk A/S v. Caraco Pharm. Labs., Ltd., 601 F.3d 1359, 1364–67 (Fed.Cir.2010) (holding that a generic competitor had no right to seek an injunction ordering the patent holder to ask the FDA to remove its allegedly overbroad "use code" form the *Orange Book*), cert. granted, 131

S.Ct. 3057 (2011). See generally Stephanie Greene, A Prescription for Change: How the Medicare Act Revises Hatch–Waxman to Speed Market Entry of Generic Drugs, 30 J. Corp. L. 309 (2005); Matthew Avery, Note, Continuing Abuse of the Hatch–Waxman Act by Pharmaceutical Patent Holders and the Failure of the 2003 Amendments, 60 Hastings L.J. 171 (2008); Natalie M. Derzko, Comment, The Impact of Recent Reforms of the Hatch–Waxman Scheme on Orange Book Strategic Behavior and Pharmaceutical Innovation, 45 IDEA 165 (2005); Henry H. Gu, Note, The Hatch–Waxman Act and the Declaratory Judgment Action: Constitutional and Practical Implications, 57 Rutgers L. Rev. 771 (2005); Ankur N. Patel, Comment, Delayed Access to Generic Medicine: A Comment on the Hatch–Waxman Act and the "Approval Bottleneck," 78 Fordham L. Rev. 1075 (2009).

4. *Industry consolidation*. Mergers continue in the pharmaceutical industry. See, e.g., Scott Hensley, Biggest Drug Firm Faces Generics but Has an Edge: Its Very Bigness, Wall St. J., Apr. 23, 2004, at A1; Gautam Naik & Jeanne Whalen, Sanofi–Aventis Deal Could Spur Other Mergers, Wall St. J., Apr. 27, 2004, at A6. For instance, the world's largest drug company at the moment, Pfizer (U.S.), grew through acquisitions of manufacturers such as Warner–Lambert, Pharmacia–Upjohn, and Wyeth. The top ten also includes companies such as GlaxoSmithKline (U.K.), which combined Glaxo, Burroughs–Wellcome, and SmithKline Beecham; Roche (Switzerland), which recently bought Genentech; Merck (U.S.), which recently merged with Schering–Plough; and Sanofi–Aventis (France), which combined a pair of companies that themselves had combined a number of other drug manufacturers. In addition, established companies often look to successful biotechnology start ups as attractive targets for acquisition. See Jonathan D. Rockoff & Ron Winslow, Drug Makers Refill Parched Pipelines, Wall St. J., July 11, 2011, at A1 ("The pharmaceutical industry as a whole has spent more than $130 billion acquiring small biotechs since 2006."); see also David T. Robinson & Toby E. Stuart, Financial Contracting in Biotech Strategic Alliances, 50 J.L. & Econ. 559 (2007); Andrew Sorkin, Bristol Buying Drug Unit of DuPont for $7.8 Billion, N.Y. Times, June 8, 2001, at C5 (describing a major acquisition made by Bristol–Myers Squibb). The medical device industry has remained more decentralized but is not immune to the pressure for mergers. See William M. Brown, Grandfathering Can Seriously Damage Your Wealth: Due Diligence in Mergers and Acquisitions of Medical Device Companies, 36 Gonz. L. Rev. 315 (2000).

5. *Antitrust issues*. This pattern of consolidation has raised a host of antitrust concerns. See Steven K. Bernstein & Jeff L. White, Federal Antitrust Review of Generic Drug Mergers: A Proposal for a More Flexible Approach, 4 N.Y.U. J.L. & Bus. 465 (2008); Thomas B. Marcotullio, Note, The Battle Against Drugmakers: An Analysis of European Union and United States Merger Enforcement in the Pharmaceutical Industry, 32 Law & Pol'y Int'l Bus. 449 (2001); see also Paul Feldstein, Health Care Economics 442 (3d ed. 1988) (explaining that the four-firm concentration ratio has been relatively low in the pharmaceutical industry, but adding that concentration may be high in sub-markets defined by therapeutic categories); Michael A. Carrier, Two Puzzles Resolved: Of the Schumpeter–Arrow Stalemate and Pharmaceutical Innovation Markets, 93 Iowa L. Rev. 393 (2008); Frank R. Lichtenberg & Tomas J. Philipson, The Dual Effects of Intellectual Property Regulations: Within– and Between–Patent Competition in the U.S. Pharmaceuticals Industry, 45 J.L. & Econ. 643 (2002); Symposium, Antitrust Enforcement in the Pharmaceutical Industry, 41 Rutgers L.J. 1 (2009). For instance, joint marketing agreements may pose antitrust questions. Cf. McDonald v. Johnson & Johnson, 722 F.2d 1370, 1376–79 (8th Cir.1983) (discussing antitrust claim brought against analgesic drug manufacturer that had acquired and then restricted the sales of a competitor's medical device used for pain relief, but rejecting the claim for lack of standing); Kurt Saunders, Patent Nonuse and the Role of Public Interest as a Deterrent to Technology Suppression, 15 Harv. J.L. & Tech. 389, 411–12 (2002) (discussing this litigation). Separately, some product approvals have required adjuvant therapies in a way that raised concerns about unlawful tying arrangements. See Mark A. Hurwitz, Note, Bundling Patented Drugs and Medical Services: An Antitrust Analysis, 91 Colum. L. Rev. 1188 (1991); see also Ortho Diagnostic Sys., Inc. v. Abbott Lab., Inc., 920 F.Supp. 455, 463–74 (S.D.N.Y.1996) (rejecting various antitrust claims brought by a competitor against the seller of five blood testing products sold at a discount to blood banks when purchased together). Would bundling two active ingredients into a single drug product (and securing FDA approval) dodge questions about tying?

6. *Medical specialty associations*. In some instances, competitors have complained that suppliers of medical technologies have conspired with professional organizations to recommend use of certain therapies. See Scott Hensley, Johnson & Johnson Settles Antitrust Suit over Contact Lenses, Wall St. J., May 23, 2001, at B2; see also Schachar v. American Acad. Ophthalmology, 870 F.2d 397 (7th Cir.1989) (rejecting antitrust claim against medical society for characterizing radial keratotomy as an experimental treatment); Tammy Asher, Unprecedented Antitrust Investigation into the Lyme Disease Treatment Guidelines Development Process, 46 Gonz. L. Rev. 117 (2011); Clark C. Havighurst, Applying Antitrust Law to Collaboration in the Production of Information: The Case of Medical Technology Assessment, Law & Contemp. Probs., Spring 1988, at 341, 357–60.

FTC v. Mylan Laboratories, Inc.

62 F.Supp.2d 25 (D.D.C.1999).

■ HOGAN, DISTRICT JUDGE:

* * * The first action is brought by the Federal Trade Commission (FTC) under § 13(a) of the Federal Trade Commission Act, 15 U.S.C. § 53(a), to secure a permanent injunction and other relief against the defendants. Defendants are Mylan Laboratories, Inc., Cambrex Corporation, Profarmaco S.R.L. and Gyma Laboratories of America, Inc. The FTC

alleges that the defendants engaged and are engaging in unfair methods of competition in or affecting commerce in violation of § 5(a) of the FTC Act, 15 U.S.C. § 45(a). * * * The second case is an action brought by thirty-two states against defendants for violations of §§ 1 and 2 of the Sherman Act as well as various state antitrust laws. * * *

For purposes of the instant motions to dismiss, the allegations of the complaints are taken as true. The facts below are presented accordingly, and do not constitute factual findings. * * * Typically, the generic manufacturer purchases the active pharmaceutical ingredient (API) from a specialty chemical manufacturer. The generic manufacturer combines the API with inactive fillers, binders, colorings and other chemicals to produce a finished product. To sell an API in the United States, the API supplier must file a drug master file (DMF) with the FDA. The DMF explains the processes that the API supplier uses to make the API and to test chemical equivalence and bioequivalence to the brand product. To use an API, the generic manufacturer's ANDA must refer to the API supplier's DMF filed with the FDA. More than one drug manufacturer can reference the DMF of the same API supplier. A generic manufacturer that wants or needs to change its API supplier must obtain FDA approval of an ANDA supplement which includes a reference to the new supplier's DMF and test results regarding the generic manufacturer's product using the new API. This process averages about 18 months, though it can take as long as three years.

Lorazepam and clorazepate are two of the approximately 91 generic drugs that Mylan currently manufactures and sells in tablet form. Lorazepam is used to treat anxiety, tension, agitation, insomnia, and as a preoperative sedative. Doctors issue over 18 million prescriptions a year for lorazepam tablets. Because lorazepam is used to treat chronic conditions and is heavily prescribed for nursing home and hospice patients, lorazepam users tend to stay on the drug for long periods of time. Clorazepate is used to treat anxiety and in adjunct therapy for nicotine and opiate withdrawal. Doctors issue over three million prescriptions a year for clorazepate tablets.

Profarmaco (which is a wholly owned subsidiary of Cambrex) manufactures APIs in Italy. Profarmaco holds DMFs for lorazepam API and clorazepate API, and has supplied such APIs to drug manufacturers in the United States. Foreign firms, like Profarmaco, that supply APIs to the United States typically have distributors in the United States who purchase APIs and resell them to generic drug manufacturers in the United States. Mylan purchases its lorazepam and clorazepate API from Gyma, Profarmaco's U.S. distributor of these products. Several other drug manufacturers have purchased API from SST Corporation, another U.S. distributor of this product.

The plaintiffs in these two cases allege the following anti-competitive conduct on the part of the defendants. Mylan sought from its API suppliers long-term exclusive licenses for the DMFs of certain APIs selected because of limited competition. If Mylan obtained such an exclusive license, no other generic drug manufacturer could use that supplier's API to make the drug in the U.S. Mylan sought exclusive licenses for the DMFs for lorazepam API and clorazepate API as well as one other drug not the subject of these lawsuits.

Mylan entered into contracts with Profarmaco and Gyma such that these companies would license exclusively to Mylan for 10 years. The exclusive licenses would provide Mylan with complete control over Profarmaco's entire supply of lorazepam API and clorazepate API entering the U.S. With complete control of Profarmaco's supply of these products and by refusing to sell to any of its competitors, Mylan would deny its competition access to the most important ingredient for producing lorazepam and clorazepate tablets.

In return for the 10–year exclusive licenses, Mylan offered to pay Cambrex, Profarmaco and Gyma a percentage of gross profits on sales of lorazepam and clorazepate tablets, regardless of who Mylan purchased the API from. Mylan also tried to execute an exclusive licensing arrangement with SST for control of its lorazepam supply. This is significant because Mylan was not authorized by the FDA to sell lorazepam manufactured with SST API (i.e., Mylan's ANDA did not reference SST's DMF). Thus, the States allege that Mylan was entering into a deal for exclusive rights even though it would not have been able to use SST API until after an ANDA supplement had been completed, which usually takes around 18 months. The plaintiffs' argue that Mylan's attempt to obtain control over SST's supply, when Mylan could not even use SST API, demonstrates the anticompetitive nature of Mylan's actions.

On or around January 12, 1998, Mylan raised its price of clorazepate tablets to State Medicaid programs, wholesalers, retail pharmacy chains and other customers by amounts ranging approximately from 1,900 percent to over 3,200 percent, depending on the size of the bottle and the strength. On March 3, 1998, Mylan raised its price of lorazepam tablets by amounts ranging from approximately 1,900 to 2,600 percent. Shortly thereafter, SST raised the price of lorazepam API by approximately 19,000 percent. SST sold the lorazepam API to Geneva, one of Mylan's competitors, which raised its prices to approximately the price of Mylan's tablets. * * *

In addition to an injunction prohibiting defendants' conduct and rescission of defendants' unlawful licensing arrangements, the FTC asks this court to "order other equitable relief, including the disgorgement of $120 million plus interest." Defendants object to the FTC's request on the ground that § 13(b) does not authorize disgorgement or any other form of monetary relief. It is true that the plain language of § 13(b) does not authorize the FTC to seek monetary remedies. The FTC argues, however, that monetary relief is a natural extension of the remedial powers authorized under § 13(b). * * * As defendant cites no relevant case law that prohibits the FTC from seeking disgorgement or any other form of equitable ancillary relief, the court denies defendants' motion on this issue. * * *

The State complaint seeks to recover damages not only for direct purchases from Mylan, but also for purchases from Mylan's competitors. The premise of the States' request is that Mylan's competitors in the generic drug industry, though not parties to the exclusive licenses nor members of the alleged conspiracy, raised their prices as a consequence of Mylan's actions. The States argue that defendants should be liable for the difference between the prices charged by Mylan's competitors and what those prices would have been had Mylan not raised its prices pursuant to an illegal agreement. * * *

The main difficulty with the umbrella theory is that, even in the context of a single level of distribution, ascertaining the appropriate measure of damages is a highly speculative endeavor. There are numerous pricing variables which this court would be bound to consider to approximate the correct measure of damages, including the cost of production, marketing strategy, elasticity of demand, and the price of comparable items (i.e., the brand versions of lorazepam and clorazepate). The interaction of these variables is uncertain. * * * Accordingly, this court will decline the States' invitation to consider umbrella damages and dismiss the States' complaint insofar as it requests such relief. * * *

In light of the court's ruling on the above issues, the States' federal claims against defendant are narrowed to the following cause of action: the States may sue the defendants under § 4 of the Clayton Act for any direct purchases that state entities or state citizens may have made of generic clorazepate and lorazepam from the defendants. Defendants contend that the States' amended complaint fails to allege direct purchases of generic lorazepam or clorazepate tablets from Mylan, and that none of the persons on whose behalf the States purport to sue made such direct purchases from Mylan. Defendants therefore seek dismissal of the States' complaint under Rule 12(b)(6). Although defendants are correct that the States' case is dependent on facts supporting direct purchases by the States, the States have sufficiently alleged direct purchases for the purposes of a motion to dismiss. * * *

To state a Section 2 monopolization claim, a plaintiff must allege facts sufficient to establish both "(1) the possession of monopoly power in the relevant market and (2) the willful acquisition or maintenance of that power as distinguished from growth or development as a consequence of a superior product, business acumen, or historic accident." Mylan alleges that the complaints fail this legal standard in two ways: (1) they fail to sufficiently identify a relevant market; and (2) the complaints fail to allege facts sufficient to show monopoly power.

On the first issue, the complaints specifically identify four relevant markets: (1) generic lorazepam tablets; (2) generic clorazepate tablets; (3) lorazepam API; and (4) clorazepate API. Each of the relevant markets includes only those products approved for sale in the United States. This level of definition is sufficient to survive a motion to dismiss, as it is entirely plausible that plaintiffs will prove a set of facts that supports those market definitions.

Mylan's second claim is that the amended complaint fails to establish the monopoly power element of the monopolization claim. In economic terms, "[m]onopoly power is the power to raise prices well above competitive levels before customers will turn elsewhere." The complaints meet this standard by alleging that Mylan instituted massive and successful price increases for lorazepam and clorazepate. Furthermore, the complaints allege that Mylan constricted the supply of generic lorazepam and clorazepate tablets by denying its competitors the APIs to manufacture these products. Like the ability to control prices, this is evidence of monopoly power. * * *

CHAPTER 11

EVOLVING MEDICAL TECHNOLOGIES

This chapter reprises many of the concepts and problems encountered in earlier chapters. How well do new medical technologies fit the molds for drugs, devices, or biologics? Will traditional mechanisms of control, such as FDA regulation, tort liability, and insurance coverage, work effectively to manage these new technologies, or is a different approach needed? Finally, this chapter considers how medical technologies influence the bioethics discourse.

A. OVERVIEW: DEFINING NOVEL TECHNOLOGIES AND COPING WITH CHANGE

Lars Noah, *Managing Biotechnology's [R]evolution: Has Guarded Enthusiasm Become Benign Neglect?*

11 VA. J.L. & TECH. 4 (2006).

The term "biotechnology" gets bandied about a good deal, but its precise meaning remains somewhat elusive. Dictionaries provide a sense for this ambiguity. For instance, the *Oxford English Dictionary* offers both a broad definition of older vintage ("The branch of technology concerned with the development and exploitation of machines in relation to the various needs of human beings.") as well as a narrower and newer definition ("The branch of technology concerned with modern forms of industrial production utilizing living organisms, esp. micro-organisms, and their biological processes."), which the *American Heritage Dictionary* provides as the sole definition. *Webster's* provides a still narrower meaning of the term: "biological science when applied especially in genetic engineering and recombinant DNA technology."

Common usages of the term "biotechnology" also reflect this range of possible meanings. For instance, the President's Council on Bioethics (PCB) recently issued a report expressing concerns about potential adverse consequences of biotechnological interventions that lack a therapeutic purpose, which it took to include such disparate things as sex selection, lifespan extension, and conventionally produced drugs intended to enhance the body or mind, but this usage conflates biotechnology and biomedical technology. Conversely, other technophobes may focus on its more controversial core, treating biotechnology as synonymous with the use of genetically modified (GM) organisms (GMOs or "transgenics") * * * *

Entrepreneurs (technophiles) looking for venture capital or deals with potential investors—or to secure patent protection, which requires a showing of novelty—may seek to appropriate the once and still fashionable "biotechnology" moniker to characterize their plans. In 2004, the shortage of flu vaccine drew public attention to the antiquated method of producing this product (namely, incubating strains of the influenza virus in specially purified, fertilized chicken eggs as the first step in deriving the vaccine) coupled with calls for more efficient "biotechnology" approaches (namely, infecting cell cultures with the virus and then multiplying these cells in fermentation tanks). Absent a genetic modification, however, the biotechnology label appears to rest on the use of living organisms in the production process, but then it seems that the label would apply with equal justification to the much older chicken egg method or, indeed, all types of vaccines.

Scientists also may have ulterior motives for embracing the term "biotechnology," hoping to attract grants to support their work. More recently, and in a similar vein, "researchers in search of funding have tended to define 'nanotechnology' rather broadly, including such things as molecular electronics and even high-resolution photolithography."

> [A]s with any new technology, nanotechnologies are defined officially by the community of people who would like to be funded and by the people who are funding them. The broader definition now in use has nothing to do with atomic precision or molecular machinery .... It merely requires that some part of the thing in question be small, less than 100 nanometers in some significant dimension. Molecules have always been small, so chemistry is now called nanotechnology. Biomolecules are small, so biotechnology is being relabeled as nanotechnology.

Indeed, the broader usages of the term biotechnology would encompass many genuinely innovative advances in the emerging field of nanomedicine, but this Article treats recombinant DNA (a.k.a. "gene splicing") and similar genetic engineering techniques as representing the core of modern biotechnology * * * *

Conversely, regulatory officials anxious to deploy their existing delegations of authority may contend that the fruits of biotechnology fit within statutory definitions enacted in an earlier era. Then, when agencies purport to act within their jurisdiction and announce the types of activities that they intend to subject to closer scrutiny, regulated entities may seek to narrow the definition or downplay the distinctiveness of their products. For instance, the Food and Drug Administration (FDA) has formulated rules that would subject "more than minimally manipulated" human tissue and cellular products to the full panoply of rules governing drugs, devices, or biologics, which would encourage regulated entities to argue that their manipulations did not exceed this ill-defined *de minimis* threshold. Again, a similar tendency already has appeared in the context of nanotechnology. * * *

[One commentator] identified five federal agencies exercising regulatory jurisdiction under at least a dozen different statutes, most of which predated the advent of genetic engineering. This frequent observation [of a patchwork regulatory system] does not, however, distinguish biotechnology from other fields; rather, it mistakenly treats biotechnology as a monolithic enterprise when it makes more sense to appreciate its multiplicity. In short, the multifaceted regulatory response to biotechnology reflects the potentially vast and varied reach of these innovative techniques. No doubt the products and processes of the petrochemical revolution (from plastics to pesticides) witnessed an equally fragmented exercise of regulatory authority. * * *

Disagreements persist about the wisdom and success of this incremental regulatory approach. The European Union (EU) has taken a decidedly different tack from the United States, focusing on the process rather than the end products and adopting restrictions specifically geared toward biotechnology. As one commentator explained:

> In its cruder forms, biotechnology has been used to produce beer, wine, and cheeses, as well as to selectively breed plants and livestock. Genetic engineering can thus be viewed either as a step in the long evolution of biotechnology or a radical break, or revolution, in that process. The tension between these two perspectives accounts for much of the controversy surrounding the regulation of biotechnology.

This Article will review some of the recent technological challenges and regulatory responses in an effort to gauge such assessments. At a more fundamental level, a number of commentators have emphasized the distinctiveness of biotechnology and the consequent need for appropriately tailored responses by legal institutions. This Article seeks to test that broad proposition, offering a decidedly contrarian take on the subject. * * *

Traditionally, the pharmaceutical industry focused on small molecule drugs. Biotechnology offered a pair of advances: a new method for synthesizing such drugs and techniques for producing protein-based and other large molecule drugs. A third application, which deviates even more profoundly from the conventional drug model, would correct certain diseases at their source by introducing bioengineered viruses into a patient's cells as a way of overwriting some genetic defect, but, after fifteen years of clinical trials, "gene therapy" has not yet lived up to expectations—it has not worked for most genetic diseases (e.g., cystic fibrosis), and, in the one rare condition that it apparently has succeeded in curing (i.e., X-linked severe combined immunodeficiency), the technique triggered leukemia. Although scientists remain hopeful that switching to different viruses to use as vectors will avoid such side effects in the future, the FDA has once again put an indefinite hold on this research.

Taking gene therapy one speculative step further, some commentators fear that the final frontier of biotechnology will usher in genetically modified human beings. Stem cell research, which simply creates cell lines from blastocysts, represents the latest craze in biomedicine, but it does not seem to fit within the narrow definition of biotechnology, and even eventual therapeutic applications would seem little different from organ transplants between different people. Preimplantation genetic diagnosis, which uses amplification techniques to read the genome of an in vitro fertilized embryo before transfer into the uterus, arguably facilitates a form of population-wide engineering even if it does not alter the genetic characteristics of the particular embryo. Germ-line therapies would, however, involve fundamental alterations in a human being and his or her progeny. Once they become feasible, these techniques will raise a host of serious legal and ethical questions.

In the meantime, after something of a slow start, biotechnology has begun to deliver the goods in the pharmaceutical field. The ever growing list of FDA-approved biotech drugs (now numbering more than 150) includes the following products: insulin (Eli Lilly's Humulin®) for diabetes, human growth hormone (hGH) (Eli Lilly's Humatrope® and Genentech's Nutropin®) for short stature, erythropoietin (EPO) (Johnson & Johnson's Procrit® and Amgen's Epogen®) for anemia (particularly in patients receiving kidney dialysis), tissue plasminogen activator (tPA) (Genentech's Activase® (alteplase)) for heart attack and stroke, granulocyte-colony stimulating factor (G–CSF) (Amgen's Neupogen® (filgrastim)) for infections after chemotherapy, interferon beta (Biogen's Avonex®) for multiple sclerosis (MS), imiglucerase (Genzyme's Cerezyme®) for Gaucher's disease, tumor-necrosis factor (TNF) inhibitors (Amgen's Enbrel®, Johnson & Johnson's Remicade®, Abbott Laboratories' Humira®, Biogen's Amevive®, and Genentech's Raptiva®) for autoimmune diseases such as rheumatoid arthritis and psoriasis, and various novel treatments for cancer (including Genentech's Avastin®, Herceptin®, and Rituxan®). Several of these products have become blockbusters and the focus of mass marketing campaigns. Like manufacturers of conventional pharmaceuticals, however, some biotech drug companies have discovered serious adverse events after receiving FDA approval, which may necessitate revised risk labeling or market withdrawal.

In most cases, the FDA classifies a biotech drug as a "biological product," which the statute defines as "a virus, therapeutic serum, toxin, antitoxin, vaccine, blood, blood component or derivative, allergenic product, or analogous product . . . applicable to the prevention, treatment, or cure of a disease or condition of human beings." Although this differentiates biotech drugs from most other "drugs" under the agency's jurisdiction, the FDA subjects them to a nearly identical review process, and a few years ago it shifted those responsibilities from its smaller Center for Biologics Evaluation & Research (CBER) to its Center for Drug Evaluation & Research (CDER). * * *

During the first decade of widespread biotech commercialization, therapeutic products made the greatest impact while agricultural applications may have drawn the most public attention. In some respects, the biopharmaceutical industry now shows signs of retrenchment as it has matured, while agricultural biotech companies finally may see the unfulfilled possibilities of their work reach fruition. Indeed, with the growing prospect of molecular farming, the two sectors have begun to coalesce, and, as a consequence, the FDA continues to encounter new regulatory challenges. * * *

[B]iotechnology has generated some genuine therapeutic breakthroughs. These pharmaceutical advances have, however, not come cheaply. Whether because of the special difficulties in manufacturing these products or because of the narrow markets offered by orphan diseases (or some combination of these and perhaps other reasons), biotech drugs have triggered sticker shock for carrying annual price tags in the tens of thousands of dollars. Medicare's tab just for EPO exceeds $1 billion annually. At the same time, several of the successful first generation biotech drugs have lost or will soon lose their patent protection and market exclusivity periods.

In the case of conventional pharmaceuticals, makers of generic copies would have already positioned themselves to enter the market * * * * In the case of biotech drugs, however, the ANDA mechanism does not offer generic sellers the same ease of market entry. First, apart from those few products (i.e., insulin and growth hormone) approved as new drugs, the FDA has used its biologics premarket review process for most biotech pharmaceutical products, which does not at present include the same statutory provisions governing approval of generic copies. Second, sponsors of "biogenerics" may find it impossible to satisfy the standard of proof normally required for ANDAs because large molecule drugs are derived through a complex and somewhat mysterious production process. For this reason, innovator biotech firms have argued strenuously that generic competitors cannot establish bioequivalence.

Again, one might note some amount of hypocrisy insofar as these same companies have criticized the FDA's excessive preoccupation with licensing biologics manufacturing facilities, arguing that they now have enough precision in characterizing their end-products to ensure that production processes at different facilities will generate essentially identical agents. These companies also embraced a more capacious notion of similarity, at least when hoping to block approvals of competing orphan drug products, than they do after their period of market exclusivity expires and generics become a threat.

In fact, after recently finding no deficiencies in an ANDA submission for a generic version of r-hGH, the FDA announced that it would have to delay further action on the application until it had an opportunity to resolve these sorts of fundamental regulatory and policy issues. The technical question about bioequivalence may not pose an insurmountable obstacle for products that replace natural proteins in the body (e.g., EPO for treating anemia), though it may present an insuperable barrier for more complex products used to treat autoimmune diseases and cancer.

The FDA recently suggested use of an alternative mechanism for approving generic versions of early biotech drugs. Sometimes referred to as a "paper NDA," this route allows a company to bring a slightly modified version of a pioneer drug to market by cross-referencing the contents of the original NDA and filing supplemental research as deemed necessary. This approach has triggered controversy because it essentially appropriates confidential safety and effectiveness data submitted by the sponsor of the innovator drug and may lead to FDA marketing approval even before the expiration of the patent term and exclusivity periods. Congress ultimately may have to resolve the issue. Although biotech generics probably would not offer the same dramatic reductions in price seen with conventional drugs because of the need to invest in complex manufacturing facilities, they still promise substantial cost savings to patients and providers. * * *

After successfully bioengineering plants to serve agronomic purposes or to produce new and improved versions of raw agricultural commodities, scientists have begun pursuing the possibility of manufacturing entirely novel compounds by genetically engineering food crops. Instead of using bioreactors (fermentation tanks) filled with engineered microorganisms to manufacture proteins and other drug substances, pharmaceutical companies could move some of their production process into the field—hence, the use of terms such as "pharming," "biopharming," or "molecular farming." For instance, scientists have engineered corn plants to produce substances with therapeutic uses—in one case, gastric lipase, an enzyme used to treat digestive problems in patients with cystic fibrosis, and, in another case, trypsin, a protein used to make insulin. * * * [G]iven the importance of precision in the production of large molecule drugs and the seemingly inevitable variability seen in agricultural commodities caused by sometimes minor differences in growing conditions (e.g., soil, moisture, temperature, and light), non-pharmaceutical applications may have greater commercial plausibility in the short-term.

The biggest objections to pharming focus, however, on the possible environmental impacts of "genetic pollution." In contrast to the containment achieved with fermentation tanks and other industrial production processes, cultivation in the field would amount to a deliberate release. As with GM foods, opponents fear cross-pollination with native plants and food crops, which could imperil both people and wildlife, or contamination of human food stuffs during distribution. More vigorous GMOs could crowd out other species, or cross-pollination could make those species more susceptible to damage from pests and disease. In the event of contamination with plants engineered to produce human proteins, allergic reactions would represent the primary adverse effect, not any pharmacological activity (after all, large molecule drugs generally require injection because digestion breaks down the proteins). Nonetheless, fearing adverse public reaction to contamination cases, major food processors that had embraced biotechnology when it served agronomic purposes now have allied themselves with environmentalists and consumer activists in expressing opposition to pharming. * * *

In an effort to curb public fears and head off a regulatory response, the biotechnology industry recently adopted a voluntary moratorium on pharming anywhere near food crops. Members of Congress have introduced bills to address the problem, and federal agencies have taken a more serious look at the issue. For instance, the FDA issued a draft guidance that asserted, among other things, that it would apply GMP requirements to pharming operations, and USDA has formulated amendments to its rules governing field testing.

Pharming represents the confluence of a pair of biotechnological advances—namely, the development of large molecule drugs and the capacity for modifying food crops—and no doubt magnifies the regulatory concerns that accompanied each of those earlier breakthroughs. Although the FDA has dealt with combination products in the past, harvesting therapeutic raw materials from a field introduces a whole new complexity. In effect, are the regulatory approaches to first-generation biotech products able to accommodate these latest innovations? Again, however, one needs to ask whether such concerns arise exclusively with pharming, or whether they represent just the latest facet of broader concerns about the environmental impacts of intensive agricultural practices or, for that matter, pharmaceutical manufacturing. In fact, only recently have scientists and regulators become aware of comparable environmental consequences associated with the production and use of conventional drugs, particularly the risk of water pollution. * * *

Transgenic animals incorporating human genes raise still additional worries. Scientists may develop such hybrids in order to create closer models of human diseases in laboratory animals for research purposes, to engineer livestock capable of producing human proteins such as insulin or clotting factors needed by hemophiliacs, and to produce closer tissue matches for organs harvested from animals for transplantation into humans (so-called "xenotransplants"). Although scientists have made "humanized" animals for some time, questions have begun to arise about the point where more substantial transfers of human genes might cross the line and create a part-human organism (sometimes designated as a "chimera"). For instance, at what point do the more stringent federal guidelines for human research subjects trump the more lenient protections governing laboratory animals? In addition, when does the non-patentability of human organisms trump the patentability of genetically engineered animals? * * *

Not unlike the emergence of biotechnology three decades ago, many observers have begun to hail nanotechnology as the next big thing. This fairly new field involves feats of engineering at the extremely small scales occupied by atoms and simple molecules—a nanometer represents one-billionth of a meter. Nanotechnology essentially allows scientists to engineer novel molecules, and it offers more than sheer miniaturization: at these scales, quantum forces come into operation and chemical reactivity increases. Using advanced electron microscopes and other tools of molecular engineering, scientists have, for instance, formed carbon atoms into unusually strong and conductive hollow tubular or spherical structures—

nanotubes and fullerenes (named after Buckminster Fuller for their resemblance to his geodesic domes and nicknamed "buckyballs"). Engineers then can assemble these and other nanomaterials into various nanoscale devices.

Many of nanotechnology's most promising applications may appear in medicine. As a result, the FDA again will have to play a significant role in supervising this emerging field. In fact, one of the first practical uses of nanotechnology, in sunscreens and cosmetics, unmistakably falls under this agency's jurisdiction. In the future, however, nanomedicine will present the FDA with far more difficult scientific, legal, and policy challenges. Possible innovations that may defy traditional regulatory classifications include nanofoam that could enhance diagnostic imaging, more precise drug delivery vehicles, and hemoglobin-carrying nanotubes as a blood substitute. If biotechnology rendered untenable the traditional distinction between drugs and biologics, then nanomedicine may do the same to the line separating devices and biologics.

Nanotechnology can expect to share some of biotechnology's successes and growing pains, including uncertainty about consumer acceptance and possible adverse impacts. For instance, it appears that some nanomaterials may persist in the environment and prove toxic to wildlife. In addition, because of their extreme chemical reactivity and ability to enter cells (and pass the blood-brain barrier), legitimate concerns about adverse health consequences have arisen—like asbestos fibers, for example, nanomaterials may become dangerous when inhaled. Finally, nanotechnology may provide another potent weapon in the arsenal of bioterrorists. Given the fact that legal institutions once again may have to play catch up, some commentators have looked for lessons about appropriate regulatory strategies from the experience with biotechnology. * * *

Even when more narrowly defined to encompass only processes and products using genetic alterations, biotechnology has come to include a vast and varied landscape, one that continues to evolve. Technological revolutions do not come in neat packages, and they defy simple attempts at management. Is it any more productive to comprehend the far-reaching revolutions ushered in by silicon chips, or, to go further back in time, petrochemicals and plastics? These component materials have remade society in pervasive and sometimes unexpected ways, and they have forced any number of legal institutions to adapt old strategies to new challenges, but no one now would express surprise or disappointment that regulatory officials or courts initially failed to appreciate these forces or design uniform and coherent (and perhaps counterproductive) responses.

Occasionally, commentators suggest that we find ourselves in the midst of more than just a technological revolution, drawing parallels to profound leaps in the development of civilization such as the Stone Age and the Iron Age. Perhaps in hindsight this transition will deserve equal billing with the likes of such epochs, but in the present we need to take care not to exaggerate the supposed profundity of scientific progress occurring at this moment. Otherwise, society may become excessively enamored with—or frightened by—the latest domain of undoubtedly significant innovation.

Biotechnology has ushered in profound changes at some levels (and may require special attention from regulators), but, in other respects, it has shown remarkable continuity with the techniques that preceded it. * * * Legal institutions must try to avoid getting blinded by the hype and inappropriately sweeping in—and perhaps overregulating—both the novel and the mundane applications of this still young science and newer ones just on the horizon.

NOTES AND QUESTIONS

1. *Coming attractions.* Many of the issues raised in the above excerpt receive more sustained attention in the remainder of this chapter. For other overviews of the general area, see Dan L. Burk, The Problem of Process in Biotechnology, 43 Hous. L. Rev. 561 (2006); Phil B. Fontanarosa & Catherine D. DeAngelis, Medical Applications of Biotechnology, 293 JAMA 866 (2005) (introducing a theme issue); W. Christopher Matton & F. Scott Thomas, The Continuing Balance: Federal Regulation of Biotechnology, 44 Jurimetrics J. 283 (2004); Gerald R. Prettyman, Jr., Ethical Reforms in Biotechnology Research Regulations, 15 Va. J. Soc. Pol'y & L. 51 (2007); Sheryl Lawrence, Comment, What Would You Do with a Fluorescent Green Pig?: How Novel Transgenic Products Reveal Flaws in the Foundational Assumptions for the Regulation of Biotechnology, 34 Ecology L.Q. 201 (2007); Rob Stein, Concerns in "Synthetic Biology," Wash. Post, Dec. 16, 2010, at A4 (discussing the first report from the new Presidential Commission for the Study of Bioethical Issues). For more on the patent issues, see Thomas M. Mackey, Nanobiotechnology, Synthetic Biology, and RNAi: Patent Portfolios for Maximal Near–Term Commercialization and Commons for Maximal Long–Term Medical Gain, 13 Marq. Intell. Prop. L. Rev. 123 (2009); Joyce Tam, Note, Biologics Revolution: The Intersection of Biotechnology, Patent Law, and Pharmaceutical Regulation, 98 Geo. L.J. 535 (2010); see also Chap. 10(A)(1).

2. *Biotech drugs and generic competition.* In terms of producing therapeutic breakthroughs, the biotechnology industry appears to have eclipsed the traditional pharmaceutical industry. See Justin Gillis, Biotech's Gains Again Outstrip Drug Giants', Wash. Post, Apr. 12, 2006, at D1. In connection with passage of health reform legislation, Congress created a pathway for the introduction of generic biologics, though subject to an exclusivity period of twelve years for the innovator. See Biologics Price Competition and Innovation Act, Pub. L. No. 111–148, tit. VII(A), 124 Stat. 804 (2010); see also David E. Adelman & Christopher M. Holman, Misplaced Fears in the Legislative Battle over Affordable Biotech Drugs, 50 IDEA 565 (2010); Krista H. Carver et al., An Unofficial Legislative History of the Biologics Price Competition and Innovation Act of 2009, 65 Food & Drug L.J. 671 (2010); Richard A. Epstein, The Constitutional Protection of Trade Secrets and Patents Under the Biologics Price Competition and Innovation Act of 2009, 66 Food & Drug L.J. 285 (2011); Steven Kozlowski et al., Developing the Nation's Biosimilars Program, 365 New Eng. J. Med. 385 (2011); John A. Vernon et al., Exploration of Potential Economics of Follow-on Biologics and Implications for Data Exclusivity Periods for Biologics, 16 B.U. J. Sci. & Tech. L. 55 (2010); John A. Little, Jr., Note, Taking from Trailblazers: Learning from Those Who Have Gone Before When Approving Biosimilars, 44 Ga. L. Rev. 1097 (2010); Sarah Sorscher, Note, A Longer Monopoly for Biologics?: Considering the Implications of Data Exclusivity as a Tool for Innovation Policy, 23 Harv. J.L. & Tech. 285 (2009); Symposium, Follow–On Biologics: Implementation Challenges and Opportunities, 41 Seton Hall L. Rev. 501 (2011); Bruce Japsen, Biotech Clones: New Health Care Rules Mean Price Wars on the Horizon, Balt. Sun, May 25, 2011, at 16A (reporting that the FDA is still drafting guidance to implement the law).

3. *Pharming in flux.* Molecular farming could revolutionize pharmaceutical production. See Lisa Krieger, Implanted Gene Can Be Passed from Hen to Egg: Procedure Could Lead to Feathered Medicine Factories, Hous. Chron., June 8, 2006, at A16; Shankar Vedantam, Drug Made in Milk of Altered Goats Is Approved, Wash. Post, Feb. 7, 2009, at A5; Aaron Zitner, Fields of Gene Factories, L.A. Times, June 4, 2001, at A1. Questions about contamination with food crops or adverse environmental consequences remain unanswered. See Center for Food Safety v. Johanns, 451 F.Supp.2d 1165 (D.Haw.2006) (resolving a challenge brought by public interest groups opposed to field testing authorized by the USDA); Justin Gillis, Farmers Grow a Field of Dilemma: Drug–Making Crops' Potential Hindered by Fear of Tainted Food, Wash. Post, Dec. 23, 2002, at A1; Rick Weiss, USDA Backs Production of Rice with Human Genes, Wash. Post, Mar. 2, 2007, at A2. Assuming that these sorts of issues get resolved, separate questions would arise about the quality of raw materials destined for therapeutic products. How exactly will the FDA apply its drug GMPs to pharming? See 67 Fed. Reg. 57,828 (2002). See generally Margaux Birdsall, Biopharming, Bananas and Bureaucracy: The Banana Vaccine as a Case Study for Products That Straddle the Definitional Food/Drug Divide, 66 Food & Drug L.J. 265 (2011). Would rules governing investigational new drugs give the agency authority to restrict research and development involving pharmed therapeutic products?

4. *Nanomedicine.* "More than 60 drugs and drug delivery systems based on nanotechnology, and more than 90 medical devices or diagnostic tests, are already being tested." Rick Weiss, Nanomedicine's Promise Is Anything but Tiny, Wash. Post, Jan. 31, 2005, at A8 (examples include quantum dots for diagnostics, amphiphiles that promote the regeneration of neurons, implanted nanotubes as biosensors that test blood, and photo-thermal nanospheres that facilitate the targeted destruction of tumors); see also Barnaby J. Feder, Doctors Use Nanotechnology to Improve Health Care, N.Y. Times, Nov. 1, 2004, at C4 (discussing the potential for improving the surfaces and other features of implanted devices); Ronald Kotulak, Tiny Battlefield in the War on Disease: Devices as Small as Genes Detect, Fight Illnesses, Chi. Trib., Sept. 14, 2004, at C10. In the field of oncology, for instance, researchers hope to use nanotechnology for improved imaging and targeted drug delivery. See Stephen Heuser, In Medicine, Small Is About to Become Big, Boston Globe, May 8, 2006, at E1; Liz Szabo, Pinpointing Cancer Fight, USA Today, Sept. 13, 2004, at 6D. Invoking images from

Isaac Asimov's sci-fi classic "Fantastic Voyage" (and the 1966 film adaptation starring Raquel Welch), hypothetical medical applications include "respirocytes" (mechanical red blood cells) and "microbivores" (nanorobotic phagocytes patrolling the bloodstream). So far, at least, these and other breakthroughs remain on the drawing board. See Rick Weiss, For Now, Consumer Nanotech Concentrates on the Little Things, Wash. Post, Mar. 10, 2006, at A3 (reporting that commercially available nanotech products serve entirely trivial purposes). See generally 76 Fed. Reg. 34,715 (2011) (announcing the availability of a draft FDA guidance governing nanotech); Jordan Paradise et al., Evaluating Oversight of Human Drugs and Medical Devices: A Case Study of the FDA and Implications for Nanobiotechnology, 37 J.L. Med. & Ethics 598 (2009); Jessica K. Fender, Note, The FDA and Nano: Big Problems with Tiny Technology, 83 Chi.–Kent. L. Rev. 1063 (2008); Emilee S. Preble, Note, Preemptive Legislation in the European Union and the United States on the Topic of Nanomedicine: Examining Questions Raised by Smart Medical Technology, 7 Ind. Health L. Rev. 397 (2010); Symposium, Governing Nanomedicine: Lessons from Within, and for, the EU Medical Technology Regulatory Framework, 33 Law & Pol'y 215 (2011).

5. *Devices catch the wave.* Putting aside whatever nanotech may promise for the future, the medical device field has witnessed some dramatic breakthroughs made possible by advances in materials science, computer and imaging technologies, and miniaturization. See, e.g., Sandra G. Boodman, Lasik's Next Revision: Can a New Eye–Mapping Technology Reduce Bad Outcomes?, Wash. Post, Apr. 29, 2003, at F1 (reporting that the FDA approved a custom ablation device that allows "wavefront-guided" Lasik vision correction surgery); Justin Gillis, New Devices May Free Diabetics from Constant Monitoring, Wash Post, Apr. 23, 2006, at A1; Rob Stein, Patients Find Technology Easy to Swallow, Wash. Post, Dec. 30, 2002, at A1 (describing the "gut cam," an FDA approved diagnostic device that patients swallow); Christian Torres, Dr. da Vinci Will See You Now: As Robotic Devices Grow More Popular, Some Question Their Cost and Claimed Value, Wash. Post, July 18, 2011, at E1 ("In 2010, an estimated 220,000 U.S. procedures were assisted by a robotic device called the da Vinci surgical system . . . , with more than 1,300 systems installed across the country."); Rita Zeidner, More Clarity Wanted, Wash. Post, Mar. 30, 2004, at F1 (reporting that the FDA approved a new type of intraocular lens for cataract patients that uses a hinge to allow natural focusing); see also Brian Libby, Pushing to Build a Better Bandage, N.Y. Times, Mar. 4, 2003, at D7 (reporting that the FDA approved a hemostatic bandage constructed of chitosan, derived from a biodegradable carbohydrate found in the exoskeleton of shrimp and other invertebrates that promotes clotting); Lisa B. Mann, When You Need Closure: Sutures Are Being Replaced by Glues, Organic Tissues, Zippers, Wash. Post, July 8, 2003, at F1; Daniel Rosenberg, Injectable Graft Offered to Fix Broken Bones, Wall St. J., Sept. 24, 2003, at B4; Rob Stein, Video Robots Redefine "TV Doctor": Machines Let Physicians Make Rounds from a Distance, Wash. Post, July 6, 2005, at

A1 (describing advances in telemedicine technologies, some of which would not fall within the FDA's jurisdiction).

6. *Back to the future.* In some instances, older technologies that have fallen out of favor mount a comeback. See, e.g., Rita Rubin, Maggots and Leeches: Good Medicine, USA Today, July 8, 2004, at 4D. In the 1930s, before penicillin became widely available, major pharmaceutical companies marketed viral agents called bacteriophages to treat infections. With the arrival of broad-spectrum antibiotics (and the inability to identify the bacteria that caused a patient's infection), "phages" faded from the scene, though they continued to be sold in parts of Eastern Europe. With the spread of antibiotic resistance (and better techniques for identifying infectious agents), researchers have begun to reconsider the antimicrobial power of targeted phages, which enjoy the added benefit of avoiding some of the adverse effects associated with newer and more powerful classes of antibiotics. See Karl Thiel, Old Dogma, New Tricks—21st Century Phage Therapy, 22 Nature Biotech. 31 (2004); Jascha Hoffman, Revival of an Old Cure: Bacteria–Eating Viruses, N.Y. Times, May 18, 2004, at F7 (reporting that one company wants to genetically engineer phages to enhance their safety and effectiveness).

B. Biologics and Human Tissue Products

United States v. Loran Medical Systems, Inc.

25 F.Supp.2d 1082 (C.D.Cal.1997).

■ WILSON, DISTRICT JUDGE:

On June 20, 1996, this court granted a temporary restraining order enjoining defendants Loran Medical Systems, Inc., Bent Formby and Ernest Thomas, M.D. from importing neonatal rabbit and human fetal cells (the "Cell Product") from Russia for use in the treatment of human diabetes. Defendants claim that injection of the Cell Product into diabetic patients can stimulate the body's production of insulin. * * *

The gravamen of this case is whether the Cell Product falls within the regulatory ambit of the FDA. The government argues that it does, pointing to regulations defining "biological product," which the FDA regulates pursuant to its authority under the Public Health Service Act; and regulations involving "drugs" and "new drugs," which the FDA regulates under its Food and Drug Act authority. * * * A biological product is any "virus, therapeutic serum, toxin, antitoxin, [vaccine, blood, blood component or derivative, allergenic product,] or analogous product applicable to the prevention, treatment or cure" of human diseases or injuries. A product is analogous to a toxin or anti-toxin if, irrespective of its source or origin, it can be used in the treatment of disease through a "specific immune process." 21 C.F.R. § 600.3(h)(5)(iii).

The human immune system will naturally react to the injection of any cellular material, whether obtained from a human or non-human source.

Defendants inject the Cell Product into an area of the abdomen selected specifically to evade this response and thus reduce the chance that the cells will be rejected. This procedure purportedly allows the rabbit cells to begin producing insulin immediately while the human fetal cells mature.

The government argues that this attempt at evading the body's natural immune system is a "specific immune process" as required by the FDA's regulations. Defendants * * * argue that the PHS Act only authorizes the FDA to regulate products which immunize against a specific disease, such as polio or smallpox. The court disagrees. As described in greater detail below, Congress conferred upon the FDA the broad statutory authority to regulate products analogous to toxins, antitoxins, vaccines, blood, etc. The FDA's assertion of authority over immunological agents such as the Cell Product is a reasonable construction of the PHS Act. * * *

Defendants argue that the Cell Product cannot be a biological product under 42 U.S.C. § 262(a) because it is not biologically or genetically altered in any way. Somatic cell therapy—medical treatment using biologically altered cells—is regulated under the FDA's authority to regulate biological products. See 58 Fed. Reg. 53,250; FDA, Points to Consider in Human Cell Therapy and Gene Therapy (1991). But nothing in the regulation requires alteration before a product is to fall under the FDA's purview. Accordingly, the court finds that the FDA's conclusion that the Cell Product is a biological product that uses a specific immune process is reasonable, and thus the Cell Product is properly under the FDA's authority.

The FD & C Act defines drugs as, inter alia, "articles intended for use in the diagnosis, cure, mitigation, treatment or prevention of disease in [humans]." 21 U.S.C. § 321. The Cell Product was developed for use in the treatment of diabetes. Thus, it meets the statutory definition of a drug. * * * Classifying the Cell Product as a drug is consistent with Congress' intent to give the FDA broad authority in this important area.

All new drugs must undergo premarket review by the FDA. A new drug is any drug that is not already generally recognized among medical experts as safe and effective for its intended use. The exception for "generally recognized" drugs is very narrow. The court's task is to determine whether the drug has a general reputation in the scientific community for safety and effectiveness, not to make an independent determination of these characteristics. * * * While defendants make sweeping arguments about the worldwide acceptance of the product, they fail to provide specific examples of successful clinical trials or published studies. Moreover, while defendants provide anecdotal evidence of clinical success, the declarations of plaintiffs' experts demonstrate that there is a marked lack of consensus in the medical community as to the effectiveness of the Cell Product. Accordingly, the court finds that the FDA has acted reasonably in classifying the Cell Product as a new drug.

The court disposes quickly of defendants' argument that the FDA's exercise of authority over the Cell Product is an attempt to regulate the practice of medicine—an area traditionally left to the states. While the FD & C Act "was not intended to regulate the practice of medicine, it was obviously intended to control the availability of drugs for prescribing by physicians." The court has already determined that the Cell Product is a drug. Accordingly, the FDA has the authority to regulate its use. * * *

CareToLive v. von Eschenbach

525 F.Supp.2d 938 (S.D.Ohio 2007), aff'd, 290 F.App'x 887 (6th Cir.2008).

■ FROST, DISTRICT JUDGE:

* * * For unapproved biological products, the sponsor seeks FDA approval by submitting a BLA [biologics license application] pursuant to the PHSA. 42 U.S.C. § 262(a). The FDA will approve a BLA for an unapproved biological product if the BLA demonstrates that the product is safe, pure, and potent, id. § 262(a)(2)(C)(i)(I), and that the facility in which the product is manufactured "meets standards designed to assure that the biological product continues to be safe, pure, and potent," id. § 262(a)(2)(C)(i)(II). Generally, when the sponsor of a biological product has completed the clinical trial process, it can submit a BLA in accordance with 21 C.F.R. § 601.2(a). The required documentation in a BLA provides information for the FDA evaluation of the biological product, including the results of clinical trials, the composition of the drug, manufacturing information, and sample labeling. * * * [I]f there are deficiencies in the BLA, the FDA may send a complete response letter declining to approve the BLA as it was presented and requesting additional information from the sponsor.

Provenge is a biological product intended to treat a particular type of metastatic prostate cancer. Provenge uses a patient's own cells to prepare a final product designed for infusion back into the patient's bloodstream to activate his or her immune system against the cancer cells. Provenge is referred to as an active cellular immunotherapy, designed to elicit a patient's specific immune response to a target antigen expressed in prostate cancer tissue, i.e., to train a patient's immune system to recognize cancer cells and to fight them. Because it is designed to act in this manner, Provenge is a vaccine and thus a "biological product" subject to FDA regulation under the PHSA. 42 U.S.C. § 262(i).

Dendreon [Corporation] has been studying Provenge's safety and effectiveness in clinical trials pursuant to an investigational new drug application it submitted to the FDA in 1996. Dendreon submitted its BLA for Provenge in late 2006, and the FDA considered it to be filed in January 2007. Because Provenge is an immunotherapy vaccine, regulatory responsibility for reviewing and, ultimately, approving or denying approval of the BLA rests with the Office of Cellular, Tissue, and Gene Therapies in the FDA Center for Biologics Research and Evaluation (CBER). 68 Fed. Reg. 38,067, 38,068 (2003). * * * *

On May 8, 2007, CBER issued a complete response letter to Dendreon, Provenge's sponsor, declining to approve the BLA in its current form because of various deficiencies. The FDA requested that Dendreon submit additional information with respect to the chemistry, manufacturing, and controls section of the BLA; such information is required to demonstrate that the facility in which the product would be manufactured "meets standards designed to assure that the biological product continues to be safe, pure, and potent." 42 U.S.C. § 262(a)(2)(C)(i)(II). The FDA also requested that Dendreon submit additional clinical data in support of its effectiveness claim. Dendreon has since met with the FDA to discuss the additional data required to support licensure and indicated that it intends to proceed with its new Phase 3 study designed to measure survival and to submit such data to the FDA when it becomes available.

Plaintiff [an association of "cancer patients, patient families, doctors, investors, and advocates"] submitted a citizen petition to the FDA dated July 26, 2007 * * * urg[ing] the Commissioner of Food and Drugs to "reverse [the FDA's] decision to deny immediate approval to Provenge." * * * [T]he FDA acknowledged receipt of the citizen petition, but otherwise has not yet responded. * * * Plaintiff claims that defendants * * * violated [its] rights under the Administrative Procedure Act (APA), 5 U.S.C. §§ 702, 704. * * * In their motion to dismiss, defendants argue that this court lacks subject matter jurisdiction over this action * * * *

"Final agency action" is both a critical prerequisite to Article III justiciability, namely ripeness, and a necessary element of a cause of action under the APA. * * * Defendants correctly contend that plaintiff faces no greater hardship from waiting for a final agency decision before bringing suit than the patients who might potentially benefit from many other biologics or drugs intended to treat life-threatening conditions that are under review by the FDA at any given time. Indeed, Congress balanced such hardships against the risks and dangers of using unsafe and ineffective drugs when it set the statutory standards for approval of drugs and biologics. The FDA's issuance of the complete response letter, at most, potentially prevents access to an unproven and speculative future benefit. Moreover, immediate consideration of the administrative record by this court could not speed patients' access to Provenge, because the only remedy that this court could issue is a remand to the FDA to continue its review of Dendreon's BLA. * * *

Defendants have convincingly shown that issuance of a complete response letter does not constitute final agency action. A complete response letter is an established mechanism for the FDA to request additional information from the sponsor of a BLA. 69 Fed. Reg. 43,351, 43,352 (2004). A complete response letter is meant to "ensure a consistent approach to informing sponsors of needed changes before [the FDA] can approve an application, with no implication as to the ultimate approvability of the application." A complete response letter does not signal the end for a product; rather, it is a step the FDA takes to assure that it has sufficient data to establish safety and effectiveness prior to licensure. The FDA continues to work with sponsors to resolve any outstanding issues. Indeed, the complete response letter made clear that it was not "the consummation of the agency's decisionmaking process" and instead was an interlocutory step in the agency's administrative process. The letter affirmatively requests Dendreon to submit additional evidence to support its BLA. * * * Because the Provenge BLA administrative process is ongoing, the FDA may ultimately approve the application, which would render plaintiff's claims moot. * * *

In addition, the complete response letter did not determine any legal rights or obligations, or trigger a process "from which legal consequences will flow." To be sure, makers of biologic products cannot market them without an approved BLA. But the complete response letter neither approved, nor denied, Dendreon's BLA. * * * Finally, the complete response letter was the ruling of a subordinate official. It was signed by Dr. Ashok Batra, who is the Director of the Division of Clinical Evaluation and Pharmacology/Toxicology within the Office of Cellular, Tissue, and Gene Therapies, which is in turn within CBER. CBER has delegated to officials at Dr. Batra's level the authority to issue complete response letters, but not the authority to approve BLAs. * * * Accordingly, because the complete response letter does not constitute final agency action under the APA, this court lacks subject matter jurisdiction over this action and must dismiss it. * * *

NOTES AND QUESTIONS

1. *Pro[state re]venge?* Normally, the FDA follows approval recommendations from its advisory committees, so the demand for an additional efficacy trial came as an unpleasant surprise to Provenge's sponsor and its investors, as recounted in a note in Chapter 2(D). Although Dendreon might have satisfied justiciability requirements had it declined to supply the requested information (thereby triggering a final agency rejection letter), sponsors rarely mount judicial challenges to nonapproval decisions, knowing them to be largely futile and preferring to find a way to address the FDA's concerns. See Chaps. 1(D)(3) & 3(A)(1). It took almost three years before the agency approved the product based on an additional clinical trial that found an average gain of four months relative to placebo (less than two months better than standard chemotherapy though safer). See Andrew Pollack, F.D.A. Approves "Vaccine" That Uses Immune System to Fight Prostate Cancer, N.Y. Times, Apr. 30, 2010, at A13 ("Getting the immune system to attack cancer has tantalized scientists for decades, because it promises to have fewer side effects than the harsh chemotherapy now used.... Provenge is not a preventive vaccine like those for ... cervical cancer, which prevent a viral infection that causes the cancer."); id. ("Dendreon hopes to use the same technique to make other cancer vaccines, including one for bladder cancer. There are dozens of other cancer vaccines in development by other companies."); Ron Winslow, Novel Cancer Treatment Cleared—Dendreon's "Therapeutic Vaccine" Prompts Body to Attack Prostate Tumors; High Cost Is a Hurdle, Wall St. J., Apr. 30, 2010, at B1. As recounted in a note in Chapter 9(A)(1), however, CMS initially threw a monkey wrench into Dendreon's commercialization plans by questioning whether Medicare would cover the $93,000 tab per patient.

2. *Regulating biologics*. For more on the definitional question, see Edward L. Korwek, What Are Biologics? A Comparative Legislative, Regulatory and Scientific Analysis, 62 Food & Drug L.J. 257 (2007). In 1997, Congress amended the FDCA to call on the agency "to take measures to minimize differences in the review and approval of products required to have approved biologics license applications under [the PHSA] and products required to have approved new drug applications under [the FDCA]." FDAMA, Pub. L. No. 105–115, § 123(c), 111 Stat. 2324 (1997). Two years later, the FDA did so by replacing the requirement for separate product and establishment licensing applications with a single biologics license application (BLA). See 64 Fed. Reg. 56,441 (1999) (codified at 21 C.F.R. pt. 601). A few year later, it transferred some of the premarket approval functions to CDER. See Marc Kaufman, FDA Seeks to Hasten Review of Biotech Drugs, Wash. Post, Sept. 7, 2002, at A3 ("FDA officials said the move makes sense because the testing, evaluation and use of the pharmaceuticals is similar, whether the drugs are created through traditional chemical means or through newer biotechnology.... [CBER] will maintain control over vaccines, blood safety, gene therapy and tissue transplantation."). See generally Martha J. Carter, The Ability of Current Biologics Law to Accommodate Emerging Technologies, 51 Food & Drug L.J. 375 (1996); Gary E. Gamerman, Regulation of Biologics Manufacturing: Questioning the Premise, 49 Food & Drug L.J. 213 (1994).

3. *Vaccines*. The FDA regulates vaccines as both drugs and biologics, which means that, in addition to satisfying new drug approval requirements, manufacturers must test each lot for potency and sterility according to the terms of a BLA and submit samples of each vaccine lot to CBER for pre-release approval. In producing the vaccine against influenza, the government must decide well in advance of each year's season which of several circulating strains to target. See David Brown, For Health Officials, Flu Shot Is an Annual Gamble, Wash. Post, Jan. 12, 2004, at A3; see also David Brown, Researchers Race to Boost Supply of Bird Flu Vaccine: Additives Studied as Way to Help Fight Potential Pandemic, Wash. Post, Feb. 12, 2006, at A3 (describing challenges encountered in vaccine development and the use of adjuvants to stretch inadequate supplies); Donald G. McNeil, Jr., Vaccination Graduates to an Older Crowd, N.Y. Times, July 1, 2003, at F1 (discussing some of the difficulties in recommending the use of new vaccines targeted for adolescents). Once approved for marketing, vaccines also may be required to undergo additional safety and efficacy studies. CBER and the Centers for Disease Control and Prevention (CDC) jointly administer the Vaccine Adverse Event Reporting System (VAERS), a postmarket safety surveillance program.

4. *Blood*. Suppliers of blood and certain blood-derivatives must comply with facility registration requirements, and blood banks also must operate in compliance with special GMPs. See 21 C.F.R. pts. 606–607. As the FDA has explained:

> CBER works closely with other parts of the Public Health Service (PHS) to identify and respond to potential threats to blood safety, to

> develop safety and technical standards, to monitor blood supplies and to help industry promote an adequate supply of blood and blood products. While a blood supply with zero risk of transmitting infectious disease may not be possible, the blood supply is safer than it has ever been. Over a period of years, FDA has progressively strengthened the overlapping safeguards that protect patients from unsuitable blood and blood products .... Blood donations are now tested for seven different infectious agents. In addition to strengthening these safeguards, FDA has significantly increased its oversight of the blood industry. The agency inspects all blood facilities at least every two years, and "problem" facilities are inspected more often. Blood establishments are now held to quality standards comparable to those expected of pharmaceutical manufacturers.

FDA, Blood Safety, available at www.fda.gov/cber/blood.htm. Sometimes, highly publicized infectious disease threats (e.g., West Nile virus) fade from the scene almost as quickly as they arrived. See Donald G. McNeil, Jr., Rare Infection Threatens to Spread in Blood Supply, N.Y. Times, Nov. 18, 2003, at F1 (reporting that "Hepatitis and AIDS were followed by mad cow disease, West Nile virus" and now Chagas disease). Putting aside concerns about disease transmission, shortages of whole blood arise with regularity, in part because of its limited shelf life. See Brian Reid, Out for Blood, but Prudently, Wash. Post, Sept. 17, 2002, at F1. This has prompted efforts to develop blood substitutes. See Ross Kerber, FDA Puts Biopure Study on Hold: Agency Cites Safety Risks, Seeks More Data on Artificial Blood, Boston Globe, July 13, 2005, at D1 (reporting regulatory problems encountered with Hemopure, which uses bovine hemoglobin suspended in a saline solution and remains the subject of a BLA submitted in 2002).

5. *Regulatory oversight of the tissue banking industry.* A report from the HHS Office of the Inspector General criticized the FDA's lack of oversight of tissue banks:

> Some tissue banks have never been inspected by FDA. We found at least 36 tissue banks that have never been inspected, out of 154 tissue establishments that we were able to identify. FDA has indicated that regulation of tissue banks is an unfunded mandate, and that in order to carry out these inspections, the agency has had to borrow resources from other programs, such as blood and plasma. Of the 118 tissue banks that FDA has inspected, 68 have been inspected only once.... Information is lacking about the number of tissue banks in operation and the products they produce and distribute. FDA has proposed a regulation to require tissue banks to register and list their products. The regulation would address directly this limitation in knowledge about tissue banking. Because the agency's current regulation focuses on donor screening and testing to prevent transmission of [disease], other important aspects of tissue bank quality are not monitored. Until FDA's good tissue practices rule is finalized, tissue banks have no external requirements for quality and handling of tissue if they are not accredited by [the American Association of Tissue Banks] or licensed

by New York or Florida. Of the 154 tissue banks we identified, 67 are neither accredited by AATB nor inspected by Florida or New York.

Office of Inspector Gen., HHS, Oversight of Tissue Banking (2001), at ii–iii, available at oig.hhs.gov/oei/reports/oei-01-00441.pdf; see also Barbara Indech, The International Harmonization of Human Tissue Regulation: Regulatory Control over Human Tissue Use and Tissue Banking in Select Countries and the Current State of International Harmonization Efforts, 55 Food & Drug L.J. 343 (2000). One patient who received a contaminated bone and cartilage transplant during knee surgery died from a rare bacterial infection. See Robert Pear, FDA Delays Regulation of Tissue Transplants, N.Y. Times, May 14, 2003, at A18. In 2004, after lengthy delays that had attracted congressional criticism, the FDA finalized a set of rules designed to address these sorts of concerns, though some criticized the agency for issuing "watered down" requirements and failing to ensure compliance. See Marilynn Marchione & Seth Borenstein, Cadaver–Tissue Transplants May Put Recipients at Risk, Orlando Sent., June 11, 2006, at A5 ("[M]any experts think the rules the FDA enacted last year as a long-promised overhaul fall short of providing the level of oversight needed.").

FDA, Final Rule, *Human Cells, Tissues, and Cellular and Tissue–Based Products; Establishment Registration and Listing*

66 Fed. Reg. 5447 (2001).

* * * The goal of the new approach is to improve protection of the public health without imposing unnecessary restrictions on research, development, or the availability of new products. Under the new system, the regulation of different types of human cells, tissues, and cellular and tissue-based products [HCT/Ps] will be commensurate with the public health risks presented, enabling us to use our resources more effectively. Consolidating the regulation of human cells, tissues, and cellular and tissue-based products into one regulatory program is expected to lead to increased consistency and greater efficiency. Together, these planned improvements will increase the safety of human cells, tissues, and cellular and tissue-based products, and public confidence in their safety, while encouraging the development of new products.

In 1997, we announced our regulatory plans for human cells, tissues, and cellular and tissue-based products in two documents: "A Proposed Approach to the Regulation of Cellular and Tissue–Based Products" and "Reinventing the Regulation of Human Tissue." The proposed approach described a comprehensive plan for regulating human cells, tissues, and cellular and tissue-based products that would include establishment registration and product listing, donor-suitability requirements, good tissue practice regulations, and other requirements. Under this tiered, risk-based approach, we proposed to exert only the type of government regulation necessary to protect the public health. To accomplish this goal, we planned to issue new regulations under the communicable disease provisions of the

Public Health Service Act (the PHS Act). Some human cellular and tissue-based products would be regulated only under these new regulations, while other human cellular and tissue-based products would also be regulated as drugs, devices, and/or biological drugs. * * *

Since 1997, we have published three proposed rules to implement the proposed approach. * * * Together, these three rules when finalized would establish a comprehensive regulatory program for human cellular and tissue-based products * * * The definition of "human cells, tissues, or cellular or tissue-based product" is intended to cover HCT/Ps at all stages of their manufacture, from recovery through distribution. Some examples of HCT/Ps include skin, tendons, bone, heart valves, corneas, hematopoietic stem cells, manipulated autologous chondrocytes, epithelial cells on a synthetic matrix, and semen or other reproductive tissue. * * *

Several comments asserted that we are proposing to regulate the practice of medicine, especially with respect to reproductive tissue and hematopoietic stem cells. We disagree with this comment. This final rule sets out registration and listing requirements for establishments that recover, process, store, label, package, or distribute HCT/Ps, or screen or test cell and tissue donors. HCT/Ps, including hematopoietic stem cells and reproductive tissues, fall within our jurisdiction. Some HCT/Ps will be regulated under the [FDCA] and/or the PHS Act, while other HCT/Ps will be effectively regulated solely by regulations issued under our authority to prevent the spread of communicable disease. We are not attempting to govern practitioners' use of HCT/Ps, but rather to ensure that HCT/Ps that would be used by practitioners in their treatment of patients are in compliance with applicable regulations, including regulations designed to prevent the transmission or spread of communicable disease. * * *

Several comments questioned the need for the regulation of reproductive cells and tissues, citing current oversight from professional organizations, other federal agencies, and States. Comments opposed registration for programs involved in egg donation, egg retrieval, semen processing, semen evaluation, or in vitro fertilization (IVF) in assisted reproductive technologies. * * * Although we recognize the value of professional efforts to self-regulate, and of regulatory efforts of other agencies and the States, we disagree that these piecemeal, often voluntary, efforts are adequate. * * * State regulation varies from state to state and does not consistently address our concerns about the transmission of communicable disease. The model certification program for embryo laboratories developed by the Centers for Disease Control and Prevention (CDC) is a voluntary program that States may or may not choose to adopt; its primary focus is not on preventing the transmission of communicable disease. No State has yet adopted CDC's model certification program. * * *

Several comments objected to the word "product" in the term human cellular or tissue-based product, defined in proposed § 1271.3(e). These comments asserted that human cells and tissues are donations, not goods manufactured for sale. Some comments argued that the use of the word "product" might have legal implications; e.g., subjecting eye banks to inappropriate product liability litigation. Comments also noted that the word "product" is inconsistent with terms used in the tissue and eye banking field. We also received an objection to describing embryos and germ cells as "products."

In choosing "human cellular or tissue-based product," we were seeking a term that would describe everything that will be subject to the regulations in part 1271. We needed a term broad enough to cover both cells and tissues, and one that would include within its scope such diverse articles as unprocessed tissue, highly processed cells, and tissues that are combined with certain drugs or devices. Although we have considered removing the word "product" from the definition, we are concerned that another term (e.g., "human cells and tissues") would not be understood to include many of the highly manufactured products to which the regulations apply, or might be misconstrued to apply only to the cell or tissue component of such a product. * * *

In proposed § 1271.10, we set out the criteria for regulating certain HCT/Ps solely under section 361 of the PHS Act and the regulations to be contained in part 1271. An HCT/P would be subject to this level of regulation if it: (1) was minimally manipulated; (2) was not promoted or labeled for any use other than a homologous use; (3) was not combined with or modified by the addition of any component that is a drug or a device; and (4) either does not have a systemic effect, or has a systemic effect and is for autologous, family-related allogeneic, or reproductive use. * * * Our ability to regulate an HCT/P as a drug, device, and/or biological product derives from the [FDCA] and section 351 of the PHS Act, authorities that are distinct from our authority to issue regulations to prevent the transmission of communicable disease under section 361 of the PHS Act. If an HCT/P does not meet the criteria in § 1271.10 for regulation solely under section 361 of the PHS Act, and the establishment does not qualify for any of the exceptions in final § 1271.15, the HCT/P will be regulated under the [FDCA] and/or the PHS Act and applicable regulations. * * *

For example, the use of bone for repair, replacement, or reconstruction anywhere in the skeleton of the recipient (including the vertebral column) would be considered homologous use. However, it should be understood that, for the use of a structural tissue to be considered homologous, the HCT/P must perform the same basic function or functions in the recipient as it did in the donor; the use of structural tissue in a location where it does not perform the same basic function as it did in the donor would not be homologous. We intend to interpret "nonhomologous" narrowly. Examples of uses that would be considered nonhomologous include: The use of dermis as a replacement for dura mater, the use of amniotic membrane in the eye, and the use of cartilage in the bladder. * * * [A]n HCT/P that is intended by the manufacturer for one of these uses would not be regulated solely under section 361 of the PHS Act and these regulations, but as a drug, device, and/or biological product. * * *

After further consideration, we agree that the term "systemic effect" may not cover all of the HCT/Ps that we intended to cover. Because the effect of implanted neurons or neural tissue into the brain would likely be restricted to the site where the tissue/cells were placed, this effect might not be included within the meaning of systemic. However, as discussed in the proposed approach, HCT/Ps that rely on living cells for their primary function, such as neuronal tissue, raise clinical safety and effectiveness concerns that are not appropriately addressed solely under section 361 of the PHS Act. Such concerns include viability, efficacy, malignant transformation, or rejection after transplantation. Thus, although neuronal cells may not be considered to have a systemic effect, they nonetheless require regulation under the [FDCA] and/or section 351 of the PHS Act.

Therefore, we have clarified § 1271.10(a)(4) to indicate that an HCT/P that either has systemic effect or depends upon the metabolic activity of living cells for its primary function would not be appropriately regulated solely under section 361 of the PHS Act, and therefore will be regulated as a drug, device, and/or biological product. Cells or tissues such as pancreatic islet cells, which have effects on many different organs throughout the body through the secretion of insulin, are appropriately characterized by the term "systemic effect." Neurons for implantation in the brain would fall into the category of HCT/Ps that depend upon the metabolic activity of living cells for their primary function. In contrast, some HCT/Ps (such as corneas, skin, or osteochondral allografts) may contain living cells, but do not depend on them for their primary function, which is structural. * * *

FDA, Final Rule, *Eligibility Determination for Donors of Human Cells, Tissues, and Cellular and Tissue–Based Products*

69 Fed. Reg. 29,786 (2004).

* * * Because of their nature as derivatives of the human body, HCT/Ps pose a risk of transmitting communicable diseases. For this reason, this final rule requires that most cell and tissue donors be tested and screened for evidence of relevant communicable disease infection. It also contains other related requirements (e.g., on records, quarantine, storage, and labeling). * * *

Communicable diseases include, but are not limited to, those transmitted by viruses, bacteria, fungi, parasites, and transmissible spongiform encephalopathy agents. Certain diseases are transmissible through the implantation, transplantation, infusion, or transfer of HCT/Ps derived from donors infected with those diseases. To prevent the introduction, transmission, or spread of such diseases, we consider it necessary to take appropriate measures to prevent the use of cells or tissues from infected donors. Thus, these regulations require that, before the use of most HCT/Ps, the cell or tissue donor must be determined to be eligible to donate, based on the results of screening and testing for relevant communicable diseases. In most cases, a donor who tests reactive for a particular disease, or who possesses clinical evidence of or risk factors for such a disease, would be considered ineligible, and cells and tissues from that donor would not ordinarily be used.

In addition to regulations governing the testing and screening of donors for relevant communicable disease and quarantine and storage of HCT/Ps, FDA has also determined that regulations requiring establishments to maintain certain records related to HCT/Ps and to establish standard operating procedures are necessary to prevent the introduction, transmission, or spread interstate of communicable disease. * * * Since some diseases, such as transmissible spongiform encephalopathies (TSEs), appear to have a long latency period, FDA has determined that a 10-year record retention period is necessary.

Similarly, it is necessary for establishments to establish, maintain, and follow procedures related to the prevention of communicable disease. The agency has determined that these provisions are necessary to ensure that the important protections created by these regulations are actually effected and are not simply empty promises. Only manufacturing conducted in accordance with established procedures can assure that HCT/Ps meet the standards in these rules. If standardized processes are not developed and used, mistakes, inevitably, are made. Moreover, review of procedures can be critical to determining the cause of a disease transmission. Without that analysis, it would be impossible to prevent a future occurrence, with possibly fatal consequences. * * *

[A]ll HCT/Ps pose some risk of carrying pathogens that could cause disease in health-care personnel, other handlers of tissue, recipients, and family members or other contacts of recipients. This broader concern for the spread of communicable disease is reflected in certain labeling requirements in these regulations and in the criteria for identifying a relevant communicable disease. We recognize that regulations exist that are specifically designed to protect employees who may come in contact with infectious materials, and we do not consider these regulations to be in conflict with those other regulations currently in effect. However, we have made an effort to be consistent with the terminology used in these other regulations; e.g., "Infectious Substances" and the Biohazard legend.

Under section 361 of the PHS Act, FDA is authorized to enforce the regulations it issues to prevent the introduction, transmission, or spread of communicable diseases interstate through such means as inspection, disinfection, sanitation, destruction of animals or articles found to be so infected or contaminated as to be sources of dangerous infection in human beings, and other measures that may be necessary. In addition, under section 368(a) of the PHS Act, any person who violates a regulation prescribed under section 361 of the PHS Act may be punished by imprisonment for up to 1 year. Individuals may also be punished for violating such a regulation by a fine of up to $100,000 if death has not resulted from the violation or up to $250,000 if death has resulted. For organizational defendants, fines range up to $200,000 and $500,000. * * *

The authorities supporting the CGMP and QS [Quality System] regulations are also applicable when the CGMP and QS regulations apply to an

HCT/P regulated as a drug, biological product, or device. Currently, the CGMP and QS regulations applicable to HCT/Ps regulated as drugs or devices do not delineate testing and screening procedures for communicable diseases. Nevertheless, we consider communicable-disease testing and screening to be steps in the manufacturing process that are crucial to the safety of such products. As a result, we are amending the existing CGMP regulations for drugs in parts 210 and 211 and the QS regulations for devices in part 820, which include CGMP requirements, to make clear that the testing and screening provisions of part 1271 subpart C apply to HCT/Ps regulated as drugs, devices, and/or biological products. * * *

The donor-eligibility draft guidance that may be found elsewhere in this *Federal Register* is intended to assist establishments in complying with the requirements of this final rule and contains details that are not in the regulation. Although not binding, the draft guidance presents the agency's current thinking on the topics covered. For example, whereas the regulation requires an establishment to screen donors for risk factors, the draft guidance specifies what we consider those risk factors to be. Similarly, the draft guidance contains recommendations on which tests to use to comply with the testing requirements * * * [and] also identifies several additional disease agents or diseases that we believe meet the definition of relevant communicable disease agent or disease. We welcome comments on the draft guidance. As scientific knowledge is developed, new tests are introduced, and additional relevant communicable disease agents and diseases are identified, we intend * * * to modify the donor-eligibility guidance so that it remains current. * * *

In the process of developing this final rule, we have reviewed standards from other countries and met with representatives from the European Union, Australia, Japan, and other nations. The requirements in place in other countries are diverse and rarely static, reflecting the fact that other countries may have screening needs different from those in the United States and different tests available to them. The challenge of achieving consistency is underscored by the European Commission's announcement of the need for a new directive on human tissue, intended to replace the current myriad of 15 differing—and sometimes nonexistent—national laws on the subject. On June 19, 2002, the Commission of European Communities put forth a "Proposal for a Directive of the European Parliament and of the Council on setting standards of quality and safety for the donation, procurement, testing, processing, storage, and distribution of human tissues and cells." Completion of this directive is expected to take several years. We applaud this effort and will continue to follow developments in tissue regulation throughout the world. However, at this time, our primary goal is to put into place the basic safeguards set out in this rule, an effort that may provide a starting point for further harmonization efforts. * * *

One comment stated that we had not sufficiently demonstrated the need to expand agency oversight to include diseases in addition to HIV and hepatitis. Another comment asserted that transmission of CJD [Creutzfeldt–Jakob Disease] and syphilis (*Treponema pallidum*) via cornea transplants is rare or nonexistent. When we issued part 1270 as an interim rule in 1993, among other reasons, we were acting swiftly to counter the transmission of three serious disease agents, HIV, HBV and HCV [hepatitis B and C]. One reason for the inclusion of more diseases and disease agents in the proposed rule and this final rule is that the new rules cover more types of cells and tissues than were subject to part 1270. These additional cells and tissues pose additional risks of transmitting communicable disease. For example, we are now requiring you to test donors of viable, leukocyte-rich tissue for HTLV [human T-lymphotropic virus] and CMV [cytomegalovirus]; this requirement did not previously exist, because part 1270 did not cover such viable, leukocyte-rich HCT/Ps as semen and hematopoietic stem/progenitor cells. Similarly, we are now requiring that you test donors of reproductive tissue for *Neisseria gonorrhea* and *Chlamydia trachomatis*, a requirement that did not exist under part 1270, which did not cover reproductive tissue.

We proposed to add TSE (including CJD and v[ariant]CJD) and syphilis to the list of disease agents and diseases for which donors of all types of cells and tissues would be required to undergo screening and/or testing, because these two diseases present significant health risks. We disagree with the assertion that testing is unnecessary due to the infrequency of transmission. With respect to CJD, there have been over 100 transmissions of CJD from dura mater worldwide (including 3 in the United States) and 1 transmission from cornea (in addition to 2 possible transmissions), and the number of cases of vCJD is rising. With respect to syphilis, several factors could be responsible for the lack of reports of syphilis transmission via organs, tissues, or cells, including the use of antibiotics during tissue processing and the storage of tissues at low temperature. (*Treponema pallidum* does not survive when stored at 4C for more than 48 to 72 hours.) However, these factors might not always be in place; i.e., antibiotics might not be used, and fresh bone grafts might not be stored under time and temperature conditions that would kill the organism, if present. Because of the potential for transmission by cells and tissue, including cornea, of both CJD and syphilis, we are maintaining the screening and testing requirements in the final rule. * * *

Many comments opposed any quarantine requirement for embryos. These comments disputed the communicable disease risks associated with embryos. They also cited increased costs from a quarantine; decreased success rates through use of frozen embryos; adverse effects on patients from a quarantine requirement; logistical concerns associated with retesting; and other possible consequences of a quarantine requirement, including loss of embryos. Some comments asserted that current screening practices are adequate. Others asserted that FDA was interfering with the practice of medicine or criticized our approach as having a potentially negative effect on the field of reproductive medicine. * * * In the preamble to the proposed rule, we stated that reproductive cells and tissues that can reliably be stored are those that maintain function and integrity during storage. As examples, we listed spermatozoa and sperm progenitor cells. Given technologies at the time, we did not assert that embryos or oocytes could reliably be stored. Thus, we did not intend the quarantine and retesting requirement to apply to embryos or oocytes.

We disagree with comments that minimize the communicable disease risks associated with reproductive cells and tissue. Among other things, these comments assert that there have been no known transmissions of disease by ova or embryos or that there is no compelling evidence to indicate that human gametes or embryos are capable of transmitting infectious disease. Each cell in the human body has receptors for viruses and bacteria and is thus capable of transmitting communicable disease. Even avascular tissue has been known to transmit disease (e.g., corneas have transmitted HBV). Semen is known to have transmitted HBV and HIV. Because embryos are a result of the combining of sperm and ova, they have the potential of being contaminated by communicable disease agents transmitted by the sperm. Moreover, bacterial contamination and transmission of HCV has occurred in assisted reproduction procedures. * * *

It is essential that the patient who chooses to use a directed donation from an ineligible donor be fully informed of the risks involved. * * * [T]he HCT/P must be labeled prominently with the Biohazard legend and must bear the statement "WARNING: Advise patient of communicable disease risks," and, in the case of reactive test results, "WARNING: Reactive test results for (name of disease agent or disease)." In the case of reproductive HCT/Ps, this includes risk to the baby. We have removed the proposed requirement for the establishment to document that the physician agreed to explain the communicable disease risks associated with the use of the HCT/P to the recipient or the recipient's legally authorized representative and that the physician agreed to obtain from the recipient or the recipient's legally authorized representative consent to use the HCT/P. We decline to require a written contract between physician and patient. We know that physicians are under legal and ethical restrictions, requiring them to discuss the risks of communicable disease transmission stemming from the use of HCT/Ps. We rely on physicians to meet these obligations when obtaining consent to procedures involving HCT/Ps from patients and their legal representatives. * * *

[W]e have defined "donor medical history interview" as a documented dialog about the donor's medical history and relevant social behavior, including activities, behaviors, and descriptions considered to increase the donor's relevant communicable disease risk. If the donor is not living or able to participate in the interview, the interview must take place with an individual or individuals who are able to provide the information sought in the interview. * * * Examples of these individuals who could possibly provide the appropriate information include the donor's next-of-kin, the nearest available relative, a member of the donor's household, an individual with an affinity relationship, or the primary treating physician. * * *

[T]his final rule may have an effect on the ability of medical examiners and coroners to recover corneas under State legislative consent laws. But, given the known transmission by corneas of HBV and CJD, and the potential for corneas to transmit other communicable diseases, including

TSE, we have concluded that making an exception from the requirement for a donor medical history interview in the case of corneas obtained under legislative consent is not justified. We disagree with the comment that urged us to interpret the definition to include an interview with the medical examiner or pathologist who performs the autopsy. Although the medical examiner or pathologist will have useful clinical information that should bear on the donor-eligibility determination, it is unlikely that this person will know the donor well enough to answer questions about his or her medical history, travel history, and/or social behavior. * * *

Some comments disagreed with considering homosexual men to be "high risk donors" and disputed the scientific basis for excluding these men as donors. Many comments cited the efficacy of the blood test for HIV, with retesting after a 6–month quarantine, although one comment noted that HIV antibody testing is imperfect. * * * Other comments asserted that the regulations would abridge the reproductive, civil, or constitutional rights of both donor and recipient * * * *

Although it is reasonable to expect that more sensitive nucleic acid amplification testing (NAT) will be available soon for reproductive tissue donors, even that testing may fail to detect early stage HIV and other infections, particularly because the level of viremia may be extremely low in the early stages of infection. Moreover, even the best test may fail to provide an accurate test result due to human error in running the test or in linking the test result to the correct donor. Accordingly, FDA believes that, based on the current state of testing and current knowledge about disease transmission, it is necessary to screen for risk factors as well as to test for diseases such as HIV. * * * [T]his final rule does not specify risk factors. Risk factors and other information about screening are contained in the donor-eligibility draft guidance announced elsewhere in this *Federal Register*. * * *

We have reviewed relevant legal authorities and disagree that these regulations discriminate or improperly abridge donor or recipient rights. We further note that, since FDA has tailored the rule's requirements to take into account an existing relationship between a donor and recipient (for example, FDA has not required quarantine and retesting for directed reproductive donors, permits the use of reproductive tissue from ineligible directed reproductive donors, and requires no testing for sexually intimate partners), the comments' remaining objections relate almost exclusively to anonymous donations of reproductive tissue. We will continue to examine the data on risk factors and, as new data are developed that justify changes to our guidance, we will make those changes * * * *

The final rule requires screening for "communicable disease risks associated with xenotransplantation." The donor-eligibility draft guidance that accompanies this final rule describes those risks. Because, at this time, so few xenotransplantations have been performed, and much is unknown about the actual risks of xenotransplantation, the risks for which you must screen may be potential or hypothetical risks. We currently consider both the xenotransplantation product recipient and the intimate contact of a xenotransplantation product recipient to be at risk for acquiring zoonoses, and, as in the proposed rule, these individuals would be ineligible to donate HCT/Ps. * * * Given the potential risks associated with the spread of diseases from live animal cells, tissues, and organs, we believe that the most prudent course at this time is to defer intimate contacts * * * *

[E]xpansion of blood donor screening and improved laboratory testing has dramatically reduced the risk of blood transfusion-transmitted disease. The risk of HIV infection has dropped from a reported 1 in 100 units in some U.S. cities to approximately 1 in 1,930,000 units. The risk of transmission of HBV has been reduced from 1 in 2,100 to 1 in 137,000 units, and the transmission risk for HCV has been lowered from 1 in 200 units in the early 1980s to the current level of 1 in 1,000,000 units. The levels of risk reduction associated with blood donation offer an illustration of the kind of improvements in safety that might be achieved through improved and expanded screening and testing of HCT/P donors. * * *

[M]ost nonreproductive tissue establishments are assumed to be already compliant with this final rule and, therefore, have already achieved much of the potential risk reduction. However, some reduction in communicable disease transmission risk may still be realized under this final rule for firms that are not currently in compliance with the voluntary standards established by their respective professional associations. * * *

FDA, Final Rule, *Current Good Tissue Practice for Human Cell, Tissue, and Cellular and Tissue–Based Product Establishments; Inspection and Enforcement*

69 Fed. Reg. 68,612 (2004).

* * * This rule represents the culmination of FDA's efforts to establish a comprehensive new system for regulating HCT/Ps. The regulations now being issued require certain HCT/Ps to be manufactured in compliance with CGTP [current good tissue practice]. The rule also contains provisions relating to establishment inspection and enforcement, as well as certain labeling and reporting requirements, which are applicable to those HCT/Ps regulated solely under the authority of section 361 of the PHS Act (42 U.S.C. § 264) and the regulations in part 1271 (21 C.F.R.), and not as drugs, devices, and/or biological products under the [FDCA]. * * *

FDA is issuing these new regulations under the authority of section 361 of the PHS Act. Under that section, * * * FDA may make and enforce regulations necessary to prevent the introduction, transmission, or spread of communicable diseases between the States or from foreign countries into the States. It is important to recognize that HCT/P manufacturing inevitably has interstate effects. HCT/Ps recovered in one State may be sent to another for processing, then shipped for use throughout the United States, or beyond. FDA has been involved in many recalls where HCT/Ps processed in a single establishment have been distributed in many States. In any event, intrastate transactions affecting interstate communicable disease transmission may also be regulated under section 361 of the PHS Act. * * *

[D]onor screening and testing, although crucial, are not sufficient to prevent the transmission of disease by HCT/Ps. Rather, each step in the manufacturing process needs to be appropriately controlled. Errors in labeling, mixups of testing records, failure to adequately clean work areas, and faulty packaging are examples of improper practices that could produce a product capable of transmitting disease to its recipient. Similarly, as noted in the proposed approach document, improper handling of an HCT/P can lead to bacterial or other pathogenic contamination of the HCT/P, or to cross-contamination between HCT/Ps, which in turn can endanger recipients. * * *

The record requirements of this rule are similarly necessary. A single donor may be the source of a large number of HCT/Ps. It may be discovered, long after the donation and transplantations have been completed, that, due to an error in processing, the donor tissue was infected and capable of spreading communicable disease. Although it might be too late to prevent infections in the recipients, it would not be too late for the recipient to obtain treatment and take steps to avoid infecting others, such as close family members. Unless adequate records were maintained, and maintained for the period of time throughout which infections may be identified, it would be impossible to identify the recipients potentially infected by the donor's HCT/Ps. This would be a critical breakdown in the prevention of disease transmission.

Moreover, a single processing error, such as an improper practice that permitted bacterial contamination of all tissue processed at a location during a limited period of time, may also have wide ranging effects. Without reporting and study of adverse events involving the transmission of communicable disease, or involving the release of HCT/Ps presenting an increased risk of such transmission, common causes of seemingly isolated incidents would never come to light. Affected HCT/Ps would continue to place patients at risk of communicable disease. Accordingly, FDA has also determined that HCT/P tracking, maintenance and retention of records, and reporting of adverse reactions and HCT/P deviations are necessary to prevent the transmission of communicable disease through HCT/Ps.

The CGTP regulations govern the methods used in, and the facilities and controls used for, the manufacture of HCT/Ps. CGTP requirements are a fundamental component of FDA's risk-based approach to regulating HCT/Ps. * * * The CGTP regulations supplement the current good manufacturing practice (CGMP) and quality system (QS) regulations applicable to drugs, devices, and biological products * * * *

In drafting this rule, we have re-evaluated each requirement of the proposed rule to ensure that it either directly prevents the introduction, transmission, or spread of communicable diseases (e.g., the requirement to store HCT/Ps at an appropriate temperature), or that it supports such a requirement (e.g., the requirement to periodically review recorded temperatures to ensure that the temperatures have been within acceptable limits).

We have removed requirements where the connection to the prevention of the introduction, transmission, or spread of communicable diseases may be more attenuated. * * * [A]t this time, we are issuing a more limited set of requirements than proposed. These requirements represent minimum expectations, but an establishment may decide to do more than this minimum. * * *

A 2002 Morbidity and Mortality Weekly Report (MMWR) discusses 26 cases of bacterial infection associated with musculoskeletal allografts and reinforces the importance of following CGTP to prevent the contamination of HCT/Ps with such communicable disease agents. In the MMWR, the Centers for Disease Control and Prevention (CDC) make several significant recommendations on preventing bacterial contamination. Among other things, the CDC states that "[s]terilization of tissue that does not adversely affect the functioning of tissue when transplanted into patients is the best way to reduce the risk for allograft-associated infections." Throughout this final rule, we discuss the CDC's recommendations and note the applicability of specific provisions of the final rule to the prevention of bacterial contamination. * * *

[Several] comments opposed our proposal to prohibit the pooling of cells or tissues. Several comments argued that the proposed regulation is too restrictive and could stifle new technologies. Although we are aware of promising new technologies that involve the pooling of cells from two or more donors, we remain concerned about the infectious disease risks inherent in pooling. * * * Screening and testing of donors, although crucial, does not completely eliminate infectious disease risk, for several reasons. The donor may be in the "window period" during which he or she may be infectious (i.e., have viral marker levels that are below detection by current tests). Chronic carriers of a disease may be immuno-silent; i.e., they do not mount an antibody response. In addition, laboratory errors may be made, or an HCT/P may be released improperly. Moreover, current tests may not detect all genetic variants of a particular virus, or a donor may be infected with an "emerging infectious disease," for which screening measures or tests have not been developed. Finally, there may be questions about the accuracy of current tests that are not approved by FDA for use with cadaveric specimens and about the reliability of donor histories obtained from another person (not the donor). Each of these risks is small, and presents a small chance of leading to communicable disease transmission to a single HCT/P recipient. However, the risk is magnified when HCT/Ps from different donors are pooled during manufacture. * * *

For some biological products, e.g., plasma derivatives, the benefits of pooling outweigh the risks. In the case of plasma derivatives, pooling contributes to product consistency. In fact, 21 C.F.R. § 640.102(d) requires that material from not less than 1,000 donors be pooled to make immune globulin. For plasma derivatives, it is necessary to pool plasma from many donors to obtain an adequate amount of product to treat one recipient (i.e., a sufficient dose). In addition, pooling plasma may dilute the viral burden or provide neutralizing antibodies that may inactivate any virus present in the pool. However, these benefits of pooling do not apply, in general, to the pooling of HCT/Ps from many donors. For instance, tendons from different donors would not need to be pooled to provide consistency or to obtain a sufficient dose. Neither would bones pooled from different donors provide neutralizing antibodies to inactivate any virus present in the pool, since neutralizing antibodies are present in plasma. * * *

The HCT/P industry is currently growing and evolving rapidly. Since the CGTP proposed rule was published in January 2001, there have been significant increases in both the number of tissue donors and manufacturing establishments, as well as the number of HCT/Ps processed, distributed, and transplanted. * * * The agency is aware of numerous reports of adverse health events and several patient deaths that have been linked to HCT/Ps. Transplantation of tissue has resulted in transmission of viral, bacterial, fungal, and other diseases, although such instances are rare. Some of these adverse events have been associated with HCT/Ps produced by large entities that do not follow voluntary industry standards and are not accredited by their respective professional associations. * * *

Problems due to inadequate product processing and quality controls, contributing to post-operative infection and/or graft failure, are one category of the many potential causes of the reported adverse health events associated with HCT/Ps. Implementation of the CGTP final rule, by establishing an enforceable set of product quality assurance procedures and standards, is expected to reduce the risk of communicable disease transmission as well as the incidence of other types of adverse health events associated with HCT/Ps. * * * [T]he limited information presented in this analysis of impacts is not likely representative of the true risks associated with HCT/Ps, because no mandatory adverse event reporting requirements exist, the information that is available is reported voluntarily and, in some sectors of the tissue industry, the necessary information is not available because it is not collected by any source. * * *

Although voluntary industry standards exist for most of the affected products, FDA finds that public safety cannot be assured or effectively protected through reliance on these informal mechanisms. The existing industry standards also vary to some extent in their comprehensiveness, and there are variations in the extent to which firms in the affected industry sectors follow these voluntary standards. * * * A regulatory requirement for quality systems and recordkeeping would provide the incentives needed to bring marginal establishments to a more uniform and appropriately high standard of quality in HCT/P processing. * * *

Recent clinical literature indicates that each type of HCT/P affected by the CGTP final rule has documented communicable disease transmission risk that may be the result of contamination or other problems resulting from processing, or other steps in manufacturing. Although the limited number of adverse events reported in the clinical literature suggests a relatively low risk of communicable disease transmission associated with HCT/Ps, it is important to note that this evidence is generally based on analysis of a limited number of voluntarily reported incidents. * * *

In some cases involving eye tissue, conventional tissue, or hematopoietic stem/progenitor cell products, HCT/P problems have required medical intervention to treat infection, or to replace an implanted HCT/P. In some clinical applications, HCT/P related problems have increased the risk of patient morbidity or mortality. * * * Conventional tissue refers to a wide range of HCT/Ps including pericardium, dura mater, heart valves, skin allograft, bone allograft, fascia, tendons, and ligaments. FDA's survey of the clinical literature indicates that bone, skin and heart valve allografts each present a different potential for communicable disease transmission risk and graft failure, and thus different levels of potential benefits from improved processing procedures and quality assurance steps in HCT/P manufacture. * * *

NOTES AND QUESTIONS

1. *Types of tissue products*. How would the following products fit into the FDA's approach to tissue regulation: pulverized and purified human bone mixed with an inactive liquid base and delivered in pre-filled syringes; human bone sculpted into the shape of a screw for use in joint repair surgery; stem cells harvested from human fat tissue to treat anemia in an unrelated donor; a human kidney grown from genetically manipulated stem cells on a biologically-based matrix?

2. *Cascading responsibility for compliance with CGTPs*. In some cases, one establishment might make a donor-suitability determination, a second might recover tissue from a cadaver, a third might process the tissue, and a fourth might finally distribute that tissue. The FDA considered several mechanisms for allocating responsibility among the various establishments involved in the production of HCT/Ps and tried to balance issues of flexibility with concerns about product safety. The agency decided to assign ultimate responsibility to the establishment that distributes the finished product. See 69 Fed. Reg. at 68,623–24 (obligating the distributor to review and maintain the relevant records for each of the previous steps); see also Tissue for Transplant Is Recalled After FDA Shuts Down N.C. Firm, Wash. Post, Aug. 23, 2006, at A5. Is it reasonable for the FDA to expect the final link in the chain of distribution to assume the primary responsibility for compliance with good tissue practice requirements when multiple establishments may have been involved?

3. *Reproductive tissues*. Until 1998, the FDA had not asserted regulatory jurisdiction over in vitro fertilization (IVF) or other fertility treatments. Indeed, agency officials previously testified before Congress that it had no such authority. See Henry T. Greely, Banning "Human Cloning": A Study in the Difficulties of Defining Science, 8 S. Cal. Interdisc. L.J. 131, 151 (1998). The Fertility Clinic Success Rate and Certification Act of 1992, 42 U.S.C. § 263a–1, suggested no role for the FDA; instead, Congress directed the CDC to collect information and to develop a model program (for states to implement) to inspect laboratories that work with human embryos. In its proposed CGTP rule, the FDA announced that the requirements would apply to sperm banks and assisted reproductive technology (ART) facilities. See 66 Fed. Reg. 1508, 1525, 1542–43 (2001). After it published this proposal, the agency sent warning letters to several fertility clinics ordering them to cease performing fertility procedures that entail any kind of alteration of human genetic material, including cloning, genetic engineering and "ooplasmic transfer." This last technique involves the transfer of genetic material from one woman's egg into another's, typically to aid an older women in achieving pregnancy. See Rick Weiss, FDA to Regulate Certain Fertilization Procedures, Wash. Post, July 11, 2001, at A2 (reporting that the FDA now requires physicians performing experimental fertility procedures to file an IND); see also Lars Noah, Assisted Reproductive Technologies and the Pitfalls of Unregulated Biomedical Innovation, 55 Fla. L. Rev. 603, 648–52 (2003); Dorothy E. Roberts, Privatization and Punishment in the New Age of Reprogenetics, 54 Emory L.J. 1343 (2005); Symposium, Assisted Reproduction Technology, 39 Fam. L.Q. 573 (2005); Rick Weiss, Greater Regulation of Fertility Encouraged: Bioethics Council Seeking Changes, Wash. Post, Apr. 2, 2004, at A8. In its final CGTP rule, the FDA left for another day the question of its applicability to ART facilities. See 69 Fed. Reg. at 68,612; id. at 68,653 ("ART establishments and semen banks are subject only to the inspection and enforcement provisions of the CGTP final rule as they apply to donor eligibility requirements ...."). The agency subsequently amended its final donor screening and labeling rules to cover cryopreserved embryos later donated to someone else. See 70 Fed. Reg. 29,949, 29,950–51, 29,952 (2005) (codified at 21 C.F.R. § 1271.90); see also Shari Roan, On the Cusp of Life, and of Law: Half a Million Embryos Sit in Clinic Freezers in the U.S., L.A. Times, Oct. 6, 2008, at A1 (reporting increased state efforts to regulate the disposition of unused embryos).

4. *Donor screening*. The FDA's decision to treat gay men as ineligible donors because of concerns about heightened HIV risks continued to attract criticism after publication of the final rule. See Marc Kaufman, Gay Groups Assail Sperm Bank Rule, Wash. Post, May 7, 2005, at A2; cf. Rob Stein, FDA to Review Ban on Gay Men Donating Blood, Wash. Post, Mar. 18, 2006, at A6 (noting that "the accuracy of testing has improved substantially" since the mid–1980s); cf. Stefanie Shulman–Cutler, Comment, The AABB's Autologous Blood Suggested Guidance: Autologous Blood, HIV, and the Americans with Disabilities Act, 46 Jurimetrics J. 407 (2006). Did the agency's preamble persuasively respond to these sorts of objections? For earlier critiques of the lack of federal supervision over sperm banks, see Karen M. Ginsberg, Note, FDA Approved? A Critique of the Artificial Insemination Industry in the United States, 30 U. Mich. J.L. Reform 823 (1997); Kathleen M. Peterson, Comment, Federal Regulation of Artificial Insemination Donor Screening Practices: An Opportunity for Law to Co–Evolve with Medicine, 96 Dick. L. Rev. 59 (1991). In the case of reproductive tissues, should donors also get screened for potential genetic diseases? See Yaniv Heled, The Regulation of Genetic Aspects of Donated Reproductive Tissue—The Need for Federal Regulation, 11 Colum. Sci. & Tech. L. Rev. 243 (2010); Denise Grady, Sperm Donor Seen as Source of Disease in

Five Children, N.Y. Times, May 19, 2006, at A16 (reporting that "sperm donors are routinely tested for most common genetic diseases, like cystic fibrosis and sickle cell anemia, but not for extremely rare ones like severe congenital neutropenia"). More generally, are these matters better left to tort litigation? See Stiver v. Parker, 975 F.2d 261, 268–72 (6th Cir.1992) (concluding that an attorney who acted as a surrogacy broker owed the surrogate mother a heightened duty of care to ensure full testing of the sperm donor for sexually transmitted diseases); Donovan v. Idant Labs., 625 F.Supp.2d 256, 273–76 (E.D.Pa.2009) (holding that strict products liability applied to a sperm bank accused of failing to screen donors for Fragile X mutation, but dismissing the child's claim as an impermissible effort to collect damages for wrongful life), aff'd mem., 374 F.App'x 319, 324 (3d Cir.2010); Johnson v. Superior Ct., 95 Cal.Rptr.2d 864 (Ct.App. 2000) (resolving a discovery dispute in tort litigation against a clinic for using sperm from a donor with a family history of serious kidney disease); Suriya E. P. Jayanti, Comment, Guarantors of Our Genes: Are Egg Donors Liable for Latent Genetic Disease?, 58 Am. U. L. Rev. 405 (2008); Jennifer M. Vagle, Comment, Putting the "Product" in Reproduction: The Viability of a Products Liability Action for Genetically Defective Sperm, 38 Pepp. L. Rev. 1175 (2011).

5. *Solid organs*. The FDA does not regulate solid human organs. See 21 C.F.R. § 1271.3(d)(1) (excluding "vascularized human organs for transplantation" from the definition of HCT/Ps). The Health Resources and Services Administration (HRSA) of HHS provides the primary federal oversight and funding support for the nation's organ procurement and allocation system. Under the National Organ Transplant Act (NOTA), HHS exercises most of the regulatory control over solid organs for transplantation. It has contracted with the United Network for Organ Sharing (UNOS) to run the federal Organ Procurement Transplant Network (OPTN). See 42 U.S.C. § 274. Although UNOS is a private nonprofit organization, it creates policies for the OPTN, and, under NOTA, all transplant centers and organ procurement organizations must comply with UNOS policies and rules. See id. § 1320b–8(a); see also Charles Ornstein & Tracy Weber, Transplant Monitor Lax in Oversight, L.A. Times, Oct. 22, 2006, at A1.

6. *What's a body worth?* Although federal law forbids the sale of tissues or organs, it allows harvesters to recover the "reasonable costs" associated with collecting human tissues. Tissue banks and processing companies currently avoid the statutory prohibition on sale by charging fees that ostensibly cover the costs of processing and handling the harvested tissue. Many of these fees appear inflated in light of the actual amount of processing involved. Tendons that are cut from cadavers in minutes are resold to sports medicine surgeons for reconstructive surgery at $2,500 each, and valves recovered from donated hearts sell for approximately $7,000. See Stephen J. Hedges & William Gaines, Donor Bodies Milled into Growing Profits: Little–Regulated Industry Thrives on Unsuspecting Families, Chi. Trib., May 21, 2000, at 1; see also Stephanie Armour, Illegal Trade in Bodies Shakes Loved Ones, USA Today, Apr. 27, 2006, at 1A; William Sherman, Shocking Details as Probe into Theft of Corpse Parts

Expands: Body Count Near 1,000, N.Y. Daily News, Oct. 8, 2005, at 7 (reporting that "the full retail price of dissected corpse parts exceeds $100,000"). See generally Traci McKee, Note, Resurrecting the Rights of the Unclaimed Dead: A Case for Regulating the New Phenomenon of Cadaver Trafficking, 36 Stetson L. Rev. 843 (2007). More seriously, safety concerns may arise when unscrupulous brokers procure potentially contaminated tissue. See Michael Powell & David Segal, In New York, a Grisly Traffic in Body Parts: Illegal Sales Worry Dead's Kin, Tissue Recipients, Wash. Post, Jan. 28, 2006, at A3.

7. *Further commentary*. See Jonathan Kahn, Biotechnology and the Legal Constitution of the Self: Managing Identity in Science, the Market, and Society, 51 Hastings L.J. 909 (2000); Russell Korobkin, Buying and Selling Human Tissues for Stem Cell Research, 49 Ariz. L. Rev. 45 (2007); Julia D. Mahoney, The Market for Human Tissue, 86 Va. L. Rev. 163 (2000); John J. Zodrow, The Commodification of Human Body Parts: Regulating the Tissue Bank Industry, 32 Sw. U. L. Rev. 407 (2003); Laura A. Buck, Comment, Regulating Human Tissue Banks, 20 St. Thomas L. Rev. 121 (2007); Matthew W. Coryell, Note, Patent Law as an Incentive to Innovate Not Donate: The Role of the U.S. Patent System in Regulating Ownership of Human Tissue, 36 J. Corp. L. 449 (2011); Lisa C. Edwards, Note, Tissue Tug-of-War: A Comparison of International and U.S. Perspectives on the Regulation of Human Tissue Banks, 41 Vand. J. Transnat'l L. 639 (2008); Michael Leachman, Comment, Regulation of the Human Tissue Industry: A Call for Fast-Track Regulations, 65 La. L. Rev. 443 (2004); Symposium, Precious Commodities: The Supply and Demand of Body Parts, 55 DePaul L. Rev. 793 (2006).

1. Tissue Engineering and Stem Cells

Laurel R. Siegel, Comment, *Re–Engineering the Laws of Organ Transplantation*

49 Emory L.J. 917 (2000).

* * * Researchers have developed new methods of organ production to better combat the supply and rejection problems: tissue engineering. Eventually, these techniques may allow scientists to have access to an unlimited supply of organs. Today, scientists use novel technologies to combine the concepts of biotechnology, molecular and cell biology, materials science, and engineering to better understand the relationship among tissues and to create alternatives for the repair and reconstruction of tissues and organs. The new organs are initially comprised of cells growing and maintaining structure and support on a scaffolding device. To provide scaffolding support, bioartificial organs consist of a biological component: cells or tissues, as well as a biomaterial scaffolding component made of a natural or synthetic material. Allowing the growth of the original tissue without remnants of foreign biomaterials is the primary challenge to this technology. The concept of seeding the patient's own cells onto the scaffolds to

control their proliferation forms the basis of tissue engineering. After a period of weeks or months, synthesis of the new tissue replaces the scaffold.

Scientists work with two kinds of cells in tissue engineering: human adult cells and embryonic stem cells ("ES cells"). * * * [W]ith human adult cells, [i]t is theoretically possible to expand, for example, a urothelial strain from a single specimen covering 1 cm squared to a surface area greater than 4000 m squared within eight weeks. One group of physicians has expanded urothelial and muscle cells in vitro (in a petri dish), seeded them onto a matrix, and allowed them to attach to form sheets of cells, before implanting them in vivo (in a living organism). Cell matrices implanted with human bladder muscle cells showed nearly complete replacement of the matrix with sheets of smooth muscle within fifty days, marking the first time composite tissue-engineered structures had been newly created. * * *

Scientists are currently revolutionizing biology with work involving embryonic stem cells. A stem cell is a cell which has not yet differentiated into a specialized cell, such as hair, blood, organ, tissue, or bone. An ES cell, derived from a blastocyst, can be maintained in an undifferentiated state indefinitely and can develop into any of 210 types of cells under certain conditions. When removed from such conditions, the ES cells spontaneously differentiate to form embryoid bodies that contain elements of all germ layers: ectoderm, mesoderm, and endoderm. November 1998 marked the first successful culture of pluripotent [meaning capable of producing multiple different kinds of specialized cells] human stem cells, but it is unknown whether the cells are totipotent [meaning capable of producing every kind of human cell]. Many scientists believe the ability to program the development of cells that could be transplanted into humans will not occur for at least ten years, and even longer before stem cells can be coaxed into creating complex organs such as kidneys or livers.

Each ES cell line contains the genome of a specific individual and can essentially reprogram an adult cell to become an ES cell through at least three principal methods. First, "therapeutic cloning" involves replacing the genetic material of the human egg with the nucleus of the adult cell and cultivating it in vitro until the ES cell-producing blastocyst stage. The ethical objection to this approach lies in the concept of creating a potential human being and then halting its development. A second method entails using any mammalian egg as the recipient of the nucleic material. Scientists first did this in November 1998, using a cow egg as the host for the human genetic material. This approach poses ethical problems of combining human and animal tissue. A third approach entails reprogramming the nuclei of adult cells using ES cell cytoplasm.

Theoretically, embryoid bodies could provide an unlimited supply of specific cell types for transplantation. Researchers must overcome certain obstacles before conducting clinical experiments with human cells. First, donor/recipient compatibility must be researched; possible solutions entail banking cell lines or creating cells genetically identical to the patient's cells by utilizing cloning techniques. Second, scientists need to more clearly understand cell differentiation in culture and whether genetic mutations are introduced during differentiation. Scientists have not yet been able to direct development of embryonic stem cells into specific, differentiated cell types. They are learning, however, to control the differentiation of stem-cell populations into desired cell types, such as cartilage, bone, or liver.

Turning human ES cells into replacement tissues and organs for transplantation without rejection is the ultimate goal. Additionally, researchers hope to manipulate a patient's own cells in culture to replace damaged tissues and avoid the ethical and legal issues of using human embryonic stem cells or creating cells. An alternative involves generating "universal donors" of several cell lines so that everybody could find a match. Existing organs, whether human or otherwise, could potentially be used as scaffolding. * * *

NOTES AND QUESTIONS

1. *Tissue engineering.* The scarcity of human organs and tissues for transplant has encouraged researchers to search for alternatives to improve the supply. "Regenerative medicine" involves using human proteins and cells, rather than foreign substances or objects, to repair injured body parts and cure illnesses, and it may combine stem cell research with genetic manipulation techniques. See Terence Chea, Regenerating Approaches in Medicine, Wash. Post, Dec. 4, 2000, at E5. Researchers have grown skin, blood vessels, bone, cartilage and other living cells on synthetic "scaffolding" comprised of substances such as coral and porous ceramic. See Thomas H. Petersen et al., Tissue–Engineered Lungs for in Vivo Implantation, 329 Science 538, 541 (2010) (noting that other researchers had reported a successful human airway transplant using decellularized tracheal matrix reseeded with the patient's own epithelial cells); Elizabeth Agnvall, Joint Initiatives: Surgeons Race to Find Better Ways to Replace Damaged Knee Cartilage, Wash. Post, Dec. 4, 2007, at F1 (discussing Genzyme's autologous chondrocyte implantation process (Carticel®), which starts by harvesting a few cells from a patient's injured knee to grow millions of new cells in the lab and costs $35,000); Anne Eisenberg, Replacement Bones, Grown to Order in the Lab, N.Y. Times, Mar. 28, 2010, at BU5 ("Engineered bones are being tested in animals and in a few people, and may be common in operating rooms within a decade ...."). Some researchers have focused on an entirely different mechanism for regeneration—based on findings that, in certain animals, a cluster of mature cells can revert to an immature state (called a "blastema") and regrow an organ or limb, they have suggested that, even though humans display such a regenerative powers only in the liver, it might be possible to trigger this capacity in other organs because the genome retains the necessary instructions. See Nicholas Wade, Regrow Your Own, N.Y. Times, Apr. 11, 2006, at F1; Ron Winslow, Matrix Reloaded: Doctors Try New Techniques to Regrow Human Tissue, Wall St. J., Feb. 12, 2007, at A1.

Several challenges still exist for tissue engineering in reconstructive surgery. Techniques for isolating and culturing cells need to be refined, and researchers continue to experiment with different growth factors. In addition, the cultured cells must proliferate continuously until enough tissue has been generated to accomplish the intended goal. Because cells cultured from a biopsied specimen cease reproducing after a time, scientists have experimented with autologous pluripotent stem cells harvested from bone marrow and, more recently, fat tissue. See Bruce Japsen, Market for Adult Stem Cells Multiplies: Progress Made, Sales Rising Away from Political Spotlight, Chi. Trib., Mar. 16, 2008, at C1. Finding appropriate scaffolding poses another scientific challenge; many materials work well initially but eventually break down, interfering with cell proliferation. These sorts of difficulties are magnified for more complex tissue generation attempts, such as the creation of muscle cells, nerve cells, and multi-tissue solid organs. See Vincent R. Hentz & James Chang, Tissue Engineering for Reconstruction of the Thumb, 344 New Eng. J. Med. 1547 (2001); see also Maria Cheng, Doctors Create Urethras with Patients' Own Cells for First Time: "Layer Cake" Process Used for Implants, Boston Globe, Mar. 9, 2011, at A4; Rick Weiss, First Bladders Grown in Lab Transplanted: Breakthrough Shows Promise for Creating Other Human Organs, Wash. Post, Apr. 4, 2006, at A1 (reporting that researchers took muscle and urothelium cells from the malfunctioning bladders of young patients, grew these in separate dishes for one week, seeded the cells onto a synthetic polymer and collagen scaffold, incubated the structure for a couple of months while the cells colonized it, and then implanted the "neo-bladders," which continued to grow and reconfigure in the patients); cf. Lawrence K. Altman, Team Creates Rat Heart Using Cells of Baby Rats, N.Y. Times, Jan. 14, 2008, at A12.

One possible technique employs three-dimensional "printers" to stack layers of different types of cells in precise patterns to replicate human tissues. See Bonnie Berkowitz, Living Body Parts, Hot off the Printer, Wash. Post, May 10, 2011, at E1 ("Bioprinting technology is years and possibly decades from producing such complex organs [as livers or kidneys], but scientists have already printed skin and vertebral disks . . . [which] could be ready for human trials in two to five years. . . . [M]aking such things as vertebral disks and knee cartilage, which largely just cushion bones, is far easier than constructing a complicated organ that filters waste, pumps blood or otherwise keeps a body alive. Scientists say the biggest technical challenge is not making the organ itself, but replicating its intricate internal network of blood vessels . . . ."); see also id. ("Once scientists get over the financial and technical hurdles of bioprinting, they will have to square the process with the [FDA], which will have to decide how to regulate something that is not simply a device, a biological product or a drug, but potentially all three.").

2. *Therapeutic use of stem cells.* Stem cell therapies also remain many years away. See Howard A. Chapman, Editorial, Toward Lung Regeneration, 364 New Eng. J. Med. 1867 (2011); Andrew Pollack, After Stem–Cell Breakthrough, the Real Work Begins, N.Y. Times, Nov. 27, 2007, at F1;

Nicholas Wade, Some Scientists See Shift in Stem Cell Hopes, N.Y. Times, Aug. 14, 2006, at A18. Although further along than work with embryonic stem cells, clinical trials of adult stem cell therapies have not panned out so far. See Andrew Pollack, First Stem Cell Drug Fails 2 Late–Stage Clinical Trials, N.Y. Times, Sept. 9, 2009, at B4 (reporting poor results with Osiris Therapeutics' Prochymal—a preparation of mesenchymal stem cells obtained from the bone marrow of healthy adults—in a pair of trials to treat graft-versus-host disease, adding that the company had abandoned another trial of the drug in Crohn's disease); see also Rob Waters, Gene Experiment May Offer Hope for Those with Cardiac Failure, Boston Globe, Aug. 6, 2010, at A11 (describing efforts to convert fibroblasts into heart muscle, which transplants of adult stem cell have failed to accomplish so far). Phase I trials using cells derived from embryonic stem cells have just begun. See Jill U. Adams, Stem Cell Trial Sets Sight on Blindness: The FDA Has OKd a New Study Aimed at Fighting Age-related Macular Degeneration, L.A. Times, Jan. 10, 2011, at E3; Rob Stein, Human Tests Set for Stem Cells, Wash. Post, Aug. 30, 2010, at A1 (explaining that, after numerous delays, the FDA cleared Geron's study in subjects with spinal cord injuries). Questions about the source (as opposed to the potential therapeutic uses) of human embryonic stem cells receive more sustained attention in the last part of this chapter.

3. *The FDA's regulatory authority over stem cell treatments*. The FDA asserts that stem cells fall within its regulatory authority under the PHS Act or over biological drugs and devices, depending on the scientific or medical context in which the cells are used. See Jason Blevins, Stem–Cell Scuffle, Denv. Post, Aug. 20, 2010, at B1 (reporting that Regenerative Sciences questioned the agency's assertion of jurisdiction after it sought to enjoin the pain clinic's autologous transplantation of cultured bone marrow cells into patients' joints); Antonio Regalado, FDA Holds up Hospital's Work with Stem Cells, Wall St. J., June 12, 2003, at B1; see also Steve Sternberg, Underground Market for Stem Cells Is a Concern, USA Today, June 1, 2011, at 3A (reporting that patients sometimes go overseas or receive treatments in this country from physicians who claim that the FDA has no regulatory jurisdiction over their practice of medicine). When desperate patients venture abroad in search of stem cell therapies, officials can do little other than warn of the dangers associated with unproven treatments. See Ariana E. Cha, On the Frontiers of Stem Cell Treatment: With Therapies Limited in the United States, Other Countries Offer the Ailing New Hope—and Risks, Wash. Post, June 6, 2010, at A12; Brian Vastag, Injections of Hope: Doctors Promote Offshore Stem Cell Shots, but Some Patients Cry Foul, Wash. Post, Sept. 2, 2008, at F1.

4. *Umbilical cord blood*. Stem cells from umbilical cord blood are used as an alternative to bone marrow transplantation to treat children and adults with blood disorders or blood cancers. When these patients receive chemotherapies that destroy their blood cell producing bone marrow, antigen-matched cord blood transplants can restore blood cell production. See Mary J. Laughlin et al., Hematopoietic Engraftment and Survival in Adult Recipients of Umbilical–Cord Blood from Unrelated Donors, 344 New Eng.

J. Med. 1815 (2001) (concluding that cord blood is more effective than bone marrow at regenerating blood cells, with a lower incidence of graft-versus-host disease, so long as it comes from a donor with identical human leukocyte antigens); see also Kimberly J. Cogdell, Saving the Leftovers: Models for Banking Cord Blood Stem Cells, 39 U. Mem. L. Rev. 229 (2009); Jennifer Kulynych, Blood as Biological "Drug": Scientific, Legal, and Policy Issues in the Regulation of Placental and Umbilical Cord Stem Cell Transplantation, 32 U. Rich. L. Rev. 407 (1998); David A. Suski, Note, Frozen Blood, Neonates, and FDA: The Regulation of Placental–Umbilical Cord Blood, 84 Va. L. Rev. 715 (1998); Reed Abelson, Group Urges Program to Promote Use of Umbilical Cord Blood, N.Y. Times, Apr. 15, 2005, at A12 (describing recommendations issued by the Institute of Medicine); Sandra G. Boodman, Study Questions Value of Private Cord–Blood Banks, Wash. Post, Apr. 14, 2009, at F6; Andrew Pollack, Questioning the Allure of Putting Cells in the Bank, N.Y. Times, Jan. 29, 2008, at F1 (contrasting other approaches such as storing pulp from baby teeth).

2. CLONING FOR THERAPEUTIC AND REPRODUCTIVE PURPOSES

Gregory J. Rokosz, *Human Cloning: Is the Reach of FDA Authority Too Far a Stretch?*

30 SETON HALL L. REV. 464 (2000).

* * * The term "cloning" has been used differently in various research settings. A strict scientific definition of cloning, however, describes the process of producing a "precise genetic copy of a molecule, cell, plant, animal, or human being." * * * At the molecular level, cloning of deoxyribonucleic acid (DNA) fragments containing genes has been ongoing for several decades. The process of using bacteria to copy and amplify human DNA fragments and manufacture proteins coded from these fragments has been the foundation for recombinant DNA technology. This technology has led to the production of commercially available quantities of valuable medicines to treat human disease.

Culturing somatic (i.e., body) cells in a laboratory is another form of cloning that results in a cell line genetically identical to the original cell. This cellular cloning technique has been used to test and produce new medicines. In addition, primordial stem-cell therapy, based on cellular cloning techniques, has the potential to revolutionize health care. Clinical trials are already being conducted utilizing nonprimordial stem cells for therapeutic purposes such as cancer treatment.

Attempts to clone genetically identical animals are typically classified as one of two separate methodologies: blastomere separation, or embryo splitting, and nuclear transplantation techniques. Blastomere separation involves the splitting of an early embryo, allowing each split blastomere cell to develop into a separate organism. These cells, considered totipotent, are capable of producing multiple genetically identical organisms when split. This technique exhibits great potential in the area of cattle and livestock breeding. Since 1993, embryo splitting has also been successfully performed with human embryos.

Nuclear transplantation cloning is a more sophisticated cloning method and involves removing the haploid nucleus from an egg cell and replacing it with the diploid nucleus of a donor somatic cell. Early experiments using this technique in frogs, mice, cattle, and rhesus monkeys were successful when embryonic cells served as the donor cell. Dolly's birth, which resulted from the use of an adult cell nucleus donor, was astonishing proof that "cell differentiation and specialization are reversible" and that a fully differentiated adult cell nucleus could be reprogrammed to produce an entire, viable mammal.

It also seems possible to pair somatic cell nuclear transfer techniques with primordial stem-cell research to produce "customized" stem cells reflecting the DNA of a particular patient. A physician might want to generate primordial stem cells containing DNA identical to the recipient patient, thereby ensuring that the "therapy would be compatible with, and not be rejected by, the person for whom the therapy is created." To accomplish this, researchers would use somatic cell nuclear transfer technology to "reprogram somatic cell nuclei to generate more undifferentiated primordial stem cells for that patient."

There are many reasons to permit animal cloning research to continue. Cloning technologies may be used to produce groups of genetically identical animals for research purposes, thus eliminating genetic differences that often lead to experimental variation. Cloning research also has the potential to provide a means of expanding the number of livestock with desirable traits such as enhanced meat or milk production. The use of nuclear transfer technology is also apt to bring about major advances in the production of transgenic livestock, resulting in a wide array of medical benefits for humans. * * * [R]esearch on nuclear transfer cloning techniques used to generate targeted gene alterations in laboratory animals has proven invaluable in studying normal gene function and in developing accurate models of human genetic disease. It is also anticipated that ongoing animal cloning research will further scientific knowledge on cell differentiation. Finally, continued research on nuclear transfer procedures should find significant application in the field of assisted reproduction.

Despite the myriad potential benefits of nuclear transfer cloning research in animals, this technology is not without risks and safety concerns, especially when applied to humans. One concern is for the safety of a surviving clone. Due to the accumulation of genetic mutations throughout life, the older the organism, the greater the predisposition to cancer. Thus, a donor somatic cell used for cloning may contain the accumulated mutations acquired during years of cell division, which may possibly lead to a predisposition for cancer, premature aging, or immunological disease in the resulting clone. In addition, the possibility that some instability in genetic imprinting may exist, particularly in cultured cells, could limit the efficiency of somatic cell nuclear transfer. Researchers have learned "that disturbances in imprinting lead to growth abnormalities in mice and are associated with cancer and rare genetic conditions in children." Other safety concerns would apply to human egg donors, recipients of cloned embryos for gestation, and the nonsurviving cloned embryos. The fact that only 1 live birth resulted from 29 implanted embryos [in the sheep cloning experiment], which in themselves resulted from 277 cellular attempts at cloning, attests to the unresolved safety issues applicable to human cloning. * * *

The scientific community overwhelmingly believes that any legislative action should be limited to the cloning of human beings, should not include language that impedes important ongoing or potential new research, and should clearly recognize the distinction between the cloning of an entire human being and the healing potential that is derived from biomedical research. Scientific organizations generally do not support the cloning of human beings, but do oppose overly broad legislation that goes beyond this narrow issue and threatens biomedical research that is vital to the discovery of cures for deadly and debilitating diseases. * * * The current federal legislative stalemate over human cloning prohibitions exemplifies the virtually impossible task of devising statutory language acceptable to both the scientific community and the pro-life constituency. The biotechnology industry, believing that the FDA has clear authority over human cloning attempts, asserts that there is no need to enact legislation in this area. On the other hand, right-to-life organizations would likely prefer the issue to be debated publicly and resolved through the political process, which may allow these organizations to wield more influence.

In February 1998, the FDA, based on safety and efficacy concerns, announced that it had authority to regulate human cloning under its biologics regulations, which deal primarily with human gene therapy and techniques that involve the "material manipulation of human cells that are then reinserted for medical purposes." These regulations and their commentary do not discuss human reproduction, and the FDA had not previously claimed authority over other human reproductive technologies. On October 26, 1998, in a "Dear Colleague" letter issued by Associate Commissioner Stuart L. Nightingale, M.D., the FDA reaffirmed its authority under the PHSA and FFDCA to regulate clinical cloning research for the creation of human beings. According to Nightingale, any such attempts at human cloning would require submission of an IND application and IRB oversight. Support for FDA regulatory authority over human cloning is less certain outside of the scientific community. Serious questions remain regarding whether the FDA does indeed possess the requisite jurisdiction to regulate the practice of human cloning.

The FDA's assertion of jurisdiction over human cloning is sure to elicit various constitutional challenges, such as the violation of the freedom of scientific inquiry under the First Amendment and the violation of a couple's right of privacy or liberty interest in making procreative decisions. A further constitutional challenge to FDA authority over cloning might be based on a lack of authority under the Commerce Clause. * * * Human cloning clinics may well assert that their activities are conducted entirely intrastate and are therefore beyond the reach of FDA jurisdiction. * * *

The FDA includes within its definition of "human cellular and tissue-based products" a variety of "medical products derived from the human body and used for replacement, reproductive, or therapeutic purposes." For example, semen, ova, and embryos used for reproductive purposes fall within this definition. * * * If the proposed regulations are adopted and found to be an appropriate exercise of FDA authority, human cloning products may fall within the category of the rule requiring premarket approval of cellular or tissue-based products that are more than minimally manipulated. Notwithstanding this possibility, the more difficult question is whether such cellular and tissue-based products are sufficiently analogous to other biological products delineated in the statute such that the FDA regulations could survive a judicial challenge. Human embryos produced by cloning technology, however, do not seem to "fit" within the same scientific or medical category as viruses, toxins, antitoxins, vaccines, serums, allergenic products, or blood products.

The statutory background, legislative history, and resulting language of the FFDCA, the PHSA, and the Biologics Act clearly demonstrate that Congress neither contemplated the potential ramifications of human cloning procedures nor drafted the statutory language broadly enough to encompass such a radically new technology. Although embryos produced by cloning techniques and the other biologicals enumerated in the statute are all biologically based, there are significant differences between them. * * * It seems unlikely that a strict interpretation of the plain language of the statute itself would allow the FDA expansive jurisdiction to regulate human cloning, even though the FDA has been inching toward this authority in the administrative arena through its biologicals and gene therapy rules.

In addition, the FDA itself fails to support its claim of cloning jurisdiction with any prior assertion of regulatory authority over either in vitro fertilization or other more aggressive fertility techniques that carry a high-risk profile. Furthermore, the FDA regulations and commentary dealing with human gene therapy do not mention human reproduction despite the fact that, in February 1998, the FDA announced that these same regulations extended to human cloning. The FDA has not generally claimed jurisdiction over human reproductive methods. If human cloning is construed as a new variant of a treatment for infertility, the FDA may have an even weaker argument for regulatory authority because "the FDA is not supposed to regulate the practice of medicine," a power traditionally entrusted to the states.

If the courts do ultimately recognize that human cloning products are sufficiently analogous to viruses, serums, toxins, antitoxins, vaccines, blood products, and allergenic products such that they fall within the statutory envelope of regulatory consideration, the FDA first must demonstrate that these products are "applicable to the prevention, treatment, or cure of a disease or condition of human beings." The resolution of this issue is unclear; however, it is probably more easily addressed than the "analogous product'' analysis, and more likely to be resolved in the FDA's favor. The issue then becomes whether human cloning products are utilized to treat or to cure a disease or condition of human beings.

If the statutory interpretation focuses on the use of cloning products to create a pregnancy, then assertion of regulatory jurisdiction would fail because pregnancy is not considered a disease, and although pregnancy arguably could be considered a human condition, such products are not applicable to the prevention, treatment, or cure of the ''pregnancy.'' Human cloning procedures would attempt to create a pregnancy—not to prevent, treat, or cure it.

The FDA could proffer a compelling argument to establish that human cloning products would be used in many instances to treat another disease or human condition—infertility. Under the Americans with Disabilities Act (ADA), courts have already considered infertility to be a physical condition affecting the reproductive system in the context of a disability determination. Although ''pregnancy'' cannot be classified as a disease, and cloning products cannot be considered applicable to the prevention, treatment, or cure of pregnancy as a human condition, an implanted human embryo created by a cloning procedure could be classified as a biological product that is used to treat the disease or condition of infertility. * * *

NOTES AND QUESTIONS

1. *The FDA's assertion of authority over human cloning.* For other assessments of the agency's announcement, see Gail H. Javitt & Kathy Hudson, Regulating (for the Benefit of) Future Persons: A Different Perspective on the FDA's Jurisdiction to Regulate Human Reproductive Cloning, 2003 Utah L. Rev. 1201; Richard A. Merrill & Bryan J. Rose, FDA Regulation of Human Cloning: Usurpation or Statesmanship?, 15 Harv. J.L. & Tech. 85 (2001); Pratheep Sevanthinathan, Heavy Regulation of Human Cloning as an Alternative to a Complete Ban, 10 Quinnipiac Health L.J. 219 (2007). In response to claims by a couple of scientists that they would begin human cloning work, the FDA sent them warning letters. See Rick Weiss, Legal Barriers to Human Cloning May Not Hold up, Wash. Post, May 23, 2001, at A1; see also Rick Weiss, Scientists Testify on Human Cloning Plans, Wash. Post, Mar. 29, 2001, at A10 (describing statements by an obscure religious group that had announced its intent to begin cloning research at an undisclosed location in the U.S., and noting that the FDA received strident criticism from members of Congress for doing ''too little too late to regulate the quickly evolving field of cloning research''). The first reported success of therapeutic cloning with human embryos proved to be a hoax, see Choe Sang–Hun, Discredited Cloning Expert Is Convicted of Fraud in South Korea, N.Y. Times, Oct. 27, 2009, at A12, but other researchers continue to try it. See Rob Stein, Scientists Use Cloning to Make Genetically Tailored Stem Cells, Wash. Post, Oct. 6, 2011, at A1.

2. *Cloning products as ''drugs'' or ''devices.''* How would you frame an argument that cloning products are drugs under the FDCA? Does your answer depend on whether you are talking about cloned somatic cells for therapeutic purposes or cloned human embryos for reproductive purposes? Can these products be considered "articles" under the drug definition? Would cloning products fit the category of "implant . . . or other similar or related article" within the device definition? Can the FDA reasonably argue that these articles are either "intended for use in the diagnosis, cure, mitigation, treatment or prevention of disease" or "intended to affect the structure or function of the body"? If treatment of infertility provided the basis for jurisdiction, that would limit the FDA's authority to situations in which reproductive cloning were used by infertile couples; it would not appear to reach situations in which a fertile woman or man wants to clone herself or himself for some other reason. Suppose a couple with a high risk of genetic disease wanted to improve their chances of achieving pregnancy with a healthy embryo, and that their embryologist was able to harvest eight eggs from the woman, fertilize them with the man's sperm, and then screen each embryo for the presence of the unwanted genetic disease. If the embryologist found only one healthy embryo in the lot, the couple might wish to clone that healthy fertilized egg in order to create two or three additional "twins" for implantation in the woman's uterus, in order to maximize the chances of achieving pregnancy in a single IVF cycle. Should the FDA be able to regulate such a procedure (or, more likely, because it involves "cloning a human being," ban it outright)? How would the arguments about FDA's regulatory authority under the different statutory sections differ if the agency were attempting to assert control over cloning processes for other therapeutic purposes such as stem cell therapy or customized tissue products designed to match the recipient's DNA?

3. *Legislative efforts to prohibit human cloning.* Congress considered a number of bills that would have banned human cloning. See, e.g., Human Cloning Prohibition Act of 2001, S. 790 (prohibiting "human cloning," which is defined as "human asexual reproduction accomplished by introducing the nuclear material of a human somatic cell into a fertilized or unfertilized oocyte whose nucleus has been removed . . . to produce a living organism (at any stage of development) with a human or predominantly human genetic constitution," and providing for civil and criminal penalties including up to ten years in prison); see also Rick Weiss, An Uncertain Year for Cloning Laws: Ban on Embryo Research Seen as Unlikely, Wash. Post, Dec. 26, 2002, at A1. At least two states (California and Michigan) enacted laws banning cloning. In California, the statute defines cloning as "creating children by the transfer of nuclei from any type of cell to enucleated eggs," Cal. Health & Safety Code § 24185, though it also has the effect of banning certain infertility treatments unrelated to cloning. For additional discussion, see Alexander M. Capron, Placing a Moratorium on Research Cloning to Ensure Effective Control over Reproductive Cloning, 53 Hastings L.J. 1057 (2002); Russell Korobkin, Stem Cell Research and the Cloning Wars, 18 Stan. L. & Pol'y Rev. 161 (2007); Catherine D. Payne, Comment, Stem Cell Research and Cloning for Human Reproduction: An Analysis of the Laws, the Direction in Which They May Be Heading in Light of Recent Developments, and Potential Constitutional Issues, 61 Mercer L. Rev. 943

(2010). Of course, when controversial research encounters restrictions in one state or country, it may simply migrate to a more permissive jurisdiction. See Richard F. Storrow, Travel into the Future of Reproductive Technology, 79 UMKC L. Rev. 295 (2010); Daniel R. Peterson, Comment, Policing Future Nontherapeutic Applications of Genetic Enhancement Through International Agreement, 30 Hous. J. Int'l L. 743 (2008); Symposium, International Arbitrage of Controversial Medical Technologies, 35 Case W. Res. J. Int'l L. 363 (2003).

4. *The ethics of cloning*. Commentators have made a variety of ethical arguments against reproductive cloning, including concerns about psychological harm to cloned offspring, the commodification of human beings, and the use of cloning technologies to accomplish eugenic goals. See, e.g., Andre P. Rose, Note, Reproductive Misconception: Why Cloning Is Not Just Another Assisted Reproductive Technology, 48 Duke L.J. 1133 (1999); Symposium, Embryonic Stem Cells, Clones, and Genes: Science, Law, Politics, and Values, 37 Hofstra L. Rev. 313 (2008); Symposium, Manufactured Humanity: The Ethics and Legality of Stem Cell Research, Bioengineering, and Human Cloning, 65 Alb. L. Rev. 587 (2002).

5. *Scientific concerns surrounding cloning*. Apart from questions of ethical propriety or the FDA's regulatory authority over human cloning, many scientists have expressed concerns about the safety of human cloning, noting a poor track record in cloned animals. See, e.g., Brian Vastag, At the Cloning Circus Sideshows Abound, While Scientists Seek a Wider Audience, 286 JAMA 1437 (2001) (describing controversy at an NAS scientific workshop on the safety of animal and human cloning); Gina Kolata, Researchers Find Big Risk of Defect in Cloning Animals, N.Y. Times, Mar. 25, 2001, at A1 (reporting that fewer than 3% of all animal cloning attempts succeed, and recounting experts' opinions that—ethical objections aside—it would be reckless to clone a human being given the rate of abnormalities that occur in animals); Rick Weiss, Human Cloning Bid Stirs Experts' Anger, Wash. Post, Mar. 7, 2001, at A1 (describing concern in the scientific community about the safety of human cloning based on "cloning's dismal safety record" in animals).

3. XENOTRANSPLANTATION

FDA, Guidance, *Source Animal, Product, Preclinical, and Clinical Issues Concerning the Use of Xenotransplantation Products in Humans*

<http://www.fda.gov/cber/gdlns/clinxeno.htm> (2003).

* * * Recent advances in technology and pharmacology, which have been important for achieving success in allotransplantation, have led to the proposal that xenotransplantation, initially attempted nearly a century ago, may provide a solution to the shortage of human allografts. Proposed xenotransplantation protocols include implantation in humans of live organs, tissues, or cells from a nonhuman animal source, and procedures in

which human cells or fluids that are intended for administration to human recipients have had ex vivo contact with live nonhuman cells, tissues, or organs. Examples of procedures involving xenotransplantation products include: transplantation of xenogeneic hearts, kidneys, or pancreatic tissue to treat organ failure; implantation of neural cells to ameliorate neurological degenerative diseases; administration of human cells previously cultured ex vivo with live nonhuman animal antigen-presenting or feeder cells; and extracorporeal perfusion of a patient's blood or blood component perfused through an intact animal organ or isolated cells contained in a device to treat liver failure.

The use of the different xenotransplantation products has the potential for transmission of infectious disease from nonhuman animals to humans. Potential public health risks posed by the use of xenotransplantation products include: transmission of infectious agents that are pathogenic for humans but may not be pathogenic or even detectable in the source animal host; transmission of organisms that may not normally be pathogenic in humans but can become so in the immunosuppressed or immunocompromised individual; and recombination or reassortment of infectious agents, particularly viruses, with nonpathogenic or endogenous human infectious agents to form new pathogenic entities.

Furthermore, it is difficult to predict the infectious agents that may cause disease in a recipient of a xenotransplantation product solely on the basis of analysis of naturally occurring zoonoses because there are major differences between normal contact of humans with animals and contact of a recipient with a xenotransplantation product. For example, the physical barrier or distance is eliminated in the recipient due to transplantation and vascularization of xenotransplantation products, or even due to implantation of nonvascularized cells or tissues, or ex vivo manipulations that cause intimate proximity or contact of xenotransplantation product materials with recipient cells, tissues, or fluids. The potential for viral adaptation in immunocompromised or iatrogenically immunosuppressed hosts and the potential for undetected spread of previously latent viral infections are of particular concern. * * *

The United States Public Health Service (PHS) has previously made recommendations regarding the infectious disease risks posed by use of xenotransplantation in humans. In 1996, the PHS published a "Draft Guideline on Infectious Disease Issues in Xenotransplantation." Based on comments received and advances in fields relating to xenotransplantation, the PHS updated and revised the draft guideline. This FDA guidance document reiterates many of the concepts in the PHS Guideline, but in addition includes specific advice regarding all aspects of xenotransplantation product development and production, and xenotransplantation clinical trials.

FDA anticipates that its approach to regulation of xenotransplantation products will evolve as the scientific knowledge in the area of xenotransplantation continues to accumulate. Thus, this document, as with other guidance documents, will change as knowledge and experience pertinent to xenotransplantation accumulates. In addition, FDA realizes that it may not be appropriate to apply every aspect of the guidance to every xenotransplantation product. For example, some of the recommendations for animal husbandry may not be needed for xenotransplantation products consisting of well-characterized, long-established animal cell culture lines or human cells co-cultured with such lines. * * *

FDA has regulatory oversight of xenotransplantation products, including live organs, tissues, or cells from a nonhuman source, or xenotransplantation product materials used in encapsulated form or in which nonhuman live organs, tissues or cells have ex vivo contact with human body fluids, cells, tissues or organs that are subsequently given to a human recipient. If xenotransplantation products are to be used in clinical investigation, they require an appropriate investigational application be in place. FDA will regulate most xenotransplantation products as biological products. CBER regulates biological products, including cellular therapies, under authority of section 351 of the PHS Act and the [FDCA]. * * * Some products may be combination products consisting of a biologic and a device, such as xenogeneic cells contained in a device used for extracorporeal hemoperfusion. * * *

Although testing of the final xenotransplantation product for infectious agents is crucial, appropriate control of animal sources and husbandry provides important additional assurance for the safety of such products by controlling infections by both known and potentially even unknown agents. Therefore, the specific information supplied by the sponsor regarding animal husbandry including housing, feeding, veterinary care, drug and biologic treatment of source animal herds and individual source animals, will be crucial for FDA evaluation of the potential for safe use of cells, tissues, or organs from such source animals. * * * Individuals with expertise in infectious diseases of the species involved should develop a list of viruses, bacteria (including the rickettsiae), mycoplasma, fungi, transmissible spongiform encephalopathies (TSEs), and parasites for which the herd is screened and supply this information to FDA as part of the application to FDA (e.g., IND). * * *

FDA has considered how this guidance relates to human embryonic stem (hES) cell lines that were in existence prior to August 9, 2001 [the cut-off date specified by the Bush administration's federal funding restriction]. These hES cell lines had used murine feeder layer cells and thus fit the definition of xenotransplantation used in this guidance and the PHS guideline. FDA has had several meetings with some of the derivers of certain of these hES cell lines. FDA does not intend that the agency's regulation of xenotransplantation will preclude the use of these hES cell lines. It may be necessary for a sponsor who wishes to investigate a stem cell product derived from existing hES cell lines in a clinical trial to demonstrate to FDA that the hES cell line is free from infectious agents, including murine infectious agents. Given current technology, a sponsor should be able to do this without undue burden. * * *

In procedures in which the xenotransplantation product is transplanted immediately after removal from the source animal, such as xenotransplantation of whole organs, results of testing of the xenotransplantation product may not be available before its clinical use. In such cases, testing of the source animal itself may be all the testing that is possible before the procedure. Testing of samples taken from such xenotransplantation products or appropriate relevant biological surrogates, e.g., adjacent tissues or contra-lateral organs, is also warranted even though the results will not be available before use of the xenotransplantation product because results may contribute to patient management and to development of a scientific data base. * * *

We understand that the lack of other therapeutic options and the severity of disease may raise the benefit-to-risk ratio for some individuals. However, consideration and evaluation of risks and benefits of xenotransplantation should address both recipient and public health concerns. * * * Transmission of microbial agents from xenotransplantation products could lead to systemic disease (for example, infection or neoplasia) or failure of the xenotransplantation product in the recipient. In addition, transmission of infectious agents could result in outbreaks of zoonotic disease, silent transmission of latent viruses, or emergence of new strains of pathogens. Experience has shown that widespread horizontal or vertical transmission of new pathogens is possible before the pathogens are recognized (e.g., Human Immunodeficiency Virus). * * *

Because the zoonotic, opportunistic, and xenogeneic infectious risks to the recipient may extend to the recipient's family or intimate contacts, the patient should consent to inform his or her current and future intimate contacts of their potential risks from the source animal species, and of their deferral from blood donation. Intimate contacts of xenotransplantation product recipients include persons who have engaged repeatedly in activities that could result in intimate exchange of body fluids, including blood or saliva, with a xenotransplantation product recipient. * * * The informed consent document should contain information about the proposed life-long surveillance for all recipients and the need for clinical and laboratory monitoring throughout. * * *

NOTES AND QUESTIONS

1. *This little piggie went to market.* Several types of xenotransplantation procedures already have been attempted in experimental settings. Researchers have implanted neurons from pigs into patients with degenerative neurological disorders. See J. Stephen Fink et al., Porcine Xenografts in Parkinson's Disease and Huntington's Disease Patients: Preliminary Results, 9 Cell Transplant. 273 (2000). Researchers also are attempting to cure diabetes with infusions of pancreatic cells from pigs, see Carl–Gustave Groth et al., Transplantation of Porcine Fetal Pancreas to Diabetic Patients, 344 Lancet 1402 (1994), and they are using cells cultured ex vivo on a murine (mouse) cell line to create skin to aid in wound healing for burn victims. Some recipients of these experimental xenotransplantation technologies have survived for several years after the procedure. As the FDA's guidance document suggests, however, problems with recipient immune rejection and concerns about infectious disease transmission pose the biggest obstacles to continued work with xenotransplantation products. Scientists anticipate that engineering of these products and cloning of preferred strains may help to reduce such risks. See Louisa E. Chapman & Eda T. Bloom, Clinical Xenotransplantation, 285 JAMA 2304 (2001); see also Rick Weiss, Gene Alteration Boosts Pig–Human Transplant Feasibility, Wash. Post, Jan. 4, 2002, at A11. Some animal tissues have a long record of successful use: for instance, surgeons have used bovine and porcine heart valves for over a quarter of a century. See Rhonda L. Rundle, Edwards Lifesciences Says FDA Is to Clear Cow–Tissue Heart Valve, Wall St. J., Nov. 18, 2003, at D6. Are these biologic devices not considered xenotransplants because the tissues have been rendered inert through cryopreservation and other processing?

2. *Current state of regulatory oversight.* The FDA has issued several other guidance documents dealing with various aspects of xenotransplantation. See, e.g., 64 Fed. Reg. 73,562 (1999) ("Precautionary Measures to Reduce the Possible Risk of Transmission of Zoonoses by Blood and Blood Products from Xenotransplantation Product Recipients and Their Contacts"); 64 Fed. Reg. 16,743 (1999) ("Public Health Issues Posed by the Use of Nonhuman Primate Xenografts in Humans"); see also Campaign for Responsible Transplantation v. FDA, 511 F.3d 187 (D.C.Cir.2007) (resolving FOIA litigation initiated by a public interest organization that had sought access to agency records regarding clinical trials of xenotransplantation procedures); Fritz H. Bach et al., Ethical and Legal Issues in Technology: Xenotransplantation, 27 Am. J.L. & Med. 283 (2001); Patrik S. Florencio & Erik D. Ramanathan, Are Xenotransplantation Safeguards Legally Viable?, 16 Berkeley Tech. L.J. 937 (2001); Jocelyn A. Holland, Comment, The "Catch–22" of Xenotransplantation: Compelling Compliance with Long–Term Surveillance, 7 Hous. J. Health L. & Pol'y 151 (2006). As with its assertion of regulatory jurisdiction over other novel medical technologies, the agency has provided a very limited explanation of the precise statutory basis of its claimed authority. How would the FDA categorize the following products: pig kidneys for direct transplant into humans, pig kidneys from genetically-altered (transgenic) pigs that have been modified with human DNA to improve histocompatability, pig pancreatic islet cells that have been cultured and cleansed of pathogens for use in the treatment of diabetes, and baboon neuronal cells that have been cultured and proliferated in vitro for use in the treatment of spinal cord injuries?

3. *Chimeras.* When a person receives an organ from another source (whether human or other animal), that person becomes a "chimera" because he or she carries the genetic material from a different organism, but such blending would have no germ-line consequences (putting aside the possibility of transplanting reproductive tissues that produce gametes) because the foreign genetic material would not get integrated into the recipient's existing tissues. Scientists use recombinant DNA techniques to integrate foreign genetic material into another organism, and bacteria engineered to produce human proteins would qualify as chimeras, though the splicing of small snippets of human genetic material into bacterial germ-lines attracts little attention nowadays. Newer techniques, however, that introduce human embryonic stem cells into animal fetuses—either to create models for research into human disease (e.g., a mouse brain that is 1% human) or to produce humanized organs for transplantation purposes (e.g., a sheep liver that is 80% human)—raise much more profound questions (although cell differentiation will have progressed in the animal fetus, the introduced stem cells carry the full complement of human genetic material and will get integrated into some of the animal's developing tissues). See Rick Weiss, Of Mice, Men and In–Between: Scientists Debate Blending of Human, Animal Forms, Wash. Post, Nov. 20, 2004, at A1 (adding that the idea of introducing human stem cells into an animal embryo, which might humanize the entire organism, would raise even more serious questions); see also Stephen R. Munzer, Human–Nonhuman Chimeras in Embryonic Stem Cell Research, 21 Harv. J.L. & Tech. 123 (2007); D. Scott Bennett, Comment, Chimera and the Continuum of Humanity: Erasing the Line of Constitutional Personhood, 55 Emory L.J. 347 (2006); Tia Sherringham, Comment, Mice, Men, and Monsters: Opposition to Chimera Research and the Scope of Federal Regulation, 96 Cal. L. Rev. 765 (2008); Rick Weiss, Human Brain Cells Are Grown in Mice: Success Is Encouraging for Stem Cell Therapies, Wash. Post, Dec. 13, 2005, at A3; Rick Weiss, Stem Cell Guidelines Issued, Wash. Post, Apr. 27, 2005, at A2 ("Injection of human embryonic cells into monkey or ape embryos to make primate chimeras would be banned [under new NAS guidelines], as would the creation of any human-animal chimera in which a human-like brain would be likely to develop.").

C. THE GENOMICS REVOLUTION

It took just one decade for the Human Genome Project (HGP), which received funding from NIH and the Department of Energy, to succeed in sequencing our basic genetic makeup. See Nicholas Wade, Reading the Book of Life: A Historic Quest, N.Y. Times, June 27, 2000, at F5; see also Elizabeth Pennisi, The Human Genome, 291 Science 1177 (2001) (describing the work of Celera Corporation). Of course, this map only provided the starting point for the development of new medical technologies. In order to analyze and ultimately apply genomic data for medical purposes, scientists must "annotate" the genome—that is, provide the "punctuation" for the string of genes that comprise the ribbons of human DNA so that researchers can more readily work with genes and determine their individual functions. After tremendous early excitement (hype), the difficulty of this process has become apparent. See Nicholas Wade, A Decade Later, Gene Map Yields Few New Cures, N.Y. Times, June 13, 2010, at A1 ("While drug companies continue to pour huge amounts of money into genome research, it has become clear that the genetics of most diseases are more complex than anticipated and that it will take many more years before new treatments may be able to transform medicine."); see also Faye Flam, Nobody's Perfect: It Turns out There Is No Norm for DNA, Scientists Say, Phila. Inquirer, Mar. 13, 2006, at E1. Scientists currently are working on a variety of promising approaches to disease detection, treatment, and prevention made possible by the HGP. See, e.g., Rob Stein, Dramatic Gains from Melanoma Drug: Medication Designed to Attack Cancer's Genetic Trigger, Wash. Post, June 6, 2011, at A4 ("PLX4032 is one of a new generation of drugs that researchers hope will be more effective and less toxic because they zero in on genetic characteristics of cancer cells that are not found in healthy cells.").

Most genes code for specific proteins, which in turn may provide structure or serve some other functional purpose in the body by affecting cell metabolism. When the genes that manufacture proteins are defective, disease may result. The new discipline of "proteomics" will enable scientists to analyze simultaneously the many proteins that comprise a cell, rather than studying cell proteins one at a time, so that the role of proteins in the cell can be better understood. See Marie McCullough, Progress from Unraveling Proteins: By Studying the Complex Structures, Researchers May Be Able to Detect and Treat Such Insidious Killers as Ovarian Cancer, Phila. Inquirer, Apr. 19, 2004, at C1; see also J. Jason Williams, Note, Protecting the Frontiers of Biotechnology Beyond the Genome: The Limits of Patent Law in the Face of the Proteomics Revolution, 58 Vand. L. Rev. 955 (2005). Scientists also have used techniques learned from the HGP to determine the genomes of laboratory and other animals as well as infectious agents (as done with the virus responsible for severe acute respiratory syndrome (SARS)), which promises to assist in vaccine development and patient diagnosis.

1. Genetic Testing

Centers for Disease Control, Notice of Intent, *Genetic Testing Under the Clinical Laboratory Improvement Amendments*

65 Fed. Reg. 25,928 (2000).

The Centers for Disease Control and Prevention acts as a scientific advisor to the Health Care Financing Administration in development of requirements for clinical laboratories under the Clinical Laboratory Improvement Amendments (CLIA). The CDC is issuing this notice to advise the public that the Department of Health and Human Services will be preparing a Notice of Proposed Rule Making to revise the CLIA regulations applicable to laboratories performing human genetic testing. Before issuing the NPRM, comments are being solicited on the recommendations of the Clinical Laboratory Improvement Advisory Committee (CLIAC) to change current CLIA requirements to specifically recognize a genetic testing specialty. This new specialty area will address unique testing issues in the pre-analytic, analytic, and post-analytic phases of testing that could affect the accuracy and reliability of test results, and related issues such as informed consent, confidentiality, counseling, and the clinical appropriateness of a genetic test. * * *

Human genetic testing is expected to lead to a whole new era in health care. Some tests may determine not only whether an individual has a particular disease or condition, but also may determine their risk of developing a disease or condition in the future. However, along with the tremendous potential for improving health and preventing disease, genetic testing can also do great harm if errors occur in: (1) the selection of an appropriate test, (2) the performance of the test, (3) the interpretation of the test results, or (4) the clinical application of the test results. False-positive or false-negative results can be especially troublesome when the test is being used to predict future risk of disease in an individual without any current symptoms of disease.

The process of performing a genetic test can be broken into three distinct phases: (1) the pre-analytic phase, which encompasses such events as determining which genetic test, if any, is appropriate to answer the clinical question being asked and collecting an appropriate sample and transporting it to the test site; (2) the analytical phase, which involves steps taken to perform the analysis and analyze the results; and (3) the post-analytic phase, which includes reporting and interpretation of the results. It is important to recognize that the laboratory may need to be involved in carrying out or assisting with all three phases of testing and that errors can occur either within the laboratory or at the interface between the laboratory and the care provider.

In the pre-analytic phase, one recent study found that 20 percent of adenomatous polyposis coli (APC) genetic tests were ordered for inappropriate indications and 19 percent of patients received genetic counseling before testing occurred. See Francis M. Giardiello et al., The Use and Interpretation of Commercial APC Gene Testing for Familial Adenomatous Polyposis, 336 New Eng. J. Med. 823 (1997). Another recent survey of 245 molecular genetic testing laboratories found that 55 percent of the laboratories did not require informed consent prior to testing and 31 percent did not have a written policy on confidentiality. See Margaret M. McGovern et al., Quality Assurance in Molecular Genetic Testing Laboratories, 281 JAMA 835 (1999). This same study found what the authors considered to be substandard laboratory practice, which could lead to adverse clinical outcomes, in 15 percent of the laboratories. In the post-analytic phase of testing, the Giardiello study reported that 31 percent of the cases were misinterpreted by the physician. The McGovern study found that 30 percent of laboratories did not provide access to genetic counseling.

These and other studies point to the need for improvements in laboratory practice and better coordination between the care provider, laboratory, genetic counselor, and the patient to ensure quality in genetic testing. The HHS has sought the advice of experts in laboratory medicine and genetic testing to help identify places in the testing process where testing problems are most likely to occur, and to determine what modifications to current CLIA regulations could provide greater assurance of accurate and reliable testing. Issues for which the laboratory might provide additional assistance to the laboratory user such as informed consent, counseling, and protecting confidentiality were also considered. * * *

In considering whether to create a genetic specialty under CLIA and whether to include the provisions recommended by the CLIAC, it is important to understand the current roles of government and professional organizations in genetic testing, and to note that no single agency or organization is likely to be able to address all of the issues raised by genetic testing. Genetic tests are currently regulated at the federal level through three mechanisms: (1) the Clinical Laboratory Improvement Amendments; (2) the federal Food, Drug, and Cosmetic Act; and (3) during investigational phases of test development, under applicable regulations for the protection of human subjects. * * *

Testing devices and tests that are packaged and sold as kits to multiple laboratories require premarket approval or clearance by the FDA. This premarket review involves an analysis of the device's accuracy as well as its analytical sensitivity and specificity. * * * The majority of new genetic tests are being developed by laboratories for their own use, that is, in-house tests. The FDA established a measure of regulation of in-house tests by instituting controls over the active ingredients (analyte-specific reagents) used by laboratories to perform tests. This regulation subjects reagent manufacturers to certain general controls, such as good manufacturing practices; however, with few exceptions, the current regulatory process does not require a premarket review of these reagents. The regulation requires that the sale of reagents be only to laboratories capable of performing high-complexity tests and requires that certain information accompany both the reagents and the test results. The labels for the reagents must also state that "analytical and performance characteristics are not established." Also, the test results must identify the laboratory that developed the test and its performance characteristics and must include a statement that the test "has not been cleared or approved by the U.S. FDA." In addition, the regulation prohibits direct marketing of in-house developed tests to consumers. * * *

Some state agencies may monitor laboratories performing genetic testing, including licensure of personnel and facilities. In some instances, the state Public Health Laboratory and state-operated CLIA program are responsible for quality assurance activities. A few states, such as New York, have promulgated regulations that go beyond the requirements of CLIA. States also administer newborn screening programs and provide other genetic services through maternal and child health programs. Private-sector organizations, in partnership with HCFA and CDC may also develop laboratory and clinical guidelines and standards. A number of organizations are involved in helping to assure the quality of laboratory practices and in developing clinical practice guidelines to ensure the appropriate use of genetic tests. * * *

Michael J. Malinowski & Robin J.R. Blatt, *Commercialization of Genetic Testing Services: The FDA, Market Forces, and Biological Tarot Cards*

71 TUL. L. REV. 1211 (1997).

* * * Concern about the impact of [genetic] testing on society inspired James Watson, codiscoverer of the double-helix structure of DNA and the first head of the HGP, to insist at the outset of the HGP that a respectable percentage of the annual budget be committed to addressing the project's ethical, legal, and social implications [ELSI]. Nevertheless, most public health officials and other regulators, both federal and state, are only beginning to become aware of the full implications of new genetic technologies. * * * As a result, the regulatory infrastructure necessary for responsible commercialization of genetic technology is being developed in response to, rather than in anticipation of, its commercialization. * * *

Generally, when a gene or biological marker linked to a physical or mental condition is discovered, the basic scientific capability to test for the presence of that marker is a given. Thousands of such linkages have been made subsequent to the commencement of the HGP, and at a rate accelerating with the passage of time, to the point that linkages are being identified almost on a weekly (if not daily) basis. * * * Biotech companies are using such discoveries to develop and commercialize predictive screening tests for an abundance of health conditions in addition to breast and ovarian cancer. Recent discoveries include genetic links to Alzheimer's, bladder cancer, cervical cancer, colon cancer, obesity, prostate cancer, and tumor growth associated with a spectrum of common cancers. Researchers are even developing an "Ides of March" genetic test to serve as a crude indicator of a person's life span. * * *

Unfortunately, the discovery of genetic alterations linked to many health conditions comes well before those discoveries can be turned into therapeutics and reliable predictors of disease in specific individuals. Although the availability of therapeutics to offset genetic predispositions will make genetic testing much less controversial, that time is years away for most conditions. * * * Nevertheless, a deluge of fully commercialized genetic testing services and kits is well within sight. * * * Many developers and manufacturers of genetic tests now are making investigatory, predictive genetic testing available to the public. * * *

In 1994, the Committee on Assessing Genetic Risks assembled by the Institutes of Medicine documented pervasive informal genetic testing by research laboratories, and the ELSI Task Force on Genetic Testing has reached similar conclusions regarding both research and commercial laboratories that report results to patients. The emergence of predictive genetic tests with implications for broad segments of the population, such as the APOE–4 (Alzheimer's) test, is raising concern among public health officials and providers who understand the limitations of this technology and are sensitive to its potential impact on the lives of patients and their families. However, with such understanding comes appreciation for the difficulty of introducing a satisfactory regulatory response to the multitude of genetic technologies approaching and entering commerce.

Predictive genetic testing services, performed in-house by the tests' developers and manufacturers, are square pegs in the rubric of federal regulation. The FDA regulates the production of reagents, probes, or test kits manufactured for use by others in laboratories and, therefore, genetic tests manufactured and sold for others to perform. However, manufacturers and private laboratories may avoid the routine FDA review process for diagnostics and comply with applicable federal regulations by manufacturing and using their own reagents in-house and selling testing services through primary care physicians. Such reagents are called "home brews" because they are manufactured and used within the same facility, and a number of such tests are being developed and made available to the public. * * *

Private laboratories performing genetic testing services also are essentially immune to federal laboratory-quality assurances imposed by the Health Care Finance Administration through the Clinical Laboratory Improvement Amendments. Under CLIA, a laboratory must demonstrate analytical validity of its tests and their components, but there is no clinical validity requirement. In other words, the CLIA validity requirement is satisfied when a genetic test to determine the presence of a specific genetic alteration does so accurately, even though the test may offer no clinical predictability. There is no required express showing that the alteration tested for has any bearing on the subject's health. * * *

The general lack of regulatory quality control on genetic tests, which raises questions about their fundamental reliability, is exacerbated by the fact that very few specific guidelines for these tests have been formally developed and introduced by the medical profession. "Lack of consensus about what type of screening should be offered means that there is also no clear guidance for state policy makers adopting mandatory screening plans" even on issues such as the testing of fetuses for BRCA1 and BRCA2 variations. Also, reliance on state regulation to monitor (in the ongoing manner necessitated by the research nature of the technology) the quality of genetic testing services is misplaced for, there too, "the field of laboratory licensure and monitoring remains in a state of flux." * * *

Predictive genetic testing services are, in the aggregate, biological tarot cards subject to misinterpretation by both patients and their physicians. The predictive capability of many genetic tests remains scientifically undefined for the general population. This type of testing must be conclusively distinguished from presymptomatic genetic testing. The latter constitutes a reliable and meaningful predictor only for a small number of conditions—conditions usually caused by a single genetic mutation. Only these few conditions, such as Huntington's and Tay Sachs disease, can be diagnosed conclusively through genetic testing. Even when such conditions can be diagnosed through genetic testing, the rate of expression may vary; with many genetic conditions, severity remains an open question. Most often there is no available treatment, or treatment exists but is price-prohibitive.

In addition, in the absence of uniform federal regulatory oversight, the quality of laboratory performance is questionable.

More troubling, due to the absence of adequate clinical data, health care providers cannot interpret the results of predictive genetic tests for most of their patients with any reliability even when they are knowledgeable about genetics. This interpretation problem is exacerbated because the current generation of health care providers does not possess such knowledge. Their lack of genetics education and the novelty of the technology makes providers dependent upon the developers and manufacturers of these tests (both commercial and academic laboratories) for information. This dependency suggests that neither consumers nor their health care providers can reasonably evaluate the technology. * * *

The information generated by predictive genetic tests, regardless of its clinical reliability, will deeply impact people's lives. Some of those who have opted to undergo the presymptomatic test for Huntington's, a clinically valid test that conclusively determines future onset, have experienced detrimental psychological reactions to the results even when they are negative. For those whose results are positive, the suicide rate is approximately thirty-five percent higher than among the general population. Further, it appears that genetic information already is disrupting the lives of individuals and their families by subjecting them to discrimination from employers and insurers. * * *

NOTES AND QUESTIONS

1. *Genetic testing and CLIA.* Testing for genetic diseases has expanded rapidly. See Ariana E. Cha, Labs Turn DNA into Personal Health Forecasts, Wash. Post, Apr. 7, 2005, at A1 ("There are now tests for more than 1,100 ailments, double what was on the market five years ago .... Until recently, genetic testing was limited to pinpointing mutations associated with diseases such as Huntington's or cystic fibrosis."). CLIA regulations set out criteria under which HHS assigns an in vitro diagnostic (IVD) test to a "complexity category," which in turn determines the level of regulation: laboratories that perform only "waived tests" are subject to minimal regulation, whereas those labs that perform moderate or high complexity tests must meet regulatory standards dealing with personnel, proficiency testing, quality assurance, and inspections. See 42 C.F.R. pt. 493; see also 64 Fed. Reg. 73,561 (1999) (transferring to FDA various functions under CLIA); Michele Schoonmaker et al., Coordination of Federal Regulation and Payment for New Diagnostic Tests: A Proposed New Approach, 57 Food & Drug L.J. 195 (2002); Rob Stein, Quick Tests for Diabetes Raise Concerns, Wash. Post, Dec. 7, 2010, at A1 (reporting that the A1c test, which helps to monitor diabetic patients, now gets used to screen for the disease (in lieu of the more accurate glucose fasting test) but, because it is categorized as "waived" under CLIA, largely escapes regulation).

2. *FDA regulation of genetic testing.* Diagnostic kits qualify as medical devices. The complexity of genetic diagnostic products (and lack of pre–

1976 predicate devices) frequently leads to Class III designation, requiring the submission of a PMA. As explained above, however, many laboratories were circumventing the premarket approval process by manufacturing and using their own diagnostic analyte specific reagents (ASRs) in house (so-called "home brews") and then marketing the test process as a service. In 1996, the FDA announced that "at a future date, the agency may reevaluate whether additional controls over the in house tests developed by such laboratories may be needed to provide an appropriate level of consumer protection. Such controls may be especially relevant as testing for the presence of genes associated with cancer or dementing diseases becomes more widely available." 61 Fed. Reg. 10,484 (1996) (declaring the agency's intent to regulate the reagents used for in-house genetic testing as Class III devices and a sub-group of these as "restricted" devices). The FDA finalized the proposed rule a year later, regulating all ASRs as restricted (though not Class III) medical devices:

> The final rule restricts ordering the use of in-house developed tests using ASRs to physicians or other health care practitioners authorized by applicable state law to access such tests. The final rule also restricts the sale of ASRs to those clinical laboratories regulated under Clinical Laboratory Improvement Amendments of 1988 (CLIA) as qualified to perform high complexity testing.... FDA does not intend, at this time, to regulate ASRs used in genetic testing differently from other restricted class I medical devices that are exempt from premarket notification requirements. The ASR regulations are drafted to classify most ASRs used to develop in-house tests as class I devices because FDA believes this degree of regulatory control is commensurate with the need to bring consistency to the manufacture of these devices and to assure their safety and effectiveness when used by health and scientific personnel trained in laboratory practices.
>
> FDA considered identifying a subset of ASRs that are used to develop tests intended for predictive genetic diagnosis as ASRs that pose unique risks to the public health because of the substantial clinical impact of the information generated using these devices. For the genetic tests currently in use, FDA is aware that both the genetic test and the ASR used in the genetic test are developed by the laboratory in-house. Because these ASRs are not being commercially marketed independently of the tests, they do not currently fall within the scope of this regulation. Nonetheless, FDA considered designating as class III devices those ASRs that would be marketed independently for use in tests intended for use in overtly healthy people to identify a genetic predisposition to a dementing disease, or to fatal or potentially fatal medical disorders (e.g., cancers or Alzheimer's disease), in situations where penetrance is poorly defined or variable and latency is 5 years or longer. However, after reviewing the comments and currently available information, FDA has not yet identified criteria that would logically distinguish among genetic tests in order to determine which have the requisite impact to trigger more stringent controls. FDA has determined that the special issues related to genetic testing or pre-

> dictive genetic testing do not warrant establishing a more stringent degree of regulatory control over ASRs used in these tests at this time. FDA believes that regulating most ASRs as restricted class I devices exempt from premarket notification establishes appropriate initial controls in the event more stringent requirements are later determined to be necessary for ASRs used in genetic tests.

62 Fed. Reg. 62,243, 62,244–46 (1997); see also 75 Fed. Reg. 34,463 (2010) (announcing a public meeting on "Oversight of Laboratory Developed Tests," and requesting comments on tentative proposals to change the agency's generally lax policy in this area). Why are ASRs, which are complex chemicals, regulated as any sort of "devices" under the FDCA? How can the FDA argue that it's appropriate to regulate any class of ASRs as "restricted" devices? Finally, how can the agency assert regulatory jurisdiction over home brews, which never leave the laboratory where they are manufactured? See Gregorio M. Garcia, The FDA and Regulation of Genetic Tests: Building Confidence and Promoting Safety, 48 Jurimetrics J. 217 (2008); Gail H. Javitt, In Search of a Coherent Framework: Options for FDA Oversight of Genetic Tests, 62 Food & Drug L.J. 617 (2007); Bruce Patsner, New "Home Brew" Predictive Genetic Tests Present Significant Regulatory Problems, 9 Hous. J. Health L. & Pol'y 237 (2009); Juliana Han, Note, The Optimal Scope of FDA Regulation of Genetic Tests: Meeting Challenges and Keeping Promises, 20 Harv. J.L. & Tech. 423 (2007); see also Andrew Pollack, F.D.A. Seeks to Regulate New Types of Diagnostic Tests, N.Y. Times, Sept. 6, 2006, at C4; Rob Stein, Genetic Test Is Predictor of Breast Cancer Relapse: Results May Let Some Skip Chemotherapy, Wash. Post, Dec. 11, 2004, at A1 (reporting that the FDA had approved OncotypeDX, a test costing $3,450).

3. *OTC gene screening*. The growing availability of genetic tests that consumers can order directly has raised particular concerns. See Gaia Bernstein, Direct-to-Consumer Genetic Testing: Gatekeeping the Production of Genetic Information, 79 UMKC L. Rev. 283 (2010); Jennifer A. Gniady, Note, Regulating Direct-to-Consumer Genetic Testing: Protecting the Consumer Without Quashing a Medical Revolution, 76 Fordham L. Rev. 2429 (2008); Deepthy Kishore, Comment, Test at Your Own Risk: Your Genetic Report Card and the Direct-to-Consumer Duty to Secure Informed Consent, 59 Emory L.J. 1553 (2010); Molly C. Novy, Note, Privacy at a Price: Direct-to-Consumer Genetic Testing and the Need for Regulation, 2010 U. Ill. J.L. Tech. & Pol'y 157; Andrew S. Robertson, Note, Taking Responsibility: Regulations and Protections in Direct-to-Consumer Genetic Testing, 24 Berkeley Tech. L.J. 213 (2009); Lauren B. Solberg, Note, Over the Counter but Under the Radar: Direct-to-Consumer Genetics Tests and FDA Regulation of Medical Devices, 11 Vand. J. Ent. & Tech. L. 711 (2009); Rob Stein, Genetic Testing Mix-up Reignites Debate over Degree of Federal Regulation Needed, Wash. Post, July 17, 2010, at A1; Rick Weiss, Genetic Testing Gets Personal: Firms Sell Answers on Health, Even Love, Wash. Post, Mar. 25, 2008, at A1.

4. *Limitations of genetic testing.* With the mapping of the human genome, the identification of genes that contribute to the development of a wide variety of diseases, traits, and conditions continues to accelerate. Once identified, it is usually possible to test an individual's genome for the presence of a mutation on a gene or genes associated with a disease or trait. Although the current state of technology permits identification of such mutations, it offers little in the way of prevention or treatment (though, like a family history, such information may lead to greater vigilance by patients). See Jeffrey N. Weitzel & Laurence E. McCahill, The Power of Genetics to Target Surgical Prevention, 344 New Eng. J. Med. 1942, 1943 (2001) (suggesting that "[t]he risks and benefits of prophylactic surgery must be balanced against the efficacy of screening, the risk of cancer, and the lethality of the particular form of cancer"). Many physicians cannot accurately calculate and convey a genetic test's "positive predictive value"—the likelihood that a person who tests positive for a mutation will actually get the disease. Thus, many patients tested receive false reassurance or become inappropriately worried about their future risk of disease. A test's predictive value depends in part on the degree of penetrance of the genetic condition; in other words, the presence of some mutations indicates a high likelihood that the disease will develop, while, for other mutations, the likelihood of disease is far lower, or more subject to influence by other genes and non-genetic factors such as environment. Similar difficulties may attend testing for antigens associated with a disease. See David Armstrong, Prostate Test Often Misses Cancer, Wall St. J., July 24, 2003, at D1 (reporting on some of the controversy over PSA testing); cf. Gina Kolata, Rapid Rise and Fall for Body–Scanning Clinics, N.Y. Times, Jan. 23, 2005, § 1, at 1 (telling "one of the most remarkable stories yet of a medical technology bubble that burst").

5. *Guarding against discrimination.* Healthy people whose genetic test results indicate that they are at increased risk for future disease may be subject to discrimination by employers or health insurers. See Deborah Hellman, What Makes Genetic Discrimination Exceptional?, 29 Am. J.L. & Med. 77 (2003); Sonia M. Suter, Disentangling Privacy from Property: Toward a Deeper Understanding of Genetic Privacy, 72 Geo. Wash. L. Rev. 737 (2004). In 2008, Congress sought to address these sorts of concerns by enacting the Genetic Information Nondiscrimination Act (GINA). See Pub. L. No. 110–233, 122 Stat. 881 (2008); see also Jessica L. Roberts, The Genetic Information Nondiscrimination Act as an Antidiscrimination Law, 86 Notre Dame L. Rev. 597 (2011); Patricia Alten, Note, GINA: A Genetic Information Nondiscrimination Solution in Search of a Problem, 61 Fla. L. Rev. 379 (2009); Joanne Barken, Note, Judging GINA: Does the Genetic Information Nondiscrimination Act of 2008 Offer Adequate Protection?, 75 Brook. L. Rev. 545 (2009); Michael S. Blackwell, Comment, Insurance, Employment, and the Genetic Information Nondiscrimination Act of 2008, 55 Loy. L. Rev. 125 (2009); Amy Foster, Comment, Critical Dilemmas in Genetic Testing: Why Regulations to Protect the Confidentiality of Genetic Information Should Be Expanded, 62 Baylor L. Rev. 537 (2010). In addition, the health reform legislation enacted in 2010 would prevent insurers from discriminating against applicants with pre-existing conditions. What do you think about a new NCAA mandate for genetic screening of student-athletes? See Rob Stein, Colleges Mandate Sickle Cell Testing, Wash. Post, Sept. 20, 2010, at A1 ("Since 2000, as many as 10 Division I college football players who had the trait without knowing it have died suddenly following workouts.").

6. *Gene expression chips*. Another new technology enables scientists to assess which among thousands of genes are active within a cell at any given time, which will facilitate understanding of how gene activity switches on and off within cells and how cell function changes over time. See Hadley C. King & Animesh A. Sinha, Gene Expression Profile Analysis by DNA Microarrays: Promise and Pitfalls, 286 JAMA 2280 (2001). Gene chips are glass slides with microscopic pieces of genetic material attached to them. When biological samples come into contact with the chips, the attached genetic material binds with complementary material in the sample. The resulting patterns of binding allow researchers to understand the precise mechanism of disease and protein production at the genetic level. See Bernadette Tansey, Study Backs Microarray Data, S.F. Chron., Sept. 10, 2006, at F1. Gene chips also may prove useful in testing with more speed and accuracy the toxic effects of chemicals and drugs on the body—a new technique called toxicogenomics. See Andrew Pollack, DNA Chip May Help Usher in a New Era of Product Testing, N.Y. Times, Nov. 28, 2000, at F2. Finally, genetic testing could allow physicians to select optimal medications for individuals based on their particular sensitivities. See Lisa B. Mann, Liver Success: Emerging Enzyme Test Can Predict Drug Side Effects, Wash. Post, Apr. 18, 2006, at F1; Bernadette Tansey, Power Tools for the Gene Age: New Test Can Help Doctors in Prescribing Medications, S.F. Chron., Feb. 7, 2005, at E1 (reporting that the FDA approved the Ampli-Chip CYP450, the first DNA microarray device, which identifies patients with variations in a critical liver enzyme that affects drug metabolism).

2. THERAPEUTIC APPLICATIONS

Edward A. Marshall, Note, *Medical Malpractice in the New Eugenics: Relying on Innovative Tort Doctrine to Provide Relief When Gene Therapy Fails*

35 GA. L. REV. 1277 (2001).

Mapping the human genome, the 3.12 billion nucleotide "letter" sequence that makes up human DNA, has taken place years ahead of even the most optimistic estimates of the scientific community. Isolating a protein that corresponds with one of the 30,000 human genes, which years ago could have taken up to a decade, now can be done in a matter of seconds simply by searching a computer database. Even more remarkable than the present advances in genetic biotechnology, however, is the inevitable transformation that genetic research will effectuate on the practice of medicine in the future. * * *

The basic premise behind gene therapy is deceptively simple: after determining what gene or genes are "defective" within a given individual's genome, a "normal" copy of the imperfect gene is inserted in an individual to alter the production of proteins within the cell. This alteration, if successful, would prevent the manifestation of a "genetic" disorder by repairing the malfunctioning sequence of nucleotides on the strands of DNA. This section explores the basic procedural model of how gene therapy "works," describes different categories of human gene therapy, and explores obstacles to successful gene therapy that must be overcome before it is available for widespread application in humans.

1. *Inserting a More Perfect Gene.* For gene therapy to be effective as a treatment for a "genetic" disorder, a physician must not only identify the defective gene or genes within a patient, but must also devise a method for inserting a "normal" copy of the gene (the transgene) into a patient's cells. No microscopic tweezers have yet been developed that can accomplish this task. Instead, geneticists have developed, and continue to develop, transgenic "vectors" that act as vehicles, carrying the transgenic materials into the patient and penetrating the patient's cells.

The "vectors" studied and employed thus far in human genetic alteration are genetically altered viruses—with the viral component replaced with the transgene sought to be introduced into the patient's cells. In fact, the genetically manipulated cold virus, also known as the adenovirus, is the most common transgenic vector currently being used. When vectors penetrate the cell, the transgene is then integrated with the patient's genome, and the process of transcription then produces the mRNA that, through transcription, should produce the same proteins that would have been synthesized from a "normal" gene.

2. *Types of Human Gene Therapy.* The process of gene therapy could theoretically be employed to manipulate two types of human cells. The first, somatic cells, are cells that are "component[s] of the body," such as white blood cells or bone marrow stem cells, that are incapable of being fertilized and, thus, not involved in the process of reproduction. Due to the non-reproductive nature of somatic cells, somatic cell gene therapy is analogous to conventional enzyme therapy or organ transplants in that the effects extend only to the patient herself. This is significant as, even after a successful somatic cell gene therapy procedure, any preexisting defect in the patient's genes could still be passed on to her children. More importantly, after a negligently performed somatic gene therapy, there is essentially no direct effect on subsequent generations.

The opposite is true when the manipulated cells are germ-line cells, which produce eggs and sperm. These cells, unlike somatic cells, are involved in the process of reproduction, and genes contained in these cells are thus capable of being passed on to the offspring of an individual. Since a negligent germ-line gene therapy procedure could detrimentally affect a patient's offspring, the ramifications of the procedure present a multigenerational problem as well as ethical considerations not involved in somatic cell gene therapy.

Somatic gene therapy has been available for treatment in humans affected by ADA–SCID (an immune disorder resulting in the death of white blood cells) since 1990, and geneticists expect human somatic gene therapy treatments for various other diseases to become available in the near future. Germ-line therapy, however, has not yet been performed in humans. Looking to the future, the widespread use of germ-line therapy in humans is questionable as, despite the efficacy of being able to "cure" multiple generations of a given defect with a single treatment, the moral and ethical controversy surrounding germ-line therapy may prove an insurmountable barrier.

3. *Biological Obstacles to Widespread Use of Gene Therapy in Humans.* Despite the success gene therapy has achieved in limited contexts, it remains to a large extent a "hellishly difficult" procedure. The first challenge is to identify an adequate vector in which to transport the transgene. The most common vector currently being employed by geneticists to transport transgenes into human cells is the adenovirus. While capable of carrying the therapeutic gene into the human body, the adenovirus often triggers an immune response that can destroy the needed gene, and may endanger the patient. In fact, complications resulting from the use of an adenovirus vector can be fatal. Researchers continue to experiment with other vectors that may prove superior in effectuating the gene replacement while creating fewer risks.

The second barrier facing the practice of eugenics that may stall widespread use of gene therapy involves establishing more site-specific gene insertion procedures. Integration of a transgene into the human genome ideally would involve target gene-replacement, with the transgene actually taking the place of the defective gene on the patient's chromosome. At present, however, gene therapy technology only allows for gene-addition procedures, which "simply add functional copies of the gene that is defective in the patient to the genomes of the recipient cells ... [with] the introduced genes ... inserted at random or nearly random sites in the chromosomes of the host cells." The problem with this type of gene therapy is twofold. First, the distance between the inserted transgene and the location along the chromosome where the "normal" gene is ordinarily present may disrupt the interaction with the surrounding genes that send signals initiating and halting protein synthesis. Second, placing the transgene at random along the chromosome increases the probability that it will alter the structure of another, "normal" gene, thereby disrupting an essential genetic process. Fortunately, these problems of gene addition may soon be resolved through recently developed targeting and selection strategies, which have already produced limited success in inserting a transgene at the appropriate place along the genetic sequence. * * *

NOTES AND QUESTIONS

1. *Dimming prospects for gene therapy.* Researchers have tried gene therapy for a variety hereditary disorders such as hemophilia, cystic fibrosis, and Parkinson's disease. See W. French Anderson, The Best of Times, the Worst of Times, 288 Science 627 (2000); Daniel G. Miller & George Stamatoyannopoulos, Gene Therapy for Hemophilia, 344 New Eng. J. Med. 1782 (2001) (offering an optimistic account about the future of gene therapy for hemophilia); David Brown, Gene Therapy Shows Progress, Wash. Post, Sept. 1, 2006, at A4 (reporting that researchers have tried it with cancer patients). So far, however, gene therapy has worked only in patients with rare immune system disorders. See Sharon Begley, Why Gene Therapy Still Hasn't Produced Major Breakthroughs, Wall St. J., Feb. 18, 2005, at B1; Gautam Naik, Gene Therapy Is Successfully Used to Treat Two with Rare Disease, Wall St. J., Apr. 3, 2006, at B6 (reporting success in treating a form of chronic granulomatous disease); see also Rick Weiss, Boy's Cancer Prompts FDA to Halt Gene Therapy, Wash. Post, Mar. 4, 2005, at A2 ("After thousands of efforts, the treatments appear to have cured only about a dozen patients, all of them children in Europe who were born with a severe immune system disorder. With three of those children having developed cancer from the treatment and one recently dying of it, even the field's most ardent supporters are discouraged.").

2. *Federal jurisdiction over gene and somatic cell therapy.* For protocols that receive public funding, the researcher must comply with NIH requirements. See 59 Fed. Reg. 34,496 (1994) (superseding all previous guidelines). In addition, the FDA has asserted the power to regulate both gene therapy and somatic cell therapy:

> Existing FDA statutory authorities, although enacted prior to the advent of somatic cell and gene therapies, are sufficiently broad in scope to encompass these new products and require that areas such as quality control, safety, potency, and efficacy be thoroughly addressed prior to marketing.... [S]omatic cell therapy products are defined as autologous (i.e., self), allogeneic (i.e., intra-species), or xenogeneic (i.e., inter-species) cells that have been propagated, expanded, selected, pharmacologically treated, or otherwise altered in biological characteristics ex vivo to be administered to humans and applicable to the prevention, treatment, cure, diagnosis, or mitigation of disease or injuries. Cellular products intended for use as somatic cell therapy are biological products subject to regulation pursuant to the PHS Act and also fall within the definition of drugs in the FDCA.

58 Fed. Reg. 53,248 (1993); see also Shane M. Ward, Global Harmonization of Regulatory Requirements for Premarket Approval of Autologous Cell Therapies, 55 Food & Drug L.J. 225 (2000); Wilder J. Leavitt, Note, Regulating Human Gene Therapy: Legislative Overreaction to Human Subject Protection Failures, 53 Admin. L. Rev. 315 (2001); Christine Wilgoos, Note, FDA Regulation: An Answer to the Questions of Human Cloning and Germline Therapy, 27 Am. J.L. & Med. 101 (2001). What problems exist with the FDA's assertion of jurisdiction over gene therapy and somatic cell therapy? Is the fact that most of these "products" are actually complex scientific *processes*, frequently customized for the individ-

ual patient, fatal to the claimed categorization of these therapies as a biologic or a drug?

3. *Eugenic fears*. Most gene therapy protocols at this point affect only the patient's somatic cells; these therapies do not modify reproductive cells and therefore cannot affect the genome of a patient's future children. In contrast, germ-line therapies could eradicate genetic disease in later generations, though some ethicists and scientists have expressed concern about a resurgence of eugenics. See George J. Annas, The Man on the Moon, Immortality, and Other Millennial Myths: The Prospects and Perils of Human Genetic Engineering, 49 Emory L.J. 753 (2000); Nancy Pham, Note, Choice v. Chance: The Constitutional Case for Regulating Human Germline Genetic Modification, 34 Hastings Const. L.Q. 133 (2006); Note, Regulating Eugenics, 121 Harv. L. Rev. 1578 (2008); see also Nicole Baffi, Comment, The Good, the Bad, and the Healthy: How Spindle-chromosomal Complex Transfer Can Improve the Future, 74 Alb. L. Rev. 361 (2011) (focusing on a technique used to guard against mitochondrial disease); cf. Michael Bliss, The Discovery of Insulin 245 (1982) ("Because insulin enabled diabetics to live and propagate, and because the disease had a strong hereditary component, the effect of the discovery of insulin was to cause steady increase in the number of diabetics."). As asked in the next part, what if we could go beyond treating genetic diseases and use germline techniques for nontherapeutic purposes—indeed, unlike problems encountered with gene therapy, genetic enhancement could proceed through the insertion of whole new chromosome pairs. Cf. Andrew Pollack, Engineering by Scientists on Embryo Stirs Criticism, N.Y. Times, May 13, 2008, at A14 (reporting that researchers "have created what is believed to be the first genetically engineered human embryo" by successfully putting a gene for a fluorescent marker protein into an unviable fertilized ovum so that, after three days of mitosis, "all the cells in the embryo glowed").

4. *Trying to make antisense*. A different type of genetic therapy hopes to use a precise chain of base pairs designed to link with the messenger RNA produced by oncogenes, viruses, or other disease-causing genes in an effort to block protein synthesis. See Justin Gillis, After Years of Failure, a Code for Cures? DNA Advances Lift Promise of Antisense Technologies, Wash. Post, June 24, 2003, at E1; Andrew Pollack, Drugmakers' Fever for the Power of RNA Interference Has Cooled, N.Y. Times, Feb. 8, 2011, at D1; see also Reese McKnight, Note, RNA Interference: A Critical Analysis of the Regulatory and Ethical Issues Encountered in the Development of a Novel Therapy, 15 Alb. L.J. Sci. & Tech. 73 (2004).

5. *Pharmacogenomics*. The improved understanding of the human genome promises advances in personalized medicine. "Pharmacogenomics" refers to the science of utilizing information about genetic variations to facilitate drug development and to create optimal patient treatments. See Helen M. Berman & Rochelle C. Dreyfuss, Reflections on the Science and Law of Structural Biology, Genomics, and Drug Development, 53 UCLA L. Rev. 871 (2006). Because human beings exhibit a great deal of variation, better understanding of individual differences presents an opportunity for physicians to tailor drugs to suit their patients' individual genetic quirks and minimize the risk of side effects. See Wylie Burke & Bruce M. Psaty, Personalized Medicine in the Era of Genomics, 298 JAMA 1682 (2007); Yusuke Nakamura, Editorial, Pharmacogenomics and Drug Toxicity, 359 New Eng. J. Med. 856 (2008); Susan B. Shurin & Elizabeth G. Nabel, Pharmacogenomics—Ready for Prime Time?, 358 New Eng. J. Med. 1061 (2008); Ron Winslow & Marilyn Chase, Genetic Research May Help Pick Patients' Best Cancer Drugs: Aid for Physicians May Narrow Market for Blockbusters, Wall St. J., June 2, 2008, at B4; cf. Gina Kolata, How Bright Promise in Cancer Testing Fell Apart, N.Y. Times, July 8, 2011, at A1. The FDA has issued guidance for the submission of pharmacogenomic data. See 70 Fed. Reg. 14,698 (2005).

How might pharmacogenomics pose a challenge to existing regulatory mechanisms? Taken to an improbable extreme of complete customization, drug manufacturing would come to resemble pharmacy compounding and, in products liability terms, represent the provision of a service rather than sale of a product. Even the more probable fragmentation of patient populations into smaller subsets may pose challenges: Will clinical trials become even larger (or might some patient populations lose out)? Will more drugs qualify for orphan status (and should they do so in order to counteract the financial disincentives resulting from smaller market shares)? Will labeling suffice to educate physicians about pharmacogenomic data (and will diagnostic tests have to be bundled with these drug products)? How will health insurers react to the idea of paying a premium for greater precision in pharmacotherapy? For tentative answers to these sorts of questions, see Lars Noah, The Coming Pharmacogenomics Revolution: Tailoring Drugs to Fit Patients' Genetic Profiles, 43 Jurimetrics J. 1 (2002); see also id. at 11 ("Federal regulators—accustomed to large clinical trials using a diverse subject population and designed to test drugs with significant market potential, centralized manufacturing facilities, and uniform labeling—will have to cope with a radically altered model of drug development and use. In addition, tort doctrines and reimbursement policies will have to adjust to this new model."); id. at 26–27 ("Pharmacogenomics may result in a steep escalation of drug prices. Unlike 'off the rack' drugs, customized medications will need to recover R & D expenses from among a smaller population of users . . . [and] will require additional health care expenditures, for genetic testing and the like, not presently associated with drug prescribing."); id. at 27 ("Ultimately, payers may have limited enthusiasm for pharmacogenomics. After all, in the past they have adopted economizing mechanisms such as restricted drug formularies and therapeutic substitution that work in precisely the opposite direction of tailoring pharmaceutical therapies.").

In 2007, the FDA announced revisions in the labeling of the anticoagulant warfarin (Coumadin®) to alert physicians that genetic testing might help to identify those patients who risk serious bleeding reactions because they metabolize the drug more slowly than normal—or are more sensitive to its effects—and therefore should receive a lower initial dose. See David Brown, For the First Time, FDA Recommends Gene Testing, Wash. Post,

Aug. 17, 2007, at A10; Bernadette Tansey, A Specific Test for What Ails You, S.F. Chron., Sept. 9, 2007, at E1; see also Susan A. Fuchs, Will the FDA's 2010 Warfarin Label Changes Finally Provide the Legal Impetus for Warfarin Pharmacogenetic Testing?, 12 N.C. J.L. & Tech. 99 (2010); cf. Andrew Pollack, F.D.A. Urges Genetic Test Before Giving AIDS Drug, N.Y. Times, July 24, 2008, at C3 (reporting the addition of a black box warning in the labeling for abacavir with instructions to screen for a particular gene variation found in approximately 5% of patients because they may suffer severe allergic reactions). The value of such routine screening remains unclear. See Mark H. Eckman et al., Cost–Effectiveness of Using Pharmacogenetic Information in Warfarin Dosing for Patients with Nonvalvular Atrial Fibrillation, 150 Annals Internal Med. 73, 80–81 (2009); Andrew Pollack, Gene Test for Dosage of Warfarin Is Rebuffed, N.Y. Times, May 5, 2009, at B3; cf. Marie McCullough, Hopes Rising on Finding a Better Blood Thinner, Phila. Inquirer, Oct. 20, 2009, at A1 (describing new and safer substitutes).

For further commentary, see Matthew Avery, Personalized Medicine and Rescuing Unsafe Drugs with Pharmacogenomics: A Regulatory Perspective, 65 Food & Drug L.J. 37 (2010); Barbara J. Evans, Seven Pillars of a New Evidentiary Paradigm: The Food, Drug, and Cosmetic Act Enters the Genomic Era, 85 Notre Dame L. Rev. 419 (2010); Dov Greenbaum, Incentivizing Pharmacogenomic Drug Development: How the FDA Can Overcome Early Missteps in Regulating Personalized Medicine, 40 Rutgers L.J. 97 (2008); Jeffrey L. Moe, Commercialization Considerations for Individualized Diagnostic and Drug Therapies Resulting from Pharmacogenomics, 66 La. L. Rev. 103 (2005); Scott Sasjack, Demanding Individually Safe Drugs Today: Overcoming the Cross–Labeling Legal Hurdle to Pharmacogenomics, 34 Am. J.L. & Med. 7 (2008); Jennifer E. Spreng, The Food and Drug Administration and the Pharmacy Profession: Partners to Ensure the Safety and Efficacy of Pharmacogenomic Therapy, 13 J. Health Care L. & Pol'y 77 (2010); Margaret Crews, Comment, Pharmacogenomics: Tailoring the Drug Approval Process for Designer Drugs, 24 J. Contemp. Health L. & Pol'y 363 (2008); David Loughnot, Note, Potential Interactions of the Orphan Drug Act and Pharmacogenomics: A Flood of Orphan Drugs and Abuses?, 31 Am. J.L. & Med. 365 (2005); Randy J. Prebula, Note, The Promise of Personalized Medicine: Regulatory Controls and Tort Influences in the Context of Personalized Risks and Benefits, 26 J. Contemp. Health L. & Pol'y 343 (2010); Symposium, Law and the New Era of Personalized Medicine, 48 Jurimetrics J. 131 (2008); Hester Plumridge, Pharmaceutical Sector Remains Genetically Challenged, Wall St. J., Jan. 22, 2011, at B18.

6. *Racial profiling in medicine?* In 2005, the FDA approved the vasodilator BiDil® for heart failure, an unprecedented step because the drug was studied and labeled for use only in African–American patients. See Sylvia P. Westphal, Heart Medication Approved for Blacks Faces Uphill Battle, Wall St. J., Oct. 16, 2006, at A1. Although physicians have long known that members of certain racial or ethnic groups respond differently to some drugs (or have higher rates of certain diseases), some critics vocally assail any use of race as a rough proxy for genetic variabilities relevant to medical research or treatment. See Jonathan Kahn, Race-ing Patents/Patenting Race: An Emerging Political Geography of Intellectual Property in Biotechnology, 92 Iowa L. Rev. 353 (2007); Dorothy E. Roberts, What's Wrong with Race-based Medicine?: Genes, Drugs, and Health Disparities, 12 Minn. J.L. Sci. & Tech. 1 (2011); see also Rob Stein, Role of Race Reemerges in DNA–Testing Debate, Wash. Post, Aug. 1, 2011, at A1 (reporting that even the PTO has weighed in on the question); cf. Marc Kaufman, Crestor May Pose Risk of Muscle Damage: FDA Issues Warning on Use of Cholesterol Drug, Especially by Asians, Wash. Post, Mar. 3, 2005, at A14. Until pharmacogenomics allows physicians to tailor therapy to each individual's peculiar genetic makeup, should a patient's race or ethnicity (or gender, or age) ever get factored into drug selection? See generally Rene Bowser, Race as a Proxy for Drug Response: The Dangers and Challenges of Ethnic Drugs, 53 DePaul L. Rev. 1111 (2004); Sharona Hoffman, "Racially–Tailored" Medicine Unraveled, 55 Am. U. L. Rev. 395 (2005); Jonathan D. Kahn, How a Drug Becomes "Ethnic": Law, Commerce, and the Production of Racial Categories in Medicine, 4 Yale J. Health Pol'y L. & Ethics 1 (2004); Michael D. Ruel, Comment, Using Race in Clinical Research to Develop Tailored Medications: Is the FDA Encouraging Discrimination or Eliminating Traditional Disparities in Health Care for African Americans?, 27 J. Legal Med. 225 (2006). Are the issues different when drugs target diseases that occur almost exclusively in certain racial or ethnic groups? Cf. David Brown, Anti–Cancer Drug Greatly Reduces Sickle Cell Mortality, Wash. Post, Apr. 2, 2003, at A11 (reporting that the FDA previously had approved this added indication for hydroxyurea).

PROBLEM #15. *HURDLES TO CUSTOMIZED MEDICINES*

There are several classes of antihypertensives currently on the market, including calcium channel blockers (CCBs), ACE inhibitors, and diuretics. Some patients respond well to one type of blood pressure drug, some to another, but individual response is unpredictable. Until now, physicians have had to prescribe by trial and error until they find a drug that will reduce their patient's blood pressure without causing unwanted side effects. For some patients, none of the available drugs is both safe and effective. Trial and error prescribing suggests that approximately one-third of hypertension patients ("the BP subpopulation") experience adverse reactions to CCBs and ACE inhibitors, and at the same time find that diuretics do not control their condition adequately.

Bio–Orb Corp., a small biotech company, has used molecular biology coupled with an improved understanding of genetics to target the precise biochemical mechanism responsible for elevating blood pressure. Its researchers isolated the gene responsible for the adverse reactions in the BP subpopulation, and they used this information to develop Lodropol—a drug that is closely related in chemical structure to CCBs but theoretically should not cause the same adverse reactions. The company's scientists also developed a genetic test to predict which patients fall into the BP subpopulation. Bio–Orb believes that Lodropol will control hypertension with virtually no side effects in this patient subpopulation. (It is less certain how effective the drug will be for other patients with high blood pressure.)

Bio–Orb plans to seek FDA permission to conduct large-scale Phase III clinical trials on Lodropol. The scientific director wants your advice about how to design a protocol that will produce the best evidence of Lodropol's effectiveness within the bounds of regulatory constraints on human subjects research. He asks you to look at the patient selection issues (for example, should they test the product on all hypertension patients or just the BP subpopulation?), placebo controls, and the risk-benefit assessment, among other things.

Assuming that the clinical trials go well, the scientific director also wants to know what sorts of problems to expect during the drug licensing process: how will the agency assess risk and benefit for this unusual product, and what other problems might arise? Finally, the company is exploring the possibility of separately commercializing the genetic test to predict which patients can most benefit from Lodropol, and the director wonders whether there are any pitfalls in marketing such a test?

D. Bioethical Challenges Posed by Technology

The preface to this casebook refers to broad and narrow definitions of "technology." The advent of new medical technologies, in both senses of the term, has shaped ethical debates in a variety of ways. The field of "bioethics" emerged in the 1960s in response to controversies about new medical research and technologies such as hemodialysis. Of course, physicians have a long tradition of recognizing ethical norms, but bioethics purports to offer a still more encompassing perspective than provided by a code of professional conduct. It relies on a set of core principles—including beneficence, patient autonomy, nonmaleficence, and justice—to help make medical choices for individual patients and for society as a whole. See John C. Fletcher et al., Introduction to Clinical Ethics 4–12 (2d ed. 1997) (explaining that beneficence refers to the obligation to further the patient's best interests, and nonmaleficence requires the caregiver to avoid harming the patient or to minimize the harm when it is unavoidable). The following sections introduce some scenarios in which the intersection of technology and medicine has posed new ethical problems, and it examines some challenges for the future, but first one must ask whether bioethics has anything useful to bring to the table. Cf. Roger B. Dworkin, Limits: The Role of the Law in Bioethical Decision Making 18 (1996) (criticizing the law's role in bioethics, and opining that "our [legal institutional] tools for dealing with social problems posed by rapid change in biology and medicine are limited at best"); Dov Fox, Safety, Efficacy, and Authenticity: The Gap Between Ethics and Law in FDA Decisionmaking, 2005 Mich. St. L. Rev. 1135; Lars Noah, Coerced Participation in Clinical Trials: Conscripting Human Research Subjects, 62 Admin. L. Rev. 329, 354–56 (2010).

Michael H. Shapiro, *Is Bioethics Broke?: On the Idea of Ethics and Law "Catching Up" with Technology*

33 IND. L. REV. 17 (1999).

* * * Debates about technology and how we manage it often seem to shift without notice between critiques of ethical and legal evaluation, on the one hand, and critiques of the technological uses that draw our attention and dismay, on the other. Those who object to acquiring or using certain kinds of knowledge may criticize those who secured or applied it. * * * If the critical reactions derive from a failure within bioethics to deal with material problems, or from infirm perception or reasoning, then the criticisms are at least partly well taken. However, if the disagreement stems from deep differences in values, it is misleading and question-begging to say that the discipline, or some segment of it, is at fault for anything other than taking a different position from that of its critics. Of course, those in deep moral disagreement are very likely to find their opponents guilty of material omissions and failures of insight. Although it is sometimes hard to separate critiques of applied technology from critiques of technology assessment, complaints about a technological use and complaints about how we morally and legally assess it are not the same. * * *

The complaint that current ethical analysis is a turtle chasing a hare often rests on a simple matter: such analysis may not provide answers, at least definitive this-is-the-way-it-is-and-must-be answers, to difficult moral issues. If a medical laboratory can determine cell counts within a narrow range of uncertainty, or that the fibula is fragmented, or that your zorch is inflamed, why is ethics unable to yield definitive answers? If it cannot, what good is it? * * *

Although some may think that ethics experts have special knowledge about rightness and goodness, that view is doubted by many, including most ethical theorists and "ethicists." Indeed, some modern democratic movements seem to reject the very possibility of special moral insight or expertise. Perhaps it would be too strong to call it a mass delusion, but many within democratic systems think that one person's views on most matters are as good as another's. In particular, bottom-line moral conclusions are thought to be as fit for one citizen as for another if one assumes that the relevant situational facts are available to all. It may well be true, for example, as Professor Robert Holmes urges, that neither meta-, normative, nor applied ethicists can "make better moral judgments in particular situations than anyone else." * * *

There is at least one sense in which the claim that "technology has outrun ethics and law" is not that puzzling. People often complain of having too much information or too much choice and perhaps even too many ethical theories on the philosophy supermarket shelves. The "too much" label is a somewhat tendentious description; we may well be better off overall with more information and opportunities. Nevertheless, increased choice and knowledge bear certain costs, at least for some decision makers—e.g., a sense of oppression from a felt responsibility to assure the best outcome by canvassing all options and considering all information. * * *

The problem with biomedical technology, however, is not simply that we have more options and information of the same sort that we had before * * * * We have new kinds of choices: choices over the traits of offspring (prenatal and preconception testing; cloning); choices concerning control of mind and behavior (antipsychotic drugs; intellect-enhancing drugs); choices about lifesaving efforts (organ transplantation); and so on. Furthermore, we have new, possibly exaggerated visions of ourselves, our powers, and our progression. We may see our thought and behavior as less "free" and more "determined," and worry over the blurring of the boundaries between ourselves and other forms of life, or even machines. We encounter new difficulties of description and evaluation that may seem deeper and reflect far greater dangers than do those arising from choice in other contexts. The fact that we cannot get a precise fix on what these dangers might be makes matters worse because of the very namelessness of the risks. The range and difficulty of choice over matters we have never or only marginally dealt with before may seem to exceed our capacities for rational choice. What is that wretched state in which one permanently loses all faculties of thought and feeling, but one's bodily functions continue? Should we choose to say it is death because the person we knew seems irretrievably gone, despite his body's endurance? Who is the natural parent of a cloned offspring, or is there even any such thing?

This expanded range of choice reflects moral/conceptual difficulties, not just an increase in things to choose from. However, this is not what prevents moral and legal analysis from gaining on technology. Such analysis does not progress or advance in the same way as technology. They are not even on the same race track. Determining how Sarah Jr. shall be constructed when we have her germ line in hand in an early embryo cannot be answered just by gathering more information, or running brilliant experiments, or even by getting smarter. * * *

Consider the debate about objectification, an important idea concerning a central premise of bioethical analysis. We are rightly concerned with the risk of transforming our view of ourselves as persons into a view of ourselves as manipulable objects. It is said that bioethics undervalues risks of objectification—our descent from persons to objects. Objectification, however, is one of the most heavily discussed issues in bioethics. Indeed, in bioethics more people credit the risk of objectification than discount it. If something is wrong with bioethics here, it is that it overestimates that risk. In any case, search the literature for articles that do more than throw the term around. You will find some—but they do not characterize the field.

Instead, you will find material suggesting that simply using the term "products" to refer to children born of artificial technology indicates that we have already plunged into the abyss and are treating, say, babies born of in vitro fertilization (IVF) as things to be used as we wish. There is zero evidence to back this up; there is not even evidence to support the colorable view that investing heavy monetary, physical, and psychic resources in creating the child will result in intrusive parental control designed to assure a proper return on the investment. Even the term "objectification," used to describe a legitimate concern of bioethics, has itself been reduced to an analytically used slogan. * * *

The indictment of applied biology is often accompanied by claims that bioethics is infirm because it has failed to stop or even slow the onslaught of personhood-impairing technological advances. It has failed because its intellectual structure is impoverished or beholden to the wrong groups or values and so hastens our decline. This is so whether bioethics is viewed as a scholarly discipline, a body of law and legal practices, a set of customs and clinical practices, a set of attitudes and perspectives held by various groups, or any or all of these. Whatever it is, it is said to lack relevant perspectives, embrace the wrong values and value priorities, use the wrong paradigms and models and other modes of thought, and to be patriarchal and too oriented toward establishment culture.

The task here is to expose the vulnerabilities of these attacks. In this "critique of the critique" of biological technology and bioethics, I will complain, among other things, about how debates on the uses of life science technologies are framed and pursued in confused, confusing, and often misleading terms. * * * The explanation lies largely in a showing of how practices which radically rearrange life processes to suit specific wants generate conceptual and normative monsters: persons, entities, relationships, situations, and behaviors that escape the major abstractions we use to describe, explain, and evaluate human actions and circumstances. Of course, we encounter daily anomalies that do not fit nicely into our conceptual bins, but the failures recited here are special not only because they fit so poorly, but because they deal with foundational matters: whether we will come into or continue our existence, in what form, and under what constraints and circumstances. * * *

Our conceptual system is not assaulted because we cannot identify a clear boundary between negligence and due care, or between due and undue process. Nor is everyday language fatally flawed because there is no clear border between being tall and not being tall. Few would claim that we should abandon all concepts and distinctions because some of their applications are unclear, indeterminate, or change with time. Even simple conceptual vagueness, however, can lead to serious normative/conceptual problems as the world changes. Six-footers used to be giants and still are among some groups, but among other groups—think of the N.B.A.—six feet is pretty short. Do persons projected to be no more than six feet tall need growth hormone? Do early embryos from short people require genetic enhancement?

Similarly, * * * it is no garden-variety puzzle to be unable to identify a single natural mother when a fertilized ovum from one woman is gestated by another woman, who of course has no genetic connection to it. Here, the very structure of elemental notions like "mother" is in question. The concept itself has been fragmented as a result of our reconfiguration of the reproductive process.

This divide-conquer-and-confuse aspect of some biological technologies leads us to other characteristics of bioethical problems. Among the more notable are the reinforcement of the idea of the determinate, predictable, controllable, algorithmic person; the introduction of new purposes for our old life processes, as in producing fetuses to provide transplantable tissue rather than to reproduce; providing opportunities to further existing purposes with greater precision, as in controlling behavior with psychotropic drugs; and, more generally, substantially increasing our control over life processes, enabling greater predictability of traits and behavior. The very existence of such choice over matters not previously under our control is itself something of a conceptual anomaly.

Think, for example, of being able to determine the entire genome of a person-to-be through cloning, or of being able to heavily influence particular traits. If we can "construct" a person through technological alteration of her physiological system or her germ line, what sort of being should we construct? What new or strengthened purposes ought to be installed for life functions? What purposes for reproduction should be added or extended? The possibility of bone marrow transplantation suggests having babies—not just fetuses—to provide compatible tissue for transplantation. The prospect of cloning may inspire reproductive acts resting on the (mistaken) view that clones are locked into some common fate shared by all who have their defining genome. A given act of cloning may thus reflect the novel purpose, not simply of having children, but of perpetuating a line of identical persons raised to pursue some sharply bounded set of tasks requiring that their talents be matched to their assigned roles in life. Here, then, biological technology restructures reproductive processes in a way that generates anomalous lineage relationships, reinforces the images of persons as determinate entities, and provides us with additional reasons, possibly mistaken or objectionable, for using procreational mechanisms.

So, the arguably distinctive features of classic bioethical problems are that they involve, at the most abstract level, the directed revision of life processes and what this entails: the idea of the determinate person; the substitution of new purposes in using human capacities; and the general expansion of choice in constructing, controlling, and predicting life processes, in partial displacement of the natural randomness of life. These distinctive features of bioethics are not fully independent. The core idea is still the reordering of life processes into unclassified forms, giving us relationships (e.g., gestational mothers and "their" children and the children's "genetic parents"); entities (such as cryopreserved embryos); and powers (over our own fundamental structures, individually and collectively) that we often do not know how to deal with. Some believe that this transforms our vision of persons as free into an anti-vision of persons as machine-like or lower-animal-like—predictable, explainable, and controllable. * * *

One can plausibly criticize a discipline as conceptually and normatively impoverished because it fails to consider all material matters; that it proceeds illogically, incoherently, or otherwise carelessly or irrationally; that it is beset by conflicts of interest and imbalances of power; that it is biased, rigidly constrained by ideology, afflicted with false consciousness; and so on. It is less plausible, however, to complain because one simply disagrees with an outcome, without express regard to the approach used; or because (unthinkingly) the critic and the criticized assign different meanings to the same terms or concepts used in the decision making process. For example, rights-talk by one party may be at a different level of generality from that used by another; or a claim about prima facie rights might be taken as an absolute claim by another; or a claim about non-interference rights might be conflated with a claim about rights to affirmative assistance. * * *

Consider, for example, the idea of a commercial transaction as applied to human reproduction. A surrogacy arrangement can be as much a commercial exchange as the purchase of a clothes dryer. But saying this and abruptly ending the analysis is an immense descriptive and normative/conceptual error. Some indeed use the comparison to attack surrogacy as causing or constituting human commodification (the commercial version of objectification) by stressing the similarities between the two transactions—and then stopping without considering their differences. It is hard to see how the analysis could possibly be complete without doing both; there is no other rational way to deal with a purported parallelism. Moreover, the analogy is mishandled if one does not see that what even counts as "similarity" or "difference" may be contested. If a commentator or a discipline characteristically fail to confront both similarities and differences and the difficulties in recognizing them as such, then its decision making processes are indeed infirm. Making comparisons with blinders on may reflect lack of time for reflection, or lack of acuity. Disagreement about the results of the comparison, of course, does not nullify its worth; one's final judgment, however, is far better informed.

Moreover, an analogy may be useful in some contexts and not in others. For example, some nontrivial constitutional value probably applies to most forms of assisted sexual reproduction—artificial insemination (AI), IVF, etc.: with respect to sexual union in the general biological sense, they are identical. The social relationships involved may vary, but few doubt the status of these processes as human reproduction entitled to some constitutional protection. Some commentators, however, think that human asexual reproduction is so radically different that all constitutional bets are off: it is outside the Fourteenth Amendment's procreational autonomy ballpark. Its distance from paradigmatic sexual reproduction cannot be measured because the notion of "distance" does not readily apply. What is contested here is the very status of sexual recombination as a defining characteristic of human reproduction; the birth of a child is, for some, not enough to trigger constitutional protections of procreation.

For such observers then, comparison to a paradigm may work pretty well for AI, IVF, and even posthumous reproduction, but not for human cloning. The paradigm does not help establish anything one way or the other, or so one might argue. The asexual nature of cloning drives some critics to say, in effect, that it makes no sense to talk of the linear distance between sexual and asexual reproduction: they are utterly distinct and rival processes that should not bear the same designation—"procreation." The upshot is that use of analogy or comparison to a paradigm need not be universally serviceable; the processes are not completely worthless merely because they sometimes fail. Much the same applies to entire disciplines: if the discipline reaches a decision different from yours, it will take a lot more beyond this bare fact to establish a failure of process and an impeachment of its practitioners. * * *

In general, the talk about law and ethics being behind science and technology has to be reconstructed to make sense. Law and ethics are categorically different from science and technology and from each other, despite isomorphisms in argument structure and the "fuzziness" of the fact/value distinction. They concern science and technology, they are about science and technology (and everything else), but they are a different order of existence, and it is thus impossible to apply the same sense of progress to both domains. Their canons of verification differ strongly, despite the structural similarities. There is no race between law and ethics on the one hand, and science and technology on the other. In many instances, indecision, paradox, and indeterminacy are not usefully considered flaws in law or in ethics because they are inherent in them. One is not deficient for failing to come up with a certainly correct answer when it is impossible to find one. * * *

I am not even remotely suggesting that progress is simply a function of process. The temptation to forego substance because of its uncertainties in favor of choosing fair procedures is understandable, and in various situations resort to procedural solutions may be the only available pragmatic strategy for securing an acceptable bottom-line decision. However, there can be no assurance that the process will culminate in a morally convincing answer or a situation that all would say is the best of the alternatives. Indeed, conscientious decisionmakers who find themselves planted within some procedural scheme, say, a committee to distribute scarce medical resources, will experience precisely the same difficulties encountered by those who, not knowing how to generate a right answer, established the procedure in the first place. What would be clearly amiss, then, is to assert that because we cannot resolve a matter definitively, something is wrong with moral and legal theory generally and bioethics in particular. There are many who cannot abide such uncertainty and the shortage of answers it entails. The only sensible response is: get used to it, because there is no honest alternative.

NOTES AND QUESTIONS

1. *"Normal" height and above-average aspirations*. Controversy has emerged over the use of human growth hormone in children of short stature. See Vita M. Salvemini, Idiopathic Short Stature or Just Plain Short: Why the Federal Government Should Regulate the Administration of Human Growth Hormone to Healthy Children, 38 Ga. L. Rev. 1105

(2004); Cecilia C. Simon, Big on HGH? Human Growth Hormone Helps Small Kids Grow, but Some Call Its Wider Use Shortsighted, Wash. Post, Sept. 30, 2003, at F1; see also Michael H. Shapiro, The Technology of Perfection: Performance Enhancement and the Control of Attributes, 65 S. Cal. L. Rev. 11 (1991); Alice Dreger, When Medicine Goes Too Far in the Pursuit of Normality, N.Y. Times, July 28, 1998, at F4 ("Instead of constantly enhancing the norm—forever upping the ante of the 'normal' with new technologies—we should work on enhancing the concept of normal by broadening appreciation of anatomical variation."). In athletics, the use of performance enhancing drugs continues to cause scandals. See Amy Shipley, Tests Suggest Revival of Well–Known Drugs, Wash. Post, Aug. 22, 2006, at E1; see also Joshua H. Whitman, Note, Winning at All Costs: Using Law and Economics to Determine the Proper Role of Government in Regulating the Use of Performance–Enhancing Drugs in Professional Sports, 2008 U. Ill. L. Rev. 459; cf. Blair Tindall, Better Playing Through Chemistry, N.Y. Times, Oct. 17, 2004, § 2, at 1 (explaining that professional musicians use beta blockers such as propranolol to combat stage fright). Is the use of testosterone, steroids, or EPO fundamentally different from Lasik surgery, which sometimes leaves patients with better-than-normal ("eagle eye") vision?

2. *Build-a-baby workshops?* In the relatively near future, parents may be able to use preimplantation genetic selection (or manipulation) to choose (or create) "better" children—apart from the medical side-effects of such interventions, what other consequences would result if they became routine? See Peter Braude, Preimplantation Diagnosis for Genetic Susceptibility, 355 New Eng. J. Med. 541 (2006); Dov Fox, Silver Spoons and Golden Genes: Genetic Engineering and the Egalitarian Ethos, 33 Am. J.L. & Med. 567 (2007); Anne D. Lyerly, Marking the Fine Line: Ethics and the Regulation of Innovative Technologies in Human Reproduction, 11 Minn. J. L. Sci. & Tech. 685 (2010); Kerry L. Macintosh, Brave New Eugenics: Regulating Assisted Reproductive Technologies in the Name of Better Babies, 2010 U. Ill. J.L. Tech. & Pol'y 257; Michael J. Malinowski, Choosing the Genetic Makeup of Children: Our Eugenics Past, Present, and Future?, 36 Conn. L. Rev. 125 (2003); Sonia M. Suter, A Brave New World of Designer Babies?, 22 Berkeley Tech. L.J. 897 (2007); Lindsey A. Vacco, Comment, Preimplantation Genetic Diagnosis: From Preventing Genetic Disease to Customizing Children—Can the Technology Be Regulated Based on the Parents' Intent?, 49 St. Louis U. L.J. 1181 (2005); Note, Regulating Preimplantation Genetic Diagnosis: The Pathologization Problem, 118 Harv. L. Rev. 2770 (2005); see also Jaime S. King, And Genetic Testing for All .... The Coming Revolution in Prenatal Genetic Testing, 42 Rutgers L.J. (forthcoming 2011) (explaining that such techniques may be used even without undergoing IVF); Rob Stein, "Embryo Bank" Stirs Ethics Fears: Firm Lets Clients Pick Among Fertilized Eggs, Wash. Post, Jan. 6, 2007, at A1.

3. *All in the eye of the beholder?* What about the possibility that parents will select children with traits that many people would regard as disabilities? See Karen E. Schiavone, Comment, Playing the Odds or Playing God?

Limiting Parental Ability to Create Disabled Children Through Preimplantation Genetic Diagnosis, 73 Alb. L. Rev. 283 (2009); Symposium, Creating Children with Disabilities: Commentaries on Parental Tort Liability for Preimplantation Genetic Interventions, 60 Hastings L.J. 297 (2008); see also Alicia Ouellette, Hearing the Deaf: Cochlear Implants, the Deaf Community, and Bioethical Analysis, 45 Val. U. L. Rev. 1247 (2011); Amy E. Brusky, Comment, Making Decisions for Deaf Children Regarding Cochlear Implants: The Legal Ramifications of Recognizing Deafness as a Culture Rather Than a Disability, 1995 Wis. L. Rev. 235.

4. *Medicine for the mind.* The burgeoning use of antidepressants and other psychotropic drugs in this country has attracted attention. See Colleen Cebuliak, Life as a Blonde: The Use of Prozac in the '90s, 33 Alta. L. Rev. 611 (1995) (discussing emotional enhancement and cosmetic pharmacology); Shankar Vedantam, British Officials Advise Less Use of Antidepressants, Wash. Post, Dec. 7, 2004, at A1; see also Rob Stein, The Potential of "Brain Pacemakers": Implanted Devices May Alter Treatment of Many Disorders, Wash. Post, Mar. 6, 2004, at A1. With hopes of developing pharmacological treatments for cognitive impairments associated with aging, will otherwise healthy individuals use such drugs for memory enhancement purposes? See Maxwell J. Mehlman, Cognition–Enhancing Drugs, 82 Milbank Q. 483 (2004); Joel Garreau, Dose of Genius: "Smart Pills" Are on the Rise, Wash. Post, June 11, 2006, at D1; see also Benedict Carey, Memory Implant Gives Rats Sharper Recollection, N.Y. Times, June 17, 2011, at A23 (calling this research "a crucial first step in the development of so-called neuroprosthetic devices to repair deficits from dementia, stroke and other brain injuries in humans"). A growing number of students cramming for tests take ADHD drugs, which some have dubbed "academic steroids." See Shankar Vedantam, Millions Have Misused ADHD Stimulant Drugs, Wash. Post, Feb. 25, 2006, at A9; see also James Pavisian, Note, The Case for Human Ingenuity: How Adderall Has Sullied the Game, 48 Washburn L.J. 175 (2008).

How about memory cleansing as a treatment for post-traumatic stress disorder (PTSD)? See Adam J. Kolber, Therapeutic Forgetting: The Legal and Ethical Implications of Memory Dampening, 59 Vand. L. Rev. 1561 (2006); Benedict Carey, So You Just Want to Forget? Science Is Working on Eraser, N.Y. Times, Apr. 6, 2009, at A1; Rob Stein, Is Every Memory Worth Keeping? Controversy over Pills to Reduce Mental Trauma, Wash. Post, Oct. 19, 2004, at A1 (describing experiments using the antihypertensive propranolol, which appears to block the action of stress hormones on the amygdala and thereby blunt the etching or reconsolidation of painful memories, but noting concerns that such treatments might alter a fundamental part of a person's identity as well as society's collective memory); see also Anahad O'Connor, Wakefulness Finds a Powerful Ally, N.Y. Times, June 29, 2004, at F1 (discussing the use of Provigil®, a drug approved for narcolepsy, by healthy but sleep-deprived individuals seeking to stay alert); Rick Weiss, "Ecstasy" Use Studied to Ease Fear in Terminally Ill, Wash. Post, Dec. 27, 2004, at A11 ("MDMA has been referred to by psychiatrists as an 'empathogen,' a drug especially good at putting people in touch with their emotions. Some believe it [as well as another psychedelic drug, psilocybin] could help patients come to terms with the biggest emotional challenge of all: the end of life.'').

5. *Bioethical expertise?* What should decisionmakers do when faced with such conundrums? See Arthur C. D'Andrea, Note, Federalizing Bioethics, 83 Tex. L. Rev. 1663 (2005). As explained in Chapter 5(C), courts have become more scrupulous about admitting expert testimony. How would a judge determine whether to allow a bioethicist to testify? See Edward J. Imwinkelried, Expert Testimony by Ethicists: What Should Be the Norm?, 76 Temp. L. Rev. 91 (2003); Bethany Spielman & George Agich, The Future of Bioethics Testimony: Guidelines for Determining Qualifications, Reliability, and Helpfulness, 36 San Diego L. Rev. 1043 (1999); see also Sheryl G. Stolberg, Bioethicists Find Themselves the Ones Being Scrutinized, N.Y. Times, Aug. 2, 2001, at A16 (explaining that just about anyone can call themselves a ''bioethicist'').

6. *Further commentary*. See Carl Elliott, Better Than Well: American Medicine Meets the American Dream (2004); Joel Garreau, Radical Evolution: The Promise and Peril of Enhancing Our Minds, Our Bodies—and What it Means to Be Human (2005); Henry T. Greely, Remarks on Human Biological Enhancement, 56 U. Kan. L. Rev. 1139 (2008); Maxwell J. Mehlman, The Law of Above Averages: Leveling the New Genetic Enhancement Playing Field, 85 Iowa L. Rev. 517 (2000); Michael H. Shapiro, Constitutional Adjudication and Standards of Review Under Pressure from Biological Technologies, 11 Health Matrix 351 (2001); Michael H. Shapiro, Illicit Reasons and Means for Reproduction: On Excessive Choice and Categorical and Technological Imperatives, 47 Hastings L.J. 1081 (1996); Adnan K. Husain, Note, Spillage from the Fountain of Youth: The Regulation of Prospective Anti–Aging Molecular and Genetic Therapies, 2006 U. Ill. J.L. Tech. & Pol'y 159; Curtis A. Kin, Note, Coming to the ''Genetic Supermarket'' Near You, 48 Stan. L. Rev. 1573 (1996).

1. Death and Technology

In re Bowman

617 P.2d 731 (Wash.1980).

■ Utter, Judge:

* * * Death is both a legal and medical question. * * * Until recently, the definition of death was both medically and legally a relatively simple matter. When the heart stopped beating and the lungs stopped breathing, the individual was dead according to physicians and according to the law. The traditional definition did not include the criterion of lack of brain activity because no method existed for diagnosing brain death. Moreover, until recently, no mechanical means have been available to maintain heart and lung action; and respiration, heart action, and brain function are so closely related that without artificial support, the cessation of any one of them will bring the other two to a halt within a very few minutes. Thus,

Black's Law Dictionary 488 (4th ed. 1951), based upon older medical technology, defines death as:

> The cessation of life; the ceasing to exist; defined by physicians as a total stoppage of the circulation of the blood, and a cessation of the animal and vital functions consequent thereon, such as respiration, pulsation, etc.

With the recent advancement of medical science, the traditional common law "heart and lungs" definition is no longer adequate. Some of the specific factors compelling a more refined definition are: (1) modern medicine's technological ability to sustain life in the absence of spontaneous heartbeat or respiration, (2) the advent of successful organ transplantation capabilities which creates a demand for viable organs from recently deceased donors, (3) the enormous expenditure of resources potentially wasted if persons in fact dead are being treated medically as though they were alive, and (4) the need for a precise time of death so that persons who have died may be treated appropriately.

The numerous legal issues which look to the time and presence of death as determining factors require a legal response to these new developments. Inheritance, liability for death claims under an insurance contract, proximate cause and time of death in homicide cases, and termination of life support efforts are but a few of the areas in which legal consequences follow from a determination of whether death has occurred. * * *

While 20 years ago a victim of cardiac arrest had little chance of survival, now, however, up to one in five victims returns to productive life. This advance in technology has produced a tragic problem not known before, of those whose cardiorespiratory systems may be kept functioning but whose brains have suffered massive and irreversible damage resulting in brain death. * * *

The determination by a physician that the symptoms of brain death are present, in accordance with acceptable medical standards, emphasizes that cessation of brain function is a symptom of the loss that makes a person dead, rather than the loss itself. It is the law's determination that brain death is the legal equivalent of death because—under current medical science—the capacity for life is irretrievably lost when the entire brain, including the brain stem, has ceased functioning. * * *

The medical profession has established criteria by which to measure whether brain death has occurred. * * * In 1968, a Harvard Medical School committee developed criteria which now constitute the basis of accepted medical standards for the determination of brain death. Ad Hoc Committee of the Harvard Medical School to Examine the Definition of Brain Death, A Definition of Irreversible Coma, 205 JAMA 337 (1968). These "Harvard criteria" require (1) unreceptivity and unresponsivity to even the most intensely painful stimuli; (2) no spontaneous movements or spontaneous breathing for at least 1 hour; (3) no reflexes, as shown by no ocular movement, no blinking, no swallowing, and fixed and dilated pupils. The report further recommended flat electroencephalograms (EEGs) as a confirmatory test, and that hypothermia and use of central nervous system depressants as causes be eliminated. * * * More recently, refinements in the criteria have been proposed. See Refinements in Criteria for the Determination of Death: An Appraisal, 221 JAMA 48 (1972); An Appraisal of the Criteria of Cerebral Death: A Summary Statement, 237 JAMA 982 (1977). * * *

Both courts and legislatures have responded to these medical advances and adopted brain death as a standard of death. * * * [We] adopt the provisions of the Uniform Determination of Death Act which state:

> An individual who has sustained either (1) irreversible cessation of circulatory and respiratory functions, or (2) irreversible cessation of all functions of the entire brain, including the brain stem, is dead. A determination of death must be made in accordance with accepted medical standards.

This standard reflects both the former common law standard and the evolutionary change in medical technology. * * *

Steven Goldberg, *The Changing Face of Death: Computers, Consciousness, and Nancy Cruzan*

43 STAN. L. REV. 659 (1991).

The law of death and dying is exquisitely sensitive to our notion of what it means to be human. When the crucial aspects of "personhood" are irretrievably lost, we feel that an individual has died. But what are those crucial aspects? Changes in the legal definition of death over time suggest that our sense of what is unique to the human experience alters as science progresses. * * *

[T]he next few decades may bring a dramatic change in our sense of human uniqueness and a corresponding change in the definition of death. The engine of change will be developments in artificial intelligence, the field of study devoted to building thinking computers. It is not the rational power of those computers that will shake us but rather the prospect that they might become self-aware. * * * [T]he current heated debate over whether such a thing is possible demonstrates the centrality of self-awareness to our sense of human uniqueness. * * *

In terms of legal doctrine, the centrality of human self-consciousness is best demonstrated by the modern approach to the definition of death. As Robert Veatch notes, any concept of human death depends directly on those qualities thought to make humans unique. By that standard, the modern trend is clear. In the space of a few decades, technology has pushed us from a world in which a beating heart symbolizes life to a world in which circulation, breathing, eating, and even responding to external stimuli are less important than human consciousness.

The interdependence of respiration, circulation, and brain function, coupled with the inability of technology to replace essential bodily functions, made the determination of death relatively uncontroversial in the first half of this century. The absence of respiration and heart function signified death. Beginning in the 1950s, however, artificial respirators and other life-support systems began to change the situation. It became possible to keep the body alive even though the brain had ceased functioning. It eventually became possible to replace virtually every part of the body except the brain with an artificial substitute.

These revolutionary technological developments caused a tremor in mankind's sense of self. A government commission, the Artificial Heart Assessment Panel at the National Heart and Lung Institute, responded by discussing "the problem of the 'man-machine symbiosis'—that is, the extent to which technological processes should be imposed upon, or substituted for, the natural processes of human beings." The panel focused its discussion on the artificial heart. As the panel put it, "[t]he heart has held pre-eminence in poetry and in common speech as the seat of bravery, love, joy, and generosity. Will its replacement by a mechanical pump and motor not merely place technology deep in man's bosom but place man more deeply in the bosom of technology?"

The development of the artificial heart and other mechanical life-support devices hardly forced mankind to admit equivalence with machines. The human thirst for uniqueness was easily satisfied by transferring all important characteristics to what was now the one remaining irreplaceable organ, the brain. A focus on the heart was dismissed as "symbolism" and "irrational." * * *

But the transfer of focus to the brain left difficult problems for medicine and law. Confronted for the first time with comatose individuals who had essential bodily functions sustained by machines, members of neither profession were certain of how to proceed. On the one hand, no one wanted to end the existence of someone who was likely to regain brain function, but on the other hand, the sense of respect for human dignity, the cost of medical treatment, and the need for transplant organs counseled for ending life support in certain cases. The result was a growing interest in "brain death," a concept that permitted death to be declared while the heart was still beating.

In this country, an influential step toward defining death in terms of the brain was the report of an ad hoc committee at the Harvard Medical School (the Committee) in 1968. The Committee emphasized that with modern technology, respiration and a heartbeat could be maintained "even when there is not the remotest possibility of an individual recovering consciousness following massive brain damage." Accordingly, the Committee believed that it was essential to try to redefine the point at which death occurs. The Committee proposed standards for determining when a patient should be declared dead because his or her brain was permanently nonfunctioning.

It became apparent, however, that the word "brain" itself was too broad for the purpose of defining death. The Committee recognized that a distinction must be made between "higher" brain and "lower" brain functions. Generally speaking, consciousness and cognition are carried on in the higher brain, that is, in the cerebrum, particularly the neocortex. By contrast, vegetative functions such as breathing and blood pressure are carried out by the brain stem, a portion of the lower brain. The distinction is critical because in many heart attacks and accidents the disturbance of circulatory or respiratory functions is too brief to destroy the brain stem, but it is sufficient to destroy the neocortex. The result of such a disturbance is an individual who is alive under a "whole brain" definition of death, because the lower part of the brain still works, but who would not be alive if a "higher brain" definition were used. Such individuals are in what is often termed a "persistent vegetative state." They can be kept alive with intravenous feeding and antibiotics, but they are unlikely to ever recover further. These individuals often need no mechanical aid to breathe; they maintain a heartbeat, react to light, and respond with other merely physical reflexes, but they lack all awareness and cognition. * * *

It is important to keep in mind the rapidity of these developments in order to understand the legal regime that grew out of them. In the space of a few decades, the centuries-old identification of death with the cessation of heartbeat and respiration was giving way to a brain-centered definition. Fundamental moral issues were being addressed at the same time that new diagnostic techniques were being developed. * * * [T]he net result was that the legal definition of death moved to a recognition that death of the whole brain meant death of the human being, even if the heart and lungs were still being artificially maintained. But the formal definition of death does not tell the whole story. For while death was defined in terms of the whole brain, legal decisions on the cessation of treatment, including that of mechanical feeding, recognized that treatment could end not only when the whole brain was dead, but also when the higher brain alone was destroyed.

The legal definition of death moved quickly to reflect the considerations set forth in the report of the Committee. An influential step in this direction was the 1972 article by Alexander Capron and Leon Kass proposing a model brain-death statute. Drawing in part on the Committee's report, the authors proposed that if artificial means were needed to keep respiration and circulation going, a person would be considered dead if "he has experienced an irreversible cessation of spontaneous brain functions." The authors emphasized that by "brain functions" they meant the whole brain, so that someone who had lost only higher brain functions would not be defined as dead. But the authors did not defend the proposition that lower brain functioning alone—a condition marked by spontaneous reflexes but no consciousness—constituted human life. On the contrary, they stipulated that "the exclusion of patients without neocortical function from the category of death may appear somewhat arbitrary." They defended the exclusion on the ground that they were taking a "modest" step to bring the definition of death in line with modern medicine and emphasized that modern medicine was not yet able to routinely diagnose irreversible higher brain death as clearly as whole brain death. Significantly, they left the door open to the notion that individuals with higher brain death should be allowed to die by stressing in a footnote to the article that they were distinguishing the question "is he dead?," from the question "should he be allowed to die?"

Two influential reports by the Presidents' Commission for the Study of Ethical Problems in Medicine and Biomedical and Behavioral Research took the same tack. The first, a 1981 report entitled *Defining Death*, opted for a whole-brain rather than a higher-brain definition of death. The second, a 1983 report entitled *Deciding to Forego Life–Sustaining Treatment*, stated that families could justifiably remove artificial feeding tubes from patients with no higher brain functions thus causing the death of those patients.

The law has generally paralleled these approaches. In most jurisdictions, statute or common law provides that an individual is dead if her whole brain has ceased functioning, even if breathing and circulation are artificially maintained. At the same time, prior to the *Cruzan* decision, "an unbroken stream of cases ha[d] authorized procedures for the cessation of treatment of patients in persistent vegetative states," that is, patients who suffered higher-brain death. Many of these cases involve the removal of feeding tubes from these patients. The courts' opinions have employed various theories, ranging from an assessment of the patient's previously expressed wishes to an analysis of the benefits of continued treatment, but the results have been the same. * * * So in the space of just a few decades, a remarkable consensus has developed in the medical and legal communities that those who have been permanently deprived of self-awareness by cessation of higher brain functioning can be allowed to die. Clearly, the emphasis on the higher brain has been driven by a concern for those qualities that make humans special. * * *

NOTES AND QUESTIONS

1. *Withdrawal of life-sustaining treatment.* In *Cruzan v. Director, Missouri Department of Health*, 497 U.S. 261 (1990), the petitioner sustained permanent brain damage that left her in a persistent vegetative state (PVS). Her family sought court permission to withdraw life-sustaining nutrition and hydration that was delivered through a tube. The Supreme Court framed the question very narrowly, asking only whether the state could constitutionally require a health care surrogate decisionmaker to present "clear and convincing evidence" of Ms. Cruzan's wishes in order to permit the withdrawal of treatment, and it concluded that this standard did not impermissibly infringe on the petitioner's 14th Amendment liberty interests. Although the decision explicitly recognizes a constitutional right to refuse unwanted medical treatment by competent patients, it does not stand for the more general proposition that there is a constitutional "right to die." See Washington v. Glucksberg, 521 U.S. 702 (1997) (physician-assisted suicide); Yale Kamisar, When Is There a Constitutional "Right to Die"? When Is There No Constitutional "Right to Live"?, 25 Ga. L. Rev. 1203 (1991); Thomas W. Mayo, Constitutionalizing the "Right to Die," 49 Md. L. Rev. 103 (1990). More than a decade later, the plight of a PVS patient in Florida attracted national attention. After the courts had concluded that she would have wanted her feeding tube removed, the state legislature attempted to overrule this judicial determination. See Abby Goodnough, Governor of Florida Orders Woman Fed in Right-to-Die Case, N.Y. Times, Oct. 22, 2003, at A1; see also Bush v. Schiavo, 885 So.2d 321 (Fla.2004) (holding the law unconstitutional). After this move failed, Congress passed special legislation to intervene in the dispute, but the federal courts rebuffed this unprecedented effort. See Schiavo ex rel. Schindler v. Schiavo, 403 F.3d 1289 (11th Cir.2005) (affirming denial of motion for temporary restraining order that would have permitted reinsertion of the feeding tube); see also Abby Goodnough, U.S. Judge Denies Feeding–Tube Bid in Schiavo's Case, N.Y. Times, Mar. 23, 2005, at A1. See generally Symposium, Reflections on and Implications of Schiavo, 35 Stetson L. Rev. 1 (2005); Symposium, The Law of Death and Dying, 37 Loy. U. Chi. L.J. 279 (2006).

2. *Where do LVADs fit in this scheme?* Fully implanted heart-assist devices (e.g., pacemakers, ICDs) may pose tricky bioethical questions. See Rob Stein, Devices Can Interfere with Peaceful Death: Implants Repeatedly Shock Hearts of Patients Who Cannot Be Saved, Wash. Post, Dec. 17, 2006, at A1. Imagine that, after the implantation of a left ventricular assist device (LVAD) for a failing heart, an ambulatory but miserable patient asks a physician to deactivate it—would that fall within the constitutional right to request the removal of ventilators or other forms of artificial (though external) life-support equipment, or is it more akin to requesting physician-assisted suicide (after all, a heart transplant patient who fares poorly and regrets his choice presumably would have no right to ask a surgeon simply to remove the new organ or perhaps try to "deactivate" it by applying a strong electrical current)? See Rob Stein, Heart Pump Creates Life–Death Ethical Dilemmas, Wash. Post, Apr. 24, 2008, at A1 ("The debate illustrates how new medical technologies often proliferate before society has resolved the issues they raise, such as what to do when a patient has had enough.").

3. *Further commentary.* See David R. Smith, Legal Recognition of Neocortical Death, 71 Cornell L. Rev. 850 (1986) (noting that advances in medical technology make it essential to examine the legal issues raised by cardiopulmonary, whole brain, and neocortical definitions of death); Eelco F.M. Wijdicks, The Diagnosis of Brain Death, 344 New Eng. J. Med. 1215 (2001) (reviewing the criteria for establishing brain death, including techniques for excluding conditions that mimic brain death); Jason L. Goldsmith, Note, Wanted! Dead and/or Alive: Choosing Among the Not-so-Uniform Statutory Definitions of Death, 61 U. Miami. L. Rev. 871 (2007); Rob Stein, In "Vegetative State" Patients, Brain Scanners Show Some Alert Minds, Wash. Post, Feb. 4, 2010, at A1.

4. *Technology's impact on changing conceptions of viability.* Advances in medical technology also impact medical decisionmaking at the beginning of life. As the Supreme Court explained in *Planned Parenthood v. Casey*, 505 U.S. 833, 871 (1992), "[t]he woman's right to terminate her pregnancy before viability is the most central principle" of *Roe v. Wade*, 410 U.S. 113

(1973). The Court rejected *Roe*'s approach, however, in part because advances in neonatology had undercut the "rigid" trimester framework and made babies born before the end of the second trimester viable. See Webster v. Reproductive Health Serv., 492 U.S. 490 (1989); see also Christine Hauser, For the Tiniest Babies, the Closest Thing to a Cocoon, N.Y. Times, May 29, 2007, at F1 (reporting that the record for viability had dropped below 22 weeks of gestation); cf. Jack M. Balkin, How New Genetic Technologies Will Transform Roe v. Wade, 56 Emory L.J. 843 (2007); Jessica H. Schultz, Note, Development of Ectogenesis: How Will Artificial Wombs Affect the Legal Status of a Fetus or Embryo?, 84 Chi.–Kent. L. Rev. 877 (2010); John Leland, Abortion Might Outgrow Its Need for Roe v. Wade, N.Y. Times, Oct. 2, 2005, § 4, at 14 (explaining that, "while combatants focus on the law, technology is already changing the future of abortion," particularly with the off-label use of misoprostol to induce a miscarriage). For suggestions to borrow brain death criteria for the other end of the human life cycle, see Hans–Martin Sass, Brain Life and Brain Death: A Proposal for a Normative Agreement, 14 J. Med. & Phil. 45 (1989); Gary B. Gertler, Note, Brain Birth: A Proposal for Defining When a Fetus Is Entitled to Human Life Status, 59 S. Cal. L. Rev. 1061 (1986).

2. TECHNOLOGY, RATIONING, AND FUTILITY

With the continuing advance of medical technology, patients and physicians have more treatment options than ever. Yet, at the same time, many available interventions appear to be of questionable therapeutic value. The proliferation of medical technology requires that physicians and society think seriously about what constitutes medically appropriate care. Previous chapters in this casebook presented the question of medical benefit at a different level of generality. For example, Chapter 3 described how the FDA makes risk-benefit evaluations when it decides whether to approve a medical technology for marketing, Chapter 6 discussed the risk-utility standard courts apply to design defect claims, and Chapter 9 considered the process by which payers make cost-benefit determinations when deciding whether to reimburse providers and patients for the use of particular technologies. The FDA generally does not evaluate the appropriateness of new technology as part of the available array of medical interventions for a particular condition. See Jonathan D. Rockoff, Critics Weigh in on FDA's Decisions: Some Say Ethics, Finances Should Be Factors for Product Approval, Balt. Sun, Jan. 9, 2006, at 1A. The agency may approve a new type of neonatal incubator for very premature infants because the product works without ever pausing to consider whether providing the incubator for such infants is appropriate. Insurers may decide to reimburse patients for an extremely expensive oncology drug because it permits the average patient to live a couple of months longer without pausing to evaluate whether the treatment provides a genuine benefit to the dying patient. Considerations of medical futility ask whether a technological intervention is medically appropriate for a particular patient apart from its safety or cost.

Mark A. Hall, *Rationing Health Care at the Bedside*

69 N.Y.U. L. Rev. 693 (1994).

When we are ill, we desperately want our doctors to do everything within their power to heal us, regardless of the costs involved. Medical technology has advanced so far, however, that literal adherence to this credo for everyone would consume the entire gross domestic product. Therefore, the fundamental problem of how best to ration limited medical resources among competing beneficial uses must be resolved in order for this country to construct a workable system for financing and delivering health care.

This axiomatic statement of the problem assumes the necessity of rationing, which some policy analysts and most politicians continue to dispute. President Clinton adamantly asserted that his 1993 health care reform proposal would not cause rationing, a claim disputed by his critics. Both sides of the political debate assume, then, that it is desirable and feasible to avoid rationing. As a few politicians and most policy analysts recognize, however, it is a fundamental law of the psychology of human wants that rationing in some form is inevitable. Every spending decision is necessarily a rationing decision simply because resources devoted to one person or one use are not available for someone or something else. Therefore, the question cannot be put whether rationing is avoidable, since we have always rationed health care resources on a massive scale, only according to irrational and unethical principles. * * * [F]or those who are fully insured, we devote vast resources to save lives and restore health once an illness or accident occurs, but we spend relatively little on safety, health education, and health prevention measure. Even within traditional medicine, care is rationed by limiting benefits for mental health, dental, and nursing home services. * * *

In searching for an acceptable form of rationing, we are plagued by two basic questions: (1) Who should decide what care is not worth the costs, and (2) What criteria of benefit should be used to make this determination? The substantive criteria problem is the one that has received more attention to date in the health care rationing literature. Numerous volumes have been written on questions such as whether the short supply of transplantable organs should be distributed based on simple queue or lottery systems or on elaborate concepts of medical need or medical benefit, and whether social worth factors can be prevented from tainting these concepts. Extensive literature has also developed around routine medical technologies asking whether medical resources generally should be rationed according to age or instead according to some more quantitative formula for cost-benefit or cost effectiveness. In the latter case, the literature discusses whether medical benefit should be defined in terms of lengths of life, quality of life, or some more intermediate end point such as diagnostic certainty.

These are tremendously important questions deserving of continuing inquiry, but they avoid what I see as the more fundamental question: Who should be the rationing decision maker? This question is more basic for three reasons. First, some decisionmaking mechanisms would obviate the need for an explicit consensus on criteria. For instance, the competitive market mechanism leaves the substantive criteria to individual choice as in other sectors of the economy where rationing is largely hidden. Second, even if we adopt more collective forms of rationing, it is highly unlikely that we will agree on a single, substantive criterion, or a lexical ordering of several rationing criteria. Therefore, the criteria question inevitably will be influenced by whatever decisionmaking framework we choose, whether political, medical professional, or market oriented. Third, even if agreement on general criteria were reached, their precise definition and application would depend on the broad range of discretion exercised by whomever implemented the criteria.

Fundamentally, three different rationing mechanisms are conceivable. Cost-sensitive treatment decisions can be made by patients, by physicians, or by third parties, primarily private and governmental insurers, but also various regulatory or review organizations. Although patient and third-party rationing are each systematically flawed, legal doctrine and ethical theory have leveled their strongest attack against physician rationing. * * *

Elsewhere in our economy, cost-benefit trade-offs are usually made through the purchasing decisions of individual consumers. For example, nutrition resources are allocated at both the macro and micro levels through the aggregation of countless, individual decisions of how much food to buy, of what quality, and from what source. This simple market mechanism, however, is not generally available or desirable for health care because of the unpredictability of illness and the complexities of medical judgment. We purchase insurance rather than pay out of pocket because we want to protect ourselves from the uncertain costs of health care and the anxiety of making spending decisions under the strain of serious illness. Moreover, even without insurance, we make few of our medical decisions ourselves because the complexity of treatment compels us to delegate extensive authority to our doctors.

These two structural elements—insurance and physician agency—make consumer rationing untenable for many health care purchasing decisions. Some role for consumer rationing may be preserved to the extent that insurance is incomplete, requiring, for instance, patients to pay deductibles and co-insurance. Consumer rationing may also occur to the extent that informed consent requirements place the ultimate authority in the hands of patients. But because consumers will always rely on insurance to insulate themselves from some health care costs, and because patients will always rely to a significant degree on their physicians' recommendations, medical spending decisions are necessarily made through the agency of insurance and the agency of physicians.

Insurers can ration through cost-sensitive rules about what treatment they will pay for, although to date this has seldom happened, either by private or governmental insurers. Oregon became the first state to attempt explicit rule-based rationing when it ranked over 600 condition-treatment pairings—e.g., surgery for appendicitis—according to medical effectiveness for purposes of allocating limited Medicaid funding. Other efforts are under way to develop a host of much more detailed and nuanced clinical practice guidelines, which could also serve as rule-based rationing tools.

As important as these efforts are, they will never produce a wholly satisfactory rationing scheme. The complexities of human mental and biological functioning and the state of medical science are such that no set of rules could possibly be detailed enough to capture all of the judgmental and value-laden aspects of medical decision making. A complete and scientifically valid set of rationing rules would entail the impossible task of developing rigorous empirical information for each of the almost 10,000 diagnostic entries in the World Health Organization's *International Classification of Diseases* and the almost 10,000 medical interventions listed in the AMA's *Current Procedural Terminology*. Moreover, even if such rules were completed and continuously updated, they would fail to reflect varying consumer preferences for different medical risks and health outcomes. Since these preferences cannot be fully captured in either patient-generated decisions or in third-party rules, we necessarily must resort to some degree of physician rationing * * * *

Despite the imperfections of rule-based third-party rationing, no one disputes that those who foot the bill for health care have a right to set some external limits on the particular items of service they will fund. Thus, for third-party rationing, the debate is only over establishing appropriate limits for its role and scope. In contrast, physician-based rationing remains controversial at a level of fundamental principle that questions whether it may occur at all. * * *

[T]he dominant position among medical ethicists and the medical profession in general is a nearly absolute moral prohibition against physicians ever considering the costs of treatment to any degree. This Article refers to this cost-is-no-object position as the physician's ethic of absolute quality. This ethic advocates that from the physician's perspective literally any marginal medical benefit, no matter how small, is worth absolutely any price because doctors in their role as healers should behave as if each of our lives is priceless. Adherents believe that rationing either is not necessary or that it must be imposed from external, societal sources. * * *

A divergent wing of less absolutist physicians and ethicists are more accommodating to bedside rationing. They recognize the necessity of rationing, are willing to contemplate that physicians will incorporate economic costs into their clinical judgments to some extent, and see this as preferable in some instances to rationing by market forces or by insurer or governmental fiat. Still, most adherents to this minority view impose the constraint that physicians be strictly insulated from any personal financial gain from their economizing decisions. These adherents believe that physicians should be allowed to mediate among the health care needs within a group of patients, but that they should not be financially rewarded for rationing. * * *

[M]uch of the opposition to bedside rationing can be explained by the fear that doctors will play God by overtly sacrificing life or health for some social agenda. Thus, many of the critics of physician rationing cited above focus on dramatic, life-or-death decisions such as terminating all treatment for the elderly or for severely injured children. But it is possible to support some measure of incremental bedside rationing and also to agree with the notion that it would be too corrosive of the treatment relationship for physicians to make high stakes, high drama rationing decisions without consulting their patients or relying on explicit regulatory or contractual authority. A more useful picture of bedside rationing involves physicians declining to order a confirming diagnostic test or an extra day in the hospital, prescribing a less expensive drug, or avoiding a referral to a specialist when the stakes are low or when their confidence in diagnosis and prognosis is fairly high already. * * *

[B]edside rationing would not require explicit cost-benefit calculations, although such calculations would not be prohibited. Instead, various mechanisms—education, peer influence, and financial incentives—would cause physicians to internalize cost consideration within their intuitive clinical judgment, encouraging them to adopt a more conservative, less interventionist practice style. Cost-benefit trade-offs would be largely subliminal in physicians' thought process, just as medical risk-benefit calculations at present are more often made through heuristic judgment rather than with rigorous calculation. * * * We will never know which mixes are acceptable until the merits and flaws of each approach and their proper domains receive rigorous empirical inquiry and analytical debate. The problem is that in order to even broach this subject in a constructive manner, we must overcome the ethical and legal taboo against physicians ever considering the costs of their treatment decisions. * * *

Paul C. Sorum, *Limiting Cardiopulmonary Resuscitation*

57 Alb. L. Rev. 617 (1994).

Cardiopulmonary resuscitation (CPR) is the treatment for cardiac arrest. Cardiac arrest is the loss of an effective pumping action of the heart, so that blood flow ceases to the vital organs (including the brain, the kidneys, and the heart itself). * * * The aim of CPR is twofold: first, to maintain a sufficient flow of oxygenated blood to the vital organs to prevent damage or, more accurately, to delay its onset; second, to restore effective cardiac function. The patient will usually receive the following interventions: manual compressions of the chest ("closed-chest cardiac massage"); one or more jolts of electricity to the chest ("defibrillation") designed to interrupt the disorganized activity so that an orderly heartbeat can reemerge; artificial ventilation of the lungs through a mask over the patient's mouth or through a tube inserted through the mouth down into the windpipe; and intravenous medications and fluids. These procedures usually last from a few minutes to a half an hour, until the patient's cardiac function has been restored or until he or she has been declared dead.

CPR has a history similar to that of many other medical technologies. It was invented at the end of the 1950s primarily for patients who, because of shocks from electrical lines, the effects of anesthesia, or heart attacks, developed ventricular fibrillation—the sudden onset of chaotic electrical activity in the muscle wall of the ventricle, leading to disorganized quivering of the heart with no forward movement of blood. But quickly it was used, even by its inventors, on patients without ventricular fibrillation as well, that is, on types of patients for whom it was not originally intended. Soon everyone in the hospital was, unless declared otherwise, a candidate for CPR, even when the cause of the arrest was chronic, not acute. CPR became a right for all patients, although a rite of passage to death for most. As a result, the hospital house staff who trained in the 1970s and 1980s, who were called on to perform most of the attempted resuscitations, were—as I have personally experienced—frequently disturbed, even revolted, by what seemed cruel and fruitless assaults on severely ill and demented patients. By the end of the 1980s, many physicians and ethicists were proposing in the medical journals that physicians should limit the use of CPR. They have advanced three types of arguments to justify restricting CPR: 1) its lack of effectiveness (in particular, its "futility" for certain categories of patients); 2) the high cost of its consequences; and 3) the wish of many patients to forgo it. * * *

The results of CPR in adults are not encouraging. Most patients die either immediately or within a few days. Only about a tenth of recipients live long enough to leave the hospital. It seems, therefore, that CPR is a highly atypical medical procedure in that most patients are worse off after it than before it. Yet the patients' condition just before CPR is cardiac arrest, and the results of no CPR are, most people believe, even worse than those of CPR: every patient who suffers a true cardiac arrest and does not receive CPR dies. The issue seems to be how many patients will hang on to meaningful life.

Yet some groups of patients have worse results than others. Patients who are gravely ill at the time of their cardiac arrests almost never survive to be discharged from the hospital. Numerous physicians and ethicists * * * have, therefore, argued that CPR is, for these groups of patients, a "futile" treatment (in the sense that it offers them no benefit). Under such circumstances, because a physician is not obligated to undertake or even offer a treatment that is clearly futile, the physician can and should decide to exclude these patients from receiving CPR, i.e., declare them DNR ("do not resuscitate"). The physician needs to inform them or their surrogates of this decision but does not need to consult with them about it. * * *

Two objections can be offered to declaring that CPR is futile for patients with little or no hope of subsequently leaving the hospital. First, when a variety of studies of the outcomes of CPR are examined, no category of patients is without some survivors to discharge. It would be very difficult, if not impossible, therefore, to draw the line between those for whom CPR is futile and those for whom it is not. Second, and more importantly, it is, in my opinion, illegitimate for a physician to deny the option of CPR to his or her patient on the grounds that the patient is going to die soon anyway. In doing this, the physician either is declaring, without consulting the patient or his or her surrogate, that the patient's life is no longer worth living or, at least, would no longer be worth living after the arrest and resuscitation, or is deciding that the meager benefit to the patient and others of keeping the patient alive for a short time is not worth the expected enormous monetary and psychological costs.

In the first case, the physician is substituting his or her own values or estimation of the worth of a particular form of living for the patient's. Yet patients frequently adjust to and find some benefit in even painful and restricted modes of existence. Physicians tend, therefore, to underestimate how the patient rates his or her quality of life. In the second case, the physician is placing the interests of society, the institution, or another group (such as personnel in the intensive care unit) above the patient's interests. In both cases the physician would, in my judgment, be acting contrary to the current dictates of medical ethics and the law, which obligate the physician to act primarily in accordance with the patient's values, not his or her own, and in accordance with the interests of the patient, not of others.

The second argument used to justify restricting the use of CPR focuses on cost. The increasingly high cost of health care in the United States alarms the public and politicians alike. Theoretically, no particular percentage of the Gross National Product (GNP) spent on health care is intrinsically too high. * * * Although restraining the costs, development, and use of new and more expensive medical technologies will be difficult, if not impossible, a number of medical economists, ethicists, and policymakers have concluded that some system of rationing of health services is necessary. * * * [Chapter 9(B) excerpts this discussion.]

[E]ven if we still believe that CPR should be restricted for economic reasons, we need to realize that this rationing should be done by society (or its representatives), not by individual physicians. The patient-physician relationship in America is based on the premise that the physician will act primarily in the individual patient's best interests, not in the interests of society. Society may decide to establish rules for rationing or to appoint agents to impose rationing (such as directors or triage officers of intensive care units), but it cannot, in the current American climate, expect individual physicians to withhold CPR from their patients in order to save money. This seems to be the position of most physicians and would likely be upheld by most judges and juries. Many commentators thus argue that, to resolve the dilemmas of futility and cost, society—in the form, for example, of proposals by presidential commissions, statements by religious authorities, state laws, and judicial rulings—needs to take a clearer stand. The conclusion of my consideration of the rationales of ineffectiveness and cost for restricting the use of CPR is that patient (or surrogate) choice provides the only legitimate ground for physicians to withhold CPR from their patients. * * *

NOTES AND QUESTIONS

1. *Defining medical futility.* For more on the debate about how to define the medically appropriate use of CPR and other expensive medical technologies, see Kathleen M. Boozang, Death Wish: Resuscitating Self–Determination for the Critically Ill, 35 Ariz. L. Rev. 23 (1993); Nancy M.P. King & Gail Henderson, Treatments of Last Resort: Informed Consent and the Diffusion of New Technology, 42 Mercer L. Rev. 1007 (1991); Patrick Moore, Note, An End-of-Life Quandary in Need of a Statutory Response: When Patients Demand Life–Sustaining Treatment That Physicians Are Unwilling to Provide, 48 B.C. L. Rev. 433 (2007); Alicia Seibel, Comment, The Limits to Life: What the D.C. Circuit's Decision in Abigail Alliance v. von Eschenbach Means for Medical Futility Statutes, 53 St. Louis U. L.J. 1321 (2009). As the excerpts above suggest, concepts of medical futility are closely linked with the process of technology assessment. See Ezekiel J. Emanuel & Linda L. Emanuel, The Economics of Dying: The Illusion of Cost Savings at the End of Life, 330 New Eng. J. Med. 540 (1994); Holly M. Holmes et al., Reconsidering Medication Appropriateness for Patients Late in Life, 166 Archives Internal Med. 605 (2006) (offering guidance for withholding or discontinuing the use of otherwise indicated drugs in patients with only a short remaining life expectancy); Jeff Donn, Can You Afford to Die?, Cin. Post, Aug. 15, 2006, at B6. For instance, artificial hearts can sustain critically ill patients for a few extra months, but, given the persistent shortage of donor hearts, these very expensive devices cannot hope to reduce the aggregate number of deaths in this group of patients (though they may give any particular patient a better shot at securing a permanent transplant), leading some to ask whether they serve any purpose. See Rob Stein, Artificial Heart Gets FDA Panel Approval, Wash. Post, Mar. 18, 2004, at A1; see also David Brown, Artificial Heart Gets Limited FDA Approval, Wash. Post, Sept. 6, 2006, at A8.

2. *Medical futility and the care of premature infants.* Questions of medical futility also arise at the beginning of life, with decisions about the care of premature or severely handicapped infants. Physicians and families often find it difficult to make decisions about appropriate levels of medical intervention because the ethical principle of autonomy does not apply. Instead, decisionmakers must attempt to determine what is in the infant's best interest—a difficult task because the outcome of any treatment remains uncertain. See, e.g., In re Baby K, 16 F.3d 590 (4th Cir.1994); In re K.I., 735 A.2d 448 (D.C.1999); Iafelice v. Zarafu, 534 A.2d 417 (N.J.App. Div.1987); see also Thomas A. Warnock, Comment, Scientific Advancements: Will Technology Make the Unpopular Wrongful Birth/Life Causes of Action Extinct?, 19 Temp. Envtl. L. & Tech. J. 173 (2001).

Lars Noah, *Triage in the Nation's Medicine Cabinet: The Puzzling Scarcity of Vaccines and Other Drugs*

54 S.C. L. REV. 741 (2003).

* * * One might understand the problem [of shortages in childhood vaccines and other critical pharmaceuticals] as the flipside of rationing

expensive health care interventions: if prices become sufficiently depressed as a result of government efforts to ensure inexpensive access for patients, manufacturers may no longer bother to produce the product or at least devote fewer resources to it than more lucrative lines of business, which then creates a problem of scarcity. Along similar lines, declining insurance reimbursements for mammograms, which may no longer cover the cost of performing this diagnostic test, have caused several mammography centers to close their doors. * * *

A vast literature exists about health care rationing, but it focuses almost exclusively on scarcity of financial resources that requires trade-offs among patients, choice of interventions, and other uses of the money. Commentators have paid relatively little attention to the "microallocation" questions that arise when, no matter the ability to pay, there are not enough units of a health care intervention to go around. The one major exception to this lack of attention is the field of organ transplantation, which actually poses both sets of rationing difficulties. Given the high costs and sometimes poor chances of success associated with organ transplantation, some have questioned whether this intervention represents a sensible expenditure of scarce health care resources. If society answers that macroallocational question in the affirmative, then, at least as long as shortages persist, it becomes necessary to face the microallocational question and decide which patients will receive the available organs.

Microallocation problems pose particularly difficult choices. How does one select among various patients when inadequate supplies prevent treating all of those in need? The federal government has established an elaborate allocation system for donated organs, but no similar framework exists for the rationing of critical pharmaceuticals when shortages arise. One could distribute such medications on a first-come, first-served basis or using some other random allocation system. In 1953, for instance, "the British Ministry of Health instituted a national lottery in order to allocate the scarce supplies of polio vaccine." Half a century later, initial shortages of a new treatment for hepatitis C required the establishment of a special patient registration system.

Most rationing schemes emphasize relying solely on medical criteria, but even these may point in different directions. Should the scarce resource go to the sickest patient or the one most likely to recover completely if treated at an early stage? When the vaccine against hepatitis B first became available, the combination of limited supplies and high costs led to recommendations for its use only in "high-risk groups." * * *

Although medical ethicists generally reject using social worth criteria, should the patient's age (or perhaps ability to pay) factor into the choice? In recent years, recurring shortages of the annual vaccines against influenza have resulted in recommendations that otherwise healthy adults delay seeking inoculations so as to ensure adequate doses for the elderly. In the face of concerns about shortages of the DTP vaccine in the mid–1980s, the CDC recommended that pediatricians delay administering booster shots. It has taken similar steps to cope with the latest round of shortages, resulting, for instance, in an inability among adults to get tetanus shots.

Finally, should purely medical criteria give way in the face of a national emergency? During World War II, the inability to synthesize penicillin coupled with a sudden surge in demand resulted in serious supply shortages and required rationing to facilitate the war effort. At present, some controversy exists about providing initial doses of scarce vaccines to public health and emergency response officials.

Rationing difficulties often arise because of macroallocational decisions or, more typically, indecision. Aside from insuperable technological barriers, we could avoid microallocation problems by devoting greater resources to securing adequate supplies. For the most part, vaccines and antibiotics do not represent expensive or exotic life-saving technologies. On the contrary, they are among the most cost-effective health care interventions available today, but their very success may have bred public complacency, and the resulting failure to give sufficient priority to ensuring the continued availability of these older medical technologies may imperil the public health. In the case of rare diseases, the federal government has extended special incentives designed to encourage the development of so-called "orphan" drugs. Notwithstanding narrow patient populations, a steady demand for certain orphan drugs coupled with generous market exclusivity provisions have resulted in several commercially successful products. Off-patent pediatric vaccines, antibiotics, and other critical pharmaceuticals designed for only occasional use by large patient populations may represent the real orphans in need of additional protection. * * *

NOTES AND QUESTIONS

1. *Organ allocation.* As noted in the above excerpt, the government has developed methods for rationing whole organs. See Christopher T. Robertson, From Free Riders to Fairness: A Cooperative System for Organ Transplantation, 48 Jurimetrics J. 1 (2007); Gail L. Daubert, Note, Politics, Policies, and Problems with Organ Transplantation: Government Regulation Needed to Ration Organs Equitably, 50 Admin. L. Rev. 459 (1998); Laura E. McMullen, Comment, Equitable Allocation of Human Organs: An Examination of the New Federal Regulation, 20 J. Legal Med. 405 (1999). One suggestion for responding to scarcity involves the salvage of diseased or defective (so-called "extended criteria") organs for patients who otherwise would receive a low priority because of their poor prognosis. See Paul Engstrom, "Marginal" Organs Can Be Another Shot at Life, L.A. Times, July 16, 2001, at S6; see also Rob Stein, Under Kidney Transplant Proposal, Younger Patients Would Get the Best Organs, Wash. Post, Feb. 24, 2011, at A1 ("If adopted, the approach could have implications for other decisions about how to allocate scarce medical resources, such as expensive cancer drugs and ventilators during ... emergencies ....").

2. *Dealing with spot shortages.* When acute shortages of childhood vaccines have arisen, public health officials sometimes responded by announcing temporary revisions in the recommended schedule of vaccinations. See, e.g., Anita Manning, Not Enough Meningitis Vaccine to Go Around, USA Today, July 19, 2006, at 5D (explaining that the CDC had recommended deferral of immunizations for pre-teens); Don Sapatkin, Hib Disease Deaths Put Focus on Vaccine Shortage, Phila. Inquirer, Apr. 1, 2009, at A1 ("Health officials believe the [sporadic recent] outbreaks [of Haemophilus influenzae type b] likely were triggered by a vaccine shortage .... [T]he government has issued guidelines to conserve supplies. The recommendations direct providers to delay giving the 'booster' shot ... except for children with specific known risk factors."). What (if any) role should manufacturers of scarce pharmaceuticals play when rationing becomes necessary? See Thomas Gryta, Genzyme Plans to End Fabry Drug Rationing, Wall St. J., Sept. 16, 2010, at B4; Andrew Pollack, The Savior That Faltered, N.Y. Times. Apr. 16, 2010, at B1 ("Genzyme, in consultation with doctors and patient advocacy groups, has allowed those with more severe Gaucher disease to get a full dose of [Cerezyme®]. But about 80 percent of the patients got no drug at all for several months late last year [because of a shortage caused by GMP problems]. With Fabry [disease], the company decided that there was no easy way to determine which cases were the most severe. So everyone recently has been getting only 30 percent of their usual doses [of Fabrazyme®]."); cf. Jennifer C. Dooren, Drug for Leukemia in Shorter Supply, Wall St. J., Apr. 14, 2011, at A5 (reporting that hospitals have begun rationing cytarabine).

3. *Rationing in the event of a national emergency.* Allocating scarce supplies of critical drugs in the event of a bioterrorist attack will pose serious challenges. See Ross D. Silverman & Thomas May, Terror and Triage: Prioritizing Access to Mass Smallpox Vaccination, 36 Creighton L. Rev. 359 (2003); Anthrax Attacks Leave States Little Better Prepared, USA Today, Jan. 3, 2002, at 10A (reporting that "no state has rules for rationing antibiotics or vaccines when there are not enough to go around"). Officials have confronted these questions more directly in connection with recent flu pandemic scares. See Ceci Connolly, Flu Vaccine Priorities Test Pandemic Planning, Wash. Post, May 12, 2006, at A10 ("In the event of a global flu pandemic, federal officials have said they intend to give vaccine first to health-care workers, followed by the oldest, sickest patients .... Below them on the priority list would be pregnant women, first responders and 'key government leaders,' followed by healthy seniors, people with one risk factor and people employed in the utility, transportation and telecommunications industries."); Denise Grady, Swine Flu Plan Would Put Some at Head of Line for Vaccine, N.Y. Times, July 30, 2009, at A20 (The CDC's Advisory Committee on Immunization Practices "decided that if there was a severe shortage of the [H1N1] vaccine, healthy children over 4 would not be vaccinated, nor would any adults except pregnant women, health and emergency workers and people caring for infants under 6 months.... The last to be eligible for vaccine will be healthy people over 65, who are least likely to contract swine flu."); Anita Manning, Pandemic Vaccine to Be Given in Order: Group Comes up with Guidelines for Inoculation, USA Today, Oct. 22, 2007, at 7D (reporting that, before the novel H1N1 virus emerged as a threat, the National Vaccine Advisory Committee had drafted a somewhat different set of recommendations); see also Ezekiel J. Emanuel & Alan Wertheimer, Who Should Get Influenza Vaccine When Not All Can?, 312 Science 854 (2006) (proposing, in descending order: health care workers; healthy individuals ages 13 to 40, ages 7 to 12 and 41 to 50, ages 6 months to 6 years and 51 to 64, over age 64 (and, within these tiers, sub-rankings for "critical" workers, such as police and utility crews); unhealthy individuals ages 6 months to 64 years, and unhealthy individuals over age 64); cf. David Brown & Rob Stein, Honor Rules, CDC Urges Vendors of H1N1 Vaccine: Some Worry Priority Is Not Being Given to At-Risk Groups, Wash. Post, Nov. 6, 2009, at A4 (noting "reports that employees of Wall Street banks and other well-connected firms were jumping the line and getting pandemic flu shots, even as many of the 159 million people in the priority groups await their turn"). See generally Benjamin E. Berkman, Incorporating Explicit Ethical Reasoning into Pandemic Influenza Policies, 26 J. Contemp. Health L. & Pol'y 1 (2009); Wendy F. Hensel & Leslie E. Wolf, Playing God: The Legality of Plans Denying Scarce Resources to People with Disabilities in Public Health Emergencies, 63 Fla. L. Rev. 719 (2011). How about sharing with other nations (after all, a "pandemic" will mean an international emergency)?

3. DEFINING CATEGORIES OF DISEASE

Lars Noah, *Pigeonholing Illness: Medical Diagnosis as a Legal Construct*

50 HASTINGS L.J. 241 (1999).

* * * The concept of disease, which is so fundamental to medical practice, has numerous important applications in the law. It helps to inform or delineate reimbursable illnesses covered by health insurance, risk-benefit calculations performed by regulatory agencies charged with licensing therapeutic products, the scope of compensable injuries in tort actions, the potential relevance of psychiatric evidence in criminal trials, and impairments subject to antidiscrimination laws and disability benefit programs. Diagnostic judgments have become so pervasive and readily accepted in these varied contexts that we may lose sight of their overall significance. Novel diseases occasionally attract critical scrutiny, as has happened recently with the perceived proliferation of psychiatric syndrome evidence in criminal trials, but commentators invariably advocate doctrinal responses designed to assist decisionmakers in properly assimilating such information. Little or no attention is paid to the ways in which medical professionals react to the external pressures emanating from, or mediated by, legal institutions with regard to defining and diagnosing disease conditions. * * *

Traditionally, medical professionals defined categories of diseases (nosology) and identified such conditions in particular patients (diagnosis) for purposes of selecting appropriate treatments and predicting the likely course of the patient's illness (prognosis). Increasingly, however, diagnostic judgments have come to serve other purposes. Perhaps such a development is neither surprising nor worrisome, at least so long as these diagnoses do not interfere with therapeutic purposes. But once the definition and identification of illness begin primarily to serve the needs of non-medical decisionmakers such as insurers, regulatory agencies, and litigants, closer scrutiny of the diagnostic process is warranted. In at least some situations, researchers apparently cater to patient demands for useful new disease categories, and physicians authenticate complaints, certifying to bureaucrats that particular patients suffer from a qualifying illness. * * *

"Diseases" are not things awaiting discovery by researchers and physicians. Instead, they are convenient short-hand descriptions of illnesses experienced by patients that facilitate investigating and selecting possible courses of treatment. But conceptions of illness do not serve only medical purposes; scholars and physicians alike have recognized that diseases are socially constructed and mutable. Nosology and diagnosis can describe a patient's health or illness experience only imperfectly. * * *

Patients seek out medical care in hopes of finding a treatment for some bothersome condition. They usually care little about the name of their affliction. Similarly, physicians diagnose patients as a means to the end of identifying the most appropriate therapy. It may be that, if there are several plausible diagnoses for a condition but further specification would serve no purpose given the nature of available treatments, the health care professional will not pursue additional diagnostic inquiries for their own sake. Similarly, physicians may have to revisit their initial diagnosis in the event that the patient's condition does not improve with the prescribed therapy. * * *

[T]he FDA's decision to approve a new drug or other medical product will entail a risk-benefit calculation, so the perceived importance of the therapeutic benefit naturally will influence the agency's licensing judgments. In this manner, the FDA takes into account the significance of a targeted health condition, or the status of that condition as a treatable disease, when making product approval decisions. * * * Asymptomatic conditions may pose difficult questions for the FDA when it reviews new drugs intended to manage these conditions. An asymptomatic condition does not really qualify as an "illness" because the patient cannot perceive any complaints, though it may still represent a disease condition detected by a physician. For example, hypertension, hypercholesterolemia, and hyperlipidemia generally do not manifest symptoms, but they are viewed as risk-factors in coronary heart disease and stroke. * * *

[T]he agency usually demands that an applicant demonstrate a drug's effectiveness in achieving clinical endpoints rather than surrogate markers associated with those clinical endpoints. By reconceptualizing hypertension as a freestanding disease entity, however, a pharmaceutical manufacturer would only have to demonstrate that its new drug product effectively reduced blood pressure without also having to show that this resulted in reduced morbidity or mortality. Classifying asymptomatic conditions as diseases may, however, also undermine the prospects for approval of a drug whose side effects include one of these conditions—for instance, a drug intended to treat some other condition may fare less well in the agency's risk-benefit calculus if it causes the "disease" of hypertension than if it merely causes elevated blood pressure.

The status of obesity as a condition or a disease has been a recurrent issue for the FDA. In approving the fat-substitute olestra, the agency noted that it had received several comments supporting this novel food additive as a useful response to the adverse health effects of obesity. The FDA also has approved prescription weight loss drugs in recent years based in part on the assumption that obesity represents a disease. Indeed, historically, the FDA did not regard obesity as a disease, leading Congress to expand the drug definition so that the agency could assert its regulatory authority over weight loss products. Although obese individuals face a variety of health problems, some scientists regard most types of obesity as a symptom of one among several possible underlying disorders rather than a disease process itself. If only regarded as a symptom, proposed new obesity treatments will fare less well in the agency's risk-benefit calculus and product approval decisions in the future. * * *

[D]efining a condition as a disease may help secure insurance coverage for treatments, improve the odds that the FDA will approve new therapeutic products for marketing, allow tort plaintiffs to side-step tricky causation questions, assist criminal defendants in avoiding conviction, and expand eligibility for disability programs and workers' compensation benefits. For instance, pharmaceutical companies seeking FDA approval of new drugs (or hoping to guarantee the availability of insurance reimbursement for prescriptions) care whether the scientific community categorizes hypertension, obesity, or premenstrual syndrome as diseases. * * *

What does it mean to be ill? It depends in part on whom you ask. Physicians, historians, philosophers, and sociologists have struggled to answer this important question. It also depends on why you want to know. The traditional response would emphasize therapeutic purposes, in which case the medical model of disease made perfect sense. If, however, non-therapeutic motives underlie the question, then the range of possible answers might proliferate and depart substantially from the medical model. Legal institutions, by looking to medical professionals for answers to non-therapeutic questions about disease, have failed to appreciate these distinctions.

Why should we care that legal institutions misunderstand the answers that they receive to their non-therapeutic questions about the meaning of disease? At one level, it may distort decisions having important personal, financial, and societal consequences, and legal decisionmakers may wish to reorient their understandings of illness for that reason alone. At another level, * * * the misunderstanding and distortion may rebound in various ways that influence the behavior of medical professionals. In this respect, legal institutions do more than make a mistake in relying on diagnostic judgments for their own non-therapeutic purposes; by becoming dependent on these medical judgments, they also distort nosology and diagnosis in ways that may threaten clinical research and patient care. * * *

Courts and agencies can try to delink themselves from an overreliance on the gatekeeping role traditionally placed on treating physicians, and the medical profession should insist on a clearer demarcation between diagnostic judgments for therapeutic purposes and forensic diagnoses. Organized medicine should not unnecessarily multiply nosologies in response to reimbursement pressures or perceived forensic opportunities, and physicians should not feel pressured into becoming zealous advocates for their patients outside of the therapeutic relationship. Otherwise, health care professionals risk losing sight of the primary purpose for making a diagnosis, namely, caring for a patient with an illness.

NOTES AND QUESTIONS

1. *Expanding diagnostic categories.* Physicians have begun to diagnose patients with conditions such as osteopenia (pre-osteoporosis), pre-hypertension and pre-diabetes. See Elizabeth Agnvall, Making Us (Nearly) Sick: A Majority of Americans Are Now Considered to Have at Least One "Pre–Disease" or "Borderline" Condition, Wash. Post, Feb. 10, 2004, at F1 (reporting that disease-specific associations, which receive funding from the drug industry, frequently offer more aggressive treatment recommendations than panels of independent experts); Susan Kelleher & Duff Wilson, Suddenly Sick: The Hidden Big Business Behind Your Doctor's Diagnosis (five part series), Seattle Times, June 26–30, 2005, at A1; see also Frank Greve, Diseases Are Everywhere—or Are They?, Miami Herald, Apr. 14, 2005, at 1A ("Add up the published claims about disease prevalence and the average American has at least two ailments at a time. Who's pushing the high numbers? Skeptical biostatisticians blame drug companies and reporters for much of the hype. They also blame research institutes and disease foundations seeking more public spending on particular diseases."); cf. January W. Payne, Guidelines: Treat Nearly All Women as Pre–Pregnant, Wash. Post, May 16, 2006, at F1. In the course of granting summary judgment to the manufacturer of the injectable contraceptive drug Depo–Provera® on failure-to-warn claims, a pair of courts concluded that "osteopenia" does not qualify as an injury or disease. See Colville v. Pharmacia & Upjohn Co., 565 F.Supp.2d 1314, 1322–23 (N.D.Fla.2008); Lorenzi v. Pfizer Inc., 519 F.Supp.2d 742, 751 (N.D.Ohio 2007) (crediting expert testimony that it "is no more than a statistical indicator" or diagnosis of low bone density that does not necessarily correlate to any higher risk of eventual fracture).

2. *"Lifestyle" drugs and the medicalization of aging.* The discovery of serious risks associated with hormone replacement therapy raised questions in some minds about the value of symptomatic treatment using products containing estrogen. See Sandra G. Boodman, Hormones Weather "the Change": Three Years After a Landmark Study Hammered Sales, Use of Hormone Therapy for Menopause May Be Inching up, Wash. Post, Sept.

20, 2005, at F1 ("Earlier this year an independent state-of-the-science panel convened by the National Institutes of Health (NIH) called for the 'demedicalization of menopause'.... It's been nearly 40 years since New York gynecologist Robert Wilson published 'Feminine Forever,' a book that fueled the popularity of estrogen and the notion that menopause is a medical problem that needs to be fixed."); Marc Kaufman, Hormone Replacement Gets New Scrutiny, Wash. Post, Aug. 14, 2002, at A1 (reporting that "federal officials want to explore whether hormone therapies and their producers have encouraged women to believe menopause is a condition to be treated, rather than an inevitable and natural set of changes to be managed," noting "the FDA's discomfort with the way that hormone treatments have been widely presented as an antidote to menopause"); see also Ray Moynihan et al., Selling Sickness: The Pharmaceutical Industry and Disease Mongering, 324 Brit. Med. J. 886 (2002); Andrew Pollack, A Drug's Second Act: Battling Jet Lag, N.Y. Times, Jan. 7, 2010, at B1 ("A jet-lag antidote might seem to be the latest lifestyle drug, a further step in the 'medicalization' of something that is not an illness. But sleep specialists, who call the affliction 'jet lag disorder,' say that while not exactly a disease, it is a condition that can be dangerous—as when someone tries to drive a car right after arriving in a distant time zone."); Rob Stein, Marketing the Illness and the Cure? Drug Ads May Sell People on the Idea That They Are Sick, Wash. Post, May 30, 2006, at A3; Fiona Walsh, Glaxo Denies Pushing "Lifestyle" Treatments, Guardian (London), Apr. 28, 2006, at 28 (restless leg syndrome); Critics Say Drugmakers Push Pills for Murky Illness, Newsday, Feb. 9, 2009, at A23 (fibromyalgia).

3. *Expanding waistlines.* It is one thing for researchers to develop more precise measures of obesity (shifting from set percentages over a person's ideal weight to body mass index (BMI) thresholds); it is quite another to shift from designating obesity as a symptom (of certain metabolic diseases or, more typically, inactivity coupled with excessive caloric intake), or as a risk factor (in the development of a variety of other diseases such as Type II diabetes), to calling it a disease in its own right. A variety of pressures external to the research enterprise have influenced this redefinition, and a number of entities have now jumped on the bandwagon, proclaiming that we are in the midst of an "epidemic" of obesity. See Rob Stein, Is Obesity a Disease?, Wash. Post, Nov. 10, 2003, at A1 (explaining that several federal regulatory agencies—including the FDA, IRS, and CMS—now accept the notion that obesity qualifies as a disease and have begun to modify their applicable rules accordingly); see also Rob Stein, Seeking a Slim Victory, Drugmakers Press FDA, Wash. Post, Sept. 17, 2004, at A1; cf. Scott Allen, In Fat War, Doctors Have Few Options, Boston Globe, Apr. 1, 2004, at A1 (reporting that, according to some critics, FDA reviewers "subject weight-loss drugs to tougher safety standards than other drugs because they do not regard obesity as a true disease"). Whatever lies behind this trend, device manufacturers have begun to respond by "supersizing" certain hospital equipment. See Susan Levine, Obese Patients Increase Need for Specialized Medical Care, Wash. Post, Jan. 3, 2006, at A1.

4. *Psychoactive medications and behavior modification*. The diagnosis and treatment of ADHD continue to generate controversy in the medical and educational communities. See Lawrence H. Diller, The Run on Ritalin: Attention Deficit Disorder and Stimulant Treatment in the 1990s, 26 Hastings Ctr. Rep. 12 (1996); Gina Kolata, Boom in Ritalin Sales Raises Ethical Issues, N.Y. Times, May 15, 1996, at C8; Shankar Vedantam, Debate over Drugs for ADHD Reignites: Long–Term Benefit for Children at Issue, Wash. Post, Mar. 27, 2009, at A1; see also House Panel Hears Tales of Ritalin Excesses in Schools, Chi. Trib., May 17, 2000, at 12 (reporting that one in five college students abuse ADHD drugs). These questions pale by comparison with concerns about the escalating use of powerful antipsychotic drugs to treat other behavioral problems in children. See Joseph T. Coyle, Psychotropic Drug Use in Very Young Children, 283 JAMA 1059 (2000); Duff Wilson, Child's Ordeal Reveals Risks of Psychiatric Drugs in Young, N.Y. Times, Sept. 2, 2010, at A1 ("More than 500,000 children and adolescents in America are now taking antipsychotic drugs .... Their use is growing not only among older teenagers, when schizophrenia is believed to emerge, but also among tens of thousands of preschoolers.... [I]t is cheaper to medicate children than to pay for family counseling ...."). The International Narcotics Control Board of the United Nations has "expressed concern about the inappropriate medicalization of social problems in developed countries and the widespread use of drugs to treat behavioral symptoms instead of treating the underlying causes." Joseph T. Coyle, Drug Treatment of Anxiety Disorders in Children, 344 New Eng. J. Med. 1326 (2001); see also Angela O. Burton, "They Use It Like Candy": How the Prescription of Psychotropic Drugs to State–Involved Children Violates International Law, 35 Brook. J. Int'l L. 453 (2010). What about the notion of inoculating children to guard against the development of addictive behaviors? See Alexis Osburn, Note, Immunizing Against Addiction: The Argument for Incorporating Emerging Anti–Addiction Vaccines into Existing Compulsory Immunization Statutes, 56 Clev. St. L. Rev. 159 (2008); see also Douglas Quenqua, An Addiction Vaccine, Tantalizingly Close, N.Y. Times, Oct. 4, 2011, at D1.

5. *PMS, PMDD, and Prozac*. Eli Lilly, the makers of Prozac®, obtained FDA approval to market the drug under the brand name Sarafem® for treatment of "premenstrual dysphoric disorder" (PMDD), an allegedly more severe and distinct form of premenstrual syndrome (PMS). See Peter D. Kramer, The Way We Live Now: Female Troubles, N.Y. Times Mag., Oct. 1, 2000, at 17 (commenting that "the pill is a pretty pink-and-lavender capsule, available in a light blue box ... sold under the liltingly soft name Sarafem, which sounds like the angels known for the quality of their spiritual love," and pointing out that it "isn't a new drug at all, only Prozac in drag"). Repackaging and marketing the drug for this new indication provided Lilly with market exclusivity through 2007—an attractive proposition for the company because it lost patent protection on Prozac in 2001. Other manufacturers of antidepressants, including Pfizer (Zoloft®) and GlaxoSmithKline (Paxil®) also pursued approval to market their products for the treatment of PMDD. Many members of the medical community have expressed skepticism, however, about whether PMDD is in fact a real disease, or "simply a way for drug companies to cast a wider net in search of new customers." Tara Parker–Pope, Drug Companies Push Use of Antidepressants to Treat Severe PMS, Wall St. J., Feb. 23, 2001, at B1; see also Elizabeth Lambdin, Note, A New Disease Born Every Minute: The Marketing of Pathology and the Exploitation of Gender–Based Insecurities and Sexuality to Sell Drugs, 13 Cardozo J.L. & Gender 145 (2006); Shankar Vedantam, Renamed Prozac Fuels Women's Health Debate, Wash. Post, Apr. 29, 2001, at A1; cf. David Segal, A Dose of Desire: The Race Is on to Create "Pink Viagra," but Some Women Aren't in the Mood for It, Wash. Post, Mar. 12, 2008, at C1.

The marketing of drugs to treat arguably normal personality variations is also escalating. See Shankar Vedantam, Drug Use, and Concern, Is on the Rise, Phila. Inquirer, Mar. 19, 2001, at C1 (describing burgeoning prescribing of antidepressants, antipsychotic medications, and anti-anxiety medications). Pharmaceutical companies employ promotional strategies intended to medicalize common personality traits, such as "social anxiety disorder" (shyness) in order to create a demand for a pharmacological intervention. See Jeff Donn, Are We Taking Too Many Drugs?, Newsday, Apr. 19, 2005, at B13 ("In a recent report, the Centers for Disease Control voiced concern about huge off-label growth of antidepressants to treat such loosely defined syndromes as compulsion, panic or anxiety and PMS. Drug makers, doctors and patients have all been quick to medicate some conditions once accepted simply as part of the human condition."); Shankar Vedantam, Drug Ads Hyping Anxiety Make Some Uneasy, Wash. Post, July 16, 2001, at A1 (describing the very successful marketing of Paxil®, and noting that "pharmaceutical companies, traditionally in the business of finding new drugs for existing disorders, are increasingly in the business of seeking new disorders for existing drugs"); see also Christopher Lane, Shyness: How Normal Behavior Became a Sickness (2007).

6. *Right back at you.* The process also may work in reverse, with the arrival of powerful therapeutic agents promising to alter the way that we think about a particular disease. See Andrew Pollack, Considering Longer Chemotherapy, N.Y. Times, July 21, 2009, at D1 (discussing research into "maintenance therapy" to guard against relapse); Rob Stein, From Killer to Chronic Disease: Drugs Redefine Cancer for Many, Wash. Post, Jan. 29, 2003, at A1; Abigail Zuger, Rediscovering the First Miracle Drug, N.Y. Times, Oct. 5, 2010, at D4 ("What insulin did was turn a brief, deadly illness into a long, chronic struggle ...."). For instance, thanks to the widespread use of vaccines and antibiotics, many of the most frightening scourges of previous centuries have become medical curiosities (though fears that terrorists might unleash smallpox demonstrate the fragility of our confidence in conquering the health threats of a bygone era—in any event, something new often stands ready to take their place). In addition, the development of anti-retroviral cocktails fundamentally changed the bleak outlook for many AIDS patients (at least those able to secure access to these expensive drugs and to tolerate their side effects). See Rochelle P. Walensky et al., The Survival Benefits of AIDS Treatment in the United

States, 194 J. Infect. Dis. 11 (2006) (concluding that the latest drugs should add an average of more than 13 years to the life expectancy of HIV-positive patients); Lawrence K. Altman, 30 Years In, We Are Still Learning from AIDS, N.Y. Times, May 31, 2011, at D1 ("[M]ore than 30 licensed drugs widely available in the developed world have turned AIDS from a death sentence to a chronic disease, though not necessarily an easy one to live with."); cf. id. ("[I]t has been almost a quarter century since federal health officials confidently predicted that a vaccine would be available in the late 1980s—a promise that has yet to be fulfilled."); David Brown, AIDS Vaccine Testing at Crossroads: After Little Progress in 25 Years, Scientists Urge Return to Basic Research, Wash. Post, Mar. 26, 2008, at A4.

7. *Contingency of disability.* As suggested by the excerpt, medical definitions of disability predominate. See Bradley A. Areheart, When Disability Isn't "Just Right": The Entrenchment of the Medical Model of Disability and the Goldilocks Dilemma, 83 Ind. L.J. 181 (2008); Adam M. Samaha, What Good Is the Social Model of Disability?, 74 U. Chi. L. Rev. 1251 (2007); Deirdre M. Smith, Who Says You're Disabled? The Role of Medical Evidence in the ADA Definition of Disability, 82 Tul. L. Rev. 1 (2007). Does the growing ability to "treat" normal conditions such short stature, see Chap. 11(D), expand what qualifies as a "disability"? Conversely, new technologies allow for surgical interventions, pharmaceutical treatments, or sophisticated assistance devices that manage to work around previously permanent "disabilities" in ways that arguably render such persons no longer genuinely disabled. See Jeannette Cox, "Corrective" Surgery and the Americans with Disabilities Act, 46 San Diego L. Rev. 113 (2009); Collin R. Bockman, Note, Cybernetic–Enhancement Technology and the Future of Disability Law, 95 Iowa L. Rev. 1315 (2010); see also Lars Noah, Comfortably Numb: Medicalizing (and Mitigating) Pain-and-Suffering Damages, 42 U. Mich. J.L. Reform 431 (2009).

E. Postscript: Defining Novel Technologies and Coping with Change

Sherley v. Sebelius

644 F.3d 388 (D.C.Cir.2011).

■ Ginsburg, Circuit Judge:

* * * [S]tem cells have the potential of yielding treatments for a wide range of afflictions because scientists can cause them to function as any one of a number of specific types of cell. * * * [There are] two different classes of human stem cells: adult stem cells, which are somewhat specialized, and ESCs [embryonic stem cells], which are pluripotent, meaning they can develop into nearly any of the 200 types of human cell. In addition to these two established categories, we note the recent development of induced pluripotent stem cells, which are adult stem cells reprogrammed to a stage of development at which they are pluripotent. There is some debate as to

which type of stem cell holds more promise of yielding therapeutic applications.

Adult stem cells can be found in the various tissues and organs of the human body. ESCs, by contrast, can be found only in a human embryo; isolating an ESC requires removing the "inner cell mass" of the embryo, a process that destroys the embryo. The stem cells among the 30 or so cells in the inner cell mass are then placed in a culture, where they will divide continuously without differentiating, thus forming a "stem cell line" of identical cells. An individual ESC may be removed from the line without disrupting either the multiplication process or the durability of the line. The removed cell may then be used in a research project—either by the investigator who extracted it or by another—in which the ESC will be caused to develop into the type of cell pertinent to that research. Most stem cell lines are maintained by one or another of several research universities, which make them available for scientific use, usually for a small fee.

The plaintiffs in this case, Drs. James Sherley and Theresa Deisher, are scientists who use only adult stem cells in their research. They contend the NIH has, by funding research projects using ESCs, violated the Dickey–Wicker Amendment, which the Congress has included in the annual appropriation for the Department of Health and Human Services each year since 1996. Dickey–Wicker prohibits the NIH from funding: "(1) the creation of a human embryo or embryos for research purposes; or (2) research in which a human embryo or embryos are destroyed" * * * [W]hen the Congress first passed Dickey–Wicker, scientists had taken steps to isolate ESCs but had not yet been able to stabilize them for research in the laboratory. The historical record suggests the Congress passed the Amendment chiefly to preclude President Clinton from acting upon an NIH report recommending federal funding for research using embryos that had been created for the purpose of in vitro fertilization. Dickey–Wicker became directly relevant to ESCs only in 1998, when researchers at the University of Wisconsin succeeded in generating a stable line of ESCs, which they made available to investigators who might apply for NIH funding.

For that reason, on January 15, 1999, the general counsel of [HHS] issued a memorandum addressing whether Dickey–Wicker permits federal funding of research using ESCs that had been derived before the funded project began; she concluded such funding is permissible because ESCs are not "embryos." After notice and comment, the NIH issued funding guidelines consistent with this opinion, 65 Fed. Reg. 51,976 (2000), but the NIH did not fund any ESC research project while President Clinton was in office. Early in 2001, President Bush directed the NIH not to fund any project pursuant to President Clinton's policy; later that year he decided funding for ESC research would be limited to projects using the approximately 60 then-extant cell lines derived from "embryos that ha[d] already been destroyed." * * *

Upon assuming office in 2009, President Obama lifted the temporal restriction imposed by President Bush and permitted the NIH to "support and conduct responsible, scientifically worthy human stem cell research, including human embryonic stem cell research, to the extent permitted by law." Exec. Order 13,505, 74 Fed. Reg. 10,667 (2009). The NIH, after notice-and-comment rulemaking, then issued the 2009 guidelines, 74 Fed. Reg. 32,170 (2009), which * * * instituted specific ethical restrictions upon ESC research funded by the NIH: Such research may be conducted only upon stem cell lines derived from embryos that "were created using in vitro fertilization for reproductive purposes and were no longer needed for this purpose," and that "were donated by individuals who sought reproductive treatment . . . who gave voluntary written consent for the human embryos to be used for research purposes," and who were not paid therefor. Id. at 32,174. Moreover, the research may use stem cell lines derived from an embryo donated after the effective date of the guidelines only if the in vitro clinic had fully informed the donor of all possible options for disposing of the embryo and had taken other specified procedural steps to separate reproductive treatment from donation.

After the 2009 guidelines were issued, the Congress once again reenacted Dickey–Wicker as part of the appropriations bill for fiscal year 2010. The Congress has not enacted an appropriations bill for FY 2011, adopting instead a series of continuing resolutions that have carried Dickey–Wicker forward to the present. * * *

The district court held, and the plaintiffs argue on appeal, [that the Dickey–Wicker Amendment] unambiguously bars funding for any project using an ESC. They reason that, because an embryo had to be destroyed in order to yield an ESC, any later research project that uses an ESC is necessarily "research" in which the embryo is destroyed. For its part, the government argues the "text is in no way an unambiguous ban on research using embryonic stem cells" because Dickey–Wicker is written in the present tense, addressing research "in which" embryos "are" destroyed, not research "for which" embryos "were destroyed." The use of the present tense in a statute strongly suggests it does not extend to past actions. * * * NIH funding decisions are forward-looking, requiring the NIH to "determine whether what is proposed to be funded meets with its requirements." Therefore, a grant application to support research that includes the derivation of stem cells would have to be rejected. * * *

The plaintiffs also argue we must read the term "research" broadly because the Congress, had it intended a narrower reading, would have used a term identifying a particular action, as it did in subsection (1) of Dickey–Wicker, which specifically bars the "creation" of an embryo for "research purposes." We see no basis for that inference. The definition of research is flexible enough to describe either a discrete project or an extended process, but this flexibility only reinforces our conclusion that the text is ambiguous. * * * In the 2009 guidelines the NIH expressly distinguished between the derivation of ESCs and "research involving [ESCs] that does not involve an embryo nor result in an embryo's destruction." 74 Fed. Reg. at 32,173. Thus, although the guidelines do not define the term "research," they do make clear the agency's understanding that "research involving [ESCs]" does not necessarily include the antecedent process of deriving the cells. * * * The plaintiffs' objection that the NIH has not explicitly defined a word in the statute—an important word, to be sure—is mere cavil; it disregards the agency's use of the term, which implicitly but unequivocally gives "research" a narrow scope, thus ensuring no federal funding will go to a research project in which an embryo is destroyed.

To this point the plaintiffs apparently respond that the NIH has, by treating derivation as part of "research," shown its understanding of Dickey–Wicker is unreasonable. Their argument is that, because the standard definition of "research" requires some kind of scientific inquiry, and deriving ESCs, standing alone, involves no such inquiry, the act of derivation can be deemed "research" only if it is part of a larger project. * * * The plaintiffs' premise is valid in part: Because the guidelines state Dickey–Wicker bans funding for the derivation of ESCs and Dickey–Wicker bans only "research," it is clear the NIH treats the act of derivation as "research." The government expressly confirmed this much at oral argument when counsel flatly stated "derivation is research." Less clear is whether the act of derivation, by itself, comes within a standard definition of research, that is, whether it involves any investigation or inquiry. On that score, the government pointed out at oral argument that "stem cells are not pre-labeled cells that you can simply extract," and argued "the scientific process" of derivation, in which cells are "extracted and put into mediums where [they] can grow" before being examined and chemically treated, "itself involves experimentation."

Rather than rely upon that account of derivation qualifying as research, let us assume for the sake of the plaintiffs' argument derivation involves no scientific inquiry; it does not follow that the NIH may define derivation as "research" only if or insofar as the derivation is tethered to some later project using the derived cells. Although an understanding of "research" that includes the derivation of stem cells is not the ordinary reading of that term, it is surely as sensible as the plaintiffs' alternative, in which the derivation of a cell line is deemed part of every one of the scores if not hundreds of subsequent research projects—although pursued by different scientists, perhaps many years later—to use one of the derived cells. To define derivation as "research," in other words, makes at least as much sense as to treat the one-off act of derivation as though it had been performed anew each time a researcher, however remote in time or place, uses a stem cell from the resulting line. The fact is the statute is not worded precisely enough to resolve the present definitional contest conclusively for one side or the other.

Broadening our focus slightly, however, we can see the words surrounding "research" in the statute support the NIH's reading. Because the Congress wrote with particularity and in the present tense—the statute says "in which" and "are" rather than "for which" and "were"—it is entirely reasonable for the NIH to understand Dickey–Wicker as permitting funding for research using cell lines derived without federal funding, even as it bars funding for the derivation of additional lines. * * *

Congress has reenacted Dickey–Wicker unchanged year after year "with full knowledge that HHS has been funding [ESC] research since 2001," 74 Fed. Reg. at 32,173, when President Bush first permitted federal funding for ESC projects, provided they used previously derived ESC lines. As the plaintiffs conceded at oral argument, because this policy permitted the NIH to fund projects using ESCs, it would have been prohibited under their proposed reading of Dickey–Wicker. So, too, with the policy the Clinton Administration announced in 1999 and, of course, with the 2009 guidelines promulgated by the Obama Administration. The plaintiffs have no snappy response to the agency's point that the Congress's having reenacted Dickey–Wicker each and every year provides "further evidence . . . [it] intended the agency's interpretation, or at least understood the interpretation as statutorily permissible." * * *

[B]ecause the plaintiffs bring solely a facial challenge to the guidelines, we have no occasion to consider their suggestion that the NIH might grant the researcher who derived an ESC line federal funds for research using it, which would link the act of derivation more closely to subsequent research and test the distinction between them drawn by the NIH. However that case—were it ever to materialize—might play out is irrelevant here. To prevail in their challenge to the guidelines on their face the plaintiffs "must establish that no set of circumstances exists under which the [guidelines] would be valid;" it is not enough for the plaintiffs to show the guidelines could be applied unlawfully. * * *

The district court reasoned the "balance of hardships weighs in favor of an injunction" because, for ESC researchers, "the injunction would simply preserve the *status quo* and would not interfere with their ability to obtain private funding." On the other hand, the court thought it certain that increased competition would "threaten [the plaintiffs'] very livelihood." As we see it, however, a preliminary injunction would in fact upend the status quo. True, the plaintiffs compete with ESC researchers for funding—indeed, that is why they have standing to bring this case*—but they have been competing with ESC researchers since 2001. The 2009 guidelines inflict some incremental handicap upon the plaintiffs' ability to compete for NIH money—they point to the additional time and money they must expend and have had to expend since 2001 to meet the additional competition from researchers proposing to use ECCS—but it is necessarily uncertain whether invalidating the guidelines would result in the plaintiffs getting any more grant money from the NIH. Accordingly, we cannot say that, if the plaintiffs are to litigate this case without the benefit of interim relief, then the 2009 guidelines will place a significant additional burden upon their ability to secure funding for their research.

The hardship a preliminary injunction would impose upon ESC researchers, by contrast, would be certain and substantial. The injunction entered by the district court would preclude the NIH from funding new

* Cf. Doe v. Obama, 631 F.3d 157 (4th Cir.2011) (rejecting for lack of standing a class action lawsuit putatively brought on behalf of all frozen embryos—as well as persons wishing to "adopt" some of these spare embryos—challenging the NIH guideline).

ESC projects it has or would have deemed meritorious, thereby inevitably denying other scientists funds they would have received. Even more problematic, the injunction would bar further disbursements to ESC researchers who have already begun multi-year projects in reliance upon a grant from the NIH; their investments in project planning would be a loss, their expenditures for equipment a waste, and their staffs out of a job. The record shows private funding is not generally available for stem cell research but even if, as the district court thought, private donors or investors would provide a reasonable alternative source of funds for ESC researchers, it remains unclear why such donors or investors would not similarly support the plaintiffs' research using adult stem cells and why the plaintiffs' "very livelihood" instead depends upon obtaining grants from the NIH. All this is to say the balance of equities tilts against granting a preliminary injunction. That, combined with our conclusion the plaintiffs have not shown they are likely to succeed on the merits, leads us to hold the district court abused its discretion in awarding preliminary injunctive relief. * * *

■ HENDERSON, CIRCUIT JUDGE (dissenting):

The majority opinion has taken a straightforward case of statutory construction and produced a result that would make Rube Goldberg tip his hat. Breaking the simple noun "research" into "temporal" bits, narrowing the verb phrase "are destroyed" to an unintended scope, dismissing the definition section of implementing regulations promulgated by [HHS] (in case the plain meaning of "research" were not plain enough), my colleagues perform linguistic jujitsu. * * *

Determining whether ESC research is "research in which a human embryo or embryos are destroyed" requires determining the meaning of "research." The plaintiffs contend that all ESC research constitutes research in which human embryos are destroyed and that the Amendment accordingly prohibits federal funding thereof. The government counters that the derivation of ECCS and the subsequent use of those cells, although both research, are not part of the same—and prohibited—research. * * * The district court correctly looked to the dictionary definition of "research" as "diligent and systematic inquiry or investigation into a subject in order to discover or revise facts, theories, applications, etc." Research, then, comprises a systematic inquiry or investigation. And "systematic" connotes sequenced action. The first sequence of ESC research is the derivation of stem cells from the human embryo. The derivation of stem cells destroys the embryo and therefore cannot be federally funded, as the government concedes. I believe the succeeding sequences of ESC research are likewise banned by the Amendment because, under the plain meaning of "research," they continue the "systematic inquiry or investigation."

That the intent of the 1996 Congress, in enacting the Amendment, is to prohibit all ESC research—not just research attendant on the derivation of the cells—is clear by comparing the language used to ban federal funding for the creation of an embryo with the language the plaintiffs rely on. While the Amendment prohibits federal financing of the "creation of a human embryo . . . for research purposes,'' it does *not* use parallel language in addressing the destruction of embryos. It bans federal funding of "research" rather than the "destruction of human embryos for research purposes." Research, then, is the express target of the ban the Congress imposed with respect to the destruction of a human embryo. This makes perfect sense because in 1996, according to the record, ESC research had barely begun. The Congress, recognizing its scant knowledge about the feasibility/scope of ESC research, chose broad language with the plain intent to make the ban as complete as possible. * * *

If there were any uncertainty about the extent of the Amendment's ban, it would be erased by reading the Amendment's language in full * * * * Congress unambiguously manifested its intent that "research" as used in the Amendment is to have the same meaning as "research" used in [45 C.F.R. §] 46.204(b). * * * [These regulations] confirms that research involves sequenced action by defining it to include "development, testing and evaluation" sequences. "Research development" perfectly describes the first sequence of ESC research, that is, the derivation of the cells. The testing and evaluation sequences of ESC research cannot be performed without first conducting the research involved in deriving ECCS from the human embryo. The derivation of ECCS is, thus, the *sine qua non* developmental sequence on which all subsequent sequences of ESC research rest. Moreover, nothing in the record suggests that ECCS are derived for any purpose other than the testing and evaluation of those cells. That ECCS cannot be tested and evaluated unless and until they are derived from a human embryo, combined with the fact that derivation of ECCS is done solely as part of a "systematic investigation" of those cells, demonstrates that derivation is the necessary first sequence of ESC research. Because derivation of ECCS necessarily destroys a human embryo or embryos, and because derivation constitutes at least ESC research development under the Amendment, all ESC research is "research in which a human embryo or embryos are destroyed." * * *

[T]he majority opinion strains mightily to find the ambiguity the government presses. Treating "research" as composed of free-standing pieces, it concludes that the only piece that is banned is the derivation of the ECCS. The authority for this novel reading of "research" is not the dictionary but the Amendment's use of the phrase "in which a human embryo or embryos *are* destroyed" rather than "for which a human embryo or embryos *were* destroyed."[3] * * * There is no question that, here, context manifests that the present tense includes both the past as well as the future.[4] * * * But it is not only the majority opinion's view of verb tenses that is wrong. My colleagues rest their *Chevron* step two analysis on the

3. The government's suggested change in inflection can fairly be described as Clinton-esque ("It depends upon what the meaning of the word 'is' is.").

4. Moreover, the Amendment combines the present tense "are" with the past participle "destroyed," that is, with "[a] verb form indicating past or completed action or time that is used as a verbal adjective." Other statutes similarly use the present tense, especially a combination of "is" with a past participle, to signify conduct that has already occurred.

transformation of "research" into "research project" in the Amendment's text. In other words, it reads "research" as if it were synonymous with "research project." But "research" is the overall "systematic investigation or inquiry" in a field—here, ESCs—of which each project is simply a part. Webster's Third New International Dictionary 1813 (1993) ("project" means "a definitely formulated piece of research"). * * * Because I believe the government's reading of the Amendment contravenes the Amendment's plain meaning, I am unpersuaded that the Congress, by simply reenacting the Amendment, has sanctioned that reading. Accordingly, the plaintiffs have demonstrated to me a strong likelihood that they will prevail on the merits. * * * I cannot say the district court abused its discretion in balancing all of the factors in favor of granting preliminary injunctive relief. * * *

Lars Noah, *A Postmodernist Take on the Human Embryo Research Debate*

36 CONN. L. REV. 1133 (2004).

Ann Kiessling's contribution to this symposium, titled *What Is an Embryo?*, poses an important and difficult question. Of course, as she concedes somewhat belatedly, this question serves as a stand-in for a still more contentious debate over when human life begins or, at least, when the potential for life has progressed to the point that interference with its further development becomes morally objectionable. Although Kiessling usefully identifies inconsistencies among the various answers offered by other sources, she ultimately dodges even her more limited question.

The answer depends, of course, on who is asking such a question and for what purposes they want to know. Kiessling asks the question from the position of a scientist who apparently resents federal funding limitations on stem cell research, and, in common with the methods of science, her search for an answer strikes a decidedly modernist chord. Although I fully share her preference for an environment that encourages rather than hinders embryonic stem cell work, this essay criticizes Kiessling's arguments and offers a far more cynical (hence "postmodern") account of the debate. * * *

It should surprise no one that the word "embryo" lacks a fixed meaning among legal institutions, much less that the confusion only increases when the question gets presented to a wider audience. In fact, the question has received a wide range of answers from research scientists, lawyers and bioethicists, religious leaders, courts, and state legislatures. * * *

[S]ome states (including North Dakota and Virginia) define an "embryo" as existing immediately after conception, at least one state (Florida) uses the term "preembryo" for the earliest stages of embryological development, and at least one state (Oklahoma) opts for the term "unborn child" from the point of conception even though it appears to concede that the zygote, morula, and blastocyst stages precede the embryo; in addition, some states (Louisiana and South Dakota) limit their definition of "embryo" to a conceptus *ex utero*, while at least one state (Idaho) limits its definition to a conceptus *in utero*. As revealed in Kiessling's review of state court decisions, some judges (in cases from New Jersey and Tennessee) opt for the term "preembryo," while other judges (in a case from New York) use the term "pre-zygote," whatever that means. * * * Kiessling evidently applauds recent legislation in Australia that had displaced inconsistent definitions of the term "embryo" adopted by different states within that country, but what if the uniform answer selected by our federal government was one that she regarded as incorrect?

Indeed, Kiessling never mentions that Congress already has adopted a definition of the term "embryo." Although her article excerpts language from the appropriations rider that prohibits federal funding of embryo research, she astonishingly fails to make any reference to the definitional clause that immediately follows the funding restriction:

> For purposes of this section, the term "human embryo or embryos" includes any organism, not protected as a human subject under 45 CFR 46 as of the date of the enactment of this Act, that is derived by fertilization, parthenogenesis, cloning, or any other means from one or more human gametes or human diploid cells.

This provision does not lose the force of law simply because it has a temporary character by virtue of its status as a rider to an annual appropriations bill, and Congress has included precisely the same language for every fiscal year since 1996.

Kiessling also complains that the appropriations rider "has not been publicly debated nor debated in Congress." Even if true when originally inserted, the rider has gotten significant attention since 1996, though the majority in Congress has not seen fit to rethink its policy. For instance, after the National Institutes of Health (NIH) adopted what some members of Congress regarded as a strained interpretation of the funding prohibition (by narrowly construing the term "organism" that appeared in the above-quoted definition), the rider triggered some sharp exchanges with the Secretary of Health and Human Services (HHS) and also drew public attention to the subject. It attracted still greater attention after President George W. Bush announced his plans to revisit NIH's implementing guidelines.

In addition, although Congress explicitly cross-referenced this regulation in its appropriations rider, Kiessling fails to mention the relevant definitions adopted by HHS and other federal agencies. The existing rules on protecting human research subjects cover "fetuses," though these are defined to include the conceptus from the point of implantation, which Kiessling and others would prefer to call "embryos" until the eighth week. When HHS revised these rules in 2001, it specifically rejected suggestions calling for a more precise definition of the term "fetus" as a stage distinct from "embryo." In effect, the appropriations rider—when read in tandem with the federal regulation as Congress intended—defines as an "embryo" every stage of human development from fertilization to implantation but not thereafter.

Statutes and judicial opinions do not, of course, purport to adopt comprehensive definitions of terms in the manner of a dictionary. On the contrary, these sources often explicitly limit their definitions narrowly to the particular dispute or activity at issue (as Congress did in prefacing the definitional clause in the appropriations rider with "For purposes of this section"). Most of the state statutes that include definitions of the term "embryo" pre-date successful efforts at human embryonic stem cell research and focus instead on issues related to abortion or fetal tissue research. Of the statutes in Kiessling's survey, only the legislature in South Dakota specifically had stem cell research in mind, and it codified a peculiar definition designed to buttress its effort to prohibit any such work. In contrast, and without bothering to define the term "embryo," the legislatures in both California and New Jersey recently passed laws that expressly authorize research using stem cells derived from whatever source. * * *

[C]ourts long have recognized that scientific or technical terms absorbed into legislation become terms of art that intentionally may deviate from their original meanings. In the appropriations rider, Congress undoubtedly cared less about codifying a scientifically nuanced definition of the term "embryo" than drafting language broadly enough to encompass all embryo-like things in order to minimize any opportunities for researchers to use loopholes that would circumvent its intent. The real question, however, is whether we should, as Kiessling does, bemoan this inconsistent state of affairs as unproductively chaotic or instead applaud it as reflecting a healthy pluralism.

Kiessling also fails to discuss definitions utilized by other federal agencies, which is not surprising insofar as these regulatory bodies generally have not adopted explicit definitions of the relevant terms. Even so, a close look at announcements from such agencies reveals informal or implicit definitions. In particular, the U.S. Food and Drug Administration (FDA), which is a unit of HHS, appears to have interpreted the term "embryo" in a fashion that differs from the definition adopted by its parent agency. For instance, in its medical device classification regulations for instruments used during IVF, the agency refers separately to zygotes, preembryos, and embryos, though without explicitly defining any of these terms.

In regulating "contraceptive" drugs and devices, the FDA focuses on implantation rather than fertilization as the critical milestone in embryological development. Even though their primary mode of action is interference with the process of fertilization, some intrauterine devices (IUDs) evidently also may prevent implantation of a fertilized ovum. Nonetheless, because it focuses on the point where "pregnancy" starts, the FDA consistently has treated IUDs as contraceptives. Whatever one chooses to call the conceptus during the period after fertilization but prior to implantation in the uterine wall, the agency views as essentially equivalent those products that interfere with ovulation, fertilization, and implantation, reserving the category of "abortifacient" (and somewhat different standards of safety and effectiveness) for those products that interfere with an established pregnancy.

These same issues have arisen more recently with pharmaceutical contraceptive products. Efforts are currently underway to make the prescription "morning after" pill available over-the-counter (OTC). Because the pill interferes with implantation of a fertilized egg, some critics argue that these products do not qualify as contraceptives and instead view them as abortifacients. The FDA long ago concluded otherwise, and some researchers have responded to these sorts of objections by coining the term "contragestive" to describe products that operate during the window between fertilization and implantation, reserving the label abortifacient for those products that work after the completion of implantation. If, however, the current administration views fertilization rather than implantation as the critical juncture, then it would surely scuttle these efforts at expanding the availability of emergency contraception.

Lastly, the FDA's curious assertion of authority over human cloning research implies that the fruits of such work would resemble products akin to pharmaceuticals, medical devices, or biologics. The agency has begun to issue rules governing human tissue products, and these purport to include *ex utero* "embryos" as reproductive tissues. Previously, the agency had promulgated rules governing tissue transplants that explicitly had excluded reproductive tissues, but treating zygotes and early embryos as human tissue products undoubtedly will make some people uneasy about viewing these entities as nothing more than commodities. Although the use of reproductive tissue for non-clinical research purposes would escape the FDA's jurisdiction, stem cells derived from embryos and intended for therapeutic use would fall within the agency's regulatory ambit. In short, although even this single regulatory agency has failed to settle on a precise definition of the term "embryo," the FDA (in common with HHS) has not yet suggested that preimplantation stages of embryological development merit any special regard.

Kiessling offers an extended description of the recommendations and terminological choices of three advisory committees established by the federal government. None of them evidently used the term "preembryo;" the 1994 and 1999 panels preferred "pre-implantation embryo" for the earliest stages of embryological development, while the 2002 panel did not draw any distinctions; the 1994 and 2002 panels defined an "embryo" as existing from the moment of fertilization, while the 1999 panel denominated the conceptus as a "zygote" during the first week of development after fertilization and as an "embryo" during the second week.

Kiessling does not provide much explanation for the fairly dramatic shift from 1999 to 2002. Although researchers had made some further advances during the interim, the new information did not alter fundamentally the predicates underlying the recommendations of the earlier panel. Nor did the new panel have a different view of the scientific issues so much as a profoundly different set of ideological commitments. Not long after taking office, George W. Bush replaced the NBAC [National Bioethics

Advisory Commission] with the President's Council on Bioethics (PCB), a group dominated by so-called "neo-conservatives." In particular, critics have argued that a set of draft documents recently circulated by the PCB "signaled an ongoing effort by conservative members of the council to create new protections for human embryos."

The Bush administration also altered the composition and direction of some scientific advisory committees. First, it sought to name Dr. David Hager, a religious fundamentalist and vocal pro-lifer, as the chairman of the FDA's Reproductive Health Drugs Advisory Committee. After joining the committee (though not as chairman), Hager voted in opposition to the proposed OTC switch of the morning after pill, and undoubtedly he can be counted on to champion a citizen petition currently pending before the FDA that seeks to withdraw the approval of the abortifacient mifepristone.

Second, the Bush administration created the HHS Secretary's Advisory Committee on Human Research Protections (SACHRP) to replace a similar panel set up during the Clinton administration, but the new charter for the reconstituted committee expanded its scope to include "embryos" as potential human research subjects. In response to critics who "called the move an inappropriate political and religious intrusion into a scientific advisory committee," an HHS official explained that this decision amounted to nothing more than an effort to take into account the tendency to conflate the terms fetus and embryo. This effort to downplay the significance of such a change makes absolutely no sense: In the appropriations rider that prevents federal funding of any research involving human embryos, Congress unmistakably foreclosed the suggested reinterpretation of the existing human subjects protection rules. Moreover, any such surreptitious effort at reinterpreting the current regulations would have the rather dramatic effect of halting all embryo research occurring at institutions that receive any sort of federal funding, even if only for entirely unrelated research. After HHS announced the names of SACHRP members, one bioethicist who had served on the predecessor committee declined the invitation to join at least in part because of "the committee's new embryo-oriented charter."

Administration officials, of course, strenuously deny that they use any sort of a litmus test when selecting members for their scientific advisory committees. Anecdotal reports suggest otherwise:

> At least one nationally renowned academic, who was recently called by an administration official to talk about serving on an HHS advisory committee, disagreed with that assessment. To the candidate's surprise, the official asked for the professor's views on embryo cell research, cloning and physician-assisted suicide. After that, the candidate said, the interviewer told the candidate that the position would have to go to someone else because the candidate's views did not match those of the administration.

Moreover, the administration recently removed two PCB members who had expressed their disagreement with the party line on human embryonic stem cell research.

In addition to selecting ideologues to help shape federal science policy, the Bush administration has established a pattern of selective invocation of science to suit its views on policy—akin to "cooking the intel" in order to justify military objectives—on issues ranging from reproductive medicine to global climate change. In fact, the President's policy on embryonic stem cell research attracted criticism for its misleading account of the number of available cell lines. Although viewed as a politically astute compromise, even this initial gesture of limited and qualified support for the research may amount to nothing if it is quietly unraveled over time.

Apart from questions about how it may influence pending FDA initiatives related to emergency contraceptives and human tissue product rules, the Bush administration has taken a number of other small steps that in the aggregate signal a significant change in the federal position on the status of "embryos." For instance, a new federal rule treats conception as the point where public insurance coverage for a child could begin. In addition, the latest omnibus spending legislation includes an appropriations rider that codifies an existing policy of treating embryos as unpatentable. Taken in isolation, each of these choices may not attract much public scrutiny, but the recurring pattern of extending protection to the earliest products of fertilization reflects an unmistakable shift in the prevailing political winds. * * *

Similarly, although improved understandings about early development may help to explain the apparent shift in scientific definitions of the word "embryo," one cannot dismiss the possibility that non-scientific factors have influenced the ways in which scientists have chosen to define the term. When and why did the scientific community begin differentiating between the earliest stages of embryonic development? One prominent biologist offered the following account:

> It is rare that scientists change well-established terminology, and such changes normally occur only in response to new scientific understanding that invalidates the use of earlier terms. Yet our scientific understanding of early embryonic development has remained essentially unchanged for more than half a century .... The term pre-embryo has been embraced wholeheartedly by IVF practitioners for reasons that are political, not scientific.

Kiessling points to the rapidly increasing sophistication of assisted reproductive technologies, particularly IVF, but she fails to mention that, from the beginning, researchers have used the phrase "embryo transfer" to describe the introduction of the conceptus a couple of days after fertilization into a woman's uterus. * * *

Perhaps the scientific community can reach some consensus on the question of embryo status, though even that seems unlikely insofar as scientists do not stand in isolation from the influences and pressures that create inconsistent answers in other settings, but any such consensus would do little to resolve the controversy. Scientists can and do inform public debates, but they cannot settle "trans-scientific" questions. To think otherwise demonstrates a combination of hubris and naiveté. * * *

Kiessling finishes her article by recognizing that the time may have passed for reconceiving (or banishing altogether?) the term "embryo," though she rejects the view that an embryo exists from the moment of conception and prefers a definition that coincides with implantation. As Kiessling explains, however, any number of things can go wrong even after this juncture, and an embryo at two weeks differs substantially from an embryo at eight weeks, so the implantation threshold suffers from its own degree of arbitrariness but one that researchers who focus on stem cell research or IVF need not really confront.

In addition, Kiessling urges differentiating "embryos" from parthenotes and ova activated by means other than the entry of sperm (e.g., somatic cell nuclear transfer (SCNT)), which she would label as "ovasomes." A parthenote is an egg that activates and cleaves without fertilization. In the future, it may be possible for a laboratory to generate parthenotes from mature human ova for purposes of deriving stem cells. Similarly, in order to minimize the risk of transplant rejection, scientists in the future may derive stem cells from eggs activated by SCNT.

Kiessling's strategy of distinguishing parthenotes and "ovasomes" from "embryos" suffers from a number of flaws, to say nothing of the fact that it flies directly in the face of the expansive definition that Congress has selected for the moment. First, is not the ceaseless expansion of terminology just going to confuse matters still further, shrouding the relevant issues in scientific jargon or a semantic sleight of hand? The scientific community opted for "therapeutic cloning" in order to differentiate embryonic stem cell research from "reproductive cloning," then it began to shy away from any use of the loaded term cloning in favor of the more technical terminology SCNT. Is Kiessling simply adding to the embryological Tower of Babel? Where, for instance, would intracytoplasmic sperm injection (ICSI), a technique that circumvents the normal process of sperm fusion with an egg cell, fit into her terminological scheme? Perhaps we should try adopting new nomenclature that encompasses both early (pre-implantation) "embryos" and "ovasomes," calling them "ovanoma" (a reference to mysteriously proliferating mature eggs, which may result from fertilization, parthenogenesis, SCNT, or perhaps tumorogenesis). Other fanciful options include "(n)ova," "sporsicle," and "zygotisome."

Second, Kiessling argues that spontaneous human parthenotes have never reached viability and therefore cannot qualify for embryo status. A few paragraphs later, however, she anticipates the possibility of deriving pluripotent stem cells from parthenotes in "the near future," which also suggests the possibility of totipotent cells that could develop into a viable embryo. After all, when researchers first succeeded at extracorporeal fertilization of a human egg, they had no idea whether this could result in a live birth—it took almost a decade before the birth of the first IVF child. Or, in the case of fertilized ova with profound chromosomal abnormalities that will halt development short of viability (or embryos that implant in a fallopian tube and cause an ectopic pregnancy), does Kiessling mean to suggest that an implanted but doomed conceptus does not qualify as an "embryo" after all?

Third, perhaps in recognition of future developments, she argues that there is no need for special terminology describing an implanted parthenote because "there is no reason to transfer a parthenote to a uterus." This is a non sequitur—one might say with equal force that there is no reason to transfer an extracorporeal fertilized ovum to a uterus, except, of course, to see if one can establish a pregnancy. Kiessling makes the same point about ovasomes. Although she admits that they could qualify as "embryos" if transferred to the uterus for implantation, Kiessling argues that researchers would derive stem cells from these reconstructed ova at the equivalent of the blastocyst stage, so "they will never achieve 'embryo' status." In fact, one fertility researcher recently reported establishing a successful pregnancy after nuclear transfer into an unfertilized ovum.

If intent defined status in this fashion, then ova fertilized solely for use in stem cell or other research would never qualify as "embryos" either (certainly not given a definition of embryo that depended on implantation), but that hardly makes the ethical, legal, and social issues magically evaporate. On the contrary, it flies in the face of suggested answers to these concerns—most defenders of embryonic stem cell research strongly oppose the creation of embryos solely for research purposes, preferring to use embryos originally created with reproductive intent but then not so used. What, for example, would Kiessling label a totipotent cell derived from a fertilized ovum (or, for that matter, an ovum activated by other means)—she clearly prefers to call such blastomere separation "twinning" rather than "cloning," but will the resulting twin not count as an "embryo" (or even a nascent embryo) if intended solely for research? * * *

Fourth, whatever the future potential for deriving pluripotent stem cells from parthenotes and "ovasomes," research on fertilized ova will need to continue in the meantime. Kiessling's preference for defining "embryo" to exclude pre-implantation stages would allow such research to proceed, but such an effort simply to define away the problem does not stand much chance of quelling the existing objections to embryonic stem cell work. Those who view life as beginning at conception (whether or not they care to attach the label "embryo" right off the bat)—as well as those who reject this view while embracing an intermediate position of according special respect even to the earliest stages of human embryological development—will find little satisfaction in Kiessling's beguiling terminological solution. Instead of trying to grapple with the core question, she simply argues that stem cells can be derived from things that, "strictly speaking," are not (yet) "embryos."

Finally, Kiessling's approach suffers from the contingency of the baseline that she criticizes. Imagine that, as a consequence of imprecise drafting, a more enlightened Congress had enacted an appropriations rider that authorized federal funding of research involving stem cells, though only when derived from spare human "embryos." Would Kiessling still insist that unimplanted fertilized eggs, parthenotes, and ovasomes did not count as "embryos," or would she now embrace the more encompassing current definitions of that term? In the United Kingdom, which authorizes research on "embryos" (defined as the products of fertilization), a pro-life group initially succeeded in persuading the courts that stem cell work using ova activated by SCNT fell outside of the terms of the statute. Conversely, even without a change in the existing restrictions on federal funding, a privately-financed researcher may prefer to characterize his or her work as using spare "embryos" (or their near equivalents) instead of emphasizing the extent to which the source of stem cells departs from minimally manipulated reproductive tissue lest the FDA's regulatory ears perk up. Then again, this same researcher may not mind enhanced scrutiny by the FDA as the price of admission into the patent system given the non-patentability of mere "embryos." * * *

NOTES AND QUESTIONS

1. *Contrasting embryo biopsy.* What if, instead of using pluripotent cells from the inner cell mass of the blastocyst (which necessitates destruction of the surrounding trophoblastic layer), scientists could derive stem cells from totipotent cells extracted more easily at the earlier morula stage—would this silence the critics? See id. at 1160 n.125 (hypothesizing such an end-run); see also Mieke Geens et al., Human Embryonic Stem Cell Lines Derived from Single Blastomeres of Two 4–Cell Stage Embryos, 24 Hum. Reprod. 2709 (2009); Karen Kaplan, Stem Cells Created, with Embryos Intact, L.A. Times, Jan. 11, 2008, at A15 (reporting the first successful use of such a technique); cf. Rick Weiss, Future of Stem Cell Tests May Hang on Defining Embryo Harm, Wash. Post, July 29, 2007, at A8 (discussing initial NIH rejection of a proposal involving blastomere separation). After all, apparently no one has objected to preimplantation genetic diagnosis (PGD), which requires removing a blastomere from a pre-embryo, on these grounds (because the embryo remains intact and capable of development, though the totipotent cell removed from that pre-embryo itself could have developed as a twin had it not been destroyed in the process of performing the diagnostic tests). Researchers continue to look for ways of getting around the federal funding restrictions and the accompanying political controversy. See Carolyn Y. Johnson, Scientists See New Hurdles in Push to Make Stem Cells, Boston Globe, July 19, 2010, at C5 ("[S]cientists have found that [induced pluripotent stem (iPS)] cells ... contain subtle differences that affect their biology and therapeutic potential."); Rob Stein, Cell Technique Works Without Embryos, Wash. Post, Oct. 1, 2010, at A2 (summarizing recent advances in the creation of iPS cells); Rick Weiss, Contentious Hearing Focuses on Stem Cells, Wash. Post, July 13, 2005, at A19 (discussing suggestions to develop "embryos that might not pass muster as 'human' because they have been engineered to lack a gene crucial for development into a baby").

2. *Embryonic stem cell research.* Earlier in this chapter, we saw some of the questions that arise when putting stem cells—whatever their source—to therapeutic uses. Before this technique for regenerative medicine can mature, however, much basic research remains to be done, which explains the continuing importance of the evolving federal funding policy. See Gardiner Harris, Obama Plans to Retain Some Limits on Stem Cells, N.Y. Times, Apr. 18, 2009, at A13; Rob Stein, NIH Rejects Stem Cell Request: Director Says Use of Dozens of Colonies Would Break New Rules, Wash. Post, June 22, 2010, at A17 (reporting that 75 cell lines have been deemed eligible for federal research funding); Rick Weiss, Long Fight Has Slowed Progress on Stem Cells, Wash. Post, July 19, 2006, at A4; see also Robert L. Hotz, Cell Labs Take Private Path, L.A. Times, June 11, 2006, at A4; Sheryl G. Stolberg, Bush Vetoes Bill Removing Stem Cell Limits, N.Y. Times, June 21, 2007, at A21 (reporting that on two separate occasions Congress had passed bills to loosen the restrictions). After remand in *Sherley*, the district court rejected all of the plaintiffs' claims on the merits. See Sherley v. Sebelius, 776 F.Supp.2d 1 (D.D.C.2011). Even when researchers get funding from non-federal sources, they still must confront a variety of ethical considerations. See Karen Kaplan, New Stem Cell Ethics Issue Emerges, L.A. Times, Sept. 13, 2006, at A1; Rick Weiss, Stem Cell Guidelines Issued, Wash. Post, Apr. 27, 2005, at A2 (describing an NAS report designed to fill the void created by the lack of any meaningful federal oversight beyond the funding restriction and the inapplicability of requirements for scrutiny by IRBs).

3. *State-level initiatives*. See Tricia Bishop, In the High–Stakes World of Stem Cell Research, Success or Failure Can Hinge on the Turn of a Phrase: It's All About Word Choices, Balt. Sun, Mar. 11, 2007, at 1C; Stephanie Simon, Stem Cell Dissent Roils States: Even Where Voters Have Moved to Support the Embryonic Research, Opposition Is Fierce, L.A. Times, Aug. 1, 2007, at A12 ("[This] has quickly become one of the hottest, and most divisive, topics in state legislatures nationwide. More than 100 bills on the subject have been introduced in the last seven months alone.... Six states ban most or all embryonic research of this type: Arkansas, Indiana, Louisiana, Michigan, North Dakota and South Dakota. Seven states subsidize the emerging science ...."); see also Michael S. Mireles, Jr., States as Innovation System Laboratories: California, Patents, and Stem Cell Technology, 28 Cardozo L. Rev. 1133 (2006); Gary R. Tulp, Comment, Whose Cell Line Is it Anyway? Intellectual Property Implications of New Jersey's Policy on Stem Cell Research, 38 Seton Hall L. Rev. 1167 (2008); Symposium, California's Stem Cell Initiative: Confronting the Legal and Policy Challenges, 21 Berkeley Tech. L.J. 1017 (2006). Meanwhile, in tort claims brought against fertility clinics for destroying cryopreserved pre-embryos, state courts continue trying to grapple with these questions. See Jeter v. Mayo Clinic Ariz., 121 P.3d 1256 (Ariz.Ct.App.2005); Patrick Rucker, Judge Says Lost Embryo a Human, Chi. Trib., Feb. 6, 2005, at 1.

4. *Further commentary*. See Ronald Chester & Robert Sackstein, Embryonic Stem Cell-based Therapeutics: Balancing Scientific Progress and Bioethics, 20 Health Matrix 203 (2010); Gregory Dolin, A Defense of Embryonic Stem Cell Research, 84 Ind. L.J. 1203 (2009); James W. Fossett, Beyond the Low–Hanging Fruit: Stem Cell Research Policy in an Obama Administration, 9 Yale J. Health Pol'y L. & Ethics 523 (2009); Yaniv Heled,

On Presidents, Agencies, and the Stem Cells Between Them: A Legal Analysis of President Bush's and the Federal Government's Policy on the Funding of Research Involving Human Embryonic Stem Cells, 60 Admin. L. Rev. 65 (2008); Russell Korobkin, Recent Developments in the "Stem Cell Century": Implications for Embryo Research, Egg Donor Compensation, and Stem Cell Patents, 49 Jurimetrics J. 51 (2008); Philip G. Peters, Jr., The Ambiguous Meaning of Human Conception, 40 U.C. Davis L. Rev. 199 (2006); Debora Spar & Anna Harrington, Selling Stem Cell Science: How Markets Drive the Law Along the Technological Frontier, 33 Am. J.L. & Med. 541 (2007); David E. Winickoff et al., Opening Stem Cell Research and Development: A Policy Proposal for the Management of Data, Intellectual Property, and Ethics, 9 Yale J. Health Pol'y L. & Ethics 52 (2009); Kristin M. Hicks, Note, Embryonic Stem Cell Research and the Theory of Medical Self–Defense, 21 Harv. J.L. & Tech. 547 (2008); Elizabeth A. Holman, Note, Charity Starts in the Womb: New Research Should Allow Healthy Embryos and Federally Funded Stem Cell Research to Coexist, 85 Wash. U. L. Rev. 161 (2007); James M. Kramer, Note, Stemming the Tide: A Call for Reinterpretation of Embryonic Rights in Light of Emerging Alternatives in Medical Research and Conflicting Areas of Law, 39 Rutgers L.J. 703 (2008); Jody Schechter, Note, Promoting Embryonic Stem Cell Research: A Comparison of Policies in the United States and the United Kingdom and Factors Encouraging Advancement, 45 Tex. Int'l L.J. 603 (2010).

INDEX

References are to pages.

†